P9-EJK-547

KIBBLE AND TIDBITS FROM
Vacationing With Your Pet

WHERE TO STAY

A comprehensive guide to pet-friendly accommodations, Eileen's award-winning directory includes more than 23,000 hotels, motels, inns and B&Bs in the United States and Canada that welcome you and your pet.

- Fluff Fido's pillow at the Four Seasons Hotel in Beverly Hills (page 141).

- Whisk your wagger away for a relaxing stay at the Plaza San Antonio in Texas (page 536).

- Fill your eyes with starry skies in Tucson at the Westward Look Resort (page 122).

- Window shop till you drop on 5th Avenue and then rest your weary paws at the Regency Hotel in New York City (page 418).

- Fall hard for autumn colors with furface in Vermont at the award-winning Top Notch at Stowe Resort (page 555).

- Take your sun-loving pet on a journey to the Sheraton in Tampa Bay (page 236).

WHERE TO STAY

- Green Acres Motel is the place to be with Frisky in Paw Paw, Michigan (page 336).

- Enjoy a winter wonderland with your snow-sniffing wagalong at the The Little Nell in Aspen (page 196).

- Go for the gold with Digger in Knoxville and get your money's worth at the Scottish Inns North (page 502).

- Don't be sleepless in Seattle, hightail it to the Alexis Hotel (page 586).

- People and pooch watch under the famous clock at San Francisco's historic Westin St. Francis Hotel (page 181).

- Give Bowser something to bark home about from the Four Seasons Inn on the Park in Toronto, Ontario (page 686).

- Have a howl of a good time at a Holiday Inn in Montreal, Quebec (page 694).

HOW TO DO IT

Increase your travel know-how with some handy traveling tips.

- How to Pack For Your Pet (page 38).
- 29 Tips For Travel Safety (page 57).
- 27 "On-the-Road Tips" (page 61).

Old dogs can learn new tricks.

- Training Do's and Don'ts (page 33).
- Prevent Aggression in Your Dog (page 36).
- Get Crate Smart (page 34).

Make a night of it.

- Hotel and Motel Policies (page 17).
- Travel by Car (page 42).
- Travel by Plane (page 49).

Kitty comes along.

- What About Cats (page 25).
- Cat Travel Tips (page 27).

Directories by Eileen Barish

DOIN' ARIZONA WITH YOUR POOCH

DOIN' CALIFORNIA WITH YOUR POOCH

DOIN' NEW YORK WITH YOUR POOCH

DOIN' TEXAS WITH YOUR POOCH

VACATIONING WITH YOUR PET

Novels by Eileen Barish

ARIZONA TERRITORY

Eileen's Directory of Pet-Friendly Lodging
United States & Canada

Vacationing
With Your Pet

Over 23,000 Listings of
Hotels, Motels, Inns, Ranches
and B&Bs that Welcome
Guests with Pets

Pet-Friendly Publications
P.O. Box 8459, Scottsdale, AZ 85252

VACATIONING WITH YOUR PET
by Eileen Barish

Pet-Friendly Publications
P.O. Box 8459, Scottsdale, AZ 85252
Tel: (800) 638-3637

ISBN #1-884465-07-2
Library of Congress Catalog Card Number:96-070502
Printed and bound in the United States of America.

While due care has been exercised in the compilation
of this directory, we are not responsible for errors or omis-
sions. We are sorry for any inconvenience. Inclusion in this
directory does not constitute endorsement or recommendation
by the author or publisher. It is intended as a guide to assist in
providing information to the public and the listings are
offered as an aid to travelers.

Eileen's directories are available at special discounts when purchased in
bulk for premiums and special sales promotions as well as for fund-
raising or educational use. Special editions or book excerpts can also be
created to specification. For details, call 1-800-638-3637.

CREDITS

Author & Managing Editor — Eileen Barish

Associate Editor — Harvey Barish

Lodging & Research Editor — Phyllis Holmes

Research/Writing Staff — Alison Dufner
Tiffany Geoghegan
Courtney Mechling

Illustrator — Gregg Myers

Graphic Designer — Tawni Hensley

Photographer — Ken Friedman

ACKNOWLEDGEMENTS

Phyllis, I am grateful for your tireless dedication and extraordinary thoroughness. Your efforts meant the difference between good and great.

Tiffany, thank you for your uncompromising, dogged determination and hardworking ethic to do it right.

Thanks to Tawni for being there when we needed you and for understanding the importance "of the look."

Thanks Courtney for your admirable attention to detail.

As always, to Sam, the"Best Friend"who started it all

And especially for Harvey who makes it all come together, who's always up for the often demanding challenge and more than ready for the next adventure.

TABLE OF CONTENTS

TRAVELING BY PLANE (cont.)

How will my pet feel about a kennel?
What about identification?
How can I make plane travel comfortable for my pet?
Will there automatically be room on board for my pet?
What will pet travel cost?
What about food and water?
What about tranquilizers?
What about after we land?
Pets who shouldn't fly.
Health certificates - will I need one?

Allergies.
Bites and stings.
Bleeding.
Burns.
Earache.
Eye scratches or inflammation.
Falls or impact injuries.
Fleas.
Heatstroke.

UNITED STATES DIRECTORY OF
PET-FRIENDLY LODGING

CANADIAN DIRECTORY OF
PET-FRIENDLY LODGING

Traveling With Your Pet Can Be A Rewarding Experience

You never have to leave your best friend home or kenneled in a small cage while you vacation. Bring your four-legged buddy along. Double your enjoyment and increase your safety. If your pet is a great companion at home, he can be just as companionable when you travel.

HOW TO USE THIS DIRECTORY

No more sneaking Snoopy

Whether you're a seasoned pet traveler or a first-time explorer, *Vacationing With Your Pet* will make traveling with your pet easier and more enjoyable.

At a glance, you'll locate thousands of accommodations in the United States and Canada that welcome people traveling with their pets.

Choose lodging from hotels, B&Bs (aka Bed & Biscuits), motels, resorts, inns and ranches that welcome you and your pet *through the front door*. Arranged in an easy-to-use alphabetical format, *Vacationing With Your Pet* covers the United States and Canada. Within each state or province, cities are also arranged in alphabetical order. Each listing includes the name of the lodging, address, zip code and phone number. Wherever available, the high/low range of room rates and toll-free 800-numbers are provided.

Do hotel and motel policies differ regarding pets?

Yes, but all the accommodations in *Vacationing With Your Pet* allow pets. Policies can vary on charges and sometimes on pet size or type. Some might require a damage deposit while some combine their deposit with a daily and/or one-time charge. Others may restrict pets to specific rooms, perhaps cabins or cottages. Residence-type inns which cater to long-term guests often charge a long-term fee.

Some also require advance notice. But most accommodations do not charge a fee or have restrictive policies. As with all travel arrangements, it is recommended that you call in advance to confirm policies and room availability. **Be aware that hotel policies may change. At the time your reservations are made, determine the pet-policy of your lodging choice.**

Not just for vacationers, this is a "must-have" reference for anyone who has a pet.

Increase your travel horizons and give your best friend a new leash on life. Owning a copy of *Vacationing With Your Pet* means you won't have to leave your trusted companion at home when you travel. Whether you're planning your annual vacation or taking off on an unexpected weekend getaway, you'll know where you and your pet are welcome to spend the night. Outfitted with this directory, people who love their pets can now travel together throughout the United States and Canada.

Containing a comprehensive overview of practical, hands-on information, this directory will make your travel experiences safer and more pleasurable. Training do's and don'ts, crate use and selection, driving tips, pet etiquette, travel manners, what and how to pack for your pet, first-aid advice and a pet identification form are just some of the topics covered. See the Table of Contents for a complete listing of travel, training and pet care information.

Lodging Guidelines For You and Your Pet

Conduct yourself in a courteous manner and you'll continue to be welcome anywhere you travel. Never do anything on vacation with your pet that you wouldn't do at home. Some quick tips follow that can make traveling with your pet more pleasurable.

1. If your pet is accustomed to sleeping on the bed with you, take along a sheet or favorite blanket and put that on top of the bedding provided by your lodging.

2. Place a towel or small mat under your pet's food and water dishes. Feed your pet in the bathroom where clean-up is easier should an accident occur.

3. Try to keep your pet off the furniture. Pack a lint and hair remover to eliminate unwanted hairs.

4. Always keep your dog on a leash on the hotel and motel grounds and carry plastic bags and/or paper towels for clean-up.

5. Keep your cat's litter box in the bathroom. Clean it often, flushing away waste.

Can my dog be left alone in the room?

Only you know the answer to that. If your dog isn't destructive, if he doesn't bark incessantly and if the hotel allows unattended dogs, try leaving him in the room for short periods of time — say when you dine out. Hang the "Do Not Disturb" sign on your door to alert the chambermaid or hotel staff members that your room shouldn't be entered.

Before leaving your dog unattended, the following suggestions might prove helpful:

1. Walk or otherwise exercise your pooch. An exercised dog will fall asleep more easily.

2. Provide a favorite toy as a distraction.

3. Turn on the TV or radio for audio/ visual companionship.

4. Be certain that there is an ample supply of fresh water available.

5. Calm your dog with a reassuring goodbye and a stroke of your hand.

Pooch Rules & Regulations

BE A RESPONSIBLE DOG OWNER AND OBEY THE RULES.

- Clean up after your dog even if no one has seen him do his business.
- Leash your dog in areas that require leashing.
- Train your dog to be well behaved.
- Control your dog in public places so that he's not a nuisance to others.

Note: When leashes are required, they must be six feet or less in length. Leashes should be carried at all times. They are prudent safety measures .

<u>FIDO FACT:</u>

- *Problems with dogs in many recreation areas have increased in recent years. The few rules that apply to dogs are meant to assure that you and other visitors have enjoyable outdoor experiences.*

INTRODUCTION

Vacationing with your pet can be a fun-filled adventure. It doesn't require special training or expertise. Just a little planning and a little patience. This directory is filled with information to make traveling with your pet easier and more satisfying. From training tips to what to take along, to the do's and don'ts of travel, virtually all of your questions will be answered.

Vacationing with pets.

Not something I thought I'd ever do. But as the adage goes, necessity is the mother of invention. What began as a necessity turned into a lifestyle. A lifestyle that has improved every aspect of my vacation and travel time.

Although my family had dogs on and off during my childhood, it wasn't until my early thirties that I decided it was time to bring another dog into my life. And the lives of my young children. I wanted them to grow up with a dog; to know what it was like to have a canine companion, a playmate, a friend who would always be there, to love you, no questions asked. A four-legged pal who would be the first to lick a teary face or a bloody knee. Enter Samson, our family's first Golden Retriever.

Samson.

For nearly fifteen years, Sammy was everything a family could want from their dog. Loyal, forgiving, sweet, funny, neurotic, playful, sensitive, smart, too smart, puddle loving, fearless, strong and cuddly. He could melt your heart with a woebegone expression or make your hair stand on end with one of his pranks. Like the time he methodically opened the seam on a bean bag chair and then cheerfully spread the beans everywhere. Or when he followed a jogger and ended up in a shelter more than 20 miles from home.

As the years passed, Sam's face turned white and one by one our kids headed off to college. Preparing for the inevitable, my husband Harvey and I decided that when Sam died, no other dog would take his place. We wanted our freedom, not the responsibility of another dog.

Sammy left us one sunny June morning with so little fanfare that we couldn't believe he was actually gone. Little did we realize the void that would remain when our white-faced Golden Boy was no longer with us.

Life goes on...Rosie and Maxwell.

After planning a two-week vacation through California, with an ultimate destination of Lake Tahoe, Harvey and I had our hearts stolen by two Golden Retriever puppies, Rosie and Maxwell. Two little balls of fur that would help to fill the emptiness Sam's death had created. The puppies were ready to leave their mom and come home with us only weeks before our scheduled departure. What to do? Kennel them? Hire a pet sitter? Neither felt right.

Sooo...we took them along.

Oh, the fun we had. And the friends we made. Both the two-legged and four-legged variety. Having dogs on our trip made us more a part of the places we visited. We learned that dogs are natural conversation starters. Rosie and Maxwell were the prime movers in some lasting friendships we made during that first trip together. Now when we revisit Lake Tahoe, we have old friends to see as well as new ones to make. The locals we met made us feel at home, offering insider information on little known hikes, wonderful restaurants and quiet neighborhood parks. This knowledge enhanced our vacation and filled every day with wonder.

Since that first trip, our travels have taken us to many places. We've visited national forests, mountain resorts, seaside villages, island retreats, big cities and tiny hamlets. We've shared everything from luxury hotel rooms to rustic cabin getaways. We've experienced good times together and always come home with wonderful memories. I can't imagine travel that doesn't include our dogs.

When I watch Rosie and Maxwell frolic in a lake or when they accompany us on a hike, I stop and think of Sammy and remember the legacy of love and friendship he left behind. So for those of you who regularly take your pet along and those who would if you knew how, come share my travel knowledge. And happy trails and tails to you.

Is my pet vacation-friendly?

Most pets can be excellent traveling companions. It stands to reason that if you accustom your pet to travel at an early age, he will adapt more quickly. That doesn't mean that an older pet won't love vacationing with you. And it doesn't mean that the training period has to be a difficult one.

Even if your dog hasn't traveled with you in the past, chances are he'll make a wonderful companion. And chances are that this unique time will result in a closer relationship with your animal and fill your travels with memories to last a lifetime.

A socialized pooch is a sophisticated traveler.

Of course, every dog is different. And you know yours better than anyone. To be sure that he will travel like a pro, accustom him to different situations. Take him for long walks around your neighborhood. Let him accompany you while you do errands. If your chores include stair climbing or using an elevator, take him with you. The more exposure to people, places and things, the better. Make your wagger worldly. The sophistication will pay off in a better behaved, less frightened pet. It won't be long until he will happily share travel and vacation times with you.

Just ordinary dogs.

Rosie and Maxwell, my traveling companions, are not exceptional dogs to anyone but me. Their training was neither intensive nor professionally rendered. They were trained with kindness, praise, consistency and love. And not all of their training came about when they were puppies. I too had a lot to learn. And as I learned what I wanted of them, their training continued. It was a sharing and growing experience. Old dogs (and humans too) can learn new tricks. Rosie and Maxwell never fail to surprise me. Their ability to adapt to new situations has never stopped. So don't think you have to start with a puppy. Every dog, young and old, can be taught to be travel friendly.

Rosie and Maxwell know when I begin putting their things together that another holiday is about to begin. Their excitement mounts with every phase of preparation. They stick like glue - remaining at my side as I organize their belongings. By the time I've finished, they can barely contain their joy. Rosie grabs her leash and prances about the kitchen holding it in her mouth while Max sits on his haunches and howls. If they could talk, they'd tell you how much they enjoy traveling. But since they can't, trust this directory to lead you to a different kind of experience. One that's filled with lots of love and an opportunity for shared adventure. So with an open mind and an open heart, pack your bags and pack your pooch. Slip this handy book into your suitcase or the glove compartment of your car and let the fun begin.

WHAT ABOUT CATS?

When people learn about my book and the fact that I travel with my two Golden Retrievers, they often say, "well, you travel with dogs, but I have cats."

Well cat lovers, rejoice! You too can enjoy the companionship of your feline when you vacation or travel. Of course, not every cat is going to adapt to travel. That's a decision only you can make. But if you'd like to give it a try, the following should prove helpful.

A walk in the park!

Perhaps one of the biggest obstacles cat owners face when they think of taking their cats along is what to do with them; how to include a feline friend on something as simple as a walk in the park. Although you don't often see people walking cats, it's not because it can't be done. It can. According to my cat-loving friends, it's not that difficult and they maintain it's worth the effort; not to mention the novelty of the sight and the friendly encounters it can provoke.

One step at a time.

Walking your kitty is not something that can be hurried. Before you begin, you'll need a well-made, light-weight harness and leash. Don't even think of using a collar with just a piece of rope. Too tight and your cat will be uncomfortable and dread her walks. Too loose and she might squirm away. A properly fitted harness is a necessity. As a rule of thumb, if you can slip the width of two fingers between the harness and your cat's neck and between the harness and her belly, you've got a good fit.

Begin slowly...as you would with a baby. Once you buy the harness and leash, let her sniff it. Leave it next to her until she becomes accustomed to its sight and smell. When she appears relaxed, gently slip on the harness. Let her wear it. You'll know when she's feeling comfortable. At that point, attach the leash and again wait for her to feel at ease. Let her walk around with it, feel the weight trailing behind. During these times, remain with your cat to supervise her. You know her better than anyone. When you sense she's ready, pick up the leash and walk around the house. Take along a handful of treats. As you walk, talk reassuringly to her, stopping every so often to praise her efforts. Give her a treat to reinforce your pleasure. Let her know how happy you are with her progress. Continue this "practice walking" until you feel confident she's up to the next step...the great outdoors. Remember she is apt to feel ill at ease and somewhat vulnerable. She'll look to you for protection. Once you're outdoors, be alert to your surroundings. If you sense anything that might frighten your cat, scoop her up in your arms. Reinforce the sense of security that being with you provides.

Follow the leader.

Make your outings fun. Praise your feline and reward her with a treat as she follows your lead. Or if you prefer, let her choose the direction and pace of your walk. Or try a combination of both approaches.

Training kitty to walk can be the first step to more shared times and a closer relationship. Not only will you be getting exercise and fresh air, but you'll be spending unique, quality time together. And don't overlook the social benefits that having your cat with you can mean. You're bound to attract other cat lovers who share the same interests.

Once you make the decision to try, proceed slowly and be generous with praise. Patience, love and a treat or two can mean success as well as a new way of life for you and your furry friend.

CAT TRAVEL TIP #1:

Several weeks before your journey, have your cat examined by your vet. If shots are due, have them done early and avoid the possibility of side effects at the time of your trip. If your cat has a tendency to carsickness, ask your vet about sedatives.

CAT TRAVEL TIP #2:

Cats should always be confined to a kennel when in a car — for their safety and yours. Cats love to jump and perch and a kennel will eliminate the potential for accidents. Make your cat's kennel as comfortable as you can by including a small scratch post or a favorite toy. Put some soft bedding on the floor of the kennel as well. Shortly before you plan to leave on your vacation, fill your cat's home litter box with fresh litter. Generally this will prompt your cat to answer nature's call before your departure. You can then begin your trip knowing your cat has already voided.

CAT TRAVEL TIP #3:

If you have more than one cat and they're companionable, buy a larger carrier and let them share the accommodations. At home or on the road, it's comforting for friendly felines to curl up together. Being in the same crate also means that your cats can continue to groom one another, a sure antidote to anxiety.

TRAVEL TRAINING

A well-trained, well-behaved dog is easy to live with and especially easy to travel with. There are basics other than sit, down and stay which you might want to incorporate into your training routine. Whenever you begin a training session, remember that your patience and your dog's attention span are the key elements to success. Training sessions should be 5-10 minutes each. Even if the results are initially disappointing, don't become discouraged. Stick with it. After just a few lessons, your canine will respond. Dogs love to learn, to feel productive and accomplished. Training isn't punishment. It's a gift. A gift of love. You'll quickly see the difference training can make in your animal. Most of all, keep a sense of humor. It's not punishment for you either.

Throughout this section, several references are made to puppies. But it's never too late for training to begin. The adage that you can't teach an old dog new tricks just isn't true. Patience and consistency combined with a reward system will provide excellent results.

Let's get social.

When it comes to travel training, not enough can be said about the benefits of socialization. The lessons of socialization are the foundation of a well-trained, well-behaved dog.

Socialize your dog at an early age. Allow your puppy to be handled by different people. Include men and children since puppies are inherently more fearful of both. When your puppy is three months old, join an obedience/training class. These classes are important because they provide puppies with the experience of being with other dogs. Your puppy will have the opportunity of putting down other dogs without inflicting harm and he'll also learn how to bounce back after being put down himself. Socialization can continue with walks around your neighborhood, visits to parks frequented by other dogs and children and by working with friends who have dogs they want to socialize.

<u>FIDO FACT:</u>

- *Dog ownership is a common bond and the basis of impromptu conversations as well as lasting friendships.*

Walking on a leash.

It's very natural for a puppy to pull at his leash. Instead of just pulling back, stop walking. Hold the leash to your chest. If your dog lets the leash slacken, say GOOD DOG. If he sits, say GOOD SIT. Then begin your walk again. Stop every ten feet or so and tell your dog to sit. Knowing he'll only be told to sit if he pulls, he'll eventually learn to pay attention to the next command. It makes sense to continue your training while on walks because your dog will learn to heed your commands under varying conditions. This will prove especially important when traveling together. Eliminating the "tug of war" factor can mean the difference between enjoying or disliking the company of your pooch at home or away.

Chewing.

Most dogs chew out of boredom. Eliminate destructive chewing by teaching your dog to chew on chew toys. An easy way to interest him in chewing is to stuff a hollow, nonconsumable chew toy with treats such as peanut butter, kibble or a piece of hard cheese. Once the toy is stuffed, attach a string to it and tempt your dog's interest by pulling the toy along. He'll take it from there.

Until you're satisfied that he won't be destructive, consider confining your pooch to one room or to his crate with a selection of chew toys. This is a particularly important training tool for dogs who must be left alone for long periods of time, and for dogs who travel with their owners. If your pooch knows not to chew destructively at home, those same good habits will remain with him on the road.

Bite inhibition.

The trick here is to keep a puppy from biting in the first place, not break the bad habit after it's formed, although that too can be accomplished. Your puppy should be taught to develop a soft mouth by inhibiting the force of his bites. As your dog grows into adolescence, he should continue to be taught to soften his bite and as an adult dog should learn never to mouth at all.

Allow your puppy to bite but whenever force is exhibited, say OUCH! If he continues to bite, say OUCH louder and then leave the room. When you return to the room, let the puppy come to you. Your pup will begin to associate the bite and OUCH with the cessation of playtime and will learn to mouth more softly. Even when your puppy's bites no longer hurt, pretend they do. Once this training is finished, you'll have a dog that will not mouth. A dog who will not accidentally injure people you meet during your travels.

Jumping dogs.

Dogs usually jump on people to get their attention. A fairly simple way to correct this habit is to teach your dog to sit and stay until released. When your dog is about to meet new people, put him in the sit/stay position. Be sure to praise your dog for obeying the command and then pet him to provide the attention he craves. Ask friends and visitors to help reinforce the command.

Come.

The secret to this command is to begin training at an early age. But older dogs can also learn. It might just take a little longer. From the time your pup's brought home, call him by name and say COME every time you're going to feed him. The association will be simple. He'll soon realize that goodies await if he responds to your call. Try another approach as well. During training sessions, call to your dog every few minutes. Reward him with praise and sometimes with a treat. And take advantage of normally occurring circumstances, such as your dog approaching you. Whenever you can anticipate that your dog is coming toward you, command COME as he nears you. Then reward him with praise for doing what came naturally.

NEVER order your dog to COME for punishment. If he's caught in the act of negative behavior, walk to him to reprimand.

Pay attention.

Train your dog to listen to you. For example, when your dog is at play in the yard, call him to you. When he comes, have him sit and praise him. Then release him to play again. Your dog will soon understand that obeying does not mean the end of playtime. Instead it means that he'll be petted and praised and then allowed to resume play.

Communication - talking to your dog.

Training isn't just about teaching your dog to sit or give his paw. Training is about teaching your pooch to become an integral part of your life. To fit into your daily routine and into your leisure time. Take notice of how your dog studies you, anticipates your next move. Incorporate his natural desire to please into your training. Let him know what you're thinking, how you're feeling. Talk to him as you go about your daily chores. He'll eventually recognize and understand changes in your voice, facial expressions, hand movements and body language. He'll know when you're happy or angry with him or with anyone else. If you want him to do something, get his attention and then speak to him. For example, if you want him to fetch his ball, ask him in an emphatic way, stressing the word ball. He won't understand at first, so fetch it yourself and tell him ball. Put the ball down and then repeat the command. This training method can be used in both play related activities and general obedience. It won't be long until you increase your dog's vocabulary and his understanding of numerous commands.

Training do's & don'ts.

- Never hit your dog.

- Praise and reward your dog for good behavior. Don't be embarrassed to lavish praise upon a dog who's earned it.

- Unless you catch your dog in a mischievous act, don't punish him. He will not understand what he did wrong. And when you do punish, go to your dog. Never use the command COME for punishment.

- Don't repeat a command. Dogs have excellent hearing. Say the command once in a firm voice. If he doesn't obey it's not because he hasn't heard you. Return to the training method for the disobeyed command.

- Don't be too eager or too reticent to punish. Most of all, be consistent.

- Don't encourage fearfulness. If your dog has a fear of people or places, work with him to overcome this fear rather than ignoring it, or believing it can't be changed.

- Don't ignore or encourage aggression.

- Don't use food excessively as a reward.

- Don't become discouraged if your initial attempts at training are unsuccessful. Try other approaches. Every dog can be trained.

CRATE TRAINING IS GREAT TRAINING

Many people erroneously equate the crate to jail. But that's only a human perspective. To a dog who's been properly crate trained, the crate represents a private place where your dog will feel safe and secure. It is much better to prevent behavioral problems by crate training than to give up on an unruly dog.

4 reasons why crate training is good for you.

1. You can relax when you leave your dog home alone. You'll know that he is safe, comfortable and incapable of destructive behavior.

2. You can housebreak your pooch faster. Confinement to a crate encourages control and helps establish a regular walk time routine.

3. You can safely confine your dog to prevent unforeseen situations. For example, if he's sick, if you have workers or guests that are either afraid of or allergic to dogs, or if your canine becomes easily excited or confused when new people enter the scene, the crate provides a reasonable method of containment.

4. You can travel with your pooch. Use of a crate in your automobile eliminates the potential for distraction. It also assures that your dog will not get loose during your trip.

FIDO FACT:

- ***Want to register your puppy or locate a breeder? The American Kennel Club's customer service line is (919) 233-9767.***

5 reasons why crate training is good for your dog.

1. He'll have an area for rest when he's tired, stressed or sick.

2. He'll be exposed to fewer bad behavior temptations which can result in punishment.

3. He'll have an easier time learning to control calls of nature.

4. He'll feel more secure when left alone.

5. He'll be able to join you in your travels.

Some do's and don'ts.

- DO exercise your dog before and after crating.

- DO place the crate in a well-used, well-ventilated area of your home.

- DO make sure that you can always approach your dog while he is in his crate. This will insure that he does not become overly protective of his space.

- DON'T punish your dog in his crate or banish him to the crate.

- DON'T leave your pooch in the crate for more than four hours at a time.

- DON'T let curious kids invade his private place. This is his special area.

- DON'T confine your dog to a crate if he becomes frantic or completely miserable.

- DON'T use a crate without proper training.

10

Ways To Prevent Aggression in Your Dog

1. Socialize him at an early age.

2. Set rules and stick to them.

3. Under your supervision, expose him to children and other animals.

4. Never be abusive towards your dog by hitting or yelling at him.

5. Offer plenty of praise when he's behaving himself.

6. Be consistent with training. Make sure your dog responds to your commands before you do anything for him.

7. Don't handle your dog roughly or play aggressively with him.

8. Neuter your dog.

9. Contact your veterinarian to deal with persistent behavior problems.

10. Your dog is a member of the family. Treat him that way. Tied to a pole is not a life.

Take your dog's temperament into account.

- Is he a pleaser?
- Is he the playful sort?
- Does he love having tasks to perform?
- Does he like to retrieve? To carry?

Dogs, like people, have distinct personalities...mellow, hyper, shy or outgoing. Take advantage of your dog's unique characteristics. A hyper dog can amuse you with hours of playful frolicking. A laid-back pooch will cuddle beside you offering warm companionship. An outgoing dog will help you make friends.

If you can combine what you know of your dog's personality with what you want to teach, your dog will train more easily. Together you will achieve a fulfilling compatibility.

<u>FIDO FACT:</u>

- *Staying at a hotel for a few days or more? Here's an easy way to identify your pet's temporary home. Staple one of the hotel's matchbook covers to your pet's collar. Be sure to remove the matches first.*

WHAT AND HOW
TO PACK FOR YOUR POOCH

Be prepared.

Dogs enjoy the adventure of travel. If your dog is basically well behaved and physically fit, he should make an excellent traveling companion. But traveling times will be more successful with just a little common sense and preparation.

Just as many children (and adults I might add) travel with their own pillow, your pooch will also enjoy having his favorites with him. Perhaps you'll want to include the blanket he sleeps with or his favorite toy. Not only will a familiar item or toy make him feel more at ease, but it will keep him occupied as well.

I restock Max and Rosie's travel bags at the end of each trip. That way I'm always prepared for our next adventure. "My Pooch's Packing List" is found on page 41. Consider including some or all of the items that follow.

- A blanket to cover the back seat of your vehicle.
- Two or three old towels for emergencies.
- Two bowls, one for water, the other for food.
- Plastic clean-up bags (supermarket produce bags work well).
- Paper towels — for spills, clean-up and everything in between.
- A long line of rope. You'll be surprised how often you'll use this very handy item.
- An extra collar and lead.
- Can opener and spoon.
- Flashlight.
- An extra flea and tick collar.
- Dog brush.
- Small scissors.
- Blunt end tweezers — great for removing thorns and cactus needles.
- Chew toys, balls, frisbees, treats — whatever your pooch prefers.
- Nightlight.
- A room deodorizer.
- A handful of zip-lock bags in several sizes.
- Pre-moistened towelettes. Take along two packs. Put one in your suitcase, the other in the glove compartment of your car.
- Dog food, enough for a couple of days. Although most brands are available throughout the country, either at pet stores, supermarkets or veterinary offices, you'll want to pack enough and eliminate having to find dog food the first night or two of your vacation.
- Water — a full container from home. Top off as needed and gradually accustom your dog to his new water supply.

People packing made easy...12 tips.

No matter where your travels take you, whether it's to the local park or on a cross-country trip, never leave home without your dog's leash and a handful of plastic bags or pooper scooper. I clearly remember those awful moments when I ended up without one or both.

1. Consolidate. Even if you're traveling as a family, one tube of toothpaste and one hair dryer should suffice.

2. Avoid potential spills by wrapping perfume, shampoo and other liquids together and placing them in large zip-lock plastic bags.

3. When packing, layer your clothing using interlocking patterns. You'll fit more into your suitcase and have less shifting and wrinkling.

4. Write out your itinerary, including flight info, car rental confirmation numbers, travel agent telephone numbers and lodging info. Keep one copy with you and put a duplicate in a safe place.

5. Take along a night light, especially if you're traveling with a child. A flashlight always comes in handy too.

6. Stash a supply of zip-lock plastic bags, moist towelettes, trash bags, an extra leash (or rope) and a plastic container in an accessible place.

7. If you plan to hike with children, give each a whistle; they're great for signaling help.

8. Include a can opener and some plastic utensils.

9. Comfortable walking shoes are a must. If you plan on hiking, invest in a sturdy pair of hiking boots, but be sure to break them in before your trip. Take an extra pair of socks with you whenever you hike.

10. Don't forget to include first aid-kits. One for dogs and one for people.

11. Pack an extra pair of glasses or contact lenses.

12. Keep medications in separate, clearly marked containers.

MY POOCH'S PACKING LIST

1 _____   16 _____

2 _____   17 _____

3 _____   18 _____

4 _____   19 _____

5 _____   20 _____

6 _____   21 _____

7 _____   22 _____

8 _____   23 _____

9 _____   24 _____

10 _____   25 _____

11 _____   26 _____

12 _____   27 _____

13 _____   28 _____

14 _____   29 _____

15 _____   30 _____

GET READY TO TRAVEL BY CAR

"Kennel Up"…the magical, all-purpose command.

When Rosie's and Maxwell's training began, I used a metal kennel which they were taught to regard as their spot, their sleeping place. Whenever they were left at home and then again when they were put to bed at night, I used the simple command, "Kennel Up," as I pointed to and tapped their kennel. They quickly learned the command. As they outgrew the kennel, the laundry room became their "kennel up" place. As full-grown dogs, the entire kitchen became their "kennel up" area. Likewise, when they began accompanying me on trips, I reinforced the command each time I told them to jump into the car. They soon understood that being in their "kennel up" place meant that I expected them to behave, whether they were at home, in the car or in a hotel room. Teaching your dog the "kennel up" command will make travel times easier and more pleasurable.

Old dogs can learn new tricks.

When we first began vacationing with Rosie and Max, some friends decided to join us on a few of our local jaunts. Their dog Brandy, a ten year-old Cocker Spaniel, had never traveled with them. Other than trips to the vet and the groomer, she'd never been in the car. The question remained... would Brandy adjust? We needn't have worried. She took to the car immediately. Despite her small size, she quickly learned to jump in and out of the rear of the station wagon. She ran through the forests with Rosie and Max, playing and exploring as if she'd always had free run. To her owners and to Brandy, the world took on new meaning. Nature as seen through the eyes of their dog became a more exciting place of discovery.

Can my dog be trained to travel?

Dogs are quite adaptable and responsive and patience will definitely have its rewards. Your pooch loves nothing more than to be with you. If it means behaving to have that privilege, he'll respond.

Now that you've decided to travel and vacation with your dog, it's probably a good idea to get him started with short trips. Before you go anywhere, remember two of the most important items for happy dog travel, a leash for safety and the proper paraphernalia for clean-up. There's nothing more frustrating or scary than a loose, uncontrolled dog. And nothing more embarrassing than being without clean-up essentials when your dog unexpectedly decides to relieve himself.

Make traveling a pleasant experience. Stop every so often and do fun things. But when you do stop to let him out, leash him before you open the car doors. When the walk or playtime is over, remember the "Kennel Up" command when you tell your pooch to get into the car or into his kennel. And use lots of praise when he obeys.

You'll find that your dog will most likely be lulled to sleep by the motion of the car. Rosie and Maxwell fall asleep after less than fifteen minutes. I stop every few hours, give them water and let them "stretch their legs." They've become accustomed to these short stops and anticipate them. The moment the car is turned off and the hatch-back popped open, they anxiously await their leashes. When our romping time is over and we're back at the car, a simple "kennel up" gets them into their travel area.

To kennel or not to kennel.

Whether or not you use a kennel for car travel is a personal choice. Safety should be your primary concern. Yours and your dog's. Whatever method of travel you choose, be certain that your dog will not interfere with your driving. If you plan to use a kennel, line the bottom with an old blanket, towel or shredded newspaper and include a favorite toy. When you're vacationing by car and not using a kennel, consider a car harness.

If you're not going to use a kennel or harness, consider confining your dog to the back seat and commanding him to "kennel up." Protect your upholstery by covering the seat with an old blanket. This will make clean-up easier at the end of your trip. To keep my car fresh smelling and free from doggie odors, I stash a deodorizer under the front seat.

How often should I stop?

Many people think that when their dogs are in the car, they have to "go" more often. Not true. Whenever you stop for yourself, let your pooch have a drink and take a walk. It's not necessary to make extra stops along the way unless your dog has a physical problem and must be walked more often. Always pull your car out of the flow of traffic so you can safely care for your pooch. Never let your dog run free. Use a leash at all times.

Can my pet be left alone in the car?

Weather is the main factor to consider in this situation. Even if you think you'll only be gone a few minutes, that's all it takes for an animal to become dehydrated in warm weather. Even if all the windows are open, even if your car is parked in the shade, even when the outside temperature is only 85°, the temperature in a parked car can reach 100° to 120° in just minutes. Exposure to high temperatures, even for short periods, can cause your pet's body temperature to skyrocket.

NEVER LEAVE YOUR DOG UNATTENDED IN WARM WEATHER.

During the winter months, be aware of hypothermia, a life threatening condition when an animal's body temperature falls below normal. In particular, short-haired dogs and toys are very susceptible to illness in extremely cold weather.

What about carsickness?

Just like people, some dogs are queasier than others. And for some reason, puppies suffer more frequently from motion sickness. It's best to wait a couple of hours after your dog has eaten before beginning your trip. Or better yet, feed your dog after you arrive at your destination. Keep the windows open enough to allow in fresh air. If your pooch has a tendency to be carsick, sugar can help. Give your dog a tablespoon of  honey or a small piece of candy before beginning your trip (**NO CHOCOLATE**). That should help settle his stomach. If you notice that he still looks sickly, stop and allow him some additional fresh air or take him for a short walk. In time most dogs will outgrow carsickness.

What about identification if my dog runs off?

As far as identification, traveling time is no different than staying at home. Never allow your pooch to be anywhere without proper identification. ID tags should provide your dog's name, your name, address and phone number. Most states require dog owners to purchase a license every year. The tag usually includes a license number that is registered with your state. If you attach the license tag to your dog's collar and you become separated, your dog can be traced. There are also local organizations that help reunite lost pets and owners. The phone numbers of these organizations can be obtained from local police authorities.

Use the form on the following page to record your pooch's description so that the information will be handy should the need arise.

MY PET'S IDENTIFICATION

In the event that your pet is lost or stolen, the following information will help describe your animal. Before leaving on your first trip, take a few minutes to fill out this form, make a duplicate, and then keep them separate but handy.

Answers to the name of: _____

Breed or mix: _____

Sex: _____ Age: _____ Tag ID#: _____

Description of hair (color, length and texture): _____

_____

Indicate unusual markings or scars: _____

_____

_____

TAIL: ( ) Short ( ) Screw-type ( ) Bushy ( ) Cut

EARS: ( ) Clipped ( ) Erect ( ) Floppy

Weight: _____ Height: _____

If you have a recent photo of your pet, attach it to this form.

TRAVELING BY PLANE

Quick takes:

- Always travel on the same flight as your pet. Personally ascertain that your pet has been put on board before you board the plane.
- Book direct, nonstop flights.
- Upon boarding, inform a flight attendant that your pet is traveling in the cargo hold.
- Early morning or late evening flights are best in the summer, while afternoon flights are best in the winter.
- Fill the water tray of your pet's travel carrier with ice cubes rather than water. This will prevent spillage during loading.
- Clip your pet's nails to prevent them from hooking in the crate's door, holes or other openings.

Carriers/kennels.

Most airlines require pets to be in specific carriers. Airline regulations vary and arrangements should be made well in advance of travel. Some airlines allow small pets to accompany their owners in the passenger cabins. The carrier must fit under the seat and the pet must remain in the carrier for the duration of the flight. These regulations also vary and prior arrangements should be made.

Airlines run hot and cold on pet travel.

Many airlines won't allow pets to travel in the cargo hold if the departure or destination temperatures are over 80°. The same holds true if the weather is too cold. Check with the airlines to ascertain specific policies.

What about the size of the carrier?

Your pet should have enough room to stand, lie down, sit and turn around comfortably. Larger doesn't equate to more comfort. If anything, larger quarters only increase the chances of your pet being hurt because of too much movement. Just as your pet's favorite place is under your desk, a cozy, compact kennel will suit him much better than a spacious one.

Should anything else be in the carrier?

Cover the bottom with newspaper sheets and cover that with shredded newspaper. This will absorb accidents and provide a soft, warm cushion for your pet. Include a blanket or an old flannel shirt of yours; some article that will remind your pet of home and engender a feeling of security. You might want to include a hard rubber chew, but forget toys, they increase the risk of accidents.

How will my pet feel about a kennel?

Training and familiarization are the key elements in this area. If possible, buy the kennel (airlines and pet stores sell them) several weeks before your trip. Leave it in your home in the area where your animal spends most of his time. Let him become accustomed to its smell, feel and look. After a few days, your pet will become comfortable around the kennel. You might even try feeding him in the kennel to make it more like home. Keep all the associations friendly. Never use the kennel for punishment. Taking the time to accustom your pet to his traveling quarters will alleviate possible problems and make vacationing more fun.

What about identification?

The kennel should contain a tag identifying your pet and provide all pertinent information including the pet's name, age, feeding and water requirements, your name, address and phone number and your final destination. In addition, it should include the name and phone number of your pet's vet. A "luggage-type" ID card will function well. Use a waterproof marker. Securely fasten the ID tag to the kennel. Your pet should also wear his state ID tag. Should he somehow become separated from his kennel, the information will travel with him. Using a waterproof pen, mark the kennel "LIVE ANIMAL" in large letters of at least an inch or more. Indicate which is the top and bottom with arrows and more large lettering of "THIS END UP."

How can I make plane travel comfortable for my pet?

If feasible make your travel plans for weekday rather than weekend travel. Travel during off hours. Direct and nonstop flights reduce the potential for problems and delays. Check with your airline to determine how much time they require for check in. Limiting the amount of time your pet will be in the hold section will make travel time that much more comfortable. Personally ascertain that your pet has been put on board your flight before you board the aircraft.

Will there automatically be room on board for my pet?

Not always. Airline space for pets is normally provided on a first-come, first-served basis. As soon as your travel plans are decided, contact the airline and confirm your arrangements.

What will pet travel cost?

Prices vary depending on whether your pet travels in the cabin or whether a kennel must be provided in the hold. Contact the airlines to determine pricing policies.

What about food and water?

It's best not to feed your pet at least six hours before departure; water two hours.

What about tranquilizers?

Opinions vary on the subject. Discuss this with your vet. But don't give your pet any medication not prescribed by a vet. And be aware that dosages for animals and humans are not the same.

What about after we land?

If your pooch has not flown in the passenger cabin with you, you will be able to pick him up in the baggage claim area. Since traveling in a kennel aboard a plane is an unusual experience, your dog may react strangely. Leash him before you let him out of the kennel to avoid mishaps. Once he's leashed, provide a cool drink of water and walk him ASAP. Cats should remain in their kennel until you arrive at your destination, but provide water upon landing.

Pets who shouldn't fly.

In general, very young puppies, females in heat, sickly, frail or pregnant pets should not be flown. In addition to the stress of flying, changes in altitude and cabin pressure might adversely effect your animal. Also, pug-nosed pets are definite "no flys" in the cargo section. These pets have short nasal passages and the noxious fumes in the cargo area can severely limit their supply of oxygen, leaving them highly susceptible to illness.

Health certificates - will I need one?

Although you may never be asked to present a health certificate, it's a good idea to have one with you. Your vet can supply a certificate listing the inoculations your pet has received, including rabies. Keep this information with your travel papers.

Airlines have specific regulations regarding animal flying rights. Make certain you know your pet's rights.

37

WAYS TO HAVE A BETTER VACATION WITH YOUR PET

Some tips and suggestions to increase your enjoyment when you and your pet hit the road.

1. Don't feed or water your animal just before starting on your trip. Feed and water your pet at least two hours before you plan to depart. Better still, if it's a short trip, wait until you arrive at your destination.

2. Exercise your dog before you leave. A tired pet will fall off to sleep more easily and adapt more readily to new surroundings.

3. Take a large container of water to avoid potential stomach upset. Your pet will do better drinking from his own water supply for the first few days. Having water along also means you can stop wherever you like and not worry about finding water. Gradually accustom your pet to the new water source by topping off the container with local water.

4. Plan stops along the way. Just like you, your animal will enjoy stretching his legs. As you travel, you'll find many areas conducive to a leisurely walk or a bit of playtime. If you make the car ride an agreeable part of the journey, your vacation will begin the moment you leave home - not just when you reach your ultimate destination.

5. While driving, keep windows open enough to allow the circulation of fresh air but not enough for your dog to jump out. If you have air conditioning, that will keep your pet cool enough.

6. Don't let your dog hang his head out of the window. Eyes, ears and throats can become inflamed.

7. Use a short leash when walking your pooch through public areas — he'll be easier to control.

8. Pack your pet's favorite toy or chew. If it entertains him at home, it'll entertain him on the road.

9. Before any trip, allow your pooch to relieve himself.

10. Cover your back seat with an old blanket or towel to protect the upholstery.

11. A room freshener under the seat of your car will keep it smelling fresh. Take an extra one for your room.

12. If your dog has a tendency to be carsick, keep a packet of honey in the glove compartment or carry a roll of hard candy like Lifesavers. Either remedy might help offset queasiness.

13. Use a flea and tick collar on your pet.

14. When traveling in warm weather months, drape a damp towel over your pet's crate. Adding moisture to the air will reduce the heat.

15. Before you begin a trip, expose your animal to experiences he will encounter while traveling; such as crowds, noise, people, elevators, walks along busy streets and stairs (especially those with open risers).

16. Shade moves. If you must leave your pet in the car for a short period of time, make sure the shade that protects him when you park will be there by the time you return. As a general rule though, it's best not to leave your pet in a parked car. NEVER LEAVE YOUR PET IN THE CAR DURING THE WARM SUMMER MONTHS. In the colder months, beware of hypothermia, a life threatening condition that occurs when an animal's body temperature falls below normal. Short-haired dogs and toys are very susceptible to illness in extremely cold weather.

17. Pack a clip-on minifan for airless hotel rooms.

18. When packing, include a heating pad, ice pack and a few safety pins.

19. A handful of clothespins will serve a dozen purposes, from clamping together motel curtains to sealing a bag of potato chips.

20. A night light will help you find the bathroom in the dark.

21. Don't forget that book you've been meaning to read.

22. Include a journal and record your travel memories.

23. Pack a roll of duct tape. Use it to repair shoes, patch suitcases or strap lunch onto the back of a rented bicycle.

24. Never begin a vacation with a new pair of shoes.

25. Pooper scoopers make clean-up simple and sanitary. Plastic vegetable bags from the supermarket are great too.

26. FYI, in drier climates, many lodging accommodations have room humidifiers available for guest use. Arrange for one when you make your reservation.

27. Use unbreakable bowls and storage containers for your pet's food and water.

28. Don't do anything on the road with your pet that you wouldn't do at home.

29. Brown and grey tinted sun lenses are the most effective for screening bright light. Polarized lenses reduce the blinding glare of the sun.

30. Before you leave on vacation, safeguard your home. Ask a neighbor to take in your mail and newspapers, or arrange with your mail carrier to hold your mail and stop newspaper delivery. Use timers so that a couple of lights go on and off. Unplug small appliances and electronics. Lock all doors and windows. Place steel bars or wooden dowels in the tracks of sliding glass doors and windows. Ladders or other objects that can be used to gain entry into your home should be stored in your garage or inside your home. Arrange to have your lawn mowed. And don't forget to take out the garbage.

31. Pack some snacks and drinks in a small cooler.

32. As a precaution when traveling, once you arrive at your final destination, check the yellow pages for the nearest vet and determine emergency hours and location.

33. It is unsafe for your dog to travel in the bed of a pickup truck. If you must use this means of transportation, there are safety straps available at auto supply stores that can offset the danger to your animal. Never use a choke chain, rope or leash around your dog's neck to secure him in the bed of a pickup.

34. Pack a spray bottle of water. A squirt in your dog's mouth will temporarily relieve his thirst.

35. Heavy duty zip-lock type bags make terrific traveling water bowls. Just roll down the edges to form a bowl and fill with water. They fold up into practically nothing. Keep one in your purse, jacket pocket or fanny pack and another in your glove compartment.

36. Arrange with housekeeping at your lodging choice to have your room cleaned either while you're in the room to supervise your pet or while you're out with your pet.

37. Traveling with children too? Keep them occupied with colored pencils and markers. Avoid crayons — they can melt in the sun. Question cards from trivia games as well as a pack of playing cards are handy amusements. Travel size magnetic games like checkers and chess are also good diversions. Don't forget those battery operated electronic games either. Include a book of crossword puzzles, a pair of dice and a favorite stuffed animal for cuddling time. In the car, games can include finding license plates from different states, spotting various makes or colors of cars, saying the alphabet backwards, or completing the alphabet from roadsigns.

29
TIPS FOR TRAVEL SAFETY

Whether you're just running errands at home or on a travel adventure, practice travel safety. A healthy dose of common sense can go a long way towards preventing you from becoming a statistic, no matter where you are.

1. When returning to your room late at night, use the main entrance of your hotel.

2. Don't leave your room key within sight in public areas, particularly if it's numbered instead of coded.

3. Store valuables in your room safe or in a safety-deposit box at the front desk.

4. Don't carry large amounts of cash, use traveler's checks and credit cards instead.

5. Avoid flaunting expensive watches and jewelry.

6. When visiting a public attraction like a museum or amusement park, decide where to meet should you become separated from your traveling companions.

7. Use a fanny pack and not a purse when touring.

8. Make use of the locks provided in your room. In addition to your room door, be certain all sliding glass doors, windows and connecting doors are locked.

9. If someone comes to your room, the American Hotel and Motel Association advises guests to ascertain the identity of the caller before opening the door. If you haven't arranged for room service or requested a delivery, call the front desk and determine if someone has been sent to your room before opening the door.

10. Carry your money (or preferably traveler's checks) separately from credit cards.

11. Use your business address on luggage tags, not your home address.

12. Be alert in parking lots and underground garages.

13. Check the back seat of your car before getting inside.

14. In your car, always buckle up. Seatbelts save lives.

15. Keep car doors locked.

16. When you stop at traffic lights, leave enough room (one car length) between your vehicle and the one in front so you can quickly pull away.

17. AAA recommends that if you're hit from behind by another vehicle, motion the other driver to a public place before getting out of your car.

18. When driving at night, stay on main roads.

19. Fill your tank during daylight hours. If you must fill up at night, do so at a busy, well-lit service station.

20. If your vehicle breaks down, tie a white cloth to the antenna or the raised hood of your car to signal other motorists. Turn on your hazard lights. Remain in your locked car until police or road service arrive.

21. Don't pull over for flashing headlights. Police cars have red or blue lights.

22. Lock video cameras, car phones and other expensive equipment in your trunk. Don't leave them in sight.

23. Have car keys ready as you approach your car.

24. At an airport, allow only uniformed airport personnel to carry your bags or carry them yourself. Refuse offers of transportation from strangers. Use the airport's ground transportation center or a uniformed taxi dispatcher.

25. Walk purposefully.

26. When using an ATM, choose one in a well-lit area with heavy foot traffic. Look for machines inside establishments - they're the safest.

27. Avoid poorly lit areas, shrubbery or dark doorways.

28. When ordering food from an outside source, have it delivered to the front desk rather than to your room.

29. Trust your instincts. If a situation doesn't feel right - it probably isn't.

11
WAYS TO TAKE THE STRESS OUT OF VACATIONS

Vacations are intended to be restful occasions but sometimes the preparations involved in "getting away from it all" can prove stressful. The tips on the following page are proven stress reducers to help you cope before, during and after your trip.

1. Awaken fifteen minutes earlier each day for a couple of weeks before your trip and use that extra time to plan your day and do vacation chores.

2. Write down errands to be done. Don't rely on your memory. The anticipation of forgetting something important can be stressful.

3. Don't procrastinate. Whatever has to be done tomorrow, do today. Whatever needs doing today, do now.

4. Take stock of your car. Get car repairs done. Have your car washed, your journey will be more pleasant in a clean car. Fill up with gas the day before your departure and check your tires and oil gauge. Summertime travel, check your air conditioning. In the winter, be certain your heater and defroster work. Make sure wiper blades are also in good working condition.

5. Learn to be more flexible. Not everything has to be perfect. Compromise, you'll have a happier life.

6. If you have an unpleasant task to do, take care of it early in the day.

7. Ask for help. Delegating responsibility relieves pressure and stress. It also makes others feel productive and needed.

8. Accept that we are all part of this imperfect world. An ounce of forgiveness will take you far.

9. Don't assume responsibility for more tasks than you can readily accomplish.

10. Think positive thoughts and eliminate negativism, like, "I'm too fat, I'm too old, I'm not smart enough."

11. Take 5-10 minutes to stretch before you begin your day or before bedtime. Breathe deeply and slowly, clearing your mind as you do.

27
ON-THE-ROAD TIPS

1. Keep your pet confined with either a crate, barrier or harness.

2. To avoid sliding in the event of sharp turns or sudden stops, be certain that your luggage, as well as your pet's crate are securely stored or fastened.

3. Ascertain that your vehicle is in good working order. Check brakelights, turn signals, hazard and headlights. Clean the windshield and top off washer fluid whenever you fill up. Since you'll be driving in unfamiliar territory, so keep an eye on the gas gauge. Fill up during daylight hours or at well-lit service stations.

4. When packing, include a flashlight, tool kit, paper towels, an extra leash, waterproof matches, a first-aid kit, blanket and a supply of plastic bags. During the winter months, keep an ice scraper, snow brush and small shovel in your trunk.

5. Never drive tired. Keep the music on and the windows open. Fresh air can help you remain alert.

6. Keep your windshield clean, inside and out.

7. Avoid using sedatives or tranquilizers when driving.

8. Don't drink and drive.

9. Never drive and read a map at the same time. If you're driving alone, pull off at a well-lit gas station or roadside restaurant and check the map. If you're unsure of directions, ask for assistance from a safe source.

10. Wear your seatbelt, they save lives.

11. Keep car doors locked.

12. Good posture is especially important when driving. Do your back a favor and sit up straight. For lower back pain, wedge a small pillow between your back and the seat.

13. If you're the driver, eat frequent small snacks rather than large meals. You'll be less tired that way.

14. Don't use high beams in fog. The light will bounce back into your eyes as it reflects off the moisture.

15. When pulling off to the side of the road, use your flashers to warn away other cars.

16. Before beginning your drive each day, do a car check. Tire pressure okay? Leakage under car? Windows clean? Signals working? Mirrors properly adjusted? Gas tank full?

17. Roads can become particularly slippery at the onset of rain, the result of water mixing with dust and oil on the pavement. Slow down and exercise caution in wet weather.

18. Every so often, turn off your cruise control. Overuse can lull you into inattention.

19. If you'll be doing a lot of driving into the sun, put a towel over the dashboard. It will provide some relief from the heat and brightness.

20. Even during the cooler months, your car can become stuffy. Keep the windows or sun roof open and let fresh air circulate.

21. Kids coming along? A small tape or CD player can amuse youngsters. Hand-held video games are also entertaining. And action figures are a good source for imaginary games. Put together a travel container and include markers or colored pencils, stamps, stickers, blunt safety scissors, and some pads of paper, both colored and lined.

22. If your car trip requires an overnight stay on route to your destination, pack a change of clothing and other necessities in a separate bag. Keep it in an accessible location.

23. When visiting wet and/or humid climates, take along insect repellent.

24. Guard against temperature extremes. Protect your skin from the effects of the sun. Hazy days are just as dangerous to your skin as sunny ones. Pack plenty of sunscreen. Apply in the morning and then again in the early afternoon. The sun is strongest midday so avoid overexposure at that time. To remain comfortable in warm weather, wear lightweight, loose fitting cotton clothing. Choose light colors, dark ones attract the sun. In dry climates, remember to drink lots of liquids. Because the evaporation process speeds up in arid areas, you won't be aware of how much you're perspiring.

25. In cold climes, protect yourself from frostbite. If the temperature falls below 32° fahrenheit and the wind chill factor is also low, frostbite can occur in a matter of minutes. Layer your clothing. Cotton next to your skin and wool over that is the best insulator. Wear a hat to keep warm - body heat escapes very quickly through your head.

26. Changes in altitude can cause altitude sickness. Whenever possible, slowly accustom yourself to an altitude change. Don't overexert yourself either. Symptoms of high altitude sickness occur more frequently over 8,000 feet and include dizziness, shortness of breath and headaches.

27. Store your maps, itinerary and related travel information in a clear plastic container (shoe box storage type with a lid works best). Keep it in the front of your vehicle in an easy-to-reach location.

<u>FIDO FACT:</u>

• *If your pooch is becoming too aggressive or is misbehaving, try startling him. Dogs dislike loud, grating noises. Load an empty soda can with pebbles or coins and keep it handy. When your pooch starts to act up, a firm "No" and a vigorous shaking of the can should prove to be an excellent deterrent to bad behavior. Be firm but not terrifying. And remember, corrective training must be administered immediately following the offending act.*

WHAT YOU SHOULD KNOW ABOUT DRIVING IN THE DESERT

Water: Check your radiator before journeying into the desert. Other than metropolitan areas, service stations are few and far between, even on major roads. Always carry extra water.

Gasoline: Since you'll be traveling through sparsely populated areas, fill up before beginning any desert adventure. When your vehicle has half a tank or less, refuel at the first service station.

Flash floods: Summer thunderstorms in the desert can wreak havoc, especially where roads dip into washes. The runoff quickly fills the washes, creating hazardous driving conditions and impassable roads. Heed the warning signs which pinpoint flash flood areas.

Dust storms: When a dust storm approaches, pull your vehicle off the road as far as possible, switch off your headlights and wait until the storm passes.

Breakdowns: Use your hazard lights or raise the hood. Remain in your vehicle until help arrives. Keep doors locked and do not open doors except for police officers. If you break down on a secluded back road and must seek help, retrace your route. Don't take any short cuts.

<u>FIDO FACT:</u>

- ***Never leave your dog unattended in the car during very warm or very cold weather.***

Desert survival.

Anyone can end up lost or stranded in the desert. All it takes is a flat tire or a wrong turn and suddenly you're faced with a dire situation which requires survival skills. Remain calm. Think through your options. Use common sense and keep focused. Survivalists recommend that you stay with your vehicle. Do not attempt to walk through the desert. Dehydration, exposure and exhaustion are killers.

Prepare yourself before traveling into a desert environment by considering the following:

- Plan your excursion and familiarize yourself with the area.
- Know where water sources exist.
- Determine local weather conditions and forecasts before hand.
- If you're hiking, carry a topographical map of the area and avoid the intense desert heat with an early morning outing.
- Never overestimate your hiking abilities - know your limits.
- Don't take sidetrips, they may cause you to lose your bearings.
- Carry as much drinking water as possible, it can save your life.
- If you're planning an overnight, establish camp near water.
- Inform a third party of your plans and when you'll be home. Contact that person upon your return.

Heat Stroke / Exhaustion.

Early heat exhaustion indicators include weakness, pale skin, dizziness, nausea, dehydration, muscle cramping and profuse sweating. Heat stroke symptoms include the preceding as well as hot, dry, red skin. In either case, seek shade, cool off by fanning yourself and apply damp cloths to face, neck and ears. Cases of heat stroke demand immediate medical attention.

Hypothermia.

Although hypothermia is a serious medical condition most commonly associated with mountain hiking, desert hikers and campers are also susceptible. Temperatures do not have to dip below freezing for exposure to occur. In fact, hypothermia strikes most often in the 30-50° temperature range - a common temperature for winter nights in the desert. Damp clothing and a cool breeze can sometimes be enough to cause the body to lose heat faster than it can be replaced - causing cold shivers. If you experience unstoppable shivering, it's imperative that you put on dry clothes, wrap yourself in a blanket and drink hot liquids. Without these precautions, you can lapse into the second, and sometimes fatal stage of hypothermia. When that occurs, there is little chance of the body rewarming itself without the aid of conventional heating methods and immediate medical attention.

Keep your cool.

- When traveling with your animal, it's a good idea to keep a cooler of cold towels in the car. Cold towels can help to bring down a dog's body temperature after a long afternoon of hiking.

- A wet bandana wrapped around your neck, and another around your dog's neck, can keep you both comfortably cool while hiking.

FIRST-AID EMERGENCY TREATMENT

Having a bit of the Girl Scout in me, I like being prepared. Over the years, I've accumulated information regarding animal emergency treatment. Although I've had only one occasion to use this information, once was enough. I'd like to share my knowledge with you.

Whether you're the stay-at-home type who rarely travels with your pet, or a gadabout who can't sit still, every pet owner should know these simple, but potentially lifesaving procedures.

The following are only guidelines to assist you during emergencies. Whenever possible, seek treatment from a vet if your animal becomes injured and you are unprepared to administer first aid.

Allergies: One in five pets suffers from some form of allergy. Sneezing and watery eyes can be an allergic reaction caused by pollen and smoke. Inflamed skin can indicate a sensitivity to grass or to chemicals used in carpet cleaning. See your vet.

Bites and stings: Use ice to reduce swelling. If your animal has been stung in the mouth, immediately take him to the vet. Swelling can close the throat. If your pet experiences an allergic reaction, an antihistamine may be needed. For fast relief from a wasp or bee sting, dab the spot with plain vinegar and then apply baking soda. If you're in the middle of nowhere, a small mud pie plastered over the sting will provide relief. Snake bites, seek veterinary attention ASAP.

Bleeding: If the cut is small, use tweezers to remove hair from the wound. Gently wash with soap and water and then bandage (not too tightly). Severe bleeding, apply direct pressure and seek medical attention ASAP.

Burns: <u>First degree burns:</u> Use an ice cube or apply ice water until the pain is alleviated. Then apply vitamin E, swab with honey or cover with a freshly brewed teabag.

<u>Minor burns:</u> Use antibiotic ointment.

<u>Acid:</u> Apply dampened baking soda.

<u>Scalds:</u> Douse with cold water. After treatment, bandage all burns for protection.

Earache: A drop of warm eucalyptus oil in your pet's ear can help relieve the pain.

Eye scratches or inflammation: Make a solution of boric acid and bathe eyes with soft cotton.

Falls or impact injuries: Limping, pain, grey gums or prostration need immediate veterinary attention. The cause could be a fracture or internal bleeding.

Fleas: Patches of hair loss, itching and redness are common signs of fleas, particularly during warm months. Use a flea bath and a flea collar to eliminate and prevent infestation. Ask your vet about new oral medication now available for flea control.

Heatstroke: Signs include lying prone, rapid or difficult breathing and heartbeat, rolling eyes, panting, high fever, a staggering gait. Quick response is essential. Move your animal into the shade. Generously douse with cold water or if possible, partially fill a tub with cold water and immerse your pet. Remain with him and check his temperature. Normal for dogs and cats: 100°-102°. Don't let your pet's temperature drop below that.

Prevent common heatstroke by limiting outdoor exercise in hot or humid weather and providing plenty of fresh, cool water and access to shade. Never leave your pet in a car on a warm day, even for "just a few minutes."

Heartworm: Mosquitos can be more than pests when it comes to the health of your dog. They are the carriers of heartworm disease, which can be life threatening to your furry friend. There is no vaccine. However, daily or monthly pills can protect your pet from infection. In areas with high mosquito populations, use a heartworm preventative. Contact your local veterinarian about testing and medication. In the case of heartworm, "an ounce of prevention equals a pound of cure."

Poisons: Gasoline products, antifreeze, disinfectants, and insecticides are all poisonous. Keep these products tightly closed and out of reach. Vomiting, trembling and convulsions can be symptoms of poisoning. If your pet suffers from any of these symptoms, get veterinary attention. (See listings on Poison Control Centers in section "Everything You Want to Know About Pet Care...")

Poison ivy: Poison ivy or oak on your pet's coat will not bother him. But the poison can be passed on to you. If you believe your pet has come in contact with poison ivy or oak, use rubber gloves before handling your animal. Rinse him in salt water, then follow with a clear water rinse. Shampoo and rinse again.

Shock: Shock can occur after an accident or severe fright. Your animal might experience shallow breathing, pale gums, nervousness or prostration. Keep him still, quiet and warm and have someone drive you to a vet.

<u>FIDO FACT:</u>

- *Got a fussy eater?*

Although missing a meal isn't unhealthy, you don't want meal times to become problem times. Never beg your dog to eat. Put the food down and leave the area. If the food hasn't been eaten in an hour, pick it up and save it for the next feeding. Your dog will eventually get the message. And no table scraps, they only encourage bad eating habits.

Skunks: The following might help you avoid a smelly encounter.

1. Don't try to scare the skunk away. Your actions might provoke a spray.

2. Keep your dog quiet. Skunks have an unforgettable way of displaying their dislike of barking.

3. Begin an immediate retreat.

If you still end up in a stinky situation, try one of these three home remedies.

1. Saturate your pet's coat with tomato juice. Allow to dry, then brush out and shampoo.

2. Combine 5 parts water with one part vinegar. Pour solution over your pet's coat. Let soak 10-15 minutes. Rinse with clear water and then shampoo.

3. Combine 1 quart of 3% hydrogen peroxide with 1/4 cup of baking soda and a squirt of liquid soap. Pour solution over your pet's coat. Let soak 10-15 minutes. Rinse with clear water and then shampoo.

Snake bites: Immobilization and prompt medical attention are the key elements in handling a poisonous snake bite. Immediate veterinary care (within 2 hours) is essential to recovery. If the bite occurs in a remote area, immediately immobilize the bitten area and carry your pet to the vehicle. Don't allow your pet to walk, the venom will spread more quickly. Most snake bites will be to the head or neck area, particularly the nose. The second most common place will be a pet's front leg.

Severe swelling within 30 to 60 minutes of the bite is the first indication that your pet is suffering from a venomous snake bite. Excessive pain and slow, steady bleeding are other indicators. Hemotoxins in the venom of certain snakes prevent blood from clotting. If your pet goes into shock or stops breathing, begin CPR. Cardiopulmonary resuscitation for pets is the same as for humans. Push on your pet's chest to compress his heart and force blood to the brain. Then hold his mouth closed and breathe into his nose.

When treating a snake bite:

- DO NOT apply ice to the bite - venom constricts the blood vessels and ice only compounds the constriction.

- DO NOT use a tourniquet - the body's natural immune system fights off the venom. By cutting off the blood flow, you'll either minimize or completely eliminate the body's natural defenses.

- DO NOT try to clean the bite or administer medication.

Ticks: Use lighter fluid (or other alcohol) and loosen by soaking. Then gently tweeze out. Make sure you get the tick's head.

Winter woes: Rock salt and other commercial chemicals used to melt ice can be very harmful to your animal. Not only can they burn your pet's pads, but ingestion by licking can result in poisoning or dehydration. Upon returning from a walk through snow or ice, wash your pet's feet with a mild soap and then rinse. Before an outdoor excursion, spray your pet's paws with cooking oil to deter adherence.

FITNESS FOR FIDO

A daily dose of exercise is as important for the pooch's health as it is for yours. A 15-30 minute walk twice daily is a perfect way to build muscles and stamina and get you and the dogster in shape for more aerobic workouts. In the summertime, beat the heat by walking in the early hours of the morning or after sundown. Keep in mind that dogs don't sweat, so if you notice your pooch panting excessively or lagging behind, stop in a cool shaded area for a water break.

If your dog is overweight or still a puppy, consult with your vet to determine an appropriate exercise program. Overweight canines may have other health problems which must be considered. Young dogs are still developing their bone structure and may not be ready for a rigorous program.

<u>FIDO FACT:</u>
- *Fido's fitness counts towards insuring a longer, healthier life. The most common cause of ill health in canines is obesity. About 60% of all adult dogs are or will become overweight due to lack of physical activity and overfeeding.*

MASSAGE, PETTING WITH A PURPOSE

Treat your dog to some special quality time. Give him the attention he craves while also doing something healthful for him. The simple procedures that follow require only 10 to 15 minutes of your time.

1. Gently stroke your animal's head.

2. Caress around his ears in a circular fashion.

3. Rub down both his neck and shoulders, first on one side of the spine, and then the other, continuing down to the rump.

4. Turn your dog over and gently knead his abdominal area.

5. Rub his legs.

6. Caress the area between his paw pads.

After the massage, offer your pooch plenty of fresh, cool water which will flush out the toxins released from the muscles.

Massages are also therapeutic for dogs recovering from surgery and/or suffering from hip dysplasia, circulatory disorders, sprains, chronic illness and old age. Timid and hyperactive pooches can benefit as well.

F_IDO_ F_ACT_:
- *Is your pooch pudgy? Place both thumbs on your dog's backbone and then run your fingers along his rib cage. If the bony part of each rib cannot be easily felt, your dog may be overweight. Another quickie test - stand directly over your dog while he's standing. If you can't see a clearly defined waist behind his rib cage, he's probably too portly.*

STEPS TO BETTER GROOMING

Grooming is another way of saying "I love you" to your pooch. As pack animals, dogs love grooming rituals. Make grooming time an extension of your caring relationship. Other than some breeds which require professional grooming, most canines can be kept well-groomed in about 10 minutes a day.

1. Designate a grooming place, preferably one that is not on the floor. If possible, use a grooming table. Your dog will learn to remain still and you won't trade a well-groomed pooch for an aching back.

2. End every grooming session with a small treat. When your dog understands that grooming ends with a goodie, he'll behave better.

3. Brush out your dog's coat before washing. Wetting a matted coat only tightens the tangles and makes removal more difficult.

4. Using a soft tissue, wipe around your dog's eyes daily, especially if his eyes tend to be teary.

5. When bathing a long-haired dog, squeeze the coat, don't rub. Rubbing can result in snarls.

6. To gently clean your dog's teeth, slip your hand into a soft sock and go over each tooth.

FIDO FACT:
- *Stroke a dog instead of patting it. Stroking is soothing. Patting can make a dog nervous.*

Grooming tips...sticky problems

Chewing gum: There are two methods you can try. Ice the gum for a minimum of ten minutes to make it more manageable and easier to remove. Or use peanut butter. Apply and let the oil in the peanut butter loosen the gum from the hair shaft. Leave on about 20 minutes before working out the gum.

Tar: This is a tough one. Try soaking the tarred area in vegetable or baby oil. Leave on for an hour or more and then bathe your dog. The oil should cause the tar to slide off the hair shaft. Since this method can be messy, shampoo your dog with Dawn dishwashing soap to remove the oil. Follow with pet shampoo to restore the pH balance.

Oil: Apply baby powder or cornstarch to the oily area. Leave on 20 minutes. Shampoo with warm water and Dawn. Follow with pet shampoo to restore the pH balance.

Burrs:

1. Burrs in your dog's coat may be easier to remove if you first crush the burrs with pliers.

2. Slip a kitchen fork under the burr to remove.

3. Soften the burrs with vegetable or baby oil before working them out.

Keep cleaning sessions as short as possible. Your dog will not want to sit for hours. If your dog's skin is sensitive, you might want to simply remove the offending matter with a scissors. If you don't feel competent to do the removal yourself, contact a grooming service in your area and have them do the job for you.

FIDO FACT:
- *Inflamed skin can indicate a sensitivity to grass or chemicals used in carpet cleaning. Patches of hair loss, itching and redness are common signs of fleas, particularly during warm months.*

12
TIPS ON MOVING WITH YOUR PET

Every year, one out of five Americans will move. Of those, nearly half will be moving with their pets. If you're part of the "pet half", be aware that your pet can experience the same anxiety as you. The following tips can make moving less stressful for you and your animal.

1. Although moving companies provide information on how to move your pet, they are not permitted to transport animals. Plan to do so on your own.

2. Begin with a visit to your vet. Your vet can provide a copy of your pet's medical records and possibly recommend a vet in the city where you'll be moving.

3. If you'll be traveling by plane, contact the airlines ASAP. Many airlines offer in-cabin boarding for small pets but only on a first-come, first-served basis. The earlier you make your reservations, the better chance you'll have of securing space.

4. If you'll be driving to your new home, *Vacationing With Your Pet* will assist you with your lodging reservations. By planning ahead, your move will proceed more smoothly .

5. Buy a special toy or a favorite chew that's only given to your pet when you're busy packing.

6. Don't feed or water your animal for several hours before your departure. The motion of the ride might cause stomach upset.

7. Keep your pet kenneled up on moving day to avoid disasters. Never allow your pet to run free when you're in unfamiliar territory.

8. Pack your pet's dishes, food, water, treats, toys, leash and bedding in an easy-to-reach location. Take water and food from home. Drinking unfamiliar water or eating a different brand of food can cause digestion problems. And don't forget those plastic bags for clean-up.

9. Once you're moved in and unpacked, be patient. Your animal may misbehave. Like a child, he may resent change and begin acting up. Deal with problems in a gentle and reassuring manner. Spend some extra time with your pet during this upheaval period and understand that it will pass.

10. If your pet requires medication or prescription diet, pack plenty for your journey and keep a copy of your pet's medical records with you.

11. Always carry your current veterinarian's phone number. You never know when an emergency may arise or when your new veterinarian will need additional health information

12. Learn as much as you can about your new area, including common diseases, local laws and required vaccinations.

10

REASONS WHY PETS ARE GOOD FOR YOUR HEALTH

Adding a pet to your household can improve your health and that of your family. In particular, pets seem to help the very young and seniors. The following is based on various studies.

1. People over 40 who own pets have lower blood pressure. 20% have lower triglyceride levels. Talking to pets has been shown to lower blood pressure as well.

2. People who own pets see their doctor less than those who don't.

3. Pets have been shown to reduce depression, particularly in seniors.

4. It's easier to make friends when you have a pet. Life is more social with them.

5. It's healthier too. Seniors with pets are generally more active because they walk more.

6. Pets are friends. Here again, seniors seem to benefit most.

7. Pets can help older people deal with the loss of a spouse. Seniors are less likely to experience the deterioration in health that often follows the stressful loss of a mate.

8. Pets ease loneliness.

9. Perhaps because of the responsibility of pet ownership, seniors take better care of themselves.

10. Pets provide a sense of security to people of all ages.

FIDO FACTS

The following facts, tidbits and data will enhance your knowledge of our canine companions.

- Gain the confidence of a worried dog by avoiding direct eye contact or by turning away, exposing your back or side to the dog.

- When dogs first meet, it's uncommon for them to approach each other head on. Most will approach in curving lines. They'll walk beyond each other's noses sniffing at rear ends while standing side by side.

- Dog ownership is a common bond and the basis of impromptu conversations as well as lasting friendships.

- Chemical salt makes sidewalks less slippery but can be harmful to your dog's footpads. Wash your dog's paws after walks to remove salt. Don't let him lick the salt either, it's poisonous.

- Vets warn that removing tar with over-the-counter petroleum products can be highly toxic.

- Although a dog's vision is better than humans in the dark, bright red and green are the easiest colors for them to see.

- Puppies are born blind. Their eyes open and they begin to see at 10 to 14 days.

- The best time to separate a pup from his mother is seven to ten weeks after birth.

- It's a sign of submission when a dog's ears are held back close to his head.

- Hot pavement can damage your dog's sensitive footpads. In the summer months, walk your pooch in the morning or evening or on grassy areas and other cool surfaces.

- Never leave your dog unattended in the car during the warm weather months or extremely cold ones.

- Always walk your dog on a leash on hotel/motel grounds.

- Want to register your puppy, or locate a breeder in your area? The American Kennel Club has a new customer service line at (919) 233-9767. Their interactive voice processing telephone system is open twenty-four hours a day, seven days a week. Information is available on dog and litter registrations. You can also use the number to order registration materials, certified pedigrees, books and videos. If you want to speak with a customer service rep, call during business hours.

- Stroke a dog instead of patting it. Stroking is soothing. Patting can make some dogs nervous.

- If your dog is lonely for you when he's left alone, try leaving your voice on a tape and let it play during your absence.

- When a dog licks you with a straight tongue, he's saying "I Love You."

- Don't do anything on the road with your dog that you wouldn't do at home.

- Never put your dog in the bed of a pickup truck as a means of transportation.

- Black dogs and dark colored ones are more susceptible to the heat.

- When traveling, take a spray bottle of water with you. A squirt in your dog's mouth will temporarily relieve his thirst.

- Changing your dog's water supply too quickly can cause stomach upset. Take along a container of water from home and replenish with local water, providing a gradual change.

- One in five dogs suffers from some form of allergy. Sneezing and watery eyes can be an allergic reaction caused by pollen or smoke.

- Inflamed skin can indicate a sensitivity to grass or chemicals used in carpet cleaning.

- Patches of hair loss, itching and redness are common signs of fleas, particularly during warm months.

- Normal temperature for dogs: 100° to 102°.

- No matter how much your dog begs, do not overfeed him.

- Housebreaking problems can sometimes be attributed to diet. Consult with your vet about one good dog food and be consistent in feeding. A change in your dog's diet can lead to digestive problems.

- Spay/neuter your dog to prevent health problems and illnesses that plague the intact animal. Contrary to popular belief, spaying/neutering your canine will not result in weight gain. Only overfeeding and lack of exercise can do that.

- Spend ample quality time with your canine every day. Satisfy his need for social contact.

- Obedience train your dog; it's good for his mental well being and yours.

- If you make training fun, your dog will learn faster.

- Always provide cool fresh drinking water for your dog.

- If your pooch lives outdoors, make sure he has easy access to shade and plenty of water.

- If your pooch lives indoors, he'll need access to cool moving air and ample fresh water.

- In the summertime, avoid exercising your dog during the hottest parts of the day.

- Never tie your dog or let him run free while he's wearing a choke collar. Choke collars can easily hook on something and strangle him.

- The Chinese Shar-Pei and the Chow have blue-black tongues instead of pink ones.

- The smallest breed of dog is the Chihuahua.

- Poodles, Bedlington Terriers, Bichon Frises, Schnauzers and Soft-Coated Wheaten Terriers don't shed.

- Terriers and toy breeds usually bark the most.

- The Basenji is often called the barkless dog.

- Labs and Golden Retrievers are fast learners, making them easy to train.

- Climate counts when deciding on a breed. Collies and Pugs will be unhappy in hot, humid climates. But the Italian Greyhound and Chihuahua originated in hot climes. The heat won't bother them, but winter will. They'll need insulation in the form of dog apparel to protect them from the cold. And as you might think, heavy-coated dogs like the Saint Bernard, Siberian Husky and the Newfy thrive in cooler weather.

- Apartment dwellers, consider the Dachshund and Cairn Terrier. Both can be content in small quarters.

- Fido's fitness counts towards insuring a longer, healthier life. In this arena, you're the one in control. The most common cause of ill health in canines is obesity. Approximately 60% of all adult dogs are overweight or will become overweight due to lack of physical activity and overfeeding. Much like humans, the medical consequences of obesity include liver, heart and orthopedic problems. As little as a few extra pounds on a small dog can lead to health-related complications.

- Is your pooch pudgy? Place both thumbs on your dog's backbone and then run your fingers along his rib cage. If the bony part of each rib cannot be easily felt, your dog may be overweight. Another quickie test - stand directly over your dog while he's standing. If you can't see a clearly defined waist behind his rib cage, he's probably too portly.

- The infamous Red Baron owned a Great Dane named Moritz who lived on the military base with the pilot. The Red Baron fondly referred to Moritz as his "little lapdog."

- Frederick the Great owned an estimated 30 Greyhounds. His love of these animals led him to coin the saying: "The more I see of men, the more I love my dogs."

- It's easier than you might think to help your dog lose those extra pounds. Begin by eliminating unnecessary table scraps. Cut back a small amount on the kibble or canned dog food you normally feed your pooch. If he's accustomed to two full cups each day, reduce that amount to 1 3/4 cups instead. If you normally give your pooch biscuits every day, cut the amount in half. And don't feel guilty. Stick with the program and you'll eventually see a reduction in weight. Slow and steady is the best approach. And don't let yourself imagine that your dog is being deprived of anything. Even when he looks at you with a woebegone expression, remember you're doing him a favor by helping him reduce and you're adding years of good health to his life.

- Exercise. Not enough can be said about the benefits. Establish a daily exercise routine. Awaken twenty minutes earlier every morning and take a brisk mile walk. Instead of watching TV after dinner, walk off some calories. Your pooch's overall good health, as well as your own, will be greatly enhanced.

- According to a survey, 90% of dog owners speak to their dogs like humans, walk or run with their dogs and take pictures of them; 72% take their pups for car rides; 51% hang Christmas stockings for their dogs; 41% watch movies and TV with their pooches; 29% sign Rover's name to greeting cards and more than 20% buy homes with their dogs in mind, carry photos of Fido with them and arrange the furniture so FiFi can see outside.

- Lewis and Clark traveled with a 150-pound Newfoundland named "Seamen." The pooch was a respected member of the expedition and his antics were included in the extensive diaries of these famous explorers.

- The English have a saying: The virtues of a dog are its own, its vices those of its master.

- Lord Byron, in his eulogy to his dog Boatswain, wrote, "One who possessed beauty without vanity, strength without insolence, courage without ferocity, and all the virtues of man without his vices."

- "Be Kind To Animals Week" (May 7-13) was established in 1915. Recognized by Congress, it is the oldest week of its kind in the nation.

- The "Always Faithful" Memorial, which honors Dogs of War, was unveiled on June 20, 1994. It now stands on the US Naval Base in Orote Point, Guam.

- During WWII, Dobermans were official members of the US Marine Corps combat force.

- The domestic dog dates back more than 50,000 years.

- Ghandi once said, "The greatness of a nation and its moral progress can be judged by the way its animals are treated."

- England's Dickin Medal is specifically awarded to dogs for bravery and outstanding behavior in wartime.

- Napoleon's wife, Josephine, had a Pug named Fortune. She relied on the animal to carry secret messages under his collar to Napoleon while she was imprisoned at Les Carnes.

- Former First Lady Barbara Bush said: "An old dog that has served you long and well is like an old painting. The patina of age softens and beautifies, and like a master's work, can never be replaced by exactly the same thing, ever again."

- Dogs and Halloween don't mix. Even the mellowest of pooches can become frightened and overexcited by all the commotion. Save the candy collecting and chocolate for the kids and leave the dog at home.

- Most outdoor dogs suffer from unnoticed parasites like fleas.

- In winter, the water in an outdoor dog dish can freeze within an hour.

- In summer, dogs consume large quantities of water. Bowls need frequent refilling.

EVERYTHING YOU WANT TO KNOW ABOUT PET CARE AND WHO TO ASK

Whether you've always had a pet or you're starting out with your first, the following organizations and hotlines can provide information on the care, feeding and protection of your loyal companion.

Pet behavior information.

Tree House Animal Foundation: If you are concerned with canine aggression, nipping, biting, housebreaking or other behavioral problems, the Tree House Animal Foundation will try to help. But don't wait until the last minute. Call for advice early on and your animal's problems will be easier to correct. Consultation is free, except for applicable long distance charges. Call (312) 784-5488, 9AM to 5PM CST, seven days a week.

Dial-Pet: Health and care topics for pets including dogs, cats, horses, small animals, exotics and fish. Call (630) 844-2862 any time. (You must have a touch-tone phone to use the service). Basically, it's a hotline sponsored by the Chicago Veterinary Medical Association. Vets who belong to the organization write and then record 5-7 minute messages on subjects ranging from ear problems to training tips. There's no charge except applicable long distance charges. Or, if you prefer, write for a list of topics to: DIAL-PET, Chicago Veterinary Medical Association, 161 S. Lincolnway, North Aurora, IL 60542.

Animal Behavior Helpline: This organization is sponsored by the San Francisco Society for the Prevention of Cruelty to Animals. It will assist you in solving canine behavioral problems. Staffed by volunteers, you may reach a recorded message. However, calls are returned within 48 hours by volunteers trained in animal behavior. Problems such as chewing, digging and barking are cited as the most common reasons dog owners call. Housebreaking tips, how to deal with aggression and other topics are covered. Callers are first asked to speak about the problem and describe what steps have been taken to correct inappropriate behavior. After evaluating the information, specific advice is given to callers. The consultation is free, except for applicable long distance charges or collect call charges when a counselor returns your call. Messages can be left any time. Call (415) 554-3075.

Poison Control Center: There are two telephone numbers for this organization. The 800 number is an emergency line for both veterinarians and pet owners for poisoning control information. Calls are taken by the veterinarian-staffed National Animal Poison Control Center at the University of Illinois. When calling the 800 number, there is a charge of $30 per case. Every call made to the 800 number is followed up by the NAPCC. The 900 number is for non-emergency questions and there is no follow up. Callers to the 900 line pay $20 for the first 5 minutes and $2.95 for every minute thereafter with a minimum charge of $20 and a maximum of $30.

When calling the NAPCC, be prepared to provide your name and address and the name of the suspected poison (be specific). If the product is manufactured by a company that is a member of the Animal Product Safety Service - the company may pay the charge.

In all other cases, you pay for the consultation. You must also provide the animal species, breed, sex, and weight. You will be asked to describe symptoms as well as unusual behavior. This detailed information is critical - it can mean the difference between life or death for your animal.

For emergencies only, call (800) 548-2423. Major credit cards are accepted. For non-emergency questions, call (900) 680-0000. The Poison Control Center offers poison control information by veterinarians 24 hours a day, 7 days a week.

Poinsettias and other toxic plants... pretty but deadly.

During the Christmas holidays, the risk of poisoning and injury is greater for your pet. If eaten, poinsettias and holly berries for example, can be fatal. Although there are conflicting reports on the effects of mistletoe, play it safe and keep your pet away from this plant. Be alert - swallowed tree ornaments, like ribbon and tinsel can cause choking and/or intestinal problems.

Christmas wiring is another potential problem. Your pet can be electrocuted by chewing on it. And don't forget about the dangers of poultry bones. The same goes for aluminum foil including the disposable pans that are used at holiday time.

Keep your trash inaccessible. And remember that the holidays are a source of excitement and stress to both people and animals. Maintain your pet's feeding and walking schedules and provide plenty of TLC and playtime. Then everyone, including your animal, will find the holidays more enjoyable.

FYI...

common plants* that are toxic to pets

Amaryllis (bulbs)
Appleseeds (cyanide)
Azalea
Boxwood
Caladium
Cherry Pits (cyanide)
Climbing Lily
Daffodil (bulb)
Delphinium
Dumb Cane
English Ivy
Foxglove
Holly
Hydrangea
Japanese Yew
Jerusalem Cherry
Laburnum
Laurel
Marigold
Mistletoe (berries)
Mushrooms
Nightshade
Peach
Poinsettia
Privet
Rhubarb
Stinging Nettie
Tobacco
Walnuts
Yew

Andromeda
Arrowgrass
Bittersweet
Buttercup
Castor Bean
Chokecherry
Crown of Thorns
Daphne
Dieffenbachia
Elephant Ear
Elderberry
Hemlock
Hyacinth (bulbs)
Iris (bulb)
Jasmine (berries)
Jimsonweed
Larkspur
Locoweed
Marijuana
Monkshood
Narcissus (bulb)
Oleander
Philodendron
Poison Ivy
Rhododendron
Snow on the Mountain
Toadstool
Tulip (bulb)
Wisteria

NOTE: This is only a partial list.

PET POEMS, PROCLAMATIONS, PRAYERS...& DOG BISCUITS

Ode to Travel with Pets

We're all set to roam

Going far from home

With doggies in tow

Off shall we go

To wander and gadabout

Since travel we're mad about

With Rosie and Max by my side

We'll all go for a ride

As we travel for miles

And bring about smiles

Rosie will grin

Max will chime in

Driving into the sunset

Odometers all set

But enough of these word rhymes

Let's roll with the good times!

— Eileen Barish, November 1994

Alone Again

I wish someone would tell me what it is
    That I've done wrong.
Why I have to stay chained up and
    Left alone so long.
They seemed so glad to have me
    When I came here as a pup.
There were so many things we'd do
    While I was growing up.
They couldn't wait to train me as a
    Companion and a friend.
And told me how they'd never fear
    Being left alone again.
The children said they'd feed me and
    Brush me every day.
They'd play with me and walk me
    If only I could stay.
But now the family "Hasn't time,"
    They often say I shed.
They do not even want me in the house
    Not even to be fed.
The children never walk me.
    They always say "Not now!"
I wish that I could please them.
    Won't someone tell me how?
All I had, you see, was love.
    I wish they would explain
Why they said they wanted me
    Then left me on a chain?

                — Anonymous

A Dogs Bill of Rights

I have the right to give and receive
    unconditional love.
I have the right to a life that is beyond
    mere survival.
I have the right to be trained so I do not become
    the prisoner of my own misbehavior.
I have the right to adequate food and
    medical care.
I have the right to fresh air and green grass.
I have the right to socialize with people
    and dogs outside my family.
I have the right to have my needs
    and wants respected.
I have the right to a special time with
    my people .
I have the right to only be bred
    responsibly if at all.
I have the right to be foolish and silly, and
    to make my person laugh.
I have the right to earn my person's trust
    and be trusted in return.
I have the right to be forgiven.
I have the right to die with dignity.
I have the right to be remembered well.

A Dog's Prayer

Treat me kindly, my beloved master, for no heart in all the world is more grateful for kindness, than the loving heart of mine.

Do not break my spirit with a stick, for though I should lick your hand between the blows, your patience and understanding will more quickly teach me the things you would have me do.

Speak to me often, for your voice is the world's sweetest music as you must know by the fierce wagging of my tail when your footstep falls up on my waiting ear.

When it is cold and wet, please take me inside...for I am now a domesticated animal, no longer used to bitter elements...and I ask no greater glory than the privilege of sitting at your feet beside the hearth...though had you no home, I would rather follow you through ice and snow, than rest upon the softest pillow in the warmest home in all the land...for you are my God...and I am your devoted worshipper.

Keep my pan filled with fresh water, for although I should not reproach you were it dry, I cannot tell you when I suffer thirst. Feed me clean food, that I may stay well, to romp and play and do your bidding, to walk by your side, and stand ready willing and able to protect you with my life, should your life be in danger.

And beloved master, should the Great Master see fit to deprive me of my health or sight, do not turn away from me. Rather hold me gently in your arms, as skilled hands grant me the merciful boon of eternal rest...and I will leave you knowing with the last breath I draw, my fate was ever safest in your hands.

Rainbow Bridge

There is a bridge connecting Heaven and Earth. It is called the Rainbow Bridge because of its many colors. Just this side of the Rainbow Bridge there is a land of meadows, hills and valleys with lush green grass.

When a beloved pet dies, the pet goes to this place. There is always food and water and warm spring weather. The old and frail animals are young again. Those who are maimed are made whole again. They play all day with each other.

There is only one thing missing. They are not with their special person who loved them on Earth. So each day they run and play until the day comes when one suddenly stops play-ing and looks up! The nose twitches! The ears are up! The eyes are staring! And this one suddenly runs from the group!

You have been seen, and when you and your special friend meet, you take him or her in your arms and embrace. Your face is kissed again and again, and you look once more into the eyes of your trusting pet.

Then you cross Rainbow Bridge together, never again to be separated.

— Anonymous

FIDO FACT:
• **Lord Byron, in his eulogy to his dog Boatswain, wrote, "One who possessed beauty without vanity, strength without insolence, courage without ferocity, and all the virtues of man without his vices."**

Homemade dog biscuits

(Makes about 8 dozen biscuits)

<u>Ingredients</u>
3 1/2 cups all-purpose flour
2 cups whole wheat flour
1 cup rye flour
1 cup cornmeal
2 cups cracked wheat bulgur
1/2 cup nonfat dry milk
4 tsp. salt
1 package dry yeast
2 cups chicken stock or other liquid
1 egg and 1 tbsp. milk (to brush on top)

Combine all the dry ingredients except the yeast. In a separate bowl, dissolve the yeast in 1/4 cup warm water. To this, add the chicken stock. (You can use bouillon, pan drippings or water from cooking vegetables.) Add the liquid to the dry ingredients. Knead mixture for about 3 minutes. Dough will be quite stiff. If too stiff, add extra liquid or an egg. Preheat oven to 300 degrees. Roll the dough out on a floured board to 1/4" thickness, then immediately cut into shapes with cookie cutters. Place on an ungreased cookie sheet and brush with a wash of egg and milk. Place in oven. After 45 minutes, turn off the heat and leave biscuits overnight in the oven to get bone hard.

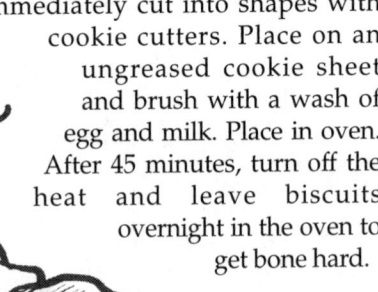

UNITED STATES DIRECTORY OF PET-FRIENDLY LODGING

ALABAMA

ABBEVILLE

BEST WESTERN INN
Hwy 431 S, Rt 2
(36310)
Rates: $34-$98
Tel: (334) 585-5060
(800) 528-1234

ALABASTER

**SHELBY
MOTOR LODGE**
Hwy 31 S,
P. O. Box 279 (35007)
Rates: $33-$35
Tel: (205) 663-1070

ALBERTVILLE

**KINGS INN
MOTOR MOTEL**
7080 Hwy 431 N
(35950)
Rates: $30-$45
Tel: (205) 878-6550
(800) 490-8589

ALEXANDER
CITY

BOB WHITE MOTEL
1020 Airport Dr
(35010)
Rates: $26-$33
Tel: (205) 234-4215

ANDALUSIA

DAYS INN
1604 E Bypass (36420)
Rates: $46-$100
Tel: (334) 427-0050
(800) 329-7466

**CHARTER HOUSE
INN**
US 84 Bypass E
(36420)
Rates: $47-$49
Tel: (334) 222-7511

TOWN LINE MOTEL
US 29 Bypass W
(36420)
Rates: $32-$35
Tel: (334) 222-3191

ANNISTON

MOTEL 6
202 Grace St (36203)
Rates: $25-$29
Tel: (205) 831-5463
(800) 466-8356

RAMADA INN
300 Quintard Ave
(36201)
Rates: $40-$105
Tel: (205) 237-9777
(800) 272-6232

SUPER 8 MOTEL
6220 McLellan Blvd
(36206)
Rates: $33-$55
Tel: (205) 820-1000
(800) 800-8000

ARDMORE

THE COUNTRY INN
I-65 AL53 Exit 365
(35620)
Rates: n/a
Tel: (205) 423-6699

ATHENS

BEST WESTERN INN
P. O. Box 816 (35611)
Rates: $37-$53
Tel: (205) 233-4030
(800) 321-0122

BUDGET INN
606 Hwy 31 S
(35611)
Rates: $28-$35
Tel: (205) 232-0131

DAYS INN
1322 Hwy 72 E
(35611)
Rates: $32-$80
Tel: (205) 233-7500
(800) 329-7466

THE MARK MOTEL
210 Hwy 31 St
(35611)
Rates: $27-$31
Tel: (205) 232-6200

**TOWN & COUNTRY
MOTEL**
2414 Hwy 31 S
(35611)
Rates: $20-$29
Tel: (205) 232-2700

WELCOME INN
1101 Hwy 31 S
(35611)
Rates: $34-$41
Tel: (205) 233-6944
(800) 824-6834

ATTALLA

COLUMBIA INN
915 E Fifth Ave
(35954)
Rates: $29-$70
Tel: (205) 570-0117

ECONO LODGE
507 Cherry St
(35954)
Rates: $47-$59
Tel: (205) 538-9925
(800) 424-4777

HOLIDAY INN EXP
801 Cleveland Ave
(35954)
Rates: $52-$58
Tel: (205) 538-7861
(800) 465-4329

AUBURN

**AUBURN CONF CTR
& MOTOR LODGE**
P. O. Box 3467
(36830)
Rates: $36-$59
Tel: (334) 821-7001

**AUBURN UNIVERSITY
HOTEL & CONF CTR**
241 S College St
(36830)
Rates: $49-$105
Tel: (334) 821-8200
(800) 228-2876

HAMPTON INN
2430 S College St
(36830)
Rates: $46-$56
Tel: (334) 821-4111
(800) 426-7866

**HEART OF AUBURN
MOTEL**
333 South College
(36830)
Rates: $37-$49
Tel: (334) 887-3462
(800) 843-5634

**QUALITY INN
UNIVERSITY CTR**
1577 S College St
(36830)
Rates: $59-$200
Tel: (334) 821-7001
(800) 221-2222

BESSEMER

**BEST WESTERN
BESSEMER INN**
1098 9th Ave SW
(35021)
Rates: $36-$45
Tel: (205) 424-0880
(800) 528-1234

MOTEL 6
1000 Shiloh Ln
(35020)
Rates: $25-$29
Tel: (205) 426-9646
(800) 440-6000

RAMADA INN
1021 9th Ave SW
(35021)
Rates: $51-$150
Tel: (205) 272-6232
(800) 272-6232

BIRMINGHAM

**BEST SUITES
OF AMERICA**
140 State Farm Pkwy
(35209)
Rates: $75-$81
Tel: (205) 940-9990
(800) 237-8466

ALABAMA 97

BEST WESTERN CIVIC CENTER
2230 Civic Center Blvd (35203)
Rates: $55-$105
Tel: (205) 328-6320
(800) 528-1234

BUDGETEL INN
513 Cahaba Park Cir (35242)
Rates: $49+
Tel: (205) 995-9990
(800) 428-3438

CROWN STERLING SUITES
2300 Woodcrest Pl (35209)
Rates: n/a
Tel: (205) 879-7400
(800) 433-4600

ECONO LODGE
103 Green Springs Hwy (35209)
Rates: $37-$47
Tel: (800) 424-4777

HAMPTON INN MOUNTAIN BROOK
2731 US Hwy 280 (35223)
Rates: $61-$75
Tel: (205) 870-7822
(800) 426-7866

HAMPTON INN SOUTH
1466 Montgomery Hwy (35216)
Rates: $59-$73
Tel: (205) 822-2224
(800) 426-7866

HOWARD JOHNSON
275 Oxmoor Rd (35209)
Rates: $33-$49
Tel: (205) 942-0919
(800) 446-4656

HOWARD JOHNSON MOTOR LODGE
1485 Montgomery Hwy (35216)
Rates: $42-$70
Tel: (205) 823-4300
(800) 446-4656

LA QUINTA INN
905 11th Ct W (35204)
Rates: $45-$56
Tel: (205) 324-4510
(800) 531-5900

MICROTEL
251 Summit Pkwy (35209)
Rates: $29-$39
Tel: (205) 945-5550
(800) 275-8047

MOTEL BIRMINGHAM
7905 Crestwood Blvd (35210)
Rates: $45-$56
Tel: (205) 956-4440
(800) 338-9275

MOUNTAIN BROOK INN
2800 Hwy 280 (35223)
Rates: $89-$99
Tel: (205) 870-3100
(800) 523-7771

PARLIAMENT HOUSE HOTEL
420 S 20th St (35233)
Rates: $55-$65
Tel: (205) 322-7000
(800) 579-5464

RED ROOF INN
151 Vulcan Rd (35209)
Rates: $42-$49
Tel: (205) 942-9414
(800) 843-7663

RESIDENCE INN BY MARRIOTT
3 Green Hill Pkwy (35242)
Rates: $69-$170
Tel: (205) 991-8686
(800) 331-3131

SUPER 8 MOTEL
1813 Crestwood Blvd (35210)
Rates: $40+
Tel: (205) 956-3650
(800) 800-8000

SUPER 8 BIRMINGHAM NORTH
624 Decatur Hwy (35068)
Rates: $39-$89
Tel: (205) 841-2200
(800) 800-8000

THE TUTWILER
2021 Park Place N (35205)
Rates: $109
Tel: (205) 322-2100
(800) 845-1787

BOAZ

BEST WESTERN BOAZ OUTLET CENTER
751 US 431 S (35957)
Rates: $38-$50
Tel: (205) 593-8410
(800) 528-1234

BOAZ INN MOTEL
Rt 5, Box 218
Hwy 431 N (35957)
Rates: $30-$40
Tel: (205) 593-2874
(800) 443-9096

KEY WEST INN
10535 Alabama Hwy (35957)
Rates: $43-$53
Tel: (205) 593-0800
(800) 833-0555

CAMDEN

BASSMASTER MOTEL
125 Broad St (36726)
Rates: n/a
Tel: (334) 682-4254

DAYS INN
39 Camden Bypass (36726)
Rates: $40-$83
Tel: (334) 682-4555
(800) 329-7466

CEDAR BLUFF

CEDAR BLUFF MOTEL
Hwy 9 (35959)
Rates: $40
Tel: (205) 779-6868

JR'S MARINA & MOTEL
Country Rd 102 (35959)
Rates: n/a
Tel: (205) 779-6461

RIVERSIDE CAMPGROUND & MOTEL
Rt 1, Box 83-H (35959)
Rates: $30-$60
Tel: (205) 779-6117
(800) 292-9324

CHILDERSBURG

DAYS INN
33669 US Hwy 280 (35044)
Rates: $39-$55
Tel: (205) 378-6007
(800) 329-7466

CLANTON

BEST WESTERN INN
109 Bradberry Ln (35045)
Rates: $40-$56
Tel: (800) 528-1234

HOLIDAY INN
2000 Holiday Inn Dr (35045)
Rates: $45-$55
Tel: (205) 755-0510
(800) 465-4329

KEY WEST INN
2045 7th St (35045)
Rates: $46
Tel: (205) 755-8500
(800) 833-0555

RODEWAY INN
2301 7th St (35045)
Rates: $30-$45
Tel: (205) 755-4049
(800) 228-2000

SHONEY'S INN
946 Lake Mitchell Rd (35045)
Rates: $41-$55
Tel: (205) 280-0306
(800) 222-2222

COLLINSVILLE

HOJO INN
Hwy 68 W (35961)
Rates: $46-$52
Tel: (205) 524-2114
(800) 446-4656

CULLMAN

ANDERSON MOTEL
1834 Second Ave NW (35055)
Rates: $35+
Tel: (205) 734-0122

BEST WESTERN FAIRWINDS INN
1917 Commerce Ave NW (35055)
Rates: $45-$75
Tel: (205) 737-5009
(800) 528-1234

DAYS INN
1841 4th St SW (35055)
Rates: $35-$60
Tel: (205) 739-3800
(800) 329-7466

FRIENDLY VILLAGE MOTEL
607 2nd Ave NW (35055)
Rates: n/a
Tel: (205) 734-2770

HOLIDAY INN EXP
I-65 Exit 304 (35055)
Rates: n/a
Tel: (800) 465-4329

HOWARD JOHNSON LODGE
I-65 & US 278 W (35056)
Rates: $40-$54
Tel: (205) 739-4603
(800) 446-4656

MOTEL I-65
14466 Hwy 91 (35077)
Rates: $26
Tel: (205) 287-1114

RAMADA INN
I-65 & Hwy 69 (35056)
Rates: $48-$80
Tel: (205) 737-7275
(800) 446-4656

SUPER 8 MOTEL
Hwy 157 & I-65 Exit 310 (35057)
Rates: $40-$55
Tel: (205) 734-8854
(800) 800-8000

DALEVILLE

ECONO LODGE
444 N Daleville Ave (36322)
Rates: $45-$55
Tel: (334) 598-6304
(800) 424-4777

GREEN HOUSE INN & LODGE
761 S Daleville Ave (36322)
Rates: $28-$38
Tel: (334) 598-1475

DAPHNE

EASTERN SHORE MOTEL
29070 Hwy 98 (36526)
Rates: $35
Tel: (334) 626-6601

LEGACY INN
70 Hwy 90 (36526)
Rates: $41-$48
Tel: (334) 626-3500

DECATUR

DAYS INN
810 6th Ave NE (35602)
Rates: $40-$50
Tel: (205) 355-3520
(800) 329-7466

DECATUR MOTOR LODGE
3429 Hwy 31 S (35601)
Rates: $36-$44
Tel: (205) 355-0190
(800) 660-0730

HOLIDAY INN
1101 6th Ave NE (35601)
Rates: $49-$74
Tel: (205) 355-3150
(800) 465-4329

RAMADA LIMITED
1317 E Hwy 67 (35602)
Rates: $37-$63
Tel: (205) 353-0333
(800) 272-6232

DEMOPOLIS

HERITAGE MOTEL
1324 Hwy 80 (36732)
Rates: $25
Tel: (334) 289-1175

RIVERVIEW INN
Hwy 45 N (36732)
Rates: $35-$37
Tel: (334) 289-0690

DOTHAN

COMFORT INN
3595 Ross Clark Cir (36303)
Rates: $50-$79
Tel: (334) 793-9090
(800) 221-2222

DAYS INN
2841 Ross Clark Cir (36301)
Rates: $36-$45
Tel: (334) 793-2550
(800) 329-7466

EASTGATE INN
1885 E Main St (36302)
Rates: $27-$34
Tel: (334) 794-6643

HAMPTON INN
3071 Ross Clark Cir (36301)
Rates: $50-$75
Tel: (334) 671-3700
(800) 426-7866

HOLIDAY INN
3053 Ross Clark Cir (36301)
Rates: $40-$62
Tel: (334) 794-6601
(800) 465-4329

HOLIDAY INN SOUTH
2195 Ross Clark Cir (36301)
Rates: $48-$58
Tel: (334) 794-8711
(800) 465-4329

MOTEL 6
2907 Ross Clark Cir (36301)
Rates: $29-$35
Tel: (334) 793-6013
(800) 440-6000

OLYMPIA SPA GOLF RESORT
P.O. Box 6108 (36302)
Rates: $39
Tel: (334) 677-3321

RAMADA INN
3011 Ross Clark Cir (36301)
Rates: $50-$68
Tel: (334) 692-0031
(800) 272-6232

TOWN TERRACE MOTEL
251 N Oates St (36303)
Rates: $25-$29
Tel: (334) 792-1135

ELBA

RIVIERA MOTEL
154 Yelverton (36323)
Rates: $28-$35
Tel: (334) 897-2204

ENTERPRISE

COMFORT INN
615 Hwy 84 Bypass (36330)
Rates: $48
Tel: (334) 395-2304
(800) 221-2222

RAMADA INN
630 Glover Ave (36330)
Rates: $40-$50
Tel: (334) 347-6262
(800) 272-6232

EQUALITY

REAL ISLAND MARINA
2700 Real Island Rd (36026)
Rates: $69
Tel: (334) 857-2741

EUFAULA

BEST WESTERN EUFAULA INN
1337 Hwy 431S (36027)
Rates: $32-$52
Tel: (334) 687-3900
(800) 528-1234

DAYS INN
1521 Eufaula Ave (36027)
Rates: $40-$70
Tel: (334) 687-1000
(800) 329-7466

HOLIDAY INN
631 E Barbour St (36027)
Rates: $48-$65
Tel: (334) 687-2021
(800) 465-4329

EUTAW

**KIRKWOOD
BED & BREAKFAST**
111 Kirkwood Dr
(35462)
Rates: $75
Tel: (205) 372-9009

EVERGREEN

DAYS INN
901 Liberty Hill Dr
(36401)
Rates: $35-$60
Tel: (334) 578-2100
(800) 329-7466

ECONO LODGE
Bates Rd (36401)
Rates: $38-$45
Tel: (334) 578-4701
(800) 424-4777

FAIRHOPE

**BARONS
ON THE BAY MOTEL**
701 S Mobile Ave
(36532)
Rates: $29-$85
Tel: (334) 929-8000

**MARCELLA'S TEA
ROOM & INN B&B**
114 Fairhope Ave
(36532)
Rates: $80
Tel: (334) 990-8520

**OAK HAVEN
COTTAGES**
355 S Mobile St
(36532)
Rates: $40-$50
Tel: (334) 928-5431

FAYETTE

JOURNEY'S INN
2502 Temple Ave N
(35555)
Rates: $39-$42
Tel: (205) 932-6727

FLORENCE

**BEST WESTERN
EXECUTIVE INN**
504 S Court St
(35630)
Rates: $39-$54
Tel: (205) 766-2331
(800) 528-1234

COMFORT INN
400 S Court St
(35630)
Rates: $40-$45
(800) 221-2222

HO JO INN
1241 Florence Blvd
(35630)
Rates: n/a
Tel: (205) 764-5421
(800) 446-4656

SUPER 8 MOTEL
P.O. Box 1457
(35631)
Rates: $35-$47
Tel: (205) 757-2167
(800) 800-8000

FOLEY

**BEST WESTERN
RIVIERA INN**
1504 S McKenzie St
(36535)
Rates: $50-$99
Tel: (800) 528-1234

KEY WEST INN
2520 S McKenzie St
(36535)
Rates: $36-$78
Tel: (334) 943-1241
(800) 833-0555

FORT PAYNE

ADAMS OUTDOORS
6102 Mitchell Rd NE
(35967)
Rates: $20-$60
Tel: (205) 845-2988

**MOUNTAIN VIEW
MOTEL**
2302 Gault Ave S
(35967)
Rates: n/a
Tel: (205) 845-2303

GADSDEN

BROADWAY INN
2704 W Meighan
Blvd (35904)
Rates: $29-$39
Tel: (205) 543-3790

DAYS INN
1600 Rainbow Dr
(35901)
Rates: $52-$62
Tel: (205) 543-1105
(800) 329-7466

**FRIENDLY
VILLAGE INN**
2110 Rainbow Dr
(35901)
Rates: $30-$45
Tel: (205) 547-3041

**GADSDEN
AIRPORT MOTEL**
1612 West Grand
Ave (35901)
Rates: n/a
Tel: (800) 441-7344

RODEWAY INN
2110 Rainbow Dr
(35901)
Rates: $35-$45
Tel: (205) 547-9053
(800) 228-2000

TRAVEL 8 MOTEL
3909 W Meighan
Blvd (35904)
Rates: $30-$34
Tel: (205) 543-7261

GAYLESVILLE

THE LIGHTHOUSE
Hwy 68,
P. O. Box 167 (35973)
Rates: n/a
Tel: (205) 779-8400

GREENVILLE

BEST WESTERN INN
106 Cahaba Rd
(36037)
Rates: $40-$55
Tel: (334) 344-3410
(800) 528-1234

ECONO LODGE
946 Fort Dale Rd
(36037)
Rates: $42-$49
Tel: (334) 382-3118
(800) 424-4777

HOLIDAY INN
941 Fort Dale Rd
(36037)
Rates: $40-$53
Tel: (334) 382-2651
(800) 465-4329

THRIFTY INN
105 Bypass (36037)
Rates: $38+
Tel: (334) 382-6671

GULF SHORES

BEST WESTERN
P.O. Box 398 (36547)
Rates: $59-$275
Tel: (334) 948-2711
(800) 788-4557

**BON SECOUR
LODGE**
16730 Oyster Bay Pl
(36542)
Rates: n/a
Tel: (334) 968-7814

GULF PINES MOTEL
245 E 22nd Ave
(36542)
Rates: n/a
Tel: (334) 968-7911

**LIGHTHOUSE
MOTEL**
P. O. Box 233 (36542)
Rates: $55-$110
Tel: (334) 948-6188

RAMADA LIMITED
610 W Beach Blvd
(36547)
Rates: $35-$135
Tel: (334) 948-8141
(800) 272-6232

**ROGERS' CASTLE
BY THE SEA**
P. O. Box 1038
(36547)
Rates: $145
Tel: (334) 948-6954

**WADE WARD
RENTALS**
1709 Gulf Shore
Pkwy (36542)
Rates: n/a
Tel: (334) 968-8423
(800) 634-1429

**YOUNG'S
BY THE SEA**
401 E Beach Blvd
(36547)
Rates: $29-$100
Tel: (334) 948-4181
(800) 245-0032

GUNTERSVILLE

DAYS INN
14040 Hwy 431 S
(35976)
Rates: $40-$65
Tel: (205) 582-3200
(800) 329-7466

HOLIDAY INN
2140 Gunter Ave
(35976)
Rates: n/a
Tel: (205) 582-2220
(800) 465-4329

**MAC'S LANDING
MOTEL**
7001 Val-Monte Dr
(35976)
Rates: $47-$93
Tel: (205) 582-1000

**OVERLOOK
MOUNTAIN LODGE**
13045 Hwy 431
(35976)
Rates: $34-$36
Tel: (205) 582-3256

HAMILTON

BEST WESTERN
2031 Military St S
(35570)
Rates: $54-$64
Tel: (205) 921-7831
(800) 528-1234

**HAMILTON
HOLIDAY MOTEL**
Bexar Ave, Hwy 78 W
(35570)
Rates: $30
Tel: (205) 921-2171

HANCEVILLE

MOTEL I-65
14466 Hwy 91
(35077)
Rates: n/a
Tel: (205) 287-1114

HALEYVILLE

HALEYVILLE MOTEL
Rt 6, Box 449 (35565)
Rates: $32
Tel: (205) 486-2263

HEFLIN

HOJO INN
Rt 2, Box 44T (36264)
Rates: $32-$50
Tel: (205) 463-2900
(800) 446-4656

HOOVER

DAYS INN-SOUTH
1535 Montgomery
Hwy (35216)
Rates: $36-$125
Tel: (205) 822-6030
(800) 329-7466

HOPE HULL

DAYS INN
7725 Mobile Hwy
(36043)
Rates: $35-$39
Tel: (800) 329-7466

HUNTSVILLE

BUDGETEL
4890 University Dr
(35816)
Rates: $37-$54
Tel: (205) 830-8999
(800) 428-3438

**CARRIAGE INN/
MASTER HOST INNS**
3911 Univeristy Dr
(35816)
Rates: $30
Tel: (205) 722-0880
(800) 251-1962

**ECONO LODGE-
PARKWAY**
1304 N Memorial
Pkwy (35801)
Rates: $25-$30
Tel: (800) 424-4777

**EXECUTIVE LODGE
SUITE HOTEL**
1535 Sparkman Dr
(35816)
Rates: $39-$89
Tel: (205) 830-8600
(800) 248-4772

HILTON INN
401 Williams Ave
(35801)
Rates: $91-$103
Tel: (205) 533-1400
(800) 445-8667

**HOLIDAY INN
EXPRESS**
5808 Univeristy Dr
(35816)
Rates: $53-$62
Tel: (205) 721-1000
(800) 465-4329

**HOLIDAY INN
SPACE CENTER**
3810 University Dr
(35816)
Rates: $49-$71
Tel: (205) 837-7171
(800) 465-4329

HOWARD JOHNSON
4404 University Dr
(35816)
Rates: $30-$46
Tel: (205) 837-3250
(800) 446-4656

**LA QUINTA INN
RESEARCH PARK**
4870 Univeristy Dr
(35816)
Rates: $41-$47
Tel: (205) 830-2070
(800) 531-5900

**LA QUINTA INN
SPACE CENTER**
3141 Univeristy Dr
(35816)
Rates: $41-$47
Tel: (205) 533-0756
(800) 531-5900

MARRIOTT HOTEL
Tranquility Base
(35805)
Rates: $94-$104
Tel: (205) 830-2222
(800) 228-9290

MOTEL 6
3200 University Dr
(35816)
Rates: $24-$28
Tel: (205) 539-8448
(800) 440-6000

**RADISSON
SUITE HOTEL**
6000 Memorial
Pkwy S (35802)
Rates: $65-$107
Tel: (205) 882-9400
(800) 333-3333

RAMADA INN
3502 Memorial
Pkwy SW (35801)
Rates: $48-$71
Tel: (205) 881-6120
(800) 272-6232

RED CARPET INN
2700 Memorial
Pkwy SW (35801)
Rates: $28-$35
Tel: (205) 536-6661

**RESIDENCE INN
BY MARRIOTT**
4020 Independence
Dr (35816)
Rates: $80-$100
Tel: (205) 837-8907
(800) 331-3131

VILLAGER LODGE
3100 University Dr
(35816)
Rates: $29-$35
Tel: (205) 533-0610
(800) 328-7829

JASPER

TRAVEL-RITE INN
200 Mallway Dr
(35501)
Rates: $33-$36
Tel: (205) 221-1161

LAFAYETTE

**HILL-WARE-
DOWDELL
MANSION**
203 2nd Ave SW
(36862)
Rates: n/a
Tel: (205) 864-7861

LEEDS

SUPER 8 MOTEL
2451 Moody Pkwy
(35004)
Rates: $33-$39
Tel: (800) 800-8000

LINDEN

COUNTRY INN
705 S Main St
(36748)
Rates: n/a
Tel: (334) 295-8704

LOXLEY

WIND CHASE INN
13156 N Hickory
(36551)
Rates: $46
Tel: (334) 964-4444

MADISON

DAYS INN AIRPORT
102 Arlington Dr
(35758)
Rates: $40-$46
Tel: (205) 772-9550
(800) 329-7466

**FEDERAL SQUARE
MOTEL & SUITES**
8781 Hwy 20 W
(35758)
Rates: $40
Tel: (205) 772-8470
(800) 458-1639

MOTEL 6
8995 Hwy 20 (35758)
Rates: $29-$33
Tel: (205) 772-7479
(800) 440-6000

MILLBROOK

HOLIDAY INN
P. O. Box A (36054)
Rates: $43-$55
Tel: (334) 285-3420
(800) 465-4329

MOBILE

**ADAM'S MARK
OF MOBILE**
64 Water St (36602)
Rates: $59-$145
Tel: (334) 438-4000
(800) 444-2326

**BEST INNS
OF MOBILE**
156 Beltline Hwy S
(36608)
Rates: $47+
Tel: (334) 343-4911
(800) 237-8466

**BEST SUITES
OF AMERICA**
150 Beltline Hwy S
(36608)
Rates: $78-$81
Tel: (334) 343-4949
(800) 237-8466

**BEST WESTERN
BATTLESHIP INN**
2701 Battleship
Pkwy (36601)
Rates: $56-$61
Tel: (334) 432-2703
(800) 528-1234

**THE CLARION
HOTEL**
3101 Airport Blvd
(36606)
Rates: $59-$99
Tel: (334) 476-6400
(800) 221-2222

DAYS INN
5480 Inn Dr (36619)
Rates: $36-$44
Tel: (334) 661-8181
(800) 329-7466

DAYS INN AIRPORT
3650 Airport Blvd
(36608)
Rates: $40-$90
Tel: (334) 344-3410
(800) 329-7466

DRURY INN
824 Beltline Hwy S
(36609)
Rates: $55-$62
Tel: (334) 344-7700
(800) 325-8300

**ECONO LODGE-
MIDTOWN**
1 Beltline Hwy S
(36606)
Rates: $46-$48
Tel: (334) 479-5333
(800) 424-4777

ECONOMY INN
1119 Government St
(36604)
Rates: $33-$35
Tel: (334) 433-8800
(800) 826-0778

**FIESTA PLAZA
HOTEL**
4101 Airport Blvd
(36606)
Rates: $65-$200
Tel: (334) 476-6400

HOLIDAY INN
I-10 Tillmans Corner
(36619)
Rates: $51-$95
Tel: (334) 666-5600
(800) 465-4329

**HOLIDAY INN
DOWNTOWN**
301 Government St
(36602)
Rates: $60-$125
Tel: (334) 694-0100
(800) 465-4329

HOLIDAY INN I-65
850 S Beltline (36616)
Rates: $60-$75
Tel: (334) 342-3220
(800) 465-4329

HOWARD JOHNSON
3132 Government
Blvd (36606)
Rates: $45-$65
Tel: (334) 471-2402
(800) 446-4656

LA QUINTA INN
816 S Beltline (36609)
Rates: $51-$75
Tel: (334) 343-4051
(800) 531-5900

MOTEL 6
5488 Inn Rd (36619)
Rates: $33-$37
Tel: (334) 660-1483
(800) 440-6000

MOTEL 6-AIRPORT
400 Beltline Hwy S
(36608)
Rates: $36-$40
Tel: (334) 343-8448
(800) 466-8356

MOTEL 6-EAST
1520 Matzenger Dr
(36605)
Rates: $29-$33
Tel: (334) 473-1603
(800) 466-8356

MOTEL 6-WEST
5470 Tillmans
Corner Pkwy
(36619)
Rates: $28-$34
Tel: (334) 660-1483

OAK TREE INN
255 Church St
(36602)
Rates: n/a
Tel: (334) 433-6923

OLSSON'S MOTEL
4137 Government
Blvd (36693)
Rates: $25-$29
Tel: (334) 661-5331
(800) 332-1004

**RAMADA INN
ON THE BAY**
1525 Battleship
Pkwy (36633)
Rates: $45-$100
Tel: (334) 626-7200
(800) 272-6232

RED ROOF INN-N.
33 Beltline Hwy S
(36606)
Rates: $37-$46
Tel: (334) 476-2004
(800) 843-7663

RED ROOF INN-S.
5450 Coca Cola Rd
(36619)
Rates: $38-$47
Tel: (334) 666-1044
(800) 843-7663

SHONEY'S INN
5472-A Tillmans
Corner Pkwy (36619)
Rates: $52-$65
Tel: (334) 660-1520
(800) 222-2222

MONROEVILLE

DAYS INN
Rt 3, Hwy 21 S
(36460)
Rates: $40-$48
Tel: (334) 243-3257
(800) 329-7466

KNIGHTS INN
Rt 3, Box 227 (36460)
Rates: $34-$42
Tel: (334) 743-3154
(800) 553-2666

MONTEVALLO

**RAMSAY
CONFERENCE CNTR**
6280 Vine St (35115)
Rates: n/a
Tel: (205) 665-6280

MONTGOMERY

**BEST SUITES
OF AMERICA**
5155 Carmichael Rd
(36106)
Rates: $81
Tel: (334) 270-3223
(800) 237-8466

**BEST WESTERN
LODGE**
977 W South Blvd
(36105)
Rates: $37-$69
Tel: (334) 288-5740
(800) 528-1234

**BEST WESTERN
MONTICELLO INN**
5835 Monticello Dr
(36117)
Rates: $47-$55
Tel: (334) 288-0876
(800) 528-1234

BUDGETEL
5225 Carmichael Rd
(36106)
Rates: $35-$45
Tel: (334) 277-6000
(800) 428-3438

CAPITOL INN
205 N Goldthwaite St
(36104)
Rates: $32-$38
Tel: (334) 265-3844

COLISEUM INN
1550 Federal Dr
(36107)
Rates: $35
Tel: (334) 265-0586
(800) 876-6835

**COLONEL'S REST
BED & BREAKFAST**
11091 Atlanta Hwy
(36117)
Rates: n/a
Tel: (334) 215-0380

DAYS INN
2625 Zelda Rd
(36107)
Rates: $44-$110
Tel: (334) 269-9611
(800) 329-7466

DAYS INN-SOUTH
1150 South Blvd
(36105)
Rates: $30-$49
Tel: (334) 281-8000
(800) 329-7466

ECONO LODGE
4135 Troy Hwy
(36116)
Rates: $39-$45
Tel: (334) 284-3400
(800) 424-4777

EMBASSY SUITES
300 Tallapoosa St
(36104)
Rates: $99
Tel: (334) 269-5055
(800) 362-2779

**HOLIDAY INN
AIRPORT I-65**
1100 W South Blvd
(36105)
Rates: $52-$54
Tel: (334) 281-1660
(800) 465-4329

**HOLIDAY INN
EAST HOLIDOME**
1185 Eastern Blvd
(36117)
Rates: $81
Tel: (334) 272-0370
(800) 465-4329

**HOLIDAY INN
HOTEL & SUITES**
120 Madison Ave
(36104)
Rates: $69-$75
Tel: (334) 264-2231
(800) 465-4329

INN SOUTH HOTEL
4243 Inn South Ave
(36105)
Rates: $33-$35
Tel: (334) 288-7999
(800) 642-0890

LA QUINTA INN
1280 East Blvd
(36117)
Rates: $56
Tel: (334) 271-1620
(800) 531-5900

MOTEL 6
1051 Eastern Bypass
(36117)
Rates: $36-$40
Tel: (334) 277-6748
(800) 466-8356

RED CARPET INN
1015 W South Blvd
(36105)
Rates: $30
Tel: (334) 281-6111
(800) 251-1962

REGENCY INN
1771 Congressman
Dickinson Dr
(36109)
Rates: $43
Tel: (334) 260-0444
(800) 824-0737

**RESIDENCE INN
BY MARRIOTT**
1200 Hilmar Ct
(36109)
Rates: $94-$119
Tel: (334) 270-3300
(800) 331-3131

SCOTTISH INNS
7237 Troy Hwy
(36064)
Rates: $28-$38
Tel: (334) 288-1501
(800) 251-1962

STATEHOUSE INN
924 Madison Ave
(36104)
Rates: $51
Tel: (334) 265-0741
(800) 552-7099

VILLAGER INN
2750 Chestnut St
(36107)
Rates: $34-$40
Tel: (334) 834-4055
(800) 328-7829

MOODY

SUPER 8 MOTEL
2451 Moody Pkwy
(35004)
Rates: $39-$45
Tel: (205) 640-7091
(800) 800-8000

MUSCLE SHOALS

DAYS INN
2700 Woodward Ave
(35651)
Rates: $34-$47
Tel: (205) 383-3000
(800) 329-7466

NORTHPORT

**BEST WESTERN
CATALINA INN**
2015 Hwy 82 W
(35476)
Rates: $40-$50
Tel: (205) 339-5200
(800) 528-1234

OPELIKA

**BEST WESTERN
MARINER INN**
1002 Columbus
Pkwy (36801)
Rates: $29-$46
Tel: (334) 749-1461
(800) 528-1234

DAYS INN
1014 Anand Ave
(36801)
Rates: $45-$100
Tel: (334) 749-5080
(800) 329-7466

ECONO LODGE
1105 Columbus
Pkwy (36081)
Rates: $28-$44
Tel: (334) 745-0988
(800) 424-4777

MOTEL 6
1015 Columbus
Pkwy (36801)
Rates: $24-$28
Tel: (334) 745-0988
(800) 440-6000

ORANGE BEACH

**ISLAND DUNES
RESORT**
P. O. Box 9 (36561)
Rates: n/a
Tel: (334) 981-4255

ISLAND & RENTALS
26021 Perdido Beach
Blvd (36561)
Rates: $35-$120
Tel: (334) 981-2909
(800) 450-2909

OXFORD

DAYS INN
#1 Recreation Dr
(36203)
Rates: $43-$90
Tel: (205) 835-0300
(800) 329-7466

ECONO LODGE
25 Elm St (36203)
Rates: $39-$99
Tel: (205) 831-9480
(800) 424-4777

HOLIDAY INN
P. O. Box 3308
(36203)
Rates: $38-$60
Tel: (205) 831-3410
(800) 465-4329

HOWARD JOHNSON
P. O . Box 3308
(36203)
Rates: $32-$42
Tel: (205) 835-3988
(800) 446-4656

RAMADA INN
900 Hwy 21 S
(36203)
Rates: n/a
Tel: (800) 272-6232

SAVE INN
25 Elm St (36203)
Rates: $21-$28
Tel: (205) 831-9480

OZARK

BEST WESTERN OZARK INN
Hwy 231 S (36361)
Rates: $42-$46
Tel: (334) 774-5166
(800) 528-1234

CANDLELIGHT MOTEL
2015 Hwy 231 S
(36360)
Rates: $25-$30
Tel: (334) 774-4947

HOLIDAY INN
151 US 231 N
(36360)
Rates: $42-$54
Tel: (334) 774-7300
(800) 465-4329

PELL CITY

BEST WESTERN RIVERSIDE INN
11900 Hwy 78
(35125)
Rates: $45-$79
Tel: (205) 338-3381
(800) 528-1234

PHENIX CITY

BEST WESTERN AMERICAN MOTOR LODGE
1600 Hwy 280
Bypass (36867)
Rates: $40-$49
Tel: (334) 298-8000
(800) 528-1234

PINE APPLE

TURKEY HOLLOW "MAN" HUNTING LODGE
Rt 2, Box 57 (36768)
Rates: n/a
Tel: (334) 746-2159

PINE HILL

PINE FOREST MOTOR LODGE
Hwy 5 & 10,
P. O. Box 400 (36769)
Rates: $31
Tel: (334) 963-4375

PRATTVILLE

DAYS INN
I-65 & Hwy 31 N,
P. O. Box 388 (36067)
Rates: $44-$61
Tel: (334) 365-3311
(800) 329-7466

ROGERSVILLE

SECOND CREEK COUNTRY
Rt 4, Box 341-B
(35652)
Rates: n/a
Tel: (205) 247-1183

SCOTTSBORO

DAYS INN
1106 John T Reid
Pkwy (35768)
Rates: $39-$65
Tel: (205) 574-1212
(800) 329-7466

RAINBOW INN
1401 E Willow St
(35768)
Rates: $33-$39
Tel: (205) 574-1115

SELMA

BEST WESTERN INN
1915 W Highland
Ave (36701)
Rates: $46-$62
Tel: (334) 872-1900
(800) 528-1234

GRACE HALL B&B
506 Lauderdale St
(36701)
Rates: $75-$110
Tel: (334) 875-5744

GRAYSTONE MOTEL
1200 W Highland
Ave (36701)
Rates: $29-$39
Tel: (334) 874-6681

HOLIDAY INN
1806 US 80W (36701)
Rates: $48-$58
Tel: (334) 872-0461
(800) 465-4329

PASSPORT INN
601 Highland Ave
(36701)
Rates: $35
Tel: (334) 872-3451
(800) 251-1962

TRAVELERS INN OF SELMA
2006 W Highland
Ave (36701)
Rates: $35-$49
Tel: (334) 875-1200

SHEFFIELD

HOLIDAY INN
4900 Hatch Blvd
(35660)
Rates: $58-$72
Tel: (205) 381-4710
(800) 465-4329

RAMADA INN
4205 Hatch Blvd
(35660)
Rates: $45-$125
Tel: (205) 381-3743
(800) 272-6232

SHORTER

DAYS INN
327 Shorter Depot
Rd (36075)
Rates: $43-$85
Tel: (334) 727-6034
(800) 329-7466

SPANISH FORT

RAMADA INN ON THE BAY
1525 Battleship
Pkwy (36633)
Rates: $45-$65
Tel: (334) 626-7200
(800) 272-6232

THOMASVILLE

BEST WESTERN INN
1200 Mosley Dr
(36784)
Rates: $37-$44
Tel: (334) 636-0614
(800) 528-1234

OPINE B & B
HC 4, Box 222
(36784)
Rates: $60-$85
Tel: (334) 636-5206

TROY

ECONO LODGE
1013 Hwy 231
(36081)
Rates: $42-$52
Tel: (334) 566-4960
(800) 424-4777

HOLIDAY INN EXPRESS
Hwy 231,
P. O. Box 564 (36081)
Rates: $44
Tel: (334) 670-0012
(800) 465-4329

SCOTTISH INNS
186 Hwy 231 N
(36081)
Rates: $35
Tel: (334) 566-4090
(800) 251-1962

TUSCALOOSA

LA QUINTA INN
4122 McFarland
Blvd E (35405)
Rates: $56
Tel: (205) 349-3270
(800) 531-5900

MASTERS ECONOMY INN
3600 McFarland
Blvd (35405)
Rates: $34
Tel: (205) 556-2010

MOTEL 6
4700 McFarland
Blvd E (35405)
Rates: $35
Tel: (205) 759-4942
(800) 440-6000

RAMADA INN
631 Skyland Blvd E
(35405)
Rates: $37-$125
Tel: (205) 759-4431
(800) 272-6232

TUSCUMBIA

KEY WEST INN
1800 Hwy 72 W
(35674)
Rates: $41-$46
Tel: (205) 383-0700
(800) 833-0555

UNION SPRINGS

MASTER RACK LODGE
Rt 1, Box 95-A
(36089)
Rates: n/a
Tel: (334) 738-4000
(800) 489-2825

WETUMPKA

WESTUMPKA INN
8534 Hwy 231 N
(36092)
Rates: $24
Tel: (334) 567-9316

YORK

DAYS INN
17700 Hwy 17
(36925)
Rates: $59-$64
Tel: (205) 392-5485
(800) 329-7466

ALASKA

ANCHOR POINT

ANCHOR RIVER INN
P. O. Box 154 (99556)
Rates: $50-$85
Tel: (800) 435-8531

ANCHORAGE

A COMFORT B & B
8501 Brookridge Dr
(99504)
Rates: n/a
Tel: (907) 338-0453

A COUSIN OF MINE
4406 Forest Rd
(99517)
Rates: n/a
Tel: (907) 248-3462

ADAMS PLACE B & B
5701 E 97th Ave
(99516)
Rates: n/a
Tel: (907) 346-3604

**ALASKAN
FRONTIER B & B**
1011 E Tudor Rd
#160 (99503)
Rates: $85-$150
Tel: (907) 345-6556

**ANCHORAGE
EAGLE NEST HOTEL**
4110 Spenard Rd
(99517)
Rates: $40-$170
Tel: (907) 243-3433
(800) 848-7852

ARCTIC INN MOTEL
842 W Int'l Airport
Rd (99518)
Rates: n/a
Tel: (907) 561-1328

**AURORA WINDS
B & B RESORT**
7501 Upper
O'Malley (99516)
Rates: $55-$95
Tel: (907) 346-2533

BEAR DEN B & B
3002 154th St (99516)
Rates: n/a
Tel: (907) 345-4012

**BEST WESTERN
BARRATT INN**
4616 Spenard Rd
(99517)
Rates: $84-$166
Tel: (907) 243-3131
(800) 528-1234

BIG TIMBER MOTEL
2037 E 5th Ave
(99501)
Rates: n/a
Tel: (907) 272-2541

BLACK ANGUS INN
1430 Gambell St
(99501)
Rates: n/a
Tel: (907) 272-7503
(800) 770-0707

BONANZA LODGE
4455 Juneau St
(99503)
Rates: n/a
Tel: (907) 563-3590

CHELSEA INN
3836 Spenard Rd
(99517)
Rates: $40-$100
Tel: (907) 276-5002
(800) 934-9106

**COMFORT INN
HERITAGE SUITES**
111 Ship Creek Ave
(99501)
Rates: $75-$250
Tel: (907) 277-6887
(800) 221-2222

**DAYS INN
DOWNTOWN**
321 E 5th Ave
(99501)
Rates: $59-$125
Tel: (907) 276-7226
(800) 329-7466

8TH AVENUE HOTEL
P. O. Box 200089
(99520)
Rates: $79-$145
Tel: (907) 274-6213
(800) 478-4837

**EXECUTIVE SUITE
HOTEL**
4360 Spenard Rd
(99517)
Rates: $69-$259
Tel: (907) 243-6366
(800) 770-6366

GLACIER WAY B & B
2051 Glacier St
(99508)
Rates: n/a
Tel: (907) 244-7148

**HILLSIDE ON
GAMBELL**
2150 Gambell St
(99503)
Rates: $46-$100
Tel: (907) 258-6006
(800) 478-6008

JENSEN B & B
6450 Downey Finch
Dr (99516)
Rates: n/a
Tel: (907) 345-4840

**MERRILL FIELD
MOTEL**
420 Sitka St (99501)
Rates: $50-$85
Tel: (907) 276-4547

MUSH INN MOTEL
333 Concrete St
(99501)
Rates: n/a
Tel: (907) 277-4554
(800) 478-4554

PUFFIN INN
4400 Spenard Rd
(99517)
Rates: $60-$116
Tel: (907) 243-4044
(800) 478-3346

QUPQUIGIAQ B & B
3801 Spenard Rd
(99517)
Rates: n/a
Tel: (907) 562-5681

**REGAL ALASKAN
HOTEL**
4800 Spenard Rd
(99517)
Rates: $89-$260
Tel: (907) 243-2300
(800) 544-0553

**SIXTH & B
BED & BREAKFAST**
145 W Sixth Ave
(99501)
Rates: $38-$105
Tel: (907) 279-5293

6 BAR E RANCH B & B
11401 Totem Rd
(99516)
Rates: n/a
Tel: (907) 346-2665

**SOURDOUGH
VISITORS LODGE**
801 E Erickson St
(99520)
Rates: $69-$125
Tel: (907) 279-4148
(800) 777-3716

SPENARD MOTEL
3960 Spenard Rd
(99517)
Rates: n/a
Tel: (907) 243-6917

SUPER 8 MOTEL
3501 Minnesota Dr
(99503)
Rates: $68-$88
Tel: (907) 276-8884
(800) 800-8000

VALARIAN VISIT B & B
1536 Valarian St
(99508)
Rates: $50-$75
Tel: (907) 274-5760

BETTLES

**BETTLES LODGE
WILDERNESS TRIPS
& CABINS**
P. O. Box 27-VP
(99726)
Rates: $95-$145
Tel: (907) 692-5111
(800) 770-5111

BIG LAKE

BIG LAKE MOTEL
P. O. Box 520728
(99652)
Rates: $65-$75
Tel: (907) 892-7976

CANTWELL

REINDEER MOUNTAIN LODGE
MP 210 Parks Hwy (99729)
Rates: n/a
Tel: (907) 768-2420

CIRCLE SPRINGS

CIRCLE HOT SPRINGS RESORT
P. O. Box 254 (99730)
Rates: n/a
Tel: (907) 520-5113

COOK INLET WEST SIDE

CHINITNA BAY LODGE
P. O. Box 233032
(Anchorage 99523)
Rates: $1100 3 days)
Tel: (907) 522-2715

COOPER LANDING

SUNRISE INN MOTEL
MP 45-A, Sterling Hwy (99572)
Rates: $39-$99
Tel: (907) 595-1222

DELTA JUNCTION

ALASKA 7 MOTEL
3548 Richardson Hwy (99737)
Rates: n/a
Tel: (907) 895-4848

BLACK SPRUCE LODGE
2740 Old Richardson Hwy (99737)
Rates: n/a
Tel: (907) 895-4668

DELTA INTERNATIONAL HOSTEL
Main St. USA North (99737)
Rates: n/a
Tel: (907) 895-5074

SUMMIT LAKE LODGE
Mile 195 Richardson Hwy(99737)
Rates: n/a
Tel: (907) 822-3969

DENALI NATL PARK AND PRESERVE

DENALI GRIZZLY BEAR CABINS & CAMPGROUND
P. O. Box 7 (99755)
Rates: $49-$99
Tel: (907) 683-2696

EARTHSONG LODGE
P. O. Box 89
(Healy 99743)
Rates: $95-$115
Tel: (907) 683-2863

MCKINLEY/DENALI PRIVATE CABINS
P. O. Box 90 (99755)
Rates: $65-$115
Tel: (907) 683-2733

MT. MCKINLEY MOTOR LODGE
P. O. Box 77 (99755)
Rates: $98
Tel: (907) 683-1240

SOURDOUGH CABINS
P. O. Box 118 (99755)
Rates: $80-$144
Tel: (907) 683-2773

EAGLE RIVER

MOUNTAIN AIR BED & BREAKFAST
HC83, Box 1652 (99577)
Rates: $40-$60
Tel: (907) 696-3116

SHOOTING STAR BED & BREAKFAST
19211 Upper Skyline Dr (99577)
Rates: n/a
Tel: (907) 696-1748

ELFIN COVE

TANAKU LODGE
P. O. Box 72 (99825)
Rates: n/a
Tel: (800) 482-6258

FAIRBANKS

AAAA CARE BED & BREAKFAST
557 Fairbanks St (99709)
Rates: $65-$125
Tel: (907) 479-2447
(800) 478-2705

A PIONEER B & B
1119 Second Ave (99701)
Rates: $55-$85
Tel: (907) 452-5393

ALASKA MOTEL
1546 Cushman St (99701)
Rates: $45-$70
Tel: (907) 456-6393

CAPTAIN BARTLETT INN
1411 Airport Way (99701)
Rates: $130-$139
Tel: (907) 452-1888
(800) 544-7528

CHENA HOT SPRINGS RESORT
P. O. Box 73440 (99707)
Rates: $65-$160
Tel: (907) 452-7867
(800) 478-4681 (AK)

CHENA RIVER B & B
1001 Dolly Varden Ln (99709)
Rates: $45-$100
Tel: (907) 479-2532

FOX CREEK B & B
2498 Elliott Hwy (99712)
Rates: $54-$70
Tel: (907) 457-5494

HILLSIDE B & B
310 Rambling Road (99712)
Rates: $35-$55
Tel: (907) 457-2664

NORTH WOODS LODGE
P. O. Box 83615 (99708)
Rates: $20-$87
Tel: (907) 479-5300
(800) 478-5305

OLD F. E. GOLD CAMP
5550 Old Steese Hwy N (99712)
Rates: n/a
Tel: (907) 389-2414

REGENCY FAIRBANKS HOTEL
95 Tenth Ave (99701)
Rates: $70-$250
Tel: (907) 452-3200
(800) 348-1340

SOURDOUGH B & B
1146 Gilmore Tr. (99708)
Rates: $75-$90
Tel: (907) 457-6684

SUCH A DEAL B & B
P. O . Box 82527 (99708)
Rates: $45-$65
Tel: (907) 474-8159

SUPER 8 MOTEL
1909 Airport Rd (99701)
Rates: $68-$88
Tel: (907) 451-8888
(800) 800-8000

GAKONA

GAKONA JUNCTION VILLAGE
P. O. Box 222 (99586)
Rates: $55-$98
Tel: (800) 962-1933

GIRDWOOD

THE RESORT INN
NHN Crystal Ave (99587)
Rates: $75
Tel: (907) 783-2492

GLENNALLEN

THE NEW CARIBOU HOTEL
P. O. Box 329 (99588)
Rates: $79-$115
Tel: (907) 822-3302
(800) 478-3302

GUSTAVUS

BEAR TRACK INN
255 Rink Creek Rd
(99826)
Rates: $2395/week
Tel: (907) 697-3017
(888) 697-2284

A PUFFIN'S B & B
(1/4 Mile Logging Rd)
Box 3 (99826)
Rates: $85-$125
Tel: (907) 697-2260

TRI BED & BREAKFAST
P. O. Box 214 (99826)
Rates: $90
Tel: (907) 697-2425

HAINES

CAPTAIN'S CHOICE MOTEL
P. O. Box 392 (99827)
Rates: $67-$150
Tel: (907) 766-3111
(800) 247-7153

EAGLE'S NEST MOTEL
P. O. Box 250 (99827)
Rates: $60-$95
Tel: (907) 766-2891
(800) 354-6009

FORT SEWARD LODGE & SALOON
P. O. Box 307 (99827)
Rates: $45-$85
Tel: (907) 766-2009
(800) 478-7772

FORT WM. H. SEWARD BED & BREAKFAST
P. O. Box 5 (99827)
Rates: $58-$125
Tel: (907) 766-2856

MOUNTAIN VIEW MOTEL
P. O. Box 62 (99827)
Rates: $50-$81
Tel: (907) 766-2900
(800) 478-2902

THUNDERBIRD MOTEL
242 Dalton St (99827)
Rates: $58-$68
Tel: (800) 327-2556

HATCHER PASS

HATCHER PASS LODGE
P.O. Box 763 (99645)
Rates: $95-$110
Tel: (907) 745-5897

HEALY

DOME HOME B & B
P. O. Box 262 (99743)
Rates: $35-$90
Tel: (907) 683-1239

HOMER

BEST WESTERN BIDARKA INN
575 Sterling Hwy
(99603)
Rates: $78-$108
Tel: (907) 235-8148
(800) 528-1234

BRIGITTE'S BAVARIAN BED & BREAKFAST
P. O. Box 2391
(99603)
Rates: $95
Tel: (907) 235-6620

DRIFTWOOD INN
135 W Bunnell Ave
(99603)
Rates: $40-$128
Tel: (907) 235-8019
(800) 478-8019

HERITAGE HOTEL/LODGE
147 E. Pioneer Ave
(99603)
Rates: $50-$80
Tel: (907) 235-7787

HOME B & B/ SEEKINS
P. O. Box 1264
(99603)
Rates: $50-$80
Tel: (907) 235-8996

LAKEWOOD INN
984 Ocean Dr #1
(99603)
Rates: n/a
Tel: (907) 235-6144

LAND'S END RESORT
4786 Homer Spit Rd
(99603)
Rates: $46-$140
Tel: (907) 235-2500

OCEAN SHORES MOTEL
3500 Crittenden Dr
(99603)
Rates: $45-$95
Tel: (800) 770-7775

PATCHWORK FARM B & B
P. O. Box 1654
(99603)
Rates: n/a
Tel: (907) 235-7368

SEASIDE FARM RETREAT LODGING
58335 E End Rd
(99603)
Rates: $55
Tel: (907) 235-7850

SUNDMARKS B & B
East Hill Rd (99603)
Rates: n/a
Tel: (907) 235-5188

INDIAN

CABIN COMFORT BED & BREAKFAST
HC 52, Box 8802
(99540)
Rates: n/a
Tel: (907) 653-7726

JUNEAU

BLUEBERRY LODGE BED & BREAKFAST
9436 N Douglas
Hwy (99801)
Rates: $65-$75
Tel: (907) 463-5886

THE DRIFTWOOD LODGE
435 Willoughby Ave
(99801)
Rates: $62-$98
Tel: (907) 586-2280
(800) 544-2239

JAN'S VIEW B & B
P. O. Box 32245
(99803)
Rates: $40-$65
Tel: (907) 463-5897

PROSPECTOR HOTEL
375 Whittier St
(99801)
Rates: $74-$144
Tel: (907) 586-3737
(800) 331-2711

SUPER 8 MOTEL
2295 Trout St (99801)
Rates: $68-$88
Tel: (907) 789-4858
(800) 800-8000

KENAI

CAPT. BLIGH'S BEAVER CREEK LODGE & GUIDES
P. O.Box 4300
(Soldotna 99669)
Rates: Package
Tel: (907) 262-7919
(907) 283-7550

KENAI KINGS INN
P. O. Box 1080
(99611)
Rates: $74-$104
Tel: (907) 283-6060

KENAI PENINSULA

ALASKA MOUNTAIN VIEW CABINS
P. O. Box 423
(Sterling 99672)
Rates: $50-$145
Tel: (907) 262-4827

ANGLER'S LODGE & FISH CAMP
P. O. Box 508-VG
(Sterling 99672)
Rates: $49-$150
Tel: (907) 262-1747

KENAI MAGIC LODGE & FISHING
2440 E Tudor Rd
#205
(Anchorage 99507)
Rates: $99-$158
Tel: (888) 262-6644

KENAI PENINSULA CONDOS
P. O. Box 3416
(Soldotna 99669)
Rates: $79-$99
Tel: (800) 362-1383

KENAI WILDERNESS LODGE
3074 Commercial Dr
(Anchorage 99501)
Rates: $40
Tel: (907) 262-4390

MORGAN'S LANDING CABIN RENTALS
P. O. Box 422
(Sterling 99672)
Rates: $75-$125
Tel: (907) 262-8343

KETCHIKAN

BEST WESTERN THE LANDING
3434 Tongass Ave
(99901)
Rates: $85-$150
Tel: (907) 225-5166
(800) 528-1234

THE GILMORE HOTEL
P. O. Box 6814
(99901)
Rates: $51-$102
Tel: (907) 225-9423
(800) 275-9423

INGERSOLL HOTEL
303 Mission St
(99901)
Rates: $57-$99
Tel: (907) 225-2124
(800) 478-2124

MILLAR STREET HOUSE B & B
P. O. Box 7281
(99901)
Rates: $55-$80
Tel: (907) 225-1258
(800) 287-1607

SUPER 8 MOTEL
2151 Sea Level Dr
(99901)
Rates: $68-$88
Tel: (907) 225-9058
(800) 800-8000

KODIAK

BUSKIN RIVER INN
1395 Airport Way
(99615)
Rates: $100-$110
Tel: (907) 487-2700
(800) 544-2202

KALSIN BAY INN
P. O. Box 1696
(99615)
Rates: n/a
Tel: (907) 486-2659

KODIAK B & B
308 Cope St (99615)
Rates: $72
Tel: (907) 486-5367

NORTHLAND RANCH RESORT
P. O. Box 2376
(99615)
Rates: n/a
Tel: (907) 486-5578

PALMER

HATCHER PASS B & B
HC01, Box 6797-D
(99645)
Rates: $55
Tel: (907) 745-4210

PETERSBURG

NARROWS INN
P. O. Box 1048
(99833)
Rates: $70
Tel: (907) 772-4284

SCANDIA HOUSE
110 Nordic Dr
(99833)
Rates: n/a
Tel: (907) 772-4281

SALCHA

SALCHA RIVER LODGE
P. O. Box 111 (99714)
Rates: n/a
Tel: (907) 488-2233

SEWARD

AROKA INN
P. O. Box 2448
(99664)
Rates: $45-$105
Tel: (907) 224-8975

"THE FARM" B & B
P. O. Box 305 (99664)
Rates: $40-$95
Tel: (907) 224-2300

SITKA

BARANOF WILDERNESS LODGE
P. O. Box 2187-VP
(99835)
Rates: $995
(Two night package)
Tel: (916) 582-8132
(CA)

SUPER 8 MOTEL
404 Sawmill Creek
Rd (99835)
Rates: $78-$104
Tel: (907) 747-8804
(800) 800-8000

SKAGWAY

GOLDEN NORTH HOTEL
P. O. Box 431 (99840)
Rates: $54-$81
Tel: (907) 983-2294

WIND VALLEY LODGE
P. O. Box 354 (99840)
Rates: $62-$72
Tel: (907) 983-2236

SOLDOTNA

BEST WESTERN KING SALMON MOTEL
33546 Kenai Spur
Hwy (99669)
Rates: $89-$119
Tel: (907) 262-5857
(800) 528-1234

KENAI RIVER LODGE
393 Riverside Dr
(99669)
Rates: $50-$100
Tel: (907) 262-4292

RAVEN MT. FARM B & B
P. O. Box 344
(Kasilof 99610)
Rates: $45-$76
Tel: (907) 262-9186

SOARING EAGLE LODGE
HC01, Box 1203
(99669)
Rates: $50-$100
Tel: (907) 337-1223

TALKEETNA

ALASKA LOG CABIN B & B
#1A Beaver Rd
(99676)
Rates: $55-$85
Tel: (907) 733-2668

LATITUDE 62 LODGE
P. O. Box 478 (99676)
Rates: n/a
Tel: (907) 733-2262

TOK

CLEFT OF THE ROCK BED & BREAKFAST
Sundog Trail
Box 122 (99780)
Rates: $48-$65
Tel: (907) 883-4219

SNOWSHOE MOTEL
P. O. Box 559 (99780)
Rates: $42-$77
Tel: (907) 883-4511

STAGE STOP B & B
P. O. Box 69 (99780)
Rates: $40-$85
Tel: (907) 883-5338

TOK LODGE
P. O. Box 135 (99780)
Rates: $85
Tel: (907) 883-2851

YOUNG'S MOTEL
Mile 1313
Alaska Hwy (99780)
Rates: $55-$78
Tel: (907) 883-4411

TRAPPER CREEK

MCKINLEY FOOTHILLS BED & BREAKFAST
P. O. Box 13089
(99683)
Rates: $80+
Tel: (907) 773-1454

WRANGELL

HARDING'S OLD SOURDOUGH LODGE
P. O. Box 1062 (99929)
Rates: $45-$150
Tel: (800) 874-3613

VALDEZ

**TIEKEL RIVER
LODGE**
Richardson Hwy
Mile 56, (99686)
Rates: $45-$85
Tel: (907) 822-3259

TOTEM INN
P. O. Box 648 (99686)
Rates: $59-$114
Tel: (907) 835-4443

WILLOW

**SHEEP CREEK
LODGE**
Mile 88, Parks Hwy
(99688)
Rates: n/a
Tel: (907) 495-6227

WOOD-TIKCHIK
STATE PARK

**MAURICE'S
FLOATING LODGE**
P. O. Box 1261
(Dillingham 99576)
Rates: n/a
Tel: (800) FLOAT44

ARIZONA

AJO

A SIESTA MOTEL
2561 N Ajo-Gila
Bend Hwy (85321)
Rates: $26-$38
Tel: (520) 387-6569

MARINE MOTEL
1966 N 2nd Ave
(85321)
Rates: $30-$69
Tel: (520) 387-7626

ALPINE

**CORONADO TRAILS
CABINS & RV PARK**
25302 Hwy 191(85920)
Rates: $45+
Tel: (520) 339-4772

TAL-WI-WI LODGE
40 County Road 2220
(85920)
Rates: $49-$89
Tel: (520) 339-4319

APACHE LAKE

**APACHE LAKE
MARINA & RESORT**
Hwy 88 (85290)
Rates: $39-$64
Tel: (520) 467-2511

ASH FORK

**STAGECOACH
MOTEL**
823 Park Ave (86320)
Rates: $20-$30
Tel: (520) 637-2278

BENSON

**BEST WESTERN
QUAIL HOLLOW INN**
699 N Ocotillo St
(85602)
Rates: $38-$48
Tel: (520) 586-3646
(800) 528-1234

BISBEE

THE BISBEE INN B & B
45 OK St (85603)
Rates: $29-$45
Tel: (520) 432-5131

MAIN STREET INN
26 Main St (85603)
Rates: $40-$95
Tel: (520) 432-5237
(800) 467-5237

**MILE HIGH COURT
TRAVEL LODGE**
901 Tombstone
Canyon (85603)
Rates: $35-$50
Tel: (520) 432-4636

PARK PLACE B & B
200 E Vista in
Warren (85603)
Rates: $40-$60
Tel: (520) 990-0682
(800) 456-0682

**SAN JOSE LODGE
& RV PARK**
1002 Naco Hwy
(85603)
Rates: $35+
Tel: (520) 432-5761

BULLHEAD CITY

ARIZONA BLUFFS
2220 Karis Dr (86442)
Rates: $192/week
Tel: (520) 763-3839

**COLORADO RIVER
RESORT**
434 Riverglen Dr
(86440)
Rates: $25-$65
Tel: (520) 754-4101

DAYS INN
2200 Karis Dr (86442)
Rates: $38-$125
Tel: (520) 758-1711
(800) 225-6903 (AZ)

**DESERT RANCHO
MOTEL**
1041 Hwy 95 (86430)
Rates: $30-$45
Tel: (520) 754-2578

LA PLAZA INN
1978 Hwy 95 (86442)
Rates: $26-$35
Tel: (520) 763-8080

**LAKE MOHAVE
RESORT & MARINA**
At Katherine
Landing (86430)
Rates: $60-$83
Tel: (520) 754-3245
(800) 752-9669

MOTEL 6
1616 Hwy 95 (86442)
Rates: $26-$36
Tel: (520) 763-1002
(800) 440-6000

**RIVER QUEEN
RESORT**
125 Long Ave
(86430)
Rates: $35-$53
Tel: (520) 754-3214

SUNRIDGE HOTEL
839 Landon Dr
(86429)
Rates: $59+
Tel: (520) 754-4700

TRAVELODGE
2360 4th St (86429)
Rates: $40-$45
Tel: (520) 754-3000
(800) 578-7878

CAMERON

**CAMERON
TRADING POST**
Hwy 89, P. O. Box 83
(86020)
Rates: $49-$79
Tel: (520) 679-2231

CAMP VERDE

**BEST WESTERN
CLIFF CASTLE
LODGE**
Middle Verde Rd,
P. O. Box 3430
(86322)
Rates: $42-$150
Tel: (520) 567-6611
(800) 528-1234

FORT VERDE MOTEL
628 S Main St
(86322)
Rates: $35+
Tel: (520) 567-3486

CAREFREE

THE BOULDERS
34631 N Tom
Darlington Rd
(85377)
Rates: $240-$525
Tel: (602) 488-9009
(800) 553-1717

CASA GRANDE

**BEST WESTERN
CASA GRANDE
SUITES**
665 Via Del Cielo
(85222)
Rates: $59-$99
Tel: (520) 836-1600
(800) 528-1234

**FRANCISCO
GRANDE RESORT
& GOLF CLUB**
26000 Gila Bend Hwy
(85222)
Rates: $56-$196
Tel: (520) 836-6444
(800) 237-4238

**HOLIDAY INN
CASA GRANDE**
777 N Pinal Ave
(85222)
Rates: $58-$72
Tel: (520) 426-3500
(800) 858-4499 (AZ)
(800) 465-4329 (US)

MOTEL 6
4965 N Sunland Gin
Rd (85222)
Rates: $35-41
Tel: (520) 836-3323
(800) 466-8356

SE-TAY MOTEL
901 N Pinal Ave
(85222)
Rates: $29-$40
Tel: (520) 836-7489

SUNLAND INN
7190 S Sunland Gin
Rd (85222)
Rates: $32-$38
Tel: (520) 836-5000

CHAMBERS

**BEST WESTERN
CHIEFTAIN INN**
P. O. Box 39 (86502)
Rates: $54-$69
Tel: (520) 688-2754
(800) 528-1234

CHANDLER

ALOHA MOTEL
445 N Arizona Ave
(85224)
Rates: $79-$200
Tel: (602) 963-3403

SUPER 8 MOTEL
7171 W Chandler
Blvd (85226)
Rates: $41-$66
Tel: (602) 961-3888
(800) 800-8000

**WYNDHAM GARDEN
HOTEL**
7475 W Chandler
Blvd (85226)
Rates: $73-$115
Tel: (602) 961-4444
(800) 822-4200

CHINLE

**HOLIDAY INN-
CANYON
DE CHELLEY/CHINLE**
BIA Rt 7, P. O. Box
1889 (86503)
Rates: $59-$109
Tel: (520) 674-5000
(800) 465-4329

CLARKDALE

**BIRD'S EYE VIEW
BED & BREAKFAST/
GUEST COTTAGES**
Hwy 89A (86324)
Rates: $55-$75
Monthly: $600
Tel: (602) 990-0682
(800) 456-0682

COTTONWOOD

**BEST WESTERN
COTTONWOOD INN**
993 S Main St (86326)
Rates: $50-$99
Tel: (520) 634-5576
(800) 528-1234 (US)
(800) 350-0025 (AZ)

**LITTLE DAISY
MOTEL**
34 S Main St (86326)
Rates: $36-$40
Tel: (520) 634-7865

THE VIEW MOTEL
818 S Main St (86326)
Rates: $34-$48
Tel: (520) 634-7581

DOUGLAS

MOTEL 6
111 16th St (85607)
Rates: $27-$33
Tel: (520) 364-2457
(800) 440-6000

**PRICE CANYON
GUEST RANCH**
P. O. Box 1065
(85607)
Rates: $85-$170
Tel: (520) 558-2383

THRIFTLODGE
1030 19th St (85607)
Rates: $32-$45
Tel: (520) 364-8434
(800) 578-7878 (US)
(800) 525-9055 (AZ)

DRAGOON

**KELLY'S WHISTLESTOP
BED & BREAKFAST**
I-10 & Hwy 191 (85609)
Rates: $50-$60
Tel: (602) 990-0682
(800) 456-0682

EAGAR

**BEST WESTERN
SUNRISE INN**
128 N Main St (85925)
Rates: $42-$99
Tel: (520) 333-2540
(800) 528-1234

EHRENBERG

**BEST WESTERN
FLYING J MOTEL**
P. O. Box 801 (85334)
Rates: $40-$60
Tel: (520) 923-9711
(800) 528-1234 (US)
(800) 292-9711 (AZ)

FLAGSTAFF

ARIZONA MT. INN
685 Lake Mary Rd
(86001)
Rates: $65-$100
Tel: (520) 774-8959
(800) 239-5236

**BEST WESTERN
KINGS HOUSE
MOTEL**
1560 Santa Fe
(86001)
Rates: $42-$85
Tel: (520) 774-7186
(800) 528-1234

COMFORT INN
914 S Milton Rd
(86001)
Rates: $38-$88
Tel: (520) 774-7326
(800) 221-2222

DAYS INN HWY 66
1000 W Route 66
(86001)
Rates: $48-$85
Tel: (520) 774-5221
(800) 329-7466

DAYS INN I-40
2735 S Woodlands
Village
Blvd (86001)
Rates: $60-$90
Tel: (520) 779-1575
(800) 329-7466

FLAGSTAFF INN
2285 E Butler (86001)
Rates: $30-$75
Tel: (520) 774-1821
(800) 533-8992

FRONTIER MOTEL
1700 E Route 66
(86001)
Rates: $18-$80
Tel: (520) 774-8993

**HALEY'S HIDEAWAY
BED & BREAKFAST**
5705 Townsend-
Winona Rd (86004)
Rates: $85
Tel: (800) 526-1780

**HIGHLAND
COUNTRY INN**
223 S Milton Rd
(86001)
Rates: $46-$93
Tel: (520) 774-5041
(800) 642-4186

HOLIDAY INN
2320 E Lucky Ln
(86004)
Rates: $79-$109
Tel: (520) 526-1150
(800) 465-4329

HOWARD JOHNSON
2200 E Butler Ave
(86004)
Rates: $60-$119
Tel: (520) 779-6944
(800) 446-4656

**INNSUITES OF
FLAGSTAFF**
1008 E Route 66
(86001)
Rates: $29-$69
Tel: (520) 774-7356
(800) 842-4242

**KNIGHTS INN
SUITES**
602 W Route 66
(86001)
Rates: $33-$110
Tel: (520) 774-4581
(800) 654-4667

**MASTER HOSTS INNS
FIVE FLAGS INN**
2610 E Route 66
(86004)
Rates: $42-$65
Tel: (520) 526-1399
(800) 251-1962

MOTEL 6
2010 E Butler Ave
(86004)
Rates: $30-48
Tel: (520) 774-1801
(800) 466-8356

MOTEL 6
2440 E Lucky Ln
(86001)
Rates: $30-$36
Tel: (520) 774-8756
(800) 440-6000

MOTEL 6
2745 S .Woodlands
Village Blvd (86001)
Rates: $32-$43
Tel: (520) 779-3757
(800) 440-6000

MOTEL 6
2500 E Lucky Ln
(86004)
Rates: $34-$40
Tel: (520) 779-6164
(800) 440-6000

PINECREST MOTEL
2818 E Route 66
(86001)
Rates: $24-$54
Tel: (520) 526-1950

QUALITY INN
2000 S Milton Rd
(86001)
Rates: $59-$105
Tel: (520) 774-8771
(800) 228-5151

RAMADA LIMITED SUITES
2755 S Woodlands
Village Blvd (86001)
Rates: $59-$135
Tel: (520) 773-1111
(800) 272-6232 (US)
(800) 255-3050 (AZ)

RELAX INN MOTEL
1416 E Santa Fe
(86001)
Rates: $35-$44
Tel: (520) 774-5123

RESIDENCE INN BY MARRIOTT
3440 N Country
Club Dr (86004)
Rates: $99-$189
Tel: (520) 526-5555
(800) 331-3131

RODEWAY INN
2650 E SR 66 (86004)
Rates: $25-49
Tel: (520) 526-2200
(800) 228-2000

RODEWAY INN EAST
2350 E Lucky Ln
(86004)
Rates: $30-$98
Tel: (520) 779-3614
(800) 424-4777

ROYAL INN
2140 E Route 66
(86001)
Rates: $52-$120
Tel: (520) 774-7308

SKI LIFT LODGE
6355 Hwy 180
(86001)
Rates: $20-$65
Tel: (520) 774-0729
(800) 472-3599

SUPER 8 MOTEL
3725 Kasper Ave
(86004)
Rates: $48-$68
Tel: (520) 526-0818
(800) 800-8000

TOWN HOUSE MOTEL
122 W Route 66
(86001)
Rates: $24-$49
Tel: (520) 774-5081

TRAVELODGE
801 W Route 66
(86001)
Rates: $28-99
Tel: (520) 774-3381
(800) 578-7878

TRAVELODGE-FLAGSTAFF
2520 E Lucky Ln
(86004)
Rates: $69-$75
Tel: (520) 779-5121
(800) 578-7878

WESTERN HILLS MOTEL
1580 E Route 66
(86001)
Rates: $20-$65
Tel: (520) 774-6633

FLORENCE

BLUE MIST MOTEL
40 S Pinal Pkwy
(85232)
Rates: $28-$45
Tel: (520) 868-5875

FREDONIA

CRAZY JUG MOTEL
465 S Main (86022)
Rates: $38-$49
Tel: (520) 643-7752

GILA BEND

BEST WESTERN SPACE AGE LODGE
401 E Pima St (85337)
Rates: $46-$76
Tel: (520) 683-2273
(800) 528-1234

YUCCA MOTEL
836 E Pima St (85337)
Rates: $20-$33
Tel: (520) 683-2211

GLENDALE

BEST WESTERN SAGE INN
5940 NW Grand Ave
(85301)
Rates: $40-$77
Tel: (602) 939-9431
(800) 528-1234

GLOBE

CLOUD NINE MOTEL
1649 E Ash St
(85501)
Rates: $47-$69
Tel: (520) 425-5741

EL REY MOTEL
1201 E Ash St (85501)
Rates: $20-$36
Tel: (520) 425-4427

GOODYEAR

BEST WESTERN
1100 N Litchfield Rd
(85338)
Rates: $39-$89
Tel: (602) 932-3210
(800) 528-1234

SUPER 8 MOTEL
1710 N Dysart Rd
(85338)
Rates: $37-$53
Tel: (602) 932-9622
(800) 800-8000

GRAND CANYON NATIONAL PARK- (S. RIM)

(Canyon Hotels
Provide Kennels)

BRIGHT ANGEL LODGE & CABINS
P. O. Box 699 (86023)
Rates: $55-$95
Tel: (520) 638-6284

EL TOVAR HOTEL
P. O. Box 699 (86023)
Rates: $115-$175
Tel: (520) 638-6384

KACHINA LODGE
P. O. Box 699 (86023)
Rates: $99-$109
Tel: (520) 638-6284

MASWIK LODGE
P. O. Box 699 (86023)
Rates: $75-$104
Tel: (520) 638-6784

QUALITY INN
Hwy 64,
P. O. Box 520 (86023)
Rates: $68-$138
Tel: (520) 638-2673
(800) 221-2222

RED FEATHER LODGE
Hwy 64,
P. O. Box 1460 (86023)
Rates: $49-$150
Tel: (520) 638-2414
(800) 538-2345

THUNDERBIRD LODGE
P. O. Box 699 (86023)
Rates: $99-$109
Tel: (520) 638-2631

YAVAPAI LODGE
P. O. Box 699 (86023)
Rates: $82-$92
Tel: (520) 638-7584

GREEN VALLEY

QUALITY INN
111 S La Canada Dr
(85614)
Rates: $69-$115
Tel: (520) 625-2250
(800) 221-2222

GREER

**MOLLY BUTLER
LODGE & CABINS**
P. O. Box 70 (85927)
Rates: $30-$80
Tel: (520) 735-7232

HOLBROOK

**BEST WESTERN
ADOBE INN**
615 W Hopi Dr
(86025)
Rates: $40-$58
Tel: (520) 524-3948
(800) 528 1234

**BEST WESTERN
ARIZONAN INN**
2508 E Navajo Blvd
(86025)
Rates: $40-$62
Tel: (520) 524-2611
(800) 528-1234

BUDGET HOST INN
235 W Hopi Dr
(86025)
Rates: $18-$28
Tel: (520) 524-3809
(800) 283-4678

COMFORT INN
2602 E Navajo Blvd
(86025)
Rates: $44-$72
Tel: (520) 524-6131
(800) 221-2222

ECONO LODGE
2596 E Navajo Blvd
(86025)
Rates: $38-$50
Tel: (520) 524-1448
(800) 424-4777

**HOLIDAY INN
EXPRESS**
1308 E Navajo Blvd
(86025)
Rates: $45-$59
Tel: (520) 524-1466
(800) 465-4329

MOTEL 6
2514 E Navajo Blvd
(86025)
Rates: $30-$36
Tel: (520) 524-6101
(800) 440-6000

RAINBOW INN
2211 E Navajo Blvd
(86025)
Rates: $30-$47
Tel: (520) 524-2654
(800) 551-1923

RAMADA INN
2608 E Navajo Blvd
(86025)
Rates: $40-$65
Tel: (520) 524-2566
(800) 272-6232

TRAVELODGE
2418 E Navajo Blvd
(86025)
Rates: $30-$46
Tel: (520) 524-6815
(800) 578-7878

JEROME

**THE SURGEON'S
HOUSE B & B**
101 Hill St (86331)
Rates: $75-$110
Tel: (602) 990-0682
(800) 456-0682

KAYENTA

**GOULDING'S
TRADING POST
& LODGE**
P. O. Box 360001
(Monument Valley,
UT 84536)
Rates: $72-$102
Tel: (801) 727-3231

KEARNY

**GENERAL
KEARNY INN**
P. O. Box 188 (85237)
Rates: $40
Tel: (520) 363-5505

KINGMAN

**BEST WESTERN
A WAYFARER'S INN**
2815 E Andy Devine
(86401)
Rates: $43-$61
Tel: (520) 753-6271
(800) 528-1234

**BEST WESTERN
KING'S INN**
2930 E Andy Devine
(86401)
Rates: $43-$64
Tel: (520) 753-6101
(800) 528-1234

DAYS INN EAST
3381 E Andy Devine
(86401)
Rates: $60+
Tel: (520) 757-7337
(800) 329-7466

DAYS INN WEST
3023 E Andy Devine
(86401)
Rates: $45-$65
Tel: (520) 753-7500
(800) 329-7466

HIGH DESERT INN
2803 E Andy Devine
(86401)
Rates: $19-$29
Tel: (520) 753-2935

HILL TOP MOTEL
1901 E Andy Devine
(86401)
Rates: $22-$36
Tel: (520) 753-2198

HOLIDAY INN
3100 E Andy Devine
(86401)
Rates: $39-$54
Tel: (520) 753-6262
(800) 465-4329

MOTEL 6
424 W Beale St
(86401)
Rates: $29-$38
Tel: (520) 753-9222
(800) 440-6000

MOTEL 6
3351 W Andy Devine
(86401)
Rates: $32-$38
Tel: (520) 757-7151
(800) 440-6000

MOTEL 6
3270 E Andy Devine
(86401)
Rates: $27-$34
Tel: (520) 757-7121
(800) 440-6000

QUALITY INN
1400 E Andy Devine
(86401)
Rates: $40-$69
Tel: (520) 753-4747
(800) 424-6423

RODEWAY INN
411 W Beale St
(86401)
Rates: $26-$45
Tel: (520) 753-5521
(800) 424-4777

**SILVER QUEEN
MOTEL**
3285 E Andy Devine
(86401)
Rates: $24-$34
Tel: (520) 757-4315

SUPER 8 MOTEL
3401 E Andy Devine
(86401)
Rates: $32-$49
Tel: (520) 757-4808
(800) 800-8000

LAKE HAVASU CITY

**BEST WESTERN
LAKE PLACE INN**
31 Wing's Loop
(86403)
Rates: $45-$89
Tel: (520) 855-2146
(800) 528-1234 (US)
(800) 258-8558 (AZ)

BRIDGEVIEW MOTEL
101 London Bridge
Rd (86403)
Rates: $35-$110
Tel: (520) 855-5559

EZ-8 MOTEL
41 S Acoma Blvd
(86403)
Rates: $25-$40
Tel: (520) 855-4023
(800) 326-6835

**HAVASU MOTEL
ALL-SUITE INN**
2035 Acoma Blvd
(86403)
Rates: $20-$45
Tel: (520) 855-2311

HOLIDAY INN
245 London Bridge
Rd (86403)
Rates: $45-$70
Tel: (520) 855-4071
(800) 465-4329

ISLAND INN HOTEL
1300 W McCulloch
Blvd (86403)
Rates: $65-$85
Tel: (520) 680-0606
(800) 243-9955

LAKEVIEW MOTEL
440 London Bridge
Rd (86403)
Rates: $25-$45
Tel: (520) 855-3605

LONDON BRIDGE RESORT
1477 Queens Bay Rd (86403)
Rates: $75-$150
Tel: (520) 855-0888
(800) 624-7939

PECOS II CONDOMINIUMS
451 B Lake Havasu Ave (86403)
Rates: $385/week
Tel: (520) 855-7444

PIONEER HOTEL LAKE HAVASU CITY
271 Lake Havasu Ave (86403)
Rates: $54-$64
Tel: (520) 855-1111
(800) 528-5169

SANDMAN INN
1700 N McCulloch Blvd (86403)
Rates: $30-$90
Tel: (520) 855-7841
(800) 835-2410

SUPER 8 MOTEL
305 London Bridge Rd (86403)
Rates: $36-$63
Tel: (520) 855-8844
(800) 800-8000

WINDSOR INN
451 London Bridge Rd (86403)
Rates: $26-$49
Tel: (520) 855-4135
(800) 245-4135

LAKE MONTEZUMA

BEAVER CREEK INN
462 S Montezuma Ave (86342)
Rates: $39-$48
Tel: (520) 567-4475

LAKESIDE

BARTRAM'S WHITE MOUNTAIN B & B
Rt 1, Box 1014 (85929)
Rates: $60-$75
Tel: (520) 367-1408
(800) 257-0211

LAKE OF THE WOODS
2244 W White Mtn Blvd (85929)
Rates: $43-$83
Tel: (520) 368-5353

LAZY OAKS RESORT COTTAGES
Rt 2, Box 1215 (85929)
Rates: $50-$65
Tel: (520) 368-6203

MOONRIDGE LODGE & CABINS
P. O. Box 1058 (85929)
Rates: $35-$135
Tel: (520) 367-1906

THE PLACE RESORT CABINS
Rt 3, Box 2675 (85929)
Rates: $66-$74
Tel: (520) 368-6777

LITCHFIELD PARK

THE WIGWAM RESORT
Indian School & N Litchfield Rds (85340)
Rates: $90-$420
Tel: (602) 935-3811
(800) 327-0396

MARBLE CANYON

LEES FERRY LODGE
HC67, Box 1 (Vermillion Cliffs 86036)
Rates: $47+
Tel: (520) 355-2231

MARBLE CANYON LODGE
Box 1, Hwy 89A (86036)
Rates: $40-$50
Tel: (520) 355-2225
(800) 726-1789

MESA

ARIZONA GOLF RESORT
425 S Power Rd (85206)
Rates: $85-$165
Tel: (602) 832-3202
(800) 528-8282

BEST WESTERN MESA INN
1625 E Main St (85203)
Rates: $34-$80
Tel: (520) 964-8000
(800) 528-1234

BEST WESTERN SUPERSTITION SPRINGS INN
1342 S Power Rd (85206)
Rates: $49-$150
Tel: (602) 641-1164
(800) 528-1234

HAMPTON INN
1563 S Gilbert Rd (85204)
Rates: $53-$83
Tel: (602) 926-3600
(800) 426-7866

HOLIDAY INN
1600 S Country Club Dr (85210)
Rates: $49-$99
Tel: (602) 964-7000
(800) 465-4329

MARICOPA INN MOTOR HOTEL
3 E Main St (85201)
Rates: $28-$49
Tel: (602) 834-6060
(800) 627-2144

MOTEL 6
336 W Hampton Ave (85210)
Rates: $32-$38
Tel: (602) 844-8899
(800) 440-6000

MOTEL 6
1511 S Country Club Dr (85210)
Rates: $34-$40
Tel: (602) 834-0066
(800) 440-6000

MOTEL 6
630 W Main St (85201)
Rates: $32-$38
Tel: (602) 969-8111
(800) 440-6000

RAMADA INN SUITES
1410 S Country Club Dr (85201)
Rates: $35-$99
Tel: (602) 964-2897
(800) 272-6232

RAMADA LIMITED EAST VALLEY
1750 E Main St (85203)
Rates: $39-$79
Tel: (602) 969-3600
(800) 272-6232

RODEWAY INN
5700 E Main St (85205)
Rates: $36-$99
Tel: (602) 985-3600
(800) 424-4777 (US)
(800) 888-3561 (AZ)

SAN DEE MOTEL
6649 E Apache Tr (85205)
Rates: $45-$58
Tel: (602) 985-1912

SUPER 8 MOTEL
1550 Gilbert Rd (85204)
Rates: $49-74
Tel: (602) 545-0888
(800) 800-8000

TRAVELODGE MESA
22 S Country Club Dr (85202)
Rates: $20-$69
Tel: (602) 964-5694
(800) 255-3050

MIAMI

BEST WESTERN COPPER HILLS INN
Rt 1, Box 506 (85539)
Rates: $54-$74
Tel: (520) 425-7151
(800) 528-1234

MUNDS PARK

MOTEL IN THE PINES
P. O. Box 18171 (86017)
Rates: $35-$65
Tel: (520) 286-9699

NOGALES

AMERICANA MOTOR HOTEL
639 N Grand Ave
(85621)
Rates: $44-$67
Tel: (520) 287-7211
(800) 874-8079

BEST WESTERN SIESTA MOTEL
673 N Grand Ave
(85621)
Rates: $36-$60
Tel: (520) 287-4671
(800) 528-1234

BEST WESTERN TIME MOTEL
921 N Grand Ave
(85621)
Rates: $34-$50
Tel: (520) 287-4627
(800) 528-1234

MOTEL 6
141 W Mariposa Rd
(85621)
Rates: $32-$38
Tel: (520) 281-2951
(800) 440-6000

ORACLE

VILLA CARDINALE B&B
1315 W Oracle
Ranch Rd (85623)
Rates: $45-$60
Tel: (520) 896-2516

PAGE

BEST WESTERN WESTON INN
207 N Lake Powell
Blvd (86040)
Rates: $34-$91
Tel: (520) 645-2451
(800) 528-1234 (US)
(800) 637-9183 (AZ)

ECONO LODGE
121 S Lake Powell
Blvd (86040)
Rates: $35-$90
Tel: (520) 645-2488
(800) 424-4777

EMPIRE HOUSE MOTEL
100 S Lake Powell
Blvd (86040)
Rates: $50-$62
Tel: (520) 645-2406

HOLIDAY INN PAGE/LAKE POWELL
287 N Lake Powell
Blvd (86040)
Rates: $52-$106
Tel: (520) 645-8851
(800) 465-4329 (US)
(800) 232-0011 (AZ)

INN AT LAKE POWELL
716 Rim View Dr
(86040)
Rates: $35-$92
Tel: (520) 645-2466
(800) 826-2718

LAKE POWELL MOTEL
Highway 89 N
(86040)
Rates: $54-$65
Tel: (520) 645-2477

WAHWEAP LODGE & MARINA RESORT
100 Lake Shore Dr
(86040)
Rates: $65-$127
Tel: (520) 645-2433
(800) 528-6154

PARKER

BUDGET INN MOTEL
912 Agency Rd
(85344)
Rates: $35-$45
Tel: (520) 669-2566

EL RANCHO MOTEL
709 California Ave
(85344)
Rates: $35+
Tel: (520) 669-2231

HAVASU SPRINGS RESORT
Rt 2, Box 624 (85344)
Rates: $75-$85
Tel: (520) 667-3361

HOLIDAY KASBAH
604 California Ave
(85344)
Rates: $39-$63
Tel: (520) 669-2133

STARDUST MOTEL
700 California Ave
(85344)
Rates: $30-$75
Tel: (520) 669-2278

PATAGONIA

STAGE STOP INN
Box 777 (85624)
Rates: $49-$95
Tel: (520) 394-2211

PAYSON

CHRISTOPHER CREEK LODGE/MOTEL
Star Rt Box 119
(85541)
Rates: $40-$75
Tel: (520) 478-4300

GREY HACKLE LODGE
Star Rt Box 145
(85541)
Rates: $40-$95
Tel: (520) 478-4392

KOHL'S GUEST RANCH RESORT
E Hwy 260 (85541)
Rates: $49-$79
Tel: (520) 478-4211
(800) 331-5645

MAJESTIC MT INN
602 E Hwy 260
(85541)
Rates: $36-$140
Tel: (520) 474-0185
(800) 408-2442

PAYSON PUEBLO INN
809 E Hwy 260
(85541)
Rates: $34-$135
Tel: (520) 474-5241
(800) 888-9828

SWISS VILLAGE LODGE
801 N Beeline Hwy
(85541)
Rates: $59-$109
Tel: (520) 474-3241
(800) 247-9477

TRAVELODGE
101 W Phoenix St
(85541)
Rates: $50-$85
Tel: (520) 474-4526
(800) 578-7878

PHOENIX
(and vicinity)

ARIZONA BILTMORE
24th St & Missouri
(85016)
Rates: $330-$475
Tel: (602) 955-6600
(800) 228-3000

BEST WESTERN AIRPORT INN
2425 S 24th St (85034)
Rates: $55-$105
Tel: (602) 273-7251
(800) 528-1234

BEST WESTERN BELL MOTEL
17211 N Black
Canyon Hwy (85023)
Rates: $39-$75
Tel: (602) 993-8300
(800) 528-1234

COMFORT INN AIRPORT
4120 E Van Buren St.
(85008)
Rates: $28-$58
Tel: (602) 275-5746
(800) 221-2222

COMFORT INN TURF PARADISE
1711 W Bell Rd
(85023)
Rates: $42-$89
Tel: (602) 866-2089
(800) 221-2222

DAYS INN
2420 W Thomas Rd
(85015)
Rates: $45-$95
Tel: (602) 257-0801
(800) 329-7466

DAYS INN-COLISEUM
2420 W Thomas Rd
(85015)
Rates: $39-$69
Tel: (602) 257-0801
(800) 329-7466

DAYS INN PHOENIX AIRPORT
3333 E Van Buren St
(85008)
Rates: $65-$119
Tel: (602) 244-8244
(800) 329-7466

ECONO LODGE
3541 E Van Buren St
(85008)
Rates: $35-$51
Tel: 602-273-7121
(800) 424-4777

ECONO LODGE
1520 N 84th Dr
(Tolleson 85353)
Rates: $79-$89
Tel: (602) 936-4667
(800) 424-4777

**EMBASSY SUITES
PHOENIX WEST**
3210 NW Grand Ave
(85017)
Rates: $64-$134
Tel: (602) 279-3211
(800) 362-2779

**EMBASSY SUITES-
AIRPORT WEST**
2333 E Thomas Rd
(85016)
Rates: $59-$109
Tel: (602) 957-1910
(800) 362-2779

E-Z 8 MOTEL
1820 S 7th St (85034)
Rates: $26-$33
Tel: (602) 254-9787

**FOUNTAINS SUITE
HOTEL**
2577 W Greenway
Rd (85023)
Rates: $69-$129
Tel: (602) 375-1777
(800) 338-1338

HAMPTON INN I-17
8101 N Black
Canyon Hwy (85021)
Rates: $66-$79
Tel: (602) 864-6233
(800) 426-7866

**HOLIDAY INN
AIRPORT EAST**
4300 E Washington
St (85034)
Rates: $49-$119
Tel: (602) 273-7778
(800) 465-4329

**HOLIDAY INN
CROWNE PLAZA/
OMNI ADAMS HOTEL**
P. O. Box 1000
(85001)
Rates: $59-$164
Tel: (602) 257-1525
(800) 227-6963

**HOLIDAY INN &
HOLIDOME-
PHX CORP CENTER**
2532 W Peoria Ave
(85029)
Rates: $59-$149
Tel: (602) 943-2341
(800) 465-4329

**HOLIDAY INN
NORTH CENTRAL**
4321 N Central Ave
(85012)
Rates: $39-$109
Tel: (602) 277-6671
(800) 465-4329

HOWARD JOHNSON
3400 NW Grand Ave
(85017)
Rates: $48-$80
Tel: (602) 264-9164
(800) 446-4656

HOWARD JOHNSON
124 S 24th St (85034)
Rates: $64-$89
Tel: (602) 244-8221
(800) 446-4656

KNIGHTS COURT
5050 N Black
Canyon Hwy
(85017)
Rates: $45-$80
Tel: (602) 242-8011
(800) 843-5644

**KNIGHTS INN
AIRPORT**
2201 S 24th St
(85034)
Rates: $45-$50
Tel: (602) 267-0611
(800) 843-5644

**LA QUINTA INN-
COLISEUM**
2725 N Black
Canyon Hwy
(85009)
Rates: $45-$72
Tel: (602) 258-6271
(800) 221-4731

**LA QUINTA
PHOENIX NORTH**
2510 W Greenway
Rd (85023)
Rates: $54-$91
Tel: (602) 993-0800
(800) 221-4731

**LEXINGTON HOTEL
& CITY SQUARE
SPORTS CLUB**
100 W Clarendon
(85013)
Rates: $69-$149
Tel: (602) 279-9811
(800) 537-8483

**LOS OLIVOS
EXECUTIVE HOTEL**
202 E McDowell Rd
(85004)
Rates: $59-$99
Tel: (602) 258-6911
(800) 776-5560

MOTEL 6
214 S 24th St (85034)
Rates: $36-$42
Tel: (602) 244-1155
(800) 440-6000

MOTEL 6
2323 E Van Buren St
(85006)
Rates: $30-$36
Tel: (602) 267-7511
(800) 440-6000

MOTEL 6
5315 E Van Buren St
(85008)
Rates: $30-$36
Tel: (602) 267-8555
(800) 440-6000

MOTEL 6
1530 N 52nd Dr
(85043)
Rates: $38-$44
Tel: (602) 272-0220
(800) 440-6000

MOTEL 6
2548 W Indian
School Rd (85017)
Rates: $37-$43
Tel: (602) 248-8881
(800) 440-6000

MOTEL 6
8152 N Black
Canyon Hwy
(85051)
Rates: $37-$43
Tel: (602) 995-7592
(800) 440-6000

MOTEL 6
4130 N Black
Canyon Hwy (85017)
Rates: $32-$38
Tel: (602) 277-5501
(800) 440-6000

MOTEL 6
2330 W Bell Rd (85023)
Rates: $37-$43
Tel: (602) 993-2353
(800) 440-6000

MOTEL 6
2735 W Sweetwater
Ave (85029)
Rates: $36-$42
Tel: (602) 942-5030
(800) 440-6000

**PHOENIX SUNRISE
MOTEL**
3644 E Van Buren St
(85008)
Rates: $33+
Tel: (602) 275-7661
(800) 432-6483

PREMIER INN
10402 N Black
Canyon Hwy (85051)
Rates: $49-$99
Tel: (602) 943-2371
(800) 786-6835

**QUALITY HOTEL
CENTRAL PHOENIX**
3600 N 2nd Ave (85013)
Rates: $59-$99
Tel: (602) 248-0222
(800) 424-6423

**QUALITY INN
AIRPORT**
3541 E Van Buren St
(85008)
Rates: $29-$69
Tel: (602) 273-7121
(800) 228-5151

**QUALITY INN
SOUTH MOUNTAIN**
5121 E La Puente
Ave (85044)
Rates: $49-$99
Tel: (602) 893-3900
(800) 228-5151 (US)
(800) 562-3332 (AZ)

**RADISSON
PHOENIX AIRPORT
HOTEL/SOUTHBANK**
3333 E University Dr
(85034)
Rates: $169-$189
Tel: (602) 437-8400
(800) 333-3333

**RAMADA INN-
METRO CENTER**
12027 N 28th Dr
(85029)
Rates: $42-$110
Tel: (602) 866-7000
(800) 272-6232

RESIDENCE INN BY MARRIOTT
8242 N Black Canyon Hwy (85051)
Rates: $119-$199
Tel: (602) 864-1900
(800) 331-3131

RITZ CARLTON
2401 E Camelback Rd (85016)
Rates: $95-$225
Tel: (602) 468-0700
(800) 241-3333

ROYAL PALMS INN
5200 E Camelback Rd (85018)
Rates: $60-$210
Tel: (602) 840-3610
(800) 672-6011 (US)
(800) 548-1202 (CAN)

SHERATON CRESCENT HOTEL
2620 W Dunlap Ave (85021)
Rates: $109-$185
Tel: (602) 943-8200
(800) 423-4126

SUPER 8 MOTEL PHOENIX CENTRAL
4021 N 27th Ave (85017)
Rates: $32-$54
Tel: (602) 248-8880
(800) 800-8000

TRAVELODGE METRO CENTER
8617 N Black Canyon Hwy (85021)
Rates: $38-$90
Tel: (602) 995-9500
(800) 578-7878

TRAVELODGE SUITES
3101 N 32nd St (85018)
Rates: $58-$150
Tel: (602) 956-4900
(800) 578-7878

UPTOWN B & B
7th Ave & Thomas Rd (85007)
Rates: $60-$75
Tel: (602) 990-0682
(800) 456-0682

WYNDHAM GARDEN HOTEL
2641 W Union Hills Dr (85027)
Rates: $65-$105
Tel: (602) 978-2222
(800) 996-3426

WYNDHAM WESTCOURT/ METROCENTER
10220 N Metro Pkwy (85051)
Rates: $59-$109
Tel: (602) 997-5900
(800) 996-3426

PINETOP

BEST WESTERN INN
404 S White Mountain Blvd (85935)
Rates: $50-$89
Tel: (520) 367-6667
(800) 528-1234

BUCK SPRINGS RESORT COTTAGES
P. O. Box 130 (85935)
Rates: $48-$65
Tel: (520) 369-3554

DOUBLE B LODGE & CABINS
P. O. Box 747 (85935)
Rates: $34-$62
Tel: (520) 367-2747

ECONO LODGE OF PINETOP
458 E White Mountain Blvd (85935)
Rates: $49-$99
Tel: (520) 367-3636
(800) 424-4777

MEADOW VIEW LODGE
P. O. Box 325 (85935)
Rates: $48+
Tel: (520) 367-4642

NORTHWOODS RESORT
165 E White Mountain Blvd (85935)
Rates: $62-$99
Tel: (520) 367-2966

PRESCOTT

ANTELOPE RESORT ESTATES
6200 N Hwy 89 (86301)
Rates: 2 month rental/$2950.00
Tel: (520) 776-2600

ANTELOPE HILLS INN SUITES
6000 Willow Creek Rd (86301)
Rates: $48-$64
Tel: (520) 778-6000

APACHE MOTEL
1130 E Gurley St (86301)
Rates: $39-$59
Tel: (520) 445-1422

BEST WESTERN PRESCOTTONIAN MOTEL
1317 E Gurley St (86301)
Rates: $44-$125
Tel: (520) 445-3096
(800) 528-1234

CASCADE MOTEL
805 White Spar Rd (86303)
Rates: $30-$80
Tel: (520) 445-1232

DAYS INN
7875 E Hwy 69 (86314)
Rates: $52-$99
Tel: (520) 772-8600
(800) 329-7466

FOREST VILLAS HOTEL
3645 Lee Cir (86301)
Rates: $69-$119
Tel: (520) 717-1200
(800) 223-3449

HERITAGE HOUSE
819 E Gurley St (86301)
Rates: $36-$85
Tel: (520) 445-9091

HI-ACRE RESORT
1001 White Spar Rd (86303)
Rates: $29-$110
Tel: (520) 445-0588

LYNX CREEK FARM BED &BREAKFAST
P. O. Box 4301, SR 69 (86302)
Rates: $75-$140
Tel: (520) 778-9573

MOTEL 6
1111 E Sheldon St (86301)
Rates: $37-$45
Tel: (520) 776-0160
(800) 440-6000

MT. VERNON INN B&B & COUNTRY COTTAGES
204 N Mt Vernon Ave (86301)
Rates: $110-$130
Tel: (520) 778-0886
(602) 990-0682
(800) 456-0682

NINE PINES COTTAGE
P. O. Box 2099 (86302)
Rates: $55-$85
Tel: (520) 778-3620

PINE VIEW MOTEL
500 Copper Basin Rd (86303)
Rates: $20-$60
Tel: (520) 445-4660

PRESCOTT SIERRA INN
809 White Spar Rd (86303)
Rates: $34-$95
Tel: (520) 445-1250

SENATOR INN
1117 E Gurley St (86301)
Rates: $35-$145
Tel: (520) 445-1440

SKYLINE MOTEL
523 E Gurley St (86301)
Rates: $32-$65
Tel: (520) 445-9963

SUPER 8 MOTEL
1105 E Sheldon St (86301)
Rates: $42-64
Tel: (520) 776-1282
(800) 800-8000

PRESCOTT VALLEY

PRESCOTT VALLEY MOTEL
8350 East Hwy 69 (86314)
Rates: $35+
Tel: (520) 772-9412

RIO RICO

RIO RICO RESORT & COUNTRY CLUB
1069 Camino Caralampi (85648)
Rates: $95-$150
Tel: (520) 281-1901
(800) 288-4746

SAFFORD

BEST WESTERN-DESERT INN OF SAFFORD
1391 W Thatcher Blvd (85546)
Rates: $57-$80
Tel: (520) 428-0521
(800) 528-1234

COMFORT INN
1578 W Thatcher Blvd (85546)
Rates: $42-$64
Tel: (520) 428-5851
(800) 221-2222

RAMADA INN
420 E Hwy 70 (85546)
Rates: $50-$100
Tel: (800) 272-6232

SANDIA MOTEL
520 E Hwy 70 (85546)
Rates: $46+
Tel: (520) 428-5000
(800) 578-2151

SCOTTSDALE

ADOBE APARTMENT HOTEL
3635 N 68th St (85251)
Rates: $54-$89
Tel: (602) 945-3544

DAYS INN-SCOTTSDALE FASHION SQUARE RESORT
4710 N Scottsdale Rd (85251)
Rates: $42-$125
Tel: (602) 947-5411
(800) 329-7466

EMBASSY SUITES
5001 N Scottsdale Rd (85250)
Rates: $155+
Tel: (602) 949-1414
(800) 528-1456

GARDINER'S RESORT
5700 E McDonald Dr (85253)
Rates: $195+
Tel: (602) 948-2100
(800) 245-2051

HOLIDAY INN OLD TOWN SCOTTSDALE
7353 E Indian School Rd (85251)
Rates: $69-$149
Tel: (602) 994-9203
(800) 465-4329 (US)
(800) 695-6995 (AZ)

HOSPITALITY SUITE RESORT
409 N Scottsdale Rd (85257)
Rates: $49-$149
Tel: (602) 949-5115
(800) 445-5115

HOWARD JOHNSON
5101 N Scottsdale Rd (85250)
Rates: $43-$88
Tel: (602) 945-4392
(800) 446-4656

INN AT THE CITADEL
8700 E Pinnacle Peak Rd (85255)
Rates: $89-$265
Tel: (602) 585-6133
(800) 927-8367

INN SUITES OF SCOTTSDALE AT EL DORADO PARK
7707 E McDowell Rd (85257)
Rates: $62-$86
Tel: (602) 941-1202
(800) 238-8851

MARRIOTT'S CAMELBACK INN
5402 E Lincoln Dr (85253)
Rates: $130-$340
Tel: (602) 948-1700
(800) 242-2635

MARRIOTT'S MT SHADOWS RESORT
5641 E Lincoln Dr (85253)
Rates: $175-$325
Tel: (602) 948-7111
(800) 228-9290 (US)
(800) 835-6205 (AZ)

MOTEL 6
6848 E Camelback Rd (85251)
Rates: $38-$44
Tel: (602) 946-2280
(800) 440-6000

PARK INN INTERNATIONAL
2934 N Scottsdale Rd (85251)
Rates: $35-$98
Tel: (602) 947-5885
(800) 599-5885

THE PHOENICIAN RESORT
6000 E Camelback Rd (85251)
Rates: $160-$445
Tel: (602) 941-8200
(800) 888-8234

RAMADA HOTEL VALLEY HO
6850 E Main St (85251)
Rates: $45-$135
Tel: (602) 945-6321
(800) 272-6232

RED LION'S LA POSADA RESORT & INN
4949 E Lincoln Dr (85253)
Rates: $99-$229
Tel: (602) 952-0420
(800) 547-8010

RESIDENCE INN BY MARRIOTT
6040 N Scottsdale Rd (85253)
Rates: $129-$210
Tel: (602) 948-8666
(800) 331-3131

SAFARI RESORT
4611 N Scottsdale Rd (85251)
Rates: $42-$150
Tel: (602) 945-0721
(800) 845-4356

SCOTTSDALE PIMA MOTEL SUITES
7330 N Pima Rd (85258)
Rates: $45-$229
Tel: (602) 948-3800
(800) 344-0262

STOUFFER RENAISSANCE COTTONWOODS RESORT
6160 N Scottsdale Rd (85253)
Rates: $109-$295
Tel: (602) 991-1414
(800) 468-3571

SEDONA

BEST WESTERN INN OF SEDONA
1200 Hwy 89A (86336)
Rates: $70-$120
Tel: (520) 282-3072
(800) 528-1234 (US)
(800) 292-6344 (AZ)

CANYON MESA COUNTRY CLUB
500 Jacks Canyon Rd (86351)
Rates: $125-$200
Tel: (520) 284-2176

COURTHOUSE BUTTE VILLA B & B
2451 Red Rock Loop Rd (86336)
Rates: $70-$95
Tel: (520) 204-1505

DESERT QUAIL INN
6626 Hwy 179 (86336)
Rates: $49-$140
Tel: (520) 284-1433
(800) 385-0927

FOREST HOUSE RESORT-OAK CREEK CANYON
HC 30, Box 250 (86336)
Rates: $75-$120
Tel: (520) 282-2999

GREYFIRE FARM B & B
1240 Jacks Canyon
Rd (86351)
Rates: $80-$200
Tel: (520) 284-2340
(800) 579-2340

LO LO MAI SPRINGS
Page Springs Rd
(86340)
Rates: $40-$50
Tel: (520) 634-4700

**MATTERHORN
MOTOR LODGE**
230 Apple Ave
(86336)
Rates: $49-$89
Tel: (520) 282-7176

**NEW EARTH LODGE
VACATION COTTAGES**
665 Sunset Dr (86336)
Rates: $75-$100
Tel: (520) 282-2644

**OAK CREEK
TERRACE RESORT**
Star Rt 3, Box 1100
(86336)
Rates: $65-$160
Tel: (520) 282-3562
(800) 224-2229

**QUAIL RIDGE
RESORT**
120 Canyon Circle
Dr (86351)
Rates: $64-$93
Tel: (520) 284-9327

**QUALITY INN-
KING'S RANSOM
MOTOR HOTEL**
771 SR 179 (86336)
Rates: $75-$120
Tel: (520) 282-7151
(800) 221-2222

**RAILROAD INN
AT SEDONA**
2545 W Hwy 89A
(86336)
Rates: $45-$66
Tel: (520) 282-1533
(800) 858-7245

**SKY RANCH LODGE
MOTEL**
SR 89A, Airport Rd
(86336)
Rates: $55-$135
Tel: (520) 282-6400

**SUGAR LOAF
LODGE**
1870 W Hwy 89A
(86340)
Rates: $36-$60
Tel: (520) 282-9451

WHITE HOUSE INN
2986 W Hwy 89A
(86336)
Rates: $35-$95
Tel: (520) 282-6680

SELIGMAN

**CANYON SHADOWS
MOTEL**
114 E Chino (86337)
Rates: $35+
Tel: (520) 422-3255

SUPAI MOTEL
134 W Chino (86337)
Rates: $35+
Tel: (520) 422-3663

SHOW LOW

DAYS INN
480 W Deuce of
Clubs Ave (85901)
Rates: $49-$69
Tel: (520) 537-4356
(800) 329-7466

**HOLIDAY INN
EXPRESS**
151 W Deuce of
Clubs Ave (85901)
Rates: $70-$75
Tel: (520) 537-5115
(800) 465-4329

KIVA MOTEL
261 E Deuce of
Clubs Ave (85901)
Rates: $32-$48
Tel: (520) 537-4542

**SNOWY RIVER
MOTEL**
13640 E Deuce of
Clubs Ave (85901)
Rates: $34-$38
Tel: (520) 537-2926

SUPER 8 MOTEL
1941 E Deuce of
Clubs Ave (85901)
Rates: $45+
Tel: (520) 537-7694
(800) 800-8000

SIERRA VISTA

MOTEL 6
1551 E Fry Blvd
(85635)
Rates: $27-$33
Tel: (520) 459-5035
(800) 440-6000

RAMADA INN
2047 S Hwy 92
(85635)
Rates: $55-$86
Tel: (520) 458-1347
(800) 272-6232 (US)
(800) 825-4645 (AZ)

SIERRA SUITES
391 E Fry Blvd
(85635)
Rates: $44-$77
Tel: (520) 459-4221

SUN CANYON INN
260 N Garden Ave
(85635)
Rates: $50-$55
Tel: (520) 459-0610
(800) 822-6966

SUPER 8 MOTEL
100 Fab Ave (85635)
Rates: $42-$62
Tel: (520) 459-5380
(800) 800-8000

THUNDER MT INN
1631 S Hwy 92
(85635)
Rates: $44-$70
Tel: (520) 458-7900
(800) 222-5811

VISTA INN
201 W Fry Blvd
(85635)
Rates: $29+
Tel: (520) 458-6711

WYNDMERE HOTEL
2047 S Hwy 92
(85635)
Rates: $74
Tel: (520) 459-5900

SPRINGERVILLE

EL-JO MOTOR INN
425 E Main St (85938)
Rates: $24-$36
Tel: (520) 333-4314

**REED'S
MOTOR LODGE**
514 E Main St (85938)
Rates: $24-$40
Tel: (520) 333-4323

ST. JOHNS

DAYS INN
185 E Commercial St
(85936)
Rates: $34-$46
Tel: (520)-337-4422
(800) 329-7466

SUPER 8 MOTEL
75 E Commercial St
(85936)
Rates: $33-$44
Tel: (520) 337-2990
(800) 800-8000

STRAWBERRY

**THE STRAWBERRY
LODGE**
HCR 1, Box 331
(85544)
Rates: $42-$52
Tel: (520) 476-3333

SUMMERHAVEN

**SUMMERHAVEN
SUITES & SWEETS**
P. O. Box 757 (85619)
Rates: $135
Tel: (520) 576-1542

SUN CITY

**BEST WESTERN
INN OF SUN CITY**
11201 Grand Ave
(85373)
Rates: $38-$88
Tel: (602) 933-8211
(800) 528-1234

SURPRISE

**WINDMILL INN AT
SUN CITY WEST**
12545 W Bell Rd
(85374)
Rates: $50-$99
Tel: (602) 583-0133
(800) 547-4747

TAYLOR

**WHITING
MOTOR INN**
825 North Hwy 77
(85939)
Rates: $48-$52
Tel: (520) 536-2600

TEMPE

THE BUTTES
2000 Westcourt Way
(85282)
Rates: $100-$235
Tel: (602) 225-9000
(800) 843-1986

COMFORT INN
5300 S Priest Dr
(85283)
Rates: $40-$90
Tel: (602) 820-7500
(800) 228-5150

**COUNTRY SUITES
BY CARLSON**
1660 W Elliot Rd
(85283)
Rates: $49-$92
Tel: (602) 345-8585
(800) 456-4000

**EMBASSY SUITES
HOTEL**
4400 S Rural Rd
(85282)
Rates: $65-$145
Tel: (602) 897-7444
(800) 362-2779

FIESTA INN
2100 S Priest Dr
(85282)
Rates: $55-$138
Tel: (602) 967-1441
(800) 528-6481

**HOLIDAY INN
TEMPE/ASU**
915 E Apache Blvd
(85281)
Rates: $55-$82
Tel: (602) 968-3451
(800) 465-4329 (US)
(800) 238-5754 (AZ)

**INNSUITES HOTEL
AIRPORT**
1651 W Baseline Rd
(85283)
Rates: $52-$119
Tel: (602) 897-7900
(800) 841-4242

**LA QUINTA
MOTOR INN**
911 S 48th St (85281)
Rates: $44-$74
Tel: (602) 967-4465
(800) 531-5900

MOTEL 6
513 W Broadway Rd
(85282)
Rates: $30-$32
Tel: (602) 967-8696
(800) 440-6000

MOTEL 6
1720 S Priest Dr
(85281)
Rates: $35-$41
Tel: (602) 968-4401
(800) 440-6000

MOTEL 6
1612 N Scottsdale
Rd (85281)
Rates: $36-$42
Tel: (602) 945-9506
(800) 440-6000

**PARAMOUNT
HOTEL**
225 E Apache Blvd
(85281)
Rates: $42-$99
Tel: (602) 967-9431

**RAMADA SUITES
TEMPE/SCOTTSDALE**
1635 N Scottsdale
Rd (85281)
Rates: $39-$139
Tel: (602) 947-3711
(800) 272-6232

**RESIDENCE INN
BY MARRIOTT**
5075 S Priest Dr
(85282)
Rates: $145-$195
Tel: (602) 756-2122
(800) 331-3131

**RODEWAY INN
AIRPORT EAST**
1550 S 52nd St
(85281)
Rates: $49-$129
Tel: (602) 967-3000
(800) 228-2000

SUPER 8 MOTEL
1020 E Apache Blvd
(85281)
Rates: $65-$87
Tel: (602) 967-8891
(800) 800-8000

**TEMPE MISSION
PALMS HOTEL**
60 E Fifth St (85281)
Rates: $109+
Tel: (602) 894-1400

**TRAVELODGE
UNIVERSITY**
1005 E Apache Blvd
(85281)
Rates: $46-$85
Tel: (602) 968-7871
(800) 578-7878

TOLLESON

ECONO LODGE
1520 N 84th Dr
(85353)
Rates: $44-$79
Tel: (602) 936-4667
(800) 424-4777

TOMBSTONE

**BEST WESTERN
LOOKOUT LODGE**
Hwy 80 W (85638)
Rates: $51-$75
Tel: (520) 457-2223
(800) 528-1234

TUBA CITY

TUBA CITY MOTEL
P.O. Box 247 (86045)
Rates: $85-$90
Tel: (520) 283-4545

TUBAC

**TUBAC GOLF
RESORT**
1 Otero Rd (85646)
Rates: $62-$142
Tel: (520) 398-2211
(800) 848-7893

TUCSON

**BEST WESTERN
EXECUTIVE INN**
333 W Drachman
(85705)
Rates: $40-$115
Tel: (520) 791-7551
(800) 528-1234 (US)
(800) 255-3371 (AZ)

**BEST WESTERN
GHOST RANCH
LODGE**
801 W Miracle Mile
(85705)
Rates: $39-$98
Tel: (520) 791-7565
(800) 528-1234

**BEST WESTERN
INNSUITES
CATALINA
FOOTHILLS**
6201 N Oracle Rd
(85704)
Rates: $49-$149
Tel: (520) 297-8111
(800) 528-1234

**BEST WESTERN
TANQUE VERDE INN**
7007 E Tanque Verde
Rd (85715)
Rates: $40-$99
Tel: (520) 298-2300
(800) 528-1234

CANDLELIGHT SUITES
1440 S Craycroft Rd
(85711)
Rates: $39-$69
Tel: (520) 747-1440
(800) 223-1440

**THE CAT AND THE
WHISTLE B & B**
22nd St & Kolb Rd
(85710)
Rates: $65-$75
Monthly: $850-$1000
Tel: (602) 990-0682
(800) 456-0682

CHATEAU SONATA
550 S Camino Seco
(85710)
Rates: $39-$111
Tel: (520) 886-2468

**CLARION HOTEL
TUCSON AIRPORT**
6801 S Tucson Blvd
(85706)
Rates: $49-$106
Tel: (520) 746-3932
(800) 221-2222 (US)
(800) 526-0550 (AZ)

**COUNTRY SUITES
BY CARLSON**
7411 N Oracle Rd
(85704)
Rates: $49-$100
Tel: (520) 575-9255
(800) 456-4000

THE COVE B & B
Tucson Blvd &
Norton (85713)
Rates: $60-$80
Weekly: $350-$400
Tel: (602) 990-0682
(800) 456-0682

**DAYS INN-
PALOVERDE/
TUCSON AIRPORT**
3700 E Irvington Rd
(85714)
Rates: $45-$90
Tel: (520) 571-1400
(800) 329-7466

**DOUBLETREE
HOTEL**
445 S Alvernon Way
(85711)
Rates: $64-$101
Tel: (520) 881-4200
(800) 222-8733

ECONO LODGE
3020 S 6th Ave
(85713)
Rates: $30-$85
Tel: (520)-623-5881
(800) 424-4777

**EMBASSY SUITES
HOTEL & CONF.
CENTER/AIRPORT**
7051 S Tucson Blvd
(85706)
Rates: $89-$139
Tel: (520) 573-0700
(800) 362-2779 (US)
(800) 262-8866 (AZ)

**EMBASSY SUITES
HOTEL TUCSON**
5335 E Broadway
(85711)
Rates: $79-$139
Tel: (520) 745-2700
(800) 362-2779

FLYING V RANCH
6800 N Flying V
Ranch Rd (85715)
Rates: $50-$110
Tel: (520) 299-4372

FRANCISCAN INN
1165 N Stone Ave
(85705)
Rates: $26-$60
Tel: (520) 622-7763

HAMPTON INN
1365 W. Grant Rd
(85745)
Rates: $55-$79
Tel: (800) 426-7866

**HAMPTON INN
AIRPORT**
6971 S Tucson Blvd
(85706)
Rates: $55-$79
Tel: (520) 889-5789
(800) 426-7866

**HOLIDAY INN
CITY CENTER**
181 W Broadway
(85701)
Rates: $50-$160
Tel: (520) 624-8711
(800) 465-4329 (US)
(800) 448-8276 (AZ)

**HOLIDAY INN-
PALOVERDE**
4550 S Paloverde
Blvd (85714)
Rates: $52-$128
Tel: (520) 746-1161
(800) 465-4329

LA QUINTA INN-E.
6404 E Broadway
(85710)
Rates: $40-$74
Tel: (520) 747-1414
(800) 531-5900

LA QUINTA INN-W.
665 N Freeway (85745)
Rates: $40-$74
Tel: (520) 622-6491
(800) 531-5900

**THE LODGE
ON THE DESERT**
306 N Alvernon Way
(85711)
Rates: $54-$177
Tel: (520) 325-3366
(800) 456-5634

MOTEL 6
1031 E Benson Hwy
(85713)
Rates: $29-$35
Tel: (520) 628-1264
(800) 440-6000

MOTEL 6
755 E Benson Hwy
(85713)
Rates: $29-$35
Tel: (520) 622-4614
(800) 440-6000

MOTEL 6
960 S Freeway
(85745)
Rates: $32-$38
Tel: (520) 628-1339
(800) 440-6000

MOTEL 6
4950 S Outlet Ctr Dr
(85706)
Rates: $35-$41
Tel: (520) 746-0030
(800) 440-6000

MOTEL 6
4630 W Ina Rd (85741)
Rates: $38-$44
Tel: (520) 744-9300
(800) 440-6000

MOTEL 6
1222 S Freeway
(85713)
Rates: $32-$38
Tel: (520) 624-2516
(800) 440-6000

MT. VIEWS B & B
E Tanque Verde Rd
(85749)
Rates: $65-$75
Weekly: $390-$450
Tel: (520) 990-0682
(800) 456-0682

**PARK INN
CLUB & BREAKFAST-
SANTA RITA**
88 E Broadway (85701)
Rates: $41-$45
Tel: (520) 622-4000
(800) 437-7275

PUEBLO INN
350 S Freeway (85745)
Rates: $68-$76
Tel: (520) 622-6611

**QUALITY INN
UNIVERSITY
& CONF CENTER**
1601 N Oracle Rd
(85705)
Rates: $45-$88
Tel: (520) 623-6666
(800) 228-5151

**RADISSON SUITE
HOTEL**
6555 E Speedway
Blvd (85710)
Rates: $59-$165
Tel: (520) 721-7100
(800) 333-3333

**RAMADA INN
FOOTHILLS**
6944 E Tanque Verde
Rd (85715)
Rates: $50-$120
Tel: (520) 886-9595
(800) 272-6232

**RAMADA INN
PALOVERDE 1**
5251 S Julian Dr
(85706)
Rates: $70-$120
Tel: (520) 294-5250
(800) 272-6232

RED ROOF INN
3700 E Irvington Rd
(85714)
Rates: $100+
Tel: (520) 571-1400
(800) 843-7663

**RESIDENCE INN
BY MARRIOTT**
6477 E Speedway
Blvd (85710)
Rates: $85-$174
Tel: (520) 721-0991
(800) 331-3131

RODEWAY INN
810 E Benson Hwy
(85713)
Rates: $49-$99
Tel: (520) 884-5800
(800) 228-2000

RODEWAY INN
1365 W Grant Rd
(85745)
Rates: $55-$95
Tel: (520) 622-7791
(800) 228-2000

**SHERATON
EL CONQUISTADOR
GOLF & TENNIS
RESORT**
10000 N Oracle Rd
(85737)
Rates: $130-$260
Tel: (520) 544-5000
(800) 325-7832

**SMUGGLER'S INN
HOTEL**
6350 E Speedway
Blvd (85710)
Rates: $42+
Tel: (520) 296-3293
(800) 525-8852

SUPER 8 MOTEL
1248 N Stone St
(85705)
Rates: $39-$90
Tel: (520) 622-6446
(800) 800-8000

THE TILLINGHAST PLACE B & B
N Oracle Rd & Rt 89 (85705)
Rates: $65-$105
Tel: (520) 990-0682
(800) 456-0682

TRAVELODGE-FLAMINGO
1300 N Stone Ave (85705)
Rates: $47-$142
Tel: (520) 770-1910
(800) 578-7878 (US)
(800) 300-3533 (AZ)

TRAVELODGE SUITES
401 W Lavery Ln (85704)
Rates: $57-$145
Tel: (520) 797-1710
(800) 578-7878

TUCSON EAST HILTON
7600 E Broadway (85710)
Rates: $49-$89
Tel: (520) 721-5600
(800) 648-7177

UNIVERSITY INN
950 N Stone Ave (85705)
Rates: $32-$59
Tel: (520) 791-7503

WAYWARD WINDS LODGE
707 W Miracle Mile (85705)
Rates: $39-$89
Tel: (520) 791-7526
(800) 791-9503

WESTWARD LOOK RESORT
245 E Ina Rd (85704)
Rates: $70-$130
Tel: (520) 297-1151
(800) 722-2500

WINDMILL INN AT ST. PHILLIP'S PLAZA
4250 N Campbell Ave (85718)
Rates: $60-$103
Tel: (520) 577-0007
(800) 547-4747

WICKENBURG

BEST WESTERN RANCHO GRANDE MOTOR HOTEL
293 E Wickenburg Way (85358)
Rates: $53-$95
Tel: (520) 684-5445
(800) 528-1234

WESTERNER MOTEL
680 W Wickenburg Way (85358)
Rates: $35-$50
Tel: (520) 684-2493

SUPER 8 MOTEL
1021 N Tegner (85930)
Rates: $45-$65
Tel: (800) 800-8000

WILLCOX

BEST WESTERN PLAZA INN
1100 W Rex Allen Dr (85643)
Rates: $50-$80
Tel: (520) 384-3556
(800) 528-1234

DAYS INN
724 N Bisbee Ave (85643)
Rates: $35-$90
Tel: (520) 384-4222
(800) 329-7466

ECONO LODGE
724 N Bisbee Ave (85643)
Rates: $46-$80
Tel: (520) 384-4222
(800) 221-2222

MOTEL 6
921 N Bisbee Ave (85643)
Rates: $28-$34
Tel: (520) 384-2201
(800) 440-6000

ROYAL WESTERN LODGE
590 S Haskell Ave (85643)
Rates: $24-$38
Tel: (520) 384-2266

WILLIAMS

BIG SIX MOTEL
134 E Bill Williams Ave (86046)
Rates: $25+
Tel: (520) 635-4591

BUDGET HOST INN
620 W Bill Williams Ave (86046)
Rates: $20-$79
Tel: (520) 635-4415
(800) 283-4678

CANYON MOTEL
Old E Hwy 66 (86046)
Rates: $20-$45
Tel: (520) 635-9371

DOWNTOWNER HOTEL
201 E Bill Williams Ave (86046)
Rates: $30+
Tel: (520) 635-4041

FAMILY INN
200 E Bill Williams Ave (86046)
Rates: $17-$50
Tel: (520) 635-2562

GATEWAY MOTEL
219 E Bill Williams Ave (86046)
Rates: $25-$40
Tel: (520) 635-4601

GRAND MOTEL
234 E Bill Williams Ave (86046)
Rates: $24-$40
Tel: (520) 635-4601

HIGHLANDER MOTEL
533 W Bill Williams Ave (86046)
Rates: $25-$48
Tel: (520) 635-2541

HOWARD JOHNSON
511 Grand Canyon Rd (86046)
Rates: $45-$69
Tel: (520) 635-9561
(800) 446-4656

9 ARIZONA MOTEL
831 W Bill Williams Ave (86046)
Rates: n/a
Tel: (520) 635-4552

PARK INN INTERNATIONAL
710 W Bill Williams Ave (86046)
Rates: $35-$85
Tel: (520) 635-4464
(800) 733-4814

QUALITY INN-MOUNTAIN RANCH & RESORT
Rt 1, Box 35 (86046)
Rates: $65-$102
Tel: (520) 635-2693
(800) 221-2222

RAMADA INN
642 E Route 66 (86046)
Rates: $50-$85
Tel: (520) 635-4431
(800) 272-6232

SUPER 8 MOTEL
2001 E Bill Williams Ave (86406)
Rates: $45-$100
Tel: (520) 635-4700
(800) 800-8000

TRAVELODGE
430 E Bill Williams Ave (86046)
Rates: $29-$169
Tel: (520) 635-2651
(800) 578-7878

WESTERNER MOTEL
530 W Bill Williams Ave (86046)
Rates: $85+
Tel: (520) 635-4312
(800) 385-8608

WINDOW ROCK

NAVAJO NATION INN
48 W Hwy 264 (86515)
Rates: $55-$70
Tel: (520) 871-4108
(800) 662-6189

WINSLOW

BEST WESTERN ADOBE INN
1701 N Park Dr (86047)
Rates: $47-$66
Tel: (520) 289-4638
(800) 528-1234

BEST WESTERN TOWN HOUSE LODGE
1914 W Third St
(86047)
Rates: $36-$56
Tel: (520) 289-4611
(800) 528-1234

COMFORT INN
520 Desmond St
(86047)
Rates: $44-$68
Tel: (520) 289-9581
(800) 221-2222

ECONO LODGE
1706 N Park Dr
(86047)
Rates: $48-$80
Tel: (520) 289-4687
(800) 424-4777

SUPER 8 MOTEL
1916 W Third St
(86047)
Rates: $37-$57
Tel: (520) 289-4606
(800) 800-8000

YOUNGSTOWN

MOTEL 6
11133 Grand Ave
(85363)
Rates: $37-$43
Tel: (602) 977-1318
(800) 440-6000

YUMA

BEST WESTERN CHILTON INN & CONF CENTER
300 E 32nd St
(85364)
Rates: $59-$99
Tel: (520) 344-1050
(800) 528-1234

BEST WESTERN CORONADO MOTOR HOTEL
233 4th Ave (85364)
Rates: $35-$90
Tel: (520) 783-4453
(800) 528-1234

BEST WESTERN INNSUITES HOTEL
1450 S Castle Dome Ave (85365)
Rates: $59-$119
Tel: (520) 783-8341
(800) 528-1234 (US)
(800) 922-2034 (AZ)

CARAVAN OASIS MOTEL
10574 Fortuna Rd
(85365)
Rates: $25-$43
Tel: (520) 342-1292

HOLIDAY INN EXPRESS
3181 S 4th Ave
(85364)
Rates: $55-$85
Tel: (520) 344-1402
(800) 465-4329

INTERSTATE 8 INN
2730 S 4th Ave
(85364)
Rates: $33+
Tel: (520) 726-6110
(800) 821-7465

MOTEL 6
1640 S Arizona Ave
(85364)
Rates: $25-$31
Tel: (520) 782-6561
(800) 440-6000

MOTEL 6
1445 E 16th St
(85365)
Rates: $27-$33
Tel: (520) 782-9521
(800) 440-6000

PARK INN INTERNATIONAL
2600 S 4th Ave
(85364)
Rates: $66-$96
Tel: (520) 726-4830
(800) 437-7275

ROYAL MOTOR INN
2941 S 4th Ave
(85364)
Rates: $40-$110
Tel: (520) 344-0550
(800) 729-0550

SHILO INNS-YUMA CONV RESORT
1550 S Castle Dome Rd (85365)
Rates: $83-$105
Tel: (520) 782-9511
(800) 222-2244

TRAVELODGE AIRPORT
711 East 32nd St
(85365)
Rates: $41-$65
Tel: (520) 726-4721
(800) 578-7878

YUMA CABANA MOTEL
2151 S 4th Ave
(85364)
Rates: $25-$65
Tel: (520) 783-8311
(800) 874-0811

ARKANSAS

ARKADELPHIA

BEST WESTERN-CONTINENTAL INN
I-30, Exit 78 (71923)
Rates: $41-$57
Tel: (501) 246-5592
(800) 528-1234

COLLEGE INN
1015 Pine (71923)
Rates: n/a
Tel: (501) 246-2404

DAYS INN
137 Valley Dr
(71923)
Rates: $40-$52
Tel: (501) 246-3031
(800) 329-7466

ECONO LODGE
106 Crystal Palace Dr
(71923)
Rates: $47-$55
Tel: (501) 246-8026
(800) 424-4777

HOLIDAY INN
Hwy 67 & 7 N
(71923)
Rates: $65-$75
Tel: (501) 246-5831
(800) 465-4329

QUALITY INN
I-30 & Hwy 7
(71923)
Rates: $40-$50
Tel: (501) 246-5855
(800) 221-2222

ASHDOWN

BUDGET INN
Hwy 71 (71822)
Rates: n/a
Tel: (501) 898-3357

BATESVILLE

ECONOMY INN
Hwy 233 N (72501)
Rates: n/a
Tel: (501) 793-3871
(800) 826-0778

RAMADA INN
1325 N St. Louis St
(72501)
Rates: $45-$90
Tel: (501) 698-1800
(800) 272-6232

BEEBE

ADAMS MOTEL
2110 Devil Hive
(72012)
Rates: n/a
Tel: (501) 882-6473

BENTON

BEST WESTERN INN
17036 I-30 (72015)
Rates: $34-$49
Tel: (501) 778-9695
(800) 528-1234

CAPRI MOTEL
15631 I-30 (72015)
Rates: n/a
Tel: (501) 778-8216

DAYS INN
17701 I-30 (72015)
Rates: $39-$49
Tel: (501) 776-3200
(800) 329-7466

ECONO LODGE
1221 Hot Springs Rd
(72015)
Rates: $35-$48
Tel: (501) 776-1515
(800) 424-4777

RAMADA INN
16732 I-30 (72015)
Rates: $37-$80
Tel: (501) 776-1900
(800) 272-6232

SCOTTISH INNS
17900 I-30 (72015)
Rates: n/a
Tel: (501) 778-4591
(800) 251-1962

SLEEP CHEAP
Cedarwood I-30,
Exit 117 (72015)
Rates: n/a
Tel: (501) 778-2305

TROUTT MOTEL
15348 I-30 (72015)
Rates: $19-$29
Tel: (501) 778-3633

BENTONVILLE

BEST WESTERN INN
2307 SE Walton Blvd
(72712)
Rates: $39-$52
Tel: (501) 273-9727
(800) 528-1234

HARTLAND MOTEL
1002 S Walton Blvd
(72712)
Rates: n/a
Tel: (501) 273-3444

BISMARCK

DEGRAY LAKEVIEW COTTAGES
Rt 3, Box 450 (71929)
Rates: n/a
Tel: (501) 865-3389

MORRISON'S COTTAGES
Rt 3 (71929)
Rates: n/a
Tel: (501) 865-4872

BLYTHEVILLE

BEST BUDGET INN
357 S Division
(72315)
Rates: n/a
Tel: (501) 763-4588

BEST WESTERN COTTON INN
I-15 & Hwy 18
(72315)
Rates: $37-$50
Tel: (501) 763-5220
(800) 528-1234

COMFORT INN
1520 E Main (72316)
Rates: $37-$45
Tel: (501) 763-7081
(800) 221-2222

DAYS INN
P. O. Box 1342
(72316)
Rates: $39-$59
Tel: (501) 763-1241
(800) 329-7466

DELTA K MOTEL
P. O. Box 1472
(72316)
Rates: $25-$36
Tel: (501) 763-1410

DRURY INN
201 N I-55 (72315)
Rates: $48-$61
Tel: (501) 763-2300
(800) 325-8300

HOLIDAY INN
Hwy 18 E (72316)
Rates: $46-$56
Tel: (501) 763-5800
(800) 465-4329

BOLES

Y-C MOUNTAIN INN & CAMPGROUND
HCR 69, Box 199
(72926)
Rates: n/a
Tel: (501) 577-2211

BRINKLEY

BEST WESTERN FULLER INN
1306 Hwy 17 N
(72021)
Rates: $45-$56
Tel: (501) 734-1650
(800) 528-1234

BRINKLEY INN
1124 S Main (72021)
Rates: n/a
Tel: (501) 734-3141

DAYS INN
I-40 & SR 49 N
(72021)
Rates: n/a
Tel: (800) 329-7466

ECONO LODGE
I-40 & Hwy 49 NE
(72021)
Rates: $40-$100
Tel: (501) 734-2035
(800) 424-4777

HERITAGE INN
1507 Hwy 17 N
(72021)
Rates: $29-$42
Tel: (501) 734-2121

SUPER 8 MOTEL
I-40 & Hwy 49 N
(72021)
Rates: $39-$54
Tel: (501) 734-4680
(800) 800-8000

BULL SHOALS

**BULL SHOALS
WHITE RIVER
LANDING**
P. O. Box 748 (72619)
Rates: n/a
Tel: (501) 445-4166

DOGWOOD LODGE
Shorecrest Dr (72619)
Rates: n/a
Tel: (501) 445-4311

DRIFTWOOD RESORT
P. O. Box 75 (72619)
Rates: n/a
Tel: (501) 445-4455
(800) 424-1129

MAR-MAR RESORT
Shorecrest Dr &
Hwy 178 (72619)
Rates: n/a
Tel: (501) 445-4444
(800) 332-2855

CABOT

DAYS INN
1114 W Main (72023)
Rates: $42-$65
Tel: (501) 843-0145
(800) 329-7466

CADDO GAP

ARROWHEAD CABINS
HC 65, Box 2 (71935)
Rates: n/a
Tel: (501) 356-2944

CALICO ROCK

**FOREST HOME LODGE
& LOG CABINS**
HC 61, Box 72
(72519)
Rates: n/a
Tel: (501) 297-8211

JENKINS MOTEL
605 Hwy 56 E
(72519)
Rates: n/a
Tel: (501) 297-8987

WISEMAN MOTEL
Box 546, Hwy 5
(72519)
Rates: n/a
Tel: (501) 297-3733

CAMDEN

AIRPORT INN
2115 Hwy 79 N
(71701)
Rates: n/a
Tel: (501) 574-0400

**AMERICAN
FAMILY INN**
Hwy 7 S &
Goodgame (71701)
Rates: n/a
Tel: (501) 231-6661

DAYS INN
942 Adams Ave SW
(71701)
Rates: $41-$45
Tel: (800) 329-7466

CARLISLE

**BEST WESTERN
INTERSTATE INN**
I-40 & Hwy 13
(72024)
Rates: $40-$58
Tel: (501) 552-7566
(800) 528-1234

CLARKRIDGE

**TREASURE COVE
RESORT**
902 County Rd 470
(72623)
Rates: n/a
Tel: (501) 425-4325

CLARKSVILLE

**BEST WESTERN
SHERWOOD
MOTOR INN**
P. O. Box 146 (72830)
Rates: $36-$65
Tel: (501) 754-7900
(800) 528-1234

COMFORT INN
1167 S Rogers Ave
(72830)
Rates: n/a
Tel: (501) 754-3000
(800) 221-2222

DAYS INN
2600 W Main St
(72830)
Rates: $33-$72
Tel: (501) 754-8555
(800) 329-7466

TAYLOR MOTEL
Hwy 64 E (72830)
Rates: n/a
Tel: (501) 754-2106

CLINTON

**BEST WESTERN
HILLSIDE INN**
P. O. Box 308 (72031)
Rates: $31-$49
Tel: (501) 745-4700
(800) 528-1234

SUPER 8 MOTEL
Hwy 65 S (72031)
Rates: $40-$52
Tel: (501) 754-8800
(800) 800-8000

COLTER

**WHITE SANDS
MOTEL**
P. O. Box 216 (72626)
Rates: n/a
Tel: (501) 435-2244

CONWAY

BEST WESTERN INN
P. O. Box 1619
(72032)
Rates: $34-$52
Tel: (501) 329-9855
(800) 528-1234

COMFORT INN

150 Hwy 65 N
(72033)
Rates: $42-$55
Tel: (501) 329-0300
(800) 221-2222

**CONTINENTAL
MOTEL**
134 Harkrider St
(72032)
Rates: n/a
Tel: (501) 327-7736

DAYS INN
1002 E Oak St
(72032)
Rates: n/a
Tel: (501) 450-7575
(800) 329-7466

ECONOMY INN
P. O. Box 606 (72033)
Rates: $32-$46
Tel: (501) 327-4800
(800) 826-0778

HOLIDAY INN
P. O. Box 998 (72032)
Rates: $47-$59
Tel: (501) 329-2961
(800) 465-4329

MOTEL 6
1105 Hwy 65 N
(72032)
Rates: $28-$32
Tel: (501) 327-6623
(800) 440-6000

RAMADA INN
815 E Oak St (72032)
Rates: $46-$59
Tel: (501) 329-8392
(800) 272-6232

COTTER

**CHAMBERLAIN'S
TROUT DOCK**
Denton Ferry Rd,
Rt 1, Box 620 (72626)
Rates: n/a
Tel: (501) 435-6535

**RAINBOW DRIVE
RESORT**
Rainbow Dr,
Rt 1, Box 1185
(72626)
Rates: n/a
Tel: (501) 430-5217

WHITE SANDS MOTEL
P. O. Box 116 (72626)
Rates: n/a
Tel: (501) 435-2244

CROSSETT

THE ASHLEY INN
Hwy 72 E (71635)
Rates: n/a
Tel: (501) 364-4911
(800) 276-7738

RAMADA INN
1400 S Florida
(71635)
Rates: $54-$146
Tel: (501) 364-4101
(800) 272-6232

DARDANELLE

BEST WESTERN FRONTIER MOTEL
P. O. Drawer 490
(72834)
Rates: $34-$44
Tel: (501) 229-4118
(800) 528-1234

DEER

THE PINEY INN
Hwy 7, P. O. Box 10
(72628)
Rates: n/a
Tel: (501) 428-5878

DERMOTT

ECONOMY INN
Rt 1, Box 60,
Hwy 65 N (71638)
Rates: n/a
Tel: (501) 222-4017

DEQUEEN

SCOTTISH INNS
1314 US Hwy 71 W
(71832)
Rates: $22-$32
Tel: (501) 642-2721
(800) 251-1962

DEVALLS BLUFF

PALAVER PLACE BED & BREAKFAST
Rt 1, Box 29-A
(72041)
Rates: n/a
Tel: (501) 998-7206

DEWITT

SAHARA MOTEL
Hwy 1, Box 309
(72042)
Rates: n/a
Tel: (501) 946-3581

DOGPATCH

ERBIE LODGE
HCR 73, Box 145
(72648)
Rates: $90+
Tel: (501) 446-5851

DOVER

MACK'S PINES
22816 SR 7 N (72837)
Rates: n/a
Tel: (501) 331-3261

DRASCO

TANNEBAUM RESORT & CABINS
1329 Tannebaum
(72530)
Rates: n/a
Tel: (501) 362-3075

DUMAS

EXECUTIVE INN
310 Hwy 65 S
(71639)
Tel: (501) 382-5115

PENDLETON INN
Rt 1 (71639)
Rates: n/a
Tel: (501) 382-4215

RAMADA LIMITED
722 Hwy 65 S
(71639)
Rates: $34-$46
Tel: (501) 382-2707
(800) 272-6232

EL DORADO

BEST WESTERN KINGS INN
1920 Junction City Rd
(71730)
Rates: $52-$56
Tel: (501) 862-5191
(800) 528-1234

COMFORT INN
2303 Junction City Rd
(71730)
Rates: $42-$59
Tel: (501) 863-6677
(800) 221-2222

EL DORADO INN MOTEL
3019 N West Ave
(71730)
Rates: n/a
Tel: (501) 862-6676

FLAMINGO MOTEL
420 S West Ave
(71730)
Rates: n/a
Tel: (501) 862-4201

WHITEHALL MOTEL
840 W Hillsboro
(71730)
Rates: n/a
Tel: (501) 863-4136

ELIZABETH

HOLIDAY HILLS RESORT
Rt 1, Box 22 (72531)
Rates: n/a
Tel: (501) 488-5303

KELLER'S KOVE RESORT
Rt 1, Box 45 (72531)
Rates: n/a
Tel: (501) 488-5360

EUREKA SPRINGS

ALPEN-DORF MOTEL
Rt 4, Box 580 (72632)
Rates: $48-$89
Tel: (501) 253-9475
(800) 776-9865

BASIN PARK HOTEL
12 Spring St (72632)
Rates: n/a
Tel: (501) 253-7837
(800) 643-4972

BEST WESTERN INN OF THE OZARKS
Hwy 62 W (72632)
Rates: $35-$84
Tel: (501) 552-3785
(800) 528-1234

BEST WESTERN SWISS HOLIDAY
P. O. Box 430 (72632)
Rates: $30-$71
Tel: (501) 253-9501
(800) 528-1234

BRACKENRIDGE LODGE
Rt 4, Box 60 (72632)
Rates: n/a
Tel: (501) 253-6803

CARRIAGE HOUSE
75 Lookout Ln (72632)
Rates: n/a
Tel: (501) 253-5259

CHALET INN
Rt 6, Box 156 (72632)
Rates: $32-$48
Tel: (501) 253-9687

COTTAGE INN B & B
Rt 6, Box 115 (72632)
Rates: $65
Tel: (501) 253-5282

DAYS INN
102 Kings Hwy
(72632)
Rates: $39-$120
Tel: (501) 253-8863
(800) 329-7466

DOGWOOD COTTAGES
RR 1, Box 168
(72632)
Rates: n/a
Tel: (501) 253-8897

DOGWOOD INN
Rt 6, Box 20 (72632)
Rates: $20-$54
Tel: (501) 253-7200

1876 INN
Rt 6, Box 247 (72632)
Rates: $30-$71
Tel: (501) 253-7183
(800) 643-3030

EUREKA SUNSET COTTAGES
10 Dogwood Ridge (72632)
Rates: n/a
Tel: (501) 253-9565

FOUR RUNNERS INN
RR 4, Box 306 (72632)
Rates: n/a
Tel: (501) 253-6000

HARVEST HOUSE BED & BREAKFAST
104 Wall (72632)
Rates: n/a
Tel: (501) 253-9363

HIDDEN VALLEY GUEST RANCH
777 Hidden Valley Ranch (72632)
Rates: n/a
Tel: (501) 253-9777

HILLSIDE COTTAGE BED & BREAKFAST
23 Hillside (72632)
Rates: n/a
Tel: (501) 253-8688

INDIAN MOUNTAIN LODGE & CABINS
Rt 4, Box 570 (72632)
Rates: n/a
Tel: (501) 253-5221

KATIE WILLOW COTTAGES
Rt 6, Box 354 (72632)
Rates: n/a
Tel: (501) 253-8199

KINGS HI-WAY INN
92 Kings Hwy (72632)
Rates: n/a
Tel: (501) 253-7311

LAKE LEATHER-WOOD PARK
Hwy 62 W (72632)
Rates: n/a
Tel: (501) 253-8624

LAKE LUCERNE RESORT
P. O. Box 441 (72632)
Rates: n/a
Tel: (501) 253-8085

LAZEE DAZE LOG CABIN RESORT
Rt 1, Box 196 (72632)
Rates: n/a
Tel: (501) 253-7026

LOG CABIN INN MOTEL
42 Kings Hwy (72632)
Rates: n/a
Tel: (501) 253-9400
(800) 254-9411

MARIPOSA INN
3 Echols (72632)
Rates: n/a
Tel: (501) 253-9169

OAK CREST COTTAGES
Rt 6, Box 126 (72632)
Rates: $30-$45
Tel: (501) 253-9493
(800) 262-6255

OLD HOMESTEAD
82 Armstrong St (72632)
Rates: n/a
Tel: (501) 253-7501

PINE LODGE
Rt 2, Box 18 (72632)
Rates: n/a
Tel: (501) 253-8065

PINE TOP LODGE
Rt 6, Box 265 (72632)
Rates: $24-$56
Tel: (501) 253-7331
(800) 643-2233

POINTE WEST RESORT
Rt 2, Box 87 (72632)
Rates: n/a
Tel: (501) 253-9050

POTTER'S HOUSE MOTEL
Passion Play Rd (72632)
Rates: n/a
Tel: (501) 253-7398

PURPLE IRIS INN
RR 6, Box 339 (72632)
Rates: n/a
Tel: (800) 831-4747

RED CARPET INN
Rt 4, Box 309A (72632)
Rates: $24-$40
Tel: (501) 253-6665
(800) 251-1962

REGENCY 7
62E Passion Play Rd (72632)
Rates: n/a
Tel: (800) 470-5959

ROADRUNNER INN
RR 2, Box 158 (72632)
Rates: $39+
Tel: (501) 253-8166

ROGUE'S MANOR AT SWEET SPRINGS BED & BREAKFAST
124 Spring St (72632)
Rates: n/a
Tel: (501) 253-4911
(800) 764-8376

SCANDIA INN B & B
33 Avo, Hwy 62 W (72632)
Rates: n/a
Tel: (501) 253-8922
(800) 523-8922

SHERWOOD COURT
27 Glenn Ave (72632)
Rates: n/a
Tel: (501) 253-8920
(800) 268-8920

SOUTHERN COUNTRY INN
Rt 1, Box 460 (72632)
Rates: n/a
Tel: (501) 253-5600
(800) 264-9565

STATUE ROAD INN MOTEL
Rt 1, Box 965 (72632)
Rates: n/a
Tel: (501) 253-9163
(800) 501-7666

STUDIO GUEST HOUSE
120 N Main (72632)
Rates: n/a
Tel: (501) 253-8773

SWISS VILLAGE INN
Rt 6, Box 5 (72632)
Rates: $44-$65
Tel: (501) 253-9541
(800) 447-6525

TAYLOR-PAGE INN BED & BREAKFAST
33 Benton St (72632)
Rates: n/a
Tel: (501) 253-7315

TRADEWINDS MOTEL
77 Kings Hwy (72632)
Rates: $26-$80
Tel: (501) 253-9774
(800) 242-1615

TRAVELERS INN
Rt 1, Box 269 (72632)
Rates: $22-$48
Tel: (501) 253-8386
(800) 643-5566

WHISPERING OAKS MOTEL
Rt 6, Box 338 (72632)
Rates: n/a
Tel: (501) 253-9459

WHITE DOVER MANOR B & B
8 Washington St (72632)
Rates: n/a
Tel: (501) 253-6151
(800) 261-6151

WILDFLOWER COTTAGES
22 Hale St (72632)
Rates: n/a
Tel: (501) 253-9173

EVENING SHADE

THE TURMAN HOUSE B & B
P. O. Box 146 (72532)
Rates: n/a
Tel: (501) 266-3405
(800) 257-3405

FAYETTEVILLE

CHIEF MOTEL
1818 N College Ave (72703)
Rates: n/a
Tel: (501) 442-7326

DAYS INN
2402 N College Ave (72703)
Rates: $45-$69
Tel: (501) 443-4323
(800) 329-7466

HILTON HOTEL
70 N East Ave
(72701)
Rates: $58-$84
Tel: (501) 442-5555
(800) 445-8667

HOLIDAY INN EXP
1251 N Shiloh Dr
(72701)
Rates: $39-$66
Tel: (501) 444-6006
(800) 465-4329

**THE INN
OF FAYETTEVILLE**
1000 Hwy 71 (72701)
Rates: $38-$44
Tel: (501) 442-3041
(800) 290-3041

MOTEL 6
2980 N College Ave
(72703)
Rates: $30-$34
Tel: (501) 443-4351
(800) 440-6000

RAMADA INN
3901 N College Ave
(72703)
Rates: $53-$75
Tel: (501) 443-3431
(800) 272-6232

TWIN ARCH MOTEL
521 N College Ave
(72701)
Rates: n/a
Tel: (501) 521-9452

FLIPPIN

**SEAWRIGHT'S
MOTEL**
1st & Sunset Sts
(72634)
Rates: n/a
Tel: (501) 453-2555

**SHADY OAKS
COTTAGES**
HC 62, Box 128 (72634)
Rates: $50-$65
Tel: (501) 626-5474
(800) 467-6257

**SPORTSMAN'S
RESORT**
HCR 62, Box 96
(72634)
Rates: n/a
Tel: (501) 453-2424
(800) 626-5474

**WHITE HOLE
RESORT**
HCR 62, Box 100
(72634)
Rates: n/a
Tel: (501) 453-2913

**WILDCAT SHOALS
RESORT**
P. O. Box 1032
(72634)
Rates: n/a
Tel: (501) 453-2321

FORDYCE

A-OK MOTEL
2403 Hwy 167 & 79
(71742)
Rates: n/a
Tel: (501) 352-3197

**ANTLERS INN
MOTEL**
2400 Bypass (71742)
Rates: n/a
Tel: (501) 352-5174

FORREST CITY

**BEST WESTERN
COLONY INN**
2333 N Washington
(72335)
Rates: $48-$72
Tel: (501) 633-0870
(800) 528-1234

ECONO LODGE
204 Holiday Dr
(72335)
Rates: $34-$49
Tel: (800) 424-4777

HOLIDAY INN
Hwy 1 N & I-40
(72335)
Rates: $41-$49
Tel: (501) 633-6300
(800) 465-4329

LUXURY INN
315 Barrow Wheel
Rd (72335)
Rates: $33-$39
Tel: (501) 633-8990

REGENCY INN
907 E Broadway
(72335)
Rates: n/a
Tel: (501) 633-4433

SAVE INN
105 NW St, Hwy 70
W (72335)
Rates: n/a
Tel: (501) 633-3214

FORT SMITH

**BEST WESTERN
KINGS ROW INN**
5801 Rogers Ave
(72901)
Rates: $44-$50
Tel: (501) 452-4200
(800) 528-1234

**BEST WESTERN
TRADE WINDS INN**
101 N 11th St (72901)
Rates: $41-$68
Tel: (501) 785-4121
(800) 528-1234

BUDGETEL INN
2123 Burnham Rd
(72903)
Rates: $38-$54
Tel: (501) 484-5770

DAYS INN
1021 Garrison Ave
(72901)
Rates: $35-$49
Tel: (501) 783-0548
(800) 329-7466

DENNIS MOTEL
5100 Midland Blvd
(72904)
Rates: n/a
Tel: (501) 782-4064

**ECONO LODGE-
HISTORIC DISTRICT**
301 N 11th St (72902)
Rates: $37-$49
Tel: (800) 424-4777

**FIFTH SEASON
MOTOR INN**
2219 S Waldron Rd
(72903)
Rates: $48-$69
Tel: (501) 452-4880
(800) 643-4567

**HOLIDAY INN
CIVIC CENTER**
700 Rogers Ave
(72901)
Rates: $72-$88
Tel: (501) 783-1000
(800) 465-4329

MOTEL 6
6001 Rogers Ave
(72903)
Rates: $32-$38
Tel: (501) 484-0576
(800) 440-6000

SHERATON INN
5711 Rogers Ave
(72901)
Rates: $55-$65
Tel: (501) 452-4110
(800) 356-7046

GAMALIEL

BAYOU RESORT
HC 66, Box 390
(72537)
Rates: n/a
Tel: (501) 467-5277

**CASTAWAYS
RESORT & CAFE**
Hwy 101 (72537)
Rates: n/a
Tel: (501) 467-5348

**DRIFTWOOD
RESORT**
HC 66, Box 6000
(72537)
Rates: n/a
Tel: (501) 467-5330

LAKESIDE RESORT
Koeller Rd, CR 801
(72537)
Rates: n/a
Tel: (501) 467-5196

LUCKY 7 RESORT
HC 66, Box 1345
(72537)
Rates: n/a
Tel: (501) 467-5451

**SHADY VALLEY
RESORT**
HC 66, Box 220
(72537)
Rates: n/a
Tel: (501) 467-5350

**TWIN GABLES
RESORT**
HC 66, Box 1385
(72537)
Rates: n/a
Tel: (501) 467-5686

GASSVILLE

RED BUD DOCK MOTEL
Rt 2, Box 541 (72635)
Rates: n/a
Tel: (501) 435-6303

GATEWAY

HOLIDAY HILL MOTEL
Hwy 62 E Gateway (72733)
Rates: n/a
Tel: (501) 656-3395

GENTRY

GENTRY MOTEL
P. O. Box 177 (72734)
Rates: n/a
Tel: (501) 736-8006

GILBERT

BUFFALO CAMPING & CANOEING
P. O. Box 504 (72636)
Rates: n/a
Tel: (501) 439-2888

GENERAL STORE CABINS
1 Frost St (72636)
Rates: n/a
Tel: (501) 439-2386

GILLETT

RICE PADDY MOTEL
P. O. Box 536 (72055)
Rates: n/a
Tel: (501) 548-2223

GLENWOOD

CADDO RIVER MOTEL
Rt 2, Box 786 (71943)
Rates: n/a
Tel: (501) 356-4117

OUACHITA MT INN
Box 32, Hwy 70
Bypass (71943)
Rates: n/a
Tel: (501) 356-3737

GREERS FERRY

COLE'S OZARK MOTEL
7650 Edgemont Rd (72067)
Rates: n/a
Tel: (501) 825-6607

NARROW'S INN
7910 Edgemont Rd (72067)
Rates: n/a
Tel: (501) 825-6246

RED BIRD INN
9174 Edgemont Rd (72067)
Rates: n/a
Tel: (501) 825-6256

HAMPTON

SMITH'S MOTEL
P. O. Box 823 (71744)
Rates: n/a
Tel: (501) 798-2755

HARDY

FRONTIER MOTOR LODGE
Rt 1, Box 62 (72542)
Rates: n/a
Tel: (501) 966-3377

HIDEAWAY INN
Rt 1, Box 199 (72542)
Rates: n/a
Tel: (501) 966-4770

MOTOR CENTER MOTEL
Rt 1, Box 57-A (72542)
Rates: n/a
Tel: (501) 856-3282

RAZORBACK MOTEL
Rt 1, Box 234 (72542)
Rates: n/a
Tel: (501) 856-2465

WEAVER MOTEL
Rt 1, Box 2 (72542)
Rates: n/a
Tel: (501) 856-3224

HARRISON

AIRPORT MOTEL
1605 Hwy 62-65 N (72601)
Rates: n/a
Tel: (501) 741-5900

CRESTHAVEN INN
825 N Main (72601)
Rates: n/a
Tel: (501) 741-9522

HOLIDAY INN
816 N Main (72601)
Rates: $46-$58
Tel: (501) 741-2391
(800) 465-4329

LITTLE SWITZERLAND
Jasper Star Rt,
Hwy 7 (72601)
Rates: n/a
Tel: (501) 446-2693
(800) 510-0691

MERRY OTTER B & B
103 W South St (72601)
Rates: n/a
Tel: (501) 743-9010

RAMADA INN
1222 N Main (72601)
Rates: $35-$56
Tel: (501) 741-7611
(800) 272-6232

ROCK CANDY MT
Hwy 7 South (72601)
Rates: n/a
Tel: (501) 743-1531

SCENIC 7 MOTEL
Rt 1, Box 16 (72601)
Rates: n/a
Tel: (501) 741-9648

SUPER 8 MOTEL
1330 Hwy 62/65 N (72601)
Rates: $42-$60
Tel: (501) 741-1741
(800) 800-8000

HEBER SPRINGS

ARKANSAS INN
2233 Hwy 25 NB (72543)
Rates: n/a
Tel: (501) 362-2500
(800) 530-7740

BARNETT MOTEL
616 W Main St (72543)
Rates: $36-$47
Tel: (501) 362-8111

LAKE & RIVER INN
2322 Hwy 25B (72543)
Rates: $35-$45
Tel: (501) 362-3161

LAKESHORE RESORT MOTEL
801 Case Ford Rd (72543)
Rates: $42+
Tel: (501) 362-2315

OZARK TRAIL MOTEL
1631 Hwy 25 B (72543)
Rates: n/a
Tel: (501) 362-3102

PINES MOTEL
1819 25 B (72543)
Rates: n/a
Tel: (501) 362-3176

HENDERSON

CRYSTAL COVE RESORT
HC 66, Box 845 (72544)
Rates: n/a
Tel: (501) 488-5373

RODEWAY INN
US 62 E (72544)
Rates: $35-$74
Tel: (501) 488-5144
(800) 424-4777

HELENA

RIVERBLUFF HOTEL
Box 730 (72342)
Rates: $40-$75
Tel: (501) 338-6431
(800) 543-5352

HETH

**BEST WESTERN
LAKE SIDE INN**
P. O. Box 151 (72346)
Rates: $36-$50
Tel: (501) 657-2101
(800) 528-1234

HINDSVILLE

**FOXFIRE CAMP
RESORT**
Rt 1, Box 198 (72738)
Rates: n/a
Tel: (501) 789-2122

HOPE

**BEST WESTERN
INN OF HOPE**
Jct I-30 & SR 4,
Exit 30 (71801)
Rates: $40-$55
Tel: (501) 777-9222
(800) 528-1234

DAYS INN
1500 N Hervey (71801)
Rates: $35-$80
Tel: (501) 722-1904
(800) 329-7466

FRIENDLY INN
P. O. Box 930 (71801)
Rates: n/a
Tel: (501) 777-4665

HOLIDAY INN
I-30 & Hwy 4 (71801)
Rates: $32-$46
Tel: (800) 465-4329

QUALITY INN
I-30 & Hwy 29 (71801)
Rates: $29-$40
Tel: (501) 777-0777
(800) 424-6423

HORSESHOE BEND

**BOXHOUND
RESORT, MARINA
& RV PARK**
1313 Tri-Lake Dr
(72512)
Rates: n/a
Tel: (501) 670-4496

HOT SPRINGS

APPLE TREE INN
805 E Grand (71901)
Rates: n/a
Tel: (501) 624-4672
(800) 782-7753

**BEST WESTERN
STAGECOACH INN**
2520 Central Ave
(71901)
Rates: n/a
Tel: (501) 624-2531
(800) 643-8722

EL RANCHO MOTEL
1611 Central Ave
(71901)
Rates: n/a
Tel: (501) 624-1273

FOUNTAIN MOTEL
1622 Central Ave
(71901)
Rates: n/a
Tel: (501) 624-1262

**HOT SPRINGS
RESORT**
1871 E Grand (71901)
Rates: n/a
Tel: (501) 623-8824
(800) 238-4891

KING'S INN MOTEL
2101 Central Ave
(71901)
Rates: n/a
Tel: (501) 623-8824
(800) 235-8824

MAJESTIC HOTEL
Park & Central Ave
(71901)
Rates: $45-$65
Tel: (501) 623-5511

MT SPRINGS INN
1127 Central Ave
(71901)
Rates: n/a
Tel: (501) 624-7131

PARK HOTEL
211 Fountain (71901)
Rates: n/a
Tel: (501) 624-5323

**PATTON'S LAKE
RESORT**
100 San Carlos Point
(71913)
Rates: n/a
Tel: (501) 525-1678

ROYALE VISTA INN
2204 Central Ave
(71901)
Rates: n/a
Tel: (501) 624-5551

SHAMROCK MOTEL
508 Albert Pike
(71913)
Rates: n/a
Tel: (501) 624-3833

**TAYLOR ROSAMOND
MOTEL**
316 Park Ave (71901)
Rates: n/a
Tel: (501) 624-1255

**TOWN HOUSE
MOTEL**
100 Cove (71901)
Rates: n/a
Tel: (501) 624-9271

**TRAVELIER
MOTOR LODGE**
1045 E Grand Ave
(71901)
Rates: n/a
Tel: (501) 624-4681

VAGABOND MOTEL
4708 Central Ave
(71913)
Rates: n/a
Tel: (501) 525-2769

**WILDWOOD
1884 B & B**
8 Park Ave (71901)
Rates: n/a
Tel: (501) 624-4275

**WILLIAMS HOUSE
INN B & B**
420 Quapaw Ave
(71901)
Rates: n/a
Tel: (501) 624-4275

**WILLOW BEACH
RESORT**
260 Lake Hamilton
(71913)
Rates: n/a
Tel: (501) 525-1362
(800) 874-1385

**WOODBINE
HOLLOW B & B**
213 Woodbine
(71901)
Rates: n/a
Tel: (501) 624-3646

HOT SPRINGS NATIONAL PARK

**AVANELLE
MOTOR LODGE**
1204 Central Ave
(71901)
Rates: $44-$70
Tel: (501) 321-1332

**BEST WESTERN
HOT SPRINGS INN**
P. O. Box CC (71902)
Rates: $19-$69
Tel: (800) 528-1234

**BUENA VISTA
RESORT**
201 Abernia (71913)
Rates: $45-$120
Tel: (800) 255-9030

**HAMILTON INN
RESORT**
106 Lookout Point
(71913)
Rates: $45-$58
Tel: (501) 525-5666

HILL WHEATLEY INN
400 W Grand Ave
(71901)
Rates: $30-$50
Tel: (800) 999-4441

**HOLIDAY INN
LAKE HAMILTON**
4813 Central Ave
(71902)
Rates: $56-$95
Tel: (501) 525-1391
(800) 465-4329

**LAKE HAMILTON
RESORT**
2803 Albert Pike Rd
(71913)
Rates: $75-$135
Tel: (501) 767-5511

MARGARETE MOTEL
217 Fountain St
(71901)
Rates: $26-$45
Tel: (501) 623-1192

QUALITY INN
1125 E Grand Ave
(71901)
Rates: $50-$60
Tel: (501) 624-3321
(800) 221-2222

RAMADA INN TOWERS
218 Park Ave (71901)
Rates: $62-$72
Tel: (501) 623-3311
(800) 272-6232

SHORECREST RESORT
360 Lakeland Dr
(71901)
Rates: $41-$52
Tel: (800) 447-9914

TRAVELIER MOTOR LODGE
1045 E Grand Ave
(71901)
Rates: $27-$49
Tel: (501) 624-4681

HUTTIG

TRACKS INN MOTEL
1141 K Ave (71747)
Rates: n/a
Tel: (501) 943-2943

JACKSONVILLE

DAYS INN
1414 John Harden
Dr (72076)
Rates: $40-$60
Tel: (501) 982-1543
(800) 329-7466

OXFORD INN
920 Hwy 161 (72076)
Rates: n/a
Tel: (501) 982-1976

RAMADA INN
200 Hwy 67N
(72076)
Rates: $49-$62
Tel: (501) 982-2183
(800) 272-6232

SANDS MOTEL
1008 S Hwy 161
(72076)
Rates: n/a
Tel: (501) 985-0266

SCOTTISH INNS
1414 John Harden
Dr (72076)
Rates: $30-$38
Tel: (501) 982-1543
(800) 251-1962

JASPER

LOOKOUT MT LOG CABINS
HCR 31, Box 90
(72641)
Rates: n/a
Tel: (501) 446-6224
(800) 596-5409

MOCKINGBIRD MOTEL
HCR 31, Box 64-B
(72641)
Rates: n/a
Tel: (501) 446-2643

JESSIEVILLE

OUACHITA MOTEL
6127 N Hwy 7
(71949)
Rates: n/a
Tel: (501) 984-5363

JONESBORO

AUTUMN INN MOTEL
2406 Phillips Dr
(72401)
Rates: $30-$40
Tel: (501) 932-9339
(800) 227-9345

BEST WESTERN INN
2901 Phillips Dr
(72401)
Rates: $45-$85
Tel: (501) 932-6600
(800) 528-1234

COMFORT INN
2904 Phillips Dr
(72401)
Rates: $38-$50
Tel: (501) 972-8686
(800) 221-2222

HOLIDAY INN
3006 S Caraway Rd
(72401)
Rates: $40-$95
Tel: (501) 935-2030
(800) 465-4329

JAMI BEE MOTEL
3423 E Nettleton Ave
(72401)
Rates: n/a
Tel: (501) 932-1611

JONESBORO MOTEL
403 S Gee St (72401)
Rates: n/a
Tel: (501) 932-6615

MOTEL 6
2300 S Caraway Rd
(72401)
Rates: $30-$48
Tel: (501) 932-1050
(800) 440-6000

PARK PLACE INN
1421 S Caraway Rd
(72401)
Rates: n/a
Tel: (501) 935-8400

RAMADA INN
3000 Apache Dr
(72401)
Rates: $48-$67
Tel: (501) 932-5757
(800) 272-6232

SCOTTISH INNS MOTEL
3116 Mead Dr
(72401)
Rates: $30-$35
Tel: (501) 972-8300
(800) 251-1962

SUPER 8 MOTEL
2500 S Caraway Rd
(72401)
Rates: $32-$50
Tel: (501) 972-1849
(800) 800-8000

WILSON INN
2911 Gilmore Dr
(72401)
Rates: $35-$55
Tel: (501) 972-9000

KIRBY

DAISY MOTEL
HC 71, Box 255
(71950)
Rates: n/a
Tel: (501) 398-5173

LAKESIDE GROCERY & MOTEL
HC 71, Box 67
(71950)
Rates: n/a
Tel: (501) 398-5304

LAKE VILLAGE

LA VILLA MOTEL
Hwys 65 & 82
(71653)
Rates: n/a
Tel: (501) 265-2277

LAKE SHORE MOTEL
P. O. Box 231 (71653)
Rates: n/a
Tel: (501) 265-2238

PLAZA MOTEL
Hwys 65 & 82 S
(71653)
Rates: n/a
Tel: (501) 265-5341

LAKEVIEW

BAY BREEZE RESORT
Box 185, Hwy 178
(72642)
Rates: n/a
Tel: (501) 431-5261

CEDAR OAKS RESORT
Rt 1, Box 694 (72642)
Rates: $45-$75
Tel: (501) 431-5351

GASTON'S WHITE RIVER RESORT
1 River Rd (72642)
Rates: $57-$105
Tel: (501) 431-5202

LAST RESORT
P. O. Box 144 (72642)
Rates: n/a
Tel: (501) 431-5681
(800) 799-5253

NEWLAND FLOAT TRIPS & LODGE
Rt 1, River Rd
(72642)
Rates: n/a
Tel: (501) 431-8620
(800) 334-5604

TWIN FIN RESORT
P. O. Box 218T (72642)
Rates: n/a
Tel: (501) 431-5377

LEAD HILL

BON TERRE INN
Hwy 281 N (72644)
Rates: n/a
Tel: (501) 436-7318

HILL TOP COTTAGES
Rt 1, Box 280 (72644)
Rates: n/a
Tel: (501) 436-5365

LITTLE ROCK

BUDGET INN
9351 I-30 (72209)
Rates: n/a
Tel: (501) 565-0111

BUDGETEL INN
1010 Breckenridge
Rd (72205)
Rates: $44-$66
Tel: (501) 225-7007

**THE CARRIAGE
HOUSE B&B**
1700 Louisiana
(72206)
Rates: $89
Tel: (501) 374-7032

CIMARRON INN
10200 I-30 (72209)
Rates: n/a
Tel: (501) 565-1181

COMFORT INN
3200 Bankhead Dr
(72206)
Rates: $40-$54
Tel: (501) 490-2010
(800) 221-2222

COMFORT INN
8219 I-30 (72209)
Rates: $45-$60
Tel: (800) 221-2222

**COURTYARD
BY MARRIOTT**
10900 Financial Ctr
Pkwy (72211)
Rates: n/a
Tel: (501) 227-6000
(800) 321-2211

DAYS INN SOUTH
2600 W 65th St
(72209)
Rates: $32-$60
Tel: (501) 562-1122
(800) 329-7466

**DOUBLETREE
HOTEL**
424 W Markham
(72201)
Rates: n/a
Tel: (501) 372-4371
(800) 937-2789

HAMPTON INN
500 W 29th (72114)
Rates: $56-$64
Tel: (501) 771-2090
(800) 426-7866

**HERITAGE HOUSE
INN**
7500 S University
(72209)
Rates: n/a
Tel: (501) 565-2055

**HOLIDAY INN
CITY CENTER**
617 S Broadway
(72201)
Rates: $60-$70
Tel: (501) 376-4000
(800) 465-4329

**HOLIDAY INN
EXPRESS**
3121 Bankhead
Dr.(72206)
Rates: $58-$68
Tel: (501) 490-4000
(800) 465-4329

HOLIDAY INN WEST
201 S Shackelford
(72211)
Rates: $73-$94
Tel: (501) 223-3000
(800) 465-4329

JACK'S MOTEL
9515 Hwy 365
(72206)
Rates: n/a
Tel: (501) 897-4951

LA QUINTA INN
11701 I-30/I-430
(72209)
Rates: $55-$125
Tel: (501) 455-2300
(800) 531-5900

LA QUINTA INN
901 Fair Park Blvd
(72204)
Rates: $44-$46
Tel: (501) 664-7000
(800) 531-5900

LA QUINTA INN
2401 W 65th St
(72209)
Rates: $41-$54
Tel: (501) 568-1030
(800) 531-5900

LA QUINTA INN
200 Shackelford Rd
(72211)
Rates: $45-$58
Tel: (501) 224-0900
(800) 531-5900

LEGACY HOTEL
625 W Capitol
(72201)
Rates: n/a
Tel: (501) 374-0100

MARKHAM INN
5120 W Markham
(72205)
Rates: n/a
Tel: (501) 666-0161
(800) 654-0161

MOTEL 6
400 W 29th St (72114)
Rates: $30-$36
Tel: (501) 758-5100
(800) 466-8356

MOTEL 6-SOUTH
9525 I-30 S (72209)
Rates: $26-$32
Tel: (501) 565-1388
(800) 440-6000

MOTEL 6-S. EAST
7501 I-30 (72209)
Rates: $32-$38
Tel: (501) 568-8888

MOTEL 6-WEST
10524 Markham St
(72205)
Rates: $32-$38
Tel: (501) 225-7366
(800) 440-6000

RAMADA LIMITED
9709 Hwy I-30
(72209)
Rates: n/a
Tel: (501) 568-6800
(800) 272-6232

RED ROOF INN
7900 Scott Hamilton
Dr (72209)
Rates: $28-$42
Tel: (501) 562-2694
(800) 843-7663

WILSON INN
4301 E Roosevelt
(72206)
Rates: $34-$54
Tel: (501) 376-2466

LONOKE

ECONOMY INN
Hwy 31 N & I-40
(72086)
Rates: n/a
Tel: (501) 676-3116
(800) 826-0778

PERRY'S MOTEL
200 Nathan Dr
(72086)
Rates: n/a
Tel: (501) 676-3181

MAGNOLIA

**BEST WESTERN-
COACHMAN'S INN**
420 E Main (71753)
Rates: $44-$59
Tel: (501) 234-6122
(800) 528-1234

CASTLE INN MOTEL
912 E Main (71753)
Rates: n/a
Tel: (501) 234-2262

FLAMINGO MOTEL
100 N Vine (71753)
Rates: n/a
Tel: (501) 234-4752

KING'S INN MOTEL
411 E Main (71753)
Rates: n/a
Tel: (501) 234-3612
(800) 444-3612

MALVERN

ECONOMY INN
Hwy 270 N (71204)
Rates: n/a
Tel: (501) 332-2487
(800) 826-0778

SUPER 8 MOTEL
Rt 8, Box 719-6
(72104)
Rates: n/a
Tel: (501) 332-5755
(800) 800-8000

TOWN HOUSE MOTEL
304 E Page Ave
(72104)
Rates: n/a
Tel: (501) 332-5437

MAMMOTH SPRING

RIVERVIEW MOTEL
P. O. Box 281 (72554)
Rates: n/a
Tel: (501) 625-3218

MARION

BEST WESTERN REGENCY MOTOR INN
Rt 2, Box 398C
(72364)
Rates: $36-$50
Tel: (501) 739-3278
(800) 528-1234

MARKED TREE

DAYS INN
201 Hwy 63 S (72365)
Rates: $36-$65
Tel: (501) 358-2700
(800) 329-7466

MARSHALL

ROSE MOTEL
P. O. Box 913 (72650)
Rates: n/a
Tel: (501) 448-2596

SUNSET MOTEL
P. O. Box 205 (72650)
Rates: n/a
Tel: (501) 448-3348

McGEHEE

SENATOR MOTEL
222 Hwy 65 (71654)
Rates: n/a
Tel: (501) 222-5511

MENA

AERIE BED & BREAKFAST
Hwy 375 (71953)
Rates: n/a
Tel: (501) 394-6473

BEST WESTERN LIMETREE INN
804 Hwy 71 N
(71953)
Rates: $37-$80
Tel: (501) 394-6350
(800) 528-1234

HOLIDAY MOTEL
1162 US 71 S (71953)
Rates: n/a
Tel: (501) 394-2611

NANA'S COUNTRY INN
203 US 71 N (71953)
Rates: n/a
Tel: (501) 394-6433

OZARK INN
P. O. Box 1071
(71953)
Rates: n/a
Tel: (501) 394-1100

MIDWAY

HOLIDAY SHORES RESORT
Rt 1, Box 283 (72651)
Rates: n/a
Tel: (501) 431-5370
(800) 365-4089

HOWARD CREEK RESORT
RR 1, Box 282
(72651)
Rates: n/a
Tel: (501) 431-5371

RED ARROW RESORT
Rt 1, Box 281 (72651)
Rates: n/a
Tel: (501) 431-5375
(800) 548-8724

SUNSET POINT RESORT
Rt 1, Box 290 (72651)
Rates: n/a
Tel: (501) 431-5372
(800) 336-8113

MONTICELLO

HIWAY HOST INN
617 W Gaines
(71655)
Rates: n/a
Tel: (501) 367-8555

MORRILTON

BEST WESTERN
365 Hwy 425 N
(71655)
Rates: $38-$54
Tel: (501) 354-0181
(800) 528-1234

ECONO LODGE
1506 N Hwy 95
(72110)
Rates: $36-$48
Tel: (501) 354-5101
(800) 424-4777

SUPER 8 MOTEL
1420 N Business 9
(72110)
Rates: n/a
Tel: (501) 354-8188
(800) 800-8000

MOUNT IDA

COLONIAL MOTEL
HC 63, Box 306 (71957)
Rates: n/a
Tel: (501) 867-2431

DENBY POINT LODGE & MARINA
SR 1, Box 241 (71957)
Rates: $35-$90
Tel: (501) 867-3651

MOUNT IDA MOTEL
HC 67, Box 67-X
(71957)
Rates: n/a
Tel: (501) 867-3456

MOUNTAIN HOME

BEST WESTERN-CARRIAGE INN
963 US 62 E (72653)
Rates: $35-$67
Tel: (501) 425-6001
(800) 528-1234

BLACKBURNS RESORT
Rt 6, Box 280 (72653)
Rates: n/a
Tel: (501) 492-5115

BLUE PARADISE RESORT
Rt 6, Box 379-CC
(72653)
Rates: $29-$46
Tel: (501) 492-5113

BUNGALOW RESORT
Rt 4, Box 439 (72653)
Rates: n/a
Tel: (501) 492-5105

CHIT-CHAT-CHAW RESORT
Rt 1, Box 157 (72653)
Rates: n/a
Tel: (501) 431-5584

DURBON'S NOE CREEK RESORT
Rt 1, Box 128 (72653)
Rates: n/a
Tel: (501) 431-5574
(800) 264-5574

EDGEWATER RESORT & LODGE
Rt 1, Box 150 (72653)
Rates: n/a
Tel: (501) 431-5222

FISH & FIDDLE RESORT
Rt 10, Box 430
(72653)
Rates: n/a
Tel: (501) 491-5161

GENE'S TROUT FISHING RESORT
Rt 3, Box 348 (72653)
Rates: n/a
Tel: (501) 499-5381
(800) 256-3625

HOLIDAY INN
1350 Hwy 62 SW
(72653)
Rates: $42-$56
Tel: (501) 425-5101
(800) 465-4329

LASALLE RESORT
Rt 4, Box 485-C
(72653)
Rates: n/a
Tel: (501) 492-5133

MOCKINGBIRD BAY RESORT
Rt 3, Box 183-MH
(72653)
Rates: n/a
Tel: (501) 491-5112

MT HOME MOTEL
411 S Main (72653)
Rates: n/a
Tel: (501) 425-2171
(800) 413-2171

OZARKS OAKS MOTEL
147 S Main (72653)
Rates: n/a
Tel: (501) 425-4881

PEAL'S RESORT
Rt 3, Box 252 (72653)
Rates: n/a
Tel: (501) 499-5215

PROMISE LAND RESORT
Rt 1, Box 140 (72653)
Rates: n/a
Tel: (501) 431-5576

RIM SHOALS TROUT RESORT
Rt 2, Box 594 (72653)
Rates: n/a
Tel: (501) 435-6695

ROCKING CHAIR RANCH
Rt 6, Box 445 (72653)
Rates: $39-$95
Tel: (501) 492-5157

ROCKY RIDGE RESORT
Rt 10, Box 610 (72653)
Rates: n/a
Tel: (501) 491-5665

ROYAL MOTEL RESORT
Rt 6, Box 500 (72653)
Rates: $33-$80
Tel: (501) 492-5288

SCOTT VALLEY DUDE RANCH
P. O. Box 1447 (72653)
Rates: $77-$175
Tel: (501) 425-5136

SILVER LEAF LODGE
Rt 9, Box 544 (72653)
Rates: $35
Tel: (501) 492-5187

SILVER SADDLE APARTMENTS & MOTEL
128 N College St (72653)
Rates: n/a
Tel: (501) 425-9998

SISTER CREEK RESORT
Rt 1, Box 147 (72653)
Rates: n/a
Tel: (501) 531-5587

SPRING VALLEY MOTEL
548 Hwy 62 NE (72653)
Rates: n/a
Tel: (501) 425-3717

SUNRISE POINT RESORT
Rt 10, Box 620-CC (72653)
Rates: n/a
Tel: (501) 491-5188

TEAL POINT RESORT
Rt 6, Box 369 (72653)
Rates: $45-$95
Tel: (501) 492-5145

WATERTREE INN
Rt 4, Box 495 (72653)
Rates: n/a
Tel: (501) 492-6477

WIMPY'S RESORT
RR 1, Box 141 (72653)
Rates: n/a
Tel: (501) 431-5325

Y CABINS
Hwy 5 S & Hwy 177 (72653)
Rates: n/a
Tel: (501) 499-5294

MOUNTAIN VIEW

BEST WESTERN FIDDLER'S INN
Hwys 5, 9 & 14 (72560)
Rates: n/a
Tel: (501) 269-2828
(800) 528-1234

DAYS INN
Hwys 5, 9 & 14 (72560)
Rates: n/a
Tel: (501) 269-3287
(800) 329-7466

HIDDEN VALLEY CABINS
P. O. Box 740 (72560)
Rates: n/a
Tel: (501) 269-2655

JACK'S FISHING RESORT & MOTEL
Hwy 5 N (72560)
Rates: n/a
Tel: (501) 585-2211

SYLAMORE LODGES
P. O. Box 1378 (72560)
Rates: n/a
Tel: (501) 585-2221
(800) 538-2221

MURFREESBORO

AMERICAN HERITAGE INN
705 N Washington (71958)
Rates: n/a
Tel: (501) 285-2131

LITTLE SHAMROCK MOTEL
919 N Washington (71958)
Rates: n/a
Tel: (501) 285-2342

RIVERSIDE COTTAGE MOTEL
RFD 1 (71958)
Rates: n/a
Tel: (501) 285-2255

NASHVILLE

HOLIDAY MOTOR LODGE
Hwy 27-B S (71852)
Rates: n/a
Tel: (501) 845-2953

NEWPORT

DAYS INN
101 Olivia Dr (72112)
Rates: $36-$46
Tel: (501) 523-6411
(800) 329-7466

LAKESIDE INN
203 Malcolm Ave (72112)
Rates: n/a
Tel: (501) 523-2787

NEWPORT MOTEL
1504 Hwy 67 N (72112)
Rates: n/a
Tel: (501) 523-2768

PARK INN INTERNATIONAL
901 Hwy 67 N (72112)
Rates: $37-$49
Tel: (501) 523-5851
(800) 437-7275

NORFOLK

WOODSMAN'S SPORT SHOP & MOTEL
HC 61, Box 461 (82658)
Rates: n/a
Tel: (501) 499-7454

NORTH LITTLE ROCK

BUDGETEL INN NORTH
4311 Warden Rd (72116)
Rates: $44-$63
Tel: (501) 758-8888

HAMPTON INN
500 W 29th St (72114)
Rates: $41-$52
Tel: (501) 771-2090
(800) 426-7866

HOLIDAY INN
111 W Pershing Blvd (72114)
Rates: $45-$65
Tel: (501) 758-1440
(800) 465-4329

LA QUINTA INN
4100 E McCain Blvd (72117)
Rates: $43-$56
Tel: (501) 945-0808
(800) 531-5900

MASTERS ECONOMY INN
2508 Jacksonville Hwy (72117)
Rates: $27-$34
Tel: (501) 945-4167

MOTEL 6-NORTH
400 W 29th St (72114)
Rates: $29-$35
Tel: (501) 758-5100
(800) 440-6000

SUPER 8 MOTEL
1 Grey Rd (72117)
Rates: $36-$40
Tel: (501) 945-0141
(800) 800-8000

OAKLAND

BLACK OAK RESORT
P. O. Box 100 (72661)
Rates: n/a
Tel: (501) 431-8363

FIN 'N' FEATHER RESORT
Rt 1, Box 14 (72661)
Rates: n/a
Tel: (501) 431-5621

HENRY'S RESORT
Rt 1, Box 16 (72661)
Rates: n/a
Tel: (501) 431-5626

HIDDEN BAY RESORT
Rt 1, Box 320 (72661)
Rates: n/a
Tel: (501) 431-8121

PERSIMMON POINT RESORT
Rt 1, Box 169 (72661)
Rates: n/a
Tel: (501) 431-8877

SOUTHERN COMFORT RESORT
Rt 1, Box 40 (72661)
Rates: n/a
Tel: (501) 431-8470

OLA

MIMA'S MOTEL
P. O. Box 157 (72853)
Rates: n/a
Tel: (501) 489-5611

OMAHA

AUNT SHIRLEY'S SLEEPING LOFT
Rt 1, Box 84-D (72662)
Rates: n/a
Tel: (501) 426-5408

OSCEOLA

BEST WESTERN INN
P. O. Box 648 (72370)
Rates: $40-$49
Tel: (501) 563-3222
(800) 528-1234

OZARK

BUDGET HOST MOTEL
1711 W Commercial
(72949)
Rates: $28-$34
Tel: (501) 667-2166

PARAGOULD

LINWOOD MOTEL
1611 Linwood Dr
(72450)
Rates: n/a
Tel: (501) 236-7671

PARIS

BLAKELY INN
2010 E Walnut St
(72855)
Rates: n/a
Tel: (501) 963-2400

PARTHENON

A CABIN IN THE WOODS
HCR 72, Box 134
(72666)
Rates: n/a
Tel: (501) 446-2293

PEA RIDGE

BATTLEFIELD INN MOTEL & RV PARK
14753 Hwy 62 E
(72751)
Rates: n/a
Tel: (501) 451-1188

PERRYVILLE

COFFEE CREEK MOTEL
Harrisbrake (72126)
Rates: n/a
Tel: (501) 889-2745

PIGGOTT

OPEN ROADS MOTEL
148 Independent St
(72454)
Rates: n/a
Tel: (501) 598-5941

PINE BLUFF

ADMIRAL BENBOW MOTEL
Box 5009 (71611)
Rates: $35-$48
Tel: (501) 535-8300

BEST WESTERN PINES
2700 E Harding
(71601)
Rates: $49-$59
Tel: (501) 535-8640
(800) 528-1234

CLASSIC INN
4125 Rhinehart Rd
(71601)
Rates: n/a
Tel: (501) 535-1200

DAYS INN
8006 Sheridan Rd
(White Hall, 71602)
Rates: $42-$67
Tel: (501) 247-1339
(800) 329-7466

ECONO LODGE
321 W 5th Ave
(71601)
Rates: $38-$48
Tel: (800) 424-4777

HOLIDAY INN
2 Convention Center
Plaza (71601)
Rates: $69-$94
Tel: (501) 535-3111
(800) 465-4329

POCAHONTAS

SCOTTISH INNS
1501 Hwy 67 N
(72455)
Rates: $30-$38
Tel: (501) 892-4527
(800) 251-1962

PONCA

LOST VALLEY CANOE & LODGING
Hwy 43, Buffalo
National River (72670)
Rates: n/a
Tel: (501) 861-5522

PRESCOTT

BROADWAY HOTEL
123 W 1st (71857)
Rates: n/a
Tel: (501) 887-5446

COMFORT INN
1703 Hwy 24 W
(71857)
Rates: $32-$43
Tel: (800) 221-2222

ROGERS

BEAVER LAKE LODGE
14733 Dutchman Dr
(72756)
Rates: $50-$56
Tel: (501) 925-2313
(800) 367-4513

DAYS INN
2102 S 8th St (72756)
Rates: $38-$125
Tel: (501) 636-3820
(800) 329-7466

HARTLAND LODGE
2931 W Walnut
(72756)
Rates: n/a
Tel: (501) 631-6000
(800) 451-1588

HIWAY HOST INN
915 S 8th (72756)
Rates: n/a
Tel: (501) 636-9400

JAN-LIN MOTOR INN
1601 71-B S (72756)
Rates: n/a
Tel: (501) 636-1733

PARK INN INTERNATIONAL
3714 W Walnut
(72756)
Rates: n/a
Tel: (501) 631-7000
(800) 437-7275

RAMADA INN
1919 Hwy 71-B S
(72756)
Rates: $45-$89
Tel: (501) 636-5850
(800) 272-6232

SECOND HOME BEAVER LAKE
100 W Locust (72756)
Rates: n/a
Tel: (501) 530-1773

SUPER 8 MOTEL
915 S 8th St (72756)
Rates: $37-$45
Tel: (501) 636-9600
(800) 800-8000

TANGLEWOOD LODGE
Rt 6 (72756)
Rates: n/a
Tel: (501) 925-2100

RUSSELLVILLE

BEST WESTERN INN
P. O. Box 2006
(72801)
Rates: $42-$50
Tel: (501) 967-1000
(800) 528-1234

BUDGET INN
2200 N Arkansas
Ave (72801)
Rates: $27-$42
Tel: (501) 968-4400

HOLLEY JOHNSON MOTEL
1206 E Main St
(72801)
Rates: n/a
Tel: (501) 968-4959

HOLIDAY INN
I-40 & Hwy 7 (72801)
Rates: $48-$64
Tel: (501) 958-4300
(800) 465-4329

LAKESIDE RESORT MOTEL
3320 N Arkansas
Ave (72801)
Rates: n/a
Tel: (501) 968-9715

MERRICK MOTEL
1320 E Main St (72801)
Rates: n/a
Tel: (501) 968-6332

MOTEL 6
215 W Birch St (72801)
Rates: $24-$30
Tel: (501) 968-3666
(800) 440-6000

PARK MOTEL
2615 W Main St
(72801)
Rates: $23-$33
Tel: (501) 968-4862

RAMADA INN
Hwy 7 & I-40
(72801)
Rates: $30-$52
Tel: (501) 968-1450

SOUTHERN INN MOTEL
704 W Dyke Rd (72801)
Rates: $30-$42
Tel: (501) 968-5511

SUNRISE INN
154 E Aspen Rd
(72801)
Rates: n/a
Tel: (501) 968-7200

WOODY'S CLASSIC INN
1522 E Main St
(72801)
Rates: n/a
Tel: (501) 968-7774

SEARCY

COMFORT INN
107 S Rand St
(72143)
Rates: $34-$45
Tel: (501) 279-9100
(800) 221-2222

HAMPTON INN
3204 E Race St
(72143)
Rates: $48-$61
Tel: (501) 268-0654
(800) 426-7866

KING'S INN
3109 E Race St
(72143)
Rates: $35-$65
Tel: (501) 268-6171

SILOAM SPRINGS

EASTGATE MOTOR LODGE
1951 Hwy 412
(72761)
Rates: n/a
Tel: (501) 524-5157

HARTLAND LODGE
1801 Hwy 412W
(72761)
Rates: $38-$44
Tel: (501) 524-2025

SPRINGDALE

BUDGETEL INN
1300 S 48th (72764)
Rates: n/a
Tel: (501) 451-2626

ECONO LODGE
2001 S Thompson
Ave (72764)
Rates: $32-$90
Tel: (800) 424-4777

EXECUTIVE INN
2005 Hwy 71-B S
(72764)
Rates: $44-$49
Tel: (501) 756-6101

HAMPTON INN
1700 S 48th (72762)
Rates: $64-$90
Tel: (501) 756-3500
(800) 426-7866

HOLIDAY INN
1500 S 48th St (72762)
Rates: $74-$89
Tel: (501) 751-8300
(800) 465-4329

ST. JOE

MAPLEWOOD MOTEL
P. O. Box 1 (72675)
Rates: n/a
Tel: (501) 439-2525

STAMPS

LAFAYETTE MOTEL
Hwy 72 E (71860)
Rates: n/a
Tel: (501) 533-4333

STORY

AQUA MOTEL
HC 64, Box 105 (71970)
Rates: n/a
Tel: (501) 867-2123

STUTTGART

BEST WESTERN DUCK INN
704 W Michigan
(72160)
Rates: $39-$85
Tel: (501) 774-3851
(800) 528-1234

HOLIDAY INN EXP
708 W Michigan
(72160)
Rates: n/a
Tel: (501) 673-3616

TOWN HOUSE MOTEL
701 W Michigan
(72160)
Rates: $26-$33
Tel: (501) 673-2611

WALKER MOTOR INN
405 E Michigan
(72160)
Rates: n/a
Tel: (501) 673-2671

TEXARKANA

BEST WESTERN-KINGS ROW INN
4200 N State Line
Ave (75502)
Rates: $42-$48
Tel: (501) 774-3851
(800) 528-1234

BUDGETEL INN
5012 N State Line
Ave (75502)
Rates: $32-$53
Tel: (501) 773-1000
(800) 428-3438

FOUR STATES INN
4300 N State Line
Ave (75502)
Rates: $34-$42
Tel: (501) 773-3144

HOLIDAY INN EXPRESS
5401 N State Line Ave (75503)
Rates: $48-$53
Tel: (501) 797-3366
(800) 465-4329

HOWARD JOHNSON
200 Realtor Rd (75502)
Rates: n/a
Tel: (501) 774-3151
(800) 446-4656

LA QUINTA INN
5201 N State Line Ave (75503)
Rates: $46-$59
Tel: (501) 794-1900
(800) 531-5900

MOTEL 6-EAST
900 Realtor Ave (75502)
Rates: $27-$33
Tel: (501) 772-0678
(800) 440-6000

RAMADA INN
I-30 & Summerhill Rd (75503)
Rates: $36-$54
Tel: (501) 794-3131

SHERATON BUSINESS HOTEL
5301 N State Line Ave (75503)
Rates: $49-$71
Tel: (501) 792-3222

SHONEY'S INN
5210 N State Line Ave (75504)
Rates: $38-$60
Tel: (501) 772-0070
(800) 222-2222

SUPER 8 MOTEL
325 E 51st St (75502)
Rates: $33-$49
Tel: (501) 774-8888
(800) 800-8000

TRUMANN

WEEM'S MOTEL
404 Hwy 63 N (72472)
Rates: n/a
Tel: (501) 483-6331

VAN BUREN

BEST WESTERN BUTTERFIELD TRAIL INN
P. O. Box 648 (72956)
Rates: $39-$45
Tel: (800) 528-1234

MOTEL 6
1716 Fayetteville Rd (72956)
Rates: $32-$38
Tel: (501) 474-8001
(800) 440-6000

SUPER 8 MOTEL
106 N Plaza Ct (72956)
Rates: $41-$49
Tel: (501) 471-8888
(800) 800-8000

WALNUT RIDGE

ALAMO COURT MOTEL
Hwy 67 S (72476)
Rates: $30-$95
Tel: (501) 886-2441
(800) 633-9575

PHILLIPS MOTEL
501 Hwy 67 N (72476)
Rates: n/a
Tel: (501) 886-6767

WARREN

ECONOMY INN
108 E Church St (71671)
Rates: n/a
Tel: (501) 226-5881

TOWN HOUSE MOTEL
201 E Church St (71671)
Rates: n/a
Tel: (501) 226-5822

WEST HELENA

HARBOR INN MOTEL
Hwy 49-B (72390)
Rates: n/a
Tel: (501) 572-2597

SANDS MOTEL
Hwy 49-B (72390)
Rates: n/a
Tel: (501) 572-6774

WEST MEMPHIS

BEST WESTERN WEST MEMPHIS INN
3401 Service Loop W (72361)
Rates: $35-$75
Tel: (501) 735-7185
(800) 528-1234

DAYS INN
1100 Ingram Blvd (72301)
Rates: $40-$50
Tel: (501) 735-8600
(800) 329-7466

ECONO LODGE
2315 S Service Rd (72303)
Rates: $28-$38
Tel: (501) 732-2830
(800) 424-4777

EXPRESS INN
3700 E Service Rd (72301)
Rates: n/a
Tel: (501) 732-5688

MOTEL 6
2501 S Frontage Rd (72301)
Rates: $30-$36
Tel: (501) 735-0100
(800) 440-6000

RAMADA INN
210 W Service Rd (72301)
Rates: n/a
Tel: (501) 735-3232
(800) 272-6232

SUPER 8 MOTEL
901 N Club Rd (72301)
Rates: $42-$68
Tel: (501) 735-8818
(800) 800-8000

WHEATLEY

COMFORT INN
Rt 2, Box 107A (72392)
Rates: $33-$38
Tel: (800) 221-2222

WOOSTER

PATTON HOUSE B & B
Hwy 25, P. O. Box 61 (72181)
Rates: n/a
Tel: (501) 679-2975

WYNNE

NATION WIDE 9 MOTEL
706 Hwy 64 E (72396)
Rates: n/a
Tel: (501) 238-9399

YELLVILLE

SILVER RUN CABINS
HCR 66, Box 364A (72687)
Rates: n/a
Tel: (501) 449-6355
(800) 741-1022

WILD BILL'S OUTFITTERS & CABINS
HCR 66, Box 380 (72687)
Rates: n/a
Tel: (501) 449-6235
(800) 554-8657

CALIFORNIA

ADELANTO

DAYS INN
11628 Bartlett Ave
(92301)
Rates: $39-$89
Tel: (619) 246-8777
(800) 329-7466

AGOURA HILLS

RADISSON HOTEL
30100 Agoura Rd
(91301)
Rates: $59
Tel: (818) 707-1220
(800) 333-3333

AHWAHNEE

SILVER SPUR B & B
44625 Silver Spur Tr
(93601)
Rates: $45-$60
Tel: (209) 683-2896

ALAMEDA

ISLANDER LODGE MOTEL
2428 Central Ave
(94501)
Rates: $44-$59
Tel: (510) 865-2121

ALTURAS

BEST WESTERN TRAILSIDE INN
343 N Main St
(96101)
Rates: $36-$46
Tel: (800) 528-1234

DRIFTERS INN
395 Lake View Rd
(96101)
Rates: $40+
Tel: (916) 233-2428

ESSEX MOTEL
1216 N Main St
(96101)
Rates: $36-$42
Tel: (916) 233-2821

FRONTIER MOTEL
1033 N Main St
(96101)
Rates: $28-$43
Tel: (916) 233-3383

HACIENDA MOTEL
201 E 12th St (96101)
Rates: $26-$45
Tel: (916) 233-3459

SUPER 8 MOTEL
511 N Main St
(96101)
Rate: $46-$63
Tel: (916) 233-3545
(800) 800-8000

ANAHEIM

ANAHEIM ANGEL INN
1800 E Katella Ave
(92805)
Rates: $31-$60
Tel: (714) 634-9121

ANAHEIM HARBOR INN
2171 S Harbor Blvd
(92802)
Rates: $44-$59
Tel: (714) 750-3100

ANAHEIM INN AT THE PARK
1855 S Harbor Blvd
(92802)
Rates: $31-$60
Tel: (714) 750-1811
(800) 421-6662

ANAHEIM PLAZA HOTEL
1700 S Harbor Blvd
(92802)
Rates: $79-$117
Tel: (800) 228-1357

BEST WESTERN RAFFLES INN
2040 S Harbor Blvd
(92802)
Rates: $59-$99
Tel: (714) 750-6100
(800) 528-1234

CAVALIER INN & SUITES
11811 S Harbor Blvd
(92802)
Rates: $36-$65
Tel: (714) 750-1000
(800) 821-2768

CROWN STERLING SUITES
3100 E Frontera St
(92806)
Rates: $170-$180
Tel: (714) 632-1221
(800) 433-4600

DESERT PALM INN& SUITES
631 W Katella Ave
(92802)
Rates: $49-$64
Tel: (714) 535-1133
(800) 635-5423

ECONO LODGE-EAST
871 S Harbor Blvd
(92805)
Rates: $42-$62
Tel: (714) 535-7878
(800) 424-4777

FRIENDSHIP INN-SUNRISE
705 S Beach Blvd
(92804)
Rates: $32-$38
Tel: (800) 424-4777

GRAND HOTEL
7 Greedman Way
(92802)
Rates: $85-$235
Tel: (800) 421-6662

HAMPTON INN
300 E Katella Way
(92802)
Rates: $55-$65
Tel: (714) 772-8713
(800) 426-7866

HILTON AND TOWERS
777 Convention Way
(92802)
Rates: $170-$255
Tel: (800) 233-6904

HOLIDAY INN ANA-HEIM AT THE PARK
1221 S Harbor Blvd
(92805)
Rates: $75-$89
Tel: (714) 758-0900
(800) 465-4329

MARRIOTT HOTEL
700 W Convention Way (92802)
Rates: $160-$189
Tel: (714) 750-8000
(800) 228-9290

MOTEL 6-PREMIER
100 W Freedman Way (92801)
Rates: $42-$46
Tel: (714) 520-9696
(800) 440-6000

MOTEL 6
921 S Beach Blvd
(92804)
Rates: $32
Tel: (714) 220-2866
(800) 440-6000

THE PAN PACIFIC
1717 S West St
(92802)
Rates: $135-$175
Tel: (714) 999-0990
(800) 321-8976

QUALITY HOTEL-MAINGATE
616 Convention Way
(92802)
Rates: $47-$95
Tel: (714) 750-3131
(800) 231-6215

RAFFLES INN & SUITES
2040 S Harbor Blvd
(92802)
Rates: $44-$74
Tel: (800) 654-0196

RED ROOF INN
1251 N Harbor Blvd
(92801)
Rates: $31-$60
Tel: (714) 635-6461
(800) 843-7663

RESIDENCE INN BY MARRIOTT
1700 S Clementine St (92802)
Rates: $79-$195
Tel: (714) 533-3555
(800) 331-3131

RODEWAY INN
800 S Beach Blvd (92804)
Rates: $44-$68
Tel: (800) 424-4777

STATION INN & SUITES
989 W Ball Rd (92802)
Rates: $35-$65
Tel: (800) 874-6265

TRAVELODGE AT THE PARK
1166 W Katella Ave (92802)
Rates: $35-$59
Tel: (714) 774-7817
(800) 578-7878

ANAHEIM HILLS

TRAVELODGE ANAHEIM HILLS
5710 E La Palma (92807)
Rates: $59-$116
Tel: (714) 779-0252
(800) 578-7878

ANDERSON

ANDERSON VALLEY INN
2661 McMurry Dr (96007)
Rates: $40-$60
Tel: (916) 365-2566

BEST WESTERN KNIGHTS INN
2688 Gateway Dr (96007)
Rates: $42-$54
Tel: (916) 365-2753
(800) 528-1234

ANGELS CAMP

ANGELS INN MOTEL
600 N Main St (95221)
Rates: $50-$85
Tel: (209) 736-4242
(800) 225-3764

GOLD COUNTRY INN
720 S Main St (95222)
Rates: $46-$76
Tel: (209) 736-4611
(800) 225-3764

ANTIOCH

RAMADA INN
2436 Mahogany Way (94509)
Rates: $71-$116
Tel: (510) 754-6600
(800) 272-6232

APPLEGATE

THE ORIGINAL FIREHOUSE MOTEL
17855 Lake Arthur Rd (95703)
Rates: $34-$43
Tel: (916) 878-7770

APTOS

APPLE LANE INN BED & BREAKFAST
6265 Soquel Dr (95003)
Rates: $70-$175
Tel: (408) 475-6868
(800) 649-8988

MANGELS HOUSE BED & BREAKFAST
570 Aptos Creek Rd (95003)
Rates: $105-$135
Tel: (408) 688-7982

ARCADIA

EMBASSY SUITES HOTEL
211 E Huntington Dr (91006)
Rates: $107-$122
Tel: (818) 445-8525
(800) 362-2779

HAMPTON INN
311 E Huntington Dr (91006)
Rates: $65-$83
Tel: (818) 574-5600
(800) 426-7866

MOTEL 6
225 Colorado Pl (91006)
Rates: $36-$42
Tel: (818) 446-2660
(800) 440-6000

RESIDENCE INN BY MARRIOTT
321 E Huntington Dr (91006)
Rates: $112-$142
Tel: (818) 446-6500
(800) 331-3131

ARCATA

BEST WESTERN ARCATA INN
4827 Valley West Blvd (95521)
Rates: $52-$83
Tel: (707) 826-0313
(800) 528-1234

COMFORT INN
4701 Valley West Blvd (95521)
Rates: $35-$85
Tel: (707) 826-2827
(800) 221-2222

HOTEL ARCATA
708 9th St (95521)
Rates: $45-$120
Tel: (707) 826-0217
(800) 344-1221

MOTEL 6
4755 Valley West Blvd (95521)
Rates: $32-$38
Tel: (707) 822-7061
(800) 440-6000

QUALITY INN MAD RIVER
3535 Janes Rd (95521)
Rates: $45-$76
Tel: (707) 822-0409
(800) 221-2222

SUPER 8
4887 Valley West Blvd (95521)
Rates: $32-$57
Tel: (800) 800-8000

ARNOLD

EBBETT'S PASS LODGE
1173 Hwy 4, P. O. Box 2591 (95223)
Rates: $42-$59
Tel: (209) 795-1563
(800) 225-3764

SIERRA VACATION RENTALS
P. O. Box 1080 (95223)
Rates: $130-$170
Tel: (800) 995-2422
(800) 225-3764 CA

WEHE'S MEADOWMONT LODGE
2011 Hwy 4 (95223)
Rates: $47-$58
Tel: (209) 795-1394
(800) 225-3764

ARROYO GRANDE

BEST WESTERN CASA GRANDE INN
850 Oak Park Rd (93420)
Rates: $58-$95
Tel: (805) 481-7398
(800) 528-1234

ECONO LODGE
611 E Camino Real (93420)
Rates: $40-$110
Tel: (805) 489-9300
(800) 424-4777

ATASCADERO

BEST WESTERN COLONY INN
3600 El Camino Real (93422)
Rates: $46-$83
Tel: (805) 466-4449
(800) 528-1234

MOTEL 6
9400 El Camino Real (93422)
Rates: $29-$35
Tel: (805) 466-6701
(800) 440-6000

RANCHO TEE MOTEL
6895 El Camino Real (93422)
Rates: $46-$95
Tel: (805) 466-2231

SUPER 8 MOTEL
6505 Morro Rd (93422)
Rates: $39-$95
Tel: (805) 466-0794
(800) 800-8000

AUBURN

**BEST WESTERN
GOLDEN KEY MOTEL**
13450 Lincoln Way
(95603)
Rates: $54-$82
Tel: (916) 885-8611
(800) 528-1234

**COUNTRY SQUIRE
INN**
13480 Lincoln Way
(95603)
Rates: $37-$52
Tel: (916) 885-7025

**HOLIDAY INN
AUBURN**
120 Grass Valley
Highway (95603)
Rates: $64-$78
Tel: (800) 814-8787

AVALON
(Catalina Island)

HOTEL MONTEREY
108 Sumner Ave,
P. O. Box 1372
(90704)
Rates: $65-$165
Tel: (310) 510-0264
(800) 858-0035

BAKER

**ARNE'S ROYAL
HAWAIIAN MOTEL**
200 W Baker Blvd
(92309)
Rates: $49
Tel: (619) 733-4326

BUN BOY MOTEL
P. O. Box 130 (92309)
Rates: $29-$44
Tel: (619) 733-4363

BAKERSFIELD

**BEST WESTERN
HERITAGE INN**
253 Trask St (93312)
Rates: $45-$62
Tel: (805) 764-6268
(800) 528-1234

**BEST WESTERN
HILL HOUSE**
700 Truxtun Ave
(93301)
Rates: $50-$65
Tel: (805) 327-4064
(800) 528-1234

BEST WESTERN INN
2620 Pierce Rd
(93308)
Rates: $63-$76
Tel: (805) 327-9651
(800) 528-1234

**BEST WESTERN
OAK INN**
889 Oak St (93304)
Rates: $56-$77
Tel: (805) 324-9686
(800) 528-1234

**COMFORT INN-
CENTRAL**
830 Wible Rd (93304)
Rates: $36-$55
Tel: (800) 221-2222

DAYS INN
2100 Panama Ln
(93307)
Rates: $50-$90
Tel: (800) 329-7466

ECONO LODGE
200 Trask St (93312)
Rates: $44-$54
Tel: (805) 764-5221
(800) 424-4777

**ECONOMY INNS
OF AMERICA**
6100 Knudsen Dr
(93308)
Rates: $22-$37
Tel: (800) 826-0778

**ECONOMY INNS
OF AMERICA**
6501 Colony St
(93307)
Rates: $24-$40
Tel: (800) 826-0778

LA QUINTA INN
3232 Riverside Dr
(93308)
Rates: $47-$50
Tel: (805) 325-7400
(800) 531-5900

LONE OAK INN
10614 Rosedale Hwy
(93312)
Rates: $49
Tel: (805) 589-6600

MOTEL 6
2727 White Lane
(93304)
Rates: $28-$34
Tel: (805) 834-2828
(800) 440-6000

MOTEL 6
5241 Olive Tree Ct
(93308)
Rates: $24-$28
Tel: (805) 392-9700
(800) 440-6000

MOTEL 6
1350 Easton Dr (93309)
Rates: $26-$32
Tel: (805) 327-1686
(800) 440-6000

MOTEL 6-EAST
8223 E Brundage Ln
(93307)
Rates: $27-$33
Tel: (805) 366-7231
(800) 440-6000

**QUALITY INN
AIRPORT**
4500 Pierce Rd
(93308)
Rates: $45-$65
Tel: (800) 221-2222

QUALITY INN
1011 Oak St (93304)
Rates: $42-$62
Tel: (800) 221-2222

RED LION HOTEL
3100 Camino
Del Rio Ct (93308)
Rates: $105-$140
Tel: (805) 323-7111
(800) 547-8010

**RESIDENCE INN
BY MARRIOTT**
4241 Chester Ln
(93309)
Rates: $65-$95
Tel: (800) 331-3131

REGENCY INN
818 Real Rd (93309)
Rates: $40-$50
Tel: (805) 324-6666

**RIO BRAVO
TENNIS & FITNESS
RESORT**
11200 Lake Ming Rd
(93306)
Rates: $68-$78
Tel: (805) 872-5000
(800) 282-5000

SHERATON INN
5101 California Ave
(93309)
Rates: $85-$110
Tel: (805) 325-9700
(800) 500-5399

BALDWIN PARK

MOTEL 6
14510 Garvey Ave
(91706)
Rates: $30-$34
Tel: (818) 960-5011
(800) 440-6000

BANNING

SUPER 8 MOTEL
1690 W Ramsey St
(92220)
Rates: $29-$37
Tel: (800) 800-8000

TRAVELODGE
1700 W Ramsey St
(92220)
Rates: $65-$90
Tel: (909) 849-1000
(800) 578-7878

BARSTOW

**ASTRO BUDGET
MOTEL**
1271 E Main St
(92311)
Rates: $22-$38
Tel: (619) 256-2204

BARSTOW INN
1261 E Main St
(92311)
Rates: $26-$34
Tel: (619) 256-7581

BEST MOTEL
1281 E Main St
(92311)
Rates: $24-$32
Tel: (619) 256-6836

DESERT INN MOTEL
1100 E Main St
(92311)
Rates: $28-$38
Tel: (619) 256-2146

ECONO LODGE
1230 E Main St
(92311)
Rates: $30-$56
Tel: (619) 256-2133
(800) 424-4777

**ECONOMY INNS
OF AMERICA**
1590 Coolwater Ln
(92311)
Rates: $24-$37
Tel: (800) 826-0778

**EL RANCHO MOTEL
& RESTAURANT**
112 E Main St
(92311)
Rates: $19-$31
Tel: (619) 256-2401

GATEWAY MOTEL
1630 E Main St
(92311)
Rates: $22-$40
Tel: (619) 256-8931

GOOD NITE INN
2551 Commerce
Pkwy (92311)
Rates: $42
Tel: (619) 253-2121

HILLCREST MOTEL
1111 E Main St
(92311)
Rates: $24-$30
Tel: (619) 256-1063

HOLIDAY INN
1511 E Main St
(92311)
Rates: $68
Tel: (619) 256-5673
(800) 465-4329

**HOLIDAY INN
EXPRESS**
1861 W Main St
(92311)
Rates: $40-$60
Tel: (800) 465-4329

HOWARD JOHNSON
1431 E Main St (92311)
Rates: $49-$69
Tel: (800) 446-4656

MOTEL 6
31951 E Main St
(92311)
Rates: $24-$28
Tel: (619) 256-0653
(800) 440-6000

MOTEL 6
150 N Yucca Ave
(92311)
Rates: $25-$29
Tel: (619) 246-1752
(800) 440-6000

QUALITY INN
1520 E Main St (92311)
Rates: $49-$68
Tel: (619) 256-6891
(800) 221-2222

STARDUST INN
901 E Main St
(92311)
Rates: $24-$45
Tel: (619) 256-7116

SUNSET INN
1350 W Main St
(92311)
Rates: $24-$35
Tel: (619) 256-8921

SUPER 8 MOTEL
170 Coolwater Ln
(92311)
Rates: $46
Tel: (619) 256-8443
(800) 800-8000

VAGABOND INN
1243 E Main St (92311)
Rates: $36-$55
Tel: (619) 234-9607
(800) 522-1555

BASS LAKE

FORK'S RESORT
39150 Rd 222 (93604)
Rates: $75-$125
Tel: (209) 642-3737

**THE LAKEHOUSE
BED & BREAKFAST**
39131 Lake Dr (93604)
Rates: $125-$195
Tel: (209) 683-8220

BAYWOOD PARK

BACK BAY INN
1391 Second St
(93402)
Rates: $45-$110
Tel: (805) 528-1233

BEAUMONT

**GOLDEN WEST
MOTEL**
625 E 5th St (92223)
Rates: $32-$40
Tel: (909) 845-2185

WINDSOR MOTEL
1265 E 6th St (92223)
Rates: $26-$30
Tel: (909) 845-1436

BELLFLOWER

MOTEL 6
17220 Downey Ave
(90706)
Rates: $36-$40
Tel: (310) 531-3933
(800) 440-6000

BELMONT

MOTEL 6
1101 Shoreway Rd
(94002)
Rates: $48-$54
Tel: (415) 591-1471
(800) 440-6000

BENECIA

**BEST WESTERN
HERITAGE INN**
1955 E 2nd St
(94510)
Rates: $60-$95
Tel: (707) 746-0401
(800) 528-1234

**THE PAINTED LADY
BED & BREAKFAST**
141 East F St (94510)
Rates: $70-$85
Tel: (707) 746-1646

BENNETT VALLEY

**COOPERS GROVE
RANCH
BED & BREAKFAST**
5763 Sonoma
Mountain Rd (95404)
Rates: $100-$150
Tel: (707) 571-1928

BERKELEY

BEAU SKY HOTEL
2520 Durant Ave
(94704)
Rates: $60-$85
Tel: (510) 540-7688

**GOLDEN BEAR
MOTEL**
1620 San Pablo Ave
(94702)
Rates: $45-$49
Tel: (510) 525-6770
(800) 252-6770

**MARRIOTT
BERKELEY MARINA**
200 Marina Blvd
(94710)
Rates: $100-$155
Tel: (510) 548-7920
(800) 228-9290

**RAMADA INN
BERKELEY**
920 University Ave
(94710)
Rates: $45-$55
Tel: (800) 272-6232

BERMUDA DUNES

MOTEL 6
78100 Varner Rd
(92203)
Rates: $32-$36
Tel: (619) 345-0550
(800) 440-6000

BEVERLY HILLS

**THE BEVERLY
HILTON HOTEL**
9876 Wilshire Blvd
(90210)
Rates: $215-$700
Tel: (800) 922-5432

**FOUR SEASONS
BEVERLY HILLS**
300 S Doheny Dr
(90048)
Rates: $325-$510
Tel: (310) 273-2222
(800) 332-3442

**HOTEL NIKKO AT
BEVERLY HILLS**
465 S La Cienega
Blvd (90048)
Rates: $220-$350
Tel: (310) 247-0400
(800) 645-5687

**HOTEL SOFITEL
MA MAISON**
8555 Beverly Blvd
(90048)
Rates: $190-$230
Tel: (310) 278-5444
(800) 763-4835
(800) 521-7772 (CA)

LOWELL HOTEL
9291 Burton Way
(90210)
Rates: $290-$630
Tel: (800) 800-2113

THE PENINSULA
9882 Little Santa
Monica Blvd (90212)
Rates: $300-$3000
Tel: (310) 551-2888
(800) 462-7899

**THE REGENT
BEVERLY WILSHIRE**
9500 Wilshire Blvd
(90212)
Rates: $255-$600
Tel: (310) 275-5200
(800) 421-4354

BIG BEAR CITY

**GOLD MTN MANOR
HISTORIC B & B**
P.O. Box 2027 (92314)
Rates: n/a
Tel: (909) 866-2010

BIG BEAR LAKE

BEAR CLAW CABINS
586 Main St (92315)
Rates: $55-$94
Tel: (909) 866-2666

BIG BEAR CABINS
39774 Big Bear Blvd
(92315)
Rates: $59-$149
Tel: (909) 866-2723

**BLACK FOREST
LODGE**
P. O. Box 156 (92315)
Rates: $38-$110
Tel: (909) 866-2166
(800) 255-4378

**BOULDER CREEK
RESORT**
Box 92 (92315)
Rates: $45-$300
Tel: (909) 866-2665
(800) 244-2327

CAL-PINE CHALETS
41545 Big Bear Blvd
(92315)
Rates: $59-$175
Tel: (909) 866-2574

**COZY HOLLOW
LODGE**
40409 Big Bear Blvd,
P. O. Box 1288
(92315)
Rates: $79-$139
Tel: (909) 866-9694
(800) 882-4480

**CREEK RUNNER'S
LODGE**
374 Georgia St
(92315)
Rates: $50-$200
Tel: (909) 866-7473

EAGLE'S NEST B & B
41675 Big Bear Blvd
(92315)
Rates: $75-$165
Tel: (909) 866-6465

EDGEWATER INN
40570 Simonds Dr
(92315)
Rates: $75-$85
Tel: (909) 866-4161

**FRONTIER
LODGE & MOTEL**
40472 Big Bear Blvd
(92315)
Rates: $50-$165
Tel: (909) 866-5888
(800) 457-6401

**GOLDEN BEAR
COTTAGES**
39367 Big Bear Blvd
(92315)
Rates: $89
Tel: (909) 866-2010

**GREY SQUIRREL
RESORT**
39372 Big Bear Blvd
(92315)
Rates: $75-$155
Tel: (909) 866-4335

GRIZZLY INN
39756 Big Bear Blvd
(92315)
Rates: $55+
Tel: (800) 423-2742

HAPPY BEAR VILLAGE
40154 Big Bear Blvd
(92315)
Rates: $59-$195
Tel: (909) 866-2350
(800) 352-8581

HONEY BEAR LODGE
40994 Pennsylvania
(92315)
Rates: $29-$259
Tel: (909) 866-7825
(800) 628-8714

MOTEL 6
42899 Big Bear Blvd
(92315)
Rates: $38-$42
Tel: (909) 585-6666
(800) 440-6000

**QUAIL COVE
LODGE**
39117 N Shore Dr
(92315)
Rates: $69-$99
Tel: (909) 866-5957
(800) 595-3683

**ROBINHOOD
INN & LODGE**
P. O. Box 3706
(92315)
Rates: $69-$109
Tel: (909) 866-4643
(800) 990-9956

**SHORE ACRES
LODGE**
40090 Lakeview Dr
(92315)
Rates: $60-$250
Tel: (909) 866-8200
(800) 524-6600

**SMOKETREE
RESORT**
40210 Big Bear Blvd
(92315)
Rates: $49-$167
Tel: (909) 866-2415
(800) 352-8581

**SNUGGLE CREEK
LODGE**
40440 Big Bear Blvd
(92315)
Rates: $79-$109
Tel: (909) 866-2555

**TIMBER HAVEN
LODGE**
877 Tulip Ln (92315)
Rates: $79-$149
Tel: (909) 866-7207

TIMBERLINE LODGE
P. O. Box 2801
(92315)
Rates: $49-$69
Tel: (800) 352-8581

**WISHING WELL
MOTEL**
540 Pine Knot
(92315)
Rates: $49-$89
Tel: (909) 866-3505
(800) 541-3505

BIG PINE

BIG PINE MOTEL
370 S Main (93515)
Rates: $30-$42
Tel: (619) 938-2282

BISHOP

**BEST WESTERN
CREEKSIDE INN**
725 N Main St
(93514)
Rates: $84-$129
Tel: (619) 872-3044
(800) 528-1234

**BEST WESTERN
HOLIDAY SPA
LODGE**
1025 N Main St
(93514)
Rates: $50-$85
Tel: (619) 873-3543
(800) 528-1234

**COMFORT INN-
BISHOP**
805 N Main St (93514)
Rates: $64-$75
Tel: (619) 873-4284
(800) 576-4080

PARADISE LODGE
Lower Rock Creek
Rd (93514)
Rates: $55-$75+
Tel: (619) 387-2370

RODEWAY INN
150 E Elm St (93514)
Rates: $50-$65
Tel: (800) 424-4777

**SIERRA FOOTHILLS
MOTEL**
535 S Main St (93514)
Rates: $33-$48
Tel: (619) 872-1386

**SPORTSMAN'S
LODGE**
636 N Main St (93514)
Rates: $25-$70
Tel: (619) 872-2423

SUNRISE MOTEL
262 W Grove St
(93514)
Rates: $33+
Tel: (619) 873-3656

THUNDERBIRD MOTEL
190 W Pine St
(93514)
Rates: $34-$54
Tel: (619) 873-4215

VAGABOND INN
1030 N Main St
(93514)
Rates: $44-$66
Tel: (619) 873-6351
(800) 522-1555

VILLAGE MOTEL
286 W Elm St (93514)
Rates: $35+
Tel: (619) 873-3545

BLAIRSDEN

FEATHER RIVER PARK RESORT
Hwy 89, Box 37
(96103)
Rates: $82-$182
Tel: (916) 836-2328

GRAY EAGLE LODGE
Gold Lake Rd,
Box 38 (96103)
Rates: $155+
Tel: (916) 836-2511
(800) 635-8778 (CA)

LAYMAN RESORT
Hwy 70, Box 8 (96103)
Rates: $48-$55
Tel: (916) 836-2356

RIVER PINES RESORT
Box 117 (96103)
Rates: $50-$75
Tel: (916) 836-2552
(800) 696-2551 (CA)

BLYTHE

ASTRO MOTEL
801 E Hobsonway
(92225)
Rates: $25-$42
Tel: (619) 922-6101

BEST WESTERN SAHARA MOTEL
825 W Hobsonway
(92225)
Rates: $44-$64
Tel: (619) 922-7105
(800) 528-1234

BEST WESTERN TROPICS MOTOR HOTEL
9274 E Hobsonway
(92225)
Rates: $48-$84
Tel: (619) 922-5101
(800) 528-1234

COMFORT INN
903 W Hobsonway
(92225)
Rates: $40-$95
Tel: (619) 922-4146
(800) 221-2222

ECONO LODGE
1020 W Hobsonway
(92225)
Rates: $40-$95
Tel: (619) 922-3161
(800) 424-4777

HAMPTON INN
900 W Hobsonway
(92225)
Rates: $50-$69
Tel: (800) 426-7866

HOLIDAY INN EXPRESS
600 W Donlon St
(92225)
Rates: $85-$139
Tel: (619) 921-2300
(800) 465-4329

MOTEL 6
500 W Donlon St
(92225)
Rates: $27-$33
Tel: (619) 922-6666
(800) 440-6000

SUPER 8 MOTEL
550 W Donlon St
(92225)
Rates: $41-$58
Tel: (800) 800-8000

TRAVELODGE
850 W Hobsonway
(92225)
Rates: $42-$60
(800) 367-2250 (CA)
(800) 578-7878

BODEGA BAY

HOLIDAY INN BODEGA BAY RESORT
521 Coast Highway 1
(94923)
Rates: $60-$180
Tel: (707) 875-2217
(800) 465-4329

BOLINAS

ELFRIEDE'S BEACHHAUS BED & BREAKFAST
59 Brighton Ave
(94924)
Rates: $75-$120
Tel: (800) 982-2545

BOULDER CREEK

MERRYBROOK LODGE
13420 Big Basin Way
(95006)
Rates: $64-$80
Tel: (408) 338-6813

BRAWLEY

TOWN HOUSE LODGE
135 Main St (92227)
Rates: $43-$47
Tel: (619) 344-5120

BREA

HYLAND MOTEL
727 S Brea Blvd
(92621)
Rates: $36-$40
Tel: (714) 990-6867

WOODFIN SUITE HOTEL-BREA
3100 E Imperial
Highway (92621)
Rates: $75-$109
Tel: (714) 579-3200
(800) 237-8811

BRIDGEPORT

BEST WESTERN RUBY INN
333 Main St (93517)
Rates: $55-$150
Tel: (619) 932-7241
(800) 528-1234

SILVER MAPLE INN
310 Main St (93517)
Rates: $45-$80
Tel: (619) 932-7383

WALKER RIVER LODGE
1 Main St,
P. O. Box 695 (93517)
Rates: $75-$120
Tel: (619) 932-7021

BROOKDALE

BROOKDALE LODGE
11570 Hwy 9 (95007)
Rates: $44-$60
Tel: (408) 338-6433

BUELLTON

MOTEL 6
333 McMurray Rd
(93427)
Rates: $34-$43
Tel: (805) 688-7797
(800) 440-6000

BUENA PARK

BEST WESTERN BUENA PARK INN
8580 Stanton Ave
(90620)
Rates: $36-$52
Tel: (800) 528-1234

COVERED WAGON MOTEL
7830 Crescent Ave
(90620)
Rates: $28-$32
Tel: (714) 995-0033

EMBASSY SUITES HOTEL-BUENA PARK/DISNEYLAND
7762 Beach Blvd
(90620)
Rates: $99-$119
Tel: (714) 739-5600
(800) 362-2779

HOLIDAY INN BUENA PARK
7000 Beach Blvd
(90620)
Rates: $89-$250
Tel: (714) 522-7000
(800) 522-7006

MOTEL 6
7051 Valley View
(90620)
Rates: $32-$36
Tel: (714) 522-1200
(800) 440-6000

**TRAVELODGE
BUENA PARK**
7640 Beach Blvd
(90620)
Rates: $35-$45
Tel: (714) 522-8461
(800) 578-7878

BURBANK

**HILTON-BURBANK
AIRPORT &
CONV CENTER**
2500 Hollywood
Way (91505)
Rates: $106-$176
(800) 468-3576
(800) 643-6400 (CA)

**HOLIDAY INN
BURBANK**
150 E Angeleno
(91510)
Rates: $96-$135
Tel: (800) 465-4329

**RAMADA INN
BURBANK AIRPORT**
2900 N San
Fernando Blvd
(91504)
Rates: $75-$95
Tel: (800) 272-6232

SCOTTISH INNS
8365 Lehigh Ave.
(Sun Valley, 91352)
Rates: $40+
Tel: (818) 504-2671
(800) 251-1962

BURLINGAME

**DOUBLETREE
HOTEL-
SAN FRANCISCO
AIRPORT**
835 Airport Blvd
(94010)
Rates: $79-$139
Tel: (415) 344-5500
(800) 222-8733

**MARRIOTT
SAN FRANCISCO
AIRPORT**
1800 Old Bayshore
Highway (94010)
Rates: $125-$138
Tel: (415) 692-9100
(800) 228-9290

**RADISSON HOTEL-
SAN FRANCISCO
AIRPORT**
1177 Airport Blvd
(94010)
Rates: $125
Tel: (415) 342-9200
(800) 333-3333

**RED ROOF INN-
SAN FRANCISCO
AIRPORT**
777 Airport Blvd
(94010)
Rates: $72-$82
Tel: (415) 342-7772
(800) 843-7663

**VAGABOND INN-
SAN FRANCISCO
AIRPORT**
1640 Old Bayshore
Highway (94010)
Rates: $60-$100
Tel: (415) 692-4040
(800) 522-1555

BURNEY

CHARM MOTEL
37363 Main St
(96013)
Rates: $46-$74
Tel: (916) 335-2254

**GREEN GABLES
MOTEL**
37385 Main St
(96013)
Rates: $45-$75
Tel: (916) 335-2264

**SHASTA PINES
MOTEL**
37386 Main St
(96013)
Rates: $32-$58
Tel: (916) 335-2201

**SLEEPY HOLLOW
LODGE**
36898 Main St,
P. O. Box 1105
(96013)
Rates: $30-$65
Tel: (916) 335-2285

BUTTON WILLOW

GOOD NITE INN
20645 Tracy Ave
(93206)
Rates: $26-$32
Tel: (805) 764-5121

MOTEL 6
3810 Tracy Ave
(93206)
Rates: $23-$29
Tel: (805) 764-5207
(800) 440-6000

MOTEL 6
20638 Tracy Ave
(92306)
Rates: $23-$29
Tel: (805) 764-5153
(800) 440-6000

SUPER 8 MOTEL
20681 Tracy Ave
(93206)
Rates: $31-$49
Tel: (805) 764-5117
(800) 800-8000

CALIMESA

**CALIMESA INN
MOTEL**
1205 Calimesa Blvd
(92320)
Rates: $35-$47
Tel: (909) 795-2536

CALIPATRIA

CALIPATRIA INN
SR111, P. O. Box 30
(92233)
Rates: $46-$52
Tel: (619) 348-7348

CALISTOGA

**MEADOWLARK
COUNTRY HOUSE**
601 Petrified Forest
Rd (94515)
Rates: $125-$150
Tel: (707) 942-5651

PINK MANSION
1415 Foothill Blvd
(94515)
Rates: $85-$160
Tel: (707) 942-0558

TRIPLE "S" RANCH
4600 Mountain Home
Ranch Rd (94515)
Rates: $42-$59
Tel: (707) 942-6730

**WASHINGTON
STREET LODGING**
1605 Washington St
(94515)
Rates: $80-$90
Tel: (707) 942-6968

CALPINE

**SIERRA VALLEY
LODGE**
Box 115 (96124)
Rates: $38-$42
Tel: (916) 994-3367
(800) 858-0322

CAMARILLO

COMFORT INN
984 Ventura Blvd
(93010)
Rates: $34-$42
Tel: (800) 221-2222

COUNTRY INN
1405 Del Norte Rd
(93010)
Rates: $62+
Tel: (805) 983-7171

MOTEL 6
1641 E Daily Dr
(93010)
Rates: $34-$40
Tel: (805) 388-3467
(800) 440-6000

CAMBRIA

**BEST WESTERN
MARINERS INN**
6180 Moonstone
Beach Dr (93428)
Rates: $32-$89
Tel: (805) 927-4624
(800) 528-1234
(800) 344-0407 (CA)

**CAMBRIA PINES
LODGE**
2905 Burton Dr
(93428)
Rates: $65-$115
Tel: (805) 927-4200
(800) 445-6868

CAMBRIA SHORES INN
6276 Moonstone Beach Dr (93428)
Rates: $45-$110
Tel: (805) 927-8644
(800) 433-9179

FOGCATCHER INN
6400 Moonstone Beach Dr (93428)
Rates: $80-$145
Tel: (800) 425-4121

CAMERON PARK

BEST WESTERN CAMERON PARK INN
3361 Coach Ln (95682)
Rates: $58-$71
Tel: (916) 677-2203
(800) 528-1234

CAMPBELL

CAMPBELL INN
675 E Campbell Ave (95008)
Rates: $89-$175
Tel: (408) 374-4300,
(800) 852-4300

EXECUTIVE INN SUITES
1300 Camden Ave (95008)
Rates: $68-$85
Tel: (800) 888-3611

MOTEL 6
1240 Camden Ave (95008)
Rates: $44-$50
Tel: (408) 371-8870
(800) 440-6000

RESIDENCE INN BY MARRIOTT-SAN JOSE/CAMPBELL
2761 S Bascom Ave (95008)
Rates: $79-$154
Tel: (800) 331-3131

CANOGA PARK

BEST WESTERN CANOGA PARK MOTOR INN
20122 Vanowen St (91306)
Rates: $55-$85
Tel: (818) 883-1200
(800) 528-1234

DAYS INN SAN FERNANDO VALLEY
20128 Roscoe Blvd (91306)
Rates: $50-$95
Tel: (818) 341-7200
(800) 329-7466

SUPER 8 MOTEL
7631 Topanga Canyon Blvd (91304)
Rates: $50-$60
Tel: (818) 883-8888
(800) 800-8000

WARNER CENTER MOTOR INN
7132 DeSoto Ave (91303)
Rates: $40-$70
Tel: (818) 346-5400

CAPISTRANO BEACH

CLARION SUITES INN
23734 Pacific Coast Highway (92624)
Rates: $49-$149
Tel: (800) 221-2222

CAPITOLA

CAPITOLA INN
822 Bay Ave (95010)
Rates: $55-$135
Tel: (408) 462-3004

EL SALTO BY THE SEA B & B
620 El Salto Dr (95010)
Rates: $100-$185
Tel: (408) 462-6365

SUMMER HOUSE B&B
216 Monterey Ave (95010)
Rates: $75
Tel: (408) 475-8474

CARLSBAD

ECONOMY INNS OF AMERICA
751 Raintree Dr (92009)
Rates: $30-$55
Tel: (619) 931-1185
(800) 826-0778

MOTEL 6
1006 Carlsbad Village Dr (92008)
Rates: $30-$38
Tel: (619) 434-7135
(800) 440-6000

MOTEL 6
750 Raintree Dr (92009)
Rates: $30-$38
Tel: (619) 431-0745
(800) 440-6000

MOTEL 6
6117 Paseo del Norte (92009)
Rates: $30-$38
Tel: (619) 438-1242
(800) 440-6000

RAMADA INN
751 Macadamia Dr (92009)
Rates: $79-$119
Tel: (619) 438-2285
(800) 272-6232

TRAVELODGE
760 Macadamia Dr (92009)
Rates: $35-$54
(800) 367-2250 (CA)
(800) 578-7878

CARMEL

BEST WESTERN CARMEL MISSION INN
3665 Rio Rd (93923)
Rates: $69-$179
Tel: (408) 624-1841
(800) 528-1234

CARMEL TRADEWINDS INN
P. O. Box 3403,
Mission between 3rd & 4th (93921)
Rates: $69-$225
Tel: (408) 624-2776
(800) 624-6665

COACHMAN'S INN
P. O. Box C-1,
San Carlos & 7th Sts (93921)
Rates: $75-$150
Tel: (408) 624-6421
(800) 336-6421

CYPRESS INN
P. O. Box Y,
Lincoln & 7th Sts (93921)
Rates: $97-$250
Tel: (408) 624-3671
(800) 443-7443

DOLORES LODGE
P. O. Box 3756 (93921)
Rates: $80-$125
Tel: (408) 625-3263

FOREST LODGE BED & BREAKFAST
P. O. Box 1316 (93921)
Rates: $80-$240
Tel: (408) 624-7023

HIGHLANDS INN
Highway 1 (93921)
Rates: $265-$695
Tel: (408) 624-3801
(800) 682-4811

QUAIL LODGE RESORT & GOLF CLUB
8205 Valley Green Dr (93923)
Rates: $195-$860
Tel: (408) 624-1581
(800) 538-9516

VAGABOND HOUSE INN
P. O. Box 2747,
Dolores & 4th Sts (93921)
Rates: $79-$135
Tel: (408) 624-7738
(800) 262-1262

WAYSIDE INN
P. O. Box 1900,
Mission & 7th Sts (93921)
Rates: $95-$225
Tel: (408) 624-5336
(800) 433-4732

CARMEL VALLEY

BLUE SKY LODGE
Flight Rd (93924)
Rates: $72-$93
Tel: (408) 659-2935

CARMEL VALLEY INN
P. O. Box 115,
Carmel Valley Rd (93924)
Rates: $49-$119
Tel: (800) 541-3113

VALLEY LODGE
8 Ford Rd (93924)
Rates: $99-$249
Tel: (408) 659-2261
(800) 641-4646

CARNELIAN BAY

LAKESIDE CHALETS
5240 N Lake Blvd
(96140)
Rates: $95-$125
Tel: (916) 546-5857
(800) 294-6378
(CA/NV)

CARPINTERIA

**BEST WESTERN
CARPINTERIA INN**
4558 Carpinteria Ave
(93013)
Rates: $91-$135
Tel: (800) 528-1234

MOTEL 6
4200 Via Real (93013)
Rates: $35-$41
Tel: (805) 684-6921
(800) 440-6000

MOTEL 6
5550 Carpinteria Ave
(93013)
Rates: $35-$41
Tel: (805) 684-8602
(800) 440-6000

CASTAIC

CASTAIC INN
31411 Ridge Rd
(91384)
Rates: $35-$69
Tel: (805) 257-0229
(800) 628-5252

COMFORT INN
31558 Castaic Rd
(91384)
Rates: $36-$85
Tel: (805) 295-1100
(800) 221-2222

CASTRO VALLEY

**HOLIDAY INN
EXPRESS**
2532 Castro Valley
Blvd (94546)
Rates: $48-$95
Tel: (510) 538-9501
(800) 465-4329

CASTROVILLE

**CASTROVILLE
MOTEL**
11656 Merritt St
(95012)
Rates: $36-$48
Tel: (408) 633-2502

CATALINA ISLAND

HOTEL MONTEREY
108 Sumner Ave,
P. O. Box 1372
(90704)
Rates: $65-$165
Tel: (310) 510-0264
(800) 858-0035

CATHEDRAL CITY

**CHARLEENE
APTS MOTEL**
37112 Palo Verde Dr
(92234)
Rates: $40-$65
Tel: (619) 328-5427

DAYS INN SUITES
69-151 E Palm
Canyon Dr (92234)
Rates: $62-$179
Tel: (619) 324-5939
(800) 329-7466

**DOUBLETREE RESORT
AT DESERT PRINCESS**
67-967 Vista Chino
(92234)
Rates: $59-$245
Tel: (619) 322-7000
(800) 637-0577

**EMERALD COURT
HOTEL**
69375 Ramon Rd
(92234)
Rates: $35-$70
Tel: (619) 324-4521

CAYUCOS

**CYPRESS TREE
MOTEL**
125 S Ocean Ave
(93430)
Rates: $60
Tel: (805) 995-3917

DOLPHIN INN
399 S Ocean Ave
(93430)
Rates: $45-$110
Tel: (805) 995-3810
(800) 540-4276 (CA)

ESTERO BAY MOTEL
25 S Ocean Ave
(93430)
Rates: $30-$85
Tel: (805) 995-3614
(800) 736-1292

CAZADERO

CAZANOMA LODGE
100 Kid Creek Rd
(95421)
Rates: $80-$115
Tel: (707) 632-5255

CEDARVILLE

SUNRISE MOTEL
Highway 299
(96104)
Rates: $35-$45
Tel: (916) 279-2161

CERRITOS

**SHERATON
CERRITOS HOTEL-
TOWNE CENTER**
12725 Center Court
Dr (90703)
Rates: $59-$300
Tel: (310) 809-1500
(800) 325-3535

CHATSWORTH

**SUMMERFIELD
SUITES HOTEL**
21902 Lassen St
(91311)
Rates: $85-$158
Tel: (818) 773-0707
(800) 833-4353.

CHESTER

**CEDAR LODGE
MOTEL**
Hwy 36, Box 677
(96020)
Rates: $29-$53
Tel: (916) 258-2904

SENECA MOTEL
Box 504 (96020)
Rates $35-$47
Tel: (916) 258-2815

**TIMBER HOUSE
LODGE**
First & Main Sts
(96020)
Rates: $35-$60
Tel: (916) 258-2729

CHICO

DELUXE INN
2507 Esplanade
(95926)
Rates: $38+
Tel: (916) 342-8386

THE ESPLANADE B&B
620 Esplanade (95926)
Rates: $45-$60
Tel: (916) 345-8084

**HOLIDAY INN
OF CHICO**
685 Manzanita Ct
(95926)
Rates: $69-$85
Tel: (916) 345-2491
(800) 465-4329

MATADOR MOTEL
1934 Esplanade
(95926)
Rates: $30-$45
Tel: (916) 342-7543

MOTEL ORLEANS
655 Manzanita Ct
(95926)
Rates: $32-$39
Tel: (916) 345-2533

MOTEL 6
665 Manzanita Ct
(95926)
Rates: $30-$36
Tel: (916) 345-5500
(800) 440-6000

**O'FLAHERTY HOUSE
BED & BREAKFAST**
1462 Arcadian
(95926)
Rates: $65+
Tel: (916) 893-5494

OXFORD SUITES
2035 Business Ln
(95928)
Rates: $59-$102
Tel: (916) 899-9090
(800) 870-7848

SAFARI GARDEN MOTEL
2352 Esplanade (95926)
Rates: $32-$44
Tel: (916) 343-3201

TOWN HOUSE MOTEL
2231 Esplanade (95926)
Rates: $28-$42
Tel: (916) 343-1621

VAGABOND INN
630 Main St (95928)
Rates: $40-$65
Tel: (916) 895-1323
(800) 522-1555

CHINO

MOTEL 6
12266 Central Ave (91710)
Rates: $29-$34
Tel: (909) 591-3877
(800) 440-6000

CHOWCHILLA

DAYS INN
220 E Robertson Blvd (93610)
Rates: $40-$54
Tel: (209) 665-4821
(800) 329-7466

CHULA VISTA

GOOD NITE INN
225 Bay Blvd (91910)
Rates: $49-$79
Tel: (619) 425-8200
(800) 648-3466

LA QUINTA INN
150 Bonita Rd (91910)
Rates: $49-$54
Tel: (619) 691-1211
(800) 531-5900

MOTEL 6
745 E St (91910)
Rates: $34-$40
Tel: (619) 422-4200
(800) 440-6000

RODEWAY INN
778 Broadway (91910)
Rates: $35-$56
Tel: (800) 424-4777

TRAVELER MOTEL KITCHEN SUITES
235 Woodlawn Ave (91910)
Rates: $29-$59
Tel: (619) 427-9170
(800) 748-6998

TRAVELODGE-CHULA VISTA
394 Broadway (91910)
Rates: $43-$69
Tel: (619) 420-6600
(800) 578-7878

VAGABOND INN
230 Broadway (91910)
Rates: $36-$55
Tel: (619) 422-8305
(800) 522-1555

CLAREMONT

CLAREMONT INN
555 W Foothill Blvd (91711)
Rates: $49-$59
Tel: (800) 854-5733

HOWARD JOHNSON
721 S Indian Hill Blvd (91711)
Rates: $40-$65
Tel: (909) 626-2431
(800) 446-4656

RAMADA INN & TENNIS CLUB
840 S Indian Hill Blvd (91711)
Rates: $54-$58
Tel: (800) 228-2828

CLEAR CREEK

CLEAR CREEK MOTEL
667-150 Hwy 147 (96137)
Rates: $35-$45
Tel: (916) 256-3166

CLEARLAKE

SUNSET LODGE
13961 Lakeshore Dr (95422)
Rates: $40-$85
Tel: (707) 994-6642

TRAVELODGE-CLEARLAKE
4775 Old Hwy 53 (95422)
Rates: $34-$48
Tel: (707) 994-1499
(800) 578-7878

CLEARLAKE OAKS

LAKE HAVEN MOTEL
100 Short St (95423)
Rates: $36-$53
Tel: (707) 998-3908

LAKE POINT LODGE
13440 E Hwy 20 (95423)
Rates: $45-$78
Tel: (707) 998-4350

TWENTY OAKS COURT
10503 E Hwy 20 (95423)
Rates: $40
Tel: (707) 998-3012

COALINGA

BIG COUNTRY INN
25020 W Dorris Ave (93210)
Rates: $44-$60
Tel: (209) 935-0866
(800) 836-6835

THE INN AT HARRIS RANCH
24505 W Dorris Ave (93210)
Rates: $86-$111
Tel: (209) 935-0717
(800) 942-2333

MOTEL 6
25278 W Dorris Ave (93210)
Rates: $28-$34
Tel: (209) 935-2063
(800) 440-6000

MOTEL 6
25008 W Dorris Ave (93210)
Rates: $28-$34
Tel: (209) 935-1536
(800) 440-6000

COFFEE CREEK

BONANZA KING RESORT
Rt 2, Box 4790 (96091)
Rates: $65-$70
Tel: (916) 266-3305

COFFEE CREEK RANCH
Coffee Creek Rd (96091)
Rates: $124-$278
Tel: (916) 266-3343
(800) 624-4480

COLEVILLE

ANDRUSS MOTEL
Walker Rte, Box 64 (96107)
Rates: $36-$42
Tel: (916) 495-2216

MEADOWCLIFF MOTEL
Rte 1, Box 126 (96107)
Rates: $32-$45
Tel: (916) 495-2255

COLTON

DAYS INN
2830 Iowa St (92324)
Rates: $42-$120
Tel: (909) 788-9900
(800) 329-7466

THRIFTLODGE
225 E Valley Blvd (92324)
Rates: $32-$42
Tel: (909) 824-1520
(800) 578-7878

COLUMBIA

COLUMBIA GEM MOTEL
22131 Parrotts Ferry Rd (95310)
Rates: $25-$70
Tel: (209) 532-4508

COLUMBIA INN MOTEL
22646 Broadway St (95310)
Rates: $32-$76
Tel: (209) 533-0446

COMMERCE

RADISSON CITY OF COMMERCE HOTEL
6300 Telegraph Rd (90040)
Rates: $60-$105
Tel: (800) 333-3333

RAMADA INN
7272 Gage Ave (90040)
Rates: $51-$64
Tel: (310) 806-4777
(800) 547-4777

WYNDHAM GARDEN HOTEL
5757 Telegraph Rd (90040)
Rates: $119-$129
Tel: (213) 887-8100
(800) 996-3426

COMPTON

RAMADA INN 16
1919 W Artesia Blvd (90220)
Rates: $46-$80
Tel: (800) 272-6232

CONCORD

BEST WESTERN HERITAGE INN
4600 Clayton Rd (94521)
Rates: $55-$60
Tel: (510) 686-4466
(800) 528-1234

COMFORT INN
1370 Monument Blvd (94520)
Rates: $54-$80
Tel: (510) 827-8996
(800) 221-2222

EL MONTE MOTOR INN
3555 Clayton Rd (94519)
Rates: $43-$55
Tel: (510) 682-1601

HOLIDAY INN CONCORD
1050 Burnett Ave (94520)
Rates: $60-$95
Tel: (510) 687-5500
(800) 465-4329

SHERATON CONCORD HOTEL
45 John Glen Dr (94520)
Rates: $60-$95
Tel: (510) 825-7700
(800) 325-3535

CORCORAN

BUDGET INN
1224 Whitley Ave (93212)
Rates: $47-$60
Tel: (209) 992-3171

CORNING

CORNING OLIVE INN MOTEL
2165 Solano St (96021)
Rates: $28-$40
Tel: (916) 824-2468
(800) 221-2230

DAYS INN
3475 Highway 99 W (96021)
Rates: $33-$60
Tel: (916) 824-2000
(800) 329-7466

SHILO INNS
3350 Sunrise Way (96021)
Rates: $54-$61
Tel: (916) 824-2940
(800) 222-2244

CORONA

MOTEL 6
200 N Lincoln Ave (91720)
Rates: $28-$32
Tel: (909) 735-6408
(800) 440-6000

TRAVELODGE
1701 W 6th St (91720)
Rates: $33-$41
Tel: (909) 735-5500
(800) 578-7878

CORONADO

EL CORDOVA MOTEL
1351 Orange Ave (92118)
Rates: $70-$148
Tel: (619) 435-4131
(800) 229-2032

LOEWS CORONADO BAY RESORT
4000 Coronado Bay Rd (92118)
Rates: $195-$245
Tel: (619) 424-4000
(800) 815-6397

COSTA MESA

ANA MESA SUITES
3597 Harbor Blvd (92626)
Rates: $59-$84
Tel: (714) 662-3500
(800) 767-2519

BEST WESTERN NEWPORT MESA INN
2642 Newport Blvd (92627)
Rates: $49-$79
Tel: (714) 650-3020
(800) 528-1234

COMFORT INN
2430 Newport Blvd (92627)
Rates: $42-$58
Tel: (714) 631-7840
(800) 221-2222

LA QUINTA INN
1515 S Coast Dr (92626)
Rates: $45-$55
Tel: (714) 957-5841
(800) 531-5900

MARRIOTT SUITES
500 Anton Blvd (92626)
Rates: $59-$178
Tel: (714) 957-1100
(800) 228-9290

MOTEL 6
1441 Gisler Ave (92626)
Rates: $33-$37
Tel: (714) 957-3063
(800) 440-6000

NEWPORT BAY INN
2070 Newport Blvd (92627)
Rates: $33-$69
Tel: (714) 631-6000
(800) 284-3229

RAMADA LIMITED
1680 Superior Ave (92627)
Rates: $44-$125
Tel: (714) 645-2221
(800) 228-2828
(800) 345-8025 (CA)

RED LION HOTEL/ ORANGE COUNTY AIRPORT
3050 Bristol St (92626)
Rates: $104-$400
Tel: (714) 540-7000
(800) 547-8010

RESIDENCE INN BY MARRIOTT
881 W Baker St (92626)
Rates: $79-$156
Tel: (714) 241-8800
(800) 331-3131

VAGABOND INN
3205 Harbor Blvd (92626)
Rates: $40-$60
Tel: (714) 557-8360
(800) 522-1555

THE WESTIN SOUTH COAST PLAZA HOTEL
686 Anton Blvd (92626)
Rates: $189-$209
Tel: (714) 540-2500
(800) 228-3000

COVELO

WAGON WHEEL MOTEL
75860 Covelo Rd (95428)
Rates: $32-$39
Tel: (707) 983-6717

COVINA

EMBASSY SUITES HOTEL
1211 E Garvey (91724)
Rates: $79-$89
Tel: (818) 915-3441
(800) 362-2779

CRESCENT CITY

ECONO LODGE
119 L St (95531)
Rates: $32-$55
Tel: (707) 464-2181
(800) 424-4777

**EL PATIO
BUDGET MOTEL**
725 Hwy 101 N
(95531)
Rates: $32-$55
Tel: (707) 464-6106

**PACIFIC
MOTOR HOTEL**
440 Hwy 101 N
(95531)
Rates: $42-$65
Tel: (707) 464-4141
(800) 323-7917

ROYAL INN
102 L St (95531)
Rates: $33-$70
Tel (707) 464-4113

SUPER 8 MOTEL
685 Hwy 101 S
(95531)
Rates: $43-$70
Tel: (707) 464-4111
(800) 800-8000

CRESTLINE

**CREST LODGE
MOUNTAIN RESORT**
23508 Lake Dr (92325)
Rates: $55-$150
Tel: (909) 338-2418

CULVER CITY

**RAMADA HOTEL-
LAX NORTH**
6333 Bristol Pkwy
(90230)
Rates: $89
Tel: (310) 670-3200
(800) 272-6232

**RED LION HOTEL-
LOS ANGELES
AIRPORT**
6161 Centinela Ave
(90230)
Rates: $95-$135
Tel: (310) 649-1776
(800) 547-8010

SUNBURST MOTEL
3900 Sepulveda Blvd
(90230)
Rates: $55-$65
Tel: (310) 398-7523

CUPERTINO

CUPERTINO INN
10889 N De Anza
Blvd (95014)
Rates: $79-$138
Tel: (408) 996-7700

CYPRESS

**RAMADA HOTEL
CYPRESS**
5865 Katella Ave
(90630)
Rates: $82-$96
Tel: (714) 827-1010
(800) 228-2828

**WOODFIN SUITE
HOTEL**
5905 Corporate Ave
(90630)
Rates: $119-$179
Tel: (714) 828-4000
(800) 237-8811

DANA POINT

DANA POINT RESORT
25135 Park Lantem
(92629)
Rates: $170-$280
Tel: (714) 661-5000
(800) 533-9748

DANVILLE

DANVILLE INN
803 Camino Ramon
(94526)
Rates: $65-$80
Tel: (510) 838-8080
(800) 654-1050

DARDANELLE

**DARDANELLE
RESORT**
Highway 108 (95314)
Rates: $49-$65
Tel: (209) 965-4355

DAVIS

**BEST WESTERN
UNIVERSITY LODGE**
123 B St (95616)
Rates: $64-$70
Tel: (916) 756-7890
(800) 528-1234

DAVIS INN
4100 Chiles Rd
(95616)
Rates: $37-$109
Tel: (916) 757-7378
(800) 771-7378

ECONO LODGE
221 D St (95616)
Rates: $50-$55
Tel: (916) 756-1040
(800) 424-4777

MOTEL 6
4835 Chiles Rd
(95616)
Rates: $30-$38
Tel: (916) 753-3777
(800) 440-6000

DEATH VALLEY NATIONAL PARK

**STOVE PIPE WELLS
VILLAGE**
SR 190 (92328)
Rates: $53-$76
Tel: (619) 786-2387

DEL MAR

**DEL MAR HILTON
NORTH SAN DIEGO**
15575 Jimmy
Durante Blvd
(92014)
Rates: $75-$140
Tel: (619) 792-5200
(800) 445-8667

**DOUBLETREE
HOTEL
DEL MAR**
11915 El Camino
Real (92130)
Rates: $119-$154
Tel: (619) 481-5900
(800) 222-8733

DELANO

COMFORT INN
2211 Girard St
(93215)
Rates: $51-$65
Tel: (800) 221-2222

SHILO INNS
2231 Girard St
(93215)
Rates: $51-$65
Tel: (805) 725-7551
(800) 222-2244

DESERT HOT SPRINGS

ATLAS HI LODGE
18-336 Avenida
Hermosa (92240)
Rates: $28-$39
Tel: (619) 329-5446

BROADVIEW LODGE
12-672 Eliseo Rd
(92240)
Rates: $25-$45
Tel: (619) 329-8006

CARAVAN SPA
66-810 E 4th St
(92240)
Rates: $38+
Tel: (619) 329-7124

EL REPOSO MOTEL
66-334 W 5th St
(92240)
Rates: $35-$75
Tel: (619) 329-6632

KISMET LODGE
13-340 Mountain
View Rd (92240)
Rates: $45-$65
Tel: (619) 329-6451

**LAS PRIMAVERAS
RESORT SPA**
66-659 6th St (92240)
Rates: 45-$75
Tel: (619) 251-1677
(800) 400-1677

MINERAL SPRINGS RESORT
11000 Palm Dr (92240)
Rates: $29-$125
Tel: (619) 329-6484
(800) 922-6484

MIRACLE MANOR
12-589 Reposo Way (92240)
Rates: $45-$50
Tel: (619) 329-6641

MOTEL 6
63-950 20th Ave (92258)
Rates: $34-$41
Tel: (619) 251-1425
(800) 440-6000

PONCE DE LEON MOTEL
11-000 Palm Dr (92240)
Rates: $39-$135
Tel: (619) 329-6484
(800) 922-6484 (CA)

ROYAL PALMS INN BED & BREAKFAST
12-885 Eliseo Rd (92240)
Rates: $45-$65
Tel: (619) 329-7975
(800) 755-9538

SAN MARCUS INN
66-540 San Marcus Rd (92240)
Rates: $32-$64
Tel: (619) 329-5304

STARDUST SPA MOTEL
66-634 5th St (92240)
Rates: $37-$58
Tel: (619) 329-5443
(800) 482-7835

SUNSET INN
67-585 Hacienda Ave (92240)
Rates: $45-$125
Tel: (619) 329-4488

SWISS HEALTH RESORT & RETREAT
66-729 8th St (92240)
Rates: $49-$74
Tel: (619) 329-6912
(800) 794-7743

TAMARIX SPA MOTEL
66-185 Acoma (92240)
Rates: $25-$60
Tel: (619) 329-6615

DIAMOND BAR

BEST WESTERN DIAMOND BAR
259 Gentle Springs Ln (91765)
Rates: $59-$89
Tel: (800) 528-1234

RADISSON INN DIAMOND BAR
21725 E Gateway Dr (91765)
Rates: $59-$79
Tel: (800) 333-3333

DINUBA

BEST WESTERN AMERICANA
Alta Ave & Kamm Rd (93618)
Rates: $45-$70
Tel: (209) 595-8401
(800) 528-1234

DIXON

BEST WESTERN INN
1345 Commercial Way (95620)
Rates: $55-$85
Tel: (916) 678-1400
(800) 528-1234

DOUGLAS CITY

INDIAN CREEK LODGE
Hwy 299 E (96024)
Rates: $28-$75
Tel: (916) 623-6294

DOWNEY

EMBASSY SUITES HOTEL
8425 Firestone Blvd (90241)
Rates: $109-$160
Tel: (310) 861-1900
(800) 362-2779

DOWNIEVILLE

SAUNDRA DYER'S RESORT
P. O. Box 406 (95936)
Rates: $54-$125
Tel: (916) 289-3308
(800) 696-3308

DOYLE

MIDWAY CAFE & MOTEL
Doyle Loop (96109)
Rates: $28+
Tel: (916) 827-2208

7W CAFE & MOTEL
434-455 Doyle Loop (96109)
Rates: $22-$33
Tel: (916) 827-3331

DUARTE

TRAVELODGE
1200 E Huntington Dr (91010)
Rates: $39-$69
Tel: (818) 357-0907
(800) 578-7878

DUBLIN

BEST WESTERN DUBLIN PARK HOTEL
6680 Regional St (94568)
Rates: $89-$175
Tel: (510) 828-7750
(800) 223-4656
(800) 422-4656 (CA)

DUNNIGAN

BEST WESTERN COUNTRY
3930 Rd 89 (95937)
Rates: $50-$85
Tel: (916) 724-3471
(800) 528-1234

VALUE LODGE-IMA
Rd 89 & Rd 6 (95937)
Rates: $39-$56
Tel: (916) 724-3333
(800) 341-8000

DUNSMUIR

ABBOTTS RIVER-WALK INN B & B
4300 Dunsmuir Ave (96025)
Rates: $35-$55
Tel: (916) 235-4300
(800) 954-4300

CABOOSE MOTEL
100 Railroad Park Rd (96025)
Rates: $45-$80
Tel: (916) 235-4440
(800) 974-7245 (CA)

CAVE SPRINGS RESORT
4727 Dunsmuir Ave (96025)
Rates: $37-$49
Tel: (916) 235-2721

CEDAR LODGE
4201 Dunsmuir Ave (96025)
Rates: $28-$50
Tel: (916) 235-4331

SHASTA ALPINE INN
4221 Siskiyou Ave (96025)
Rates: $30-$80
Tel: (916) 235-0930
(800) 880-0930

TRAVELODGE
5400 Dunsmuir Ave (96025)
Rates: $40-$60
Tel: (916) 235-4395
(800) 578-7878

EL CAJON

BEST WESTERN COURTESY INN
1355 E Main St (92021)
Rates: $40-$110
Tel: (619) 440-7378
(800) 528-1234

BUDGET HOST HACIENDA
588 N Mollison Ave (92021)
Rates: $31-$36
Tel: (800) 283-4678

DAYS INN-LA MESA
1250 El Cajon Blvd (92020)
Rates: $35-$49
Tel: (800) 329-7466

MOTEL 6
550 Montrose Ct (92020)
Rates: $30-$36
Tel: (619) 588-6100
(800) 440-6000

THRIFTLODGE
1220 W Main St
(92020)
Rates: $35-$85
Tel: (619) 442-2576
(800) 578-7878

VILLA EMBASADORA
1556 E Main St
(92021)
Rates: $25-$42
Tel: (619) 442-9617

EL CENTRO

**BEST WESTERN
JOHN JAY INN**
2352 S Fourth
(92243)
Rates: $50-$75
Tel: (619) 337-8677
(800) 528-1234

BRUNNER'S MOTEL
215 N Imperial Ave
(92243)
Rates: $46-$55
Tel: (619) 352-6431

**DEL CORONADO
CROWN MOTEL**
330 N Imperial Ave
(92243)
Rates: $38-$58
Tel: (619) 353-0030
(800) 653-3226

**EXECUTIVE INN
OF EL CENTRO**
725 State St (92243)
Rates: $27-$40
Tel: (619) 352-8500

LAGUNA INN
2030 Cottonwood
Cir (92243)
Rates: $53
Tel: (619) 353-7750

MOTEL 6
395 Smoketree Dr
(92243)
Rates: $27-$33
Tel: (619) 353-6766
(800) 440-6000

SANDS MOTEL
611 N Imperial Ave
(92243)
Rates: $30-$44
Tel: (619) 352-0715

TRAVELODGE
1464 Adams Ave
(92243)
Rates: $36-$50
Tel: (619) 352-7333
(800) 578-7878

VACATION INN
2000 Cottonwood
Cir (92243)
Rates: $43-$48
Tel: (619) 352-9523
(800) 328-6289

EL CERRITO

FREEWAY MOTEL
11645 San Pablo Ave
(94530)
Rates: $38-$58
Tel: (510) 234-5581

EL MONTE

MOTEL 6
3429 Peck Rd (91731)
Rates: $27-$31
Tel: (818) 448-6660
(800) 440-6000

EL SEGUNDO

**CROWN STERLING
SUITES**
1440 E Imperial Ave
(90245)
Rates: $124-$149
Tel: (310) 640-3600
(800) 433-4600

**SUMMERFIELD
SUITES-LAX**
810 S Douglas Ave
(90245)
Rates: $179-$189
Tel: (310) 725-0100,
(800) 833-4353

**TRAVELODGE
AT LAX SOUTH**
1804 E Sycamore St
(90245)
Rates: $45-$62
Tel: (310) 615-1073
(800) 578-7878

ELK

**THE GREENWOOD
PIER INN**
Box 36, 5938
Highway 1 (95432)
Rates: $100-$225
Tel: (707) 877-9997

EMERYVILLE

**HOLIDAY INN
SAN FRANCISCO
BAYBRIDGE**
1800 Powell St
(94608)
Rates: $75-$130
Tel: (800) 465-4329

EMIGRANT GAP

**RANCHO SIERRAS
RESORT**
43440 Laing Rd
(95715)
Rates: $45-$85
Tel: (916) 389-8572

ENCINITAS

**BUDGET MOTELS
OF AMERICA**
133 Encinitas Blvd
(92024)
Rates: $31-$57
Tel: (619) 944-0260
(800) 795-6044

**FRIENDSHIP INN
ENCINITAS**
410 N Hwy 101
(92024)
Rates: $35-$55
Tel: (619) 436-4999
(800) 424-4777

ESCONDIDO

**BEST WESTERN
ESCONDIDO**
1700 Seven Oaks Rd
(92026)
Rates: $59-$116
Tel: (619) 740-1700
(800) 528-1234

**CASTLE CREEK INN
RESORT & SPA**
29850 Circle "R"
Way (92026)
Rates: $80
Tel: (619) 751-8800
(800) 253-5341

ECONO LODGE
1250 W Valley Pkwy
(92029)
Rates: $44-$49
Tel: (800) 424-4777

**LAWRENCE WELK
RESORT**
8860 Lawrence Welk
Dr (92026)
Rates: $90-$220
Tel: (619) 749-3000
(800) 932-9355

MOTEL MEDITERANIAN
2336 S Escondido
Blvd (92025)
Rates: $34-$75
Tel: (619) 743-1061

MOTEL 6
509 W Washington
Ave (92025)
Rates: $25-$29
Tel: (619) 743-6669
(800) 440-6000

MOTEL 6
900 N Quince St
(92025)
Rates: $32-$38
Tel: (619) 745-9252
(800) 440-6000

PINE TREE LODGE
425 W Mission
(92025)
Rates: $44
Tel: (619) 740-7613

THE SHERIDAN INN
1341 N Escondido
Blvd (92026)
Rates: $51-$57
Tel: (619) 743-8338
(800) 258-8527

SUNSHINE MOTEL
1107 S Escondido
Blvd (92025)
Rates: $29-$95
Tel: (619) 743-3111

SUPER 7 MOTEL
515 W Washington
Ave (92025)
Rates: $21-$72
Tel: (619) 743-7979

**SUPER 8 MOTEL-
ESCONDIDO**
528 W Washington
Ave (92025)
Rates: $35-$55
Tel: (619) 747-3711
(800) 800-8000

EUREKA

**A WEAVER'S INN
BED & BREAKFAST**
1440 B St (95501)
Rates: $65-$100
Tel: (707) 443-8119

BAYVIEW MOTEL
Hwy 101 (95501)
Rates: $42-$60
Tel: (707) 442-1673

**BUDGET HOST
TOWN HOUSE
MOTEL**
933 4th St (95501)
Rates: $34-$85
Tel: (800) 445-6888

**CARSON HOUSE
INN**
1209 4th St (95501)
Rates: $65-$115
Tel: (707) 443-1601
(800) 772-1622

EUREKA INN
518 7th St (95501)
Rates: $70-$140
Tel: (707) 442-6441
(800) 862-4906

FIRESIDE INN
5th & R Sts (95501)
Rates: $30-$55
Tel: (707) 443-6312

MATADOR MOTEL
129 4th St (95501)
Rates: $33-$53
Tel: (707) 443-9751

MOTEL 6
1934 Broadway
(95501)
Rates: $29-$43
Tel: (707) 445-9631
(800) 440-6000

NENDELS VALU INN
2223 4th St (95501)
Rates: $40-$65
Tel: (707) 442-3261

RED LION INN
1929 4th St (95501)
Rates: $78-$125
Tel: (707) 445-0844
(800) 547-8010

**SAFARI BUDGET 6
MOTEL**
801 Broadway
(95501)
Rates: $30-$58
Tel: (707) 443-4891

SANDPIPER MOTEL
4055 Broadway
(95501)
Rates: $34-$45
Tel: (707) 443-7394

**TOWN HOUSE
MOTEL**
933 4th St (95501)
Rates: $32-$75
Tel: (707) 443-4536
(800) 445-6888

TRAVELODGE
4 4th St (95501)
Rates: $35-$90
Tel: (707) 443-6345
(800) 578-7878
(800) 255-3050

VAGABOND INN
1630 4th St (95501)
Rates: $35-$60
Tel: (707) 443-8041
(800) 522-1555
(800) 424-4777

FAIRFIELD

**BEST WESTERN
CORDELIA INN**
4373 Central Pl
(94585)
Rates: $50-$68
Tel: (707) 864-2029
(800) 528-1234

HOLIDAY INN
1350 Holiday Ln
(94533)
Rates: $59-$86
Tel: (707) 422-4111
(800) 465-4329

MOTEL 6-NORTH
1473 Holiday Ln
(94533)
Rates: $30-$38
Tel: (707) 425-4565
(800) 440-6000

MOTEL 6-SOUTH
2353 Magellan Rd
(94533)
Rates: $28-$34
Tel: (707) 427-0800
(800) 440-6000

FALL RIVER
MILLS

HI-MONT MOTEL
43021 Hwy 299
(96028)
Rates: $43-$65
Tel: (916) 336-5541

FALLBROOK

**BEST WESTERN
FRANCISCAN INN**
1635 S Mission Rd
(92028)
Rates: $67-$85
Tel: (619) 728-6174
(800) 528-1234

LA ESTANCIA INN
3135 S Old Hwy 395
(92028)
Rates: $48-$78
Tel: (619) 723-2888

FERNDALE

FERNDALE MOTEL
632 Main St (95536)
Rates: $48-$53
Tel: (707) 786-9471

FIREBAUGH

**APRICOT INN/
SHILO INNS**
46290 W Panoche Rd
(93622)
Rates: $42-$58
Tel: (209) 659-1444
(800) 222-2244

FISH CAMP

**MARRIOTT'S
TENAYA LODGE**
1122 Hwy 41 (93623)
Rates: $199-$259
Tel: (209) 683-6555
(800) 635-5807

FOLSOM

**RADISSON INN
AT LAKE NATOMA**
720 Gold Lake Dr
(95630)
Rates: $79-$135
Tel: (916) 351-1500
(800) 333-3333

FONTANA

MOTEL 6
10195 Sierra Ave
(92335)
Rates: $31-$35
Tel: (909) 823-8686
(800) 440-6000

FORT BIDWELL

**FORT BIDWELL
HOTEL**
Main St,
P. O. Box 100 (96112)
Rates: $35-$45
Tel: (916) 279-2050

FORT BRAGG

**BEACHCOMBER
MOTEL**
1111 N Main St
(95437)
Rates: $59-$275
Tel: (707) 964-2402
(800) 400-7873

**CLEONE LODGE INN
& BEACH HOUSE
BED & BREAKFAST**
24600 N Hwy 1
(95437)
Rates: $72-$130
Tel: (707) 964-2788

COAST MOTEL
18661 Hwy 1 (95437)
Rates: $38-$64
Tel: (707) 964-2852

EBB TIDE LODGE
250 S Main St (95437)
Rates: $45-$75
Tel: (707) 964-5321
(800) 974-6730

**THE RENDEZVOUS
INN**
647 N Main St (95437)
Rates: $55-$95
Tel: (800) 491-8142

WISHING WELL COTTAGES
Hwy 20 (95437)
Rates: $60-$70
Tel: (800) 362-9305

FORTUNA

BEST WESTERN COUNTRY INN
1528 Kenmar Rd (95540)
Rates: $45-$99
Tel: (707) 725-6822
(800) 528-1234

ECONO LODGE
275 12th St (95540)
Rates: $39-$59
Tel: (707) 725-6993
(800) 424-4777

HOLIDAY INN EXP.
1859 Alamar Way (95540)
Rates: $35-$70
Tel: (707) 725-5500
(800) 465-4329

NATIONAL 9 MOTEL
819 Main St (95540)
Rates: $30-$52
Tel: (707) 725-5136

SUPER 8 MOTEL
1805 Alamar Way (95540)
Rates: $40-$60
Tel: (707) 725-2888
(800) 800-8000

FOUNTAIN VALLEY

FOUNTAIN VALLEY INN
9125 Recreational Circle Dr (92708)
Rates: $40-$65
Tel: (714) 847-3388
(800) 826-1964 (CA)

RAMADA INN
9125 Recreation Cir Dr (92708)
Rates: $49-$89
Tel: (714) 847-3388
(800) 272-6232

RESIDENCE INN BY MARRIOTT
9930 Slater Ave (92708)
Rates: $136-$149
Tel: (714) 965-8000
(800) 331-3131

FREESTONE

GREEN APPLE INN
520 Bohemian Hwy (95472)
Rates: $85-$92
Tel: (707) 874-2526

FREMONT

BEST WESTERN THUNDERBIRD INN
5400 Mowry Ave (94538)
Rates: $65-$75
Tel: (510) 792-4300
(800) 528-1234

GOOD NITE INN
4135 Cushing Pkwy (94538)
Rates: $42-$49
Tel: (510) 656-9307

ISLANDER MOTEL
4101 Mowry Ave (94538)
Rates: $35-$53
Tel: (510) 796-8200

LORD BRADLEY'S INN BED & BREAKFAST
43344 Mission Blvd (94539)
Rates: $65-$75
Tel: (510) 490-0520

MISSION PEAK LODGE
43643 Mission Blvd (94539)
Rates: $29-$50
Tel: (510) 656-2366

MOTEL 6-NORTH
34047 Fremont Blvd (94536)
Rates: $34-$40
Tel: (510) 793-4848
(800) 440-6000

MOTEL 6-SOUTH
46101 Research Ave (94539)
Rates: $34-$40
Tel: (510) 490-4528
(800) 440-6000

RESIDENCE INN BY MARRIOTT
5400 Farwell Pl (94536)
Rates: $69-$158
Tel: (510) 794-5900
(800) 331-3131

FRESNO

BEST WESTERN TRADEWINDS MOTOR INN
2141 N Parkway Dr (93705)
Rates: $49-$62
Tel: (209) 237-1881
(800) 528-1234

BLACKSTONE PLAZA INN
4061 N Blackstone Ave (93726)
Rates: $36-$48
Tel: (209) 222-5641

BROOKS RANCH INN
4278 W Ashian Ave (93722)
Rates: $31-$44
Tel: (209) 275-2727

DAYS INN
1101 N Parkway Dr (93728)
Rates: $39-$75
Tel: (209) 268-6211
(800) 329-7466

ECONOMY INNS OF AMERICA
2570 S East St (93706)
Rates: $26-$33
Tel: (800) 826-0778

ECONOMY INNS OF AMERICA
5021 N Barcus Ave (93722)
Rates: $27-$41
Tel: (800) 826-0778

EXECUTIVE SUITES OF FRESNO
P. O. Box 42 (93707)
Rates: $650-$1495/ monthly
Tel: (209) 237-7444

HILTON HOTEL-FRESNO
1055 Van Ness Ave (93721)
Rates: $74-$119
Tel: (209) 485-9000
(800) 445-8667

HOLIDAY INN CENTRE PLAZA
2233 Ventura St (93709)
Rates: $72-$86
Tel: (209) 268-1000
(800) 465-4329

HOLIDAY INN FRESNO AIRPORT
5090 E Clinton Ave (93727)
Rates: $74-$110
Tel: (209) 252-3611
(800) 465-4329

HOWARD JOHNSON
4071 N Blackstone Ave (93726)
Rates: $36-$48
Tel: (800) 654-2000

LA QUINTA INN
2926 Tulare St (93721)
Rates: $50-$65
Tel: (209) 442-1110
(800) 531-5900

MOTEL 6
445 N Pkwy Dr (93706)
Rates: $26-$32
Tel: (209) 485-5011
(800) 440-6000

MOTEL 6
4245 N Blackstone Ave (93726)
Rates: $32-$38
Tel: (209) 221-0800
(800) 440-6000

MOTEL 6
4080 N Blackstone Ave (93726)
Rates: $32-$38
Tel: (209) 222-2431
(800) 440-6000

MOTEL 6
933 N Pkwy Dr (93728)
Rates: $26-$32
Tel: (209) 233-3913
(800) 440-6000

MOTEL 6
1240 Crystal Ave
(93728)
Rates: $26-$32
Tel: (209) 237-0855
(800) 440-6000

RESIDENCE INN
5322 N Diana Ave
(93710)
Rates: n/a
Tel: (209) 222-8900
(800) 331-3131

RODEWAY INN
949 N. Parkway
Drive (93728)
Rates: $35-$49
Tel: (209) 268-0363
(800) 228-2000

SUPER 8 MOTEL
1087 N Parkway Dr
(93728)
Rates: $42
Tel: (209) 268-0741
(800) 800-8000

TRAVELODGE
2345 N Parkway Dr
(93705)
Rates: $36-$40
Tel: (209) 268-0711
(800) 578-7878

FULLERTON

FULLERTON INN
2601 W Orangethorpe
Ave (92633)
Rates: $35-$45
Tel: (714) 773-4900

**HOLIDAY INN-
FULLERTON/
DISNEYLAND**
222 W Houston Ave
(92632)
Rates: $61-$90
Tel: (714) 992-1700
(800) 465-4329
(800) 553-3441 (CA)

**MARRIOTT HOTEL/
CAL STATE UNIV**
2701 E Nutwood
Ave (92631)
Rates: $79-$89
Tel: (714) 738-7800
(800) 228-9290

MOTEL 6-EAST
1440 N State College
(92631)
Rates: $32-$36
Tel: (714) 956-9690
(800) 440-6000

MOTEL 6-WEST
1415 S Euclid St
(92632)
Rates: $30-$34
Tel: (714) 992-0660
(800) 440-6000

GARBERVILLE

BENBOW INN
445 Lake Benbow Dr
(95542)
Rates: $110-$295
Tel: (707) 923-2124
(800) 355-3301

**BEST WESTERN
HUMBOLDT HOUSE
INN**
701 Redwood Dr
(95542)
Rates: $56-$120
Tel: (707) 923-2771
(800) 528-1234

**GARBERVILLE
MOTEL**
948 Redwood Dr
(95542)
Rates: $38-$56
Tel: (707) 923-2422

**HEART OF THE RED-
WOODS RESORT**
900 Hwy 101 (95542)
Rates: $55-$110
Tel: (707) 247-3305

**SHERWOOD
FOREST MOTEL**
814 Redwood Dr
(95542)
Rates: $50-$88
Tel: (707) 923-2721

GARDEN GROVE

**HIDDEN VILLAGE
BED & BREAKFAST**
9582 Halekulani Dr
(92641)
Rates: $55
Tel: (714) 636-8312

GARDENA

**CARSON PLAZA
HOTEL**
111 W Albertoni St
(90248)
Rates: $32-$50
Tel: (310) 329-0651

GEORGETOWN

**AMERICAN RIVER
INN B & B**
P. O. Box 43, Main &
Orleans Sts (95643)
Rates: $89-$105
Tel: (916) 333-4499
(800) 245-6566

GILROY

BEST WESTERN INN
360 Leavesley Rd
(95020)
Rates: $48-$71
Tel: (408) 848-1467
(800) 528-1234

LEAVESLEY INN
8430 Murray Ave
(95020)
Rates: $38-$50
Tel: (408) 847-5500
(800) 624-8225

MOTEL 6
6110 Monterey Hwy
(95020)
Rates: $30-$36
Tel: (408) 842-6061
(800) 440-6000

SUNREST INN
8292 Murray Ave
(95020)
Rates: $42-$50
Tel: (408) 848-3500
(800) 526-4489

SUPER 8 MOTEL
8435 San Ysidro
(95020)
Rates: $35-$48
Tel: (408) 848-4108
(800) 800-8000

GLEN AVON

CIRCLE INN MOTEL
9220 Granite Hill Dr
(92509)
Rates: n/a
Tel: (714) 360-1132

GLEN ELLEN

BIG DOG INN B & B
15244 Arnold Dr
(95442)
Rates: $100-$135
Tel: (707) 996-4319

GLENDALE

DAYS INN
600 N Pacific Ave
(91203)
Rates: $64-$74
Tel: (818) 956-0202
(800) 329-7466

RED LION HOTEL
100 W Glenoaks
Blvd (91203)
Rates: $128-$155
Tel: (818) 956-5468
(800) 547-8010

VAGABOND INN
120 W Colorado St
(91204)
Rates: $48-$65
Tel: (818) 240-1700
(800) 522-1555

GLENHAVEN

**INDIAN BEACH
RESORT**
9945 E Hwy 20,
Box 648 (95443)
Rates: $35-$100
Tel: (707) 998-3760

GOLETA

MOTEL 6
5897 Calle Real
(93117)
Rates: $42-$48
Tel: (805) 964-3596
(800) 440-6000

GRASS VALLEY

**ALTA SIERRA
RESORT MOTEL**
135 Tammy Way
(95949)
Rates: $40-$90
Tel: (916) 273-9102

**BEST WESTERN
GOLD COUNTRY
INN**
11972 Sutton Way
(95945)
Rates: $69-$76
Tel: (916) 273-1393
(800) 528-1234

**GOLDEN CHAIN
RESORT MOTEL**
13363 SR 49 (95949)
Rates: $34-$70
Tel: (916) 273-7279

HOLIDAY LODGE
1221 E Main St
(95945)
Rates: $38-$75
Tel: (916) 273-4406
(800) 742-7125

SWAN-LEVINE HOUSE
328 S Church St
(95945)
Rates: $65-$95
Tel: (916) 272-1873

GREEN VALLEY LAKE

LODGE AT GREEN VALLEY BED & BREAKFAST
33655 Green Valley Lake Rd (92341)
Rates: $65-$95
Tel: (909) 867-4281

GREENVILLE

HIDEAWAY RESORT MOTEL
101 Hideaway Rd
(95947)
Rates: $42-$45
Tel: (916) 284-7915

OAK GROVE MOTOR LODGE
700 Hwy 89,
Box 827 (95947)
Rates: $40-$47
Tel: (916) 284-6671

SIERRA LODGE
303 Main St,
Box 578 (95947)
Rates: $24-$40
Tel: (916) 284-6565

SPRING MEADOW RESORT MOTEL
18964 Hwy 89 (95947)
Rates: $53+
Tel: (916) 284-6768

GROVELAND

BUCKMEADOWS LODGE
7647 Hwy 120 (95321)
Rates: $45-$85
Tel: (209) 962-5281
(800) 253-9673

GROVELAND HOTEL/YOSEMITE NATIONAL PARK
18767 Main St
(95321)
Rates: $75-$155
Tel: (209) 962-4000
(800) 273-3314

MOUNTAIN RIVER MOTEL
12655 Jacksonville Rd (95321)
Rates: $30
Tel: (209) 984-5071

SUGAR PINE RANCH
P. O. Box 784 (95321)
Rates: $69-$95
Tel: (209) 962-7823

YOSEMITE INN
31191 Hardin Flat Rd (95321)
Rates: $28-$55
Tel: (209) 962-0103

YOSEMITE WESTGATE MOTEL
7366 Hwy 120 (95321)
Rates: $49-$150
Tel: (209) 962-5281
(800) 253-9673

GROVER BEACH

OAK PARK INN
775 N Oak Park Blvd
(93433)
Rates: $50-$100
Tel: (805) 481-4448
(800) 549-4448

GUALALA

GUALALA COUNTRY INN
Hwy 1 (95445)
Rates: $71-$145
Tel: (707) 884-4343
(800) 564-4466

SURF MOTEL AT GUALALA
39170 Hwy 1 (95445)
Rates: $79-$145
Tel: (707) 884-3571

GUERNEVILLE

AVALON INN
16484 4th St (95446)
Rates: $50-$125
Tel: (707) 869-9566

CREEKSIDE INN & RESORT
16180 Neeley Rd
(95446)
Rates: $60-$150
Tel: (707) 869-3623
(800) 776-6586

THE HIGHLANDS
14000 Woodland Dr
(95446)
Rates: $55-$105
Tel: (707) 869-0333

HACIENDA HEIGHTS

MOTEL 6
1154 S 7th Ave (91745)
Rates: $30-$34
Tel: (818) 968-9462
(800) 440-6000

HALF MOON BAY

HOLIDAY INN EXP
230 Cabrillo Hwy
(94019)
Rates: $69-$85
Tel: (415) 726-3400
(800) 465-4329

RAMADA LIMITED
3020 Hwy 1 N
(94019)
Rates: $75-$150
Tel: (415) 726-9700
(800) 272-6232
(800) 350-9888 (CA)

ZABALLA HOUSE BED & BREAKFAST
324 Main St (94019)
Rates: $65-$170
Tel: (415) 726-9123

HANFORD

DOWNTOWN MOTEL
101 N Redington St
(92320)
Rates: $30-$42
Tel: (209) 582-9036

IRWIN STREET INN
522 N Irwin (93230)
Rates: $69-$110
Tel: (209) 583-8791

HAPPY CAMP

FOREST LODGE MOTEL
63712 Hwy 96 (96039)
Rates: $40-$55
Tel: (916) 493-5424

HARBOR CITY

MOTEL 6
820 W Sepulveda Blvd (90710)
Rates: $36-$40
Tel: (310) 518-2034
(800) 440-6000

TRAVELODGE
1665 W Pacific Coast Hwy (90710)
Rates: $38-$46
Tel: (310) 326-9026
(800) 578-7878

HAYFORK

BIG CREEK LODGE
Big Creek Rd (96041)
Rates: $25-$65
Tel: (916) 628-5521

HAYWARD

BEST WESTERN INN OF HAYWARD
360 West A St
(94541)
Rates: $55-$63
Tel: (510) 785-8700
(800) 528-1234

EXECUTIVE INN
20777 Hesperian Blvd (94541)
Rates: $72-$88
Tel: (510) 732-6300
(800) 553-5083

HAYWARD ISLANDER MOTEL
29083 Mission Blvd
(94544)
Rates: $34-$49
Tel: (510) 538-8700

MOTEL 6
30155 Industrial Pkwy SW (94544)
Rates: $32-$38
Tel: (510) 489-8333
(800) 440-6000

PHOENIX LODGE
2286 Industrial
Pkwy W (94545)
Rates: $36-$42
Tel: (510) 786-2844

PHOENIX LODGE
500 West A St
(94541)
Rates: $36-$44
Tel: (510) 786-0417

VAGABOND INN
20455 Hesperian
Blvd (94541)
Rates: $49-$64
Tel: (510) 785-5480
(800) 522-1555

HEALDSBURG

**BEST WESTERN
DRY CREEK INN**
198 Dry Creek Rd
(95448)
Rates: $55-$79
Tel: (707) 433-0300
(800) 528-1234

FAIRVIEW MOTEL
74 Healdsburg Ave
(95448)
Rates: $38-$60
Tel: (707) 433-5548

**MADRONA MANOR-
A WINE COUNTRY
INN**
1001 Westside Rd
(95448)
Rates: $130-$240
Tel: (707) 433-4231
(800) 258-4003

HEMET

**BEST WESTERN
HEMET MOTOR INN**
2625 W Florida Ave
(92545)
Rates: $46-$60
Tel: (909) 925-6605
(800) 528-1234

**COACHLIGHT
MOTEL**
1640 W Florida Ave
(92543)
Rates: $28-$40
Tel: (909) 658-3237
(800) 678-0124

QUALITY INN
800 W Florida Ave
(92543)
Rates: $45-$61
Tel: (909) 929-6366
(800) 221-2222

SUPER 8 MOTEL
3510 W Florida Ave
(92543)
Rates: $39-$65
Tel: (909) 658-2281
(800) 800-8000

TRAVELODGE
1201 W Florida Ave
(92543)
Rates: $38-$42
Tel: (909) 766-1902
(800) 578-7878

HESPERIA

DAYS INN SUITES
14865 Bear Valley
Rd (92345)
Rates: $42-$90
Tel: (619) 948-0600
(800) 329-7746

HIGHLAND

SUPER 8 MOTEL
26667 E Highland
Ave (92346)
Rates: $32-$36
Tel: (909) 864-0100
(800) 800-8000

HOLLISTER

**BEST WESTERN
SAN BENITO INN**
660 San Felipe Rd
(95023)
Rates: $45-$70
Tel: (408) 637-9248
(800) 528-1234

**CINDERELLA
MOTEL-IMA**
110 San Felipe Rd
(95023)
Rates: $52-$66
Tel: (408) 637-5761
(800) 341-8000

**RIDGEMARK
GUEST COTTAGES**
3800 Airline Hwy
(95023)
Rates: $70-$105
Tel: (408) 637-8151
(800) 637-8151

HOLLYWOOD

**BEST WESTERN
HOLLYWOOD
MOTEL**
6141 Franklin Ave
(90028)
Rates: $55-$85
Tel: (213) 464-5181
(800) 528-1234

HOLIDAY INN
1755 N Highland
Ave (90028)
Rates: $89-$169
Tel: (213) 462-7181
(800) 465-4329

OBAN HOTEL
6364 Yucca St
(90028)
Rates: $25-$45
Tel: (213) 466-0524

HOLTVILLE

**BARBARA WORTH
COUNTRY CLUB &
HOTEL**
2050 Country Club
Dr (92250)
Rates: $48-$75
Tel: (619) 356-2806
(800) 356-3806

HOMEWOOD

HOMESIDE MOTEL
5205 W Lake Blvd
(96141)
Rates: $222 (3 nights)
Tel: (800) 824-6348

HOPE VALLEY

**SORENSEN'S
RESORT**
14255 Hwy 88
(96120)
Rates: $55-$120
Tel: (916) 694-2203
(800) 423-9949

HUNTINGTON
BEACH

**BEACH COMFORT
MOTEL**
118 11th St (92647)
Rates: $50-$75
Tel: (714) 536-4170

**BEST WESTERN
REGENCY INN**
19360 Beach Blvd
(92648)
Rates: $63-$120
Tel: (800) 528-1234

MOTEL EUROPA
7561 Center Ave 46
(92647)
Rates: $36-$50
Tel: (714) 892-7336

HYAMPOM

**ZIEGLER'S
TRAILS' END**
#1 Main St (96046)
Rates: $50-$80
Tel: (916) 628-4929
(800) 566-5266

IDYLLWILD

FIRESIDE INN
54540 N Circle Dr
(92549)
Rates: $55-$80
Tel: (909) 659-2966

IDYLLWILD INN
P. O. Box 515 (92549)
Rates: $47-$124
Tel: (909) 659-2552

**KNOTTY PINE
CABINS**
54340 Pine Crest Dr
(92549)
Rates: $42-$120
Tel: (909) 659-2933

MILE HIGH LODGE
54635 N Circle Dr
(92549)
Rates: $70-$110
Tel: (909) 659-2931

IMPERIAL

**BEST WESTERN
IMPERIAL VALLEY
INN**
1093 Airport Blvd
(92251)
Rates: $42-$60
Tel: (619) 355-4500
(800) 528-1234

IMPERIAL BEACH

HAWAIIAN GARDENS SUITE-HOTEL
1031 Imperial Beach Blvd (91932)
Rates: $60-$125
Tel: (619) 429-5303
(800) 334-3071

INDIAN WELLS

ERAWAN GARDEN RESORT
76-477 Hwy 111 (92210)
Rates: $49-$140
Tel: (619) 346-8021
(800) 237-2926

STOUFFER RENAISSANCE ESMERELDA RESORT
44-400 Indian Wells Ln (92210)
Rates: $145-$390
Tel: (619) 773-4444
(800) 552-4386

INDIO

BEST WESTERN DATE TREE HOTEL
81-909 Indio Blvd (92201)
Rates: $56-$150
Tel: (619) 347-3421
(800) 528-1234
(800) 292-5599 (CA)

COMFORT INN
43-505 Monroe St (92201)
Rates: $39-$99
Tel: (619) 347-4044
(800) 221-2222

INDIO HOLIDAY MOTEL
44-301 Sun Gold St (92201)
Rates: $45-$65
Tel: (619) 347-6105

MOTEL 6
82-195 Indio Blvd (92201)
Rates: $28-$32
Tel: (619) 342-6311
(800) 440-6000

PALM SHADOW INN
80-761 Hwy 111 (92201)
Rates: $39-$97
Tel: (619) 347-3476

PENTA INN
84-115 Indio Blvd (92201)
Rates: $29-$42
Tel: (619) 342-4747
(800) 897-9555

RODEWAY INN AT BIG AMERICA
84-096 Indio Springs Dr (92201)
Rates: $39-$76
Tel: (800) 424-4777

ROYAL PLAZA INN
82-347 Hwy 111 (92201)
Rates: $52-$79
Tel: (619) 347-0911
(800) 228-9559

SUPER 8 MOTEL
81-753 Hwy 111 (92201)
Rates: $36-$60
Tel: (619) 342-0264
(800) 800-8000

THUNDERBIRD MOTEL
84-115 Indio Blvd (92201)
Rates: $30-$35
Tel: (619) 342-4747

INDUSTRY

INDUSTRY HILLS SHERATON RESORT & CONF. CENTER
1 Industry Hills Pkwy (91744)
Rates: $115-$150
Tel: (818) 965-0861
(800) 325-3535

INGLEWOOD

BEST WESTERN AIRPORT PLAZA INN
1730 Centinela Ave (90302)
Rates: $56-$95
Tel: (310) 568-0071
(800) 528-1234
(800) 233-8061 (CA)

ECONO LODGE-AIRPORT
439 W Manchester Blvd (90301)
Rates: $45-$60
Tel: (800) 424-4777

ECONO LODGE LAX
4123 W Century Blvd (90304)
Rates: $35-$50
Tel: (310) 672-7285
(800) 424-4777

HAMPTON INN-LAX
10300 La Cienega Blvd (90304)
Rates: $65-$85
Tel: (310) 337-1000
(800) 426-7866

MOTEL 6
5101 W Century Blvd (90304)
Rates: $42-$45
Tel: (310) 419-1234
(800) 466-7356

INVERNESS

MANKA'S INVERNESS LODGE
P. O. Box 1110 (94937)
Rates: $65-$160
Tel: (415) 669-1034

MOTEL INVERNESS
12718 Sir Francis Drake Blvd (94937)
Rates: $59-$79
Tel: (415) 669-1081

ROSEMARY COTTAGE BED & BREAKFAST
75 Balboa Ave (94937)
Rates: $112-$175
Tel: (415) 663-9338
(800) 878-9338

INYOKERN

THREE FLAGS INN
1233 Brown Rd (93527)
Rates: $30-$120
Tel: (619) 377-3300

IRVINE

ATRIUM MARQUIS HOTEL
18700 MacArthur Blvd (92715)
Rates: $75-$190
Tel: (714) 833-2770
(800) 854-3012

HOLIDAY INN SELECT-COUNTY AIRPORT
17941 Von Karman Ave (92714)
Rates: $89-$149
Tel: (714) 863-1999
(800) 465-4329

LA QUINTA INN
14972 Sand Canyon Ave (92718)
Rates: $58-$76
Tel: (714) 551-0909
(800) 531-5900

MARRIOTT HOTEL
18000 Von Karman Ave (92715)
Rates: $79-$160
Tel: (714) 553-0100
(800) 228-9290

MOTEL 6 AIRPORT
1717 E Dyer Rd (92705)
Rates: $42-$48
Tel: (714) 261-1515
(800) 440-6000

RESIDENCE INN BY MARRIOTT
10 Morgan (92718)
Rates: $74-$159
Tel: (714) 380-3000
(800) 331-3131

JACKSON

AMADOR MOTEL
12408 Kennedy Flat Rd (95642)
Rates: $27-$57
Tel: (209) 223-0970

BEST WESTERN AMADOR INN
200 S Hwy 49 (95642)
Rates: $46-$74
Tel: (209) 223-0211
(800) 528-1234

EL CAMPO CASA RESORT MOTEL
12548 Kennedy Flat Rd (95642)
Rates: $33-$70
Tel: (209) 223-0100

JACKSON HOLIDAY LODGE
850 N Hwy 49 (95642)
Rates: $46-$70
Tel: (209) 223-0486

LINDA VISTA MOTEL
10708 N Hwy 49 (95642)
Rates: $28-$47
Tel: (209) 223-1096

JAMESTOWN

HISTORIC NATIONAL HOTEL B & B
77 Main St,
P. O. Box 502 (95327)
Rates: $65-$80
Tel: (209) 984-3446
(800) 446-1333
(800) 894-3446 (CA)

SONORA COUNTRY INN
18755 Charbroullian Ln (95327)
Rates: $49-$69
Tel: (800) 847-2211

JENNER

STILLWATER COVE RANCH
22555 Coast Hwy 1 (95450)
Rates: $50-$80
Tel: (707) 847-3227

TIMBER COVE INN
21780 Coast Hwy 1 (95450)
Rates: $68-$110
Tel: (707) 847-3231

JOSHUA TREE

JOSHUA TREE INN BED & BREAKFAST
61259 29 Palms Hwy (92252)
Rates: $95-$150
Tel: (619) 366-1188

JULIAN

EDEN CREEK ORCHARD BED & BREAKFAST
1052 Julian Orchards Dr (92036)
Rates: $90-$100
Tel: (619) 765-2102

PINE HILLS LODGE
2960 La Posada, Box 2260 (92036)
Rates: $60-$125
Tel: (619) 765-1100

JUNCTION CITY

BIGFOOT CAMPGROUND
Hwy 299 (96048)
Rates: $69
Tel: (916) 623-6088

STEELHEAD COTTAGES
Hwy 299 (96048)
Rates: $43-$76
Tel: (916) 623-6325

JUNE LAKE

GULL LAKE LODGE
P. O. Box 25 (93529)
Rates: $59-$75
Tel: (619) 648-7516

JUNE LAKE MOTEL & CABINS
P. O. Box 98 (93529)
Rates: $50-$80
Tel: (619) 648-7547
(800) 648-6835

REVERSE CREEK LODGE
4479 Hwy 158 (93529)
Rates: $45-$100
Tel: (619) 648-7535
(800) 762-6440

KELSEYVILLE

CREEKSIDE LODGE
79901 Hwy 29 (95451)
Rates: $34-$50
Tel: (707) 279-9258
(800) 279-1380

JIM'S SODA BAY RESORT
6380 Soda Bay Rd (95451)
Rates: $49-$59
Tel: (707) 279-4837

KENWOOD

THE LITTLE HOUSE BED & BREAKFAST
255 Adobe Canyon Rd (95452)
Rates: $130
Tel: (707) 833-2536

KERNVILLE

HI-HO RESORT LODGE
11901 Sierra Way (93238)
Rates: $60-$80
Tel: (619) 376-2671

KERN LODGE MOTEL
67 Valley View (93238)
Rates: $50-$95
Tel: (619) 376-2223

LAZY RIVER LODGE
15729 Sierra Way (93238)
Rates: $36-$65
Tel: (619) 376-2242

RIVER VIEW LODGE
2 Sirretta St (93238)
Rates: $65-$85
Tel: (619) 476-6019

KETTLEMAN CITY

BEST WESTERN OLIVE TREE INN
33410 Powers Dr (93239)
Rates: $56-$65
Tel: (209) 386-9530
(800) 528-1234

KING CITY

BEST WESTERN KING CITY INN
1190 Broadway (93930)
Rates: $42-$55
Tel: (408) 385-6733
(800) 528-1234

COURTESY INN
4 Broadway Cir (93930)
Rates: $42-$94
Tel: (408) 385-4646
(800) 350-5616

MOTEL 6
3 Broadway Cir (93930)
Rates: $27-$33
Tel: (408) 385-5000
(800) 440-6000

PALM MOTEL
640 Broadway (93930)
Rates: $27-$49
Tel: (408) 385-3248

SAGE MOTEL
633 Broadway (93930)
Rates: $29+
Tel: (408) 385-3274

KINGS BEACH

FALCON LODGE
8258 N Lake Blvd (96143)
Rates: $61-$99
Tel: (916) 546-2583

NORTH LAKE LODGE
8716 North Lake Blvd (96143)
Rates: $60
Tel: (800) 824-6348

STEVENSON'S HOLIDAY INN
8742 N Lake Blvd (96143)
Rates: $45-$95
Tel: (916) 546-2269
(800) 634-9141

KINGSBURG

SWEDISH INN
401 Conejo St (93631)
Rates: $42-$52
Tel: (209) 897-1022
(800) 834-1022

KLAMATH

CAMP MARIGOLD MOTEL
16101 Hwy 101
(95548)
Rates: $32-$55
Tel: (707) 482-3585

KNIGHTS FERRY

KNIGHTS FERRY RESORT COTTAGE
17525 Sonora Rd
(95361)
Rates: $95
Tel: (209) 881-3349

LA HABRA

LA HABRA INN
700 N Beach Blvd
(90631)
Rates: $42-$50
Tel: (310) 694-1991

MOTEL 6
870 N Beach Blvd
(90631)
Rates: $30-$34
Tel: (310) 694-2158
(800) 440-6000

LA JOLLA

COLONIAL INN
910 Prospect St
(92037)
Rates: $120-$220
Tel: (619) 454-2181

THE INN AT LA JOLLA
5440 La Jolla Blvd
(92037)
Rates: $53-$83
Tel: (800) 525-6552

LA JOLLA PALMS INN
6705 La Jolla Blvd
(92037)
Rates: $69-$149
Tel: (619) 454-7101

MARRIOTT HOTEL-LA JOLLA
4240 La Jolla Village
Dr (92037)
Rates: $115-$135
Tel: (619) 587-1414
(800) 228-9290

RESIDENCE INN BY MARRIOTT
8901 Gilman Dr
(92037)
Rates: $95-$139
Tel: (619) 587-1770
(800) 331-3131

SCRIPPS INN
555 Coast Blvd S
(92037)
Rates: $90-$165
Tel: (619) 454-3391

U.S. SUITES OF SAN DIEGO
3262 Holiday Ct
#205 (92037)
Rates: $84-$107
Tel: (800) 877-8483

LA MESA

COMFORT INN LA MESA
8000 Parkway Dr
(91942)
Rates: $39-$99
Tel: (619) 698-7747
(800) 221-2222

E-Z 8 MOTEL
7851 Fletcher Pkwy
(92041)
Rates: $35-$50
Tel: (619) 698-9444
(800) 326-6835

LA MESA SPRINGS HOTEL
4210 Spring St
(91941)
Rates: $29-$39
Tel: (619) 589-7288

MOTEL 6
7621 Alvarado Rd
(92041)
Rates: $30-$36
Tel: (619) 464-7151
(800) 440-6000

TRAVELODGE-GROSSMONT
9550 Murray Dr
(91942)
Rates: $30-$50
Tel: (619) 466-0200
(800) 578-7878

LA MIRADA

RESIDENCE INN BY MARRIOTT
14419 Firestone Blvd
(90638)
Rates: $69-$119
Tel: (714) 523-2800
(800) 331-3131

LA PALMA

LA QUINTA INN
3 Centerpointe Dr
(90623)
Rates: $50-$60
Tel: (714) 670-1400
(800) 531-5900

LA QUINTA

LA QUINTA HOTEL GOLF & TENNIS RESORT
49-499 Eisenhower
Dr (92253)
Rates: $220-$2300
Tel: (619) 564-4111
(800) 854-1271

LAGUNA BEACH

CARRIAGE HOUSE BED & BREAKFAST
1322 Catalina St
(92651)
Rates: $95-$150
Tel: (714) 494-8945

CASA LAGUNA INN B & B
2510 S Coast Hwy
(92651)
Rates: $69-$225
Tel: (714) 494-2996
(800) 233-0449 (CA)

COMFORT INN
23061 Ave de la
Carlota (92653)
Rates: $49-$69
Tel: (714) 850-0166
(800) 221-2222

QUALITY INN
1404 N Coast Hwy
(92651)
Rates: $49-$119
Tel: (714) 494-6464
(800) 221-2222

TRADE WINDS MOTOR LODGE
2020 S Coast Hwy
(92651)
Rates: $35-$120
Tel: (714) 494-5450

VACATION VILLAGE
647 S Coast Hwy
(92651)
Rates: $80-$285
Tel: (714) 494-8566
(800) 843-6895

LAGUNA HILLS

HOLIDAY INN LAGUNA HILLS
25205 La Paz Rd
(92653)
Rates: $69-$99
Tel: (714) 586-5000
(800) 465-4329

LAGUNA HILLS LODGE
23932 Paseo De
Valencia (92653)
Rates: $50-$70
Tel: (714) 830-2550
(800) 782-1188

LAKE ALMANOR

ALMANOR LAKESIDE LODGE
3747 Eastshore Dr
(96137)
Rates: $70
Tel: (916) 284-7376
(800) 238-3924

LAKE ALMANOR RESORT
2706 Big Springs Rd
(96137)
Rates: $47-$90
Tel: (916) 596-3337

LASSEN VIEW RESORT
7457 Eastshore Dr
(96137)
Rates: $42-$92
Tel: (916) 596-3437

LITTLE NORWAY RESORT
432 Peninsula Dr
(96137)
Rates: $50-$100
Tel: (916) 596-3225

LAKE ARROWHEAD

ARROWHEAD TREE TOP LODGE
P. O. Box 186 (92352)
Rates: $59-$125
Tel: (909) 337-2311
(800) 358-8733

LAKE ARROWHEAD RESORT
27984 Hwy 189
(92352)
Rates: $99-$329
Tel: (909) 336-1511
(800) 800-6792

PROPHETS' PARADISE BED & BREAKFAST
26845 Modoc Ln
(92352)
Rates: $90-$160
Tel: (909) 336-1969
(800) 987-2231

STORYBOOK INN BED & BREAKFAST
28717 Hwy 19
(92385)
Rates: $60-$145
Tel: (909) 336-1483

LAKE ELSINORE

LAKEVIEW INN
31808 Casino Dr
(92530)
Rates: $38-$48
Tel: (909) 674-6749

LAKE TAHOE AREA

(Also see South Lake Tahoe)

ALDER INN
1072 Ski Run Blvd
(S Lake Tahoe 96150)
Rates: $38-$95
Tel: (916) 544-4485

BEESLEY'S COTTAGES
6674 N Lake Blvd
(Tahoe Vista 96148)
Rates: $70-$140
Tel: (916) 546-2448

BLUE JAY LODGE
4133 Cedar Ave
(S Lake Tahoe 96150)
Rates: $39-$99
Tel: (800) 258-3529

CAPTAIN'S ALPENHAUS
6941 W Lake Blvd
(Tahoma 96142)
Rates: $100-$150
Tel: (916) 525-5000

DAYS INN STATELINE
968 Park Ave
(S Lake Tahoe 96150)
Rates: $60-$92
Tel: (916) 541-4800
(800) 329-7466

EMBASSY SUITES RESORT
4130 Lake Tahoe Blvd
(S Lake Tahoe 96150)
Rates: $139-$500
Tel: (800) 362-2779

HIGH COUNTRY LODGE
1227 Emerald Bay Rd
(S Lake Tahoe 96150)
Rates: $30-$70
Tel: (916) 541-0508

HOLIDAY HOUSE LAKESIDE CHALETS
7276 N Lake Blvd
(Tahoe Vista 96148)
Rates: $75-$115
Tel: (916) 546-2369

LA BAER INN
4133 Lake Tahoe Blvd
(S Lake Tahoe 96150)
Rates: $40-$53
Tel: (916) 544-2139

LAKEPARK LODGE
4081 Cedar Ave
(S Lake Tahoe 96150)
Rates: $40-$65
Tel: (916) 541-5004

LAKESIDE CHALETS
5240 N Lake Blvd
(96140)
Rates: $95-$125
Tel: (916) 546-5857
(800) 294-6378

MATTERHORN MOTEL
2187 Lake Tahoe Blvd
(S Lake Tahoe 96157)
Rates: $38-$58
Tel: (916) 541-0367

THE MONTGOMERY INN
966 Modesto Ave
(S Lake Tahoe 96151)
Rates: $28-$40
Tel: (916) 544-3871

RAVEN WOOD HOTEL
4075 Manzanita Ave
(S Lake Tahoe 96150)
Rates: $79-$99
Tel: (800) 659-4185

RODEWAY INN
4082 Lake Tahoe Blvd
(S Lake Tahoe 96150)
Rates: $39-$79
Tel: (916) 541-7900
(800) 228-2000

SCOTTISH INNS
930 Park Ave
(S Lake Tahoe 96150)
Rates: $33-$58
Tel: (800) 251-1962

SUPER 8 MOTEL
3600 Highway 50
(S Lake Tahoe 96150)
Rates: $53-$78
Tel: (800) 800-8000

TAHOE MARINA INN
930 Bal Bijou Rd
(S Lake Tahoe 96150)
Rates: $56-$140
Tel: (916) 541-2180

TAHOE VALLEY MOTEL
2241 Lake Tahoe Blvd
(S Lake Tahoe 96150)
Rates: $85-$150
Tel: (916) 541-0353

TATAMI COTTAGE RESORT
7449 N Lake Blvd
(Tahoe Vista 96148)
Rates: $69-$129
Tel: (916) 546-3523

TORCHLITE INN
965 Park Ave
(S Lake Tahoe 96150)
Rates: $38-$78
Tel: (916) 541-2363

TRADE WINDS MOTEL
944 Friday Ave
(S Lake Tahoe 96150)
Rates: $35-$125
Tel: (916) 544-6459

WOODVISTA LODGE
7699 N Lake Blvd
(Tahoe Vista 96148)
Rates: $35-$75
Tel: (916) 546-3839

LAKEHEAD

ANTLERS RESORT & MARINA
P. O. Box 140 (96051)
Rates: $90-$170
Tel: (800) 238-3924

O'BANION'S SUGARLOAF COTTAGES RESORT
19667 Lakeshore Dr
(96051)
Rates: $59-$122
Tel: (916) 238-2448

TSASDI RESORT
19990 Lakeshore Dr
(96051)
Rates: $47-$175
Tel: (916) 238-2575
(800) 995-0291

LAKEPORT

CHALET MOTEL
2802 Lakeshore Blvd
(95453)
Rates: $35-$45
Tel: (707) 263-5040

COVE RESORT
2812 Lakeshore Blvd
(95453)
Rates: $50-$85
Tel: (707) 263-6833

RAINBOW LODGE MOTEL
2569 Lakeshore Blvd
(95453)
Rates: $30-$36
Tel: (707) 263-4309

LAKESHORE

LAKEVIEW COTTAGES
58374 Huntington Lodge Rd (93634)
Rates: $45-$80
Tel: (310) 697-6556
(209) 893-2330

LAKEWOOD

CRAZY 8 MOTEL
11535 E Carson St
(90715)
Rates: $34-$42
Tel: (310) 860-0546

LANCASTER

**BEST WESTERN
ANTELOPE VALLEY
INN**
44055 N
Sierra Hwy (93534)
Rates: $59-$81
Tel: (805) 948-4651
(800) 528-1234

MOTEL 6
43540 17th St W
(93534)
Rates: $29-$33
Tel: (805) 948-0435
(800) 440-6000

LASSEN VOLCANIC NATIONAL PARK

**DRAKESBAD GUEST
RANCH RESORT
COMPLEX**
CR Chester-Warner
Valley (96020)
Rates: $110-$190
Tel: (916) 529-1512

LAYTONVILLE

**GENTLE VALLEY
RANCH COTTAGES**
P. O. Box 1535
(95454)
Rates: $65-$150
Tel: (707) 984-8456

THE RANCH MOTEL
P. O. Box 1535
(95454)
Rates: $26-$45
Tel: (707) 984-8456

LEBEC

FLYING J INN
42810 Frazier Mtn
Park Rd (93243)
Rates: $50-$65
Tel: (805) 248-2700
(800) 766-9009

LEE VINING

MURPHEY'S MOTEL
P. O. Box 57 (93541)
Rates: $38-$73
Tel: (619) 647-6316
(800) 334-6316

LEGGETT

**REDWOODS
RIVER RETREAT**
75000 Hwy 101
(95585)
Rates: $20-$55
Tel: (707) 925-6249

LEMON GROVE

E-Z 8 MOTEL
7458 Broadway
(92045)
Rates: $35-$50
Tel: (619) 462-7022
(800) 326-6835

LEMOORE

**BEST WESTERN
VINEYARD INN**
877 East D St (93245)
Rates: $44-$46
Tel: (209) 924-1950
(800) 528-1234

LEWISTON

**LAKEVIEW TERRACE
RESORT**
Star Rt, Box 250
(96052)
Rates: $36-$82
Tel: (916) 778-3803

**LEWISTON VALLEY
MOTEL**
Trinity Dam Blvd
(96052)
Rates: $35-$43
Tel: (916) 778-3942

LINDSAY

OLIVE TREE INN
390 N Highway 65
(93247)
Rates: $45-$56
Tel: (209) 562-5188
(800) 366-4469

LITTLERIVER

**S. S. SEAFOAM
LODGE**
6751 N Hwy 1
(95456)
Rates: $85-$175
Tel: (707) 937-1827
(707) 937-1022

**VICTORIAN FARM
HOUSE B & B**
7001 N Hwy 1
(95456)
Rates: $85-$130
Tel: (707) 937-0697
(800) 264-4723

LIVERMORE

HOLIDAY INN
720 Las Flores Rd
(94550)
Rates: $53-$65
Tel: (510) 443-4950
(800) 465-4329

MOTEL 6
4673 Lassen Rd
(94550)
Rates: $34-$40
Tel: (510) 443-5300
(800) 440-6000

**RESIDENCE INN
BY MARRIOTT**
1000 Airway Blvd
(94550)
Rates: $69-$130
Tel: (510) 373-1800
(800) 331-3131

**SPRINGTOWN
MOTEL**
933 Bluebell Dr
(94550)
Rates: $37+
Tel: (510) 449-2211

LODI

**BEST WESTERN
ROYAL HOST INN**
710 S Cherokee Ln
(95240)
Rates: $45-$75
Tel: (209) 369-8484
(800) 528-1234

COMFORT INN
118 N Cherokee Ln
(95240)
Rates: $69-$89
Tel: (209) 367-4848
(800) 221-2222

LODI MOTOR INN
1140 S Cherokee Ln
(95240)
Rates: $65-$72
Tel: (209) 334-6322

LOMITA

**ELDORADO COAST
HOTEL**
2037 PCH (90717)
Rates: $44-$58
Tel: (310) 534-0700
(800) 536-7236

LOMPOC

**BEST WESTERN
VANDENBERG INN**
940 E Ocean Ave
(93436)
Rates: $45-$75
Tel: (805) 735-7731
(800) 528-1234

INN OF LOMPOC
1122 North H St
(93436)
Rates: $51-$57
Tel: (800) 548-8231

MOTEL 6
1521 North H St
(93436)
Rates: $25-$31
Tel: (805) 735-7631
(800) 440-6000

**QUALITY INN &
EXECUTIVE SUITES**
1621 North H St
(93436)
Rates: $44-$79
Tel: (800) 221-2222

REDWOOD INN
1200 North H St
(93436)
Rates: $40-$45
Tel: (805) 735-3737

**TALLY HO
MOTOR INN**
1020 E Ocean Ave
(93436)
Rates: $29-$40
Tel: (805) 735-6444
(800) 332-6444

LONE PINE

ALABAMA HILLS INN
1920 S Main St (93545)
Rates: $38-$60
Tel: (619) 876-8700
(800) 800-5026

BEST WESTERN FRONTIER MOTEL
1008 S Main St (93545)
Rates: $39-$80
Tel: (619) 876-5571
(800) 528-1234

DOW VILLA MOTEL
310 S Main St,
P. O. Box 205 (93545)
Rates: $56-$70
Tel: (619) 876-5521
(800) 824-9317

NATIONAL 9 TRAILS MOTEL
633 S Main St (93545)
Rates: $34-$54
Tel: (619) 876-5555

LONG BEACH

BEST WESTERN LONG BEACH
1725 Long Beach Blvd (90813)
Rates: $58-$88
Tel: (310) 599-5555
(800) 528-1234

CLARION HOTEL EDGEWATER
6400 E Pacific Coast Highway (90803)
Rates: $63
Tel: (310) 434-8451

COMFORT INN
3201 E Pacific Coast Highway (90804)
Rates: $50-$54
Tel: (800) 221-2222

DAYS INN LONG BEACH
1500 E Pacific Coast Highway (90806)
Rates: $45-$85
Tel: (310) 591-0088
(800) 329-7466

HILTON LONG BEACH AT WORLD TRADE CENTER
Two World Trade Center (90831)
Rates: $110-$170
Tel: (310) 983-3400
(800) 445-8667

HOLIDAY INN-CONVENTION & WORLD TRADE CENTER
500 E First St (90802)
Rates: $79-$104
Tel: (800) 465-4329

HOLIDAY INN LONG BEACH AIRPORT
2640 Lakewood Blvd (90815)
Rates: $59-$125
Tel: (310) 597-4400
(800) 465-4329

HOWARD JOHNSON
1133 Atlantic Ave (90813)
Rates: $71-$87
Tel: (800) 654-2000

MARRIOTT LONG BEACH
4700 Airport Plaza Dr (90815)
Rates: $69-$119
Tel: (510) 425-5210
(800) 228-9290
(800) 321-5642 (CA)

MOTEL 6
5665 E 7th St (90804)
Rates: $38-$42
Tel: (310) 597-1311
(800) 440-6000

RAMADA INN
5325 E Pacific Coast Highway (90804)
Rates: $79-$139
Tel: (310) 597-1341
(800) 272-6232
(800) 990-9991 (CA)

RESIDENCE INN BY MARRIOTT
4111 E Willow St (90815)
Rates: $79-$149
Tel: (800) 331-3131

SHERATON LONG BEACH
333 E Ocean Blvd (90802)
Rates: $139-$165
Tel: (510) 436-3000
(800) 325-3535

TRAVELODGE HOTEL RESORT & MARINA
700 Queensway Dr (90802)
Rates: $59-$150
Tel: (510) 435-7676
(800) 578-7878

TRAVELODGE LONG BEACH CONVENTION CENTER
80 Atlantic Ave (90802)
Rates: $50-$65
Tel: (510) 435-2471
(800) 578-7878

VAGABOND INN
185 Atlantic Ave (90802)
Rates: $45-$55
Tel: (510) 435-7621
(800) 522-1555

LOS ALAMOS

SKYVIEW MOTEL
9150 Highway 101 (93440)
Rates: $75-$125
Tel: (805) 344-3770

LOS ANGELES
(Also see Hollywood and West Hollywood)

BEST WESTERN DRAGON GATE INN
818 N Hill St (90012)
Rates: $59-$70
Tel: (213) 617-3077
(800) 528-1234

BEST WESTERN HOLLYWOOD HILLS
6141 Franklin Ave (90028)
Rates: $50-$85
Tel: (213) 464-5181
(800) 287-1700

BEVERLY HILLS PLAZA HOTEL
10300 Wilshire Blvd (90024)
Rates: $105-$310
Tel: (310) 275-5575

BEVERLY LAUREL MOTOR HOTEL
8018 Beverly Blvd (90048)
Rates: $51-$57
Tel: (213) 651-2441
(800) 962-3824

BRENTWOOD MOTOR HOTEL
12200 Sunset Blvd (90049)
Rates: $55-$85
Tel: (310) 476-9981

BRENTWOOD SUITES HOTEL
199 N Church Ln (90049)
Rates: $85-$105
Tel: (310) 476-6255

CENTURY PLAZA HOTEL & TOWER
2025 Ave of the Stars (90067)
Rates: $215-$290
Tel: (310) 277-2000
(800) 228-3000

CENTURY WILSHIRE HOTEL
10776 Wilshire Blvd (90029)
Rates: $65-$85
Tel: (800) 421-7223

CHATEAU MARMONT HOTEL
8221 Sunset Blvd (90046)
Rates: $160-$550
Tel: (213) 656-1010
(800) 242-8328

CONTINENTAL PLAZA LOS ANGELES AIRPORT
9750 Airport Blvd (90045)
Rates: $85-$130
Tel: (310) 645-4600
(800) 529-4683

DOUBLETREE LOS ANGELES AIRPORT
5400 W Century Blvd (90045)
Rates: $89-$114
Tel: (800) 528-0444

ECONO LODGE
3400 W 3rd St (90020)
Rates: $40-$54
Tel: (213) 385-0061
(800) 553-2666

EMBASSY SUITES HOTEL-LAX/CENTURY
9801 Airport Blvd (90045)
Rates: $99
Tel: (800) 362-2779

HALLMARK HOTEL
7023 Sunset Blvd (90028)
Rates: $56-$75
Tel: (213) 464-8344

HOLIDAY INN BRENTWOOD/ BEL AIR
170 N Church Ln (90049)
Rates: $98-$210
Tel: (310) 476-6411
(800) 465-4329

HOLIDAY INN CITY CENTER
1020 S Figueroa St (90015)
Rates: $89-$129
Tel: (213) 748-1291
(800) 465-4329

HOLIDAY INN CROWNE PLAZA-LAX
5985 W Century Blvd (90045)
Rates: $124-$154
Tel: (800) 465-4329

HOLIDAY INN-DOWNTOWN
750 Garland Ave (90017)
Rates: $69-$79
Tel: (800) 465-4329

HOLIDAY INN-INTERNATIONAL AIRPORT
9901 S La Cienega Blvd (90045)
Rates: $89-$109
Tel: (310) 649-5151
(800) 465-4329

HOLIDAY SELECT INN
1150 S Beverly Dr (90035)
Rates: $85+
Tel: (310) 553-6561

HOLLYWOOD CELEBRITY HOTEL
1775 Orchid Ave (90028)
Rates: $65-$83
Tel: (800) 222-7090

HOTEL BEL-AIR
701 Stone Canyon Rd (90077)
Rates: $285-$435
Tel: (800) 648-4097

HOTEL INTER-CONTINENTAL AT CALIFORNIA PLAZA
251 S Olive St (90012)
Rates: $175-$265
Tel: (213) 617-3300
(800) 442-5251

HOWARD JOHNSON
8620 Airport Blvd (90045)
Rates: $55-$99
Tel: (310) 645-7700
(800) 446-4656

KAWADA HOTEL
200 S Hill St (90012)
Rates: $75-$109
Tel: (800) 752-9232

MARRIOTT-LOS ANGELES AIRPORT
5855 W Century Blvd (90045)
Rates: $105-$154
Tel: (800) 228-9290

OMNI HOTEL & CENTRE
930 Wilshire Blvd (90017)
Rates: $129-$169
Tel: (800) 445-8667

QUALITY HOTEL-AIRPORT
5249 W Century Blvd (90045)
Rates: $55-$125
Tel: (800) 266-2200

RADISSON WILSHIRE PLAZA HOTEL
3515 Wilshire Blvd (90010)
Rates: $129-$139
Tel: (213) 381-7411
(800) 333-3333

SKYWAYS KNIGHTS INN AIRPORT HOTEL
9250 Airport Blvd (90045)
Rates: $40-$55
Tel: (800) 336-0025

TRAVELODGE
1903 W Olympic Blvd (9006)
Rates: $59-$99
Tel: (213) 385-7141
(800) 578-7878

TRAVELODGE
5547 W Century Blvd (90045)
Rates: $54-$74
Tel: (310) 649-4000
(800) 578-7878

VAGABOND INN FIGUEROA
3101 S Figueroa St (90007)
Rates: $59-$76
Tel: (213) 746-1531
(800) 522-1555

VAGABOND INN
1904 W Olympic Blvd (90006)
Rates: $45-$55
Tel: (213) 380-9393
(800) 522-1555

THE WESTIN BONAVENTURE HOTEL & SUITES
404 S Figueroa St (90071)
Rates: $159-$199
Tel: (213) 624-1000
(800) 228-3000

WILSHIRE MOTEL
12023 Wilshire Blvd (90025)
Rates: $50-$60
Tel: (310) 478-3545

WYNDHAM CHECKERS HOTEL-LOS ANGELES
535 S Grand Ave (90071)
Rates: $95-$205
Tel: (213) 624-0000
(800) 822-4200

LOS BANOS

BEST WESTERN JOHN JAY INN
301 W Pacheco Blvd (93635)
Rates: $45-$55
Tel: (209) 827-0954
(800) 528-1234

REGENCY INN
349 W Pacheco Blvd (93635)
Rates: $30-$42
Tel: (209) 826-3871

LOS GATOS

LOS GATOS MOTOR INN
55 Saratoga Ave (95032)
Rates: $58-$70
Tel: (408) 356-9191

TOLL HOUSE MOTOR HOTEL
140 S Santa Cruz Ave (95030)
Rates: $79-$158
Tel: (408) 395-7070
(800) 238-6111

LOS OSOS

BACK BAY INN
1391 Second St (93402)
Rates: $29-$110
Tel: (805) 528-1233

LOST HILLS

ECONOMY INNS OF AMERICA
14684 Aloma St (93249)
Rates: $23-$36
Tel: (800) 826-0778

MOTEL 6
14685 Warren St (93249)
Rates: $24-$30
Tel: (805) 797-2346
(800) 440-6000

LOTUS

GOLDEN LOTUS B & B INN
1006 Lotus Rd (95651)
Rates: $80-$95
Tel: (916) 621-4562

LUCERNE

BEACHCOMBER RESORT
6345 E Hwy 20,
Box 358 (95458)
Rates: $40-$85
Tel: (707) 274-6639

LAKE SANDS RESORT
6335 E Hwy 20,
Box 48 (95458)
Rates: $50
Tel: (707) 274-7732

STARLITE MOTEL
5960 E Hwy 20,
Box 467 (95458)
Rates: $40-$85
Tel: (707) 274-5515

MADERA

BEST WESTERN MADERA VALLEY INN
317 North G St
(93637)
Rates: $56-$64
Tel: (209) 673-5164
(800) 528-1234

ECONOMY INNS OF AMERICA
1855 W Cleveland
Ave (93637)
Rates: $26-$42
Tel: (800) 826-0778

GATEWAY INN
25327 Avenue 16
(93637)
Rates: $46-$60
Tel: (209) 674-8817

MALIBU

MALIBU COUNTRY INN
6506 Westward
Beach Road (90265)
Rates: $95-$155
Tel: (310) 457-9622
(800) 386-6787

MALIBU RIVIERA MOTEL
28920 Pacific Coast
Highway (90265)
Rates: $50-$70
Tel: (310) 457-9503

MAMMOTH LAKES

AUSTRIA HOF LODGE
924 Canyon Blvd,
P. O. Box 607 (93546)
Rates: $50-$115
Tel: (619) 934-2764
(800) 922-2966

CONVICT LAKE RESORT
Rt 1, Box 204 (93546)
Rates: $65-$350
Tel: (619) 934-3800
(800) 992-2260

CRYSTAL CRAG LODGE
307 Crystal Crag Dr
(93546)
Rates: $55-$195
Tel: (619) 934-2436

ECONO LODGE WILDWOOD INN
3626 Main St (93546)
Rates: $69-$99
Tel: (619) 934-6855
(800) 424-4777

ENGLEHOF LODGE
6156 Minaret Rd
(93546)
Rates: $35-$80
Tel: (619) 934-2416

EXECUTIVE INN
54 Sierra Blvd
(93546)
Rates: $39-$89
Tel: (619) 934-8892

INTERNATIONAL INN
3554 Main St (93546)
Rates: $45-$65
Tel: (619) 934-2542
(800) 457-1997

MOTEL 6
3372 Main St (93546)
Rates: $39-$48
Tel: (619) 934-6660
(800) 440-6000

NORTH VILLAGE INN
103 Lake Mary Rd
(93546)
Rates: $70-$115
Tel: (619) 934-2925
(800) 257-3781

ROYAL PINES RESORT
3814 Viewpoint Rd,
P. O. Box 348 (93546)
Rates: $49-$59
Tel: (619) 934-2306

SHILO INNS
2963 Main St (93546)
Rates: $69-$115
Tel: (619) 934-4500
(800) 222-2244

THRIFTLODGE
6209 Minaret Rd
(93546)
Rates: $49-$95
Tel: (619) 934-8576
(800) 525-9055
(800) 578-7878

ZWART HOUSE THE FAMILY LODGE
76 Lupin St, P. O.
Box 174 (93546)
Rates: $50-$80
Tel: (619) 934-2217

MANHATTAN BEACH

RADISSON PLAZA HOTEL-LAX SOUTH
1400 Parkview Ave
(90266)
Rates: $129-$159
Tel: (800) 333-3333

RESIDENCE INN BY MARRIOTT
1700 N Sepulveda
Blvd (90266)
Rates: $89-$189
Tel: (310) 546-7627
(800) 331-3131

MANTECA

BEST WESTERN INN OF MANTECA
1415 E Yosemite Ave
(95336)
Rates: $59-$99
Tel: (209) 825-1415
(800) 528-1234

MARINA

MOTEL 6
100 Reservation Rd
(93933)
Rates: $35-$46
Tel: (408) 384-1000
(800) 440-6000

TRAVELODGE
3290 Dunes Dr
(93933)
Rates: $59-$114
Tel: (408) 883-0300

MARINA DEL REY

FOGHORN HARBOR INN
4140 Via Marina
(90292)
Rates: $60-$109
Tel: (310) 823-4626

MARINA DEL REY HOTEL
13534 Bali Way
(90292)
Rates: $79-$325
Tel: (310) 301-1000
(800) 882-4000
(800) 862-7462 (CA)

MARRIOTT MARINA DEL REY
13480 Maxella Ave
(90291)
Rates: $139-$159
Tel: (800) 228-9290

MARIPOSA

BEST WESTERN YOSEMITE WAY STATION
499 Hwy 140 (95338)
Rates: $59-$87
Tel: (209) 966-7545
(800) 528-1234

THE CLUBB'S
5060 Charles St
(95338)
Rates: $45-$75
Tel: (209) 966-5085

THE GUEST HOUSE INN
4962 Triangle Rd
(95338)
Rates: $68-$98
Tel: (209) 742-6869

IMA MARIPOSA LODGE
5052 Hwy 140,
Box 733 (95338)
Rates: $35-$82
Tel: (209) 966-3607
(800) 341-8000

MINERS INN
P. O. Box 1989
(95338)
Rates: $70
Tel: (209) 742-7777

MOTHERLODE LODGE
5051 Hwy 140,
P. O. Box 986 (95338)
Rates: $29-$65
Tel: (209) 966-2521
(800) 398-9770

MOUNTAIN OAKS GUEST HOUSE
5070 Allred Rd
(95338)
Rates: $45-$95
Tel: (209) 966-6033

THE PELENNOR BED & BREAKFAST
3871 Hwy 49 S
(95338)
Rates: $35-$45
Tel: (209) 966-2832

TWELVE OAKS CARRIAGE HOUSE
4877 Wildwood Dr
(95338)
Rates: $65+
Tel: (209) 966-3231

MARKLEEVILLE

J. MARKLEE TOLL STATION HOTEL
14856 Highway 89,
P. O. Box 395 (96120)
Rates: $40
Tel: (916) 694-2507

MARYSVILLE

HOLIDAY LODGE
530 10th St (95901)
Rates: $29-$38
Tel: (916) 742-7147

MARYSVILLE MOTOR LODGE
904 E St (95901)
Rates: $32-$40
Tel: (916) 743-1531

McCLOUD

STONEY BROOK INN B & B
309 W Colombero
Dr (96057)
Rates: $20-$70
Tel: (916) 964-2300
(800) 369-6118

McKINLEYVILLE

SEA VIEW MOTEL
1186 Central Ave
(95521)
Rates: $35-$125
Tel: (707) 839-1321

MENDOCINO

BLACKBERRY INN
44951 Larkin Road
(95460)
Rates: $90-$160
Tel: (707) 937-5281

BLAIR HOUSE B & B
45110 Little Lake St
(95460)
Rates: $75-$130
Tel: (707) 937-1800

L.L. MENDOCINO COTTAGES & B&B
10940 Lansing St
(95460)
Rates: $131-$191
Tel: (800) 944-3278

MENDOCINO VIL-LAGE COTTAGES
45320 Little Lake St
(95460)
Rates: $50-$100
Tel: (707) 937-0866

1021 MAIN STREET INN
44781 Main St
(95460)
Rates: $130-$175
Tel: (707) 937-5150

SALLIE & EILEEN'S PLACE FOR WOMEN ONLY
P.O. Box 409 (95460)
Rates: $65-$80
Tel: (619) 937-2028

SEARS HOUSE
44840 Main St (95460)
Rates: $55-$110
Tel: (707) 937-4076

STANFORD INN BY THE SEA B & B
P. O. Box 487,
Comptche-Ukiah Rd
& Highway 1 (95460)
Rates: $195-$275
Tel: (707) 937-5026
(800) 331-8884

MERCED

BEST WESTERN PINE CONE INN
1213 V St (95340)
Rates: $49-$69
Tel: (209) 723-3711
(800) 528-1234

DAYS INN-MERCED
1199 Motel Dr (95340)
Rates: $38-$60
Tel: (209) 722-2726
(800) 329-7466

MOTEL 6-CENTRAL
1215 R St (95340)
Rates: $26-$32
Tel: (209) 722-2737
(800) 440-6000

MOTEL 6-NORTH
1410 V St (95340)
Rates: $28-$34
Tel: (209) 384-2181
(800) 440-6000

MOTEL 6-SOUTH
1983 E Childs Ave
(95340)
Rates: $26-$32
Tel: (209) 384-3702
(800) 440-6000

SANDPIPER LODGE
1001 Motel Dr
(95340)
Rates: $36-$58
Tel: (209) 723-1034

MI-WUK VILLAGE

MI-WUK MOTOR LODGE
24680 Highway 108
(95346)
Rates: $45-$95
Tel: (209) 586-3031
(800) 341-8000

MIDPINES

HOMESTEAD GUEST RANCH
P. O. Box 113 (95345)
Rates: $95-$130
Tel: (209) 966-2820

LION'S DEN RETREAT
5125 Chamberlain
Rd (95345)
Rates: $75-$110
Tel: (209) 966-5254

MUIR LODGE HOTEL
6833 Highway 140
(95345)
Rates: $28-$78
Tel: (209) 966-2468

MILL VALLEY

HOLIDAY INN EXPRESS
160 Shoreline Hwy
(94941)
Rates: $77-$95
Tel: (415) 332-5700
(800) 465-4329

MILLBRAE

BEST WESTERN EL RANCHO INN
1100 El Camino Real
(94030)
Rates: $79-$135
Tel: (415) 588-8500
(800) 826-5500

CLARION HOTEL-AIRPORT
401 E Millbrae Ave
(94030)
Rates: $99-$119
Tel: (415) 692-6363
(800) 223-7111

COMFORT INN AIRPORT WEST
1390 El Camino Real
(94030)
Rates: $99-$109
Tel: (415) 952-3200
(800) 221-2222

THE WESTIN SAN FRANCISCO AIRPORT
1 Old Bayshore Hwy
(94030)
Rates: $205-$245
Tel: (415) 692-3500
(800) 228-3000

MILPITAS

BEST WESTERN BROOKSIDE INN
400 Valley Way (95035)
Rates: $60-$80
Tel: (408) 263-5566
(800) 528-1234

BEVERLY HERITAGE HOTEL
1820 Barber Ln (95033)
Rates: $98
Tel: (408) 943-9080

ECONOMY INNS OF AMERICA
270 S Abbott Ave (95035)
Rates: $39-$49
Tel: (408) 946-8889
(800) 826-0778

HOLIDAY INN SAN JOSE NORTH
777 Bellew Dr (95035)
Rates: $95-$145
Tel: (408) 321-9500
(800) 465-4329

MIRANDA

MIRANDA GARDENS RESORT
6766 Ave of the Giants (95553)
Rates: $45-$155
Tel: (707) 943-3011

WHISPERING PINES
Avenue of the Giants (95553)
Rates: $40-$65
Tel: (707) 943-3182

MISSION HILLS

BEST WESTERN MISSION HILLS INN
10621 Sepulveda Blvd (91345)
Rates: $61-$78
Tel: (818) 891-1771
(800) 528-1234

MISSION VIEJO

FAIRFIELD INN BY MARRIOTT
26328 Oso Pkwy (92691)
Rates: $57-$64
Tel: (714) 582-7100
(800) 228-2800

MODESTO

BEST WESTERN MALLARDS INN
1720 Sisk Rd (95350)
Rates: $65-$95
Tel: (209) 577-3825
(800) 528-1234

BEST WESTERN TOWN HOUSE LODGE
909 16th St (95354)
Rates: $44-$58
Tel: (209) 524-7621
(800) 528-1234

CHALET MOTEL
115 Downey Ave (95354)
Rates: $36-$48
Tel: (209) 529-4370

HOLIDAY INN HOLIDOME
1612 Sisk Rd (95350)
Rates: $65-$150
Tel: (800) 334-2030

MOTEL 6-NORTH
1920 W Orangeburg Ave (95350)
Rates: $30-$34
Tel: (209) 522-7271
(800) 440-6000

MOTEL 6-SOUTH
722 Kansas Ave (95351)
Rates: $29-$33
Tel: (209) 524-3000
(800) 440-6000

RED LION HOTEL
1150 9th St (95354)
Rates: $98-$141
Tel: (209) 526-6000
(800) 547-8010

TROPICS MOTOR HOTEL
936 McHenry Ave (95350)
Rates: $32-$48
Tel: (209) 523-7701

VAGABOND INN
1525 McHenry Ave (95350)
Rates: $38-$57
Tel: (209) 521-6340
(800) 522-1555

MOJAVE

MOTEL 6
16958 Hwy 58 (93501)
Rates: $26-$30
Tel: (805) 824-4571
(800) 440-6000

SCOTTISH INNS
16352 Sierra Highway (93501)
Rates: $35-$55
Tel: (805) 824-9317
(800) 251-1962

VAGABOND INN
2145 Highway 58 (93501)
Rates: $29-$48
Tel: (805) 824-2463
(800) 522-1555

WESTERN INN
16200 Sierra Highway (93501)
Rates: $33-$45
Tel: (805) 824-3601

MONROVIA

COMFORT INN
1125 E Huntington Dr (91016)
Rates: $30-$40
Tel: (800) 221-2222

HOLIDAY INN
924 W Huntington Dr (91016)
Rates: $60-$125
Tel: (818) 357-1900
(800) 465-4329

OAK TREE INN
788 W Huntington Dr (91016)
Rates: $54-$105
Tel: (818) 358-8981

WYNDHAM GARDEN HOTEL
700 W Huntington Dr (91016)
Rates: $59-$128
Tel: (818) 357-5211
(800) 996-3426

MONTARA

FARALLONE INN BED & BREAKFAST
1410 Main St (94037)
Rates: $75-$150
Tel: (415) 728-8200
(800) 350-9777

MONTE RIO

ANGELO'S RESORT
20285 River Blvd (95462)
Rates: $50-$150
Tel: (707) 865-9080

HIGHLAND DELL INN B & B
21050 River Blvd, P.O. Box 370 (95462)
Rates: $85-$250
Tel: (707) 865-1759
(800) 767-1759

MONTEBELLO

HOWARD JOHNSON
7709 Telegraph Rd (90640)
Rates $55-$79
Tel: (213) 721-4410
(800) 446-4656

MONTECITO

SAN YSIDRO RANCH
900 San Ysidro Ln (93108)
Rates: $195-$995
Tel: (805) 969-5046

MONTEREY/ MONTEREY PENINSULA

ARBOR INN
1058 Munras Ave (94930)
Rates: $79-$119
Tel: (408) 372-3381

BAY PARK HOTEL
1425 Munras Ave (93940)
Rates: $69-$129
Tel: (408) 649-1020
(800) 338-3564

BAYSIDE INN
2055 Fremont St (93940)
Rates: $35+
Tel: (408) 372-8071

BEST WESTERN MONTEREY BEACH HOTEL
2600 Sand Dunes Dr (93940)
Rates: $69-$179
Tel: (408) 394-3321
(800) 528-1234

BEST WESTERN VICTORIAN INN
487 Foam St (93940)
Rates: $89-$369
Tel: (408) 373-8000
(800) 528-1234
(800) 232-4141 (CA)

CANNERY ROW INN
200 Foam St (93940)
Rates: $65-$150
Tel: (408) 649-8580

COLTON INN
707 Pacific St (93940)
Rates: $69-$110
Tel: (408) 649-6500
(800) 848-7007

CYPRESS GARDENS INN
1150 Munras Ave (93940)
Rates: $63-$225
Tel: (408) 373-2761
(800) 433-4732

CYPRESS TREE INN
2227 N Fremont St (93940)
Rates: $52-$185
Tel: (408) 372-7586

DRIFTWOOD MOTEL
2362 N Fremont St (93940)
Rates: $60-$129
Tel: (408) 372-5059

EL ADOBE INN
936 Munras Ave (93940)
Rates: $59-$99
Tel: (408) 372-5409
(800) 433-4732

HOLIDAY INN RESORT
1000 Aquajito Rd (93940)
Rates: $89-$220
Tel: (408) 373-6141
(800) 234-5697

MONTEREY BAY LODGE
55 Camino Aquajito (93940)
Rates: $49-$139
Tel: (408) 372-8057
(800) 558-1900

MONTEREY FIRESIDE LODGE
1131 10th St (93940)
Rates: $55-$99
Tel: (408) 373-4172

MONTEREY MARRIOTT
350 Calle Principal (93940)
Rates: $150-$170
Tel: (408) 649-4232
(800) 228-9290

MOTEL 6
2124 N Fremont St (93940)
Rates: $42-$50
Tel: (408) 646-8585
(800) 440-6000

MUNRAS LODGE
1010 Munras Ave (93940)
Rates: $79-$149
Tel: (408) 646-9696

SCOTTISH FAIRWAY MOTEL
2075 N Fremont St (93940)
Rates: $35-$84
Tel: (408) 373-5551
(800) 373-5571

WESTERNER MOTEL
2041 Fremont St (93940)
Rates: $35+
Tel: (408) 373-2911

MONTEREY PARK

DAYS INN & SUITES HOTEL
434 Potrero Grande Dr (91755)
Rates: $65
Tel: (213) 728-8444
(800) 329-7466

MORENO VALLEY

MOTEL 6-NORTH
24630 Sunnymead Blvd (92553)
Rates: $30-$34
Tel: (909) 243-0075
(800) 440-6000

MOTEL 6-SOUTH
23581 Alessandro Blvd (92553)
Rates: $27-$31
Tel: (909) 656-4451
(800) 440-6000

MORGAN HILL

BEST WESTERN COUNTRY INN
16525 Condit Rd (95037)
Rates: $60-$85
Tel: (408) 779-0447
(800) 528-1234

BUDGET INN
19240 Monterey Hwy (95037)
Rates: $30-$55
Tel: (408) 778-3341

EXECUTIVE INN
16505 Condit Rd (95037)
Rates: $70
Tel: (408) 778-0404

INN AT MORGAN HILL
16115 Condit Rd (95037)
Rates: $83-$108
Tel: (408) 779-7666

MORGAN HILL INN
16250 Monterey Rd (95037)
Rates: $36-$65
Tel: (408) 779-1900

MORRO BAY

ADVENTURE INN ON THE SEA
1148 Front St (93442)
Rates: $40-$125
Tel: (805) 772-5607

BEST VALUE INN
220 Beach St (93442)
Rates: $28-$98
Tel: (805) 772-3333
(800) 549-2022 (CA)

BEST WESTERN-EL RANCHO
2460 Main St (93442)
Rates: $49-$109
Tel: (805) 772-2212
(800) 528-1234

BEST WESTERN TRADEWINDS MOTEL
225 Beach St (93442)
Rates: $38-$110
Tel: (805) 772-7376
(800) 528-1234

BREAKERS MOTEL
780 Market St (93442)
Rates: $60-$120
Tel: (805) 772-7317
(800) 932-8899

COFFEE BREAK BED & BREAKFAST
213 Dunes St (93442)
Rates: $75-$125
Tel: (805) 772-4378

ECONO LODGE
1100 Main St (93442)
Rates: $38-$105
Tel: (800) 424-4777

GOLD COAST MOTEL
670 Main St (93442)
Rates: $30-$85
Tel: (805) 772-7740

GOLDEN PELICAN INN
3270 N Main St (93442)
Rates: $40-$125
Tel: (805) 772-7135

MORRO HILLTOP HOUSE
1200 Morro Ave (93442)
Rates: $40-$75
Tel: (805) 772-1890

MOTEL 6
298 Atascadero Rd (93442)
Rates: $35-$42
Tel: (805) 772-5641
(800) 440-6000

SUNDOWN MOTEL
640 Main St (93442)
Rates: $30-$75
Tel: (805) 772-7381
(800) 696-6928

SUNSET TRAVELODGE
1080 Market Ave (93442)
Rates: $39-$125
Tel: (805) 772-1259
(800) 578-7878

MOUNT SHASTA

ALPINE LODGE MOTEL
908 S Mount Shasta Blvd (96067)
Rates: $31-$89
Tel: (916) 926-3145
(800) 500-3145

BEST WESTERN TREE HOUSE MOTOR INN
P.O. Box 236, I-5 & Lake St (96067)
Rates: $70-$99
Tel: (916) 926-3101
(800) 545-7164
(800) 528-1234

CEDAR POND CHALET
1701 N Old Stage Rd (96067)
Rates: $95+
Tel: (916) 926-3200

EVERGREEN LODGE
1312 S Mount Shasta Blvd (96067)
Rates: $28-$60
Tel: (916) 926-2143

MOUNTAIN AIR LODGE
1121 S Mount Shasta Blvd (96067)
Rates: $36-$125
Tel: (916) 926-3411

PINE NEEDLES MOTEL
1340 S Mount Shasta Blvd (96067)
Rates: $34-$58
Tel: (916) 926-4811

SHASTA LODGE MOTEL
724 N Mount Shasta Blvd (96067)
Rates: $29-$55
Tel: (916) 926-2815
(800) 742-7821

SWISS HOLIDAY LODGE
2400 S Mount Shasta Blvd (96067)
Rates: $33-$90
Tel: (916) 926-3446

TRAVEL INN
504 S Mount Shasta Blvd (96067)
Rates: $24-$60
Tel: (916) 926-4617

VILLAS VACATION RENTAL CABINS
P. O. Box 344 (96067)
Rates: $30-$125
Tel: (916) 926-3313

WAGON CREEK INN BED & BREAKFAST
1239 Woodland Park Dr (96067)
Rates: $55-$65
Tel: (916) 926-0838
(800) 995-9260

MOUNTAIN VIEW

BEST WESTERN TROPICANA LODGE
1720 El Camino Real (94040)
Rates: $70-$95
Tel: (415) 961-0220
(800) 528-1234

RESIDENCE INN BY MARRIOTT
1854 El Camino Real (94040)
Rates: $89-$139
Tel: (415) 940-1300
(800) 331-3131

NAPA

BUDGET INN
3380 Solano Ave (94558)
Rates: $40-$96
Tel: (707) 257-6111

ELM HOUSE B & B
800 California Blvd (94559)
Rates: $60-$130
Tel: (800) 788-4356

SHERATON INN NAPA VALLEY
3425 Solano Ave (94558)
Rates: $65-$120
Tel: (800) 325-3535

NATIONAL CITY

E-Z 8 MOTEL
607 Roosevelt St (92050)
Rates: $35-$50
Tel: (619) 575-8808
(800) 326-6835

E-Z 8 MOTEL
1700 E Plaza (92050)
Rates: $35-$50
Tel: (619) 474-6491
(800) 326-6835

HOLIDAY INN-SOUTH BAY
700 National City Blvd (91950)
Rates: $55
Tel: (619) 474-2800
(800) 465-4329

RADISSON SUITES NATIONAL CITY
810 National City Blvd (91950)
Rates: $55-$69
Tel: (619) 336-1100
(800) 333-3333

NEEDLES

BEST MOTEL
1900 W Broadway (92363)
Rates: $21-$30
Tel: (619) 326-3824

BEST WESTERN COLORADO RIVER INN
2371 W Broadway (92363)
Rates: $40-$150
Tel: (619) 326-4552
(800) 528-1234

DAYS INN
1111 Pashard St (92363)
Rates: $40-$65
Tel: (619) 326-5660
(800) 329-7446

IMPERIAL 400 MOTOR INN
644 Broadway (92363)
Rates: $28-$38
Tel: (619) 326-2145

MOTEL 6-NORTH
1420 J St (92363)
Rates: $25-$29
Tel: (619) 326-3399
(800) 440-6000

MOTEL 6-SOUTH
1215 Hospitality Ln (92363)
Rates: $25-$29
Tel: (619) 326-5131
(800) 440-6000

OLD TRAILS INN BED & BREAKFAST
304 Broadway (92363)
Rates: $40-$65
Tel: (619) 326-3523

RIVER VALLEY MOTOR LODGE
1707 W Broadway (92363)
Rates: $21-$34
Tel: (619) 326-3839
(800) 346-2331 (CA)

SUPER 8 MOTEL
1102 E Broadway (92363)
Rates: $35-$55
Tel: (619) 326-4501
(800) 800-8000

NEVADA CITY

NEVADA STREET COTTAGES
690 Nevada St (95959)
Rates: $60-$100
Tel: (916) 265-8071

NEWARK

MOTEL 6
5600 Cedar Ct (94560)
Rates: $34-$40
Tel: (510) 791-5900
(800) 440-6000

WOODFIN SUITES
39150 Cedar Blvd (94560)
Rates: $79-$84
Tel: (510) 795-1200
(800) 237-8811

NEWBURY PARK

MOTEL 6
1516 Newbury Rd (91320)
Rates: $30+
Tel: (805) 499-0711
(800) 440-6000

NEWPORT BEACH

BALBOA INN
105 Main St (92661)
Rates: $90-$160
Tel: (714) 675-3412

FOUR SEASONS HOTEL-NEWPORT BEACH
690 Newport Center Dr (92660)
Rates: $205-$305
Tel: (714) 759-0808
(800) 332-3442
(800) 268-6282 (CAN)

NEWPORT BEACH MARRIOTT HOTEL
900 Newport Center Dr (92660)
Rates: $109-$139
Tel: (714) 640-4000
(800) 228-9290

NEWPORT BEACH MARRIOTT SUITES
500 Bayview Cir (92660)
Rates: $119-$139
Tel: (714) 854-4500
(800) 228-9290

OAKWOOD CORPORATE HOUSING
880 Irvine Ave (92663)
Rates: $31-$60
Tel: (714) 574-3725
(800) 456-9351

NICE

TALLEY'S FAMILY RESORT
3827 E Hwy 20 (95464)
Rates: $50-$85
Tel: (707) 274-1177

NORTH HIGHLANDS

MOTEL 6
4600 Watt Ave (95660)
Rates: $36-$42
Tel: (916) 973-8637
(800) 440-6000

RODEWAY INN
3425 Orange Grove Ave (95660)
Rates: $40-$65
Tel: (800) 424-4777

NORWALK

ECONO LODGE
12225 E Firestone Blvd (90650)
Rates: $39-$65
Tel: (310) 868-0791
(800) 424-4777

MOTEL 6
10646 E Rosecrans Ave (90650)
Rates: $32-$36
Tel: (310) 864-2567
(800) 440-6000

NOVATO

DAYS INN
8141 Redwood Blvd (94945)
Rates: $49-$84
Tel: (415) 897-7111
(800) 329-7466

RUSH CREEK TRAVELODGE
7600 Redwood Blvd (94945)
Rates: $55-$65
Tel: (415) 892-7500
(800) 578-7878

OAK VIEW

OAKRIDGE INN
780 N Ventura Ave (93022)
Rates: $50-$100
Tel: (805) 649-4018

OAKHURST

BEST WESTERN-YOSEMITE GATEWAY INN
40530 Hwy 41 (93644)
Rates: $44-$125
Tel: (209) 683-2378
(800) 528-1234

COMFORT INN
40489 Hwy 41 (93644)
Rates: $80
Tel: (209) 683-8282
(800) 221-2222

PINE ROSE INN BED & BREAKFAST
41703 Road 222 (93644)
Rates: $40-$100
Tel: (209) 642-2800

RAMADA LIMITED
48800 Royal Oaks Dr (93644)
Rates: $40-$115
Tel: (209) 658-5500
(800) 272-6232

OAKLAND

BROWN'S YOSEMITE CABIN
7187 Yosemite Pkwy (94605)
Rates: $55-75
Tel: (510) 430-8466

CLARION SUITES HOTEL LAKE MERRITT
1800 Madison St (94612)
Rates: $89-$169
Tel: (510) 832-2300
(800) 933-4683

DAYS INN OAKLAND AIRPORT
8350 Edes Ave (94621)
Rates: $58-$98
Tel: (510) 568-1880
(800) 329-7466

HAMPTON INN OAKLAND AIRPORT
8485 Enterprise Way (94621)
Rates: $64-$75
Tel: (800) 426-7866

HILTON-OAKLAND AIRPORT
1 Hegenberger Rd (94621)
Rates: $115-$595
Tel: (510) 635-5000
(800) 445-8667

HOLIDAY INN OAKLAND AIRPORT
500 Hegenberger Rd (94621)
Rates: $79-$105
Tel: (510) 562-5311
(800) 465-4329

MOTEL 6
8480 Edes Ave (94621)
Rates: $38-$46
Tel: (510) 638-1180
(800) 440-6000

MOTEL 6
1801 Embarcadero (94606)
Rates: $46-$56
Tel: (510) 436-0103
(800) 440-6000

PARC LANE HOTEL
1001 Broadway (94607)
Rates: 105-$150
Tel: (800) 338-1338

TRAVELODGE OAKLAND AT CHINATOWN
423 7th St (94607)
Rates: $45-$159
Tel: (800) 578-7878

OCCIDENTAL

NEGRI'S OCCIDENTAL LODGE
3610 Bohemian Hwy (95465)
Rates: $38-$56
Tel: (707) 874-3623

UNION HOTEL
3731 Main St (95465)
Rates: $30-$40
Tel: (707) 874-3555

OCEANSIDE

MOTEL 6-EAST
3708 Plaza Dr (92056)
Rates: $33-$39
Tel: (619) 941-1011
(800) 440-6000

MOTEL 6-NORTH
1403 Mission Ave (92054)
Rates: $32-$38
Tel: (619) 721-6662
(800) 440-6000

SANDMAN MOTEL
1501 Carmelo Dr
(92054)
Rates: $36-$49
Tel: (619) 722-7661

OJAI

**BEST WESTERN
CASA OJAI**
1302 E Ojai Ave
(93023)
Rates: $56-$110
Tel: (805) 646-8175
(800) 528-1234

LOS PADRES INN
1208 E Ojai Ave
(93023)
Rates: $50-$115
Tel: (805) 646-4365
(800) 228-3744

**OJAI MANOR
HOTEL**
210 E Matilija St
(93023)
Rates: $50-$100
Tel: (805) 646-0961

OJAI VALLEY INN
SR 150 (93023)
Rates: $99-$189
Tel: (805) 646-5511
(800) 422-6524

OLEMA

**RIDGETOP INN
& COTTAGES**
9865 Sir Francis
Drake Blvd (94950)
Rates: $95-$150
Tel: (415) 663-1500

ONTARIO

COUNTRY INN
2359 S Grove Ave
(91761)
Rates: $39-$49
Tel: (800) 770-1887

**COUNTRY SUITES
BY CARLSON**
231 N Vineyard Ave
(91764)
Rates: $62-$72
Tel: (909) 983-8484
(800) 456-4000

**DOUBLETREE CLUB
HOTEL**
429 N Vineyard Ave
(91764)
Rates: $65-$69
Tel: (800) 582-2946

GOOD NITE INN
1801 East G St
(91764)
Rates: $67-$80
Tel: (909) 983-3604
(800) 724-8822

**HOLIDAY INN
ONTARIO AIRPORT**
3400 Shelby St
(91764)
Rates: $62-$76
Tel: (909) 466-9600
(800) 465-4329

**HOWARD JOHN-
SON ONTARIO
AIRPORT SOUTH**
2425 S Archibald
Ave (91761)
Rates: $40-$53
Tel: (909) 923-2728
(800) 446-4656

**MARRIOTT HOTEL-
ONTARIO**
2200 E Holt Blvd
(91764)
Rates: $59-$79
Tel: (800) 284-8811

MOTEL 6-EAST
1560 E 4th St (91764)
Rates: $27-$31
Tel: (909) 984-2424
(800) 440-6000

MOTEL 6-WEST
1515 N Mountain
Ave (91762)
Rates: $27-$33
Tel: (909) 986-6632
(800) 440-6000

ONTARIO INN
5361 W Holt Ave
(91763)
Rates: $25-$35
Tel: (909) 625-3806

RAMADA INN
1120 E Holt Blvd
(91761)
Rates: $30-$50
Tel: (909) 984-9655
(800) 272-6232

RED LION HOTEL
222 N Vineyard Ave
(91764)
Rates: $62-$82
Tel: (909) 983-0909
(800) 547-8010

RED ROOF INN
1818 E Holt Blvd
(91761)
Rates: $51
Tel: (909) 988-8466
(800) 843-7663

**RESIDENCE INN
BY MARRIOTT**
2025 East D St
(91764)
Rates: $99-$129
Tel: (909) 983-6788
(800) 331-3131

TRAVELODGE
755 N Euclid Ave
(91762)
Rates: $35-$46
Tel: (909) 984-1775
(800) 578-7878

ORANGE

**DOUBLETREE HOTEL-
ORANGE COUNTY**
100 The City Dr
(92668)
Rates: $130-$170
Tel: (714) 634-4500
(800) 222-8733

GOOD NITE INN
101 N State College
Blvd (92668)
Rates: $31-$60
Tel: (714) 634-9500
(800) 544-6991

**HILTON SUITES-
ORANGE**
400 N State College
Blvd (92668)
Rates: $130-$180
Tel: (714) 938-1111
(800) 445-8667

**RESIDENCE INN
BY MARRIOTT**
201 N State College
Blvd (92668)
Rates: $89-$145
Tel: (714) 978-7700
(800) 331-3131

ORICK

**ROLF'S PARK CAFE &
PRAIRIE CREEK MOTEL**
Davidson Rd (95555)
Rates: $28-$35
Tel: (707) 488-3841

ORLAND

**AMBER LIGHT INN
MOTEL**
828 Newville Rd
(95963)
Rates: $26-$36
Tel: (916) 865-7655

ORLAND INN
1052 South St
(95963)
Rates: $26-$36
Tel: (916) 865-7632

**ORLANDA INN
MOTEL**
827 Newville Rd
(95963)
Rates: $27+
Tel: (916) 865-4162

OROSI

MAMA BEAR'S B & B
42723 Rd 128 (93647)
Rates: $45-$120
Tel: (209) 528-3614
(800) 530-2327

OROVILLE

**BEST WESTERN
GRAND MANOR
INN**
1470 Feather River
Blvd (95965)
Rates: $53-$91
Tel: (916) 553-9673
(800) 528-1234

DAYS INN
1745 Feather River
Blvd (95965)
Rates: $47-$70
Tel: (916) 533-3297
(800) 329-7466

ECONO LODGE
1835 Feather River
Blvd (95965)
Rates: $42-$58
Tel: (916) 533-8201
(800) 424-4777

JEAN'S RIVERSIDE BED & BREAKFAST
45 Cabana Dr (95965)
Rates: $55-$125
Tel: (916) 533-1413

MOTEL 6
505 Montgomery St (95965)
Rates: $29-$35
Tel: (916) 532-9400
(800) 440-6000

TRAVELODGE
580 Oro Dam Blvd (95965)
Rates: $45-$50
Tel: (916) 533-7070
(800) 578-7878

OXNARD

AMBASSADOR MOTEL
1631 S Oxnard Blvd (93030)
Rates: $49
Tel: (805) 486-8404

BEST WESTERN OXNARD INN
1156 S Oxnard Blvd (93030)
Rates: $49
Tel: (805) 483-9581
(800) 528-1234

CITY CENTER MOTEL
550 S Oxnard Blvd (93030)
Rates: $49
Tel: (805) 486-2522

HILTON INN
600 Esplanade Dr (93030)
Rates: $65
Tel: (805) 485-9666
(800) 445-8667

RADISSON SUITE HOTEL AT RIVER RIDGE
2101 W Vineyard (93030)
Rates: $85-$129
Tel: (805) 988-0130
(800) 333-3333

VAGABOND INN
1245 N Oxnard Blvd (93030)
Rates: $40-$60
Tel: (805) 983-0251
(800) 522-1555

VILLA MOTEL
1715 S Oxnard Blvd (93030)
Rates: $49
Tel: (805) 487-1370

PACIFIC GROVE

ANDRIL FIREPLACE COTTAGES
569 Asilomar Blvd (93950)
Rates: $64-$100
Tel: (408) 375-0994

BEST WESTERN LIGHTHOUSE LODGE & SUITES
1150 Lighthouse Ave (93950)
Rates: $79-$288
Tel: (408) 655-2111
(800) 528-1234

BID-A-WEE MOTEL & COTTAGES
221 Asilomar Blvd (93950)
Rates: $49-$95
Tel: (408) 372-2330

OLD ST. ANGELA'S INN
321 Central Ave (93950)
Rates: $90-$150
Tel: (408) 372-3246

OLYMPIA MOTOR LODGE
1140 Lighthouse Ave (93950)
Rates: $50-$90
Tel: (408) 373-2777

PACIFICA

DAYS INN
200 Rockaway Beach Ave (94044)
Rates: $75
Tel: (800) 329-7466

LIGHTHOUSE HOTEL
105 Rockaway Beach Ave (94044)
Rates: $55-$295
Tel: (415) 355-6300
(800) 832-4777

PALM DESERT

ALADDIN LODGE
73-793 Shadow Mtn Dr (92260)
Rates: $35-$75
Tel: (619) 346-6816

CASA LARREA RESORT
73-811 Larrea St (92260)
Rates: $47-$98
Tel: (619) 568-0311

DESERT PATCH INN
73-758 Shadow Mtn Dr (92260)
Rates: $47-$94
Tel: (619) 346-9161
(800) 350-9758

EMBASSY SUITES
74-700 Hwy 111 (92260)
Rates: $69-$219
Tel: (619) 340-6600
(800) 633-2843
(800) 223-1679 (CA)

INN AT DEEP CANYON
74-470 Abronia Tr (92260)
Rates: $29-$179
Tel: (619) 346-8061
(800) 253-0004

MOTEL 6
78100 Varner Rd (92211)
Rates: $30-$34
Tel: (619) 345-0550
(800) 440-6000

PALM DESERT LODGE
74-527 Hwy 111 (92260)
Rates: $40-$75
Tel: (619) 346-3875
(800) 300-3875

PALM SPRINGS

AMERICAN HOTEL
1200 S Palm Canyon Dr (92264)
Rates: $30-$54
Tel: (619) 320-4399

A CASA BELLA HOTEL
650 San Lorenzo Rd (92264)
Rates: $40-$70
Tel: (619) 325-1487

A SUNBEAM INN
291 Camino Monte Vista (92262)
Rates: $35-$75
Tel: (619) 323-3812
(800) 328-3812

BAHAMA HOTEL
2323 N Palm Canyon Dr (92262)
Rates: $30-$150
Tel: (619) 325-8190

BERMUDA PALMS RESORT
650 E Palm Canyon Dr (92264)
Rates: $39-$98
Tel: (619) 323-1839
(800) 869-1132

BEST WESTERN HOST MOTOR HOTEL
1633 S Palm Canyon Dr (92264)
Rates: $39-$98
Tel: (619) 325-9177
(800) 528-1234

BEST WESTERN ROYAL SUN HOTEL
1700 S Palm Canyon Dr (92264)
Rates: $60-$100
Tel: (619) 327-1564
(800) 528-1234

BILTMORE HOTEL
1000 E Palm Canyon Dr (92264)
Rates: $60-$250
Tel: (619) 323-1811

CABANA CLUB RESORT
970 Parocela (92264)
Rates: $50-$150
Tel: (619) 323-8842

CASA CODY COUNTRY INN
175 S Cahuilla Rd (92262)
Rates: $49-$185
Tel: (619) 320-9346
(800) 231-2639

CASA DE CAMERO HOTEL
1480 N Indian Canyon Dr (92262)
Rates: $40+
Tel: (619) 320-1678

DESERT RIVIERA HOTEL
610 E Palm Canyon Dr (92264)
Rates: $22-$85
Tel: (619) 327-5314

DUESENBERG MOTOR LODGE
269 Chuckwalla Rd (92262)
Rates: $45-$65
Tel: (619) 326-2567

THE DUNES HOTEL
390 S Indian Canyon Dr (92262)
Rates: $29-$79
Tel: (619) 322-8789

ESTRELLA INN AT PALM SPRINGS
415 S Belardo Rd (92262)
Rates: $79-$300
Tel: (619) 320-4117
(800) 237-3687

HILTON RESORT PALM SPRINGS
400 E Tahquitz Canyon Way (92262)
Rates: $65-$235
Tel: (619) 320-6868
(800) 445-8667

HOLIDAY OASIS
117 W Tahquitz Canyon Way (92264)
Rates: $29-$69
Tel: (619) 320-7205

HOWARD JOHNSON
701 E Palm Canyon Dr (92264)
Rates: $46-$86
Tel: (619) 320-2700
(800) 446-4656

HYATT REGENCY SUITES PALM SPRINGS
285 N Palm Canyon Dr (92262)
Rates: $69-$229
Tel: (619) 322-9000
(800) 233-1234

INGLESIDE INN
200 W Ramon Rd (92264)
Rates: $76-$375
Tel: (619) 325-0046
(800) 772-6655

INN AT THE RACQUET CLUB
2743 N Indian Canyon Dr (92263)
Rates: $69-$395
Tel: (619) 325-1281
(800) 367-0946

IRONSIDE HOTEL
310 E Palm Canyon Dr (92264)
Rates: $35-$75
Tel: (619) 325-1995

KORAKIA PENSIONE
257 S Patencio Rd (92262)
Rates: $79-$165
Tel: (619) 864-6411

LA SERENA VILLAS
339 S Belardo Rd (92262)
Rates: $55-$180
Tel: (619) 325-3216

LOS DOLORES HOTEL
312 Camino Monte Vista (92264)
Rates: $45-$85
Tel: (619) 327-4000
(800) 445-8916

MOTEL 6 DOWNTOWN
660 S Palm Canyon Dr (92262)
Rates: $34-$41
Tel: (619) 327-4200
(800) 440-6000

MOTEL 6-EAST
595 E Palm Canyon Dr (92264)
Rates: $34-$41
Tel: (619) 325-6129
(800) 440-6000

MUSICLAND HOTEL
1342 S Palm Canyon Dr (92264)
Rates: $29-$99
Tel: (619) 325-1326
(800) 428-3939

PEPPER TREE INN
645 N Indian Canyon Dr (92262)
Rates: $20-$55
Tel: (619) 325-9505

PLACE IN THE SUN
754 San Lorenzo Rd (92264)
Rates: $49-$99
Tel: (619) 325-0254
(800) 779-2254

QUALITY INN RESORT
1269 E Palm Canyon Dr (92264)
Rates: $39-$169
Tel: (619) 323-2775
(800) 221-2222

RAMADA INN
1800 E Palm Canyon Dr (92264)
Rates: $79-139
Tel: (619) 323-1711
(800) 272-6232

RIVIERA RESORT & RACQUET CLUB
1600 N Indian Canyon Dr (92262)
Rates: $45-$195
Tel: (619) 327-8311
(800) 444-8311

RODEWAY INN
390 S Indian Canyon Dr.(92262)
Rates: $29-$39
Tel: (619) 322-8789
(800) 228-2000

ROYAL SUN
1700 S Palm Canyon Dr (92264)
Rates: $35-$99
Tel: (619) 327-1564

SMOKE TREE VILLA
1586 E Palm Canyon Dr (92264)
Rates: $75-$115
Tel: (619) 323-2231

SUPER 8 MOTEL
1900 N Palm Canyon Dr (92262)
Rates: $46-$76
Tel: (619) 322-3757
(800) 800-8000

TUSCANY GARDEN RESORT
350 W Chino Canyon Rd (92262)
Rates: $49-$80
Tel: (619) 325-2349

PALMDALE

HOLIDAY INN PALMDALE/ LANCASTER
38630 5th St W (93551)
Rates: $50-$70
Tel: (805) 947-8055
(800) 465-4329

MOTEL 6
407 W Palmdale Blvd (93551)
Rates: $27-$31
Tel: (805) 272-0660
(800) 440-6000

PALO ALTO

CARDINAL HOTEL
235 Hamilton Ave (94301)
Rates: $60-$125
Tel: (415) 323-5101

CORONET MOTEL
2455 El Camino Real (94306)
Rates: $38-$40
Tel: (415) 326-1081

DAYS INN
4238 El Camino Real (94306)
Rates: $55-$125
Tel: (415) 493-4222
(800) 329-7466

HOLIDAY INN PALO ALTO/STANFORD
625 El Camino Real (94301)
Rates: $124-$152
Tel: (415) 328-2800
(800) 874-3516

HYATT RICKEYS
4219 El Camino Real (94306)
Rates: $75-$195
Tel: (415) 493-8000
(800) 233-1234

MOTEL 6
4301 El Camino Real (94306)
Rates: $43-$49
Tel: (415) 949-0833
(800) 440-6000

PARADISE

LANTERN MOTEL
5799 Wildwood Ln
(95969)
Rates: $37-$46
Tel: (916) 877-5553

LIME SADDLE MARINA
3428 Pentz Rd
(95969)
Rates: $225
Tel: (916) 877-2414
(800) 834-7571

PALOS VERDES MOTEL
5423 Skyway (95969)
Rates: $35-$39
Tel: (916) 877-2127

PONDEROSA GARDENS MOTEL
7010 Skyway (95969)
Rates: $50-$95
Tel: (916) 872-9094

PARKFIELD

PARKFIELD INN
First & Oak Sts
(93451)
Rates: $41-$65
Tel: (805) 463-2323

PASADENA

HOLIDAY INN
303 E Cordova St
(91101)
Rates: $79-$189
Tel: (818) 449-4000
(800) 457-7940

HOLIDAY INN EXPRESS
2321 E Colorado
Blvd (91107)
Rates: $75
Tel: (818) 796-9261
(800) 465-4329

PASADENA HILTON
150 S Los Robles Ave
(91101)
Rates: $119-$175
Tel: (818) 577-1000
(800) 445-8667

PASADENA INN
400 S Arroyo Pkwy
(91105)
Rates: $50-$70
Tel: (818) 795-8401

RAMADA INN
3500 E Colorado
Blvd (91107)
Rates: $50-$75
Tel: (818) 792-1363
(800) 272-6232

VAGABOND INN
2863 E Colorado
Blvd (91107)
Rates: $42-$62
Tel: (818) 449-3020
(800) 522-1555

VAGABOND INN
1203 E Colorado
Blvd (91106)
Rates: $36-$48
Tel: (818) 449-3170
(800) 522-1555

WESTWAY INN
1599 E Colorado
Blvd (91106)
Rates: $44-$56
Tel: (818) 304-9678

PASO ROBLES

BUDGET INN
2745 Spring St
(93446)
Rates: $60-$120
Tel: (805) 238-2770

COUNTRY GARDENS INN B & B
2430 Genesco Rd
(93446)
Rates: $66-$100
Tel: (805) 238-6639

FARMHOUSE MOTEL
425 Spring St (93446)
Rates: $25+
Tel: (805) 238-1720

MOTEL 6
1134 Black Oak Dr
(93446)
Rates: $30-$36
Tel: (805) 239-9090
(800) 440-6000

SHAMROCK INN BED & BREAKFAST
1640 Circle B Rd
(93446)
Rates: $41-$65
Tel: (805) 239-8585

SUBURBAN LODGE
1955 Theatre Dr
(93446)
Rates: $40-$65
Tel: (805) 238-3814

TRAVELODGE PASO ROBLES
2701 Spring St (93446)
Rates: $34-$75
Tel: (805) 238-0078
(800) 578-7878

PEBBLE BEACH

THE LODGE AT PEBBLE BEACH
1700 17-Mile Dr
(93953)
Rates: $295-$450
Tel: (408) 624-3811
(800) 654-9300

PERRIS

BEST WESTERN LAKE PERRIS INN
480 S Redlands Ave
(92376)
Rates: $45-$53
Tel: (909) 943-5577
(800) 528-1234

PETALUMA

MOTEL 6-NORTH
5135 Montero Way
(94954)
Rates: $30-$37
Tel: (707) 664-9090
(800) 440-6000

MOTEL 6-SOUTH
1368 N McDowell
Blvd (94952)
Rates: $33-$39
Tel: (707) 765-0333
(800) 440-6000

QUALITY INN-PETALUMA
5100 Montero Way
(94954)
Rates: $59-$155
Tel: (707) 664-1155
(800) 221-2222

PETROLIA

MATTOLE RIVER RESORT
42354 Mattole Rd
(95558)
Rates: $45-$90
Tel: (707) 629-3445
(800) 845-4607

PHELAN

ECONOMY INN
8317 Hwy 138
(Cajon Pass 92371)
Rates: $48-$57
Tel: (619) 249-6777
(800) 826-0778

PIERCY

HARTSOOK INN
900 Hwy 101 (95587)
Rates: $39-$100
Tel: (707) 247-3305

PINECREST

PINECREST CHALET
500 Dodge Ridge Rd
(95364)
Rates: $33-$225
Tel: (209) 965-3276

PINOLE

MOTEL 6
1501 Fitzgerald Dr
(94564)
Rates: $42-$48
Tel: (510) 222-8174
(800) 440-6000

PISMO BEACH

KNIGHT'S REST MOTEL
2351 Price St (93449)
Rates: $45-$129
Tel: (805) 773-4617

MOTEL 6
860 4th St (93449)
Rates: $27-$36
Tel: (805) 773-2665
(800) 440-6000

OCEAN PALMS MOTEL
390 Ocean View
(93449)
Rates: $28-$85
Tel: (805) 773-4669

QUALITY SUITES
651 Five Cities Dr
(93449)
Rates: $83-$136
Tel: (805) 773-3773
(800) 982-7848

SANDCASTLE INN
100 Stimson Ave
(93449)
Rates: $105-$130
Tel: (805) 773-2422
(800) 822-6606

SEA VIEW MOTEL
230 Five Cats Dr
(93499)
Rates: $29-$49
Tel: (805) 773-1841

PITTSBURG

MOTEL 6
2101 Loveridge Rd
(94565)
Rates: $32-$38
Tel: (510) 427-1600
(800) 440-6000

PLACENTIA

**RESIDENCE INN
BY MARRIOTT**
700 W Kimberly Ave
(92670)
Rates: $69-$145
Tel: (714) 996-0555
(800) 331-3131

PLACERVILLE

**BEST WESTERN
PLACERVILLE INN**
6850 Greenleaf Dr
(95667)
Rates: $58-$74
Tel: (916) 622-9100
(800) 528-1234

**GOLD TRAIL
MOTOR LODGE**
1970 Broadway
(95667)
Rates: $36-$51
Tel: (916) 622-2906

**MOTHER LODE
MOTEL**
1940 Broadway
(95667)
Rates: $34-$51
Tel: (916) 622-0895

PLEASANT HILL

**RESIDENCE INN
BY MARRIOTT
PLEASANT HILL**
700 Ellinwood Way
(94523)
Rates: $89-$119
Tel: (510) 689-1010
(800) 331-3131

PLEASANTON

**DOUBLETREE CLUB
HOTEL**
5990 Stoneridge
Mall Rd (94588)
Rates: $69-$139
Tel: (510) 463-3330
(800) 222-8733

**HILTON
PLEASANTON**
7050 Johnson Dr
(94588)
Rates: $99-$149
Tel: (510) 463-8000
(800) 445-8667

HOLIDAY INN
11950 Dublin
Canyon Rd (94588)
Rates: $95-$115
Tel: (510) 847-6000
(800) 465-4329

MOTEL 6
5102 Hopyard Rd
(94588)
Rates: $40-$46
Tel: (510) 463-2626
(800) 440-6000

PLYMOUTH

SHENANDOAH INN
17674 Village Dr
(95669)
Rates: $53-$71
Tel: (209) 245-4491
(800) 542-4549

POINT REYES STATION

**BERRY PATCH
COTTAGE B & B**
P. O. Box 712 (94956)
Rates: $110
Tel: (415) 663-1942

GRAY'S RETREAT
P. O. Box 547 (94956)
Rates: $135
Tel: (415) 663-2000
(800) 887-2880

JASMINE COTTAGE
P. O. Box 547 (94956)
Rates: $125
Tel: (415) 663-2000
(800) 887-2880

KNOB HILL COTTAGE
P. O. Box 1108
(94956)
Rates: $55-$95
Tel: (415) 663-1784

**THIRTY-NINE
CYPRESS B & B**
39 Cypress Rd,
P. O. Box 176 (94956)
Rates: $110-$130
Tel: (415) 663-1709

POLLOCK PINES

**STAGECOACH
MOTOR INN**
5940 Pony Express
Tr (95726)
Rates: $50-$68
Tel: (916) 644-2029

POMONA

MOTEL 6
2470 S Garey Ave
(91766)
Rates: $30-$34
Tel: (909) 591-1871
(800) 440-6000

**SHERATON SUITES
FAIRPLEX**
600 W McKinley Ave
(91768)
Rates: $95-$115
Tel: (909) 622-2220
(800) 722-4055

**SHILO INNS HOTEL-
DIAMOND BAR/
POMONA**
3200 Temple Ave
(91768)
Rates: $90-$100
Tel: (909) 598-0073
(800) 222-2244

PORT HUENEME

COUNTRY INN
350 E Hueneme Rd
(93041)
Rates: $72+
Tel: (805) 986-5353

SURFSIDE MOTEL
615 E Hueneme Rd
(93041)
Rates: $49
Tel: (805) 488-3686

PORTERVILLE

MOTEL 6
935 W Morton Ave
(93257)
Rates: $24-$28
Tel: (209) 781-7600
(800) 440-6000

PORTOLA

**SLEEPY PINES
MOTEL**
74631 Hwy 70
(96122)
Rates: $40+
Tel: (916) 832-4291

POWAY

**POWAY COUNTRY
INN**
13845 Poway Rd
(92064)
Rates: $40-$56
Tel: (619) 748-6320
(800) 648-6320

QUINCY

GOLD PAN MOTEL
200 Crescent St
(95971)
Rates: $38-$64
Tel: (916) 283-3686
(800) 804-6541

RAMONA

**LAKE SUTHERLAND
LODGE B & B**
24901 Dam Oaks Dr
(92065)
Rates: $110-$165
Tel: (619) 789-6483

RAMONA VALLEY INN
416 Main St (92065)
Rates: $40-$78
Tel: (619) 789-6433
(800) 648-4618

RANCHO BERNARDO

CARMEL HIGHLAND DOUBLETREE GOLF RESORT
14455 Penasquitos Dr (92129)
Rates: $100-$179
Tel: (619) 672-9100
(800) 622-9223

HOLIDAY INN
17065 W Bernardo Dr (92127)
Rates: $59-$69
Tel: (619) 485-6530
(800) 465-4329

LA QUINTA INN
10185 Paseo Montril (92129)
Rates: $49-$59
Tel: (619) 484-8800
(800) 531-5900

RADISSON SUITE HOTEL
11520 W Bernardo Ct (92127)
Rates: $79-$119
Tel: (619) 451-6600
(800) 333-3333

RANCHO BERNARDO INN
17550 Bernardo Oaks (92128)
Rates: $79-$149
Tel: (619) 487-1611
(800) 542-6096

RESIDENCE INN BY MARRIOTT
11002 Rancho Carmel Dr (92128)
Rates: $79-$149
Tel: (619) 673-1900
(800) 331-3131

TRAVELODGE
16929 W Bernardo Dr (92127)
Rates: $47-$62
Tel: (619) 487-0445
(800) 578-7878

RANCHO CORDOVA

BEST WESTERN HERITAGE INN
11269 Point East Dr (95742)
Rates: $59-$69
Tel: (916) 635-4040
(800) 528-1234

COMFORT INN
3240 Mather Field Rd (95670)
Rates: $45-$79
Tel: (916) 363-3344
(800) 221-2222

DAYS INN
11131 Folsom Blvd (95670)
Rates: $49-$75
Tel: (800) 329-7466

ECONOMY INNS OF AMERICA
12249 Folsom Blvd (95670)
Rates: $34-$42
Tel: (916) 351-1213
(800) 826-0778

MOTEL 6-EAST
10694 Olson Dr (95670)
Rates: $30-$36
Tel: (916) 635-8784
(800) 440-6000

MOTEL 6-WEST
10271 Folsom Blvd (95670)
Rates: $29-$35
Tel: (916) 362-5800
(800) 440-6000

RANCHO MIRAGE

MARRIOTT'S RANCHO LAS PALMAS RESORT
41000 Bob Hope Dr (92270)
Rates: $69-$280
Tel: (619) 568-2727
(800) 458-8786

MOTEL 6
69-570 Hwy 111 (92270)
Rates: $34-$41
Tel: (619) 324-8475
(800) 440-6000

WESTIN MISSION HILLS RESORT
71-333 Dinah Shore Dr (92270)
Rates: $310-$350
Tel: (619) 328-5955
(800) 228-3000

RANCHO SANTA FE

INN AT RANCHO SANTA FE
5951 Linea del Cielo (92067)
Rates: $95-$510
Tel: (619) 756-1131
(800) 654-2928

MORGAN RUN RESORT & CLUB
5690 Cancha de Golf (92067)
Rates: $139-$339
Tel: (619) 756-2471

RAVENDALE

RAVENDALE LODGE
Highway 395 (96123)
Rates: $25-$30
Tel: (916) 728-0028

RED BLUFF

CINDERELLA RIVERVIEW MOTEL
600 Rio St (96080)
Rates: $32-$48
Tel: (916) 527-5490

FLAMINGO HOTEL
250 S Main St (96080)
Rates: $22-$52
Tel: (916) 527-3454

IMA VALUE LODGE
30 Gilmore Rd (96080)
Rates: $37-$60
Tel: (916) 529-2028
(800) 341-8000

KINGS LODGE
38 Antelope Blvd (96080)
Rates: $35-$41
Tel: (916) 527-6020
(800) 426-5655

MOTEL 6
20 Williams Ave (96080)
Rates: $30-$36
Tel: (916) 527-9200
(800) 440-6000

SUPER 8 MOTEL
203 Antelope Blvd (96080)
Rates: $40-$50
Tel: (916) 527-8882
(800) 800-8000

REDDING

AMERICANA LODGE
1250 Pine St (96001)
Rates: $27-$34
Tel: (916) 241-7020
(800) 626-1900

BEL AIR MOTEL
540 N Market St (96003)
Rates: $24-$49
Tel: (916) 243-5291

BEST WESTERN HOSPITALITY HOUSE
532 N Market St (96003)
Rates: $44-$70
Tel: (916) 241-6464
(800) 528-1234

BEST WESTERN PONDEROSA INN
2220 Pine St (96001)
Rates: $44-$66
Tel: (916) 241-6300
(800) 528-1234

BRIDGE BAY RESORT
10300 Bridge Bay Rd (96003)
Rates: $55-$150
Tel: (916) 241-6464
(800) 752-9669

CAPRI MOTEL
4620 Hwy 90 S (96001)
Rates: $30-$40
Tel: (916) 241-1156
(800) 626-1900

CEDAR LODGE
513 N Market St (96003)
Rates: n/a
Tel: (916) 244-3251

COMFORT INN
2059 Hilltop Dr
(96002)
Rates: $44-$48
Tel: (916) 221-6530
(800) 221-2222

ECONOMY INN
525 N Market St
(96003)
Rates: $35+
Tel: (916) 246-9803

**FAWNDALE LODGE
& RV RESORT**
15215 Fawndale Rd
(96003)
Rates: $30-$75
Tel: (916) 275-8000

IMA RIVER INN
1835 Park Marina Dr
(96001)
Rates: $40-$70
Tel: (916) 241-9500
(800) 995-4341

LA QUINTA INN
2180 Hilltop Dr
(96002)
Rates: $54-$89
Tel: (916) 221-8200
(800) 531-5900

MOTEL 6-CENTRAL
1640 Hilltop Dr
(96002)
Rates: $36-$42
Tel: (916) 221-1800
(800) 440-6000

MOTEL 6-NORTH
1250 Twin View
Blvd (96003)
Rates: $33-$39
Tel: (916) 246-4470
(800) 440-6000

MOTEL 6-SOUTH
2385 Bechelli Ln
(96002)
Rates: $33-$39
Tel: (916) 221-0562
(800) 440-6000

MOTEL 99
533 N Market St
(96003)
Rates: $35+
Tel: (916) 241-4942

**NORTH GATE
LODGE**
1040 Market St
(96001)
Rates: $30
Tel: (916) 243-4900

OXFORD SUITES
1967 Hilltop Dr
(96002)
Rates: $65-$105
Tel: (916) 221-0100
(800) 762-0133

PARK TERRACE INN
1900 Hilltop Dr
(96002)
Rates: $68-$75
Tel: (916) 221-7500

RED LION INN
1830 Hilltop Dr
(96002)
Rates: $84-$121
Tel: (916) 221-8700
(800) 547-8010

REDDING LODGE
1135 Market St
(96001)
Rates: $32-$36
Tel: (916) 243-5141

SARATOGA MOTEL
3025 S Market St
(96001)
Rates: $25+
Tel: (916) 243-8586

**SHASTA DAM
EL RANCHO MOTEL**
1529 Cascade Blvd
(Shasta Lake City
96079)
Rates: $28-$38
Tel: (916) 275-1065

SHASTA LODGE
1245 Pine St (96001)
Rates: $28-$45
Tel: (916) 243-6133

STAR DUST MOTEL
1200 Pine St (96001)
Rates: $30-$35
Tel: (916) 241-6121

**THRIFTLODGE &
CASA BLANCA
MOTEL**
413 N Market St
(96003)
Rates: $25+
Tel: (916) 241-3010

VAGABOND INN
536 E Cypress Ave
(96002)
Rates: $40-$65
Tel: (916) 223-1600
(800) 522-1555

VAGABOND INN
2010 Pine St (96001)
Rates: $32-$45
Tel: (916) 243-3336
(800) 522-1555

REDLANDS

**BEST WESTERN
SANDMAN MOTEL**
1120 W Colton Ave
(92373)
Rates: $39-$58
Tel: (909) 793-2001
(800) 528-1234

GOOD NITE INN
1675 Industrial Park
Ave (92374)
Rates: $37
Tel: (909) 793-3723

REDLANDS INN
1235 W Colton Ave
(92373)
Rates: $28-$33
Tel: (909) 793-6648

SUPER 8 MOTEL
1160 Arizona St
(92374)
Rates: $26-$32
Tel: (909) 335-1612
(800) 800-8000

REDONDO
BEACH

**PORTOFINO HOTEL
& YACHT CLUB**
260 Portofino Way
(90277)
Rates: $129-$159
Tel: (310) 379-8481
(800) 468-4292

**TRAVELODGE-
REDONDO BEACH
PIER**
206 S Pacific Coast
Hwy (90277)
Rates: $65
Tel: (310) 318-1811
(800) 578-7878

VAGABOND INN
6226 Pacific Coast
Hwy (90277)
Rates: $45-$54
Tel: (310) 378-8555
(800) 522-1555

REDWAY

**BUDGET WEST
REDWAY INN**
3223 Redwood Dr
(95560)
Rates: $36
Tel: (707) 923-2660
(800) 732-5380 (CA)

REDWOOD CITY

GOOD NITE INN
485 Veterans Blvd
(94063)
Rates: $40-$71
Tel: (415) 365-5500

SUPER 8 MOTEL
2526 Camino Real
(94061)
Rates: $39-$59
Tel: (415) 366-0880
(800) 800-8000

REEDLEY

EDGEWATER INN
1977 W Manning
Ave (93654)
Rates: $52
Tel: (209) 637-7777

RESEDA

**HOWARD
JOHNSON**
7432 Reseda Blvd
(91335)
Rates: $49-$99
Tel: (818) 344-0324
(800) 446-4656

RIALTO

**BEST WESTERN
EMPIRE INN**
475 W Valley Blvd
(92376)
Rates: $56-$65
Tel: (909) 877-0690
(800) 528-1234

RICHARDSON
GROVE

HARTSOOK INN
900 Hwy 101 (95542)
Rates: $50-$125
Tel: (707) 247-3305

RIDGECREST

EL DORADO MOTEL
400 S China Lake
Blvd (93555)
Rates: $28-$95
Tel: (619) 375-1354

EL RANCHO
507 S China Lake
Blvd (93555)
Rates: $37-$49
Tel: (619) 375-9731

HACIENDA COURT
150 W Miguel
(93555)
Rates: $50-$70
Tel: (619) 375-5066

HERITAGE INN
1050 N Norma Dr
(93555)
Rates: $75-$95
Tel: (619) 446-6543
(800) 843-0693

HERITAGE SUITES
919 N Heritage Dr
(93555)
Rates: $90-$150
Tel: (619) 446-7951

MOTEL 6
535 S China Lake
Blvd (93555)
Rates: $27-$31
Tel: (619) 375-6866
(800) 440-6000

PANAMINT SPRINGS RESORT
Hwy 190 (93555)
Rates: $46-$65
Tel: (619) 764-2010

RIDGECREST MOTOR INN
329 E Ridgecrest
Blvd (93555)
Rates: $30-$50
Tel: (619) 371-1695

RIO DELL

HUMBOLT GABLES MOTEL
40 W Davis St
(95562)
Rates: $30-$70
Tel: (707) 764-5609

RIO NIDO

RIO NIDO LODGE RESORT
1458 River Rd
(95471)
Rates: $50-$80
Tel: (707) 869-0821

RIVERSIDE

COURTYARD BY MARRIOTT
1510 University Ave
(92507)
Rates: $59
Tel: (909) 276-1200
(800) 443-6000

DYNASTY SUITES
3735 Iowa Ave (92507)
Rates: $39-$49
Tel: (909) 369-8200
(800) 842-7899

ECONO LODGE
1971 University Ave
(92507)
Rates: $38-$58
Tel: (909) 684-6363
(800) 424-4777

HAMPTON INN
1590 University Ave
(92507)
Rates: $39
Tel: (909) 683-6000
(800) 426-7866

MOTEL 6 DOWNTOWN
4045 University Ave
(92501)
Rates: $26-$30
Tel: (909) 686-6666
(800) 440-6000

MOTEL 6-EAST
1260 University Ave
(92507)
Rates: $27-$31
Tel: (909) 784-2131
(800) 440-6000

MOTEL 6-SOUTH
3663 La Sierra Ave
(92505)
Rates: $27-$31
Tel: (909) 351-0764
(800) 440-6000

SUPER 8 MOTEL
1199 University Ave
(92507)
Rates: $32-$39
Tel: (909) 682-9011
(800) 800-8000

TRAVELODGE LA SIERRA
11043 Magnolia Ave
(92505)
Rates: $39-$69
Tel: (909) 688-5000
(800) 578-7878

ROCKLIN

FIRST CHOICE INNS
4420 Rocklin Rd
(95677)
Rates: $62-$125
Tel: (916) 624-4500
(800) 462-2400

ROHNERT PARK

BEST WESTERN INN
6500 Redwood Dr
(94928)
Rates: $44-$76
Tel: (707) 584-7435
(800) 528-1234

MOTEL 6
6145 Commerce
Blvd (94928)
Rates: $32-$38
Tel: (707) 585-8888
(800) 440-6000

RED LION HOTEL SONOMA COUNTY
1 Red Lion Dr (94928)
Rates: $105-$145
Tel: (707) 584-5466
(800) 547-8010

ROHNERT PARK INN
6288 Redwood Dr
(94928)
Rates: $28-$34
Tel: (707) 584-1005

ROSAMOND

DEVONSHIRE INN MOTEL
P. O. Box 2080 (93560)
Rates: $49-$59
Tel: (805) 256-3454

ROSEMEAD

MOTEL 6
1001 S San Gabriel
Blvd (91770)
Rates: $34-$38
Tel: (818) 572-6076
(800) 440-6000

VAGABOND INN
3633 N Rosemead
Blvd (91770)
Rates: $42-$57
Tel: (818) 288-6661
(800) 522-1555

ROSEVILLE

BEST WESTERN ROSEVILLE INN
220 Harding Blvd
(95678)
Rates: $49-$80
Tel: (916) 782-4434
(800) 528-1234

ROWLAND HEIGHTS

MOTEL 6
18970 E Labin Ct
(91748)
Rates: $29-$33
Tel: (818) 964-5333
(800) 440-6000

RUNNING SPRINGS

GIANT OAKS MOTEL & CABINS
32180 Hilltop Blvd
(92382)
Rates: $49-$119
Tel: (800) 786-1689

SACRAMENTO

AAA RESIDENCE INN
3721 Watt Ave
(95821)
Rates: $46
Tel: (916) 485-7125
(800) 786-4926

AMERICANA LODGE
818 15th St (95814)
Rates: $35-$45
Tel: (916) 444-8085
(800) 645-7318

BEST WESTERN JOHN JAY INN
15 Massie Ct (95823)
Rates: $53-$90
Tel: (916) 689-4425
(800) 528-1234

BEVERLY GARLAND HOTEL & CONFERENCE CENTER
1780 Tribute Rd (95815)
Rates: $74-$145
Tel: (916) 929-7900
(800) 972-3976

CANTERBURY INN
1900 Canterbury Rd (95815)
Rates: $55-$65
Tel: (916) 927-3492
(800) 932-3492

CLARION HOTEL
700 16th St (95814)
Rates $79-$109
Tel: (916) 444-8000
(800) 443-0880

CORAL REEF LODGE
2700 Fulton Ave (95814)
Rates: $45-$80
Tel: (916) 483-6461
(800) 995-6460

CROSSROADS INN
221 Jibboom St (95814)
Rates: $38-$60
Tel: (916) 442-7777

DAYS INN DISCOVERY PARK
350 Bercut Dr (95814)
Rates: $54-$73
Tel: (916) 442-6971
(800) 329-7746
(800) 952-5516 (CA)

ECONO LODGE
711 16th St (95814)
Rates: $40-$60
Tel: (916) 443-6631
(800) 553-2666

EXPO INN
1413 Howe Ave (95825)
Rates: $65
Tel: (916) 922-9833

GOLDEN TEE INN
3215 Auburn Blvd (95821)
Rates: $25-$40
Tel: (916) 482-7440

GUEST SUITES
2806 Grassland Dr (95833)
Rates: $45-$80
Tel: (916) 641-2617
(800) 227-4903

HILTON INN SACRAMENTO
2200 Harvard St (95815)
Rates: $99-$109
Tel: (916) 922-4700
(800) 344-4321

HOLIDAY INN CAL EXPO
1780 Tribute Rd (95815)
Rates: $69-$89
Tel: (800) 465-4329

HOLIDAY INN NORTH EAST
5321 Date Ave (95841)
Rates: $56-$74
Tel: (916) 338-5800
(800) 465-4329

HOWARD JOHNSON
3343 Bradshaw Rd (95827)
Rates: $50-$60
Tel: (916) 366-1266
(800) 446-4656

INNS OF AMERICA
25 Howe Ave (95826)
Rates: $35-$50
Tel: (916) 386-8408
(800) 826-0778

LA QUINTA INN
4604 Madison Ave (95841)
Rates: $52-$65
Tel: (916) 348-0900
(800) 531-5900

LA QUINTA INN
200 Jibboom St (95814)
Rates: $52-$68
Tel: (916) 448-8100
(800) 531-5900

MANSION VIEW LODGE
771 16th St (95814)
Rates: $36-$42
Tel: (916) 443-6631
(800) 409-9595

MOTEL ORLEANS
228 Jibboom St (95814)
Rates: $40-$62
Tel: (916) 443-4811
(800) 626-1900

MOTEL 6
7407 Elsie Ave (95828)
Rates: $32-$38
Tel: (916) 689-6555
(800) 440-6000

MOTEL 6-CENTRAL
7850 College Town Dr (95826)
Rates: $34-$40
Tel: (916) 383-8110
(800) 440-6000

MOTEL 6 DOWNTOWN
1415 30th St (95816)
Rates: $39-$45
Tel: (916) 457-0777
(800) 440-6000

MOTEL 6-NORTH
5110 Interstate Ave (95842)
Rates: $33-$39
Tel: (916) 331-8100
(800) 440-6000

MOTEL 6-OLD SACRAMENTO
227 Jibboom St (95814)
Rates: $34-$40
Tel: (916) 441-0733
(800) 440-6000

MOTEL 6-SOUTHWEST
7780 Stockton Blvd (95823)
Rates: $32-$38
Tel: (916) 689-9141
(800) 440-6000

POINT WEST APARTMENTS
1761 Heritage Ln (95815)
Rates: $80+
Tel: (916) 922-5882

RADISSON HOTEL
500 Leisure Ln (95815)
Rates: $72-$82
Tel: (916) 922-2020
(800) 333-3333

RAMADA INN
2600 Auburn Blvd (958221)
Rates: $52-$83
Tel: (916) 487-7600
(800) 272-6232

RED LION HOTEL
2001 Point West Way (95815)
Rates: $85-$145
Tel: (916) 929-8855
(800) 547-8010

RED LION'S INN
1401 Arden Way (95815)
Rates: $68-$120
Tel: (916) 922-8041
(800) 547-8010

RESIDENCE INN BY MARRIOTT
2410 W El Camino (95833)
Rates: $59-$129
Tel: (916) 649-1300
(800) 331-3131

SIERRA INN
2600 Auburn Blvd (95821)
Rates: $36-$125
Tel: (916) 482-4770
(800) 757-4377

SKY RIDERS MOTEL
6100 Freeport Blvd (95822)
Rates: $45-$80
Tel: (916) 421-5700

SUPER 8 MOTEL
7216 55th St (95823)
Rates: $40-$56
Tel: (916) 427-7925
(800) 800-8000

TRAVELODGE CAPITOL CENTER
1111 H St (95814)
Rates: $39-$79
Tel: (916) 444-8880
(800) 578-7878

VAGABOND INN-MIDTOWN
1319 30th St (95816)
Rates: $39-$49
Tel: (916) 454-4400
(800) 522-1555

SALINAS

**BEST WESTERN
JOHN JAY INN**
175 Kern St (93905)
Rates: $53-$75
Tel: (800) 528-1234

DAYS INN
1226 De La Torre
Blvd (93905)
Rates: $35-$90
Tel: (800) 329-7466

EL DORADO MOTEL
1351 N Main St
(93906)
Rates: $28-$60
Tel: (408) 449-2442
(800) 523-6506

MOTEL 6-CENTRAL
1010 Fairview Ave
(93905)
Rates: $30-$36
Tel: (408) 758-2122
(800) 440-6000

MOTEL 6-NORTH
140 Kern St (93901)
Rates: $28-$35
Tel: (408) 753-1711
(800) 440-6000

MOTEL 6-SOUTH
1275 De La Torre
Blvd (93905)
Rates: $30-$36
Tel: (408) 757-3077
(800) 440-6000

RAMADA INN
808 N Main St
(93906)
Rates: $49-$89
Tel: (800) 272-6232

**TRAVELODGE
OF SALINAS**
555 Airport Blvd
(93905)
Rates: $36-$99
Tel: (408) 424-1741
(800) 578-7878

VAGABOND INN
131 Kern St (93905)
Rates: $45-$95
Tel: (408) 758-4693
(800) 522-1555

SAMOA

**SAMOA AIRPORT
BED & BREAKFAST**
3000 New Navy
Base Rd (95501)
Rates: $60
Tel: (707) 445-0765

SAN ANDREAS

**BLACK BART INN
& MOTEL**
35 Main St (95249)
Rates: $47-$55
Tel: (209) 754-3808
(800) 225-3764

SAN BERNARDINO

**BEST WESTERN
SANDS MOTEL**
606 North H St
(92410)
Rates: $52-$60
Tel: (909) 889-8391
(800) 528-1234
(800) 331-4409 (CA)

**HILTON-SAN
BERNARDINO**
285 E Hospitality Ln
(92408)
Rates: $85-$95
Tel: (909) 889-0133
(800) 445-8667
(800) 446-1065 (CA)

LA QUINTA INN
205 E Hospitality Ln
(92408)
Rates: $52-$67
Tel: (909) 888-7571
(800) 531-5900

MOTEL 6-NORTH
1960 Ostrems Way
(92407)
Rates: $30-$34
Tel: (909) 887-8191
(800) 440-6000

MOTEL 6-SOUTH
111 Redlands Blvd
(92408)
Rates: $29-$33
Tel: (909) 825-6666
(800) 440-6000

SAN BRUNO

**SUMMERFIELD
SUITES HOTEL**
1350 Huntington
Ave (94066)
Rates: $129-$189
Tel: (800) 833-4353

SAN CLEMENTE

**HOLIDAY INN-SAN
CLEMENTE RESORT**
111 S Avenida de
Estrella (92672)
Rates: $70-$95
Tel: (714) 361-3000
(800) 465-4329

SAN DIEGO

ARENA INN
3330 Rosecrans St
(92110)
Rates: $44-$78
Tel: (619) 224-8266
(800) 742-4627

**BEST WESTERN
HANALEI HOTEL**
2270 Hotel Circle N
(92108)
Rates: $69-$109
Tel: (619) 297-1101
(800) 882-0858

DAYS INN
9350 Kearny Mesa
Dr (92126)
Rates: $40-$70
Tel: (619) 578-4350
(800) 329-7466

ECONO LODGE
445 S Hotel Circle
(92108)
Rates: $33-$78
Tel: (619) 692-1288
(800) 553-2666

**EMBASSY SUITES-
SAN DIEGO BAY**
601 Pacific Hwy
(92101)
Rates: $119-$169
Tel: (619) 239-2400
(800) 362-2779

E-Z 8 MOTEL
2484 Hotel Circle Pl
(92018)
Rates: $35-$50
Tel: (619) 291-8252
(800) 326-6835

**E-Z 8 MOTEL
OLD TOWN**
4747 Pacific Hwy
(92110)
Rates: $35-$50
Tel: (619) 294-2512
(800) 326-6835

**E-Z 8 MOTEL
SPORTS ARENA**
3325 Midway Dr
(92110)
Rates: $35-$50
Tel: (619) 223-9500
(800) 326-6835

GOOD NITE INN
4545 Waring Rd
(92120)
Rates: $35-$53
Tel: (619) 286-7000
(800) 648-3466

**GOOD NITE INN
SEA WORLD**
3880 Greenwood St
(92110)
Rates: $46-$70
Tel: (619) 543-9944
(800) 648-3466

**GROSVENOR INN
DOWNTOWN**
810 Ash St (92101)
Rates: $40-$50
Tel: (619) 233-8826
(800) 232-1212

**HOLIDAY INN
ON THE BAY**
1355 N Harbor Dr
(92101)
Rates: $68-$98
Tel: (619) 232-3861
(800) 465-4329

**THE HORTON
GRAND HOTEL**
311 Island Ave
(92101)
Rates: $99-$129
Tel: (619) 544-1886
(800) 542-1886

**HOTEL CIRCLE INN
& SUITES**
2201 S Hotel Circle
(92108)
Rates: $49-$99
Tel: (619) 291-2711
(800) 772-7711

HOWARD JOHNSON
1430 17th Ave (92101)
Rates: $55-$90
Tel: (619) 696-0911
(800) 446-4656

LAMPLIGHTER INN & SUITES
6474 El Cajon Blvd (92115)
Rates: $39-$64
Tel: (619) 582-3088
(800) 545-0778

MARRIOTT HOTEL & MARINA- SAN DIEGO
333 W Harbor Dr (92101)
Rates: $149-$179
Tel: (619) 234-1500
(800) 228-9290

MARRIOTT SUITES DOWNTOWN
701 A St (92101)
Rates: $170-$180
Tel: (619) 696-9800
(800) 962-1367

MOTEL 6 HOTEL CIRCLE
2424 N Hotel Circle (92108)
Rates: $40-$46
Tel: (619) 296-1612
(800) 440-6000

MOTEL 6-NORTH
5592 Clairemont Mesa Blvd (92117)
Rates: $37-$43
Tel: (619) 268-9758
(800) 440-6000

OLD TOWN INN
4444 Pacific Hwy (92110)
Rates: $35-$50
Tel: (619) 260-8024

OUTRIGGER MOTEL
1370 Scott St (92106)
Rates: $35-$50
Tel: (619) 223-7105

PACIFIC SANDS MOTEL & CONDOMINIUMS
4449 Ocean Blvd (92109)
Rates: $40-$60
Tel: (619) 483-7555

PACIFIC SHORES INN
4802 Mission Blvd (92109)
Rates: $58-$95
Tel: (619) 483-6300
(800) 826-0715

PARK MANOR SUITES
525 Spruce St (92103)
Rates: $69-$149
Tel: (619) 291-0999
(800) 874-2649

PICKWICK HOTEL
132 W Broadway (92101)
Rates: $35-$50
Tel: (619) 234-0141

RADISSON HOTEL- SAN DIEGO
1433 Camino Del Rio S (92108)
Rates: $79-$135
Tel: (619) 260-0111
(800) 333-3333

RED LION INN
7450 Hazard Center Dr (92108)
Rates: $130-$165
Tel: (619) 297-5466
(800) 547-8010

RESIDENCE INN
11002 Rancho Carmel Dr (92128)
Rates: n/a
Tel: (619) 673-1900
(800) 331-3131

RESIDENCE INN BY MARRIOTT
5400 Kearny Mesa Rd (92111)
Rates: $69-$175
Tel: (619) 278-2100
(800) 331-3131

SAN DIEGO HILTON BEACH & TENNIS RESORT
1775 E Mission Bay Dr (92109)
Rates: $145-$225
Tel: (619) 276-4010
(800) 445-8667

SAN DIEGO MARRIOTT MISSION VALLEY
8757 Rio San Diego Dr (92108)
Rates: $99-$149
Tel: (619) 692-3800
(800) 228-9290

SAN DIEGO MISSION VALLEY HILTON
901 Camino Del Rio S (92108)
Rates: $109-$179
Tel: (619) 543-9000
(800) 445-8667
(800) 733-2332 (CA)

SAN DIEGO PRINCESS RESORT
1404 W Vacation Rd (92109)
Rates: $130-$345
Tel: (619) 274-4630
(800) 344-2626

SHERATON INN SAN DIEGO CENTRAL
8110 Aero Dr (92123)
Rates: $89-$122
Tel: (619) 277-8888
(800) 325-3535

SOUTH BAY LODGE
1101 Hollister St (92154)
Rates: $27-$47
Tel: (619) 428-7600

SUPER 8 MISSION BAY
4540 Mission Bay Dr (92109)
Rates: $45-$58
Tel: (619) 274-7888
(800) 800-8000

U.S. GRANT HOTEL
326 Broadway (92101)
Rates: $135-$195
Tel: (619) 232-3121
(800) 237-5029

VAGABOND INN BY THE BAY
1655 Pacific Hwy (92101)
Rates: $38-$67
Tel: (619) 232-6391
(800) 522-1555

VAGABOND INN MISSION VALLEY
625 S Hotel Circle (92108)
Rates: $50-$73
Tel: (619) 297-1691
(800) 522-1555

VAGABOND INN POINT LOMA
1325 Scott St (92106)
Rates: $47-$70
Tel: (619) 224-3371
(800) 522-1555

VAGABOND INN UNIVERSITY
6440 El Cajon Blvd (92115)
Rates: $38-$53
Tel: (619) 286-2040
(800) 522-1555

WAYFARER'S INN
3275 Rosecrans St (92110)
Rates: $32-$60
Tel: (619) 224-2411
(800) 266-2411

SAN DIMAS

MOTEL 6
502 W Arrow Hwy (91773)
Rates: $30-$34
Tel: (909) 592-5631
(800) 440-6000

RED ROOF INN
204 N Village Ct (91773)
Rates: $65-$85
Tel: (909) 599-2362
(800) 843-7663

SAN FRANCISCO

ALEXANDER INN
415 O'Farrell St (94102)
Rates: $48-$84
Tel: (415) 928-6800
(800) 843-8709

BERESFORD ARMS
701 Post St (94109)
Rates: $89-$150
Tel: (415) 673-2600
(800) 533-6533

BERESFORD HOTEL
635 Sutter St (94102)
Rates: $89-$114
Tel: (415) 673-9900
(800) 533-6533

**BEST WESTERN
CIVIC CENTER
MOTOR INN**
364 9th St (94103)
Rates: $65-$115
Tel: (415) 621-2826
(800) 528-1234

**CAMPTON PLACE
HOTEL**
340 Stockton St
(94108)
Rates: $185-$320
Tel: (415) 781-5555
(800) 235-4300

CHANCELLOR HOTEL
433 Powell St (94102)
Rates: $69-$250
Tel: (415) 362-2004
(800) 428-4748

EXECUTIVE SUITES
One St Francis Pl
(94107)
Rates: $125-$189
Tel: (415) 495-5151

**GRAND HERITAGE
HOTEL**
495 Geary St (94102)
Rates: $215-$360
Tel: (415) 775-4700
(800) 437-4824

**GROSVENOR
HOUSE**
899 Pine St (94108)
Rates: $99-$169
Tel: (415) 421-1899
(800) 999-9189

**HAUS KLEEBAUER
BED & BREAKFAST**
225 Clipper (Noe
Valley 94114)
Rates: $65-$85
Tel: (415) 821-3866

**HOLIDAY INN
FINANCIAL
DISTRICT**
750 Kearny St
(94108)
Rates: $125-$170
Tel: (415) 433-6600
(800) 465-4329

**HOLIDAY LODGE &
GARDEN HOTEL**
1901 Van Ness Ave
(94109)
Rates: $89-$139
Tel: (800) 738-7477

**HOTEL BERESFORD
MANOR**
860 Sutter St (94102)
Rates: $60-$70
Tel: (415) 673-3330
(800) 533-6533

HOTEL NIKKO
222 Mason St (94102)
Rates: $225-$1300
Tel: (415) 394-1111
(800) 645-5687

**THE INN SAN
FRANCISCO B & B**
943 Van Ness Ave
(94110)
Rates: $75-$195
Tel: (415) 641-0188
(800) 359-0913

THE JULIANA HOTEL
590 Bush St (94108)
Rates: $125-$185
Tel: (415) 392-2540
(800) 328-3880

**LAUREL
MOTOR INN**
444 Presidio Ave
(94115)
Rates: $75-$99
Tel: (415) 567-8467
(800) 928-1866

**THE MANSIONS
HOTEL**
2220 Sacramento St
(94115)
Rates: $114-$350
Tel: (415) 929-9444
(800) 826-9398

**MARRIOTT-FISHER-
MAN'S WHARF**
1250 Columbus Ave
(94133)
Rates: $148-$450
Tel: (415) 775-7555
(800) 228-9290

**MARRIOTT
SAN FRANCISCO**
55 Fourth St (94103)
Rates: $140-$185
Tel: (415) 896-1600
(800) 228-9290

**OCEAN PARK
MOTEL**
2690 46th Ave
(94116)
Rates: $53-$65
Tel: (415) 566-7020

**PACIFIC HEIGHTS
INN**
1555 Union St
(94123)
Rates: $65-$105
Tel: (415) 776-3310
(800) 523-1801

**THE PAN PACIFIC
HOTEL**
500 Post St (94102)
Rates: $185-$350
Tel: (415) 771-8600
(800) 327-8585

**THE PHILLIPS
HOTEL**
205 Ninth St (94109)
Rates: $23-$35
Tel: (415) 863-7652

THE PHOENIX INN
601 Eddy St (94109)
Rates: $79-$99
Tel: (415) 776-1380
(800) 248-9466

**RENAISSANCE
STANFORD COURT-
NOB HILL**
905 California St
(94108)
Rates: $205-$2000
Tel: (800) 227-4736

**RODEWAY INN
BY THE BAY**
1450 Lombard St
(94123)
Rates: $49-$125
Tel: (415) 673-0691
(800) 424-4777

**SAN FRANCISCO
AIRPORT HILTON**
P. O. Box 8355,
San Francisco
International Airport
(94128)
Rates: $139-$175
Tel: (415) 589-0770
(800) 445-8667

SHEEHAN HOTEL
620 Sutter St (94102)
Rates: $40-$99
Tel: (415) 775-6500
(800) 848-1529

THE STEINHART
952 Sutter St (94109)
Rates: $70-$135
Tel: (415) 928-3855

TRAVELODGE
1450 Lombard St
(94123)
Rates: $55-135
Tel: (415) 673-0691
(800) 578-7878

**THE WESTIN
ST. FRANCIS**
335 Powell St (94102)
Rates: $195-$345
Tel: (415) 397-7000
(800) 228-3000

SAN GABRIEL

QUALITY INN
1114 E Las Tunas Dr
(91776)
Rates: $50-$110
Tel: (818) 285-0921
(800) 221-2222

SAN JACINTO

CROWN MOTEL
138 S Ramona Blvd
(92583)
Rates: $36-$54
Tel: (909) 654-7133

SAN JOSE

**AIRPORT INN
INTERNATIONAL**
1355 N 4th St (95112)
Rates: $49-$64
Tel: (408) 453-5340

**BEST WESTERN
GATEWAY INN**
2585 Seaboard Ave
(95131)
Rates: $59-$79
Tel: (408) 435-8800
(800) 528-1234

**BEST WESTERN
SAN JOSE LODGE**
1440 N First St
(95112)
Rates: $56-$68
Tel: (408) 453-7750
(800) 528-1234

COMFORT INN AIRPORT
1310 N First St
(95112)
Rates: $65
Tel: (408) 453-1100
(800) 221-2222

EXECUTIVE INN SUITES
3930 Monterey Rd
(94111)
Rates: $65
Tel: (408) 281-8700

FRIENDSHIP INN
2188 The Alameda
(95126)
Rates: $35-$45
Tel: (408) 248-8300
(800) 424-4777

HOLIDAY INN PARK CENTER PLAZA
282 Almaden Blvd
(95113)
Rates: $72-$89
Tel: (408) 998-0400
(800) 465-4329

HOMEWOOD SUITES
10 W Trimble Rd
(95131)
Rates: $144-$189
Tel: (408) 428-9900
(800) 225-5466

MOTEL 6-SOUTH
2560 Fontaine Rd
(95121)
Rates: $40-$46
Tel: (408) 270-3131
(800) 440-6000

MOTEL 6-AIRPORT
2081 N First St
(95131)
Rates: $44-$50
Tel: (408) 436-8180
(800) 440-6000

RED LION HOTEL
2050 Gateway Pl
(95110)
Rates: $135-$600
Tel: (408) 453-4000
(800) 547-8010

SAN JOSE HILTON & TOWERS
300 Almaden Blvd
(95110)
Rates: $80-$600
Tel: (408) 287-2100
(800) 445-8667

SUMMERFIELD SUITES
1602 Crane Ct
(95122)
Rates: $119-$149
Tel: (408) 436-1600
(800) 833-4353

VAGABOND INN
1488 N First St
(95112)
Rates: $54-$64
Tel: (408) 453-8822
(800) 522-1555

SAN JUAN BAUTISTA

SAN JUAN INN
410 The Alameda
(95045)
Rates: $42-$60
Tel: (408) 623-4380

SAN JUAN CAPISTRANO

BEST WESTERN INN
27174 Ortega Hwy
(92675)
Rates: $63-$120
Tel: (714) 493-5661
(800) 441-9438

SAN LEANDRO

ISLANDER LODGE MOTEL
2398 E 14th St
(94577)
Rates: $33-$45
Tel: (510) 352-5010

SAN LUIS OBISPO

AVILA HOT SPRINGS SPA
250 Avila Beach Dr
(93405)
Rates: $35+
Tel: (805) 595-2359
(800) 332-2359

BEST WESTERN OLIVE TREE INN
1000 Olive St (93405)
Rates: $49-$185
Tel: (805) 544-2800
(800) 528-1234

BEST WESTERN ROYAL OAK MOTOR HOTEL
214 Madonna Rd
(93405)
Rates: $45-$95
Tel: (805) 544-4410
(800) 528-1234

BEST WESTERN SOMERSET MANOR
1895 Monterey St
(93401)
Rates: $38-$72
Tel: (805) 544-0973
(800) 528-1234

CAMPUS MOTEL
404 Santa Rosa St
(93405)
Rates: $44-$89
Tel: (805) 544-0881
(800) 447-8080

DAYS INN
2050 Garfield St
(93401)
Rates: $42-$135
Tel: (805) 549-9911
(800) 329-7466

HERITAGE INN BED & BREAKFAST
978 Olive St (93405)
Rates: $65-$150
Tel: (805) 544-7440

HOWARD JOHNSON
1585 Calle Joaquin
(93405)
Rates: $69-$109
Tel: (805) 544-5300
(800) 446-4656

MOTEL 6-NORTH
1433 Calle Joaquin
(93401)
Rates: $32-$38
Tel: (805) 549-9595
(800) 440-6000

MOTEL 6-SOUTH
1625 Calle Joaquin
(93401)
Rates: $32-$38
Tel: (805) 541-6992
(800) 440-6000

SANDS MOTEL & SUITES
1930 Monterey St
(93401)
Rates: $54-$109
Tel: (805) 544-0500
(800) 441-4657

TRAVELODGE
1825 Monterey St
(93401)
Rates: $39-$99
Tel: (805) 543-5110
(800) 578-7878

TRAVELODGE SOUTH
950 Olive St (93405)
Rates: $40-$115
Tel: (805) 544-8886
(800) 578-7878

VAGABOND INN
210 Madonna Rd
(93401)
Rates: $48-$74
Tel: (805) 544-4710
(800) 522-1555

SAN MARCOS

QUAILS INN LAKE SAN MARCOS RESORT
1025 La Bonita Dr
(92069)
Rates: $85-$225
Tel: (619) 744-0120
(800) 447-6556

SAN MATEO

BEST WESTERN LOS PRADOS
2940 S Norfolk St
(94403)
Rates: $81-$109
Tel: (415) 341-3300
(800) 528-1234

DUNFEY SAN MATEO HOTEL
1770 S Amphlett Blvd (94402)
Rates: $59-$89
Tel: (415) 573-7661

HOLIDAY INN SAN MATEO
330 N Bayshore Blvd (94401)
Rates: $79-$200
Tel: (800) 465-4329

HOWARD JOHNSON
2110 S El Camino Real (94403)
Rates: $65-$95
Tel: (415) 341-9231
(800) 446-4656

RESIDENCE INN BY MARRIOTT
2000 Winward Way (94404)
Rates: $129-$155
Tel: (800) 331-3131

VILLA HOTEL AIRPORT
4000 S El Camino Real (94403)
Rates: $56-$149
Tel: (415) 341-0966
(800) 341-2345

SAN MIGUEL

SAN MIGUEL MISSION INN
P. O. Box 58 (93451)
Rates: $30-$45
Tel: (805) 467-3674

SAN PEDRO

SHERATON L A HARBOR
601 S Palos Verdes St (90731)
Rates: $95-$695
Tel: (310) 519-8200
(800) 325-3535

VAGABOND INN
215 S Gaffey St (90731)
Rates: $50-$60
Tel: (310) 831-8911
(800) 522-1555

SAN RAFAEL

CASA SOLDAVINI GUESTHOUSE
531 C St (94901)
Rates: n/a
Tel: (415) 454-3140

VILLA INN
1600 Lincoln Ave (94901)
Rates: $62-$85
Tel: (415) 456-4975
(800) 228-2000

WYNDHAM GARDEN HOTEL-MARIN/ SAN RAFAEL
1010 Northgate Dr (94903)
Rates: $79-$109
Tel: (415) 479-8800
(800) 996-3426

SAN RAMON

RESIDENCE INN BY MARRIOTT
1071 Market Pl (94583)
Rates: $69-$179
Tel: (510) 277-9292
(800) 331-3131

SAN RAMON MARRIOTT AT BISHOP RANCH
2600 Bishop Dr (94583)
Rates: $72-$125
Tel: (800) 228-9290

SAN SIMEON

BEST WESTERN CAVALIER INN
9415 Hearst Dr (93452)
Rates: $62-$154
Tel: (805) 927-4688
(800) 826-8168

BEST WESTERN COURTESY INN
9450 Castillo Dr (93452)
Rates: $50-$125
Tel: (805) 927-4691
(800) 528-1234

MOTEL 6
9070 Castillo Dr (93452)
Rates: $40-$46
Tel: (805) 927-8691
(800) 440-6000

RAGGED POINT INN
Hwy 1 (93452)
Rates: $40-$120
Tel: (805) 927-4502

SILVER SURF MOTEL
9390 Castillo Dr (93452)
Rates: $39-$99
Tel: (805) 927-4661
(800) 621-3999

SAN YSIDRO

ECONOMY INNS OF AMERICA
230 Via de San Ysidro (92173)
Rates: $25-$40
Tel: (800) 826-0778

INTERNATIONAL MOTOR INN
190 E Calle Primera (92173)
Rates: $39-$42
Tel: (619) 428-4486

MOTEL 6
160 E Calle Primera (92173)
Rates: $27-$33
Tel: (619) 690-6663
(800) 440-6000

SANTA ANA

CROWN STERLING SUITES
1325 E Dyer Rd (92705)
Rates: $79-$99
Tel: (800) 433-4600

HOLIDAY INN EXPRESS
1600 E First St (92701)
Rates: $55-$75
Tel: (714) 835-3051
(800) 959-4654

HOWARD JOHNSON MOTOR LODGE
939 E 17th St (92701)
Rates: $55-$75
Tel: (714) 558-3700
(800) 654-8778

MOTEL 6
1623 E First St (92701)
Rates: $32-$38
Tel: (714) 558-0500
(800) 440-6000

RADISSON HOTEL
2720 Hotel Terrace Dr (92705)
Rates: $85-$105
Tel: (714) 556-3838
(800) 333-3333

RED ROOF INN
2600 N Main St (92701)
Rates: n/a
Tel: (714) 542-0311
(800) 843-7663

TRAVELODGE-ORANGE COUNTY AIRPORT
1400 SE Bristol St (92707)
Rates: $43-$47
Tel: (714) 557-8700
(800) 578-7878

SANTA BARBARA

ALPINE MOTEL
2824 State St (93105)
Rates: $75
Tel: (805) 687-2821

BAYBERRY INN BED & BREAKFAST
111 W Valerio St (93101)
Rates: $85-$135
Tel: (805) 682-3199
(800) 528-9691

BEACH HOUSE INN
320 W Yanonali St
(93101)
Rates: $75-$125
Tel: (805) 966-1126

BLUE SANDS MOTEL
421 S Milpas (93103)
Rates: $75
Tel: (805) 965-1624

CASA DEL MAR INN
18 Bath St (93101)
Rates: $59-$194
Tel: (805) 963-4418
(800) 433-3097

EAST BEACH LODGE
1029 Orilla Del Mar St (93103)
Rates: $75-$125
Tel: (805) 965-0546

FESS PARKER'S RED LION RESORT
633 E Cabrillo Blvd (93103)
Rates: $195-$295
Tel: (805) 564-4333
(800) 879-2929

FOUR SEASONS BILTMORE HOTEL
1260 Channel Dr (93108)
Rates: $290-$595
Tel: (805) 969-2261
(800) 332-3442

HOTEL STATE STREET
121 State St (93101)
Rates: $75
Tel: (805) 966-6586

IVANHOE INN B & B
1406 Castillo St (93101)
Rates: $95-$195
Tel: (805) 963-8832

LA PLAYA INN
212 W Cabrillo Blvd (93102)
Rates: $45-$150
Tel: (805) 962-6436

MOTEL 6
443 Corona Del Mar (93103)
Rates: $47-$53
Tel: (805) 564-1392
(800) 440-6000

MOTEL 6
3505 State St (93105)
Rates: $47-$53
Tel: (805) 687-5400
(800) 440-6000

OCEAN PALMS RESORT HOTEL
232 W Cabrillo Blvd (93101)
Rates: $75-$125
Tel: (805) 966-9133

PACIFICA SUITES
5490 Hollister Ave (93111)
Rates: $120-$180
Tel: (805) 683-6722
(800) 338-6722

PLAZA INN
3885 State St (93105)
Rates: $75
Tel: (805) 687-3217

SAHARA MOTEL
2800 State St (93105)
Rates: $75-$125
Tel: (805) 687-2500

SANDY BEACH INN
122 W Cabrillo Blvd (93102)
Rates: $55-$150
Tel: (805) 963-0405
(800) 662-1451

TRAVELER'S MOTEL
3222 State St (93105)
Rates: $75-$125
Tel: (805) 687-6009

SANTA CLARA

BUDGET INN
2499 El Camino Real (95051)
Rates: $44-$52
Tel: (408) 244-9610

DAYS INN
4200 Great America Pkwy (95054)
Rates: $59-$89
Tel: (408) 980-1525
(800) 329-7466

DAYS INN SANTA CLARA
859 El Camino Real (95050)
Rates: $59-$89
Tel: (408) 255-2840
(800) 329-7466

ECONO LODGE SILICON VALLEY
2930 El Camino Real (95051)
Rates: $62-$134
Tel: (408) 241-3010
(800) 424-4777

HOWARD JOHNSON LODGE
5405 Stevens Creek Blvd (95051)
Rates: $75-$120
Tel: (408) 257-8600
(800) 446-4656

MARRIOTT HOTEL
2700 Mission College Blvd (95054)
Rates: $69-$400
Tel: (408) 988-1500
(800) 228-9290

MOTEL 6
3208 El Camino Real (95051)
Rates: $38-$48
Tel: (408) 241-0200
(800) 440-6000

VAGABOND INN
3580 El Camino Real (95051)
Rates: $44-$55
Tel: (408) 241-0771
(800) 522-1555

THE WESTIN HOTEL SANTA CLARA
5101 Great America Pkwy (95054)
Rates: $199-$234
Tel: (408) 986-0700
(800) 228-3000

SANTA CLARITA

BEST WESTERN RANCH HOUSE INN
27143 N Tourney Rd (91355)
Rates: $70-$100
Tel: (800) 528-1234

HAMPTON INN MAGIC MOUNTAIN
25259 The Old Rd (91381)
Rates: $74-$89
Tel: (805) 253-2400
(800) 426-7866

RESIDENCE INN
25320 The Old Rd (91381)
Rates: n/a
Tel: (805) 290-2800
(800) 331-3131

SANTA CRUZ

CANDLELITE INN
1101 Ocean St (95060)
Rates: $35-$140
Tel: (408) 427-1616

EDGEWATER BEACH MOTEL
525 Second St (95060)
Rates: $48-$100
Tel: (408) 423-0440

HOLIDAY INN EXPRESS
600 Riverside Ave (95060)
Rates: $45-$175
Tel: (408) 458-9660
(800) 465-4329

THE INN AT PASATIEMPO
555 Hwy 17 (95060)
Rates: $74-$175
Tel: (408) 423-5000
(800) 834-2546

MISSION INN
2250 Mission St (95060)
Rates: $110
Tel: (408) 425-5455

MOTEL CONTINENTAL
414 Ocean St (95060)
Rates: $38-$98
Tel: (408) 429-1221

OCEAN FRONT HOUSE
1600 W Cliff Dr (95060)
Rates: $850-$1320 /weekly
Tel: (408) 266-4453
(800) 801-4453

OCEAN PACIFIC LODGE
120 Washington (95060)
Rates: $55-$185
Tel: (408) 457-1234
(800) 995-0289

PACIFIC INN
330 Ocean St (95060)
Rates: $38-$98
Tel: (408) 425-3722

SANTA CRUZ INN
2950 Soquel Ave (95062)
Rates: $32-$85
Tel: (408) 475-6322

SUNNY COVE MOTEL
2-1610 E Cliff Dr (95062)
Rates: $40-$95
Tel: (408) 475-1741

SUNSET INN
2424 Mission St (95060)
Rates: $40-$95
Tel: (408) 423-3471

TERRACE COURT MOTEL
125 Beach St (95060)
Rates: $62-$105
Tel: (408) 423-3031

TRAVELODGE RIVIERA MOTEL
619 Riverside Ave (95060)
Rates: $34-$129
Tel: (408) 423-9515
(800) 578-7878

SANTA FE SPRINGS

DYNASTY SUITES
13530 E Firestone Blvd (90670)
Rates: $35-$40
Tel: (310) 921-8571
(800) 842-7899

MOTEL 6
13412 Excelsior Dr (90670)
Rates: $30-$34
Tel: (310) 921-0596
(800) 440-6000

SANTA MARIA

BEST WESTERN BIG AMERICA
1725 N Bway (93454)
Rates: $55-$90
Tel: (805) 922-5200
(800) 426-3213

HOWARD JOHNSON LODGE
210 S Nicholson Ave (93454)
Rates: $39-$64
Tel: (805) 922-5891
(800) 446-4656

HUNTER'S INN
1514 S Bway (93454)
Rates: $49-$95
Tel: (805) 922-2123
(800) 950-2123

MOTEL 6-NORTH
2040 N Preisker Ln (93454)
Rates: $30-$34
Tel: (805) 928-8111
(800) 440-6000

MOTEL 6-SOUTH
839 E Main St (93454)
Rates: $26-$32
Tel: (805) 925-2551
(800) 440-6000

RAMADA SUITES
2050 N Preisker Ln (93454)
Rates: $60-$139
Tel: (805) 928-6000
(800) 272-6232

ROSE GARDEN INN
1007 E Main St (93454)
Rates: $49-$79
Tel: (805) 922-4505

SANTA MONICA

THE GEORGIAN
1415 Ocean Ave (90401)
Rates: $125
Tel: (310) 395-9945

LOEWS SANTA MONICA BEACH HOTEL
1700 Ocean Ave (90401)
Rates: $195-$450
Tel: (310) 458-6700
(800) 223-0888

SANTA NELLA

BEST WESTERN ANDERSEN'S INN
12367 S Hwy 33 (95322)
Rates: $55-$65
Tel: (209) 826-5534
(800) 527-5534

HOLIDAY INN MISSION DE ORO
13070 S Hwy 33 (95322)
Rates: $45-$72
Tel: (209) 826-5555
(800) 465-4329

MOTEL 6
12733 S Hwy 33 (95322)
Rates: $33-$39
Tel: (209) 826-6644
(800) 440-6000

RAMADA INN
13070 S Hwy 33 (95322)
Rates: $40-$80
Tel: (209) 826-4444
(800) 272-6232

SUPER 8 MOTEL
28821 W Gonzaga Rd (95322)
Rates: $40-$56
Tel: (209) 827-8700
(800) 800-8000

SANTA PAULA

TRAVELODGE
350 S Peck Rd (93060)
Rates: $46-$62
Tel: (805) 525-1561
(800) 578-7878

SANTA ROSA

BEST WESTERN GARDEN INN
1500 Santa Rosa Ave (95404)
Rates: $52-$81
Tel: (707) 546-4031
(800) 528-1234

BEST WESTERN HILLSIDE INN
2901 4th St (95409)
Rates: $44-$54
Tel: (707) 546-9353
(800) 528-1234

ECONO LODGE
1800 Santa Rosa Ave (95407)
Rates: $36-$66
Tel: (800) 424-4777

HERITAGE INN
870 Hopper Ave (95403)
Rates: $47-$68
Tel: (707) 545-9000

LOS ROBLES LODGE
1985 Cleveland Ave (95401)
Rates: $65-$95
Tel: (707) 545-6330
(800) 255-6330

MOTEL 6-NORTH
3145 Cleveland Ave (95403)
Rates: $32-$38
Tel: (707) 525-9010
(800) 440-6000

MOTEL 6-SOUTH
2760 Cleveland Ave (95403)
Rates: $35-$41
Tel: (707) 546-1500
(800) 440-6000

RAMADA LIMITED
866 Hopper Ave (95403)
Rates: $49-$95
Tel: (707) 575-0945
(800) 272-6232

TRAVELODGE
1815 Santa Rosa Ave
(95407)
Rates: $48-$65
Tel: (707) 542-3472
(800) 578-7878

TRAVELODGE-DOWNTOWN
635 Healdsburg Ave
(95401)
Rates: $45-$70
Tel: (707) 544-4141
(800) 578-7878

SANTA YNEZ

SANTA COTA MOTEL
3099 Mission Dr
(93460)
Rates: $75-$125
Tel: (805) 688-5525

SANTA YSABEL

APPLE TREE INN
4360 Hwy 78 (92070)
Rates: $45-$79
Tel: (619) 765-0222

SANTEE

CARLTON OAKS COUNTRY CLUB
9200 Inwood Dr
(92071)
Rates: $40-$75
Tel: (619) 448-4242

SCOTTS VALLEY

BEST WESTERN INN SCOTTS VALLEY
6020 Scotts Valley Dr
(95066)
Rates: $65-$85
Tel: (408) 438-6666
(800) 528-1234

SEAL BEACH

RADISSON INN SEAL BEACH
600 Marina Dr
(90740)
Rates: $89-$109
Tel: (310) 493-7501
(800) 333-3333

SEASIDE

BAY BREEZE INN
2049 Fremont Blvd
(93955)
Rates: $33-$102
Tel: (408) 899-7111

DAYS INN
1400 Del Monte Blvd
(93955)
Rates: $69-$109
Tel: (408) 394-5335
(800) 329-7466

SEASIDE MOTEL
81131 Fremont Blvd
(93955)
Rates: $50-$95
Tel: (408) 394-8881

THUNDERBIRD MOTEL
1933 Fremont Blvd
(93955)
Rates: $29-$95
Tel: (408) 394-6797
(800) 848-7841

SELMA

BEST WESTERN JOHN JAY INN
2799 Floral Ave
(93662)
Rates: $45-$55
Tel: (209) 891-0300
(800) 528-1234

SUPER 8 MOTEL
3142 S Highland Ave
(93662)
Rates: $44-$48
Tel: (800) 800-8000

SEPULVEDA

COMFORT INN
8657 Sepulveda Blvd
(91343)
Rates: $35-$65
Tel: (800) 221-2222

MOTEL 6
15711 Roscoe Blvd
(91343)
Rates: $33-$39
Tel: (818) 894-9341
(800) 440-6000

SEQUOIA/KINGS CANYON NATL PARKS

GRANT GROVE LODGE
SR 180 (93633)
Rates: $33-$90
Tel: (209) 561-3314

SHASTA LAKE

BRIDGE BAY RESORT
10300 Bridge Bay Rd
(Redding 96003)
Rates: $55-$150
Tel: (916) 241-6464
(800) 752-9669

SHELL BEACH

THE CLIFFS AT SHELL BEACH
2757 Shell Beach Rd
(93449)
Rates: $70+
Tel: (805) 773-5000
(800) 826-7827

SPYGLASS INN
2705 Spyglass Dr
(93449)
Rates: $64-$124
Tel: (805) 773-4855
(800) 824-2612 (CA)

SHELTER COVE

MARINA MOTEL
533 Machi Rd
(95589)
Rates: $52-$62
Tel: (707) 986-7595

SHELTER COVE MOTOR INN
205 Wave Dr (95589)
Rates: $63-$78
Tel: (707) 986-7521

SIERRA CITY

HERRINGTON'S SIERRA PINES
SR 49 (96125)
Rates: $55-$75
Tel: (916) 862-1151

SIMI VALLEY

MOTEL 6
2566 N Erringer Rd
(93065)
Rates: $36-$42
Tel: (805) 526-3533
(800) 440-6000

RADISSON HOTEL SIMI VALLEY
999 Enchanted Way
(93065)
Rates: $69-$109
Tel: (805) 583-2000
(800) 333-3333

SMITH RIVER

BEST WESTERN SHIP ASHORE RESORT
12370 Hwy 101 N
(95567)
Rates: $44-$83
Tel: (707) 487-3141
(800) 528-1234

CASA RUBIO BEACH HOUSE
17285 Crissey Rd
(95567)
Rates: $78-$88
Tel: (800) 357-6199

SEA ESCAPE MOTEL
15370 Hwy 101 N
(95567)
Rates: $40-$60
Tel: (707) 487-7333

SOLEDAD

MOTEL 8-SOLEDAD
1013 S Front St
(93960)
Rates: $39-$64
Tel: (408) 678-3814

PARAISO HOT SPRINGS LODGE
Paraiso Springs Rd
(93960)
Rates: $110-$160
Tel: (408) 678-2882

SOLVANG

BEST WESTERN KRONBORG INN
1440 Mission Dr (93463)
Rates: $65-$90
Tel: (805) 688-2383
(800) 528-1234

ECONO LODGE
630 Ave of Flags (93427)
Rates: $40-$70
Tel: (805) 688-0022
(800) 424-4777

HAMLET MOTEL
1532 Mission Dr (93463)
Rates: $35-$95
Tel: (805) 688-4413
(800) 253-5033

MEADOWLARK MOTEL
2644 Mission Dr (93463)
Rates: $40-$70
Tel: (805) 688-4631
(800) 549-4658

VIKING MOTEL
1506 Mission Dr (93463)
Rates: $32-$85
Tel: (805) 688-1337
(800) 368-5611

SOMES BAR

MARBLE MOUNTAIN RANCH CABINS
92520 Hwy 96 (95568)
Rates: $27-$200
Tel: (800) 552-6284

SONOMA

BEST WESTERN SONOMA VALLEY INN
550 2nd St W (95476)
Rates: $75-$179
Tel: (707) 938-9200
(800) 334-5784

MARTHA'S COTTAGE B & B
19377 Orange Ave (95476)
Rates: $110-$125
Tel: (707) 996-6918

SPARROW'S NEST INN B & B
425 Denmark St (95476)
Rates: $85-$105
Tel: (707) 996-3750

STONE GROVE BED & BREAKFAST
240 2nd St E (95476)
Rates: $65-$115
Tel: (707) 939-8249

TREE HOUSE B & B
431 2nd St E (95476)
Rates: $125-$150
Tel: (707) 938-1628

VILLA CASTILLO BED & BREAKFAST
1100 Castle Rd (95476)
Rates: $150
Tel: (707) 996-4616

SONORA

ALADDIN MOTOR INN
14260 Mono Way (95370)
Rates: $49-$67
Tel: (209) 533-4971

BEST WESTERN SONORA OAKS MOTOR HOTEL
19551 Hess Ave (95370)
Rates: $56-$80
Tel: (209) 553-4400
(800) 528-1234

KENNEDY MEADOWS RESORT CABINS
P. O. Box 4010 (95370)
Rates: $52-$105
Tel: (209) 965-3900

MINERS MOTEL
18740 Hwy 108 (95370)
Rates: $40-$75
Tel: (209) 532-7850
(800) 451-4176 (CA)

RAIL FENCE MOTEL
19950 Hwy 108 (95370)
Rates: $35-$47
Tel: (209) 532-9191

SONORA INN HOTEL
160 S Washington St (95370)
Rates: $49-$59
Tel: (209) 532-7468

SOUTH EL MONTE

RAMADA SUITES
1089 Santa Anita Ave (91733)
Rates: $79-$107
Tel: (818) 350-9588
(800) 272-6232

SOUTH LAKE TAHOE
(Also see Lake Tahoe Area)

ALDER INN
1072 Ski Run Blvd (96150)
Rates: $42-$95
Tel: (916) 544-4485
(800) 544-0056

BEACHSIDE INN & SUITES
930 Park Ave (96150)
Rates: $30-$125
Tel: (916) 544-2400
(800) 884-4920

BEST WESTERN LAKE TAHOE INN
4110 Lake Tahoe Blvd (96150)
Rates: $65-$165
Tel: (916) 541-2010
(800) 528-1234

BLUE JAY LODGE
4133 Cedar Ave (96150)
Rates: $39-$99
Tel: (916) 544-5232
(800) 258-3529

BLUE LAKE MOTEL
1055 Ski Run Blvd (96150)
Rates: $50-$80
Tel: (916) 541-2399

CARNEY'S CABINS
P. O. Box 601748 (96153)
Rates: $70-$100
Tel: (916) 542-3361

DAYS INN-STATELINE/SOUTH LAKE TAHOE
968 Park Ave (96150)
Rates: $49-$120
Tel: (916) 541-4800
(800) 329-7466

ECHO CREEK RANCH
P. O. Box 20088 (96151)
Rates: $101+
Tel: (916) 544-5397
(800) 462-5397

EMBASSY SUITES RESORT
4130 Lake Tahoe Blvd (96150)
Rates: $139-$500
Tel: (916) 544-5400
(800) 362-2779

HEAVENLY VALLEY MOTEL & SPA
1261 Ski Run Blvd (96150)
Rates: $101+
Tel: (916) 544-4244
(800) 692-2246

HIGH COUNTRY LODGE
1227 Emerald Bay Rd (96150)
Rates: $30-$70
Tel: (916) 541-0508

LA BAER INN
4133 Lake Tahoe Blvd (96150)
Rates: $40-$53
Tel: (916) 544-2139
(800) 544-5575

LAKEPARK LODGE
4081 Cedar Ave (96150)
Rates: $40-$65
Tel: (916) 541-5004

LAMPLITER MOTEL
4143 Cedar Ave (96150)
Rates: $45-$70
Tel: (916) 544-2936

MATTERHORN MOTEL
2187 Lake Tahoe Blvd (96150)
Rates: $39-$150
Tel: (916) 541-0367

MOTEL 6
2375 Lake Tahoe
Blvd (96150)
Rates: $30-$42
Tel: (916) 542-1400
(800) 440-6000

THE MONTGOMERY INN
966 Modesto Ave
(96150)
Rates: $49-$69
Tel: (916) 544-3871
(800) 624-8224

PARK AVENUE/ MEADOWOOD LODGE
904 Park Ave (96150)
Rates: $70-$100
Tel: (916) 544-3503

RAVEN WOOD HOTEL
4075 Manzanita Ave
(96150)
Rates: $52-$169
Tel: (800) 659-4185

RED CARPET INN
4100 Lake Tahoe
Blvd (96150)
Rates: $40-$70
Tel: (916) 544-2261
(800) 851-7952

RIVIERA INN
890 Stateline Ave
(96150)
Rates: $40-$70
Tel: (916) 544-3448
(800) 358-2463

RODEWAY INN
4082 Lake Tahoe
Blvd (96150)
Rates: $39-$79
Tel: (916) 541-7900
(800) 424-4777

SAFARI MOTEL
966 LaSalle St
(96150)
Rates: $70-$100
Tel: (916) 544-2912

SIERRA-CAL LODGE
3838 Lake Tahoe
Blvd (96150)
Rates: $70-$100
Tel: (916) 541-5400
(800) 245-6343

SLEEPY RACCOON MOTEL
1180 Ski Run Blvd
(96150)
Rates: $40-$70
Tel: (916) 544-5890

SUPER 8 MOTEL
3600 Lake Tahoe
Blvd (96150)
Rates: $53-$78
Tel: (916) 544-3476
(800) 237-8882

TAHOE COLONY INN
3794 Montreal
(96157)
Rates: $40-$70
Tel: (916) 655-6481

TAHOE KEYS RESORT
599 Tahoe Keys Blvd
(96150)
Rates: $200-$300
Tel: (916) 544-5397
(800) 438-8246

TAHOE MARINA INN
930 Bal Bijou Rd
(96150)
Rates: $56-$140
Tel: (916) 541-2180

TAHOE QUEEN MOTEL
932 Poplar St (96150)
Rates: $40-$70
Tel: (916) 544-2291

TAHOE TROPICANA LODGE
4132 Cedar Ave
(96150)
Rates: $40-$70
Tel: (916) 541-3911

TAHOE VALLEY MOTEL
2241 Lake Tahoe
Blvd (96150)
Rates: $85-$150
Tel: (916) 541-0353
(800) 669-7544

TORCHLITE INN
965 Park Ave (96150)
Rates: $38-$78
Tel: (916) 541-2363
(800) 455-6060

TRADE WINDS MOTEL
944 Friday Ave
(96150)
Rates: $35-$125
Tel: (916) 544-6459
(800) 628-1829

SOUTH SAN FRANCISCO

LA QUINTA INN
20 Airport Blvd
(94080)
Rates: $64-$70
Tel: (415) 583-2223
(800) 531-5900

RADISSON HOTEL
275 S Airport Blvd
(94080)
Rates: $85-$160
Tel: (800) 333-3333

RAMADA INN NORTH
245 S Airport Blvd
(94080)
Rates: $82-$150
Tel: (415) 589-7200
(800) 272-6232

TRAVELODGE- AIRPORT NORTH
326 S Airport Blvd
(94080)
Rates: $55-$80
Tel: (415) 583-9600
(800) 578-7878

VAGABOND INN- AIRPORT
222 S Airport Blvd
(94080)
Rates: $48-$95
Tel: (415) 692-4040
(800) 522-1555

SPRING VALLEY

SUPER 8 MOTEL SPRING VALLEY
9603 Campo Rd
(91977)
Rates: $37-$49
Tel: (619) 589-1111
(800) 800-8000

ST. HELENA

EL BONITA MOTEL
195 Main St (94574)
Rates: $46-$115
Tel: (707) 963-3216
(800) 541-3284

HARVEST INN
1 Main St (94574)
Rates: $100-$350
Tel: (707) 963-9463
(800) 950-8466

HYPHEN INN
P. O. Box 190 (94574)
Rates: $135
Tel: (707) 942-0434

STANTON

MOTEL 6
7450 Katella Ave
(90680)
Rates: $28-$32
Tel: (714) 891-0717
(800) 440-6000

STOCKTON

BEST WESTERN CHARTER WAY INN
550 W Charter Way
(95206)
Rates: $46-$61
Tel: (209) 948-0321
(800) 528-1234

DAYS INN
33 N Center St (95202)
Rates: $45-$65
Tel: (209) 931-3131
(800) 329-7466

ECONO LODGE
2210 Manthey Rd
(95206)
Rates: $32-$69
Tel: (209) 466-5741
(800) 553-2666

HOLIDAY INN STOCKTON
111 E March Ln
(95207)
Rates: $85-$93
Tel: (209) 474-3301
(800) 465-4329
(800) 633-3737

LA QUINTA INN
2710 W March Ln
(95219)
Rates: $46-$72
Tel: (209) 952-7800
(800) 531-5900

MOTEL 6
4100 Waterloo Rd
(95205)
Rates: $28-$42
Tel: (209) 931-9511
(800) 440-6000

MOTEL 6
1625 French Camp
Tpk (95206)
Rates: $28-$34
Tel: (209) 467-3600
(800) 440-6000

MOTEL 6
817 Navy Dr (95206)
Rates: $28-$34
Tel: (209) 946-0923
(800) 440-6000

MOTEL 6
6717 Plymouth Rd
(95207)
Rates: $30-$36
Tel: (209) 951-8120
(800) 440-6000

SUNSHINE INN
8009 N Hwy 99
(95212)
Rates: $25-$50
Tel: (209) 956-5200

STRAWBERRY

THREE RIVERS RESORT
P. O. Box 81 (95375)
Rates: $85-$185
Tel: (209) 965-3278
(800) 514-6777

SUISUN CITY

ECONOMY INNS OF AMERICA
4376 Central Pl
(94585)
Rates: $30-$42
Tel: (707) 864-1728
(800) 826-0778

SUN CITY

SUNSET INN
27955 Encanto
(92586)
Rates: $20-$35
Tel: (909) 679-1133

TRAVELODGE
27955 Encanto Dr
(92586)
Rates: $35-$53
Tel: (909) 679-1133
(800) 578-7878

SUN VALLEY

SCOTTISH INNS
8365 Lehigh Ave
(91352)
Rates: $40+
Tel: (818) 504-2671
(800) 251-1962

SUNNYVALE

BEST WESTERN SUNNYVALE INN
940 Weddell Dr
(94089)
Rates: $75-$99
Tel: (408) 734-3742
(800) 528-1234

CAPTAIN'S COVE MOTEL
600 N Mathilda Ave
(94086)
Rates: $59-$61
Tel: (800) 322-2683

COMFORT INN
820 E El Camino
Real (94087)
Rates: $49-$65
Tel: (800) 221-2222

MAPLE TREE INN
711 E El Camino
Real (94087)
Rates: $72-$83
Tel: (408) 720-9700
(800) 423-0243

MOTEL 6
775 N Mathilda Ave
(94086)
Rates: $46-$52
Tel: (408) 736-4595
(800) 440-6000

MOTEL 6
806 Ahwanee Ave
(94086)
Rates: $40-$46
Tel: (408) 720-1222
(800) 440-6000

RESIDENCE INN BY MARRIOTT
750 Lakeway Dr
(94086)
Rates: $78-$157
Tel: (408) 720-1000
(800) 331-3131

RESIDENCE INN BY MARRIOTT
1080 Stewart Dr
(94086)
Rates: $78-$157
Tel: (408) 720-8893
(800) 331-3131

SUMMERFIELD SUITES
900 Hamlin Ct (94089)
Rates: $79-$159
Tel: (800) 833-4353

VAGABOND INN
816 Ahwanee Ave
(94086)
Rates: $40-$55
Tel: (408) 734-4607
(800) 522-1555

WOODFIN SUITES MOTOR HOTEL
635 E El Camino
Real (94087)
Rates: $79-$152
Tel: (408) 738-1700
(800) 237-8811

SUSANVILLE

BEST WESTERN TRAILSIDE INN
2785 Main St (96130)
Rates: $44-$83
Tel: (916) 257-4123
(800) 528-1234

COZY MOTEL
2829 Main St (96130)
Rates: $25-$30
Tel: (916) 257-2319

DIAMOND VIEW MOTEL
1529 Main St (96130)
Rates: $27-$34
Tel: (916) 257-4585

FRONTIER INN MOTEL
2685 Main St (96130)
Rates: $30-$55
Tel: (916) 257-4141

KNIGHTS INN MOTEL
1705 Main St (96130)
Rates: $37-$49
Tel: (916) 257-2168

MT. LASSEN HOTEL
27 S Lassen St
(96130)
Rates: $37+
Tel: (916) 257-6609

RIVER INN MOTEL
1710 Main St (96130)
Rates: $32-$45
Tel: (916) 257-6051

SIERRA VISTA MOTEL
1067 Main St (96130)
Rates: $29-$34
Tel: (916) 257-6721

SUPER BUDGET MOTEL
2975 Johnstonville
Rd (96130)
Rates: $36-$44
Tel: (916) 257-2782

SYLMAR

MOTEL 6
12775 Encinitas Ave
(91342)
Rates: $28-$34
Tel: (818) 362-9491
(800) 440-6000

TAHOE VISTA

BEESLEY'S COTTAGES
6674 N Lake Blvd
(96148)
Rates: $70-$140
Tel: (916) 546-2448

HOLIDAY HOUSE LAKESIDE CHALETS
7276 N Lake Blvd
(96148)
Rates: $85-$125
Tel: (916) 546-2369
(800) 294-6378

TATAMI COTTAGE RESORT
7449 N Lake Blvd (96148)
Rates: $69-$129
Tel: (916) 546-3523

TAHOMA

CAPTAIN'S ALPENHAUS
6941 W Lake Blvd (96142)
Rates: $100-$150
Tel: (916) 525-5000

NORFOLK WOODS COUNTRY INN
6941 W Lake Blvd (96142)
Rates: $100-$150
Tel: (916) 525-5000

TAHOE LAKE COTTAGES
7030 W Lake Blvd (96142)
Rates: $237 (3 nights)
Tel: (800) 824-6348

TAHOMA LODGE
7018 W Lake Blvd (96142)
Rates: $60-$213
Tel: (800) 824-6348

TEHACHAPI

BEST WESTERN MOUNTAIN INN
416 W Tehachapi Blvd (93561)
Rates $48-$54
Tel: (805) 822-5591
(800) 528-1234

GOLDEN HILLS MOTEL
22561 Woodford-Tehachapi Rd (93561)
Rates: $25+
Tel: (805) 822-4488
(800) 434-1118

TRAVELODGE-TEHACHAPI SUMMIT
500 Steuber Rd (93581)
Rates: $46-$60
Tel: (805) 823-8000
(800) 578-7878

TEMECULA

COMFORT INN
27338 Jefferson Ave (92590)
Rates: $39-$75
Tel: (909) 699-5888
(800) 221-2222

MOTEL 6
41900 Moreno Dr (92590)
Rates: $30-36
Tel: (909) 676-7199
(800) 440-6000

RAMADA INN
28980 Front St (92592)
Rates: $39-$54
Tel: (909) 676-8770
(800) 272-6232

TEMECULA CREEK
44501 Rainbow Canyon Rd (92592)
Rates: $115-$150
Tel: (909) 694-1000

THOUSAND OAKS

BEST WESTERN OAKS LODGE
12 Conejo Blvd (91360)
Rates: $52-$57
Tel: (805) 495-7011
(800) 528-1234

E-Z 8 MOTEL
2434 W Hillcrest Dr (91360)
Rates: $31+
Tel: (805) 499-0755
(800) 326-6835

HOLIDAY INN
495 N Ventu Park Rd (91360)
Rates: $69+
Tel: (805) 498-6733
(800) 465-4329

MOTEL 6
1516 Newbury Rd (91360)
Rates: $30-$36
Tel: (805) 499-0711
(800) 440-6000

THOUSAND OAKS INN
75 W Thousand Oaks Blvd (91360)
Rates: $47-$70
Tel: (805) 497-3701
(800) 600-6878

THREE RIVERS

BEST WESTERN HOLIDAY LODGE
40105 Sierra Dr (93271)
Rates: $65-$85
Tel: (209) 561-4119
(800) 528-1234

BUCKEYE TREE LODGE
46000 Sierra Dr (93271)
Rates: $39-$61
Tel: (209) 561-5900

IMA LAZY J RANCH MOTEL
39625 Sierra Dr (93271)
Rates: $50-$68
Tel: (209) 561-4449
(800) 341-8000

THE RIVER INN
45176 Sierra Dr (93271)
Rates: $35-$59
Tel: (209) 561-4367

SEQUOIA VILLAGE INN
45971 Sierra Dr (93271)
Rates: $35-$90
Tel: (209) 561-3652

SIERRA LODGE
43175 Sierra Dr (93271)
Rates: $35-$65
Tel: (209) 561-3681

TORRANCE

DAYS INN
4111 Pacific Coast Hwy (90505)
Rates: $55-$70
Tel: (800) 329-7466

HOLIDAY INN TORRANCE DEL AMO
21333 Hawthorne Blvd (90503)
Rates: $89-$119
Tel: (800) 465-4329

HOWARD JOHNSON LODGE
2880 Pacific Coast Hwy (90505)
Rates: $79-$94
Tel: (310) 325-0660
(800) 446-4656

RESIDENCE INN BY MARRIOTT
3701 Torrance Blvd (90503)
Rates: $124-$162
Tel: (310) 543-4566
(800) 331-3131

SUMMERFIELD SUITES HOTEL
19901 Prairie Ave (90503)
Rates: $89-$159
Tel: (310) 371-8525

TRACY

BEST WESTERN JOHN JAY INN
811 Clover Rd (95376)
Rates: $53-$65
Tel: (209) 832-0271
(800) 528-1234

MOTEL 6
3810 Tracy Blvd (95376)
Rates: $32-$36
Tel: (209) 836-4900
(800) 440-6000

PHOENIX LODGE
3511 Tracy Blvd (95376)
Rates: $45
Tel: (209) 835-1335

TRINIDAD

BISHOP PINE LODGE
1481 Patricks Point Dr (95570)
Rates: $60-$90
Tel: (707) 677-3314

SHADOW LODGE
687 Patricks Point Dr (95570)
Rates: $39-$89
Tel: (707) 677-0532

TRINIDAD INN
1170 Patricks Point Dr (95570)
Rates: $50-$100
Tel: (707) 677-3349

VIEW CREST LODGE
3415 Patricks Point Dr (95570)
Rates: $50-$120
Tel: (707) 677-3393

TRINITY CENTER

BECKER'S BOUNTY LODGE
HCR 3, Box 4659 (96091)
Rates: $400-$650/weekly
Tel: (916) 266-3277

CEDAR STOCK RESORT
45810 Hwy 3 (96091)
Rates: $350-$2300/weekly
Tel: (916) 286-2225
(800) 982-2279

ENRIGHT GULCH CABINS & MOTEL
3500 Hwy 3, P. O Box 244 (96091)
Rates: $30-$35
Tel: (916) 266-3600

RIPPLE CREEK CABINS
Rt 2, Box 4020 (96091)
Rates: $60-$115
Tel: (916) 266-3505

WYNTOON RESORT
Hwy 3, P. O. Box 70 (96091)
Rates: $16-$110
Tel: (916) 266-3337
(800) 715-3337

TRONA

DESERT ROSE MOTEL
84368 Trona Rd (93562)
Rates: $30-$42
Tel: (619) 372-4572

TRUCKEE

ALPINE VILLAGE MOTEL
12660 Deerfield Dr (96161)
Rates: $50-$79
Tel: (916) 587-3801
(800) 933-1787

RICHARDS MOTEL
15758 Donner Pass Rd (96160)
Rates: $60-$110
Tel: (916) 587-3662

SUPER 8 LODGE
11506 Deerfield Dr (96161)
Rates: $57-$94
Tel: (916) 587-8888
(800) 800-8000

TULARE

BEST WESTERN TOWN & COUNTRY LODGE
1051 N Blackstone (93274)
Rates: $47-$52
Tel: (209) 688-7537
(800) 528-1234

FRIENDSHIP INN
26442 SR 99 (93274)
Rates: $35-$45
Tel: (800) 424-4777

GREEN GABLE INN
1010 E Prosperity Ave (93274)
Rates: $42
Tel: (209) 686-3432

INNS OF AMERICA
1183 N Blackstone (93274)
Rates: $29-$35
Tel: (209) 686-1611
(800) 826-0778

MOTEL 6
1111 N Blackstone (93274)
Rates: $29-$35
Tel: (209) 686-1611
(800) 440-6000

TULARE INN MOTEL
1301 E Paige (93274)
Rates: $29-$38
Tel: (800) 333-8571

TURLOCK

BEST WESTERN THE GARDENS
1119 Pedras Rd (95380)
Rates: $48-$95
Tel: (209) 634-9351
(800) 528-1234

BEST WESTERN ORCHARD INN
5025 N Golden State Blvd (95380)
Rates: $54-$99
Tel: (209) 667-2827
(800) 528-1234

COMFORT INN
200 W Glenwood Ave (95380)
Rates: $40-$50
Tel: (209) 668-3400
(800) 221-2222

MOTEL 6
250 S Walnut Ave (95380)
Rates: $28-$34
Tel: (209) 667-4100
(800) 440-6000

TWAIN HARTE

ELDORADO MOTEL
P. O. Box 368 (95383)
Rates: $40-$60
Tel: (209) 586-4479

TWENTYNINE PALMS

CIRCLE "C" MOTEL
6340 El Rey Ave (92277)
Rates: $85
Tel: (619) 367-7615

MOTEL 6
72562 Twentynine Palms Hwy (92277)
Rates: $32-$36
Tel: (619) 367-2833
(800) 440-6000

TWIN PEAKS

ARROWHEAD PINE ROSE CABINS
Hwy 189 at Grand View (92391)
Rates: $49-$69
Tel: (909) 337-2341
(800) 429-7463

UKIAH

DAYS INN-REDWOODS/WINE COUNTRY
950 N State St (95482)
Rates: $55-$85
Tel: (707) 462-7584
(800) 329-7466

HOLIDAY LODGE
1050 S State St (95482)
Rates: $27-$40
Tel: (707) 462-2906
(800) 300-2906

MOTEL 6
1208 S State St (95482)
Rates: $32-$38
Tel: (707) 468-5404
(800) 440-6000

TRAVELODGE
406 S State St (95482)
Rates: $39-$58
Tel: (707) 462-8611
(800) 578-7878

WESTERN TRAVELER MOTEL
693 S Orchard Ave (95482)
Rates: $32-$56
Tel: (707) 468-9167

UPPER LAKE

NARROWS LODGE RESORT
5690 Blue Lakes Rd (95485)
Rates: $50-$85
Tel: (707) 275-2718

PINE ACRES BLUE LAKE RESORT
5328 Blue Lakes Rd (95485)
Rates: $85+
Tel: (707) 275-2811

VACAVILLE

BEST WESTERN HERITAGE INN
1420 E Monte Vista Ave (95688)
Rates: $50-$68
Tel: (707) 448-8453
(800) 528-1234

DAYS INN
1571 E Monte Vista Ave (95688)
Rates: $45-$75
Tel: (800) 329-7466

MOTEL 6
107 Lawrence Dr (95687)
Rates: $30-$36
Tel: (707) 447-5550
(800) 440-6000

VALENCIA

HILTON GARDEN INN
27710 The Old Rd (91355)
Rates: $99-$129
Tel: (805) 254-8800
(800) 445-8667

VALLEJO

DAYS INN
300 Fairgrounds Dr (94590)
Rates: $45-$75
Tel: (707) 554-8000
(800) 329-7466

E-Z 8 MOTEL
4 Mariposa St (94590)
Rates: $25-$32
Tel: (800) 326-6835

HOLIDAY INN-MARINE WORLD/ USA
1000 Fairgrounds Dr (94590)
Rates: $55-$80
Tel: (707) 644-1200
(800) 465-4329

IMA ROYAL BAY INN
44 Admiral Callaghan Ln (94594)
Rates: $35-$68
Tel: (707) 643-1061
(800) 643-8887

MOTEL 6
458 Fairgrounds Dr (94589)
Rates: $32-$38
Tel: (707) 642-7781
(800) 440-6000

MOTEL 6
1455 Marine World Pkwy (94589)
Rates: $32-$38
Tel: (707) 643-7611
(800) 440-6000

MOTEL 6
597 Sandy Beach Rd (94590)
Rates: $30-$36
Tel: (707) 552-2912
(800) 440-6000

RAMADA INN
1000 Admiral Callaghan Ln (94591)
Rates: $61-$98
Tel: (707) 643-2700
(800) 228-2828

THRIFTLODGE
160 E Lincoln (94591)
Rates: $43+
Tel: (800) 255-3050

VALU INN BY NENDELS
300 Fairgrounds Dr (94590)
Rates: $32-$59
Tel: (707) 554-8000

WINDMILL INN-MARINE WORLD/ USA
1596 Fairgrounds Dr (94589)
Rates: $45-$69
Tel: (707) 554-9655
(800) 547-4747

VALLEY SPRINGS

10TH GREEN INN BED & BREAKFAST
14 St. Andrews Rd (95252)
Rates: $59-$89
Tel: (209) 772-1084

VENICE

LINCOLN INN
2447 Lincoln Blvd (90291)
Rates: $86
Tel: (310) 822-0686

MARINA MOTEL
3130 Washington Blvd (90291)
Rates: $45-$50
Tel: (310) 821-5086

VENTURA

COUNTRY INN
298 Chestnut St (93001)
Rates: $62+
Tel: (805) 653-1434

LA QUINTA INN
5818 Valentine Rd (93003)
Rates: $48-$60
Tel: (805) 658-6200
(800) 531-5900

MOTEL 6
2145 E Harbor Blvd (93001)
Rates: $34-$38
Tel: (805) 643-5100
(800) 440-6000

MOTEL 6
3075 Johnson Dr (93003)
Rates: $38-$42
Tel: (805) 650-0080
(800) 440-6000

PACIFIC INN
350 E Thompson Blvd (93001)
Rates: $35-$63
Tel: (805) 653-0879

PIERPONT INN
550 Sanjon Rd (93001)
Rates: $99
Tel: (805) 658-6200
(800) 285-4667

RAMADA CLOCKTOWER INN
181 E Santa Clara (93001)
Rates: $75-$80
Tel: (805) 652-0141
(800) 272-6232

VAGABOND INN
756 E Thompson Blvd (93001)
Rates: $43-$65
Tel: (805) 648-5371
(800) 522-1555

VICTORIA MOTEL
2350 S Victoria Ave (93003)
Rates: $33-$60
Tel: (805) 642-2173

VICTORVILLE

BEST WESTERN GREEN TREE INN
14173 Green Tree Rd (92392)
Rates: $50-$80
Tel: (619) 245-3461
(800) 528-1234

BUDGET INN
14153 Kentwood Blvd (92392)
Rates: $30-$42
Tel: (619) 241-8010

HI DESERT/ RED ROOF INN
13409 Mariposa Rd (92392)
Rates: $45-$51
Tel: (619) 241-1577
(800) 843-7663

HOLIDAY INN MOTOR HOTEL
15494 Palmdale Rd (92392)
Rates: $51-$61
Tel: (619) 245-6565
(800) 465-4329

MOTEL 6
16901 Stoddard Wells Rd (92392)
Rates: $25-$29
Tel: (619) 243-0666
(800) 440-6000

RED ROOF INN
13409 Mariposa Rd (92392)
Rates: n/a
Tel: (619) 241-1577
(800) 843-7663

SCOTTISH INNS
15499 Village Dr (92392)
Rates: $22-$36
Tel: (800) 251-1962

SUNSET INN
15765 Mojave Dr (92392)
Rates: $25-$36
Tel: (619) 243-2342

TRAVELODGE NORTH MOTEL
16868 Stoddard Wells Rd (92392)
Rates: $31-$39
Tel: (619) 243-7700
(800) 578-7878

VISALIA

BEST WESTERN VISALIA INN MOTEL
623 W Main St (93277)
Rates: $55-$64
Tel: (209) 732-4561
(800) 528-1234

HOLIDAY INN PLAZA PARK
9000 W Airport Dr (93277)
Rates: $74-$94
Tel: (209) 651-5000
(800) 465-4329

OAK TREE INN
401 Woodland Dr (93277)
Rates: $30-$36
Tel: (209) 732-8861
(800) 554-7664

THRIFTLODGE
4645 W Mineral King Ave (93277)
Rates: $35-$75
Tel: (209) 732-5611
(800) 578-7878

VISTA

HILLTOP MOTOR LODGE
330 Mar Vista Dr (92083)
Rates: $36-$44
Tel: (619) 726-7010

LA QUINTA INN
630 Sycamore Ave (92083)
Rates: $46-$61
Tel: (619) 727-8180
(800) 531-5900

WALNUT CREEK

EMBASSY SUITES HOTEL
1345 Treat Blvd (94596)
Rates: $119-$134
Tel: (415) 934-2500
(800) 362-2779

MOTEL 6
2389 N Main St (94596)
Rates: $43-$53
Tel: (415) 935-4010
(800) 440-6000

WALNUT CREEK MOTOR LODGE
1960 N Main St (94596)
Rates: $65-$90
Tel: (415) 932-2811
(800) 824-0334

WATSONVILLE

BEST WESTERN INN
740 Freedom Blvd (95076)
Rates: $44-$118
Tel: (408) 724-3367
(800) 528-1234

COUNTRY SUNRISE BED & BREAKFAST
3085 Freedom Blvd (95076)
Rates: $70-$95
Tel: (408) 722-4793

EL RANCHO MOTEL
976 Salinas Rd (95076)
Rates: $30-$69
Tel: (408) 722-2766

MONTEREY BAY/ SANTA CRUZ RESORT
1186 San Andreas Rd (95076)
Rates: $26-$39
Tel: (408) 722-0551

MOTEL 6
125 Silver Leaf Dr (95076)
Rates: $35-$41
Tel: (408) 728-4144
(800) 440-6000

NATIONAL 9 MOTEL
1 Western Dr (95076)
Rates: $55-$80
Tel: (408) 724-1116

WEAVERVILLE

49ER MOTEL
718 Main St (96093)
Rates: $34-$50
Tel: (916) 623-4937

MOTEL TRINITY
1112 Main St (96093)
Rates: $30-$65
Tel: (916) 623-2129

VICTORIAN INN
1709 Main St (96093)
Rates: $49-$80
Tel: (916) 623-4432

WEED

GRAND MANOR INN
1844 Shastina Dr (96094)
Rates: $64-$92
Tel: (916) 938-1982

MOTEL 6
466 N Weed Blvd (96094)
Rates: $30-$36
Tel: (916) 938-4101
(800) 440-6000

SIS-Q-INN MOTEL
1825 Shastina Dr (96094)
Rates: $29-$46
Tel: (916) 938-4194

STEWART MINERAL SPRINGS CABINS
4617 Stewart Springs Rd (96094)
Rates: $25-$65
Tel: (916) 938-2222
(800) 322-9223

TOWN HOUSE MOTEL
157 S Weed Blvd (96094)
Rates: $36-$33
Tel: (916) 938-4431

Y MOTEL
90 N Weed Blvd (96094)
Rates: $27-$40
Tel: (916) 938-4481

WEST HOLLYWOOD

LE MONTROSE SUITE HOTEL DE GRAN LUXE
900 Hammond St (90069)
Rates: $185-$300
Tel: (310) 855-1115
(800) 776-0666

LE PARC DE GRAN LUXE HOTEL
733 N West Knoll Dr (90069)
Rates: $165-$205
Tel: (310) 855-8888
(800) 578-4837

MONDRIAN HOTEL
8440 Sunset Blvd (90069)
Rates: $185-$325
Tel: (213) 650-8999
(800) 525-8029

RAMADA PLAZA HOTEL
8585 Santa Monica Blvd (90069)
Rates: $80
Tel: (310) 652-6400
(800) 272-6232

SUMMERFIELD SUITES HOTEL
1000 Westmount Dr (90069)
Rates: $149-$179
Tel: (310) 657-7400
(800) 833-4353

WYNDHAM BELAGE MOTEL
1020 N San Vicente Blvd (90069)
Rates: $149-$175
Tel: (310) 854-1111
(800) 996-3426

WEST SACRAMENTO

BEST WESTERN- HARBOR INN & SUITES
1250 Halyard Dr (95691)
Rates: $59-$159
Tel: (916) 922-9833
(800) 528-1234

MOTEL 6
1254 Halyard Dr (95691)
Rates: $31-$37
Tel: (916) 372-3624
(800) 440-6000

WESTLEY

DAYS INN
7144 McCracken Rd (95387)
Rates: $38-$65
Tel: (209) 894-5500
(800) 329-7466

WESTMINSTER

**BEST WESTERN
WESTMINSTER INN**
5755 Westminster
Ave (92683)
Rates: $42-$57
Tel: (714) 898-4043
(800) 528-1234

MOTEL 6
6266 Westminster
Ave (92683)
Rates: $32-$36
Tel: (714) 891-5366
(800) 440-6000

MOTEL 6
13100 Goldenwest
(92683)
Rates: $32-$36
Tel: (714) 895-0042
(800) 440-6000

WESTPORT

**BLUE VICTORIAN
INN**
38921 N Hwy 1
(95488)
Rates: $75-$130
Tel: (707) 964-6310
(800) 400-6310

**HOWARD CREEK
RANCH B & B**
40501 N Hwy 1
(95488)
Rates: $55-$145
Tel: (707) 964-6725

WESTWOOD

HOTEL DEL CAPRI
10587 Wilshire Blvd
(90024)
Rates: $85-$140
Tel: (800) 444-6835

**WESTWOOD
MARQUIS HOTEL
GARDENS**
930 Hilgard Ave
(90024)
Rates: $220-$325
Tel: (310) 208-8765
(800) 421-2317

WHITTIER

BEST WHITTIER INN
14226 Whittier Blvd
(90606)
Rates $34-$80
Tel: (310) 698-0323

MOTEL 6
8221 S Pioneer Blvd
(90606)
Rates: $30-$34
Tel: (310) 692-9101
(800) 440-6000

VAGABOND INN
14125 E Whittier
Blvd (90605)
Rates: $35-$55
Tel: (310) 698-9701
(800) 522-1555

WILLIAMS

MOTEL 6
455 4th St (95987)
Rates: $30-$36
Tel: (916) 473-5337
(800) 440-6000

STAGE STOP MOTEL
330 7th St (95987)
Rates: $33-$50
Tel: (916) 473-2281

WOODCREST INN
400 C St (95987)
Rates: $54
Tel: (916) 473-2381

WILLITS

**BAECHTEL CREEK
INN**
101 Gregory Ln
(95490)
Rates: $65-$105
Tel: (707) 459-9063
(800) 459-9911

HOLIDAY LODGE
1540 S Main St (95490)
Rates: $45-$65
Tel: (707) 459-5361

LARK MOTEL
1411 S Main St (95490)
Rates: $30-$40
Tel: (707) 459-2421

**PEPPERWOOD
MOTEL**
452 S Main St
(95490)
Rates: $30-$40
Tel: (707) 459-2231

PINE CONE MOTEL
1350 S Main St
(95490)
Rates: $29-$32
Tel: (707) 459-5044

**SKUNK TRAIL
MOTEL**
500 S Main St
(95490)
Rates: $38+
Tel: (707) 459-2302

**WESTERN VILLAGE
INN**
1440 S Main St
(95490)
Rates: $34+
Tel: (707) 459-4011

WILLOWS

**BEST WESTERN
GOLDEN PHEASANT
INN**
249 N Humboldt
Ave (95988)
Rates: $56-$150
Tel: (916) 934-4603
(800) 528-1234

BLUE GUM INN
Rt 2, Hwy 99 W
(95988)
Rates: $26-$42
Tel: (916) 934-5401

**CROSS ROADS
WEST INN**
452 N Humboldt
Ave (95988)
Rates: $26-$36
Tel: (916) 934-7026

DAYS INN
475 N Humboldt
Ave (95988)
Rates: $42-$70
Tel: (916) 934-4444
(800) 329-7466

ECONOMY INN
435 N Tehama
(95988)
Rates: $30+
Tel: (916) 934-4224

GROVE MOTEL
Rt 2, Hwy 99 W
(95988)
Rates: $30+
Tel: (916) 934-5067

SUPER 8 MOTEL
457 N Humboldt
Ave (95988)
Rates: $36-$38
Tel: (916) 934-2871
(800) 800-8000

WESTERN MOTEL
601 N Tehama
(95988)
Rates: $27+
Tel: (916) 934-3856

WISHON

MILLER'S LANDING
37976 Rd 222 (93669)
Rates: $40-$125
Tel: (209) 642-3633

WOODLAND

CINDERELLA MOTEL
99 W Main St
(95695)
Rates: $35-$42
Tel: (916) 662-1091
(800) 782-9403

COMFORT INN
1562 E Main St
(95695)
Rates: $45-$65
Tel: (916) 666-3050
(800) 221-2222

MOTEL 6
1564 E Main St
(95695)
Rates: $32-$38
Tel: (916) 666-6777
(800) 440-6000

WOODLAND
HILLS

VAGABOND INN
20157 Ventura Blvd
(91364)
Rates: $47-$67
Tel: (818) 347-8080
(800) 522-1555

YORKVILLE

**SHEEP DUNG
ESTATES
COTTAGES**
P. O. Box 49 (95494)
Rates: $75
Tel: (707) 894-5322

YOSEMITE AREA

DEER VALLEY INN
45013 Hwy 49
(Nipinnawasee
93601)
Rates: $49-$175
Tel: (209) 683-2155

YOSEMITE NATIONAL PARK

**THE REDWOODS
GUEST COTTAGES**
P. O. Box 2085
(Wawona Station
95389)
Rates: $88-$365
Tel: (209) 375-6666

**YOSEMITE VIEW
LODGE**
11159 Hwy 140,
P. O. Box D
(El Portal 95318)
Rates: $95-$135
Tel: (209) 379-2681
(800) 321-5261

YOUNTVILLE

VINTAGE INN
6541 Washington St
(94599)
Rates: $134-$204
Tel: (707) 944-1112
(800) 351-1133

YREKA

**BEST WESTERN
MINER'S INN**
122 E Miner St
(96097)
Rates: $46-$100
Tel: (916) 842-4355
(800) 528-1234

MOTEL ORLEANS
1804-B Fort Jones Rd
(96097)
Rates: $32-$39
Tel: (916) 842-1612
(800) 626-1900

MOTEL 6
1785 S Main St
(96097)
Rates: $30-$36
Tel: (916) 842-4111
(800) 440-6000

SUPER 8 MOTEL
136 Montegue Rd
(96097)
Rates: $40-$60
Tel: (916) 842-5781
(800) 800-8000

**THUNDERBIRD
LODGE**
526 S Main St
(96097)
Rates: $32-$76
Tel: (916) 842-4404
(800) 554-4339

WAYSIDE INN
1235 S Main St
(96097)
Rates: $30-$150
Tel: (916) 842-4412
(800) 795-7974

YUBA CITY

**GARDEN COURT
INN**
4228 S Hwy 99
(95991)
Rates: $26-$38
Tel: (916) 674-0210

**MOTEL ORLEANS-
YUBA CITY**
730 Palora Ave
(95991)
Rates: $32-$40
Tel: (916) 674-1592
(800) 626-1900

MOTEL 6
700 N Palora Ave
(95991)
Rates: $30-$36
Tel: (916) 674-1710
(800) 440-6000

YUCCA VALLEY

**OASIS OF EDEN
INN & SUITES**
56377 Twentynine
Palms Hwy (92284)
Rates: $44-$80
Tel: (619) 365-6321

SUPER 8 MOTEL
57096 Twentynine
Palms Hwy (92284)
Rates: $42-$46
Tel: (619) 228-1773
(800) 800-8000

YUCCA INN
7500 Camino Del
Cielo (92284)
Rates: $39-$55
Tel: (619) 365-3311

COLORADO

ALAMOSA

LAMPLIGHTER MOTEL
425 Main St (81101)
Rates: n/a
Tel: (800) 359-2138

BEST WESTERN ALAMOSA INN
1919 Main St (81101)
Rates: $45-$95
Tel: (719) 589-2567
(800) 528-1234

ARVADA

ON GOLDEN POND
7831 Eldridge
(80005)
Rates: n/a
Tel: (303) 424-2296

ASPEN

CRESTAHAUS LODGE
1301 E Cooper Ave
(81611)
Rates: $80-$235
Tel: (970) 925-7081
(800) 344-3853

HOTEL JEROME
330 E Main St
(81611)
Rates: $189-$499
Tel: (970) 920-1000

LIMELITE LODGE
228 E Cooper St
(81611)
Rates: $58-$210
Tel: (970) 925-3025
(800) 433-0832

THE LITTLE NELL
675 E Durant Ave
(81611)
Rates: $240-$425
Tel: (970) 920-4600
(800) 525-6200

AURORA

HOLIDAY INN-SOUTHEAST
3200 S Parker Rd
(80014)
Rates: $83
Tel: (800) 465-4329

LA QUINTA INN
1011 S Abilene
(80012)
Rates: $45-$58
Tel: (800) 531-5900

AVON

COMFORT INN-VAIL/BEAVER CREEK
P. O. Box 5510
(81620)
Rates: $87-$205
Tel: (970) 949-5511
(800) 423-4374

BOULDER

BEST WESTERN BOULDER INN
770 28th St (80303)
Rates: $72-$103
Tel: (303) 449-3800
(800) 528-1234

BOULDER MOUNTAIN LODGE
91 Four Mile
Canyon Rd (80302)
Rates: $40-$90
Tel: (303) 444-0882
(800) 458-0882

BOULDER BROKER INN
555 30th St (80303)
Rates: $69-$115
Tel: (303) 444-3330
(800) 338-5407

DAYS INN BOULDER
5397 S Boulder Rd
(80303)
Rates: $54-$84
Tel: (303) 499-4422

FOOT OF THE MOUNTAIN MOTEL
200 Arapahoe Ave
(80302)
Rates: $55-$70
Tel: (303) 442-5688

HIGHLANDER INN MOTEL
970 28th St (80303)
Rates: $45-$83
Tel: (303) 443-7800

HOLIDAY INN
800 28th St (80303)
Rates: $65-$84
Tel: (303) 443-3322

HOMEWOOD SUITES
4950 Baseline Rd
(80303)
Rates: $112-$155
Tel: (303) 499-9922
(800) 225-5466

PEARL STREET INN
1820 Pearl St (80302)
Rates: $78-$103
Tel: (800) 232-5949

RESIDENCE INN BY MARRIOTT
3030 Center Green
Dr (80301)
Rates: $109-$129
Tel: ((303) 449-5545
(800) 331-3131

BRUSH

BEST WESTERN BRUSH
1208 N Colorado
Ave (80723)
Rates: $51-$76
Tel: (970) 842-5146
(800) 528-1234

BUENA VISTA

COTTONWOOD INN
18999 County Rd
306 (81211)
Rates: n/a
Tel: (719) 395-6434

TOPAZ LODGE MOTEL
115 N US 24 (81211)
Rates: $40-$70
Tel: (719) 395-2427

BURLINGTON

CHAPARRAL BUDGET HOST
405 S Lincoln (80807)
Rates: $28-$44
Tel: (719) 346-5361

ECONO LODGE
450 S Lincoln (80807)
Rates: $31-$45
Tel: (719) 346-5555

SLOAN'S MOTEL
1901 Rose Ave
(80807)
Rates: $26-$39
Tel: (719) 346-5333

BYERS

LONGHORN MOTEL
457 N Main (80103)
Rates: $25-$40
Tel: (303) 822-5205

CANON CITY

BEST WESTERN ROYAL GORGE MOTEL
1925 Fremont Dr
(81212)
Rates: $50-$80
Tel: (719) 275-3377
(800) 231-7317

CANON INN
3075 E Hwy 50
(81212)
Rates: $45-$90
Tel: (719) 275-8676

HOLIDAY MOTEL
1502 Main St (81212)
Rates: $22-$40
Tel: (719) 275-3317

PARK LANE MOTEL
1401 Main St (81212)
Rates: $38-$55
Tel: (719) 275-7240

TRAVELODGE
2990 E Main St
(81212)
Rates: $35-75
Tel: (719) 275-0461
(800) 578-7878

CARBONDALE

THUNDER RIVER LODGE
Hwy 133 (81623)
Rates: $40-$62
Tel: (970) 963-2543

CASTLE ROCK

SUPER 8 MOTEL
1020 Park St (80104)
Rates: $37-$49
Tel: (303) 688-0880
(800) 800-8000

COLORADO CITY

GREENHORN MOUNTAIN RESORT
I-25 Exit 74 (81019)
Rates: $44-$49
Tel: (719) 676-3315

COLORADO SPRINGS

ANTLERS DOUBLETREE HOTEL
4 S Cascade (80903)
Rates: $79-$170
Tel: (719) 473-5600
(800) 222-8733

APOLLO PARK EXECUTIVE SUITES
805 S Circle Dr, 2-B
(80910)
Rates: $54-$65
Tel: (800) 666-1955

BEST WESTERN PALMER HOUSE
3010 N Chestnut
(80907)
Rates: $49-$77
Tel: (719) 636-5201
(800) 223-9127

CHIEF MOTEL
1624 S Nevada Ave
(80906)
Rates: $26-$45
Tel: (719) 473-5228

DAYS INN
2850 S Circle Dr
(80906)
Rates: $40-80
Tel: (719) 527-0800
(800) 329-7466

HILTON INN
505 Pope's Bluff Tr
(80907)
Rates: $55-$89
Tel: (719) 598-7656

HOWARD JOHNSON
5056 N Nevada Ave
(80918)
Rates: $40-110
Tel: (719) 598-7793
(800) 446-4656

COMFORT INN
8280 Hwy 83 (80920)
Rates: $40-$75
Tel: (719) 598-6700

DRURY INN-PIKES PEAK
8155 N Academy
Blvd (80920)
Rates: $49-$84
Tel: (719) 598-2500

ECONOMY INN
1231 S Nevada Ave
(80903)
Rates: $23-$50
Tel: (719) 634-1545

EMBASSY SUITES HOTEL
7290 Commerce Ctr
Dr (80919)
Rates: $79-$119
Tel: (719) 599-9100

HAMPTON INN-NORTH
7245 Commerce
Center Dr (80919)
Rates: $52-$78
Tel: (719) 593-9700

HOLIDAY INN NORTH
3125 Sinton Rd
(80907)
Rates: $40-$95
Tel: (719) 633-5541

HOLIDAY INN-EXPRESS
8th & Cimarron Sts
(80905)
Rates: $35-$87
Tel: (719) 473-5530

LA QUINTA INN
4385 Sinton Rd
(80907)
Rates: $38-$74
Tel: (719) 528-5060

MOTEL 6
3228 N Chestnut St
(80907)
Rates: $32-$38
Tel: (719) 520-5400
(800) 440-6000

RADISSON INN AIRPORT
1645 Newport Dr
(80916)
Rates: $59-$77
Tel: (800) 333-3333

RADISSON INN-NORTH
8110 N Academy
Blvd (80920)
Rates: $65-$100
Tel: (719) 598-5770
(800) 333-3333

RAINTREE INN-WEST
2625 Ore Mill Rd
(80904)
Rates: $28-$60
Tel: (719) 632-4600

RAMADA INN-EAST
520 N Murray Blvd
(80915)
Rates: $40-$96
Tel: (719) 596-7660
(800) 272-6232

RAMADA INN NORTH
4440 I-25 N (80907)
Rates: $40-$90
Tel: (719) 594-0700
(800) 272-6232

RED LION HOTEL
1775 E Cheyenne
Mtn Blvd (80906)
Rates: $110-$170
Tel: (719) 576-8900
(800) 547-8010

RESIDENCE INN BY MARRIOTT
3880 N Academy
Blvd (80917)
Rates: $99-$129
Tel: (719) 574-0370
(800) 331-3131

RODEWAY INN
2409 E Pikes Peak
Ave (80909)
Rates: $43-$70
Tel: (719) 471-0990
(800) 228-2000

SHERATON HOTEL
2886 S Circle Dr
(80906)
Rates: $74-$129
Tel: (800) 635-3304

STAGECOACH MOTEL
1647 S Nevada Ave
(80906)
Rates: $28-$42
Tel: (719) 633-3894

SWISS CHALET
3410-3420 W
Colorado Ave
(80904)
Rates: $24-$61
Tel: (719) 471-2260

TRAVELERS UPTOWN MOTEL
220 E Cimarron St
(80903)
Rates: $25-$42
Tel: (719) 473-2774

CORTEZ

ANASAZI MOTOR INN
640 S Broadway
(81321)
Rates: $40-$63
Tel: (970) 565-3773

**ANETH LODGE-
BUDGET 6**
645 E Main St
(81321)
Rates: $24-$51
Tel: (970) 565-3453

**ARROW NATIONAL
9 INN**
440 S Broadway
(81321)
Rates: $24-$58
Tel: (970) 565-7778
(800) 727-7692

BEL RAU LODGE
2040 E Main St
(81321)
Rates: $34-$70
Tel: (970) 565-3738

**BEST WESTERN
TURQUOISE
MOTOR INN**
535 E Main St
(81321)
Rates: $52-$110
Tel: (970) 565-3778
(800) 528-1234

COMFORT INN
2321 E Main St
(81321)
Rates: $49-$109
Tel: (970) 565-3400
(800) 221-2222

DAYS INN
Jct US 160 & 145
(81321)
Rates: $39-$69
Tel: (970) 565-8577
(800) 329-7466

**HOLIDAY INN
EXPRESS**
2121 E Main St
(81321)
Rates: $42-$88
Tel: (970) 565-6000

**NORTH BROADWAY
MOTEL**
510 N Broadway
(81321)
Rates: $23+
Tel: (970) 565-2481

RAMADA LIMITED
2020 E Main (81321)
Rates: $34-$65
Tel: (970) 565-3474
(800) 272-6232

SAND CANYON INN
301 W Main St
(81321)
Rates: $38+
Tel: (800) 258-3699

TOMAHAWK LODGE
728 S Broadway
(81321)
Rates: $27-$47
Tel: (970) 565-8521

**UTE MOUNTAIN
MOTEL**
531 S Broadway
(81321)
Rates: $26-$40
Tel: (970) 565-8507

CRAIG

A BAR Z MOTEL
2690 W Hwy 40
(81625)
Rates: $35-$39
Tel: (800) 458-7228

**BEST WESTERN
INN OF CRAIG**
755 E Victory Way
(81625)
Rates: $30-$65
Tel: (970) 824-8101
(800) 528-1234

**BLACK NUGGET
MOTEL**
2855 W Victory Way
(81625)
Rates: $30-$34
Tel: (970) 824-8161

CRAIG MOTEL
894 Yampa Ave
(81625)
Rates: $22-$36
Tel: (970) 824-4491

**HOLIDAY INN-
CRAIG**
300 S Hwy 13
(81625)
Rates: $49-$57
Tel: (970) 824-4000

RAMADA INN
262 Commerce St
(81625)
Rates: $49-99
Tel: (800) 272-6232

SUPER 8 MOTEL
200 Hwy 13 S
(81625)
Rates: $35-$73
Tel: (970) 824-3471
(800) 800-8000

CREEDE

**BROADACRES
RANCH**
P. O. Box 39 (81130)
Rates: n/a
Tel: (719) 658-2291

DEL NORTE

DEL NORTE MOTEL
1050 Grand Ave
(81132)
Rates: n/a
Tel: (719) 657-3581
(800) 372-2331

DELTA

**BEST WESTERN
SUNDANCE**
903 Main St (81416)
Rates: $37-$55
Tel: (970) 874-9781
(800) 626-1994

SOUTHGATE INN
2124 S Main St
(81416)
Rates: $25-$50
Tel: (970) 874-9726

DENVER
(and Vicinity)

**BEST BUDGET
MOTOR BAR X**
5001 W Colfax Ave
(80204)
Rates: $32-$37
Tel: (303) 534-7191

**BEST WESTERN
EXECUTIVE INN**
4411 Peoria St
(80239)
Rates: $69-$79
Tel: (303) 373-5730
(800) 528-1234

**BEST WESTERN
LANDMARK INN**
455 S Colorado Blvd
(80222)
Rates: $59-$84
Tel: (303) 388-5561
(800) 528-1234

BURNSLEY HOTEL
1000 Grant St
(80203)
Rates: $65-$135
Tel: (303) 830-1000

**THE CAMBRIDGE
INN**
1560 Sherman St
(80203)
Rates: $79-$139
Tel: (303) 831-1252
(800) 877-1252

CAMERON MOTEL
4500 E Evan Ave
(80222)
Rates: $34-$42
Tel: (303) 757-2100

**COMFORT INN
AIRPORT**
7201 E 36th Ave
(80207)
Rates: $48-$73
Tel: (303) 393-7666

**CONCORDE
AIRPORT HOTEL**
6090 Smith Rd
(80216)
Rates: n/a
Tel: (303) 388-4051

**DAYS HOTEL
AIRPORT**
4590 Quebec St
(80216)
Rates: $49-$55
Tel: (303) 320-0260
(800) 329-7466

**DAYS INN -
CENTRAL**
620 Federal Blvd
(80204)
Rates: $32-54
Tel: (303) 571-1715
(800) 329-7466

DRURY INN
4400 Peoria St
(80239)
Rates: $49-$61
Tel: (303) 373-1983

EMBASSY SUITES-AIRPORT
4444 N Havana
(80239)
Rates: $84-$120
Tel: (303) 375-0400
(800) 345-0087

EXECUTIVE TOWER INN
1405 Curtis St
(80202)
Rates: $142-$162
Tel: (303) 571-0300
(800) 525-6651

HOLIDAY CHALET HOTEL APARTMENTS
1820 E Colfax Ave
(80218)
Rates: $49-$67
Tel: (303) 321-9975

HOLIDAY INN-AIRPORT
4040 Quebec St
(80216)
Rates: $69-$79
Tel: (303) 321-6666

HOLIDAY INN DENVER I-70 EAST & TRADE CENTER
15500 40th Ave
(80239)
Rates: $66-$78
Tel: (800) 465-4329

HOLIDAY INN-DOWNTOWN
1450 Glenarm Pl
(80202)
Rates: $75-$150
Tel: (303) 573-1450
(800) 523-5128

HOLIDAY INN-NORTH
4849 Bannock St
(80216)
Rates: $70-$95
Tel: (800) 465-4329

HOLIDAY INN SPORTS CENTER
1975 Bryant St
(80204)
Rates: $62-$72
Tel: (800) 465-4329

HOLIDAY INN-WEST
14707 W Colfax Ave
(80401)
Rates: $52-$62
Tel: (800) 465-4329

HOWARD JOHNSON MOTOR LODGE SOUTH
6300 E Hampden Ave (80222)
Rates: $60-$67
Tel: (800) 446-4656

LA QUINTA INN-AIRPORT
3975 Peoria Way
(80239)
Rates: $47-$60
Tel: (800) 531-5900

LA QUINTA INN-CENTRAL
3500 Fox St (80216)
Rates: $44-$54
Tel: (800) 531-5900

LA QUINTA INN-SOUTH
1975 S Colorado Blvd (80222)
Rates: $47-$60
Tel: (800) 531-5900

LA QUINTA INN
8701 Turnpike Dr
(80030)
Rates: $65-$79
Tel: (303) 425-9099
(800) 531-5900

LAKEWOOD INN
7150 Colfax (80215)
Rates: $35-$50
Tel: (303) 238-1251

LOEWS GIORGIO HOTEL
4150 E Mississippi Ave (80222)
Rates: $170-$450
Tel: (303) 782-9300
(800) 345-9172

MARRIOTT HOTEL CITY CENTER
1701 California St
(80202)
Rates: $99-$129
Tel: (303) 297-1300
(800) 228-9290

MARRIOTT HOTEL SOUTHEAST
6363 E Hampden Ave (80222)
Rates: $59-$129
Tel: (303) 758-7000
(800) 228-9290

MOTEL 6-CENTRAL
3050 W 49th Ave
(80221)
Rates: $32-$38
Tel: (303) 455-8888
(800) 440-6000

MOTEL 6-EAST
12020 E 39th Ave
(80239)
Rates: $37-$43
Tel: (303) 371-1980
(800) 440-6000

901 PENN HOUSE
901 Pennsylvania St
(80203)
Rates: $172-$335
Tel: (303) 831-8060

QUALITY INN SOUTH
6300 E Hampden Ave (80222)
Rates: $62-$98
Tel: (303) 758-2211
(800) 617-1986

RADISSON HOTEL
1550 Court Pl
(80202)
Rates: $59-$140
Tel: (303) 893-3333

RAMADA INN AIRPORT
3737 Quebec St
(80207)
Rates: $72-$86
Tel: (303) 388-6161
(800) 272-6232

RAMADA INN DOWNTOWN DENVER 2
1150 E Colfax Ave
(80218)
Rates: $70-$85
Tel: (303) 831-7700
(800) 272-6232

RED LION HOTEL
3203 Quebec St
(80207)
Rates: $134-$164
Tel: (303) 321-3333
(800) 547-8010

REGENCY INN
3900 Elati St (80216)
Rates: $39
Tel: (303) 458-0808

RESIDENCE INN BY MARRIOTT DOWNTOWN
2777 Zuni St (80211)
Rates: $99-$129
Tel: (303) 458-5318
(800) 331-3131

ROCKIES LODGE
4760 E Evans Ave
(80222)
Rates: $26-$48
Tel: (303) 757-7601

SHERATON DENVER TECH CENTER
4900 DTC Pkwy
(80237)
Rates: $69-$159
Tel: (303) 779-1100

SHERATON INN-AIRPORT
3535 Quebec St
(80207)
Rates: $69-$84
Tel: (303) 333-7711

SUPER 8 MOTEL
2601 Zuni St (80211)
Rates: $33-$69
Tel: (303) 433-6677
(800) 800-8000

SUPER 8 MOTEL
5888 N Broadway
(80216)
Rates: $37-$75
Tel: (303) 296-3100
(800) 800-8000

VICTORIA OAKS INN
1575 Race St (80206)
Rates: $39-$79
Tel: (303) 355-1818

WARWICK HOTEL
1776 Grant St
(80203)
Rates: $89-$240
Tel: (303) 861-2000
(800) 525-2588

THE WESTIN HOTEL
1672 Lawrence St
(80202)
Rates: $207-$242
Tel: (303) 572-9100
(800) 228-3000

DILLON

**BEST WESTERN
PTARMIGAN LODGE**
P. O. Box 218 (80435)
Rates: $45-$130
Tel: (970) 468-2341
(800) 528-1234

DAYS INN
580 Silvershorne Ln
(80435)
Rates: $70-$200
Tel: (800) 329-7466

**HOLIDAY INN
SUMMIT COUNTY**
Box 10 (80435)
Rates: $89-$175
Tel: (800) 465-4329

DOLORES

**DOLORES
MOUNTAIN INN**
701 Railroad Ave
(81323)
Rates: $34-$54
Tel: (970) 882-7203
(800) 842-8113

**LOST CANYON
LAKE LODGE**
P. O. Box 1289
(81323)
Rates: $75
Tel: (970) 882-4913

OUTPOST MOTEL
1800 Central Ave
(81323)
Rates: $32-$38
Tel: (970) 882-7271
(800) 382-4892

**PRIEST GULCH
RANCH CAMP**
2670 Hwy 145
(81323)
Rates: $54-$59
Tel: (970) 562-3810

**RAG O'MUFFIN
RANCH**
26030 Hwy 145
(81323)
Rates: $75+
Tel: (970) 562-3803

DURANGO

ADOBE INN
2178 Main Ave
(81301)
Rates: $38-$102
Tel: (970) 247-2743

ALPINE MOTEL
3515 Main Ave
(81301)
Rates: $28-$84
Tel: (970) 247-4042
(800) 818-4042

**BEST WESTERN
LODGE AT
PURGATORY**
49617 Hwy 550 N
(81301)
Rates: $85-$170
Tel: (970) 247-9669
(800) 528-1234

BUDGET INN
3077 Main Ave
(81301)
Rates: $38-$74
Tel: (970) 247-5222
(800) 257-2222

CABOOSE MOTEL
3363 Main Ave
(81301)
Rates: $24-$64
Tel: (970) 247-1191

EDELWEISS INN
689 Animas View Dr
(81301)
Rates: $48-$58
Tel: (970) 247-5685

HOLIDAY INN
800 Camino Del Rio
(81301)
Rates: $49-$99
Tel: (970) 247-5393

IRON HORSE INN
5800 N Main Ave
(81301)
Rates: $70-$110
Tel: (970) 259-1010

**JARVIS SUITE
HOTEL**
125 W 10th St
(81301)
Rates: $69-$129
Tel: (970) 259-6190
(800) 824-1024

**NATIONAL 9
SUNSET**
2855 N Main Ave
(81301)
Rates: $29-$79
Tel: (970) 247-2653

RED LION INN
501 Camino Del Rio
(81301)
Rates: $79-$194
Tel: (970) 259-6580
(800) 547-8010

RODEWAY INN
2701 N Main Ave
(81301)
Rates: $39-$98
Tel: (970) 259-2540
(800) 424-4777

SIESTA MOTEL
3475 N Main Ave
(81301)
Rates: $52-$84
Tel: (970) 247-0741

TRAVELODGE
2970 Main Ave
(81301)
Rates: $36-$136
Tel: (970) 247-1741
(800) 578-7878

**WESTERN STAR
MOTEL**
3310 N Main Ave
(81301)
Rates: $28-$58
Tel: (970) 247-4895

EADS

**COUNTRY MANOR
MOTEL**
609 East 15th St
(81036)
Rates: $27-$36
Tel: (719) 438-5451

EAGLE

**BEST WESTERN
EAGLE LODGE**
P. O. Box 128 (81631)
Rates: $49-$120
Tel: (800) 528-1234

ENGLEWOOD

**CLARION HOTEL
SOUTHEAST**
7770 S Peoria St
(80112)
Rates: $73-$95
Tel: (303) 790-7770

EMBASSY SUITES
10250 E Costilla Ave
(80112)
Rates: $94-$159
Tel: (303) 792-0433
(800) 654-4810

HAMPTON INN
9231 E Arapahoe Rd
(80112)
Rates: $56-$72
Tel: (800) 426-7886

**RESIDENCE INN
BY MARRIOTT**
6565 S Yosemite St
(80111)
Rates: $59-$155
Tel: (303) 740-7177
(800) 331-3131

SUPER 8 MOTEL
5150 S Quebec St
(80111)
Rates: $49-70
Tel: (303) 771-8000
(800) 800-8000

ESTES PARK

**AMERICAN
WILDERNESS
LODGE**
481 W Elkhorn
(80517)
Rates: $45-$70+
Tel: (970) 586-4402
(800) 762-7968

**CASTLE MOUNTAIN
LODGE**
1520 Fall River Rd
(80517)
Rates: $45-$270
Tel: (970) 586-3664

**FOUR WINDS
MOTOR LODGE**
1120 Big Thompson
Ave (80517)
Rates: $31-$75
Tel: (970) 586-3313

MACHIN'S COTTAGES IN THE PINES
P. O. Box 2867-CW (80517)
Rates: $70-$108
Tel: (970) 586-4276

OLYMPUS LODGE
P. O. Box 547 (80517)
Rates: $28-$125
Tel: (970) 586-8141

TRIPLE R COTTAGES
1000 Riverside Dr (80517)
Rates: $45-$125
Tel: (970) 586-5552

EVANS

MOTEL 6
3015 8th Ave (80620)
Rates: $29-$35
Tel: (970) 351-6481
(800) 466-8356

WINTERSET INN
800 31 St (80620)
Rates: $26-$76
Tel: (970) 339-2493

FAIRPLAY

THE WESTERN INN
P. O. Box 187 (80440)
Rates: $39-$52
Tel: (719) 836-2026

FORT COLLINS

DAYS INN
3625 E Mulberry St (80524)
Rates: $40-$70
Tel: (970) 221-5490
(800) 329-7466

HAMPTON INN
1620 Oakridge Dr. (80525)
Rates: $59-81
Tel: (970) 229-5927
(800) 426-7866

HOLIDAY INN I-25
3836 E Mulberry St (80524)
Rates: $62-$70
Tel: (800) 465-4329

MOTEL 6
3900 E Mulberry (80524)
Rates: $28-$34
Tel: (970) 482-6466
(800) 466-8356

MONTCLAIR MOTEL
1405 N College Ave (80524)
Rates: $24-$45
Tel: (970) 482-5452

MULBERRY INN
4333 E Mulberry St (80524)
Rates: $39-$55
Tel: (970) 493-9000

SLEEP INN
3808 Mulberry St (80524)
Rates: $32-$48
Tel: (800) 221-2222

SUPER 8 MOTEL
409 Centro Way (80524)
Rates: $41-$58
Tel: (970) 493-7701
(800) 800-8000

UNIVERSITY PARK HOLIDAY INN
425 W Prospect Rd (80526)
Rates: $90
Tel: (970) 482-2626

FORT GARLAND

THE LODGE MOTEL
P. O. Box 160 (81133)
Rates: $29-$33
Tel: (719) 379-3434

FORT MORGAN

BEST WESTERN PARK TERRACE MOTEL
725 Main (80701)
Rates: $43-$68
Tel: (970) 867-8256
(800) 528-1234

CENTRAL MOTEL
201 W Platte Ave (80701)
Rates: $37-$57
Tel: (970) 867-2401

ECONO LODGE
1409 Barlow Rd (80701)
Rates: $43-$50
Tel: (970) 867-9481
(800) 424-4777

MADISON HOTEL
14378 Hwy 34 (80701)
Rates: $36-$42
Tel: (970) 867-8208

FRISCO

BEST WESTERN LAKE DILLON LODGE
1202 Summit Blvd (80443)
Rates: $67-$184
Tel: (800) 528-1234

HOLIDAY INN SUMMIT COUNTY
1129 N Summit Blvd (80443)
Rates: $55-$135
Tel: (970) 668-5000

LUXURY INN
1205 N Summit Blvd (80443)
Rates: $33-$100
Tel: (970) 668-3220

GEORGETOWN

GEORGETOWN MOTOR INN
1100 Rose St (80444)
Rates: $36-$57
Tel: (970) 569-3201
(800) 884-3201

GLENWOOD SPRINGS

AFFORDABLE INNS
51823 Hwys 6 & 24 (81601)
Rates: $29-$79
Tel: (970) 945-8888

BEST WESTERN CARAVAN INN
1826 Grand Ave (81601)
Rates: $46-$91
Tel: (970) 945-7451
(800) 528-1234

HOLIDAY INN
51359 Hwys 6 & 24 (81601)
Rates: $58-$68
Tel: (800) 465-4329

HOMESTEAD INN NATIONAL 9
52039 Hwys 6 & 24 (81601)
Rates: $30-$70
Tel: (800) 456-6685

RAMADA INN
124 W 6th St (81601)
Rates: $47-$145
Tel: (970) 945-2500
(800) 272-6232

SILVER SPRUCE MOTEL
162 W 6th St (81601)
Rates: $39-$84
Tel: (970) 945-5458

GOLDEN

DAYS INN SUITES-WEST
15059 W Colfax Ave (80401)
Rates: $47-$59
Tel: (800) 329-7466

GOLDEN MOTEL
510 24th St (80401)
Rates: n/a
Tel: (303) 279-5581

LA QUINTA INN
3301 Youngfield Service Rd (80401)
Rates: $45-$58
Tel: (800) 531-5900

MARRIOTT-WEST
1717 Denver West Blvd (80401)
Rates: $75-$120
Tel: (303) 279-9100
(800) 228-9290

GRANBY

BROKEN ARROW MOTEL
Box 143 (80446)
Rates: $25-$40
Tel: (970) 887-3532

LITTLETREE INN
P. O. Box 800 (80446)
Rates: $66-$72
Tel: (970) 887-2551

GRAND JUNCTION

BEST WESTERN SANDMAN MOTEL
708 Horizon Dr
(81506)
Rates: $38-$64
Tel: (970) 243-4150
(800) 528-1234

DAYS INN
733 Horizon Dr
(81506)
Rates: $42-76
Tel: (970) 245-7200
(800) 329-7466

FRIENDSHIP INN
733 Horizon Dr
(81506)
Rates: $36-$48
Tel: (800) 424-4777

HILTON HOTEL
743 Horizon Dr
(81506)
Rates: $79-$129
Tel: (970) 241-8888
(800) 445-8667

HOLIDAY INN
P. O. Box 1725
(81502)
Rates: $48-$58
Tel: (800) 465-4329

HOWARD JOHNSON
752 Horizon Dr
(81506)
Rates: $42-$49
Tel: (970) 243-5150
(800) 446-4656

MOTEL 6
776 Horizon Dr
(81506)
Rates: $28-$34
Tel: (970) 243-2628
(800) 466-8356

PEACHTREE INN
1600 North Avenue
(81501)
Rates: $27-$42
Tel: (970) 245-5770
(800) 525-0030

SUPER 8 MOTEL
728 Horizon Dr
(81506)
Rates: $35-$55
Tel: (970) 248-8080
(800) 800-8000

VALUE LODGE
104 White Ave
(81501)
Rates: $30-$42
Tel: (970) 242-0651

WEST GATE INN
2210 Hwys 6 & 50
(81505)
Rates: $35-$42
Tel: (970) 241-3020

GRAND LAKE

RIVERSIDE GUESTHOUSES
P. O. Box 1469
(80447)
Rates: n/a
Tel: (970) 627-3619

GREELEY

BEST WESTERN RAMKOTA INN
701 8th St (80631)
Rates: $52-$75
Tel: (970) 353-8444
(800) 528-1234

HOLIDAY INN OF GREELEY
609 8th Ave (80631)
Rates: $55-$72
Tel: (970) 356-3000

WINTERSET INN OF GREELEY
800 31st St (Evans 80620)
Rates: $29-$45
Tel: (970) 339-2492

GREENWOOD VILLAGE

DAYS INN
5150 S Quebec St
(80111)
Rates: $48-80
Tel: (303) 721-1144
(800) 329-7466

MOTEL 6
9201 E Arapahoe Rd
(80112)
Rates: $38-44
Tel: (303) 790-8220
(800) 466-8356

GUNNISON

DAYS INN
701 Hwy 50W
(81230)
Rates: $35-$60
Tel: (970) 641-0608

HARMEL'S GUEST RANCH
Box 955M (81230)
Rates: $110-$170
Tel: (970) 641-1740

HYLANDER INN
412 E Tomichi Ave
(81230)
Rates: $30-$68
Tel: (970) 641-0700

HESPERUS

CANYON MOTEL
Hwy 160 & CR 124
(81326)
Rates: n/a
Tel: (303) 259-6277

HOTCHKISS

COMFORT LODGE
P. O. Box 37 (81419)
Rates: $34-$57
Tel: (970) 872-2200

HOTCHKISS INN
406 Hwy 133 (81419)
Rates: $39-$51
Tel: (970) 872-2200

IDAHO SPRINGS

H & H MOTOR LODGE
2445 Colorado Blvd
(80452)
Rates: $38-$65
Tel: (303) 567-2838
(800) 445-2893

PEORIANA MOTEL
2901 Colorado Blvd
(80452)
Rates: $25-$35
Tel: (303) 567-2021

6 & 40-NATIONAL 9 INN
2920 Colorado Blvd
(80452)
Rates: $27-$45
Tel: (303) 567-2691

JULESBURG

PLATTE VALLEY INN
I-76 and US 385
(80737)
Rates: $34-$71
Tel: (970) 474-3336
(800) 563-5166

KIT CARSON

STAGE STOP MOTEL
P. O. Box 207 (80825)
Rates: $26-$34
Tel: (719) 962-3277

LA JUNTA

QUALITY INN
1325 E 3rd St (81050)
Rates: $37-$54
Tel: (719) 384-2571
(800) 221-2222

STAGECOACH INN
905 W 3rd St (81050)
Rates: $28-$42
Tel: (719) 384-5476

LAKE CITY

CINNAMON INN
426 Gunnison Ave
(81235)
Rates: $60-$85
Tel: (303) 944-2641

WESTERN BELLE LODGE
1221 Hwy 149 N
(81235)
Rates: n/a
Tel: (303) 944-2415

LAKEWOOD

CHALET MOTEL
6051 W Alameda
Ave (80226)
Rates: $31-$38
Tel: (303) 237-7775

COMFORT INN-SOUTHWEST
3440 S Vance St
(80227)
Rates: $48-$80
Tel: (800) 221-2222

FOOTHILLS EXECUTIVE LODGING
7150 W Colfax Ave
(80215)
Rates: $40-$65
Tel: (303) 232-2932
(800) 456-0425

HAMPTON INN-SOUTHWEST
3605 S Wadsworth
Blvd (80235)
Rates: $48-$62
Tel: (800) 426-7886

HOLIDAY INN
7390 W Hampden
Ave (80227)
Rates: $69-$79
Tel: (800) 465-4329

MOTEL 6
480 Wadsworth
Blvd (80226)
Rates: $32-42
Tel: (303) 232-4924
(800) 466-8356

RESIDENCE INN BY MARRIOTT
6565 S Yosemite St
(80111)
Rates: $59-$135
Tel: (800) 331-3131

RODEWAY INN
7150 W Colfax Ave
(80215)
Rates: $45-$70
Tel: (303) 238-1251
(800) 321-7187
(800) 228-2000

SHERATON HOTEL & CONFERENCE CENTER
360 Union Blvd
(80228)
Rates: $65-$139
Tel: (303) 987-2000

SUPER 8 MOTEL
Wadsworth &
Hampden (80215)
Rates: $59-69
Tel: (800) 800-8000

LAMAR

ECONOMY INN
1201 N Main St
(81052)
Rates: $19-$34
Tel: (719) 336-7471

LAS ANIMAS

BEST WESTERN BENT'S FORT INN
P. O. Box 108 (81054)
Rates: $42-$60
Tel: (719) 456-0011
(800) 528-1234

LEADVILLE

ALPS MOTEL
Hwy 24 S at Elm
(80461)
Rates: n/a
Tel: (719) 486-1223

BEL-AIR MOTEL
Hwy 24 S at Elm
(80461)
Rates: n/a
Tel: (719) 486-0881

CLUB LEAD
500 E 7th St (80461)
Rates: n/a
Tel: (719) 486-2202

LEADVILLE INN
25 Jacktown Pl
(80461)
Rates: $40-$50
Tel: (719) 486-3637

MOUNTAIN PEAKS MOTEL
1 Harrison Ave
(80461)
Rates: n/a
Tel: (719) 486-3178

SILVER KING MOTOR INN
2020 N Poplar
(80461)
Rates: $42-$59
Tel: (719) 486-2610
(800) 871-2610

TIMBERLINE MOTEL
216 Harrison Ave
(80461)
Rates: n/a
Tel: (719) 486-1876
(800) 352-1876

LIMON

BEST WESTERN LIMON INN
P.O. Box 1361 (80828)
Rates: $35-79
Tel: (719) 775-0277
(800) 528-1234

DAYS INN
250 E Main St
(80828)
Rates: $38-75
Tel: (719) 775-2821
(800) 329-7466

ECONO LODGE OF LIMON
985 Hwy 24 (80828)
Rates: $46-$56
Tel: (719) 775-2867
(800) 424-4777

LIMON INN 4 LESS EAST
250 E Main St
(80828)
Rates: $42-$61
Tel: (719) 775-2821

SAFARI MOTEL
637 Main St (80828)
Rates: $32-$46
Tel: (719) 775-2363

SUPER 8 MOTEL
P.O. Box 1202 (80828)
Rates: $34-50
Tel: (719) 775-2889
(800) 800-8000

LONGMONT

BUDGET HOST LONGMONT INN
3815 Hwy 119
(80504)
Rates: $33-$48
Tel: (303) 776-8700

FIRST INTERSTATE INN
3940 Hwy 119
(80504)
Rates: n/a
Tel: (303) 772-6000
(800) 462-4667

RAINTREE PLAZA HOTEL & CONFERENCE CENTER
1900 Ken Pratt Blvd
(80501)
Rates: $94-$133
Tel: (303) 776-2000
(800) 843-8240

SUPER 8 MOTEL
10805 Turner Ave
(80504)
Rates: $42-59
Tel: (303) 772-0888
(800) 800-8000

SUPER 8 MOTEL-TWIN PEAKS
2446 N Main St
(80501)
Rates: $43-$64
Tel: (303) 772-8106
(800) 800-8000

LOVELAND

BEST WESTERN COACH HOUSE
5542 Hwy 34E
(80537)
Rates: $45-$75
Tel: (970) 667-7810
(800) 528-1234

BUDGET HOST EXIT 254 INN
2716 SE Frontage Rd
(80537)
Rates: $30-$44
Tel: (970) 667-5202

MANCOS

BLUE SPRUCE MOTEL
40700 Hwy 160 West
(81328)
Rates: $27-$50
Tel: (970) 533-7073

PONDEROSA CABINS
Cty Road 37 &
Hwy 184 (81328)
Rates: $40+
Tel: (970) 882-7396

MESA

WAGON WHEEL MOTEL
1090 Hwy 65 (81643)
Rates: $40-$45
Tel: (970) 268-5224

MESA VERDE NATIONAL PARK

FAR VIEW LODGE IN MESA VERDE
P. O. Box 277
(Mancos 81328)
Rates: $72-$84
Tel: (970) 529-4421
(800) 449-2288

MONARCH

MONARCH MOUNTAIN LODGE
#1 Power Pl (81227)
Rates: $50-$169
Tel: (719) 539-2581
(800) 332-3668

MONTE VISTA

COMFORT INN
P. O. Box 781 (81144)
Rates: $60-$85
Tel: (719) 852-0612
(800) 221-2222

MONTROSE

BLACK CANYON MOTEL
1605 E Main (81401)
Rates: $33-$76
Tel: (970) 249-3495

SUPER 8 MOTEL
1705 E Main (81401)
Rates: $35-$53
Tel: (970) 249-9294
(800) 800-8000

NATURITA

RAY MOTEL
123 Main St (81422)
Rates: $26-$46
Tel: (970) 865-2235

NEDERLAND

NEDERHAUS MOTEL
686 Hwy 119 South
(80466)
Rates: $38-$90
Tel: (303) 444-4705
(800) 422-4629

NORTHGLENN

DAYS INN-NORTH
36 E 120th Ave
(80233)
Rates: $37-$52
Tel: (303) 457-0688
(800) 329-7466

HOLIDAY INN
10 E 120th Ave
(80233)
Rates: $66-$75
Tel: (800) 465-4329

RAMADA INN
110 W 104th Ave
(80234)
Rates: $65-75
Tel: (303) 451-1234
(800) 272-6232

OURAY

OURAY COTTAGE MOTEL
4th & Main Sts
(81427)
Rates: $45-$115
Tel: (970) 325-4370

OURAY VICTORIAN INN
50 3rd Ave (81427)
Rates: $49-$75
Tel: (970) 325-7222
(800) 84-OURAY

TIMBER RIDGE MOTEL
1515 North Main St
(81427)
Rates: n/a
Tel: (970) 325-4523

PAGOSA SPRINGS

SUPER 8 MOTEL
34 Piedra Rd (81147)
Rates: $39-$59
Tel: (970) 731-4005
(800) 800-8000

PARACHUTE

SUPER 8 MOTEL
252 Green Motel
(81635)
Rates: $43-$60
Tel: (970) 285-7936
(800) 800-8000

PUEBLO

HAMPTON INN
4703 N Frwy (81108)
Rates: $54-$66
Tel: (800) 426-7866

HOLIDAY INN
4001 N Elizabeth
(81108)
Rates: $63-$80
Tel: (800) 465-4329

MOTEL 6
960 Hwy 50 W
(81008)
Rates: $29-$35
Tel: (719) 543-8900
(800) 466-8356

MOTEL 6
4103 N Elizabeth
(81008)
Rates: $29-$35
Tel: (719) 543-6221
(800) 466-8356

NATIONAL 9 INN
4400 N Elizabeth
(81008)
Rates: $28-$49
Tel: (719) 543-4173

PUEBLO INN
800 Hwy 50 W
(81008)
Rates: $32-$48
Tel: (719) 543-6820

RAMADA INN
2001 N Hudson
(81008)
Rates: $60-90
Tel: (719) 542-3750
(800) 272-6232

PURGATORY

BEST WESTERN LODGE AT PURGATORY
49617 US 550 N
(81301)
Rates: $70-$170
Tel: (970) 247-9669
(800) 637-7727

REDSTONE

AVALANCHE RANCH B & B
12863 Hwy 133
(81623)
Rates: $85-$135
Tel: (970) 963-2846

CLEVEHOLM MANOR
58 Redstone Blvd
(81623)
Rates: $95-$180
Tel: (970) 963-3463
(800) 643-4837

RIFLE

RED RIVER INN
718 Taughenbaugh
Blvd (81650)
Rates: $22-$42
Tel: (970) 625-3050

RUSTY CANNON MOTEL
701 Taughenbaugh
Blvd (81650)
Rates: $32-$55
Tel: (970) 625-4004
(800) 341-8000

ROCKY FORD

MELON VALLEY INN
1319 Elm Ave
(81067)
Rates: $30-$45
Tel: (719) 254-3306

SALIDA

ASPEN LEAF LODGE
7350 Hwy 50W
(81201)
Rates $30-$60
Tel: (719) 539-6733
(800) 759-0338

BUDGET LODGE
1146 E Hwy 50
(81201)
Rates: $27-$47
Tel: (719) 539-6695
(800) 933-4823 (CO)

CIRCLE R MOTEL
304 E Rainbow Blvd
(81201)
Rates: $24-$64
Tel: (719) 539-6296

RAINBOW INN
105 Hwy 50E (81201)
Rates: $24-$52
Tel: (719) 539-4444

SALIDA MOTEL
1310 E Hwy 50
(81201)
Rates: $25-$60
Tel: (719) 539-2895

WESTERN HOLIDAY MOTEL
545 W Rainbow Blvd (81201)
Rates: $35-$60
Tel: (719) 539-2553

WOODLAND MOTEL
903 W 1st (81201)
Rates: $26-$71
Tel: (719) 539-4980
(800) 488-0456

SILVER CREEK

THE INN AT SILVER CREEK
P. O. Box 4222 (80446)
Rates: $37-$218
Tel: (800) 926-4386

SILVERTHORNE

I-70 INN
361 Blueriver Pkwy (80498)
Rates: n/a
Tel: (970) 468-5170

DAYS INN
580 Silverthorne Ln (80498)
Rates: $45-160
Tel: (970) 468-8661
(800) 329-7466

SILVERTON

ALMA HOUSE INN
220 E 10th St (81433)
Rates: $48-$80
Tel: (970) 387-5336

WYMAN HOTEL & INN
1370 Greene St (81433)
Rates: $45-$83
Tel: (970) 387-5372
(800) 609-7845

SNOWMASS VILLAGE

SILVERTREE HOTEL
P. O. Box 5009 (81615)
Rates: $145-$500
Tel: (303) 923-3520

SOUTH FORK

THE INN MOTEL
30362 West Hwy 160 (81154)
Rates: n/a
Tel: (719) 873-5514

WOLF CREEK SKI LODGE
31042 Hwy W 160 (81154)
Rates: $48-$55
Tel: (719) 873-5547
(800) 874-0416

STEAMBOAT SPRINGS

THE ALPINER LODGE
424 Lincoln Ave (80477)
Rates: $54-$115
Tel: (970) 879-1430

HARBOR HOTEL & HOTEL HARBOR CONDOS
P. O. Box 774109 (80477)
Rates: $40-$180
Tel: (970) 879-1522

HOLIDAY INN OF STEAMBOAT
3190 S Lincoln Ave (80477)
Rates: $55-$205
Tel: (800) 465-4329

RABBIT EARS MOTEL
201 Lincoln Ave (80477)
Rates: $50-$136
Tel: (970) 879-1150
(800) 828-7702

SKY VALLEY LODGE
P. O. Box 773132 (80477)
Rates: $55-$195
Tel: (970) 879-7749

SUPER 8 MOTEL
US Hwy 40 E (80477)
Rates: $50-$99
Tel: (970) 879-5230
(800) 800-8000

STERLING

BEST WESTERN SUNDOWNER
Overland Trail St (80751)
Rates: $69-$110
Tel: (970) 522-6265
(800) 528-1234

COLONIAL MOTEL
915 S Division (80751)
Rates: $24-$38
Tel: (970) 522-3382

DAYS INN
12881 Hwy 61 (80751)
Rates: $30-$47
Tel: (970) 522-6660
(800) 329-7466

FIRST INTERSTATE INN
20930 Hwy 6 (80751)
Rates: $25-$43
Tel: (970) 522-7274

RAMADA INN
I-76 & Hwy 6 (80751)
Rates: $64-$87
Tel: (970) 522-2625
(800) 272-6232

SUPER 8 MOTEL
12883 Hwy 61 (80751)
Rates: $43-53
Tel: (970) 522-0300
(800) 800-8000

STRATTON

BEST WESTERN GOLDEN PRAIRIE INN
700 Colorado Ave (80836)
Rates: $43-$79
Tel: (719) 348-5311
(800) 528-1234

TELLURIDE

DORAL TELLURIDE RESORT & SPA
145 Country Club Dr (81435)
Rates: $335-$800
Tel: (800) 443-6725

THE PEAKS AT TELLURIDE
136 Country Club Dr (81435)
Rates: $235-$1750
Tel: (970) 728-6800

THORNTON

MOTEL 6
6 W 83rd Pl (80221)
Rates: $30-40
Tel: (303) 429-1550
(800) 466-8356

TRINIDAD

BEST WESTERN COUNTRY CLUB INN
900 W Adams St (81082)
Rates: $45-$89
Tel: (719) 846-2215
(800) 528-1234

BUDGET HOST TRINIDAD
10301 Santa Fe Trail Dr (81082)
Rates: $24-$69
Tel: (800) 283-4678

BUDGET SUMMIT INN
I-25 Exit 11 (81082)
Rates: n/a
Tel: (719) 846-2251

DAYS INN
702 W Main St (81082)
Rates: $45-59
Tel: (719) 846-2271
(800) 329-7466

HOLIDAY INN
Rt 1, I-25 exit 11 (81082)
Rates: $38-$90
Tel: (800) 465-4329

SUPER 8 MOTEL
1924 Freedom Rd (81082)
Rates: $37-55
Tel: (719) 846-8280
(800) 800-8000

VAIL

ANTLERS AT VAIL
680 W Lionshead Pl
(81657)
Rates: $105-$365
Tel: (970) 476-2471
(800) 843-8245

L'OSTELLO
704 W Lionshead Cir
(81657)
Rates: $49-$245
Tel: (970) 476-2050

VICTOR

VICTOR HOTEL
4th & Victor Ave
(80860)
Rates: $85-$99
Tel: (970) 689-3553
(800) 748-0870 (CO)

WALDEN

**NORTH PARK
MOTEL**
625 Main St (80480)
Rates: $30-$60
Tel: (970) 723-4271

WALSENBURG

ANCHOR MOTEL
1001 Main St (81089)
Rates: $28-$55
Tel: (719) 738-2800

**BEST WESTERN
RAMBLER MOTEL**
P. O. Box 48 (81089)
Rates: $49-$89
Tel: (719) 738-1121
(800) 528-1234

WESTCLIFFE

WESTCLIFFE INN
S Hwy 69 &
Hermit Rd (81252)
Rates: $33-$75
Tel: (719) 783-9275
(800) 284-0850

WESTMINSTER

**LA QUINTA INN-
NORTH**
345 W 120th Ave
(80234)
Rates: $56-$68
Tel: (800) 531-5900

SUPER 8 MOTEL
12055 Melody Dr
(80234)
Rates: $37-$57
Tel: (303) 451-7200
(800) 800-8000

WHEAT RIDGE

**HOLIDAY INN
EXPRESS**
4700 Kipling St
(80033)
Rates: $34-$52
Tel: (303) 423-4000
(800) 465-4329

MOTEL 6
9920 W 49th Ave
(80033)
Rates: $28-38
Tel: (303) 424-0658
(800) 466-8356

MOTEL 6
10300 S I-70
Frontage Rd
(80033)
Rates: $28-$38
Tel: (303) 467-3172
(800) 466-8356

QUALITY INN
12100 W 44th Ave
(80033)
Rates: $34-$69
Tel: (800) 221-2222

WINTER PARK

**ALPENGLO
MOTOR LODGE**
US Hwy 40, Box 35
(80482)
Rates: $42-$160
Tel: (970) 726-5294

**SITZMARK LODGE
CHALETS & CABINS**
Hwy 40 at King's
Crossing (80482)
Rates: $40-$80
Tel: (970) 726-5453

VINTAGE HOTEL
P. O. Box 1369
(80482)
Rates: $65-$500
Tel: (970) 726-8801
(800) 472-7017

CONNECTICUT

AVON

AVON OLD FARMS HOTEL
P.O. Box 1295
(06001)
Rates: $79-$129
Tel: (203) 677-1651

BERLIN

HAWTHORNE INN
2387 Wilbur Cross
Hwy (06037)
Rates: $51-$75
Tel: (860) 828-4181

BRANFORD

BRANFORD MOTOR INN
P. O. Box 449 (06405)
Rates: $50-$74
Tel: (203) 488-8314

DAYS INN
375 E Main St
(06405)
Rates: $65-225
Tel: (203) 488-8314
(800) 329-7466

MOTEL 6
320 E Main St
(06405)
Rates: $36-48
Tel: (203) 483-5828
(800) 466-8356

BRIDGEPORT

BRIDGEPORT HOLIDAY INN
1070 Main St (06604)
Rates: $69-$129
Tel: (800) 465-4329

BROOKFIELD

DAYS INN
1030 Federal Rd
(06804)
Rates: n/a
Tel: (800) 329-7466

CHAPLIN

PLEASANT VIEW LODGE MOTEL
Rt 6 (06235)
Rates: $30-$50
Tel: (860) 455-9588

CHESTER

INN AT CHESTER
318 W Main St
(06412)
Rates: $95-$105
Tel: (203) 526-9541
(800) 949-7829

CLINTON

CLINTON MOTEL
163 East Main St
(06413)
Rates: $48-$78
Tel: (860) 669-8850

CORNWALL BRIDGE

THE CORNWALL INN
Route 7 (06754)
Rates: $50-$150
Tel: (800) 786-6884

CROMWELL

COMFORT INN
111 Berlin Rd (06416)
Rates: $45-$72
Tel: (800) 221-2222

HOLIDAY INN
4 Sebethe Dr (06416)
Rates: $69-$78
Tel: (800) 465-4329

RADISSON HOTEL & CONFERENCE CTR
100 Berlin Rd
(06416)
Rates: $69-$109
Tel: (203) 635-2000

SUPER 8 MOTEL
1 Industrial Park Rd
(06416)
Rates: $44-$65
Tel: (860) 632-8888
(800) 800-8000

DANBURY

DANBURY HILTON & TOWERS
18 Old Ridgebury
Rd (06810)
Rates: $85-$95
Tel: (203) 794-0600
(800) 445-8667

ETHAN ALLEN INN
21 Lake Ave
Extension (06811)
Rates: $67-$109
Tel: (203) 744-1776

HOLIDAY INN
80 Newtown Rd
(06810)
Rates: $59-$104
Tel: (800) 465-4329

RAMADA INN
I-84 at Exit 8 (06810)
Rates: $59-$125
Tel: (203) 792-3800
(800) 272-6232

DARIEN

COMFORT INN
50 Ledge Rd (06820)
Rates: $59-$79
Tel: (800) 221-2222

EAST HARTFORD

ECONO LODGE
927 Main St (06108)
Rates: $35-$60
Tel: (800) 424-4777

HOLIDAY INN
363 Roberts St
(06108)
Rates: $79-$83
Tel: (800) 465-4329

WELLESLY INN
333 Roberts St
(06108)
Rates: $45-$75
Tel: (203) 289-4950

EAST LYME

HOWARD JOHNSON
265 Flanders Rd
(06333)
Rates: $70-$130
Tel: (203) 739-6921

EAST WINDSOR

BEST WESTERN COLONIAL INN
161 Bridge St (06088)
Rates: $57-150
Tel: (860) 623-9411
(800) 528-1234

COMFORT INN
260 Main St (06088)
Rates: $44-$60
Tel: (800) 221-2222

RAMADA INN
161 Bridge St (06088)
Rates: $55-$72
Tel: (800) 272-6232

ENFIELD

MOTEL 6
11 Hazard Ave
(06082)
Rates: $33-$39
Tel: (860) 741-3685
(800) 440-6000

RED ROOF INN
5 Hazard Ave
(06082)
Rates: $38-$46
Tel: (860) 741-2571
(800) 843-7663

FAIRFIELD

**FAIRFIELD
MOTOR INN**
417 Post Rd (06430)
Rates: $63-$70
Tel: (800) 257-0496

FARMINGTON

**CENTENNIAL
INN SUITES**
5 Spring Ln (06032)
Rates: $76-$99
Tel: (860) 677-4647
(800) 852-2052

FARMINGTON INN
827 Farmington Ave
(06032)
Rates: $79-$120
Tel: (860) 677-2821

MARRIOTT HOTEL
15 Farm Springs Rd
(06032)
Rates: $99-$125
Tel: (860) 678-1000

GROTON

GOLD STAR INN
156 Kings Hwy
(06340)
Rates: $69-$90
Tel: (860) 446-0660

**TRAILS CORNER
MOTOR INN**
580 Poquannock Rd
(06340)
Rates: n/a
Tel: (860) 445-0220

GUILFORD

B & B AT B
279 Boston St (06437)
Rates: $76-$99
Tel: (203) 453-6490

HARTFORD

DAYS INN
207 Brainard Rd
(06114)
Rates: $39-89
Tel: (860) 247-3297
(800) 329-7466

CLARION HOTEL
5 Constitution Plaza
(06103)
Rates: $59-$69
Tel: (860) 278-2000

ECONO LODGE
7 Weston St (06120)
Rates: $39-$65
Tel: (800) 424-4777

HOLIDAY INN
363 Roberts St
(06108)
Rates: n/a
Tel: (800) 465-4329

**HOLIDAY INN
DOWNTOWN**
50 Morgan St (06120)
Rates: $86-$119
Tel: (800) 465-4329

**RAMADA INN-
DOWNTOWN-
CAPITOL HILL**
440 Asylum St
(06103)
Rates: $50-$75
Tel: (860) 246-6591
(800) 272-6232

RED ROOF INN
100 Weston St
(06120)
Rates: $36-$62
Tel: (860) 724-0222
(800) 843-7663

SUPER 8 MOTEL
57 W Service Rd
(06120)
Rates: $42-$58
Tel: (860) 246-8888
(800) 800-8000

WELLESLEY INN
333 Roberts St
(06018)
Rates: n/a
Tel: (860) 289-4950
(800) 444-8888

LAKEVILLE

**INTERLAKEN
INN RESORT &
CONF CENTER**
74 Interlaken Rd
(06039)
Rates: $85-$169
Tel: (860) 435-9878

**IRON MASTERS
MOTOR INN**
229 Main St (06039)
Rates: $59-$120
Tel: (860) 435-9844

LITCHFIELD

TOLLGATE HILL INN
P. O. Box 1339
(06759)
Rates: $100-$175
Tel: (860) 567-4545
(800) 445-3903

MANCHESTER

**CLARION
SUITES INN**
191 Spencer St
(06040)
Rates: $89-$167
Tel: (800) 221-2222

**MANCHESTER
VILLAGE MOTOR INN**
100 E Center St
(06040)
Rates: $49-$57
Tel: (860) 646-2300

MERIDEN

HAMPTON INN
10 Bee St (06450)
Rates: $48-$64
Tel: (203) 235-5154
(800) 426-7866

**RAMADA PLAZA
HOTEL &
CONFERENCE CENTER**
275 Research Pkwy
(06450)
Rates: $69-$125
Tel: (203) 238-2380
(800) 272-6232

**RESIDENCE INN
BY MARRIOTT**
390 Bee St (06450)
Rates: $65-$125
Tel: (203) 634-7770
(800) 331-3131

MILFORD

**COMFORT INN-
MILFORD**
278 Old Gate Ln
(06460)
Rates: $54-$60
Tel: (800) 221-2222

HAMPTON INN
129 Plains Rd
(06460)
Rates: $54-$65
Tel: (800) 426-7866

HOLIDAY INN
1212 Boston Post Rd
(06460)
Rates: $65-$112
Tel: (800) 465-4329

HOWARD JOHNSON
1052 Boston Post Rd
(06460)
Rates: $58-90
Tel: (203) 878-4611
(800) 446-4656

RED ROOF INN
10 Rowe Ave (06460)
Rates: $44-$55
Tel: (203) 877-6060
(800) 843-7663

MONTVILLE

**CHESTERFIELD
LODGE**
1596 Rt 85 (06370)
Rates: $30-$50
Tel: (860) 442-0039

MYSTIC

**CHARLEY'S HARBOR
INNE & COTTAGE**
15 Edgemont St
(06355)
Rates: $55-250
Tel: (860) 572-9253

MYSTIC-
LEDYARD

**APPLEWOOD
FARMS INN**
528 Col Ledyard
Hwy (06339)
Rates: n/a
Tel: (203) 536-2022

NEW BRITAIN

**RAMADA INN
CONFERENCE
CENTER**
65 Columbus Blvd
(06051)
Rates: $39-$99
Tel: (860) 224-9161
(800) 272-6232

NEW HAVEN

MOTEL 6
270 Foxon Blvd
(06513)
Rates: $46-$52
Tel: (203) 469-0343
(800) 440-6000

QUALITY INN
100 Pond Lily Ave
(06525)
Rates: $60-$130
Tel: (800) 221-2222

NEW LONDON

RED ROOF INN
707 Colman St
(06320)
Rates: $29-$67
Tel: (860) 444-0001
(800) 843-7663

NEW MILFORD

**THE HERITAGE INN
OF LITCHFIELD
COUNTY**
34 Bridge St (06776)
Rates: $59-$94
Tel: (860) 354-8883

NEW PRESTON

**ATHA HOUSE
COTTAGE**
Wheaton Rd off Rt
202 (06777)
Rates: $76-$99
Tel: (203) 355-7387

NIANTIC

**CONNECTICUT
YANKEE MOTEL**
Box 479 (06357)
Rates: $38-$68
Tel: (800) 942-8466

HOWARD JOHNSON
265 Flanders Rd
(06357)
Rates: $32-$105
Tel: (800) 446-4656

MOTEL 6
269 Flanders Rd
(06357)
Rates: $33-$39
Tel: (860) 739-6991
(800) 440-6000

NORTH HAVEN

HOLIDAY INN
201 Washington Ave
(06473)
Rates: $63
Tel: (800) 465-4329

NORTH STONINGTON

STATE LINE MOTEL
593 Providence-New
London Tpke (06359)
Rates: $30-$50
Tel: (203) 535-0680

NORWALK

**GARDEN PARK
MOTEL**
351 Westport Ave
(06851)
Rates: $51-$75
Tel: (203) 847-7303

RAMADA INN
789 Connecticut Ave
(06854)
Rates: $69-91
Tel: (203) 853-3477
(800) 272-6232

OLD LYME

OLD LYME INN
85 Lyme St (06371)
Rates: $85-$140
Tel: (203) 434-2600
(800) 434-5352

OLD SAYBROOK

COMFORT INN
100 Essex Rd (06475)
Rates: $30-$90
Tel: (800) 221-2222

**SANDPIPER
MOTOR INN**
1750 Boston Post Rd
(06475)
Rates: $56-$110
Tel: (860) 399-7973

PLAINFIELD

PLAINFIELD MOTEL
Box 101, RR 2
(Moosup 06354)
Rates: $37-$64
Tel: (203) 564-2791

PLAINVILLE

**HOWARD
JOHNSON LODGE**
400 New Britain Ave
(06062)
Rates: $55-$60
Tel: (860) 747-6876
(800) 446-4656

PUTNAM

KING'S INN
5 Heritage Rd
(06260)
Rates: $62-$78
Tel: (860) 928-7961

RIVERSIDE

HOWARD JOHNSON
1114 Boston Post Rd
(06878)
Rates: $49-99
Tel: (203) 637-3691
(800) 446-4656

ROCKY HILL

HOWARD JOHNSON
1499 Silas Deane
Hwy (06067)
Rates: $39
Tel: (800) 446-4656

SHELTON

**RESIDENCE INN
BY MARRIOTT**
1001 Bridgeport Ave
(06484)
Rates: $63-$160
Tel: (203) 926-9000
(800) 331-3131

SIMSBURY

THE EXECUTIVE INN
969 Hopmeadow St
(06070)
Rates: $59-$75
Tel: (860) 658-2216

**THE SIMSBURY
1820 HOUSE**
731 Hopmeadow St
(06070)
Rates: $85-$135
Tel: (860) 658-7658

SOUTHINGTON

HOWARD JOHNSON
30 Laning St (06489)
Rates: $36-$69
Tel: (800) 446-4656

MOTEL 6
625 Queen St (06489)
Rates: $33-$39
Tel: (860) 621-7351
(800) 440-6000

RED CARPET INN
580 Poquonnock Rd.
(06384)
Rates: n/a
Tel: (203) 445-0220
(800) 251-1962

STAMFORD

**BUDGET HOST
HOSPITALITY INN**
19 Clarks Hill Ave
(06902)
Rates: $52-$75
Tel: (203) 327-4300

DAYS INN
135 Harvard Ave
(06902)
Rates: $50-$65
Tel: (800) 329-7466

SUPER 8 MOTEL
32 Grenhart Rd
(06902)
Rates: n/a
Tel: (800) 800-8000

STRATFORD

HOJO INN
360 Honeyspot Rd
(06497)
Rates: $32-$60
Tel: (800) 446-4656

TRUMBULL

TRUMBULL MARRIOTT
180 Hawley Lane
(06611)
Rates: n/a
Tel: (203) 378-1400
(800) 228-9290

VERNON

HOWARD JOHNSON LODGE
451 Hartford Tpk
(06066)
Rates: $40-$70
Tel: (203) 875-0781
(800) 446-4656

VOLUNTOWN

TAMARACK LODGE
10 Rod Rd (06384)
Rates: $51-$75
Tel: (860) 376-0640

WATERBURY

HOLIDAY INN WATERBURY AT BUCKINGHAM SQ
63 Grand St (06702)
Rates: $59-$65
Tel: (800) 465-4329

HOWARD JOHNSON LODGE
2636 S Main St
(06706)
Rates: $42-$52
Tel: (203) 756-7961
(800) 446-4656

QUALITY INN OF WATERBURY
88 Union St (06702)
Rates: $49-$55
Tel: (800) 221-2222

RAMADA INN
Schrafft's Dr (06705)
Rates: $55-$93
Tel: (800) 272-6232

WATERFORD

LAMPLIGHTER MOTEL
211 Parkway N
(06385)
Rates: $76-$99
Tel: (860) 442-7227

OAKDELL MOTEL
983 Hartford Tpke
(06385)
Rates: n/a
Tel: (860) 442-9446

WESTBROOK

MAPLES MOTEL
1935 Boston Post Rd
(06498)
Rates: $36-$55
Tel: (860) 399-9345

WEST GOSHEN

GOSHEN MOTEL
Rt 4 W (06756)
Rates: $30-$50
Tel: (860) 491-9989

WEST HAVEN

DAYS HOTEL NEW HAVEN/WEST HAVEN
490 Sawmill Rd
(06516)
Rates: $64-$87
Tel: (203) 933-0344

ECONO LODGE
370 Highland St
(06516)
Rates: $40-$50
Tel: (203) 934-6611
(800) 424-4777

SUPER 8 MOTEL
7 Kimberly Ave
(06516)
Rates: $46-75
Tel: (203) 932-8338
(800) 800-8000

WETHERSFIELD

MOTEL 6
1341 Silas Deane
Hwy (06109)
Rates: $33-39
Tel: (860) 563-5900
(800) 466-8356

RAMADA INN
1330 Silas Deane
Hwy (06109)
Rates: $55-$85
Tel: (860) 563-2311
(800) 272-6232

WINDSOR

RESIDENCE INN BY MARRIOTT
100 Dunfey Ln
(06095)
Rates: $75-$155
Tel: (860) 688-7474
(800) 331-3131

WINDSOR LOCKS

BUDGETEL INN
64 Ella Grasso Tpk
(06096)
Rates: $33-$49
Tel: (860) 623-3336
(800) 428-3438

HOMEWOOD SUITES
65 Ella Grasso Tpke
(06096)
Rates: $99-109
Tel: (860) 627-8463
(800) 225-5466

MOTEL 6
3 National Dr
(06096)
Rates: $33-39
Tel: (860) 292-6200
(800) 466-8356

SHERATON HOTEL AT BRADLEY INTL AIRPORT
1 Bradley Intl
Airport
(06096)
Rates: $145-$160
Tel: (860) 627-5311

THE WINDSOR COURT HOTEL & CONFERENCE CTR
383 S Center St
(06096)
Rates: $55-$78
Tel: (860) 623-9811

DELAWARE

BETHANY BEACH

WESTWARD PINES MOTEL
10 Kent Ave (19930)
Rates: $75-$90
Tel: (302) 539-7426

BRIDGEVILLE

TEDDY BEAR B & B
303 Market St
(19933)
Rates: $45-$65
Tel: (302) 337-3134

CLAYMONT

HILTON HOTEL
630 Naamans Rd
(19703)
Rates: $74-$129
Tel: (302) 792-2700
(800) 445-8667

DEWEY BEACH

ATLANTIC OCEANSIDE
1700 Hwy 1 (19971)
Rates: $29-$119
Tel: (302) 227-8811
(800) 422-0481

BELLBUOY MOTEL
21 Van Dyke St
(19971)
Rates: $39-$135
Tel: (302) 227-6000

BEST WESTERN GOLD LEAF
1400 Hwy One
(19971)
Rates: $118-$178
Tel: (302) 226-1100
(800) 528-1234

SEA ESTA MOTEL
2306 Hwy 1 (19971)
Rates: $60-$105
Tel: (800) 436-6591

SEA ESTA MOTEL III
1409 Hwy 1 (19971)
Rates: $79-$119
Tel: (800) 436-6591

DOVER

BUDGET INN
1426 N DuPont Hwy
(19901)
Rates: $38-$47
Tel: (302) 734-4433

COMFORT INN
222 S DuPont Hwy
(19901)
Rates: $55-$69
Tel: (302) 674-3300

DAYS INN
272 N DuPont Hwy
(19901)
Rates: $39-$60
Tel: (302) 674-8002
(800) 329-7466

HAYNIE'S MOTEL
1760 N DuPont Hwy
(19901)
Rates: $26-$35
Tel: (302) 734-4042

QUALITY INN
348 N DuPont Hwy
(19901)
Rates: $59-$93
Tel: (302) 734-5701
(800) 221-2222

SHERATON INN
1570 N DuPont Hwy
(19901)
Rates: $73-$80
Tel: (302) 678-8500

FENWICK ISLAND

ATLANTIC BUDGET INN
Ocean Hwy & Rt 54
(19944)
Rates: $71-$97
Tel: (302) 539-7673

ISKANDER'S ISLAND INN
Rt 1 (19944)
Rates: $99-$169
Tel: (302) 537-1900

SANDS MOTEL & APARTMENTS
Rt 1 & James St
(19944)
Rates: $67+
Tel: (302) 539-7745

LEWES

COUNTRY LANE BED & BREAKFAST
7 Country Ln (19958)
Rates: $85-$95
Tel: (302) 945-1586

FIRST PORT OF CALL
28 Cape Henlopen
(19958)
Rates: $55+
Tel: (302) 645-7266

VESUVIO MOTEL
105 Savannah Rd
(19958)
Rates: $71-$81
Tel: (302) 645-2224

MILLSBORO

ATLANTIC BUDGET INN
210 W DuPont Hwy
(19966)
Rates: $47-$99
Tel: (302) 934-6711

NEW CASTLE

DAYS INN
3 Memorial Dr
(19720)
Rates: $45-$55
Tel: (302) 654-5400
(800) 329-7466

ECONO LODGE
232 S DuPont Hwy
(19720)
Rates: $30-$42
Tel: (800) 424-7777

HOWARD JOHNSON MOTOR LODGE
2162 New Castle Ave
(19720)
Rates: $50-$80
Tel: (800) 446-4656

MOTEL 6
1200 West Ave
(19720)
Rates: $39
Tel: (302) 571-1200
(800) 440-6000

NEW CASTLE MOTEL
196 S DuPont Hwy
(19720)
Rates: $30+
Tel: (302) 328-1836

QUALITY INN SKYWAYS
147 N DuPont Hwy
(19720)
Rates: $46-$92
Tel: (302) 328-6666
(800) 221-2222

RAMADA INN
Rt 13 & I-295 (19720)
Rates: $67-$99
Tel: (302) 658-8511
(800) 272-6232

RODEWAY INN
111 S DuPont Hwy
(19720)
Rates: $54-$67
Tel: (302) 328-6246
(800) 424-7777

TRAVELODGE
1213 West Ave
(19720)
Rates: $42-$100
Tel: (302) 654-5544
(800) 578-7878

NEWARK

BEST WESTERN INN
260 Chapman Rd
(19702)
Rates: $55-$70
Tel: (302) 738-3400
(800) 528-1234

COMFORT INN
1120 S College Ave
(19713)
Rates: $50-$60
Tel: (302) 368-8715
(800) 221-2222

HAMPTON INN
3 Concord Ln
(19713)
Rates: $65-$69
Tel: (302) 737-3900
(800) 426-7866

HOWARD JOHNSON MOTOR LODGE
1119 S College Ave
(19713)
Rates: $45-$65
Tel: (302) 368-8521
(800) 446-4656

RED ROOF INN
415 Stanton
Christiana Rd
(19713)
Rates: $39+
Tel: (302) 292-2870
(800) 843-7663

RESIDENCE INN BY MARRIOTT
240 Chapman Rd
(19702)
Rates: $79-$129
Tel: (302) 453-9200
(800) 331-3131

TRAVELODGE
268 E Main St
(19711)
Rates: $42-52
Tel: (302) 737-5050
(800) 578-7878

REHOBOTH BEACH

AIRPORT MOTEL
Rt 14 (19971)
Rates: $55-$96
Tel: (302) 227-6737

ATLANTIC BUDGET INN
154 Rehoboth Ave
(19971)
Rates: $95-$179
Tel: (302) 227-9446

ATLANTIC SANDS HOTEL
101 N Boardwalk
(19971)
Rates: $145-$178
Tel: (302) 227-2511

CAPE SUITES
47 Baltimore Ave
(19971)
Rates: $110-$130
Tel: (302) 226-3342

CORNER CUPBOARD INN
50 Park Ave (19971)
Rates: $155-$240
Tel: (302) 227-8553

LORD BALTIMORE LODGE
16 Baltimore Ave
(19971)
Rates: $35-$65
Tel: (302) 227-2855

LOVE CREEK MOTEL
Rt 24 (19971)
Rates: $48+
Tel: (302) 945-8909

RENEGADE MOTEL
Hwy 1 (19971)
Rates: $70-$120
Tel: (302) 227-1222

SEA ESTA MOTEL II
140 Rehoboth Ave
(19971)
Rates: $85-$119
Tel: (800) 436-6591

SEAFORD

COMFORT INN
225 N Dual Hwy
(19973)
Rates: $49-$125
Tel: (302) 629-8385

WILMINGTON

BEST WESTERN BRANDYWINE VALLEY INN
1807 Concord Pike
(19803)
Rates: $65-$110
Tel: (302) 656-9436
(800) 528-1234

DAYS INN
1102 West St (19801)
Rates: $79-$119
Tel: (302) 654-5400
(800) 329-7466

GUEST QUARTERS SUITE HOTEL
707 N King St
(19801)
Rates: $89-$99
Tel: (302) 656-9300

HOLIDAY INN DOWNTOWN
700 King St (19801)
Rates: $79-$99
Tel: (302) 655-0400
(800) 465-4329

HOLIDAY INN NORTH
4000 Concord Pike
(19803)
Rates: $79+
Tel: (302) 478-2222

RADISSON HOTEL
4727 Concord Pike,
Rt 202 (19803)
Rates: $59-$129
Tel: (302) 478-6000

SHERATON SUITES
422 Delaware Ave
(19801)
Rates: $109-$130
Tel: (302) 654-8300
(800) 325-3535

TALLY-HO MOTOR LODGE
5209 Concord Pike
(19803)
Rates: $42-$48
Tel: (302) 478-0300
(800) 445-0852

DISTRICT OF COLUMBIA

WASHINGTON
(Downtown and vicinity)

ANA HOTEL
2401 M St NW (20037)
Rates: $129-$295
Tel: (202) 429-2400

BEST WESTERN-NEW HAMPSHIRE
1121 New Hampshire Ave NW (20037)
Rates: $145-$210
Tel: (202) 457-0565
(800) 528-1234

CAPITAL HILTON
16th & K Sts NW (20036)
Rates: $225-$295
Tel: (202) 393-1000

THE CARLTON
923 16th St at K St NW (20006)
Rates: $160-$325
Tel: (202)638-2626

CARLYLE SUITES HOTEL
1731 New Hampshire Ave (20009)
Rates: $55-$119
Tel: (202) 234-3200

COMFORT INN DOWNTOWN
500 H St NW (20001)
Rates: $69-$139
Tel: (202) 289-5959

DAYS INN
2700 New York Ave NE (20002)
Rates: $52-$115
Tel: (202) 832-5800
(800) 329-7466

ECONO LODGE
4502 NW Crain Hwy (Bowie, MD 20718)
Rates: $49-69
Tel: 301-464-2200
(800) 424-4777

ECONO LODGE
7851 Malcolm Rd (Clinton, MD 20735)
Rates: $40-60
Tel: 301-856-2800
(800) 424-4777

ECONO LODGE NORTH EAST
1600 New York Ave NE (20002)
Rates: $48-$55
Tel: (800) 424-4777

FOUR SEASONS HOTEL
2800 Pennsylvania Ave NW (20007)
Rates: $205-$320
Tel: (202) 342-0444

GEORGETOWN DUTCH INN
1075 Thomas Jefferson NW (20007)
Rates: n/a
Tel: (202) 337-0900

GEORGETOWN MEWS
1111 20th St NW (20007)
Rates: n/a
Tel: (202) 298-7731

THE GRAND HOTEL
2350 M St NW (20037)
Rates: $155-$300
Tel: (202) 429-0100

GUEST QUARTERS-PENNSYLVANIA AVENUE
2500 Pennsylvania Ave NW (20037)
Rates: $99
Tel: (800) 424-2900

GUEST QUARTERS SUITE HOTEL-NH
801 New Hampshire Ave NW (20037)
Rates: $180-$195
Tel: (202) 785-2000

THE HAY-ADAMS HOTEL
1 Lafayette Sq NW (20006)
Rates: $210-$420
Tel: (202) 638-6600

HOLIDAY INN-CAPITOL
550 C St SW (20024)
Rates: $99-$109
Tel: (800) 465-4329

HOLIDAY INN-CENTRAL
1501 Rhode Island Ave NW (20005)
Rates: $59-$143
Tel: (800) 465-4329

HOLIDAY INN-THOMAS CIRCLE
1155 14th St NW (20005)
Rates: $79-$130
Tel: (800) 465-4329

HOTEL WASHINGTON
Pennsylvania Ave NW at 15th St (20004)
Rates: $148-$200
Tel: (202) 638-5900

THE JEFFERSON HOTEL
1200 16th St NW (20036)
Rates: $210-$950
Tel: (202) 347-2200

LE MERIDIEN WATERGATE
2650 Virginia Ave (20037)
Rates: n/a
Tel: (202) 965-2300

LOEWS L'ENFANT PLAZA HOTEL
480 L'Enfant Plaza SW (20024)
Rates: $185-$225
Tel: (202) 484-1000

THE MADISON HOTEL
1177 15th St NW (20005)
Rates: $225-$395
Tel: (202) 862-1600

MASTER HOSTS INN
6711 Georgia Ave. NW (20012)
Rates: n/a
Tel: (202) 722-1600
(800) 251-1962

MASTER HOSTS INN
1917 Bladensburg Rd (20002)
Rates: n/a
Tel: (202) 832-8600

OMNI SHOREHAM HOTEL
2500 Calvert St NW (20008)
Rates: $175-$235
Tel: (202) 234-0700

ONE WASHINGTON CIRCLE HOTEL
One Washington Cir NW (20037)
Rates: $75-$290
Tel: (202) 872-1680

PARK HYATT WASHINGTON D.C.
1201 124th St NW (20037)
Rates: $159-$330
Tel: (202) 789-1234

PULLMAN HIGH-LAND HOTEL
1914 Connecticut Ave NW (20009)
Rates: $185-$285
Tel: (202) 797-2000

QUALITY HOTEL-CENTRAL
1900 Connecticut Ave NW (20009)
Rates: $110-$155
Tel: (202) 332-9300

RADISSON PARK TERRACE HOTEL
1515 Rhode Island Ave NW (20005)
Rates: $99
Tel: (800) 333-3333

RAMADA INN
6711 Georgia Ave (20012)
Rates: n/a
Tel: (800) 272-6232

RAMADA INN
4050 Powder Mill Rd (Beltsville, MD 20705)
Rates: $59-99
Tel: (301) 572-7100
(800) 272-6232

RAMADA INN
8400 Wisconsin Ave (Bethesda, MD 20814)
Rates: $99-119
Tel: (301) 654-1000
(800) 272-6232

RAMADA INN
6868 Springfield Blvd
(Springfield, VA 22150)
Rates: $49-119
Tel: (703) 644-5311
(800) 272-6232

RED ROOF INN
7306 Parkway Dr (Hanover, MD 21076)
Rates: n/a
Tel: (410) 712-4070
(800) 843-7663

RED ROOF INN
8000 Washington Blvd
(Jessup, MD 20794)
Rates: n/a
Tel: (410) 796-0380
(800) 843-7663

RED ROOF INN
497 Quince Orchard Rd
(Gaithersburg, MD 20878)
Rates: n/a
Tel: (301) 977-3311
(800) 843-7663

THE SAVOY SUITES HOTEL
2505 Wisconsin Ave NW (20007)
Rates: $69-$129
Tel: (202) 337-9700

SHERATON HOTEL
923 16th St NW (20006)
Rates: n/a
Tel: (202) 638-2626

SHERATON WASHINGTON HOTEL
2660 Woodley Rd NW (20008)
Rates: $186-$266
Tel: (202) 328-2000

STOUFFER MAYFLOWER HOTEL
1127 Connecticut Ave NW (20036)
Rates: $159-$320
Tel: (202) 347-2000

SWISS INN HOTEL NORTHWEST
1204 Massachusetts Ave (20005)
Rates: n/a
Tel: (202) 371-1816

TRAVELODGE CENTER CITY HOTEL
1201 13th St NW (20005)
Rates: $69-$105
Tel: (202) 682-5300
(800) 578-7878

WASHINGTON COURT CAPITAL HILL
525 New Jersey Ave NW (20001)
Rates: n/a
Tel: (202) 628-2100

WASHINGTON HILTON & TOWERS
1919 Connecticut Ave NW (20009)
Rates: $97-$260
Tel: (202) 483-3000

WASHINGTON HOTEL
515 15th St NW (20004)
Rates: $149-$589:
Tel: (800) 424-9540

WASHINGTON MARRIOTT HOTEL
1221 22nd St at M St NW (20037)
Rates: $109-$189
Tel: (202) 872-1500

WASHINGTON PLAZA HOTEL
10 Thomas Circle (20005)
Rates: n/a
Tel: (202) 842-1300

WASHINGTON RENAISSANCE HOTEL
999 9th St NW (20001)
Rates: $205-$245
Tel: (202) 898-9000

THE WATERGATE HOTEL
2650 Virginia Ave NW (20037)
Rates: $235-$495
Tel: (202) 965-2300

WESTIN HOTEL
24th & M St NW (20037)
Rates: $185-$550
Tel: (202) 429-2400

THE WILLARD INTER-CONTINENTAL
1401 Pennsylvania Ave NW (20004)
Rates: $199-$330
Tel: (202) 628-9100

WYNDHAM BRISTOL HOTEL
2430 Pennsylvania Ave NW (20037)
Rates: $235-$255
Tel: (202) 955-6400

WASHINGTON
(West and South and vicinity)

BEST WESTERN ARLINGTON INN & TOWER
2480 S Glebe Rd (Arlington, VA 22206)
Rates: $59-$149
Tel: (703) 979-4400
(800) 528-1234

BEST WESTERN KEY BRIDGE
1850 N Fort Meyer Dr (22209)
Rates: $69-150
Tel: (703) 522-0400
(800) 539-2743

COMFORT INN DULLES INTL AIRPORT
4050 Westfax Dr (Chantilly, VA 22021)
Rates: $49-$88
Tel: (703) 818-2222
(800) 221-2222

COMFORT INN MOUNT VERNON
7212 Richmond Hwy
(Alexandria, VA 22306)
Rates: $50-$80
Tel: (703) 765-9000
(800) 221-2222

COMFORT INN-UNIVERISTY CENTER
11180 Main St (Fairfax, VA 22030)
Rates: $49-$70
Tel: (800) 221-2222

DAYS INN-ALEXANDRIA
110 S Bragg St (Alexandria, VA 22312)
Rates: $46-$61
Tel: (703) 354-4950
(800) 329-7466

DAYS INN-RICHMOND HIGHWAY
6100 Richmond Hwy
(Alexandria, VA 22303)
Rates: $51-$67
Tel: (703) 329-0500
(800) 329-7466

DOUBLETREE HOTEL NATIONAL AIRPORT
300 Army Navy Dr
(Arlington, VA 22202)
Rates: $65-$155
Tel: (800) 222-8733

ECONO LODGE-MOUNT VERNON
8849 Richmond Hwy
(Alexandria, VA 22309)
Rates: $45-$65
Tel: (703) 780-0300
(800) 424-4777

DOUBLETREE SUITES
100 S Reynolds St
(Alexandria, VA 22304)
Rates: $89-$99
Tel: (703) 370-9600

ECONO LODGE-NORTH
3335 Lee Hwy
(Arlington, VA 22207)
Rates: $35-$65
Tel: (800) 424-4777

ECONO LODGE-OLD TOWN
700 N Washington St
(Alexandria, VA 22314)
Rates: $55-$80
Tel: (703) 836-5100
(800) 424-4777

ECONO LODGE-PENTAGON
5666 Columbia Pike
(Baileys Crossroads, VA 22041)
Rates: $55-$75
Tel: (703) 820-5600
(800) 424-4777

ECONO LODGE-SPRINGFIELD
6868 Springfield Blvd
(Springfield, VA 22150)
Rates: $51-$70
Tel: (703) 491-5196
(800) 424-4777

ECONO LODGE-WOODBRIDGE
13317 Gordon Blvd
(Woodbridge, VA 22191)
Rates: $48-$70
Tel: (703) 491-5196
(800) 424-4777

FAIRVIEW PARK MARRIOTT HOTEL
3111 Fairview Park Dr
(Falls Church, VA 22042)
Rates: $79-$145
Tel: (703) 849-9400
(800) 228-9290

FRIENDSHIP INN-WOODBRIDGE
13964 Jefferson Davis Hwy
(Woodbridge, VA 22191)
Rates: $43-$58
Tel: (703) 494-4144
(800) 453-4511

HAMPTON INN DULLES AIRPORT
45440 Holiday Dr
(Sterling, VA 22170)
Rates: $77-$85
Tel: (703) 471-4300
(800) 426-7866

HOLIDAY INN
1489 Jefferson Davis Hwy (Arlington, VA 22202)
Rates: n/a
Tel: (800) 465-4329

HOLIDAY INN
1850 St. Myers Dr
(Arlington, VA 22209)
Rates: n/a
Tel: (800) 465-4329

HOLIDAY INN ARLINGTON
4610 N Fairfax Dr
(Arlington, VA 22203)
Rates: $79-$132
Tel: (800) 465-4329

HOLIDAY INN EISENHOWER METRO
2460 Eisenhower Ave (Alexandria, VA 22314)
Rates: $72-$118
Tel: (800) 465-4329

HOLIDAY INN EXP WASHINGTON/ DULLES
485 Eden St
(Herndon, VA 22070)
Rates: $52-$75
Tel: (703) 478-9777
(800) 465-4329

HOLIDAY INN-FAIR OAKS
11787 Lee Jackson Hwy
(Fairfax, VA 22033)
Rates: $69-$115
Tel: (703) 352-2525
(800) 465-4329

HOLIDAY INN FAIRFAX CITY
3535 Chain Bridge Rd
(Fairfax, VA 22030)
Rates: $65-$95
Tel: (703) 591-5500
(800) 465-4329

HOLIDAY INN-OLD TOWN
480 King St
(Alexandria, VA 22314)
Rates: $99-$250
Tel: (703) 549-6080
(800) 465-4329

HOLIDAY INN WASHINGTON-DULLES
1000 Sully Rd
(Sterling, VA 22170)
Rates: $71-$125
Tel: (703) 471-7411
(800) 465-4329

HOWARD JOHNSON
5821 Richmond Hwy (Alexandria, VA 22303)
Rates: $59-$99
Tel: (703) 329-1400
(800) 446-4656

HOWARD JOHNSON NATL AIRPORT
2650 Jefferson Davis Hwy (Arlington, VA 22202)
Rates: $79-$145
Tel: (703) 684-7200
(800) 446-4656

HYATT ARLINGTON AT KEY BRIDGE
1325 Wilson Blvd
(Arlington, VA 22209)
Rates: $69-$181
Tel: (703) 525-1234

HYATT FAIR LAKES
12777 Fair Lakes Cir
(Fairfax, VA 22033)
Rates: $59-$79
Tel: (703) 818-1234

MARRIOTT CRYSTAL GATEWAY HOTEL
1700 Jefferson Davis Hwy (Arlington, VA 22202)
Rates: $105-$192
Tel: (703) 920-3230

MARRIOTT KEY BRIDGE
1401 Lee Hwy
(Arlington 22209)
Rates: $164-$184
Tel: (703) 524-6400

QUALITY INN
6461 Edsall Rd
(Alexandria, VA 22312)
Rates: $55-$99
Tel: (800) 221-2222

QUALITY INN EXECUTIVE
6111 Arlington Blvd
(Falls Church, VA 22044)
Rates: $60-$70
Tel: (703) 534-9100

RAMADA PLAZA HOTEL
901 N Fairfax St
(Alexandria, VA 22314)
Rates: $80-$135
Tel: (703) 683-6000
(800) 272-6232

RAMADA PLAZA HOTEL-PENTAGON
4641 Kenmore Ave
(Alexandria, VA 22304)
Rates: $106-$250
Tel: (703) 751-4510
(800) 272-6232

RAMADA HOTEL-TYSONS CORNER
7801 Leesburg Pike
(Falls Church, VA 22043)
Rates: $99-$129
Tel: (703) 893-1340

RAMADA RENAISSANCE ARLINGTON HOTEL
950 N Stafford St
(Arlington, VA 22203)
Rates: $120-$180
Tel: (703) 528-6000

RED ROOF INN
10610 Automotive Dr
(Manassas, VA 22110)
Rates: $38-47
Tel: (703) 335-9333
(800) 843-7663

RED ROOF INN
5975 Richmond Hwy
(Alexandria, VA 22303)
Rates: $50-$62
Tel: (703) 960-5200
(800) 843-7663

RENAISSANCE HOTEL DULLES INTL AIRPORT
13869 Park Center Rd
(Herndon, VA 22071)
Rates: $59-$79
Tel: (703) 478-2900

RESIDENCE INN HERNDON
315 Elden St
(Herndon, VA 22070)
Rates: $57-$145
Tel: (703) 435-0044
(800) 331-3131

RESIDENCE INN TYSONS CORNER
8616 Westwood Center Dr
(Vienna, VA 22182)
Rates: $129-$169
Tel: (800) 331-3131

THE RITZ-CARLTON TYSONS CORNER
1700 Tysons Blvd
(McLean, VA 22102)
Rates: $135-$210
Tel: (703) 506-4300

SHERATON SUITES ALEXANDRIA
801 N St. Asaph St
(Alexandria, VA 22314)
Rates: $99-$164
Tel: (703) 836-4700

SPRINGFIELD HILTON
6550 Loisdale Rd
(Springfield, VA 22150)
Rates: $70-$130
Tel: (703) 971-8900

STOUFFER CONCOURSE HOTEL
2399 Jefferson Davis Hwy (Arlington, VA 22202)
Rates: $89-$240
Tel: (703) 418-6800

TYSONS CORNER MARRIOTT HOTEL
8028 Leesburg Pike
(Vienna, VA 22182)
Rates: $136-$172
Tel: (703) 734-3200

WASHINGTON DULLES AIRPORT MARRIOTT
333 W Service Rd
(Chantilly, VA 22021)
Rates: $59-$110
Tel: (703) 471-9500

WELLESLEY INN OF FAIRFAX
10327 Lee Hwy
(Fairfax, VA 22030)
Rates: $46-$70
Tel: (703) 359-2888
(800) 444-8888

WASHINGTON
(West and North and vicinity)

COMFORT INN
16216 Frederick Rd
(Gaithersburg, MD 20877)
Rates: $53-$79
Tel: (800) 221-2222

COMFORT INN GERMANTOWN
20260 Goldenrod Ln
(Germantown, MD 20876)
Rates: $54-$63
Tel: (800) 221-2222

DAYS INN ROCKVILLE/GAITHE RSBURG
16001 Shady Grove Rd (Rockville, MD 20850)
Rates: $50-$79
Tel: (301) 948-4300
(800) 329-7466

ECONO LODGE
18715 N Frederick Ave
(Gaithersburg, MD 20879)
Rates: $49-$51
Tel: (301) 963-3840
(800) 424-4777

ECONO LODGE
7990 Georgia Ave
(Silver Spring, MD 20910)
Rates: $56-$79
Tel: (301) 565-3444
(800) 424-4777

EMBASSY SUITES CHEVY CHASE PAVILLION
4300 Military Rd NW (20015)
Rates: $119-$165
Tel: (202) 362-9300

HOLIDAY INN BETHESDA
8120 Wisconsin Ave
(Bethesda, MD 20814)
Rates: $109-$134
Tel: (800) 465-4329

HOLIDAY INN CHEVY CHASE
5520 Wisconsin Ave
(Chevy Chase, MD 20815)
Rates: $95-$129
Tel: (800) 465-4329

HOLIDAY INN-GAITHERSBURG
2 Montgomery Village Ave
(Gaithersburg, MD 20879)
Rates: $69-$101
Tel: (800) 465-4329

HOLIDAY INN-SILVER SPRING PLAZA
8777 Georgia Ave
(Silver Spring, MD 20910)
Rates: $80-$115
Tel: (800) 465-4329

MARRIOTT SUITES BETHESDA
6711 Democracy Blvd
(Bethesda, MD 20817)
Rates: $99-$160
Tel: (301) 897-5600

RESIDENCE INN-BETHESDA
7335 Wisconsin Ave
(Bethesda, MD 20814)
Rates: $145-$165
Tel: (301) 718-0200

WOODFIN SUITES HOTEL
1380 Piccard Dr
(Rockville, MD 20850)
Rates: $69-$136
Tel: (301) 590-9880

WASHINGTON
(Eastern and vicinity)

COMFORT SUITES-LAUREL LAKES
14402 Laurel Pl
(Laurel, MD 20707)
Rates: $59-$150
Tel: (800) 221-2222

DAYS INN ANDREWS AFB
5001 Mercedes Blvd
(Camp Springs, MD 20746)
Rates: 39-$73
Tel: (800) 329-7466

DAYS INN CAPITAL CENTRE
55 Hampton Park Blvd
(Capitol Heights, MD 20743)
Rates: $39-$71
Tel: (800) 329-7466

ECONO LODGE
100 Hampton Park
Blvd
(Capitol Heights,
MD 20743)
Rates: $33-$55
Tel: (800) 424-4777

**THE GREENBELT
MARRIOTT**
6400 Ivy Ln
(Greenbelt, MD
20770)
Rates: $69-$119
Tel: (301) 441-3700

HOJO INN
600 New York Ave
NE (20002)
Rates: $50-$62
Tel: (800) 446-4656

**HOLIDAY INN-
CALVERTON**
4095 Powder Mill Rd
(Beltsville, MD
20705)
Rates: $69-$86
Tel: (800) 465-4329

**HOLIDAY INN
CAPITAL BELTWAY
EAST**
5910 Princess
Garden Pkwy
(Lanham, MD 20706)
Rates: $50-$69
Tel: (800) 465-4329

**HOLIDAY INN-
GREENBELT**
7200 Hanover Dr
(Greenbelt, MD
20770)
Rates: $63-$88
Tel: (800) 465-4329

**HOWARD JOHN-
SON LODGE**
5811 Annapolis Rd
(Cheverly, MD
20784)
Rates: $49-$78
Tel: (301) 779-7700
(800) 446-4656

MASTER HOST INN
1917 Bladensburg
Rd NE (20002)
Rates: $50-$66
Tel: (202) 832-8600

MOTEL 6
75 Hampton Park
Blvd
(Capitol Heights,
MD 20743)
Rates: $46-$52
Tel: (301) 499-0800
(800) 440-6000

**PARK VIEW INN-
COLLEGE PARK**
9020 Baltimore Blvd
(College Park, MD
20740)
Rates: $50-$60
Tel: (301) 441-8110

RED ROOF INN
12525 Laurel Bowie
Rd
(Laurel, MD 20708)
Rates: n/a
Tel: (301) 498-8811
(800) 843-7663

RED ROOF INN
9050 Lanham Severn
Rd
(Lanham, MD 20706)
Rates: $44-$54
Tel: (301) 731-8830
(800) 843-7663

RED ROOF INN
6170 Oxon Hill Rd
(Oxon Hill, MD
20745)
Rates: $30-$49
Tel: (301) 567-8030
(800) 843-7663

**SHERATON
GREENBELT HOTEL**
8500 Annapolis Rd
(New Carrollton,
MD 20784)
Rates: $72-$112
Tel: (301) 459-6700

FLORIDA

ALACHUA

DAYS INN
16301 MLK Blvd
(32615)
Rates: $42-$140
Tel: (904) 462-3251
(800) 329-7466

RAMADA INN
16305 NW 163rd Ln
(32615)
Rates: $50-$105
Tel: (904) 462-4200
(800) 272-6232

TRAVELODGE
Rt 1, Box 229A
(32615)
Rates: $40-$50
Tel: (904) 462-2244
(800) 578-7878

ALTAMONTE SPRINGS

EMBASSY SUITES ORLANDO NORTH
225 E Altamonte Dr
(32701)
Rates: $99-$105
Tel: (407) 834-2400

HOLIDAY INN
230 W Hwy 436
(32714)
Rates: n/a
Tel: (407) 862-4455
(800) 465-4329

LA QUINTA INN
150 S Westmonte Dr
(32714)
Rates: $53-$70
Tel: (800) 531-5900

RESIDENCE INN BY MARRIOTT
270 Douglas Ave
(32714)
Rates: $73-$110
Tel: (407) 788-7991
(800) 331-3131

APALACHICOLA

RAINBOW INN & MARINA
123 Water St (32320)
Rates: n/a
Tel: (904) 653-8139

RANCHO INN
240 Hwy 98 (32320)
Rates: $32-$38
Tel: (904) 653-9435

APOLLO BEACH

RAMADA INN BAYSIDE
6414 Surfside Blvd
(33572)
Rates: $55-$110
Tel: (813) 645-3271
(800) 272-6232

APOPKA

CROSBY'S MOTOR INN
1440 W Orange
Blossom Tr (32712)
Rates: $39-$69
Tel: (800) 821-6685

ARCADIA

BEST WESTERN ARCADIA INN
504 S Brevard
(34265)
Rates: $51-$75
Tel: (941) 494-4884
(800) 528-1234

BARTOW

DAVIS BROS MOTEL
1035 N Broadway
Ave (33830)
Rates: $38-$48
Tel: (941) 533-0711

EL JON MOTEL
1460 E Main St
(33830)
Rates: $39-$59
Tel: (941) 533-8191

BASEBALL CITY

DAYS INN
I-4 & US 27 (33837)
Rates: $29-$99
Tel: (941) 424-2596
(800) 329-7466

BOCA RATON

RADISSON SUITE HOTEL
7920 Glades Rd
(33434)
Rates: $89-$169
Tel: (407) 483-3600
(800) 333-3333

RESIDENCE INN BY MARRIOTT
525 NW 77th St
(33487)
Rates: $68-$155
Tel: (407) 994-3222
(800) 331-3131

RAMADA INN
2901 N Federal Hwy
(33431)
Rates: $35-$115
Tel: (407) 395-6850
(800) 272-6232

BONIFAY

BEST WESTERN-TIVOLI INN
2004 S Waukesha St
(32425)
Rates: $40-$75
Tel: (904) 547-4251
(800) 528-1234

ECONO LODGE
2210 S Waukesha St
(32425)
Rates: $38-$80
Tel: (904) 547-9345
(800) 424-4777

BRADENTON

DAYS INN
3506 1st St W (34208)
Rates: $59-$95
Tel: (941) 746-1141
(800) 329-7466

HOJO INN

6511 14th St W
(34207)
Rates: $30-$46
Tel: (941) 756-8399
(800) 446-4656

MOTEL 6
660 67 St Cir E
(34208)
Rates: $29-$35
Tel: (941) 747-6005
(800) 440-6000

PARK INN CLUB
4450 47th St W
(34210)
Rates: $52-$102
Tel: (941) 795-4633

BRANDON

BEHIND THE FENCE BED &BREAKFAST
1400 Viola Dr (33511)
Rates: $40-$65
Tel: (813) 685-8201

BROOKSVILLE

HOLIDAY INN
30307 Cortez Blvd
(34602)
Rates: $65-$70
Tel: (800) 465-4329

BUSHNELL

BEST WESTERN GUEST HOUSE INN
2224 W-CR 48
(33513)
Rates: $39-$56
Tel: (352) 793-5010
(800) 528-1234

CALLAHAN

FRIENDSHIP INN
US I-301 & 23 North
(32011)
Rates: $33-$36
Tel: (904) 879-3451
(800) 453-4511

CAPE CORAL

DEL PRADO INN
1502 Miramar St
(33904)
Rates: $60-$75
Tel: (941) 542-3151
(800) 231-6818

CAPTIVA ISLAND

TWEEN WATERS INN
15951 Captiva Rd
(33924)
Rates: n/a
Tel: (941) 472-5161
(800) 223-5865

CARRABELLE

THE MOORINGS AT CARRABELLE
1000 US 98 (32322)
Rates: $48-$55
Tel: (904) 697-2800

CEDAR KEY

DOCKSIDE MOTEL
11 Dock St (32625)
Rates: $45-$65
Tel: (352) 543-5432

PARK PLACE MOTEL
P. O. Box 613 (32625)
Rates: $65-$80
Tel: (352) 543-5737

CHATTA-HOOCHEE

MORGAN MOTEL
E US 90 (32324)
Rates: $27-36
Tel: (904) 663-4336

CHIPLEY

DAYS INN
1593 Main St (32428)
Rates: $38-$95
Tel: (904) 638-7335
(800) 329-7466

CLEARWATER

AGEAN SANDS MOTEL
421 S Gulfview Blvd
(34630)
Rates: $55-$130
Tel: (800) 942-3432

HOLIDAY INN EXPRESS
13625 Icot Blvd
(34620)
Rates: $80-$105
Tel: (813) 536-7275
(800) 465-4329

HOWARD JOHNSON
21030 US Hwy 19 N
(34625)
Rates: $59-$67
Tel: (813) 797-8173
(800) 446-4656

LA QUINTA INN
3301 Ulmerton Rd
(34622)
Rates: $41-$57
Tel: (800) 531-5900

RESIDENCE INN BY MARRIOTT
5050 Ulmerton Rd
(34620)
Rates: $130-$185
Tel: (813) 573-4444
(800) 331-3131

CLEARWATER BEACH

BEST WESTERN INN
691 S Gulfview Blvd
(34630)
Rates: $73-$150
Tel: (813) 443-7652
(800) 444-1919

CLEARWATER BEACH HOTEL
500 Mandalay Ave
(34630)
Rates: n/a
Tel: (813) 441-2425
(800) 292-2295

COCOA

BEST WESTERN COCOA INN
4225 W King St
(32926)
Rates: $42-$65
Tel: (407) 632-1065
(800) 528-1234

DAYS INN
5600 Hwy 524 (32926)
Rates: $42-$69
Tel: (407) 636-6500
(800) 329-7466

ECONO LODGE
3220 N Cocoa Blvd
(32926)
Rates: $54-$75
Tel: (407) 632-4561
(800) 424-4777

RAMADA INN COCOA-KENNEDY SPACE CENTER
900 Friday Rd (32926)
Rates: $40-$80
Tel: (407) 631-1210
(800) 272-6232

COCOA BEACH

ECONO LODGE OCEAN VIEW
1275 N Atlantic Ave
(32931)
Rates: $55-$85
Tel: (407) 783-2252
(800) 424-4777

MOTEL 6
3701 N Atlantic Ave
(32931)
Rates: $42-$46
Tel: (407) 783-3103
(800) 440-6000

SURF STUDIO BEACH RESORT
1801 S Atlantic Ave
(32931)
Rates: $40-$110
Tel: (407) 783-7100

CORAL GABLES

HOWARD JOHNSON
1430 S Dixie Hwy
(33146)
Rates: $58-$72
Tel: (305) 665-7501
(800) 446-4656

CORAL SPRINGS

WELLESLEY INNS-CORAL SPRINGS
3100 N University Dr (33065)
Rates: $45-$90
Tel: (954) 344-2200
(800) 444-8888

CRESTVIEW

DAYS INN
4255 S Ferdon Blvd
(32536)
Rates: $39-$59
Tel: (904) 682-8842
(800) 329-7466

HOLIDAY INN
4050 S Ferdon Blvd
(32536)
Rates: $50-$58
Tel: (800) 465-4329

SUPER 8 MOTEL
3925 S Ferdon Blvd
(32539)
Rates: $35-$50
Tel: (904) 682-9649
(800) 800-8000

CROSS CITY

CARRIAGE INN
280 E Main (32628)
Rates: $38-$42
Tel: (352) 498-3910
(800) 682-4816

CRYSTAL RIVER

COMFORT INN
4486 N Suncoast Blvd (32629)
Rates: $45-$65
Tel: (800) 221-2222

DAYS INN RESORT
2380 NW Hwy 19
(32629)
Rates: $39-$85
Tel: (352) 795-2111
(800) 329-7466

PLANTATION INN & GOLF RESORT
9301 W Fort Island Tr
(34429)
Rates: $79-$125
Tel: (352) 795-4211
(800) 632-6262

CYPRESS GARDENS

BEST WESTERN ADMIRAL'S INN
5665 Cypress Gardens Blvd (33884)
Rates: $42-$89
Tel: (941) 324-5950
(800) 528-1234

DANIA BEACH

**HILTON-
FT LAUDERDALE**
1870 Griffin Rd
(33004)
Rates: $79-$175
Tel: (800) 445-8667

MOTEL 6
825 E Dania Beach
Blvd (33004)
Rates: $36-$44
Tel: (954) 921-5505
(800) 466-8356

SHERATON DESIGN CENTER
1825 Griffin Rd
(33004)
Rates: $85-$195
Tel: (954) 920-3500

DAVENPORT

DAYS INN-SOUTH OF MAGIC KINGDOM
2425 Frontage Rd
(33837)
Rates: $38-$79
Tel: (800) 329-7466

MOTEL 6
5620 US Hwy 27 N
(33837)
Rates: $36+
Tel: (941) 424-2521
(800) 440-6000

DAYTONA BEACH

ARUBA INN
1254 N Atlantic Ave
(32118)
Rates: $30-$65
Tel: (904) 253-5643

BUDGET HOST INN-THE CANDLELIGHT
1305 S Ridgewood
Ave (32114)
Rates: $22-$38
Tel: (800) 283-4678

COMFORT INN INTERSTATE
1567 N. US 1
(Ormond Beach
32174)
Rates: $33-$139
Tel: (800) 221-2222

COMFORT INN ON THE BEACH
507 S Atlantic Ave
(Ormond Beach
32074)
Rates: $43-$110
Tel: (800) 221-2222

DAYS INN
1909 S Atlantic Ave
(32118)
Rates: $29-$135
Tel: (904) 255-4492
(800) 329-7466

DAYS INN-OCEANFRONT NORTH
839 S Atlantic Ave
(Ormond Beach,
32074)
Rates: $39-$215
Tel: (904) 677-6600
(800) 329-7466

DAYS INN SPEEDWAY
2900 W International
Speedway Blvd
(32124)
Rates: $49-$199
Tel: (904) 255-0541
(800) 329-7466

DRIFTWOOD BEACH MOTEL
657 S Atlantic Ave
(Ormond Beach
32176)
Rates: $30-$62
Tel: (904) 677-1331

HOWARD JOHNSON
701 S Atlantic Ave
(32118)
Rates: $59-$109
Tel: (904) 258-8522
(800) 446-4656

HOWARD JOHNSON DAYTONA NORTH
1633 N US 1
(Ormond Beach
32174)
Rates: $35-$140
Tel: (800) 446-4656

JAMAICAN BEACH MOTEL
505 S Atlantic Ave
(Ormond Beach
32176)
Rates: $28-$125:
Tel: (904) 677-3353

LA QUINTA INN
2725 International
Speedway Blvd
(32114)
Rates: $50-$62
Tel: (800) 221-4731

RAMADA INN
1798 W International
Speedway Blvd
(32114)
Rates: $69-$229
Tel: (904) 255-2422
(800) 272-6232

RED CARPET INN
1855 S Ridgewood
Ave (32119)
Rates: $26-$130
Tel: (904) 767-6681
(800) 251-1962

SCOTTISH INNS
1515 S Ridgewood
Ave (32114)
Rates: $26-$95
Tel: (904) 258-5742
(800) 251-1962

SUPER 8 MOTEL
2992 W Int.
Speedway Blvd
(32124)
Rates: $39-69
Tel: (904) 253-0643
(800) 800-8000

TRAVELERS REST INN
749 Ridgewood Ave
(Holly Hill 32117)
Rates: $39-$100
Tel: (904) 255-6511

DAYTONA BEACH SHORES

CASA MARINA MOTEL
828 N Atlantic Ave
(32118)
Rates: n/a
Tel: (800) 225-3691

INTERNATIONAL MOTOR INN
313 S Atlantic Ave
(32118)
Rates: $29-$89
Tel: (904) 255-7491

PARADISE INN
333 S Atlantic Ave
(32118)
Rates: $89-$99
Tel: (904) 255-8827

SAND CASTLE MOTEL
3619 S Atlantic Ave
(32127)
Rates: $28-$65
Tel: (800) 967-4757

SCOTTISH INNS-DESERT ISLE
133 S Ocean Ave
(32118)
Rates: $18-$60
Tel: (800) 251-1962

SEA OATS BEACH MOTEL
2539 S Atlantic Ave
(32118)
Rates: $39-$119
Tel: (904) 767-5684
(800) 732-6287

DE FUNIAK SPRINGS

BEST WESTERN CROSSROADS INN
2343 Freeport Rd
(32433)
Rates: $45-$65
Tel: (904) 892-5111
(800) 528-1234

COMFORT INN
1326 S Freeport Rd
(32433)
Rates: $40-$95
Tel: (800) 221-2222

DAYS INN
472 Hugh Adams Rd
(32433)
Rates: $34-$95
Tel: (904) 892-6115
(800) 329-7466

ECONO LODGE
1325 S Freeport Rd
(32433)
Rates: $32-$100
Tel: (800) 424-4777

DEERFIELD BEACH

COMFORT SUITES HOTEL
1040 E Newport Center Dr (33442)
Rates: $49-$99
Tel: (954) 570-8887
(800) 538-2777

DAYS INN
1250 Hillsboro Blvd (33442)
Rates: $45-$110
Tel: (800) 329-7466

DAYS INN OCEANSIDE
50 SE 20th Ave (33441)
Rates: $89-$115
Tel: (954) 427-2200
(800) 329-7466

LA QUINTA INN
351 W Hillsboro Blvd (33441)
Rates: $49-$73
Tel: (954) 421-1004
(800) 531-5900

QUALITY SUITES HOTEL
1050 E Newport Center Dr (33341)
Rates: $59-$129
Tel: (954) 570-8888
(800) 538-2777

RAMADA INN
1401 S Fed Hwy US 1(33441)
Rates: $75-$115
Tel: (954) 421-5000
(800) 272-6232

WELLESLEY INN
100 SW 12th Ave (33442)
Rates: $60-$100
Tel: (954) 428-0661
(800) 444-8888

DELAND

HOLIDAY INN
350 E International Speedway Blvd (32724)
Rates: $65-$145
Tel: (904) 738-5200
(800) 465-4329

QUALITY INN
2801 E New York Ave (32724)
Rates: $34-$150
Tel: (800) 221-2222

DELRAY BEACH

COLONY HOTEL
525 E Atlantic Ave (33483)
Rates: $60-$160
Tel: (561) 276-4123
(800) 552-2363

DESTIN

DAYS INN
1029 Hwy 98E (32541)
Rates: $40-$130
Tel: (904) 837-2599
(800) 329-7466

FRANGISTA BEACH INN
1860 Old Hwy 98 E (32541)
Rates: $50-$195
Tel: (904) 654-5501
(800) 382-2612

HOWARD JOHNSON
713 Hwy 98E (32541)
Rates: $39-$69
Tel: (904) 837-5455

DUNEDIN

ECONO LODGE-WATERFRONT
1414 Bayshore Blvd (34698)
Rates: $85-$170
Tel: (813) 734-8851
(800) 424-4777

EAST PALATKA

THE OAKS MOTEL
Rt 3 Box 50, Hwy 17 (32131)
Rates: n/a
Tel: (904) 328-1545

EASTPOINT

SPORTSMAN'S LODGE MOTEL & MARINA
99 N Bayshore Dr (32328)
Rates: $34-$44
Tel: (904) 670-8423

ELKTON

COMFORT INN
2625 SR 207 (32033)
Rates: $36-$99
Tel: (800) 221-2222

ELLENTON

BEST WESTERN INN
5218 17th St E (34222)
Rates: $55-$150
Tel: (941) 729-8505
(800) 528-1234

ENGLEWOOD

DAYS INN
2540 S McCall Rd (34224)
Rates: $53-$125
Tel: (941) 474-5544
(800) 329-7466

VERANDA INN
2073 S McCall Rd (34224)
Rates: $85-$100
Tel: (941) 475-6533
(800) 633-8115

FERNANDINA BEACH

SHONEY'S INN
2707 Sadler Rd (32034)
Rates: $61-$73
Tel: (800) 222-2222

FLAGLER BEACH

TOPAZ MOTEL
1224 S Oceanshore Blvd (32136)
Rates: $45-$90
Tel: (904) 439-3301

FLORIDA CITY

HAMPTON INN
124 E Palm Dr (33034)
Rates: $60-$90
Tel: (305) 247-8833
(800) 426-7866

FORT LAUDERDALE

ADMIRAL'S COURT RESORT MOTEL
21 Hendricks Isle (33301)
Rates: $195-$795/Weekly
Tel: (954) 462-5072
(800) 248-6669

BAY PALMS VILLAS
8 Isle of Venice
Rates: $290-$540/Weekly
Tel: (954) 552-2821

BUDGETEL INN-FORT LAUDERDALE
3800 W Commercial Blvd (33309)
Rates: $39-$64
Tel: (954) 485-7900

DAYS INN FT LAUERDALE AIRPORT NORTH
1700 W Broward Blvd (33312)
Rates: $69-$89
Tel: (954) 463-2500
(800) 329-7466

FORT LAUDERDALE INN
5727 N Federal Hwy (33308)
Rates: $46-$74
Tel: (954) 491-2500

FORT LAUDERDALE YACHT & BEACH CLUB
341 N Birch Rd
(33304)
Rates: $48-$170
Tel: (954) 463-2821

GUEST QUARTERS SUITE HOTEL
2670 E Sunrise Blvd
(33304)
Rates: $109-$179
Tel: (954) 565-3800
(800) 331-3131

HOWARD JOHNSON
501 SE 17th St
(33316)
Rates: $55-$75
Tel: (954) 525-5194
(800) 446-4656

HOWARD JOHNSON
700 N Atlantic Blvd
(33304)
Rates: $51-$72
Tel: (954) 563-2451
(800) 446-4656

MARK 2100 RESORT HOTEL
2100 N Atlantic Blvd
(33305)
Rates: $45-$199
Tel: (954) 566-8383
(800) 334-6275

MOTEL 6
1801 SR 84 (33315)
Rates: $42-$46
Tel: (954) 760-7999
(800) 440-6000

RAMADA INN
2275 SR 84 (33312)
Rates: $99-$119
Tel: (954) 584-4000
(800) 272-6232

RED CARPET INN
2440 SR 84 (33312)
Rates: n/a
Tel: (954) 792-8181
(800) 251-1962

RIVIERA SUITES
501 Breakers Ave
(33304)
Rates: $28-$53
Tel: (954) 564-2525

THREE SUNS MOTEL
3016 Windamar St
(33304)
Rates: $33-$109
Tel: (954) 563-7926
(800) 758-8884

TREVERS AT THE BEACH
552 N Birch Rd
(33304)
Rates: $36-$145
Tel: (954) 564-4341
(800) 533-4744

WELLESLEY INNS-FT LAUDERDALE WEST
5070 N SR 7 (33319)
Rates: $40-$150
Tel: (954) 484-6909
(800) 444-8888

THE WESTIN HOTEL CYPRESS CREEK
400 Corporate Dr
(33334)
Rates: $229-$269
Tel: (954) 772-1331
(800) 228-3000

WISH YOU WERE HERE INN
7 N Birch Rd (33304)
Rates: $30-$90
Tel: (954) 462-0531
(800) 462-0531

FORT MYERS

BUDGETEL INN
2717 Colonial Blvd
(33907)
Rates: $43-$73
Tel: (941) 275-3500

COMFORT SUITES
13651 Indian Paint
Ln (33912)
Rates: $70-$130
Tel: (941) 768-0005
(800) 435-8234

DAYS INN
11435 S Cleveland
Ave (33907)
Rates: $39-$111
Tel: (941) 936-1311
(800) 329-7466

DAYS INN-NORTH FORT MYERS/CAPE CORAL
13353 N Cleveland
Ave
(N Ft Myers 33903)
Rates: $35-$80
Tel: (800) 329-7466

ECONO LODGE
13301 N Cleveland
Ave (33903)
Rates: $35-$75
Tel: (800) 424-4777

GOLF VIEW MOTEL
3523 Cleveland Ave
(33901)
Rates: $39-$75
Tel: (941) 936-1858

LA QUINTA MOTOR INN
4850 Cleveland Ave
(33907)
Rates: $42-$71
Tel: (941) 275-3300

MOTEL 6
3350 Marina Town
Ln (33903)
Rates: $30-$34
Tel: (941) 656-5544
(800) 440-6000

RADISSON INN SANIBEL GATEWAY
20091 Summerlin Rd
SW (33908)
Rates: $59-$124
Tel: (941) 466-1200

ROCK LAKE MOTEL
2930 Palm Beach
Blvd (33916)
Rates: n/a
Tel: (941) 334-3242

SLEEP INN
13651 Indian Paint
Ln (33912)
Rates: $45-$105
Tel: (941) 561-1117
(800) 435-8234

TRAVELODGE
2038 W First St
(33901)
Rates: $32-$69
Tel: (941) 334-2284
(800) 578-7878

FORT MYERS BEACH

ANCHOR INN COTTAGES
285 Virginia Ave
(33931)
Rates: $330-$1000
Tel: (941) 463-2630

BEST WESTERN BEACH RESORT
684 Estero Blvd
(33931)
Rates: $109-$199
Tel: (941) 463-6000
(800) 528-1234

FORT PIERCE

DAYS INN-FORT PIERCE
6651 Darter Ct
(34945)
Rates: $45-$80
Tel: (407) 466-4066
(800) 329-7466

HOLIDAY INN-SUNSHINE PARKWAY
7151 Okeechobee Rd
(34945)
Rates: $46-$65
Tel: (800) 465-4329

HOWARD JOHNSON LODGE
7150 Okeechobee Rd
(34945)
Rates: $39-$48
Tel: (407) 464-4500
(800) 446-4656

MOTEL 6
2500 Peters Rd
(34945)
Rates: $29-$33
Tel: (407) 461-9937
(800) 440-6000

FORT WALTON BEACH

ECONO LODGE
1284 Marler Dr
(32548)
Rates: $55-$65
Tel: (904) 243-7123
(800) 424-4777

MARINA MOTEL & EFFICIENCIES
1345 US 98 E
Okaloosa Isl. (32548)
Rates: $35-$69
Tel: (904) 244-1129

PARK INN INTERNATIONAL
100 Miracle Strip
Pkwy W (32548)
Rates: $37-$69
Tel: (904) 244-0121

GAINESVILLE

APARTMENT INN MOTEL
4401 SW 13th St
(32608)
Rates: $165
Tel: (352) 371-3811

DAYS INN
7516 Newberry Rd
(32606)
Rates: $39-$99
Tel: (352) 332-3033
(800) 329-7466

DAYS INN - UNIVERSITY
2820 NW 13th St
(32609)
Rates: $36-$90
Tel: (352) 376-1211
(800) 329-7466

ECONO LODGE-U OF FL
2649 SW 13th St
(32608)
Rates: $38-$75
Tel: (352) 373-7816
(800) 424-4777

FAIRFIELD INN
6901 NW 4th Blvd
(32607)
Rates: $40-$55
Tel: (800) 348-6000

HOJO INN
1900 SW 13th St
(32608)
Rates: $32-$45
Tel: (800) 228-2800

LA QUINTA INN
920 NW 69th Terr
(32601)
Rates: $45-$53
Tel: (352) 332-6466

MOTEL 6-U OF FL
4000 SW 40th Blvd
(32608)
Rates: $28-$32
Tel: (352) 373-1604
(800) 440-6000

RAMADA INN
4021 SW 40th Blvd
(32608)
Rates: $50-$125
Tel: (352) 373-0392
(800) 272-6232

RESIDENCE INN BY MARRIOTT
4001 SW 13th St
(32608)
Rates: $95-$160
Tel: (352) 371-2101
(800) 331-3131

SCOTTISH INNS
Rt 2, Box 804
(Micanopy, 32667)
Rates: $21-$25
Tel: (352) 466-3163
(800) 251-1962

SUPER 8 MOTEL
4202 SW 40th Blvd
(32608)
Rates: $40-$58
Tel: (352) 378-3888
(800) 800-8000

TRAVELODGE
3103 NW 13th St
(32609)
Rates: $40-$75
Tel: (352) 372-4319
(800) 578-7878

HAHIRA

RAMADA INN
I-75 Exit 7 (31632)
Rates: $34-$52
Tel: (912) 794-3000
(800) 272-6232

HAINES CITY

BEST WESTERN LAKE HAMILTON
605 B Moore Rd
(33844)
Rates: $42-$75
Tel: (941) 421-6929
(800) 421-6928

ECONO LODGE-DISNEYWOLD RESORT
1504 US 27 S (33844)
Rates: $40-$70
Tel: (941) 422-8621
(800) 424-4777

HALLANDALE

RAMADA INN
2080 S Ocean Dr
(33009)
Rates: $95-$150
Tel: (800) 272-6232

HOBE SOUND

RED CARPET INN
8605 SE Federal
Hwy. (33455)
Rates: n/a
Tel: (407) 546-3600
(800) 251-1962

HOLIDAY

BEST WESTERN TAHITIAN RESORT
2337 US 19 (34691)
Rates: $51-$88
Tel: (813) 937-4121
(800) 528-1234

HOLLYWOOD

COMFORT INN-HOLLYWOOD AIRPORT
2520 Stirling Rd
(33020)
Rates: $45-$105
Tel: (954) 922-1600
(800) 333-1492

DAYS INN-FT AIRPORT SOUTH
2601 N 29th Ave
(33020)
Rates: $59-$150
Tel: (954) 923-7300
(800) 329-7466

GREEN SEAS MOTEL
1419 S Federal Hwy
(33020)
Rates: $37-$99
Tel: (954) 923-6564
(305) 927-5707

HOJO INN-AIRPORT SOUTH
2900 Polk St (33020)
Rates: $41-$70
Tel: (954) 923-1516
(800) 446-4656

MIRADOR RESORT MOTEL
901 S Ocean Dr
(33019)
Rates: $195-$860
(Weekly)
Tel: (305) 922-7581

MONTREAL INN AT HOLLYWOOD BEACH
324-336 Balboa St
(33019)
Rates: $30-$79
Tel: (954) 925-4443

THREE PALM MOTEL
930 N 17th Ct (33020)
Rates: n/a
Tel: (954) 923-7683

HOLMES BEACH

THE INN BETWEEN
105 66th St (34217)
Rates: $305-$500
Tel: (941) 778-0751

HOMESTEAD

DAYS INN-HOMESTEAD
51 S Homestead
Blvd (33030)
Rates: $55-$99
Tel: (305) 245-1260
(800) 329-7466

EVERGLADES MOTEL
605 S Krome Ave
(33030)
Rates: $39-$52
Tel: (305) 247-4117

HOWARD JOHNSON LODGE
1020 N Homestead
Blvd (33030)
Rates: $44-$56
Tel: (305) 248-2121
(800) 446-4656

HOMOSASSA SPRINGS

HOMOSASSA LODGE
P. O. Box 8 (34447)
Rates: $45-$75
Tel: (352) 628-4311

RAMADA INN
4076 S Suncoast Blvd (34446)
Rates: $69-$109
Tel: (352) 628-4311
(800) 272-6232

RIVERSIDE INN
P. O. Box 258
(Homosassa 34487)
Rates: $59-$79
Tel: (800) 442-2040

INDIALANTIC

QUALITY SUITES MELBOURNE OCEANFRONT
1665 N SR A1A (32903)
Rates: $89-$109
Tel: (800) 221-2222

INDIAN SHORES

EDGEWATER BEACH RESORT
19130 Gulf Blvd (34635)
Rates: $50-$100
Tel: (813) 595-4028

HOLIDAY VILLAS II
19610 Gulf Blvd (34635)
Rates: n/a
Tel: (813) 596-4852
(800) 428-4852

INVERNESS

CENTRAL MOTEL
721 US 41S (32651)
Rates: $45-$50
Tel: (352) 726-4515

THE CROWN HOTEL
109 N Seminole Ave (34450)
Rates: $40-$70
Tel: (352) 344-5555

ISLAMORADA

BED & BREAKFAST ISLAMORADA
81175 Old Hwy (33036)
Rates: $40-60
Tel: (305) 664-9321

COCONUT COVE RESORT
84801 Old Hwy (33036)
Rates: $35-$125
Tel: (305) 664-0123

GAME FISH RESORT
Rt 1, Box 70 (33036)
Rates: $55-$75
Tel: (305) 664-5568

LOOKOUT LODGE
87770 Overseas Hwy (33036)
Rates: n/a
Tel: (305) 852-9915
(800) 870-1772

OCEAN DAWN LODGE
82885 Old Highway (33036)
Rates: $65-$115
Tel: (305) 664-4844

SANDS OF ISLAMORADA
80051 Overseas Hwy (33036)
Rates: $55-$150
Tel: (305) 664-2791

JACKSONVILLE

ADMIRAL BENBOW INN-AIRPORT
14691 Duval Rd (32218)
Rates: $39-$49
Tel: (904) 741-4254

BEST INNS OF AMERICA
8220 Dix Ellis Tr (32256)
Rates: $34-$43
Tel: (904) 739-3323

BUDGETEL INN
3199 Hartley Rd (32257)
Rates: $32-$48
Tel: (904) 268-9999

COMFORT SUITES HOTEL
8333 Dix Ellis Tr (32256)
Rates: $56-$85
Tel: (904) 739-1155

DAYS INN WEST
460 S Lane Ave
Rates: $29-$65
Tel: (904) 786-7550
(800) 329-7466

ECONO LODGE-CENTRAL
5221 University Blvd W (32216)
Rates: $30-$36
Tel: (800) 424-4777

ECONOMY INNS OF AMERICA
4300 Salisbury Rd (32216)
Rates: $29
Tel: (904) 281-0198

ECONOMY INNS OF AMERICA
5959 Youngerman Cir E (32244)
Rates: $27-$34
Tel: (904) 777-0160

HAMPTON INN
1170 Airport Entrance Rd (32218)
Rates: $59-$69
Tel: (904) 741-4980
(800) 425-7866

HOMEWOOD SUITES
8737 Baymeadows Rd (32256)
Rates: $120-$130
Tel: (904) 733-9299
(800) 225-5466

LA QUINTA INN
8255 Dix Ellis Tr (32256)
Rates: $45-$74
Tel: (904) 731-9940
(800) 531-5900

LA QUINTA INN
8555 Blanding Blvd (32244)
Rates: $35-$45
Tel: (800) 531-5900

LA QUINTA INN-NORTH
812 Dunn Ave (32218)
Rates: $38-$45
Tel: (800) 531-5900

MOTEL 6-SOUTH-EAST
8286 Dix Ellis Tr (32256)
Rates: $33-$37
Tel: (904) 731-8400
(800) 440-6000

MOTEL 6-SOUTH-WEST
6107 Youngerman Cir (32244)
Rates: $31-$39
Tel: (904) 777-6100
(800) 440-6000

RAMADA INN MANDARIN SOUTH
3130 Hartley Rd (32257)
Rates: $52-$95
Tel: (8904) 268-8080
(800) 272-6232

RAMADA INN-SOUTH
5624 Cagle Rd (32216)
Rates: $36-$89
Tel: (904) 737-8000
(800) 272-6232

RED ROOF INN-AIRPORT
14701 Airport Entrance Rd (32218)
Rates: $31-$38
Tel: (904) 741-4488
(800) 843-7663

RED ROOF INN-SOUTH
6099 Youngerman Cir (32244)
Rates: $30-$37
Tel: (904) 777-1000
(800) 843-7663

RESIDENCE INN BY MARRIOTT
8365 Dix Ellis Rd (32256)
Rates: $80-$125
Tel: (904) 733-8088
(800) 331-3131

SUPER 8 MOTEL
10901 Harts Rd
(32218)
Rates: $39-$57
Tel: (904) 751-3888
(800) 800-8000

JACKSONVILLE BEACH

DAYS INN OCEANFRONT RESORT
1031 S 1st St (32250)
Rates: $45-$85
Tel: (800) 329-7466

JASPER

DAYS INN
Rt 3, Box 133 (32052)
Rates: $35-$50
Tel: (904) 792-1987
(800) 329-7466

SCOTTISH INNS
Rt 3, Box 136 (32052)
Rates: $20-$25
Tel: (904) 792-1234
(800) 251-1962

JENNINGS

QUALITY INN
I-75 & SR 143 (32053)
Rates: $40-$50
Tel: (800) 465-4329

JENNINGS HOUSE INN
P. O. Box 179 (32053)
Rates: $20-$25
Tel: (904) 938-3305

JUNO BEACH

HOWARD JOHNSON
13930 US Hwy 1
(33408)
Rates: $39-$49
Tel: (407) 626-1531
(800) 446-4656

KENDALL

HOWARD JOHNSON
10201 S Dixie Hwy
(33156)
Rates: $66-$72
Tel: (305) 666-2531
(800) 446-4656

KEY LARGO

FLAMINGO LODGE
#1 Flamingo Lodge
Hwy
(Everglades, 33030)
Rates: $59-$102
Tel: (305) 253-2241

HOWARD JOHNSON RESORT
P.O. Box 1024 (33037)
Rates: $89-$250
Tel: (305) 451-1400
(800) 446-4656

KELLY'S MOTEL
104220 Overseas
Hwy (33037)
Rates: $55-$75+
Tel: (305) 451-1622

LOOKOUT LODGE
87770 Overseas Hwy
(Plantation Key,
33070)
Rates: $69-$159
Tel: (305) 852-9915

SEA TRAIL MOTEL
Route 5, Box 91
(33037)
Rates: $30-$45
Tel: (305) 852-8001

TROPIC VISTA MOTEL
90701 Overseas Hwy
(Plantation Key,
33070)
Rates: $38-$95
Tel: (305) 852-8799

KEY WEST

ALEXANDER PALMS COURT
715 South St (33040)
Rates: $75-$295
Tel: (305) 296-6413

ANDREW'S INN
Whalton Ln (33040)
Rates: $98-$278
Tel: (305) 294-7730

CARIBBEAN HOUSE MOTEL
226 Petronia St
(33040)
Rates: $39-$79
Tel: (305) 296-1600

CASA ALANTE GUEST COTTAGES
1435 S Roosevelt
Blvd
Rates: $60-$150
Tel: (305) 293-0702

CASABLANCA AT BOGART'S
916 Center St (33040)
Rates: $85-$155
Tel: (305) 296-0637

CENTER COURT HISTORIC INN & COTTAGES B&B
916 Center St (33040)
Rates: $78-$268
Tel: (305) 296-9292

COURTNEY'S PLACE
720 Whitmarsh Ln
(33040)
Rates: $59-$169
Tel: (305) 294-3480

CUBAN CLUB SUITES
1102-A Duval St
(33040)
Rates: $100-$300
Tel: (305) 296-0465

CURRY MANSION INN B & B
511 Caroline St
(33040)
Rates: $110-$200
Tel: (305) 294-5349
(800) 253-3466

DAYS INN
3852 N Roosevelt
Blvd (33040)
Rates: $88-$240
Tel: (305) 294-3742
(800) 329-7466

DOUGLAS GUEST HOUSE
419 Amelia St
(33040)
Rates: $88-$275
Tel: (305) 294-5269

EDEN HOUSE
1015 Fleming St
(33040)
Rates: $55-$250
Tel: (305) 296-6868

FLEMING STREET INN
618 Fleming St
(33040)
Rates: $75-$225
Tel: (305) 294-5181

HALFRED MOTEL
512 Truman Ave
(33040)
Rates: $65-$143
Tel: (305) 296-5565

HAMPTON INN
2801 N Roosevelt
Blvd (33040)
Rates: $109-$179
Tel: (305) 294-2917
(800) 426-7866

INCENTRA CARRIAGE HOUSE INN
729 Whitehead St
(33040)
Rates: $59-$290
Tel: (305) 296-5565

KEY LODGE MOTEL
1004 Duval St
(33040)
Rates: $70-$163
Tel: (305) 296-9915
(800) 458-1296

LA CASA DE LUCES
422 Amelia St
(33040)
Rates: $55-$155
Tel: (305) 296-0582

MAHOGANY HOUSE
812 Simongton St
(33040)
Rates: $45-$175
Tel: (305) 293-9464

MERLINN GUEST HOUSE
811 Simonton St (33040)
Rates: $65-$150
Tel: (305) 296-3336

NASSAU HOUSE
1016 Fleming St (33040)
Rates: $49-$199
Tel: (305) 296-8513

OLD CUSTOMS HOUSE INN
124 Duval St (33040)
Rates: $50-$200
Tel: (305) 294-8507

RAMADA INN
3420 N Roosevelt Blvd (33040)
Rates: $70-$220
Tel: (305) 294-5541
(800) 272-6232

SEA ISLE RESORT
915 Windsor Ln (33040)
Rates: $65-$140
Tel: (305) 294-5188

SEA SHELL MOTEL
718 South St (33040)
Rates: $45-$95
Tel: (305) 296-5719

SOUTHERN CROSS MOTEL
326 Duval St (33040)
Rates: $80-$115
Tel: (305) 294-3200

SPEAK EASY INN
1117 Duval St (33040)
Rates: $70-$163
Tel: (305) 296-2680

SUGAR LOAF LODGE RESORT
Box 148
(Sugar Loaf Key 33044)
Rates: $65-$100
Tel: (305) 745-3211

TRAVELERS PALM GARDEN COTTAGES
815 Catherine St (33040)
Rates: $650-$950 (Weekly)
Tel: (305) 294-9560

WHISPERS B & B INN
409 William St (33040)
Rates: $69-$150
Tel: (305) 294-5969

WICKER GUEST HOUSE
913 Duval St (33040)
Rates: $45-$140
Tel: (305) 296-4275

WILLIAM HOUSE
1317 Duval St (33040)
Rates: $83-$170
Tel: (305) 294-8233

KISSIMMEE

BEST WESTERN EASTGATE
5565 W Irlo Bronson Memorial Hwy (34746)
Rates: $43-$109
Tel: (407) 396-0707
(800) 528-1234

COMFORT INN-MAIN GATE
7571 W Irlo Bronson Memorial Hwy (34746)
Rates: $27-$41
Tel: (800) 221-2222

DAYS INN
5820 W Irlo Bronson Hwy (34746)
Rates: $49-$159
Tel: (407) 396-7900
(800) 329-7466

DAYS INN-WEST
7980 W Irlo Bronson Memorial Hwy (34746)
Rates: $35-$89
Tel: (407) 396-7969
(800) 329-7466

FANTASY WORLD CLUB VILLAS
2935 Hart Ave (34746)
Rates: $130-$180
Tel: (800) 874-8047

FORTUNE PLACE RESORT
1475 Astro Lake Dr N (34744)
Rates: $109-$189
Tel: (407) 348-0330

HOLIDAY INN-MAIN GATE EAST
5678 W Irlo Bronson Memorial Hwy (34746)
Rates: $75-$126
Tel: (407) 396-4488
(800) 465-4656

HOMEWOOD SUITES MAIN GATE/PARKWAY
3100 Parkway Blvd (34746)
Rates: $94-$189
Tel: (407) 396-2229

HOWARD JOHNSON
4643 W Hwy 192 (34706)
Rates: $28-$90
Tel: (407) 396- 1340
(800) 446-4656

HOWARD JOHNSON LODGE
2323 Hwy 192 E (34744)
Rates: $25-$89
Tel: (407) 846-4900
(800) 446-4656

INNS OF AMERICA
2945 Entry Point Blvd (34746)
Rates: $32-$48
Tel: (407) 396-7743

LARSON'S LODGE-MAIN GATE
6075 US Hwy 192 (34747)
Rates: $36-$85
Tel: (407) 396-6100
(800) 327-9074

MOTEL 6
5731 W Bronson Hwy (34746)
Rates: $23-$29
Tel: (407) 396-6333
(800) 440-6000

MOTEL 6 DISNEYWORLD MAIN GATE
7455 W Bronson Hwy (34747)
Rates: $28+
Tel: (407) 396-6422
(800) 440-6000

RAMADA INN
4559 W Hwy 192 (34746)
Rates: $26-$55
Tel: (407) 396-1212
(800) 272-6232

RAMADA LIMITED
5055 W Hwy 192 (34746)
Rates: $32-$59
Tel: (407) 396-2212
(800) 272-6232

RED ROOF INN
4970 Kyng's Heath Rd (34746)
Rates: $33-$39
Tel: (407) 396-0065
(800) 843-7663

TRAVELODGE
2050 E Irlo Bronson Mem Hwy (34744)
Rates: $30-$90
Tel: (407) 846-4545
(800) 578-7878

LABELLE

THE RIVER'S EDGE MOTEL
285 N River Rd (33935)
Rates: $45
Tel: (941) 675-6062

LAKE BUENA VISTA

CASA ADOBE
9107 South Rt 535 (32819)
Rates: n/a
Tel: (407) 876-5432

COMFORT INN AT LAKE BUENA VISTA
8442 Palm Pkwy (32830)
Rates: $35-$55
Tel: (800) 221-2222

CONTEMPORARY RESORT HOTEL
P. O. Box 10000
(32830)
Rates: n/a
Tel: (407) 824-1000

HOWARD JOHNSON
8501 Palm Parkway
(32836)
Rates: $59-$140
Tel: (407) 239-6900
(800) 446-4656

LAKE CITY

BEST WESTERN INN
Rt 13, Box 1077
(32055)
Rates: $33-$48
Tel: (800) 528-1234

COMFORT INN
4515 US 90 W(32056)
Rates: $49-$69
Tel: (904) 755-1344

CYPRESS INN
Rt 13, Box 180A
(32055)
Rates: $25-$39
Tel: (904) 752-9369

DAYS INN
Rt 13, Box 1140
(32055)
Rates: $35-$65
Tel (904) 752-9350
(800) 329-7466

ECONO LODGE
I-75 & US 90 (32055)
Rates: $31-$65
Tel: (904) 752-7891
(800) 424-4777

ECONO LODGE SOUTH
Rt 3, Box 173 (32055)
Rates: $34-$38
Tel: (800) 424-4777

HOLIDAY INN
Drawer 1239 (32055)
Rates: $53-$60
Tel: (904) 752-3901
(800) 465-4329

HOWARD JOHNSON LODGE
Rt 13, Box 1082
(32055)
Rates: $32-$52
Tel: (904) 752-6262
(800) 446-4656

MOTEL 6
1 Hall of Fame Dr
(32055)
Rates: $25-$29
Tel: (904) 755-4664
(800) 440-6000

PINEY WOODS LODGE
Rt 13, Box 1224
(32055)
Rates: $19-$40
Tel: (904) 752-8334

RAMADA INN
Exit 82 on I-75
(32055)
Rates: $35-$69
Tel: (904) 752-7550
(800) 272-6232

RED CARPET INN
I-75 & US Hwys. 441
& 41
(Ellisville, 32055)
Rates: n/a
Tel: (904) 752-7582
(800) 251-1962

RED CARPET INN
Rt 13, Box 631
(32055)
Rates: $22-$26
Tel: (904) 755-1707

RODEWAY INN
Rt 18, Box 35 (32056)
Rates: $28-$34
Tel: (904) 755-5203
(800) 228-2000

SCOTTISH INNS
Rt 13, Box 1150
(32055)
Rates: $24-$33
Tel: (904) 755-0230
(800) 251-1962

TRAVELODGE HOTEL
I-75 & US 90 W
(32055)
Rates: $29-$69
Tel: (904) 755-9306
(800) 578-7878

WELLESLEY INN & SUITES
3420 US Hwy 98 N
(33805)
Rates: n/a
Tel: (813) 859-3399

LAKE PLACID

BEST WESTERN LAKE PLACID INN
2165 US 27 S (33852)
Rates: $49-$100
Tel: (941) 465-3133
(800) 528-1234

LAKE WALES

CHALET SUZANNE
3800 Chalet Suzanne
Ln (33853)
Rates: $125-$209
Tel: (941) 676-6011
(800) 288-6011

EMERALD MOTEL
530 S Scenic Hwy
(33853)
Rates: $30-$50
Tel: (941) 676-3310

KNIGHTS INN
541 W Central Ave
(33853)
Rates: $31-$55
Tel: (941) 676-7925

LANTERN MOTEL
3949 Hwy 27 North
(33853)
Rates: n/a
Tel: (941) 676-4821

LAKE WORTH

LAGO MOTOR INN
714 S Dixie Hwy
(33460)
Rates: $32-$66
Tel: (561) 585-5246

MARTINIQUE MOTOR LODGE
801 S Dixie Hwy
(33460)
Rates: $28-$75
Tel: (407) 585-2502

WHITE MANOR MOTEL
1618 S Federal Hwy
(33460)
Rates: $32-$58
Tel: (407) 582-7437

LAKELAND

COMFORT INN
1817 E Memorial
Blvd (33801)
Rates: $30-$55
Tel: (800) 221-2222

DAYS INN
508 E Memorial
Blvd(33801)
Rates: $30-$85
Tel: (941) 682-0303
(800) 329-7466

HOLIDAY INN
4645 Socrum Loop
Rd (33809)
Rates: $54-$64
Tel: (941) 858-1411
(800) 465-4329

MOTEL 6
3120 US Hwy 98 N
(33809)
Rates: $29-$33
Tel: (941) 682-0643
(800) 440-6000

TRAVELODGE HOTEL
3223 Hwy 98 N
(33805)
Rates: $30-$90
Tel: (941) 688-6031
(800) 578-7878

WELLESLEY INN
3420 US Hwy 98 N
(33805)
Rates: $50-$89
Tel: (941) 859-3399
(800) 444-8888

LANTANA

MOTEL 6
1310 W Lantana Rd
(33462)
Rates: $33-$37
Tel: (407) 585-5833
(800) 440-6000

SUPER 8 MOTEL
1255 Hypoluxo Rd
(33462)
Rates: $49-$64
Tel: (407) 585-3970
(800) 800-8000

LEESBURG

SCOTTISH INNS
1321 N 14th St
(34748)
Rates: $29-$40
Tel: (904) 787-3343
(800) 251-1962

SHONEY'S INN
1308 N 14th St
(34748)
Rates: $38-$60
Tel: (904) 787-1210
(800) 222-2222

SUPER 8 MOTEL
1392 North Blvd W
(34748)
Rates: $41-$65
Tel: (352) 787-6363
(800) 800-8000

LIVE OAK

ECONO LODGE
US 129 & I-10
(32060)
Rates: $37-$75
Tel: (904) 362-7459
(800) 424-4777

LONGBOAT KEY

HOLIDAY INN
4949 Gulf of Mexico
Dr (34228)
Rates: $123-$290
Tel: (941) 383-3771
(800) 465-4329

**RIVIERA BEACH
MOTEL**
5451 Gulf of Mexico
Dr (34228)
Rates: $450-$750
Tel: (941) 383-2552

LONGWOOD

RAMADA INN
2025 W SR 434
(32750)
Rates: $54-$72
Tel: (407) 862-4000
(800) 272-6232

MacCLENNY

ECONO LODGE
I-10 & SR 121 (32063)
Rates: $35-$75
Tel: (904) 259-3000
(800) 424-4777

MADEIRA BEACH

**SANDY SHORES
CONOMINIUMS**
12924 Gulf Blvd
(33708)
Rates: $77-$101
Tel: (813) 392-1281

SEA DAWN MOTEL
13733 Gulf Blvd
(33708)
Rates: $27-$60
Tel: (813) 391-7500

MARATHON

BONEFISH RESORT
Rt 1, Box 343 (33050)
Rates: $29-$77
Tel: (305) 743-7107

**CAPT. PIPS
VACATION SUITES**
1410 Overseas Hwy
(33050)
Rates: $760-$1100
(Weekly)
Tel: (305) 743-4403

**CORAL LAGOON
RESORT**
12399 US1 Hwy
(33050)
Rates: $65-$130
Tel: (305) 289-0121

**FARO BLANCO
MARINE RESORT**
1996 Overseas Hwy
(33050)
Rates: $55-$233
Tel: (305) 743-2918

**GRASSY KEY BEACH
MOTEL**
Rt 1, Box 357 (33050)
Rates: $45-$95
Tel: (305) 743-0533

**HOWARD JOHNSON
RESORT**
13351 Overseas Hwy
(33050)
Rates: $70-$150
Tel: (305) 743-8550
(800) 446-4656

LAGOON RESORT
7200 Aviation Blvd
(33050)
Rates: $49-$129
Tel: (305) 743-5463

PEACE INN
7931 US1 Hwy
(33050)
Rates: $30-$55+
Tel: (305) 743-5124

PELICAN MOTEL
Rt 1, Box 528 (33050)
Rates: $34-$78
Tel: (305) 289-0011

**RAINBOW BEND
RESORT**
Rt 1, Box 159 (33050)
Rates: $120-$210
Tel: (305) 289-1505
(800) 929-1505

SEA COVE MOTEL
12685 Overseas Hwy
(33050)
Rates: $24-$99
Tel: (305) 289-0800

**SEASHELL BEACH
RESORT**
Rt 1, Box 154 (33050)
Rates: $39-$49+
Tel: (305) 289-0265

**SEAWARD RESORT
MOTEL**
8700 US1 Hwy
(33050)
Rates: $35-$80
Tel: (305) 743-5711

YARDARM MOTEL
6200 Overseas Hwy
(33050)
Rates: $45-$50
Tel: (305) 743-2541

YELLOWTAIL INN
Rt 1, Box 355B
(33050)
Rates: $50-$95
Tel: (305) 743-8400

MARIANNA

**BEST WESTERN
MARIANNA INN**
2086 Hwy 71 (32446)
Rates: $44-$50
Tel: (904) 526-5666
(800) 528-1234

DAYS INN
4132 Lafayette St
(32446)
Rates: $35-$65
Tel: (904) 526-4311
(800) 329-7466

RAMADA LIMITED
4655 Hwy 90 E
(32446)
Rates: $44-$53
Tel: (800) 272-6232

MELBOURNE

**HILTON
AT RIALTO PLACE**
200 Rialto Pl (32901)
Rates: $109-$119
Tel: (407) 768-0200
(800) 445-8667

**HOLIDAY INN-
WEST I-95**
4500 W New Haven
Ave (32904)
Rates: $69-$85
Tel: (800) 465-4329

RIO VISTA MOTEL
1046 S Harbor City
Blvd (32901)
Rates: n/a
Tel: (407) 727-2818

**TRAVELODGE
HOTEL**
4505 W New Haven
Ave (32904)
Rates: $31-$60
Tel: (407) 724-5450
(800) 578-7878

MEXICO BEACH

**THE SURFSIDE
MOTEL**
Hwy 98 & 38th St
(32410)
Rates: $40-$45
Tel: (904) 648-5771

MIAMI
(and Vicinity)

BUDGETEL INN-MIAMI AIRPORT
3501 NW Le Jeune Rd (33142)
Rates: $46-$68
Tel: (305) 871-1777

HAMPTON INN-DOWNTOWN
2500 Brickell Ave (33129)
Rates: $83-$100
Tel: (305) 854-2070
(800) 426-7866

HOLIDAY INN-AIRPORT LAKES SOUTH
1101 NW 57th Ave (33126)
Rates: $75-$105
Tel: (800) 465-4329

HOWARD JOHNSON
1850 NW LeJeune Rd (33126)
Rates: $39-$85
Tel: (305) 871-4350
(800) 446-4656

HOWARD JOHNSON
16500 NW 2nd Ave (33169)
Rates: $45-$110
Tel: (305) 945-2621
(800) 446-4656

HOWARD JOHNSON MOTOR LODGE AIRPORT
7330 NW 36th St (33166)
Rates: $65-$100
Tel: (305) 592-5440
(800) 446-4656

LA QUINTA INN
7401 NW 36th St (33166)
Rates: $55-$71
Tel: (305) 599-9902

MIAMI AIRPORT HILTON
5101 Blue Lagoon Dr (33126)
Rates: $145-$210
Tel: (305) 262-1000
(800) 445-8667

MIAMI AIRPORT MARRIOTT
1201 NW Le Jeune Rd (33126)
Rates: $115-$500
Tel: (305) 649-5000
(800) 228-9290

QUALITY INN-SOUTH
14501 S Dixie Hwy (33176)
Rates: $61-$99
Tel: (800) 221-2222

RAMADA LIMITED
7600 N Kendall Dr (33156)
Rates: $59-$109
Tel: (305) 595-6000
(800) 272-6232

RESIDENCE INN BY MARRIOTT
1212 NW 82nd Ave (33126)
Rates: $133-$159
Tel: (305) 591-2211
(800) 331-3131

SOFITEL HOTEL
5800 Blue Lagoon Dr (33126)
Rates: $125-$500
Tel: (305) 264-4888

WELLESLEY INN
11750 Mills Dr (Kendall, 33183)
Rates: $49-$99
Tel: (305) 270-0359
(800) 444-8888

MIAMI BEACH
(and Vicinity)

BAY HARBOR INN
9660 E Bay Harbor Dr (Bay Harbor Is. 33154)
Rates: $80-$115
Tel: (305) 868-4141

BEST WESTERN BEACH RESORT
4333 Collins Ave (33140)
Rates: $79-$129
Tel: (305) 532-3311
(800) 832-8332

DAYS INN
4299 Collins Ave (33140)
Rates: $69-$119
Tel: (305) 673-1513
(800) 329-7466

DAYS INN
100-21st (33139)
Rates: $79-$139
Tel: (305) 538-6631
(800) 329-7466

FONTAINEBLEAU HILTON RESORT & SPA
4441 Collins Ave (33140)
Rates: $165-$355
Tel: (305) 538-2000

HOWARD JOHNSON
4000 Alton Rd (33140)
Rates: $61-$120
Tel: (305) 532-4411
(800) 446-4656

HOWARD JOHNSON
6261 Collins Ave (33140)
Rates: $69-$99
Tel: (305) 868-1200
(800) 446-4656

NEWPORT BEACH-SIDE CROWNE PLAZA RESORT
16701 Collins Ave (33160)
Rates: $109-$205
Tel: (305) 949-1300
(800) 327-5476

OCEAN FRONT HOTEL
1230 Ocean Dr (33139)
Rates: $125-$335
Tel: (305) 672-2579

SEACOAST SUITE HOTEL
5151 Collins Ave (33160)
Rates: $170-$315
Tel: (305) 865-5152
(800) 523-3671

SHERATON BAL HARBOUR RESORT
9701 Collins Ave (Bal Harbour 33154)
Rates: $165-$320
Tel: (305) 865-7511

NAPLES

HOWARD JOHNSON
221 9th St S (33940)
Rates: $50-$85
Tel: (941) 262-6181
(800) 446-4656

KNIGHTS INN
6600 Dudley Dr (33999)
Rates: $46-$90
Tel: (800) 843-5644

RED ROOF INN
1925 Davis Blvd (33942)
Rates: $42-$130
Tel: (941) 774-3117
(800) 843-7663

WELLESLEY INN
1555 5th Ave S (33942)
Rates: $40-$130
Tel: (941) 793-4646
(800) 444-8888

WORLD TENNIS CENTER & RESORT
4800 Airport Rd (33942)
Rates: $145
Tel: (800) 292-6663

NAVARRE

COMFORT INN
8680 Navarre Pkwy (32566)
Rates: $44-$78
Tel: (800) 221-2222

NEPTUNE BEACH

DAYS INN
1401 Atlantic Blvd (32266)
Rates: $36-$81
Tel: (904) 249-3952
(800) 329-7466

NEW PORT RICHEY

QUALITY INN
5316 US 19 (34652)
Rates: $45-$55
Tel: (800) 221-2222

NEW SMYRNA BEACH

BUENA VISTA MOTEL AND APARTMENTS
500 N Causeway
(32169)
Rates: $35-$60
Tel: (904) 428-5565

SMYRNA MOTEL
1050 N Dixie Frwy
(32168)
Rates: $25-$37
Tel: (904) 428-2495

NICEVILLE

COMFORT INN
101 Hwy 85 N
(32578)
Rates: $56-$61
Tel: (904) 678-8077
(800) 221-2222

OCALA

BUDGET HOST-WESTERN MOTEL
4013 NW Blitchton
Rd (34482)
Rates: $25-$35
Tel: (800) 283-4678

DAYS INN
3811 NW Blichton
Rd (34482)
Rates: $40-75
Tel: (352) 629-7041
(800) 329-7466

DAYS INN
3620 W Silver
Springs Blvd (34475)
Rates: $34-$75
Tel: (352) 629-0091
(800) 329-7466

HOLIDAY INN-OCALA
3621 W Silver
Springs Blvd (34478)
Rates: $39-$45
Tel: (904) 629-0381
(800) 465-4329

QUALITY INN I-75
3767 NW Blitchton
Rd (34475)
Rates: $28-$40
Tel: (800) 424-6423

RAMADA INN & CONFERENCE CENTER
3810 NW Blitchton
Rd (34482)
Rates: $39-$65
Tel: (352) 732-3131
(800) 272-6232

SCOTTISH INNS
3520 W Silver
Springs
Blvd (34470)
Rates: $21-$25
Tel: (352) 629-7961
(800) 251-1962

SOUTHLAND MOTEL
1260 E Silver Springs
Blvd (34470)
Rates: $19-$39
Tel: (352) 351-0113

SUPER 8 MOTEL
3924 W Silver
Springs Blvd (34482)
Rates: $30-$57
Tel: (352) 629-8794
(800) 800-8000

WESTERN MOTEL
4013 NW Blitchton
Rd (34482)
Rates: n/a
Tel: (352) 732-6940
(800) 283-4678

OKEECHOBEE

BUDGET INN MOTEL
201 S Parrott Ave
(34974)
Rates: $32-$55
Tel: (941) 763-3185

DAYS INN PIER II
2200 SE Hwy 441
(34974)
Rates: $39-$125
Tel: (941) 775-4522
(800) 329-7466

OLD TOWN

SUWANNEE GABLES
Rt 3, Box 208 (32680)
Rates: $36-$48
Tel: (352) 542-7752

ORANGE CITY

COMFORT INN
445 S Volusia Ave
(32763)
Rates: $40-$69
Tel: (800) 221-2222

ORANGE PARK

BEST WESTERN OF ORANGE PARK
300 Park Ave N
(32073)
Rates: $55-150
Tel: (904) 264-1211
(800) 528-1234

HOLIDAY INN
150 Park Ave (32073)
Rates: $55-$70
Tel: (904) 264-9513
(800) 465-4329

ORLANDO
(and Vicinity)

BUDGETEL INN
2051 Consulate Dr
(32837)
Rates: $36-$59
Tel: (407) 240-0500

BEST WESTERN
2014 W Colonial Dr
(32804)
Rates: $39-$85
Tel: (407) 841-8600
(800) 528-1234

DAYS INN ORLANDO AIRPORT
2323 McCoy Rd
(32809)
Rates: $35-$58
Tel: (407) 859-6100
(800) 329-7466

DAYS INN EAST OF UNIVERSAL STUDIOS
5827 Caravan Ct
(32819)
Rates: $39-$129
Tel: (407) 351-3800
(800) 327-2111

DAYS INN-INTERNATIONAL DRIVE
7200 International
Dr (32819)
Rates: $48-$98
Tel: (407) 351-1200
(800) 329-7466

DAYS INN LODGE-FLORIDA MALL
1851 W Landstreet
Rd (32809)
Rates: $32-$109
Tel: (407) 859-7700
(800) 329-7466

DAYS INN ORLANDO 33RD STREET
2500 W 33rd St
(32839)
Rates: $29-$110
Tel: (407) 841-3731
(800) 329-7466

DAYS INN
235 S Wymore Rd
(Altamonte Springs,
32714)
Rates: $76-$96
Tel: (407) 862-2800
(800) 329-7466

DAYS INN
3300 S Orange
Blossom Trail
(32839)
Rates: $49-$89
Tel: (407) 442-4521
(800) 329-7466

DAYS INN
12490 Apopka-Vineland Rd (32836)
Rates: $45-$145
Tel: (407) 239-4646
(800) 329-7466

DAYS INN
12799 Apopka-Vineland Rd (32836)
Rates: $86-$140
Tel: (407) 239-4441
(800) 329-7466

DELTA ORLANDO RESORT
5715 Major Blvd
(32819)
Rates: $120-$150
Tel: (407) 351-3340

ECONO LODGE CENTRAL
3300 W Colonial Dr (32808)
Rates: $38-$58
Tel: (407) 293-7221
(800) 424-4777

GATEWAY INN
7050 Kirkman Rd (32819)
Rates: $52-$96
Tel: (407) 351-2000
(800) 327-3808

HOMEWOOD SUITES
3100 Parkway Blvd (34747)
Rates: n/a
Tel: (407) 396-2229
(800) 225-5466

HOWARD JOHNSON
5905 International Dr (32819)
Rates: $39-$99
Tel: (407) 351-2100
(800) 446-4656

HOWARD JOHNSON
6603 International Dr (32819)
Rates: $40-$90
Tel: (407) 351-2900
(800) 446-4656

HOWARD JOHNSON
3835 McCoy Rd (82812)
Rates: $49-$69
Tel: (407) 859-2711
(800) 446-4656

HOWARD JOHNSON
9956 Hawaiian Ct (32819)
Rates: $69-$89
Tel: (407) 351-5100
(800) 446-4656

HOWARD JOHNSON LODGE
8700 S Orange Blossom Tr (32809)
Rates: $30-$85
Tel: (407) 851-2330
(800) 446-4656

INNS OF AMERICA
8222 Jamaican Ct (32819)
Rates: $34-$50
Tel: (407) 345-1172

KNIGHTS INN
221 E Colonial Dr (32801)
Rates: $40-$54
Tel: (800) 843-5644

LA QUINTA INTERNATIONAL DRIVE
8300 Jamaican Ct (32819)
Rates: $39-$84
Tel: (800) 531-5900

LA QUINTA MOTOR INN AIRPORT
7931 Daetwyler Dr (32812)
Rates: $53-$62
Tel: (800) 531-5900

MOTEL 6
5300 Adanson Rd (32810)
Rates: $28-$32
Tel: (407) 647-1444
(800) 440-6000

MOTEL 6
5909 American Way (32819)
Rates: $35
Tel: (407) 351-6500
(800) 440-6000

RAMADA INN
736 Lee Rd (32810)
Rates: $49-$99
Tel: (407) 647-1112
(800) 272-6232

RED ROOF INN
9922 Hawaiian Ct (32819)
Rates: $33-$65
Tel: (407) 352-1507
(800) 843-7663

RODEWAY INN
6327 International Dr (32819)
Rates: $55-$65
Tel: (407) 351-4444
(800) 228-2000

THRIFTLODGE
6119 S Orange Blossom Tr (32809)
Rates: $30-$46
Tel: (407) 855-1356
(800) 578-7878

TRAVELODGE
7101 S Orange Blossom Tr (32809)
Rates: $35-$59
Tel: (407) 851-4300
(800) 578-7878

WELLESLEY INN & SUITES
5635 Windhover Dr (32819)
Rates: $70-$100
Tel: (407) 345-0026
(800) 444-8888

ORMOND BEACH

BEST WESTERN PLANTATION INN
2251 S Old Dixie Hwy
(Bunnell, 32110)
Rates: $50-$170
Tel: (904) 437-3737
(800) 528-1234

DAYS INN
1608 N US Hwy 1 (32174)
Rates: $29-$169
Tel: (904) 672-7341
(800) 329-7466

MAKAI MOTEL
707 S Atlantic Ave (32174)
Rates: n/a
Tel: (904) 677-8060

OSPREY

RAMADA INN
1660 S Tamiami Trl (34229)
Rates: $79-$115
Tel: (941) 966-2121
(800) 272-6232

PALM BAY

KNIGHTS INN-SPACE COAST
1170 Malabar Rd (32905)
Rates: $30-$40
Tel: (407) 951-8222

PALM BEACH

FOUR SEASONS OCEAN GRAND
2800 S Ocean Blvd (33480)
Rates: $140-$525
Tel: (407) 582-2800
(800) 432-2335

HEART OF PALM BEACH MOTEL
160 Royal Palm Way (33480)
Rates: $69-$199
Tel: (407) 655-5600
(800) 523-5377

HOWARD JOHNSON HOTEL
2870 S Ocean Blvd (33480)
Rates: $59-$76
Tel: (407) 582-2581
(800) 446-4656

PLAZA INN
215 Brazilian Ave (33480)
Rates: $75-$165
Tel: (407) 832-8666

PALM BEACH GARDENS

EMBASSY SUITES
4350 PGA Blvd (33410)
Rates: $115-$195
Tel: (407) 622-1000
(800) 333-3333

MACARTHUR'S HOLIDAY INN
4431 PGA Blvd (33410)
Rates: $49-$130
Tel: (800) 465-4329

PALM BEACH SHORES

BEST WESTERN SEASPRAY INN-SINGER ISLAND
123 S Ocean Dr (33404)
Rates: $69-$149
Tel: (561) 844-0233
(800) 528-1234

PALM HARBOR

KNIGHTS INN
34106 US 19 N
(34684)
Rates: $31-$52
Tel: (813) 789-2002

TRAVELODGE HOTEL
32000 US 19 N
(34684)
Rates: $35-$60
Tel: (813) 786-2529
(800) 578-7878

PANACEA

OAKS MOTEL
US 98 (32346)
Rates: n/a
Tel: (904) 984-5370

PANAMA CITY

BEST WESTERN BAYSIDE INN
711 W Beach Dr
(32401)
Rates: $45-$110
Tel: (904) 763-4622
(800) 528-1234

DAYS INN 23RD STREET
301 W 23rd St
(32405)
Rates: $30-$60
Tel: (800) 329-7466

DAYS INN
4111 W Hwy 98
(32401)
Rates: $33-$85
Tel: (904) 784-1777
(800) 329-7466

HOWARD JOHNSON
4601 US Hwy 98 W
(32401)
Rates: $52-$65
Tel: (904) 785-0222
(800) 446-4656

PASSPORT INN
5003 W Hwy 98
(34201)
Rates: $25-$60
Tel: (904) 769-2101
(800) 251-1962

SCOTTISH INNS
4907 W Hwy 98
(32401)
Rates: $20-$40
Tel: (904) 769-2432
(800) 251-1962

SUPER 8 MOTEL
207 Hwy 231 N
(32405)
Rates: $36-$76
Tel: (904) 784-1988
(800) 800-8000

PANAMA CITY BEACH

ADMIRAL IMPERIAL INN MOTEL
16819 Front Beach
Rd (32413)
Rates: n/a
Tel: (904) 234-2142

SURF HIGH INN ON THE GULF
10611 Front Beach
Rd (32407)
Rates: $35-$55
Tel: (904) 234-2129

PENSACOLA

COMFORT INN
6919 Pensacola Blvd
(32505)
Rates: $30-$60
Tel: (800) 221-2222

COMFORT INN-NAS CORRY
3 New Warrington
Rd (32506)
Rates: $40-$45
Tel: (800) 221-2222

DAYS INN NORTH
7051 Pensacola Blvd
(32505)
Rates: $40-$59
Tel: (904) 476-9090
(800) 329-7466

HOWARD JOHNSON
4126 Mobile Hwy
(32506)
Rates: $28-$65
Tel: (904) 456-5731
(800) 446-4656

HOWARD JOHNSON
6911 Pensacola Blvd
(32505)
Rates: $45-$55
Tel: (904) 479-3800
(800) 446-4656

LA QUINTA INN
7750 N Davis Hwy
(32514)
Rates: $42-$49
Tel: (800) 531-5900

MOTEL 6-EAST
7226 Plantation Rd
(32504)
Rates: $34-$40
Tel: (904) 474-1060
(800) 440-6000

MOTEL 6-NORTH
7827 N Davis Hwy
(32514)
Rates: $36-$42
Tel: (904) 476-5386
(800) 440-6000

MOTEL 6-WEST
5829 Pensacola Blvd
(32505)
Rates: $29-$33
Tel: (904) 477-7522
(800) 440-6000

PENSACOLA GRAND
200 E Gregory St
(32501)
Rates: $80-$100
Tel: (904) 433-3336

RAMADA INN
8060 Lavelle Way
(32526)
Rates$ 50-$100
Tel: (904) 944-0333
(800) 272-6232

RED ROOF INN
7340 Plantation Rd
(32504)
Rates: $33-$47
Tel: (904) 476-7960
(800) 843-7663

RODEWAY INN
8500 Pine Forest Rd
(32534)
Rates: $38-$48
Tel: (904) 477-9150
(800) 228-2000

SHONEY'S INN
8080 N Davis Hwy
(32514)
Rates: $66-$85
Tel: (904) 484-8070
(800) 222-2222

SUPER 8 MOTEL
7220 Plantation Rd
(32504)
Rates: $37-$60
Tel: (904) 476-8038
(800) 800-8000

PERRY

BEST BUDGET INN
2220 Byron Butler
Pkwy (32347)
Rates: $29
Tel: (904) 584-6231

SOUTHERN INN MOTEL
2238 S Byron Butler
Pkwy (32347)
Rates: $30-$45
Tel: (904) 584-4221

PLANT CITY

DAYS INN
301 S Frontage Rd
(33566)
Rates: $40-$85
Tel: (813) 584-5311
(800) 329-7466

RAMADA INN
2011 N Wheeler St
(33566)
Rates: $60-$125
Tel: (813) 752-3141
(800) 272-6232

POMPANO BEACH

DAYS INN
1411 NW 31st Ave
(33069)
Rates: $34-$99
Tel: (954) 972-3700
(800) 329-7466

HOWARD JOHNSON
9 N Pompano Beach
Blvd (33062)
Rates: $62-$98
Tel: (954) 781-1300
(800) 446-4656

SEA CASTLE RESORT MOTEL
730 N Ocean Blvd (33062)
Rates: $31-$119
Tel: (305) 941-2570

PONTE VEDRA BEACH

MARRIOTT AT SAWGRASS
1000 TPC Blvd (32082)
Rates: $115-$245
Tel: (904) 285-7777
(800) 228-9290

PORT CHARLOTTE

DAYS INN
1941 Tamiami Tr (33948)
Rates: $39-$105
Tel: (941) 627-8900
(800) 329-7466

QUALITY INN DOWNTOWN
3400 Tamiami Tr (33952)
Rates: $39-$89
Tel: (800) 377-8414

PORT RICHEY

DAYS INN
11736 US 19 (34668)
Rates: $40-$90
Tel: (813) 863-1502
(800) 329-7466

PORT SALERNO

PIRATES COVE RESORT & MARINA
4307 SE Bayview St (34992)
Rates: $60-$130
Tel: (407) 287-2500

PUNTA GORDA

DAYS INN
26560 N Jones Loop Rd (33950)
Rates: $35-$73
Tel: (800) 329-7466

HOLIDAY INN
300 Retta Esplanade (33950)
Rates: $54-$129
Tel: (800) 465-4329

HOWARD JOHNSON RIVERSIDE LODGE
33 Tamiami Tr (33950)
Rates: $38-$47
Tel: (941) 639-2167
(800) 446-4656

MOTEL 6
9300 Knights Dr (33950)
Rates: $30-$34
Tel: (941) 639-9585
(800) 440-6000

QUINCY

QUINCY MOTOR LODGE
368 E Jefferson (32351)
Rates: $n/a
Tel: (904) 627-8929

RIVIERA BEACH

BEST WESTERN
123 Ocean Ave (33404)
Rates: n/a
Tel: (407) 844-0233
(800) 528-1234

MOTEL 6
3651 W Blue Heron Blvd (33404)
Rates: $32-$36
Tel: (407) 863-1011
(800) 440-6000

ROCKLEDGE

SPITZER'S SWISS MOTEL
3220 S Fiske Blvd (32955)
Rates: $40-$50
Tel: (407) 631-9445

ST. AUGUSTINE

ANCHORAGE MOTOR INN
1 Dolphin Dr (32084)
Rates: n/a
Tel: (904) 829-9041

BEST WESTERN I-95
2445 SR 16 (32092)
Rates: $39-$59
Tel: (904) 829-1999
(800) 528-1234

DAYS INN HISTORIC
2800 N Ponce de Leon Blvd (32084)
Rates: $35-$90
Tel: (904) 829-6581
(800) 329-7466

DAYS INN
2560 SR 16 (32092)
Rates: $35-$65
Tel: (904) 824-4341
(800) 329-7466

ECONO LODGE
2535 SR 16 (32092)
Rates: $39-$89
Tel: (904) 829-5643
(800) 424-4777

HOWARD JOHNSON
2550 SR 16 (32092)
Rates: $29-$43
Tel: (904) 829-5686
(800) 446-4656

PONCE DE LEON GOLF & CONFERENCE RESORT
4000 US Hwy 1 N (32095)
Rates: $75-$130
Tel: (904) 824-2821
(800) 228-2821

RAMADA INN
116 San Marco Ave (32084)
Rates: $49-$120
Tel: (904) 824-4352
(800) 272-6232

SCOTTISH INNS DOWNTOWN
110 San Marco Ave (32084)
Rates: $27-$45
Tel: (904) 824-2871
(800) 251-1962

SEABREEZE MOTEL
208 Anastasia Blvd (32084)
Rates: $59-$140
Tel: (904) 829-8122

ST. AUGUSTINE BEACH

BEST WESTERN OCEAN INN
3955 Hwy A1A S (32084)
Rates: $39-$69
Tel: (904) 471-8010
(800) 528-1234

HOWARD JOHNSON
300 A1A Beach Blvd (32084)
Rates: $38-$150
Tel: (904) 471-2575
(800) 446-4656

ST. PETERSBURG
(and Vicinity)

COLONIAL GATEWAY INN
6300 Gulf Blvd (St. Pete Beach 33706)
Rates: $67-$115
Tel: (813) 367-2711
(800) 237-8918

DAYS INN
2595 54th Ave N (33714)
Rates: $35-$65
Tel: (813) 522-3191
(800) 329-7466

HOWARD JOHNSON HOTEL
3600 34th St S (33711)
Rates: $42-$69
Tel: (813) 867-6591
(800) 446-4656

LA MARK CHARLES MOTEL
6200 34th St N (Pinellas Park 34665)
Rates: $55-$90
Tel: (813) 527-7334

LA QUINTA INN
4999 34th St N
(33714)
Rates: $40-$62
Tel: (800) 531-5900

LA QUINTA INN
7500 US 19N
(Pinellas Park 34665)
Rates: $40-$62
Tel: (800) 531-5900

**VALLEY FORGE
MOTEL**
6825 Central Ave
(33710)
Rates: $30-$85
Tel: (813) 345-0135

SAFETY HARBOR

**SAFETY HARBOR
RESORT**
105 N Bayshore Dr
(34695)
Rates: $110-$185
Tel: (813) 726-1161
(800) 237-0155

SANFORD

DAYS INN
4650 SR 46 (32771)
Rates: $30-$54
Tel: (407) 323-6500
(800) 329-7466

SUPER 8 MOTEL
4750 State Rd 46 W
(32771)
Rates: $42-$65
Tel: (407) 323-3445
(800) 800-8000

SARASOTA

COMFORT INN
4800 N Tamiami Tr
(34234)
Rates: $45-$90
Tel: (800) 221-2222

**COQUINA
ON THE BEACH**
1008 Ben Franklin
Dr (34236)
Rates: $79-$219
Tel: (941) 388-2141
(800) 833-2141

**DAYS INN-
SARASOTA
AIRPORT**
4900 N Tamiami Tr
(34234)
Rates: $39-$100
Tel: (941) 955-9721
(800) 329-7466

**DAYS INN-
SARASOTA/
SIESTA KEY**
6600 S Tamiami Tr
(34231)
Rates: $53-$109
Tel: (941) 924-4900
(800) 329-7466

ECONO LODGE
6727 14th St W
(34207)
Rates: $31-$90
Tel: (941) 758-7199
(800) 424-4777

**HOLIDAY INN-
AIRPORT MARINA**
7150 N Tamiami Tr
(34243)
Rates: $54-$101
Tel: (800) 465-4329

RAMADA INN
5774 Clark Rd
(34233)
Rates: $75-100
Tel: (941) 921-7812
(800) 272-6232

WELLESLEY INNS
1803 N Tamiami Tr
(34234)
Rates: $40-$100
Tel: (941) 366-5128

SATELLITE BEACH

DAYS INN
180 Hwy A1A
(32937)
Rates: $42-$95
Tel: (407) 777-3552
(800) 329-7466

SEBRING

INN ON THE LAKES
3100 Golfview Rd
(33870)
Rates: $49-$75
Tel: (813) 471-9400

SIESTA KEY

**SURFRIDER BEACH
APARTMENTS**
6400 Midnight Pass
Rd (34242)
Rates: $63-$119
Tel: (941) 349-2121

**TROPICAL BREEZE
INN**
140 Columbus Blvd
(34242)
Rates: $75-$225
Tel: (941) 349-1125

**TURTLE BEACH
RESORT**
9049 Midnight Pass
Rd (34242)
Rates: $89-165
Tel: (941) 349-4554

SILVER SPRINGS

**DAYS INN OCALA
EAST**
5001 E Silver Springs
Blvd (32688)
Rates: $40-$60
Tel: (352) 236-2891
(800) 329-7466

HOLIDAY INN
5751 E Silver Springs
Blvd (34489)
Rates: $45-$65
Tel: (800) 465-4329

**HOWARD JOHNSON
MOTEL**
5565 E Silver Springs
Blvd (34489)
Rates: $35-$50
Tel: (352)236-2616
(800) 446-4656

SUN PLAZA MOTEL
5461 E Silver Springs
Blvd (32688)
Rates: $26-$40
Tel: (352) 236-2343

SOUTH BAY

OKEECHOBEE INN
265 N US Hwy 27
(33493)
Rates: $40-$45
Tel: (407) 996-7617

STARKE

**BEST WESTERN
MOTOR INN**
1290 N Temple Ave
(32091)
Rates: $40-$100
Tel: (904) 964-6744
(800) 528-1234

DAYS INN
1101 N Temple
(32091)
Rates: $47-$85
Tel: (904) 964-7600
(800) 329-7466

RED CARPET INN
744 N. Temple Ave.
(32091)
Rates: n/a
Tel: (904) 964-5590
(800) 251-1962

**SLEEPY HOLLOW
MOTEL**
2317 N Temple Ave
(32091)
Rates: $23-$27
Tel: (904) 964-5006

STEINHATCHEE

**STEINHATCHEE
LANDING**
Hwy 51 N (32359)
Rates: $95-$225
Tel: (352) 498-3513

STUART

HOWARD JOHNSON
950 S Federal Hwy
(34994)
Rates: $58
Tel: (407) 287-3171
(800) 446-4656

SUN CITY CENTER

SUN CITY CENTER HOTEL
1335 Rickenbacker Dr (33573)
Rates: $45-$65
Tel: (813) 634-3331

TALLAHASSEE

AMERICAN INN
2726 N Monroe St (32303)
Rates: $32-$37
Tel: (800) 307-5001

BEST INNS OF AMERICA
2738 Graves Rd (32303)
Rates: $39-$50
Tel: (904) 562-2378

COLLEGIATE VILLAGE INN
2121 W Tennessee (32304)
Rates: $40+
Tel: (904) 576-6121

DAYS INN AIRPORT SOUTH
3100 Apalachee Pkwy (32301)
Rates: $33-$41
Tel: (904) 877-6121
(800) 329-7466

ECONO LODGE
2681 N Monroe St (32303)
Rates: $35-$75
Tel: (904) 385-6155
(800) 424-4777

HOLIDAY INN
2714 Graves Rd NW (32303)
Rates: $58-$81
Tel: (904) 562-2000
(800) 465-4329

KILLEARN COUNTRY CLUB & INN
100 Tyron Cir (32308)
Rates: $54-$80
Tel: (904) 893-2186

LA QUINTA INN-NORTH
2905 N Monroe St (32303)
Rates: $42-$51
Tel: (800) 531-5900

LA QUINTA INN-SOUTH
2850 Apalachee Pkwy (32301)
Rates: $44-$57
Tel: (800) 531-5900

MOTEL 6-DOWNTOWN
1027 Apalachee Pkwy (32301)
Rates: $30-$36
Tel: (904) 877-6171
(800) 440-6000

MOTEL 6-NORTH
1481 Timberlane Rd (32312)
Rates: $29-$35
Tel: (904) 668-2600
(800) 440-6000

MOTEL 6-WEST
2738 N Monroe St (32303)
Rates: $29-$35
Tel: (904) 386-7878
(800) 440-6000

RED ROOF INN
2930 Hospitality St (32303)
Rates: $34-$41
Tel: (904) 385-7884
(800) 843-7663

SEMINOLE INN
6737 Mahan Dr (32308)
Rates: $40-$49
Tel: (904) 656-2938

TAMPA
(and Vicinity)

AMERISUITES
4811 W Main St (33607)
Rates: $65-$110
Tel: (813) 282-1037

BUDGETEL INN
4811 US Hwy 301N (33610)
Rates: $34-$57
Tel: (813) 626-0885

BUDGETEL INN-TAMPA SOUTHEAST
602 S Falkenburg Rd (33619)
Rates: $40-$56
Tel: (813) 684-4007

DAYS INN-BUSCH GARDENS EAST
2520 N 50th St (33619)
Rates: $42-$150
Tel: (813) 247-3300
(800) 329-7466

DAYS INN-TAMPA BUSCH GARDENS NORTH
701 E Fletcher Ave (33612)
Rates: $40-$88
Tel: (813) 977-1550
(800) 329-7466

ECONO LODGE BUSCH GARDENS
1701 E Busch Blvd (33612)
Rates: $35-$50
Tel: (813) 933-7681
(800) 424-4777

HOLIDAY INN STATE FAIR
2708 N 50th St (33619)
Rates: $55+
Tel: (800) 237-1510

HOWARD JOHNSON
4139 E Busch Blvd (33617)
Rates: $29-$68
Tel: (813) 988-9191
(800) 446-4656

HOWARD JOHNSON AIRPORT
2055 N Dale Mabry (33607)
Rates: $49-$79
Tel: (813) 875-8818
(800) 446-4656

LA QUINTA INN AIRPORT
4730 Spruce St (33607)
Rates: $49-$56
Tel: (800) 531-5900

LA QUINTA INN-EAST
2904 Melbourne Blvd (33605)
Rates: $30-$46
Tel: (800) 531-5900

MASTERS ECONOMY INN
6010 SR 579 (Seffner 33584)
Rates: $24-$40
Tel: (813) 621-4681

MOTEL 6-DOWNTOWN
333 E Fowler Ave (33612)
Rates: $28-$32
Tel: (813) 932-4948
(800) 440-6000

MOTEL 6-FAIRGROUNDS
6510 N Hwy 301 (33610)
Rates: $30-$34
Tel: (813) 628-0888
(800) 440-6000

RAMADA INN-USF/BUSCH GARDENS
400 E Bearss Ave (33613)
Rates: $59-$125
Tel: (813) 961-1000
(800) 272-6232

RAMADA INN STADIUM
4732 N Dale Mabry Hwy (33614)
Rates: $58-$81
Tel: (800) 272-6232

RED ROOF INN-BRANDON
10121 Horace Ave (33619)
Rates: $32-$50
Tel: (813) 681-8484
(800) 843-7663

RED ROOF INN-BUSCH GARDENS
2307 E Busch Blvd (33612)
Rates: $30-$55
Tel: (813) 932-0093
(800) 843-7663

RED ROOF INN-FAIRGROUND
5001 N US 301
(33610)
Rates: $29-$45
Tel: (813) 623-5245
(800) 843-7663

RESIDENCE INN BY MARRIOT
3075 N Rocky Point Dr (33607)
Rates: $89
Tel: (813) 281-5677
(800) 331-3131

SCOTTISH INNS
11414 Central Ave (33612)
Rates: $20-$34
Tel: (813) 933-7831
(800) 251-1962

SHERATON TAMPA EAST
7401 E Hillsborough Ave (33610)
Rates: $105-$275
Tel: (813) 626-0999
(800) 325-3535

TAHITIAN INN
601 S Dale Mabry (33609)
Rates: $44-$57
Tel: (813) 877-6721

TARPON SPRINGS

DAYS INN
40050 US Hwy 19 N (34689)
Rates: $35-$85
Tel: (813) 934-0859
(800) 329-7466

SCOTTISH INNS
110 W Tarpon Ave (34689)
Rates: $30-$55
Tel: (813) 937-6121
(800) 251-1962

TAVARES

INN ON THE GREEN
700 E Burleigh Blvd (32778)
Rates: $39-$65
Tel: (904) 343-6373

TITUSVILLE

BEST WESTERN SPACE SHUTTLE INN
3455 Cheney Hwy (32780)
Rates: $52-$80
Tel: (407) 269-9100
(800) 528-1234

DAYS INN-KENNEDY SPACE CENTER
3755 Cheney Hwy (32780)
Rates: $39-$149
Tel: (407) 269-4480
(800) 329-7466

HOWARD JOHNSON LODGE KENNEDY SPACE CENTER
1829 Riverside Dr (32780)
Rates: $44-$79
Tel: (407) 267-7900

TREASURE ISLAND

LORELEI RESORT
10273 Gulf Blvd (33706)
Rates: $40-$85
Tel: (813) 360-4351
(800) 354-6364

SEA HORSE COTTAGES & APTS
11780 Gulf Blvd (33706)
Rates: $35-105
Tel: (813) 367-2291
(800) 741-2291

VENICE

BEST WESTERN VENICE RESORT
455 US 41 Bypass N (34292)
Rates: $86-$110
Tel: (941) 485-5411
(800) 528-1234

DAYS INN
1710 S Tamiami Tr (34293)
Rates: $42-$245
Tel: (941) 493-4558
(800) 329-7466

INN AT THE BEACH RESORT
101 The Esplanade (34285)
Rates: $55-$140
Tel: (800) 255-8471

MOTEL 6
281 US Hwy 41 N (34292)
Rates: $33-$37
Tel: (941) 485-8255
(800) 440-6000

VERO BEACH

DAYS INN
8800 20th St (32966)
Rates: $44-$69
Tel: (407) 562-9991
(800) 329-7466

HOJO INN
1985 90th Ave (32966)
Rates: $30-$48
Tel: (407) 778-1985
(800) 446-4656

SUPER 8 MOTEL
8800 20th St (32966)
Rates: $39-$74
Tel: (407) 562-9996
(800) 800-8000

WEEKI WACHEE

HOLIDAY INN
6172 Commercial Way (34606)
Rates: $65-$102
Tel: (904) 596-2007
(800) 465-4329

WEST PALM BEACH

COMFORT INN-ON PALM BEACH LAKES
1901 Palm Beach Lakes Blvd (33409)
Rates: $69-$104
Tel: (800) 221-2222

DAYS INN
2700 N Ocean Dr (Singer Isl 33404)
Rates: $56-$166
Tel: (407) 848-8661
(800) 329-7466

DAYS INN-TURNPIKE
6255 Okeechobee Blvd (33417)
Rates: $49-$99
Tel: (561) 686-6000
(800) 329-7466

DAYS INN WEST PALM BEACH
2300 45th St (33407)
Rates: $39-$99
Tel: (407) 689-0450
(800) 329-7466

KNIGHTS INN
2200 45th St (33407)
Rates: $37-$63
Tel: (800) 843-5644

WELLESLEY INN
1910 Palm Beach Lakes Blvd (33409)
Rates: $40-$100
Tel: (407) 689-8540
(800) 444-8888

WHITE SPRINGS

SCOTTISH INNS
Rt 1, Box 97A-1 (32096)
Rates: $22-$26
Tel: (800) 251-1962

WILDWOOD

DAYS INN
551 E SR 44 (34785)
Rates: $30-$79
Tel: (352) 748-7766
(800) 329-7466

RED CARPET INN
US 301 & FL Tpk, Box 159 (34785)
Rates: $20-$34
Tel: (352) 748-4488
(800) 251-1962

WILLISTON

WILLISTON MOTOR INN
606 W Noble Ave (32696)
Rates: $28-$32
Tel: (352) 528-4801

WINTER HAVEN

BEST WESTERN INN
5665 Cypress
Gardens Blvd
(33884)
Rates: $39-$95
Tel: (941) 324-5950
(800) 247-2799

**BUDGET HOST
DRIFTWOOD**
970 Cypress Gardens
Blvd (33880)
Rates: $32-$62
Tel: (800) 283-4678

CYPRESS MOTEL
5651 Cypress
Gardens Rd (33884)
Rates: $30-$55
Tel: (941) 324-5867

**HOWARD JOHNSON
LODGE**
1300 US 17 SW
(33880)
Rates: $36-$95
Tel: (800) 446-4656

SCOTTISH INNS
1901 Cypress
Gardens Blvd
(33884)
Rates: $32-$62
Tel: (941) 324-3954

WINTER PARK

**DAYS INN ORLANDO
WINTER PARK**
901 N Orlando Ave
(32789)
Rates: $54-$79
Tel: (407) 644-8000
(800) 329-7466

**LANGFORD RESORT
HOTEL**
300 E New England
Ave (32789)
Rates: $39-$95
Tel: (407) 647-1072
(800) 228-7220

YULEE

DAYS INN
3250 US Hwy 17
(32097)
Rates: $39-$65
Tel: (904) 225-2011
(800) 329-7466

ZEPHYRHILLS

**CRYSTAL SPRINGS
MOTOR INN**
6736 Gall Blvd
(33541)
Rates: n/a
Tel: (813) 782-1214

GEORGIA

ACWORTH

**BEST WESTERN
FRONTIER INN**
P. O. Box 600 (30101)
Rates: $50-$75
Tel: (770) 974-0116
(800) 528-1234

DAYS INN
5035 Cowan Rd
(30101)
Rates: $35-$45
Tel: (800) 329-7466

QUALITY INN
4980 Cowan Rd
(30101)
Rates: $38-$43
Tel: (800) 221-2222

SUPER 8 MOTEL
Cowan Rd (30101)
Rates: $35-$55
Tel: (770) 966-9700
(800) 800-8000

ADEL

DAYS INN I-75
1200 W 4th St
(31620)
Rates: $30-$39
Tel: (912) 896-4574
(800) 329-7466

HOJO INN I-75
1103 W 4th St
(31620)
Rates: $28-$36
Tel: (912) 896-2244
(800) 800-8000

SCOTTISH INNS
911 W 4th St (31620)
Rates: $21-$28
Tel: (912) 896-2259
(800) 251-1962

SUPER 8 MOTEL
1102 W 4th St
(31620)
Rates: $25-$34
Tel: (800) 424-4777

ALBANY

ECONO LODGE
1806 E Oglethorpe
Blvd (31705)
Rates: $45-$60
Tel: (912) 883-5544
(800) 424-4777

HOLIDAY INN
2701 Dawson Rd
(31707)
Rates: $63-$67
Tel: (912) 883-8100
(800) 465-4325

KNIGHTS INN
1201 Schley Ave
(31707)
Rates: $35-$43
Tel: (912) 888-9600

MOTEL 6
301 S Thornton Dr
(31705)
Rates: $26-$30
Tel: (912) 439-0078
(800) 466-8356

RAMADA INN
2505 N Slappey Blvd
(31701)
Rates: $59-$85
Tel: (912) 883-3211
(800) 272-6232

SUPER 8 MOTEL
2444 N Slappey Blvd
(31701)
Rates: $40-$58
Tel: (912) 888-8388
(800) 800-8000

ALPHARETTA

**RESIDENCE INN
BY MARRIOTT**
5465 Windward
Pkwy W (30201)
Rates: $120-$159
Tel: (770) 664-0664
(800) 331-3131

AMERICUS

PATHWAY INN B & B
501 S Lee St (31709)
Rates: $70-$107
Tel: (912) 928-2078
(800) 889-1466

ASHBURN

COMFORT INN
803 Shoneys Dr
(31714)
Rates: $37+
Tel: (800) 221-2222

DAYS INN
823 E Washington
Ave (31714)
Rates: $32-$60
Tel: (912) 567-3346
(800) 329-7466

ATHENS

**BEST WESTERN-
COLONIAL INN**
170 N Milledge Ave
(30601)
Rates: $45-$59
Tel: (706) 546-7311
(800) 528-1234

DAYS INN
2741 Atlanta Hwy
(30606)
Rates: $40-$49
Tel: (800) 329-7466

**DOWNTOWNER
INNS**
1198 S Milledge Ave
(30605)
Rates: $29-$95
Tel: (706) 549-2626
(800) 251-1962

**HOWARD JOHNSON
LODGE**
2465 W Broad St
(30606)
Rates: $40-$145
Tel: (706) 548-1111
(800) 446-4656

RAMADA INN
513 W Broad St
(30601)
Rates: $57-$99
Tel: (706) 546-8122
(800) 272-6232

SCOTTISH INNS
410 Macon Hwy
(30606)
Rates: $23-$27
Tel: (706) 546-8161
(800) 251-1962

SUPER 8 MOTEL
3425 Atlanta hwy
(30606)
Rates: $33-$50
Tel: (706) 549-0251
(800) 800-8000

TRAVELODGE
898 W Broad St
(30601)
Rates: $32-$150
Tel: (706) 549-5400
(800) 578-7878

ATLANTA
(and Vicinity)

**ATLANTA MARRIOTT
GWINNETT PLACE**
1775 Pleasant Hill
Rd (Duluth 30136)
Rates: $94-$140
Tel: (970) 923-1775

**WESTIN HOTEL
INTL AIRPORT**
4736 Best Rd (30337)
Rates: $105-$600
Tel: (404) 762-7676

**BEST INNS
OF AMERICA**
1255 Franklin Rd
(Marietta 30067)
Rates: $39-$51
Tel: (404) 955-0004

**BEST WESTERN
ATLANTA SOUTH**
3509 Hwy 138
(Stockbridge 30281)
Rates: $40-$100
Tel: (770) 474-8771
(800) 528-1234

BEVERLY HILLS INN BED & BREAKFAST
65 Sheridan Dr
(30305)
Rates: $80-$140
Tel: (404) 233-8520
(800) 331-8520

BUDGETEL INN
575 Old Holcomb
Bridge Rd
(Roswell 30076)
Rates: $40-$54
Tel: (770) 552-0200

BUDGETEL INN
5395 Peachtree Ind
Blvd
(Norcross 30092)
Rates: $32-$50
Tel: (770) 446-2882

BUDGETEL INN-ATLANTA AIRPORT
2480 Old National
Pkwy
(College Park 30349)
Rates: $36-$40
Tel: (404) 766-0000

BUDGETEL INN ATLANTA LENOX
2535 Chantilly Dr
NE (30324)
Rates: $43-$63
Tel: (404) 321-0999

DAYS INN
1701 Northside Dr
(30318)
Rates: $40-$75
Tel: (404) 351-6500
(800) 329-7466

DAYS INN-GWINNETT PLACE
1948 Day Dr
(Duluth 30136)
Rates: $49-$84
Tel: (770) 476-1211
(800) 329-7466

DOUBLETREE HOTEL ATLANTA CONCOURSE
7 Concourse Pkwy
(30328)
Rates: $135-$165
Tel: (770) 395-3900
(800) 222-8733

GRANADA SUITE HOTEL
1302 W Peachtree St
(30309)
Rates: $59-$119
Tel: (800) 548-5631

HAMPTON INN
9995 Old Dogwood
Rd
(Roswell 30076)
Rates: $69-$79
Tel: (770) 587-5161
(800) 426-7866

HAWTHORN SUITES
1500 Parkwood Cir
(30339)
Rates: $69-$145
Tel: (770) 952-9595

HILTON & TOWERS
255 Courtland St NE
(30303)
Rates: $185-$400
Tel: (800) 445-8667

HOLIDAY INN AIRPORT SOUTH
5010 Old National
Hwy
(College Park 30349)
Rates: $81-$109
Tel: (800) 465-4329

HOLIDAY INN CENTRAL
418 Armour Dr NE
(30324)
Rates: $48+
Tel: (800) 465-4329

HOLIDAY INN PERIMETER DUN-WOODY
4386 Chamblee-Dunwoody Rd
(30341)
Rates: $79-$125
Tel: (800) 465-4329

HOLIDAY INN-SOUTH
6288 Old Dixie Hwy
(Jonesboro 30236)
Rates: $46-$71
Tel: (800) 465-4329

HOMEWOOD SUITES CUMBERLAND
3200 Cobb Pkwy
(30339)
Rates: $96-$106
Tel: (770) 988-9449

KNIGHTS INN-ATLANTA WEST/SIX FLAGS
1595 Blair Bridge Rd
(Austell 30001)
Rates: $40-$60
Tel: (770) 944-0824

LA QUINTA ATLANTA STONE MOUNTAIN
1819 Mountain Ind
Blvd (Tucker 30084)
Rates: $41-$49
Tel: (800) 531-5900

LA QUINTA ATLANTA WEST
7377 Six Flags Dr
(Austell 30001)
Rates: $42-$49
Tel: (800) 531-5900

LA QUINTA INN JIMMY CARTER
6187 Dawson Blvd
(Norcross 30093)
Rates: $41-$47
Tel: (800) 531-5900

LA QUINTA INN-PANOLA ROAD
2859 Panola Rd
(Lithonia 30058)
Rates: $45-$51
Tel: (800) 531-5900

LA QUINTA-PEACHTREE
5375 Peachtree Ind
Blvd
(Norcross 30092)
Rates: $41-$48
Tel: (800) 531-5900

MOTEL 6
3585 Chamblee-Tucker Rd
(30341)
Rates: $35-$41
Tel: (770) 455-8000
(800) 446-8356

OCCIDENTAL GRAND HOTEL-ATLANTA
75 14th St (30309)
Rates: $145-$1500
Tel: (800) 952-0702

RAMADA INN
70 NE John Wesley
Dobbs NE (30303)
Rates: $59-$109
Tel (404) 659-2660
(800) 272-6232

RED ROOF INN-DRUID HILLS
1960 N Druid Hills
Rd (30329)
Rates: $40-$50
Tel: (404) 321-1653
(800) 843-7663

RED ROOF INN-SIX FLAGS
4265 Shirley Dr SW
(30336)
Rates: $31-$60
Tel: (770) 696-4391
(800) 843-7663

RESIDENCE INN BY MARRIOTT
2960 Piedmont Rd
NE (30305)
Rates: $115
Tel: (404) 239-0677
(800) 331-3131

RESIDENCE INN BY MARRIOTT
1901 Savoy Dr
(30341)
Rates: $55-$125
Tel: (770) 455-4446
(800) 331-3131

SHONEY'S INN-ATLANTA NORTHEAST
2050 Willow Trail
Pkwy
(Norcross 30093)
Rates: $44-$60
Tel: (770) 564-0492

SUMMERFIELD SUITES HOTEL BUCKHEAD
505 Pharr Rd (30305)
Rates: $98-$179
Tel: (404) 262-7880

SUMMIT INN
3900 Fulton
Industrial
Blvd (30336)
Rates: $31-$49
Tel: (404) 691-2444

SUPER 8 MOTEL
2867 NE Expressway
(30345)
Rates: $50-$65
Tel: (404) 633-8451
(800) 800-8000

SUPER 8 MOTEL
111 Cone St (30303)
Rates: $59-$129
Tel: (404) 524-7000
(800) 800-8000

UNIVERSITY INN-EMORY
1767 N Decatur Rd (30307)
Rates: $69-$160
Tel: (404) 634-7327

THE WESTIN PEACHTREE PLAZA
210 NW Peachtree St (30303)
Rates: $229-$295
Tel: (404) 659-1400
(800) 228-3000

AUGUSTA

DAYS INN
444 Broad St (30901)
Rates: $35-$180
Tel: (706) 724-8100
(800) 329-7466

HOLIDAY INN GORDON HIWAY
2155 Gordon Hwy (30909)
Rates: $52-$69
Tel: (800) 465-4329

HOWARD JOHNSON
1238 Gordon Hwy (30901)
Rates: $29-$65
Tel: (706) 724-9613
(800) 446-4656

HOWARD JOHNSON LODGE
601 Bobby Jones Expwy (30907)
Rates: $30-$45
Tel: (706) 863-2882
(800) 446-4656

LA QUINTA INN
3020 Washington Rd (30907)
Rates: $33-$40
Tel: (800) 531-5900

MASTERS ECONOMY INN
3027 Washington Rd (30907)
Rates: $26-$39
Tel: (706) 863-5566

MOTEL 6
2560 Center West Pkwy (30909)
Rates: $24-$28
Tel: (404) 736-1934
(800) 466-8356

RADISSON SUITES INN
3038 Washington Rd (30907)
Rates: $59-$99
Tel: (706) 868-1800
(800) 333-3333

RADISSON RIVER-FRONT HOTEL AUGUSTA
Two 10th St (30901)
Rates: $84-$110
Tel: (800) 333-3333

RAMADA INN
640 Broad St (30901)
Rates: $72-$229
Tel: (706) 722-5541
(800) 272-6232

RED CARPET INN
1455 Walton Way (30901)
Rates: n/a
Tel: (770) 952-3365
(800) 251-1962

SHERATON AUGUSTA HOTEL
2651 Perimeter Pkwy (30909)
Rates: $59-$102
Tel: (706) 855-8100

SUPER 8 MOTEL
954 5th St (30901)
Rates: $29-$46
Tel: (706) 724-0757
(800) 800-8000

TELFAIR INN-A VACATION VILLAGE
326 Greene St (30901)
Rates: $67-$177
Tel: (706) 724-3315

BAXLEY

PINE LODGE MOTEL
500 S Main St (31513)
Rates: $32-$33
Tel: (912) 367-3622
(800) 841-6052

BLACKSHEAR

POND VIEW INN
4200 Grady St (31516)
Rates: $60-$125
Tel: (912) 449-3697
(800) 585-8659

BLAIRSVILLE

7 CREEKS HOUSEKEEPING CABINS
5109 Horseshoe Cove Rd (30512)
Rates: $50-$250
Tel: (706) 745-4753

BLUE RIDGE

BLUE RIDGE MOUNTAIN CABINS
P. O. Box 1182 (30513)
Rates: $70-$100
Tel: (706) 632-7891

DAYS INN
4970 Appalachian Hwy (30513)
Rates: $37-$80
Tel: (706) 632-2100
(800) 329-7466

BREMEN

BEST WESTERN CARROLLTON
35 Price Creek Rd (30110)
Rates: $45-$69
Tel: (770) 537-4646
(800) 528-1234

DAYS INN
1077 Alabama Ave (30110)
Rates: $45-$150
Tel: (770) 537-3833
(800) 329-7466

BRUNSWICK

BEST WESTERN BRUNSWICK INN
5323 New Jesup Hwy (31523)
Rates: $36-$53
Tel: (912) 265-8830
(800) 528-1234

BUDGETEL INN
105 Tourist Dr (31520)
Rates: $33-$50
Tel: (912) 265-7725

COMFORT INN
5308 New Jesup Hwy (31525)
Rates: $39-$59
Tel: (800) 221-2222

DAYS INN
2307 Gloucester St (31520)
Rates: $35-$55
Tel: (912) 265-8830
(800) 329-7466

HOLIDAY INN I-95
5252 New Jesup Hwy (31525)
Rates: $59-$73
Tel: (800) 465-4329

MOTEL 6
403 Butler Dr (31525)
Rates: $30-$34
Tel: (912) 264-8582
(800) 466-8356

QUALITY INN SUITES
3302 Glynn Ave (31520)
Rates: $46-$62
Tel: (800) 221-2222

RAMADA LIMITED DOWNTOWN
3241 Glynn Ave (31520)
Rates: $45-$57
Tel: (912) 264-8611
(800) 272-6232

RAMADA LIMITED I-95
3040 Scarlet St (31520)
Rates: $45-$57
Tel: (912) 264-3621
(800) 272-6232

SHONEY'S INN
3030 Scarlet St (31520)
Rates: $37-$43
Tel: (912) 264-3626
(800) 222-2222

SLEEP INN
5272 New Jesup Hwy (31525)
Rates: $39-$52
Tel: (800) 221-2222

SUPER 8 MOTEL
5280 New Jesup
Hwy (31520)
Rates: $39-$58
Tel: (912) 264-8800
(800) 800-8000

BYRON

ECONO LODGE
106 Old Mason Rd
(31008)
Rates: $32-$48
Tel: (912) 956-5600
(800) 424-4777

**MASTERS
ECONOMY INN**
Rt 3, Box 1540
(31008)
Rates: $23-$31
Tel: (912) 956-5300

PASSPORT INN
I-75 at Exit 46
(31008)
Rates: $23-$35
Tel: (912) 956-5200
(800) 251-1962

CAIRO

DAYS INN
35 US Hwy 84
(31728)
Rates: $40-$50
Tel: (912) 377-4400
(800) 329-7466

CALHOUN

**BEST WESTERN
OF CALHOUN**
2261 Hwy 41 NE
(30701)
Rates: $34-$52
Tel: (706) 629-4521
(800) 528-1234

**BUDGET HOST
SHEPHERD MOTEL**
3900 Fairmont Hwy
SE (30703)
Rates: $25-$36
Tel: (800) 283-4678

ECONO LODGE
1438 US 41 (30701)
Rates: $24-$43
Tel: (706) 625-5421
(800) 424-4777

HOLIDAY INN
1220 Red Bud Rd
(30703)
Rates: $45-$50
Tel: (800) 465-4329

QUALITY INN
915 Hwy 53 E SE
(30701)
Rates: $30-$44
Tel: (800) 221-2222

SCOTTISH INNS
1510 Red Bud Rd NE
(30701)
Rates: $23-$89
Tel: (706) 629-8271
(800) 251-1962

SUPER 8 MOTEL
1446 Hwy 41 N
(30701)
Rates: $35-$59
Tel: (706) 602-1400
(800) 800-8000

CAMILLA

**BEST WESTERN
COURTLAND CLUB**
600 US Hwy 19
(31730)
Rates: $48-$60
Tel: (912) 336-0731
(800) 528-1234

CANTON

DAYS INN
291 Ball Ground
Hwy (30114)
Rates: $39-$54
Tel: (770) 479-0301
(800) 329-7466

CARROLLTON

DAYS INN
180 Centennial Rd
(30117)
Rates: $44-$49
Tel: (770) 830-1000
(800) 329-7466

RAMADA INN
1202 S Park St
(30116)
Rates: $55-$100
Tel: (770) 834-7700
(800) 272-6232

CARTERSVILLE

BUDGET HOST INN
851 Cass-White Rd
(30120)
Rates: $22-$29
Tel: (800) 283-4678

COMFORT INN
28 Hwy 294 SE
(30120)
Rates: $34-$99
Tel: (800) 221-2222

DAYS INN
5618 Hwy 20 SE
(30120)
Rates: $35-$88
Tel: (706) 382-1824
(800) 329-7466

ECONO LODGE
25 Carson Loop
(30120)
Rates: $30-$150
Tel: (404) 386-0700
(800) 424-4777

HOLIDAY INN
2336 Hwy 411 NE
(30120)
Rates: $40-$66
Tel: (770) 386-0830
(800) 465-4329

**HOWARD JOHNSON
LODGE**
5657 Hwy 20 (30120)
Rates: $28-$155
Tel: (770) 386-1449
(800) 446-4656

KNIGHTS INN
420 E Church St
(30120)
Rates: $33-$42
Tel: (770) 386-7263

RED CARPET INN
851 Cass-White Rd
(30120)
Rates: $20-$25
Tel: (770) 382-8000
(800) 251-1962

SUPER 8 MOTEL
41 SR 20 Spur SE
(30120)
Rates: $37-$55
Tel: (770) 382-8881
(800) 800-8000

CHATSWORTH

KEY WEST INN
501 GI Maddox
Pkwy (30705)
Rates: $36-$57
Tel: (706) 517-1155

CHULA

RED CARPET INN
P. O. Box 40 (31733)
Rates: $23-$29
Tel: (912) 382-2686
(800) 251-1962

CLAYTON

**ENGLISH MANOR
INN**
P. O. Box 1605
(30525)
Rates: n/a
Tel: (706) 782-5789
(800) 782-5780

CLEVELAND

**VILLAGIO DI
MONTAGNA**
Hwy 129 N (30528)
Rates: $80-$120
Tel: (800) 367-3922

COLLEGE PARK

**LA QUINTA INN
AIRPORT**
4874 Old National
Hwy (30337)
Rates: $50-$64
Tel: (404) 768-1241
(800) 531-5900

MARRIOTT-AIRPORT
4711 Best Rd (30337)
Rates: $132-$147
Tel: (404) 766-7900
(800) 228-9290

COLUMBUS

BUDGETEL
2919 Warm Springs
Rd (31909)
Rates: $37-$54
Tel: (706) 323-4344

COMFORT INN
3443 Macon Rd
(31907)
Rates: $43-$63
Tel: (800) 221-2222

DAYS INN
3452 Macon Rd
(31907)
Rates: $51-$65
Tel: (706) 561-4408
(800) 329-7466

ECONO LODGE
4483 Victory Dr
(31903)
Rates: $38-$54
Tel: (706) 682-3803
(800) 424-4777

LA QUINTA INN
3201 Macon Rd
(31906)
Rates: $56-$69
Tel: (706) 568-1740
(800) 531-5900

MOTEL 6
3050 Victory Dr
(31903)
Rates: $27-$31
Tel: (706) 687-7214
(800) 466-8356

SUPER 8 MOTEL
2935 Warm Springs
Rd (31909)
Rates: $41-$59
Tel: (706) 322-6580
(800) 800-8000

COMMERCE

GUEST HOUSE INN
30934 US 441 S
(30529)
Rates: $26-$33
Tel: (706) 335-5147

HOJO INN
Rt 1, Box 163-D
(30529)
Rates: $36-$89
Tel: (706) 335-5581
(800) 446-4656

HOLIDAY INN
30747 US 441 S
(30529)
Rates: $38-$56
Tel: (800) 465-4329

RAMADA INN
US Hwy 441 & I-85
(30529)
Rates: $39-$48
Tel: (706) 335-5191
(800) 272-6232

CONYERS

COMFORT INN
1363 Klondike Rd
(30207)
Rates: $49-$99
Tel: (800) 221-2222

CORDELE

COLONIAL INN
2016 16th Ave E
(31015)
Rates: $33-$42
Tel: (912) 273-5420

DAYS INN
215 S. 7th St.(31015)
Rates: $40-$55
Tel: (912) 273-1123
(800) 329-7466

ECONO LODGE
1618 E 16th Ave
(31015)
Rates: $30-$46
Tel: (800) 424-4777

HOLIDAY INN
1711 16th Ave E
(31015)
Rates: $48-$62
Tel: (800) 465-4329

PASSPORT INN
1602 16th Ave
(31015)
Rates: $22-$30
Tel: (912) 273-4088
(800) 251-1962

RAMADA INN
2016 16th Ave E
(31015)
Rates: $44-$62
Tel: (912) 273-5000
(800) 272-6232

RODEWAY INN
1609 E 16th Ave
(31015)
Rates: $35-$100
Tel: (912) 273-3390
(800) 228-2000

DALTON

**BEST INNS
OF AMERICA**
1529 W Walnut Ave
(30720)
Rates: $39-$50
Tel: (706) 226-1100

**BEST WESTERN INN
OF DALTON**
2106 Chattanooga
Rd (30720)
Rates: $40-$54
Tel: (706) 226-5022
(800) 528-1234

DAYS INN
1518 W Walnut Ave
(30720)
Rates: $45-$75
Tel: (706) 278-0850
(800) 329-7466

HOLIDAY INN
515 Holiday Dr
(30720)
Rates: $60-$100
Tel: (800) 465-4329

MOTEL 6
2200 Chattanooga
Rd (30720)
Rates: $28-$32
Tel: (706) 278-5522
(800) 466-8356

SUPER 8 MOTEL
236 Connector 3 SW
(30720)
Rates: $39-$57
Tel: (706) 277-9323
(800) 800-8000

DARIEN

SUPER 8 MOTEL
Hwy 251 & 195
(31305)
Rates: $34-$48
Tel: (912) 437-6660
(800) 800-8000

DECATUR

ECONO LODGE
2574 Candler Rd
(30032)
Rates: $50-$100
Tel: (404) 243-4422
(800) 424-4777

HOLIDAY INN
4300 Snapfinger
Woods Dr (30035)
Rates: $55-$65
Tel: (770) 981-5670
(800) 465-4329

MOTEL 6
2565 Wesley Chapel
Rd (30085)
Rates: $40-46
Tel: (404) 288-6911
(800) 466-8356

DILLARD

**BEST WESTERN
DILLARD**
US 23 & 441 (30537)
Rates: $45-$119
Tel: (706) 746-5321
(800) 528-1234

**THE DILLARD
HOUSE**
P. O. Box 10 (30537)
Rates: $39-$75
Tel: (706) 746-5348

DOUGLAS

DAYS INN
907 N Peterson Ave
(31533)
Rates: $34-$46
Tel: (912) 384-5190
(800) 329-7466

DUBLIN

HOLIDAY INN
Hwy 441 & 116
(31040)
Rates: $40-$53
Tel: (800) 465-4329

DULUTH

**AMERISUITES OF
GWINNETT**
3390 Venture Pkwy
(30136)
Rates: $65-$105
Tel: (770) 623-6800

ELBERTON

GRANITE CITY MOTEL
925 Elbert Extension St (30365)
Rates: $33-$36
Tel: (706) 283-4221

FOLKSTON

DAYS INN
1201 S 2nd St (31537)
Rates: $35-$70
Tel: (912) 496-2514
(800) 329-7466

FORSYTH

BEST WESTERN HILLTOP INN
SR 42 & I-75 (31029)
Rates: $36-$58
Tel: (912) 994-9260
(800) 528-1234

DAYS INN
I-75 & Lee St (31029)
Rates: $46-$51
Tel: (912) 994-2900
(800) 329-7466

ECONO LODGE
I-75 & US 83 (31029)
Rates: $35-$44
Tel: (912) 994-5603
(800) 424-4777

HAMPTON INN
520 Holiday Cir (31029)
Rates: $46-$51
Tel: (912) 994-9697
(800) 426-7866

PASSPORT INN
I-75 & Hwy 83 (31029)
Rates: $22-$70
Tel: (912) 994-2643
(800) 251-1962

GAINESVILLE

MASTERS INN MOTEL
Hwy 129 & Monroe Dr (30507)
Rates: $33-$48
Tel: (770) 532-7531

HAPEVILLE

RESIDENCE INN BY MARRIOTT
3401 International Blvd (30354)
Rates: $100-$146
Tel: (404) 761-0511
(800) 331-3131

HAZLEHURST

THE VILLAGE INN
312 Coffee St (31539)
Rates: $36-$52
Tel: (912) 375-4527

HELEN

HELENDORF RIVER INN & TOWERS
33 Munich Strasse (30545)
Rates: $24-$150
Tel: (706) 878-2271

HINESVILLE

SHONEY'S INN
786 E Oglethorpe (31313)
Rates: $43-$47
Tel: (912) 368-5858
(800) 222-2222

JEKYLL ISLAND

CLARION BUCCA-NEER RESORT
85 S Beachview Dr (31527)
Rates: $75-$169
Tel: (912) 635-2211
(800) 204-0202

COMFORT INN ISLAND SUITES
711 N Beachview Dr (31527)
Rates: $65-$149
Tel: (912) 635-2211
(800) 204-0202

DAYS INN BEACH RESORT
60 S Beachview Dr (31527)
Rates: $42-$99
Tel: (912) 635-3319
(800) 329-7466

HOLIDAY INN BEACH RESORT
200 S Beachview Dr (31527)
Rates: $45-$63
Tel: (912) 635-3311
(800) 753-5955

SEAFARER INN
700 Beachview Dr (31527)
Rates: $46-$88
Tel: (912) 635-2202

VILLAS BY THE SEA
1175 N Beachview Dr (31527)
Rates: $74-$234
Tel: (800) 841-6262

JESUP

DAYS INN
384 US Hwy 301 S (31545)
Rates: $39-$45
Tel: (912) 427-3751
(800) 329-7466

KENNESAW

RODEWAY INN
1460 Busbee Pkwy (30144)
Rates: $25-$39
Tel: (770) 590-0519

DAYS INN
760 Cobb Place Blvd (30144)
Rates: $56-$100
Tel: (770) 419-1576
(800) 329-7466

RED ROOF INN-TOWN CENTER MALL
520 Roberts Ct NW (30144)
Rates: $32-$44
Tel: (800) 843-7663

KINGSLAND

COMFORT INN
111 Edenfield Rd (31548)
Rates: $41-$66
Tel: (800) 221-2222

DAYS INN
1050 E King Ave (31548)
Rates: $31-$75
Tel: (912) 729-5454
(800) 329-7466

LA GRANGE

DAYS INN LA GRANGE/ CALLAWAY GARDENS
2606 Whitesville Rd (30240)
Rates: $47-$150
Tel: (706) 882-8881
(800) 329-7466

LAKE PARK

HOLIDAY INN EXPRESS
1198 Lakes Blvd (31636)
Rates: $39-$42
Tel: (912) 559-5181

SHONEY'S INN
1075 Lakes Blvd (31636)
Rates: $36-$42
Tel: (912) 559-5660
(800) 424-4777

TRAVELODGE
I-75, Exit 2 (31636)
Rates: $38-$56
Tel: (912) 559-0110
(800) 578-7878

LAKEMONT

FOREST LODGES
Lake Rabun Rd (30552)
Rates: $65
Tel: (706) 782-6250

LAVONIA

SHONEY'S INN
14227 Jones St (30553)
Rates: $40+
Tel: (706) 356-8848
(800) 222-2222

LAWRENCEVILLE

DAYS INN
731 W Pike St
(30245)
Rates: $38-$100
Tel: (770) 995-7782
(800) 329-7466

LOCUST GROVE

RED CARPET INN
4829 Hampton Rd
(30248)
Rates: $22-$33
Tel: (404) 957-2601
(800) 251-1962

SCOTTISH INNS
4679 Hampton Rd
(30248)
Rates: $25-$131
Tel: (404) 957-9001
(800) 251-1962

SUPER 8 MOTEL
4605 Hampton Rd
(30248)
Rates: $37-$53
Tel: (770) 957-2936
(800) 800-8000

LOUISVILLE

**LOUISVILLE
MOTOR LODGE**
308 Hwy 1 Bypass
(30434)
Rates: $34-$48
Tel: (912) 625-7168

MACON

**COMFORT INN-
NORTH**
2690 Riverside Dr
(31204)
Rates: $49-$59
Tel: (912) 746-8855
(800) 221-2222

**CROWNE PLAZA
HOTEL**
108 1st St (31201)
Rates: $89-$99
Tel: (912) 746-1461

DAYS INN NORTH
2737 Sheraton Dr
(31204)
Rates: $45-$60
Tel: (912) 745-8521
(800) 329-7466

ECONO LODGE
4951 Romeiser Rd
(31206)
Rates: $32-$48
Tel: (912) 474-1661
(800) 424-4777

HAMPTON INN
3680 Riverside Dr
(31210)
Rates: $41-$51
Tel: (800) 426-7866

**HOLIDAY INN
EXPRESS**
2720 Riverside Dr
(31204)
Rates: $42-$46
Tel: (800) 465-4329

HOWARD JOHNSON
4709 Chambers Rd
(31206)
Rates: $32-$100
Tel: (912) 781-6680
(800) 446-4656

**HOWARD JOHNSON
LODGE**
2566 Riverside Dr
(31204)
Rates: $40-$100
Tel: (912) 746-7671
(800) 446-4656

KNIGHTS INN
4952 Romeiser Dr
(31206)
Rates: $29-$45
Tel: (912) 471-1230

**MASTERS
ECONOMY INN**
4295 Pio Nono Ave
(31206)
Rates: $23-$27
Tel: (912) 788-8910

MOTEL 6
4991 Harrison Rd
(31206)
Rates: $29-$33
Tel: (912) 474-2870
(800) 466-8356

PASSPORT INN
5022 Romeiser Dr
(31206)
Rates: $21-$30
Tel: (912) 474-2665
(800) 251-1962

QUALITY INN
4630 Chambers Rd
(31206)
Rates: $35-$55
Tel: (800) 221-2222

RED CARPET INN
4604 Chambers Rd
(31206)
Rates: n/a
Tel: (912) 781-2810
(800) 251-1962

RODEWAY INN
4999 Eisenhower
Pkwy (31206)
Rates: $42-$48
Tel: (912) 781-4343
(800) 228-2000

MADISON

BURNETT PLACE
317 Old Post Rd
(30650)
Rates: $65-$75
Tel: (706) 342-4034

DAYS INN
2001 Eatonton Hwy
(30650)
Rates: $45-$85
Tel: (706) 342-1839
(800) 329-7466

RAMADA INN
US 441 & I-20
(30650)
Rates: $39-$55
Tel: (706) 342-2121
(800) 272-6232

MARIETTA

HOWARD JOHNSON
I-75 & Delk Rd
(30067)
Rates: $48-$205
Tel: (770) 951-1144
(800) 446-4656

LA QUINTA INN
2170 Delk Rd (30067)
Rates: $85-$110
Tel: (770) 951-0026
(800) 531-5900

MOTEL 6
2360 Delk Rd (30067)
Rates: $39-$45
Tel: (770) 952-8161
(800) 466-8356

RAMADA INN
610 Franklin Rd
(30067)
Rates: $40-$95
Tel: (770) 919-7878
(800) 272-6232

SUPER 8 MOTEL
2500 Delk Rd (30067)
Rates: $42-$60
Tel: (770) 984-1570
(800) 800-8000

SUPER 8 MOTEL
610 Franklin Rd
(30067)
Rates: $40-$55
Tel: (770) 919-2340
(800) 800-8000

McDONOUGH

**THE BRITTANY
MOTOR INN**
P. O. Box 477 (30253)
Rates: $29
Tel: (770) 957-5821

DAYS INN
744 GA 155 S.(30253)
Rates: $42-$55
Tel: (770) 957-5261
(800) 329-7466

**HOLIDAY INN
MCDONOUGH**
930 Hwy 155 S
(30253)
Rates: $50-$65
Tel: (800) 465-4329

HOWARD JOHNSON
1279 Hampton Rd
(30253)
Rates: $40-$55
Tel: (770) 957-2651
(800) 446-4656

RED CARPET INN
1170 Hampton Rd
(30253)
Rates: $22-$29
Tel: (404) 957-2458
(800) 251-1962

METTER

DAYS INN
720 S Lewis St
(30349)
Rates: $35-$55
Tel: (912) 685-2700
(800) 329-7466

MILLEDGEVILLE

DAYS INN
3001 Heritage Rd
(31061)
Rates: $33-$59
Tel: (912) 453-3551
(800) 329-7466

SCOTTISH INNS
2474 N Columbia St
NW (31061)
Rates: $20-$28
Tel: (912) 453-9491
(800) 251-1962

MONROE

DAYS INN
Box 10, Hwy 11 N
(30655)
Rates: $40-$150
Tel: (770) 267-3666
(800) 329-7466

MORROW

BEST WESTERN SOUTHLAKE
907 Holcomb Bridge
Rd (30075)
Rates: $54-$99
Tel: (770) 961-6300
(800) 528-1234

NEWNAN

DAYS INN
P. O. Box 548 (30263)
Rates: $43-$99
Tel: (770) 253-8550
(800) 329-7466

NORCROSS

DAYS INN
5385 Peachtree
Industrial Blvd
(30092)
Rates: $40-$150
Tel: (800) 329-7466

MOTEL 6
6015 Oakbrook
Pkwy (30093)
Rates: $40-$46
Tel: (770) 446-2311
(800) 466-8356

TRAVELODGE NORTHEAST
6045 Oakbrook
Pkwy (30093)
Rates: $49-$129
Tel: (770) 449-7322
(800) 578-7878

PERRY

HAMPTON INN
102 Hampton Ct
(31069)
Rates: $51-$61
Tel: (912) 987-7681
(800) 426-7866

NEW PERRY HOTEL
800 Main St (31069)
Rates: $26-$46
Tel: (912) 987-1000
(800) 877-3779

PASSPORT INN
1519 Sam Nunn
Blvd (31069)
Rates: n/a
Tel: (912) 987-9709
(800) 251-1962

QUALITY INN
1504 Sam Nunn
Blvd (31069)
Rates: $35-$55
Tel: (912) 987-1345
(800) 221-2222

RAMADA INN
100 Market Place Dr
(31069)
Rates: $48-$80
Tel: (912) 987-8400
(800) 272-6232

RED CARPET INN
105 Carrol Blvd
(31069)
Rates: $20-$30
Tel: (912) 987-2200
(800) 251-1962

RODEWAY INN
103 Marshallville Rd
(31069)
Rates:$45-$49
Tel: (912) 987-3200
(800) 228-2000

SCOTTISH INNS
106 Gen. Courtney
Hodges Blvd (31069)
Rates: n/a
Tel: (912) 987-3622
(800) 251-1962

SUPER 8 MOTEL
1410 Sam Nunn
Blvd (31069)
Rates: $35-$55
Tel: (800) 800-8000

PINE MOUNTAIN

WHITE COLUMNS MOTEL
19727 S US 27
(31822)
Rates: $33-45
Tel: (706) 663-2312

POOLER

RAMADA INN
301 Governor
Teutlen Dr (31322)
Rates: $49-$89
Tel: (912) 748-6464
(800) 272-6232

RICHMOND HILL

DAYS INN
P. O. Box 519 (31324)
Rates: $42-$50
Tel: (912) 756-3371
(800) 329-7466

MOTEL 6
I-95 & Hwy 17
(31324)
Rates: $26-$30
Tel: (912) 756-3543
(800) 466-8356

RINGGOLD

FRIENDSHIP INN
Sr 11, Box 405
(30736)
Rates: $38-$50
Tel: (706) 965-3428
(800) 453-4111

SUPER 8 MOTEL
401 S Hwy 151
(30736)
Rates: $42-$52
Tel: (706) 965-7080
(800) 800-8000

ROME

BEST WESTERN EXECUTIVE INN
Hwy 411 (30161)
Rates: $45-$85
Tel: (800) 528-1234

HOLIDAY INN-SKY TOP CENTER
20 US Hwy 411E
(30161)
Rates: $60-$70
Tel: (800) 465-4329

SUPER 8 MOTEL
1590 Dodd Blvd SE
(30161)
Rates: $37-$56
Tel: (706) 234-8182
(800) 800-8000

ST. SIMONS ISLAND

ISLAND INN
301 Main St (31522)
Rates: $45-$99
Tel: (800) 673-6323

SAVANNAH

BALLASTONE INN & TOWNHOUSE
4 E Oglethorpe Ave
(31401)
Rates: $100-$215
Tel: (912) 236-1484

BUDGET INN
3702 Ogeechee Rd
(31405)
Rates: $25-$36
Tel: (800) 949-7666

BUDGETEL INN
8484 Abercorn St
(31406)
Rates: $36-$54
Tel: (912) 927-7660

EAST BAY INN
225 E Bay St (31404)
Rates: $89-$119
Tel: (800) 500-1225

ECONO LODGE GATEWAY
7 Gateway Blvd W
(31419)
Rates: $38-$95
Tel: (912) 925-2280
(800) 424-4777

HOMEWOOD SUITES
5820 White Bluff Rd
(31405)
Rates: $89-$119
Tel: (912) 353-8500

HOWARD JOHNSON I-95 SAVANNAH
1501 Butler Ave
(31328)
Rates: $35-$59
Tel: (912) 786-0700
(800) 446-4656

JOAN'S ON JONES BED & BREAKFAST
17 W Jones St
(31401)
Rates: $115-$130
Tel: (912) 234-3863

LA QUINTA INN
6805 Abercorn St
(31405)
Rates: $51-$64
Tel: (912) 355-3004

MARRIOT - SAVANNAH RIVERFRONT
100 General
McIntosh Blvd
(31401)
Rates: $129-$169
Tel: (912) 233-7722

OLDE HARBOUR INN B&B
508 E Factors Walk
(31401)
Rates: $115-$195
Tel: (912) 234-4100
(800) 553-6533

QUALITY INN-AIRPORT
Rt 5, Box 285 (31408)
Rates: $55-$150
Tel: (800) 221-2222

RED CARPET INN
1 Fort Argyle Rd
(31419)
Rates: $30-$40
Tel: (912) 925-2640
(800) 251-1962

RIVER STREET INN
115 E River St
(31401)
Rates: $75-$145
Tel: (912) 234-6400
(800) 253-4229

SCOTTISH INNS
4005 Ogeechee Rd
(31405)
Rates: n/a
Tel: (912) 236-8236
(800) 251-1962

SHONEY'S INN
17003 Abercorn St
(31419)
Rates: $48-$62
Tel: (912) 925-7050
(800) 222-2222

SUPER 8 MOTEL
15 Ft Argyle Rd
(31419)
Rates: $37-$57
Tel: (912) 927-8550
(800) 800-8000

SENOIA

CULPEPPER HOUSE BED & BREAKFAST
35 Broad St (30276)
Rates: $75
Tel: (770) 599-8182

SMYRNA

RESIDENCE INN BY MARRIOTT
2771 Hargrove
Rd(30080)
Rates: n/a
Tel: (770) 433-8877
(800) 331-3131

SPARKS

RED CARPET INN
Rt 1, Box 212 (31647)
Rates: $25+
Tel: (800) 251-1962

STATESBORO

DAYS INN
461 Main St (30458)
Rates: $34-$64
Tel: (912) 764-5666
(800) 329-7466

HOLIDAY INN
230 S Main St
(30458)
Rates: $47
Tel: (800) 465-4329

STATESBORO INN
106 S Main St
(30458)
Rates: $65-$95
Tel: (912) 489-8628

STOCKBRIDGE

MOTEL 6
7233 Davidson
Pkwy (30281)
Rates: $34-$40
Tel: (770) 389-1142
(800) 466-8356

SWAINSBORO

DAYS INN
654 S Main St
(30401)
Rates: $35-$60
Tel: (912) 237-9333
(800) 329-7466

SYLVESTER

DAYS INN
909 Franklin St
(31791)
Rates: $40-$76
Tel: (912) 776-9700
(800) 329-7466

THOMASVILLE

DAYS INN
15375 US 195 (31792)
Rates: $38-$60
Tel: (912) 226-6025
(800) 329-7466

HOLIDAY INN
15138 US 195 (31792)
Rates: $47-$55
Tel: (800) 465-4329

SHONEY'S INN
14866 US Hwy 19 S
(31792)
Rates: n/a
Tel: (912) 228-5555
(800) 222-2222

THOMSON

DAYS INN
2658 Cobbham Rd
(30824)
Rates: $32-$40
Tel: (706) 595-2262
(800) 329-7466

TIFTON

BEST WESTERN
1103 King Rd (31794)
Rates: $36-$61
Tel: (800) 528-1234

COMFORT INN
1104 King Rd (31794)
Rates: $42-$54
Tel: (800) 221-2222

DAYS INN
1008 8th St (31794)
Rates: $40-$55
Tel: (912) 382-7210
(800) 329-7466

HAMPTON INN
720 Hwy 319S
(31794)
Rates: $53-$64
Tel: (912) 382-8800
(800) 426-7866

HOLIDAY INN
I-75 & US 82 W
(31973)
Rates: $43-$48
Tel: (800) 465-4329

MASTERS ECONOMY INN
US 82 & 319 (31793)
Rates: $23-$32
Tel: (912) 382-8100

PASSPORT INN
902 W 7th St (31794)
Rates: $22-$31
Tel: (912) 382-1221
(800) 251-1962

RED CARPET INN
1025 W 2nd St
(31794)
Rates: $24-$37
Tel: (912) 382-0280
(800) 251-1962

SCOTTISH INNS
1409 Hwy 82 West
(31794)
Rates: n/a
Tel: (912) 386-2350
(800) 251-1962

SUPER 8 MOTEL
I-75 & W 2nd St
(31793)
Rates: $33-$46
Tel: (912) 382-9500
(800) 800-8000

TOCCOA

DAYS INN
Hwy 17 & Rt 5, Box
150 (30577)
Rates: $34-$60
Tel: (706) 886-9641
(800) 329-7466

TOWNSEND

DAYS INN
P.O. Box 156 (31331)
Rates: $33-$60
Tel: (912) 832-4411
(800) 329-7466

RAMADA INN
Hwy 57 & I-95
(31331)
Rates: $34-$43
Tel: (912) 832-4444
(800) 272-6232

TUCKER

**RAMADA INN
NORTHLAKE**
2180 Northlake
Pkwy (30084)
Rates: $55-$160
Tel: (770) 939-1000
(800) 272-6232

UNADILLA

**DAYS INN OF
UNADILLA**
I-75 & US 41 S
(31091)
Rates: $29-$42
Tel: (912) 627-3211
(800) 329-7466

PASSPORT INN
Rt 1, Box 184 (31091)
Rates: $20-$23
Tel: (912) 627-3258
(800) 251-1962

RED CARPET INN
101 Robert St (31091)
Rates: $19-$24
Tel: (912) 627-3261
(800) 251-1962

SCOTTISH INNS
Rt 2, Box 82 (31091)
Rates: $22-$24
Tel: (912) 627-3228
(800) 251-1962

VALDOSTA

**BEST WESTERN
KING OF THE ROAD**
1403 N St. Augustine
Rd (31601)
Rates: $30-$45
Tel: (912) 244-7600
(800) 528-1234

**COMFORT INN
CONFERENCE
CENTER**
2799 W Hill Ave
(31603)
Rates: $46-$54
Tel: (800) 221-2222

DAYS INN
4598 N Valdosta Rd
(31602)
Rates: $30-$39
Tel: (912) 244-4460
(800) 329-7466

DAYS INN
1821 West Hill Ave
(31601)
Rates: $32-$41
Tel: (912) 249-8800
(800) 329-7466

HOLIDAY INN
1309 St. Augustine
Rd (31601)
Rates: $51-$55
Tel: (912) 242-3881
(800) 465-4329

MOTEL 6
2003 West Hill Ave
(31601)
Rates: $25-$29
Tel: (912) 333-0047
(800) 466-8356

**QUALITY INN
NORTH**
1209 St. Augustine
Rd (31601)
Rates: $39-$54
Tel: (800) 221-2222

**QUALITY INN
SOUTH**
1902 W Hill Ave
(31601)
Rates: $33-$43
Tel: (800) 221-2222

RAMADA INN
2008 W Hill Ave
(31601)
Rates: $44-$49
Tel: (912) 242-1225
(800) 272-6232

SCOTTISH INNS
1114 St. Augustine
Rd (31601)
Rates: n/a
Tel: (912) 244-7900
(800) 251-1962

**SHONEY'S INN
VALDOSTA**
1828 W Hill Ave
(31601)
Rates: $38-$48
Tel: (912) 244-7711
(800) 222-2222

TRAVELODGE
4912 Timber Dr
(Lake Park 31636)
Rates: $31-$35
Tel: (912) 559-0110

VIDALIA

DAYS INN
1503 Hwy 280 E
(30474)
Rates: $35-$50
Tel: (912) 537-9251
(800) 329-7466

**HOLIDAY INN
EXPRESS**
2619 E First St
(30474)
Rates: $38-$48
Tel: (912) 537-9000
(800) 465-4329

SHONEY'S INN
2505 Lyons Hwy
(30474)
Rates: n/a
Tel: (912) 537-1282
(800) 222-2222

VILLA RICA

**AHAVA
PLANTATION B & B**
2236 S Van Wert Rd
(30180)
Rates: $65
Tel: (770) 459-2863
(800) 858-3473

SUPER 8 MOTEL
195 Hwy 61
Connector (30180)
Rates: $39-$58
Tel: (404) 459-8888
(800) 800-8000

WARNER ROBINS

SUPER 8 MOTEL
105 Woodcrest Blvd
(31093)
Rates: $36-$57
Tel: (912) 923-8600
(800) 800-8000

WAYCROSS

DAYS INN
2016 Memorial Dr
(31501)
Rates: $34-$48
Tel: (912) 285-4700
(800) 329-7466

HOLIDAY INN
1725 Memorial Dr
(30501)
Rates: $43-$52
Tel: (912) 283-4490
(800) 465-4329

PINE CREST MOTEL
Box 1357 (31501)
Rates: $25-$28
Tel: (912) 283-3580

WHITE

SCOTTISH INNS
2385 Hwy 411 NE
(30184)
Rates: $20-$100
Tel: (404) 382-7011
(800) 251-1962

HAWAII

SPECIAL NOTE: In the state of Hawaii, pets are not permitted in rooms. In addition, there is a quarantine on pets arriving from the mainland. If you intend to visit Hawaii with your pet, contact the Hawaii Visitors Bureau, (800) 464-2924 for additional information.

IDAHO

ALBION

MOUNTAIN MANOR BED & BREAKFAST
P. O. Box 128 (83311)
Rates: $35-$55
Tel: (208) 673-6642

AMERICAN FALLS

HILLVIEW MOTEL
2799 Lakeview Rd (83211)
Rates: $25-$45
Tel: (208) 226-5151

RONNEZ MOTEL
411 Lincoln (83211)
Rates: $25-$45
Tel: (208) 226-9658

ARCO

ARCO INN
540 W Grand (83213)
Rates: $32-$45
Tel: (208) 527-3100

D K MOTEL
316 S Front (83213)
Rates: $25-$55
Tel: (208) 527-8282
(800) 231-0134

LAZY A MOTEL
P. O. Box 12 (83213)
Rates: $25-$40
Tel: (208) 527-8263

LOST RIVER MOTEL
405 Hwy Dr (83213)
Rates: $22-$50
Tel: (208) 527-3600

RIVERSIDE MOTEL
P. O. Box 22 (83213)
Rates: $20-$60
Tel: (208) 527-8954
(800) 229-8954

ASHTON

FOUR SEASONS MOTEL
P. O. Box 848 (83420)
Rates: $28-$45
Tel: (208) 652-7769

ATHOL

ATHOL MOTEL
P. O. Box 275 (83801)
Rates: $22-$45
Tel: (208) 683-3476

BANKS

THE PONDEROSA
HC 76, Box 1010 (83602)
Rates: $25-$30
Tel: (208) 793-2700

TRAILS END MOTEL
HC 76, Box 1010 (83602)
Rates: $25-$40
Tel: (208) 793-2700

BAYVIEW

BAYVIEW SCENIC MOTEL & RV PARK
6th & Main Sts (83803)
Rates: $50-$60
Tel: (208) 683-2215

MACDONALD'S HUDSON BAY RESORT
P. O. Box 38 (83803)
Rates: $65-$190
Tel: (208) 683-2211

SCENIC BAY MARINA
P. O. Box 36 (83803)
Rates: $55
Tel: (208) 683-2243

BELLEVUE

HIGH COUNTRY MOTEL
P. O. Box 598 (83313)
Rates: $35-$50
Tel: (208) 788-2050

BLACKFOOT

ALDER INN B & B
384 Alder St (83221)
Rates: $50
Tel: (208) 785-6968

BEST WESTERN BLACKFOOT INN
750 Jensen Grove Dr (83221)
Rates: $39-$65
Tel: (208) 785-4144
(800) 528-1234

RIVERSIDE INN
1229 Park Way Dr (83221)
Rates: $40-$95
Tel: (208) 785-5000

BLISS

AMBER INN
HC 60, Box 1330 (83314)
Rates: $28-$48
Tel: (208) 352-4441

BOISE

BOULEVARD MOTEL
1121 S Capitol Blvd (83706)
Rates: $25-$45
Tel: (208) 342-4629

BUDGET INN
2600 Fairview Ave (83702)
Rates: $28-$55
Tel: (208) 344-8617
(800) 792-8612

CABANA INN
1600 Main St (83702)
Rates: $27-$55
Tel: (208) 343-6000

ECONO LODGE
2155 N Garden St (83706)
Rates: $36-$50
Tel: (208) 344-4030
(800) 424-4777

FAIRFIELD INN BY MARRIOTT
3300 S Shoshone (83705)
Rates: $45-$85
Tel: (208) 331-5656

**FALL CREEK
RESORT & MARINA**
6633 Overland Rd
(83709)
Rates: $45-$55
Tel: (208) 653-2242

FLYING J INN
8002 Overland Rd
(83709)
Rates: $32-$55
Tel: (208) 322-4404
(800) 733-1418

HAMPTON INN
3270 S Shoshone
(83705)
Rates: $57-$85
Tel: (208) 331-5600
(800) 426-7866

**HOLIDAY INN
AIRPORT**
3300 Vista Ave
(83705)
Rates: $74-$89
Tel: (208) 344-8375
(800) 465-4329

HOLIDAY MOTEL
5416 Fairview Ave
(83706)
Rates: $27-$45
Tel: (208) 376-4631

**MIDDLE FORK
LODGE**
P. O. Box 16278
(83715)
Rates: $400/Week
Tel: (208) 342-7888

MOTEL 6
2323 Airport Way
(83705)
Rates: $34-$44
Tel: (208) 344-3506
(800) 440-6000

NENDELS INN
2155 N Garden
(83704)
Rates: $35-$55
Tel: (208) 344-4030

**OWYHEE PLAZA
HOTEL**
1109 Main St (83702)
Rates: $58-$97
Tel: (208) 343-4611
(800) 233-4611

**QUALITY INN
AIRPORT**
2717 Vista Ave (83705)
Rates: $45-$68
Tel: (208) 343-7505
(800) 221-2222

RAMADA INN
1025 S Capitol Blvd
(83706)
Rates: $49-$175
Tel: (208) 344-7971
(800) 272-6232

**RED LION
DOWNTOWNER**
1800 Fairview (83702)
Rates: $85-$105
Tel: (208) 344-7691
(800) 547-8010

RED LION RIVERSIDE
2900 Chinden Blvd
(83714)
Rates: $99-$124
Tel: (208) 343-1871
(800) 547-8010

**RESIDENCE INN
BY MARRIOTT**
1401 Lusk (83706)
Rates: $120-$150
Tel: (208) 344-1200
(800) 331-3131

RODEWAY INN
1115 N. Curtis Rd.
(83706)
Rates: $62-$92
Tel: (208) 376-2700
(800) 228-2000

SAWTOOTH LODGE
1403 E Bannock
(83712)
Rates: n/a
Tel: (208) 344-6685

SEVEN K MOTEL
3633 Chinden Blvd
(83703)
Rates: $32-$65
Tel: (208) 343-7723

SHILO INNS AIRPORT
4111 Broadway Ave
(83705)
Rates: $62-$83
Tel: (208) 343-7662
(800) 222-2244

SHILO INNS RIVERSIDE
3031 Main St (83702)
Rates: $58-$83
Tel: (208) 344-3521
(800) 222-2244

SUPER 8 MOTEL
2773 Elder St (83705)
Rates: $42-$62
Tel: (208) 344-8871
(800) 800-8000

WEST RIVER INN
3525 Chinden Blvd
(83714)
Rates: $28-$38
Tel: (208) 338-1155

BONNERS FERRY

**BEST WESTERN
KOOTENAI
RIVER INN**
Kootenai River Plaza
(83805)
Rates: $50-$90
Tel: (208) 267-8511
(800) 345-5668

**BONNERS FERRY
RESORT**
Rt 4, Box 4700
(83805)
Rates: $20-$60
Tel: (208) 267-2422

DEEP CREEK RESORT
Rt 4, Box 628 (83805)
Rates: $37-$47
Tel: (208) 267-2729
(800) 689-2729

**IMA KOOTENAI
VALLEY MOTEL**
Hwy 955 (83805)
Rates: $45-$105
Tel: (208) 267-7567
(800) 341-8000

**TOWN N' COUNTRY
MOTEL & RV PARK**
Rt 4, Box 4664
(83805)
Rates: $35-$75
Tel: (208) 267-7915

BUHL

SIESTA MOTEL
629 Broadway S
(83316)
Rates: n/a
Tel: (208) 543-6427

BURLEY

BEST WESTERN INN
800 N Overland Ave
(83318)
Rates: $55-$79
Tel: (208) 678-3501
(800) 528-1234

BUDGET MOTEL
900 N Overland Ave
(83318)
Rates: $38-$48
Tel: (208) 678-2200
(800) 635-4952

GREENWELL MOTEL
904 E Main St (83318)
Rates: $30-$56
Tel: (208) 678-5576

LAMPLITER MOTEL
304 E Main (83318)
Rates: $20-$50
Tel: (208) 678-0031

PARISH MOTEL
721 E Main (83318)
Rates: $20-$40
Tel: (208) 678-5505

STARLITE MOTEL
510 Overland
(83318)
Rates: $25-$45
Tel: (208) 678-7766

CALDER

**ST. JOSE LODGE
& RESORT**
Rt 3, Box 350 (83808)
Rates: $50
Tel: (208) 245-3462

CALDWELL

COMFORT INN
901 Specht (83605)
Rates: $49-$105
Tel: (208) 454-2222
(800) 221-2222

HOLIDAY MOTEL
512 Frontage Rd
(83606)
Rates: $24-$50
Tel: (208) 454-3888

CAMBRIDGE

**CAMBRIDGE
HOUSE B & B**
P. O. Box 313 (83610)
Rates: n/a
Tel: (208) 257-3325

**FRONTIER MOTEL
& RV PARK**
P. O. Box 178 (83610)
Rates: $28-$60
Tel: (208) 257-3851

HUNTERS INN
P. O. Box 313 (83610)
Rates: $20-$35
Tel: (208) 257-3325

CASCADE

**ARROWHEAD
CABINS**
P. O. Box 337 (83611)
Rates: $25
Tel: (208) 382-4534

**AURORA MOTEL
& RV PARK**
P. O. Box 799 (83611)
Rates: $26-$48
Tel: (208) 382-4948
(800) 554-6175

HIGH COUNTRY INN
P. O. Box 548 (83611)
Rates: $30-$50
Tel: (208) 382-3315

**MOUNTAIN VIEW
MOTEL**
P. O. Box 1053
(83611)
Rates: $29-$49
Tel: (208) 382-4238

**NORTH SHORE
LODGE**
175 N Shorelind Dr
(83611)
Rates: $50-$85
Tel: (208) 257-2219
(800) 933-3193

SILVER PINES MOTEL
P. O. Box 70 (83611)
Rates: $32-$55
Tel: (208) 382-4370

CHALLIS

**CHALLIS
HOT SPRINGS**
HC 63, Box 1779
(83226)
Rates: $45-$55
Tel: (208) 879-4442

**CHALLIS
MOTOR LODGE**
P. O. Box 6 (83226)
Rates: $26-$42
Tel: (208) 879-2251

NORTHGATE INN
HC 63, Box 1665
(83226)
Rates: $32-$46
Tel: (208) 879-2490

THE VILLAGE INN
P. O. Box 6, Hwy 93
(83226)
Rates: $30-$50
Tel: (208) 879-2239

CHUBBUCK

**OXBOW
MOTOR INN**
4333 Yellowstone
Ave (83202)
Rates: $34-$39
Tel: (208) 237-3100

CLARK FORK

**RIVER DELTA
RESORT**
Box 128, Hwy 200
(83811)
Rates: $45-$65
Tel: (208) 266-1335

COEUR D'ALENE

BATES MOTEL
2018 Sherman Ave
(83814)
Rates: $35-$45
Tel: (208) 667-1411

BENNETT BAY INN
E 5144, I-90 (83814)
Rates: $30-$125
Tel: (208) 664-6168
(800) 368-8609

BOULEVARD MOTEL
2400 Seltice Way
(83814)
Rates: $35-$60
Tel: (208) 664-4978

**CEDAR MOTEL
& RV PARK**
319 Coeur d'Alene
Lake Dr (83814)
Rates: $29-$95
Tel: (208) 664-2278

**COEUR D'ALENE
BED & BREAKFAST**
906 Foster Ave
(83814)
Rates: $60-$100
Tel: (208) 667-7527

COEUR D'ALENE INN
414 W Appleway
Ave (83814)
Rates: $59-$119
Tel: (208) 765-3200
(800) 251-STAY

**COEUR D'ALENE
KOA & CABINS**
10700 Wolf Lodge
Bay Rd (83814)
Rates: n/a
Tel: (208) 664-4471

COMFORT INN
280 W Appleway
(83814)
Rates: $50-$150
Tel: (208) 765-5500
(800) 221-2222

**COUNTRY RANCH
BED & BREAKFAST**
1495 S Green Ferry
Rd (83814)
Rates: $85-$95
Tel: (208) 664-1189

DAYS INN
2200 NW Blvd
(83814)
Rates: $42-$110
Tel: (208) 667-8668
(800) 329-7466

EL RANCHO MOTEL
1915 E Sherman Ave
(83814)
Rates: $26-$69
Tel: (208) 664-8794
(800) 359-9791

**FLAMINGO MOTEL
& RESORT
BUNGALOWS**
718 Sherman Ave
(83814)
Rates: $65-$150
Tel: (208) 664-2159

**HOLIDAY INN
EXPRESS**
2209 E Sherman Ave
(83814)
Rates: $85-$149
Tel: (800) 465-4329

**MONTE VISTA
MOTEL & RV PARK**
320 Coeur d'Alene
Lake Dr (83814)
Rates: $40-$75
Tel: (208) 664-8201

MOTEL 6
416 W Appleway
(83814)
Rates: $37-$53
Tel: (208) 664-6600
(800) 440-6000

RODEWAY INN
1422 NW Blvd
(83814)
Rates: $51-$89
Tel: (208) 664-8244
(800) 228-2000

**SCENIC BAY
MARINA & MOTEL**
P. O. Box 36 (83814)
Rates: $55-$65
Tel: (208) 683-2243

SHILO INNS
702 W Appleway
(83814)
Rates: $72-$138
Tel: (208) 664-2300
(800) 222-2244

**SUMMER HOUSE
BY THE LAKE**
1535 Silver Beach Rd
(83814)
Rates: $125
Tel: (208) 667-9395

SUPER 8 MOTEL
505 W Appleway
(83814)
Rates: $36-$64
Tel: (208) 765-8880
(800) 800-8000

COOLIN

BISHOP'S MARINA & RESORT
Box 91 (83821)
Rates: $40-$60
Tel: (208) 443-2191

THE INN AT PRIEST LAKE
P. O. Box 189 (83821)
Rates: $50-$150
Tel: (208) 443-212
(800) 443-6240

DIXIE

LODGEPOLE PINE INN
P. O. Box 71 (83525)
Rates: n/a
Tel: (208) 842-2343

DONNELLY

LONG VALLEY MOTEL
161 S Main St (83615)
Rates: $34-$64
Tel: (208) 325-8545

DOWNEY

DOWNATA HOT SPRINGS
25900 S Downata Rd (83234)
Rates: $50-$200
Tel: (208) 897-5736

FLAG'S WEST TRUCK STOP MOTEL
Exit 31, I-15 (83234)
Rates: $24-$30
Tel: (208) 897-5238

DRIGGS

BEST WESTERN TETON WEST
476 N Main St (83422)
Rates: $38-$75
Tel: (208) 354-2363
(800) 528-1234

PINES MOTEL-GUEST HAUS
105 South Main (83422)
Rates: $30-$48
Tel: (208) 354-2774
(800) 354-2778

DUBOIS

CROSS ROADS MOTEL
391 S Reynolds (83423)
Rates: $26-$34
Tel: (208) 374-5258

ELK CITY

CANTERBURY HOUSE INN B & B
501 Elk Creek Rd (83525)
Rates: $40-$50
Tel: (208) 842-2366

ELK CITY HOTEL
P. O. Box 356 (83525)
Rates: $25-$48
Tel: (208) 842-2452

ELK CITY MOTEL & LODGE
P. O. Box 143 (83525)
Rates: $20-$30
Tel: (208) 842-2250

PROSPECTOR LODGE & CABINS
P. O. Box 270 (83525)
Rates: $32-$65
Tel: (208) 842-2557

RED RIVER HOT SPRINGS
Elk City (83525)
Rates: $40-$100
Tel: (208) 842-2587

SABLE TRAIL RANCH
Box 21, Red River Rd (83525)
Rates: $20-$50
Tel: (208) 983-1418

ELK RIVER

HUCKLEBERRY HEAVEN LODGE
P. O. Box 165 (83827)
Rates: $50-$109
Tel: (208) 826-3405

EMMETT

L & H MOTEL
720 S Johns (83617)
Rates: $20-$30
Tel: (208) 365-2482

HOLIDAY MOTEL
1111 S Washington AVe (83617)
Rates: $24-$45
Tel: (208) 365-4479

FAIRFIELD

COUNTRY INN
P. O. Box 393 (83327)
Rates: $32-$38
Tel: (208) 764-2247

MOTEL 68
P. O. Box 285 (83327)
Rates: $15
Tel: (208) 764-2211

GARDEN VALLEY

SILVER CREEK PLUNGE MOTEL
HC 76, Box 2377 (83622)
Rates: $30-$70
Tel: (208) 344-8688

GIBBONSVILLE

BROKEN ARROW CABINS
Hwy 93 N (83463)
Rates: $24
Tel: (208) 865-2241

GLENNS FERRY

REDFORD MOTEL
612 Main ST (83623)
Rates: n/a
Tel: (208) 366-2421

GOODING

GOODING HOTEL BED & BREAKFAST
112 Main St (83330)
Rates: $25-$55
Tel: (208) 934-4374

GRANGEVILLE

ELKHORN LODGE
822 SW 1st (83530)
Rates: $32-$43
Tel: (208) 983-1500

JUNCTION LODGE
HC 67, Box 98 (83530)
Rates: $34-$36
Tel: (208) 842-2459

MONTY'S MOTEL
700 W Main St (83530)
Rates: $30-$45
Tel: (208) 983-2500

HAGERMAN

HAGERMAN VALLEY INN
P. O. Box 480 (83332)
Rates: $36-$59
Tel: (208) 837-6196

ROCK LODGE RESORT & CREEKSIDE RV PARK
P. O. Box 449 (83332)
Rates: $37-$75
Tel: (208) 837-4822

HAILEY

AIRPORT INN
820 4th Ave (83333)
Rates: $58-$80
Tel: (208) 788-2477

HITCHRACK MOTEL
619 S Main (83333)
Rates: $40-$55
Tel: (208) 788-2409

HAMMETT

OASIS RANCH MOTEL
HC 63, Box 6 (83627)
Rates: $20-$25
Tel: (208) 366-2025

HARRISON

LAKEVIEW LODGE
P. O. Box 54 (83833)
Rates: $60-$110
Tel: (208) 689-3318

PEG'S BED N' BREAKFAST PLACE
202 Garfield Ave (83833)
Rates: $75-$100
Tel: (208) 689-3525

SQUAW BAY RESORT & MARINA
Rt 2, Box 130 (83833)
Rates: $84-$155
Tel: (208) 664-6450

HEYBURN

TOPS MOTEL
Rt 1, Box 1038 (83336)
Rates: $28-$44
Tel: (208) 436-4724

HOMEDALE

SUNNYDALE MOTEL
P. O. Box 935 (83628)
Rates: $22-$40
Tel: (208) 337-3302

HOPE

IDAHO COUNTRY RESORT
140 Idaho Country Rd (83836)
Rates: $75-$150
Tel: (208) 264-5505
(800) 307-3050

RED FIR RESORT
450 Red Fir Rd (83836)
Rates: $70-$120
Tel: (208) 264-5287

IDAHO CITY

IDAHO CITY HOTEL
215 Montgomery St (83631)
Rates: $21-$46
Tel: (208) 392-4290

PROSPECTOR MOTEL
517 Main St (83631)
Rates: n/a
Tel: (208) 392-4290

IDAHO FALLS

BEST WESTERN DRIFTWOOD INN
575 River Pkwy (83405)
Rates: $45-$99
Tel: (208) 523-2242
(800) 939-2242

BEST WESTERN STARDUST MOTEL
700 Lindsay Blvd (83402)
Rates: $59-$109
Tel: (208) 522-2910
(800) 527-0274

BONNEVILLE MOTEL
2000 South Yellowstone (83402)
Rates: $30-$60
Tel: (208) 522-7847

COMFORT INN
195 E Colorado Ave (83402)
Rates: $49-$80
Tel: (208) 528-2804
(800) 221-2222

LITTLETREE INN
888 N Holmes (83401)
Rates: $49-$99
Tel: (208) 523-5993
(800) 521-5993

MOTEL 6
1448 W Broadway (83402)
Rates: $29-$41
Tel: (208) 522-0112
(800) 440-6000

MOTEL WEST
1540 W Broadway (83402)
Rates: $34-$50
Tel: (208) 522-1112
(800) 582-1063

QUALITY INN
850 Lindsay Blvd (83402)
Rates: $42-$60
Tel: (208) 523-6260
(800) 221-2222

SHILO INNS
780 Lindsay Blvd (83402)
Rates: $89-$109
Tel: (208) 523-0088
(800) 222-2244

ISLAND PARK

A-BAR MOTEL
HC 66, Box 452 (83429)
Rates: $38-$90
Tel: (208) 558-7358
(800) 286-7358

ASPEN LODGE
HC 66, Box 269 (83429)
Rates: $39-$85
Tel: (208) 558-7406

ELK CREEK RANCH
P. O. Box 2 (83429)
Rates: $65
Tel: (208) 558-7404

POND'S LODGE
P. O. Box 258 (83429)
Rates: $40-$160
Tel: (208) 558-7221

STALEY SPRINGS LODGE
HC 66, Box 102 (83429)
Rates: $55-$165
Tel: (208) 558-7471

WILD ROSE RANCH
340 W 7th S (83429)
Rates: n/a
Tel: (208) 558-7201

JEROME

CREST MOTEL
2983 S Lincoln (83338)
Rates: $32-$50
Tel: (208) 324-2670

HOLIDAY MOTEL
401 W Main (83338)
Rates: $20-$60
Tel: (208) 324-2361

KAMIAH

CLEARWATER 12 MOTEL
Hwy 12 & Cedar St (83536)
Rates: $40-$50
Tel: (208) 935-2671
(800) 935-2671

LEWIS CLARK RESORT
Rt 1, Box 17X (83536)
Rates: $40-$58
Tel: (208) 935-2556

SUNDOWN MOTEL
Rt 2, Box 100 (83536)
Rates: $24-$26
Tel: (208) 935-2568

WHITEWATER OUTFITTERS GUEST RANCH
P. O. Box 642 (83536)
Rates: $65
Tel: (208) 935-0631

KELLOGG

THE INN AT SILVER MOUNTAIN
305 S Division (83837)
Rates: $20+
Tel: (208) 786-2311
(800) SNOW-FUN

MOTEL-51
206 E Cameron Ave (83837)
Rates: $25-$40
Tel: (208) 786-9441

SILVERHORN MOTOR INN
699 W Cameron Ave (83837)
Rates: $51-$69
Tel: (208) 783-1151

SUNSHINE INN
301 W Cameron Ave (83837)
Rates: $24-$40
Tel: (208) 784-1186

SUPER 8 MOTEL
601 Bunker Ave (83837)
Rates: $40-70
Tel: (208) 783-1234
(800) 800-8000

TRAIL MOTEL
206 W Cameron Ave (83837)
Rates: $25-$35
Tel: (208) 784-1161

KETCHUM

BALD MOUNTAIN LODGE
151 S Main (83340)
Rates: $45-$105
Tel: (208) 726-9963

BEST WESTERN CHRISTIANIA LODGE
651 Sun Valley Rd (83340)
Rates: $50-$90
(208) 726-3351
(800) 535-3241

BEST WESTERN TYROLEAN LODGE
260 Cottonwood
Box 802 (83340)
Rates: $70-$110
Tel: (208) 726-5336
(800) 528-1234

SAWTOOTH HOTEL
P. O. Box 52 (83340)
Rates: $27-$60
Tel: (208) 774-9947
(208) 622-7922

SKI VIEW LODGE
409 S Hwy 75
(83340)
Rates: n/a
Tel: (208) 726-3441

KINGSTON

KINGSTON 5 RANCH B & B
297 Silver Valley Rd
(83839)
Rates: $85-$125
Tel: (208) 682-4862
(800) 443-3505

KOOSKIA

BEAR HOLLOW BED & BREAKFAST
HC 75, Box 16
(83539)
Rates: $55-$85
Tel: (208) 926-7146
(800) 831-3713

IDA-LEE MOTEL
P. O. Box 592 (83539)
Rates: $25-$36
Tel: (208) 926-0166

MOUNT STUART INN MOTEL
P. O. Box 592 (83539)
Rates: $25-$48
Tel: (208) 926-0166

RYAN'S WILDERNESS INN
HC 75, Box 60-A2
(83539)
Rates: $35-$45
Tel: (208) 926-4706

THREE RIVERS RESORT
HC 75, Box 61
(83539)
Rates: $39-$97
Tel: (208) 926-4430

LAVA HOT SPRINGS

DEMPSEY CREEK LODGE
P. O. Box 600 (83246)
Rates: $29-$49
Tel: (208) 776-5000

LAVA HOT SPRINGS INN
5 Portneuf Ave
(83246)
Rates: $42-$85
Tel: (208) 776-5830

LAVA RANCH INN MOTEL & RV
9611 Hwy 30 (83246)
Rates: $35-$75
Tel: (208) 776-9917

OREGON TRAIL LODGE
119 E Main (83246)
Rates: n/a
Tel: (208) 776-5000

RIVERSIDE INN & HOT SPRINGS
255 Portneuf (83246)
Rates: $35-$85
Tel: (208) 776-5504
(800) 733-5504

TUMBLING WATERS MOTEL
359 E Main St
(83246)
Rates: $45-$55
Tel: (208) 776-5589

LEADORE

LEADORE INN
P. O. Box 68 (83464)
Rates: $25-$30
Tel: (208) 768-2647

LEWISTON

BEL AIR MOTEL
2018 N & S Hwy
(83501)
Rates: $21-$27
Tel: (208) 743-5946

CHURCHILL INNS
1021 Main St (83501)
Rates: $29-$48
Tel: (208) 743-4501
(800) 635-2225

EL RANCHO MOTEL
2240 3rd Ave N
(83501)
Rates: $26-$32
Tel: (208) 743-8517

HILLARY MOTEL
2030 N & S Hwy
(83501)
Rates: $21-$45
Tel: (208) 743-8514
(800) 856-8514

HOLLYWOOD INN
3001 N & S Hwy
(83501)
Rates: $40-$60
Tel: (208) 743-9424
(800) 210-6925

PONY SOLDIER MOTOR INN
1716 Main St (83501)
Rates: $55-$92
Tel: (208) 743-9526
(800) 634-7669

RAMADA PLAZA HOTEL
621 21st St (83501)
Rates: $59-$400
Tel: (208) 799-1000
(800) 232-6730

RIVERVIEW INN
1325 Main St (83501)
Rates: $36-$58
Tel: (208) 746-3311
(800) 806-7666

SACAJAWEA MOTOR INN
1824 Main St (83501)
Rates: $44-$78
Tel: (208) 746-1393
(800) 333-1393

SHEEP CREEK RANCH
227 Snake River Ave
(83501)
Rates: $85-$280
Tel: (208) 746-6276
(800) 262-8874

SNAKE RIVER ADVENTURES
227 Snake River Ave
(83501)
Rates: $85+
Tel: (208) 746-6276
(800) 262-8874

SUPER 8 MOTEL
3120 N South Hwy
(83501)
Rates: $39-$57
Tel: (208) 743-8808
(800) 800-8000

LOWMAN

NEW HAVEN LODGE
HC 77, Box 3608
(83637)
Rates: $38-$110
Tel: (208) 259-3344

SOURDOUGH LODGE & RV RESORT
HC 77, Box 3109
(83637)
Rates: $15-$39
Tel: (208) 259-3326

MACKAY

WAGON WHEEL MOTEL
809 W Custer
(83251)
Rates: $59
Tel: (208) 588-3331

WHITE KNOB MOTEL
Box 180 (83251)
Rates: $22-$42
Tel: (208) 588-2622

WILD HORSE CREEK RANCH
P. O. Box 398 (88251)
Rates: $50-$125
Tel: (208) 588-2575

MACK'S INN

MACK'S INN RESORT
P. O. Box 10 (83433)
Rates: $20-$110
Tel: (208) 558-7272

SAWTELL MOUNTAIN RESORT
P. O. Box 250 (83433)
Rates: $54-$74
Tel: (208) 558-9366
(800) 574-0404

MALAD

VILLAGE INN MOTEL
50 South 300 E (83252)
Rates: $32-$48
Tel: (208) 766-4761

McCALL

**BEST WESTERN
MCCALL**
415 3rd St (83638)
Rates: $50-$120
Tel: (208) 634-6300
(800) 528-1234

**BRUNDAGE
BUNGALOWS**
308 W Lake (83638)
Rates: $55-$165
Tel: (208) 634-8573

**FOREST
CONDOMINIUMS**
Box 1978 (83638)
Rates: $59-$150
Tel: (208) 634-4528

LAKEFORK LODGE
P. O. Box 4336 (83638)
Rates: $150-$175
Tel: (208) 634-3713

**RIVERSIDE MOTEL
& CONDOS**
400 W Lake (83638)
Rates: $40-$55
Tel: (208) 634-5610
(800) 326-5610

SUPER 8 MOTEL
303 S 3rd (83638)
Rates: $45-$70
Tel: (208) 634-4637
(800) 800-8000

VILLAGE INN MOTEL
P. O. Box 734 (83638)
Rates: $40-$85
Tel: (208) 634-2344
(800) 643-2009

WOODSMAN
P. O. Box 884 (83638)
Rates: $28-$55
Tel: (208) 634-7671

MONTPELIER

BEST WESTERN INN
243 N 4th St (83254)
Rates: $43-$75
Tel: (208) 847-1782
(800) 528-1234

BUDGET MOTEL
240 N 4th St (83254)
Rates: $20-$35
Tel: (208) 847-1273

MICHELLE MOTEL
401 Boise St (83254)
Rates: $20-$33
Tel: (208) 847-1772

THE PARK MOTEL
745 Washington
(83254)
Rates: $24-$50
Tel: (208) 847-1911

MOSCOW

**BEST WESTERN
UNIVERSITY INN**
1516 Pullman Rd
(83843)
Rates: $65-$350
Tel: (208) 882-0550
(800) 528-1234

HILLCREST MOTEL
706 N Main (83843)
Rates: $28-$60
Tel: (208) 882-7579
(800) 368-6564

**MARK IV
MOTOR INN**
414 N Main St
(83843)
Rates: $35-$87
Tel: (208) 882-7557
(800) 833-4240

ROYAL MOTOR INN
120 West 6th St
(83843)
Rates: $25-$65
Tel: (208) 882-2581

MOUNTAIN HOME

**BEST WESTERN
FOOTHILLS
MOTOR INN**
1080 Hwy 20 (83647)
Rates: $47-$150
Tel: (208) 587-8477
(800) 528-1234

**HILANDER MOTEL
& STEAK HOUSE**
615 S 3rd W (83647)
Rates: $29-$49
Tel: (208) 587-3311

**MOTEL
THUNDERBIRD**
910 Sunset Strip
(83647)
Rates: $23-$30
Tel: (208) 587-7927

ROSESTONE INN
495 N 3rd E (83647)
Rates: $45-$85
Tel: (208) 587-8866
(800) 717-ROSE

SLEEP INN
1180 Hwy 20 (83647)
Rates: $33-$65
Tel: (208) 587-9743
(800) 627-5337

**TOWNE CENTER
MOTEL**
410 N 2nd E (83647)
Rates: $24-$40
Tel: (208) 587-3373

MUD LAKE

B - K'S MOTEL
1073 E 1500 N (83450)
Rates: $30-$35
Tel: (208) 663-4578

**HAVEN MOTEL
& TRAILER PARK**
1079 E 1500 N (83450)
Rates: $30-$35
Tel: (208) 663-4821

NAMPA

DESERT INN MOTEL
115 9th Ave S (83651)
Rates: $34-$48
Tel: (208) 467-1161

FIVE CROWNS INN
908 3rd St South
(83651)
Rates: $30-$32
Tel: (208) 466-3594

SHILO INNS
617 Nampa Blvd
(83687)
Rates: $51-$68
Tel: (208) 466-8993
(800) 222-2244

**SHILO INNS
NAMPA SUITES**
1401 Shilo Dr (83687)
Rates: $69-$89
Tel: (208) 465-3250
(800) 222-2244

STARLITE MOTEL
320 11th Ave N
(83651)
Rates: $29-$42
Tel: (208) 466-9244

SUPER 8 MOTEL
624 Nampa Blvd
(83687)
Rates: $40-$55
Tel: (208) 467-2888
(800) 800-8000

NEW MEADOWS

HALF WAY INN
HC 75, Box 3760
(83654)
Rates: $18-$35
Tel: (208) 628-3259

**PINEHURST RESORT
COTTAGES**
5604 Hwy 95 (83654)
Rates: $25-$50
Tel: (208) 628-3323

NORDMAN

**ELKINS CABINS
ON PRIEST LAKE**
HCO 1, Box 40
(83848)
Rates: $85-$235
Tel: (208) 443-2432

KANIKSU RESORT
HCO 1, Box 152
(83848)
Rates: $60-
$695/weekly
Tel: (208) 443-2609

NORTH FORK

**INDIAN CREEK
GUEST RANCH**
HC 64, Box 105-A
(83466)
Ratees: $100-$250
Tel: (208) 394-2126

**NORTH FORK
MOTEL**
P. O. Box 100 (83466)
Rates: $32-$44
Tel: (208) 865-2412

RIVER'S FORK INN
Hwy 93 N (83466)
Rates: $42+
Tel: (208) 865-2301

OROFINO

**HELGESON PLACE
HOTEL**
P. O. Box 463 (83544)
Rates: $34-$47
Tel: (208) 476-5729

**KONKOLVILLE
MOTEL**
2000 Konkolville Rd
(83544)
Rates: $30-$46
Tel: (208) 476-5584

RIVERSIDE MOTEL
10560 Hwy 12
(83544)
Rates: $20-$40
Tel: (208) 476-5711

WHITE PINE MOTEL
222 Brown St (83544)
Rates: $33-$55
Tel: (208) 476-7093
(800) 874-2083

PIERCE

CEDAR INN
412 S Main (83546)
Rates: $15-$22
Tel: (208) 464-2704

**KEY BAR
HOTEL & CAFE**
Box 494 (83546)
Rates: $10-$15
Tel: (208) 464-2704

PIERCE MOTEL
509 Main St (83546)
Rates: $25-$40
Tel: (208) 464-2324

PINEHURST

**KELLOGG
VACATION HOMES**
P. O. Box 944 (83850)
Rates: $50-$150
Tel: (208) 786-4261

**PINEHURST KOA
& CABINS**
P. O. Box 949 (83850)
Rates: $16-$22
Tel: (208) 682-3612
(800) KOA-0799

PLUMMER

**BONNIE'S BED
& BREAKFAST**
P. O. Box 258 (83851)
Rates: $50-$60
Tel: (208) 686-1165

HIWAY MOTEL
301 10th St (83851)
Rates: $28-$50
Tel: (208) 686-1310

POCATELLO

**BEST WESTERN
COTTON TREE INN**
1415 Bench Rd
(83201)
Rates: $63-$99
Tel: (208) 237-7650
(800) 528-1234

**BEST WESTERN
WESTON INN**
745 S 5th (83201)
Rates: $40-$105
Tel: (208) 233-5530
(800) 528-1234

COMFORT INN
1333 Bench Rd
(83201)
Rates: $49-$80
Tel: (208) 237-8155
(800) 221-2222

MOTEL 6
291 W Burnside Ave
(83201)
Rates: $29-$38
Tel: (208) 237-7880
(800) 440-6000

NENDEL'S INN
4333 Yellowstone
Ave (83202)
Rates: $21-$39
Tel: (208) 237-3100

QUALITY INN
1555 Pocatello Creek
Rd (83201)
Rates: $74-$79
Tel: (208) 233-2200
(800) 221-2222

SUPER 8 MOTEL
1330 Bench Rd
(83201)
Rates: $41-$54
Tel: (208) 234-0888
(800) 800-8000

**THUNDERBIRD
MOTEL**
1415 S 5th Ave
(83201)
Rate: $26-$40
Tel: (208) 232-6330

POST FALLS

**BEST WESTERN
TEMPLIN'S RESORT
HOTEL**
414 E First Ave
(83854)
Rates: $59-$106
Tel: (208) 773-1611
(800) 528-1234

SUNTREE INN
W 3705 5th Ave
(83854)
Rates: $51-$60
Tel: (208) 773-4541
(800) 888-6630

POTLATCH

**ROLLING HILLS
BED & BREAKFAST**
Rt 1, Box 157 (83855)
Rates: $45-$55
Tel: (208) 668-1126

PRIEST LAKE

HILL'S RESORT
HCR 5, Box 162A
(83856)
Rates: $80-$250
Tel: (208) 443-2551

PRIEST RIVER

SELKIRK MOTEL
Rt 3, Box 441 (83856)
Rates: $35-$61
Tel: (208) 448-1112

PRESTON

DEER CLIFF INN
2106 N Deer Cliff
(83263)
Rates: $28-$32
Tel: (208) 852-0643

REXBURG

**BEST WESTERN
COTTONTREE INN**
450 W 4th St S
(83440)
Rates: $44-$100
Tel: (208) 356-4646
(800) 528-1234

CALAWAY MOTEL
361 S 2nd W (83440)
Rates: $25-$35
Tel: (208) 356-3217

DAYS INN
271 S 2nd W (83440)
Rates: $36-$56
Tel: (208) 356-9222
(800) 329-7466

REX MOTEL
357 W 400 S (83440)
Rates: $25-$35
Tel: (208) 356-5477

RIGGINS

BRUCE MOTEL
P. O. Box 208 (83549)
Rates: $29-$70
Tel: (208) 628-3005

THE LODGE B & B
P. O. Box 498 (83549)
Rates: $30-$60
Tel: (208) 628-3863

RIGGINS MOTEL
P. O. Box 1157
(83549)
Rates: $30-$80
Tel: (208) 628-3001
(800) 669-6739

TAYLOR MOTEL
206 S Main St
(83549)
Rates: $27
Tel: (208) 628-3914

ROGERSON

**DESERT HOT
SPRINGS MOTEL**
General Delivery
(83302)
Rates: $25-$35
Tel: (208) 857-2233

RUPERT

FLAMINGO LODGE MOTEL
Rt 1, Box 227 (83350)
Rates: n/a
Tel: (208) 436-4321

UPTOWN MOTEL
Hwy 24 (83350)
Rates: $22-$35
Tel: (208) 546-4036

SAGLE

COUNTRY INN
7360 Hwy 95 S
(83860)
Rates: $24-$49
Tel: (208) 263-3333
(800) 736-0454

ST. MARIES

BENEWAH RESORT
Rt 1, Box 50-C
(83861)
Rates: $25-$29
Tel: (208) 245-3288

SALMON

MOTEL DE LUXE DOWNTOWNER
112 S Church St
(83467)
Rates: $32-$48
Tel: (208) 756-2231

SUNCREST MOTEL
705 Challis St
(83467)
Rates: $25-$39
Tel: (208) 756-2294

SYRINGA LODGE
2000 Syringa Dr
(83467)
Rates: $40-$75
Tel: (208) 756-4424

WILLIAMS LAKE RESORT
P. O. Box 1150
(83467)
Rates: $25-$100
Tel: (208) 756-2007

SANDPOINT

BEST SPA MOTEL
521 N 3rd Ave
(83864)
Rates: $30-$130
Tel: (208) 263-3532

BOTTLE BAY RESORT & MARINA
1360 Bottle Bay Rd
(83864)
Rates: $60-$115
Tel: (208) 263-5916

IDAHO COUNTRY RESORT
141 Idaho Country
Rd (83864)
Rates: $75-$150
Tel: (208) 264-5505
(800) 307-3050

K2 MOTEL
501 N 4th Ave
(83864)
Rates: $35-$110
Tel: (208) 263-3441

LAKESIDE INN
106 Bridge St (83864)
Rates: $36-$125
Tel: (208) 263-3717
(800) 543-8126

MONARCH WEST INN
Hwy 95N (83864)
Rates: $36-$95
Tel: (208) 263-1222
(800) 543-8193

MOTEL 16
317 Marion (83864)
Rates: $30-$110
Tel: (208) 263-5323

QUALITY INN
807 N 5th Ave
(83864)
Rates: $38-$72
Tel: (208) 263-111
(800) 221-2222

SUPER 8 MOTEL
3245 Hwy 95N
(83864)
Rates: $34-$61
Tel: (208) 263-2210
(800) 800-8000

WHITAKER HOUSE BED & BREAKFAST
410 Railroad Ave
#10 (83864)
Rates: $30-$46
Tel: (208) 263-0816

SHOSHONE

GOVERNOR'S MANSION
315 S Greenwood
(83352)
Rates: $30-$65
Tel: (208) 886-2858

SHOUP

SMITH HOUSE B & B
49 Salmon River Rd
(83469)
Rates: $150
Tel: (208) 394-2121
(800) 238-5915

SILVERTON

MOLLY B'DAMM MOTEL
P. O. Box 481 (83867)
Rates: $25-$45
Tel: (208) 556-4391

SILVER LEAF MOTEL
P. O. Box 151 (83867)
Rates: $25-$30
Tel: (208) 752-0222

SODA SPRINGS

CARIBOU LODGE MOTEL
110 West 2nd S
(83276)
Rates: $25-$50
Tel: (208) 547-3377
(800) 270-9178

LAKEVIEW MOTEL
341 W 2nd S (83276)
Rates: $22-$40
Tel: (208) 547-4351

SPIRIT LAKE

SILVER BEACH RESORT CABINS
8350 W Spirit Lake
Rd (83869)
Rates: n/a
Tel: (208) 632-4842

STANLEY

CREEK SIDE LODGE
P. O. Box 110 (83278)
Rates: $70-$100
Tel: (208) 774-2213
(800) 523-0733

DANNER'S LOG CABIN MOTEL
P. O. Box 196 (83278)
Rates: $50-$100
Tel: (208) 774-3539

ELK MOUNTAIN RV RESORT
P. O. Box 115 (83278)
Rates: $50-$60
Tel: (208) 774-2202

JERRY'S COUNTRY STORE & MOTEL
HC 67, Box 300
(83278)
Rates: $38-$65
Tel: (208) 774-3566
(800) 972-4627

MOUNTAIN VILLAGE LODGE
P. O. Box 150 (83278)
Rates: $60-$120
Tel: (208) 774-3661
(800) 843-5475

REDFISH LAKE LODGE
P. O. Box 9 (83278)
Rates: $46-$132
Tel: (208) 774-3536

STANLEY OUTPOST
P. O. Box 131, Hwy
21 (83278)
Rates: $50-$75
Tel: (208) 774-3646

TRIANGLE C RANCH
P. O. Box 69 (83278)
Rates: $55
Tel: (208) 774-2266

SUN VALLEY

CLARION INN
600 N Main St
(83353)
Rates: $55-$128
Tel: (208) 726-5900
(800) 262-4833

HEIDELBERG INN
P. O. Box 5704
(83353)
Rates: $60-$125
Tel: (208) 726-5361
(800) 284-4863

RIVER STREET INN
P. O. Box 182 (83353)
Rates: $120-$175
Tel: (208) 726-3611

SWAN VALLEY

SOUTH FORK LODGE
P. O. Box 22 (83449)
Rates: $45-$105
Tel: (208) 483-2112
(800) 483-2110

TWIN FALLS

BEST WESTERN APOLLO MOTOR INN
296 Addison Ave W
(83301)
Rates: $43-$60
Tel: (208) 733-2010
(800) 528-1234

COMFORT INN
1893 Canyon
Springs Rd (83301)
Rates: $51-$69
Tel: (208) 734-7494
(800) 221-2222

ECONO LODGE
320 Main Ave S
(83301)
Rates: $30-$50
Tel: (208) 733-8770
(800) 424-4777

MOTEL 3
248 2nd Ave W
(83301)
Rates: $21-$40
Tel: (208) 733-5630

MOTEL 6
1472 Blue Lakes
Blvd N (83301)
Rates: $29-$41
Tel: (208) 734-3993
(800) 440-6000

SHILO INNS
1586 Blue Lakes
Blvd (83301)
Rates: $62-$99
Tel: (208) 733-7545
(800) 222-2244

WESTON INN
906 Blue Lakes Blvd
(83301)
Rates: $34-$54
Tel: (208) 733-6095
(800) 551-3505

WALLACE

BEST WESTERN WALLACE INN
100 Front St (83873)
Rates: $70-$82
Tel: (208) 752-1252
(800) 528-1234

MYLES MOTEL
P. O. Box 1348
(83873)
Rates: $24-$30
Tel: (208) 556-4391

STARDUST MOTEL
410 Pine St (83873)
Rates: $40-$55
Tel: (208) 752-1213
(800) N IDA FUN

WEISER

COLONIAL MOTEL
251 E Main (83672)
Rates: $30-$60
Tel: (208) 549-0150

INDIANHEAD MOTEL
747 US Hwy 95
(83672)
Rates: $30-$70
Tel: (208) 549-0331

STATE STREET MOTEL
1279 State St (83672)
Rates: $32-$52
Tel: (208) 549-1390

ILLINOIS

ALORTON

LAKESIDE MOTEL
4300 Missouri Ave
(62207)
Rates: n/a
Tel: (618) 874-4700

ALSIP

BUDGETEL INN
1208 S Cicero Ave
(60658)
Rates: $49-$58
Tel: (708) 597-3900
(800) 428-3438

ALTAMONT

**BEST WESTERN
CARRIAGE INN**
I-70 & Hwy 128
(62411)
Rates: $33-$51
Tel: (618) 483-6101
(800) 528-1234

ALTON

HOLIDAY INN
3800 Homer Adams
Pkwy (62002)
Rates: $65-$80
Tel: (800) 465-4329

SUPER 8 MOTEL
1800 Homer Adams
Pkwy (62002)
Rates: $42-$60
Tel: (618) 465-8885
(800) 800-8000

AMBOY

AMBOY MOTEL
Rts 52 & 30 (61310)
Rates: n/a
Tel: (815) 857-3916

ANNA

**ANNA PLAZA
MOTEL**
150 E Vienna S E
(62906)
Rates: n/a
Tel: (618) 883-5215

ANTIOCH

**BEST WESTERN
REGENCY INN**
350 Hwy 173 (60002)
Rates: $57-$110
Tel: (847) 395-3606
(800)528-1234

ARCOLA

**BEST WESTERN
REGENCY INN**
610 E Springfield
(61910)
Rates: $35-$59
Tel: (217) 268-4000
(800) 528-1234

BUDGET HOST INN
236 S Jacques St
(61910)
Rates: $29-$54
Tel: (217) 268-4971
(800) 283-4678

DAYS INN
640 E Springfield Rd
(61910)
Rates: $39-$53
Tel: (217) 268-3031
(800) 329-7466

ARLINGTON
HEIGHTS

**BEST WESTERN
ARLINGTON INN**
948 E Northwest
Hwy (60004)
Rates: $49-$67
Tel: (847) 255-2900
(800) 528-1234

LA QUINTA INN
1415 W Dundee Rd
(60004)
Rates: $55-$69
Tel: (847) 253-8777
(800) 531-5900

MOTEL 6
441 W Algonquin Rd
(60005)
Rates: $36-$42
Tel: (847) 806-1230
(800) 440-6000

RADISSON HOTEL
75 W Algonquin Rd
(60005)
Rates: $53-$95
Tel: (847) 364-7600
(800) 333-3333

RED ROOF INN
22 W Algonquin Rd
(60005)
Rates: $38-$51
Tel: (847) 228-6650
(800) 843-7663

ATLANTA

ROUTE 66 MOTEL
103 Empire St
(61723)
Rates: n/a
Tel: (217) 648-2322

AURORA

HOWARD JOHNSON
306 S Lincolnway
(60542)
Rates: $52-68
Tel: (708) 892-6481
(800) 446-4656

MOTEL 6
2380 N Farnsworth
Ave (60504)
Rates: $34-$40
Tel: (708) 851-3600
(800) 440-6000

RIVERWALK INN
77 S Stolp Ave
(60505)
Rates: n/a
Tel: (708) 892-0001

BARRINGTON

**BARRINGTON
MOTOR LODGE**
405 W Northwest
Hwy (60010)
Rates: $54+
Tel: (847) 381-2640
(800) 354-6605

DAYS INN
405 W Northwest
Hwy 14 (60010)
Rates: $59-75
Tel: (847) 381-2640
(800) 329-7466

BEARDSTOWN

SUPER 8 MOTEL
US 67 & Hwy 100 S
(62223)
Rates: $36-41
Tel: (217) 323-5858
(800) 800-8000

BELLEVILLE

CINDERELLA MOTEL
1438 Centreville Ave
(62223)
Rates: n/a
Tel: (618) 233-7410

DAYS INN
2120 West Main St
(62226)
Rates: $51-$81
Tel: (618) 234-9400
(800) 329-7466

**EXECUTIVE INN
MOTEL**
1234 Centreville Ave
(62223)
Rates: n/a
Tel: (618) 233-1234

SCOTT LODGE
1651 Old Hwy 158
(62223)
Rates: n/a
Tel: (618) 744-1244

BENTON

BENTON GRAY PLAZA MOTEL
706 W Main St
(62812)
Rates: n/a
Tel: (618) 439-3113

DAYS INN
711 W Main St
(62812)
Rates: $38-$52
Tel: (618) 439-3183
(800) 329-7466

BLOOMINGTON

BEST INNS OF AMERICA
1905 W Market St
(61701)
Rates: $35-$46
Tel: (309) 827-5333
(800) 237-8466

DAYS INN-EAST
1803 E Empire St
(61704)
Rates: $45-$65
Tel: (309) 663-1361
(800) 329-7466

DAYS INN WEST
1707 W Market St
(61701)
Rates: $43-$69
Tel: (309) 829-6292
(800) 329-7466

HOWARD JOHNSON EXP
401 Brock Dr (61701)
Rates: $25-$48
Tel: (309) 829-3100
(800) 446-4656

JUMER'S CHATEAU
1601 Jumer Dr
(61704)
Rates: $74-$99
Tel: (309) 662-2020
(800) 285-8637

RAMADA INN
1219 Holiday Dr
(61704)
Rates: $49-$77
Tel: (309) 662-5311
(800) 272-6232

RAMADA INN WEST
403 Brock Dr (61701)
Rates: $35-$69
Tel: (309) 829-7602
(800) 272-6232

RODEWAY INN
2419 Springfield Rd
(61701)
Rates: $50-$60
Tel: (309) 828-1505
(800) 228-2000

SUPER 8 MOTEL
818 I.A.A. Dr (61701)
Rates: $39-$58
Tel: (309) 663-2388
(800) 800-8000

BOURBONNAIS

LEES INN
1500 N SR 50 (60914)
Rates: $55-$76
Tel: (815) 932-8080
(800) 733-5337

MOTEL 6
Illinois Rt 50
& Armour Rd
(60914)
Rates: $30-$36
Tel: (815) 933-2300
(800) 440-6000

BRADLEY

LEES INN
1500 N Rt 50 (60914)
Rates: n/a
Tel: (815) 932-8080
(800) 733-5337

NORTHGATE MOTEL
Rt 50 N (60914)
Rates: n/a
Tel: (815) 933-8261

RAMADA INN
800 N Kinzie Ave
(60915)
Rates: $36-$72
Tel: (815) 939-3501
(800) 228-2828

BRAIDWOOD

SANDS MOTEL
1179 W Kennedy Rd
(60408)
Rates: n/a
Tel: (815) 458-3401

BREESE

KNOTTY PINE HOTEL
Old Rt 50 W (62230)
Rates: n/a
Tel: (618) 526-4556

BRIDGEVIEW

EXEL INN
9625 S 76th Ave
(60455)
Rates: $45-$63
Tel: (708) 430-1818

BUREAU

RANCH HOUSE LODGE
Rts 26 & 29 (61315)
Rates: n/a
Tel: (815) 659-3361

BUSHNELL

BUSHNELL INN
Rt 41 (61422)
Rates: n/a
Tel: (309) 772-3172

CACHE

MELTON'S FISHING CAMP
Rural Route (62913)
Rates: n/a
Tel: (618) 776-5504

CAIRO

DAYS INN
RR 1 Box 10 (62914)
Rates: $30-$48
Tel: (618) 734-0215
(800) 329-7466

PLAZA MOTEL
3705 Sycamore St
(62914)
Rates: n/a
Tel: (618) 734-2102

CANTON

SIESTA MOTEL
Rt 9 W (61520)
Rates: n/a
Tel: (309) 647-1915

CARBONDALE

BEST INNS OF AMERICA
1345 E Main St
(62901)
Rates: $35-$43
Tel: (618) 529-4801
(800) 237-8466

HOLIDAY INN
800 E Main St
(62901)
Rates: $59-$64
Tel: (618) 529-1100
(800) 465-4329

KNIGHTS INN
3000 W Main St
(62901)
Rates: $30-$150
Tel: (618) 529-2424
(800) 843-5644

RELAX INN
700 E Main St
(62901)
Rates: n/a
Tel: (618) 549-0889

SUPER 8 MOTEL
1180 E Main St
(62901)
Rates: $40-$58
Tel: (618) 457-8822
(800) 800-8000

CARLINVILLE

BEL-AIRE MOTEL
915 E 1st South St
(62626)
Rates: n/a
Tel: (217) 854-3287

CARLIN VILLA MOTEL
SR 4 South (62626)
Rates: $31-$99
Tel: (217) 854-3201
(800) 341-8000

HOLIDAY INN
I-55 & Rt 108 (62626)
Rates: $44-$68
Tel: (217) 324-2100
(800) 465-4329

CARTHAGE

PRAIRIE WINDS MOTEL
Hwy 136 West
(62321)
Rates: n/a
Tel: (217) 357-3101

CASEY

COMFORT INN
I-70 & Rt 49 (62420)
Rates: $45-$94
Tel: (217) 932-2212
(800) 221-2222

CASEYVILLE

BEST INNS OF AMERICA
2423 Old Country
Inn Rd (62232)
Rates: $38-$53
Tel: (618) 397-3300
(800) 237-8466

CENTRALIA

BELL TOWER INN
200 E Noleman St
(62801)
Rates: $39-$57
Tel: (618) 533-1300

CHAMPAIGN

BUDGETEL INN
302 W Anthony Dr
(61821)
Rates: $38-$56
Tel: (217) 356-8900
(800) 428-3438

CAMPUS INN
1701 S State St
(61820)
Rates: $35-$42
Tel: (217) 359-8888

CHANCELLOR HOTEL
1501 S Neil St
(61820)
Rates: $59-$64
Tel: (217) 352-7891
(800) 257-6667

COMFORT INN
305 Marketview Dr
(61821)
Rates: $39-$60
Tel: (217) 352-4055
(800) 221-2222

FAIRFIELD INN BY MARRIOTT
1807 Moreland Blvd
(61820)
Rates: $56-$73
Tel: (217) 355-0604
(800) 228-2800

HOWARD JOHNSON LODGE
1505 N Neil St
(61820)
Rates: $25-$48
Tel: (217) 359-1601
(800) 446-4656

LA QUINTA INN
1900 Center Dr
(61820)
Rates: $48-$62
Tel: (217) 356-4000
(800) 531-5900

RED ROOF INN
212 W Anthony Dr
(61820)
Rates: $32-$76
Tel: (217) 352-0101
(800) 843-7663

SUPER 8 MOTEL
202 Marketview Dr
(61820)
Rates: $38-$59
Tel: (217) 359-2388
(800) 800-8000

CHESTER

HI 3 MOTEL
Rt 3 N (62233)
Rates: n/a
Tel: (618) 826-4415

CHICAGO
(and Vicinity)

BLACKSTONE HOTEL
636 S Mighigan Ave
(60605)
Rates: $99-$109
Tel: (312) 427-4300
(800) 622-6330

BUDGETEL INN
17225 S Halsted St
(So Holland 60473)
Rates: $39-$55
Tel: (708) 596-8700

CLARIDGE HOTEL
1244 N Dearborn
Pkwy (60610)
Rates: $88-$155
Tel: (312) 787-4980
(800) 245-1258

COMFORT INN GURNEE
6080 Gurnee Mills
Blvd
(Gurnee 60030)
Rates: $45-$130
Tel: (800) 221-2222

COMFORT INN NORTHWEST
2550 Landmeier Rd
(Elk Grove Village
60007)
Rates: $52-$68
Tel: (800) 221-2222

COMFORT INN ORLAND PARK
8800 W 159th St
(Orland Park 60462)
Rates: $63-$70
Tel: (800) 221-2222

DAYS INN
5400 S Cicero Ave
(60688)
Rates: $79-$109
Tel: (312) 581-0500
(800) 329-7466

DAYS INN ELK GROVE VILLAGE
1920 E Higgins Rd
(Elk Grove Village
60007)
Rates: $41-$129
Tel: (708) 437-1650
(800) 329-7466

ESSEX INN
800 S Michigan Ave
(60605)
Rates: $89-$115
Tel: (312) 939-2800
(800) 621-6909

FOUR SEASONS HOTEL
120 E Delaware
(60611)
Rates: $235-$310
Tel: (312) 280-8800
(800) 332-3442

HILTON-O'HARE
P. O. Box 66414
(O'Hare Airport
60666)
Rates: $165
Tel: (312) 686-8000
(800) 445-8667

HOLIDAY INN-ALSIP
5000 W 127th St
(Alsip 60658)
Rates: $69-$86
Tel: (800) 465-4329

HOLIDAY INN
17040 S Halsted St
(Harvey 60426)
Rates: $49-$98
Tel: (800) 465-4329

HOLIDAY INN-MART PLAZA
350 N Orleans St
(60654)
Rates: $124-$187
Tel: (312) 836-5000
(800) 465-4329

HOWARD JOHNSON
8201 W Higgins Rd
(60631)
Rates: $59-89
Tel: (312) 693-2323
(800) 446-4656

HOWARD JOHNSON
720 N LaSalle St
(60610)
Rates: $63-85
Tel: (312) 664-8100
(800) 446-4656

THE INN AT UNIVERSITY VILLAGE
625 S Ashland Ave
(60607)
Rates: $75-$175
Tel: (312) 243-7200
(800) 662-5233

LA QUINTA INN
1 S 666 Midwest Rd
(Oakbrook Terrace
60181)
Rates: $53-$67
Tel: (800) 221-4731

MARRIOTT O'HARE
8535 W Higgins Rd
(60631)
Rates: $74-$166
Tel: (312) 693-4444
(800) 228-9290

MOTEL 6
162 E Ontario St
(60611)
Rates: $79-$89
Tel: (312) 787-3580
(800) 466-8356

PALMER HOUSE HILTON
17 E Monroe St
(60603)
Rates: $125-$230
Tel: (312) 726-7500
(800) 445-8667

QUALITY INN-DOWNTOWN
1 S Halsted (60661)
Rates: $39-$129
Tel: (312) 829-5000
(800) 221-2222

RADISSON PLAZA AMBASSADOR WEST
1300 N State Pkwy
(60610)
Rates: $109-$189
Tel: (800) 333-3333

THE RAPHAEL HOTEL
201 E Delaware Pl
(60611)
Rates: $105-$165
Tel: (312) 943-5000
(800) 821-5343

RESIDENCE INN BY MARRIOTT
201 E Walton Pl
(60611)
Rates: $120-$166
Tel: (312) 943-9800
(800) 331-3131

THE RITZ-CARLTON
160 E Pearson St
(60611)
Rates: $240-$315
Tel: (312) 266-1000
(800) 621-6906

SPA MOTEL
5414 N Lincoln Ave
(60625)
Rates: n/a
Tel: (312) 561-0313

SURF HOTEL NEIGHBORHOOD INNS
555 W Surf St
(60657)
Rates: $79-$99
Tel: (312) 528-8400
(800) SURF-108

SUTTON PLACE HOTEL
21 E Bellevue Pl
(60611)
Rates: $225-$350
Tel: (312) 266-2100
(800) 543-4300

TREMONT HOTEL
100 E Chestnut St
(60611)
Rates: $205-$225
Tel: (312) 751-1900
(800) 621-8133

WESTIN HOTEL,
909 N Michigan Ave
(60611)
Rates: $239-$294
Tel: (312) 943-7200
(800) 879-5444

CLARENDON HILLS

MAYFLOWER MOTEL
407 Ogden Ave
(60514)
Rates: n/a
Tel: (708) 325-2500

CLINTON

DAYS INN
US 51 Bypass (61727)
Rates: $38-$68
Tel: (217) 935-4140
(800) 329-7466

TOWN & COUNTRY MOTEL
1151 Rt 54W (61727)
Rates: $25-$32
Tel: (217) 935-2121

WYE MOTEL
Rt 54 & 10 E (61727)
Rates: $30-$40
Tel: (217) 935-3373

COBDEN

BLACK DIAMOND RANCH
Rt 3 (62920)
Rates: n/a
Tel: (618) 833-7629

COLLINSVILLE

BEST WESTERN BO JON INN
Rt 159 (62234)
Rates: $34-$54
Tel: (618) 345-5720
(800) 528-1234

DAYS INN
1803 Ramada Blvd
(62234)
Rates: $37-$49
Tel: (618) 345-8100
(800) 329-7466

DRURY INN
602 N Bluff Rd
(62234)
Rates: $52-$69
Tel: (618) 345-7700
(800) 325-8300

HOWARD JOHNSON LODGE
301 N Bluff (62234)
Rates: $35-$70
Tel: (618) 345-1530
(800) 446-4656

MAGGIE'S B & B
2102 N Keebler Ave
(62234)
Rates: n/a
Tel: (618) 344-8283

MOTEL 6
295A N Bluff Rd
(62234)
Rates: $33-$41
Tel: (618) 345-2100
(800) 440-6000

PEAR TREE INN BY DRURY
552 Ramada Blvd
(62234)
Rates: $42-$62
Tel: (618) 345-9500
(800) 282-8733

QUALITY INN
475 Bluff Rd (62234)
Rates: $45-$65
Tel: (618) 344-7171
(800) 221-2222

SUPER 8 MOTEL
2 Gateway Dr
(62234)
Rates: $40-$58
Tel: (618) 345-8008
(800) 800-8000

CRESTWOOD

HAMPTON INN
13330 S Cicero Ave
(60445)
Rates: n/a
Tel: (708) 597-3330
(800) 426-7866

CRYSTAL LAKE

HOLIDAY INN
800 SR 31 S (60014)
Rates: $82-$89
Tel: (815) 477-7000
(800) 465-4329

SUPER 8 MOTEL
577 Crystal Point Dr
(60014)
Rates: $46-$66
Tel: (815) 455-2388
(800) 800-8000

DANVILLE

BEST WESTERN REGENCY INN
360 Eastgate Dr
(61834)
Rates: $49-$55
Tel: (217) 446-2111
(800) 528-1234

BEST WESTERN RIVERSIDE
57 S Gilbert St
(61832)
Rates: $49-$59
Tel: (217) 431-0200
(800) 528-1234

COMFORT INN
383 Lynch Dr (61832)
Rates: $41-$54
Tel: (217) 443-8004
(800) 221-2222

FAIRFIELD INN MARRIOTT
389 Lynch Rd
(61832)
Rates: $42-$57
Tel: (217) 443-3388
(800) 228-2800

GLO MOTEL
3617 N Vermillion
(61832)
Rates: $24-$32
Tel: (217) 442-2086

RAMADA INN
338 Eastgate (61832)
Rates: $55-$76
Tel: (217) 446-2400
(800) 272-6232

**REDWOOD
MOTOR INN**
411 Lynch Dr (61832)
Rates: $35-$75
Tel: (217) 443-3690
(800) 369-1339

SUPER 8 MOTEL
377 Lynch Dr (61832)
Rates: $40-$58
Tel: (217) 443-4499
(800) 800-8000

DECATUR

**BEST WESTERN
SHELTON**
450 E Pershing Rd
(62526)
Rates: $45-$49
Tel: (217) 877-7255
(800) 528-1234

BUDGETEL INN
5100 Hickory Pt
Frontage Rd (62526)
Rates: $33-$49
Tel: (217) 875-5800

DAYS INN
333 N Wyckles Rd
(62522)
Rates: $38-$66
Tel: (217) 422-5900
(800) 329-7466

**GREEN VALLEY
MOTEL**
145 W Pershing Rd
(62526)
Rates: n/a
Tel: (217) 877-3123

HAMPTON INN
1429 Hickory Point
Rd (62526)
Rates: $58-$71
Tel: (217) 877-5577
(800) 426-7866

**HOLIDAY INN
CONFERENCE
HOTEL**
US 36W & Wyckles
Rd (62522)
Rates: $69-$81
Tel: (217) 422-8800
(800) 465-4329

INTOWN MOTEL
1013 E Eldorado St
(62526)
Rates: n/a
Tel: (217) 422-9080

RED CARPET INN
3035 N Water St
(62526)
Rates: $31-$44
Tel: (217) 877-3380
(800) 251-1962

SUPER 8 MOTEL
3140 N Water St
(62526)
Rates: $37-$62
Tel: (217) 877-8888
(800) 800-8000

DEERFIELD

EMBASSY SUITES
1445 Lake Cook Rd
(60015)
Rates: $152-$173
Tel: (847) 945-4500
(800) 362-2779

MARRIOTT SUITES
2 Parkway Blvd N
(60015)
Rates: $109-$119
Tel: (847) 405-9666
(800) 228-9290

**RESIDENCE INN
BY MARRIOTT**
530 Lake Cook Rd
(60015)
Rates: $115-$145
Tel: (847) 940-4644
(800) 331-3131

DEKALB

MOTEL 6
1116 W Lincoln Hwy
(60115)
Rates: $26-$32
Tel: (815) 756-3398
(800) 440-6000

UNIVERSITY INN
1212 W Lincoln Hwy
(60115)
Rates: n/a
Tel: (815) 758-8861
(800) 329-7466

DIX

SCOTTISH INNS
I-57 Exit 103 (62830)
Rates: $23-$34
Tel: (618) 266-7254
(800) 251-1962

DIXON

**BEST WESTERN
BRANDYWINE
LODGE**
443 State Rt 2 (61021)
Rates: $54-$175
Tel: (815) 284-1890
(800) 528-1234

DOWNERS GROVE

MARRIOTT SUITES
1500 Opus Pl (60515)
Rates: $69-$133
Tel: (708) 852-1500
(800) 228-9290

**RADISSON SUITE
HOTEL**
2111 Butterfield Rd
(60515)
Rates: $72-$120
Tel: (708) 971-2000
(800) 333-3333

RED ROOF INN
1113 Butterfield Rd
(60515)
Rates: $42-$51
Tel: (708) 963-4205
(800) 843-7663

DWIGHT

SUPER 8 MOTEL
14 E Northbrook Dr
(60420)
Rates: $39-$56
Tel: (815) 584-1888
(800) 800-8000

EAST DUBUQUE

L & L MOTEL
20170 Rt 20 W
(61025)
Rates: n/a
Tel: (815) 747-3931

EAST HAZELCREST

DAYS INN
17220 S Halsted St
(60429)
Rates: $38-$44
Tel: (708) 957-5900
(800) 329-7466

MOTEL 6
17214 Halsted St
(60429)
Rates: $34-$40
Tel: (708) 957-9233
(800) 440-6000

EAST MOLINE

SUPER 8 MOTEL
2201 John Deere Exp
(61244)
Rates: $36-44
Tel: (309) 796-1999
(800) 800-8000

EAST PEORIA

**BEST WESTERN
EASTLIGHT**
401 N Main St
(61611)
Rates: $39-$49
Tel: (309) 699-7231
(800) 528-1234

**BEST WESTERN
REGENCY INN**
360 East gate Dr
(61834)
Rates: $49-$59
Tel: (217) 446-2111
(800) 528-1234

**BUDGET HOST
COUNTRY INN**
300 N Main St
(61611)
Rates: $35-$45
Tel: (309) 694-4261
(800) 283-4678

MOTEL 6
104 W Camp St
(61611)
Rates: $32-$38
Tel: (309) 699-7281
(800) 440-6000

SUPER 8 MOTEL
725 Taylor St (61611)
Rates: $40-60
Tel: (309) 698-8889
(800) 800-8000

EFFINGHAM

ABE LINCOLN MOTEL
Jct 32, 33, 34 (62401)
Rates: n/a
Tel: (217) 342-4717

ANTHONY ACRES RESORT
RR 2 (62401)
Rates: n/a
Tel: (217) 868-2950

BEST INNS OF AMERICA
1209 N Keller Dr (62401)
Rates: $31-$46
Tel: (217) 347-5141

BEST WESTERN RAINTREE INN
I-57 & I-70 (62401)
Rates: $40-$59
Tel: (217) 342-4121
(800) 528-1234

BUDGETEL
1103 Ave of Mid-America (62401)
Rates: $33-$51
Tel: (217) 342-2525
(800) 428-3438

BUDGET HOST LINCOLN LODGE
N Rt 45 at I-57 & 70 (62401)
Rates: $25-$34
Tel: (217) 342-4133
(800) 283-4678

DAYS INN
1412 W Fayette Ave (62401)
Rates: $30-57
Tel: (217) 342-9271
(800) 329-7466

ECONO LODGE
1205 N Keller Dr (62401)
Rates: $36-$54
Tel: (217) 347-7131
(800) 424-4777

EFFINGHAM MOTEL
702 E Fayette Ave (62401)
Rates: n/a
Tel: (217) 342-3991

HAMPTON INN
1509 Hampton Dr (62401)
Rates: $53-$65
Tel: (217) 342-4499
(800) 426-7866

HOLIDAY INN
1600 W Fayette Ave (62401)
Rates: $46-$54
Tel: (217) 342-4161
(800) 465-4329

HOWARD JOHNSON LODGE
1606 W Fayette Ave (62401)
Rates: $34-$49
Tel: (217) 342-4667
(800) 446-4656

KNIGHTS INN
1000 W Fayette Ave (62401)
Rates: $23-$39
Tel: (217) 342-2165

RAMADA INN & CONVENTION CTR
I-57 & I-70 & Rt 32/33 (62401)
Rates: $49-$99
Tel: (217) 342-2131
(800) 272-6232

SUPER 8 MOTEL
1400 Thelma Keller Ave (62401)
Rates: $39-$54
Tel: (217) 342-6888
(800) 800-8000

EL PASO

SUPER 8 MOTEL
880 W Main (61738)
Rates: $40-$59
Tel: (309) 527-4949
(800) 800-8000

ELIZABETH

RIDGEVIEW B & B
8833 S Massbach Rd (61028)
Rates: n/a
Tel: (815) 598-3150

ZEAL'S COUNTRY MOTEL
2 Rt 20 W (61028)
Rates: n/a
Tel: (815) 858-2205

ELK GROVE VILLAGE

EXEL INN
1000 W Devon Ave (60007)
Rates: $51-$63
Tel: (847) 894-2085
(800) 356-8013

EXEL INN OF O'HARE
2881 Touhy Ave (6007)
Rates: $52-$70
Tel: (847) 803-9400
(800) 356-8013

HOLIDAY INN
1000 Busse Rd (60007)
Rates: $84-$95
Tel: (847) 437-6010
(800) 465-4329

LA QUINTA INN O'HARE
1900 E Oakton St (60007)
Rates: $68-$83
Tel: (847) 439-6767
(800) 531-5900

MOTEL 6
1601 Oakton St (60007)
Rates: $34-$40
Tel: (847) 981-9766
(800) 466-8356

SHERATON SUITES O'HARE
121 Northwest Point Blvd (60007)
Rates: $89-$175
Tel: (847) 290-1600
(800) 325-3535

SUPER 8 MOTEL
2951 Touhy Ave (60007)
Rates: $50-$65
Tel: (309) 663-2361
(800) 800-8000

ELMHURST

HOLIDAY INN
624 N York Rd (60126)
Rates: $80-$100
Tel: (708) 279-1100
(800) 465-4329

EVANSTON

A SOMMER PLACE BED & BREAKFAST
1213 Maple Ave (60201)
Rates: n/a
Tel: (847) 869-0543

HOMESTEAD HOTEL
1625 Hinman Ave (60201)
Rates: n/a
Tel: (847) 475-3300

FAIRVIEW HEIGHTS

BEST WESTERN CAMELOT INN
311 Salem Pl (62208)
Rates: $45-$65
Tel: (618) 624-3636
(800) 528-1234

DRURY INN
12 Ludwig Dr (62208)
Rates: $51-$65
Tel: (618) 398-8530
(800) 325-8300

FAIRFIELD INN BY MARRIOTT
140 Ludwig Dr (62208)
Rates: $53-$66
Tel: (618) 398-7124

HAMPTON INN
150 Ludwig Dr (62208)
Rates: $53-$66
Tel: (618) 397-9705
(800) 426-7866

SUPER 8 MOTEL
45 Ludwig Dr
(62208)
Rates: $42-$60
Tel: (618) 398-8338
(800) 800-8000

TRAILWAY MOTEL
10039 Lincoln Tr
(62208)
Rates: n/a
Tel: (618) 397-5757

FARMER CITY

BUDGET MOTEL
Rt 54 E (61842)
Rates: n/a
Tel: (309) 928-2157

DAYS INN
I-74 & Rt 54 (61842)
Rates: $39-69
Tel: (309) 928-9434
(800) 329-7466

FORSYTH

COMFORT INN
134 Barnett Ave
(62535)
Rates: $42-$48
Tel: (800) 221-2222

FAIRFIELD INN
1417 Hickory Point
Dr (62526)
Rates: $46-$61
Tel: (217) 875-3337

HAMPTON INN
1429 Hickory Point
Dr (62526)
Rates: $58-$71
Tel: (217) 877-5577
(800) 426-7866

FREEBURG

GABRIEL MOTEL
600 N State St
(62243)
Rates: n/a
Tel: (618) 539-5588

FREEPORT

**BEST WESTERN
STEPHENSON**
109 S Galena Ave
(61032)
Rates: $52-$70
Tel: (815) 233-0300
(800) 528-1234

**COUNTRYSIDE
MOTEL**
1535 W Galena Ave
(61032)
Rates: $27-$53
Tel: (815) 232-6148

HOLIDAY INN
1300 E South St
(61032)
Rates: $55-$69
Tel: (815) 235-3121
(800) 465-4329

**TOWN HOUSE
MOTEL**
1156 W Galena Ave
(61032)
Rates: n/a
Tel: (815) 232-2191

WEST MOTEL
2084 W Galena Ave
(61032)
Rates: n/a
Tel: (815) 232-4188

GALENA

**BEST WESTERN
QUIET HOUSE
SUITES**
9923 Hwy 20 (61036)
Rates: $84-$198
Tel: (815) 777-2597
(800) 528-1234

**CLORAN MANSION
BED & BREAKFAST**
1237 Franklin St
(61036)
Rates: n/a
Tel: (815) 777-0583

**COUNTRY GARDENS
BED & BREAKFAST**
1000 Third St (61036)
Rates: n/a
Tel: (815) 777-3062

**FARSTER'S
EXECUTIVE INN**
305 N Main St (61036)
Rates: n/a
Tel: (815) 777-9125
(800) 545-8551

TRIANGLE MOTEL
Rt 20 West (61036)
Rates: n/a
Tel: (815) 777-2897

GALESBURG

**AARON'S THRIFTY
MOTEL**
1777 Grand Ave
(61401)
Rates: n/a
Tel: (309) 343-2812

COMFORT INN
907 W Carl
Sandburg Dr (61401)
Rates: $46-$65
Tel: (309) 344-5445
(800) 221-2222

**JUMER'S
CONTINENTAL INN**
260 S Soangetaha Rd
(61401)
Rates: $62-$79
Tel: (309) 343-7151
(800) 285-8637

MOTEL 6
1475 N Henderson
St (61401)
Rates: $26-$32
Tel: (309) 344-2401
(800) 440-6000

RAMADA INN
29 Public Sq (61401)
Rates: $50-$65
Tel: (309) 343-9161
(800) 272-6232

REGENCY HOTEL
3282 N Henderson
St (61401)
Rates: n/a
Tel: (309) 344-1111
(800) 648-4707

GENESEO

DECK PLAZA MOTEL
2181 S Oakwood
Ave (61254)
Rates: $26-$41
Tel: (309) 944-4651

**THE OAKWOOD
MOTEL**
225 US Hwy 6 E
(61254)
Rates: $19-$25
Tel: (309) 944-3696

GILMAN

DAYS INN
834 Hwy 24 W (60938)
Rates: $39-75
Tel: (815) 265-7283

SUPER 8 MOTEL
1301 S Crescent St
(60938)
Rates: $44-62
Tel: (815) 265-7000
(800) 800-8000

GLEN ELLYN

**BEST WESTERN
FOUR SEASONS**
656 Taft Ave (60137)
Rates: $42-$80
Tel: (708) 469-8500
(800) 528-1234

HOLIDAY INN
1250 Roosevelt Rd
(60137)
Rates: $53-$69
Tel: (708) 629-6000
(800) 465-4329

GLENVIEW

BUDGETEL INN
1625 Milwaukee Ave
(60025)
Rates: $51-$62
Tel: (847) 635-8300
(800) 428-3438

MOTEL 6
1535 Milwaukee Ave
(60025)
Rates: $35-$41
Tel: (847) 390-7200
(800) 466-8356

GOLCONDA

**SAN DAMIANO
RETREAT**
Rt 1, P. O. Box 106
(62938)
Rates: n/a
Tel: (618) 285-3507

GRANITE CITY

CHAIN OF ROCKS MOTEL
3228 W Chain of
Rocks Rd (62040)
Rates: n/a
Tel: (618) 931-6600

GRANITE CITY LODGE
1200 19th St (62040)
Rates: n/a
Tel: (618) 876-2600

ILLINI MOTEL
1100 Niedringhaus
Ave (62040)
Rates: n/a
Tel: (618) 877-7100

GRAYVILLE

BEST WESTERN WINDSOR OAKS INN
2200 S Court St
(62844)
Rates: $50-$74
Tel: (800) 528-1234

GREENUP

FIVE STAR MOTEL
US Rt 40 & Rt 130
(62428)
Rates: n/a
Tel: (217) 923-5512

GATEWAY INN MOTEL
716 E Elizabeth St
(62428)
Rates: n/a
Tel: (217) 923-3176

GREENVILLE

BEST WESTERN COUNTRY VIEW INN
I-70 & Rt 127 (62246)
Rates: $34-$52
Tel: (618) 664-3030
(800) 528-1234

BUDGET HOST-BEL AIR MOTEL
I-70 & Rt 127 (62246)
Rates: $28-$45
Tel: (618) 664-1950
(800) 283-4678

PRAIRIE HOUSE COUNTRY INN
RR 4, Box 47-AA
(62246)
Rates: n/a
Tel: (618) 664-3003

2 ACRES MOTEL
I-70 & Rt 127 (62246)
Rates: n/a
Tel: (618) 664-3131

UPTOWN MOTEL
323 S Third St (62246)
Rates: n/a
Tel: (618) 664-3121

GURNEE

ADVENTURE INNS
3732 Grand Ave
(60031)
Rates: n/a
Tel: (847) 623-7777
(800) 373-5245

HAMPTON INN
5550 Grand Ave
(60031)
Rates: $65-$109
Tel: (847) 662-1100
(800) 426-7866

HAMEL

INNKEEPER MOTEL
I-55 & Rt 140 (62234)
Rates: n/a
Tel: (618) 633-2111

HARRISBURG

PLAZA MOTEL
411 E Poplar St
(62946)
Rates: n/a
Tel: (618) 253-7651

SUPER 8 MOTEL
100 E Seright St
(62946)
Rates: $40-$55
Tel: (800) 800-8000

HAVANA

RED LION MOTOR LODGE
136 US E (62644)
Rates: n/a
Tel: (309) 543-4407

HENRY

HENRY HARBOR INN
208 Cromwell Dr
(61537)
Rates: n/a
Tel: (309) 364-2365

HERRIN

PARK AVENUE MOTEL
900 N Park Ave
(62948)
Rates: n/a
Tel: (618) 942-3159

HIGHLAND

CARDINAL INN
101 Walnut St
(62249)
Rates: n/a
Tel: (618) 654-4433

HILLSBORO

MANOR MOTEL
1447 Vandalia Rd
(62049)
Rates: n/a
Tel: (217) 532-6144

HILLSIDE

HOLIDAY INN
4400 Frontge Rd
(60162)
Rates: $74-$84
Tel: (708) 544-9300
(800) 465-4329

HOFFMAN ESTATES

BUDGETEL INN
2075 Barrington Rd
(60195)
Rates: $37-$55
Tel: (847) 882-8848
(800) 428-3438

LA QUINTA INN
2280 Barrington Rd
(60195)
Rates: $59-$73
Tel: (847) 882-3312
(800) 531-5900

RED ROOF INN
2500 Hassell Rd
(60195)
Rates: $34-$52
Tel: (847) 885-7877
(800) 843-7663

HOOPESTON

DOWNTOWN MOTEL
200 E Main St
(60942)
Rates: n/a
Tel: (217) 283-6605

ITASCA

HOLIDAY INN
860 W Irving Park
Rd (60143)
Rates: n/a
Tel: (708) 773-2340
(800) 465-4329

JACKSONVILLE

HOLIDAY INN
1717 W Morton Ave
(62650)
Rates: $48-$107
Tel: (217) 245-9571
(800) 465-4329

MOTEL 6
1716 W Morton Dr
(62650)
Rates: $28-$34
Tel: (217) 243-7157
(800) 440-6000

STAR LITE MOTEL
1910 W Morton Ave
(62650)
Rates: $29+
Tel: (217) 245-7184

JOHNSTON CITY

FARRIS MOTEL
Rt 37 South, Box 6
(62951)
Rates: n/a
Tel: (618) 983-8086

JOLIET

**FAIRFIELD INN
BY MARRIOTT**
3239 Norman Ave
(60435)
Rates: $47-$60
Tel: (800) 348-6000

MANOR MOTEL
32926 E Eames
(60436)
Rates: n/a
Tel: (815) 467-5385

MOTEL 6
1850 McDonough
Rd (60436)
Rates: $34-$40
Tel: (815) 729-2800
(800) 440-6000

RED ROOF INN
1750 McDonough St
(60436)
Rates: $43-$45
Tel: (815) 741-2304
(800) 843-7663

JONESBORO

**TRAIL OF TEARS
SPORTS RESORT**
Rt 1, Old Cape Rd
(62952)
Rates: n/a
Tel: (618) 833-8697

KANKAKEE

AVIS MOTEL
1225 E Court (60901)
Rates: n/a
Tel: (815) 933-1717

DAYS INN
1975 E Court St
(60901)
Rates: $38-$42
Tel: (815) 939-7171
(800) 329-7466

**FAIRFIEW COURTS
MOTEL**
2745 S Rt 45-52
(60901)
Rates: n/a
Tel: (815) 933-7708

MODEL MOTEL
1245 S Washington
Ave (60901)
Rates: n/a
Tel: (815) 932-5013

**NORMA'S
BED & BREAKFAST**
429 S Fourth (60901)
Rates: n/a
Tel: (815) 937-1533

KEITHSBURG

**THE KEITHSBURG
MOTEL**
2nd & Main Sts
(61442)
Rates: n/a
Tel: (309) 374-2659

KEWANEE

**KEWANEE
MOTOR LODGE**
400 S Main St
(61443)
Rates: $38-$45
Tel: (309) 853-4000

LA GRANGE

**J C COUNTRYSIDE
MOTEL**
6401 Joliet Rd
(60525)
Rates: n/a
Tel: (708) 352-3113

LAKE FOREST

THE DEER PATH INN
255 E Illinois Rd
(60045)
Rates: n/a
Tel: (847) 234-2280

LANSING

**BEST WESTERN
SOUTH**
2505 Bernice Rd
(60438)
Rates: $42-$66
Tel: (708) 895-7810
(800) 528-1234

HOLIDAY INN
17356 Torrence Ave
(60438)
Rates: n/a
Tel: (708) 474-6300
(800) 465-4329

RED ROOF INN
2450 E 173rd St
(60438)
Rates: $34-$50
Tel: (708) 895-9570
(800) 843-7663

LA SALLE

**HOWARD JOHNSON
MOTEL**
I-80 & IL 251 (61301)
Rates: $40-$59
Tel: (815) 224-2500
(800) 446-4656

LE ROY

SUPER 8 MOTEL
1 Demma Dr (61752)
Rates: $40-$58
Tel: (309) 962-4700
(800) 800-8000

LIBERTYVILLE

**BEST INNS
OF AMERICA**
1809 W Milwaukee
Ave (60048)
Rates: $39-$57
Tel: (847) 816-8006
(800) 237-8466

LINCOLN

COMFORT INN
2811 Woodlawn Rd
(62656)
Rates: $43-$80
Tel: (217) 735-3960
(800) 221-2222

**CROSSROADS
MOTEL**
1305 Woodlawn Rd
(62656)
Rates: n/a
Tel: (217) 735-5571

DAYS INN
I-55 Business City Rt
(62656)
Rates: $30-$39
Tel: (217) 735-1202
(800) 329-7466

SUPER 8 MOTEL
2809 Woodlawn Rd
(62656)
Rates: $43-$61
Tel: (217) 732-8886
(800) 800-8000

LINCOLNSHIRE

**HAWTHORN
SUITES HOTEL**
10 Westminster Way
(60069)
Rates: $89-$135
Tel: (847) 945-9300
(800) 527-1133

MARRIOTTS RESORT
10 Marriott Dr
(60069)
Rates: $114-$129
Tel: (857) 634-0100
(800) 228-9290

LISLE

HILTON INN
3003 Corporate West
Dr (60532)
Rates: $66-$94
Tel: (708) 505-0900
(800) 445-8667

LITCHFIELD

**BEST WESTERN
GARDENS**
413 Columbian
Blvd N (62056)
Rates: $38-$53
Tel: (217) 324-2181
(800) 528-1234

66 MOTEL
621 N Sherman St
(62056)
Rates: n/a
Tel: (217) 324-2179

SUPER 8 MOTEL
Box 281 (62056)
Rates: $39-$36
Tel: (217) 324-7788
(800) 800-8000

LOMBARD

**RESIDENCE INN
BY MARRIOTT**
2001 S Highland Ave
(60148)
Rates: $115-$145
Tel: (708) 629-7800
(800) 331-3131

MACOMB

MACOMB INN
1400 N Lafayette St
(61455)
Rates: $47-$57
Tel: (309) 833-5511

MAHOMET

**HERITAGE INN
MOTEL**
I-74 & Rt 47 (61853)
Rates: n/a
Tel: (217) 586-4975

MARION

**BEST INNS
OF AMERICA**
Rt 8, Box 70 (62959)
Rates: $34-$46
Tel: (618) 997-9421
(800) 237-8466

**BEST WESTERN
AIRPORT INN**
130 Express Dr
(62959)
Rates: $39-$69
Tel: (618) 993-3222
(800) 528-1234

COURTS INN
110 S Court (62959)
Rates: n/a
Tel: (618) 993-8131

**GRAY PLAZA
MOTEL**
New Rt 13 W (62959)
Rates: n/a
Tel: (618) 993-2174

MOTEL MARION
2100 W Main St
(62959)
Rates: n/a
Tel: (618) 993-2101

MOTEL 6
1008 Halfway Rd
(62959)
Rates: $27-$33
Tel: (618) 993-2631
(800) 440-6000

OLD SQUAT INN
RR 7, Box 246 (62959)
Rates: n/a
Tel: (618) 982-2916

SHONEY'S INN
I-57 & Rt 13 (62959)
Rates: n/a
Tel: (618) 997-7900
(800) 222-2222

SUPER 8 MOTEL
2601 W De Young St
(62959)
Rates: $39-$45
Tel: (618) 993-5577
(800) 800-8000

**TOUPAL'S
COUNTRY INN**
RR 5 (62959)
Rates: n/a
Tel: (618) 995-2074

MARSHALL

HOLIDAY INN
500 Holiday Plaza
Dr (60443)
Rates: $70-$86
Tel: (708) 747-3500
(800) 465-4329

LINCOLN MOTEL
US Rt 40 (62441)
Rates: n/a
Tel: (217) 826-2941

MATTESON

BUDGETEL
5210 W Southwick
Dr (60443)
Rates: $44-$63
Tel: (708) 503-0999
(800) 428-3438

PEAKS MOTOR INN
I-70, Exit 147 (62441)
Rates: n/a
Tel: (217) 826-3031

SUPER 8 MOTEL
Rt 3, Box 116-AA
(62441)
Rates: $38-$45
Tel: (217) 826-8043
(800) 800-8000

MASON CITY

MASON CITY MOTEL
701 W Chestnut St
(62664)
Rates: n/a
Tel: (217) 482-3003

MATTOON

BUDGET INN
I-57 & SR 45, Exit
184 (61938)
Rates: n/a
Tel: (217) 235-4011

**HOWARD JOHNSON
INN**
I-57 & Exit 184 (61938)
Rates: $41-$91
Tel: (217) 235-4161
(800) 446-4656

RAMADA INN
300 Broadway E
(61938)
Rates: $53-$81
Tel: (217) 235-0313
(800) 272-6232

US GRANT MOTEL
SR 45 (61938)
Rates: n/a
Tel: (217) 235-5695

McLEAN

SUPER 8 MOTEL
South St & Elm St
(61754)
Rates: $40-$58
Tel: (309) 874-2366
(800) 800-8000

MENDOTA

SUPER 8 MOTEL
508 Hwy 34 E, Box
526 (61342)
Rates: $41-$58
Tel: (815) 539-7429
(800) 800-8000

METROPOLIS

**BEST INNS
OF AMERICA**
2055 E 5th St (62960)
Rates: $44-$60
Tel: (618) 524-8200
(800) 237-8466

ISLE OF VIEW B & B
205 Metropolis St
(62960)
Rates: n/a
Tel: (618) 524-5838

**METROPOLIS INN
MOTEL**
Rts 45 & 24, Exit 37
(62960)
Rates: n/a
Tel: (618) 524-3723

MINONK

**VICTORIAN OAKS
BED & BREAKFAST**
435 Locust (61760)
Rates: n/a
Tel: (309) 432-2771

MOLINE

HAMPTON INN
6920 27th St (61265)
Rates: $51-59
Tel: (309) 762-1711
(800) 426-7866

EXEL INN
2501 52nd Ave
(61265)
Rates: $35-$49
Tel: (309) 797-5580
(800) 356-8013

LA QUINTA INN
5450 27th St (61265)
Rates: $50-$60
Tel: (309) 762-9008
(800) 531-5900

MOTEL 6
Airport Road (61265)
Rates: $30-36
Tel: (309) 764-8711
(800) 440-6000

SUPER 8 MOTEL
2201 John Deere
Expy (61244)
Rates: $36-59
Tel: (309) 796-1999
(800) 800-8000

MONMOUTH

MELING'S MOTEL
1129 N Main St
(61462)
Rates: $27-$46
Tel: (309) 734-2196

MONTROSE

**MOTEL
MONTAROSA**
I-70, Exit 105 (62445)
Rates: n/a
Tel: (217) 924-4117

MORRIS

COMFORT INN
70 W Gore Rd
(60450)
Rates: $43-$100
Tel: (800) 221-2222

HOLIDAY INN
200 Gore Rd (60450)
Rates: $42-$48
Tel: (800) 465-4329

MORRISON

PARKVIEW MOTEL
15424 E Lincoln Rd
(61270)
Rates: n/a
Tel: (815) 772-2163

MORTON

**HOWARD JOHNSON
LODGE**
128 Queenswood Rd
(61550)
Rates: $35-$45
Tel: (309) 263-2511
(800) 446-4656

MOUNT CARROLL

**THE CAPTAINS
QUARTERS B & B**
207 S Main St (61053)
Rates: n/a
Tel: (815) 244-2692

MT. PROSPECT

RAMADA INN
200 E Rand Rd
(60056)
Rates: $69-107
Tel: (847) 255-8800
(800) 272-6232

MOUNT STERLING

**LAND OF LINCOLN
MOTEL**
403 E Main St
(62353)
Rates: n/a
Tel: (217) 773-3311

MOUNT VERNON

**BEST INNS OF
AMERICA**
222 S 44th (62864)
Rates: $33-$47
Tel: (618) 244-4343
(800) 237-8466

BEST WESTERN INN
I-57/I-64 & Rt 15
(62864)
Rates: n/a
Tel: (618) 242-6370
(800) 528-1234

DAYSTOP
750 S 10th (62864)
Rates: $28-$45
Tel: (618) 244-3224
(800) 329-7466

DRURY INN
145 N 44th St (62864)
Rates: $43-$58
Tel: (618) 244-4550
(800) 325-8300

HOLIDAY INN
I-57 & Rt 5 (62864)
Rates: $48-$65
Tel: (618) 244-3670
(800) 465-4329

MOTEL 6
333 S 44th St (62864)
Rates: $27-$33
Tel: (618) 244-2383
(800) 440-6000

RAMADA HOTEL
222 Potomac Blvd
(62864)
Rates: $50-$60
Tel: (618) 244-7100
(800) 272-6232

SUPER 8 MOTEL
401 S 44th St (62864)
Rates: $40-$55
Tel: (618) 242-8800
(800) 800-8000

THRIFTY INN
100 N 44th St (62864)
Rates: $39-$55
Tel: (618) 244-7750

MUDDY

DAYS INN
Rt 45, Box 3 (62965)
Rates: $33-43
Tel: (618) 252-6354
(800) 329-7466

MUNDELEIN

HOLIDAY INN
510 Rt 83S (60060)
Rates: $57-$63
Tel: (800) 465-4329

SUPER 8 MOTEL
1950 S Lake St
(60060)
Rates: $46-$67
Tel: (847) 949-8842
(800) 800-8000

MURPHYSBORO

APPLE TREE INN
100 North 2nd St
(62966)
Rates: $30-$40
Tel: (618) 687-2345
(800) 626-4356

NAPERVILLE

DAYS INN
1350 E Ogden Ave
(60566)
Rates: $41-$57
Tel: (708) 369-3600
(800) 329-7466

EXEL INN
1585 N Naperville/
Wheaton Rd (60563)
Rates: $38-$51
Tel: (708) 357-0022
(800) 356-8013

RED ROOF INN
1698 W Diehl Rd
(60563)
Rates: $35-$55
Tel: (708) 369-2500
(800) 843-7663

NASHVILLE

MILL CREEK INN
560 N Mill (62263)
Rates: n/a
Tel: (618) 327-8424

U.S. INN
11640 SR 27 (62263)
Rates: $29-$35
Tel: (618) 478-5341

NAUVOO

**IMA NAUVOO
FAMILY MOTEL**
150 N Warsaw
(62354)
Rates: $38-$57
Tel: (217) 453-6527

**NAUVOO VILLAGE
INN**
1350 Farley St
(62354)
Rates: $20-$30
Tel: (217) 453-6634

NEWTON

RIVER PARK MOTEL
RR 5 (62448)
Rates: n/a
Tel: (618) 783-2327

NILES

DAYS INN
6450 W Touhy Ave
(60714)
Rates: $59-225
Tel: (847) 647-7700
(800) 329-7466

TRAVELODGE
7247 N Waukegan
Rd (60714)
Rates: $46-70
Tel: (847) 647-9444
(800) 578-7878

NORMAL

**BEST WESTERN
UNIVERSITY INN**
6 Traders Cir (61761)
Rates: $55-$68
Tel: (309) 454-4070
(800) 528-1234

COMFORT SUITES
310-B Greenbriar Dr
(61761)
Rates: $65-100
Tel: (309) 452-8588
(800) 221-2222

HOLIDAY INN NORTH
8 Traders Cir (61761)
Rates: $61-$74
Tel: (309) 452-8300
(800) 465-4329

MOTEL 6
1600 N Main St
(61761)
Rates: $32-$38
Tel: (309) 452-0422
(800) 440-6000

NORTHBROOK

RED ROOF INN
340 Waukegan Rd
(60062)
Rates: $40-$62
Tel: (847) 205-1755
(800) 843-7663

OAK FOREST

THE TERRACE MOTEL
15353 S Cicero Ave
(60452)
Rates: n/a
Tel: (708) 687-7500

OAKBROOK TERRACE

COMFORT SUITES
17W445 Roosevelt
Rd (60181)
Rates: $75-$85
Tel: (708) 916-1000
(800) 221-2222

HILTON SUITES
10 Drury Ln (60181)
Rates: $99-$149
Tel: (708) 941-0100
(800) 445-8667

O'FALLON

COMFORT INN
1100 SE Gate Dr
(62269)
Rates: $42-$66
Tel: (618) 624-6060
(800) 221-2121

RAMADA INN
1313 Central Park Dr
(62269)
Rates: $45-$90
Tel: (800) 272-6232

OKAWVILLE

ORIGINAL MINERAL SPRINGS MOTEL
506 Hanover (62271)
Rates: n/a
Tel: (618) 243-5458

SUPER 8 MOTEL
I-64 & Rt 177 (62271)
Rates: $39-$63
Tel: (618) 243-6525
(800) 800-8000

OLNEY

SUPER 8 MOTEL
Rt 130 & North Ave
(62450)
Rates: $38-$53
Tel: (618) 392-7888
(800) 800-8000

OREGON

VIP MOTEL
1326 IL 2 N (61061)
Rates: $27-$32
Tel: (815) 732-6195

PALATINE

MOTEL 6
1450 E Dundee Rd
(60067)
Rates: $34-$40
Tel: (708) 359-0046
(800) 440-6000

RED GABLES MOTEL
875 W Northwest
Hwy (60067)
Rates: n/a
Tel: (847) 358-3443

RAMADA HOTEL
920 E Northwest
Hwy (60067)
Rates: $59-$69
Tel: (847) 359-6900
(800) 272-6232

PANA

ROSE BUD MOTEL
RR 2, Jct 16 & 51
(62557)
Rates: n/a
Tel: (217) 562-3929

PARIS

SCOTTISH INNS
Hwy Rt 1 & 150 N
(61944)
Rates: $30-$46
Tel: (217) 465-6441
(800) 251-1962

SUPER 8 MOTEL
Hwy 150 (61944)
Rates: $38-$51
Tel: (217) 463-8888
(800) 800-8000

PEKIN

COMFORT INN
2340 Vandever Ave
(61554)
Rates: $44-$66
Tel: (309) 353-4047
(800) 221-2222

PEKIN INN
2801 E Court St
(61554)
Rates: $42-$55
Tel: (309) 347-5533

PEORIA

BEST WESTERN MARK TWAIN HOTEL
225 NE Adams
(61602)
Rates: $57-$75
Tel: (309) 676-3600
(800) 528-1234

COMFORT SUITES
4021 War Memorial
Dr (61614)
Rates: $51-$99
Tel: (309) 688-3800
(800) 221-2222

DAYS INN
2726 Westlake Ave
(61615)
Rates: $40-$45
Tel: (309) 688-7000
(800) 329-7466

HOLIDAY INN
4400 N Brandywine
Dr (61614)
Rates: $67-$109
Tel: (309) 686-8000
(800) 465-4329

HOLIDAY INN
500 Hamilton Blvd
(61602)
Rates: $68-$86
Tel: (309) 674-2500
(800) 465-4329

JUMER'S CASTLE LODGE
117 N Western Ave
(61604)
Rates: $77-$100
Tel: (309) 673-8040
(800) 285-8637

PERE MARQUETTE HOTEL
501 Main St (61602)
Rates: $65-$500
Tel: (800) 447-1676

RED ROOF INN
4031 N War
Memorial Dr (61614)
Rates: $42-$60
Tel: (309) 684-3911
(800) 843-7663

SUPER 8 MOTEL
4025 W War
Memorial Dr (61614)
Rates: $42-$62
Tel: (309) 688-8074
(800) 800-8000

PERU

DAYS INN
P. O. Box 626 (61354)
Rates: $39-$49
Tel: (815) 224-1060
(800) 329-7466

SUPER 8 MOTEL
1851 May Rd (61354)
Rates: $37-$58
Tel: (815) 223-1848
(800) 800-8000

PINCKNEYVILLE

FOUNTAIN MOTEL
112 S Main St (62274)
Rates: $32-$34
Tel: (618) 357-2128

POCAHONTAS

TAHOE MOTEL
Rt 40 & I-70, Exit 36
(62275)
Rates: n/a
Tel: (618) 669-2404

WIKIUP MOTEL
Plant & Johnson Sts
(62275)
Rates: n/a
Tel: (618) 669-2293

POLO

VILLAGE INN MOTEL
1007 S Division St
(61064)
Rates: n/a
Tel: (815) 946-2229

PONTIAC

COMFORT INN
1821 W Reynolds St
(61764)
Rates: $43-$90
Tel: (815) 842-2777

FIESTA MOTEL
Rts 66 & 116 (61764)
Rates: n/a
Tel: (815) 844-7103

PALAMAR MOTEL
213 S Ladd St
(61764)
Rates: n/a
Tel: (815) 844-5191

SUPER 8 MOTEL
601 Deerfield Rd
(61764)
Rates: $39-$54
Tel: (815) 844-6888
(800) 800-8000

PONTOON BEACH

BEST WESTERN CAMELOT INN
1240 E Old Chain of
Rock Rd (62040)
Rates: $36-$67
Tel: (618) 931-2262
(800) 528-1234

PRINCETON

DAYS INN
2238 N Main St
(61356)
Rates: $39-$57
Tel: (815) 875-3371
(800) 329-7466

LINCOLN INN
I-80 & Rt 26 (61356)
Rates: $32-$44
Tel: (815) 875-3371

PRAIRIE HILL BARN B & B
Rt 4, Box 74 (61356)
Rates: n/a
Tel: (815) 447-2487

PRINCETON MOTOR LODGE
I-80 & Rt 26 (61356)
Rates: $30-$38
Tel: (815) 875-1121

PROPHETSTOWN

PROPHET MOTEL
201 Washington St
(61277)
Rates: n/a
Tel: (815) 537-5333

PROSPECT HEIGHTS

EXEL INN
540 Milwaukee Ave
(60070)
Rates: $34-$47
Tel: (847) 459-0545
(800) 456-8013

FOREST LODGE
1246 S River Rd
(60070)
Rates: $29-$150
Tel: (847) 537-2000

QUAD CITIES

BEST WESTERN STEEPLEGATE INN
100 W 76th St
(Davenport 52806)
Rates: $62-$85
Tel: (800) 528-1234

COMFORT INN
2600 52nd Ave
(Moline 61265)
Rates: $42-$76
Tel: (309) 762-7000

COMFORT INN-DAVENPORT
7222 Northwest Blvd
(Davenport 52806)
Rates: $38-$47
Tel: (319) 391-8222

DAYS INN OF DAVENPORT
3202 E Kimberly Rd
(Davenport 52807)
Rates: $37-$61
Tel: (319) 355-1190

ECONO LODGE
2205 Kimberly Rd
(Bettendorf 52722)
Rates: $34-$51
Tel: (319) 355-6471

EXEL INN OF DAVENPORT
6310 N Brady St
(Davenport 52806)
Rates: $31-$45
Tel: (319) 386-6350

EXEL INN OF MOLINE
2501 52nd Ave
(Moline 61265)
Rates: $29-$45
Tel: (309) 797-5580

FAIRFIELD INN
2705 48th Ave
(Moline 61265)
Rates: $44-$65
Tel: (309) 762-9083

FAIRFIELD INN BY MARRIOTT-DAVENPORT
3206 E Kimberly Rd
(Davenport 52807)
Rates: $44-$70
Tel: (319) 355-3364

HAMPTON INN-AIRPORT
6920 27th St
(Moline 61265)
Rates: $49-$58
Tel: (309) 762-1711

HAMPTON INN-DAVENPORT
3330 E Kimberly Rd
(Davenport 52807)
Rates: $42-$53
Tel: (319) 359-3921

JUMER'S CASTLE LODGE-BETTENDORF
900 Spruce Hills Dr
(Bettendorf 52722)
Rates: $76-$97
Tel: (319) 359-7141

LA QUINTA INN
5450 27th St
(Moline 61265)
Rates: $44-$58
Tel: (309) 762-9008

MOTEL 6
Airport Road
(Moline 61265)
Rates: $26-$34
Tel: (309) 764-8711

RAMADA INN-DAVENPORT
6263 N Brady
(Davenport 52806)
Rates: $55-$63
Tel: (319) 386-1940

TWIN BRIDGES MOTOR INN-BETTENDORF
221 15th St
(Bettendorf 52722)
Rates: $39-$48
Tel: (319) 355-6451

QUINCY

BEL-AIRE MOTEL
2314 North 12th St
(62301)
Rates: n/a
Tel: (217) 223-1356

COMFORT INN
4100 Broadway
(62301)
Rates: $41-$66
Tel: (217) 228-2700
(800) 221-2222

DAYS INN
200 Main St (62301)
Rates: $29-$79
Tel: (217) 223-6610
(800) 329-7466

DIAMOND MOTEL
4703 N 12th St
(62301)
Rates: n/a
Tel: (217) 223-1436

**FAIRFIELD INN
BY MARRIOTT**
4315 Broadway
(62301)
Rates: $52-$57
Tel: (217) 223-5922
(800) 228-2800

HOLIDAY INN
201 S 3rd St (62301)
Rates: $57-$74
Tel: (217) 222-2666
(800) 465-4329

SUPER 8 MOTEL
224 N 36th St (62301)
Rates: $44-$61
Tel: (217) 228-8808
(800) 800-8000

TRAVELODGE
200 S 3rd St (62301)
Rates: $40-$64
Tel: (217) 222-5620
(800) 578-7878

RANTOUL

**BEST WESTERN
HERITAGE INN**
420 S Murray Rd
(61866)
Rates: $39-$55
Tel: (217) 892-9292
(800) 528-1234

DAYS INN
801 W Champaign
(61866)
Rates: $47-$58
Tel: (217) 893-0700
(800) 329-7466

ROBINSON

DAYS INN
1500 W Main St
(62454)
Rates: $42-$96
Tel: (618) 544-8448

RED BUD

RED BUD MOTEL
1103 S Main St
(62278)
Rates: n/a
Tel: (618) 282-2123

RICHMOND

DAYS INN
11200 N Rt 12
(60071)
Rates: $45-$86
Tel: (815) 678-4711
(800) 329-7466

DRAKE MOTEL
8613 S Rt 12 (60071)
Rates: n/a
Tel: (815) 678-3501

ROCK FALLS

HOLIDAY INN
2105 S 1st Ave
(61071)
Rates: $54-$61
Tel: (815) 626-5500
(800) 465-4329

ROCKFORD

AIRPORT INN
4419 S 11th St
(61108)
Rates: n/a
Tel: (815) 397-4000

ALPINE INN
4404 E State St
(61108)
Rates: $30-$54
Tel: (815) 399-1890

**BEST WESTERN
COLONIAL INN
MOTOR LODGE**
4850 E State St
(61108)
Rates: $64-$166
Tel: (815) 398-5050
(800) 613-1234

EXEL INN
220 S Lyford Rd
(61108)
Rates: $34-$46
Tel: (815) 332-4915

MOTEL 6
3851 S 11th St
(61109)
Rates: $28-$34
Tel: (815) 398-6080
(800) 440-6000

RED ROOF INN
7434 E State St (61108)
Rates: $24-$59
Tel: (815) 398-9750
(800) 843-7663

SIXPENCE INN
4205 11th St (61109)
Rates: $25-$29
Tel: (815) 398-0066

SUPER 8 MOTEL
7646 Coloseum Dr
(61107)
Rates: $41-$60
Tel: (815) 229-5522
(800) 800-8000

**SWEDEN HOUSE
LODGE**
4605 E State St (61108)
Rates: $36-$59
Tel: (815) 398-4130
(800) 896-4138

ROCK ISLAND

PLAZA ONE HOTEL
17th St at 3rd Ave
(61201)
Rates: $80-$248
Tel: (309) 794-1212

ROLLING MEADOWS

HOLIDAY INN
3405 Algonquin Rd
(60008)
Rates: $89-$99
Tel: (847) 259-5000
(800) 465-4329

MOTEL 6
1800 Winnetka Cir
(60008)
Rates: $34-$40
Tel: (847) 818-8088
(800) 440-6000

ROSEMONT

**CLARION
INTERNATIONAL-
O'HARE**
6810 N Mannheim
Rd (60018)
Rates: $89-$119
Tel: (847) 297-1234
(800) 221-2222

**HOLIDAY INN-
O'HARE**
5540 N River Rd
(60018)
Rates: $125-$145
Tel: (847) 671-6350
(800) 465-4329

**HOTEL
SOFITEL-O'HARE**
5550 N River Rd
(60018)
Rates: $180-$195
Tel: (847) 678-4488
(800) 763-4835

**MARRIOTT SUITES-
O'HARE**
6155 N River Rd
(60018)
Rates: $89-$175
Tel: (847) 696-4400
(800) 228-9290

RUSHVILLE

**THE BOTTENBERG
BED & BREAKFAST**
505 N Liberty
(62681)
Rates: n/a
Tel: (217) 322-6100

SAINT ANNE

GEORGIAN MOTEL
Rts 1 & 17 (61964)
Rates: n/a
Tel: (815) 937-9740

SALEM

**CONTINENTAL
MOTEL**
Rt 50 E (62881)
Rates: $20-$25
Tel: (618) 548-3090

HOLIDAY INN
1812 W Main St
(62881)
Rates: $40-$52
Tel: (618) 548-4212
(800) 465-4329

MOTEL LAKEWOOD
1500 E Main St
(62881)
Rates: $18-$23
Tel: (618) 548-2785

RESTWELL MOTEL
700 W Main St
(62881)
Rates: n/a
Tel: (618) 548-2040

SUPER 8 MOTEL
118 Paragon Rd
(62881)
Rates: $39-$54
Tel: (618) 548-5882
(800) 800-8000

SAVANNA

**INDIAN HEAD
MOTEL**
3523 Rt 84 N (61074)
Rates: n/a
Tel: (815) 273-2154

LAW'S MOTEL II
Rts 52 & 64 (61074)
Rates: n/a
Tel: (815) 273-7728

PINE LODGE MOTEL
2017 Chicago Ave
(61074)
Rates: n/a
Tel: (815) 273-2291

RADKE HOTEL
422 Main St (61074)
Rates: n/a
Tel: (815) 273-3713

SAVOY

**BEST WESTERN
PARADISE INN**
1001 N Dunlap
(61874)
Rates: $45-$61
Tel: (217) 356-1824
(800) 528-1234

SCHAUMBURG

**CORPORATE SUITES
& APARTMENTS**
1813 Hemlock Pl
(60173)
Rates: n/a
Tel: (847) 397-8021

DRURY INN
600 N Martingale Rd
(60173)
Rates: $63-$75
Tel: (847) 517-7737
(800) 325-8300

HOMEWOOD SUITES
815 E American Ln
(60173)
Rates: $99-$124
Tel: (847) 605-0400
(800) 225-5466

LA QUINTA INN
1730 E Higgins Rd
(60173)
Rates: $53-$70
Tel: (847) 517-8484
(800) 531-5900

MARRIOTT HOTEL
50 N Martingale Rd
(60173)
Rates: $69-$145
Tel: (847) 240-0100
(800) 228-9290

**SUMMERFIELD
SUITES**
901 E Woodfield
Office Ct (60173)
Rates: n/a
Tel: (847) 619-6677
(800) 833-4353

SCHILLER PARK

HOWARD JOHNSON
10249 Irving Park Rd
(60176)
Rates: $74-$89
Tel: (708) 671-6000
(800) 446-4656

MOTEL 6
9408 W Lawrence
Ave (60176)
Rates: $38-$44
Tel: (847) 671-4282
(800) 466-8356

**RESIDENCE INN
BY MARRIOTT**
9450 W Lawrence
Ave (60176)
Rates: $149-$179
Tel: (847) 678-2210
(800) 331-3131

SHEFFIELD

DAYS INN
I-80 & Rt 40, Exit 45
(61361)
Rates: $30-$55
Tel: (815) 454-2361
(800) 329-7466

**HIDDEN LAKE
COUNTRY CLUB
GUEST HOUSES**
Buda on Rt 40
(61361)
Rates: n/a
Tel: (815) 454-2603

SHELBYVILLE

LITHIA RESORT
RR 4, Box 105
(62565)
Rates: $52-$109
Tel: (217) 774-2882

SPILLWAY MOTEL
Hwy 16 E (62565)
Rates: n/a
Tel: (217) 774-9591

SHOREWOOD

DAYS INN
19747 Frontage Rd
(60435)
Rates: $47-139
Tel: (815) 725-2180
(800) 329-7466

SKOKIE

**HOLIDAY INN
NORTH SHORE**
5300 W Touhy Ave
(60077)
Rates: $98-$115
Tel: (847) 679-8900
(800) 465-4329

**HOWARD JOHNSON
HOTEL**
9333 Skokie Blvd
(60077)
Rates: $77-$108
Tel: (847) 679-4200
(800) 654-2000

**HILTON & TOWERS
NORTH SHORE**
9599 Skokie Blvd
(60077)
Rates: $115-$175
Tel: (847) 679-7000
(800) 445-8667

SOUTH
HOLLAND

RED ROOF INN
17301 S Halsted St
(60473)
Rates: $39-$51
Tel: (708) 331-1621
(800) 843-7663

SPARTA

**MAC'S SPARTA
MOTEL**
700 S St. Louis St
(62286)
Rates: n/a
Tel: (618) 443-3614

POOLSIDE MOTEL
402 E Broadway
(62286)
Rates: n/a
Tel: (618) 443-3187

SPRING VALLEY

RIVIERA MOTEL
I-80 & Rt 89 (61362)
Rates: n/a
Tel: (815) 894-2225

SPRINGFIELD

**BEST INNS
OF AMERICA**
500 N 1st St (62702)
Rates: $42-$55
Tel: (217) 522-1100
(800) 237-8466

**BEST WESTERN
LINCOLN PLAZA
HOTEL**
101 E Adams St
(62701)
Rates: $55-$100
Tel: (217) 523-5661
(800) 528-1234

**CAPITOL PLAZA
HOTEL**
418 E Jefferson St
(62701)
Rates: n/a
Tel: (217) 525-1700

COMFORT INN
3442 Freedom Dr
(62704)
Rates: $44-$66
Tel: (217) 787-2250
(800) 221-2222

DAYS INN
3000 Stevenson Dr
(62703)
Rates: $44-$58
Tel: (217) 529-0171
(800) 329-7466

DRURY INN
3180 S Dirksen Pkwy
(62703)
Rates: $53-$65
Tel: (217) 529-3900
(800) 325-8300

FAIRFIELD INN
3446 Freedom Dr
(62704)
Rates: $46-$66
Tel: (217) 793-9277
(800) 228-2800

HILTON HOTEL
700 E Adams St
(62701)
Rates: $70-$137
Tel: (217) 789-1530
(800) 445-8667

HOLIDAY INN-EAST HOTEL & CONFERENCE CTR
3100 S Dirksen Pkwy
(62703)
Rates: $63-$85
Tel: (217) 529-7171

MANSION VIEW MOTEL
529 S 4th St (62701)
Rates: $38-$50
Tel: (217) 544-7411
(800) 252-1083

MOTEL 6
3125 Wide Track Dr
(62703)
Rates: $24-$35
Tel: (217) 789-1063
(800) 440-6000

MOTEL 6
6010 S 6th St (62707)
Rates: $27-$33
Tel: (217) 529-1633
(800) 440-6000

PARK INN
3751 S Sixth St
(62703)
Rates: n/a
Tel: (217) 529-5511

PEAR TREE INN
3190 S Dirksen Pkwy
(62703)
Rates: $40-$55
Tel: (217) 529-9100
(800) 282-8733

RAMADA INN
625 E St Joseph St
(62703)
Rates: $59-150
Tel: (217) 529-7131
(800) 272-6232

RED ROOF INN
3200 Singer Ave
(62703)
Rates: $30-$51
Tel: (217) 753-4302
(800) 843-7663

SLEEP IN
3470 Freedom Dr
(62704)
Rates: $40-$60
Tel: (217) 787-6200
(800) 221-2222

SUPER 8 MOTEL
1330 S Dirksen Pkwy
(62703)
Rates: $37-$57
Tel: (217) 528-8889
(800) 800-8000

SUPER 8 MOTEL
3675 S 6th St (62703)
Rates: $36-$55
Tel: (217) 529-8898
(800) 800-8000

TRAVELODGE SKY HARBOR CONF CTR
1701 Jones Pkwy
(62702)
Rates: $35-$79
Tel: (217) 753-3446
(800) 578-7878

STAUNTON

SUPER 8 MOTEL
832 E Main St
(62088)
Rates: $37-$52
Tel: (618) 635-5353
(800) 800-8000

SULLIVAN

GATEWAY INN
S Hamilton (61951)
Rates: n/a
Tel: (217) 728-4314

TAYLORVILLE

RYAN'S INN
Rt 29 S & 48 Bypass
(62568)
Rates: n/a
Tel: (217) 287-7211
(800) 252-4748

29 WEST MOTEL
709 Springfield Rd
(62568)
Rates: $27-$33
Tel: (217) 824-2216

TINLEY PARK

HAMPTON INN
18501 North Creek
Rd. (60477)
Rates: $58-$75
Tel: (708) 633-0602
(800) 426-7866

BUDGETEL INN
7255 W 183rd St
(60477)
Rates: n/a
Tel: (800) 428-3438

TONICA

KISHAUWAU ON THE VERMILION
RR 1 (61370)
Rates: n/a
Tel: (815) 442-8453

TROY

SCOTTISH INNS
909 Edwardsville Rd
(62294)
Rates: $30-$40
Tel: (618) 667-9969
(800) 251-1962

TUSCOLA

SUPER 8 MOTEL
Rt 36, Box 202
(61953)
Rates: $38-$60
Tel: (217) 253-5488
(800) 800-8000

ULLIN

BEST WESTERN CHEEKWOOD
I-57, Exit 18 (62992)
Rates: $34-$47
Tel: (618) 845-3773
(800) 528-1234

URBANA

BEST WESTERN CUNNINGHAM PLACE
1907 N Cunningham
(61801)
Rates: $58-$150
Tel: (217) 367-8331
(800) 528-1234

JUMER'S CASTLE LODGE
209 S Broadway
(61801)
Rates: $72-$125
Tel: (217) 384-8800
(800) 285-8637

MOTEL 6
1906 N Cunningham
Ave (61801)
Rates: $30-$34
Tel: (217) 344-1082
(800) 440-6000

PARK INN & CONFERENCE CTR
2408 N Cunningham
Ave (61801)
Rates: n/a
Tel: (217) 344-8000

RAMADA EXPRESS
902 W Killaraney
(61801)
Rates: $55-$80
Tel: (217) 328-4400
(800) 272-6232

VANDALIA

DAYS INN
Hwy 51 N (62471)
Rates: $32-$125
Tel: (618) 283-4400
(800) 329-7466

RAMADA LIMITED
Rt 40 W (62471)
Rates: $47-$67
Tel: (618) 283-1400
(800) 272-6232

JAY'S MOTEL
I-70 & Rt 51 (62471)
Rates: $23-$30
Tel: (618) 283-1200

TRAVELODGE
1500 N 6th St (62471)
Rates: $36-$46
Tel: (618) 283-2363
(800) 578-7878

VILLA PARK

MOTEL 6
10 W Roosevelt Rd
(60181)
Rates: $39-$45
Tel: (708) 941-9100
(800) 440-6000

MOTEL 6
10 W Roosevelt Rd
(60181)
Rates: $32-$38
Tel: (708) 941-9100
(800) 440-6000

WASHINGTON

CRESTVIEW MOTEL
1216 Peoria St
(61571)
Rates: n/a
Tel: (309) 444-4421

SUPER 8 MOTEL
1884 Washington Rd
(61571)
Rates: $38-$55
Tel: (309) 444-8881
(800) 800-8000

WATSEKA

CAROUSEL INN MOTEL
1120 E Walnut St
(60970)
Rates: $29-$40
Tel: (815) 432-4966

SUPER 8 MOTEL
710 W Walnut St
(60970)
Rates: $44-$62
Tel: (815) 432-6000
(800) 800-8000

WATSEKA MOTEL
814 E Walnut St
(60970)
Rates: n/a
Tel: (815) 432-2426

WAUKEGAN

AIRPORT INN
3651 Lewis Ave
(60087)
Rates: n/a
Tel: (708) 249-7777

BEST INNS OF AMERICA
31 N Green Bay Rd
(60085)
Rates: $39-$57
Tel: (847) 336-9000
(800) 237-8466

BEST WESTERN OF WAUKEGAN
411 S Green Bay Rd
(60085)
Rates: $39-$99
Tel: (847) 244-6100
(800) 528-1234

SLUMBERLAND MOTEL
3030 Belvidere Rd
(60085)
Rates: n/a
Tel: (847) 623-6830

TRAVELODGE
222 W Grand Ave
(60085)
Rates: $43-$66
Tel: (847) 244-8950
(800) 578-7878

WENONA

SUPER 8 MOTEL
I-39 &IL 17, Exit 35
(61377)
Rates: $39-55
Tel: (815) 853-4371
(800) 800-8000

WEST FRANKFORT

GRAY PLAZA MOTEL
1010 W Main St
(62896)
Rates: n/a
Tel: (618) 932-3116

WESTMONT

BEST WESTERN AMBASSADOR INN
669 Pasquinelli Dr
(60559)
Rates: $45-$65
Tel: (708) 323-1515
(800) 528-1234

WILLOWBROOK

BUDGETEL INN
855 W 79th St
(60521)
Rates: $48-$66
Tel: (708) 654-0077
(800) 428-3438

HOLIDAY INN
7800 S Kingery Hwy
(60521)
Rates: $74-$102
Tel: (708) 325-6400
(800) 465-4329

RED ROOF INN
7535 S Kingery Hwy
(60521)
Rates: $36-$57
Tel: (708) 323-8811
(800) 843-7663

WINDSOR

THE DEERFIELD BED & BREAKFAST
RR 1, Box 99-A
(61957)
Rates: n/a
Tel: (217) 459-2750

WINTHROP HARBOR

SANDPIPER INN
301 Sheridan Rd
(60096)
Rates: $32-$50
Tel: (847) 746-7380

WOOD RIVER

BEL AIR MOTEL
542 West Ferguson
Ave (62095)
Rates: n/a
Tel: (618) 254-0683

WOODSTOCK

BUNDLING BOARD INN
220 E South St
(60098)
Rates: n/a
Tel: (815) 338-7054

CONCORD COUNTRY INN
1122 Cass St (60098)
Rates: n/a
Tel: (815) 338-1100

INDIANA

ALEXANDRIA

COUNTRY GAZEBO INN
RR 1 Box 323 (46001)
Rates: n/a
Tel: (317) 754-8783

ANDERSON

BEST INNS
5706 Scatterfield Rd
(46013)
Rates: $38-$49
Tel: (317) 644-2000

COMFORT INN
2205 E 59th St
(46013)
Rates: $38-$53
Tel: (800) 221-2222

HOLIDAY INN
5920 Scatterfield Rd
(46013)
Rates: $57-$78
Tel: (800) 465-4329

LEES INN
2114 E 59th St
(46013)
Rates: $54-$75
Tel: (317) 649-2500
(800) 733-5337

RAMADA INN
5901 Scatterfield Rd
(46013)
Rates: $65-75
Tel: (317) 649-0451
(800) 272-6232

AUBURN

AUBURN INN
225 Touring Dr
(46706)
Rates: $55-$79
Tel: (800) 255-2541

BEDFORD

ROSEMOUNT MOTEL
1923 M St (47421)
Rates: $28-$31
Tel: (812) 275-5953

BLOOMINGTON

BEST WESTERN FIRESIDE INN
4501 E Third St
(47401)
Rates: $36-$99
Tel: (812) 332-2141
(800) 528-1234

COURTYARD INN
4501 E 3rd St (47401)
Rates: $32-$89
Tel: (800) 331-3131

DAYS INN
200 Matlock Rd
(47401)
Rates: $49-$79
Tel: (812) 336-0905
(800) 329-7466

HAMPTON INN
2100 N Walnut St
(47408)
Rates: $49-$67
Tel: (800) 426-7866

MOTEL 6
1800 N Walnut
(47401)
Rates: $28-$34
Tel: (812) 332-0820

RAMADA LTD INN
2601 N Walnut
(47402)
Rates: $35-$50
Tel: (812) 332-9453

SUPER 8 MOTEL
1000 W State Rd
(47401)
Rates: $42-$50
Tel: (800) 800-8000

BRAZIL

HOWARD JOHNSON
935 W State Rd 42
(47834)
Rates: $32-$40
Tel: (812) 446-2345
(800) 446-4656

BROOKVILLE

SULINA FARM
10052 US 52 (47012)
Rates: n/a
Tel: (317) 647-2955

CARLISLE

SUPER 8 MOTEL
Hwy 41 S, Box 205
(47838)
Rates: $34-$49
Tel: (812) 398-2500
(800) 800-8000

CENTERVILLE

SUPER 8 MOTEL
2407 N Centerville
Rd (47330)
Rates: $38-$52
Tel: (317) 855-5461
(800) 800-8000

CLARKSVILLE

BEST WESTERN GREENTREE INN
1425 Broadway
(47129)
Rates: $42-$50
Tel: (800) 528-1234

HOWARD JOHNSON
342 Eastern Blvd
(47129)
Rates: $40-$75
Tel: (812) 282-7511
(800) 446-4656

CLINTON

RENATTO INN
SR 63 & 163 (47842)
Rates: $33-$46
Tel: (317) 832-3557

COLUMBIA CITY

COLUMBIA CITY MOTEL
500 Old US 30W
(46725)
Rates: $21-$38
Tel: (219) 244-5103

LEES INN
235 Frontage Rd
(46725)
Rates: $52-$66
Tel: (219) 244-5300
(800) 733-5337

COLUMBUS

COMFORT INN
P. O. Box 506
(Taylorsville 47280)
Rates: $47-$55
Tel: (800) 221-2222

CORYDON

BEST WESTERN OLD CAPITOL INN
SR 135 (47112)
Rates: $38-$65
Tel: (800) 528-1234

CRAWFORDSVILLE

THE DAVIS HOUSE BED & BREAKFAST
1010 W Wabash Ave
(47933)
Rates: $50-$60
Tel: (317) 364-0461

GENERAL LEW WALLACE INN
309 W Pike St
(47933)
Rates: $37-$43
Tel: (317) 362-8400

HOLIDAY INN
2500 N Lafayette Rd
(47933)
Rates: $50-$73
Tel: (800) 465-4329

SUPER 8 MOTEL
1025 Carey Blvd
(47933)
Rates: $35-$50
Tel: (317) 364-9999

DALE

SCOTTISH INNS
I-64 & US 231
(47523)
Rates: $30-$39
Tel: (812) 937-2816
(800) 251-1962

DECATUR

DAYS INN
1033 N 13th St
(46733)
Rates: $36-80
Tel: (219) 728-2196
(800) 329-7466

ELKHART

DIPLOMAT MOTEL
52162 SR 19N
(46514)
Rates: $24-$42
Tel: (219) 264-4118

ECONO LODGE
3440 Cassopolis St
(46514)
Rates: $30-$70
Tel: (219) 262-0540
(800)424-4777

KNIGHTS INN
52188 SR 19 (46514)
Rates: $30-$49
Tel: (800) 843-5644

**QUALITY HOTEL
CITY CENTRE**
300 S Main St
(46516)
Rates: $49-$90
Tel: (219) 295-0280

RED ROOF INN
2902 Cassopolis St
(46514)
Rates: $33-$41
Tel: (800) 843-7663

SUPER 8 MOTEL
345 Windsor Ave
(46514)
Rates: $35-$44
Tel: (800) 800-8000

EVANSVILLE

COMFORT INN
5006 Morgan Ave
(47715)
Rates: $43-$70
Tel: (800) 221-2222

DAYS INN
4819 Tecumsen Ln
(47715)
Rates: $45-90
Tel: (812) 473-7944
(800) 329-7466

**DRURY INN-
EVANSVILLE**
3901 US 41N (47711)
Rates: $49-$58
Tel: (800) 325-8300

LEES INN
5538 E Indiana St
(47715)
Rates: $49-$70
Tel: (812) 477-6663
(800) 733-5337

SUPER 8 MOTEL
4600 Morgan Ave
(47715)
Rates: $36-$44
Tel: (800) 800-8000

FISHERS

**HOLIDAY INN
EXPRESS-
INDIANAPOLIS
NORTHEAST**
9790 North by
Northeast Blvd
(46038)
Rates: $50-$65
Tel: (800) 465-4329

RAMADA INN
9780 N by NE Blvd
(46038)
Rates: $64-$150
Tel: (317) 578-9000
(800) 272-6232

FORT WAYNE

**BEST INNS
OF AMERICA**
3017 W Coliseum
Blvd (46808)
Rates: $35-$46
Tel: (219) 483-0091

BUDGETEL INN
1005 W Washington
Center Rd (46825)
Rates: $37-$53
Tel: (219) 489-2220

COMFORT INN
2908 Goshen Rd
(46802)
Rates: $45-$67
Tel: (800) 221-2222

**DAYS INN
EAST DOWNTOWN**
3730 E Washington
Blvd (46803)
Rates: $30-$52
Tel: (219) 424-1980
(800) 329-7466

DAYS INN
I-69 Exit 111A
(46825)
Rates: $29-$39
Tel: (219) 484-9681
(800) 329-7466

ECONOMY INN
1401 W Washington
Center Rd
(46825)
Rates: $26-$37
Tel: (219) 489-3588

**FORT WAYNE
MARRIOTT**
305 E Washington
Center Rd (46825)
Rates: $65-$109
Tel: (219) 484-0411

HAMPTON INN
5702 Challenger
Pkwy (46818)
Rates: $68-$74
Tel: (219) 489-0908
(800) 426-7866

HOMETOWN INN
6910 US 30E (46803)
Rates: $29-$36
Tel: (219) 749-5058

**KNIGHT'S INN-
NORTH**
2901 Goshen Rd
(46808)
Rates: $38-$43
Tel: (800) 843-5644

LEES INN
5707 Challenger
Pkwy (46818)
Rates: $53-$74
Tel: (219) 489-8888
(800) 733-5337

RED ROOF INN
2920 Goshen Rd
(46808)
Rates: $29-$38
Tel: (800) 843-7663

**RESIDENCE INN
BY MARRIOTT**
4919 Lima Rd
(46808)
Rates: $90-$115
Tel: (800) 331-3131

FRANKLIN

DAYS INN
2180 E King St
(46131)
Rates: $47-$77
Tel: (317) 736-8000
(800) 329-7466

FREMONT

E & L MOTEL
35 W SR 120 (46737)
Rates: $25-$38
Tel: (219) 495-3300

FRENCH LICK

LANE MOTEL
Box 224 (47432)
Rates: $30-$37
Tel: (812) 936-9919

**THE PINES AT
PATOKA LAKE
VILLAGE**
RR 2, Box 255E
(47432)
Rates: $60-$75
Tel: (812) 936-9854

GOSHEN

BEST WESTERN INN
900 Lincolnway E
(46526)
Rates: $51-$59
Tel: (219) 533-0408
(800) 528-1234

COUNTRY B & B
27727 CR 36 (46526)
Rates: n/a
Tel: (219) 862-2748

GREENCASTLE

COLLEGE INN
315 Bloomington St
(46135)
Rates: $22-$33
Tel: (317) 653-4167

GREENFIELD

HOWARD HUGHES MOTOR LODGE
1310 W Main St
(46140)
Rates: $31-$38
Tel: (317) 462-4493

LEES INN
2270 N State St
(46140)
Rates: $49-$70
Tel: (317) 462-7112
(800) 733-5337

GREENSBURG

BEST WESTERN PINES INN
Rt 1, Box 61E (47240)
Rates: $46-$57
Tel: (800) 528-1234

LEES INN
2211 N State Rd 3
(47240)
Rates: $49-$63
Tel: (812) 663-9998
(800) 733-5837

GREENWOOD

COMFORT INN
P. O. Box 901 (46143)
Rates: $39-$100
Tel: (800) 221-2222

LEES INN
1281 S Park Dr
(46413)
Rates: n/a
Tel: (317) 865-0100
(800) 733-5337

HOWE

SUPER 8 MOTEL
7333 N SR 9 (46746)
Rates: $40-$50
Tel: (800) 800-8000

HUNTINGTON

DAYS INN
2996 W Park Dr
(46750)
Rates: $40-$67
Tel: (219) 359-8989
(800) 329-7466

INDIANAPOLIS

BUDGETEL INN
2650 Executive Dr
(46241)
Rates: $36-$52
Tel: (317) 244-8100

THE CANTERBURY HOTEL
123 S Illinois St
(46225)
Rates: $145-$350
Tel: (800) 538-8186

COMFORT INN-NORTH
3880 W 92nd St
(46268)
Rates: $40-$175
Tel: (800) 221-2222

COURTYARD BY MARRIOTT-DOWNTOWN
501 W Washington
St (46204)
Rates: $49-$109
Tel: (800) 331-3131

DAYS INN EAST
7314 E 21st St
(46219)
Rates: $39-$55
Tel: (317) 359-5500
(800) 329-7466

DAYS INN-NORTHWEST
3740 N High School
Rd (46224)
Rates: $39-$75
Tel: (317) 293-6550
(800) 329-7466

DAYS INN-SOUTH
450 Bixler Rd (46227)
Rates: $36-$65
Tel: (317) 788-0811
(800) 329-7466

DAYS INN
8275 Craig St (46250)
Rates: $59-$109
Tel: (317) 841-9700
(800) 329-7466

DRURY INN
9320 N Michigan Rd
(46268)
Rates: $52-$67
Tel: (800) 325-8300

HAMPTON INN-EAST
2311 N Shadeland
Ave (46219)
Rates: $50-$61
Tel: (800) 426-7866

HAMPTON INN NORTHWEST
7220 Woodland Dr
(46278)
Rates: $50-$61
Tel: (800) 426-7866

HOJO INN
2602 N High School
Rd (46224)
Rates: $35-$60
Tel: (800) 446-4656

HOLIDAY INN
2501 S High School
Rd (46241)
Rates: $99
Tel: (800) 465-4329

HOLIDAY INN-EAST
6990 E 21st St
(46219)
Rates: $61-$66
Tel: (800) 465-4329

HOMEWOOD SUITES-AT THE CROSSING
2501 E 86th St
(46240)
Rates: $89-$99
Tel: (317) 253-1919

HOWARD JOHNSON
7050 E 21st St
(46219)
Rates: $36-$48
Tel: (317) 352-0481
(800) 446-4656

KNIGHTS INN-NORTH
9402 Haver Way
(46240)
Rates: $36-$54
Tel: (800) 843-5644

KNIGHTS INN-SOUTH
4909 Knights Way
(46217)
Rates: $31-$41
Tel: (800) 843-5644

LA QUINTA INN-AIRPORT
5316 W Southern
Ave (46241)
Rates: $50-$64
Tel: (800) 531-5900

LA QUINTA INN-EAST
7304 E 21st St (46219)
Rates: $45-$52
Tel: (800) 531-5900

LEES INN
5011 N Lafayette Rd
(46254)
Rates: $55-$76
Tel: (317) 297-8880
(800) 733-5337

PICKWICK FARMS SHORT-TERM APTS.
9300 N Ditch Rd
(46260)
Rates: $50-$60
Tel: (317) 872-6506

QUALITY INN CASTLETON SUITES
8275 Craig St (46250)
Rates: $65-$210
Tel: (800) 221-2222

RADISSON PLAZA AND SUITE HOTEL
8787 Keystone
Crossing (46240)
Rates: $96-$130
Tel: (317) 846-2700

RED ROOF INN-NORTH
9520 Vaparaiso Ct
(46268)
Rates: $30-$53
Tel: (800) 843-7663

RED ROOF INN-SPEEDWAY
6415 Debonair Ln
(46224)
Rates: $30-$51
Tel: (800) 843-7663

RESIDENCE INN
9765 Cross Point
Blvd (46256)
Rates: n/a
Tel: (800) 331-3131

SUPER 8 MOTEL
4502 S Harding
(46217)
Rates: $31-$38
Tel: (800) 800-8000

SUPER 8 MOTEL
8850 E 21st St
(46219)
Rates: $39-$48
Tel: (317) 895-5402
(800) 800-8000

JASPER

DAYS INN JAPSER
272 Bruckestrasse
(47547)
Rates: $49-$68
Tel: (812) 482-6000
(800) 329-7466

JEFFERSONVILLE

DAYS INN
350 Eastern Blvd
(47130)
Rates: $33-$47
Tel: (812) 288-9331
(800) 329-7466

RAMADA HOTEL
700 W Riverside Dr
(47130)
Rates: $57-$90
Tel: (812) 284-6711

KENTLAND

TRI-WAY INN
611 E Dunlap St
(47951)
Rates: $31-$42
Tel: (219) 474-5141

KOKOMO

COMFORT INN
522 Essex Dr (46901)
Rates: $43-$56
Tel: (800) 221-2222

FAIRFIELD INN
1717 E Lincoln Rd
(46902)
Rates: $42-$53
Tel: (317) 453-8822

MOTEL 6
2808 S Reed Rd
(46902)
Rates: $32-$41
Tel: (317) 457-8211
(800) 466-8356

LAFAYETTE

DAYS INN
400 S Sagamore
Pkwy (47905)
Rates: $45-$100
Tel: (317) 447-4131
(800) 329-7466

HOLIDAY INN
201 Frontage Rd
(47905)
Rates: $40-$60
Tel: (800) 465-4329

**HOMEWOOD
SUITES**
3939 SR 26E (47905)
Rates: $75-$139
Tel: (317) 448-9700

KNIGHTS INN
4110 SR 26E (47905)
Rates: $34-$70
Tel: (800) 843-5644

RADISSON INN
4343 SR 26E (47905)
Rates: $73-$89
Tel: (800) 333-3333

RED ROOF INN
4201 SR 26E (47905)
Rates: $33-$44
Tel: (800) 843-7663

LA PORTE

PINE LAKE HOTEL
444 Pine Lake Ave
(46350)
Rates: $50-$74
Tel: (800) 465-4329

LEBANON

HOLIDAY INN
P. O. Box 582 (46052)
Rates: $48-$75
Tel: (800) 465-4329

LEES INN
1245 SR 32W (46052)
Rates: $52-$66
Tel: (317) 482-9611
(800) 733-5337

LINGONIER

MINUETTE B & B
210 S Main St
(46767)
Rates: n/a
Tel: (219) 894-4494

LOGANSPORT

HOLIDAY INN
P. O. Box 813 (46947)
Rates: $58-$75
Tel: (800) 465-4329

SUPER 8 MOTEL
P. O. Box 813 (46947)
Rates: $44-$53
Tel: (800) 800-8000

MADISON

**BEST WESTERN
OF MADISON**
700 Clifty Dr, Hwy
62 (47250)
Rates: $52-$68
Tel: (812) 273-5151
(800) 528-1234

**PRESIDENT
MADISON MOTEL**
906 E 1st St (47250)
Rates: $30-$36
Tel: (812) 265-2361

MARION

**BROADMOOR
MOTEL**
1323 N Baldwin Ave
(46952)
Rates: $31-$39
Tel: (317) 664-0501

HOLIDAY INN
501 E 4th St (46952)
Rates: $45-$48
Tel: (317) 668-8801

MARTINSVILLE

LEES INN
50 Bill's Blvd (46151)
Rates: $52-$66
Tel: (317) 342-1842
(800) 733-5337

MERRILLVILLE

CARLTON LODGE
7850 Rhode Island
Ave (46410)
Rates: $69-$130
Tel: (219) 756-1600

DAYS INN
Mississippi Ave &
82nd St (46410)
Rates: $52-$95
Tel: (800) 329-7466

KNIGHTS INN
8250 Louisiana St
(46410)
Rates: $31-$44
Tel: (800) 843-5644

LA QUINTA INN
8210 Louisiana St
(46410)
Rates: $48-$62
Tel: (800) 221-4731

MOTEL 6
8290 Louisianna St
(46410)
Rates: $32-$38
Tel: (219) 738-2701

**RADISSON HOTEL
AT STAR PLAZA**
800 E 81st Ave
(46410)
Rates: $69
Tel: (219) 769-6311

RED ROOF INN
8290 Georgia St
(46410)
Rates: $36-$55
Tel: (800) 843-7663

RESIDENCE INN
8018 Delaware Place
(46410)
Rates: n/a
Tel: (800) 331-3131

SUPER 8 MOTEL
8300 Louisianna St
(46410)
Rates: $40-$53
Tel: (800) 800-8000

METAMORA

**THORPE HOUSE
COUNTRY INN**
P.O. Box 36 (47030)
Rates: n/a
Tel: (317) 647-5425

MICHIGAN CITY

**CITY MANOR
MOTEL**
5225 Franklin St
(46360)
Rates: $29+
Tel: (219) 872-9149

KNIGHTS INN
201 W Kieffer Rd
(46360)
Rates: $29-$65
Tel: (800) 843-5644

RED ROOF INN
110 W Kieffer Rd
(46360)
Rates: $33-$50
Tel: (800) 843-7663

MIDDLEBURY

THE THAYER HOUSE
14604 CR 22 (46540)
Rates: n/a
Tel: (219) 825-7926

MISHAWAKA

HAMPTON INN
445 University Dr.
(46545)
Rates: $64-$76
Tel: (219) 273-2309
(800) 426-7866

MONTICELLO

**1887 BLACK
DOG INN**
2830 Untaluti
(47960)
Rates: n/a
Tel: (219) 583-8297

**MOUNT
VERNON**

**FOUR SEASONS
MOTEL**
2400 W 4th St
(41620)
Rates: $41-$91
Tel: (812) 838-4821

MUNCIE

COMFORT INN
4011 W Bethel Ave
(47305)
Rates: $41-$60
Tel: (800) 221-2222

DAYS INN
3509 N Everbrook
Ln (47304)
Rates: $40-$55
Tel: (317) 288-2311
(800) 329-7466

HOLIDAY INN
3400 S Madison
(47302)
Rates: $47-$52
Tel: (800) 465-4329

LEES INN
3302 Everbrook Ln
(47304)
Rates: $54-$75
Tel: (317) 282-7557
(800) 733-5337

RADISSON HOTEL
420 S High St (47305)
Rates: $54
Tel: (317) 741-7777

SUPER 8 MOTEL
3601 W Fox Ridge
Ln (47304)
Rates: $35-$46
Tel: (800) 800-8000

NAPPANEE

**VICTORIAN
GUEST HOUSE**
302 E Market (46550)
Rates: n/a
Tel: (219) 773-4383

NASHVILLE

SALT CREEK INN
Box 397 (47448)
Rates: $40-$110
Tel: (812) 988-1149

STORY INN
6404 S SR 135
(47448)
Rates: n/a
Tel: (812) 988-2273

NEW ALBANY

**HOLIDAY INN-
NORTHWEST**
411 W Spring St
(47150)
Rates: $60-$66
Tel: (812) 945-2771

NEW CASTLE

**BEST WESTERN
RAINTREE INN**
2836 S SR 3 (47362)
Rates: $32-$75
Tel: (800) 528-1234

DAYS INN
5343 S State Rd 3
(47362)
Rates: $29-$41
Tel: (317) 987-8205
(800) 329-7466

PLYMOUTH

DAYS INN
2229 Michigan St
(46563)
Rates: $39-49
Tel: (219) 935-4276
(800) 329-7466

SUPER 8 MOTEL
2150 N Oak Rd #4
(46563)
Rates: $49-$53
Tel: (800) 800-8000

PORTAGE

DAYS INN
6161 Melton Rd
(46368)
Rates: $49-$79
Tel: (219) 762-2136
(800) 329-7466

**INDIANA DUNES
MOTEL**
6200 Melton Rd
(46368)
Rates: $66-$72
Tel: (800) 437-5145

LEES INN
2300 Willowcreek
(46368)
Rates: $52-$73
Tel: (219) 763-7177
(800) 733-5337

REMINGTON

DAYS INN
4252 W Hwy 24
(47977)
Rates: $45-$49
Tel: (219) 261-2178
(800) 329-7466

RENSSELAER

INTERSTATE MOTEL
8530 W St Rd Hwy
(47978)
Rates: $30-$40
Tel: (219) 866-4164

REYNOLDS

PARK VIEW MOTEL
RR 1, Box 4 (47980)
Rates: $25-$55
Tel: (219) 984-5380

RICHMOND

**BEST WESTERN
IMPERIAL
MOTOR LODGE**
3020 E Main St
(47374)
Rates: $32-$66
Tel: (317) 966-1505
(800) 528-1234

COMFORT INN
912 Mendelson Dr
(47374)
Rates: $42-$63
Tel: (800) 221-2222

DAYS INN
540 W Eaton Pike
(47374)
Rates: $40-$66
Tel: (317) 966-7591
(800) 329-7466

HOLIDAY INN
5501 E National Rd
(47374)
Rates: $39-$125
Tel: (800) 465-4329

HOWARD JOHNSON LODGE
2525 Chester Blvd
(47374)
Rates: $32-$47
Tel: (800) 654-2000

LEES INN
6030 E National Rd
(47374)
Rates: $55-$76
Tel: (317) 966-6559
(800) 733-5337

RAMADA INN
4700 E National Rd
(47374)
Rates: $49-$59
Tel: (800) 272-6232

VILLA MOTEL
533 W Eaton Pike
(47374)
Rates: $20-$27
Tel: (317) 962-5202

ROCHESTER

ROSE DALE MOTEL
RR 1, Box 280
(46975)
Rates: $25-$32
Tel: (219) 223-3185

SCOTTSBURG

BEST WESTERN SCOTTSBURG INN
P. O. Box 129 (47170)
Rates: $51-$115
Tel: (812) 752-2212
(800) 528-1234

CAMPBELL'S MOTEL
300 N Gardner
(47170)
Rates: $20-$45
Tel: (812) 752-4401

MARIANN TRAVEL INN
P. O. Box 36 (47170)
Rates: $30-$46
Tel: (812) 752-3396

SEYMOUR

DAYS INN
302 S Commerce Dr
(47274)
Rates: $38-$100
Tel: (812) 522-3678
(800) 329-7466

KNIGHTS INN
207 N Frontage Rd
(47274)
Rates: $32-$39
Tel: (800) 722-7220

LEES INN
2075 E Tipton St
(47274)
Rates: $54-$75
Tel: (812) 523-1850
(800) 733-5337

SUPER 8 MOTEL
Hwy 65 & 50 (47274)
Rates: $39-$53
Tel: (800) 800-8000

SHELBYVILLE

HOLIDAY INN
1810 N Riley Hwy
(46176)
Rates: $55-$67
Tel: (800) 465-4329

LEES INN
2880 SR 44E (46176)
Rates: $51-$72
Tel: (317) 392-2299
(800) 733-5337

SOUTH BEND

BEST INNS OF AMERICA
425 Dixie Hwy N
(46637)
Rates: $35-$53
Tel: (219) 277-7700

DAYS INN
52757 US 31 S
(46637)
Rates: $45-$99
Tel: (219) 277-0510
(800) 329-7466

HAMPTON INN
52709 US 31 North
(46637)
Rates: $69-$155
Tel: (219) 277-9373
(800) 426-7866

HOLIDAY INN-UNIVERSITY AREA
515 Dixie Way N
(46637)
Rates: $67-$88
Tel: (800) 465-4329

KNIGHTS INN-SOUTH BEND
236 Dixie Way N
(46637)
Rates: $33-$40
Tel: (800) 843-5644

SUPER 8 MOTEL
52825 US 31-33 N
(46637)
Rates: $40-$60
Tel: (219) 272-9000
(800) 800-8000

UNIVERSITY PARK INN
52939 US 31 & 33N
(46637)
Rates: $30-$85
Tel: (219) 272-1500

SPEEDWAY

MOTEL 6
6330 Debonair Ln
(46224)
Rates: $30-$37
Tel: (317) 293-3220
(800) 466-8356

SULLIVAN

DAYS INN
P. O. Box 97 (47882)
Rates: $39-$55
Tel: (812) 268-6391
(800) 329-7466

TELL CITY

DAYSTOP
Hwy 66 & 14th St
(47586)
Rates: $32-$52
Tel: (812) 547-3474
(800) 329-7466

RAMADA INN
235 Orchard Hill Dr
(47586)
Rates: $65-$115
Tel: (812) 547-3234
(800) 272-6232

TERRE HAUTE

BEST WESTERN-LINDEN
3325 Dixie Bee Rd
(47802)
Rates: $48-$160
Tel: (800) 528-1234

KNIGHTS INN
401 Margaret Ave
(47802)
Rates: $37-$44
Tel: (800) 843-5644

MID TOWN MOTEL
400 S 3rd St (47807)
Rates: $25-$32
Tel: (812) 232-0383

PEAR TREE INN
3050 S US Hwy 41
(47802)
Rates: $37-$72
Tel: (800) 282-8733

SUPER 8 LODGE
3089 S 1st St (47802)
Rates: $38-$54
Tel: (800) 800-8000

THRIFTLODGE
530 S 3rd St (47807)
Rates: $33-$45
Tel: (812) 232-7075

WOODBRIDGE MOTEL
4545 Wabash Ave
(47803)
Rates: $26-$34
Tel: (812) 877-1571

VINCENNES

BEST WESTERN INN
2500 Old Decker Rd
(47591)
Rates: $50-$60
Tel: (800) 528-1234

HOLIDAY INN
600 Wheatland Rd
(47591)
Rates: $48-$60
Tel: (800) 465-4329

SUPER 8 MOTEL
609 Shirlee St (47591)
Rates: $41-$56
Tel: (812) 882-5101
(800) 800-8000

VINCENNES LODGE
1411 Willow St
(47591)
Rates: $28-$38
Tel: (812) 882-1282

WABASH

**AROUND
WINDOW INN**
313 W Hill St (46992)
Rates: n/a
Tel: (219) 563-6901

WALKERTON

**HESTERS CABIN
BED & BREAKFAST**
71880 SR 23 (46574)
Rates: n/a
Tel: (219) 586-2105

WARSAW

COMFORT INN
2605 E Center St
(46580)
Rates: $50-$70
Tel: (800) 221-2222

DAYS INN
3521 Lake City Hwy
(46580)
Rates: $39-$62
Tel: (219) 269-3031
(800) 329-7466

HOLIDAY INN
2519 E Center
(46580)
Rates: $63+
Tel: (800) 465-4329

*WEST
LAFAYETTE*

HOLIDAY INN
5600 SR 4 3N (47906)
Rates: $53-$68
Tel: (800) 465-4329

TRAVELODGE
200 Brown St (47906)
Rates: $45-$71
Tel: (317) 743-9661
(800) 578-7878

WHITELAND

**WISHING WELL
MOTEL**
RR 1, Box 93 (46184)
Rates: $21-$25
Tel: (317) 535-7548

ZIONSVILLE

**THE BRICK STREET
INN**
175 S Main St
(46077)
Rates: n/a
Tel: (317) 873-9177

IOWA

ALGONA

IMA BURR OAK MOTEL
Hwy 169 S (50511)
Rates: $29-$45
Tel: (515) 295-7213
(800) 341-8000

ALBIA

INDIAN HILLS INN
Rt 1 (52531)
Rates: $32-$40
Tel: (515) 932-7181

AMANA COLONIES

HOLIDAY INN
P. O. Box 187 (52203)
Rates: $60-$85
Tel: (319) 668-1175
(800) 465-4329

AMES

BEST WESTERN STARLITE VILLAGE
2601 E 13th St
(50010)
Rates: $45-$62
Tel: (515) 232-9260
(800) 528-1234

BUDGETEL INN
2500 Elwood Dr
(50010)
Rates: $48-$54
Tel: (515) 296-2500

COMFORT INN
1605 S Dayton Ave
(50010)
Rates: $40-$61
Tel: (515) 232-0689
(800) 221-2222

HEARTLAND INN
Hwy 30 & I-35
(50010)
Rates: $42-$56
Tel: (515) 233-6060
(800) 334-3277

HOLIDAY INN-GATEWAY CTR
P. O. Box X (50010)
Rates: $74-$107
Tel: (515) 292-8600
(800) 465-4329

RAMADA INN
1206 S Duff (50010)
Rates: $48-$58
Tel: (515) 232-3410
(800) 272-6232

UNIVERSITY INN
316 S Duff (50010)
Rates: $38-$75
Tel: (515) 232-0280

ANKENY

BEST WESTERN STARLITE VILLAGE
133 SE Delaware,
Box 378 (50021)
Rates: $44-$64
Tel: (515) 964-1717
(800) 528-1234

DAYS INN
103 NE Delaware
(50021)
Rates: $40-$50
Tel: (515) 965-1995
(800) 329-7466

SUPER 8 MOTEL
206 SE Delaware St
(50021)
Rates: $42-$60
Tel: (515) 964-4503
(800) 800-8000

ARNOLDS PARK

FILLENWARTH BEACH COTTAGES
87 Lake Shore Dr
(51331)
Rates: $240-$960/
weekly
Tel: (712) 332-5646

ATLANTIC

ECONO LODGE
I-80 & US 71 (50022)
Rates: $37-$46
Tel: (712) 243-4067
(800) 424-4777

AVOCA

CAPRI MOTEL
P. O. Box 699 (51521)
Rates: $30-$45
Tel: (712) 343-6301

BLOOMFIELD

SOUTHFORK INN
P. O. Box 155 (52537)
Rates: $28-$37
Tel: (515) 664-1063

BOONE

SUPER 8 MOTEL
1715 S Story St
(50036)
Rates: $39-$54
Tel: (515) 432-8890
(800) 800-8000

BURLINGTON

BEST WESTERN PZAZZ MOTOR INN
3001 Winegard Dr
(52601)
Rates: $53-$65
Tel: (319) 753-2223
(800) 528-1234

COMFORT INN
3051 Kirkwood Ave
(52601)
Rates: $30-$65
Tel: (319) 753-0000
(800) 221-2222

DAYS INN
1601 N Roosevelt
(52601)
Rates: $35-$65
Tel: (319) 754-1111
(800) 329-7466

FRIENDSHIP INN
2731 Mt. Pleasant St
(52601)
Rates: $45-$65
Tel: (319) 754-7571
(800) 453-4511

RAMADA INN
2759 Mt. Pleasant St
(52601)
Rates: $55-$75
Tel: (319) 754-5781
(800) 272-6232

CARROLL

BEST WESTERN HOLIDAY
Hwy 30 West (51401)
Rates: $30-$56
Tel: (712) 792-9214
(800) 528-1234

ECONO LODGE
1225 Plaza Dr
(51401)
Rates: $45-$59
Tel: (712) 792-5156
(800) 424-4777

71-30 MOTEL
Jct US 30 & 71
(51401)
Rates: $30-$44
Tel: (712) 792-1100

SUPER 8 MOTEL
Hwy 71 N (51401)
Rates: $38-$51
Tel: (712) 792-4753
(800) 800-8000

CEDAR FALLS

BLACKHAWK MOTOR INN
122 Washington
(50613)
Rates: $32-$38
Tel: (319) 271-1161

ECONO LODGE
4117 University Ave
(50613)
Rates: $30-$61
Tel: (319) 277-6931
(800) 424-4777

HOLIDAY INN
5826 University Ave (50613)
Rates: $59-$75
Tel: (319) 277-1161
(800) 465-4329

MARQUIS INN
4711 University Ave (50613)
Rates: $28-$49
Tel: (319) 277-1412

CEDAR RAPIDS

COLLINS PLAZA HOTEL
1200 Collins Rd NE (52402)
Rates: $87-$121
Tel: (319) 393-6600

COMFORT INN-NORTH
5055 Rockwell Dr (52402)
Rates: $42-$64
Tel: (319) 393-8247
(800) 221-2222

COMFORT INN-SOUTH
390 33rd Ave SW (52404)
Rates: $39-$54
Tel: (319) 363-7934
(800) 221-2222

DAYS INN
3245 Southgate Place SW (52404)
Rates: $45-65
Tel: (319) 365-4339
(800) 329-7466

ECONO LODGE
622 33rd Ave SW (52404)
Rates: $39-$58
Tel: (319) 363-8888
(800) 424-4777

EXEL INN
616 33rd Ave SW (52404)
Rates: $31-$90
Tel: (319) 366-8888
(800) 356-8013

FIVE SEASONS HOTEL
350 1st Ave NE (52401)
Rates: $69-$109
Tel: (319) 363-8161

HOJO INN
3233 Southridge Dr SW (52404)
Rates: $43-$56
Tel: (319) 363-9999
(800) 446-4656

HOLIDAY INN
2501 Williams Blvd SW (52404)
Rate: $50-$80
Tel: (319) 365-9441
(800) 465-4329

RAMADA INN
4011 SW 16th Ave (52404)
Rates: $48-$70
Tel: (319) 396-5000
(800) 272-6232

RED ROOF INN
3325 Southgate Ct SW (52404)
Rates: $28-$49
Tel: (319) 366-7523
(800) 843-7663

SHERATON INN
525 33rd Ave SW (52404)
Rates: $62-$76
Tel: (319) 366-8671
(800) 325-3535

CHARITON

IMA ROYAL REST MOTEL
Hwy 14 & 34 E (50049-0349)
Rates: $28-$42
Tel: (515) 774-5961
(800) 341-8000

CHARLES CITY

HARTWOOD INN
1312 Gilbert St (50616)
Rates: $33-$65
Tel: (515) 228-4352

CHEROKEE

SUPER 8 MOTEL
1400 N Second St (51012)
Rates: $38-$55
Tel: (712) 225-4278
(800) 800-8000

CLEAR LAKE

BEST WESTERN INN
US 18, Box J (50248)
Rates: $49-$68
Tel: (515) 357-5253
(800) 528-1234

BUDGET INN
1306 N 25th St (50428)
Rates: $37-$44
Tel: (515) 357-8700

HEARTLAND INN
1603 S Shore Dr (50428)
Rates: $51-$134
Tel: (515) 357-5123
(800) 334-3277

CLINTON

BEST WESTERN-FRONTIER MOTOR INN
2300 Lincolnway (52732)
Rates: $44-$77
Tel: (319) 242-7112
(800) 528-1234

RAMADA INN
1522 Lincolnway (52732)
Rates: $50-$110
Tel: (319) 243-8841
(800) 272-6232

TIMBER MOTEL
2225 Lincolnway (52732)
Rates: $27-$39
Tel: (319) 243-6901

CLIVE

BEST WESTERN-WEST
11040 Hickman Rd (50325)
Rates: $69-$99
Tel: (515) 287-6464
(800) 528-1234

BUDGETEL INN
1390 NW 188th St (50325)
Rates: $45-$69
Tel: (515) 221-9200
(800) 428-3438

COLUMBUS JUNCTION

COLUMBUS MOTEL
Hwy 92 E (52738)
Rates: $32-$45
Tel: (319) 728-8080

COOK

VERMILLION DAM LODGE
P. O. Box 1105-AA (55723)
Rates: $700-$1040/Weekly
Tel: (800) 325-5780

CORALVILLE

BEST WESTERN CANTERBURY
704 1st Ave (52241)
Rates: $55-$82
Tel: (319) 351-0400
(800) 528-1234

BEST WESTERN WESTFIELD
1895 27th Ave (52241)
Rates: $52-$73
Tel: (319) 354-7770
(800) 528-1234

BLUE TOP MOTEL
1015 5th St (52241)
Rates: $28-$47
Tel: (319) 351-0900

COMFORT INN
209 W 9th St (52241)
Rates: $41-$79
Tel: (319) 351-8144
(800) 221-2222

FAIRFIELD INN BY MARRIOTT
214 W 9th St (52241)
Rates: $44-$70
Tel: (319) 337-8382
(800) 348-6000

MOTEL 6
810 1st Ave (52241)
Rates: $30-$36
Tel: (319) 354-0030
(800) 466-8356

COUNCIL BLUFFS

BEST WESTERN INN
2216 27th Ave (51501)
Rates: $59-$74
Tel: (712) 322-3150
(800) 528-1234

DAYS INN
3619 9th Ave (51501)
Rates: $55-$65
Tel: (712) 323-2200
(800) 329-7466

HEARTLAND INN
1000 Woodbury Ave (51503)
Rates: $44-$58
Tel: (712) 322-8400
(800) 334-3277

MOTEL 6
1846 N 16th St (51501)
Rates: $26-$32
Tel: (712) 328-8300
(800) 440-6000

MOTEL 6-SOUTH
3032 S Expwy (51501)
Rates: $30-$34
Tel: (712) 366-2405
(800) 440-6000

SUPER 8 MOTEL
2712 S 24th St (51501)
Rates: $35-$43
Tel: (712) 322-2888
(800) 800-8000

DAVENPORT

DAYS INN
3202 E Kimberly Rd (52807)
Rates: $40-$115
Tel: (319) 355-1190
(800) 329-7466

HAMPTON INN
3330 E. Kimberly Rd. (52807)
Rates: $51-$59
Tel: (319) 359-3921
(800) 426-7866

MOTEL 6
6111 N Brady St (52806)
Rates: $31-$37
Tel: (319) 391-8997
(800) 466-8356

SUPER 8 MOTEL
410 E 65th St (52807)
Rates: $37-$58
Tel: (319) 388-9810
(800) 800-8000

DECORAH

DAYS INN
315 Chamberlin Dr (51442)
Rates: $32-$63
Tel: (712) 263-2500
(800) 326-7466

DENISON

BEST WESTERN INN
502 Boyer Valley Rd (51442)
Rates: $32-$48
Tel: (712) 263-5081
(800) 528-1234

DES MOINES

ADVENTURELAND INN
I-80 & Hwy 65 (50316)
Rates: $40-$70
Tel: (515) 265-7321

ARCHER MOTEL
4965 Hubbell Ave (50317)
Rates: $28-$54
Tel: (515) 265-0368

BEST WESTERN BAVARIAN INN
5220 NE 14th St (50313)
Rates: $52-$70
Tel: (515) 265-5611
(800) 528-1234

BEST WESTERN COLONIAL
5020 NE 14th St (50313)
Rates: $37-$55
Tel: (515) 265-7511
(800) 528-1234

BEST WESTERN STARLITE VILLAGE
929 3rd St (50309)
Rates: $53-$70
Tel: (515) 282-5251
(800) 528-1234

BEST WESTERN INTERNATIONAL HOTEL
1810 Army Post Rd (50315)
Rates: $59-$81
Tel: (515) 287-6464
(800) 528-1234

BROADWAY MOTEL
5100 Hubbell Ave (50317)
Rates: $30-$60
Tel: (515) 262-5659

BUDGET HOST
7625 Hickman Rd (50322)
Rates: $35-$50
Tel: (800) 283-4678

COMFORT INN
5231 Fleur Dr (50321)
Rates: $47-$76
Tel: (515) 282-5251
(800) 221-2222

DAYS INN CAPITOL CITY
3501 E 14th St (50316)
Rates: $50-$75
Tel: (515) 265-2541
(800) 329-7466

EMBASSY SUITES
101 E Locust St (50309)
Rates: $99-$149
Tel: (515) 244-1700
(800) 362-2779

FORT DES MOINES HOTEL
1000 Walnut St (50309)
Rates: $61-$160
Tel: (800) 532-1466

HICKMAN MOTOR LODGE
6500 Hickman Rd (50322)
Rates: $33-$48
Tel: (515) 276-8591

HOLIDAY INN
5000 Merle Hay Rd (50322)
Rates: $58-$99
Tel: (515) 278-0271
(800) 465-4329

THE INN ON UNIVERSITY
11001 University Ave (50325)
Rates: $45-$53
Tel: (515) 225-2222

KIRKWOOD CIVIC CENTER HOTEL
400 Walnut St (50309)
Rates: $69-$150
Tel: (515) 244-9191
(800) 798-9191

MARRIOTT HOTEL
700 Grand Ave (50309)
Rates: $92-$132
Tel: (515) 245-5500
(800) 228-9290

MOTEL 6-AIRPORT
4817 Fleur Dr (50321)
Rates: $30-$36
Tel: (515) 287-6364
(800) 440-6000

MOTEL 6-NORTH
4940 NE 14th St (50313)
Rates: $32-$38
Tel: (515) 266-5456
(800) 440-6000

RAMADA INN
1250 74th St (50266)
Rates: $60-$70
Tel: (515) 223-6500
(800) 272-6232

SAVERY HOTEL & SPA
401 Locust St (50309)
Rates: $88-$125
Tel: (515) 244-2151

SUPER 8 LODGE
4755 Merle Hay Rd (50322)
Rates: $40-$60
Tel: (515) 278-8858
(800) 800-8000

DUBUQUE

COMFORT INN
4055 Dodge St (52003)
Rates: $38-$71
Tel: (319) 557-8000
(800) 221-2222

DAYS INN
1111 Dodge St
(52001)
Rates: $47-$62
Tel: (319) 583-3297
(800) 329-7466

**FAIRFIELD INN
BY MARRIOTT**
3400 Dodge St
(52001)
Rates: $46-$67
Tel: (319) 588-2349
(800) 228-2800

MOTEL 6
2670 Dodge St
(52001)
Rates: $28-$34
Tel: (319) 556-0880
(800) 440-6000

EARLY

EARLY MOTEL
403 Hwys 71 & 20
(50535)
Rates: n/a
Tel: (712) 273-5599

ELDORA

VILLAGE MOTEL
2005 E Edgington
Ave (50627)
Rates: $28-$38
Tel: (515) 858-3441

EVANSDALE

RAMADA INN
450 Evansdale Dr
(50707)
Rates: $40-$55
Tel: (319) 235-1111
(800) 272-2632

FAIRFIELD

**BEST WESTERN
INN**
2200 W Burlington
(52556)
Rates: $55-$72
Tel: (515) 472-2200
(800) 528-1234

DREAM MOTEL
US 34 W (52556)
Rates: $28-$48
Tel: (515) 472-4161

FORT DODGE

**BEST WESTERN
STARLITE VILLAGE**
P. O. Box 1297
(50501)
Rates: $43-$62
Tel: (515) 575-7177
(800) 528-1234

BUDGET HOST INN
US 20 & 169 (50501)
Rates: $36-$70
Tel: (800) 283-4678

COMFORT INN
E 5th Ave (50501)
Rates: $46-$60
Tel: (515) 573-3731
(800) 221-2222

HOLIDAY INN
P. O. Box 1336
(50501)
Rates: $49-$74
Tel: (515) 955-3621
(800) 465-4329

FORT MADISON

**AMERICANA
MOTEL**
Hwy 61 & Hwy 2
West (52627)
Rates: n/a
Tel: (319) 372-5123

**BEST WESTERN
IOWAN
MOTOR LODGE**
P. O. Box 485 (52627)
Rates: $50-$58
Tel: (319) 372-7510
(800) 528-1234

GLENWOOD

WESTERN INN
707 S Locust (51534)
Rates: $29-$35
Tel: (712) 527-3175

GRINNELL

**BEST WESTERN
INN**
2210 West St S
(50112)
Rates: $41-$75
Tel: (515) 236-6116
(800) 528-1234

DAYS INN
I-80 & Hwy 146
(50112)
Rates: $41-$60
Tel: (515) 236-6710
(800) 329-7466

SUPER 8 MOTEL
I-80 & Hwy 146, Exit
182 (50112)
Rates: $40-$55
Tel: (515) 236-7888
(800) 800-8000

HAMPTON

GOLD KEY MOTEL
Rt 2, Box 242 (50441)
Rates: $25-$40
Tel: (515) 456-2566

HOMESTEAD

**DIE HEIMAT
COUNTRY INN**
Box 160 (52236)
Rates: $48-$70
Tel: (319) 622-3937

HUMBOLT

SUPER 8 MOTEL
Hwy 3 W (50548)
Rates: $37-$54
Tel: (515) 332-1131
(800) 800-8000

INDEPENDENCE

SUPER 8 MOTEL
2000 1st St W (50644)
Rates: $36-$53
Tel: (319) 334-7041
(800) 800-8000

INDIANOLA

WOODS MOTEL
906 South Jefferson
(50125)
Rates: n/a
Tel: (515) 961-5311

IOWA CITY

HOLIDAY INN
210 S Dubuque St
(52240)
Rates: $76-$125
Tel: (319) 337-4058
(800) 465-4329

JOHNSTON

**BEST INNS
OF AMERICA**
5050 Merle Hay Rd
(50131)
Rates: $43-$58
Tel: (515) 270-1111

**THE INN &
CONFERENCE CTR**
5055 Merle Hay Rd
(50131)
Rates: $40-$60
Tel: (515) 276-5411

KEOKUK

CHIEF MOTEL
2701 Main St Rd
(52632)
Rates: $30-$38
Tel: (319) 524-2565

**KEOKUK
MOTOR LODGE**
Hwy 218, E Main St
Rd (52632)
Rates: $35-$50
Tel: (800) 252-2256

KNOXVILLE

RED CARPET INN
1702 N Lincoln
(50138)
Rates: $23-$32
Tel: (515) 842-3191
(800) 251-1962

LE MARS

AMBER INN MOTEL
635 Eighth Ave SW
(51031)
Rates: $28-$34
Tel: (712) 546-7066

MAPLETON

MAPLE MOTEL
Rt 1, Box 1 (51034)
Rates: $29-$38
Tel: (712) 882-1271

MAQUOKETA

KEY MOTEL
Hwy 61 & 64 (52060)
Rates: $25-$40
Tel: (319) 652-5131

MARQUETTE

THE FRONTIER MOTEL
101 S 1st St (52158)
Rates: $30-$70
Tel: (319) 873-3497

MARSHALL-TOWN

BEST WESTERN REGENCY INN
3303 S Center St
(50158)
Rates: $52-$200
Tel: (515) 752-6321
(800) 528-1234

BEST WESTERN THUNDERBIRD MOTEL
2009 S Center St
(50158)
Rates: $36-$85
Tel: (515) 752-3631
(800) 528-1234

DAYS INN
403 E Church St
(50158)
Rates: $38-$48
Tel: (515) 753-7777
(800) 326-7466

MASON CITY

DAYS INN
2301 4th St SW
(50401)
Rates: $40-$95
Tel: (515) 424-0210
(800) 329-7466

HOLIDAY INN
2101 4th St SW
(50401)
Rates: $52-$72
Tel: (515) 423-1640
(800) 465-4329

THRIFTLODGE
24 5th St SW (50401)
Rates: $36-$50
Tel: (515) 424-2910
(800) 578-7878

MISSOURI VALLEY

DAYS INN
1967 Hwy 30 (51555)
Rates: $41-$55
Tel: (712) 642-4003
(800) 329-7466

MOUNT PLEASANT

HEARTLAND INN
Hwy 218 N (52641)
Rates: $40-$57
Tel: (319) 385-2102
(800) 334-3277

NEW HAMPTON

SOUTHGATE INN
2199 McCloud Ave
(50659)
Rates: $41-$54
Tel: (515) 394-4145

NEWTON

BEST WESTERN INN
P. O. Box 8 (50208)
Rates: $45-$81
Tel: (515) 792-4200
(800) 528-1234

DAYS INN
1605 W 19th St S
(50208)
Rates: $36-$65
Tel: (515) 792-2330
(800) 329-7466

RAMADA INN
I-80 & Hwy 14
(50208)
Rates: $25-$75
Tel: (515) 792-8100
(800) 272-2632

SUPER 8 MOTEL
1635 S 12th Ave W
(50208)
Rates: $40-$55
Tel: (515) 792-8868
(800) 800-8000

TERRACE LODGE MOTEL
Hwy 14 & I-80
(50208)
Rates: $46-$100
Tel: (800) 383-7722

OKOBOJI

IMA COUNTRY CLUB MOTEL
1107 Sanborn Ave
(51355)
Rates: $31-$90
Tel: (712) 332-5617
(800) 341-8000

ONAWA

SUPER 8 MOTEL
P.O. Box 56 (51040)
Rates: $41-$55
Tel: (712) 423-2101
(800) 800-8000

OSCEOLA

BEST WESTERN REGAL INN
P. O. Box 238 (50213)
Rates: $36-$49
Tel: (515) 342-2123
(800) 528-1234

BLUE HAVEN MOTEL
325 S Main St (50213)
Rates: $34-$55
Tel: (515) 342-2115

OSKALOOSA

RED CARPET INN
2278 Hwy 63 North
(52577)
Rates: n/a
Tel: (515) 673-8641
(800) 251-1962

RODEWAY INN
1315 A Ave E (52577)
Rates: $45-$60
Tel: (515) 673-8351
(800) 228-2000

TRAVELER BUDGET INN
1210 A Ave East
(52577)
Rates: $30-$44
Tel: (515) 673-8333
(800) 341-8000

OTTUMWA

COLONIAL MOTOR INN
1534 Albia Rd
(52501)
Rates: $26-$40
Tel: (515) 683-1661

DAYS INN
206 Church St
(52501)
Rates: $38-$58
Tel: (515) 682-8131
(800) 329-7466

HEARTLAND INN
125 W Joseph Ave
(52501)
Rates: $41-$60
Tel: (515) 682-8526
(800) 334-3277

PACIFIC JUNCTION

BLUFF VIEW MOTEL
RR 1 (51561)
Rates: $30-$34
Tel: (712) 622-8191

QUAD CITIES

BEST WESTERN STEEPLEGATE INN
100 W 76th St
(Davenport 52806)
Rates: $67-$93
Tel: (319) 386-6900
(800) 528-1234

COMFORT INN
2600 52nd Ave
(Moline 61265)
Rates: $47-$76
Tel: (309) 762-7000
(800) 221-2222

COMFORT INN
7222 Northwest Blvd
(Davenport 52806)
Rates: $43-$55
Tel: (319) 391-8222
(800) 221-2222

EXEL INN
6310 N Brady St
(Davenport 52806)
Rates: $31-$45
Tel: (319) 386-6350
(800) 356-8013

EXEL INN
2501 52nd Ave
(Moline 61265)
Rates: $35-$42
Tel: (309) 797-5580
(800) 356-8013

FAIRFIELD INN
2705 48th Ave
(Moline 61265)
Rates: $44-$65
Tel: (309) 762-9083
(800) 228-2800

**FAIRFIELD INN
BY MARRIOTT**
3206 E Kimberly Rd
(Davenport 52807)
Rates: $56-$70
Tel: (319) 355-2264
(800) 228-2800

**HAMPTON INN-
AIRPORT**
6920 27th St
(Moline 61265)
Rates: $49-$58
Tel: (309) 762-1711
(800) 426-7866

HAMPTON INN
3330 E Kimberly Rd
(Davenport 52807)
Rates: $46-$56
Tel: (319) 354-3921
(800) 426-7866

HOLIDAY INN
909 Middle Rd
(Bettendorf 52722)
Rates: $69-$91
Tel: (319) 395-7141
(800) 465-4329

**JUMER'S CASTLE
LODGE**
900 Spruce Hills Dr
(Bettendorf 52722)
Rates: $76-$97
Tel: (319) 359-7141

LA QUINTA INN
Airport Corners
(Moline 61265)
Rates: $50-$58
Tel: (309) 762-9008
(800) 531-5900

MOTEL 6
6111 N Brady St
(Davenport 52806)
Rates: $27-$35
Tel: (319) 391-8997
(800) 440-6000

RAMADA INN
6263 N Brady
(Davenport 52806)
Rates: $48-$63
Tel: (319) 386-1940
(800) 272-6232

**TWIN BRIDGES
INN**
221 15th St
(Bettendorf 52722)
Rates: $39-$48
Tel: (319) 355-6451

SERGEANT BLUFF

MOTEL 6
6166 Harbor Dr
(51111)
Rates: $28-$34
Tel: (712) 277-3131
(800) 440-6000

SHELDON

SHELDON MOTEL
3 Blks W on US 18
(51201)
Rates: $25-$28
Tel: (712) 324-2568

SHENANDOAH

TALL CORN MOTEL
Sheridan Ave
& US 59 (51601)
Rates: $28-$32
Tel: (712) 246-1550

SIBLEY

SUPER 8 MOTEL
1108 2nd Ave (51249)
Rates: $38-$56
Tel: (712) 754-3603
(800) 800-8000

SIOUX CENTER

COLONIAL MOTEL
1367 South Main
(51250)
Rates: n/a
Tel: (800) 762-9149

ECONO LODGE
86 9th St Circle NE
(51250)
Rate: $37-$46
Tel: (712) 722-4000
(800) 424-4777

SIOUX CITY

**BEST WESTERN
CITY CENTRE**
130 Nebraska St
(51101)
Rates: $59-$65
Tel: (712) 277-1550
(800) 528-1234

ELMDALE MOTEL
US 75 N at 22nd St
(51105)
Rates: $25-$38
Tel: (712) 277-1012

**FAIRFIELD INN
BY MARRIOTT**
4716 Southern Hills
Dr (51106)
Rates: $47-$57
Tel: (712) 276-5600
(800) 228-2800

HILTON HOTEL
707 4th St (51101)
Rates: $84-$104
Tel: (712) 277-4101
(800) 445-8667

HOLIDAY INN
1401 Zenith Dr
(51103)
Rates: $57-$74
Tel: (712) 277-3211
(800) 465-4329

MARINA INN
4th & B Sts (51101)
Rates: $64-$74
Tel: (800) 798-7980

RIVERBOAT INN
701 Gordon Dr
(51101)
Rates: $45-$63
Tel: (712) 277-9400

SUPER 8 MOTEL
4307 Stone Ave
(51106)
Rates: $38-$53
Tel: (712) 274-1520
(800) 800-8000

SLOAN

RODEWAY INN
1862 SR 141 (51055)
Rates: $41-$66
Tel: (712) 428-4280
(800) 228-2000

SPIRIT LAKE

OAKS MOTEL
1701 Chicago (51360)
Rates: $29-$69
Tel: (712) 336-2940

STORM LAKE

**CROSS ROADS
MOTEL**
Hwys 3 & 71 (50588)
Rates: $43-$53
Tel: (800) 383-1456

ECONOMY INN
1316 N Lake Ave
(50588)
Rates: $28-$36
Tel: (712) 732-2342
(800) 826-0778

PALACE MOTEL
E Lake Shore Dr
(50588)
Rates: $25-$32
Tel: (712) 732-5753

STORY CITY

**VIKING
MOTOR INN**
West of I-35, Exit 124
(50248)
Rates: $37-$46
Tel: (515) 733-4306

STUART

SUPER 8 MOTEL
I-80 (50250)
Rates: $37-$45
Tel: (515) 523-2888
(800) 800-8000

TOLEDO

SUPER 8 MOTEL
Hwy 30 W (52342)
Rates: $36-$53
Tel: (515) 484-5888
(800) 800-8000

URBANDALE

COMFORT INN
5900 Sutton Dr
(50322)
Rates: $36-$60
Tel: (515) 270-1037
(800) 221-2222

WALCOTT

SUPER 8 MOTEL
Walcott I-80 Ind Prk
(52773)
Rates: $37-$52
Tel: (319) 284-5083
(800) 800-8000

WALNUT

SUPER 8 MOTEL
Exit 46, I-80 (51577)
Rates: $38-$50
Tel: (712) 784-2221
(800) 800-8000

WASHINGTON

SUPER 8 MOTEL
Hwy 1 & 92 (52353)
Rates: $42-$60
Tel: (319) 653-6621
(800) 800-8000

WATERLOO

**BEST WESTERN
STARLITE VILLAGE**
214 Washington St
(50701)
Rates: $52-$62
Tel: (319) 235-0321
(800) 528-1234

COMFORT INN
1945 La Porte Rd
(50702)
Rates: $41-$72
Tel: (319) 234-7411
(800) 221-2222

DAYS INN
2141 La Porte Rd
(50702)
Rates: $38-$55
Tel: (319) 233-9191
(800) 329-7466

EXEL INN
3350 University Ave
(50701)
Rates: $29-$48
Tel: (319) 235-2165
(800) 356-8013

**FAIRFIELD INN
BY MARRIOTT**
2011 La Porte Rd
(50702)
Rates: $43-$61
Tel: (319) 234-5452
(800) 228-2800

HEARTLAND INN
1809 La Porte Rd
(50702)
Rates: $42-$65
Tel: (319) 235-4461
(800) 334-3277

HEARTLAND INN
3052 Marnie Ave
(50701)
Rates: $42-$57
Tel: (319) 232-7467
(800) 334-3277

SUPER 8 MOTEL
1825 La Porte Rd
(50702)
Rates: $43-$58
Tel: (319) 233-1800
(800) 800-8000

WAVERLY

**BEST WESTERN
RED FOX INN**
1900 Heritage Way
(50677)
Rates: $58-$149
Tel: (319) 352-5330
(800) 528-1234

WEBSTER CITY

**THE EXECUTIVE
INN**
1700 Superior St
(50595)
Rates: $36-$44
Tel: (515) 832-3631

WEST BEND

WEST BEND MOTEL
West of Hwy 15
(50597)
Rates: $21-$29
Tel: (515) 887-3611

WEST BRANCH

**PRESIDENTIAL
MOTOR INN**
711 S Doney (52358)
Rates: $31-$39
Tel: (319) 643-2526

WEST LIBERTY

ECONO LODGE
1943 Garfield Ave
(52776)
Rates: $36-$46
Tel: (319) 627-2171
(800) 424-4777

WEST UNION

ELMS MOTEL
Hwy 150 South
(52175)
Rates: n/a
Tel: (800) 422-3843

WILLIAMS

**BEST WESTERN
NORSEMAN INN**
I-35 Exit 144 (50271)
Rates: $37-$61
Tel: (515) 854-2281
(800) 528-1234

WILLIAMSBURG

**BEST WESTERN
QUIET HOUSE
SUITES**
Hwy 149 (52361)
Rates: $66-$153
Tel: (319) 668-9777
(800) 528-1234

CREST MOTEL
2214 U Ave (52361)
Rate: $40-$70
Tel: (319) 668-2097

DAYS INN
Rt 2, Box 182 (52361)
Rates: $39-$65
Tel: (800) 329-7466

RAMADA INN
I-80 & Hwy 149
(52361)
Rates: $37-$76
Tel: (319) 668-1000
(800) 272-6232

SUPER 8 MOTEL
1708 N Highland St
(52361)
Rates: $50-$80
Tel: (319) 668-9718
(800) 800-8000

SUPER 8 MOTEL
2228 U Ave (52361)
Rates: $36-$51
Tel: (319) 668-2800
(800) 800-8000

WYOMING

SUNSET MOTEL
RR #1 (52362)
Rates: n/a
Tel: (319) 488-2240

KANSAS

ABILENE

BALFOUR'S HOUSE BED & BREAKFAST
940 1900 Ave (67410)
Rates: $40-$65+
Tel: (913) 263-4262

BEST WESTERN ABILENE'S PRIDE
1709 N Buckeye (67410)
Rates: $40-$70
Tel: (913) 263-2800
(800) 528-1234

BEST WESTERN INN
2210 N Buckeye (67410)
Rates: $38-$58
Tel: (913) 263-2050
(800) 528-1234

DIAMOND MOTEL
1407 NW 3rd St (67410)
Rates: $20-$40
Tel: (913) 263-2360

SPRUCE HOUSE
604 N Spruce (67410)
Rates: $50-$65
Tel: (913) 263-3900

ARKANSAS CITY

BEST WESTERN HALLMARK MOTOR INN
1617 N Summit St (67005)
Rates: $44-$49
Tel: (316) 442-1400
(800) 528-1234

HERITAGE REGENCY COURT INN
3232 N Summit St (67005)
Rates: $37-$43
Tel: (316) 442-7700

ASHLAND

ROLIING HILLS BED & BREAKFAST
204 E 4th Ave (67831)
Rates: $45-$50
Tel: (316) 635-2859

ATCHISON

ATCHISON MOTOR INN
401 S 10th (66002)
Rates: $30-$45
Tel: (913) 367-7000

AUBURN

LIPPINCOTT'S FYSHE HOUSE
8720 W 85th St (66402)
Rates: $60-$75
Tel: (913) 256-2436

BAXTER SPRINGS

BAXTER INN-4-LESS
2451 Military Ave (66713)
Rates: $26-$42
Tel: (316) 856-2106

BELLEVILLE

BEST WESTERN BEL VILLA MOTEL
215 US Hwy 36 (66935)
Rates: $38-$54
Tel: (913) 527-2231
(800) 528-1234

BELOIT

MAINLINER INN
RFD 1, Box 47 A (67420)
Rates: $28-$60
Tel: (913) 738-3531

BERN

LEAR ACRES B & B
Rt 1, Box 31 (66408)
Rates: $32-$38
Tel: (913) 336-3903

CAWKER CITY

OAK CREEK LODGE
1787 Rain Road (67431)
Rates: $55-$85
Tel: (913) 263-8755

CHANUTE

GUEST HOUSE INN
1814 S Santa Fe (66720)
Rates: $25-$32
Tel: (316) 431-0600

HOLIDAY PARK MOTEL65
3030 S Santa Fe (66720)
Rates: $30
Tel: (316) 431-0850

IMA SAFARI INN
35oo S Santa Fe (66720)
Rates: $34-$49
Tel: (316) 431-9460

CLAY CENTER

CEDAR COURT MOTEL
905 Crawford (67432)
Rates: $25-$44
Tel: (913) 632-2148

COFFEYVILLE

APPLETREE INN
820 E 11th (67337)
Rates: $40-$48
Tel: (316) 251-0002

FOUNTAIN PLAZA INN
104 W 11th St (67337)
Rates: $39-$55
Tel: (316) 251-2250

COLBY

BEST WESTERN CROWN MOTEL
2320 S Range (67701)
Rates: $41-$77
Tel: (913) 462-3943
(800) 528-1234

BUDGET HOST INN
1745 W 4th St (67701)
Rates: $26-$46
Tel: (800) 283-4678

COMFORT INN
2225 S Range (67701)
Rates: $42-$60
Tel: (800) 221-2222

DAYS INN
1925 S Range (67701)
Rates: $41-$50
Tel: (800) 329-7466

ECONO LODGE
1985 S Range (67701
Rates: $32-$54
Tel: (800) 424-4777

RAMADA INN
1950 S Range (67701)
Rates: $39-$51
Tel: (800) 272-6232

CONCORDIA

BEST WESTERN THUNDERBIRD INN
89 Lincoln (66901)
Rates: $36-$60
Tel: (913) 243-4545
(800) 528-1234

COTTONWOOD FALLS

1874 STONEHOUSE ON MULBERRY HILL
Rt 1, Box 67A (66845)
Rates: $75
Tel: (316) 273-8481

COUNCIL GROVE

THE COTTAGE HOUSE HOTEL
25 N Neosho (66846)
Rates: $45-$80
Tel: (316) 767-6828
(800) 727-7903

FLINT HILLS B & B
613 W Main (66846)
Rates: $50-$65
Tel: (316) 767-6655

DODGE CITY

ASTRO MOTEL
2200 Wyatt Earp
Blvd (67801)
Rates: $42-$60
Tel: (316) 225-9000

**BEST WESTERN
SILVER SPUR LODGE**
1510 W Wyatt Earp
Blvd (67801)
Rates: $49-$67
Tel: (316) 227-2125
(800) 528-1234

**DODGE HOUSE
MOTEL**
2408 W Wyatt Earp
Blvd (67801)
Rates: $21-$120
Tel: (800) 553-9901

SUPER 8 MOTEL
1708 W Wyatt Earp
Blvd (67801)
Rates: $39-$54
Tel: (800) 800-8000

EL DORADO

**BEST WESTERN
RED COACH INN**
2525 W Central
(67042)
Rates: $40-$80
Tel: (316) 321-6900
(800) 528-1234

HERITAGE INN
2515 W Central Ave
(67042)
Rates: $26-$42
Tel: (316) 321-6800

ELLSWORTH

**BEST WESTERN
GARDEN INN**
Box 44 (67439)
Rates: $38-$57
Tel: (913) 472-3116
(800) 528-1234

ELWOOD

CAPRI MOTEL
P. O. Box 97-C
(Wathena 66090)
Rates: $17-$24
Tel: (913) 365-0209

EMPORIA

**BUDGET HOST-
SUNRISE MOTEL**
1830 E Hwy 50
(66801)
Rates: $23-$30
Tel: (800) 283-4678

COMFORT INN
2511 W 18th (66801)
Rates: $32-$42
Tel: (800) 221-2222

DAYS INN
3032 W Hwy 50
(66801)
Rates: $42-$54
Tel: (316) 342-1787
(800) 329-7466

QUALITY INN
3021 Hwy 50W
(66801)
Rates: $36-$58
Tel: (800) 424-6423

ERIE

**LAND OF AH'S
MOTOR INN**
700 W Canville &
Hwy 59
(66733)
Rates: $29-$34
Tel: (316) 244-5231

ENTERPRISE

**EHRSAM PLACE
BED & BREAKFAST**
103 S Grant (67441)
Rates: $55-$65
Tel: (913) 263-8747
(800) 470-7774

EUREKA

BLUE STEM LODGE
1314 E River St
(67045)
Rates: $28-$38
Tel: (316) 583-5531

FLORENCE

HOLIDAY MOTEL
630 W 5th (66851)
Rates: $22-$31
Tel: (316) 878-4246

FORT SCOTT

**FRONTIER INN
4 LESS**
2222 S Main (66701)
Rates: $29-$39
Tel: (316) 223-5330

**RANCH HOUSE
MOTEL**
Hwy 54 West (66701)
Rates: n/a
Tel: (316) 223-9734

RED RAM MOTEL
Hwy 54 West (66704)
Rates: n/a
Tel: (316) 223-2400

GARDEN CITY

**BEST WESTERN RED
BARON MOTOR INN**
US 50 & US 8 (67846)
Rates: $40-$65
Tel: (316) 275-4164
(800) 528-1234

**BEST WESTERN
WHEAT LANDS INN**
1311 E Fulton (67846)
Rates: $40-$66
Tel: (316) 276-2387
(800) 528-1234

BUDGET HOST
123 Honey Bee Ct
(67846)
Rates: $30-$44
Tel: (800) 283-4678

CONTINENTAL INN
1408 Jones Ave
(67846)
Rates: $27-$35
Tel: (316) 276-7691

DAYS INN
1818 Commanche
(67846)
Rates: $43-$81
Tel: (316) 275-5095
(800) 329-7466

NATIONAL 9 INN
1502 E Fulton
(67846)
Rates: $31-$42
Tel: (316) 276-2304

PLAZA INN
1911 E Kansas Ave
(67846)
Rates $48-$90
Tel: (800) 875-5201

GLASCO

**RUSTIC
REMEMBRANCES**
Rt 1, Box 68 (67445)
Rates: $25-$75
Tel: (913) 546-2552

GOODLAND

HOLIDAY INN
2218 Commerce Rd
(67735)
Rates: $49-$66
Tel: (800) 465-4329

GREAT BEND

**BEST WESTERN
ANGUS INN**
2920 10th St (67530)
Rates: $48-$68
Tel: (316) 792-3541
(800) 528-1234

INN 4 LESS
4701 10th St (67530)
Rates: $29-$39
Tel: (316) 792-8235

HOLIDAY INN
3017 W 10th St
(67530)
Rates: $39-$56
Tel: (800) 528-1234

**PEACEFUL ACRES
BED & BREAKFAST**
Rt 5, Box 153 (67530)
Rates: $25-30
Tel: (316) 793-7527

**TRAVELERS
BUDGET INN**
4200 W 10th St
(67530)
Rates: $23-$31
Tel: (316) 793-5448

GREENSBURG

**BEST WESTERN
J-HAWK MOTEL**
515 W Kansas Ave
(67054)
Rates: $40-$51
Tel: (316) 723-2121
(800) 528-1234

KANSAN INN
800 E Kansas Ave
(67054)
Rates: $26-$41
Tel: (316) 723-2141

HALLOWELL

CLAYTHORNE LODGE
Rt 1, Box 13 (66725)
Rates: n/a
Tel: (316) 597-2568

HAYS

**BEST WESTERN
VAGABOND MOTEL**
2524 Vine St (67601)
Rates: $40-$62
Tel: (913) 625-2511
(800) 528-1234

BUDGET HOST VILLA
810 E 8th (67601)
Rates: $23-$48
Tel: (800) 283-4678

DAYS INN
3205 N Vine St
(67601)
Rates: $40-$96
Tel: (913) 628-8261
(800) 329-7466

HAMPTON INN
3801 Vine St (67601)
Rates: $49-$54
Tel: (913) 625-8103
(800) 426-7866

HOLIDAY INN
3603 Vine St (67601)
Rates: $58-$63
Tel: (800) 465-4329

HIAWATHA

**HIAWATHA
HEARTLAND INN**
1100 S 1st (66434)
Rates: $35-$43
Tel: (913) 742-7401

HILL CITY

**PHEASANT RUN
BED & BREAKFAST**
609 N 4th Ave
(67642)
Rates: $35-$45
Tel: (913) 674-2955

HUTCHINSON

**BEST WESTERN
SUN DOME HOTEL**
11 Des Moines
(67505)
Rates: $60-$75
Tel: (316) 663-4444
(800) 528-1234

COMFORT INN
1621 Super Plaza
(67501)
Rates: $42-$53
Tel: (800) 221-2222

**QUALITY INN
CITY CENTER**
15 W 4th St (67501)
Rates: $37-$56
Tel: (800) 221-2222

SUPER 8 MOTEL
1315 E 11th Ave
(67501)
Rates: $37-$57
Tel: (316) 662-6394
(800) 800-8000

INDEPENDENCE

APPLETREE INN
201 N 8th St (67301)
Rates: $44-$55
Tel: (316) 331-5500

**BEST WESTERN
PRAIRIE INN**
P.O. Box 26 (67301)
Rates: $38-$56
Tel: (316) 331-7300
(800) 528-1234

JUNCTION CITY

**BEST WESTERN
JAYHAWK THIRD
MOTEL**
110 E Flint Hills
Blvd (66441)
Rates: $35-$65
Tel: (913) 238-5188
(800) 528-1234

DAYS INN
1024 S Washington
St (66441)
Rates: $38-$55
Tel: (800) 329-7466

DREAMLAND MOTEL
520 E Flint Hills
Blvd (66441)
Rates: $24-$36
Tel: (913) 238-1108

ECONO LODGE
211 E Flint Hills
Blvd (66441)
Rates: $31-$42
Tel: (800) 424-4777

HARVEST INN
1001 E 6th St (66441)
Rates: $40-$85
Tel: (800) 762-0270

KANSAS CITY

CIVIC CENTRE HOTEL
424 Minnesota Ave
(66101)
Rates: $49-$125
Tel: (800) 542-2983

**HOME & HEARTH
INN**
3930 Rainbow Blvd
(66103)
Rates: $35-$47
Tel: (913) 236-6880

KINGMAN

WELCOME INN
1101 Hwy 54 E
(67068)
Rates: $22-$33
Tel: (316) 532-3144

LAKIN

**WINDY HEIGHTS
BED & BREAKFAST**
607 Country Heights
Rd (67860)
Rates: $40-$50
Tel: (316) 355-7699

LANSING

ECONO LODGE
504 N Main St (66043)
Rates: $34-$44
Tel: (913) 727-2777
(800) 424-4777

LARNED

**BEST WESTERN
TOWNSMAN INN**
123 E 14th St (67550)
Rates: $37-$52
Tel: (316) 285-3114
(800) 528-1234

LAWRENCE

DAYS INN
2309 Iowa St (66046)
Rates: $43-$95
Tel: (913) 843-9100
(800) 329-7466

HOLIDAY INN
200 McDonald Dr
(66044)
Rates: $59-$86
Tel: (800) 465-4329

RAMADA INN
2222 W 6th St (66049)
Rates: $54-$75
Tel: (913) 842-7030
(800) 272-6232

SUPER 8 MOTEL
515 McDonald Dr
(66049)
Rates: $41-$61
Tel: (913) 842-5721
(800) 800-8000

WESTMINSTER INN
2525 W 6th St (66049)
Rates: $32-$46
Tel: (913) 841-8410

LEAVENWORTH

COMMANDER'S INN
6th and Metropolitan
(66048)
Rates: $34-$75
Tel: (913) 651-5800

LENEXA

**HOWARD JOHNSON
LODGE-SOUTHWEST**
12381 W 95th St
(66215)
Rates: $51-$65
Tel: (800) 654-2000

LA QUINTA INN
9461 Lenexa Dr
(66215)
Rates: $46-$62
Tel: (800) 221-4731

LIBERAL

**BEST WESTERN
LAFONDA MOTEL**
229 W Pancake Blvd
(67901)
Rates: $37-$62
Tel: (316) 624-5601
(800) 528-1234

CIMARRON INN
564 E Pancake Blvd
(67901)
Rates: $30-$43
Tel: (316) 624-6203

IMA WESTERN HO MOTEL
754 E Pancake
(67901)
Rates: $23-$40
Tel: (316) 624-1921
(800) 341-8000

KANSAN MOTEL
310 E Pancake Blvd
(67901)
Rates: n/a
Tel: (316) 624-7215

LIBERAL INN
603 E Pancake Blvd
(67901)
Rates: $34-$48
Tel: (316) 624-7254

RED CARPET INN
488 E Pancake Blvd
(67901)
Rates: $28-$40
Tel: (316) 624-5642
(800) 251-1962

THUNDERBIRD INN
2100 N Hwy 83
(67901)
Rates: $24-$29
Tel: (316) 624-7271

LINDSBORG

CORONADO MOTEL
305 N Harrison
(67456)
Rates: n/a
Tel: (913) 227-3943

LOUISBURG

RED MAPLE INN
201 S 11th St (66053)
Rates: $55-$75
Tel: (913) 837-2840

LYONS

LYONS INN
817 W Main (67554)
Rates: $29-$37
Tel: (316) 257-5185

MANHATTAN

BEST WESTERN CONTINENTAL INN
100 Bluemont Ave
(66502)
Rates: $48-$70
Tel: (913) 776-4771
(800) 528-1234

DAYS INN
1501 Tuttle Creek
Blvd (66502)
Rates: $45-$75
Tel: (913) 539-5391
(800) 329-7466

HOLIDAY INN/HOLIDOME
530 Richards Dr
(66502)
Rates: $69-$70
Tel: (800) 465-4329

MOTEL 6
510 Tuttle Creek
Blvd (66502)
Rates: $28-$34
Tel: (913) 537-1022

RAMADA INN
17th & Anderson
KSU (66502)
Rates: $62-$87
Tel: (800) 272-6232

MANKATO

CREST-VUE MOTEL
1/2 Mi East on US
36 (66956)
Rates: $25-$31
Tel: (913) 378-3515

DREAMLINER MOTEL
RR 2, Box 8 (66956)
Rates: $28-$34
Tel: (913) 378-3107

MARION

COUNTRY DREAMS
Rt 3, Box 82 (66861)
Rates: $50-$60
Tel: (316) 382-2250
(800) 570-0540

MARYSVILLE

BEST WESTERN SURF MOTEL
2005 Center Rd
(66508)
Rates: $30-$48
Tel: (800) 528-1234

SUPER 8 MOTEL
1155 Pony Express
Rd (66508)
Rates: $38-52
Tel: (913) 562-5588
(800) 800-8000

THUNDERBIRD MOTEL
Hwy 36W (66508)
Rates: $28-$40
Tel: (913) 562-2373

McPHERSON

BEST WESTERN HOLIDAY MANOR
2211 E Kansas Ave
(67460)
Rates: $39-$55
Tel: (316) 241-5343
(800) 528-1234

RED COACH INN
2111 E Kansas Ave
(67460)
Rates: $32-$45
Tel: (316) 241-6960

SUPER 8 MOTEL
2110 E Kansas
(67460)
Rates: $37-$57
Tel: (316) 241-8881
(800) 800-8000

MEADE

DALTON'S BEDPOST MOTEL
519 Carthage (67864)
Rates: $22-$32
Tel: (316) 873-2131

MERRIAM

COMFORT INN
6401 E Frontage Rd
(66202)
Rates: $44-$59
Tel: (800) 221-2222

DRURY INN
9009 Shawnee
Mission
Pkwy (66202)
Rates: $49-$69
Tel: (800) 325-8300

NESS CITY

DERRICK INN
Hwy 96 E (67560)
Rates: $35-$45
Tel: (913) 798-3617

NEWTON

BEST WESTERN RED COACH INN
1301 E 1st St (67114)
Rates: $43-$75
Tel: (316) 283-9120
(800) 528-1234

DAYS INN NEWTON
105 Manchester
(67114)
Rates: $36-$40
Tel: (316) 283-3300
(800) 329-7466

SUPER 8 MOTEL
1620 E 2nd St (67114)
Rates: $37-$57
Tel: (316) 283-7611
(800) 800-8000

OAKLEY

ANNIE OAKLEY MOTEL
428 Center St (67748)
Rates: $22-$33
Tel: (913) 672-3223

BEST WESTERN GOLDEN PLAINS MOTEL
3506 US 40 (67748)
Rates: $44-$60
Tel: (913) 672-3254
(800) 528-1234

FIRST TRAVEL INN
708 Center Ave
(67748)
Rates: $26-$42
Tel: (913) 672-3226

OBERLIN

FRONTIER MOTEL
207 E Frontier Pkwy
(67749)
Rates: $26-$50
Tel: (913) 475-2203

OSBORNE

CAMELOT INN
933 N 1st (67473)
Rates: $30-$36
Tel: (913) 436-5413

OTTAWA

DAYS INN
1641 S Main (66067)
Rates: $36-50
Tel: (913) 242-4842
(800) 329-7466

ECONO LODGE
2331 S Cedar Rd
(66067)
Rates: $34-$44
Tel: (800) 424-4777

ROYAL MANOR MOTEL
1641 S Main (66067)
Rates: $24-$36
Tel: (913) 242-4842

VILLAGE INN MOTEL
2520 S Main (66067)
Rates: $22-$31
Tel: (913) 242-5512

OVERBROOK

PINEMOORE INN
RR 1, Box 44 (66524)
Rates: $60
Tel: (913) 453-2304

OVERLAND PARK

DOUBLETREE HOTEL
10100 College Blvd
(66210)
Rates: $69-$89
Tel: (913) 451-6100

DRURY INN
10951 Metcalf (66210)
Rates: $58-$74
Tel: (800) 325-8300

MARRIOTT-OVERLAND PARK
10800 Metcalf (66212)
Rates: $69-$119
Tel: (913) 451-8000

RED ROOF INN
6800 W 108th St
(66211)
Rates: $34-$53
Tel: (800) 843-7663

RESIDENCE INN BY MARRIOTT
6300 W 110th St
(66211)
Rates: $69-$130
Tel: (800) 331-3131

WHITE HAVEN MOTEL
8039 Metcalf Ave
(66204)
Rates: $33-$42
Tel: (800) 752-2892

PARSONS

TOWNSMAN MOTEL
P. O. Box 813 (67357)
Rates: $28-$41
Tel: (800) 552-4008

PHILLIPSBURG

MARK V MOTEL
320 W State St (67661)
Rates: $26-$34
Tel: (800) 219-3149

PITTSBURG

SUNSET MOTEL
RR 3, Box 737 (66762)
Rates: $21-$26
Tel: (316) 231-3950

PRATT

BEST WESTERN HILLCREST MOTEL
1336 E 1st St (67124)
Rates: $33-$45
Tel: (316) 672-6407
(800) 528-1234

DAYS INN
1901 E First St (67124)
Rates: $38-$56
Tel: (316) 672-9465
(800) 329-7466

EVERGREEN INN
20001 W Hwy 54
(67124)
Rates: $27-$36
Tel: (800) 456-6424

PRATT BUDGET INN
1631 E 1st St (67124)
Rates: $18-$28
Tel: (316) 672-6468

RED CARPET INN
1401 East First St
(67124)
Rates: n/a
Tel: (316) 672-5588
(800) 251-1962

SUPER 8 MOTEL
1906 E 1st St (67124)
Rates: $25-$34
Tel: (800) 800-8000

QUINTER

"Q" MOTEL
P. O. Box 398 (67752)
Rates: $28-$38
Tel: (913) 754-3337
(800) 283-4678

ROSE HILL

QUEEN ANNE'S LACE B & B
15335 SW Queen
Anne's Lace (67133)
Rates: $40-50
Tel: (316) 733-4075

RUSSELL

RED CARPET INN
Box 489 (67665)
Rates: $34-$48
Tel: (913) 483-2107
(800) 251-1962

WINCHESTER INN
Frontage Rd, Hwy
281 S (67665)
Rates: $26-$41
Tel: (913) 483-6660

SALINA

AIRLINER MOTEL
781 N Broadway
(67401)
Rates: $20-$32
Tel: (913) 827-5586

BEST WESTERN HEART OF AMERICA
632 Westport Blvd
(67401)
Rates: $45-$80
Tel: (913) 827-9315
(800) 528-234

BEST WESTERN MID-AMERICA INN
1846 N 9th St (67401)
Rates: $45-$80
Tel: (913) 827-0356
(800) 528-1234

BUDGET INN VAGABOND MOTEL
217 S Broadway
(67401)
Rates: $26-$35
Tel: (913) 825-7265

BUDGET KING MOTEL
809 N Broadway
(67401)
Rates: $22-$30
Tel: (913) 827-4477

COMFORT INN
1820 W Crawford St
(67401)
Rates: $45-$67
Tel: (800) 221-2222

HOLIDAY INN
1616 W Crawford St
(67401)
Rates: $58-$62
Tel: (800) 465-4329

HOWARD JOHNSON
2403 S 9th St (67401)
Rates: $33-$39
Tel: (800) 446-4656

RAMADA INN
1949 N 9th St (67401)
Rates: $45-$48
Tel: (800) 272-6232

RED COACH INN
2020 W Crawford
(67401)
Rates: $34-$54
Tel: (913) 825-2111

SUPER 8 MOTEL
1640 W Crawford St
(77401)
Rates: $38-$48
Tel: (800) 800-8000

SENECA

STARLITE MOTEL
410 North St (66538)
Rates: $21-$32
Tel: (913) 336-2191

SHARON SPRINGS

HEYL'S TRAVELER MOTEL
Jct US 40 & KS27
(67758)
Rates: n/a
Tel: (913) 852-4293

SMITH CENTER

MODERN AIRE MOTEL
117 W US 36 (66967)
Rates: $23-$40
Tel: (800) 727-7332

TECUMSAH

OLD STONE HOUSE
6033 SE Hwy 40
(66542)
Rates: $45-$55
Tel: (913) 379-5568

TOPEKA

BEST WESTERN MEADOW ACRES MOTEL
2950 S Topeka Blvd
(66611)
Rates: $48-$70
Tel: (913) 267-1681
(800) 528-1234

COMFORT INN
1518 SW Wanamaker
Rd (66604)
Rates: $41-$61
Tel: (800) 221-2222

COUNTRY VIEW ESTATE
5420 SW Fairlawn
Rd (66610)
Rates: $55-$125
Tel: (913) 862-0335
(913) 862-1975

DAYS INN
1510 SW Wanamaker
Rd (66604)
Rates: $39-$75
Tel: (913) 272-8538
(800) 329-7466

ECONO LODGE
1240 SW Wanamaker
Rd (66604)
Rates: $34-$50
Tel: (800) 424-4777

FAIRFIELD INN BY MARRIOTT
1530 SW Westport
Dr (66604)
Rates: $41-$60
Tel: (800) 348-6000

LIBERTY INN
3839 S Topeka Blvd
(66609)
Rates: $37-$55
Tel: (913) 266-4700

PLAZA INN MOTEL
3802 S Topeka Blvd
(66609)
Rates: $42-$54
Tel: (913) 266-8880

SUPER 8 MOTEL
5968 SW 10th Ave
(66604)
Rates: $35-$46
Tel: (800) 800-8000

WAKEENEY

BEST WESTERN WHEEL MOTEL
I-70 & US 283
(67672)
Rates: $36-$60
Tel: (913) 743-2118
(800) 528-1234

WAMEGO

SUMMER MOTEL
1215 Hwy 24 W
(66547)
Rates: $30-$35
Tel: (913) 456-2304

WAKEFIELD

WAKEFIELD'S COUNTRY B & B
197 Sunflower Rd
(67487)
Rates: $35
Tel: (913) 461-5533

WICHITA

AIR CAP MOTEL
6075 Air Cap Dr
(67219)
Rates: n/a
Tel: (316) 744-2071

BEST WESTERN RED COACH INN
915 E 53rd St N
(67219)
Rates: $49-$69
Tel: (316) 832-9387
(800) 362-0095

DELUXE INN
8401 Hwy 54W
(67209)
Rates: $26-$42
Tel: (316) 722-4221

GRAND PALACE INN
607 E 47th St S
(67216)
Rates: $32-$38
Tel: (316) 529-4100

HAMPTON INN
9449 E. Corporate
Hills (67207)
Rates: $66-$76
Tel: (316) 686-3576
(800) 426-7866

HARVEY HOTEL
549 S Rock Rd
(67207)
Rates: $69-$90
Tel: (316) 686-7131

HOLIDAY INN-EAST
7335 E Kellogg
(67207)
Rates: $56-$81
Tel: (800) 465-4329

HOLIDAY INN WICHITA/AIRPORT
5500 W Kellogg
(67209)
Rates: $69-$85
Tel: (800) 465-4329

HOWARD JOHNSON
6575 W Kellogg Dr
(67209)
Rates: $40-$48
Tel: (316) 943-8165
(800) 446-4656

INN AT THE PARK
3751 E Douglas
(67218)
Rates: $75-$125
Tel: (316) 652-0500

LA QUINTA INN
7700 E Kellogg
(67207)
Rates: $48-$65
Tel: (800) 531-5900

MARRIOTT HOTEL
9100 Corporate Hills
Dr (67207)
Rates: $99-$275
Tel: (316) 651-0333

RED CARPET INN
607 E 47th St (67216)
Rates: $38-$46
Tel: (316) 529-4100
(800) 251-1962

WICHITA ROYALE HOTEL
125 N Market St
(67202)
Rates: $74-$250
Tel: (800) 876-0240

WINFIELD

COMFORT INN
US 77 at Quail Ridge
(67156)
Rates: $40-$53
Tel: (800) 221-2222

YATES CENTER

STAR MOTEL
206 S Fry (66783)
Rates: $25-$33
Tel: (316) 625-2175

TOWNSMAN MOTEL
609 W Mary (66783)
Rates: $25-$32
Tel: (316) 625-2131

KENTUCKY

ASHLAND

DAYS INN
12700 SR 180 (41101)
Rates: $43-$59
Tel: (606) 928-3600
(800) 329-7466

KNIGHTS INN
7216 US 60 (41102)
Rates: $33-$43
Tel: (800) 843-5644

AUBURN

AUBURN GUEST HOUSE
421 W Main St
(42206)
Rates: n/a
Tel: (502) 542-6019

AURORA

CEDAR LANE RESORT
Hwy 68, Rt 1, Box 520 (42048)
Rates: n/a
Tel: (502) 474-8042

EARLY AMERICAN MOTEL
Hwy 68, Rt 1 (42048)
Rates: $30-$58
Tel: (502) 474-2241

FIN 'N' FEATHER
Rt 1, Hwy 68 (42048)
Rates: n/a
Tel: (502) 474-2351

BARDSTOWN

BARDSTOWN-PARKVIEW MOTEL
418 E Stephen Foster Ave (40004)
Rates: $32-$48
Tel: (502) 348-5983

HOLIDAY INN CONVENTION CTR
P. O. Box 520 (40004)
Rates: $58-$70
Tel: (800) 465-4329

OLD BARDSTOWN INN
510 E Stephen Foster Ave (40004)
Rates: $30-$47
Tel: (502) 349-0776

OLD KENTUCKY HOME MOTEL
414 W Stephen Foster Ave (40004)
Rates: $31-$45
Tel: (502) 348-5979

RAMADA INN
523 N 3rd St (40004)
Rates: $50-$60
Tel: (502) 349-0363
(800) 272-6232

RED CARPET INN
1714 New Haven Rd (40004)
Rates: $36-$51
Tel: (502) 348-1112
(800) 251-1962

BENTON

COZY COVE RESORT
917 Reed Rd (42025)
Rates: $59-$1529
Tel: (502) 354-8168

HOLIDAY MOTEL
P. O. Box 227 (40403)
Rates: $34-$39
Tel: (606) 986-9311

KING CREEK RESORT & MARINA
972 King Creek Rd (42025)
Rates: $475-$850/Weekly
Tel: (502) 354-8268

SOUTHERN KOMFORT
Rt 4, Box 348 (42025)
Rates: n/a
Tel: (502) 354-6422

BEREA

BOONE TAVERN HOTEL
Main & Prospect (40404)
Rates: $52-$79
Tel: (606) 986-9358

DAYS INN/EXIT 77
1202 Walnut Meadow Rd (40403)
Rates: $39-$53
Tel: (606) 986-7373
(800) 366-9358

ECONO LODGE
1010 Paint Lick Rd (40403)
Rates: $40-$52
Tel: (800) 424-4777

HOLIDAY MOTEL
100 Jane St (40403)
Rates: $36-$39
Tel: (606) 986-9311

HOWARD JOHNSON
715 Chestnut St (40403)
Rates: $32-$50
Tel: (606) 986-2384

SUPER 8 MOTEL
196 Prince Royal Dr (40403)
Rates: $35-$47
Tel: (606) 986-8426
(800)-800-8000

BOWLING GREEN

BUDGETEL INN
165 Three Springs Rd (42104)
Rates: $36-$52
Tel: (502) 843-3200

HOLIDAY INN
3240 Scottsville Rd (42104)
Rates: $49-$90
Tel: (800) 465-4329

NEW'S INN OF BOWLING GREEN
3160 Scottsville Rd (42104)
Rates: $36-$45
Tel: (502) 781-3460

RAMADA INN
4767 Scottsville Rd (42104)
Rates: $34-$70
Tel: (502) 781-3000

SCOTTISH INNS
3140 Scottsville Rd (42104)
Rates: $30-$45
Tel: (502) 781-6550
(800) 251-1962

BURKESVILLE

RIVERFRONT LODGE
305 Keen St (42717)
Rates: $37-$43
Tel: (502) 864-3300

CADIZ

COUNTRY INN BY CARLSTON
5909 Hopkinsville Rd (42211)
Rates: $39-$55
Tel: (502) 522-7007

CAMPBELLSVILLE

LAKEVIEW MOTEL
1291 Old Lebanon Rd (42718)
Rates: $33-38
Tel: (502) 465-8139

SUPER 8 MOTEL
100 Albion Rd (42718)
Rates: $40-$47
Tel: (800) 800-8000

CARROLLTON

BLUE GABLES COURT
1501 HIghland Ave (41008)
Rates: $26-$30
Tel: (502) 732-4248

DAYS INN
61 Inn Rd (41008)
Rates: $52-$57
Tel: (502) 732-9301
(800) 329-7466

HOLIDAY INN EXPRESS
140 Inn Rd (41008)
Rates: $55
Tel: (800) 465-4329

SUPER 8 MOTEL
130 Slumber Ln (41008)
Rates: $35+
Tel: (800) 800-8000

CAVE CITY

CAVE LAND MOTEL
451 Dixie Hwy (42127)
Rates: $18-$36
Tel: (502) 773-2321

COMFORT INN
801 Mammoth Cave St (42127)
Rates: $50-$85
Tel: (502) 773-2030

DAYS INN
822 Mammoth Cave St (42127)
Rates: $28-$66
Tel: (502) 773-2151

HERITAGE INN
Box 2048 (42127)
Rates: $25-$62
Tel: (800) 264-1514

HOLIDAY INN EXPRESS
Hwy 90 & I-65 (42127)
Rates: $40-85
Tel: (502) 773-3101

QUALITY INN
Mammoth Cave Rd (42127)
Rates: $28-$68
Tel: (800) 424-6423

CORBIN

BUDGETEL INN
174 Adams Rd (40701)
Rates: $43-$60
Tel: (606) 528-9040

HOLIDAY INN
2615 Cumberland Falls Hwy (40701)
Rates: $55-$75
Tel: (800) 465-4329

HOLIDAY MOTEL
1304 S Main St (40701)
Rates: $22-$25
Tel: (606) 528-6220

KNIGHTS INN
Rte 11, Box 256 (40701)
Rates: $35-$49
Tel: (800) 843-5644

SUBURBAN MOTEL
1320 Cumberland Falls Hwy (40701)
Rates: n/a
Tel: (606) 528-1370

SUPER 8 MOTEL
171 W Cumberland Gap Pkwy (40701)
Rates: $39-$48
Tel: (800) 800-8000

CORINTH

K & T MOTEL
Hwy 330 & I-75 Exit 144 (41010)
Rates: n/a
Tel: (506) 824-4371

COVINGTON

EMBASSY SUITES AT RIVERCENTER
10 E Rivercenter Blvd (41011)
Rates: $39-$179
Tel: (606) 261-8400

QUALITY HOTEL RIVERVIEW
666 W 5th St (41011)
Rates: $79-$99
Tel: (800) 292-2079

SANDFORD HOUSE B & B
1026 Russell St (41011)
Rates: $50-$100
Tel: (606) 291-9133

DANVILLE

DAYS INN
Danville Bypass (40422)
Rates: $50-$55
Tel: (606) 236-8601
(800) 329-7466

HOLIDAY INN
96 Daniel Dr (40422)
Rates: $50-$65
Tel: (800) 465-4329

SUPER 8 MOTEL
3663 Hwy 150/127 Bypass (40422)
Rates: $34-$59
Tel: (800) 800-8000

DRY RIDGE

SUPER 8 MOTEL
88 Blackburn Ln (41035)
Rates: $38-$50
Tel: (606) 824-3700
(800) 800-8000

EDDYVILLE

EDDY BAY LODGING
75 Forest Glen Dr (42038)
Rates: $64-$110
Tel: (502) 388-9960

HOLIDAY HILLS TOWNHOUSES
Rt 1, Box 406 (42038)
Rates: $105
Tel: (502) 388-7236

ELIZABETHTOWN

BEST WESTERN CARDINAL INN
642 E Dixie Ave (42701)
Rates: $28-$54
Tel: (502) 765-6139
(800) 528-1234

COMFORT INN
1043 Executive Dr (42701)
Rates: $45-$75
Tel: (800) 221-2222

DAYS INN
2010 N Mulberry (42701)
Rates: $34-$46
Tel: (502) 769-5522
(800) 329-7466

LINCOLN TRAIL MOTEL
905 N Mulberry St (42701)
Rates: $21-$26
Tel: (502) 769-1301

THE OLDE BETHLEHEM ACADEMY INN
7051 St John Rd (42701)
Rates: $65-$150
Tel: (502) 862-9003

SUPER 8 MOTEL
2028 N Mulberry St (42701)
Rates: $35-$49
Tel: (502) 737-1088
(800) 800-8000

TRAVELODGE
2009 N Mulberry (42701)
Rates: $31-$49
Tel: (502) 765-4166

ERLANGER

COMFORT INN CINCINNATI AIRPORT
630 Donaldson Rd (41018)
Rates: $45-$80
Tel: (800) 221-2222

HOWARD JOHNSON
648 Donaldson Rd
(41018)
Rates: $39-$55
Tel: (606) 342-6200
(800) 446-4656

FLORENCE

KNIGHTS INN CINCINNATI SOUTH
8049 Dream St
(41042)
Rates: $35-$46
Tel: (800) 843-5644

MOTEL 6
7937 Dream St
(41042)
Rates: $27-$36
Tel: (606) 283-0909

SUPER 8 MOTEL
7928 Dream St
(41042)
Rates: $37-$52
Tel: (606) 283-1221
(800) 800-8000

FORT MITCHELL

HOLIDAY INN SOUTH
2100 Dixie Hwy
(41017)
Rates: $79-$89
Tel: (800) 465-4329

FORT WRIGHT

DAYS INN CINCINNATI-FT. WRIGHT
1945 Dixie Hwy
(41011)
Rates: $36-$42
Tel: (800) 329-7466

FRANKFORT

ANCHOR INN
790 E Main (40601)
Rates: n/a
Tel: (502) 227-7404

BLUEGRASS INN
635 Versailles Rd
(40601)
Rates: $34-$46
Tel: (502) 695-1800

SUPER 8 MOTEL
1225 US Hwy 127 S
(40601)
Rates: $40-$60
Tel: (502) 875-3220
(800) 800-8000

FRANKLIN

COMFORT INN
3794 Nashville Rd
(42134)
Rates: $39-$58
Tel: (800) 221-2222

HOLIDAY INN EXPRESS
3811 Nashville Rd
(42134)
Rates: $45-$65
Tel: (502) 586-5090

SUPER 8 MOTEL
2805 Scottsville Rd
(42134)
Rates: $33-$43
Tel: (502) 586-8885
(800) 800-8000

GEORGETOWN

DAYS INN
385 Delaplain Rd
(40324)
Rates: $30-$100
Tel: (502) 863-5002
(800) 329-7466

MOTEL 6
401 Delaplain Rd
(40324)
Rates: $33-$39
Tel: (502) 863-1166
(800) 466-8356

SHONEY'S INN
200 Shoney Dr
(40324)
Rates: $40-$47
Tel: (502) 868-9800
(800) 222-2222

SUPER 8 MOTEL
250 Shoney Dr
(40324)
Rates: $35-$40
Tel: (502) 863-4888
(800) 800-8000

GIBERTSVILLE

MOORS RESORT
Hwy 963 (42044)
Rates: n/a
Tel: (800) 626-5472

RAMADA INN RESORT AT KY DAM/CALVERT CITY
P. O. Box 158 (42044)
Rates: $55-$74
Tel: (502) 362-4278

GLASGOW

GLASGOW INN
1003 W Main (42141)
Rates: $30-$68
Tel: (502) 651-5191

GRAND RIVERS

BEST WESTERN BARKLEY LAKES INN
720 Complex Dr
(42045)
Rates: $38-$69
Tel: (502) 928-2700
(800) 528-1234

HARDIN

EARLY AMERICAN MOTEL
Rt 1, Hwy 68 (42048)
Rates: $26-$47
Tel: (502) 474-2241

HARLAN

SCOTTISH INNS
US 421 S, Eugene
Goss Hwy (40831)
Rates: $35-$39
Tel: (606) 573-4660
(800) 251-1962

HARRODSBURG

BEST WESTERN
1680 Danville Rd
(40330)
Rates: $46-$62
Tel: (606) 734-9431
(800) 528-1234

HAZARD

SUPER 8 MOTEL
125 Village Ln
(41701)
Rates: $43-$49
Tel: (606) 436-8888

HEBRON

RADISSON INN-CINCINNATI AIRPORT
Cincinnati-N KY
Airport (41048)
Rates: $69-$109
Tel: (606) 371-6166

HENDERSON

DAYS INN
2044 US 41N (42420)
Rates: $53-$95
Tel: (502) 826-6600
(800) 329-7466

SCOTTISH INNS
2820 US 41N (42420)
Rates: $27-$36
Tel: (502) 827-1806
(800) 251-1962

SUPER 8 MOTEL
2030 Hwy 41 N
(42420)
Rates: $39-$53
Tel: (502) 827-5611
(800) 800-8000

HOPKINSVILLE

BEST WESTERN
4101 Fort Campbell
Blvd (42240)
Rates: $44-$57
Tel: (502) 886-9000
(800) 528-1234

HOLIDAY INN
2910 Fort Campbell
Blvd (42240)
Rates: $43-$79
Tel: (800) 465-4329

RODEWAY INN
2923 Fort Campbell
Blvd (42240)
Rates: $35-$43
Tel: (502) 885-1126
(800) 228-2000

HORSE CAVE

BUDGET HOST INN
P. O. Box 332 (42749)
Rates: $24-$100
Tel: (800) 283-4678

KENLAKE STATE RESORT PARK

EARLY AMERICAN MOTEL
Rt 1 (Hardin 42048)
Rates: $30-$58
Tel: (502) 474-2241

KUTTAWA

DAYS INN
Factory Outlet Ave
(42055)
Rates: $48-$68
Tel: (502) 388-5420
(800) 329-7466

LAGRANGE

DAYS INN
I-71 & SR 53 (40031)
Rates: $33-$47
Tel: (502) 222-7192
(800) 329-7466

LEBANON

HOLLYHILL MOTEL
459 Main St (40033)
Rates: n/a
Tel: (502) 692-2175

LEITCHFIELD

COUNTRY SIDE INN
Commerce Dr & W
KY Pkwy (42754)
Rates: $29-$41
Tel: (502) 259-4021

LEXINGTON

DAYS INN
1987 N Broadway
(40505)
Rates: $39-$69
Tel: (606) 299-1202
(800) 329-7466

DAYS INN-SOUTH
5575 Athens-
Boonesboro Rd
(40509)
Rates: $35-$55
Tel: (606) 263-3100
(800) 329-7466

ECONO LODGE
5527 Athens-
Boonesboro Rd
(40509)
Rates: $30-$40
Tel: (800) 424-4777

ECONO LODGE NORTH
925 Newtown Pike
(40511)
Rates: $30-$40
Tel: (800) 424-4777

FAIRFIELD INN BY MARRIOT
3050 Lakecrest Cir
(40513)
Rates: $57-$62
Tel: (606) 224-3338

GREENLEAF MOTEL
2280 Nicholasville
Rd (40503)
Rates: $39-$48
Tel: (606) 277-1191

HAMPTON INN
3060 Lakecrest Cir
(40513)
Rates: $67-$91
Tel: (800) 426-7866

HOLIDAY INN-NORTH
1950 Newtown Pike
(40511)
Rates: $84-$102
Tel: (800) 465-4329

HOLIDAY INN SOUTH
5532 Athens-
Boonesboro Rd
(40509)
Rates: $60-$79
Tel: (800) 465-4329

HOWARD JOHNSON
2250 Elkhorn Rd
(40505)
Rates: $34-$47
Tel: (606) 299-8481
(800) 446-4656

THE KENTUCKY INN
525 Waller Ave
(40504)
Rates: $46-$52
Tel: (606) 254-1177

LA QUINTA INN
1919 Stanton Way
(40511)
Rates: $41-$60
Tel: (800) 531-5900

MARRIOTT'S GRIFFIN GATE RESORT
1800 Newtown Pike
(40511)
Rates: $125-$150
Tel: (606) 231-5100

QUALITY INN NORTHWEST
1050 Newtown Pike
(40511)
Rates: $37-$56
Tel: (800) 221-2222

RADISSON PLAZA HOTEL
369 W Vine St
(40507)
Rates: $115-$135
Tel: (800) 333-3333

RED ROOF INN-NORTH
483 Haggard Ln
(40505)
Rates: $31-$56
Tel: (800) 843-7663

RED ROOF INN-SOUTH
2651 Wilhite Dr
(40503)
Rates: $38-$48
Tel: (800) 843-7663

SUPER 8 MOTEL
2351 Buena Vista Rd
(40505)
Rates: $37-$49
Tel: (800) 800-8000

WILSON INN
2400 Buena Vista Dr
(40505)
Rates: $40-$60
Tel: (606) 293-6113

LONDON

BEST WESTERN HARVEST INN
207 W Hwy 80
(40741)
Rates: $41-$60
Tel: (606) 864-2222
(800) 528-1234

DAYS INN
285 W Hwy 80
(40741)
Rates: $35-$75
Tel: (606) 878-9800
(800) 329-7466

RAMADA INN
2035 Hwy 192 W
(40741)
Rates: $38-$46
Tel: (800) 272-6232

WESTGATE INN MOTEL
254 W Daniel Boone
Pkwy (40741)
Rates: $32-$37
Tel: (606) 878-7330

LOUISA

BEST WESTERN VILLAGE INN
117 E Madison St
(41230)
Rates: $40-$47
Tel: (606) 638-9417

LOUISVILLE
(and Vicinity)

BEST WESTERN GREEN TREE INN
1425 Broadway
(Clarksville, IN
47129)
Rates: $45-$70
Tel: (812) 288-9281
(800) 528-1234

BRECKINRIDGE INN
2800 Breckinridge
Ln (40220)
Rates: $65
Tel: (502) 456-5050

**THE CAMBERLEY
BROWN HOTEL**
335 W Broadway
(40202)
Rates: $145-$180
Tel: (502) 583-1234

DAYS INN
101 E Jefferson St
(40202)
Rates: $69-$89
Tel: (502) 585-2200

DAYS INN EAST
4621 Shelbyville Rd
(40207)
Rates: $48-$110
Tel: (502) 896-8871
(800) 329-7466

**DAYS INN SOUTH-
EAST**
1850 Embassy Sq
Blvd (40299)
Rates: $36-$55
Tel: (502) 491-1040
(800) 329-7466

EXECUTIVE WEST
830 Phillips Ln
(40209)
Rates: $72-$82
Tel: (502) 367-2251

HOLIDAY INN
1465 Gardiner Ln
(40213)
Rates: $60-$77
Tel: (800) 465-4329

**HOLIDAY INN
DOWNTOWN**
120 W Broadway
(40202)
Rates: $74-$105
Tel: (800) 465-4329

**HOLIDAY INN
SOUTHEAST**
3255 Bardstown Rd
(40205)
Rates: $55-$75
Tel: (800) 465-4329

**HOLIDAY INN
SOUTH-AIRPORT**
3317 Fern Valley Rd
(40213)
Rates: $67-$83
Tel: (800) 465-4329

**HOLIDAY INN
SOUTHWEST**
4110 Dixie Hwy
(40216)
Rates: $60-$71
Tel: (800) 465-432

**HURSTBOURNE
HOTEL &
CONFERENCE CTR**
9700 Bluegrass
Pkwy (40299)
Rates: $70-$90
Tel: (502) 491-4830

**MELROSE INN
& MOTEL**
13306 US 42
(Prospect 40059)
Rates: $39-$58
Tel: (502) 228-1136

**MOTEL 6-
JEFFERSONVILLE**
2016 Old Hwy 31 E
(Jeffersonville, IN)
(47130)
Rates: $25-$34
Tel: (612) 283-7703

**OLD LOUISVILLE INN
BED & BREAKFAST**
1359 S 3rd St (40208)
Rates: $60-$195
Tel: (502) 635-1574

RAMADA INN
4805 Brownsboro Rd
(40207)
Rates: $49-$84
Tel: (800) 272-6232

RAMADA INN
1921 Bishop Ln
(40218)
Rates: $76+
Tel: (800) 272-6232

**RED ROOF INN-
AIRPORT**
4704 Preston Hwy
(40213)
Rates: $33-$50
Tel: (800) 843-7663

RED ROOF INN-EAST
9330 Blairwood Rd
(40222)
Rates: $33-$40
Tel: (800) 843-7663

**RED ROOF INN-
SOUTHEAST**
3322 Newburg Rd
(40218)
Rates: $30-$48
Tel: (800) 843-7663

**RESIDENCE INN
BY MARRIOTT**
120 Hurstbourne
Pkwy (40222)
Rates: $92-$120
Tel: (800) 331-3131

SEELBACH HOTEL
500 Fourth Ave
(40202)
Rates: $170-$180
Tel: (800) 333-3399

**SLEEP INN -
FAIRGROUNDS**
3330 Preston Hwy
(40213)
Rates: $39-$150
Tel: (502) 368-9597

SUPER 8 MOTEL
4800 Preston Hwy
(40213)
Rates: $40-$50
Tel: (800) 800-8000

**THRIFTY DUTCH-
MAN MOTEL**
3357 Fern Valley Rd
(40213)
Rates: $30-$42
Tel: (502) 968-8124

**WILSON INN
AIRPORT**
3209 Kemmons Dr
(40218)
Rates: $37-$53
Tel: (800) 945-7667

**WILSON INN
LOUISVILLE EAST**
9802 Bunsen Way
(40299)
Rates: $40-$60
Tel: (800) 945-7667

MADISONVILLE

DAYS INN
1900 Lantaff Blvd
(42431)
Rates: $49-$100
Tel: (502) 821-8620
(800) 329-7466

*MAMMOTH CAVE
NATIONAL PARK*

**MAMMOTH CAVE
HOTEL**
11 Mi W of Jct I-65
& SR 70 (42259)
Rates: $64-$67
Tel: (502) 758-2225

MAYFIELD

SUPER 8 MOTEL
1100 Links Ln (42066)
Rates: $36-$57
Tel: (502) 247-8899
(800) 800-8000

MIDDLESBORO

PARK VIEW MOTEL
202 1/2 N 12th St
(40965)
Rates: $30-$40
Tel: (606) 248-4516

MORTONS GAP

BEST WESTERN
Pennyrile Pkwy
(42440)
Rates: $35-$47
Tel: (502) 258-5201

*MOUNT
STERLING*

DAYS INN
705 Maysville Rd
(40353)
Rates: $24-$39
Tel: (606) 498-4680
(800) 329-7466

SCOTTISH INNS
517 Maysville Rd
(40353)
Rates: $22-$28
Tel: (606) 498-3424
(800) 251-1962

MOUNT VERNON

**BEST WESTERN
KASTLE INN MOTEL**
P. O. Box 637 (40456)
Rates: $36-$42
Tel: (800) 528-1234

**DAYS INN
RENFRO VALLEY**
1630 Richmond St
(40456)
Rates: $33-$59
Tel: (800) 329-7466

ECONO LODGE
P. O. Box 1106
(40456)
Rates: $30-$50
Tel: (800) 424-4777

MULDRAUGH

GOLDEN MANOR MOTEL
346 Dixie Hwy
(40155)
Rates: $39-$50
Tel: (502) 942-2800

MURRAY

DAYS INN
517 S 12th St (42071)
Rates: $45-$95
Tel: (502) 753-6706
(800) 329-7466

MURRAY PLAZA COURT
S 12th St (42071)
Rates: $29-$35
Tel: (502) 753-2682

PARADISE RESORT
Rt 6, Box 239 (42071)
Rates: n/a
Tel: (502) 436-2767

SHONEY'S INN
1503 N 12th St
(42071)
Rates: $40-$44
Tel: (502) 753-5353
(800) 222-2222

NEW CONCORD

MISSING HILL RESORT
HC Box 215-A
(42076)
Rates: n/a
Tel: (502) 436-5519

OWENSBORO

DAYS INN
3720 New Hartford
Rd (42301)
Rates: $42-$46
Tel: (502) 684-9621
(800) 329-7466

HOLIDAY INN
3136 W 2nd St
(42301)
Rates: $55-$66
Tel: (800) 465-4329

SUPER 8 MOTEL
1027 Goetz Dr
(42301)
Rates: $36-$45
Tel: (800) 800-8000

WEATHERBERRY BED & BREAKFAST
2731 W 2nd St
(42301)
Rates: $55-$85
Tel: (502) 684-8760

PADUCAH

BEST INNS OF AMERICA
5001 Hinckleville Rd
(42002)
Rates: $40-$48
Tel: (502) 442-3334

BUDGET HOST INN
1234 Broadway
(42001)
Rates: $31-$36
Tel: (800) 283-4678

DAYS INN
3901 Hinkleville Rd
(42001)
Rates: $40-$45
Tel: (502) 442-7501

DRURY INN
3975 Hinkleville Rd
(42001)
Rates: $55-$76
Tel: (800) 325-8300

DRURY SUITES
120 McBride Ln
(42001)
Rates: $79-$89
Tel: (502) 441-0024

FARLEY PLACE B & B
166 Farley Pl (42003)
Rates: n/a
Tel: (502) 442-2488

HAMPTON INN
4930 Hinkleville Rd
(42001)
Rates: $63-$78
Tel: (502) 442-4500
(800) 426-7866

HICKORY HOUSE MOTEL
2504 Bridge St
(42003)
Rates: n/a
Tel: (502) 442-1601

PEAR TREE INN
4910 Hinkleville Rd
(42001)
Rates: $47-$65
Tel: (800) 282-8733

QUALITY INN
1380 Irvin Cobb Dr
(42001)
Rates: $40-$48
Tel: (800)424-6423

RAMADA INN
727 Joe Clifton Dr
(42001)
Rates: $39-$60
Tel: (502) 443-7521
(800) 272-6232

ROYAL INN
2160 S Beltline
(42003)
Rates: n/a
Tel: (502) 442-6171

PAINTSVILLE

DAYS INN
512 South Mayo
Trail (41240)
Rates: $38-$55
Tel: (606) 789-3551
(800) 329-7466

PARKERS LAKE

HOLIDAY MOTOR LODGE
Hwy 90, Box 300
(42634)
Rates: n/a
Tel: (606) 376-2732

PIKEVILLE

LANDMARK INN
146 S Mayo Tr
(41501)
Rates: $49-$53
Tel: (606) 432-2545

PRESTONSBURG

HOLIDAY INN
575 S US 23 (41653)
Rates: $58-$70
Tel: (800) 465-4329

RADCLIFF

ECONO LODGE
261 N Dixie Hwy
(40160)
Rates: $35-$43
Tel: (800) 424-4777

FORT KNOX INN
1400 N Dixie Hwy
(40160)
Rates: n/a
Tel: (502) 351-3199

SUPER 8 MOTEL
395 Redmar Blvd
(40160)
Rates: $36-$42
Tel: (800) 800-8000

RICHMOND

DAYS INN
2109 Belmont Dr
(40475)
Rates: $38-$55
Tel: (606) 624-5769
(800) 329-7466

ECONO LODGE
230 Eastern Bypass
(40475)
Rates: $28-$35
Tel: (800) 424-4777

HOJO INN
1688 Northgate Dr
(40475)
Rates: $32-$36
Tel: (800) 446-4656

MOTEL 6
1698 Northgate Dr
(40475)
Rates: $25-$31
Tel: (606) 623-0880

SUPER 8 MOTEL
107 N Keeneland
(40475)
Rates: $38-$58
Tel: (606) 624-1550
(800) 800-8000

WISE MOTEL
105 N Killarney Ln
(40475)
Rates: $31-$32
Tel: (606) 623-8126

RICHWOOD

DAYS INN
11177 Frontage Rd
(Walton 41094)
Rates: $30-$40
Tel: (800) 329-7466

RICHWOOD MOTEL
10805 Dixie Hwy
(41094)
Rates: n/a
Tel: (606) 525-9525

SHELBYVILLE

**BEST WESTERN
SHELBYVILLE
LODGE**
115 Isaac Shelby Dr
(40065)
Rates: $44-$58
Tel: (502) 633-4400
(800) 528-1234

DAYS INN
101 Howard Dr
(40065)
Rates: $44-$49
Tel: (502) 633-4005
(800) 329-7466

SHELBYVILLE MOTEL
Box 378 Hwy US 60
(40065)
Rates: n/a
Tel: (502) 533-3350

SHEPHERDSVILLE

**BEST WESTERN
SOUTH**
211 S Lakeview Dr
(40165)
Rates: $43-$58
Tel: (502) 543-7097
(800) 528-1234

DAYS INN
SR 44 at Jct I-65
(40165)
Rates: $40+
Tel: (800) 329-7466

MOTEL 6
144 Paroquet
Springs Dr (40165)
Rates: $36-$42
Tel: (502) 543-4400
(800) 466-8356

SMITHS GROVE

BRYCE MOTEL
592 S Main St
(42171)
Rates: $32-$45
Tel: (502) 563-5141

SOMERSET

**CUMBERLAND
MOTEL**
6050 S Hwy 27
(42501)
Rates: n/a
Tel: (606) 561-5131

SPRINGFIELD

**GLENMAR
PLANTATION B & B**
Rt 1, Box 682 (40069)
Rates: $75
Tel: (606) 284-7791

WEST SOMERSET

BECKETT MOTEL
2001 Lees Ford Dock
(42564)
Rates: n/a
Tel: (606) 636-6411

WHITESBURG

SUPER 8 MOTEL
377-A Hazard Rd
(41858)
Rates: $39-$55
Tel: (606) 633-8888

WILLIAMSBURG

**BEST WESTERN
CONVENIENT
LODGE**
P. O. Box 204 (40769)
Rates: $29-$45
Tel: (606) 549-1500
(800) 528-1234

HOLIDAY INN
30 W Hwy 92
(40769)
Rates: $36
Tel: (800) 465-4329

WILLIAMSTOWN

DAYS INN
211 SR 36 W (41097)
Rates: $36-$70
Tel: (606) 824-5025
(800) 329-7466

HOJO INN
10 Skyway Dr
(41097)
Rates: $34-$49
Tel: (800) 446-4656

WINCHESTER

HOLIDAY INN
1100 Holiday Dr
(40391)
Rates: $55
Tel: (800) 465-4329

RED CARPET INN
1510 W Lexington
Ave (40391)
Rates: $32-$50
Tel: (606) 744-9220
(800) 251-1962

LOUISIANA

ALEXANDRIA

**BEST WESTERN
OF ALEXANDRIA**
2720 W MacArthur
Dr (71303)
Rates: $48-$70
Tel: (318) 445-5530
(800) 528-1234

RODEWAY INN
742 MacArthur Dr
(71303)
Rates: $55-$70
Tel: (318) 448-1611
(800) 228-2000

TRAVELODGE
1146 MacArthur Dr
(71303)
Rates: $37-$43
Tel: (318) 443-1841

AMITE

**BLYTHEWOOD
PLANTATION B & B**
P. O. Box 155 (70422)
Rates: $75-$150
Tel: (504) 345-6419

ARCADIA

DAYS INN
1061 Hwy 151
(71001)
Rates: $40-$70
Tel: (318) 263-3555
(800) 329-7466

BASTROP

COUNTRY INN
1815 E Madison
(71220)
Rates: $33-$38
Tel: (318) 281-8100

BATON ROUGE

BUDGETEL INN
10555 Rieger Rd
(70809)
Rates: $35-$52
Tel: (504) 291-6600

COMFORT INN
2445 S Acadian
(70808)
Rates: $46-$51
Tel: (800) 221-2222

**HILTON-BATON
ROUGE**
5500 Hilton Ave
(70808)
Rates: $80-$85
Tel: (800) 445-8667

LA QUINTA INN
2333 S Acadian
Thruway (70808)
Rates: $51-$61
Tel: (800) 531-5900

MOTEL 6
9901 Gwen Adele
Ave (70816)
Rates: $34-$40
Tel: (504) 924-2130
(800) 466-8356

RED ROOF INN
11314 Boardwalk Dr
(70816)
Rates: $38-$53
Tel: (800) 843-7663

SHONEY'S INN
9919 Gwen Adele Dr
(70816)
Rates $45-$60
Tel: (800) 222-2222

BOSCO

**BOSCOBEL
COTTAGE B & B**
185 Cordell Ln
(71202)
Rates: $75-$95
Tel: (318) 325-1550

BOSSIER CITY

DAYS INN
200 John Wesley
Blvd (71112)
Rates: $25-$56
Tel: (318) 742-9200
(800) 329-7466

MOTEL 6
210 John Wesley
Blvd (71112)
Rates: $34-$44
Tel: (318) 742-3472
(800) 466-8356

RAMADA INN
750 Isle of Capri
Blvd (71111)
Rates: $51-$71
Tel: (318) 746-8410:
(800) 272-6232

RESIDENCE INN
1001 Gould Dr
(71111)
Rates: $94-$135
Tel: (318) 747-6220
(800) 331-3131

BREAUX BRIDGE

BEST WESTERN
2090 Rees St (70517)
Rates: $59-$78
Tel: (800) 528-1234

CHENEYVILLE

**LOYD HALL
PLANTATION B & B**
292 Loyd Bridge Rd
(71325)
Rates: $95-$145
Tel: (318) 776-5641
(800) 240-8135

CROWLEY

BEST WESTERN
9571 Egan Hwy
(70526)
Rates: $59-$78
Tel: (318) 783-2378
(800) 940-0003

DELHI

**BEST WESTERN
DELHI INN**
35 Snider Rd (71232)
Rates: $38-$72
Tel: (318) 878-5126
(800) 528-1234

DE RIDDER

**BEST WESTERN
DE RIDDER INN**
1213 N Pine (70634)
Rates: $44-$49
Tel: (318) 462-3665
(800) 528-1234

RED CARPET INN
806 N Pine St (70634)
Rates: $27-$39
Tel: (318) 463-8605
(800) 251-1962

EUNICE

**SEALE GUEST-
HOUSE B & B**
P. O. Box 568 (70535)
Rates: $65-$75
Tel: (318) 457-3753

FRANKLIN

**BEST WESTERN
FOREST
MOTOR INN**
1909 Main St (70538)
Rates: $50-$70
Tel: (318) 828-1810
(800) 528-1234

GRETNA

**HOWARD
JOHNSON**
100 Westbank
Expwy (70053)
Rates: $55-$95
Tel: (504) 366-8531
(800) 446-4656

HAMMOND

BEST WESTERN INN
14175 Hwy 190
(70401)
Rates: $48-$68
Tel: (504) 542-8555
(800) 528-1234

HOUMA

CROCHET HOUSE BED & BREAKFAST
801 Midland Dr (71073)
Rates: $45-$65
Tel: (504) 879-3033

QUALITY INN
1400 W Tunnel Blvd (70360)
Rates: $47-$125
Tel: (800) 221-2222

JACKSON

ASPHODEL INN
Rt 2, Box 89A (70748)
Rates: $55-$130
Tel: (504) 654-6868

JENNINGS

CREOLE ROSE MANOR B & B
214 W Plaquemine (70546)
Rates: $50-$75
Tel: (318) 824-3145

KROTZ SPRINGS

COUNTRY STORE B & B INN
P. O. Drawer 457 (70750)
Rates: $45-$75
Tel: (318) 566-2331

LAFAYETTE

BEST WESTERN HOTEL ACADIANA
1801 Pinhook Rd (70508)
Rates: $78-$88
Tel: (318) 233-8120
(800) 826-8386

BOIS DES CHENES INN B & B
338 N Sterling (70501)
Rates: $75-$105
Tel: (318) 233-7816

COMFORT INN
1421 SE Evangeline Thrwy (70501)
Rates: $48-$59
Tel: (800) 221-2222

DAYS INN
1620 N University & I-10 (70506)
Rates: $40-$50
Tel: (318) 237-8880
(800) 329-7466

LA QUINTA INN
2100 NE Evangeline Thrwy (70501)
Rates: $43-$49
Tel: (800) 531-5900

QUALITY INN
1605 N University (70501)
Rates: $39-$56
Tel: (800) 221-2222

RED ROOF INN
1718 N University Ave (70507)
Rates: $31-$39
Tel: (800) 843-7663

RODEWAY INN
1801 NW Evangeline Thrwy (70501)
Rates: $40-$68
Tel: (318) 233-5500
(800) 228-2000

SUPER 8 MOTEL
2224 NE Evangeline Thrwy (70501)
Rates: $26-$33
Tel: (800) 800-8000

LAKE CHARLES

DAYS INN
1010 Hwy 171 N (70601)
Rates: $60-$70
Tel: (318) 433-1711
(800) 329-7466

MOTEL 6
335 Hwy 171 (70601)
Rates: $34-$44
Tel: (318) 433-1773
(800) 466-8356

MINDEN

BEST WESTERN MINDEN
1411 Sibley Rd (71055)
Rates: $40-$80
Tel: (318) 377-1001

MONROE

BEST WESTERN AIRPPORT INN
1475 Garrett Rd (71202)
Rates: $54-$115
Tel: (318) 345-4000
(800) 528-1234

BOSCOBEL COTTAGE B & B
185 Cordell Lane (71202)
Rates: $65-$95
Tel: (318) 325-1550
(800) 254-3529

HOWARD JOHNSON
5650 Frontage Rd (71202)
Rates: $39-$48
Tel: (318) 345-2220
(800) 446-4656

LA QUINTA INN
1035 US 165S Bypass (71203)
Rates: $44-$50
Tel: (800) 531-5900

MOTEL 6
1501 US Hwy 165 Bypass (71202)
Rates: $29-$35
Tel: (318) 322-5430
(800) 466-8356

RED ROOF INN
102 Constitution Dr (West Monroe 71292)
Rates: $37-$45
Tel: (800) 843-7663

NATCHITOCHES

CLOUTIER TOWN-HOUSE B & B
Front St/Ducoumau Square (71457)
Rates: $50-$150
Tel: (318) 352-5242
(800) 351-7666

DAYS INN
1000 College Ave (71457)
Rates: $32-$49
Tel: (318) 352-4426
(800) 329-7466

NEW IBERIA

BEST WESTERN OF NEW IBERIA
2714 Hwy 14 (70560)
Rates: $48-$68
Tel: (318) 364-3030
(800) 528-1234

LA MAISON B & B
8317 Weeks Island Rd (70560)
Rates: $75-$140
Tel: (318) 364-2970
(800) 225-8671

MAISON MARCELINE B & B
442 E Main (70560)
Rates: $50-$175
Tel: (318) 364-5922

NEW ORLEANS
(and Vicintiy)

BEST WESTERN PATIO DOWNTOWN MOTEL
2820 Tulane Ave (70119)
Rates: $49-$105
Tel: (504) 822-0200
(800) 528-1234

DAYS INN AIRPORT
1300 Veterans Memorial Blvd (Kenner 70062)
Rates: $50-$135
Tel: (504) 469-2531
(800) 329-7466

LA QUINTA INN-CAUSEWAY
3100 I-10 Service Rd (Metairie 70001)
Rates: $53-$61
Tel: (504) 835-8511

MAISON ESPLANADE GUEST HOUSE B&B
1244 Esplanade Ave (70116)
Rates: $39-$149
Tel: (504) 523-8080

MARIGNY GUEST-HOUSE B & B
617 Kerlerec (70116)
Rates: $75-$150
Tel: (504) 944-9700

NEW ORLEANS AIRPORT HILTON
901 Airline Hwy
(70063)
Rates: $110-$155
Tel: (504) 469-5000

QUALITY HOTEL
2261 N Causeway Blvd
(Metairie 70001)
Rates: $50-$119
Tel: (504) 833-8213

QUALITY INN MARINA
5353 Paris Rd, LA 47
(Chalmette 70043)
Rates: $40-$99
Tel: (800) 424-6423

RATHBONE INN BED & BREAKFAST
1227 Esplanade
(70116)
Rates: $75-$125
Tel: (504) 947-2100
(800) 947-2101

ROBERT GORDY HOUSE B & B
2630 Bell St (70119)
Rates: $75-$95+
Tel: (504) 488-9424

SULLY MANSION
2631 Prtania St
(70130)
Rates: $50-$150
Tel: (504) 891-0457

WINDSOR COURT HOTEL
300 Gravier St
(70140)
Rate: $235-$500
Tel: (504) 523-6000

NEW ROADS

RIVER BLOSSOM INN B & B
300 N Carolina St
(70760)
Rates: $55-$75
Tel: (504) 638-8650

OPELOUSAS

BEST WESTERN OF OPELOUSAS
1635 I-49 Service Rd S (70570)
Rates: $59-78
Tel: (318) 942-5540
(800) 528-1234

PORT ALLEN

DAYS INN
215 Lobdell Hwy
(70767)
Rates: $32-50
Tel: (504) 387-0671
(800) 329-7466

NEWCOURT INN
I-10 & Hwy 415
(70767)
Rates: $39-$44
Tel: (504) 381-9134

RAYVILLE

COTTONLAND INN
P. O. Box 29 (71269)
Rates: $24-$33
Tel: (318) 728-5985

RUSTON

HOLIDAY INN
401 N Service Rd
(71270)
Rates: $44-$58
Tel: (800) 465-4329

ST. FRANCISVILLE

BUTLER GREEN-WOOD B & B
8345 US Hwy 61
(70775)
Rates: $80-$100
Tel: (504) 635-6312

LAKE ROSEMOUND INN B & B
10473 Lindsey Ln
(70775)
Rates: $70-$105
Tel: (504) 635-3176

ST. MARTINVILLE

MAISON BLEUE B&B
417 N Main St
(70582)
Rates: $65-$75
Tel: (318) 394-1215

SHREVEPORT

DAYS INN
4935 W Monkhouse Rd (71109)
Rates: $21-$55
Tel: (318) 636-0800
(800) 329-7466

MOTEL 6
4915 Monkhouse Dr
(71109)
Rates: $28-$32
Tel: (318) 631-9691
(800) 466-8356

RED ROOF INN
7296 Greenwood Rd
(71119)
Rates: $33-$50
Tel: (800) 843-7663

SUPER 8 LODGE
5204 Monkhouse Dr
(71109)
Rates: $37-$46
Tel: (800) 800-8000

SLIDELL

ECONO LODGE
58512 Tyler Dr
(70459)
Rates: $36-$75
Tel: (800) 424-4777

LA QUINTA INN
794 E I-10 Service Rd
(70461)
Rates $49-$62
Tel: (800) 531-5900

MOTEL 6
136 Taos St (70458)
Rates: $32-$40
Tel: (504) 649-7925
(800) 466-8356

RAMADA INN
798 E I-10 Service Rd
(70461)
Rates: $36-$55
Tel: (504) 653-9960

SULPHUR

LA QUINTA INN
2600 S Ruth St
(70663)
Rates: $45-$61
Tel: (800) 531-5900

TALLULAH

SUPER 8 MOTEL
1604 New Hwy 65 S
(71282)
Rates: $40-$53
Tel: (318) 574-2000
(800) 800-8000

THIBODAUX

HOWARD JOHNSON
201 N Canal Blvd
(70301)
Rates: $44-$57
Tel: (504) 447-9071

OAKES B & B
1418 Himalaya Ave
(70301)
Rates: $75-$150
Tel: (504) 447-3764

VINTON

BEST WESTERN DELTA DOWNS MOTOR INN
2267 Old Hwy 90
(70668)
Rates: $47-$68
Tel: (318) 589-7492
(800) 528-1234

WINNSBORO

BEST WESTERN WINNSBORO
4198 Front St (71295)
Rates: $45-$53
Tel: (318) 435-2000
(800) 528-1234

MAINE

AUBURN

AUBURN INN
Washington St at
exit 12 (04210)
Rates: $49-$79
Tel: (207) 777-1777

AUGUSTA

**BEST WESTERN
SENATOR INN**
284 Western Ave
(04330)
Rates: $59-$109
Tel: (207) 622-5804
(800) 528-1234

**ECHO LAKE LODGE
& COTTAGES**
Rt 17 in Fayette
(04330)
Rates: n/a
Tel: (207) 685-9550

MOTEL 6
18 Edison Dr (04330)
Rates: $36-$42
Tel: (207) 622-0000
(800) 440-6000

BANGOR

**BEST WESTERN
WHITE HOUSE**
155 Littlefield Ave
(04401)
Rates: $44-$79
Tel: (207) 862-3737
(800) 528-1234

**BUDGET TRAVELER
MOTOR LODGE**
327 Odlin Rd (04401)
Rates: $32-$50
Tel: (207) 945-0111

COMFORT INN
750 Hogan Rd
(04401)
Rates: $45-$79
Tel: (207) 942-7899
(800) 221-2222

DAYS INN
250 Odlin Rd (04401)
Rates: $48-$84
Tel: (207) 942-8272
(800) 329-7466

ECONO LODGE
327 Odlin Rd (04401)
Rates: $27-$46
Tel: (207) 945-0111
(800) 424-4777

**HOLIDAY INN-
MAIN STREET**
500 Main St (04401)
Rates: $57-$98
Tel: (207) 947-8651
(800) 465-4329

**HOLIDAY INN-
ODLIN ROAD**
404 Odlin Rd (04401)
Rates: $65-$85
Tel: (207) 947-0101
(800) 465-4329

MOTEL 6
1100 Hammond St
(04401)
Rates: $30-$36
Tel: (207) 947-6921
(800) 440-6000

PENOBSCOT INN
570 Main St (04401)
Rates: $48-$68
Tel: (207) 947-0566

**THE PHENIX INN
BED & BREAKFAST**
20 W Market Sq
(04401)
Rates: $35-$80
Tel: (207) 947-3850

RED CARPET INN
480 Main St (04401)
Rates: $32-$59
Tel: (207) 942-5282

RIVERSIDE INN
495 State St (04401)
Rates: $40-$88
Tel: (207) 947-3800

RODEWAY INN
482 Odlin Rd (04401)
Rates: $45-$100
Tel: (207) 942-6301
(800) 228-2000

SCOTTISH INNS
1476 Hammond St
(04401)
Rates: $24-$59
Tel: (207) 945-2934
(800) 251-1962

BAR HARBOR

BALANCE ROCK INN
21 Albert Meadow
(04609)
Rates: $125-$435
Tel: (207) 288-9900

**BAYVIEW HOTEL
& INN**
111 Eden St (04609)
Rates: n/a
Tel: (207) 288-5861
(800) 356-3585

**HUTCHIN'S
MOUNTAIN VIEW
MOTOR COURT**
RFD 1, Box 1190
(04609)
Rates: $38-$74
Tel: (207) 288-4833

**WONDERVIEW
MOTOR LODGE**
Box 25 (04609)
Rates: n/a
Tel: (207) 288-3358

BASS HARBOR

**BASS HARBOR
GABLES**
P.O. Box 396 (04653)
Rates: $125
Tel (207) 244-3699

BATH

FAIRHAVEN
North Bath Rd (04530)
Rates: $60-$90
Tel: (207) 443-4391

NEW MEADOWS INN
Bath Rd (West Bath
04530)
Rates: $30-$58
Tel: (207) 443-3921

BELFAST

**ADMIRAL'S OCEAN
INN**
RR 1, Box 99A
(04915)
Rates: $35-$75
Tel: (207) 338-4260

**BELFAST BAY
MEADOWS INN**
90 North port
Avenue (04915)
Rates: $75-$125
Tel: (207) 338-5715
(800) 335-2370

**BELFAST
MOTOR INN**
RR 2, Box 21 (04915)
Rates: $85-$95
Tel: (207) 338-2740

GULL MOTEL
RR 1 Box 80 (04915)
Rates: $29-$59
Tel: (207) 338-4030

BETHEL

**BETHEL INN
& COUNTRY CLUB**
On the Common
(04217)
Rates: $95-$280
Tel: (207) 824-2175
(800) 654-0125

**THE BRIAR LEA
BED & BREAKFAST**
150 Mayville Rd
(04217)
Rates: $42-$93
Tel: (207) 824-4717

**THE CAMERON
HOUSE**
Maston St Box 468
(04217)
Rates: n/a
Tel: (207) 824-3219

**L'AUBERGE
COUNTRY INN**
Mill Hill Rd (04217)
Rates: $50-$100
Tel: (207) 824-2774

BINGHAM

**BINGHAM
MOTOR INN**
Route 201 (04920)
Rates: $30-$68
Tel: (207) 672-4135

BOOTHBAY

**HILLSIDE ACRES
MOTEL**
P. O. Box 300
04537
Rates: $40-$65
Tel: (207) 633-3411

**WHITE ANCHOR
MOTEL**
RR 1 Box 438 (04537)
Rates: $29-$69
Tel: (207) 633-3788

BOOTHBAY HARBOR

**CATWALK ON
THE MILL POND**
P.O. Box 447
(E Boothbay, 04554)
Rates: $750/weekly
Tel: (207) 633-3270

**FISHERMAN'S
WHARF INN**
40 Commercial St
(04538)
Rates: $60-$170
Tel: (207) 633-5090

**HARBORSIDE
RESORT**
P. O. Box 516B
(04575)
Rates: $59-$109
Tel: (207) 633-5381
(800) 235-5402

THE LAWNMEER INN
P. O. Box 505 (04538)
Rates: $58-$168
Tel: (207) 633-2544
(800) 633-7645

LEEWARD VILLAGE
Rt 96 Ocean Point
Rd (East Boothbay
04544)
Rates: $65-$150
Tel: (207) 633-3681

**OCEAN POINT
CABIN**
HC Box 936 (East
Boothbay, 04544)
Rates: n/a
Tel: (207) 633-2981

THE PINES MOTEL
P. O. Box 693 (04538)
Rates: $60-$70
Tel: (207) 633-4555

**SMUGGLER'S COVE
MOTOR INN**
Dept A (East
Boothbay 04544)
Rates: $48-$120
Tel: (207) 633-2800

WELCH HOUSE INN
36 McKown St
(04538)
Rates: $50-$105
Tel: (207) 633-3431

BREWER

**BREWER
MOTOR INN**
359 Wilson St
(04412)
Rates: $32-$59
Tel: (207) 989-4476

RODEWAY INN
448 Wilson St
(04412)
Rates: $35-$50
Tel: (207) 989-3200
(800) 228-2999

BROWNFIELD

**FOOTHILLS FARM
BED & BREAKFAST**
RR 1, Box 598
(04010)
Rates: n/a
Tel: (207) 935-3799

BRUNSWICK

THE ATRIUM MOTEL
Cooks Corner exit
(04011)
Rates: $45-$97
Tel: (207) 729-5555

MAINLINE MOTEL
133 Pleasant St
(04011)
Rates: $59-$79
Tel: (207) 725-8761

VIKING MOTOR INN
287 Bath Rd (04011)
Rates: $35-$79
Tel: (207) 729-6661
(800) 429-6661

BUCKSPORT

**BEST WESTERN
JED PROUTY INN**
52 Main St (04416)
Rates: $59-$89
Tel: (207) 469-3113
(800) 528-1234

**BUCKSPORT
MOTOR INN**
151 Main St (04416)
Rates: $33-$55
Tel: (207) 469-3111

**SPRING FOUNTAIN
MOTEL**
RFD 2, Box 710
(04416)
Rates: $34-$75
Tel: (207) 469-3139

CAMDEN

BELOIN'S MOTEL
HCR 60, Box 3105
US 1 (04843)
Rates: n/a
Tel: (207) 236-3262

**BLUE HARBOR
HOUSE,
A COUNTRY INN**
67 Elm St (04843)
Rates: $85-$135
Tel: (207) 236-3196

**PINE GROVE
COTTAGES**
Rt 1 (Lincolnville,
04849)
Rates: $50-$115
Tel: (207) 236-2929

CAPE ELIZABETH

INN BY THE SEA
40 Bowery Beach Rd
(04107)
Rates: $95-$390
Tel: (207) 799-3134

CARIBOU

**CARIBOU INN &
CONVENTION CTR**
Rt 3 (04736)
Rates: $46-$82
Tel: (207) 498-3733

CASTINE

**THE HOLIDAY
HOUSE**
Box 215, Perkins St
(04421)
Rates: n/a
Tel: (207) 326-4335

THE MANOR
P. O. Box 276 (04421)
Rates: $65-$150
Tel: (207) 326-4861

CENTER LOVELL

**HEWNOAKS
HOUSEKEEPING
COTTAGES**
RR 1, Box 65 (04016)
Rates: n/a
Tel: (207) 925-6051

**WESTWAYS
ON KEZAR LAKE**
Rt 5 (04016)
Rates: $90+
Tel: (207) 928-2663

DAMARISCOTTA

**COUNTY FAIR
MOTEL**
RFD 1, Box 36
(04543)
Rates: $37-$61
Tel: (207) 563-3769

**OYSTER SHELL
MOTEL**
Box 267 (04543)
Rates: $85-$99
Tel: (800) 874-3747

EAST HOLDEN

THE LUCERNE INN
Bar Harbor Rd
(04429)
Rates: $59-$89
Tel: (207) 843-5123

EAST WINTHROP

LAKESIDE MOTEL CABINS & MARINA
P. O. Box 236 (04343)
Rates: $35+
Tel: (800) 532-6892

EASTPORT

TODD HOUSE
Todd's Head (04631)
Rates: $45-$80
Tel: (207) 853-2328

EDGECOMB

BAY VIEW INN
P. O. Box 117 (04556)
Rates: $60-$90
Tel: (207) 882-6911

EDGECOMB INN
Rt 1, Box 51 (04556)
Rates: $49-$110
Tel: (207) 882-6343

ELLSWORTH

BROOKSIDE MOTEL
High St (04605)
Rates: $38-$88
Tel: (207) 667-2543

COLONIAL MOTOR LODGE
Bar Harbor Rd (04605)
Rates: $40-$80
Tel: (207) 667-5548

COMFORT INN
130 High St (04605)
Rates: $89-$109
Tel: (207) 667-1345
(800) 221-2222

HOLIDAY INN
3 High St (04650)
Rates: $57-$119
Tel: (800) 465-4329

TWILITE MOTEL
US 1 & SR 3 (04605)
Rates: $30-$70
Tel: (207) 667-8165

THE WHITE BIRCHES
P.O. Box 743 (04605)
Rates: $30-$65
Tel: (207) 667-3621

FARMINGTON

MOUNT BLUE MOTEL
RFD 4, Box 5260 (04938)
Rates: $39-$54
Tel: (207) 778-6004

FREEPORT

EAGLE MOTEL
291 US 1 S (04032)
Rates: $39-$79
Tel: (207) 865-3106
(800) 334-4088

FREEPORT INN
335 US 1 S (04032)
Rates: $50-$70
Tel: (207) 865-3106
(800) 242-8838

ISAAC RANDALL BED & BREAKFAST
5 Independence Dr (04032)
Rates: n/a
Tel: (207) 865-9295
(800) 865-9295

MAINE IDYLL MOTOR CT
325 US Rt 1 North (04032)
Rates: n/a
Tel: (207) 865-4201

SUPER 8 MOTEL
218 US Rt 1 S (04032)
Rates: $39-$94
Tel: (207) 865-1408

GLEN COVE

SEA VIEW MOTEL
US 1, Box 101 (04846)
Rates: $62-$69
Tel: (207) 594-8479

GREENVILLE

KINEO VIEW MOTOR LODGE
P. O. Box 514, Rt 15 (04441)
Rates: $55
Tel: (207) 695-4470
(800) 659-8439

SPENCER POND CAMPS
Star Rt 76, Box 580 (04441)
Rates: $36-$48
Tel: (207) 695-2821

GREENVILLE JUNCTION

CHALET MOOSEHEAD MOTEL
Box 327 (04442)
Rates: $55-$65
Tel: (207) 695-2950
(800) 290-3645

GREENWOOD MOTEL
P. O. Box 307 (04442)
Rates: $40-$65
Tel: (207) 695-3321

HAMPDEN

BEST WESTERN-WHITE HOUSE
155 Littlefield Ave (04401)
Rates: $44-$79
Tel: (207) 862-9575

HOULTON

AMERICAN MOTEL
Rt 2A Bangor Rd (04730)
Rates: $24-$48
Tel: (207) 532-2236

SCOTTISH INNS
Rt 2A Bangor Rd (04730)
Rates: $38-$48
Tel: (207) 532-2236
(800) 251-1962

SHIRETOWN MOTOR INN
Rt 3, Box 30 (04730)
Rates: $50-$74
Tel: (207) 532-9421

JACKMAN

BRIARWOOD MOUNTAIN RESORT
P. O. Box 490 (04945)
Rates: $46-$54
Tel: (207) 668-7756

TUCKAWAY SHORES
Forest St (04945)
Rates: $25
Tel: (207) 668-3351

JONESBORO

WINDRISE FARM
Box 47, Evergreen Pt Rd (04648)
Rates: $250-$500 (Weekly)
Tel: (207) 434-2701

KENNEBUNK-PORT

THE COLONY
P. O. Box 511 (04046)
Rates: $165-$300
Tel: (207) 967-3331

CABOT COVE LODGE
South Maine St, Box 1082 (04046)
Rates: $70-$135
Tel: (800) 962-5424

LODGE AT TURBAT'S CREEK
P O Box 2722 (04046)
Rates: $55-$85
Tel: (207) 967-8700

SEASIDE HOUSE COTTAGES
Beach St, Gooch's Beach (04046)
Rates: $85-$160
Tel: (207) 967-4461

KINGFIELD

THE HERBERT HOTEL
Box 67 (04947)
Rates: $38-$125
Tel: (800) 843-4372

KITTERY

SUPER 8 MOTEL
85 US Rt 1 Bypass S (03904)
Rates: $35-$94
Tel: (207) 439-2000
(800) 800-8000

LEEDS

ANGELL COVE COTTAGES
Box 29, Bishop Hill Rd (04263)
Rates: $500/Weekly
Tel: (207) 524-5041

LEWISTON

HOLIDAY MOTEL
1905 Lisbon Rd (04240)
Rates: $19-$41
Tel: (207) 783-2277

MOTEL 6
516 Pleasant St (04240)
Rates: $33-$39
Tel: (207) 782-6558
(800) 440-6000

LINCOLN

BRIARWOOD MOTOR INN
P. O. Box 628 (04457)
Rates: $40-$55
Tel: (207) 794-6731

LINCOLN HOUSE MOTEL
85 Main St (04457)
Rates: $32-$42
Tel: (207) 794-3096

LUBEC

EASTLAND MOTEL
Box 220 (04652)
Rates: $36-$56
Tel: (207) 733-5501

MACHIAS

THE BLUEBIRD MOTEL
US 1, Box 45 (04654)
Rates: $42-$56
Tel: (207) 255-3332

MACHIAS MOTOR INN
26 E Main St (04654)
Rates: $46-$60
Tel: (207) 255-4861

MAINELAND MOTEL
RR 2 (East Machias 04630)
Rates: $30-$50
Tel: (207) 255-3334

MANSET

SEAWALL MOTEL
Rt 102A (04656)
Rates: $40-$85
Tel: (207) 244-9250
(800) 248-9250

MATINICUS

TUCKANUCK LODGE
Shag Hollow Rd (04851)
Rates: $40-$80
Tel: (207) 366-3830

MEDWAY

GATEWAY INN
Rt 157 (04460)
Rates: $45-$65
Tel: (207) 746-3193

KATAHDIN SHADOWS CABINS & MOTEL
P. O. Box H-I (04460)
Rates: $29-$39
Tel: (207) 746-9349
(800) 794-5267

MILLINOCKET

THE ATRIUM INN & HEALTH CLUB
740 Central St (04462)
Rates: $65-$90
Tel: (207) 723-4555

BEST WESTERN HERITAGE MOTOR INN
935 Central St (04462)
Rates: $49-$79
Tel: (207) 723-9777
(800) 528-1234

PAMOLA MOTOR LODGE
973 Central St (04462)
Rates: $29-$54
Tel: (207) 723-9746

MOODY

NE'R BEACH MOTEL
US 1, Box 389 (04054)
Rates: $39-$109
Tel: (207) 646-2636

NAPLES

AUGUSTUS BOVE HOUSE
RR 1, Box 501 (04055)
Rates: $49-$105
Tel: (207) 693-6365

NEWPORT

LOVLEY'S MOTEL
P. O. Box 147 (04953)
Rates: $30-$90
Tel: (207) 368-4311

NOBLEBORO

HOUSEKEEPING COTTAGE
RR1, Box 820 (Jefferson, 04348)
Rates: $150-$300/weekly
Tel: (207) 832-7055

NOBLEBORO CABIN
631 W Neck Rd (04555)
Rates: $500/Weekly
Tel: (207) 563-8152
(207) 563-8677

NORTH ANSON

EMBDEN LAKE RESORT
RR 1, Box 3395 (04958)
Rates: $110-$130
Tel: (207) 566-7501

NORWAY

INN TOWN MOTEL
43 Paris St (04268)
Rates: $39-$65
Tel: (207) 743-7706

LEDGEWOOD MOTEL
RFD 2, Box 30 (04268)
Rates: $38-$60
Tel: (207) 743-6347

OGUNQUIT

NORSEMAN MOTOR INN
P. O. Box 896 (03907)
Rates: $50-$185
Tel: (207) 646-7024

YELLOW MONKEY GUEST HOUSE
168 Main St (03907)
Rates: n/a
Tel: (207) 646-9056

OLD ORCHARD BEACH

BEAU RIVAGE MOTEL
54 E Grand Ave (04064)
Rates: $40-$105
Tel: (207) 934-4668

FLAGSHIP MOTEL
54 W Grand Ave (04064)
Rates: $34-$99
Tel: (207) 934-4866

GRAND BEACH INN
198 E Grand Ave (04064)
Rates: $75-$155
Tel: (800) 926-3242

OLD COLONIAL MOTEL
61 W Grand Ave (04064)
Rates: n/a
Tel: (207) 934-9862

WAVES MOTOR INN
87 W Grand Ave (04064)
Rates: $50-$150
Tel: (207) 934-4949

ORONO

UNIVERSITY MOTOR INN
5 College Ave (04473)
Rates: $36-$68
Tel: (207) 866-4921

PATTEN

MT CHASE LODGE & COUNTRY INN
Shin Pond Rd,
Box 281 (04765)
Rates: n/a
Tel: (207) 528-2183

SHIN POND VILLAGE
RR 1, Box 280-M
(04765)
Rates: $30-$62
Tel: (207) 528-2900

PORTLAND

HOLIDAY INN WEST
81 Riverside St
(04103)
Rates: $82-$109
Tel: (207) 774-5601
(800) 465-4329

HOWARD JOHNSON LODGE
155 Riverside (04103)
Rates: $60-$83
Tel: (207) 774-5861
(800) 446-4656

INN AT PORTLAND
1150 Brighton Ave
(04102)
Rates: $50-$110
Tel: (207) 775-3711

INN AT ST. JOHN
939 Congress St
(04102)
Rates: $35-$115
Tel: (207) 773-6481
(800) 636-9127

MOTEL 6
One Riverside St
(04102)
Rates: $36-$42
Tel: (207) 775-0111
(800) 440-6000

RADISSON
157 High St (04101)
Rates: $85-$150
Tel: (207) 775-5411

RAMADA INN
1230 Congress St
(04102)
Rates: $69-$115
Tel: (207) 774-5611

PRESQUE ISLE

KEDDY'S MOTOR INN
P. O. Box 270 (04769)
Rates: $49-$54
Tel: (207) 764-3321

NORTHERN LIGHTS MOTEL
692 Main St (04769)
Rates: $24-$39
Tel: (207) 764-4441

RANGELEY

RANGELEY INN & MOTOR LODGE
Box 160 (04970)
Rates: $65-$110
Tel: (207) 864-3341

TOWN & LAKE MOTEL
P. O. Box Box 47,
Main St (04970)
Rates: $40-$500
Tel: (207) 864-3755

ROCKLAND

NAVIGATOR MOTOR INN
520 Main St (04841)
Rates: $45-$95
Tel: (207) 594-2131
(800) 545-8026

OAKLAND SEASHORE
RFD 1, Box 1449
(04841)
Rates: $35-$100
Tel: (207) 594-8104

TRADE WINDS MOTOR INN
2 Park View Dr
(04841)
Rates: $39-$99
Tel: (207) 596-6661

ROCKWOOD

ABNAKI COTTAGES
Abnki Rd,
P. O. Box 6 (04478)
Rates: n/a
Tel: (207) 534-7318

THE BIRCHES RESORT
Box 81 (04478)
Rates: $35-$950
Tel: (207) 534-7305

MAYNARDS IN MAINE
P. O. Box 228 (04478)
Rates: n/a
Tel: (207) 534-7702

RUMFORD

LINNELL MOTEL & REST INN CONF CTR
2 Mi W on US 2
(04276)
Rates: $45-$65
Tel: (207) 364-4511

THE MADISON FOUR SEASON RESORT
Rt 2, P. O. Box 398
(04276)
Rates: $65-$125
Tel: (207) 364-7973
(800) 258-6234

SACO

CLASSIC MOTEL
21 Ocean Park Rd
(04072)
Rates: $50-$78
Tel: (207) 282-5569

SACO MOTEL
473 Main St (04072)
Rates: $30-$60
Tel: (207) 284-6952

TOURIST HAVEN MOTEL
757 Portland Rd
(04072)
Rates: $35-$60
Tel: (207) 284-7251

SANFORD

BAR-H MOTEL
3 Mi S on SR 109
(04073)
Rates: $32-$52
Tel: (207) 324-4662

SEARSPORT

LIGHT'S MOTEL
RFD Box 349 (04974)
Rates: $33-$46
Tel: (207) 548-2405

SKOWHEGAN

BELMONT MOTEL
P. O. Box 160 (04976)
Rates: $45-$55
Tel: (207) 474-8315

TOWNE MOTEL
248 Madison Ave
(04976)
Rates: $42-$72
Tel: (207) 474-5151

SOUTH PORTLAND

BEST WESTERN MERRY MANOR INN
700 Main St (04106)
Rates: $44-$84
Tel: (800) 528-1234

COMFORT INN
90 Maine Mall Rd
(04106)
Rates: $59-$98
Tel: (207) 775-0409
(800) 221-2222

HOWARD JOHNSON HOTEL
675 Main St (04106)
Rates: $69-$99
Tel: (207) 775-5343
(800) 446-4656

MARRIOTT HOTEL
200 Sable Oakes Dr
(04106)
Rates: $99-$144
Tel: (207) 871-8000

SOUTHPORT

THE LAWNMEER INN
Rt 27 (04576)
Rates: $40-$150
Tel: (207) 633-2544

OCEAN GATE MOTOR INN
Route 27 (04576)
Rates: n/a
Tel: (207) 633-3321
(800) 221-5924

SOUTH PRINCETON

THE HIDEAWAY ON POCOMOON-SHINE LAKE
Mary Wallace, The Hideaway (04668)
Rates: n/a
Tel: (207) 427-6183

SPRUCE HEAD

CRAIGNAIR INN
Clark Island Rd (04859)
Rates: $65-$100
Tel: (207) 594-7644

STRATTON

SPILLOVER MOTEL
P. O. Box 427 (04982)
Rates: $42-$68
Tel: (207) 246-6571

TRENTON

DAYS INN
Rt 1, Box 183 (04605)
Rates: $49-$59
Tel: (207) 667-9506
(800) 329-7466

SUNRISE MOTEL
Bar Harbor Rd (04605)
Rates: $20-$85
Tel: (207) 667-8452

WATERFORF

WATERFORD INN
Box 149, 04088
Rates: $74-$99
Tel: (207) 583-4037

WATERVILLE

THE ATRIUM MOTEL
332 Main St (04901)
Rates: $45-$80
Tel: (207) 873-2777

BEST WESTERN
356 Main St (04901)
Rates: $49-$79
Tel: (207) 873-3335
(800) 528-1234

BUDGET HOST AIRPORT INN
400 Kennedy Memorial Dr (04901)
Rates: $30-$70
Tel: (800) 876-2463

ECONO LODGE
455 Kennedy Memorial Dr (04901)
Rates: $32-$43
Tel: (207) 872-5577
(800) 424-4777

HOLIDAY INN
375 Upper Main St (04901)
Rates: $55-$98
Tel: (207) 873-0111
(800) 465-4329

HOWARD JOHNSON LODGE
356 Main St (04901)
Rates: $64-$74
Tel: (207) 873-3335
(800) 446-4656

WATERVILLE MOTOR LODGE
320 Kennedy Memorial Dr (04901)
Rates: $28-$54
Tel: (207) 873-0141

WELLS

GARRISON HOUSE MOTEL & COTTAGES
1099 Post Rd (04090)
Rates: $45+
Tel: (207) 646-3497
(800) 646-3497

WATER CREST COTTAGES & MOTEL
P.O. Box 37E (04090)
Rates: $69+
Tel: (207) 646-2202
(800) 847-4693

WESTBROOK

SUPER 8 MOTEL
208 Larrabee Rd (04092)
Rates: $29-$62
Tel: (207) 854-1881

WEST KENNEBUNK

ALEWIFE COUNTRY MOTOR INN
P. O. Box 575 (04094)
Rates: $40-$70
Tel: (207) 985-6525

WILTON

WHISPERING PINES MOTEL
P. O. Box 649 (04294)
Rates: $36-$72
Tel: (207) 645-3721

WINTERPORT

THE COLONIAL WINTERPORT INN
P. O. Box 525 (04496)
Rates: $50-$65
Tel: (207) 223-5307

YARMOUTH

DOWN-EAST VILLAGE MOTEL
31 US Rt 1 (04096)
Rates: $55-$95
Tel: (207) 846-5161

YORK

YORK COMMONS INN
Rt 1 & Brickyard Ln (03909)
Rates: $43-$95
Tel: (207) 363-8903

MARYLAND

ABERDEEN

DAYS INN
783 W Bel Air Ave
(21001)
Rates: $39-$48
Tel: (410) 272-8500
(800) 329-7466

ECONO LODGE
820 W Bel Air Ave
(21001)
Rates: $33-$40
Tel: (410) 272-5500
(800) 424-4777

HOLIDAY INN CHESAPEAKE HOUSE
1007 Beards Hill Rd
(21001)
Rates: $74-$98
Tel: (800) 465-4329

HOWARD JOHNSON LODGE
793 W Bel Air Ave
(21001)
Rates: $39-$56
Tel: (410) 272-6000
(800) 446-4656

RED ROOF INN
988 Hospitality Way
(21001)
Rates: $40-$50
Tel: (410) 273-7800
(800) 842-7663

ANNAPOLIS

DAYS INN
1542 Whitehall Rd
(21401)
Rates: $43-$95
Tel: (410) 974-4440
(800) 329-7466

ECONO LODGE
2451 Riva Rd
(21401)
Rates: $49-$100
Tel: 410-224-4317
(800) 424-4777

HOLIDAY INN & CONF. CENTER
210 Holiday Ct
(21401)
Rates: $59-$65
Tel: (800) 465-4329

LOEWS ANNAPOLIS HOTEL
126 West St (21401)
Rates: $115-$175
Tel: (410) 263-7777

RED CARPET INN
101 Ferguson Rd
(21401)
Rates: n/a
Tel: (410) 757-3030
(800) 251-1962

RESIDENCE INN BY MARRIOTT
170 Admiral
Cochrane Dr (21401)
Rates: $110-$154
Tel: (410) 573-0300
(800) 331-3131

BALTIMORE

AMANDA'S B & B RESERVATION SERVICE
1428 Park Ave (21217)
Rates: n/a
Tel: (410) 225-0001

COMFORT INN AIRPORT
6921 Baltimore
Annapolis Blvd
(21225)
Rates: $68-$80
Tel: (800) 221-2222

DOUBLETREE INN AT THE COLONNADE
4 W University
Pkwy (21218)
Rates: $119-$275
Tel: (800) 456-3396

HAMPTON INN
8225 Town Center
Dr. (21236)
Rates: $75-$85
Tel: (410) 931-2200
(800) 426-7866

HOLIDAY INN
6510 Frankford Ave
(21206)
Rates: $69-$75
Tel: (800) 465-4329

HOLIDAY INN
1800 Belmont Ave
(21244)
Rates: $59-$83
Tel: (800) 465-4329

MOTEL 6
1654 Whitehead Ct
(21207)
Rates: $43-$49
Tel: (410) 265-7660
(800) 440-6000

RADISSON PLAZA LORD BALTIMORE
20 W Baltimore St
(21201)
Rates: $85-$154
Tel: (800) 333-3333

SHERATON INNER HARBOR HOTEL
300 S Charles St
(21201)
Rates: $109-$170
Tel: (410) 962-8300

SHERATON INTL HOTEL ON BWI AIRPORT
7032 Elm Rd (21240)
Rates: $65-$150
Tel: (410) 859-3300

THE TREMONT HOTEL
8 E Pleasant St
(21202)
Rates: $89-$170
Tel: (410) 576-1200

TREMONT PLAZA HOTEL
222 St. Paul Pl
(21202)
Rates: $89-$155
Tel: (410) 727-2222

BELTSVILLE

HOLIDAY INN
4050 Powder Mill Rd
(20705)
Rates: $69-$87
Tel: (800) 465-4329

BETHESDA

HOLIDAY INN
8120 Wisconsin Ave
(20814)
Rates: $109-$250
Tel: (800) 465-4329

MARRIOTT SUITES BETHESDA
6711 Democracy Blvd
(20817)
Rates: $99-$160
Tel: (301) 897-5600

RAMADA INN
8400 Wisconsin Ave
(20814)
Rates: $99-119
Tel: (301) 654-1000
(800) 272-6232

RESIDENCE INN-
7335 Wisconsin Ave
(20814)
Rates: $145-$165
Tel: (301) 718-0200

BOWIE

ECONO LODGE
4502 NW Crain Hwy
(20718)
Rates: $49-69
Tel: (301)-464-2200
(800) 424-4777

CAMP SPRINGS

DAYS INN ANDREWS AFB
5001 Mercedes Blvd
(20746)
Rates: $39-$73
Tel: (800) 329-7466

MOTEL 6
5701 Allentown Rd
(20746)
Rates: $50-$56
Tel: (301) 702-1061
(800) 440-6000

CAPITOL HEIGHTS

DAYS INN CAPITAL CENTRE
55 Hampton Park
Blvd (20743)
Rates: $39-$71
Tel: (800) 329-7466

ECONO LODGE
100 Hampton Park
Blvd (20743)
Rates: $33-$55
Tel: (800) 424-4777

MOTEL 6
75 Hampton Park
Blvd (20743)
Rates: $46-$52
Tel: (301) 499-0800
(800) 440-6000

CHEVY CHASE

HOLIDAY INN
5520 Wisconsin Ave
(20815)
Rates: $90-$149
Tel: (800) 465-4329

CHURCH CREEK

LOBLOLLY LANDINGS & LODGE
2142 Liners Rd
(21622)
Rates: n/a
Tel: (800) 862-7452

CLINTON

ECONO LODGE
7851 Malcolm Rd
(20735)
Rates: $40-60
Tel: (301) 856-2800
(800) 424-4777

COCKEYSVILLE

ECONO LODGE
10100 York Rd
(21020)
Rates: $42-$62
Tel: (410) 667-4900
(800) 424-4777

COLUMBIA

THE COLUMBIA INN
10207 Wincopin Cir
(21044)
Rates: $124-$134
Tel: (800) 638-2817

COLLEGE PARK

PARK VIEW INN-COLLEGE PARK
9020 Baltimore Blvd
(20740)
Rates: $50-$60
Tel: (301) 441-8110

CUMBERLAND

DIPLOMAT MOTEL
17012 McMullen
(21502)
Rates: $29-$37
Tel: (301) 729-2311

EASTON

DAYS INN
P. O. Box 968 (21601)
Rates: $56-$77
Tel: (410) 822-4600
(800) 329-7466

ECONO LODGE
U S 50 (21601)
Rates: $46-$54
Tel: (800) 424-4777

GROSS' COATE PLANTATION 1658 BED & BREAKFAST
11300 Gross' Coate
Rd (21601)
Rates: $295-$395
Tel: (800) 580-0802

THE TIDEWATER INN
101 E Dover St
(21601)
Rates: $109-$150
Tel: (410) 822-1300

EDGEWOOD

BEST WESTERN INVITATION INN
1709 Edgewood Rd
(21040)
Rates: $49-$94
Tel: (410) 679-9700
(800) 528-1234

DAYS INN
2116 Emmorton Park
Rd (21040)
Rates: $45-$65
Tel: (410) 671-9990
(800) 329-7466

ELKTON

ECONO LODGE
311 Belle Hill Rd
(21921)
Rates: $32-$45
Tel: (410) 392-5010
(800) 424-4777

MOTEL 6
223 Belle Hill Rd
(21921)
Rates: $36-$42
Tel: (301) 392-5020
(800) 440-6000

FREDERICK

COMFORT INN
420 Prospect Blvd
(21701)
Rates: $49-$64
Tel: (800) 221-2222

HAMPTON INN
5311 Buckeystown
Pike (21701)
Rates: $89-$109
Tel: (301) 698-2500
(800) 426-7866

HOLIDAY INN
999 W Patrick St
(21702)
Rates: $71-$75
Tel: (800) 465-4329

KNIGHTS INN
6005 Urbana Pike
(21704)
Rates: $37-$46
Tel: (301) 698-0555

RED HORSE INN
998 W Patrick St
(21702)
Rates: $38-$60
Tel: (301) 245-6701

FROSTBURG

CHARLIE'S MOTEL
220 W Main St (21532)
Rates: n/a
Tel: (301) 689-6557

COMFORT INN
SR 36 N (21532)
Rates: $56-$61
Tel: (800) 221-2222

GAITHERSBURG

COMFORT INN
16216 Frederick Ave
(20877)
Rates: $53-$79
Tel: (800) 221-2222

ECONO LODGE
18715 Frederick Ave
(20879)
Rates: $49-$51
Tel: (301) 963-3840
(800) 424-4777

HILTON HOTEL
620 Perry Pkwy
(20877)
Rates: $64-$115
Tel: (301) 977-8900

HOLIDAY INN
2 Montgomeryey
Village Ave (20879)
Rates: $69-$105
Tel: (800) 465-4329

RED ROOF INN
497 Quince Orchard
Rd (20878)
Rates: $50-$54
Tel: (301) 977-3311
(800) 843-7663

GERMANTOWN

COMFORT INN GERMANTOWN
20260 Goldenrod Ln
(20876)
Rates: $54-$63
Tel: (800) 221-2222

GLEN BURNIE

HOLIDAY INN-NORTH
6323 Ritchie Hwy
(21061)
Rates: $69-$72
Tel: (800) 465-4329

HOLIDAY INN-SOUTH
6600 Ritchie Hwy
(21061)
Rates: $69-$72
Tel: (800) 465-4329

GRANTSVILLE

HOLIDAY INN
US 219 N (21536)
Rates: $39-$66
Tel: (800) 465-4329

GREENBELT

HOLIDAY INN-
7200 Hanover Dr
(20770)
Rates: $63-$88
Tel: (800) 465-4329

MARRIOTT HOTEL
6400 Ivy Ln (20770)
Rates: $69-$124
Tel: (301) 441-3700
(800) 228-9290

HAGERSTOWN

BEST WESTERN INN
431 Dual Hwy
(21740)
Rates: $59-$67
Tel: (301) 733-0830
(800) 528-1234

ECONO LODGE
18221 Mason-Dixon
Rd (21740)
Rates: $38-47
Tel: (301) 791-3560
(800) 424-4777

HOLIDAY INN
900 Dual Hwy
(21740)
Rates: $49-$54
Tel: (800) 465-4329

MOTEL 6
11321 Massey Blvd
(21740)
Rates: $40-$46
Tel: (301) 582-4445
(800) 440-6000

SHERATON INN
1910 Dual Hwy
(21740)
Rates: $56-$69
Tel: (301) 790-3010

STATE LINE MOTEL
Rt 6, Box 195C
(21740)
Rates: $24-$31
Tel: (301) 733-8262

SUPER 8 MOTEL
1220 Dual Hwy
(21740)
Rates: $37-$51
Tel: (301) 739-5800
(800) 800-8000

HANOVER

RED ROOF INN
7306 Parkway Dr
(21076)
Rates: $30-$41
Tel: (410) 712-4070
(800) 843-7663

HUNT VALLEY

**EMBASSY SUITES
HOTEL**
213 International Cir
(21030)
Rates: $89-$119
Tel: (410) 584-1400

HAMPTON INN
11200 York Rd
(21031)
Rates: $59-$69
Tel: (410) 527-1500
(800) 426-7866

**MARRIOTT'S
HUNT VALLEY INN**
245 Shawan Rd
(21031)
Rates: $89-$128
Tel: (410) 785-7000

**RESIDENCE INN
BY MARRIOTT**
10710 Beaver Dam
Rd (21030)
Rates: $77-$145
Tel: (410) 483-7370
(800) 331-3131

JESSUP

RED ROOF INN
8000 Washington
Blvd (20794)
Rates: $30-$54
Tel: (410) 796-0380
(800) 843-7663

LA PLATA

TRAVELODGE
P. O. Box 1661 (20646)
Rates: $29-$69
Tel: (301) 934-1400
(800) 578-7878

LANHAM

BEST WESTERN
5910 Princess
Garden Pkwy
(20706)
Rates: $57+
Tel: (800) 528-1234

**HOLIDAY INN
CAPITAL BELTWAY E**
5910 Princess
Garden Pkwy
(20706)
Rates: $50-$69
Tel: (800) 465-4329

RED ROOF INN
9050 Lanham Severn
Rd (20706)
Rates: $45-$55
Tel: (301) 731-8830
(800) 843-7663

LAUREL

**COMFORT SUITES-
LAUREL LAKES**
14402 Laurel Pl
(20707)
Rates: $59-$150
Tel: (800) 221-2222

MOTEL 6
3510 Old Annapolis
Rd (20724)
Rates: $40-$46
Tel: (301) 497-1544
(800) 440-6000

RED ROOF INN
12525 Laurel Bowie
Rd (20708)
Rates: $30-$50
Tel: (301) 498-8811
(800) 843-7663

LEXINGTON
PARK

DAYS INN
60 Main St (20653)
Rates: $49-78
Tel: (301) 863-6666
(800) 329-7466

LINTHICUM
HEIGHTS

HAMPTON INN
829 Elkridge
Landing Rd (21090)
Rates: $62-$66
Tel: (800) 426-7866

**HOLIDAY INN-
AIRPORT**
890 Elkridge
Landing Rd (21090)
Rates: $99
Tel: (800) 465-4329

MOTEL 6
5179 Raynor Ave
(21090)
Rates: $30-$40
Tel: (410) 636-9070
(800) 440-6000

**RED ROOF INN
AIRPORT**
827 Elkridge
Landing Rd (21090)
Rates: $32-$44
Tel: (800) 843-7663

McHENRY

ROYAL OAKS INN
HCR 2, Box 11 (21541)
Rates: n/a
Tel: (301) 387-4200

NEW
CARROLLTON

**SHERATON
GREENBELT HOTEL**
8500 Annapolis Rd
(20784)
Rates: $72-$112
Tel: (301) 459-6700

OAKLAND

DREAMLAND MOTEL
17848 Garrett Hwy
(21550)
Rates: n/a
Tel: (301) 387-6696

OCEAN CITY

BAYSAILS INN
102 60th St (21842)
Rates: n/a
Tel: (410) 524-5634
(800) 776-5634

**BEST WESTERN
SEA BAY INN**
6007 Coastal Hwy
(21842)
Rates: $29-$124
Tel: (410) 524-6100
(800) 528-1234

BUDGET BEACH MOTEL
32nd St & Coastal Hwy (21842)
Rates: n/a
Tel: (410) 289-1808

ECONO LODGE
6007 Coastal Hwy (21842)
Rate: $27-$114
Tel: (800) 424-4777

FENWICK INN
13801 Coastal Hwy (21842)
Rates: $40-$149
Tel: (800) 492-1873

GEORGIA BELLE SUITES AND LODGE
12000 Coastal Hwy (21842)
Rates: $29-$175
Tel: (410) 250-4000
(800) 542-4444

RODEWAY INN
2910 Baltimore Ave (21842)
Rates: $29-$140
Tel: (800) 424-4777

SHERATON FONTAINBLEAU HOTEL
10100 Ocean Hwy (21842)
Rates: $55-$200
Tel: (800) 638-2100

OXON HILL

RED ROOF INN
6170 Oxon Hill Rd (20745)
Rates: $37-$58
Tel: (301) 567-8030
(800) 843-7663

PERRYVILLE

COMFORT INN
61 Heather Ln (21903)
Rates: $44-$59
Tel: (800) 221-2222

PIKESVILLE

COMFORT INN NW
10 Wooded Way (21208)
Rates: $49-$140
Tel: (800) 221-2222

HOLIDAY INN
1721 Reisterstown Rd (21208)
Rates: $72-$75
Tel: (800) 465-4329

POCOMOKE CITY

DAYS INN
1540 Ocean Hwy (21851)
Rates: $53-$75
Tel: (410) 957-3000
(800) 329-7466

QUALITY INN
825 Ocean Hwy (21851)
Rates: $44-$75
Tel: (800) 221-2222

RED CARPET INN
912 Ocean Hwy (21851)
Rates: n/a
Tel: (410) 957-1030
(800) 251-1962

PRINCESS ANNE

ECONO LODGE
10936 Market Ln (21853)
Rates: $42-$70
Tel: (410) 651-9400
(800) 424-4777

ROCKVILLE

DAYS INN ROCKVILLE/ GAITHERSBURG
16001 Shady Grove Rd (20850)
Rates: $50-$79
Tel: (301) 948-4300
(800) 329-7466

SALISBURY

COMFORT INN
2701 N Salisbury (21801)
Rates: $36-$59
Tel: (800) 221-2222

ECONO LODGE STATESMAN
712 N Salisbury (21801)
Rates: $34-$69
Tel: (410) 749-7155
(800) 424-4777

HAMPTON INN
1735 N Salisbury (21801)
Rates: $39-$69
Tel: (800) 426-7866

HOLIDAY INN
2625 N Salisbury (21801)
Rates: $45-$90
Tel: (800) 465-4329

LORD SALISBURY MOTEL
Rt 11, Box 233 (21801)
Rates: $39-$75
Tel: (410) 742-3251

SILVER SPRING

ECONO LODGE
7990 Georgia Ave (20910)
Rates: $56-$79
Tel: (301) 565-3444
(800) 424-4777

HOLIDAY INN-SILVER SPRING PLAZA
8777 Georgia Ave (20910)
Rates: $80-$115
Tel: (800) 465-4329

SOLOMONS

HOLIDAY INN
155 Holiday Dr (20688)
Rates: $68-$140
Tel: (800) 465-4329

THURMONT

RAMBLER MOTEL
US 15 & Jct SR 550 (21788)
Rates: $42-$50
Tel: (301) 271-2424

TIMONIUM

RED ROOF INN
111 W Timonium Rd (21093)
Rates: $34-$50
Tel: (800) 843-7663

TOWSON

DAYS INN-EAST
8801 Loch Raven Blvd (21204)
Rates: $48-$56
Tel: (800) 329-7466

HOLIDAY INN
1100 Cromwell Bridge Rd (21204)
Rates: $79-$82
Tel: (800) 465-4329

QUALITY INN CONF CTR
1015 York Rd (21204)
Rates: $52-$74
Tel: (800) 221-2222

RAMADA INN
8712 Loch Raven Blvd (21204)
Rates: $52-$92
Tel: (410) 823-8750
(800) 272-6232

UPPER MARLBORO

FOREST HILLS MOTEL
2901 Crain Hwy (20772)
Rates: $42-$47
Tel: (301) 627-3969

WALDORF

DAYS INN
11370 Days Ct
(20603)
Rates: $40-$150
Tel: (301) 932-9200
(800) 329-7466

ECONO LODGE
4 Business Park Dr
(20601)
Rates: $46-$71
Tel: (301) 645-0022
(800) 424-4777

HOJO INN
3125 Crain Hwy
(20602)
Rates: $43-$51
Tel: (301) 932-5090
(800) 446-4656

HOLIDAY INN
1 St. Patrick's Dr
(20603)
Rates: $55-$63
Tel: (800) 465-4329

WESTMINSTER

THE BOSTON INN
533 Baltimore Blvd
(21157)
Rates: $27-$40
Tel: (410) 848-9095

COMFORT INN
451 WMC Dr (21158)
Rates: $43-$70
Tel: (800) 424-6423

DAYS INN
25 S Cranberry Rd
(21157)
Rates: $52-$76
Tel: (410) 857-0500
(800) 329-7466

WILLIAMSPORT

DAYS INN
310 E Potomac St
(21795)
Rates: $50-$85
Tel: (301) 582-3500
(800) 329-7466

WOLF'S END FARM
14940 Falling Waters
Rd (21795)
Rates: $60-$100
Tel: (301) 223-6888

MASSACHUSETTS

AMHERST

UNIVERSITY MOTOR LODGE
345 N Pleasant St (01002)
Rates: $42-$87
Tel: (413) 256-8111

ANDOVER

ANDOVER INN
Chapel Ave (01810)
Rates: $79-$89
Tel: (508) 475-5903

MARRIOTT HOTEL
123 Old River Rd (01810)
Rates: $79-$95
Tel: (508) 975-3600

ATTLEBORO

ARNS PARK MOTEL
515 S Washington St (02760)
Rates: $55-$70
Tel: (508) 222-0801

AUBURN

BUDGETEL INN
444 Southbridge St (01501)
Rates: $50-$60
Tel: (508) 832-7000

BARNSTABLE

LAMB & LION INN
P. O. Box 511 (02630)
Rates: $80-$105
Tel: (508) 362-6823

BARRE

JENKINS INN
7 West St (01005)
Rates: $80-$125
Tel: (508) 355-6444

BASS RIVER

WAYFARERS ALL COTTAGES
186 Seaview Ave (02664)
Rates: $600/Weekly
Tel: (508) 771-4532

BEDFORD

STOUFFER RENNAISSANCE
44 Middlesex Tpk (01730)
Rates: $115-$200
Tel: (617) 275-5500

BOSTON

BOSTON HARBOR HOTEL
70 Rowes Wharf (02110)
Rates: $195-$390
Tel: (617) 439-7000

COPLEY PLAZA HOTEL
138 St James Ave (02116)
Rates: $129-$280
Tel: (617) 267-5300

THE ELIOT SUITE HOTEL
370 Commonwealth Ave (02215)
Rates: $175-$245
Tel: (617) 267-1607

THE FOUR SEASONS
200 Boylston St (02116)
Rates: $230-$420
Tel: (800) 332-3442

HILTON-BOSTON BACK BAY
40 Dalton St (02115)
Rates: $155-$225
Tel: (800) 445-8667

HOWARD JOHNSON
200 Stuart St (02116)
Rates: $90-$200
Tel: (617) 482-1800
(800) 466-4656

HOWARD JOHNSON
575 Commonwealth Ave (02215)
Rates: $79-$155
Tel: (617) 267-3100

HOWARD JOHNSON
1271 Boylston St (02215)
Rates: $71-$115
Tel: (617) 267-8300

MARRIOTT HOTEL COPLEY PLACE
110 Huntington Ave (02116)
Rates: $155-$169
Tel: (617) 236-5800

NEWBURY GUEST HOUSE
261 Newbury St (02116)
Rates: $75-$125
Tel: (617) 437-7666

THE RITZ CARLTON
15 Arlington St (02117)
Rates: $215-$360
Tel: (617) 536-5700

SHERATON HOTEL
39 Dalton St (02199)
Rates: $190-$250
Tel: (617) 236-2000

SWISSOTEL BOSTON
One Ave de Lafayette (02111)
Rates: $235-$290
Tel: (617) 451-2600

THE WESTIN COPLEY PLACE
10 Huntington Ave (02116)
Rates: $260-$345
Tel: (617) 262-9600

BOURNE

BEST WESTERN BRIDGE-BOURNE HOTEL
100 Trowbridge Rd (02532)
Rates: $55-$149
Tel: (508) 759-0800
(800) 528-1234

YANKEE THRIFT MOTEL
114 Trowbridge Rd (02532)
Rates: n/a
Tel: (508) 759-3883

BRAINTREE

DAYS INN
190 Wood Rd (02184)
Rates: $50-$115
Tel: (617) 848-1260
(800) 329-7466

MOTEL 6
125 Union St (02184)
Rates: $50-$61
Tel: (617) 848-7890
(800) 466-8356

BREWSTER

HIGH BREWSTER INN
964 Satucket Rd (02631)
Rates: $90-$120
Tel: (508) 896-3636
(800) 202-2634

PINE HILLS COTTAGES
P.O. Box 75 (02631)
Rates: $325/(Weekly
Tel: (508) 896-1999

BURLINGTON

HOWARD JOHNSON
98 Middlesex Tpk (01803)
Rates: $69-$110
Tel: (617) 272-6550
(800) 446-4656

BUZZARDS BAY

BAY MOTOR INN
223 Main St (02532)
Rates: $40-70
Tel: (508) 759-3989

THE POND HOUSE
44 Monument
Neck Rd (02532)
Rates: $45-$95
Tel: (508) 759-1994

**SHIPSWAY MOTEL
& COTTAGES**
51 Canal Rd (02532)
Rates: n/a
Tel: (508) 888-0206

CAMBRIDGE

**CHARLES HARVARD
SQUARE**
1 Bennett St (02138)
Rates: $139-$259
Tel: (617) 864-1200

HOWARD JOHNSON
777 Memorial Dr
(02139)
Rates: $87-$185
Tel: (617) 492-7777
(800) 446-4656

CAPE COD
TOWNS

ACORN COTTAGES
927 Main St
(Dennis Port 02639)
Rates: $495-
895/Weekly
Tel: (508) 760-2101

ANGEL MOTEL
Rt 132
(Hyannis 02601)
Rates: $41-54
Tel: (508) 775-2440

**AZARIAH
SNOW HOUSE**
Rt 6A (E Sandwich)
Rates: n/a
Tel: (508) 888-6677

BARNABY INN
36 Main St
(W Harwich 02671)
Rates: n/a
Tel: (508) 432-6789

**BAY LIGHT
COTTAGES**
P. O. Box 595
(Dennis Port 02639)
Rates: n/a
Tel: (508) 398-5989
(617) 268-9788

BAY MOTOR INN
223 Main St
(Buzzards Bay 02532)
Rates: $40-70
Tel: (508) 759-3989

**BEST WESTERN
BRIDGE-BOURNE
HOTEL**
100 Trowbridge Rd
(Bourne 02532)
Rates: $55-$149
Tel: (508) 759-0800
(800) 528-1234

**BETH'S
BEACH HOUSE**
Dennis Port (02639)
Rates: $650 /weekly
Tel: (508) 385-4588

BLUE DOLPHIN INN
Rt 6, Drawer S
(N Eastham 02642)
Rates: $79-$90
Tel: (508) 255-1159
(800) 654-0504

**BRENTWOOD
COTTAGES**
961 Main St
(S Yarmouth 02664)
Rates: n/a
Tel: (508) 398-8812
(800) 328-8812

**BRENTWOOD
MOTOR INN**
Rt 28
(S Yarmouth 02664)
Rates: $35-65+
Tel: (508) 398-8812
(800) 328-8812

**BREAKWATER
MOTOR INN**
Rt 6A
(Provincetown 02657)
Rates: n/a
Tel: (508) 487-1134
(800) 487-1134

BROWN'S LANDING
P.O. Box 1017
(Wellfleet 02667)
Rates: n/a
Tel: (508) 349-6923

**CAPTAIN'S ROW
ON NANTUCKET
SOUND**
257 Old Wharf Rd
(Dennis Port 02639)
Rates: n/a
Tel: (508) 398-3117

**CAPTAIN VARRIEUR'S
COTTAGES**
P.O. Box 1332
(W Dennis 02670)
Rates: $600
Tel: (508) 394-4338
(800) 647-7126

CEDAR COTTAGES
59 Ploughed Neck
(E Sandwich 02537)
Rates: n/a
Tel: (508) 888-0464

**CENTERVILLE
CORNERS LODGE**
Craigville Beach
P. O. Box 507
(Centerville 02632)
Rates: $42-$91
Tel: (508) 775-7223
(800) 242-1137

CLADDAGH INN
77 Main St
(W. Harwich 02671)
Rates: $95-$120
Tel: (508) 432-9628

**COACHMAN
MOTOR LODGE**
774 Main St
(Harwich 02646)
Rates: $55-$98
Tel: (508) 432-0707

**COLONIAL HOUSE
INN**
277 Main St, Rt 6-A
(Yarmouth Port 02675)
Rates: $60-$95
Tel: (800) 999-3416

**COUNTRY SQUIRE
MOTOR LODGE**
206 Main St
(Hyannis 02601)
Rates: $35-89
Tel: (508) 775-5225

COZY NEST B & B
161 Maple St
(W Barnstable 02630)
Rates: n/a
Tel: (508) 362-4218

**CRANBERRY
COTTAGES**
785 State Hwy
(Eastham 02642)
Rates: $40-$72
Tel: (508) 255-0602

CRICKET COURT
130 Rt 28
(Dennis Port 02639)
Rates: $250-$500
/weekly
Tel: (508) 398-8400

**THE EARL OF
SANDWICH**
378 Rt 6A
(East Sandwich 02537)
Rates: $45-$89
Tel: (508) 888-1415

ELMWOOD INN
57 Old Main St
(W Dennis 02670)
Rates: $38+
Tel: (508) 394-2798

FALMOUTH INN
824 Main St
(Falmouth 02540)
Rates: $45-$77
Tel: (508) 540-2500
(800) 255-4157

**FRIENDSHIP
COTTAGES**
530 Chequessett
Neck Rd
(Wellfleet 02667)
Rates: n/a
Tel: (508) 349-3390

GIBSON COTTAGES
Long Pond
(Eastham 02642)
Rates: n/a
Tel: (508) 255-0882

GLO-MIN BY THE SEA
182 Sea St
(Hyannis 02601)
Rates: n/a
Tel: (508) 775-1423

**GREEN HARBOR
WATERFRONT**
134 Acapesket Rd
(E Falmouth 02536)
Rates: $80-96
Tel: (508) 548-4747
(800) 548-5556

**GREEN HAVEN
COTTAGES**
Rt 6, Box 486
(S Wellfleet 02663)
Rates: n/a
Tel: (508) 349-1715

**HANDKERCHIEF
SHOALS MOTEL**
MA 28
(S Harwich 02661)
Rates: $42-$70
Tel: (508) 432-2200

HARBOR VILLAGE
160 Marstons Ave
(Hyannis Port 02647)
Rates: $90-1300
Tel: (508) 775-7581

**HARBOR WALK
GUEST HOUSE**
6 Freeman St
(Harwich Port 02646)
Rates: n/a
Tel: (508) 432-1675

**HARGOOD HOUSE
APTS**
493 Commercial St
(Provincetown 02657)
Rates: $72-$142
Tel: (508) 487-9133

HIGH BREWSTER INN
964 Satucket Rd
(Brewster 02631)
Rates: $90-$120
Tel: (508) 896-3636
(800) 202-2634

HOLIDAY INN
Shore Dr Rt 6A
(Provincetown 02657)
Rates: $70-$140
Tel: (508) 487-1711
(800) 465-4329

HYANNIS SANDS
921 Rt 132
(Hyannis 02601)
Rates: n/a
Tel: (508) 790-1700

LAMB & LION INN
P. O. Box 511
(Barnstable 02630)
Rates: $80-$105
Tel: (508) 362-6823

LAMPLIGHTER
329 Main St
(Dennis Port 02639)
Rates: $28-55
Tel: (508) 398-8469

**MARINE LODGE
COTTAGES**
15 North St
(Dennis Port 02639)
Rates: n/a
Tel: (508) 398-2963

MARINER MOTEL
555 Main St
(Falmouth 02540)
Rates: $42-$79
Tel: (508) 548-1331
(800) 233-2939

**MORGAN WATER-
FRONT HOUSES**
444 Old Harbor Rd
(Chatham 02633)
Rates: $400-1800
/weekly
Tel: (508) 945-1870

**OCEAN BAY VIEW
COTTAGES**
Portanimicut Rd
(S Orleans 02662)
Rates: n/a
Tel: (508) 255-3344

OCEAN VIEW MOTEL
263 Grand Ave
(Falmouth Hts 02540)
Rates: $40-$120
Tel: (508) 540-4120

**OCEANFRONT
COTTAGES**
Seagull Ln
(Chatham 02633)
Rates: n/a
Tel: (508) 945-5907

**ORLEANS HOLIDAY
MOTEL**
486 Cranberry Hwy
(Orleans 02653)
Rates: $53-$105
Tel: (508) 255-1514
(800) 451-1833

**OUTER REACH
RESORT**
Rt 6 (N Truro 02652)
Rates: n/a
Tel: (508) 487-9500
(800) 942-5388

**PINE COVE INN
& COTTAGES**
Rt 28 & Main St
(W Dennis 02670)
Rates: $30-50
Tel: (508) 398-8511

**PINE GROVE
COTTAGES**
Rt 6A
(E Sandwich 02537)
Rates: n/a
Tel: (508) 888-8179

**PINE HILLS
COTTAGES**
P.O. Box 75,
(Brewster 02631)
Rates: $325 /weekly
Tel: (508) 896-1999

THE POND HOUSE
44 Monument
Neck Rd
(Buzzards Bay (02532)
Rates: $45-$95
Tel: (508) 759-1994

QUALITY INN
291 Jones Rd.
(Falmouth 02540)
Rates: $45-$119
Tel: (508) 540-2000
(800) 221-2222

**RAINBOW RESORT
MOTEL**
Rt 132
(Hyannis 02601)
Rates: $48-56
Tel: (508) 362-3217

RYAN'S COTTAGE
19 Sandy Ln
(W Yarmouth 02673)
Rates: n/a
Tel: (508) 771-6387

**SANDWICH
MOTOR LODGE**
P. O. Box 557
(Sandwich 02563)
Rates: $79-$110
Tel: (508) 888-2275
(800) 282-5353

**SEA BREEZE
COTTAGES
BY THE BEACH**
337 Sea St
(Hyannis Port 02647)
Rates: $450-$850
Tel: (508) 775-4269

**SEASCAPE
MOTOR INN**
Rt 6A
(N Truro 02652)
Rates: n/a
Tel: (508) 487-1225

**SHIPSWAY
MOTEL & COTTAGES**
51 Canal Rd
(Buzzards Bay 02532)
Rates: n/a
Tel: (508) 888-0206

**SKAKET BEACH
MOTEL**
203 Cranberry Hwy
(Orleans 02653)
Rates: $43-$104
Tel: (508) 255-1020
(800) 835-0298

**SMITH HEIGHTS
COTTAGES**
Box 111
(Eastham 02642)
Rates: n/a
Tel: (508) 255-5985

**SNUG HARBOUR
MOTOR LODGE**
48 E Main St
(Hyannis 02601)
Rates: n/a
Tel: (508) 771-0699
(800) 345-0130

**THUNDERBIRD
MOTOR LODGE**
Rt 28
(W Yarmouth 02673)
Rates: $26+
Tel: (508) 775-2692
(800) 247-3006

TOWN COTTAGES
319 Main St
(Dennis Port 02639)
Rates: $429/weekly
Tel: (508) 398-8469
(800) 328-8812

**TOWN 'N COUNTRY
MOTOR LODGE**
452 Main St
(W Yarmouth 02673)
Rates: $65+
Tel: (508) 771-0212
(800) 992-2340

TOWN CRIER MOTEL
P. O. Box 457
(Eastham 02642)
Rates: $49-$75
Tel: (508) 255-4000

**UNION WHARF
VILLAGE**
(Dennis Port 02639)
Rates: $300/weekly
Tel: (508) 881-1381

VILLAGE INN
Main St
(Yarmouth Port 02675)
Rates: $40-90
Tel: (508) 362-3182

**WAYFARERS ALL
COTTAGES**
186 Seaview Ave
(Bass River 02664)
Rates: $600/weekly
Tel: (508) 771-4532

**WHITE SANDS
MOTEL**
Rt 6A, Box 611
(Provincetown 02657)
Rates: n/a
Tel: (508) 487-0244

WHITE WIND INN
174 Commercial St
(Provincetown02657)
Rates: n/a
Tel: (508) 487-1526

WINDJAMMER MOTOR INN
192 South Shore Dr
(South Yarmouth 02664)
Rates: $49-$99
Tel: (508) 398-2370
(800) 448-9744

WINGSCORTON FARM
11 Wing Blvd
(E Sandwich02537)
Rates: n/a
Tel: (508) 888-0534

WOODBINE VILLAGE ON THE COVE
Rt 28
(W Dennis 02670)
Rates: $300/weekly
Tel: (508) 881-1381

YANKEE THRIFT MOTEL
114 Trowbridge Rd
(Bourne 02532)
Rates: n/a
Tel: (508) 759-3883

YARMOUTH SHORES
29 Lewis Bay Rd
(W Yarmouth 02673)
Rates: $190+ /weekly
Tel: (508) 775-1944

CENTERVILLE

CENTERVILLE CORNERS MOTOR LODGE
(Craigville Beach
P. O. Box 507
(02632)
Rates: $42-$91
Tel: (508) 775-7223
(800) 242-1137

OCEANFRONT COTTAGES
Seagull Ln (02633)
Rates: n/a
Tel: (508) 945-5907

CHATHAM

MORGAN WATERFRONT HOUSES
444 Old Harbor Rd
(02633)
Rates: $400-1800 /weekly
Tel: (508) 945-1870

CHELMSFORD

HOWARD JOHNSON
187 Chelmsford St
(01824)
Rates: $65-$80
Tel: (508) 256-7511
(800) 446-4656

CHICOPEE

BEST WESTERN
463 Memorial Dr
(01020)
Rates: $44-$64
Tel: (413) 592-6171
(800) 528-1234

MOTEL 6
Rt 291 (01020)
Rates: $36-$42
Tel: (413) 592-5141
(800) 440-6000

CONCORD

BEST WESTERN
740 Elm St (01742)
Rates: $70-$95
Tel: (800) 528-1234

CUMMINGTON

SWIFT RIVER INN
151 South St (01026)
Rates: $49-$99
Tel: (413) 634-5751

DANVERS

MOTEL 6
65 Newbury St
(01923)
Rates: $46-$52
Tel: (508) 774-8045
(800) 440-6000

RESIDENCE INN BY MARRIOTT
51 Newbury St
(01923)
Rates: $125-$150
Tel: (508) 777-7171
(800) 331-3131

SUPER 8 MOTEL
225 Newbury St
(01923)
Rates: $45-$68
Tel: (508) 774-6500
(800) 800-8000

DENNIS PORT

ACORN COTTAGES
927 Main St (02639)
Rates: $495-895 /weekly
Tel: (508) 760-2101

BAY LIGHT COTTAGES
P. O. Box 595 (02639)
Rates: n/a
Tel: (508) 398-5989
(617) 268-9788

BETH'S BEACH HOUSE
(02639)
Rates: $650 /weekly
Tel: (508) 385-4588

CAPTAIN'S ROW ON NANTUCKET SOUND
257 Old Wharf Rd
(02639)
Rates: n/a
Tel: (508) 398-3117

CRICKET COURT
130 Rt 28
(02639)
Rates: $250-$500 /weekly
Tel: (508) 398-8400

LAMPLIGHTER MOTOR LODGE
329 Main St
(02639)
Rates: $28-$55
Tel: (508) 398-8469

MARINE LODGE COTTAGES
15 North St
(02639)
Rates: n/a
Tel: (508) 398-2963

TOWN COTTAGES
319 Main St
(02639)
Rates: $429 /weekly
Tel: (508) 398-8469
(800) 328-8812

UNION WHARF VILLAGE
(02639)
Rates: $300 /weekly
Tel: (508) 881-1381

EAST BOSTON

HILTON-LOGAN AIRPORT
Logan Intl Airport
(02128)
Rates: $105-$200
Tel: (617) 569-9300

EAST FALMOUTH

GREEN HARBOR WATERFRONT MOTOR LODGE
134 Acapesket Rd
(02536)
Rates: $80-96
Tel: (508) 548-4747
(800) 548-5556

EAST SANDWICH

AZARIAH SNOW HOUSE
Rt 6A (02537)
Rates: n/a
Tel: (508) 888-6677

CEDAR COTTAGES
59 Ploughed Neck
(02537)
Rates: n/a
Tel: (508) 888-0464

THE EARL OF SANDWICH MOTOR MANOR
378 Rt 6A (02537)
Rates: $45-$89
Tel: (508) 888-1415

PINE GROVE COTTAGES
Rt 6A (02537)
Rates: n/a
Tel: (508) 888-8179

WINGSCORTON FARM
11 Wing Blvd
(02537)
Rates: n/a
Tel: (508) 888-0534

EASTHAM

CRANBERRY COTTAGES
785 State Hwy
(02642)
Rates: $40-$72
Tel: (508) 255-0602

GIBSON COTTAGES
Long Pond (02642)
Rates: n/a
Tel: (508) 255-0882

SMITH HEIGHTS COTTAGES
Box 111 (02642)
Rates: n/a
Tel: (508) 255-5985

TOWN CRIER MOTEL
P. O. Box 457 (02642)
Rates: $49-$75
Tel: (508) 255-4000

FALL RIVER

DAYS INN
332 Milliken Blvd
(02721)
Rates: $70-$109
Tel: (508) 676-1991
(800) 329-7466

QUALITY INN
1878 Wilbur Ave
(02725)
Rates: $60-$109
Tel: (508) 678-4545
(800) 221-2222

FALMOUTH

FALMOUTH INN
824 Main St
(02540)
Rates: $45-$77
Tel: (508) 540-2500
(800) 255-4157

MARINER MOTEL
555 Main St (02540)
Rates: $42-$79
Tel: (508) 548-1331
(800) 233-2939

OCEAN VIEW MOTEL
263 Grand Ave
(Falmouth Hts 02540)
Rates: $40-$120
Tel: (508) 540-4120

QUALITY INN
291 Jones Rd. (02540)
Rates: $45-$119
Tel: (508) 540-2000
(800) 221-2222

FENWAY

HOWARD JOHNSON
1271 Boylston St
(02215)
Rates: $87-$135
Tel: (617) 267-8300
(800) 446-4656

FITCHBURG

ROYAL PLAZA HOTEL & TRADE CENTER
150 Royal Plaza Dr
(01420)
Rates: $65-$78
Tel: (508) 342-7100

FLORIDA

WHITCOMB SUMMIT MOTEL
229 Mohawk Tr
(01247)
Rates: $45-$80
Tel: (413) 662-2625

FRAMINGHAM

MOTEL 6
1668 Worcester Rd
(01701)
Rates: $46-$52
Tel: (508) 620-0500
(800) 466-8356

RED ROOF INN
650 Cochituate Rd
(01701)
Rates: $36-$70
Tel: (508) 481-3904
(800) 843-7663

GLOUCESTER

CAPE ANN MOTOR INN
33 Rockport Rd
(01930)
Rates: $54-$95
Tel: (508) 281-2900

OCEAN VIEW INN
171 Atlantic Rd
(01930)
Rates: $69-$140
Tel: (508) 283-6200

SPRUCE MANOR MOTEL AND GUEST HOUSE
141 Essex Ave
(01930)
Rates: $40-$100
Tel: (508) 283-0614

GREAT BARRINGTON

BARRINGTON COURT MOTEL
400 Stockbridge Rd
(01230)
Rates: n/a
Tel: (413) 528-2340

BROOK COVE
30 Linda Ln
(Housatonic 01236)
Rates: $65-$85
Tel: (413) 274-6653

CHEZ GABRIELLE
320 State Rd (01230)
Rates: $85-$100
Tel: (413) 528-2799

CHICADEE COTTAGE
27 Division St
(01230)
Rates: $65-$75
Tel: (413) 528-0002

MOUNTAIN VIEW MOTEL
304 State Rd (01230)
Rates: $45-$125
Tel: (413) 528-0250

SEEKONK PINES INN
142 Seekonk Cross Rd (01230)
Rates: $70-$160
Tel: (413) 528-4192
(800) 292-4192

WAINWRIGHT INN
518 S Main St
(01230)
Rates: $65-$175
Tel: (413) 528-2062

GREENFIELD

THE BRANDT HOUSE B & B
29 Highland Ave
(01301)
Rates: $80-$150
Tel: (413) 774-3329

CANDLELIGHT MOTOR INN
208 Mohawk Tr
(01301)
Rates: $38-$84
Tel: (413) 772-0101

HADLEY

HOWARD JOHNSON
401 Russell St
(01036)
Rates: $59-$100
Tel: (413) 586-01114
(800) 446-4656

HARWICH

COACHMAN MOTOR LODGE
774 Main St (02646)
Rates: $55-$98
Tel: (508) 432-0707

HARBOR WALK GUEST HOUSE
6 Freeman St
(Harwich Port 02646)
Rates: n/a
Tel: (508) 432-1675

HAVERHILL

BEST WESTERN MERRIMACK VALLEY LODGE
401 Lowell Ave
(01832)
Rates: $50-$100
Tel: (508) 373-1511
(800) 528-1234

HOLYOKE

HOLIDAY INN
245 Whiting Farms
Rd (01040)
Rates: $76-$106
Tel: (800) 465-4329

HYANNIS

ANGEL MOTEL
Rt 132 (02601)
Rates: $41-54
Tel: (508) 775-2440

**COUNTRY SQUIRE
MOTOR LODGE**
206 Main St (02601)
Rates: $35-89
Tel: (508) 775-5225

GLO-MIN BY THE SEA
182 Sea St (02601)
Rates: n/a
Tel: (508) 775-1423

**HYANNIS SANDS
MOTOR LODGE**
921 Rt 132 (02601)
Rates: n/a
Tel: (508) 790-1700

**RAINBOW RESORT
MOTEL**
Rt 132 (02601)
Rates: $48-56
Tel: (508) 362-3217

**SNUG HARBOUR
MOTOR LODGE**
48 E Main St (02601)
Rates: n/a
Tel: (508) 771-0699
(800) 345-0130

HYANNIS PORT

HARBOR VILLAGE
160 Marstons Ave
(02647)
Rates: $90-1300
Tel: (508) 775-7581

**SEA BREEZE
COTTAGES
BY THE BEACH**
337 Sea St (02647)
Rates: $450-$850
Tel: (508) 775-4269

KENMORE

HOWARD JOHNSON
575 Commonwealth
Ave (02215)
Rates: $95-$175
Tel: (617) 267-3100
(800) 446-4656

KINGSTON

PLYMOUTH BAY INN
149 Main St (02364)
Rates: $59-$99
Tel: (617) 585-3831

LANESBORO

**ARSENAULT'S
LAKE HOUSE**
Ocean St (01237)
Rates: n/a
Tel: (413) 442-6304

**BERKSHIRE NORTH
COTTAGES**
121 S Main St
(01237)
Rates: n/a
Tel: (413) 44207469

LAMPOST MOTEL
P.O. Box 335 (01237)
Rates: n/a
Tel: (413) 443-2979

**LANESBORO
MOUNTAIN MOTEL**
P.O. Box 355 (01237)
Rates: n/a
Tel: (413) 442-6717

MT. VIEW MOTEL
499 S Main St (01237)
Rates: $30-$95
Tel: (413) 442-1009

**WEATHERVANE
MOTEL**
475 S Main St
(01237)
Rates: $32-$98
Tel: (413) 443-3230

LAWRENCE

**HAMPTON INN
NORTH**
224 Winthrop Ave
(01843)
Rates: $59-$85
Tel: (508) 975-4050
(800) 426-7866

LEE

HUNTERS MOTEL
89 Pleasant St
(01238)
Rates: $35-$95
Tel: (413) 243-0101

**MORGAN HOUSE
INN**
33 Main St (01238)
Rates: $42-$160
Tel: (413) 243-0181

RAMADA INN
165 Housatonic St
(01238)
Rates: $45-$105
Tel: (800) 272-6232

LENOX

SEVEN HILLS INN
40 Plunkett St
(01240)
Rates: n/a
Tel: (413) 637-0060
(800) 869-6518

WALKER HOUSE INN
64 Walker St (01240)
Rates: $70-$80
Tel: (413) 637-1271

LEOMINSTER

**THE INN
ON THE HILL**
450 N Main St
(01453)
Rates: $46
Tel: (508) 537-1661

MOTEL 6
Commercial St
(01453)
Rates: $36-$42
Tel: (508) 537-8161
(800) 440-6000

LEXINGTON

BATTLE GREEN INN
1720 Massachusetts
Ave (02173)
Rates: $48-$52
Tel: (617) 862-6100

LOWELL

SHERATON INN
50 Warren St (01852)
Rates: $59-$350
Tel: (508) 452-1200

LYNN

**DIAMOND DISTRICT
B & B INN**
142 Ocean St (01902)
Rates: $58-$84
Tel: (617) 599-5122
(800) 666-3076

MALDEN

**NEW ENGLANDER
MOTOR COURT**
551 Broadway
(02148)
Rates: $40-$60
Tel: (617) 321-0505

MANSFIELD

HOLIDAY INN
31 Hampshire St
(02048)
Rates: $79-$119
Tel: (800) 465-4329

MOTEL 6
60 Forbes Blvd
(02048)
Rates: $46-$52
Tel: (508) 339-2323
(800) 440-6000

MARLBOROUGH

**BEST WESTERN
ROYAL PLAZA**
181 Boston Post Rd
(01752)
Rates: $95-$295
Tel: (800) 528-1234

SUPER 8 MOTEL
880 Donald J Lynch
Blvd (01752)
Rates: $45-$49
Tel: (800) 800-8000

MARTHA'S VINEYARD

ISLAND INN
Beach Rd (02557)
Rates: $65-$235
Tel: (508) 693-2002

MIDDLEBORO

DAYS INN
Rt 105 N (02346)
Rates: $60-$80
Tel: (508) 946-4400
(800) 329-7466

MIDDLEFIELD

PEASE BLUEBERRY FARM
Skyline Trail (01243)
Rates: $100
Tel: (413) 623-5519

NANTUCKET ISLAND

BACK-A-BIT COTTAGE
4 Walsh St (02554)
Rates: n/a
Tel: (508) 228-2623

BARTLETT'S BEACH COTTAGES
P.O. Box 899 (02554)
Rates: n/a
Tel: (508) 228-3906

BOAT HOUSE
15 Old N Wharf (02554)
Rates: $250-500
Tel: (508) 228-9552
(800) 245-9552

CORKISH COTTAGES
320 Polpis Rd (02554)
Rates: n/a
Tel: (508) 228-0258

FAR ISLAND COTTAGES
41 Madaket Rd (02554)
Rates: n/a
Tel: (508) 228-4227

GREY LADY
34 Centre St (02554)
Rates: $95-$175
Tel: (508) 228-9552
(800) 245-9552

HALLIDAY'S NANTUCKET HOUSE
2 E York St (02554)
Rates: $400-$500 /weekly
Tel: (508) 228-9450

JARED COFFIN HOUSE
29 Broad St (02554)
Rates: $150-$400
Tel: (508) 228-2400
(800) 248-2405

NANTUCKET INN
27 Macy's Ln (02554)
Rates: $100-$195
Tel: (508) 228-6900

SAFE HARBOR GUEST HOUSE
2 Harbor View Way (02554)
Rates: $140-$170
Tel: (508) 228-3222

TEN HUSSEY STREET
10 Hussey St (02554)
Rates: $95-$175
Tel: (508) 228-9552
(800) 245-9552

WEST WIND COTTAGE AT MADAKET HARBOR
41 Linnaean St (01238)
Rates: n/a
Tel: (617) 868-6866

NEEDHAM

SHERATON HOTEL
100 Cabot St (02194)
Rates: $114-$159
Tel: (617) 444-1110

NEW ASHFORD

CARRIAGE HOUSE
Route 7 (01237)
Rates: n/a
Tel: (413) 458-5359

NEW BEDFORD

DAYS INN
500 Hathaway Rd (02740)
Rates: $35-$70
Tel: (508) 997-1231
(800) 329-7466

NEWBURYPORT

MORRILL PLACE INN
209 High St (01950)
Rates: $60-$80
Tel: (508) 462-2808

NEWTON

DAYS INN
399 Grove St (02162)
Rates: $79-$119
Tel: (800) 329-7466

NORTH EASTHAM

BLUE DOLPHIN INN
Rt 6, Drawer S (02642)
Rates: $79-$90
Tel: (508) 255-1159
(800) 654-0504

NORTH TRURO

OUTER REACH RESORT
Rt 6 (02652)
Rates: n/a
Tel: (508) 487-9500
(800) 942-5388

SEASCAPE MOTOR INN
Rt 6A (02652)
Rates: n/a
Tel: (508) 487-1225

NORTH-BOROUGH

FRIENDSHIP INN
At Jct SR 9 & 20 (01532)
Rates: $58-$69
Tel: (508) 842-8941
(800) 453-4511

NORTHAMPTON

DAYS INN
117 Conz St (01060)
Rates: $49-$89
Tel: (413) 586-1500
(800) 329-7466

INN AT NORTHAMPTON
Rt 5 & Rt 91 (01060)
Rates: n/a
Tel: (413) 586-1211

ORANGE

BALD EAGLE MOTEL
110 Daniel Shay Hwy (01364)
Rates: $35-$100
Tel: (508) 544-8864

ORLEANS

ORLEANS B & B ASSOCIATION
P.O. Box 1312 (02653)
Rates: n/a
Tel: (508) 255-3824
(800) 541-6226

ORLEANS HOLIDAY MOTEL
486 Cranberry Hwy (02653)
Rates: $53-$105
Tel: (508) 255-1514
(800) 451-1833

SKAKET BEACH MOTEL
203 Cranberry Hwy (02653)
Rates: $43-$104
Tel: (508) 255-1020
(800) 835-0298

OTIS

GROUSE HOUSE
P.O. Box 70 (01253)
Rates: n/a
Tel: (413) 269-4446

PEABODY

MARRIOT
8A Centennial Dr (01960)
Rates: $99-$129
Tel: (508) 977-9700

PITTSFIELD

BONNIE BRAE CABINS
108 Broadway St
(01201)
Rates: $45-$75
Tel: (413) 442-3754

HUNSTMAN MOTEL
1350 W Housatonic
St (01201)
Rates: n/a
Tel: (413) 442-8714

LAKEVIEW COTTAGE
43 Thomas Rd
(01201)
Rates: $80-$120
Tel: (413) 445-7620
(413) 445-7179

PROVINCE-TOWN

BREAKWATER MOTOR INN
Rt 6A (02657)
Rates: n/a
Tel: (508) 487-1134
(800) 487-1134

HARGOOD HOUSE APTS
493 Commercial St
(02657)
Rates: $72-$142
Tel: (508) 487-9133

HOLIDAY INN
Shore Dr Rt 6A
(02657)
Rates: $70-$140
Tel: (508) 487-1711
(800) 465-4329

WHITE SANDS MOTEL
Rt 6A, Box 611
(02657)
Rates: n/a
Tel: (508) 487-0244

WHITE WIND INN
174 Commercial St
(02657)
Rates: n/a
Tel: (508) 487-1526

RANDOLPH

HOLIDAY INN
1374 N Main St
(02368)
Rates: $82-$98
Tel: (800) 465-4329

RAYNHAM

DAYS INN
Rt 44 (02767)
Rates: $44-$59
Tel: (508) 824-8647
(800) 329-7466

REHOBOTH

FIVE BRIDGE FARM INN B & B
154 Pine St (02769)
Rates: $55-$85
Tel: (508) 252-3190

REVERE

HOWARD JOHNSON LODGE
407 Squire Rd
(02151)
Rates: $74-$130
Tel: (617) 284-7200
(800) 446-4656

RICHMOND

A B & B IN THE BERKSHIRES
1666 Dubin Rd
(01254)
Rates: $75-$125
Tel: (413) 698-2817
(800) 795-7122

MIDDLERISE B & B
Route 41 (01254)
Rates: $90-$100
Tel: (413) 698-2687

ROCKLAND

HOLIDAY INN
909 Hingham St
(02370)
Rates: $65-$89
Tel: (617) 871-5660

ROCKPORT

SANDY BAY MOTOR INN
173 Main St (01966)
Rates: $64-$136
Tel: (508) 546-7155

ROWLEY

COUNTRY GARDEN MOTEL
101 Mai St (01969)
Rates: $45-$95
Tel: (508) 948-7773

SALEM

HAWTHORNE HOTEL
18 Washington Sq
(01970)
Rates: $80-$127
Tel: (508) 744-4080

THE SALEM INN
7 Summer St (01970)
Rates: $85-$135
Tel: (508) 741-0680
(800) 446-2995

SANDISFIELD

NEW BOSTON INN
P.O. Box 166 D
(01255)
Rates: $85-$95
Tel: (413) 258-4477

SANDWICH

SANDWICH MOTOR LODGE
P. O. Box 557
(02563)
Rates: $79-$110
Tel: (508) 888-2275
(800) 282-5353

SAUGUS

COLONIAL TRAVELER MOTOR COURT
1753 Broadway
(01906)
Rates: $40-$60
Tel: (617) 233-6700

SCITUATE

CLIPPER SHIP LODGE
7 Beaver Dam Rd
(02066)
Rates: $72-$149
Tel: (617) 545-5550
(800) 368-3818

SEEKONK

MOTEL 6
821 Fall River Ave
(02771)
Rates: $46-$56
Tel: (508) 336-7800
(800) 466-8356

RAMADA INN
940 Fall River Ave
(02771)
Rates: $60-$90
Tel: (508) 336-7300

SHEFFIELD

BOW WOW ROAD INN
570 Bow Wow Rd
(01257)
Rates: n/a
Tel: (413) 229-3339

DEPOT GUEST HOUSE
P.O. Box 575 (01257)
Rates: $45-$95
Tel: (413) 229-2908

IVANHOE COUNTRY HOUSE
254 Undermountain
Rd (01257)
Rates: $55-$110
Tel: (413) 229-2143

STAGECOACH HILL INN
854 S Under-
mountain Rd (01257)
Rates: $50-$125
Tel: (413) 229-8585

SHREWSBURY

DAYS INN
889 Boston Tpk (01545)
Rates: $48-$59
Tel: (800) 329-7466

SOMERSET

QUALITY INN
1878 Wilbur Ave
(02725)
Rates: $54-$90
Tel: (508) 678-4545

SOUTH ATTLEBORO

DAYS INN
1116 Washington St
(02703)
Rates: $45-$70
Tel: (508) 761-4825

SOUTH DEERFIELD

MOTEL 6
Rt 5-10 (01373)
Rates: $40-$46
Tel: (413) 665-7161
(800) 440-6000

SOUTH EGREMONT

SWISS HUTTE
Route 23 (01258)
Rates: $75-$140
Tel: (413) 528-6200

SOUTH HARWICH

HANDKERCHIEF SHOALS MOTEL
MA 28 (02661)
Rates: $42-$70
Tel: (508) 432-2200

SOUTH ORLEANS

OCEAN BAY VIEW COTTAGES
Portanimicut Rd
(02662)
Rates: n/a
Tel: (508) 255-3344

SOUTH WELLFLEET

GREEN HAVEN COTTAGES
Rt 6, Box 486
(02663)
Rates: n/a
Tel: (508) 349-1715

SOUTH YARMOUTH

BRENTWOOD COTTAGES
961 Main St (02664)
Rates: n/a
Tel: (508) 398-8812
(800) 328-8812

BRENTWOOD MOTOR INN
Rt 28 (02664)
Rates: $35-65+
Tel: (508) 398-8812
(800) 328-8812

WINDJAMMER MOTOR INN
192 South Shore Dr
(02664)
Rates: $49-$99
Tel: (508) 398-2370
(800) 448-9744

SOUTH-BOROUGH

RED ROOF INN
367 Turnpike Rd
(01772)
Rates: $35-$48
Tel: (800) 843-7663

SPRINGFIELD

HOLIDAY INN
711 Dwight St
(01104)
Rates: $82-$125
Tel: (800) 465-4329

STOCKBRIDGE

HIGH MEADOWS
P.O. Box 976 (01262)
Rates: n/a
Tel: (413) 298-4652
(800) 817-5665

STURBRIDGE

BEST WESTERN AMERICAN MOTOR LODGE
US 20 W (01566)
Rates: $57-$87
Tel: (508) 347-9121
(800) 528-1234

ECONO LODGE
682 Main St (01518)
Rates: $50-$70
Tel: (508) 347-2324
(800) 424-4777

HOST HOTEL & CONFERENCE CTR
366 Main St (01566)
Rates: $99-$135
Tel: (800) 582-3232

PUBLICK HOUSE HISTORIC RESORT
SR 131 (01566)
Rates: $55-$145
Tel: (508) 347-3313

STURBRIDGE MOTOR INN
68 Old Rt 15 (01566)
Rates: $45-$70
Tel: (508) 347-3391

SUPER 8 MOTEL
358 Main St (01566)
Rates: $43-$73
Tel: (508) 347-9000
(800) 800-8000

TEWKSBURY

HOLIDAY INN
4 Highwood Dr
(01876)
Rates: $49-$89
Tel: (800) 465-4329

RESIDENCE INN BY MARRIOTT
1775 Andover St
(01876)
Rates: $93-$150
Tel: (508) 640-1003
(800) 331-3131

TRYINGHAM

SUNSET FARM B & B
66 Tryingham Rd
(01264)
Rates: $65-$110
Tel: (413) 243-3229

WAKEFIELD

BEST WESTERN LORD WAKEFIELD HOTEL
595 North Ave
(01880)
Rates: $55-$80
Tel: (800) 528-1234

WALTHAM

THE WESTIN HOTEL
70 Third Ave (02154)
Rates: $119-$199
Tel: (617) 290-5600

WELLFLEET

BROWN'S LANDING
P.O. Box 1017 (02667)
Rates: n/a
Tel: (508) 349-6923

FRIENDSHIP COTTAGES
530 Chequessett
Neck Rd (02667)
Rates: n/a
Tel: (508) 349-3390

WEST BARNSTABLE

COZY NEST B & B
161 Maple St
(02630)
Rates: n/a
Tel: (508) 362-4218

WEST DENNIS

CAPTAIN VARRIEUR'S COTTAGES
P.O. Box 1332 (02670)
Rates: $600
Tel: (508) 394-4338
(800) 647-7126

ELMWOOD INN
57 Old Main St
(02670)
Rates: $38+
Tel: (508) 394-2798

PINE COVE INN & COTTAGES
Rt 28 & Main St
(02670)
Rates: $30-50
Tel: (508) 398-8511

WOODBINE VILLAGE ON THE COVE
Rt 28 (02670)
Rates: $300 /weekly
Tel: (508) 881-1381

WEST HARWICH

BARNABY INN
36 Main St (02671)
Rates: n/a
Tel: (508) 432-6789

CLADDAGH INN
77 Main St (02671)
Rates: $95-$120
Tel: (508) 432-9628

WEST SPRINGFIELD

BLACK HORSE MOTEL
500 Riverdale St
(01089)
Rates: $39-$69
Tel: (413) 733-2161

ECONO LODGE
1533 Elm St (01089)
Rates: $32-$60
Tel: (413) 734-8278
(800) 424-4777

GOODLIFE INN
21 Baldwin St
(01089)
Rates: $69-$82
Tel: (413) 781-2300

HAMPTON INN
1011 Riverdale St
(01089)
Rates: $60-$66
Tel: (800) 426-7866

HOWARD JOHNSON BED & BREAKFAST
1150 Riverdale St
(01089)
Rates: $44-$90
Tel: (800) 654-2000

MOTEL 6
106 Capital Dr
(01089)
Rates: $36-$42
Tel: (413) 788-4000
(800) 440-6000

RED ROOF INN
1254 Riverdale St
(01089)
Rates: $29-$56
Tel: (413) 731-1010
(800) 843-7663

SUPER 8 MOTEL
1500 Riverdale St
(01089)
Rates: n/a
Tel: (800) 800-8000

WEST STOCKBRIDGE

PLEASANT VALLEY MOTEL
Rt 102 (01266)
Rates: $35-$125
Tel: (413) 232-8511

WEST YARMOUTH

RYAN'S COTTAGE
19 Sandy Ln
(02673)
Rates: n/a
Tel: (508) 771-6387

THUNDERBIRD MOTOR LODGE
Rt 28
(02673)
Rates: $26+
Tel: (508) 775-2692
(800) 247-3006

TOWN 'N COUNTRY MOTOR LODGE
452 Main St
(02673)
Rates: $65+
Tel: (508) 771-0212
(800) 992-2340

YARMOUTH SHORES
29 Lewis Bay Rd
(02673)
Rates: $190+ /weekly
Tel: (50≥8) 775-1944

WESTBOROUGH

COMFORT INN
399 Turnpike Rd
(01581)
Rates: $53-$68
Tel: (800) 272-6232

MARRIOTT HOTEL
5400 Computer Dr
(01581)
Rates: $79-$143
Tel: (508) 366-5511

RESIDENCE INN BY MARRIOTT
25 Connector Rd
(01581)
Rates: $73-$160
Tel: (508) 366-7700
(800) 331-3131

WESTFIELD

COUNTRY COURT MOTEL
480 Southampton Rd
(01085)
Rates: $n/a
Tel: (413) 562-9790

WESTMINSTER

TOWN CRIER MOTEL
Rt 2A & 140 (04173)
Rates: $29-$45
Tel: (508) 874-5951

WESTMINSTER VILLAGE INN
9 Village Inn Rd
(01473)
Rates: $69-$139
Tel: (508) 874-5351

WILLIAMSTOWN

COZY CORNER MOTEL
284 Sand Spring Rd
(01267)
Rates: $39-$78
Tel: (413) 458-8006

JERICHO VALLEY INN
Rt 13 (01267)
Rates: $48-$98
Tel: (413) 458-9511
(800) 537-4246

THE VILLAGER MOTEL
953 Simonds Rd
(01267)
Rates: $35-$70
Tel: (413) 458-4046

WILLIAMS INN
Rt 2 & 7 (01267)
Rates: $80-$140
Tel: (413) 458-9371

THE WILLOWS MOTEL
480 Main St (01267)
Rates: $38-$76
Tel: (413) 458-5768

WOBURN

COMFORT INN
315 Mishawum Rd
(01801)
Rates: $50-$55
Tel: (800) 221-2222

RAMADA INN
15 Middlesex Canal
Park Rd (01801)
Rates: $59-$129
Tel: (617) 935-8760
(800) 272-6232

RED ROOF INN
19 Commerce Way
(01801)
Rates: $69-$104
Tel: (800) 843-7663

WORCESTER

ECONO LODGE
531 Lincoln St
(01605)
Rates: $40-$50
Tel: (508) 852-5800
(800) 424-4777

HAMPTON INN
110 Summer St
(01608)
Rates: $79-$89
Tel: (508) 757-0400
(800) 426-7866

YARMOUTH PORT

COLONIAL HOUSE INN
277 Main St, Rt 6-A
(02675)
Rates: $60-$95
Tel: (800) 999-3416

VILLAGE INN
Main St
(02675)
Rates: $40-90
Tel: (508) 362-3182

MICHIGAN

ACME

KNOLLWOOD MOTEL
5777 US 31 N, Box 37
(49610)
Rates: $38-$88
Tel: (616) 938-2040

SUN 'N SAND MOTEL
P. O. Box 307 (49610)
Rates: n/a
Tel: (616) 938-2190

ALBION

**BEST WESTERN
ADAMS ARMS
MOTEL**
400 B Dr N (49224)
Rates: $48-$93
Tel: (517) 629-3966
(800) 528-1234

DAYS INN
P. O. Box 865 (49224)
Rates: $50-$67
Tel: (517) 629-9411
(800) 329-7466

ALLEGAN

**BUDGET HOST
SUNSET MOTEL**
1580 Lincoln Rd
(49010)
Rates: n/a
Tel: (800) 283-4678

ALMA

PETTICOAT INN
2454 W Monroe Rd
(48801)
Rates: $27-$40
Tel: (517) 681-5728

ALPENA

AMBER MOTEL
2052 State St (49707)
Rates: $35-$65
Tel: (517) 354-8573

BAY MOTEL
2107 US 23 S (49707)
Rates: $30-$150
Tel: (517) 356-6137

FIRESIDE INN
18730 Fireside Hwy
(49707)
Rates: n/a
Tel: (517) 595-6369

HOLIDAY INN
1000 Hwy 23N
(49707)
Rates: $69-$109
Tel: (517) 356-2151
(800) 465-4329

**PARKER HOUSE
MOTEL**
11505 Hwy 23N
(49707)
Rates: $40-$55
Tel: (517) 595-6484

**WATERS EDGE
MOTEL**
1000 State St (49707)
Rates: $28-$49
Tel: (517) 354-5495

ANN ARBOR

**BEST WESTERN
WOLVERINE INN**
3505 S State St
(48108)
Rates: $51-$69
Tel: (313) 665-3500
(800) 528-1234

COMFORT INN
2455 Carpenter Rd
(48108)
Rates: $69-$110
Tel: (313) 973-6100
(800) 973-6101

**HAMPTON INN-
NORTH**
2300 Green Rd
(48105)
Rates: $54-$66
Tel: (313) 996-4444
(800) 426-7866

HOJO INN
2424 E Stadium Blvd
(48104)
Rates: $45-$60
Tel: (313) 971-8000
(800) 446-4656

**HOLIDAY INN-
NORTH CAMPUS**
3600 Plymouth Rd
(48105)
Rates: $79-$89
Tel: (313) 769-9800
(800) 465-4329

MOTEL 6
3764 S State St
(48104)
Rates: $37-$43
Tel: (313) 665-9900
(800) 440-6000

RED ROOF INN
3621 Plymouth Rd
(48105)
Rates: $38-$61
Tel: (313) 996-5800
(800) 843-7663

**RESIDENCE INN
BY MARRIOTT**
800 Victors Way
(48108)
Rates: $120-$160
Tel: (313) 996-5666
(800) 331-3131

AUBURN HILLS

HILTON SUITES
2300 Featherstone
Rd (48326)
Rates: $119-$164
Tel: (810) 334-2222
(800) 445-8667

**HOLIDAY INN
SELECT**
1500 Opdyke Rd
(48326)
Rates: $69-$139
Tel: (810) 373-4550
(800) 465-4329

MOTEL 6
1471 Opdyke Rd
(48326)
Rates: $37-$43
Tel: (810) 373-8440
(800) 440-6000

AU GRES

**POINT AU GRES
HOTEL**
3279 South Point Ln
(48703)
Rates: $33-$40
Tel: (517) 876-7217

BARAGA

**CARLA'S LAKE
SHORE MOTEL**
Rt 1, Box 233 (49908)
Rates: $32-$49
Tel: (906) 353-6256

SUPER 8 MOTEL
790 Michigan Ave
(49908)
Rates: $41-$47
Tel: (906) 353-6680
(800) 800-8000

BATTLE CREEK

APPLETREE INN
4786 Beckley Rd
(49017)
Rates: $41-$85
Tel: (616) 979-3561
(800) 388-7829

BATTLE CREEK INN
5050 Beckley Rd
(49015)
Rates: $55-$68
Tel: (616) 979-1100
(800) 232-3405

ECONO LODGE
165 Capital Ave SW
(49015)
Rates: $35-$66
Tel: (616) 965 3976
(800) 424-4777

HAMPTON INN
1150 Riverside Dr
(49017)
Rates: $58-$70
Tel: (616) 979-5577
(800) 426-7866

KNIGHTS INN
2595 Capital Ave SW
(49015)
Rates: $35-$49
Tel: (616) 964-2600
(800) 843-5644

MICHIGAN MOTEL
20475 Capital Ave NE (49017)
Rates: $34-$44
Tel: (616) 963-1565

MOTEL 6
4775 Beckley Rd (49017)
Rates: $32-$38
Tel: (616) 979-1141
(800) 440-6000

SUPER 8 MOTEL
5395 Beckley Rd (49015)
Rates: $39-$49
Tel: (616) 979-1828
(800) 800-8000

BAY CITY

BAY VALLEY HOTEL & RESORT
2470 Old Bridge Rd (48706)
Rates: $65-$108
Tel: (517) 686-3500

DELTA MOTEL
1000 S Euclid Ave (48706)
Rates: $27-$60
Tel: (517) 684-4490

HOLIDAY INN
501 Saginaw St (48708)
Rates: $59-$79
Tel: (517) 892-3501
(800) 465-4329

BAY VIEW

COMFORT INN
1314 US 31N (49770)
Rates: $60-$150
Tel: (616) 347-3220
(800) 221-2222

BEAR LAKE

BELLA VISTA MOTOR LODGE
US #31 in Village (49614)
Rates: n/a
Tel: (616) 864-3000

BELLAIRE

WINDWARD SHORE MOTEL
5812 E Torch Lake Dr (49615)
Rates: n/a
Tel: (616) 377-6321

BELLEVILLE

RED ROOF INN METRO AIRPORT
45501 I-94 N Expwy (48111)
Rates: $29-$47
Tel: (313) 697-2244
(800) 843-7663

BENTON HARBOR

COMFORT INN
1598 Mall Dr (49022)
Rates: $35-$60
Tel: (616) 925-1880
(800) 221-2222

COURTYARD BY MARRIOTT
1592 Mall Dr (49022)
Rates: $59-$129
Tel: (616) 925-3000
(800) 321-2211

DAYS INN
2699 Michigan Rt 139 (49022)
Rates: $44-$67
Tel: (616) 925-7021
(800) 329-7466

MOTEL 6
2063 Pipestone Rd (49022)
Rates: $27-$33
Tel: (616) 925-5100
(800) 440-6000

RAMADA INN
798 Ferguson Dr (49022)
Rates: $49-$79
Tel: (616) 927-1172
(800) 272-6232

RED ROOF INN
1630 Mall Dr (49022)
Rates: $29-$45
Tel: (616) 927-2484
(800) 843-7663

SUPER 8 MOTEL
1950 E Napier Ave (49022)
Rates: $37-$62
Tel: (616) 926-1371
(800) 800-8000

BERGLAND

NORTHWINDS MOTEL & RESORT
1497 W M-28 (49910)
Rates: $22-69
Tel: (906) 575-3557

BEULAH

PINE KNOT MOTEL
171 N Center St (49617)
Rates: $40-$60
Tel: (616) 882-7751

SUNNYWOODS RESORT MOTEL
14065 Honor Hwy (49617)
Rates: $30-$80
Tel: (616) 325-3952
(800) 347-9728

BIRCH RUN

MARKET STREET INN
9087 Birch Run (48415)
Rates: $39-$54
Tel: (517) 624-9395
(800) 336-2486

SUPER 8 MOTEL
9235 Birch Run Rd (48415)
Rates: $40-$80
Tel: (517) 624-4440
(800) 800-8000

BLISSFIELD

H D ELLIS INN
415 West Adrian St (49228)
Rates: $50-$90
Tel: (517) 486-3155

BLOOMFIELD HILLS

HOLIDAY INN BLOOMFIELD HILLS-PONTIAC
1801 Telegraph Rd (48302)
Rates: $62-$99
Tel: (810) 334-2444
(800) 465-4329

ST. CHRISTOPHER MOTEL
3915 Telegraph Rd (48302)
Rates: $35-$45
Tel: (810) 647-1800

BOYNE FALLS

BOYNE VUE MOTEL
2711 Railroad, Box 12 (49713)
Rates: $28-$125
Tel: (616) 549-2822
(800) 549-2822

BRANCH

LAZY DAYS MOTEL
P. O. Box 104 (49402)
Rates: $32
Tel: (616) 898-2252

BREVORT

CHAPEL HILL MOTEL
4422 W US 2 (49760)
Rates: $35-$50
Tel: (906) 292-5521

BRIDGEPORT

MOTEL 6
6361 Dixie Hwy (48722)
Rates: $30-$36
Tel: (517) 777-2582
(800) 440-6000

BRIDGMAN

BRIDGMAN INN
9999 Red Arrow Hwy (49106)
Rates: $30-$70
Tel: (616) 465-3187

BURTON

WALLI'S SUPER 8 MOTEL
G-1341 S Center Rd (48509)
Rates: $33-$88
Tel: (810) 743-8850

CADILLAC

BEST WESTERN BILL OLIVER'S
845 S Mitchell Dr (49601)
Rates: $50-$96
Tel: (616) 775-2458
(800) 528-1234

CADILLAC SANDS RESORT
6319 E M115 (49601)
Rates: $39-$125
Tel: (616) 775-2407

DAYS INN
6001 E M115 (49601)
Rates: $54-$121
Tel: (616) 775-4414
(800) 329-7466

PILGRIM'S VILLAGE
181 S Lake Mitchell (49601)
Rates: $49
Tel: (616) 775-5412

PINE KNOLL MOTEL
8072 Mackinaw Tr (49601)
Rates: $35-$45
Tel: (616) 775-9471

SOUTH SHORE RESORT
1246 Sunnyside Dr (49601)
Rates: $30-$60
Tel: (616) 775-7641

SUN'N SNOW MOTEL
301 S Lake Mitchell Dr (49601)
Rates: $30-$120
Tel: (616) 775-9961

CANTON

BUDGETEL
41211 Ford Rd (48187)
Rates: $42-$65
Tel: (313) 981-1808

MOTEL 6
41216 Ford Rd (48187)
Rates: $32-$36
Tel: (313) 981-5000
(800) 440-6000

CARO

KINGS WAY INN
1057 E Caro Rd (48723)
Rates: $27-$65
Tel: (517) 673-7511

CASEVILLE

SURF N SAND MOTEL
6006 Pt Austin Rd (48725)
Rates: $36-$84
Tel: (517) 856-4400

CASCADE

BUDGETEL
41211 Ford Rd (48187)
Rates: $39-$49
Tel: (616) 956-3300

KNIGHTS INN
5175 28th St SE (49512)
Rates: $38-$51
Tel: (616) 956-6601

RED ROOF INN
5131 28th St SE (49512)
Rates: $38-$53
Tel: (616) 942-0800
(800) 843-7663

CASS CITY

WILDWOOD MOTEL
5986 E Cass City Rd (48726)
Rates: $34
Tel: (517) 872-3366

CEDARVILLE

COMFORT INN
P. O. Box 189 (49719)
Rates: $69-$89
Tel: (906) 484-2266
(800) 221-2222

CHARLEVOIX

CAPRI MOTEL
1455 S Bridge St (49720)
Rates: $60-$120
Tel: (616) 547-2545

THE LODGE MOTEL
US 31 N (49720)
Rates: $30-$160
Tel: (616) 547-6565

CHARLOTTE

SUPER 8 MOTEL
I-69 & M-50 (48813)
Rates: $44-$63
Tel: (517) 543-8288
(800) 800-8000

CHEBOYGAN

BIRCH HAUS MOTEL
1301 Mackinaw Ave (49721)
Rates: $27-$47
Tel: (616) 627-5862

CHEBOYGAN MOTOR LODGE
1355 Mackinaw Ave (49721)
Rates: $30-$75
Tel: (616) 627-3129

CONTINENTAL INN
613 N Main St (49721)
Rates: $38-$88
Tel: (616) 627-7164

MONARCH MOTEL
1257 Mackinaw Ave (49721)
Rates: $30-$55
Tel: (616) 627-2143

PINE RIVER MOTEL
102 Lafayette (49721)
Rates: $25-$50
Tel: (616) 627-5119

CLARE

BUDGET HOST CLARE MOTEL
1110 McEwan St (48617)
Rates: $35-$70
Tel: (517) 386-7201
(800) 825-2738

DOHERTY MOTOR HOTEL
604 McEwan St (48617)
Rates: $40-$75
Tel: (517) 386-3441
(800) 525-4115

LONE PINE MOTEL
1508 McEwan St (48617)
Rates: $45-$50
Tel: (517) 386-7787

CLIO

CLIO MOTEL
4254 W Vienna (48420)
Rates: $39-$56
Tel: (810) 687-0660

COLDWATER

ECONO LODGE
884 W Chicago Rd (49036)
Rates: $32-$56
Tel: (517) 278-4501
(800) 424-4777

LITTLE KING MOTEL
847 E Chicago Rd (49036)
Rates: $30-$46
Tel: (517) 278-6660

QUALITY INN
1000 Orleans Blvd (49036)
Rates: $56-$135
Tel: (517) 278-2017
(800) 221-2222

SUPER 8 MOTEL
600 Orleans Blvd (49036)
Rates: $44-$63
Tel: (517) 278-8833
(800) 800-8000

COPPER HARBOR

ASTOR HOUSE-MINNETONKA RESORT
P. O. Box 13 (49918)
Rates: $43-$85
Tel: (906) 289-4449
(800) 433-2770

BELLA VISTA MOTEL
P. O. Box 26 (49918)
Rates: $38-$50
Tel: (906) 289-4213

KING COPPER MOTELS
PO Box 68 (49918)
Rates: $40-$60
Tel: (906) 289-4214
(800) 833-2470

NORLAND MOTEL
2 Mi E on US 41
(49918)
Rates: $28-$48
Tel: (906) 289-4815

CURTIS

SEASONS MOTEL
Main St (49820)
Rates: $30-$43
Tel: (906) 586-3078

DEARBORN

BEST WESTERN GREENFIELD INN
3000 Enterprise Dr
(Allen Park 48101)
Rates: $79-$140
Tel: (800) 528-1234

HOLIDAY INN FAIRLANE
5801 Southfield
Service Dr (48228)
Rates: $94-$99
Tel: (313) 336-3340
(800) 465-4329

MARRIOTT HOTEL-DEARBORN INN
20301 Oakwood
Blvd (48124)
Rates: $89-$139
Tel: (313) 271-2700
(800) 228-9290

QUALITY INN FAIRLANE
21430 Michigan Ave
(48124)
Rates: $55-$125
Tel: (313) 565-0800
(800) 221-2222

RED ROOF INN
24130 Michigan Ave
(48124)
Rates: $42-$64
Tel: (313) 278-9732
(800) 843-7663

RESIDENCE INN BY MARRIOTT
5777 Southfield
Service Dr (48228)
Rates: $125-$175
Tel: (313) 441-1700
(800) 331-3131

DETROIT

HOTEL ST. REGIS
3071 W Grand Blvd
(48202)
Rates: $79-$115
Tel: (313) 873-3000

RAMADA INN DOWNTOWN
400 Bagley Ave
(48226)
Rates: $59-$94
Tel: (313) 962-2300
(800) 272-6232

SHORECREST MOTOR INN
1316 E Jefferson
(48207)
Rates: $48-$135
Tel: (313) 568-3000
(800) 992-9616

SUBURBAN HOUSE
16920 Telegraph
(48219)
Rates: $28-$40
Tel: (313) 535-9646

WESTIN HOTEL-RENAISSANCE CENTER
Renaissance Center
(48243)
Rates: $165-$200
Tel: (313) 568-8000
(800) 228-3000

DRUMMOND ISLAND

VECHELL'S CEDAR VIEW RESORT
P. O. Box 175 (49726)
Rates: $225-$255
Tel: (906) 493-5381

EAGLE HARBOR

SHORELINE RESORT
HYC 1, Box 262
(49950)
Rates: $48-$62
Tel: (906) 289-4441

EAST JORDAN

WESTBROOK MOTEL
218 Elizabeth St
(49727)
Rates: $45-$55
Tel: (616) 536-2674

EAST LANSING

PARK INN INTERNATIONAL
1100 Trowbridge Rd
(48823)
Rates: $42-$99
Tel: (517) 351-5500
(800) 437-7275

RESIDENCE INN BY MARRIOTT
1600 E Grand River
Ave (48823)
Rates: $99-$129
Tel: (517) 332-7711
(800) 331-3131

EAST TAWAS

CARRIAGE INN
1500 N US 23 (48730)
Rates: $30-$55
Tel: (517) 362-2831
(800) 666-8493

NORTHLAND BEACH COTTAGES
808 East Bay St
(48730)
Rates: n/a
Tel: (517) 362-2601

EASTPOINTE

EASTLAND MOTEL
21055 Gratiot Ave
(48021)
Rates: $26-$32
Tel: (810) 772-1300

ELK RAPIDS

CAMELOT INN
P. O. Box 910 (49629)
Rates: $38-$82
Tel: (616) 264-8473

EPOUFETTE

WONDERLAND MOTEL
80 West US 2 (49762)
Rates: n/a
Tel: (906) 292-5574

ESCANABA

DAYS INN
2603 N Lincoln Rd
(49829)
Rates: $42-$70
Tel: (906) 789-1200
(800) 329-7466

HIAWATHA MOTEL
2400 Ludington St
(49829)
Rates: $36-$50
Tel: (906) 786-1341

SUNSET MOTEL
P. O. Box 343 (49829)
Rates: $25-$45
Tel: (906) 786-1213

FARMINGTON HILLS

HOLIDAY INN
38123 W Ten Mile
Rd (48335)
Rates: $88-$103
Tel: (810) 477-4000
(800) 465-4329

MOTEL 6
38300 Grand River
Ave (48335)
Rates: $32-$38
Tel: (810) 471-0590
(800) 440-6000

RED ROOF INN
24300 Sinacola Ct
(48335)
Rates: $26-$42
Tel: (810) 478-8640
(800) 843-7663

FENNVILLE

HERITAGE MANOR INN B & B
2253 Blue Star Hwy
(49408)
Rates: $65-$195
Tel: (616) 561-2836

FLAT ROCK

SLEEP INN
29101 Commerce Dr (48134)
Rates: $49-$54
Tel: (313) 782-9898
(800) 627-5337

FLINT

DAYS INN
2207 W Bristol Rd (48507)
Rates: $42-$57
Tel: (810) 239-4681
(800) 329-7466

MOTEL 6
2324 Austin Pkwy (48507)
Rates: $32-$38
Tel: (810) 767-7100
(800) 440-6000

RAMADA INN
G-4300 W Pierson Rd (48504)
Rates: $59-$130
Tel: (810) 732-0400
(800) 272-6232

RED ROOF INN
G-3219 Miller Rd (48507)
Rates: $39-$50
Tel: (810) 733-1660
(800) 843-7663

SUPER 8 MOTEL
3033 Claude Ave (48507)
Rates: $36-$56
Tel: (810) 230-7888
(800) 800-8000

FOUNTAIN

CHRISTIE'S LOG CAB-INS ON ROUND LAKE
6503 E Sugar Grove (49410)
Rates: $45-$80
Tel: (616) 462-3218
(800) 209-7385

FRANKENMUTH

BED & BREAKFAST AT THE PINES
327 Ardussi St (48734)
Rates: $35-$55
Tel: (517) 652-9019

FRANKFORT

CHIMNEY CORNERS RESORT
1602 Crystal Dr (49635)
Rates: $37-$110
Tel: (616) 352-7522

HOTEL FRANKFORT BED & BREAKFAST
231 Main St (49635)
Rates: $39-230
Tel: (616) 352-4303

FREELAND

FREELAND INN MOTEL
6840 Midland Rd (48623)
Rates: n/a
Tel: (517) 695-9646

GAYLORD

BEST WESTERN ROYAL CREST MOTEL
803 S Otsego Ave (49735)
Rates: $49-$89
Tel: (517) 732-6451
(800) 876-9252

THE CEDARS MOTEL
701 North Center (49735)
Rates: $25-$30
Tel: (517) 732-4525

DOWNTOWN MOTEL
208 S Otsego Ave (49735)
Rates: $34-$58
Tel: (517) 732-5010

ECONO LODGE
2880 S Old 27 (49735)
Rates: $49-$74
Tel: (517) 732-5133
(800) 424-4777

HOLIDAY INN
P. O. Box 544 (49735)
Rates: $74-$91
Tel: (517) 732-2431
(800) 465-4329

MICHAYWE RESORT
1535 Opal Lake Rd (49735)
Rates: $65-$300
Tel: (517) 939-8914
(800) 322-6636

SUPER 8 MOTEL
1042 W Main (49735)
Rates: $54-$155
Tel: (517) 732-5193
(800) 800-8000

TIMBERLY MOTEL
881 S Old 27 (49735)
Rates: $38-$76
Tel: (517) 732-5166

GLADSTONE

NORWAY PINES MOTEL
7111 US Hwy 2 (49837)
Rates: $25-$48
Tel: (906) 786-5119

SLEEPY HOLLOW MOTEL
7156 US 2 & 41 (49837)
Rates: n/a
Tel: (906) 786-7092

GLADWIN

GLADWIN MOTOR INN
1003 W Cedar Ave (48624)
Rates: $25-$50
Tel: (517) 426-9661

GRAND BLANC

SCENIC INN
G8308 S Saginaw Rd (48439)
Rates: $35-$61
Tel: (313) 694-6611

GRAND MARAIS

ALVERSON'S MOTEL
P. O. Box 188 (49839)
Rates: $32-$41
Tel: (906) 494-2681

BUDGET HOST-WELKER'S RESORT
P. O. Box 277 (49839)
Rates: $34-$350
Tel: (800) 283-4678

HILLTOP CABINS
P. O. Box 377 (49839)
Rates: $45-$65
Tel: (906) 494-2331

GRAND RAPIDS

CASCADE INN
2865 Broadmoore (49512)
Rates: $27-$43
Tel: (616) 949-0850

DAYS INN DOWNTOWN
310 Pearl St NW (49504)
Rates: $49-$80
Tel: (616) 235-7611
(800) 329-7466

ECONO LODGE
250 28th St SW (49548)
Rates: $46-$55
Tel: (616) 452-2131
(800) 424-4777

EXEL INN
4855 28th St SE (49512)
Rates: $37-$54
Tel: (616) 957-3000

FAIRFIELD INN
3930 Stahl Dr SE (49546)
Rates: n/a
Tel: (616) 940-2700
(800) 228-2800

HAMPTON INN
4981 28th St SE (49512)
Rates: $57-$68
Tel: (616) 956-9304
(800) 426-7866

MOTEL 6
3524 28th St SE (49508)
Rates: $32-$38
Tel: (616) 957-3511
(800) 440-6000

NEW ENGLAND SUITES HOTEL
2985 Kraft Ave SE (49512)
Rates: $55-$75
Tel: (616) 940-1777
(800) 784-8371

RAMADA INN
65 28th St SW (49508)
Rates: $39-$56
Tel: (616) 452-1461
(800) 272-6232

RESIDENCE INN BY MARRIOTT
2701 E Beltline SE (49546)
Rates: $105-$140
Tel: (616) 957-8111
(800) 331-3131

RIVIERA MOTEL
4350 Rememberance Rd (49504)
Rates: $35-$50
Tel: (616) 453-2404

SUPER 8 MOTEL
727 44th St SW (49509)
Rates: $43-$65
Tel: (616) 530-8588
(800) 800-8000

SWAN INN MOTEL
5182 Alpine Ave NW (Comstock Park 49321)
Rates: $32-$50
Tel: (616) 784-1224
(800) 875-7926

GRAYLING

CEDAR MOTEL
606 N James (49738)
Rates: $26-$40
Tel: (517) 348-5884

HOLIDAY INN
P. O. Box 473 (49738)
Rates: $64-$92
Tel: (517) 348-7611
(800) 465-4329

NORTH COUNTRY LODGE
P. O. Box 290 (49738)
Rates: $40-$150:
Tel: (517) 348-8471
(800) 475-6300

POINTE NORTH OF GRAYLING
Bus Rt I-75 N (49738)
Rates: $35-$75
Tel: (517) 348-5950

RIVER COUNTRY MOTOR LODGE
N I-75 Bus Loop (49738)
Rates: $30-$65
Tel: (517) 348-8619
(800) 733-7396

SUPER 8 MOTEL
5828 NA Miles Pkwy (49738)
Rates: $44-$58
Tel: (517) 348-8888
(800) 800-8000

WOODLAND MOTEL
267 I-75 Business Loop (49738)
Rates: $30-$80
Tel: (517) 348-9094

HAGAR SHORE

SWEET CHERRY RESORT
3313 Chestnut (49038)
Rates: n/a
Tel: (616) 849-1233

HARBOR BEACH

THE TRAIN STATION MOTEL
2044 N Lakeshore Dr (48441)
Rates: $51-$62
Tel: (517) 479-3215

HARBOR SPRINGS

HARBOR SPRINGS COTTAGE INN
145 Zoll St (49740)
Rates: $50-$103
Tel: (616) 526-5431

HARPER WOODS

PARKCREST INN
20000 Harper Ave (48225)
Rates: $57-$78
Tel: (313) 884-8800

HARRISON

LAKESIDE MOTEL
South Business #27 (48625)
Rates: $32-$42
Tel: (517) 539-3796

WAGON WHEEL MOTEL
4294 North Clare Ave (48625)
Rates: $30-$40
Tel: (517) 539-7065

HARRISVILLE

WIDOW'S WATCH BED & BREAKFAST
401 Lake St (48740)
Rates: $45-$65
Tel: (517) 724-5465
(800) 868-1904

HART

HART MOTEL
715 State St (49420)
Rates: n/a
Tel: (616) 873-2151

HAZEL PARK

QUALITY INN
1 W 9 Mile Rd (48030)
Rates: $50-$65
Tel: (810) 399-5800
(800) 221-2222

HESSEL

LAKEVIEW MOTEL
P. O. Box 277 (49745)
Rates: $39-$42
Tel: (906) 484-2474

HILLSDALE

BAVARIAN INN
1728 Hudson Rd (49242)
Rates: $27-$34
Tel: (517) 437-3367
(800) 779-8033

HOLLAND

BLUE MILL INN
409 US 31S (49423)
Rates: $39-$51
Tel: (616) 392-7073

DAYS INN
717 Hastings (49423)
Rates: $50-$65
Tel: (616) 392-7001
(800) 329-7466

FAIRFIELD INN
2854 W Shore Dr (49424)
Rates: $45-$55
Tel: (616) 786-9700
(800) 228-2800

KNIGHTS COURT
422 E 32nd St (49423)
Rates: $45-$95
Tel: (616) 392-1000
(800) 843-5644

HONOR

FOUR SEASON
8841 Deadstream (49640)
Rates: $75-$125
Tel: (616) 325-6992
(800) 347-9728

HOUGHTON LAKE

HILLSIDE MOTEL
3419 W Houghton Lake Dr (48629)
Rates: $40-$52
Tel: (517) 366-5711

HOLIDAY INN
9285 W Houghton Lake Dr (48629)
Rates: $81-$97
Tel: (517) 422-5175
(800) 426-4329

HOLIDAY ON THE LAKE
100 Clearview Rd (48629)
Rates: $30-$85
Tel: (517) 422-5195

LAGOON RESORT & MOTEL
6578 W Houghton Lake Dr (48629)
Rates: $30-$70
Tel: (517) 422-5761

POPULARS RESORT
10360 West Shore Dr (48629)
Rates: $38-$72
Tel: (517) 422-5132

VALHALLA MOTEL
9869 West Shore Dr (48629)
Rates: $34-$48
Tel: (517) 422-5137

WAY NORTH MOTEL
9052 N Old US 27
(48629)
Rates: $34-$58
Tel: (517) 422-5523

HOWELL

KNIGHTS INN
124 Holiday Ln
(48843)
Rates: $38-$47
Tel: (517) 548-2900
(800) 843-5644

HUDSON

SUNSET ACRES MOTEL
400 S Meridian
US 127 (49247)
Rates: $31-$51
Tel: (517) 448-8968

HULBERT

THE LEEJA MOTEL
2000 M28 (49748)
Rates: n/a
Tel: (906) 876-2323

IMLAY CITY

SUPER 8 MOTEL
6951 Newark Rd
(48444)
Rates: $41-$60
Tel: (810) 724-8700
(800) 800-8000

INDIAN RIVER

**CARAVAN
MOTEL COTTAGES**
4904 S Straits Hwy
(49749)
Rates: $45-$65
Tel: (616) 238-7537

**NORTHWOODS
LODGE**
2390 S Straits Hwy
(49749)
Rates: $44-$98
Tel: (616) 238-7729

REIDS MOTOR COURT
3977 S Straits Hwy
(49749)
Rates: $29-$48
Tel: (616) 238-9353

STAR GATE MOTEL
4646 S Straits (49749)
Rates: $30-$48
Tel: (616) 238-7371

**WOODLANDS
LODGE**
5115 S Straits Hwy
(49749)
Rates: $39-$54
Tel: (616) 238-4137

IONIA

EVERGREEN MOTEL
2030 N State Rd
(48846)
Rates: $29
Tel: (616) 527-0930

MIDWAY MOTEL
7076 S State Rd
(48846)
Rates: $26-$51
Tel: (616) 527-2080

SUPER 8 MOTEL
7245 S State Rd
(48846)
Rates: $44-$63
Tel: (616) 527-2828
(800) 800-8000

IRON MOUNTAIN

**BEST WESTERN
EXECUTIVE INN**
1518 S Stephenson
Ave (49801)
Rates: $54-$75
Tel: (906) 774-2040
(800) 528-1234

DAYS INN
W 8176 S US 2
(49801)
Rates: $39-$99
Tel: (906) 774-2181
(800) 329-7466

**EDGEWATER
RESORT LOG CABINS**
N4128 N US 2 (49801)
Rates: $44-$70
Tel: (906) 774-6244
(800) 236-6244

HOWARD JOHNSON
1609 S Stephenson
Ave (49801)
Rates: $38-$52
Tel: (906) 774-6220
(800) 446-4656

**TIMBERS
MOTOR LODGE**
200 S Stephenson
Ave (49801)
Rates: $34-$74
Tel: (906) 774-7600
(800) 443-8533

**WOODLANDS
MOTEL**
N 3957 North US 2
(49801)
Rates: $30-$40
Tel: (906) 774-6106

IRON RIVER

IRON RIVER MOTEL
3073 East US 2
(49935)
Rates: $32
Tel: (906) 265-4212

IRONWOOD

ARMATA MOTEL
124 W Cloverland
Dr (49938)
Rates: $24-$34
Tel: (906) 932-4421

BLUE CLOUD MOTEL
105 W Cloverland
Dr (49938)
Rates: $30-$50
Tel: (906) 932-0920

BUDGET HOST INN
447 W Cloverland
Dr (49938)
Rates: $28-$65
Tel: (906) 932-1260
(800) 283-4678

SUPER 8 MOTEL
160 E Cloverland
Dr (49938)
Rates: $37-$46
Tel: (906) 932-3395
(800) 800-8000

TWILIGHT TIME MOTEL
930 E US 2 (49938)
Rates: $25-$60
Tel: (906) 932-3010

JACKSON

BUDGETEL INN
2035 N Service Dr
(49202)
Rates: $42-$55
Tel: (517) 789-6000

FAIRFIELD INN
2395 Shirley Dr
(49202)
Rates: $52-$70
Tel: (517) 784-7877
(800) 228-2800

HOLIDAY INN
2000 Holiday Inn Dr
(49202)
Rates: $75-$112
Tel: (517) 783-2681
(800) 465-4329

MOTEL 6
830 Royal Dr (49202)
Rates: $32-$38
Tel: (517) 789-7186
(800) 440-6000

RODEWAY INN
901 Rosehill Dr
(49202)
Rate4s: $40-$100
Tel: (517) 787-1111
(800) 228-2000

JONESVILLE

PINECREST MOTEL
516 W Chicago St
(49250)
Rates: $25+
Tel: (517) 849-2137

KALAMAZOO

BUDGETEL INN
2203 S 11th St
(49009)
Rates: $39-$60
Tel: (616) 372-7999

DAYS INN
1912 E Kilgore Rd
(49002)
Rates: $39-$65
Tel: (616) 382-2303
(800) 329-7466

HAMPTON INN
1550 E Kilgore R.
(49001)
Rates: $62-$74
Tel: (616) 344-7774
(800) 426-7866

**HOLIDAY INN-
AIRPORT**
3522 Sprinkle Rd
(49002)
Rates: $70-$86
Tel: (616) 381-7070
(800) 465-4329

HOLIDAY INN-WEST
2747 S 11th St
(49009)
Rates: $79-$89
Tel: (616) 375-6000
(800) 465-4329

LA QUINTA MOTOR INN
3750 Easy St (49002)
Rates: $46-$51
Tel: (616) 388-3551
(800) 221-4731

MOTEL 6
3704 Van Rick Rd
(49002)
Rates: $32-$38
Tel: (616) 344-9255
(800) 440-6000

RED ROOF INN-E
3701 E Cork St
(49001)
Rates: $35-$43
Tel: (616) 382-6350
(800) 843-7663

RED ROOF INN-W
5425 W Michigan
Ave (49009)
Rates: $30-$45
Tel: (616) 375-7400
(800) 843-7663

RESIDENCE INN BY MARRIOTT
1500 E Kilgore Rd
(49001)
Rates: $105-$130
Tel: (616) 349-0855
(800) 331-3131

SUPER 8 MOTEL
618 Maple Hill Dr
(49009)
Rates: $40-$61
Tel: (616) 345-0146
(800) 800-8000

LAKE CITY

LAKE CITY MOTEL
704 N Morey Rd
(49651)
Rates: $35
Tel: (616) 839-4857

NORTHCREST MOTEL
1341 S Lakeshore
(49651)
Rates: $41-$51
Tel: (616) 839-2075

LANSING

BEST WESTERN GOVERNOR'S INN
6133 S Pennsylvania
Ave (48911)
Rates: $53-$69
Tel: (517) 393-5500
(800) 528-1234

BEST WESTERN MIDWAY HOTEL
7711 W Saginaw
Hwy (48917)
Rates: $65-$91
Tel: (517) 627-8471
(800) 528-1234

COMFORT INN
2209 University Dr
(48864)
Rates: $45-$99
Tel: (517) 349-8700

DAYS INN LANSING-SOUTH
6501 S Pennsylvania
Ave (48911)
Rates: $47-$119
Tel: (517) 393-1650
(800) 329-7466

FAIRFIELD INN
810 Delta Commerce
Dr (48917)
Rates: n/a
Tel: (517) 886-1066
(800) 228-2800

HOJO INN
6741 S Cedar St
(48911)
Rates: $32-$95
Tel: (517) 694-0454
(800) 446-4656

KNIGHTS INN-S
1100 Ramada Dr
(48911)
Rates: $33-$42
Tel: (800) 843-5644

MOTEL 6
7326 W Saginaw
Hwy (48917)
Rates: $32-$38
Tel: (517) 321-1444
(800) 440-6000

MOTEL 6
112 E Main St
(48933)
Rates: $28-$34
Tel: (517) 484-8722
(800) 440-6000

QUALITY SUITES
901 Delta Commerce
(48917)
Rates: $84-$104
Tel: (517) 886-0600
(800) 456-6431

RED ROOF INN-EAST
3615 Dunckel Rd
(48910)
Rates: $34-$47
Tel: (517) 332-2575
(800) 843-7663

RED ROOF INN-WEST
7412 W Saginaw
Hwy (48917)
Rates: $35-$43
Tel: (517) 321-7246
(800) 843-7663

RESIDENCE INN
922 Delta Commerce
Dr (48917)
Rates: n/a
Tel: (517) 886-5030
(800) 331-3131

SHERATON LANSING HOTEL
925 S Creyts Rd
(48917)
Rates: $96-$225
Tel: (517) 323-7100
(800) 325-3535

LAPEER

TOWN AND COUNTRY MOTEL
1275 Imlay City Rd
(48446)
Rates: $35-$60
Tel: (810) 664-9132

LELAND

FALLING WATERS LODGE
200 W Cedar, Box
345 (49654)
Rates: $75-$175
Tel: (616) 256-9832

LEWISTON

FAIRWAY INN
County Rd 489
(49756)
Rates:$40-$50
Tel: (517) 786-2217

LIVONIA

MARRIOTT HOTEL
17100 Laurel Park
Dr N (48152)
Rates: $79-$134
Tel: (313) 462-3100

RAMADA INN
30375 Plymouth Rd
(48150)
Rates: $60-$75
Tel: (313) 261-6800
(800) 272-6232

LUDINGTON

NADER'S LAKE SHORE MOTOR LODGE
612 N Lakeshore Dr
(49431)
Rates: $50-$85
Tel: (616) 843-8757
(800) 968-0109

MARINA BAY MOTOR LODGE
604 W Ludington
Ave (49431)
Rates: $30-$140
Tel: (616) 845-5124
(800) 968-1440

NOVA MOTEL
472 S Old 31 Hwy
(49431)
Rates: $28-$69
Tel: (616) 843-3454

TIMBERLANE LONG LAKE RENOVA MOTEL
472 S Old 31 Hwy
(49431)
Rates: $28-$69
Tel: (616) 843-3454

TIMBERLANE LONG LAKE RESORT
7410 E US 10 (49458)
Rates: n/a
Tel: (616) 757-2142
(800) 227-2142

MACKINAC ISLAND

PINE COTTAGE BED & BREAKFAST
P.O. Box 1890
(49757)
Rates: n/a
Tel: (906) 847-3820

MACKINAW CITY

AFFORDABLE INNS OF AMERICA
206 Nicolet St (49701)
Rates: n/a
Tel: (616) 436-8961
(800) 388-9508

AMERICAN MOTEL
14351 S US 31 (49701)
Rates: $20-$55
Tel: (616) 436-5231

BEACHCOMBER MOTEL ON THE WATER
1011 S Huron (49701)
Rates: $29-$110
Tel: (616) 436-8451

THE BEACH HOUSE
1035 S Huron (49701)
Rates: $39-$110
Tel: (616) 436-5353

BELL'S MELODY MOTEL
P. O. Box 896 (49701)
Rates: $28-$73
Tel: (616) 436-5463

BUDGET HOST
517 N Huron (49701)
Rates: $30-$108
Tel: (616) 436-5543
(800) 283-4678

CAPRI MOTEL
801 S Nicolet St (49701)
Rates: $26-$65
Tel: (616) 436-5498

ECONO LODGE AT THE BRIDGE
412 Nicolet St (49701)
Rates: $29-$658
Tel: (616) 436-5026
(800) 424-4777

KNIGHTS INN
1009 S Huron (49701)
Rates: $26-$89
Tel: (616) 436-5527
(800) 843-5644

LAMPLIGHTER MOTEL
303 Jamet St (49701)
Rates: $43-$60
Tel: (616) 436-5350

LOVELAND'S LA MIRAGE
699 N Huron (49701)
Rates: $35-$98
Tel: (616) 436-5304

OTTAWA MOTEL
P. O. Box 908 (49701)
Rates: $24-$65
Tel: (616) 436-8041

PARKSIDE INN-BRIDGESIDE
102 Nicolet St (49701)
Rates: $38-$110
Tel: (616) 436-8301

QUALITY INN
917 S Huron (49701)
Rates: $36-$105
Tel: (616) 436-5051
(800) 221-2222

STARLITE BUDGET INNS
116 Old US 31 (49701)
Rates: $26-$60
Tel: (616) 436-5959
(800) 288-8190

SURF MOTEL
907 S Huron (49701)
Rates: $29-$95
Tel: (616) 436-8831

VAL-RU MOTEL
P. O. Box 521 (49701)
Rates: $21-$54
Tel: (616) 436-7691

VIN-DEL MOTEL
223 W Central Ave (49701)
Rates: $30-$65
Tel: (616) 436-5273

WA WA TAM MOTEL
219 W Jamet St (49701)
Rates: $26-$54
Tel: (616) 436-8871

MADISON HEIGHTS

HAMPTON INN
32420 Stephenson Hwy (48071)
Rates: $59-$82
Tel: (810) 585-8881
(800) 426-7866

KNIGHTS INN
26091 Dequindre Rd (48071)
Rates: $32-$39
Tel: (800) 843-5644

MOTEL 6
32700 Barrington Rd (48071)
Rates: $32-$38
Tel: (810) 583-0500
(800) 440-6000

RED ROOF INN
32511 Concord Dr (48071)
Rates: $30-$46
Tel: (810) 583-4700
(800) 843-7663

RESIDENCE INN BY MARRIOTT
32650 Stephenson Hwy (48071)
Rates: $129-$189
Tel: (810) 583-4322
(800) 331-3131

MANCELONA

MANCELONA MOTEL
8306 US 131 (49659)
Rates: $35-$76
Tel: (616) 587-8621
(800) 320-1240

RAPID RIVER MOTEL
7530 US 131 (49659)
Rates: $30-$50
Tel: (616) 258-2604

MANISTEE

CARRIAGE INN
200 Arthur St (49660)
Rates: $29-$94
Tel: (616) 723-9949

HILLSIDE MOTEL
1599 US 31S (49660)
Rates: $30-$80
Tel: (616) 723-2584
(800) 234-1250

MANISTIQUE

ECONO LODGE
E. Lakeshore Dr. (49854)
Rates: $34-$48
Tel: (906) 341-6014
(800) 424-4777

HOJO INN
726 E Lakeshore Dr (49854)
Rates: $50-$70
Tel: (906) 341-6981
(800) 446-4656

HOLIDAY MOTEL
Rt 1, Box 1514 (49854)
Rates: $26-$44
Tel: (906) 341-2710

ECONO LODGE
E US 2 (49854)
Rates: $28-$44
Tel: (906) 341-6014

RAMADA INN
US 2 E Lakeshore Dr (49854)
Rates: $49-$79
Tel: (906) 341-6911
(800) 272-6232

MANTON

GREEN MILL MOTEL
709 N US 131 (49663)
Rates: $30-$70
Tel: (616) 824-3504

IRISH INN MOTEL
415 N Michigan Ave (49663)
Rates: $31-$41
Tel: (616) 824-6988

MARINE CITY

MARINE BAY LODGE MOTEL
6000 River Rd (E China 48054)
Rates: $30-$62
Tel: (810) 765-8877
(810) 765-8878

PORT SEAWAY INN
7623 River Rd (48039)
Rates: $32-$90
Tel: (810) 765-4033

MARQUETTE

BIRCHMONT MOTEL
2090 US 41S (49855)
Rates: $34-$44
Tel: (906) 228-7538

EDGEWATER MOTEL
2050 US 41 S (49855)
Rates: $31-$47
Tel: (906) 225-1305

LAMPLIGHTER MOTEL
3600 US 41 W (49855)
Rates: $22-$44
Tel: (906) 228-4004

MARQUETTE MOTOR LODGE
1010 M-28 E (49855)
Rates: $32-$75
Tel: (906) 249-1712
(800) 939-9890

RAMADA INN
P. O. Box 464 (49855)
Rates: $75-$89
Tel: (800) 272-6232

TIROLER HOF MOTEL
150 Carp River Hill (49855)
Rates: $38-$52
Tel: (906) 226-7516
(800) 892-9376

MARSHALL

ARBOR INN
15435 W Michigan Ave (49068)
Rates: $45-$57
Tel: (616) 781-7772
(800) 424-0807

HOWARD'S MOTEL
14884 W Michigan Ave (49068)
Rates: $30-$54
Tel: (616) 781-4201

MARSHALL HEIGHTS MOTEL
16147 Old US 27 N (49068)
Rates: $24-$40
Tel: (616) 781-5659

McMILLAN

INTERLAKEN LODGE
Rt 3, Box 2542 (49853)
Rates: $65-$125
Tel: (906) 586-3545

MENOMINEE

HOJO INN
2516 10th St (49858)
Rates: $40-$70
Tel: (906) 863-4431
(800) 446-4656

MIDLAND

BEST WESTERN VALLEY PLAZA RESORT
5221 Bay City Rd (48642)
Rates: $55-$85
Tel: (517) 496-2700
(800) 528-1234

FAIRVIEW INN
2200 W Wackerly St (48640)
Rates: $50-$69
Tel: (517) 631-0070
(800) 422-2744

HOLIDAY INN
1500 W Wackerly St (48640)
Rates: $76-$116
Tel: (517) 631-4220
(800) 465-4329

RAMADA INN
1815 S Saginaw Rd (48640)
Rates: $41-$99
Tel: (517) 631-0570
(800) 272-6232

MILAN

STAR MOTEL
335 E Lewis Ave (48160)
Rates: $32-$48
Tel: (313) 439-2448

MILFORD

MILFORD'S HURON VALLEY MOTEL
640 N Milford Rd (48381)
Rates: $35-$45
Tel: (810) 685-1020

MIO

MIO MOTEL
415 N Morenci St (48647)
Rates: $40-$60
Tel: (517) 826-3248

MONROE

HOLIDAY INN
1225 N Dixie Hwy (48161)
Rates: $69-$77
Tel: (313) 242-6000
(800) 465-4329

HOMETOWN INN
1885 Welcome Way (48161)
Rates: $32-$90
Tel: (313) 289-1080

KNIGHTS INN
1250 N Dixie Hwy (48161)
Rates: $28-$35
Tel: (800) 843-5644

MOUNT PLEASANT

BUDGETEL INN
5858 E Pickard St (48858)
Rates: $45-$105
Tel: (517) 775-5555
(800) 290-7777

COMFORT INN-UNIVERSITY PARK
2424 S Mission St (48858)
Rates: $41-$125
Tel: (517) 772-4000
(800) 221-2222

HAMPTON INN
5205 E.Pickard St (48858)
Rates: $59-$74
Tel: (517) 772-5500
(800) 426-7866

HOLIDAY INN
5665 E Pickard St (48858)
Rates: $65-$130
Tel: (517) 772-2905
(800) 465-4329

MUNISING

BEST WESTERN MOTEL
P. O. Box 310 (49862)
Rates: $55-$110
Tel: (906) 387-4864
(800) 528-1234

MIRAGE
P. O. Box 276 (49862)
Rates: $64-$94
Tel: (906) 387-5292
(800) 221-2222

SCOTTY'S MOTEL
415 Cedar St (49862)
Rates: $26-$34
Tel: (906) 387-2449

STAR-LITE MOTEL
500 M-28E (49862)
Rates: $32-$38
Tel: (906) 387-2291

SUNSET MOTEL
P. O. Box 291 (49862)
Rates: $32-$49
Tel: (906) 387-4574

TERRACE MOTEL
420 Prospect (49862)
Rates: $32-$42
Tel: (906) 387-2735

YULE LOG RESORT
122 W Chocobay (49862)
Rates: $36-$78
Tel: (906) 387-3184

MUSKEGON

BEL-AIRE MOTEL
4240 Airline Rd (49444)
Rates: $38-$58
Tel: (616) 733-2196

SUPER 8 MOTEL
3380 Hoyt St (49444)
Rates: $38-$59
Tel: (616) 733-0088
(800) 800-8000

NEGAUNEE

QUARTZ MOUN-TAIN INN MOTEL
791 US 41 E (49866)
Rates: $29-$40
Tel: (906) 475-7165

NEW BALTIMORE

LODGE KEEPER INN
29101 23-Mile Rd
(48047)
Rates: n/a
Tel: (810) 949-4520
(800) 2828-5711

NEW BUFFALO

COMFORT INN
11539 O'Brien Ct
(49117)
Rates: $44-$104
Tel: (616) 469-4440

EDGEWOOD MOTEL
18716 LaPorte Rd
(49117)
Rates: $33-$43
Tel: (616) 469-3345

GRAND BEACH MOTEL
19189 US 12 (49117)
Rates: $25-$50
Tel: (616) 469-1555

SANS SOUCI EURO INN
19265 S Lakeside Rd
(49117)
Rates: $98-$185
Tel: (616) 756-3141

NEWBERRY

BEST WESTERN VILLAGE INN
P. O. Box 474 (49868)
Rates: $42-$85
Tel: (906) 293-5114
(800) 528-1234

GATEWAY MOTEL
Rt 4, Box 980 - M123
(49868)
Rates: n/a
Tel: (906) 293-5651

GREEN ACRES MOTEL
Rt 1, Box 736 (49868)
Rates: $38-$48
Tel: (800) 800-5398

PARK-A-WAY MOTEL
RR 4, Box 966
(49868)
Rates: $30-$60
Tel: (906) 293-5771

RAINBOW LODGE
County Rd 423,
P. O. Box 386 (49868)
Rates: $31-$75
Tel: (906) 658-3357

NILES

RAMADA INN
930 S 11th St (49120)
Rates: $65-$107
Tel: (616) 684-3000

NOVI

FAIRLANE MOTEL
45700 Grand River
(48374)
Rates: $28-$35
Tel: (810) 349-6410

HILTON HOTEL
21111 Haggerty Rd
(48375)
Rates: $75-$350
Tel: (810) 349-4000
(800) 445-8667

ONAWAY

LAKESIDE MOTEL
County Rd 489,
Rt 1 (49765)
Rates: n/a
Tel: (517) 733-4298

ONEKAMA

TRAVELERS MOTEL
5606 Eight Mile,
Box 97 (49675)
Rates: $30-$70
Tel: (616) 889-4342
(800) 769-0184

ONTONAGON

BEST WESTERN PORCUPINE MOUNTAIN LODGE
120 Lincoln (49953)
Rates: $63-$105
Tel: (906) 885-5311
(800) 528-1234

RAINBOW MOTEL & CHALETS
P. O. Box 2900
(49953)
Rates: $36-$70
Tel: (906) 885-5348

SUNSHINE MOTEL & CABINS
1442 M-64 (49953)
Rates: $25-$75
Tel: (906) 884-2187

SUPERIOR SHORES RESORT
1823 M-64 (49953)
Rates: $35-$115
Tel: (906) 884-2653

OSCODA

ANCHORAGE COTTAGES RESORT
3164 N US 23 (48750)
Rates: $45-$95
Tel: (517) 739-7843

ASPEN MOTOR INN
115 N Lake St
(48750)
Rates: $29-$50
Tel: (517) 739-9152
(800) 892-7736

BLUE HORIZON CT
4208 N US 23,
Box 151 (48750)
Rates: $30-$55
Tel: (517) 739-8487
(800) 524-5201

CEDAR LANE RESORT MOTEL
7404 N US 23 (48750)
Rates: $26-$68
Tel: (517) 739-9988

NORTHERN TRAVELER
5493 N US 23 (48750)
Rates: $34-$58
Tel: (517) 739-9261

RAINBOW RESORT
5764 N US 23 (48750)
Rates: $60-
$400/weekly
Tel: (517) 739-5695

SURFSIDE I & II COND. & MOTEL
6504 N US 23 (48750)
Rates: $52-$150
Tel: (517) 739-5363

OWOSSO

OWOSSO MOTOR LODGE
2247 E Main St
(48867)
Rates: $30-$50
Tel: (517) 725-7148
(800) 444-7148

PARADISE

CURLEY'S MOTEL
P. O. Box 57, M-123
(49768)
Rates: $36-$65
Tel: (906) 492-3445
(800) 236-7386

PAW PAW

GREEN ACRES MOTEL
38245 W Red Arrow
(49079)
Rates: n/a
Tel: (616) 657-4037

MROCZEK INN
139 Ampey Rd
(49079)
Rates: $31-$40
Tel: (616) 657-2578

PERRY

HEB'S INN MOTEL
2811 Lansing Rd
(48872)
Rates: $32-$42
Tel: (517) 625-7500

PETOSKEY

COACH HOUSE MOTEL
2445 Charlevoix Ave
(49770)
Rates: $50-$65
Tel: (616) 347-2593

COMFORT INN
1314 US 31 N (49770)
Rates: $48-$95
Tel: (616) 347-3220
(800) 228-5150

DAYS INN
630 W Mitchell St
(49770)
Rates: $38-$125
Tel: (616) 347-8717
(800) 329-7466

ECONO LODGE
1858 US 131 (49770)
Rates: $41-$90
Tel: (616) 348-3324
(800) 424-4777

PINCONNING

PINCONNING TRAIL HOUSE MOTEL
201 S M-13 (48650)
Rates: $32-$75
Tel: (517) 879-4219

PLAINWELL

COMFORT INN
622 Allegan St (49080)
Rates: $54-$100
Tel: (616) 685-9891
(800) 221-2222

PLYMOUTH

RED ROOF INN
39700 Ann Arbor Rd
(48170)
Rates: $28-$36
Tel: (313) 459-3300
(800) 843-7663

PORT AUSTIN

LAKESIDE MOTOR LODGE
P.O. Box 358 (48467)
Rates: $35-$60
Tel: (517) 738-5201

PORT HURON

COLONIAL BEST WESTERN INN
2908 Pine Grove
(48060)
Rates: $50-$57
Tel: (810) 984-1522
(800) 528-1234

DAYS INN
2908 Pine Grove
(48060)
Rates: $40-$160
Tel: (810) 984-1522
(800) 329-7466

KNIGHTS INN
2160 Water St
(48060)
Rates: $47-$63
Tel: (810) 982-1022
(800) 843-5644

MAINSTREET LODGE
514 Huron Ave
(48060)
Rates: $39-$72
Tel: (810) 984-3166
(800) 441-3034

PORTLAND

BEST WESTERN AMERICAN HERITAGE INN
1625 Grand River
Ave (48875)
Rates: $49-$70
Tel: (517) 647-2200
(800) 528-1234

POWERS

CANDLE LITE MOTEL
P.O. Box 195 (49874)
Rates: $22-$30
Tel: (906) 497-5413

RAPID RIVER

THE RIGHT BOWER MOTEL
9912 US 2 (49878)
Rates: $23-$36
Tel: (906) 474-6078

REDFORD

COACH & LANTERN MOTEL
25255 Grand River
Ave (48240)
Rates: $29-$42
Tel: (313) 533-4020

DORCHESTER MOTEL
26825 Grand River
Ave (48240)
Rates: $33-$75
Tel: (313) 533-8400

ROCHESTER HILLS

RED ROOF INN
2580 Crooks Rd
(48309)
Rates: $38-$61
Tel: (810) 853-6400
(800) 843-7663

ROCHESTER MOTOR LODGE
2070 S Rochester Rd
(48307)
Rates: $38-$48
Tel: (810) 651-8591

ROMULUS

BUDGETEL-METRO AIRPORT
9000 Wickham Rd
(48174)
Rates: $42-$62
Tel: (313) 722-6000

CLARION INN AIRPORT
31200 Detroit
Industrial Expy
(48174)
Rates: $44-$99
Tel: (800) 753-5956

DAYS INN - METRO-POLITAN AIRPORT
9501 Middlebelt Rd
(48174)
Rates: $64-$125
Tel: (313) 946-4300
(800) 329-7466

HOLIDAY INN CROWNE PLAZA
8000 Merriman Rd
(48174)
Rates: $115
Tel: (313) 729-2600
(800) 465-4329

HOWARD JOHNSON AIRPORT
7600 Merriman Rd
(48174)
Rates: $54-$64
Tel: (313) 728-2430
(800) 446-4656

MARRIOTT HOTEL
30559 Flynn Dr
(48174)
Rates: $94-$350
Tel: (313) 729-7555

ROSEVILLE

BUDGETEL
20675 13 Mile Road
(48066)
Rates: $37-$58
Tel: (810) 296-6910

GEORGIAN INN
31327 Gratiot Ave
(48066)
Rates: $52-$60
Tel: (810) 294-0400

RED ROOF INN
31800 Little Mack Rd
(48066)
Rates: $34-$45
Tel: (810) 296-0310
(800) 843-7663

SAGINAW

BEST WESTERN INN
3325 Davenport Ave
(48602)
Rates: $49-$61
Tel: (517) 793-2080
(800) 528-1234

COMFORT SUITES
5180 Fashion Square
Blvd (48603)
Rates: n/a
Tel: (517) 797-8000
(800) 228-2800

FAIRFIELD INN
5200 Fashion Square
Blvd (48603)
Rates: n/a
Tel: (517) 797-6100
(800) 228-2800

HAMPTON INN
2222 Tittabawassee
Rd (48604)
Rates: $54-$74
Tel: (517) 792-7666
(800) 426-7866

HOLIDAY INN I-75
1408 S Outer Dr
(48601)
Rates: $70-$98
Tel: (517) 755-0461
(800) 465-4329

KNIGHTS INN-NORTH
2225 Tittabawassee
Rd (48604)
Rates: $37-$49
Tel: (517) 791-1411
(800) 843-5644

KNIGHTS INN-SOUTH
1415 S Outer Dr
(48601)
Rates: $36-$57
Tel: (517) 754-4200
(800) 843-5644

RED ROOF INN
966 S Outer Dr
(48601)
Rates: $33-$41
Tel: (517) 754-8414
(800) 843-7663

SHERATON INN-FASHION SQUARE
4960 Towne Center
Rd (48604)
Rates: $128-$138
Tel: (517) 790-5050

SUPER 8 MOTEL
4848 Town Centre
Rd (48603)
Rates: $37-$57
Tel: (517) 791-3003
(800) 800-8000

ST. IGNACE

**BAY VIEW
BEACH FRONT
MOTEL**
1133 N State St
(49781)
Rates: $28-$65
Tel: (906) 643-9444

BLUE BAY MOTEL
1071 N State St
(49781)
Rates: $29-$79
Tel: (906) 643-7414

BUDGET HOST INN
700 N State St
(49781)
Rates: $36-$72
Tel: (906) 643-9666
(800) 283-4678

CEDAR'S MOTEL
2040 N Business
Loop I-75 (49781)
Rates: $32-$39
Tel: (906) 643-9578

**THE DRIFTWOOD
MOTEL**
590 N State St
(49781)
Rates: $30-$52
Tel: (906) 643-7744

HOWARD JOHNSON
913 Boulevard Dr
(49781)
Rates: $50-$87
Tel: (906) 643-9700
(800) 654-2000

RODEWAY INN
750 US 2 W.
P.O. Box 651 (49781)
Rates: $42-$125
Tel: (906) 643-8511
(800) 228-2000

ROCKVIEW MOTEL
2055 N Business
Loop I-75 (49781)
Rates: $32-$38
Tel: (906) 643-8839

**SILVER SANDS
RESORT**
1519 US 2 W (49781)
Rates: $50-$125
Tel: (906) 643-8635

WAYSIDE MOTEL
751 N State St (49781)
Rates: $28-$53
Tel: (906) 643-8944

ST. JOSEPH

**BEST WESTERN
GOLDEN LINK**
2723 Niles Ave (49085)
Rates: $29-$58
Tel: (616) 983-6321
(800) 528-1234

SANDUSKY

**THUMB HERITAGE
INN**
405 W Sanilac (48471)
Rates: $34-$70
Tel: (810) 648-4811

SAUGATUCK

**DOUGLAS DUNES
RESORT**
333 Blue Star Hwy
(Douglas 49406)
Rates: n/a
Tel: (616) 857-1401

PINES MOTEL
56 S Blue Star Hwy
(Douglas 49406)
Rates: $29-$98
Tel: (616) 857-5211

SHIP-N-SHORE
528 Water St (49453)
Rates: $69-$110
Tel: (616) 857-2194

SAULT STE. MARIE

ADMIRALS INN
2701 I-75 Business
Spur (49783)
Rates: $33-$40
Tel: (906) 632-1130

BAMBI MOTEL
1801 Ashmun
(49783)
Rates: $34-$65
Tel: (906) 632-7881
(800) 289-0864

**BAVARIA
MOTOR LODGE**
2006 Ashmun
(49783)
Rates $29-$69
Tel: (906) 632-6864

BILTMORE MOTEL
331 E Portage
(49783)
Rates: $34-$54
Tel: (906) 632-2119
(800) 528-0612

**CRESTVIEW
THRIFTY INNS**
1200 Ashmun
(49783)
Rates: $48-$64
Tel: (906) 635-5213

GRAND MOTEL
1100 E Portage
(49783)
Rates: $49-$110
Tel: (906) 632-2141

**IMPERIAL
MOTOR INN**
2216 Ashmun
(49783)
Rates: n/a
Tel: (906) 632-7334
(800) 859-9898

KING'S INN MOTEL
3755 I-75 Business
Spur (49783)
Rates: $28-$60
Tel: (906) 635-5061

LAKER INN
1712 Ashmun
(49783)
Rates: $42-$46
Tel: (906) 632-3581

ROYAL MOTEL
1707 Ashmun
(49783)
Rates: $32-$64
Tel: (906) 632-6323

SUPER 8 MOTEL
3826 I-75 Business
Spur (49783)
Rates: $40-$68
Tel: (906) 632-8882
(800) 800-8000

SMYRNA

**DOUBLE R RANCH
RESORT**
4424 Whites Bridge
Rd (48887)
Rates: $34-$50
Tel: (616) 794-0520

SOUTH HAVEN

COLONIAL HOTEL
532 Dyckman
(49090)
Rates: $50-$125
Tel: (616) 637-2887
(800) 608-8951

ECONO LODGE
09817 SR 140 (49090)
Rates: $60-$95
Tel: (616) 637-5141
(800) 424-4777

SOUTHFIELD

ECONO LODGE
23300 Telegraph Rd
(48034)
Rates: $55-$95
Tel: (810) 358-1800
(800) 424-4777

HILTON GARDEN INN
26000 American Dr
(48034)
Rates: $65-$109
Tel: (810) 357-1100

HOLIDAY INN
26555 Telegraph Rd
(48034)
Rates: $59-$93
Tel: (810) 353-7700
(800) 465-4329

MARRIOTT HOTEL
27033 Northwestern
Hwy (48034)
Rates: $79-$199
Tel: (313) 356-7400

**RAMADA CONVEN-
TION CENTER**
17017 W 9 Mile Rd
(48075)
Rates: $55-$95
Tel: (810) 557-4800
(800) 272-6232

RED ROOF INN
27660 Northwestern
Hwy (48034)
Rates: n/a
Tel: (810) 353-7200
(800) 843-7663

**RESIDENCE INN
BY MARRIOTT**
26700 Central Park
Blvd (48076)
Rates: $115-$159
Tel: (810) 352-8900
(800) 331-3131

SOUTHGATE

BUDGETEL
12888 Reeck Rd
(48195)
Rates: $39-$57
Tel: (313) 374-3000

STANDISH

STANDISH MOTEL
US 23 & M-76 (48658)
Rates: $30-$50
Tel: (517) 846-9571

STEPHENSON

**STEPHENSON
MOTEL**
Rt 2, Box 20, Hwy 41
(49887)
Rates: $30-$35
Tel: (906) 753-2552

STEVENSVILLE

**PARK INN
INTERNATIONAL**
4290 Red Arrow
Hwy (49127)
Rates: $40-119
Tel: (616) 429-3218
(800) 228-5885

STURGIS

THE INN OF STURGIS
1300 S Centerville
Rd (49091)
Rates: $70-$82
Tel: (616) 651-7881

SUTTONS BAY

**RED LION
MOTOR LODGE**
4290 S West Bay
Shore Rd (49682)
Rates: $45-$110
Tel: (616) 271-6694
(800) 547-8010

TAWAS CITY

**NORTH STAR
MOTEL**
1119 S US 23 (48763)
Rates: $35-$65
Tel: (517) 362-2255

TAYLOR

**HOFFMAN'S
COLONIAL HOUSE
OF TAYLOR**
10780 S Telegraph
(48180)
Rates: $27-$42
Tel: (313) 291-3000

RED ROOF INN
21230 Eureka Rd
(48180)
Rates: $32-$59
Tel: (313) 374-1150
(800) 843-7663

TECUMSEH

TECUMSEH INN
1445 W Chicago
Blvd (49286)
Rates: $38-$95
Tel: (517) 423-7401

THREE RIVERS

GREYSTONE MOTEL
59271 US 131, Box 62
(49093)
Rates: $28-$42
Tel: (616) 278-1695

THREE RIVERS INN
1200 W Broadway
(49093)
Rates: $45-$80
Tel: (616) 273-9521

TRAVERSE CITY

**COMFORT INN
BY THE BAY**
1492 US 31 N (49684)
Rates: $39-$114
Tel: (616) 929-4423

**FOX HAUS
MOTOR LODGE**
704 Munsion Ave
(49684)
Rates: $30-$175
Tel: (616) 947-4450

HOLIDAY INN
615 E Front St
(49684)
Rates: $80-$146
Tel: (616) 947-3700
(800) 465-4329

MAIN STREET INNS
618 E Front St
(49684)
Rates: $30-$185
Tel: (616) 929-0410
(800) 255-7180

OLD MISSION INN
18599 Old Mission
Rd (49684)
Rates: $250-
$500/Weekly
Tel: (616) 223-7770

RODEWAY INN
1582 US 31 N
(49686)
Rates: $30-$100
Tel: (616) 938-2080
(800) 228-2000

TROUT LAKE

**MCGOWAN FAMILY
MOTEL**
SR 123 (49793)
Rates: $38-$51
Tel: (906) 569-3366

TROY

DRURY INN
575 W Big Beaver Rd
(48084)
Rates: $69-$85
Tel: (810) 528-3330
(800) 325-8300

HILTON HOTEL
5500 Crooks Rd
(48098)
Rates: $89-$159
Tel: (810) 879-2100

HOLIDAY INN
2537 Rochester Ct
(48083)
Rates: $49-$99
Tel: (810) 689-7500
(800) 465-4329

MARRIOTT HOTEL
200 W Big Beaver Rd
(48084)
Rates: $79-$159
Tel: (810) 680-9797

RED ROOF INN
2350 Rochester Rd
(48083)
Rates: $27-$43
Tel: (810) 689-4391
(800) 843-7663

WAKEFIELD

**INDIANHEAD
MOUNTAIN RESORT**
500 Indianhead Rd
(49968)
Rates: $58-$160
Tel: (906) 229-5181
(800) 346-3426

WALKER

MOTEL 6
777 Three Mile Rd
(49544)
Rates: $32-$38
Tel: (616) 784-9375
(800) 440-6000

WARREN

BUDGETEL
30900 Van Dyke
(48093)
Rates: $39-$61
Tel: (810) 574-0550

**HOMEWOOD
SUITES**
30180 N Civic
Center Blvd (48093)
Rates: $74-$139
Tel: (810) 558-7870

MOTEL 6
8300 Chicago Rd
(48093)
Rates: $32-$38
Tel: (313) 826-9300
(800) 440-6000

RED ROOF INN
26300 DeQuindre Rd
(48091)
Rates: $29-$40
Tel: (810) 573-4300
(800) 843-7663

**RESIDENCE INN
BY MARRIOTT**
30120 Civic Center
Blvd (48093)
Rates: $104-$125
Tel: (810) 558-8050
(800) 331-3131

VAN DYKE PARK HOTEL
31800 Van Dyke (48093)
Rates: $59-$500
Tel: (800) 321-1008

WATERS

NORTHLAND INN & MOTEL
9311 Old US 27 (49797)
Rates: $40-$70
Tel: (517) 732-4470

WATERSMEET

VACATIONLAND RESORT
E 19636 Hebert Rd (49969)
Rates: $60-$160
Tel: (906) 358-4380

WEST BRANCH

LA HACIENDA MOTEL
969 W Houghton Ave (48661)
Rates: n/a
Tel: (517) 345-2345

RED ROSE MOTEL
836 S M-33 (48661)
Rates: $39
Tel: (517) 345-2136

SUPER 8 MOTEL
2596 Austin Way Box 338 (48661)
Rates: $46-$69
Tel: (517) 345-8488
(800) 800-8000

TRI-TERRACE MOTEL
2259 Business Loop I-75 (49661)
Rates: $37-$60
Tel: (517) 345-3121

WELCOME MOTEL
3308 W M-76 (48661)
Rates: $28+
Tel: (517) 345-2896

WHITE PIGEON

PLAZA MOTEL
71410 US 131 S (49099)
Rates: $23-$49
Tel: (616) 382-7285

WHITMORE LAKE

BEST WESTERN OF WHITMORE LAKE
9897 Main St (48189)
Rates: $50-$150
Tel: (313) 449-2058
(800) 528-1234

LAKES MOTEL
8365 Main St (48189)
Rates: $35-$60
Tel: (313) 449-5991

WOODHAVEN

KNIGHTS INN
21880 West Rd (48183)
Rates: $35-$48
Tel: (313) 676-8550
(800) 843-5644

WYOMING

JIM WILLIAMS MOTEL
3821 S Division (49548)
Rates: $28-$46
Tel: (616) 241-5461

YPSILANTI

MARRIOTT HOTEL
1275 Huron St S (48917)
Rates: $72-$145
Tel: (313) 487-2000

MAYFLOWER MOTEL
5610 Carpenter (48197)
Rates: $35-$90
Tel: (313) 434-2200

MINNESOTA

AITKIN

BILL'S RESORT
Rt 2, Box 521 (56431)
Rates: n/a
Tel: (218) 927-3841

40 CLUB INN
950 2nd St NW
(56431)
Rates: $45-$60
Tel: (218) 927-2903
(800) 682-8152

**RIPPLE RIVER
MOTEL**
701 Minnesota Ave
(56431)
Rates: $35-$55
Tel: (218) 927-3734

ALBERT LEA

**BEL AIRE
MOTOR INN**
700 US Hwy 69 S
(56007)
Rates: $28-$45
Tel: (507) 373-3983
(800) 373-4073

**BEST WESTERN
ALBERT LEA INN**
2301 E Main St
(56007)
Rates: $46-$69
Tel: (507) 373-8291
(800) 528-1234

DAYS INN
2306 E Main St
(56007)
Rates: $49-$74
Tel: (507) 373-6471
(800) 329-7466

LEA BUDGET INN
2210 E Main St
(56007)
Rates: $25-$55
Tel: (507) 373-1496

SUPER 8 MOTEL
2019 E Main St
(56007)
Rates: $37-$56
Tel: (507) 377-0591
(800) 800-8000

ALEXANDRIA

**CARRINGTON
HOUSE B & B**
4974 Interlachen Dr
NE (56308)
Rates: $85-$135
Tel: (612) 846-7400

DAYS INN
4810 Hwy 29 S
(56308)
Rates: $35-$47
Tel: (612) 762-1171
(800) 329-7466

"L" MOTEL
910 Hwy 27 W
(56308)
Rates: $25-$40
Tel: (612) 763-5121

RED CARPET INN
1903 Aga Dr (56308)
Rates: n/a
Tel: (612) 762-0512

SKYLINE MOTEL
605 30th Ave (56308)
Rates: n/a
Tel: (612) 763-3175
(800) 467-4096

SUPER 8 MOTEL
4620 Hwy 29 S
(56308)
Rates: $37-$46
Tel: (612) 763-6552
(800) 800-8000

ANNANDALE

THAYER INN
60 W Elm (55302)
Rates: $60-$125
Tel: (612) 274-8222
(800) 944-6595

ANOKA

SUPER 8 MOTEL
1129 W Hwy 10
(55303)
Rates: $47-$65
Tel: (612) 422-8000
(800) 800-8000

APPLETON

SUPER 8 MOTEL
900 N Munsterman
(56208)
Rates: $35-$51
Tel: (320) 289-2500
(800) 800-8000

ARDEN HILLS

RAMADA HOTEL
1201 W Country Rd
E (55112)
Rates: $53-$62
Tel: (800) 272-6232

AUSTIN

AUSTIN MOTEL
805 21st St NE
(55912)
Rates: $20-$39
Tel: (507) 433-9254
(800) 433-9254

DAYS INN
700 16th Ave NW
(55912)
Rates: $42-$58
Tel: (507) 433-8600
(800) 329-7466

HOLIDAY INN
1701 4th St NW
(55912)
Rates: $58-$85
Tel: (800) 465-4329

RODEWAY INN
3303 Oakland Ave W
(55912)
Rates: $39-$51
Tel: (507) 437-7774
(800) 228-2000

SUPER 8 MOTEL
1401 14th St NW
(55912)
Rates: $37-$56
Tel: (507) 433-1801
(800) 800-8000

AVON

AMERICINN MOTEL
304 Blattner Dr
(56310)
Rates: $32-$53
Tel: (612) 356-2211
(800) 634-3444

BABBITT

**TIMBER BAY LODGE
& HOUSEBOATS**
8347 Timber Bay Rd
(55706)
Rates: $150-$890
Tel: (218) 827-3682
(800) 846-6821

BACKUS

**PINE MOUNTAIN
INN B & B**
P.O. Box 144 (56435)
Rates: $40-$45
Tel: (218) 947-3050
(218) 682-2884

BAUDETTE

**SPORTSMAN'S
LODGE**
Rt 1, Box 167 (56623)
Rates: $45-$176
Tel: (800) 862-8602

BAXTER

TWIN BIRCH MOTEL
2300 Fairview Rd N
(56401)
Rates: $27-$46
Tel: (218) 829-2833

BECKER

SUPER 8 MOTEL
13804 First St (55308)
Rates: $35-$54
Tel: (612) 261-4440
(800) 800-8000

BEMIDJI

BEL AIR MOTEL
1350 Paul Bunyan
Dr NW (56601)
Rates: $26-$56
Tel: (218) 751-3222

**BEST WESTERN
BEMIDJI INN**
2420 Paul Bunyan
Dr NW (56601)
Rates: $37-73
Tel: (218) 751-0390
(800) 528-1234

COMFORT INN
3500 Comfort Dr
(56601)
Rates: $38-$58
Tel: (800) 221-2222

EDGEWATER MOTEL
1015 Paul Bunyan
Dr NE (56601)
Rates: $29-$68
Tel: (218) 751-3600

**RUTTER'S
BIRCHMONT LODGE**
530 Birchmont Beach
Rd NE (56601)
Rates: $66-$142
Tel: (218) 751-1630
(800) 726-3866

BENSON

MOTEL 1
620 Atlantic Ave
(56215)
Rates: $28-$38
Tel: (612) 843-4434

BLACKDUCK

AMERICINN MOTEL
US 71 & Lake Rd
(56630)
Rates: $52-$65
Tel: (218) 835-4500
(800) 634-3444

DRAKE MOTEL
305 N Pine (56630)
Rates: n/a
Tel: (218) 835-4567

BLOOMINGTON

**BEST WESTERN
HOTEL SEVILLE**
8151 Bridge Rd
(55437)
Rates: $68-$91
Tel: (612) 830-1300
(800) 528-1234

**BEST WESTERN
THUNDERBIRD
HOTEL**
2201 E 78th St
(55425)
Rates: $85-$91
Tel: (612) 854-3411
(800) 528-1234

**BUDGETEL INN
AIRPORT**
7815 Nicollet Ave S
(55420)
Rates: $42-$59
Tel: (612) 881-7311

**CROWN STERLING
SUITES**
7901 34th Ave
(55425)
Rates: $119
Tel: (612) 854-1000

EXEL INN
2701 E 78th St
(55425)
Rates: $54-$77
Tel: (612) 854-7200

HOTEL SOFITEL
5601 W 78th St
(55439)
Rates: $105
Tel: (800) 835-6303

**MARRIOTT HOTEL
AIRPORT**
2020 E 79th St
(55425)
Rates: $94-$160
Tel: (612) 854-7441
(800) 228-9290

**RADISSON HOTEL
SOUTH & PLAZA
TOWER**
7800 Normandale
Blvd (55439)
Rates: $69-$89
Tel: (612) 835-7800

SELECT INN
7851 Normandale
Blvd (55435)
Rates: $34-$44
Tel: (612) 835-7400

SUPER 8 MOTEL
7800 2nd Ave S
(55420)
Rates: $55-$69
Tel: (612) 888-8800
(800) 800-8000

**THUNDERBIRD
HOTEL**
2201 E 78th St
(55425)
Rates: $82-$360
Tel: (612) 854-3411
(800) 328-1931

**WYNDHAM GARDEN
HOTEL**
4460 W 78th St
(55435)
Rates: $59-$111
Tel: (800) 822-4200

BLUE EARTH

SUPER 8 MOTEL
1120 Grove, Box 394
(56013)
Rates: $39-$56
Tel: (507) 526-7376
(800) 800-8000

BRAINERD

AMERICINN MOTEL
600 Dellwood Dr
(56425)
Rates: $48-$95
Tel: (800) 634-3444

DAYS INN
1630 Fairview Dr N
(56401)
Rates: $34-$53
Tel: (218) 829-0391
(800) 329-7466

DELLWOOD MOTEL
1302 S 6th St (56401)
Rates: $23-$35
Tel: (218) 828-8756

ECONO LODGE
2655 SR 371 S
(56401)
Rates: $30-$60
Tel: (218) 828-0027
(800) 424-4777

HOLIDAY INN
2115 S 6th St (56401)
Rates: $53-$72
Tel: (800) 465-4329

BRECKENRIDGE

SCOTWOOD MOTEL
821 Hwy 75N
(56520)
Rates: $23-$32
Tel: (218) 643-9201

BROOKLYN CENTER

BUDGETEL INN
6415 James Cir N
(55430)
Rates: $36-$53
Tel: (612) 561-8400

BUFFALO

SUPER 8 MOTEL
303 10th Ave S
(55313)
Rates: $41-$51
Tel: (612) 682-5930
(800) 800-8000

BURNSVILLE

HOLIDAY INN
14201 Nicollet Ave S
(55337)
Rates: $71-$92
Tel: (800) 465-4329

RED ROOF INN
12920 Aldrich Ave S
(55337)
Rates: $31-$46
Tel: (800) 843-7663

SUPER 8 MOTEL
1101 Burnsville
Pkwy (55337)
Rates: $42-$62
Tel: (612) 894-3400
(800) 800-8000

CANNON FALLS

**COUNTRY QUIET
INN**
37295 112th Ave Way
(55009)
Rates: $45-100
Tel: (612) 258-4406
(800) 258-1843

CHANHASSEN

CHANHASSEN INN MOTEL
531 W 79th St (55317)
Rates: $37-$44
Tel: (612) 934-7373

COUNTRY SUITES BY CARLSON
591 W 78th St (55317)
Rates: $68-$141
Tel: (612) 937-2424

CHATFIELD

LUND'S GUEST HOUSES
218 Winona St SE
(55923)
Rates: $45-$65
Tel: (507) 867-4003

CHISAGO CITY

SUPER 8 MOTEL
11650 Lake Blvd
(55013)
Rates: $33-$47
Tel: (612) 257-8088
(800) 800-8000

CLEARWATER

BUDGET INN
945 SR 24 (55320)
Rates: $31-$41
Tel: (612) 558-2221

CLOQUET

AMERICINN MOTEL
111 Big Lake Rd
(55720)
Rates: $40-$86
Tel: (218) 879-1231
(800) 634-3444

SUPER 8 MOTEL
Hwy 33 & Big Lake
Rd (55720)
Rates: $39-$53
Tel: (218) 879-1250
(800) 800-8000

COLD SPRING

AMERICINN MOTEL
118 3rd St S (56320)
Rates: $37-$59
Tel: (612) 685-4539

COOK

VERMILLION DAM LODGE
3276 Randa Rd (55723)
Rates: $675-
$1050/Weekly
Tel: (218) 666-5418

COON RAPIDS

COUNTRY SUITES BY CARLSON
155 Coon Rapids
Blvd (55433)
Rates: $64-$80
Tel: (612) 780-3797
(800) 456-4000

COTTAGE GROVE

SUPER 8 MOTEL
7125 80th St S
(55016)
Rates: $42-$64
Tel: (612) 458-0313
(800) 800-8000

CRANE LAKE

OLSON'S BORDERLAND
7488 Crane Lake Rd
(55725)
Rates: n/a
Tel: (218) 993-2233

CROOKSTON

NORTHLAND INN OF CROOKSTON
2200 University Ave
(56716)
Rates: $42-$55
Tel: (218) 281-5210

DEER RIVER

BAHR'S MOTEL
P. O. Box 614 (56636)
Rates: $25-$39
Tel: (218) 246-8271

MILLER'S RESORT
RR 1, Box 266
(56636)
Rates: $275-
$350/Weekly
Tel: (218) 246-8951

DEERWOOD

COUNTRY INN BY CARLSON
115 Front St E
(56444)
Rates: $52-$68
Tel: (218) 534-3101

DEERWOOD MOTEL
9 W Forest Rd
(56444)
Rates: $32-60
Tel: (218) 534-3163

DETROIT LAKES

BUDGET HOST INN
895 Hwy 10E (56501)
Rates: $30-$65
Tel: (218) 847-4454
(800) 283-4678

CASTAWAY INN & RESORT
Rt 4, Box 15 (56501)
Rates: n/a
Tel: (218) 847-4449
(800) 640-3395

INN ON THE LAKE-HOLIDAY INN
Hwy 10E (56501)
Rates: $50-$86
Tel: (800) 465-4329

SUPER 8 MOTEL
400 Morrow Ave
(56501)
Rates: $37-$46
Tel: (218) 847-1651
(800) 800-8000

DEXTER

MILL INN MOTEL
P. O. Box 78A (55926)
Rates: $32-$40
Tel: (507) 584-6440

DILWORTH

HOWARD JOHNSON
701 E Center Ave
(56529)
Rates: $36-$69
Tel: (218) 287-1212
(800) 446-4656

DULUTH

ALLYNDALE MOTEL
510 N 66th Ave W
(55807)
Rates: $31-$58
Tel: (218) 628-1061
(800) 341-8000

BEST WESTERN DOWNTOWN MOTEL
131 W 2nd St (55802)
Rates: $32-$79
Tel: (218) 727-6851
(800) 528-1234

BEST WESTERN EDGEWATER EAST MOTEL
2400 London Rd
(55812)
Rates: $49-$129
Tel: (218) 728-3601
(800) 528-1234

BEST WESTERN EDGEWATER WEST MOTEL
2211 London Rd
(55812)
Rates: $44-$99
Tel: (218) 728-3601
(800) 528-1234

DAYS INN
909 Cottonwood Ave
(55811)
Rates: $42-$56
Tel: (218) 727-3110
(800) 329-7466

GRAND MOTEL
4312 Grand Ave
(55807)
Rates: n/a
Tel: (218) 624-4821
(800) 472-0841

FITGER'S INN
600 E Superior St
(55802)
Rates: $55-$110
Tel: (218) 722-8826

**PARK INN
INTERNATIONAL-
DULUTH LAKESHORE**
250 Canal Park Dr
(55802)
Rates: $59-$88
Tel: (218) 727-8821

RADISSON HOTEL
505 W Superior St
(55802)
Rates: $59-$295
Tel: (218) 727-8981
(800) 333-3333

SELECT INN
200 S 27th Ave W
(55806)
Rates: $29-$48
Tel: (218) 723-1123

**SPINNAKER INN
BED & BREAKFAST**
5427 North Shore
Scenic Dr (55804)
Rates: $50-$125
Tel: (218) 525-2838

**VOYAGEUR
LAKEWALK INN**
333 E Superior St
(55802)
Rates: $27-$150
Tel: (218) 722-3911
(800) 258-3911

**WILLARD MUNGER
INN**
7408 Grand Ave
(55807)
Rates: $36-$122
Tel: (218) 624-4814
(800) 982-2453

EAGAN

**RESIDENCE INN
BY MARRIOTT**
3040 Eagandale Pl
(55121)
Rates: $79-$147
Tel: (612) 688-0363
(800) 331-3131

EAST
GRAND FORKS

COMFORT INN
US 2-E (56721)
Rates: $45-$55
Tel: (800) 221-2222

EDEN PRAIRIE

**RESIDENCE INN
BY MARRIOTT**
7780 Flying Cloud
Dr (55344)
Rates: $59-$119
Tel: (612) 829-0033
(800) 331-3131

EDINA

**HAWTHORNE
SUITES HOTEL**
3400 Edinborough
Way (55435)
Rates: $85-$95
Tel: (612) 893-9300

ELK RIVER

AMERICINN MOTEL
17432 Hwy 10
(55330)
Rates: $39-$52
Tel: (612) 441-8554

RED CARPET INN
17291 Hwy 10
(55330)
Rates: $26-$42
Tel: (612) 441-2424
(800) 251-1962

ELY

BLUE HERON B & B
P.O. Box 466 (55731)
Rates: $68-$72
Tel: (218) 365-4720

ELY MOTEL
1047 E Sheridan St
(55731)
Rates: $34-$55
Tel: (218) 365-3237

**OLSON BAY
RESORT COTTAGES**
2279 Grant
McMahan Blvd
(55731)
Rates: $350-$600
Tel: (800) 777-4419

**SILVER RAPIDS
LODGE RESORT**
HC 1, Box 2992
(55731)
Rates: $45-$80
Tel: (218) 365-4877

THREE DEER HAVEN
1850 Deer Haven Dr
(55731)
Rates: $75-$90
Tel: (218) 365-6464

EVELETH

HOLIDAY INN
701 Hat Trick Ave
(55734)
Rates: $56-$89
Tel: (800) 465-4329

**KOKE'S
DOWNTOWN
MOTEL**
714 Fayal Rd (55734)
Rates: $25-$32
Tel: (218) 744-4500

FAIRFAX

FAIRFAX MOTEL
403 E Lincoln Ave
(55332)
Rates: n/a
Tel: (507) 426-7266

FAIRMONT

COMFORT INN
I-90 & Hwy 15
(56031)
Rates: $53-$134
Tel: (507) 238-5444
(800) 228-5150

**HIGHLAND COURT
MOTEL**
1245 Lake Ave
(56031)
Rates: $23-$49
Tel: (507) 235-6686

HOLIDAY INN
Torgerson Dr (56031)
Rates: $54-$80
Tel: (800) 465-4329

SUPER 8 MOTEL
1200 Torgerson Dr
Box 922 (56031)
Rates: $45-$64
Tel: (507) 238-9444
(800) 800-8000

FARIBAULT

**BEST WESTERN
GALAXIE
MOTOR LODGE**
1401 Hwy 60 (55021)
Rates: $39-$64
Tel: (507)334-5508
(800) 528-1234

**FARIBAULT
MOTOR LODGE**
841 Faribault Rd
(55021)
Rates: n/a
Tel: (507) 334-1841

SELECT INN
4040 Hwy 60 (55021)
Rates: $33-$53
Tel: (507) 334-2051
(800) 641-1000

FERGUS FALLS

AMERICINN MOTEL
526 Western Ave N
(56537)
Rates: $44-$100
Tel: (218) 739-3900
(800) 634-3444

MOTEL 7
616 Frontier Dr
(56537)
Rates: $32-$39
Tel: (218) 736-2554

SUPER 8 MOTEL
2454 College Way
(56537)
Rates: $35-$52
Tel: (218) 739-3261
(800) 800-8000

FINLAYSON

SUPER 8 MOTEL
2811 Hwy 23 (55735)
Rates: $41-$53
Tel: (320) 245-5284
(800) 800-8000

FOREST LAKE

FOREST MOTEL
7 NE 6th Ave (55025)
Rates: $28-$44
Tel: (612) 464-4077

FOSSTON

SUPER 8 MOTEL
Hwy 2 E (56542)
Rates: $38-$50
Tel: (218) 435-1088
(800) 800-8000

FRANKLIN

MAPLE HILL COTTAGE
RR 1, Box 12 (55333)
Rates: $45-$55
Tel: (507) 557-2403

FRIDLEY

BEST WESTERN KELLY INN
5201 Central Ave NE (55421)
Rates: $64-$98
Tel: (612) 571-9440
(800) 528-1234

GLENCOE

SUPER 8 MOTEL
717 Morningside Dr (55336)
Rates: $39-$58
Tel: (320) 864-6191
(800) 800-8000

GLENWOOD

HI-VIEW MOTEL
255 N Hwy 55 (56334)
Rates: $26-$43
Tel: (612) 634-4541

GRAND MARAIS

BEST WESTERN SUPERIOR INN
US Hwy 61 E (55604)
Rates: $59-139
Tel: (218) 387-2240
(800) 842-8439

CLEARWATER LODGE
355 Gunflint Trail (55604)
Rates: $595-$625
Tel: (800) 527-0554

ECONO LODGE
US 61 E, (55604)
Rates: $39-$99
Tel: (218) 387-2500
(800) 247-6020

GOLDEN EAGLE LODGE
325 Gunflint Trail (55604)
Rates: $89-$120
Tel: (218) 388-2203
(800) 346-2203

GUNFLINT LODGE
750 Gunflint Trail (55604)
Rates: $89-$239
Tel: (218) 388-2294

GUNFLINT PINES RESORT
755 Gunflint Trail (55604)
Rates: n/a
Tel: (800) 533-5814

HARBOR INN
207 Wisconsin St (55604)
Rates: n/a
Tel: (218) 387-1191

LITTLE OLLIE LAKE CABIN
590 Gunflint Trail (55604)
Rates: $110-$125
Tel: (218) 388-972
(800) 322-8327

MOTEL WEDGEWOOD
HC 1, Box 100 (55604)
Rates: $30-$35
Tel: (218) 387-2944

NOR' WESTER LODGE
550 Gunflint Trail (55604)
Rates: $560-$800/Weekly
Tel: (218) 388-2252

SANDGREN MOTEL
P. O. Box 1056 (55604)
Rates: $30-$45
Tel: (218) 387-2975

SEAWALL MOTEL
Hwy 61 & 3rd Ave (55604)
Rates: n/a
Tel: (218) 387-2095
(800) 245-5806

SUPER 8 MOTEL
Hwy 61 W (55604)
Rates: $43-$72
Tel: (218) 387-2448
(800) 800-8000

TOMTEBODA MOTEL
1800 Hwy 61 W (55604)
Rates: $35-$50
Tel: (218) 387-1585

GRAND RAPIDS

AMERICANA MOTEL
1915 Hwy 2 W (55744)
Rates: n/a
Tel: (218) 326-0369

BEST WESTERN RAINBOW INN
1300 US 169 E (55744)
Rates: $45-$75
Tel: (218) 326-9655
(800) 528-1234

COUNTRY INN BY CARLSON
2601 Hwy 169 S (55744)
Rates: $60-$85
Tel: (218) 327-4960
(800) 456-4000

DAYS INN
311 E Hwy 2 (55744)
Rates: $40-$69
Tel: (218) 326-3457
(800) 329-7466

SAWMILL INN
2301 S Pokegama Ave (55744)
Rates: $50-$99
Tel: (218) 326-8501

GRANITE FALLS

SUPER 8 MOTEL
845 W Hwy 212 (56241)
Rates: $40-$56
Tel: (612) 564-4075
(800) 800-8000

HASTINGS

A COUNTRY ROSE
13452 90th St S (55033)
Rates: $65-$85
Tel: (612) 436-2237

HENDRICKS

TRIPLE L FARM
Rt 1, Box 141 (56136)
Rates: $30-$55
Tel: (507) 275-3740

HIBBING

DAYS INN
1520 Hwy 37 E (55746)
Rates: $34-$54
Tel: (218) 263-8306
(800) 329-7466

KAHLER PARK HOTEL
1402 E Howard St (55746)
Rates: $65-$95
Tel: (612) 384-7751
(800) 262-3481

SUPER 8 MOTEL
1411 E 40th St (55746)
Rates: $41-$63
Tel: (218) 263-8982
(800) 800-8000

HINCKLEY

DAYS INN
104 Grindstone Ct (55037)
Rates: $41-$84
Tel: (800) 329-7466

HOLIDAY INN EXPRESS
604 Weber Ave (55037)
Rates: $47-$87
Tel: (800) 465-4329

HUTCHINSON

BEST WESTERN VICTORIAN INN
1000 Hwy 7 W (55350)
Rates: $54-$95
Tel: (320) 587-6030
(800) 369-0145

INTERNATIONAL FALLS

DAYS INN
2331 Hwy 53 S
(56649)
Rates: $36-$48
Tel: (218) 283-9441
(800) 329-7466

HILLTOP MOTEL
2002 2nd Ave W
(56649)
Rates: $33-$49
Tel: (218) 283-2505
(800) 322-6671

HOLIDAY INN
1810 Hwy 11 &
71 W (56649)
Rates: $59-$93
Tel: (800) 465-4329

ISLAND VIEW LODGE & MOTEL
HCR8, Box 411
(56649)
Rates: $60-$195
Tel: (218) 266-3511

NORTHERNAIRE FLOATING LODGES
P. O.Box 510 (56649)
Rates: $695-
$1895/Weekly
Tel: (218) 286-5221

JACKSON

BUDGET HOST PRAIRIE WINDS MOTEL
950 N US 71 (56143)
Rates: $35-$60
Tel: (507) 847-2020
(800) 283-4678

SUPER 8 MOTEL
RR 3, Box 21 (56143)
Rates: $40-$59
Tel: (800) 800-8000

KELLIHER

ROYAL SHOOKS MOTEL
Corner of 1 & 72
(56661)
Rates: n/a
Tel: (218) 647-8379

LAKE CITY

LAKE PEPIN LODGE-MOTEL
620 Central Point Rd
(55041)
Rates: $59-$139
Tel: (612) 345-5392
(800) 644-2780

LAKEVILLE

MOTEL 6
11274 210th St
(55044)
Rates: $30-$36
Tel: (612) 469-1900
(800) 440-6000

SUPER 8 MOTEL
20800 Kenrick Ave
(55044)
Rates: $48-$68
Tel: (612) 469-1134
(800) 800-8000

LITCHFIELD

IMA SCOTWOOD MOTEL
1017 E Frontage Rd
(55355)
Rates: $36-$50
Tel: (612) 693-2496
(800) 341-8000

LITTLE FALLS

PINE EDGE INN
308 1st St SE (56345)
Rates: $35-$95
Tel: (612) 632-6681
(800) 344-6681

LONG PRAIRIE

BUDGET HOST
417 Lake St (56347)
Rates: $31-$44
Tel: (612) 732-6118

LUTSEN

BEST WESTERN CLIFF DWELLER
Hwy 61, Box 26
(55612)
Rates: $44-$89
Tel: (218) 663-7273
(800) 223-2048

SOLBAKKEN RESORT
HC 3 Box 170
(55612)
Rates: $39-$191
Tel: (218) 663-7566
(800) 435-3950

THOMSONITE BEACH
R3, Box 470 (55612)
Rates: $38-$145
Tel: (218) 387-1532

LUVERNE

SUPER 8 MOTEL
I-90 & Hwy 75
(56156)
Rates: $40-$55
Tel: (507) 283-9541
(800) 800-8000

MANKATO

COMFORT INN
131 Apache Pl
(56601)
Rates: $40-$65
Tel: (800) 221-2222

DAYS INN
1285 Range St
(56001)
Rates: $38-$65
Tel: (507) 387-3332
(800) 329-7466

HOLIDAY INN-DOWNTOWN
101 E Main St
(56001)
Rates: $50-$72
Tel: (800) 465-4329

RIVERFRONT INN
1727 N Riverfront Dr
(56001)
Rates: $29-$59
Tel: (507) 388-1638

MANTORVILLE

GRAND OLD MANSION
501 Clay St (55955)
Rates: $30-$64
Tel: (507) 635-3231

MAPLEWOOD

BEST WESTERN INN
1780 E CR D (55109)
Rates: $55-$59
Tel: (800) 528-1234

HOLIDAY INN EAST
2201 Burns Ave
(55119)
Rates: $77-$112
Tel: (800) 465-4329

MARSHALL

BEST WESTERN MARSHALL INN
1500 E College Dr
(56258)
Rates: $50-$70
Tel: (507) 532-3221
(800) 528-1234

COMFORT INN
1511 E College Dr
(56258)
Rates: $45-$80
Tel: (507) 532-3070
(800) 221-2222

SUPER 8 MOTEL
1106 E Main St
(56258)
Rates: $41-$59
Tel: (507) 537-1461
(800) 800-8000

TRAVELER'S LODGE
1425 E College Dr
(56258)
Rates: $30-$44
Tel: (507) 532-5721
(800) 532-5721

McGREGOR

HILLCREST RESORT
HCR 3, Box 754
(55760)
Rates: n/a
Tel: (218) 426-3323

TOWN & COUNTRY MOTEL
Hwy 65 & 210
(55760)
Rates: n/a
Tel: (218) 768-3271

MELROSE

SUPER 8 MOTEL
231 E County Rd 173
(56352)
Rates: $36-$50
Tel: (612) 256-4261
(800) 800-8000

MILACA

RODEWAY INN
215 10th Ave.(56353)
Rates: $39-59
Tel: (320) 983-2660
(800) 228-2000

MINNEAPOLIS

AQUA CITY MOTEL
5739 Lyndale Ave S
(55419)
Rates: $25-$50
Tel: (612) 861-6061

**BEST WESTERN
NORMANDY INN**
405 S 8th St (55404)
Rates: $63-$80
Tel: (612) 370-1400
(800) 528-1234

**CROWN STERLING
SUITES**
425 S 7th St (55415)
Rates: $99-$225
Tel: (800) 433-4600

**HOLIDAY INN
METRODOME**
1500 Washington
Ave (55454)
Rates: $97-$117
Tel: (800) 465-4329

**MARQUETTE
MINNEAPOLIS**
710 Marquette Ave
(55402)
Rates: $79-$92
Tel: (612) 332-2351

METRO INN
5637 Lyndale Ave S
(55419)
Rates: $33-$59
Tel: (612) 861-6011

**MINNEAPOLIS
HILTON AND TOWERS**
1001 Marquette Ave
(55403)
Rates: $99-$210
Tel: (800) 445-8667

**MINNEAPOLIS
MARRIOTT
CITY CENTER**
30 S 7th St (55402)
Rates: $69-$179
Tel: (612) 349-4000

**RADISSON HOTEL
METRODOME**
615 Washington Ave
SE (55414)
Rates: $92-$102
Tel: (612) 379-8888

**RADISSON PLAZA
HOTEL**
35 S 7th St (55402)
Rates: $91
Tel: (612) 339-4900

**REGAL
MINNEAPOLIS
HOTEL**
1313 Nicollet Mall
(55403)
Rates: $94-$124
Tel: (612) 332-6000
(800) 777-3277

**SHERATON PARK
PLACE HOTEL**
1500 Park Place Blvd
(55416)
Rates: n/a
Tel: (612) 542-8600
(800) 542-5566

MONTEVIDEO

**BEST WESTERN
ROYALE INN**
207 N 1st St (56265)
Rates: $39-$61
Tel: (800) 528-1234

MONTICELLO

COMFORT INN
200 E Oakwood Dr
(55362)
Rates: $45-$80
Tel: (612) 295-1111
(800) 221-2222

MOORHEAD

**BEST WESTERN
RED RIVER INN**
600 30th Ave S
(56560)
Rates: $44-$72
Tel: (218) 233-6171
(800) 528-1234

**GUEST HOUSE
MOTEL**
2107 SE Main
(56560)
Rates: $25-$35
Tel: (218) 233-2471

**THE MADISON
HOTEL**
600 30 Ave S (56560)
Rates: $39-$78
Tel: (218) 233-6171

MOTEL 75
810 Belsly Blvd
(56560)
Rates: $29-$36
Tel: (218) 233-7501

MORA

ANN RIVER MOTEL
Rt 2, Box 279 (55051)
Rates: $27-$50
Tel: (612) 679-2972

MOTEL MORA
301 S Hwy 65
(55051)
Rates: $29-$42
Tel: (612) 679-3262
(800) 657-0167

MORRIS

**BEST WESTERN
PRAIRIE INN**
200 Hwy 28 (56267)
Rates: $33-$90
Tel: (320) 589-3030
(800) 528-1234

MORTON

DAYS INN
400 W Ledge (56270)
Rates: $29-$54
Tel: (507) 697-6205
(800) 329-7466

NEW ULM

**COLONIAL INN
MOTEL**
1315 N Broadway
(56073)
Rates: $22-$40
Tel: (507) 354-3128

HOLIDAY INN
2101 S Broadway
(56073)
Rates: $56-$80
Tel: (800) 465-4329

SUPER 8 MOTEL
1901 S Broadway
(56073)
Rates: $42-$57
Tel: (507) 359-2400
(800) 800-8000

NEVIS

**THE PARK STREET
INN**
254 Park St (56467)
Rates: $50-$90
Tel: (218) 652-4500
(800) 797-1778

NEW YORK MILLS

MILLS MOTEL
P. O. Box B (56567)
Rates: $29-$39
Tel: (218) 385-3600

NISSWA

DAYS INN
45 N Smiley Rd
(56468)
Rates: $37-$75
Tel: (218) 963-3500
(800) 329-7466

NISSWA MOTEL
1426 Merrill Ave
(56468)
Rates: $39-$48
Tel: (218) 963-7611

NORTH BRANCH

CROSSROADS MOTEL
1118 Main St (55056)
Rates: $33-$50
Tel: (612) 674-7074

OLIVIA

SHEEP SHEDDE INN
2425 W Lincoln Ave
(56277)
Rates: $29-$39
Tel: (612) 523-5000

ONAMIA

ECONO LODGE
40993 US 169 (56359)
Rates: $28-$50
Tel: (320) 532-3838
(800) 424-4777

OWATONNA

BUDGET HOST INN
745 State Ave (55060)
Rates: $28-$55
Tel: (507) 451-8712

**COUNTRY INN
& SUITES**
130 Allen Ave SW
(55060)
Rates: $52-81
Tel: (507) 455-9295
(800) 456-4000

OAKDALE MOTEL
1416 S Oak St
(55060)
Raes: $27-$45
Tel: (507) 451-5480

DAYS INN
205 N Oak Ave
(55060)
Rates: $32-$55
Tel: (507) 451-4620

RAMADA INN
1212 I-35 (55060)
Rates: $47-$69
Tel: (507) 455-0606
(800) 272-6232

PINE RIVER

TRAILSIDE INN
SR 371 S (56474)
Rates: $43-$65
Tel: (218) 587-4499

PIPESTONE

KINGS KOURT
821 SE 7th St (56164)
Rates: n/a
Tel: (507) 825-3314

SUPER 8 MOTEL
605 8th Ave SE
(56164)
Rates: $40-$56
Tel: (507) 825-4217
(800) 800-8000

PLYMOUTH

RADISSON HOTEL
3131 Campus Dr
(55441)
Rates: $69-$79
Tel: (612) 559-6600

RED ROOF INN
2600 Annapolis Ln
N (55441)
Rates: $30-$50
Tel: (800) 843-7663

PRESTON

INN TOWN LODGE
205 Franklin St
(55965)
Rates: $40-$65
Tel: (507) 765-4412

PRINCETON

RUM RIVER MOTEL
510 19th Ave N
(55371)
Rates: $36-$44
Tel: (612) 389-3120

RED WING

**AMERICINN
OF RED WING**
1819 Old Main W
(55066)
Rates: $55-$87
Tel: (612) 385-9060
(800) 634-3444

**BEST WESTERN
QUIET HOUSE
SUITES**
752 Withers Harbor
Dr (55066)
Rates: $74-$170
Tel: (612) 388-1577
(800) 528-1234

DAYS INN
955 E 7th St (55066)
Rates: $38-$80
Tel: (612) 388-3568
(800) 329-7466

RICHFIELD

MOTEL 6
7640 Cedar Ave S
(55423)
Rates $38-$44
Tel: (612) 861-4491
(800) 440-6000

ROCHESTER

**BEST WESTERN
FIFTH AVE**
20 5th Ave NW
(55901)
Rates: $49-$68
Tel: (507) 289-3987
(800) 528-1234

**CLINIC VIEW INN
& SUITES**
9 3rd Ave NW (55901)
Rates: $65-$75
Tel: (507) 289-8646

COLONIAL HOTEL
114 2nd St SW
(55902)
Rates: $25-$54
Tel: (507) 289-3363
(800) 533-2226

**COUNTRY INN
& SUITES**
4323 Hwy 52 N
(55901)
Rates: $50-$70
Tel: (507) 285-3335
(800) 456-4000

DAYS INN
111 28th St SE
(55904)
Rates: $39-55
Tel: (507) 286-1001
(800) 329-7466

**DAYS INN-
DOWNTOWN**
61st Ave NW (55901)
Rates: $45-$65
Tel: (507) 282-3801
(800) 329-7466

DAYS INN WEST
435 16th Ave NW
(55901)
Rates: $59-$79
Tel: (507) 288-9090
(800) 329-7466

DAYSTOP
11 17th Ave SW
(55902)
Rates: $32-$46
Tel: (507) 282-2733
(800) 329-7466

ECONO LODGE
519 3rd Ave SW
(55902)
Rates: $39-$52
Tel: (507) 288-1855
(800) 424-4777

FIKSDAL MOTEL
1215 2nd St SW
(55902)
Rates: $35-$49
Tel: (507) 288-2671

**FRIENDSHIP INN
CENTER TOWNE**
116 5th St SW
(55902)
Rates: $42-$51
Tel: (507) 289-1628
(800) 453-4511

**HOLIDAY INN
DOWNTOWN**
220 S Broadway
(55904)
Rate: $60-$92
Tel: (800) 465-4329

**HOLIDAY INN
SOUTH**
1630 S Broadway
(55904)
Rates: $54-$74
Tel: (800) 465-4329

**HOWARD
JOHNSON**
111 17th Ave SW
(55902)
Rates: $36-$58
Tel: (507) 289-1617
(800) 446-4656

IMA COLONIAL INN
114 SW 2nd St
(55902-3131)
Rates: $34-$47
Tel: (507) 289-3363
(800) 341-8000

THE KAHLER HOTEL
20 2nd Ave SW
(55903)
Rates: $58-$138
Tel: (507) 282-2581

**KAHLER PLAZA
HOTEL**
101 1st Ave SW
(55902)
Rates: $56-$350
Tel: (507) 280-6000
(800) 533-1655

MOTEL 6
2107 W Frontage Rd
(55901)
Rates: $26-$32
Tel: (507) 282-6625
(800) 440-6000

QUALITY INN
1620 1st Ave SE
(55904)
Rates: $69-$74
Tel: (507) 282-8091

RADISSON HOTEL CENTERPLACE
150 S Broadway
(55904)
Rates: $59-$105
Tel: (507) 281-8000

RAMADA INN
1625 S Broadway
(55904)
Rates: $49-$84
Tel: (507) 281-2211
(800) 272-6232

SUPER 8 MOTEL
1850 S Broadway
(55904)
Rates: $40-$55
Tel: (507) 282-9905
(800) 800-8000

SUPER 8 MOTEL-SOUTH #1
1230 S Broadway
(55904)
Rates: $48-$63
Tel: (507) 288-8288
(800) 800-8000

SUPER 8 MOTEL-W
1608 2nd St SW
(55902)
Rates: $48-$63
Tel: (507) 281-5100
(800) 800-8000

ROGERS

SUPER 8 MOTEL
21130 134th Ave N
(55374)
Rates: $42-$64
Tel: (612) 428-4000
(800) 800-8000

ROSEAU

AMERICINN MOTEL
1090 3rd St NW
(56751)
Rates: $34-$46
Tel: (218) 463-1045

SUPER 8 MOTEL
318 West Side
(56751)
Rates: $33-$47
Tel: (218) 463-2196
(800) 800-8000

ROSEVILLE

MOTEL 6
2300 Cleveland Ave
N (55113)
Rates: $33-$39
Tel: (612) 639-3988
(800) 440-6000

ST. CLOUD

BUDGETEL INN
70 37th Ave S (56301)
Rates: $28-$44
Tel: (612) 253-4444

DAYS INN
420 SE Hwy 10
(56304)
Rates: $39-$96
Tel: (612) 253-0500
(800) 329-7466

FAIRFIELD INN BY MARRIOTT
4120 South 2nd St
(56301)
Rates: $36-$62
Tel: (800) 348-6000

GATEWAY MOTEL
310 Lincoln Ave SE
(56304)
Rates: $24-$42
Tel: (612) 252-4050

HOLIDAY INN
75 37th Ave S (56302)
Rates: $50-$155
Tel: (800) 465-4329

KLEIS MOTEL
30 25th Ave S (56301)
Rates: $24-$44
Tel: (612) 251-7450

MOTEL 6
815 1st St S (56387)
Rates: $28-$36
Tel: (612) 253-7070
(800) 466-8356

SUPER 8 MOTEL
50 Park Ave S
(56301)
Rates: $36-$53
Tel: (320) 253-5530
(800) 800-8000

THRIFTY MOTEL
130 14th Ave NE
(56304)
Rates: $24-$32
Tel: (612) 253-6320

ST. LOUIS PARK

SHERATON MINNEAPOLIS METRODOME
1330 Industrial Blvd
(55413)
Rates: $83-$103
Tel: (612) 331-1900

ST. JAMES

SUPER 8 MOTEL
Hwy 60 (56081)
Rates: $39-$56
Tel: (507) 375-4708
(800) 800-8000

ST. JOSEPH

SUPER 8 MOTEL
P. O. Box 721 (56374)
Rates: $37-$58
Tel: (612) 363-7711
(800) 800-8000

ST. PAUL

BEST WESTERN KELLY INN
161 St Anthony Ave
(55103)
Rates: $74-$119
Tel: (612) 227-8711
(800) 528-1234

CROWN STERLING SUITES
175 E 10th St (55101)
Rates: $88
Tel: (612) 224-5400

DAYS INN CIVIC CENTER
175 W 7th St (55102)
Rates: $49-$169
Tel: (612) 292-8929
(800) 329-7466

EXEL INN
1739 Old Hudson Rd
(55106)
Rates: $50-$75
Tel: (612) 771-5566
(800) 356-8013

RADISSON HOTEL
11 E Kellogg Blvd
(55101)
Rates: $95-$145
Tel: (612) 292-1900

SHERATON MIDWAY
400 Hamline Ave N
(55104)
Rates: $90-$120
Tel: (612) 642-1234
(800) 535-2339

ST. PETER

AMERICINN MOTEL
700 N Minnesota
Ave (56082)
Rates: $39-$68
Tel: (507) 931-6554

VIKING JR MOTEL
169 & 90 West
(56082)
Rates: n/a
Tel: (507) 931-3081

SANBORN

SOD HOUSE ON THE PRAIRIE
Rt 2, Box 75 (56083)
Rates: $75-$135
Tel: (507) 723-5138

SAUK CENTRE

ECONO LODGE MOTEL
I-94 at Sauk Ctr
(56378)
Rates: $40-$95
Tel: (320) 352-6581
(800) 424-4777

GOPHER PRAIRIE MOTEL
I-94 & US 71 (56378)
Rates: $30-$39
Tel: (612) 352-2275
(800) 341-8000

HILLCREST MOTEL
965 S Main St
(56378)
Rates: $23-$32
Tel: (612) 352-2215

PALMER HOUSE INN
500 Sinclair Lewis
Ave (56378)
Rates: $17-$38
Tel: (612) 352-3431

SAUK RAPIDS

ECONO LODGE
1420 2nd St N
(56379)
Rates: $32-$40
Tel: (800) 251-1962

SAVAGE

COMFORT INN
4601 Hwy 13-W
(55378)
Rates: $49-$55
Tel: (800) 221-2222

SCHROEDER

LAMB'S RESORT
North Shore Dr
Hwy 61 (55613)
Rates: n/a
Tel: (218) 663-7292

SEBEKA

K'S MOTEL
Hwy 71 (56477)
Rates: n/a
Tel: (218) 837-5162

SHAKOPEE

**AMERICINN
OF SHAKOPEE**
1251 E 1st Ave
(55379)
Rates: $39-$59
Tel: (800) 634-3444

SHOREVIEW

HAMPTON INN
1000 Gramsie Rd
(55126)
Rates: $60-$81
Tel: (800) 465-4329

SILVER BAY

MARINER MOTEL
46 Outer Dr (55614)
Rates: $32-$75
Tel: (218) 226-4488
(800) 777-8452

SLEEPY EYE

**BEST WESTERN INN
OF SEVEN GABLES**
1100 E Main St
(56085)
Rates: $46-$70
Tel: (507) 794-5390
(800) 528-1234

SPICER

IMA CAZADOR INN
154 Lake St (56288)
Rates: $34-$74
Tel: (612) 796-2091
(800) 341-8000

SPRING VALLEY

66 MOTEL
612 North Huron
Ave (55975)
Rates: $22-$25
Tel: (507) 346-9993

STAPLES

SUPER 8 MOTEL
109 2nd Ave W
(56479)
Rates: $38-$54
Tel: (218) 894-3585
(800) 800-8000

STEWARTVILLE

AMERICINN MOTEL
1700 NW 2nd Ave
(55976)
Rates: $41-$50
Tel: (507) 533-4747

STILLWATER

BEST WESTERN INN
1750 Frontage Rd W
(55082)
Rates: $51-$73
Tel: ((612) 430-1300
(800) 528-1234

STURGEON LAKE

**STURGEON LAKE
MOTEL**
I-35 & County Rd 46
(55783)
Rates: n/a
Tel: (218) 372-3194

TAYLORS FALLS

SPRINGS INN
90 Government Rd
(55084)
Rates: $35-$90
Tel: (612) 465-6565
(800) 851-4243

THIEF RIVER FALLS

SUPER 8 MOTEL
Hwy 59 S (56701)
Rates: $43-$55
Tel: (218) 681-6205
(800) 800-8000

TOFTE

**ASPENWOOD
RESORT MOTEL**
130 Aspenwood
(55615)
Rates: n/a
Tel: (218) 663-7978

BLUEFIN BAY MOTEL
Box 2125 (55615)
Rates: $69-$295
Tel: (800) 258-3346

CHATEAU LE VEAUX
P.O. Box 115 (55615)
Rates: $55-$159
Tel: (218) 663-7223
(800) 445-5773

TWO HARBORS

**COUNTRY INN
BY CARLSON**
1204 7th Ave (55616)
Rates: $38-$82
Tel: (800) 456-4000

SUPERIOR SHORES
LODGE & HOMES

10 Superior Shores
(55616)
Rates: $49-$199
Tel: (218) 834-5671
(800) 242-1988

TYLER

BABETTE'S INN
308 S Tyler St (56178)
Rates: $55-$65
Tel: (507) 537-1632

VIRGINIA

**LAKESHORE MOTOR
INN DOWNTOWN**
404 N 6th Ave
(55792)
Rates: $31-$44
Tel: (218) 741-3360

SKI-VIEW MOTEL
903 N 17th St (55792)
Rates: $26-$38
Tel: (218) 741-8918

WABASHA

**THE ANDERSON
HOUSE**
333 W Main St
(55981)
Rates: $30-$125
Tel: (800) 535-5467

WACONIA

SUPER 8 MOTEL
301 E Frontage Rd
(55387)
Rates: $36-$46
Tel: (612) 442-5147
(800) 800-8000

WADENA

**BEST WESTERN
FOUR SEASONS**
500 Ash Ave NW
(56482)
Rates: $35-$60
Tel: (218) 631-3725
(800) 528-1234

WALKER

LAKEVIEW INN
P.O. Box 1359
(56484)
Rates: n/a
Tel: (218) 547-1212
(800) 252-5073

**TIANNA FARMS
BED & BREAKFAST**
Tianna Farms Rd,
Box 968 (56484)
Rates: $45-$125
Tel: (218) 547-1306
(800) 842-6620

WARROAD

**BEST WESTERN
CAN-AM INN**
406 Main Ave NE
(56763)
Rates: $34-$48
Tel: (218) 386-3807
(800) 528-1234

**HOSPITAL BAY
BED & BREAKFAST**
620 Lake St NE
(56763)
Rates: $40-$60
Tel: (218) 386-2627
(800) 568-6028

THE PATCH MOTEL
Hwy 11 W (56763)
Rates: $31-$42
Tel: (218) 386-2723

WHITE BEAR LAKE

**COUNTRY INN
BY CARLSON**
4940 Hwy 61 (55110)
Rates: $60-$80
Tel: (612) 429-5393
(800) 456-4000

WILLMAR

COLONIAL INN
1102 S 1st St (56201)
Rates: $22-$79
Tel: (612) 235-4444
(800) 396-4445

DAYS INN
225 28th St SE
(56201)
Rates: $42-$53
Tel: (612) 231-1275
(800) 528-1234

HOLIDAY INN
2100 US 12 E (56201)
Rates: $58-$85
Tel: (800) 465-4329

SUPER 8 MOTEL
US 71 S (56201)
Rates: $29-$45
Tel: (800) 800-8000

WINONA

**BEST WESTERN
RIVERPORT INN**
900 Bruski Dr
(55987)
Rates: $52-$80
Tel: (507) 452-0606
(800) 595-0606

DAYS INN
420 Cottonwood Dr
(55987)
Rates: 43-$53
Tel: (507) 454-6930
(800) 329-7466

STERLING MOTEL
1450 Gilmore Ave
(55987)
Rates: n/a
Tel: (507) 454-1120
(800) 452-1235

SUPER 8 MOTEL
1025 Sugar Loaf Rd
((55987)
Rates: $39-$57
Tel: (507) 454-6066
(800) 800-8000

WOODBURY

HAMPTON INN
1450 Weir Dr.
(55125)
Rates: $70-$86
Tel: (612) 578-2822
(800) 426-7866

RED ROOF INN
1806 Wooddale Dr
(55125)
Rates: $42-$58
Tel: (800) 843-7663

WORTHINGTON

**BEST WESTERN
WORTHINGTON**
1923 Dover St
(56187)
Rates: $37-$49
Tel: (507) 376-4146
(800) 528-1234

BUDGET HOST INN
207 Oxford St
(56187)
Rates: $34-$46
Tel: (800) 283-4678

HOLIDAY INN
2015 Humiston Ave
(56187)
Rates: $52-$77
Tel: (800) 465-4329

SUPER 8 MOTEL
P. O. Box 98 (56187)
Rates: $41-$59
Tel: (507) 372-7755
(800) 800-8000

ZUMBROTA

SUPER 8 MOTEL
P. O. Box 156 (55992)
Rates: $36-$56
Tel: (507) 732-7852
(800) 800-8000

MISSISSIPPI

ABERDEEN

**BEST WESTERN
ABERDEEN INN**
801 E Commerce St
(39730)
Rates: $40-$54
Tel: (601) 369-4343
(800) 528-1234

BATESVILLE

**BATESVILLE SKYLINE
MOTEL**
311 Hwy 51S (38606)
Rates: $26-$35
Tel: (601) 563-7671

COMFORT INN
I-55 and SR 6 (38606)
Rates: $42-$58
Tel: (800) 221-2222

BILOXI

**JULS BEACH
HOTEL RESORT**
2428 Beach Blvd
(39531)
Rates: 55-$80
Tel: (601) 385-5555

MOTEL 6
2476 Beach Blvd
(39531)
Rates: $38-$44
Tel: (601) 388-5130
(800) 440-6000

SEAVIEW RESORT
1870 Beach Blvd
(39531)
Rates: $35-$75
Tel: (601) 388-5512

BROOKHAVEN

CLARIDGE INN
1210 Brockway Blvd
(39601)
Rates: $38-$42
Tel: (601) 833-1341

CLARKSDALE

**CLEVELAND
COMFORT INN**
721 N Davis Hwy 61
N (38732)
Rates: $39-$50
Tel: (800) 221-2222

DAYS INN
1910 State St (38614)
Rates: $39-$84
Tel: (601) 624-4391
(800) 329-7466

HAMPTON INN
710 State St (38614)
Rates: $58-$66
Tel: (601) 627-9292
(800) 426-7866

CLINTON

DAYS INN
482 Springridge Rd
(39056)
Rates: $35-$100
Tel: (601) 924-7243
(800) 329-7466

CORINTH

COMFORT INN
P. O. Box 540 (38834)
Rates: $35-$45
Tel: (800) 221-2222

DURANT

SUPER 8 MOTEL
Rt 2, Box 228 (39063)
Rates: $39-$51
Tel: (601) 653-3881
(800) 800-8000

ESCATAWPS

**BEST WESTERN
FLAGSHIP INN**
P.O. Box 1280
(39552)
Rates: $50-$80
Tel: (601) 475-5000
(800) 522-5082

FOREST

BEST WESTERN INN
P. O. Box 402 (39074)
Rates: $47-$58
Tel: (601) 469-2640
(800) 528-1234

GREENVILLE

DAYS INN
P.O. Box 1139 (38701)
Rates: $35-$65
Tel: (601) 335-1999
(800) 329-7466

GREENWOOD

COMFORT INN
401 Hwy 82 W
(38930)
Rates: $42-$45
Tel: (800) 221-2222

DAYS INN
335 Hwy 82-49
(38930)
Rates: $45-$50
Tel: (601) 453-4364
(800) 329-7466

GRENADA

BEST WESTERN
1750 Sunset Dr
(38901)
Rates: $42-$64
Tel: (601) 226-7816
(800) 528-1234

HOLIDAY INN
1660 Frontage Rd
(38901)
Rates: $55
Tel: (800) 465-4329

GULFPORT

**BEST WESTERN
SEAWAY INN**
US 49 I I-10 (39503)
Rates: $60-$150
Tel: (601) 864-0050
(800) 528-1234

MOTEL 6
9355 US Hwy 49
(39503)
Rates: $36-$42
Tel: (601) 863-1890
(800) 440-6000

**RED CREEK
COLONIAL INN**
7416 Red Creek Rd
(Long Beach 39560)
Rates: $39-$69
Tel: (601) 452-3080

SHONEY'S INN
9375 Hwy 49 (39503)
Rates: $70-$89
Tel: (601) 868-8500
(800) 222-2222

HATTIESBURG

COMFORT INN
6595 Hwy 49 N
(39401)
Rates: $46-$58
Tel: (800) 272-6232

HAMPTON INN
4301 Hardy St
(39401)
Rates: $57-$68
Tel: (601) 264-8080
(800) 426-7866

HOWARD JOHNSON
6553 US Hwy 49 N
(39401)
Rates: $40-$89
Tel: (601) 268-2251
(800) 446-4656

MOTEL 6
6508 US Hwy 49
(39401)
Rates: $30-$34
Tel: (601) 544-6096
(800) 440-6000

IUKA

KEY WEST INN
189 CR 180 (38852)
Rates: $38-$58
Tel: (601) 423-9221

JACKSON

BEST WESTERN METRO INN
1520 Ellis Ave (39204)
Rates: $45-$75
Tel: (601) 355-7483
(800) 528-1234

BEST WESTERN NORTHEAST
5035 I-55 N (39206)
Rates: $49-$80
Tel: (601) 939-8200
(800) 528-1234

DAYS INN EAST
716 Hwy 80E (39208)
Rates: $30-$45
Tel: (800) 329-7466

EDISON WALTHALL HOTEL
225 E Capitol St
(39201)
Rates: $60-$185
Tel: (601) 948-6161

HARVEY HOTEL
200 E Amite St
(39201)
Rates: $57-$71
Tel: (800) 922-9222

HOLIDAY INN-SOUTHWEST
2649 Hwy 80W
(39204)
Rates: $46-$62
Tel: (800) 465-4329

LA QUINTA INN
150 Angle St (39204)
Rates: $42-$50
Tel: (800) 531-5900

LA QUINTA INN NORTH
616 Briarwood Rd
(39211)
Rates: $43-$51
Tel: (800) 531-5900

MOTEL 6
6145 I-55 N (39213)
Rates: $36-$42
Tel: (601) 956-8848
(800) 440-6000

RED ROOF INN COLISEUM
700 Larson St (39202)
Rates: $35-$48
Tel: (601) 969-5006
(800) 843-7663

RESIDENCE INN BY MARRIOTT
881 E River Pl (39202)
Rates: $99-$149
Tel: (601) 355-3599
(800) 331-3131

SCOTTISH INNS
2263 US Hwy 80 W
(39204)
Rates: $24-$36
Tel: (601) 969-1144
(800) 251-1962

SUPER 8 MOTEL
2655 I-55 S (39204)
Rates: $37-$49
Tel: (601) 372-1006
(800) 800-8000

KOSCIUSKO

BEST WESTERN PARKWAY INN
1052 Hwy 35 Bypass
(39090)
Rates: $42-$50
Tel: (601) 289-6252
(800) 528-1234

LAUREL

DAYS INN
Hwy 11 N & I-59
(39442)
Rates: $35-$45
Tel: (601) 428-8421
(800) 329-7466

McCOMB

HOLIDAY INN
1900 Delaware Ave
(39648)
Rates: $46-$52
Tel: (800) 465-4329

MAGEE

PASSPORT INN
Hwy 49 N (39111)
Rates: n/a
Tel: (601) 849-3250
(800) 251-1962

MERIDIAN

BUDGETEL INN
1400 Roebuck Dr
(39301)
Rates: $33-$40
Tel: (601) 693-2300

ECONO LODGE
2405 S Frontage Rd
(39301)
Rates: $30-$55
Tel: (601) 693-9393
(800) 424-4777

HOLIDAY INN EXPRESS
1401 Roebuck Dr
(39301)
Rates: $41-$46
Tel: (800) 465-4329

MOTEL 6
2309 S Frontage Rd
(39301)
Rates: $29-$33
Tel: (601) 482-1182
(800) 440-6000

RAMADA INN
2915 St. Paul St
(39301)
Rates: $38-$50
Tel: (601) 485-2722
(800) 272-6232

RODEWAY INN
146 US 11/80 (39301)
Rates: $35-$45
Tel: (800) 228-2000

SCOTTISH INNS
1903 S Frontage Rd
(39301)
Rates: $22-$32
Tel: (601) 482-2487
(800) 251-1962

SLEEP INN
1301 Hamilton Ave
(39301)
Rates: $35-$57
Tel: (800) 221-2222

NATCHEZ

DAYS INN
109 US Hwy 61 S
(39120)
Rates: $35-$85
Tel: (601) 445-8291
(800) 329-7466

THE GUEST HOUSE HISTORIC HOTEL BED & BREAKFAST
201 N Pearl St
(39120)
Rates: $79-$94
Tel: (601) 442-1054

HOWARD JOHNSON
45 Prentiss Dr (39120)
Rates: $42-$56
Tel: (601) 442-1691
(800) 446-4656

NATCHEZ EOLA HOTEL
110 N Pearl St
(39120)
Rates: $60-$150
Tel: (800) 888-9140

SCOTTISH INNS
40 Sgt Prentis Dr
(39120)
Rates: $29-$43
Tel: (601) 442-9141
(800) 251-1962

NEWTON

DAYS INN
I-20 & Hwy 15
(39345)
Rates: $36-$54
Tel: (601) 683-3361
(800) 329-7466

OXFORD

HOLIDAY INN
400 N Lamar Ave
(38655)
Rates: $47-$59
Tel: (800) 465-4329

PASCAGOULA

LA FONT INN
2703 Denny Ave
(39568)
Rates: $53-$78
Tel: (601) 762-7111

PHILADELPHIA

DAYS INN
1009 Holland Ave
(39350)
Rates: $55-$75
Tel: (601) 650-3590
(800) 329-7466

RAMADA INN
1011 Holland Ave
(39350)
Rates: $50-$60
Tel: (601) 656-1223
(800) 272-6232

RICHLAND

DAYS INN
1035 Hwy 49 S
(39218)
Rates: $55-$85
Tel: (601) 932-5553
(800) 329-7466

RIDGELAND

RED ROOF INN
810 Adcock St
(39157)
Rates: $39-$49
Tel: (601) 956-7707
(800) 843-7663

SARDIS

**BEST WESTERN
SARDIS INN**
P. O. Box 279 (38666)
Rates: $39-$52
Tel: (601) 487-2424
(800) 528-1234

STARKVILLE

HAMPTON INN
700 Highway 12
(39759)
Rates: $54-$64
Tel: (800) 426-7866

HOLIDAY INN
P. O. Box 751 (39759)
Rates: $42-$60
Tel: (800) 465-4329

TUPELO

HAMPTON INN
1516 McCullough
Blvd (38801)
Rate: $54-$64
Tel: (601) 840-8300
(800) 426-7866

VICKSBURG

**BELLE OF THE
BENDS B & B**
508 Klein St (39108)
Rates: $95-$150
Tel: (601) 634-0737
(800) 844-2308

THE CORNERS B&B
601 Klein St (39180)
Rates: $75-$105
Tel: (800) 444-7421

**DUFF GREEN
MANSION INN B&B**
1114 First East St
(39180)
Rates: $55-$160
Tel: (800) 992-0037

HAMPTON INN
3330 Clay St (39180)
Rates: $53-$63
Tel: (601) 636-6100
(800) 426-7866

PARK INN
4137 I-20 (39180)
Rates: $50-$70
Tel: (601) 638-5811

RAMADA INN
4216 Washington St
(39180)
Rates: $40-$105
Tel: (601) 638-5750
(800) 272-6232

SUPER 8 MOTEL
4127 I-20 Frontage
Rd (39180)
Rates: $41-$61
Tel: (601) 638-5077
(800) 800-8000

MISSOURI

AFFTON

OAK GROVE INN
6602 S Lindbergh
Blvd (63123)
Rates: $34-$42
Tel: (314) 894-9449

ALBANY

EASTWOOD MOTEL
US 136E (64402)
Rates: $22-$33
Tel: (816) 726-5208

ARNOLD

DRURY INN
1201 Drury Ln
(63010)
Rates: $49-$65
Tel: (800) 325-8300

WHITE WING RESORT
P. O. Box 840 (65616)
Rates: $42-$53
Tel: (417) 338-2318

AURORA

AURORA INN MOTEL
Rt 3, Box 200 (65605)
Rates: $36-$42
Tel: (417) 678-5035

BERKLEY

QUALITY HOTEL
9600 Natural Bridge
Rd (63134)
Rates: $58-$73
Tel: (314) 427-7600

BETHANEY

BEST WESTERN I-35 INN
Rt 1, Box 249B
(64424)
Rates: $39-$59
Tel: (816) 425-7915
(800) 528-1234

BIRCH TREE

HICKORY HOUSE MOTOR INN
P. O. Box 306 (65438)
Rates: $20-$32
Tel: (314) 292-3232

BLUE SPRINGS

MOTEL 6
901 W Jefferson St
(64015)
Rates: $23-$29
Tel: (816) 228-9133
(800) 440-6000

RAMADA LIMITED
1110 N 7 Hwy
(64014)
Rates: $50-$85
Tel: (816) 229-6363
(800) 272-6232

BOLIVAR

SUPER 8 MOTEL
1919 S Killingsworth
Ave (65613)
Rates: $38-$57
Tel: (417) 777-8888
(800) 800-8000

BOURBON

BUDGET INN MOTEL
I-44 & Hwy C (65441)
Rates: $23-$36
Tel: (314) 732-4626

BRANSON

BARRINGTON HOTEL
263 Shepherd of the
Hills Expy (65616)
Rates: n/a
Tel: (417) 334-8866

BEST WESTERN BRANSON INN
P.O. Box 676 (65615)
Rates: $45-$70
Tel: (417) 334-5121
(800) 334-5121

BEST WESTERN BRANSON RUSTIC OAK INN
403 W Main (65616)
Rates: $35-$99
Tel: (417) 334-6464
(800) 528-1234

BIG VALLEY MOTEL
2005 W Hwy 76
(65616)
Rates: $45-$76
Tel: (417) 334-7676
(800) 332-7274

BRANSON GRAND RAMADA
245 N Wildwood
(65616)
Rates: $50-$80
Tel: (417) 336-6646

BRANSON LODGE
2456 SR 165 (65616)
Rates: $40-$68
Tel: (417) 334-3105

BRIGHTON PLACE MOTEL
3514 W Hwy 76
(65616)
Rates: $40-$58
Tel: (417) 334-5510

COLONIAL MOUNTAIN INN
P. O. Box 2068
(65737)
Rates: $30-$50
Tel: (417) 272-8414

COUNTRY MUSIC INN
3060 Green Mtn Dr
(65616)
Rates: $49-$69
Tel: (417) 336-3300

DAYS INN
3524 Keeter St
(65616)
Rates: $43-$96
Tel: (417) 334-5544
(800) 329-7466

FAIRFIELD INN BY MARRIOT
220 SR 165 S (65616)
Rates: $31-$66
Tel: (417) 336-5665

GOOD SHEPHERD INN
1023 W Hwy 76
(65616)
Rates: $29-$60
Tel: (417) 334-1695

HOWARD JOHNSON
3027-A W Hwy 76
(65616)
Rates: $69-$89
Tel: (417) 336-5151
(800) 446-4656

LAKESHORE RESORT
1773 Lakeshore Dr
(65616)
Rates: $57-$135
Tel: (417) 334-6262

LIGHTHOUSE INN
2375 Green Mtn Dr
(65616)
Rates: $48-$88
Tel: (417) 336-6161

QUALITY INN
3269 Shepherd of the
Hills Expy (65616)
Rates: $59-$62
Tel: (417) 335-6776

RESIDENCE INN BY MARRIOT
280 Wildwood Dr S
(65616)
Rates: $49-$139
Tel: (417) 336-4077

RODEWAY INN - SOUTH
2422 Shepherd of the
Hills Expy (65616)
Rates: $50-$150
Tel: (417) 336-5577
(800) 228-2000

RAMADA LIMITED
2316 Shepherd of the
Hills Expy (65616)
Rates: $50-$75
Tel: (417) 337-5207
(800) 272-6232

ROCK VIEW MOTEL
1049 Park View Dr
(65672)
Rates: $40-$70
Tel: (417) 334-4678

SETTLE INN
3050 Green Mtn Dr
(65616)
Rates: $35-$72
Tel: (417) 335-4700

TANEY MOTEL
311 Hwy 65N
Business (65616)
Rates: $30-$59
Tel: (417) 334-3143

WELK RESORT CTR
1984 SR 165 (65616)
Rates: $75-$79
Tel: (417) 336-3575

WHITE WING RESORT
Lake Rd 76-60
(65616)
Rates: $28-$53
Tel: (417) 338-2318

BRANSON WEST

**RUSTIC GATE
MOTOR INN**
US 76 & SR 13
(65737)
Rates: $33-$46
Tel: (417) 272-3326

BRIDGETON

BRIDGEPORT INN
4199 N Lindbergh
Blvd (63044)
Rates: $24-$34
Tel: (314) 739-4600

ECONO LODGE
4575 N Lindbergh
Blvd (63044)
Rates: $35-$46
Tel: (314) 731-3000
(800) 424-4777

**HOLIDAY INN-
AIRPORT**
4545 N Lindbergh
Blvd (63044)
Rates: $73-$83
Tel: (800) 465-4329

KNIGHTS INN
12433 St Charles
Rock Rd (63044)
Rates: $32-$48
Tel: (800) 843-5644

MOTEL 6
3655 Pennridge Dr
(63044)
Rates: $32-$39
Tel: (314) 291-6100
(800) 466-8356

**SCOTTISH INNS-
AIRPORT**
4645 N Lindbergh
Blvd (63044)
Rates: $32-$42
Tel: (314) 731-1010
(800) 251-1962

BROOKFIELD

COUNTRY INN
800 S Main St (64628)
Rates: $31-$36
Tel: (816) 258-7262

BUTLER

SUPER 8 MOTEL
Rt 3, Box 74 (64730)
Rates: $36-$50
Tel: (816) 679-6183
(800) 800-8000

CAMDENTON

LAN-O-LAK MOTEL
P. O. Box 619 (65020)
Rates: $38-$55
Tel: (314) 346-2256

CAMERON

**BEST WESTERN
ACORN INN**
P. O. Box 436 (64429)
Rates: $38-$56
Tel: (816) 632-2187
(800) 528-1234

**BEST WESTERN
RAMBLER MOTEL**
P. O. Box 469 (64429)
Rates: $33-$45
Tel: (816) 632-6571

**COUNTRY SQUIRE
INN**
501 Northland Dr
(64429)
Rates: $25-$33
Tel: (816) 632-6623

CAPE GIRARDEAU

DRURY LODGE
104 S Vantage
(63701)
Rates: $55-$68
Tel: (314) 334-7151

DRURY SUITES
3303 Campster
(63701)
Rates: $69-$84
Tel: (314) 339-9500

HAMPTON INN
103 Cape West Pkwy
(63701)
Rates: $47-$54
Tel: (314) 651-3000
(800) 426-7866

HOLIDAY INN
P. O. Box 1570
(63701)
Rates: $74-$80
Tel: (800) 465-4329

SANDS MOTEL
1448 N Kings Hwy
(63701)
Rates: $27-$37
Tel: (314) 334-2828

PEAR TREE INN
3248 William St
(63701)
Rates: $34-$49
Tel: (314) 334-3000

VICTORIAN INN
3249 William St
(63701)
Rates: $39-$61
Tel: (314) 651-4486

CARTHAGE

DAYS INN
2244 Grand Ave
(64836)
Rates: $33-$44
Tel: (417) 358-2499

ECONO LODGE
1441 W Central
(64836)
Rates: $43-$60
Tel: (417) 358-3900
(800) 424-4777

CASSVILLE

HOLIDAY MOTEL
85 S Main St (65625)
Rates: $32-$39
Tel: (417) 847-3163

SUPER 8 MOTEL
Hwy 37 (65625)
Rates: $39-$54
Tel: (417) 847-4888
(800) 800-8000

**TOWNHOUSE
MOTEL**
HCR 81, Box 9570
(65625)
Rates: $28-$38
Tel: (417) 847-4196

CHARLESTON

CHARLESTON INN
310 S Story (63834)
Rates: $37-$40
Tel: (314) 683-2125

CHESTERFIELD

**RESIDENCE INN
BY MARRIOTT**
15431 Conway Rd
(63017)
Rates: $69-$109
Tel: (314) 537-1444l
(800) 331-3131

CHILLICOTHE

BEST WESTERN INN
1020 S Washington
(64601)
Rates: $41-$58
Tel: (816) 646-0572
(800) 528-1234

GRAND RIVER INN
606 W Business 36
(64601)
Rates: $47-$60
Tel: (816) 646-6590

TRAVEL INN
901 Hwy 36W
(64601)
Rates: $32-$42
Tel: (816) 646-0784

CLARKSVILLE

CLARKSVILLE INN
2nd & Lewis Sts
(63336)
Rates: $29-$41
Tel: (314) 242-3324

CLAYTON

THE DANIELE
216 N Meramec
(63105)
Rates: $75-$129
Tel: (314) 721-0101

SEVEN GABLES INN
26 N Meramec
(63105)
Rates: $85-$130
Tel: (314) 863-8400

CLINTON

BEST WESTERN COLONIAL
On MO 13 Bypass
(64735)
Rates: $26-$47
Tel: (800) 528-1234

SAFARI MOTEL
1505 N 2nd St
(64735)
Rates: $28-$41
Tel: (816) 885-3395

COLUMBIA

BUDGETEL INN
2500 I-70 Dr SW
(65203)
Rates: $32-$48
Tel: (314) 445-1899

BUDGET HOST CROSSWAYS INN
900 Vandiver Dr
(65202)
Rates: $27-$50
Tel: (800) 283-4678

DAYS INN CONFERENCE CENTER
1900 I-70 Dr SW
(65203)
Rates: $34-$70
Tel: (314) 445-8511
(800) 329-7466

DRURY INN
1000 Knipp St
(65203)
Rates: $59-$74
Tel: (800) 325-8300

ECONO LODGE
900 I-70 Dr SW
(65203)
Rates: $37-$55
Tel: (573) 442-1191
(800) 424-4777

HOLIDAY INN EAST- HOLIDOME
1612 N Providence
Rd (65202)
Rates: $59-$69
Tel: (314) 449-2491

HOLIDAY INN EXECUTIVE CENTER
2200 I-70 Dr SW
(65203)
Rates: $66-$92
Tel: (800) 465-4329

MOTEL 6-EAST
1718 N Providence
Rd (65202)
Rates: $24-$30
Tel: (314) 442-9390
(800) 440-6000

MOTEL 6-WEST
1800 I-70 Dr SW
(65203)
Rates: $24-$30
Tel: (314) 445-8433
(800) 440-6000

RAMADA INN
111 E Broadway
(65201)
Rates: $49-$89
Tel: (573) 443-2090
(800) 272-6232

RAMADA INN & CONF CENTER
1100 Vandiver Dr
(65202)
Rates: $51-$99
Tel: (573) 449-0051
(800) 272-6232

RED ROOF INN
201 E Texas Ave
(65202)
Rates: $31-$41
Tel: (314) 442-0145
(800) 843-7663

SCOTTISH INNS
2112 Business Loop
70 E (65201)
Rates: $25-$50
Tel: (314) 449-3771
(800) 251-1962

CONCORDIA

BEST WESTERN HEIDELBERG INN
406 W Williams St
(64020)
Rates: $40-$66
Tel: (816) 463-2114
(800) 528-1234

CONCORDIA INN
200 N West St
(64020)
Rates: $24-$42
Tel: (816) 463-7987

CUBA

BEST WESTERN INN
Rt 2, Box 284 (65453)
Rates: $34-$52
Tel: (573) 885-7707
(800) 528-1234

DEXTER

DEXTER INN
1707 Business 60W
(63841)
Rates: $34-$41
Tel: (573) 624-7465

DONIPHAN

ECONO LODGE
109 Smith Dr (63935)
Rates: $28-$36
Tel: (800) 424-4777

TIN LIZZIE MOTEL
Hwy 160 (63935)
Rates: n/a
Tel: (314) 996-2101

EAGLE ROCK

EAGLE ROCK RESORT
HCR 01, Box 1593
(65641)
Rates: n/a
Tel: (417) 271-3222

FLETCHER'S DEVIL'S DIVE RESORT
HCR 01, Box 8
(65641)
Rates: n/a
Tel: (417) 271-3396

LAZY EAGLE RESORT
P. O. Box 141 (65641)
Rates: n/a
Tel: (417) 271-3390
(800) 232-4783

EDMUNDSON

DRURY INN-AIRPORT
10490 Natural
Bridge (63134)
Rates: $69-$84
Tel: (800) 325-8300

MARRIOTT HOTEL-AIRPORT
10700 Pear Tree
(63134)
Rates: $59-$109
Tel: (314) 423-9700

EL DORADO SPRINGS

EL DORADO MOTEL
102 Hwy 54 East
(64744)
Rates: n/a
Tel: (417) 876-6888

ELLINGTON

SCENIC RIVERS MOTEL
231 N 2nd St (63638)
Rates: $29-$37
Tel: (314) 663-7722

EUREKA

DAYS INN-SIX FLAGS
15 Hilltop Village
Ctr (63025)
Rates: $39-$195
Tel: (314) 938-5565
(800) 329-7466

OAK GROVE INN
1733 W 5th St (63025)
Rates: $26-$55
Tel: (314) 938-4368

RAMADA INN-SIX FLAGS
4901 Allenton Rd (63025)
Rates: $54-$129
Tel: (314) 938-6661
(800) 272-6232

RED CARPET INN-SIX FLAGS
1725 W 5th St (63025)
Rates: $27-$39
Tel: (800) 251-1962

FARMINGTON

BEST WESTERN TRADITION INN
1627 W Columbia (63640)
Rates: $47-$58
Tel: (573) 756-8031
(800) 528-1234

FENTON

DRURY INN
1088 S Hwy Dr (63026)
Rates: $55-$71
Tel: (800) 325-8300

MOTEL 6
1860 Bowles Ave (63026)
Rates: $36-46
Tel: (314) 349-1800
(800) 466-8356

PEAR TREE INN
1100 S Hwy Dr (63026)
Rates: $50-$65
Tel: (314) 343-8820

FESTUS

BUDGETEL INN
1303 Veterans Blvd (63028)
Rates: $38-$49
Tel: (314) 937-2888

DRURY INN
1001 Veterans Blvd (63028)
Rates: $43-$58
Tel: (800) 325-8300

FLAT RIVER

ROSENER'S INN
Hwy 67 N (63601)
Rates: $29-$45
Tel: (314) 431-4241

FLORISSANT

RED ROOF INN
307 Dunn Rd (63031)
Rates: $38-$49
Tel: (800) 843-7663

FORISTELL

BEST WESTERN WEST 70 INN
Rt W, Box 10 (63348)
Rates: $30-$50
Tel: (314) 673-2900
(800) 528-1234

FREDERICK-TOWN

ECONO LODGE
740 Madison Plaza Dr (63645)
Rates: $44-$59
Tel: (573) 783-2500
(800) 424-4777

LONGHORN MOTEL
P. O. Box 721 (63645)
Rates: $19-$34
Tel: (314) 783-3363

FULTON

BUDGET HOST WESTWOODS MOTEL
422 Gaylord Dr (65251)
Rates: $28-$36
Tel: (800) 283-4678

GRAIN VALLEY

SCOTTISH INNS
105 Sunny Lane Dr (64029)
Rates: $26-$43
Tel: (816) 224-3420
(800) 251-1962

GRAVOIS MILLS

MILLSTONE LODGE RESORT
Rt 1, Box 515 (65037)
Rates: $60-$299
Tel: (314) 372-5111

HANNIBAL

DAYS INN
4070 Market St (63401)
Rates: $30-$60
Tel: (314) 248-1700
(800) 329-7466

HOWARD JOHNSON
3603 McMasters Ave (63401)
Rates: $35-$75
Tel: (314) 221-7950
(800) 446-4656

HARRISONVILLE

BEST WESTERN
P. O. Box 363 (64701)
Rates: $40-$65
Tel: (816) 884-3200
(800) 528-1234

CARAVAN MOTEL
1705 Hwy 291 N (64701)
Rates: $30-$37
Tel: (816) 884-4100

SLUMBER INN MOTEL
Rt 3, Box 611-D (64701)
Rates: $22-$35
Tel: (816) 884-3100

HAZELWOOD

BUDGETEL
318 Taylor D (63042)
Rates: $37-$55
Tel: (314) 731-4200

LA QUINTA-AIRPORT
5781 Campus St (63042)
Rates: $45-$59
Tel: (800) 531-5900

HAYTI

DRURY INN
I-55 & Rt 84 (63851)
Rates: $49-$61
Tel: (800) 325-8300

HIGGINSVILLE

BEST WESTERN CAMELOT INN
Rt 2, Box 231 (64037)
Rates: $35-$60
Tel: (816) 584-3646
(800) 528-1234

SUPER 8 MOTEL
P. O. Box 306 (64037)
Rates: $40-$53
Tel: (816) 584-7781
(800) 800-8000

HOLLISTER

ECONO LODGE
US 65 (65672)
Rates: $33-$42
Tel: (417) 334-2770
(800) 424-4777

ROCK VIEW RESORT
HCR 2, Box 870 (65672)
Rates: $46-$63
Tel: (417) 334-4678

HOLTS SUMMIT

RAMADA INN
Hwy 54 (65043)
Rates: $49-$65
Tel: (573) 896-8787

INDEPENDENCE

HOWARD JOHNSON
4200 S Noland Rd
(64055)
Rates: $51-$77
Tel: (816) 373-8856
(800) 446-4656

RED ROOF INN
13712 E 42nd Ter
(64055)
Rates: $37-$41
Tel: (800) 843-7663

SUPER 8 MOTEL
4032 S Lynn Court
Dr (64055)
Rates: $38-$60
Tel: (816) 833-1888
(800) 800-8000

ISABELLA

LAKEPOINT RESORT
HCR 1, Box 1152
(65676)
Rates: $42-$47
Tel: (417) 273-4343

JACKSON

DAYS INN
517 Jackson Blvd
(63755)
Rates: $40-$75
Tel: (314) 243-3579
(800) 329-7466

JEFFERSON CITY

**CAPITOL PLAZA
HOTEL**
415 W McCarty St
(65101)
Rates: $79-$130
Tel (314) 635-1234

HOTEL DEVILLE
319 W Miller St
(65101)
Rates: $50-$57
Tel: (314) 636-5231

HOWARD JOHNSON
422 Monroe St
(65101)
Rates: $55-$75
Tel: (314) 636-5101
(800) 446-4656

MOTEL 6-SOUTH
1624 Jefferson St
(65109)
Rates: $28-$34
Tel: (314) 634-4220
(800) 440-6000

JOPLIN

**BEST INNS
OF AMERICA**
3508 Range Line Rd
(64804)
Rates: $39-$48
Tel: (417) 781-6776

**BEST WESTERN
SANDS INN**
1611 Range Line Rd
(64801)
Rates: $43-$65
Tel: (417) 624-8300
(800) 528-1234

CAPRI MOTEL
3401 South Main
(64804)
Rates: n/a
Tel: (417) 623-0391

DRURY INN
3601 Range Line Rd
(64804)
Rates: $62-$82
Tel: (417) 781-8000

HOWARD JOHNSON
3510 Range Line Rd
(64804)
Rates: $40-$60
Tel: (417) 623-0000
(800) 446-4656

MOTEL 6
3031 Range Line Rd
(64804)
Rates: $30-$36
Tel: (417) 781-6400
(800) 440-6000

RAMADA INN
3320 Range Line Rd
(64804)
Rates: $54-$72
Tel: (417) 781-0500

SLEEP INN
I-44 & St Hwy 43 S
(64804)
Rates: $39-$59
Tel: (417) 782-1212

SUPER 8 MOTEL
2830 E 36th St
(64804)
Rates: $38-$63
Tel: (417) 782-8765
(800) 800-8000

TROPICANA MOTEL
2417 Range Line Rd
(64804)
Rates: $26-$32
Tel: (417) 624-8200

WESTWOOD MOTEL
170 W 30th St (64804)
Rates: $29-$38
Tel: (417) 782-7212

KANSAS CITY

**AMERICAN INN
MOTEL**
1211 Armour Rd
(64118)
Rates: $30-$45
Tel: (816) 471-3451

AMERICANA HOTEL
1301 Wyandotte St
(64105)
Rates: $59-$77
Tel: (816) 221-8800

**BEST WESTERN INN
AND CONF CTR**
501 Southwest Blvd
(66103)
Rates: $59-$77
Tel: (816) 677-3060

BUDGETEL INN
8601 Hillcrest Rd
(64136)
Rates: $37-$49
Tel: (816) 822-7000

**BUDGETEL INN-
NORTH**
2214 Taney St
(64116)
Rates: $35-$52
Tel: (816) 221-1200

DAYS INN-SOUTH
11801 Blueridge
Blvd (64134)
Rates: $36-$55
Tel: (816) 765-1888

DRURY INN-STADIUM
3830 Blue Ridge
Cutoff (64133)
Rates: $58-$73
Tel: (800) 325-8300

**EMBASSY SUITES
HOTEL-AIRPORT**
7640 New Tiffany
Springs Pkwy
(64153)
Rates: $89-$139
Tel: (816) 891-7788

**HISTORIC SUITES
OF AMERICA**
612 Central Ave
(64105)
Rates: $89-$190
Tel: (816) 842-6544

**HOLIDAY INN
CITY CENTRE**
1215 Wayandote St
(64105)
Rates: $63-$78
Tel: (800) 465-4329

HOLIDAY INN
11832 Plaza Circle
NW (64153)
Rates: $50-$60
Tel: (800) 465-4329

INN TOWNE LODGE
2620 NE 43rd St
(64117)
Rates: $40-$55
Tel: (816) 453-6550

**MARRIOTT HOTEL-
AIRPORT**
775 Brasilia Ave
(64153)
Rates: $54-$143
Tel: (816) 464-2200

**MARRIOTT
DOWNTOWN**
200 W 12th St
(64105)
Rates: $85-$150
Tel: (816) 421-6800

MOTEL 6
6400 E 87th St
(64138)
Rates: $32-$38
Tel: (816) 333-4468
(800) 440-6000

MOTEL 6-NORTH
8230 NW Prairie
View Rd (64152)
Rates: $30-$36
Tel: (816) 741-6400
(800) 440-6000

RADISSON SUITE HOTEL
106 W 12th St
(64105)
Rates: $89-$109
Tel: (800) 333-3333

RAMADA INN
1600 NE Parvin Rd
(64116)
Rates: $39-$54
Tel: (816) 453-5210
(800) 272-6232

RED ROOF INN-NORTH
3636 NE Randolph
Rd (64161)
Rates: $27-$50
Tel: (816) 452-8585
(800) 843-7663

RESIDENCE INN BY MARRIOTT
9900 NW Prairie
View Rd (64153)
Rates: $59-$115
Tel: (816) 891-9009
(800) 331-3131

RESIDENCE INN BY MARRIOTT
2975 Main St (64108)
Rates: $105-$145
Tel: (816) 561-3000
(800) 331-3131

RAMADA HOTEL AIRPORT
7301 New Tiffany
Spgs Rd (64153)
Rates: $32-$74
Tel: (800) 234-9501

SUPER 8 MOTEL-NW
6900 NW 83rd Terr
(64151)
Rates: $38-$61
Tel: (816) 587-0808
(800) 800-8000

TRAVELODGE
1051 N Cambridge
(64120)
Rates: $40-70
Tel: (816) 483-7900
(800) 578-7878

THE WESTIN CROWN CENTER
1 Pershing Rd
(64108)
Rates: $185-$230
Tel: (816) 474-4400
(800) 228-3000

KEARNEY

ECONO LODGE
505 Shanks Ave
(64060)
Rates: $35-$60
Tel: (816) 635-6000
(800) 424-4777

KENNETT

OXFORD INN
110 Independence
(63857)
Rates: $39-$46
Tel: (314) 888-9860

KIMBERLING CITY

KIMBERLING ARMS BEST WESTERN
P. O. Box 429 (65686)
Rates: $44-$79
Tel: (417) 739-2461
(800) 528-1234

KIMBERLING HEIGHTS RESORT MOTEL
HCR 4, Box 980
(65686)
Rates: $39-$58
Tel: (417) 779-4158

KIRKSVILLE

BEST WESTERN SHAMROCK INN
P. O. Box 1005
(63501)
Rates: $48-$56
Tel: (816) 665-8352
(800) 528-1234

BUDGET HOST VILLAGE INN
1304 S Baltimore
(63501)
Rates: $31-$38
Tel: (800) 283-4678

COMFORT INN
2209 N Baltimore
(63501)
Rates: $37-$45
Tel: (800) 221-2222

DAYS INN
P. O. Box M (63501)
Rates: $48-$60
Tel: (816) 665-8244
(800) 329-7466

KIRKWOOD

BEST WESTERN INN
1200 S Kirkwood Rd
(63122)
Rates: $57-$87
Tel: (800) 528-1234

KNOB NOSTER

WHITEMAN INN
2340 W Irish Ln
(65336)
Rates: $35-$50
Tel: (816) 563-3000

LAKE ST. LOUIS

DAYS INN
2560 S Outer Rd
(63367)
Rates: $39-$110
Tel: (314) 625-1711
(800) 329-7466

LAKEVIEW

COLONIAL MOUNTAIN INN
P. O. Box 2068 (65737)
Rates: $36-$55
Tel: (417) 272-8414

RUSTIC GATE MOTOR INN
P. O. Box 1088
(65737)
Rates: $32-$50
Tel: (417) 272-3326

LAMAR

BEST WESTERN BLUE TOP INN
65 SE 1st Ln (64759)
Rates: $32-$42
Tel: (417) 682-3333
(800) 528-1234

LEBANON

BEST WESTERN WYOTA INN
P. O. Box 9 (65536)
Rates: $36-$52
Tel: (417) 532-6171
(800) 528-1234

BRENTWOOD MOTEL
1320 S Jefferson
(65536)
Rates: $29-$36
Tel: (417) 532-6131

ECONO LODGE
P. O. Box 972 (65536)
Rates: $26-$36
Tel: (800) 424-4777

HOLIDAY INN
I-44 W Business
Loop 992 (65536)
Rates: $31-$49
Tel: (417) 588-3226
(800) 465-4329

SHEPHERD HILLS MOTEL
P. O. Box 1100
(65536)
Rates: $28-$38
Tel: (417) 532-3133

LEE'S SUMMIT

BEST WESTERN SUMMIT INN
625 N Murray Rd
(64081)
Rates: $48-$75
Tel: (816) 525-1400
(800) 528-1234

COMFORT INN
607 SE Oldham
Pkwy (64063)
Rates: $40-$59
Tel: (800) 221-2222

FAIRFIELD INN BY MARRIOTT
1301 NE Windsor Dr (64086)
Rates: $41-$59
Tel: (816) 524-7572

LEXINGTON

LEXINGTON INN
Jct US 24 & SR 13 (64067)
Rates: $32-$37
Tel: (816) 259-4641

LIBERTY

SUPER 8 MOTEL
115 N Stewart Rd (64068)
Rates: $37-$57
Tel: (816) 781-9400
(800) 800-8000

LOUISIANA

RIVER'S EDGE MOTEL
201 Mansion St (63353)
Rates: $27-$39
Tel: (314) 754-4522

MACON

BEST WESTERN INN
28933 Sunset Dr (63552)
Rates: $41-$48
Tel: (816) 385-2125
(800) 528-1234

SUPER 8 MOTEL
1420 N Rutherford St #2A (63552)
Rates: $41-$54
Tel: (816) 385-5788
(800) 800-8000

MARYLAND HEIGHTS

BEST WESTERN WESTPORT PARK
2434 Old Dorsett Rd (63043)
Rates: $64-$109
Tel: (314) 291-8700
(800) 528-1234

BUDGETEL INN
12330 Dorsett Rd (63043)
Rates: $38-$54
Tel: (314) 878-1212

DRURY INN
12220 Dorsett Rd (63043)
Rates: $59-$71
Tel: (800) 325-8300

HOLIDAY INN
1973 Craigshire (63146)
Rates: n/a
Tel: (800) 465-4329

COMFORT INN
12031 Lackland Rd (63146)
Rates: $49
Tel: (800) 272-6232

RED ROOF INN
11837 Lackland Rd (63146)
Rates: $36-$50
Tel: (314) 991-4900
(800) 843-7663

MARYVILLE

SUPER 8 MOTEL
Business Hwy 71 S (64468)
Rates: $38-$45
Tel: (816) 582-8088
(800) 800-8000

MEHLVILLE

OAK GROVE INN
6602 S Lindbergh Blvd (63123)
Rates: $38-$55
Tel: (314) 894-9449

MEXICO

BEST WESTERN STEPHENSON
1010 E Liberty St (65265)
Rates: $36-$48
Tel: (800) 528-1234

MOBERLY

KNOLL MOTEL
P. O. Box 146 (65270)
Rates: $28-$32
Tel: (816) 263-5000

RAMADA INN
Jct US 24 & 63 (65270)
Rates: $47-$57
Tel: (816) 263-6540
(800) 272-6232

MONETT

HARTLAND LODGE
929 Hwy 60E (65708)
Rates: $37-$43
Tel: (417) 235-4000

OXFORD INN
868 Hwy 60 (65708)
Rates: $42-$47
Tel: (417) 235-8039

MONROE CITY

ECONO LODGE
3 Gateway Sq.(63456)
Rates: $29-$55
Tel: (573) 735-4200
(800) 424-4777

MOUND CITY

AUDREY'S MOTEL
RR 2, Box 231 (64470)
Rates: $26-$38
Tel: (816) 442-3191

MOUNT VERNON

BEST WESTERN BELAIRE MOTOR INN
740 E Mt. Vernon (65712)
Rates: $37-$52
Tel: (417) 466-2111
(800) 528-1234

BUDGET HOST RANCH MOTEL
Rt 1, Box 68 (65712)
Rates: $32-$46
Tel: (800) 283-4678

MOUNTAIN GROVE

BEST WESTERN RANCH HOUSE INN
111 E 17th St (65711)
Rates: $36-$59
Tel: (417) 926-3152
(800) 528-1234

DAYS INN
300 E 19th St (65711)
Rates: $40-$70
Tel: (417) 926-5555
(800) 329-7466

NEOSHO

HARTLAND LODGE
1400 71 S (64850)
Rates: $38-$46
Tel: (417) 451-3784

NEOSHO INN
2500 S 71 Hwy (64850)
Rates: $42-$48
Tel: (417) 451-6500

NEVADA

BEST WESTERN RAMBLER MOTEL
1401 E Austin (64772)
Rates: $36-$48
Tel: (417) 667-3351
(800) 528-1234

COMFORT INN
2345 Marvel Dr
(64772)
Rates: $40-$50
Tel: (800) 221-2222

**RAMSEY'S
NEVADA MOTEL**
1514 E Austin
(64772)
Rates: $30-$38
Tel: (417) 667-5273

SUPER 8 MOTEL
2301 E Austin
(64772)
Rates: $36-$50
Tel: (417) 667-8888
(800) 800-8000

NIXA

SUPER 8 MOTEL
418 Massey Blvd
(65714)
Rates: $39-$52
Tel: (417) 725-0880

OAK GROVE

DAYS INN
101 N Locust (64075)
Rates: $45-$75
Tel: (816) 625-8686
(800) 329-7466

ECONO LODGE
410 SE 1st St (64075)
Rates: $32-$60
Tel: (816) 625-3681
(800) 424-4777

OVERLAND PARK

EMBASSY SUITES
10601 Metcalf Ave
(66212)
Rates: $109-$154
Tel: (913) 649-7060

OZARK

DAYS INN
900 N 18th St (65721)
Rates: $39-$69
Tel: (417) 581-5800

**HOLIDAY INN
EXPRESS**
1900 W Evangel St
(65721)
Rates: $43-$61
Tel: (417) 485-6688

SUPER 8 MOTEL
299 N 20th (65721)
Rates: $36-$61
Tel: (417) 581-8800
(800) 800-8000

PACIFIC

**HOLIDAY INN
EXPRESS**
1400 W Osage St
(63069)
Rates: $59-$110
Tel: (314) 257-8400

PALMYRA

HILLCREST INN
423 E Lafayette
(63461)
Rates: $29-$38
Tel: (314) 769-2007

PERRYVILLE

BUDGET HOST INN
221 S Kings Hwy
(63775)
Rates: $24-$38
Tel: (800) 283-4678

PLATTE CITY

**BEST WESTERN
AIRPORT INN**
P. O. Box 319 (64079)
Rates: $42-$72
Tel: (816) 858-4588
(800) 528-1234

COMFORT INN
1200 Hwy 92 (64079)
Rates: $47-$62
Tel: (800) 221-2222

POPLAR BLUFF

DRURY INN
2220 N Westwood
Blvd (63901)
Rates: $49-$59
Tel: (800) 325-8300

HOLIDAY INN
2115 N Westwood
Blvd (63901)
Rates: $45-$63
Tel: (800) 465-4329

PEAR TREE INN
2218 N Westwood
Blvd (63901)
Rates: $38-$46
Tel: (314) 785-7100

PORTAGEVILLE

TEROY MOTEL
903 Hwy 61 N
(63873)
Rates: $27-$32
Tel: (314) 379-5461

REEDS SPRING

**KING'S KOVE
RESORT**
Rt 5, Box 498A
(65737)
Rates: $60
Tel: (417) 739-4513

RICH HILL

APACHE MOTEL
Rt 3, Box 309A
(64779)
Rates: $24-$30
Tel: (417) 395-2161

ROCKAWAY BEACH

EDEN ROC RESORT
607 Beach Blvd
(65740)
Rates: $25-$38
Tel: (417) 561-4163

KENNY'S COURT
P. O. Box 87 (65740)
Rates: $29-$45
Tel: (417) 561-4131

ROCK PORT

ROCK PORT INN
Rt 4, Box 218 (64482)
Rates: $32-$41
Tel: (816) 744-6282

ROLLA

BESTWAY INN
1631 Martin Springs
Dr (65401)
Rates: $18-$29
Tel: (314) 341-2158

**BEST WESTERN
COACHLIGHT**
1403 Martin Springs
Dr (65401)
Rates: $49-$66
Tel: (573) 341-2511
(800) 528-1234

DAYS INN
1207 Kings Hwy
(65401)
Rates: $40-$60
Tel: (573) 341-3700
(800) 329-7466

DRURY INN
2006 N Bishop
(65401)
Rates: $47-$64
Tel: (800) 325-8300

ECONO LODGE
1417 Martin Springs
Dr (65401)
Rates: $30-$50
Tel: (573) 341-3130
(800) 424-4777

HOWARD JOHNSON
127 H J Dr (65401)
Rates: $44-$66
Tel: (314) 364-7111
(800) 446-4656

TRAVELODGE
1605 Martin Springs
Dr (65401)
Rates: $37-$58
Tel: (314) 341-3050
(800) 578-7878

ST. CHARLES

BUDGETEL INN
1425 S 5th St (63301)
Rates: $34-$59
Tel: (314) 946-6936

COMFORT INN-AIRPORT
2750 Plaza Way
(63303)
Rates: $44-$55
Tel: (800) 221-2222

KNIGHTS INN
3800 Harry S
Truman Blvd (63301)
Rates: $33-$50
Tel: (800) 843-5644

MONARCH BUDGET MOTEL
3717 I-70 (63303)
Rates: $22-$32
Tel: (314) 724-3717

RED ROOF INNS
2010 Zumbehl Rd
(63303)
Rates: $34-$48
Tel: (314) 947-7770
(800) 843-7663

ST. CLAIR

BUDGET LODGING
866 Service Rd
(63077)
Rates: $33-$47
Tel: (314) 629-1000

STE. GENEVIEVE

FAMILY BUDGET INNS
17030 New Bremen
(63670)
Rates: $33-$55
Tel: (314) 543-2272

ST. JOSEPH

BEST WESTERN CLASSIC INN
4502 S I-69 (64507)
Rates: $47-$65
Tel: (816) 232-2345
(800) 528-1234

DAYS INN
4312 Frederick Blvd
(64506)
Rates: $35-$50
Tel: (800) 329-7466

DRURY INN
4213 Frederick Blvd
(64506)
Rates: $44-$59
Tel: (800) 325-8300

HOLIDAY INN-DOWNTOWN
102 S Third St
(64501)
Rates: $60-$62
Tel: (800) 465-4329

MOTEL 6
4021 Frederick Blvd
(64506)
Rates: $32-$36
Tel: (816) 232-2311
(800) 440-6000

RAMADA INN
4016 Frederick Blvd
(64506)
Rates: $59-$85
Tel: (816) 233-6192
(800) 272-6232

ST. LOUIS
(and Vicinity)

BEST WESTERN 55 - SOUTH INN
6224 Heimos
Industrial Pk (63129)
Rates: $65-$120
Tel: (314) 961-1361
(800) 528-1234

COMFORT INN
12031 Lackland Rd
(63146)
Rates: $39-$69
Tel: (800) 221-2222

DAYS INN-AIRPORT
4545 Woodson Rd
(63134)
Rates: $43-$70
Tel: (314) 423-6770
(800) 329-7466

DRURY INN GATEWAY ARCH
711 N Broadway
(63102)
Rates: $79-$94
Tel: (800) 325-8300

DRURY INN UNION STATION
201 S 20th St (63103)
Rates: $84-$99
Tel: (800) 325-8300

EMBASSY SUITES
901 N 1st St (63102)
Rates: $130-$150
Tel: (314) 241-4200

HAMPTON INN AIRPORT
10800 Pear Tree Ln
(63074)
Rates: $64-$87
Tel: (314) 427-3400
(800) 426-7866

HAMPTON INN
150 Ludwig Dr,
(Fairview Heights,
IL 62208)
Rates: $61-$73
Tel: (618) 397-9705
(800) 426-7866

HAMPTON INN UNION STATION
2211 Market St
(63103)
Rates: $79-$105
Tel: (314) 241-3200
(800) 426-7866

HOLIDAY INN-RIVERFRONT
200 N 4th St (63102)
Rates: $49-$99
Tel: (800) 465-4329

HOLIDAY INN-FOREST PARK
5915 Wilson Ave
(63110)
Rates: $60-$95
Tel: (800) 465-4329

HOLIDAY INN-SOUTH I-55
4234 Butler Hill Rd
(63129)
Rates: $76-$84
Tel: (800) 465-4329

HOWARD JOHNSON
4530 N Lindbergh
(63044)
Rates: $50-$65
Tel: (314) 731-3800
(800) 446-4656p

MOTEL 6-NE
1405 Dunn Rd
(63138)
Rates: $32-$38
Tel: (314) 869-9400
(800) 440-6000

MOTEL 6-SOUTH
6500 S Lindbergh
Blvd (63123)
Rates: $33-$39
Tel: (314) 892-3664
(800) 440-6000

RAMADA INN
9600 Natural Bridge
Rd (63134)
Rates: $49-$109
Tel: (314) 427-7600
(800) 272-6232

RAMADA INN
6900 N Illinois
(Fairview Heights,
IL, 62208)
Rates: $48-$64
Tel: (618) 632-4747
(800) 272-6232

**RAMADA
HENRY VIII HOTEL**
4690 N Lindbergh
Blvd (63044)
Rates: $69-$94
Tel: (314) 731-3040

**RED ROOF INN-
HAMPTON**
5823 Wilson Ave
(63110)
Rates: $55-$68
Tel: (314) 645-0101
(800) 843-7663

**RESIDENCE INN
BY MARRIOTT-
GALLERIA**
1100 McMorrow Ave
(63117)
Rates: $59-$179
Tel: (314) 862-1900
(800) 331-3131

**RESIDENCE INN
BY MARRIOTT
WESTPORT PLAZA**
1881 Craigshire Rd
(63146)
Rates: $75-$139
Tel: (314) 469-0060
(800) 331-3131

**SHERATON-
WESTPORT INN**
191 West Port Plaza
(63146)
Rates: $70-$129
Tel: (314) 878-1500

**SUMMERFIELD
SUITES HOTEL**
1855 Craigshire Rd
(63146)
Rates: $118-$168
Tel: (314) 878-1555

**SUPER 8 MOTEL-
NORTH**
2790 Target Dr
(63136)
Rates: $39-$53
Tel: (314) 355-7808
(800) 800-8000

ST. ROBERT

ECONO LODGE
309 Hwy 7 (65583)
Rates: $33-$53
Tel: (573) 336-7272
(800) 424-4777

HOWARD JOHNSON
1083 Missouri Ave
(65583)
Rates: $42-$46
Tel: (314) 336-5115
(800) 446-4656

SALEM

SCOTTISH INNS
1005 S Main St
(65560)
Rates: $27-$38
Tel: (314) 729-4191
(800) 251-1962

SEDALIA

**BEST WESTERN
STATE FAIR
MOTOR INN**
3210 S 65 Hwy
(65301)
Rates: $45-$58
Tel: (816) 826-6100
(800) 528-1234

SHELL KNOB

**BASS HAVEN
FAMILY RESORT**
HCR 1, Box 4480E
(65747)
Rates: n/a
Tel: (417) 858-6401

SIKESTON

**BEST WESTERN
COACH HOUSE INN**
220 S Interstate Dr
(63801)
Rates: $47-$80
Tel: (573) 471-9700
(800) 528-1234

DRURY INN
2602 Rear East
Malone (63801)
Rates: $41-$54
Tel: (800) 325-8300

HAMPTON INN
1330 S Main (63801)
Rates: $47-$59
Tel: (573) 471-3930
(800) 426-7866

**HOLIDAY INN
EXPRESS**
2602 Rear E Malone
(63801)
Rates: $52-$64
Tel: (314) 471-4100

SPRINGFIELD

BASS COUNTRY INN
2610 N Glenstone
Ave (65803)
Rates: $44-$175
Rates: (417) 866-6671

**BEST WESTERN
AMBASSADOR INN**
2745 N Glenstone
Ave (65803)
Rates: $51-$58
Tel: (417) 869-0001

**BEST WESTERN
COACH HOUSE INN**
2535 N Glenstone
Ave (65803)
Rates: $42-$67
Tel: (417) 862-0701
(800) 528-1234

**BEST WESTERN
SYCAMORE INN**
203 S Glenstone Ave
(65802)
Rates: $40-$89
Tel: (417) 866-1963
(800) 528-1234

**BUDGET HOST
LOVELAND INN**
2601 N Glenstone
Ave (65803)
Rates: $30-$48
Tel: (417) 865-6565

COMFORT INN
2550 N Glenstone
Ave (65803)
Rates: $60-$85
Tel: (800) 221-2222

**COURTYARD
BY MARRIOTT**
3370 E Battlefield Rd
(65804)
Rates: $69-$74
Tel: (800) 443-6000

DAYS INN
2700 N Glenstone
Ave (65803)
Rates: $36-$55
Tel: (417) 865-5511
(800) 329-7466

DAYS INN
621 W Sunshine
(65807)
Rates: $44-$85
Tel: (417) 862-0153
(800) 329-7466

**HOLIDAY INN
UNIVERSITY PLAZA**
333 John Q
Hammons Pkwy
(65806)
Rates: $71-$84
Tel: (800) 465-4329

HOWARD JOHNSON
2815 N Glenstone
Ave (65803)
Rates: $51-$79
Tel: (417) 869-8246
(800) 446-4656

**MARKHAM INN
OF THE OZARKS**
2820 N Glenstone
Ave (65803)
Rates: $45-$49
Tel: (417) 866-3581

MOTEL 6-NORTH
3114 N Kentwood
(65803)
Rates: $26-$32
Tel: (417) 833-0880
(800) 440-6000

MOTEL 6-SOUTH
2455 N Glenstone
Ave (65803)
Rates: $26-$32
Tel: (417) 869-4343
(800) 440-6000

MOUNT VERNON MOTOR LODGE
2006 S Glenstone
(65804)
Rates: n/a
Tel: (417) 881-2833

RED ROOF INN
2655 N Glenstone
Ave (65803)
Rates: $33-$44
Tel: (417) 831-2100
(800) 843-7663

RESIDENCE INN BY MARRIOTT
1550 E Raynell Pl
(65804)
Rates: $99-$129
Tel: (417) 883-7300
(800) 331-3131

SATELLITE MOTEL
2305 N Glenstone
Ave (65803)
Rates: $25-$42
Tel: (417) 869-2527

SCOTTISH INNS
2933 N Glenstone
Ave (65803)
Rates: $34-$42
Tel: (417) 862-4301
(800) 251-1962

SHERATON HAWTHORN PARK
2431 N Glenstone
Ave (65803)
Rates: $69-$99
Tel: (417) 831-3131

SKYLINE MOTEL
2120 N Glenstone
Ave (65803)
Rates: $28-$112
Tel: (417) 866-4356

SUPER 8 MOTEL
3022 N Kentwood
Ave (65803)
Rates: $32-$58
Tel: (417) 833-9218
(800) 800-8000

STRAFFORD

SUPER 8 MOTEL
315 E Chestnut St
(65757)
Rates: $39-$50
Tel: (417) 736-3883

SULLIVAN

BEST WESTERN PENBERTHY INN
307 N Service Rd
(63080)
Rates: $41-$58
Tel: (573) 468-3136
(800) 528-1234

FAMILY MOTOR INN
209 N Service Rd
(63080)
Rates: $25-$40
Tel: (314) 468-4119

SUPER 8 MOTEL
601 N Service Rd
(63080)
Rates: $40-$56
Tel: (314) 468-8076
(800) 800-8000

SUNSET HILLS

COMFORT INN
3730 S Lindbergh
Blvd (63127)
Rates: $38-$65
Tel: (800) 221-2222

SWEET SPRINGS

PEOPLE'S CHOICE MOTEL
1001 N Locust St
(65351)
Rates: $24-$45
Tel: (816) 335-6315

THEODOSIA

THEODOSIA MARINA-RESORT
HR 5, Box 5020
(65761)
Rates: $32-$50
Tel: (417) 273-4444

TIPTON

TWIN PINE MOTEL
Hwy 50 W (65081)
Rates: $21-$30
Tel: (816) 433-5525

VAN BUREN

HAWTHORNE MOTEL
P. O. Box 615 (63965)
Rates: $24-$40
Tel: (314) 323-4275

VILLA RIDGE

BEST WESTERN DIAMOND INN
581 Hwy 100 E
(63089)
Rates: $54-$89
Tel: (314) 742-3501
(800) 528-1234

WAPPAPELLO

MILLERS MOTOR LODGE
Rt 2, Box 2900
(63966)
Rates: $34-$50
Tel: (314) 222-8579

WARRENSBURG

DAYS INN
Hwy 13 & Hwy 50
(64093)
Rates: $36-$50
Tel: (816) 429-2400
(800) 329-7466

WARRENTON

COLLIER HOSPITALITY INN
2532 W Old Hwy 40
(63383)
Rates: $22-$34
Tel: (314) 456-7272

DAYS INN
220 Arlington Way
(63383)
Rates: $32-$65
Tel: (314) 456-4301
(800) 329-7466

WAYNESVILLE

BEST WESTERN MONTIS INN
14086 Hwy Z (65583)
Rates: $45-$58
Tel: (573) 336-4299
(800) 528-1234

DAYS INN
14125 Hwy Z (65583)
Rates: $38-$60
Tel: (573) 335-5556
(800) 329-7466

ECONO LODGE
HC 6 107B (65583)
Rates: $34-$49
Tel: (314) 336-3121

RAMADA INN FORT LEONARD WOOD
I-44 & Missouri Ave
(65583)
Rates: $50-$63
Tel: (800) 272-6232

SCOTTISH INNS
25755 Hwy 17
(65583)
Rates: n/a
Tel: (314) 774-3600

SUPER 8 MOTEL
I-44 & Hwy 28
(65583)
Rates: $40-$55
Tel: (314) 336-3036
(800) 800-8000

WENTZVILLE

HERITAGE MOTEL
404 N Hwy 61,
Business Rt (63385)
Rates: $22-$26
Tel: (314) 327-6263

HOWARD JOHNSON
1500 Continal Dr
(63385)
Rates: $36-$56
Tel: (314) 327-5212
(800) 446-4656

SCOTTISH INNS
404 N Hwy 61,
Business Rt (63385)
Rates: n/a
Tel: (800) 251-1962

WEST PLAINS

**BEST WESTERN
GRAND VILLA**
220 US Hwy 63
(65775)
Rates: $50-$60
Tel: (417) 257-2711
(800) 528-1234

DAYS INN
Hwy 63 (65775)
Rates: $36-100
Tel: (417) 256-4135
(800) 329-7466

RAMADA INN
1301 Preacher Rae
Blvd (65775)
Rates: $36-$110
Tel: (417) 256-8191
(800) 272-6232

WOODSON TERRACE

DAYS INN-AIRPORT
4545 Woodson Rd
(63134)
Rates: $35-$65
Tel: (314) 423-6770

**MARRIOTT HOTEL-
AIRPORT**
I-70 at Lambert
(63134)
Rates: $125-$375
Tel: (314) 423-9700

MOTEL 6-AIRPORT
4576 Woodson Rd
(63134)
Rates: $36-$42
Tel: (314) 427-1313
(800) 440-6000

MONTANA

ALBERTON

RIVER EDGE MOTEL
P. O. Box 64 (59820)
Rates: $24-$48
Tel: (406) 722-4418

ANACONDA

**GEORGETOWN
LAKE LODGE**
Denton's Point Rd
(59711)
Rates: $40-$60
Tel: (406) 563-7020

PINTLAR INN
13902 Hwy 1 (59711)
Rates: $30-$40
Tel: (406) 563-5072

**SEVEN GABLES
RESORT**
Hwy 1 (59711)
Rates: $40-$60
Tel: (406) 563-5052
(800) 472-6940

AUGUSTA

BUNKHOUSE INN
122 Main St (59410)
Rates: $30-$40
Tel: (406) 562-3387

BABB

**THRONSON'S
MOTEL**
US 89, Box 169
(59411)
Rates: $40-$60
Tel: (406) 732-5530

**TWO SISTERS
MOTEL**
US 89, Box 262
(59411)
Rates: $40-$60
Tel: (406) 732-5535

BAKER

**ROY'S MOTEL &
CAMPGROUND**
327 W Montana Ave
(59313)
Rates: $30-$40
Tel: (406) 778-3321
(800) 552-3321

SAGEBRUSH INN
518 US 12 W (59313)
Rates: $40-$60
Tel: (406) 778-3341
(800) 638-3708

BELGRADE

HOMESTEAD INN
6261 Jackrabbit Ln
(59714)
Rates: $40-$60
Tel: (406) 338-0800
(800) 272-9500

BIG FORK

**BAYVIEW MARINA
RESORT**
543 Yenne Point Rd
(59911)
Rates: n/a
Tel: (800) 775-3536

GALLERY SUITES
537 Electric Ave
(59911)
Rates: $60-$80
Tel: (406) 837-2288

**O'DAUCH'AIN
COUNTRY INN**
675 Ferndale Dr
(59911)
Rates: $50-$95
Tel: (406) 837-6851

TIMBERS MOTEL
8540 Hwy 35 (59911)
Rates: $30-$57
Tel: (406) 837-6200
(800) 821-4546

WOODS BAY MOTEL
26481 E Shore Rt
(59911)
Rates: $40-$60
Tel: (406) 837-3333

BIG SANDY

Q's MOTEL
US 87 & Hwy 236,
Box 421 (59520)
Rates: $30-$40
Tel: (406) 378-2389

BIG SKY

**BEST WESTERN
BUCK'S T-4 LODGE**
46625 Gallatin Rd
(59716)
Rates: $69-$114
Tel: (406) 995-4111
(800) 528-1234

320 GUEST RANCH
205 Buffalo Horn
(59730)
Rates: $59-$180
Tel: (406) 995-4283

BIG TIMBER

**BIG TIMBER INN
BED & BREAKFAST**
Yellowstone River Ln,
Box 328 (59011)
Rates: $40-$60
Tel: (406) 932-4080

LAZY 3 MOTEL
Hwy 10 (59011)
Rates: $40-$60
Tel: (406) 932-5533

SUPER 8 MOTEL
Box 1441 (59011)
Rates: $39-$55
Tel: (406) 932-8888
(800) 800-8000

BILLINGS

**AIRPORT METRA
INN**
403 Main St (59105)
Rates: $31-$40
Tel: (406) 245-6611
(800) 234-6611

**BEST WESTERN
BILLINGS**
5610 S Frontage Rd
(59101)
Rates: $60-$80
Tel: (406) 248-9800
(800) 528-1234

**BEST WESTERN
PONDEROSA INN**
2511 1st Ave N
(59101)
Rates: $50-$70
Tel: (406) 259-5511
(800) 528-1234

BILLINGS INN
880 N 29th St (59101)
Rates: $40-$60
Tel: (406) 252-6800
(800) 231-7782

CHERRY TREE INN
823 N Broadway
(59101)
Rates: $30-$38
Tel: (406) 252-5603
(800) 237-5882

CLARION HOTEL
1223 Mullowney Ln
(59101)
Rates: $50-$99
Tel: (406) 248-7151

COMFORT INN
2030 Overland Ave
(59102)
Rates: $38-$49
Tel: (406) 652-5200
(800) 221-2222

DAYS INN
843 Parkway Ln
(59101)
Rates: $43-$62
Tel: (406) 252-4007
(800) 329-7466

DUDE RANCHER LODGE
415 N 29th St (59101)
Rates: $36-$58
Tel: (406) 259-5561
(800) 221-3302

FAIRFIELD INN BY MARRIOTT
2026 Overland Ave
(59102)
Rates: $40-$62
Tel: (406) 652-5330
(800) 228-2800

FIRESIDE INN
1223 Mullowney Ln
(59101)
Rates: $45-$57
Tel: (406) 248-7151
(800) 228-2828

HEIGHTS INN MOTEL
1206 Main St (59101)
Rates: $30-$40
Tel: (406) 252-8451
(800) 275-8451

HILLTOP INN
1116 N 28th St
(59101)
Rates: $37-$46
Tel: (406) 245-5000

HOLLIDAY INN BILLINGS PLAZA
5500 Midland Rd
(59101)
Rates: $58-$99
Tel: (406) 248-7701
(800) 465-4329

HOWARD JOHNSON
S 27th St (59101)
Rates $38-$62
Tel: (406) 248-4656
(800) 446-4656

JUNIPER MOTEL
1315 N 27th St
(59101)
Rates: $41-$43
Tel: (406) 245-4128
(800) 826-7530

KELLY INN
5425 Midland Rd
(59101)
Rates: $40-$60
Tel: (406) 252-2700
(800) 635-3559

LAZY KT MOTEL
1403 1st Ave N
(59101)
Rates: $40
Tel: (406) 252-6606
(800) 290-2681

MOTEL 6 NORTH
5353 Midland Rd
(59102)
Rates: $26-$38
Tel: (406) 248-7551
(800) 440-6000

MOTEL 6 SOUTH
5400 Midland Rd,
RR 9 (59101)
Rates: $26-$38
Tel: (406) 252-0093
(800) 440-6000

PICTURE COURT MOTEL
5146 Laurel Rd
(59101)
Rates: $40
Tel: (406) 252-8478
(800) 523-7379

QUALITY INN HOMESTEAD
2036 Overland Ave
(59102)
Rates: $43-$62
Tel: (406) 652-1320
(800) 221-2222

RADISSON NORTHERN HOTEL
19 N 28th St (59101)
Rates: $84-$94
Tel: (406) 245-5121
(800) 333-3333

RAMADA LIMITED
1345 Mullowney Ln
(59101)
Rates: $40-$60
Tel: (406) 252-2584
(800) 272-6232

RIMROCK INN
1203 North 27th St
(59101)
Rates: $40-$60
Tel: (406) 252-7107
(800) 624-9770

RIMVIEW INN
1025 N 27th St
(59101)
Rates: $30-$42
Tel: (406) 248-2622
(800) 551-1418

SHERATON BILLINGS HOTEL
27 N 27th St (59101)
Rates: $60-$80
Tel: (406) 252-7400
(800) 588-7666

SUPER 8 LODGE
5400 Southgate Dr
(59102)
Rates: $40-$60
Tel: (406) 248-8842
(800) 800-8000

WAR BONNET INN
2612 Belknap Ave
(59101)
Rates: $40-$60
Tel: (406) 248-7761

BOULDER

CASTORIA MOTEL
211 S Monroe
(59632)
Rates: $30-$40
Tel: (406) 225-3549

O-Z MOTEL
114 N Main St (59632)
Rates: $30-$40
Tel: (406) 225-3364

BOZEMAN

ALPINE LODGE
1017 E Main (59715)
Rates: $30-$40
Tel: (406) 586-0356

BLUE SKY MOTEL
1010 E Main (59715)
Rates: $30-$40
Tel: (406) 587-2311
(800) 845-9032

BOBCAT LODGE
2307 W Main (59715)
Rates: $40-$60
Tel: (406) 587-5241

BOZEMAN INN
1235 N 7th Ave
(59715)
Rates: $35-$57
Tel: (406) 587-3176
(800) 648-7515

DAYS INN
1321 N 7th Ave
(59715)
Rates: $36-$150
Tel: (406) 587-5251
(800) 329-7466

FAIRFIELD INN BY MARRIOTT
828 Wheat Dr
(59715)
Rates: $50-$90
Tel: (406) 587-2222
(800) 228-2800

HOLIDAY INN
5 Baxter Ln (59715)
Rates: $56-$77
Tel: (406) 587-4561
(800) 465-4329

RAINBOW MOTEL
510 N 7th Ave
(59715)
Rates: $30-$46
Tel: (406) 587-4201

RAMADA LIMITED
2020 Wheat Dr
(59715)
Rates: $39-$149
Tel: (406) 585-2626
(800) 221-2222

ROYAL "7" BUDGET INN
310 N 7th Ave
(59715)
Rates: $40-$50
Tel: (406) 587-3103

SUPER 8 MOTEL
800 Wheat Dr
(59715)
Rates: $40-$60
Tel: (406) 586-1521
(800) 800-8000

WESTERN HERITAGE INN
1200 E Main St
(59715)
Rates: $40-$70
Tel: (406) 586-8534
(800) 341-8000

BROADUS

C-J MOTEL
311 W Holt (59317)
Rates: $40-$60
Tel: (406) 436-2671

QUARTERHORSE MOTOR INN
101 N Park (59317)
Rates: $30-$40
Tel: (406) 436-2626

BROWNING

GLACIER MOTEL
US 2 (59417)
Rates: $40-$60
Tel: (406) 338-7277

WESTERN MOTEL
121 Central Ave E
(59417)
Rates: $40-$60
Tel: (406) 338-7572

BUTTE

CAPRI MOTEL
220 N Wyoming
(59701)
Rates: $40-$60
Tel: (406) 723-4391

COMFORT INN
2777 Harrison Ave
(59701)
Rates: $49-$120
Tel: (406) 494-8850
(800) 221-2222

DAYS INN
2700 Harrison Ave
(59701)
Rates: $45-$150
Tel: (406) 494-7000
(800) 329-7466

MILE HI MOTEL
3499 Harrison Ave
(59701)
Rates: $40-$60
Tel: (406) 494-2250

ROSE MOTEL
920 S Montana
(59701)
Rates: $30-$40
Tel: (406) 723-4346

SKOOKUM MOTEL
3541 Harrison Ave
(59701)
Rates: $30-$40
Tel: (406) 494-2153

SUPER 8 MOTEL
2929 Harrison Ave
(59701)
Rates: $33-$46
Tel: (406) 494-6000
(800) 800-8000

WAR BONNET INN
2100 Cornell Ave
(59701)
Rates: $55-$78
Tel: (406) 494-7800
(800) 443-1806

CAMERON

**WEST FORK
CABIN CAMP**
1475 US 287 N
(59720)
Rates: $40-$60
Tel: (406) 682-4802

CHARLO

**ALLENTOWN
MOTEL**
41000 US 93 (59824)
Rates: $30-$40
Tel: (406) 644-2588

CHINOOK

**CHINOOK
MOTOR INN**
100 Indiana Ave
(59523)
Rates: $40-$60
Tel: (406) 357-2248
(800) 642-7053

CHOTEAU

**BEST WESTERN
STAGE STOP INN**
1005 N Main St
(59422)
Rates: $45-$70
Tel: (406) 466-5900
(888) 466-5900

BIG SKY MOTEL
209 S Main Ave
(59422)
Rates: $40-$60
Tel: (406) 466-5318

**WESTERN STAR
MOTEL**
426 Main Ave S
(59422)
Rates: $30-$40
Tel: (406) 466-5737

CIRCLE

TRAVELERS INN
Hwy 200, Box 78
(59215)
Rates: $30-$40
Tel: (406) 485-3323

CLINTON

**ROCK CREEK
LODGE**
I-90 Exit 126 (59825)
Rates: $30-$40
Tel: (406) 825-4868

COLUMBUS

**GLACIER INN
MOTEL**
1401 2nd Ave E
(59912)
Rates: $40-$60
Tel: (406) 892-4341

**GLACIER
MOUNTAIN
SHADOWS RESORT**
US 2 E & Hwy 206
(59912)
Rates: $40-$60
Tel: (406) 892-7686
(800) 766-1137

SUPER 8 MOTEL
602 8th Ave N
(59019)
Rates: $31-$35
Tel: (406) 322-4101
(800) 800-8000

CONDON

SUPER 8 MOTEL
Hwy 83, Box 1278
(59826)
Rates: $40-53
Tel: (406) 754-2688
(800) 800-8000

CONRAD

CONRAD MOTEL
210 N Main (59425)
Rates: $30-$40
Tel: (406) 278-7544

NORTHGATE MOTEL
5 N Main (59425)
Rates: $30-$40
Tel: (406) 278-3516

SUPER 8 MOTEL
215 N Main St
(59425)
Rates: $35-$49
Tel: (406) 278-7676
(800) 800-8000

COOKE CITY

**ALL SEASONS MINE
COMPANY HOTEL
& CASINO**
US 212 (59020)
Rates: $50-$75
Tel: (406) 838-2251

**BIG MOOSE
RESORT**
Colter Pass,
Box 1009 (59020)
Rates: $40-$60
Tel: (406) 838-2393

ELKHORN LODGE
208 Main St (59020)
Rates: $40-$60
Tel: (406) 838-2332

**HIGH COUNTRY
MOTEL**
US 212, P. O. Box
1146 (59020)
Rates: $32-$58
Tel: (406) 838-2272

CULBERTSON

**DIAMOND WILLOW
INN**
US 2 & Hwy 16,
Box 753 (59218)
Rates: $30-$40
Tel: (406) 787-6218

CUSTER

D & L MOTEL/CAFE
3rd St, Box 105
(59024)
Rates: $30-$40
Tel: (406) 856-4128

CUT BANK

CORNER MOTEL
201 E Main St
(59427)
Rates: $30-$40
Tel: (406) 873-5588
(800) 851-5541

GLACIER GATEWAY INN
1121 E Railroad St (59427)
Rates: $39-$49
Tel: (406) 873-5544
(800) 851-5541

PARKWAY MOTEL
7 3rd Ave W (59427)
Rates: $30-$40
Tel: (406) 873-4582

POINT MOTEL
1109 E Main St (59427)
Rates: $30-$40
Tel: (406) 873-5433
(800) 851-5541

TERRACE MOTEL
11 9th Ave SE (59427)
Rates: $30-$40
Tel: (406) 873-5031

DARBY

WILDERNESS MOTEL & BUNKHOUSE
308 S Main St (59829)
Rates: $30-$40
Tel: (406) 821-3405
(800) 820-2554

DE BORGIA

HOTEL ALBERT BED & BREAKFAST
#2 Yellowstone Tr (59830)
Rates: $44-$60
Tel: (406) 678-4303

DEER LODGE

DOWN TOWNER MOTEL
506 4th St (59722)
Rates: $40-$60
Tel: (406) 846-1021

SCHARF'S MOTOR INN
819 Main St (59722)
Rates: $26-$49
Tel: (406) 846-2810
(800) 341-8000

SUPER 8 MOTEL
1150 N Main St (59722)
Rates: $40-$60
Tel: (406) 846-2370
(800) 800-8000

DILLON

BEST WESTERN PARADISE INN
650 N Montana St (59725)
Rates: $44-$62
Tel: (406) 683-4214
(800) 528-1234

COMFORT INN
450 N Interchange (59725)
Rates: $33-$45
Tel: (406) 683-6831
(800) 221-2222

CRESTON MOTEL
335 S Atlantic (59725)
Rates: $26-$39
Tel: (406) 683-2341

CROSSWINDS MOTEL
1004 S Atlantic (59725)
Rates: $30-$40
Tel: (406) 683-2378

SACAJAWEA MOTEL
775 N Montana St (59725)
Rates: $30-$40
Tel: (406) 683-2381

SUNDOWNER MOTEL
500 N Montana St (59725)
Rates: $26-$36
Tel: (406) 683-2375
(800) 524-9746

DRUMMOND

DRUMMOND MOTEL
170 W Front St (59832)
Rates: $30-$40
Tel: (406) 288-3272

SKY MOTEL
Front & Broadway (59832)
Rates: $30-$40
Tel: (406) 288-3206
(800) 559-3206

WAGON WHEEL CAFE & MOTEL
Front & C Sts (59832)
Rates: $30-$40
Tel: (406) 288-3201

EAST GLACIER PARK

JACOBSON'S SCENIC VIEW COTTAGES
1204 Hwy 49, Box 216 (59434)
Rates: $35-$50
Tel: (406) 226-4422

PORTER'S ALPINE MOTEL
P. O. Box 149 (59434)
Rates: $32-$52
Tel: (406) 226-4402

SEARS MOTEL & CAMPGROUND
1023 Hwy 49 N (59434)
Rates: $40-$60
Tel: (406) 226-4432

ELLISTON

LAST CHANCE MOTEL
Hwy 12 (59728)
Rates: $30-$40
Tel: (406) 492-7250

ENNIS

THE EL WESTERN MOTEL
US 287 S (59729)
Rates: $50-$80
Tel: (406) 682-4127
(800) 831-2773

FAN MOUNTAIN INN
207 N Main (59729)
Rates: $ 35-$50
Tel: (406) 682-5200

RIVERSIDE MOTEL & OUTFITTERS
346 Main St (59729)
Rates: $30-$40
Tel: (406) 682-4240
(800) 535-4139

SILVERTIP LODGE
301 Main St (59729)
Rates: $30-$40
Tel: (406) 682-4384

SPORTSMAN'S LODGE
310 US 287 N (59729)
Rates: $40-$60
Tel: (406) 682-4242

ESSEX

DENNY'S MOTEL
14297 US 2 (59916)
Rates: $30-$40
Tel: (406) 888-5720

EUREKA

CREEK SIDE CABINS
1333 US 93 N (59917)
Rates: $30-$40
Tel: (406) 296-2361

KSANKA MOTOR INN
US 93 & Hwy 37 (59917)
Rates: $30-$40
Tel: (406) 296-3127

FAIRVIEW

KORNER MOTEL
217 W 9th (59221)
Rates: $30-$40
Tel: (406) 747-5259
(800) 656-7637

FORSYTH

BEST WESTERN SUNDOWNER INN
1018 Front St (59327)
Rates: $49-$80
Tel: (406) 356-2115
(800) 528-1234

RAILS INN MOTEL
3rd & Front St (59327)
Rates: $40-$60
Tel: (406) 356-2242
(800) 621-3754

RESTWEL MOTEL
810 Front St (59327)
Rates: $25-$32
Tel: (406) 356-2771
(800) 548-3442

**WESTWIND
MOTOR INN**
P. O. Box 5025
(59327)
Rates: $33-$38
Tel: (406) 356-2038

**WHIT'S
ECONO LODGE**
659 Front St (59327)
Rates: $30-$40
Tel: (406) 356-7947

FORT BENTON

FORT MOTEL
1809 St Charles
(59442)
Rates: $40-$60
Tel: (406) 622-3312

FORT SMITH

**BIGHORN ANGLER
MOTEL**
Rt 313 (59035)
Rates: $40-$60
Tel: (406) 666-2233

**QUILL GORDON FLY
FISHERS MOTEL**
Box 7597 (59035)
Rates: $40-$60
Tel: (406) 666-2253

GALATA

**GALATA MOTEL
& RV OVERNITE**
Box 31 (59444)
Rates: $30-$40
Tel: (406) 432-2352

GALLATIN GATEWAY

CASTLE ROCK INN
65840 Gallatin
Gateway (59730)
Rates: n/a
Tel: (406) 763-4243

**GALLATIN
GATEWAY INN**
76405 Gallatin Rd
(59730)
Rates: $60-$105
Tel: (406) 763-4672

GARDINER

**BEST WESTERN
BY MAMMOTH
HOT SPRINGS**
Hwy 89, Box 646
(59030)
Rates: $47-$104
Tel: (406) 848-7311
(800) 528-1234

BLUE HAVEN MOTEL
Box 952 (59030)
Rates: $47-$104
Tel: (406) 848-7719

**JIM BRIDGER
COURT**
US 89, Box 325
(59030)
Rates: $40-$60
Tel: (406) 848-7371

MILE HI MOTEL
US 89, Box 1060
(59030)
Rates: $40-$60
Tel: (406) 848-7544

**WILSON'S
YELLOWSTONE
RIVER MOTEL**
US 89 (59030)
Rates: $35-$70
Tel: (406) 848-7303

GLACIER NATIONAL PARK

**APGAR VILLAGE
LODGE**
P. O. Box 398
(West Glacier 59936)
Rates: $54-$88
Tel: (406) 888-5484

GLASGOW

CAMPBELL LODGE
534 3rd Ave S
(59230)
Rates: $29-$38
Tel: (406) 228-9328

COTTONWOOD INN
US 2 E (59230)
Rates: $40-$58
Tel: (406) 228-8213
(800) 321-8213

KOSKI'S MOTEL
320 US 2 E (59230)
Rates: $30-$40
Tel: (406) 228-8282
(800) 238-8282

LACASA MOTEL
238 1st Ave N
(59230)
Rates: $30-$40
Tel: (406) 228-9311

**LAKERIDGE MOTEL
& TACKLE**
Hwy 24, HCR 1660
(59230)
Rates: $40-$60
Tel: (406) 526-3597

STAR LODGE MOTEL
US 2 W (59230)
Rates: $30-$40
Tel: (406) 228-2494

GLENDIVE

**BEST WESTERN
JORDAN INN**
222 N Kendrick
(59330)
Rates: $47-$74
Tel: (406) 365-5655
(800) 528-1234

**BUDGET HOST
RIVERSIDE INN**
HC 44, Hwy 18
(59330)
Rates: $28-$38
Tel: (406) 365-2349
(800) 283-4678

DAYS INN
2000 N Merrill Ave
(59330)
Rates: $28-$52
Tel: (406) 365-6011
(800) 329-7466

**JORDON
MOTOR INN**
223 N Merrill Ave
(59330)
Rates: $40-$60
Tel: (406) 365-3371
(800) 824-5067

KINGS INN
1903 N Merrill Ave
(59330)
Rates: $30-$40
Tel: (406) 365-5636

SUPER 8 MOTEL
1904 N Merrill Ave
(59330)
Rates: $40-$60
Tel: (406) 365-5671
(800) 800-8000

GREAT FALLS

BUDGET INN MOTEL
2 Treasure State Dr
(59404)
Rates: $41-$47
Tel: (406) 453-1602
(800) 362-4842

CENTRAL MOTEL
715 Central Ave W
(59404)
Rates: $28-$40
Tel: (406) 453-0161

**EDELWEISS
MOTOR INN**
626 Central Ave W
(59404)
Rates: $28-$40
Tel: (406) 452-9503
(800) 294-9503

**FAIRFIELD INN
BY MARRIOTT**
1000 9th Ave S
(59405)
Rates: $47-$61
Tel: (406) 454-3000
(800) 228-2800

GREAT FALLS INN
1400 28th St S
(59405)
Rates: $40-$60
Tel: (406) 453-6000
(800) 454-6010

HOLIDAY INN
400 10th Ave S
(59405)
Rates: $54-$84
Tel: (406) 727-7200
(800) 465-4329

IMPERIAL INN
601 2nd Ave N
(59401)
Rates: $30-$40
Tel: (406) 452-9581

MID-TOWN MOTEL
526 2nd Ave N
(59401)
Rates: $40-$60
Tel: (406) 453-2411
(800) 457-2411

PLAZA INN
1224 10th Ave S
(59405)
Rates: $32-$55
Tel: (406) 452-9594

**RENDEZVOUS 9
MOTOR INN**
Fox Farm Rd &
10th Ave S (59401)
Rates: $40-$60
Tel: (406) 452-9525
(800) 772-1330

**SKI'S WESTERN
MOTEL**
2420 10th Ave S
(59405)
Rates: $32-$58
Tel: (406) 453-3281

SUPER 8 MOTEL
1214 13th St (59405)
Rates: $38-$52
Tel: (406) 727-7600
(800) 800-8000

**TOWN & COUNTRY
MOTEL**
2418 10th Ave S
(59405)
Rates: $30-$40
Tel: (406) 452-5642

TOWNHOUSE INNS
1411 10th St S
(59405)
Rates: $56-$70
Tel: (406) 761-4600
(800) 442-4667

**TRIPLE CROWN
MOTOR INN**
621 Central Ave
(59401)
Rates: $34-$43
Tel: (406) 727-8300
(800) 722-8300

**VILLAGE
MOTOR INN**
726 10th Ave S
(59405)
Rates: $30-$40
Tel: (406) 727-7666
(800) 354-0868

GREENOUGH

**LORAN'S
CLEARWATER INN**
Hwy 200 & 83,
Box 20 (59836)
Rates: $30-$40
Tel: (406) 244-9535

HAMILTON

**BITTERROOT
MOTEL**
408 S 1st St (59840)
Rates: $30-$40
Tel: (406) 363-1142

CITY CENTER MOTEL
W 415 Main (59840)
Rates: $40-$60
Tel: (406) 363-1651

COMFORT INN
1115 N 1st St (59840)
Rates: $40-$60
Tel: (406) 363-6000
(800) 442-4667

**RANCH
BED & BREAKFAST**
1615 US 93 S (59840)
Rates: $40-$60
Tel: (406) 363-4739

SPORTSMAN MOTEL
410 N 1st St (59840)
Rates: $30-$40
Tel: (406) 363-2411

SUPER 8 MOTEL
1325 N 1st St (59840)
Rates: $40-$60
Tel: (406) 363-2940

HARDIN

**CAMP CUSTER
MOTEL**
303 E 4th St (59034)
Rates: $30-$40
Tel: (406) 665-2504
(800) 234-2504

LARIAT MOTEL
709 North Center
Ave (59034)
Rates: $30-$54
Tel: (406) 665-2683

WESTERN MOTEL
830 W 3rd St (59034)
Rates: $40-$60
Tel: (406) 665-2296

HARLOWTON

CORRAL MOTEL
P. O. Box 721 (59036)
Rates: $29-$34
Tel: (406) 632-4331
(800) 392-4723

COUNTRY SIDE INN
309 3rd St NE
(59036)
Rates: $30-$40
Tel: (406) 632-4119
(800) 632-4120

TROY MOTEL
US 12 & 191, Box 779
(59036)
Rates: $30-$40
Tel: (406) 632-4428

HAUGAN

SILVER $ INN
I-90 Exit 16, Box W
(59842)
Rates: $40-$60
Tel: (406) 678-4242
(800) 531-1968

HAVRE

BUDGET INN MOTEL
115 9th Ave (59501)
Rates: $30-$40
Tel: (406) 265-8625

CIRCLE INN MOTEL
3565 US 2 E (59501)
Rates: $30-$40
Tel: (406) 265-9655

EL TORO INN
521 1st St (59501)
Rates: $36-$46
Tel: (406) 265-5414
(800) 422-5414

RAILS INN
537 2nd St (59501)
Rates: $30-$40
Tel: (406) 265-1438
(800) 724-5746

TOWNHOUSE INNS
601 W 1st St (59501)
Rates: $47-$65
Tel: (406) 265-6711
(800) 442-4667

HELENA

**ALADDIN
MOTOR INN**
2101 11th Ave
(59601)
Rates: $44-$52
Tel: (406) 443-2300
(800) 541-2743

**APPLETON INN
BED & BREAKFAST**
1999 Euclid Ave
(59601)
Rates: $60-$85
Tel: (406) 449-7492

COMFORT INN
750 Fee St (59601)
Rates: $39-$73
Tel: (406) 443-1000
(800) 221-2222

DAYS INN
2001 Prospect Ave
(59601)
Rates: $40-$75
Tel: (406) 442-3280
(800) 329-7466

**JORGENSON'S
HOLIDAY MOTEL**
P. O. Box 857 (59624)
Rates: $37-$87
Tel: (406) 442-1770
(800) 272-1770

**KINGS CARRIAGE
INN**
910 N Last Chance
Gulch (59601)
Rates: $40-$60
Tel: (406) 442-6080
(800) 521-2743

**KNIGHTS REST
MOTEL**
1831 Euclid (59601)
Rates: $30-$38
Tel: (406) 442-6384
(800) 303-6384

**LAMPLIGHTER
MOTEL**
1006 Madison
(59601)
Rates: $26-$38
Tel: (406) 442-9200

PARK PLAZA HOTEL
22 N Last Chance
Gulch (59601)
Rates: $60-$80
Tel: (406) 443-2200
(800) 332-2290

SHILO INNS
2020 Prospect Ave
(59601)
Rates: $47-$60
Tel: (406) 442-0320
(800) 222-2244

SUPER 8 MOTEL
2201 11th Ave
(59601)
Rates: $42-$55
Tel: (406) 443-2450
(800) 800-8000

HOT SPRINGS

HOT SPRINGS SPA
308 N Springs St
(59845)
Rates: $30-$40
Tel: (406) 741-2283

HUNGRY HORSE

HUNGRY HORSE MOTEL
8808 US 2 E (59919)
Rates: $40-$60
Tel: (406) 387-5443

MINI GOLDEN INNS MOTEL
8955 US 2 E (59919)
Rates: $60-$80
Tel: (406) 387-4313
(800) 891-6464

HYSHAM

TREASURE VALLEY MOTEL
415 6th Ave (59038)
Rates: $30-$40
Tel: (406) 342-5627

KALISPELL

AERO INN
1830 US 93 S (59901)
Rates: $40-$60
Tel: (406) 755-3798
(800) 843-6114

BEST WESTERN OUTLAW INN
1701 Hwy 93 S
(59901)
Rates: $70-$210
Tel: (406) 755-6100
(800) 528-1234

BIG CHIEF MOTEL
1484 Hwy 35 (59901)
Rates: $40-$60
Tel: (406) 756-3434

BLUE & WHITE MOTEL
640 E Idaho (59901)
Rates: $40-$60
Tel: (406) 755-4311
(800) 382-3577

CAVANAUGH'S AT KALISPELL CENTER
20 N Main (59901)
Rates: $60-$110
Tel: (406) 752-6660
(800) 843-4667

DIAMOND LIL'S INN MOTEL
1680 US 93 S (59901)
Rates: $64-$66
Tel: (406) 752-3467
(800) 843-7301

FOUR SEASONS MOTOR INN
350 N Main St
(59901)
Rates: $45-$53
Tel: (406) 755-6123
(800) 545-6399

GLACIER GATEWAY MOTEL
264 N Main St
(59901)
Rates: $28-$75
Tel: (406) 755-3330

HILLTOP INN
801 E Idaho (59901)
Rates: $40-$60
Tel: (406) 755-4455

KALISPELL GRAND HOTEL
100 Main St (59901)
Rates: $35-$78
Tel: (406) 755-8100
(800) 858-7422

MOTEL 6
1540 Hwy 93 S
(59901)
Rates: $27-$39
Tel: (406) 752-6355
(800) 440-6000

RED LION INN
1330 Hwy 2W
(59901)
Rates: $69-$95
Tel: (406) 755-6700
(800) 547-8100

SUPER 8 MOTEL
1341 1st Ave E
(59901)
Rates: $43-$57
Tel: (406) 755-1888
(800) 800-8000

VACATIONER MOTEL
285 7th Ave NE
(59901)
Rates: $60-$80
Tel: (406) 755-7144

WHITE BIRCH MOTEL
17 Shady Ln (59901)
Rates: $25-$39
Tel: (406) 752-4008

LAUREL

RUSSELL MOTEL
711 E Main (59044)
Rates: $30-$40
Tel: (406) 628-6513

WELCOME TRAVELERS MOTEL
620 W Main (59044)
Rates: $40-$60
Tel: (406) 628-6821

LEWISTOWN

B & B MOTEL-IMA
520 E Main St
(59457)
Rates: $27-$41
Tel: (406) 538-5496
(800) 341-8000

MOUNTAIN VIEW MOTEL
1422 Main St (59457)
Rates: $30-$40
Tel: (406) 538-3457
(800) 862-5786

MOTEL SUNSET
115 NE Main (59457)
Rates: $30-$40
Tel: (406) 538-8741

TRAIL'S END MOTEL
216 NE Main (59457)
Rates: $30-$40
Tel: (406) 538-5468

YOGO INN
211 E Main St
(59457)
Rates: $47-$57
Tel: (406) 538-8721
(800) 860-YOGO

LIBBY

CABOOSE MOTEL
714 W 9th (59923)
Rates: $32-$45
Tel: (406) 293-6201
(800) 627-0206

MOUNTAIN MAGIC MOTEL
919 Mineral Ave
(59923)
Rates: $40-$50
Tel: (406) 293-7795

SUPER 8 MOTEL
448 US Hwy 2W
(59923)
Rates: $36-$53
Tel: (406) 293-2771
(800) 800-8000

VENTURE MOTOR INN
443 US Hwy 2W
(59923)
Rates: $36-$59
Tel: (406) 293-7711

LIMA

EXIT 15 INN
111 Baily St (59739)
Rates: $30-$40
Tel: (406) 276-3535

LINCOLN

BLACKFOOT RIVER INN
At 7UP Ranch, Box
295 (59639)
Rates: $40-$60
Tel: (406) 362-4255
(800) 362-4787

BLUE SKY MOTEL
328 Main St (59639)
Rates: $30-$40
Tel: (406) 362-4450
(800) 632-0952

LEEPER'S MOTEL
P. O. Box 611 (59639)
Rates: $27-$40
Tel: (406) 362-4333

THREE BEARS MOTEL
Hwy 200, Box 789
(59639)
Rates: $30-$40
Tel: (406) 362-4355

LIVINGSTON

BUDGET HOST PARKWAY MOTEL
1124 W Park (59047)
Rates: $26-$56
Tel: (406) 222-3840
(800) 727-7217

DEL MAR MOTEL
P. O. Box 636 (59047)
Rates: $28-$58
Tel: (406) 222-3120

MURRAY HOTEL
201 W Park (59047)
Rates: $40-$60
Tel: (406) 222-1350

PARADISE INN
P. O. Box 684 (59047)
Rates: $35-$49
Tel: (406) 222-6320
(800) 437-6291

RAINBOW MOTEL
5574 E Park St
(59047)
Rates: $40-$60
Tel: (406) 222-3780
(800) 788-2301

S-S MOTEL
1 View Vista Dr
(59047)
Rates: $40-$60
Tel: (406) 222-0591
(800) 339-0591

YELLOWSTONE MOTOR INN
1515 West Park
(59047)
Rates: $60-$80
Tel: (406) 222-6110
(800) 826-1214

LOLO

DAYS INN
11225 US 93 S
(59847)
Rates: $40-$60
Tel: (406) 273-2121
(800) 329-7466

FORT FIZZLE INN
US 12 W (59847)
Rates: $40-$60
Tel: (406) 273-6993

MALTA

RIVERSIDE MOTEL
8 N Central (59538)
Rates: $30-$40
Tel: (406) 654-2310
(800) 854-2310

MARTIN CITY

MIDDLE FORK MOTEL
US 2, P. O. Box
260237 (59926)
Rates: $40-$60
Tel: (406) 387-5900

MARTINSDALE

CRAZY MOUNTAIN INN
100 Main St (59053)
Rates: $30-$40
Tel: (406) 572-3307

McALLISTER

CROSSROADS MARKET & CABINS
5564 US 287 N,
Box 155 (59740)
Rates: $30-$40
Tel: (406) 682-7652

MELROSE

SPORTSMAN MOTEL
Frontage Rd, Box 86
(59743)
Rates: $40-$60
Tel: (406) 835-2141

MELSTONE

TERRI'S MOTEL
205 Main St (59054)
Rates: $30-$40
Tel: (406) 358-2470

MILES CITY

BEST WESTERN WAR BONNET INN
1015 S Haynes
(59301)
Rates: $52-$125
Tel: (406) 232-4560
(800) 528-1234

BUCKBOARD MOTEL
1006 S Haynes
(59301)
Rates: $28-$38
Tel: (406) 232-3550
(800) 525-6303

BUDGET HOST CUSTER'S INN
1209 S Haynes
(59301)
Rates: $28-$48
Tel: (406) 232-5170
(800) 456-5026

DAYS INN
1006 S Haynes
(59301)
Rates: $26-$56
Tel: (406) 232-3550
(800) 329-7466

MOTEL 6
1314 S Haynes
(59301)
Rates: $26-$32
Tel: (406) 232-7040
(800) 440-6000

RODEWAY INN
501 Main St (59301)
Rates: $41+
Tel: (406) 232-2450
(800) 228-2000

SUPER 8 MOTEL
RR 2, Hwy 59S
(59301)
Rates: $25-$39
Tel: (406) 232-5261
(800) 800-8000

MISSOULA

BEL AIRE MOTEL
300 E Broadway
(59802)
Rates: $25-$55
Tel: (406) 543-3183
(800) 543-3184

BEST WESTERN EXECUTIVE INN
201 E Main St
(59802)
Rates: $45-$70
Tel: (406) 543-7221
(800) 528-1234

BEST WESTERN-GRANT CREEK
5290 Grant Creek Rd
(59801)
Rates: $68-$175
Tel: (406) 543-0700
(800) 528-1234

BROOKS ST. MOTOR INN
3333 Brooks St
(59802)
Rates: $40-$60
Tel: (406) 549-5115

BROWNIE'S PLUS MOTEL
1540 W Broadway
(59802)
Rates: $30-$40
Tel: (406) 543-6614
(800) 543-6614

BUDGET MOTEL & LODGE-RIVERSIDE
1135 W Broadway
(59802)
Rates: $30-$40
Tel: (406) 549-2358

CAMPUS INN
744 E Broadway
(59802)
Rates: $34-$55
Tel: (800) 232-8013

CLARK FORK INN
1010 W Broadway
(59802)
Rates: $40-$60
Tel: (406) 543-6619
(800) 554-8765

CREEKSIDE INN
630 E Broadway
(59802)
Rates: $60-$80
Tel: (406) 549-2387
(800) 551-2387

DAYS INN
RR 2, US 93 N
& I-90 (59802)
Rates: $43-$76
Tel: (406) 721-9776
(800) 329-7466

DOWNTOWN MOTEL
502 E Broadway
(59802)
Rates: $28-$34
Tel: (406) 549-5191

ECONO LODGE
1609 W Broadway
(59802)
Rates: $29-$62
Tel: (406) 543-7231
(800) 424-4777

4 B'S INN NORTH
4953 N Reserve St
(59802)
Rates: $39-$60
Tel: (406) 542-7550
(800) 272-9500

4 B'S INN SOUTH
3803 Brooks St
(59801)
Rates: $39-$59
Tel: (406) 251-2665
(800) 272-9500

HAMPTON INN
4805 N Reserve St
(59802)
Rates: $63-73
Tel: (406) 549-1800
(800) 426-7866

**HOLIDAY INN-
MISSOULA
PARKSIDE**
200 S Pattee St
(59802)
Rates: $57-$73
Tel: (406) 721-8550
(800) 465-4329

**HUBBARD'S
PONDEROSA
LODGE-IMA**
800 E Broadway
(59802)
Rates: $36-$46
Tel: (406) 543-3102
(800) 341-8000

**ORANGE STREET
BUDGET
MOTOR INN**
801 N Orange St
(59802)
Rates: $43-$49
Tel: (406) 721-3610

RED LION INN
700 W Broadway
(59802)
Rates: $51-$71
Tel: (406) 728-3300
(800) 547-8010

**RED LION VILLAGE
MOTOR INN**
100 Madison (59802)
Rates: $40-$58
Tel: (406) 728-3100
(800) 547-8010

REDWOOD LODGE
8060 Hwy 93 (59802)
Rates: $39-$54
Tel: (406) 721-2110
(800) 874-9412

ROYAL MOTEL
338 Washington St
(59802)
Rates: $24-$38
Tel: (406) 542-2184

**RUBY'S RESERVE
STREET INN**
4825 N Reserve St
(59802)
Rates: $49-$74
Tel: (406) 721-0990
(800) 221-2057

SLEEPY INN MOTEL
1427 W Broadway
(59801)
Rates: $30-$40
Tel: (406) 549-6484

SWEET REST MOTEL
1135 W Broadway
(59801)
Rates: $30-$40
Tel: (406) 549-2350

**THUNDERBIRD
MOTEL**
1009 E Broadway
(59802)
Rates: $35-$55
Tel: (406) 543-7251
(800) 952-2400

**TRAVELERS INN
MOTEL**
4850 N Reserve St
(59802)
Rates: $27-$47
Tel: (406) 728-8330
(800) 862-3363

NEVADA CITY

**NEVADA CITY
HOTEL & CABINS**
US 287 W, Box 338
(59755)
Rates: $40-$60
Tel: (406) 843-5377
(800) 648-7588

NOXON

NOXON MOTEL
2 Klakken Rd
(59853)
Rates: $30-$40
Tel: (406) 847-2600

OVANDO

**LAKE UPSATA
GUEST RANCH**
135 Lake Upsala Rd
(59854)
Rates: $350-$390
Tel: (800) 594-7687

PHILIPSBURG

**THE INN
AT PHILIPSBURG**
915 W Broadway
(59858)
Rates: $30-$40
Tel: (406) 859-3959

PLAINS

TOPS MOTEL
340 E Railroad
(59859)
Rates: $40-$60
Tel: (406) 826-3412

PLENTYWOOD

SHERWOOD INN
515 W 1st Ave
(59254)
Rates: $40-$60
Tel: (406) 765-2810

POLSON

DAYS INN
914 Hwy 93 (59860)
Rates: $30-$60
Tel: (406) 883-3120
(800) 329-7466

PRAY

**CHICO HOT
SPRINGS LODGE**
P. O. Box 127 (59645)
Rate: $36-$275
Tel: (406) 333-4933

RED LODGE

**BECK'S ALPINE
MOTEL**
US 212 N, Box 471
(59068)
Rates: $40-$60
Tel: (406) 446-2213

**BEST WESTERN
LUPINE INN**
702 S Hauser (59068)
Rates: $50-$75
Tel: (406) 446-1321
(800) 528-1234

**EAGLE'S NEST
MOTEL**
702 S Broadway
(59068)
Rates: $30-$40
Tel: (406) 446-2312

SUPER 8 MOTEL
1223 S Broadway
(59068)
Rates: $35-$59
Tel: (406) 446-2288
(800) 800-8000

**VALLI HI
MOTOR LODGE**
320 S Broadway
(59068)
Rates: $28-$60
Tel: (406) 446-1414

YODELER MOTEL
601 S Broadway
(59068)
Rates: $29-$48
Tel: (406) 446-1435

RONAN

STARLITE MOTEL
18 Main St SW
(59864)
Rates: $30-$40
Tel: (406) 676-7000
(800) 823-4403

ROUNDUP

BIG SKY MOTEL
740 Main (59072)
Rates: $30-$40
Tel: (406) 323-2303

ST. IGNATIUS

SUNSET MOTEL
Main Hwy Access
(59865)
Rates: $30-$40
Tel: (406) 745-3900

ST. MARY

RED EAGLE MOTEL
Star Rt, Box 896
(59417)
Rates: $40-$60
Tel: (406) 732-4453

**ST. MARY LODGE
& RESORT**
US 89 & Going-to-
the-Sun Rd (59417)
Rates: $60-$80
Tel: (406) 732-4431
(800) 452-7275

ST. REGIS

LITTLE RIVER MOTEL
I-90 Exit 33 (59866)
Rates: $30-$40
Tel: (406) 649-2713

SUPER 8 MOTEL
9 Old Hwy 10 E
(59866)
Rates: $36-$46
Tel: (406) 649-2422
(800) 800-8000

ST. XAVIER

**ROYAL BIG HORN
LODGE**
Box 181 (59075)
Rates: $60-$80
Tel: (406) 666-2340

SCOBEY

**CATTLE KING
MOTOR INN**
Hwy 13 S, Box 750
(59263)
Rates: $40-$60
Tel: (406) 487-5332
(800) 562-2775

SEELEY LAKE

DUCK INN MOTEL
Hwy 83 at MM 15,
Box 458 (59868)
Rates: $40-$60
Tel: (406) 677-2335
(800) 237-9978

**THE EMILY A
BED & BREAKFAST**
Hwy Marker 20,
SR 83 (59868)
Rates: $95+
Tel: (406) 677-3474

**WILDERNESS
GATEWAY INN**
P. O. Box 661 (59868)
Rates: $32-$43
Tel: (406) 677-2095

SHELBY

BEACON MOTEL
722 1st St N (59474)
Rates: $40-$60
Tel: (406) 434-2721
(800) 884-5935

COMFORT INN
50 Frontage Rd
(59474)
Rates: $40-$60
Tel: (406) 434-2212
(800) 442-4667

**CROSSROADS INN
MOTEL**
1200 Hwy 2 (59474)
Rates: $40-$52
Tel: (406) 434-5134

**GLACIER MOTEL
& RV PARK**
744 US 2 (59474)
Rates: $30-$40
Tel: (406) 434-5181
(800) 764-5181

**O'HAIRE MANOR
MOTEL**
204 2nd St. (59474)
Rates: $26-$40
Tel: (406) 434-5555
(800) 541-5809

SHERIDAN

MILL CREEK INN
Box 155 (59749)
Rates: $40-$60
Tel: (406) 842-5422

SIDNEY

**LONE TREE
MOTOR INN**
900 S Central (59270)
Rates: $40-$60
Tel: (406) 482-4520

**RICHLAND
MOTOR INN**
1200 S Central
(59270)
Rates: $40-$47
Tel: (406) 482-6400

SILVER GATE

**PARK VIEW
CABINS & MOTEL**
Hwy 212, HC 84,
Box 10 (59081)
Rates: $40-$60
Tel: (406) 838-2371

STANFORD

SUNDOWN MOTEL
Hwy 200 W, Box 126
(59479)
Rates: $30-$40
Tel: (406) 566-2316
(800) 346-2316

STEVENSVILLE

**ST. MARY'S MOTEL
& RV PARK**
3889 US 93 N (59870)
Rates: $40-$60
Tel: (406) 777-2838
(800) 624-7015

SUPERIOR

**BUDGET HOST
BIG SKY MOTEL**
103 4th Ave E (59872)
Rates: $30-$44
Tel: (406) 822-4831
(800) 283-4678

**LAKE TOWNSEND
MOTEL**
413 N Pine (59644)
Rates: $30-$40
Tel: (406) 266-3461
(800) 856-3461

THREE FORKS

**BROKEN SPUR
MOTEL**
124 W Elm (59752)
Rates: $40-$60
Tel: (406) 285-3237
(800) 354-3048

**FORT THREE FORKS
MOTEL**
10776 Hwy 287
(59752)
Rates: $30-$44
Tel: (406) 285-3233
(800) 477-5690

SACAJAWEA INN
5 N Main St (59752)
Rates: $60-$90
Tel: (406) 285-6515
(800) 821-7326

TOWNSEND

MUSTANG MOTEL
412 North Front St
(59644)
Rates: $39-$40
Tel: (406) 266-3491
(800) 349-3499

TROUT CREEK

**TROUT CREEK
MOTEL & RV PARK**
Hwy 200, Box 1441
(59874)
Rates: $40-$60
Tel: (406) 827-3268

TWIN BRIDGES

KING'S MOTEL
307 S Main (59754)
Rates: $30-$40
Tel: (406) 684-5639
(800) 222-5510

**STARDUST
COUNTRY INN**
409 N Main (59754)
Rates: $30-$40
Tel: (406) 684-5648

VALIER

ATKINS INN
412 Teton (59486)
Rates: $30-$40
Tel: (406) 279-3476
(800) 551-8332

VIRGINIA CITY

DAYLIGHT CREEK MOTEL
Box 338 (59755)
Rates: $40-$60
Tel: (406) 843-5377
(800) 648-7588

FAIRWEATHER INN
315 W Wallace (59755)
Rates: $40-$60
Tel: (406) 843-5377
(800) 648-7588

NEVADA CITY HOTEL & CABINS
P. O. Box 338 (59755)
Rates: $40-$50
Tel: (406) 843-5377
(800) 648-7588

WEST GLACIER

RIVER BEND MOTEL
200 Going-to-the-Sun Rd (59936)
Rates: $60-$80
Tel: (406) 888-5662

WEST YELLOWSTONE

BEST WESTERN CROSSWINDS MOTOR INN
201 Firehole Ave (59758)
Rates: $32-$105
Tel: (406) 646-9557
(800) 528-1234

BEST WESTERN DESERT INN
133 Canyon (59758)
Rates: $32-$102
Tel: (406) 646-7376
(800) 528-1234

BEST WESTERN EXECUTIVE INN
236 Dunraven (59758)
Rates: $70-$95
Tel: (406) 646-7681
(800) 528-1234

BEST WESTERN WESTON INN
103 Gibbon (59758)
Rates: $35-$90
Tel: (406) 646-7373
(800) 528-1234

BIG WESTERN PINE MOTEL
234 Firehole (59758)
Rates: $32-$80
Tel: (406) 646-7622

BUCKBOARD MOTEL
119 Electric St (59758)
Rates: $32-$70
Tel: (406) 646-9020
(800) 548-4117

CIRCLE R MOTEL
321 Madison (59758)
Rates: $26-$85
Tel: (406) 646-7641

DAYS INN
118 Electric St (59758)
Rates: $48-$78
Tel: (406) 646-7656
(800) 548-9551

EVERGREEN MOTEL
229 Firehole (59758)
Rates: $28-$79
Tel: (406) 646-7655

HIBERNATION STATION
Box 821 (59748)
Rates: $80+
Tel: (406) 646-4200

KELLY INN
104 S Canyon St (59748)
Rates: $80+
Tel: (406) 646-4544
(800) 259-4672

LAKE VIEW CABINS
15570 Hebgen Lake Rd (59748)
Rates: $40-$60
Tel: (406) 646-7257

MID TOWN MOTEL
24 Dunraven (59758)
Rates: $60-$80
Tel: (406) 646-7394
(800) 646-7365

RANCH MOTEL
235 Canyon (59748)
Rates: $60-$80
Tel: (406) 646-7388
(800) 234-4083

THREE BEAR LODGE ANNEX
24 Dunraven (59758)
Rates: $32-$70
Tel: (406) 646-7394
(800) 646-7353

THREE BEAR MOTOR LODGE
217 Yellowstone Ave (59758)
Rates: $31-$78
Tel: (406) 646-7353
(800) 646-7353

TRAVELERS LODGE
225 Yellowstone Ave (59758)
Rates: $40-$70
Tel: (406) 646-9561
(800) 831-5741

WEARY REST MOTEL
601 US 20 (59748)
Rates: $60-$80
Tel: (406) 646-7633

WHITE SULPHUR SPRINGS

SPA HOT SPRINGS MOTEL
202 W Main (59645)
Rates: $30-$40
Tel: (406) 547-3366

TENDERFOOT/HILAND MOTEL
301 W Main (59645)
Rates: $30-$40
Tel: (406) 547-3303
(800) 898-3303

WHITEFISH

ALLEN'S MOTEL
6540 US 93 S (59937)
Rates: $40-$60
Tel: (406) 862-3995

BEST WESTERN ROCKY MOUNTAIN LODGE
6510 US 93 S (59937)
Rates: $60-$80
Tel: (406) 862-2569
(800) 528-1234

CHALET MOTEL
6430 US 93 S (59937)
Rates: $30-$70
Tel: (406) 862-5581
(800) 462-3266

COMFORT INN GLACIER PARK
6390 US 93S (59937)
Rates: $29-$199
Tel: (406) 862-4020
(800) 221-2222

MOUNTAIN HOLIDAY MOTEL
6595 US 93 S (59937)
Rates: $40-$55
Tel: (406) 862-2548
(800) 543-8064

QUALITY INN PINE LODGE
920 Spokane Ave (59937)
Rates: $50-$95
Tel: (406) 862-7600
(800) 221-2222

SUPER 8 MOTEL
800 Spokane Ave (59937)
Rates: $37-52
Tel: (406) 862-8255
(800) 800-8000

WHITEFISH ATHLETIC CLUB
224 Spokane Ave (59937)
Rates: $40-$60
Tel: (406) 862-2535

WHITEFISH MOTEL
620 8th St (59937)
Rates: $40-$60
Tel: (406) 862-3507

WHITEHALL

CHIEF MOTEL
303 E Legion (59759)
Rates: $40-$60
Tel: (406) 287-3921

SUPER 8 MOTEL
515 N Whitehall St
(59759)
Rates: $36-$48
Tel: (406) 287-5588
(800) 800-8000

WIBAUX

SUPER 8 MOTEL
P. O. Box 275 (59353)
Rates: $20-$38
Tel: (406) 795-2666
(800) 800-8000

WISDOM

NEZ PIERCE MOTEL
Hwy 43, Box 123
(59761)
Rates: $30-$40
Tel: (406) 689-3254

WOLF POINT

HOMESTEAD INN MOTEL
101 US 2 E (59201)
Rates: $25-$37
Tel: (406) 653-1300
(800) 232-0986

SHERMAN MOTOR INN
200 E Main St
(59201)
Rates: $26-$35
Tel: (406) 653-1100
(800) 952-1100

ZORTMAN

BUCKHORN STORE, CABINS & RV PARK
1st & Main Sts,
Box 501 (59546)
Rates: $30-$40
Tel: (406) 673-3162

NEBRASKA

AINSWORTH

LAZY A MOTEL
1120 East 4th St
(69210)
Rates: $35+
Tel: (402) 387-2600

REMINGTON ARMS MOTEL
1000 E 4th (69210)
Rates: $35-$55
Tel: (402) 387-2220

SUPER 8 MOTEL
1025 E 4th St (69210)
Rates: $32-$40
Tel: (402) 387-0700
(800) 800-8000

ALLIANCE

IMA McCARROLL'S MOTEL
1028 E 3rd St (69301)
Rates: $34-48
Tel: (308) 762-3680
(800) 341-8000

SUNSET MOTEL
1210 E Hwy 2
(69301)
Rates: $45-$60
Tel: (308) 762-8660

SUPER 8 MOTEL
1419 W 3rd St
(69301)
Rates: $41-$58
Tel: (308) 762-8300
(800) 800-8000

WEST WAY MOTEL
1207 W Hwy 2 & 385
(69301)
Rates: $38-$67
Tel: (308) 762-4040

ALMA

SUPER OUTPOST MOTEL
N Hwy 183 & 136
(68920)
Rates: $35+
Tel: (308) 928-2116

ARAPAHOE

ARAPAHOE MOTEL
W Hwys 6 & 34
(68922)
Rates: $35+
Tel: (308) 962-7948

AUBURN

AUBURN INN
517 J St (68305)
Rates: $30-$49
Tel: (402) 274-3143
(800) 272-3143

PALMER HOUSE MOTEL
1918 J St (68305)
Rates: $35-$55
Tel: (402) 274-3193
(800) 272-3193

AURORA

HAMILTON MOTOR INN
Rt 3, Box 41A (68818)
Rates: $35-$65
Tel: (402) 694-6961

KEN'S MOTEL
1515 11th St (68818)
Rates: $26-$32
Tel: (402) 694-3141

BEATRICE

BEATRICE INN
3500 N 6th St (68310)
Rates: $35-$48
Tel: (402) 223-4074
(800) 232-8742

HOLIDAY VILLA MOTEL
1820 N 6th St (68310)
Rates: $35-$55
Tel: (402) 223-4036

SUPER 8 MOTEL
3210 N 6th St (68310)
Rates: $35-$55
Tel: (402) 223-3536
(800) 800-8000

BELLEVUE

AMERICAN FAMILY INN
1110 Fort Crook Rd S
(68005)
Rates: $35-$47
Tel: (402) 291-0804
(800) 253-2865

OFFUTT MOTOR COURT
3618 Fort Crook Rd
(68005)
Rates: $35+
Tel: (402) 291-4333

BLAIR

BLAIR HOUSE MOTEL
W Hwy 30 (68008)
Rates: $35-$55
Tel: (402) 426-4801

BRIDGEPORT

BELL MOTOR INN
P. O. Box 854 (69336)
Rates: $29-$38
Tel: (308) 262-0557

BROKEN BOW

WM PENN LODGE
853 E South E St
(68822)
Rates: $24-$40
Tel: (308) 872-2412

BURWELL

CALAMUS COUNTRY MOTEL
HC 79, Box 18A
(68823)
Rates: $35
Tel: (308) 346-4729

RODEO INN
Hwys 91 & 11
(68823)
Rates: $35
Tel: (308) 346-4408
(800) 926-9427

CALLAWAY

MOTEL 4
106 E Kimball St
(68825)
Rates: $35
Tel: (308) 836-2205

CAMBRIDGE

BUNKHOUSE MOTEL
E Hwy 6 & 34
(69022)
Rates: $35-$55
Tel: (308) 697-4540

MEDICINE CREEK LODGE
Rt 2, Box 93 (69022)
Rates: $35
Tel: (308) 697-3774

CENTRAL CITY

CRAWFORD MOTEL
RR 1, Box 270 (68826)
Rates: $18-$25
Tel: (308) 946-3051

CREST MOTEL
E Hwy 30 (68826)
Rates: $35
Tel: (308) 946-3077

CHADRON

BEST WESTERN WEST HILLS INN
1100 W 10th St
(69337)
Rates: $42-$125
Tel: (308) 432-3305
(800) 528-1234

BLAINE MOTEL
159 Bordeaux St
(69337)
Rates: $35-$55
Tel: (308) 432-5568
(800) 788-9428

THE OLDE MAIN STREET INN B&B
115 Main St (69337)
Rates: $35-$60
Tel: (308) 432-3380

COLUMBUS

GEMBOL'S MOTEL
3220 8th St (68601)
Rates: $35-$55
Tel: (402) 564-2729

NEW WORLD INN
265 33rd Ave (68601)
Rates: $43-$61
Tel: (402) 564-1492
(800) 433-1492

**IMA SEVEN
KNIGHTS MOTEL**
2222 23rd St (68601)
Rates: $26-$41
Tel: (402) 563-3533
(800) 341-8000

COZAD

**BUDGET HOST
CIRCLE S MOTEL**
P. O. Box 85 (69130)
Rates: $26-$34
Tel: (800) 283-4678

CRAWFORD

BUTTE RANCH
803 W Ashcreek Rd
(69339)
Rates: $55
Tel: (308) 665-2364

HILLTOP MOTEL
304 McPherson St
(69339)
Rates: $55
Tel: (308) 665-1144
(800) 504-1444

TOWN LINE MOTEL
Hwys 2 & 20 (69339)
Rates: $35-$55
Tel: (308) 665-1450

CRETE

VILLA MADRID MOTEL
Hwy 33 W (68333)
Rates: $27-$35
Tel: (402) 826-4341

CROFTON

BOGNER'S MOTEL
Hwys 12 & 121
(68730)
Rates: $35
Tel: (402) 388-4626

DAVID CITY

FIESTA MOTEL
N Hwy 15 (68632)
Rates: $35
Tel: (402) 356-3129

DONIPHAN

USA INNS
Rt 2, Box 190 E
(68832)
Rates: $33-$60
Tel: (308) 381-0111

EDGAR

HOTEL EDGAR
South end Main St,
Box 217 (68935)
Rates: $35
Tel: (402) 225-3228

ELM CREEK

1ST INTERSTATE INN
I-80 & Hwy 183
(68836)
Rates: $30-$40
Tel: (308) 856-4652

ELWOOD

J. J.'S MARINA
4 Lakeview Acres
Dr 14 (68937)
Rates: $55+
Tel: (308) 785-2836

FAIRBURY

CAPRI MOTEL
1100 14th St (68352)
Rates: $28-$32
Tel: (402) 729-3317

FALLS CITY

CHECK IN MOTEL
1901 Fulton St
(68355)
Rates: $35
Tel: (402) 245-2433

STEPHENSON MOTEL
2621 Harlan St
(68355)
Rates: $35-$55
Tel: (402) 245-2459

FRANKLIN

**PLANK'S
PLUNK N BUNK**
Hwy 10 & 136
(68939)
Rates: $35-$55
Tel: (308) 425-6269

FREMONT

COMFORT INN
1649 E 23rd St
(68025)
Rates: $37-$70
Tel: (402) 721-1109
(800) 221-2222

HOLIDAY LODGE
1220 E 23rd St
(68025)
Rates: $38-$45
Tel: (402) 727-1110
(800) 743-ROOM

SUPER 8 MOTEL
1250 E 23rd St
(68025)
Rates: $39-$48
Tel: (402) 727-4445
(800) 800-800

GERING

CIRCLE S LODGE
400 M St (69341)
Rates: $35-$55
Tel: (308) 436-2157

GIBBON

5 STAR MOTEL
I-80 Exit 285 (68840)
Rates: $35-$55
Tel: (308) 468-5256

GORDON

HILLS MOTEL
107 West Hwy 20
(69343)
Rates: n/a
Tel: (308) 282-1795

GOTHENBURG

TRAVEL INN
501 S Lake (69138)
Rates: $35-$55
Tel: (308) 537-3638

**WESTERN
MOTOR INN**
1102 21st St (69138)
Rates: $35-$55
Tel: (308) 537-3622

GRAND ISLAND

**BEST WESTERN
RIVERSIDE INN**
3333 Ramada Rd
(68801)
Rates: $44-$60
Tel: (800) 528-1234

**BUDGET HOST
ISLAND INN**
2311 S Locust St
(68801)
Rates: $26-$32
Tel: (308) 382-1815
(800) 283-4678

CONOCO MOTEL
2107 W 2nd St
(68803)
Rates: $32-$36
Tel: (308) 384-2700

HOLIDAY INN I-80
P. O. Box 1501
(68802)
Rates: $45-$70
Tel: (308) 384-1330
(800) 465-4329

**HOLIDAY INN
MIDTOWN**
2503 S Locust St
(68801)
Rates: $54-$61
Tel: (800) 465-4329

IMA LAZY V MOTEL
2703 E Hwy 30
(68801)
Rates: $24-$30
Tel: (308) 384-0700
(800) 341-8000

MOTEL 6
3021 S Locust St
(68801)
Rates: $27-$31
Tel: (308) 384-4100
(800) 440-6000

OAK GROVE INN
3205 S Locust St
(68801)
Rates: $28-$37
Tel: (308) 384-1333
(800) 435-7144

SUPER 8 MOTEL
2603 S Locust St
(68801)
Rates: $40-$51
Tel: (308) 384-4380
(800) 800-8000

USA INNS
7000 S Nine Bridge
Rd (68832)
Rates: $33-$45
Tel: (308) 381-0111

GREENWOOD

DAYS INN
13006 238th St
(68366)
Rates: $32-$42
Tel: (402) 944-3313
(800) 329-7466

HASTINGS

ECONO LODGE
2903 W Osborne Dr
(68901)
Rates: $40-47
Tel: (800) 424-4777

HOLIDAY INN
P. O. Box 2089
(68901)
Rates: $60-$100
Tel: (402) 463-6721
(800) 465-4329

MIDLANDS LODGE
910 West J St (68901)
Rates: $26-$32
Tel: (402) 463-2428
(800) 237-1872

RAINBOW MOTEL
1400 West J St
(68901)
Rates: $26-$35
Tel: (402) 463-2989
(800) 825-7424

SUPER 8 MOTEL
2200 Kansas Ave
(68901)
Rates: $40-$53
Tel: (402) 463-8888
(800) 800-8000

USA INNS
2424 E Osborne Dr
(68901)
Rates: $38-$43
Tel: (402) 463-1422

WAYFAIR MOTEL
101 East J St (68901)
Rates: $35-$55
Tel: (402) 463-2434

X-L MOTEL
1400 West J St
(68901)
Rates: $27-$37
Tel: (402) 463-3148
(800) 341-8000

HAYES CENTER

MIDWAY MOTEL
Hwy 25 (69032)
Rates: $35
Tel: (308) 286-3253

HEBRON

RIVERSIDE MOTEL
S Hwy 81 (68370)
Rates: $35-$55
Tel: (402) 768-7366

WAYFARER MOTEL
104 N 13th St (68370)
Rates: $35
Tel: (402) 768-7226

HENDERSON

WAYFARER MOTEL
Jct I-80 & S-93A
(68371)
Rates: $28-$32
Tel: (800) 543-0577

HOLDREGE

IMA PLAINS MOTEL
619 W Hwy 6
(68949)
Rates: $32-$60
Tel: (308) 995-8646
(800) 341-8000

TOWER MOTEL
413 West 4th Ave
(68949)
Rates: n/a
Tel: (308) 995-4488

KEARNEY

**BEST WESTERN
TEL-STAR INN**
1010 3rd Ave (68848)
Rates: $52-$67
Tel: (308) 237-5185
(800) 528-1234

**BUDGET MOTEL
SOUTH**
411 S 2nd Ave
(68847)
Rates: $35-$65
Tel: (308) 237-5991

FORT KEARNY INN
Box 16881, I-80 Exit
272 (68848)
Rates: $33-$70
Tel: (308) 234-2541

**HOLIDAY INN-
HOLIDOME**
P. O. Box 1118
(68848)
Rates: $65-$100
Tel: (308) 237-3141
(800) 465-4329

**KEARNEY INN
4 LESS**
709 2nd Ave
(68847)
Rates: $32-$46
Tel: (308) 237-2671

SUPER 8 MOTEL
15 W 8th St (68847)
Rates: $40-$60
Tel: (308) 234-5513
(800) 800-8000

**WESTERN INN
SOUTH**
510 3rd Ave (68847)
Rates: $28-$49
Tel: (308) 234-1876
(800) 437-8457

WESTERN MOTEL
824 E 25th St (68847)
Rates: $35-$55
Tel: (308) 234-2408
(800) 234-2308

KIMBALL

FINER MOTEL
Rt 1, Box 126 (69145)
Rates: $35-$55
Tel: (308) 235-4878

**1ST INTERSTATE
INN**
Rt 1, Box 136 (69145)
Rates: $27-$60
Tel: (308) 235-4601
(800) 462-4667

MOTEL KIMBALL
Rt 1, Box 131 (69145)
Rates: $35-$55
Tel: (308) 235-4606

WESTERN MOTEL
914 W Hwy 30
(69145)
Rates: $55+
Tel: (308) 235-4622

LAUREL

BIG RED MOTEL
202 S Hwy 20
(68745)
Rates: $35-$55
Tel: (402) 256-9952

LEWELLEN

**GANDER INN
MOTEL**
S Main St (69147)
Rates: $35
Tel: (308) 778-5616

LEXINGTON

**GREEN VALLEY
MOTEL**
311 W 5th (68850)
Rates: $35
Tel: (308) 324-3216

**MINUTE MAN
MOTEL**
801 S Bridge St
(68850)
Rates: $30-$38
Tel: (308) 324-5540
(800) 973-5544

DAYS INN
Hwy 285 &
Commerce Rd
(68850)
Rates: $34-$44
Tel: (308) 324-6440
(800) 329-7466

ECONO LODGE
I-80 at US 283 (68850)
Rates: $30-$41
Tel: (308) 324-5601
(800) 424-4777

TODDLE INN MOTEL
2701 Plum Creek
Pkwy (68850)
Rates: $29-$49
Tel: (308) 324-5595

LINCOLN

AIRPORT LODGE
2410 NW 12th
(68508)
Rates: $30-$45
Tel: (402) 474-1311
(800) 747-9311

**BEST WESTERN
AIRPORT INN**
1200 W Cornhusker
Hwy (68521)
Rates: $46-$74
Tel: (402) 475-9541
(800) 528-1234

**BEST WESTERN
VILLAGER
MOTOR INN**
5200 O St (68510)
Rates: $64-$84
Tel: (402) 464-9111
(800) 528-1234

**COMFORT INN
AIRPORT**
2940 NW 12th St
(68521)
Rates: $39-$70
Tel: (402) 464-2200
(800) 221-2222

COMFORT SUITES
4231 Industrial Ave
(68521)
Rates: $46-$75
Tel: (402) 464-8080
(800) 221-2222

CONGRESS INN
2001 West O St
(68528)
Rates: $30-$63
Tel: (402) 477-4488
(800) 447-2393

ECONO LODGE
2410 NW 12th St
(68521)
Rates: $29-$56
Tel: (402) 474-1311
(800) 424-4777

**ECONO LODGE-
NORTHEAST**
5600 Cornhusker
Hwy (68529)
Rates: $35-$50
Tel: (402) 464-5971
(800) 424-4777

**FAIRFIELD INN
BY MARRIOTT**
4221 Industrial Ave
(68504)
Rates: $47-$58
Tel: (402) 476-6000
(800) 228-2800

GUESTHOUSE INN
3245 Cornhusker
Hwy (68504)
Rates: $35-$55
Tel: (402) 466-2341

**HOLIDAY INN
AIRPORT**
1101 W Bond Circle
(68521)
Rates: $54-$90
Tel: (402) 475-4971
(800) 465-4329

INN 4 LESS
1140 W Cornhusker
Hwy (68521)
Rates: $35
Tel: (402) 475-4511

KING'S INN MOTEL
3510 Cornhusker
Hwy (68504)
Rates: $30-$60
Tel: (402) 466-2324

MOTEL 6
3001 NW 12th St
(68521)
Rates: $28-$34
Tel: (402) 475-3211
(800) 440-6000

QUALITY INN
5250 Cornhusker
Hwy (68504)
Rates: $55+
Tel: (402) 464-3171
(800) 221-2222

**RAMADA INN
AIRPORT**
2301 NW 12th St
(68521)
Rates: $44-$60
Tel: (402) 475-4400
(800) 272-6232

**RESIDENCE INN
BY MARRIOTT**
200 S 68th Pl (68510)
Rates: $94-$114
Tel: (402) 483-4900
(800) 331-3131

SENATE INN MOTEL
2801 West O St
(68528)
Rates: $24-$32
Tel: (402) 475-4921

STARLITE MOTEL
5200 Cornhusker
Hwy (68504)
Rates: $55+
Tel: (402) 466-1902

STOP 'N' SLEEP
1140 Calvert St
(68502)
Rates: $40-$55
Tel: (402) 423-7111

**TOWN HOUSE
MOTEL**
1744 M St (68508)
Rates: $41-$69
Tel: (402) 475-3000
(800) 279-1744

LOUP CITY

COLONY INN
Rt 1, Box 184 (68853)
Rates: $35
Tel: (308) 745-0164

McCOOK

CEDAR MOTEL
1400 East C St
(69001)
Rates: $35-$55
Tel: (308) 345-7091
(800) 352-4489

RED HORSE MOTEL
E Hwys 6 & 34
(69001)
Rates: $35-$55
Tel: (308) 345-2800

SUPER 8 MOTEL
1103 East B St
(69001)
Rates: $34-$50
Tel: (308) 345-1141
(800) 800-8000

MINDEN

**PIONEER VILLAGE
MOTEL**
224 E Hwy 6 (68959)
Rates: $30-$55
Tel: (308) 832-2750
(800) 445-4447

NEBRASKA CITY

**AMERICAN STAR
INN**
1715 S 11th (68410)
Rates: $55+
Tel: (402) 873-6656
(800) 647-1343

APPLE INN
502 S 11th (68410)
Rates: $34-$43
Tel: (402) 873-5959
(800) 659-4446

NELIGH

DELUXE MOTEL
Hwy 275 E (68756)
Rates: $35-$55
Tel: (402) 887-4628

**WEST HILLVIEW
MOTEL**
RR 2, Box 43 (68756)
Rates: $35-$50
Tel: (402) 887-4186

NIOBRARA

**TWO RIVERS
SALOON & HOTEL**
254 - 12 Park Ave
(68760)
Rates: $35-$55
Tel: (402) 857-3340

NORFOLK

BLUE RIDGE MOTEL
916 S 13th St (68701)
Rates: $35
Tel: (402) 371-0530

**NORFOLK COUNTRY
INN**
P. O. Box 181 (68701)
Rates: $48-$54
Tel: (402) 371-4430

NORTH PLATTE

BAR X MOTEL
905 N Jeffers (69101)
Rates: $35-$55
Tel: (308) 532-0664

**BEST WESTERN
CHALET LODGE**
920 N Jeffers St
(69101)
Rates: $40-$65
Tel: (308) 532-2313
(800) 528-1234

**BLUE SPRUCE
MOTEL**
821 S Dewey (69101)
Rates: $35-$55
Tel: (308) 534-2600

**CAMINO INN
SUITES**
2102 S Jeffers (69101)
Rates: $50-$66
Tel: (308) 532-9090
(800) 760-3333

COUNTRY INN
321 S Dewey (69101)
Rates: $27-$32
Tel: (308) 532-8130

**1ST INTERSTATE
INN**
I-80 & Hwy (69101)
Rates: $35-$50
Tel: (308) 532-6980

GREEN ACRES
4601 Rodeo Rd
(69101)
Rates: $55-$65
Tel: (308) 532-6654

MOTEL 6
1520 S Jeffers (69101)
Rates: $32-$38
Tel: (308) 534-6200
(800) 440-6000

PARK MOTEL
1302 N Jeffers(69101)
Rates: $26-$37
Tel: (308) 532-6834

PIONEER MOTEL
902 S Dewey (69101)
Rates: $35-$55
Tel: (308) 532-8730

RAMBLER INN
1420 Rodeo Rd
(69101)
Rates: $25-$35
Tel: (308) 532-9290

SANDS MOTOR INN
501 Halligan Dr
(69101)
Rates: $30-$50
Tel: (308) 532-0151

STANFORD MOTEL
1400 E 4th St (69101)
Rates: $30-49
Tel: (308) 532-9380

STOCKMAN INN
1402 S Jeffers (69103)
Rates: $41-$65
Tel: (308) 534-3630

SUPER 8 MOTEL
220 Eugene Ave
(69101)
Rates: $34-$57
Tel: (308) 532-4224
(800) 800-8000

TRAVELERS INN
602 E 4th St (69101)
Rates: $28-$40
Tel: (308) 534-4020
(800) 341-8000

OGALLALA

**BEST WESTERN
STAGECOACH INN**
201 Stagecoach Tr
(69153)
Rates: $39-85
Tel: (308) 284-3656
(800) 662-2993

DAYS INN
601 Stagecoach Tr
(69153)
Rates: $34-$48
Tel: (308) 284-6365
(800) 329-7466

OMAHA

**BEN FRANKLIN
MOTEL**
10308 Frontage Rd
(68138)
Rates: $45-$60
Tel: (402) 895-2200
(800) 341-8000

**1ST INTERSTATE
INN**
108 Prospector Dr
(69153)
Rates: $25-$50
Tel: (308) 285-2056
(800) 462-4667

KINGSLEY LODGE
R 2, P. O. Box 62-0
(69153)
Rates: $35-$55
Tel: (308) 284-2775
(800) 883-2775

LAKEWAY LODGE
918 N Spruce St
(69153)
Rates: $35-$55
Tel: (308) 284-4431

PLAZA INN
311 E 1st (69153)
Rates: $55-$65
Tel: (308) 284-8416

RAMADA LIMITED
201 Chuckwagon Rd
(69153)
Rates: $49
Tel: (308) 284-3623
(800) 272-6232

SUNSET MOTEL
1021 W 1st (69153)
Rates: $35
Tel: (308) 284-4264

SUPER 8 MOTEL
500 East A South
(69153)
Rates: $33-$44
Tel: (308) 284-2076
(800) 800-8000

**WESTERN PARADISE
MOTEL**
221 E 1st (69153)
Rates: $35-$55
Tel: (308) 284-3684
(800) 733-0899

BUDGETEL INN
10760 M St (68127)
Rates: $40-$63
Tel: (402) 592-5200
(800) 428-3438

CLARION HOTEL
10909 M St (68137)
Rates: $69-$175
Tel: (402) 331-8220
(800) 221-2222

COMFORT INN
10919 J St (68137)
Rates: $50-$75
Tel: (402) 592-2882
(800) 221-2222

ECONO LODGE
7833 W Dodge
Rd(68124)
Rates: $39-$70
Tel: (402) 391-7100
(800) 424-4777

**HAMPTON INN-
SOUTHWEST**
10728 L St (68127)
Rates: $55-$64
Tel: (402) 593-2380
(800) 426-7866

HAWTHORN SUITES
11025 M Street
(68137)
Rates: $55-$65
Tel: (402) 331-0101
(800) 527-1133

LA QUINTA INN
3330 N 104th Ave
(68134)
Rates: $49-$61
Tel: (402) 493-1900
(800) 221-4731

MARRIOTT HOTEL
10220 Regency Cir
(68114)
Rates: $72-$250
Tel: (402) 399-9000
(800) 228-9290

MOTEL 6
10708 M St (68127)
Rates: $33-$39
Tel: (402) 331-3161
(800) 440-6000

**PARK INN
INTERNATIONAL**
9305 S 145th St
(68138)
Rates: $40-$65
Tel: (402) 895-2555
(800) 437-7275

RAMADA INN AIRPORT
Abbott Dr & Locust St (68110)
Rates: $58-$95
Tel: (402) 342-5100
(800) 272-6232

RAMADA INN CENTRAL I-80
7007 Grover St (68106)
Rates: $89-$135
Tel: (402) 391-7030
(800) 272-6232

RESIDENCE INN BY MARRIOTT
6990 Dodge St (68132)
Rates: $99-$130
Tel: (402) 553-8898
(800) 331-3131

SATELLITE MOTEL
6006 L St (68117)
Rates: $30-$40
Tel: (402) 733-7373

SHERATON INN
4888 S 118th St (68137)
Rates: $75-$86
Tel: (402) 895-1000
(800) 662-4280

TOWNHOUSE INN
13929 Gold Cir (68144)
Rates: $55-$65
Tel: (402) 333-3777

O'NEILL

BUDGET HOST CARRIAGE HOUSE MOTEL
929 E Douglas St (68763)
Rates: $35-$55
Tel: (402) 336-3403
(800) 345-7989

CAPRI MOTEL
1020 E Douglas St (68763)
Rates: $28-$45
Tel: (402) 336-2762

ELMS MOTEL
E Hwys 20 & 275 (68763)
Rates: $30-$45
Tel: (402) 336-3800
(800) 526-9052

GOLDEN HOTEL
406 E Douglas St (68763)
Rates: $19-$32
Tel: (402) 336-4436
(800) 658-3148

INNKEEPER
725 E Douglas St (68763)
Rates: $35-$60
Tel: (402) 336-1640

ORCHARD

ORCHARD MOTEL
E Hwy 20 (68764)
Rates: $35
Tel: (402) 893-2165

OSHKOSH

S & S MOTEL
Hwy 26 & 27 (69154)
Rates: $35
Tel: (308) 772-3350

SHADY REST MOTEL
Rt 1, Box 75 (69154)
Rates: $25-$35
Tel: (308) 772-4115

PAWNEE CITY

PAWNEE INN
1021 F St (68420)
Rates: $35-$55
Tel: (402) 852-2238

PLATTSMOUTH

BROWN'S FAMILY MOTEL
1913 Hwy 34 E (68048)
Rates: $55-$65
Tel: (402) 296-9266

RANDOLPH

CEDAR MOTEL
107 East Hwy 20 (68771)
Rates: $25-$35
Tel: (402) 337-0500

RED CLOUD

MCFARLAND HOTEL
137 West 4th Ave (68970)
Rates: $25-$35
Tel: (402) 746-3591

REPUBLICAN CITY

GATEWAY MOTEL
17 Hwy 136 (68971)
Rates: $35
Tel: (308) 799-2815

RUSHVILLE

ANTLERS MOTEL
607 East 2nd St (69360)
Rates: $30-$60
Tel: (308) 327-2444

NEBRASKALAND MOTEL
508 East 2nd, Box 377 (69360)
Rates: $35-$55
Tel: (308) 327-2277

ST. PAUL

KELLER'S KORNER MOTEL
1517 2nd St (68873)
Rates: $35
Tel: (308) 754-4451

SUPER 8 MOTEL
116 Howard Ave (68873)
Rates: $38-58
Tel: (308) 754-4554
(800) 800-8000

SCHUYLER

JOHNNIE'S MOTEL
222 W 16th (68661)
Rates: $26-$37
Tel: (402) 352-5454

VALLEY COURT MOTEL
320 W 16th St (68661)
Rates: $35
Tel: (402) 352-3326

SCOTTSBLUFF

CAPRI MOTEL
2424 Ave I (69361)
Rates: $28-$40
Tel: (308) 635-2057
(800) 642-2774

LAMPLIGHTER MOTEL
606 E 27th St (69361)
Rates: $32-$43
Tel: (308) 632-7108
(800) 341-8000

SANDS MOTEL
814 W 27th St (69361)
Rates: $27-$40
Tel: (308) 632-6191

SCOTTSBLUFF INN
1901 21st Ave (69361)
Rates: $50-$85
Tel: (308) 635-3111
(800) 597-3111

SEWARD

EAST HILL MOTEL
131 Hwy 34 E (68434)
Rates: $35
Tel: (402) 643-3679

SUPER 8 MOTEL
S Hwy 15 (68434)
Rates: $38-$51
Tel: (402) 643-3388
(800) 800-8000

SIDNEY

DAYS INN
3042 Silverberg Dr (69162)
Rates: $55-$65
Tel: (308) 254-2121
(800) 329-7466

FORT SIDNEY INN
935 9th Ave (69162)
Rates: $33-$85
Tel: (308) 254-5863

GENERIC MOTEL
11552 Hwy 30 (69162)
Rates: $35-$55
Tel: (308) 254-4527
(800) 893-5309

SIDNEY

MOTOR LODGE
2031 W Illinois St
(69162)
Rates: $32-$50
Tel: (308) 254-4581
(800) 341-8000

SUPER 8 MOTEL
2115 W Illinois St
(69162)
Rates: $37-$49
Tel: (308) 254-2081
(800) 800-8000

SOUTH SIOUX CITY

ECONO LODGE
4402 Dakota Ave
(68776)
Rates: $35-$57
Tel: (402) 494-4114
(800) 424-4777

THE MARINA INN
4th & B Sts (68776)
Rates: $60-$80
Tel: (402) 494-4000
(800) 798-7980

PARK PLAZA MOTEL
1201 1st Ave (68776)
Rates: $35-$53
Tel: (402) 494-2021
(800) 341-8000

TRAVELODGE
400 Dakota Ave
(68776)
Rates: $36-$46
Tel: (402) 494-3046
(800) 578-7878

SPENCER

SKYLINE MOTEL
Hwys 281 & 12
(68777)
Rates: $35
Tel: (402) 589-1300
(800) 917-1300

SUTHERLAND

PARK MOTEL
1110 1st St (69165)
Rates: $35
Tel: (308) 386-4384
(800) 437-2565

SUTTON

SUTTON MOTEL
208 N French (68979)
Rates: $25-$35
Tel: (402) 773-4803

THEDFORD

RODEWAY INN
HC 58, Box 1-D
(69166)
Rates: $40-$55
Tel: (308) 645-2284
(800) 424-4777

VALENTINE

BALLARD MOTEL
227 S Hall St (69201)
Rates: $35
Tel: (402) 376-2922

COMFORT INN
101 Main St (69201)
Rates: $55-$65
Tel: (402) 376-3300
(800) 221-2222

FOUNTAIN INN
237 S Cherry St
(69201)
Rates: $55
Tel: (402) 376-2300

MERRITT RESORT
HC 32, Box 23
(69201)
Rates: $60
Tel: (402) 376-3437

MOTEL RAINE
W Hwy 20 (69201)
Rates: $30-$45
Tel: (402) 376-2030
(800) 999-3066

**TRADE WINDS
LODGE-IMA**
HC 37, Box 2 (69201)
Rates: $25-$50
Tel: (402) 376-1600
(800) 341-8000

VALENTINE MOTEL
Hwy 20 & 83 (69201)
Rates: $35-$55
Tel: (402) 376-2450
(800) 376-2450

WAHOO

**BILL'S WAHOO
MOTEL**
Hwys 77, 92 & 109
(68066)
Rates: $35
Tel: (402) 443-9933

WAUSA

**COMMERCIAL
HOTEL**
Main St (68786)
Rates: $35-$55
Tel: (402) 586-2377

WAYNE

K-D INN MOTEL
311 East 7th St
(68787)
Rates: n/a
Tel: (402) 375-1770

WEST POINT

SUPER 8 MOTEL
1211 N Lincoln
(68788)
Rates: $40-52
Tel: (402) 372-3998
(800) 800-8000

WISNER

MIDWEST MOTEL
1612 Ave E (68791)
Rates: $35-$55
Tel: (402) 529-6910

WOOD RIVER

**WOOD RIVER
MOTEL**
11774 S Hwy 11
(68883)
Rates: $35
Tel: (308) 583-2256
(800) 587-2256

WYMORE

D & M MOTEL
601 S 14th St (68466)
Rates: $35
Tel: (402) 645-3801

YORK

**BEST WESTERN
PALMER INN**
2426 S Lincoln Ave
(68467)
Rates: $39-$69
Tel: (402) 362-5585
(800) 528-1234

STAEHR MOTEL
RR 4, Box 49 (68467)
Rates: $35-$55
Tel: (402) 362-4804

SUPER 8 MOTEL
Box 532 (68467)
Rates: $39-$54
Tel: (402) 362-3388
(800) 800-8000

USA INNS
4817 S Lincoln Ave
(68467)
Rates: $34-$40
Tel: (402) 362-6885
(800) 348-0427

NEVADA

ALAMO

MEADOW LANE MOTEL
US Hwy 93 (89001)
Rates: $27-$45
Tel: (702) 725-3371

AMARGOSA VALLEY

LONGSTREET INN & CASINO
Hwy 373 (89020)
Rates: $48-$79
Tel: (702) 372-1777

AUSTIN

MOUNTAIN MOTEL
Hwy 50, P. O. Box 91 (89310)
Rates: $30-$55
Tel: (702) 964-2471

PONY CANYON MOTEL
Hwy 50,
P. O. Box 209 (89310)
Rates: $32-$52
Tel: (702) 964-2605

THE PONY EXPRESS HOUSE
115 NW Main St (89310)
Rates: $35
Tel: (702) 964-2306

BAKER

BORDER INN
Hwys 50 & 6 (89311)
Rates: n/a
Tel: (702) 234-7300

SILVERJACK MOTEL
Main St,
P. O. Box 166 (89311)
Rates: $31-$54
Tel: (702) 234-7323

BATTLE MOUNTAIN

BEL COURT MOTEL
292 E Front St (89820)
Rates: $19-$30
Tel: (702) 635-2569

BEST WESTERN BIG CHIEF MOTEL
434 W Front St (89820)
Rates: $49-$87
Tel: (702) 635-2416
(800) 528-1234

COLT SERVICE CENTER
650 W Front St (89820)
Rates: $37-$51
Tel: (702) 635-5424
(800) 343-0085

HO MOTEL
150 W Front St (89820)
Rates: $20
Tel: (702) 635-5101

HOLIDAY INN EXPRESS
521 E Front St (89820)
Rates: $44-$49
Tel: (800) 465-4329

NEVADA HOTEL
36 E Front St (89820)
Rates: $17-$60
Tel: (702) 635-2453

BEATTY

STAGECOACH HOTEL & CASINO
SR 95, P. O. Box 836 (89003)
Rates: $25-$48
Tel: (702) 553-2419
(800) 4BIG-WIN

BOULDER CITY

DESERT INN OF BOULDER CITY
800 Nevada Hwy (89005)
Rates: $30-$100
Tel: (702) 293-2827

FLAMINGO INN MOTEL
804 Nevada Hwy (89005)
Rates: $27-$60
Tel: (702) 293-3565

LAKE MEAD RESORT & MARINA
322 Lakeshore Rd (89005)
Rates: $50-$125
Tel: (702) 293-2074
(800) 752-9669

STARVIEW MOTEL
1017 Nevada Hwy (89005)
Rates: $25-$75
Tel: (702) 293-1658

CALIENTE

CALIENTE HOT SPRINGS MOTEL
Hwy 93 N (89008)
Rates: $34-$75
Tel: (702) 726-3777
(800) 748-4785

LONGHORN CATTLE COMPANY GUEST RANCH
Rainbow Canyon Rd (89008)
Rates: $100+
Tel: (702) 388-9955

RAINBOW CANYON MOTEL
884 A St (89008)
Rates: $31-$40
Tel: (702) 726-3291

SHADY MOTEL
450 Front St (89008)
Rates: $33-$40
Tel: (702) 726-3274

CARSON CITY

BEST WESTERN TRAILSIDE INN
1300 N Carson St (89701)
Rates: $46-$150
Tel: (702) 883-7300
(800) 528-1234

CARSON MOTOR LODGE
1421 N Carson St (89701)
Rates: $30-$42
Tel: (702) 882-3572

DAYS INN
3103 N Carson St (89701)
Rates: $40-$100
Tel: (702) 883-3343
(800) 329-7466

DESERT HILLS MOTEL
1010 S Carson St (89701)
Rates: n/a
Tel: (702) 882-1932

MOTEL ORLEANS
2731 S Carson St (89701)
Rates: $29-$70
Tel: (702) 882-2007
(800) 626-1900

MOTEL 6
2749 S Carston St (89701)
Rates: $29-$36
Tel: (702) 885-7710
(800) 440-6000

PIONEER MOTEL
907 S Carson St (89701)
Rates: $28-$65
Tel: (702) 882-3046
(800) 882-3046

ROUND HOUSE INN
1400 N Carson St (89701)
Rates: $29-$99
Tel: (702) 882-3446

ROYAL CREST INN
1930 N Carson
(89701)
Rates: n/a
Tel: (702) 882-1785

SIERRA SAGE MOTEL
801 S Carson St
(89701)
Rates: $25-$60
Tel: (702) 882-1419

SIERRA VISTA MOTEL
711 S Plaza St
(89701)
Rates: $30-$75
Tel: (702) 883-9500
(800) NEVADA-1

DENIO

DENIO JUNCTION MOTEL
P. O. Box 10 (89404)
Rates: $27-$44
Tel: (702) 941-0371

ECHO BAY

ECHO BAY RESORT
On Lake Mead
(Overton 89040)
Rates: $69-$84
Tel: (702) 394-4000
(800) 752-9669

ELKO

BEST WESTERN AMERITEL INN EXPRESS
837 Idaho St (89801)
Rates: $49-$69
Tel: (702) 738-7261
(800) 528-1234

BEST WESTERN GOLD COUNTRY MOTOR INN
2050 Idaho St
(89801)
Rates: $69-$94
Tel: (702) 738-8421
(800) 528-1234

CENTRE MOTEL
475 Third St (89801)
Rates: $30-$48
Tel: (702) 738-3226

ELKO MOTEL
1243 Idaho St
(89801)
Rates: $27-$59
Tel: (702) 738-4433

ESQUIRE MOTEL LODGE
505 Idaho St (89801)
Rates: $28-$65
Tel: (702) 738-3157
(800) 822-7473

HOLIDAY INN
3015 Idaho St
(89801)
Rates: $53-$75
Tel: (800) 465-4329

JIGGS GUEST RANCH
HC 30, Box 197
(89801)
Rates: $150+
Tel: (702) 744-2277

LOUIS MOTEL
2100 Idaho St
(89801)
Rates: $25-$50
Tel: (702) 738-3536

MOTEL 6
3021 Idaho St
(89801)
Rates: $28-$34
Tel: (702) 738-4337

RED LION INN & CASINO
2065 Idaho St
(89801)
Rates: $65-$83
Tel: (800) 547-8010

RUBY CREST GUEST RANCH
HC 30, Box 197
(89801)
Rates: 150+
Tel: (702) 744-2277

RUBY MARSHES GUEST RANCH
HC 30, Box 197
(89801)
Rates: $150+
Tel: (702) 744-2277

SHILO INNS
2401 Mountain City
Hwy (89801)
Rates: $65-$89
Tel: (800) 222-2244

THUNDERBIRD MOTEL
345 Idaho St (89801)
Rates: $39-$57
Tel: (702) 738-7115

TOWNE HOUSE MOTEL
500 W Oak St
(89801)
Rates: $30-$46
Tel: (702) 738-7269

TRAVELERS MOTEL
1181 Idaho St (89801)
Rates: $28-$65
Tel: (702) 738-4048

ELY

BEST WESTERN MAIN MOTEL
1101 Aultman St
(89301)
Rates: $41-$65
Tel: (702) 289-4529
(800) 528-1234

BEST WESTERN PARK VUE
930 Aultman St
(89301)
Rates: $43-$65
Tel: (702) 289-4497
(800) 528-1234

EL RANCHO MOTEL
1400 Aultman St
(89301)
Rates: $25-$40
Tel: (702) 289-3644

FIRESIDE INN
McGill Hwy (89301)
Rates: $34-$41
Tel: (702) 289-3765

GRAND CENTRAL MOTEL
1498 Lyons Ave
(89301)
Rates: $26+
Tel: (702) 289-6868

GREAT BASIN INN
701 Ave F (89301)
Rates: $32-$60
Tel: (702) 289-4468

HOTEL NEVADA
501 Aultman St
(89301)
Rates: $28-$95
Tel: (702) 289-6665

IDLE INN MOTEL
150 Fourth St (89301)
Rates: $22-$35
Tel: (702) 289-4411

LANE'S RANCH MOTEL
HC 34, Box 34145
(89301)
Rates: $27-$43
Tel: (702) 238-5246

RAMADA INN COPPER QUEEN HOTEL & CASINO
701 Ave I (89301)
Rates: $50-$84
Tel: (702) 289-4884
(800) 851-9526

MOTEL 6
7th St & Ave O
(89301)
Rates: $28-$34
Tel: (792) 289-6671
(800) 440-6000

RUSTIC INN
1555 Aultman St
(89301)
Rates: $25-$50
Tel: (702) 289-4404

SURE REST MOTEL
1550 High St (89301)
Rates: $28-$38
Tel: (702) 289-2512

WHITE PINE MOTEL
1301 Aultman St
(89301)
Rates: $33-$45
Tel: (702) 289-3800

EUREKA

COLONNADE HOTEL
Clark & Monroe Sts
(89316)
Rates: $23-$32
Tel: (702) 237-9988

EUREKA MOTEL
10289 Main St
(89316)
Rates: $25-$41
Tel: (702) 237-5247

JACKSON HOUSE BED & BREAKFAST
10200 Main St
(89316)
Rates: $30-$57
Tel: (702) 237-5577

RUBY HILL MOTEL
Hwy 50, P. O. Box
281 (89316)
Rates: $25-$38
Tel: (702) 237-5339

SUNDOWN LODGE
Main St, P. O. Box
324 (89316)
Rates: $31-$45
Tel: (702) 237-5334

FALLON

BUDGET INN
1705 S Taylor (89406)
Rates: $35-$55
Tel: (702) 423-2277

COMFORT INN
1830 W Williams
Ave (89406)
Rates: $47-$65
Tel: (702) 423-5554
(800) 221-2222

**NEVADA BELLE
MOTEL**
25 N Taylor St
(89406)
Rates: $29-$52
Tel: (702) 423-4648

WESTERN MOTEL
125 S Carson St
(89406)
Rates: $32-$38
Tel: (702) 423-5118

FERNLEY

**BEST WESTERN
FERNLEY INN**
1405 E Newlands Dr
(89408)
Rates: $42-89
Tel: (702) 575-6776
(800) 528-1234

**REST RANCHO
MOTEL**
350 Main (89408)
Rates: n/a
Tel: (702) 575-4452

TRUCK INN
485 Truck Inn Way
(89408)
Rates: $30-$50
Tel: (702) 351-1000

GABBS

GABBS MOTEL
100 S Main St
(89409)
Rates: $28-$45
Tel: (702) 285-4019

GARDNERVILLE

**THE NENZEL
MANSION**
1431 Ezell St (89410)
Rates: $80-$95
Tel: (702) 782-7644

TOPAZ LODGE
1979 US 395S (89410)
Rates: $39-$48
Tel: (702) 266-3338

WESTERNER MOTEL
1353 US 395S (89410)
Rates: $30-$43
Tel: (702) 782-3602

GERLACH

**BRUNO'S
COUNTRY CLUB**
300 Main St (89412)
Rates: $30-$45
Tel: (702) 557-2220

HAWTHORNE

ANCHOR MOTEL
965 Sierra Way
(89415)
Rates: $27-$32
Tel: (702) 945-2573

**BEST WESTERN
DESERT LODGE**
1402 E Fifth St
(89415)
Rates: $55-$75
Tel: (702) 945-2600
(800) 528-1234

**CLIFF HOUSE
LAKESIDE RESORT**
1 Cliff House Rd
(89415)
Rates: $30-$34
Tel: (702) 945-2444

**EL CAPITAN
MOTOR LODGE**
540 F St (89415)
Rates: $28-$42
Tel: (702) 945-3321

**HAWTHORNE
MOTEL**
720 Sierra Hwy 95
(89415)
Rates: $25-$30
Tel: (702) 945-2544

HOLIDAY LODGE
Fifth & J Sts (89415)
Rates: $26-$32
Tel: (702) 945-3316

MONARCH MOTEL
1291 E Fifth St
(89415)
Rates: $25-$30
Tel: (702) 945-3117

ROCKET MOTEL
694 Sierra Way
(89415)
Rates: $22-$25
Tel: (702) 945-2143

**SAND N SAGE
MOTEL**
P. O. Box 2325
(89415)
Rates: $28-$40
Tel: (702) 945-3352

WRIGHT MOTEL
W Fifth & I Sts
(89415)
Rates: $28-$38
Tel: (702) 945-2213

HENDERSON

BOBY MOTEL
2100 S Boulder Hwy
(89015)
Rates: $30-$45
Tel: (702) 565-9711

OUTPOST MOTEL
1104 N Boulder Hwy
(89015)
Rates: $36-$54
Tel: (702) 564-2664

SKY MOTEL
1713 N Boulder
Hwy (89015)
Rates: $32-$48
Tel: (702) 564-1534

INDIAN
SPRINGS

**INDIAN SPRINGS
MOTOR HOTEL**
P. O. Box 270 (89018)
Rates: $35-$37
Tel: (702) 879-3700

JACKPOT

BARTON'S CLUB 93
Hwy 93, P. O. Box
523 (89825)
Rates: $35-$65
Tel: (702) 755-2341
(800) 258-2937

**HORSESHU
HOTEL & CASINO**
Hwy 93, Dice Rd
(89825)
Rates: $30-$75
Tel: (702) 755-7777

JARBIDGE

OUTDOOR INN
Main St (89826)
Rates: n/a
Tel: (702) 488-2311

LAKE TAHOE

**HORIZON CASINO
RESORT**
P. O. Box C (89449)
Rates: $69-$169
Tel: (702) 588-6211
(800) 322-7723

LAMOILLE

**BREITENSTEIN
HOUSE
BED & BREAKFAST**
P. O. Box 281381
(89828)
Rates: $55-$125
Tel: (702) 753-6356

**PINE LODGE-HOTEL
LAMOILLE**
Lamoille Hwy,
P. O. Box 281208
(89828)
Rates: $55-$85
Tel: (702) 753-6363

LAS VEGAS

BEST WESTERN HERITAGE INN
4975 S Valley View Blvd (89118)
Rates: $59-$150
Tel: (702) 798-7736
(800) 528-1234

BEST WESTERN MAIN STREET INN
1000 N Main St (89101)
Rates: $50-$85
Tel: (702) 382-3455
(800) 528-1234

BEST WESTERN NELLIS MOTOR INN
5330 E Craig Rd (89115)
Rates: $40-$59
Tel: (702) 643-6111
(800) 528-1234

BESTERN WESTERN PARKVIEW INN
905 Las Vegas Blvd N (89101)
Rates: $45-$72
Tel: (702) 385-1213
(800) 528-1234

CENTER STRIP INN
3688 Las Vegas Blvd S (89109)
Rates: $30-$150
Tel: (702) 739-6066
(800) 777-7737

CITY CENTER MOTEL
700 E Fremont St (89101)
Rates: $30-$70
Tel: (702) 382-4766

COMFORT INN NORTH
910 E Cheyenne (89030)
Rates: $59-$125
Tel: (702) 399-1500

CONVENTION INN
735 E Desert Inn Rd (89109)
Rates: $55
Tel: (702) 737-1555

CROWNE PLAZA
4255 S Paradise Rd (89109)
Rates: $95-$185
Tel: (702) 369-4400
(800) 465-4329

DAISY MOTEL & APARTMENTS
415 S Main St (89101)
Rates: $35-$55
Tel: (702) 382-0707

DESERT STAR MOTEL
1210 Las Vegas Blvd S (89104)
Rates: $35-$150
Tel: (702) 382-1066

E-Z 8 MOTEL
5201 S Industrial Rd (89118)
Rates: $28-$43
Tel: (702) 735-9513
(800) 326-6835

FERGUSONS MOTEL
1028 E Fremont St (89101)
Rates: $27-$65
Tel: (702) 382-3500

GATEWAY MOTEL
928 Las Vegas Blvd S (89101)
Rates: $25-$50
Tel: (702) 382-2146

GATEWOOD MOTEL
3075 E Fremont St (89104)
Rates: $35-$75
Tel: (702) 457-3600

GLASS POOL INN
4613 Las Vegas Blvd S (89119)
Rates: n/a
Tel: (800) 527-7118

GOLDEN INN
120 Las Vegas Blvd N (89101)
Rates: n/a
Tel: (702) 384-8204

HOLIDAY INN EXPRESS
8669 W Sahara Ave (89117)
Rates: $59-$150
Tel: (702) 256-3766
(800) 465-4329

HOLIDAY ROYALE APARTMENT SUITES
4505 Paradise Rd (89109)
Rates: $120-$215/Weekly
Tel: (702) 733-7676
(800) 732-7676

IMPERIAL MOTEL
1326 S Main St (89104)
Rates: $95 Weekly
Tel: (702) 384-8069

KNOTTY PINE MOTEL
1900 Las Vegas Blvd N (89030)
Rates: $32-$40
Tel: (702) 642-8300

LA QUINTA INN
3970 Paradise Rd (89109)
Rates: $65-$200
Tel: (702) 796-9000
(800) 531-5900

LA QUINTA INN
3782 Las Vegas Blvd S (89109)
Rates: $49-$67
Tel: (800) 531-5900

MEADOWS INN
525 E Bonanza Rd (89101)
Rates: $22-$80
Tel: (702) 366-0456

MOTEL MONACO
3072 Las Vegas Blvd S (89109)
Rates: $24-$46
Tel: (702) 735-9222

MOTEL REGENCY
700 N Main St (89101)
Rates: n/a
Tel: (702) 382-2332

MOTEL 6
194 E Tropicana Ave (89109)
Rates: $28-$46
Tel: (702) 798-0728
(800) 440-6000

MOTEL 6
4125 Boulder Hwy (89121)
Rates: $28-$46
Tel: (702) 457-8051
(800) 440-6000

MOTEL 6
5085 S Industrial Rd (89118)
Rate: $28-$36
Tel: (702) 739-6747
(800) 440-6000

NORMANDIE MOTEL
708 Las Vegas Blvd S (89101)
Rates: $30-$45
Tel: (702) 382-1002

PARADISE RESORT INN
3450 Paradise Rd (89109)
Rates: $37-$49
Tel: (702) 733-3900

REGENCY MOTEL
700 N Main St (89101)
Rates: $35-$49
Tel: (702) 382-2332

RESIDENCE INN BY MARRIOTT
3225 S Paradise Rd (89109)
Rates: $95-$199
Tel: (800) 331-3131

SITA INN
1322 E Fremont St (89101)
Rates: $35-$68
Tel: (702) 385-1150
(800) 356-5329

TAM O'SHANTER MOTEL
3317 Las Vegas Blvd S (89109)
Rates: $38-$64
Tel: (702) 735-7331
(800) 727 DICE

VACATION VILLAGE HOTEL CASINO
6711 Las Vegas Blvd S (89119)
Rates: $29-$65
Tel: (702) 897-1700
(800) 658-5000

VAGABOND INN-CENTER STRIP
3265 Las Vegas Blvd S (89109)
Rates: $45-$139
Tel: (702) 735-5102
(800) 828-8032

VAGABOND MOTEL
1919 E Fremont St (89101)
Rates: $30-$40
Tel: (702) 387-1650

VALLEY MOTEL
1313 E Fremont St
(89101)
Rates: $30-$40
Tel: (702) 384-6890

VEGAS CHALET MOTEL
2401 Las Vegas Blvd N (89030)
Rates: $29-$35
Tel: (702) 642-2115

LAUGHLIN

BAYSHORE INN
1955 Casino Dr
(89029)
Rates: $45-$85
Tel: (702) 299-9010

RIVERSIDE RESORT HOTEL & CASINO
1650 Casino Dr
(89029)
Rates: $17-$109
Tel: (702) 298-2535
(800) 227-3849

LOVELOCK

BEST WESTERN STURGEONS MOTEL CASINO
1420 Cornell Ave
(89419)
Rates: $35-$80
Tel: (702) 273-2971
(800) 528-1234

CADILLAC INN
1395 Cornell Ave
(89419)
Rates: $20-$38
Tel: (702) 273-2798

COVERED WAGON MOTEL
945 Dartmouth Ave
(89419)
Rates: $38-$45
Tel: (702) 273-2961

DESERT HAVEN MOTEL
885 Dartmouth Ave
(89419)
Rates: $30-$40
Tel: (702) 273-2339

DESERT PLAZA INN
1435 Cornell Ave
(89419)
Rates: n/a
Tel: (702) 273-2500

LOVELOCK INN
55 Cornell Ave
(89419)
Rates: $39-$65
Tel: (702) 273-2937

NATIONAL 9 MOTEL
1390 Cornell Ave
(89419)
Rates: $26-$36
Tel: (702) 273-2224

THE SAGE MOTEL
1335 Cornell Ave
(89419)
Rates: $17-$29
Tel: (702) 273-0444

SIERRA MOTEL
14th & Dartmouth Sts (89419)
Rates: $20-$38
Tel: (702) 273-2798

SUNSET MOTEL
1145 Cornell Ave
(89419)
Rates: n/a
Tel: (702) 273-7366

McDERMITT

DIAMOND A MOTEL
140 S US 95 (89421)
Rates: $27-$35
Tel: (702) 532-8551

MCDERMITT MOTEL
US Hwy 95 S (89421)
Rates: n/a
Tel: (702) 532-8588

MESQUITE

DESERT PALMS MOTEL
Mesquite Blvd
(89024)
Rates: $27-$50
Tel: (702) 346-5756

VALLEY INN MOTEL
791 W Mesquite Blvd (89024)
Rates: $30-$50
Tel: (702) 346-5281

VIRGIN RIVER HOTEL & CASINO
P. O. Box 1620 (89024)
Rates: $20-$45
Tel: (702) 346-7777

MILL CITY

SUPER 8 MOTEL
Hwy I-80 (89418)
Rates: $34-49
Tel: (702) 538-7311
(800) 800-8000

MINDEN

BEST WESTERN INN
1795 Ironwood Dr
(89410)
Rates: $55-$95
Tel: (702) 782-7766
(800) 528-1234

HOLIDAY LODGE
1591 US 395N (89423)
Rates: $32-$47
Tel: (702) 782-2288

MT. CHARLESTON

MT. CHARLESTON RESORT B&B
Kyle Canyon Rd
(89124)
Rates: $125-$220
Tel: (702) 872-5408
(800) 955-1314

MOUNTAIN CITY

CHAMBERS' MOTEL
P. O. Box 188 (89831)
Rates: $28-$34
Tel: (702) 763-6626

MOUNTAIN CITY MOTEL
Hwy 225 (89831)
Rates: n/a
Tel: (702) 763-6622

NORTH LAS VEGAS

BARKER MOTEL
26001 Las Vegas Blvd N (89030)
Rates: n/a
Tel: (702) 642-1138

OASIS

OASIS MOTEL
I-80, Exit 378 (89835)
Rates: $23-$45
Tel: (702) 478-5113

OLD NEVADA

BONNIE SPRINGS MOTEL
1 Bonnie Springs Rd
(89004)
Rates: n/a
Tel: (702) 875-4191

PAHRUMP

CHARLOTTA INN MOTEL
1201 S Hwy 160
(89041)
Rates: $28-$34
Tel: (702) 727-5445

DAYS INN
Hwy 160 N (89041)
Rates: $39-$89
Tel: (702) 727-5100
(800) 329-7466

HUTCHINGS MOTEL
Hwy 93,
P. O. Box 353 (89043)
Rates: $30+
Tel: (702) 962-5404

MOTEL PIOCHE
100 LaCour St
(89043)
Rates: $35
Tel: (702) 962-5551

RACHEL

LITTLE A'LE'INN
HCR Box 45,
Hwy 375 (89001)
Rates: $30+
Tel: (702) 729-2515

RENO

BONANZA INN
215 W Fourth St
(89501)
Rates: n/a
Tel: (702) 322-8632

CASTAWAY INN
525 W Second St
(89503)
Rates: $150-
$250/Weekly
Tel: (702) 329-2555

COACH INN
500 N Center St
(89501)
Rates: $25-$55
Tel: (702) 323-3222

DAYS INN
701 E 7th St (89512)
Rates: $32-$105
Tel: (702) 786-4070
(800) 329-7466

DONNER INN MOTEL
720 W 4th St (89503)
Rates: $25-$50
Tel: (702) 323-1851

DOWNTOWNER MOTOR LODGE
150 Stevenson St
(89503)
Rates: $30-$75
Tel: (702) 322-1188

EL PATIO MOTEL
3495 S Virginia St
(89502)
Rates: $30-$50
Tel: (702) 825-6666

EL RAY MOTEL
330 N Arlington
(89501)
Rates: $30-$120
Tel: (702) 329-6669

EL TAVERN MOTEL
1801 W Fourth St
(89503)
Rates: $32-$50
Tel: (702) 322-4504

FARRIS MOTEL
1752 E Fourth St
(89512)
Rates: $85-
$145/Weekly
Tel: (702) 322-3190

GATEWAY INN
1275 Stardust St
(89503)
Rates: n/a
Tel: (702) 747-4220

GOLD COIN MOTEL
2555 E Fourth St
(89512)
Rates: $28-$50
Tel: (702) 323-0237

HAMPTON INN
175 Second St
(89501)
Rates: $59-$94
Tel: (702) 788-2300
(800) 426-7866

HARRAH'S RENO CASINO HOTEL
219 N Center St
(89504)
Rates: $84-$375
Tel: (702) 786-3232
(800) 427-7247

HOLIDAY INN-CONVENTION CTR
5851 S Virginia St
(89502)
Rates: $45-$65
Tel: (702) 825-2940
(800) 465-4329

HOLIDAY INN-DOWNTOWN
1000 E 6th St (89512)
Rates: $59-$99
Tel: (702) 786-5151
(800) 465-4329

IN-TOWN MOTEL
260 W Fourth St
(89501)
Rates: $30-$60
Tel: (702) 323-1421

KENO MOTEL
322 N Arlington Ave
(89501)
Rates: $25-$60
Tel: (702) 322-6281

LA QUINTA INN
4001 Market St
(89502)
Rates: $46-$66
Tel: (702) 348-6100
(800) 531-5900

MARTIN LODGE
6950 S Virginia St
(89511)
Rates: $35-$75
Tel: (702) 853-6504

MOTEL 500
500 S Center St
(89501)
Rates: $25-$59
Tel: (702) 786-2777

MOTEL 6
1901 S Virginia St
(89502)
Rates: $26-$36
Tel: (702) 827-0255
(800) 440-6000

MOTEL 6
1400 Stardust St
(89503)
Rates: $26-$36
Tel: (702) 747-7390
(800) 440-6000

MOTEL 6
866 N Wells Ave
(89512)
Rates: $26-$36
Tel: (702) 786-9852
(800) 440-6000

MOTEL 6
666 N Wells Ave
(89512)
Rates: $26-$36
Tel: (702) 329-8681
(800) 440-6000

OLYMPIC APARTMENT HOTEL
195 W Second St
(89501)
Rates: $42-$90
Tel: (702) 323-0726

OX-BOW MOTOR LODGE
941 S Virginia St
(89509)
Rates: $29-$69
Tel: (702) 786-3777

PLAZA MOTOR LODGE
11 E Plaza (89501)
Rates: $30-$75
Tel: (702) 786-1077

PONDEROSA MOTEL
595 Lake St (89501)
Rates: $35-$70
Tel: (702) 786-3070

RAMADA INN
567 W 4th St (89503)
Rates: $39-$79
Tel: (702) 322-8181
(800) 583-3370

RENO INN & SUITES
5851 S Virginia St
(89502)
Rates: $45-$75
Tel: (702) 825-2940

RIVER HOUSE MOTOR HOTEL
P. O. Box 2425
(89505)
Rates: $30-$60
Tel: (702) 329-0036

RODEWAY INN
2050 Market St
(89502)
Rates: $39-$109
Tel: (702) 786-2500
(800) 424-4777

SEASONS INN
495 West St (89503)
Rates: $34-$75
Tel: (702) 322-6000

SILVER STATE LODGE
1791 W Fourth St
(89503)
Rates: $135-
$240/Weekly
Tel: (702) 322-1380

SUNDANCE MOTEL
850 N Virginia St
(89501)
Rates: $30-$50
Tel: (702) 329-9248
(800) 438-5660

TRAVELODGE DOWNTOWN
655 W 4th St (89503)
Rates: $39-$89
Tel: (702) 329-3451
(800) 578-7878

TRUCKEE RIVER LODGE
501 W 1st St (89503)
Rates: $31-$53
Tel: (800) 635-8950

VAGABOND INN
3131 S Virginia St
(89502)
Rates: $40-$59
Tel: (702) 825-7134
(800) 522-1555

SEARCHLIGHT

EL REY MOTEL
430 S Hobson Box
1235 (89046)
Rates: n/a
Tel: (702) 297-1144

SPARKS

BLUE FOUNTAIN INN
1590 B St (89431)
Rates: n/a
Tel: (702) 359-0359

INNCAL
255 N McCarran
Blvd (89431)
Rates: $29-$99
Tel: (702) 358-2222
(800) 550-0055

MOTEL 6
2405 Victorian Ave
(89431)
Rates: $27-$37
Tel: (702) 358-1080
(800) 440-6000

PONY EXPRESS LODGE
2406 Prater Way
(89431)
Rates: $28-$46
Tel: (702) 358-7110

SUPER 8 MOTEL
E Greg St (89431)
Rates: $42-$58
Tel: (800) 800-8000

STATELINE

HARRAH'S LAKE TAHOE HOTEL CASINO
Hwy 50, P. O. Box 8
(89449)
Rates: $119-$239
Tel: (702) 588-6611
(800) 427-7247

TONOPAH

BEST WESTERN HI-DESERT INN
320 Main St (89049)
Rates: $40-$62
Tel: (702) 482-3511
(800) 528-1234

GOLDEN HILLS MOTEL
826 E Main St
(89049)
Rates: n/a
Tel: (702) 482-6238

JIM BUTLER MOTEL
100 S Main St
(89049)
Rates: $30-$36
Tel: (800) 635-9455

MIZPAH HOTEL & CASINO
100 Main St (89049)
Rates: $27-$32
Tel: (702) 482-6202

OK CORRAL INN
Hwy 95 N (89049)
Rates: $24-$47
Tel: (702) 482-8202

SILVER QUEEN MOTEL
P. O. Box 311 (89049)
Rates: $28-$38
Tel: (702) 482-6291

SUNDOWNER MOTEL
700 Hwy 95 (89049)
Rates: $26-$39
Tel: (702) 482-6224

TONOPAH MOTEL
325 Main St (89049)
Rates: $20+
Tel: (702) 482-3987

UNIONVILLE

OLD PIONEER GARDEN
Main 79 (89418)
Rates: n/a
Tel: (702) 538-7585

VIRGINIA CITY

COMSTOCK LODGE
875 South C St
(89440)
Rates: $45-$68
Tel: (702) 847-0233

SUGAR LOAF MOTEL
430 South C St
(89440)
Rates: $40-$60
Tel: (702) 857-0505

VIRGINIA CITY MOTEL
675 South C St
(89440)
Rates: n/a
Tel: (702) 847-0277

WELLS

BEST WESTERN SAGE INN
576 6th St (89835)
Rates: $35-$88
Tel: (702) 752-3353
(800) 528-1234

COTTONWOOD GUEST RANCH
HC 62, Box 1300
(89835)
Rates: $95+
Tel: (702) 752-3604

LONE STAR MOTEL
676 6th St (89835)
Rates: n/a
Tel: (702) 752-3632

MOTEL 6
US 40 & US 93
(89835)
Rates: $26-$32
Tel: (702) 752-2116
(800) 440-6000

OVERLAND HOTEL
P. O. Box 79 (89835)
Rates: $19-$27
Tel: (702) 752-3373

RESTINN SUITES MOTEL
1250 E 6th St (98935)
Rates: $37-$57
Tel: (702) 752-2277

SHARON MOTEL
633 6th St (89835)
Rates: $19-$50
Tel: (702) 752-3232

SHELLCREST MOTEL
575 6th St (89835)
Rates: n/a
Tel: (702) 752-3755

SUPER 8 MOTEL
930 6th St (98935)
Rates: $37-$57
Tel: (702) 752-3384
(800) 800-8000

WAGON WHEEL MOTEL
326 Sixth St (89835)
Rates: $19-$37
Tel: (702) 752-2151

WELLS CHINATOWN
455 S Humboldt Ave
(89835)
Rates: $30-$45
Tel: (702) 752-2101

WEST WENDOVER

SUPER 8 MOTEL
1325 Wendover Blvd
(89883)
Rates: $35-$80
Tel: (702) 664-2888
(800) 800-8000

WINNEMUCCA

BEST WESTERN GOLD COUNTRY INN
921 W Winnemucca
Blvd (89445)
Rates: $54-69
Tel: (702) 623-6999
(800) 528-1234

BEST WESTERN HOLIDAY MOTEL
670 W Winnemucca
Blvd (89445)
Rates: $54-$69
Tel: (702) 623-3684
(800) 528-1234

BULL HEAD MOTEL
500 E Winnemucca
Blvd (89445)
Rates: $26-$51
Tel: (702) 623-3636

COZY MOTEL
344 E Winnemucca
Blvd (89445)
Rates: $28-$30
Tel: (702) 623-2615

DAYS INN
511 E Winnemucca
Blvd (89445)
Rates: $45-$70
Tel: (702) 625-1818
(800) 800-8000

DOWNTOWN MOTEL
251 E Winnemucca
Blvd (89445)
Rates: $27-$39
Tel: (702) 623-2394

FRONTIER MOTEL
410 E Winnemucca
Blvd (89445)
Rates: $38-$65
Tel: (702) 623-2915

LA VILLA MOTEL
390 Lay St (89445)
Rates: $38-$65
Tel: (702) 623-2334

MOTEL 6
1600 Winnemucca
Blvd (89445)
Rates: $28-$40
Tel: (702) 623-1180
(800) 440-6000

MODEL T MOTEL
1122 Winnemucca
Blvd (89445)
Rates: $29-$80
Tel: (702) 623-0222
(800) 645-5658

NEVADA MOTEL
635 W Winnemucca
Blvd (89445)
Rates: $20-$70
Tel: (702) 623-5281

PARK MOTEL
740 W Winnemucca
Blvd (89445)
Rates: $30-$40
Tel: (702) 623-2810

PONDEROSA MOTEL
705 W Winnemucca
Blvd (89445)
Rates: $28-$59
Tel: (702) 623-4898

PYRENES MOTEL
714 W Winnemucca
Blvd (89445)
Rates: $45-$58
Tel: (702) 623-1116

SCOTT SHADY COURT
400 First St (89445)
Rates: $35-$75
Tel: (702) 623-3646

SCOTTISH INNS
333 N Winnemucca
Blvd (89445)
Rates: n/a
Tel: (702) 623-3703
(800) 251-1962

SUPER 8 MOTEL
1157 W Winnemucca
Blvd (89445)
Rates: $40-$90
Tel: (702) 625-1818
(800) 800-8000

THUNDERBIRD MOTEL
511 W Winnemucca
Blvd (89445)
Rates: $60-$75
Tel: (702) 623-3661

VAL-U INN
125 E Winnemucca
Blvd (89445)
Rates: $39-$55
Tel: (702) 623-5248

WINNERS HOTEL & CASINO
185 W Winnemucca
Blvd (89445)
Rates: $36-$75
Tel: (702) 623-2511
(800) 648-4770

YERINGTON

CASINO WEST
11 N Main St (89447)
Rates: $38-$58
Tel: (702) 463-2481
(800) 227-4661

IN TOWN MOTEL
111 S Main St (89447)
Rates: $35-$45
Tel: (702) 463-2164

RANCH HOUSE MOTEL
311 W Bridge St
(89447)
Rates: $29-$41
Tel: (702) 463-2200

ZEPHYR COVE

ZEPHYR COVE RESORT
760 Hwy 50 (89448)
Rates: n/a
Tel: (702) 588-6644

NEW HAMPSHIRE

ALTON

EYE JOY COTTAGES
Roberts Cove Rd
(03809)
Rates: n/a
Tel: (603) 569-4973

ALTON BAY

**HORSE & BUGGY
COTTAGES**
Bay Hill Rd (03810)
Rates: $50-$390
Tel: (603) 875-5600

**LEMAY'S
BY THE BAY**
Rt 28A, Box 127
(03810)
Rates: n/a
Tel: (603) 875-3629

ANTRIM

MAPLEHURST INN
155 Main St (03440)
Rates: $60-$85
Tel: (603) 588-8000

ASHLAND

**BLACK HORSE
MOTOR COURT**
RFD 1, Box 46, Rt 3
(03217)
Rates: n/a
Tel: (603) 968-7116

BARTLETT

**NORTH COLONY
MOTEL**
P. O. Box 1 (03812)
Rates: $25-$59
Tel: (603) 374-6679
(800) 685-4895

**THE VILLAGER
MOTEL**
P. O. Box 427 (03812)
Rates: $25-$69
Tel: (603) 356-2878
(800) 334-6988

BENNINGTON

ECONO LODGE
634 Francistown Rd
(03442)
Rates: $50-70
Tel: (603) 588-2777
(800) 424-4777

BERLIN

TRAVELER MOTEL
25 Pleasant St (03570)
Rates: $32-$68
Tel: (603) 752-2500
(800) 365-9391

BRADFORD

BRADFORD INN
RFD 1, Box 40 (03221)
Rates: n/a
Tel: (603) 938-5309

CENTER HARBOR

**LAKE SHORE
MOTEL &COTTAGES**
RR 2, Box 16T
(03226)
Rates: n/a
Tel: (603) 253-6244

**THE MEADOWS
LAKESIDE LODGING**
P. O. Box 204 (03226)
Rates: $44-$88
Tel: (603) 253-4347

**SACO RIVER
MOTOR LODGE**
Rt 302, P. O. Box 9A
(03813)
Rates: $39-$139
Tel: (603) 447-3720

CLAREMONT

**CLAREMONT
MOTOR LODGE**
Beauregard St
(03743)
Rates: $35-$50
Tel: (603) 542-2540

DEL-E-MOTEL
24 Sullivan St
(03743)
Rates: $28-$52
Tel: (603) 542-9567

COLEBROOK

**NORTHERN
COMFORT MOTEL**
RFD 1, Box 520
(03576)
Rates: $50-$66
Tel: (603) 237-4440

CONCORD

**BRICK TOWER
MOTOR INN**
414 S Main St (03301)
Rates: $39-$64
Tel: (603) 224-9565

COMFORT INN
71 Hall St (03301)
Rates: $59-$185
Tel: (603) 226-4100
(800) 221-2222

ECONO LODGE
Gulf St (03301)
Rates: $40-$63
Tel: (603) 224-4011
(800) 424-4777

HOLIDAY INN
172 N Main St
(03301)
Rates: $79-$109
Tel: (603) 224-4011
(800) 465-4329

CONWAY

**SUNNY BROOK
PLACE COTTAGES**
Rt 16, P. O. Box 1429
(03818)
Rates: n/a
Tel: (603) 447-3922

**TANGLEWOOD
MOTEL**
Rt 16, Box 108 (03818)
Rates: n/a
Tel: (603) 447-5932

DIXVILLE NOTCH

**THE BALSAMS
GRAND RESORT
HOTEL**
Off SR 26 (03576)
Rates: $195-$400
Tel: (603) 255-3400
(800) 255-0600

DOVER

DAYS INN
481 Central Ave
(03820)
Rates: $54-130
Tel: (603) 742-0400
(800) 329-7466

EAST SWANZEY

**COACH AND FOUR
MOTOR INN**
755 Monadnock
Hwy (03446)
Rates: n/a
Tel: (603) 357-3705

EXETER

**BEST WESTERN
HEARTHSIDE
MOTOR INN**
137 Portsmouth Ave
(03833)
Rates: $60-$90
Tel: (603) 772-3794
(800) 528-1234

EXETER INN
P. O. Box 508 (03833)
Rates: $65-$125
Tel: (603) 772-5901

FRANCESTOWN

**THE INN AT
CROTCHED
MOUNTAIN**
Mountain Rd
(03043)
Rates: $45-$120
Tel: (603) 588-6840

FRANCONIA

GALE RIVER MOTEL
1 Main St (03580)
Rates: $40-$75
Tel: (603) 823-5655
(800) 255-7989

THE HORSE & HOUND INN
205 Wells Rd (03580)
Rates: $65-$120
Tel: (603) 823-5501

LOVETT'S INN BY LAFAYETTE BROOK
Route 18 (03580)
Rates: $86-$156
Tel: (800) 356-3802

GILMANTON

TEMPERANCE TAVERN HISTORIC BED & BREAKFAST
SR 140 & 107 (03237)
Rates: $40-$85
Tel: (603) 267-7349

GLEN

THE RED APPLE INN
P.O. Box 103 (03838)
Rates: $39-$99
Tel: (603) 383-9680

GORHAM

GORHAM MOTOR INN
324 Main St (03581)
Rates: $42-$64
Tel: (603) 466-3381

NORTHERN PEAKS MOTEL
289 Main St (03581)
Rates: $32-$62
Tel: (603) 466-3374

ROYALTY INN
130 Main St (03581)
Rates: $49-$76
Tel: (603) 466-3312

TOP NOTCH MOTOR INN
265 Main St (03581)
Rates: $32-$74
Tel: (603) 466-5496

TOWN & COUNTRY MOTOR INN
P. O. Box 220 (03581)
Rates: $48-$84
Tel: (800) 325-4386

HAMPTON

LAMIE'S INN & TAVERN
490 Lafayette Rd (03842)
Rates: $49-$99
Tel: (603) 926-0330

THE VILLAGER MOTOR INN
308 Lafayette Rd (03842)
Rates: $29-$69
Tel: (603) 926-3964

HAMPTON FALLS

HAMPTON FALLS INN
11 Lafayette Rd (03844)
Rates: $58-$88
Tel: (603) 926-9545
(800) 356-1729

HANOVER

HANOVER INN
Center on Dartmouth College Campus (03755)
Rates: $179-$229
Tel: (603) 643-4300
(800) 443-7024

HENNIKER

HENNIKER MOTEL
P. O. Box 622 (03242)
Rates: $44-$72
Tel: (603) 428-3536

HILLSBORO

1830 HOUSE MOTEL
626 W Main St (03244)
Rates: $45+
Tel: (603) 478-3135

HOLDERNESS

OLDE COLONIAL EAGLE ON SQUAM
P. O. Box R (03245)
Rates: $62
Tel: (603) 968-3233

INTERVALE

RIVERSIDE INN
Rt 16A (03845)
Rates: $45-$95
Tel: (603) 356-9060

SWISS CHALETS MOTEL
Rt 16A (03845)
Rates: $38-$115
Tel: (800) 831-2727

JACKSON

DANA PLACE INN
P. O. Box L (03846)
Rates: $75-$105
Tel: (603) 383-6822
(800) 537-9276

WENTWORTH RESORT HOTEL
P. O. Box M (03846)
Rates: $69-$169
Tel: (603) 383-9700
(800) 637-0013

WHITNEY'S INN
P. O. Box 822 (03846)
Rates: $59-$126
Tel: (603) 383-8916
(800) 677-5737

JAFFREY

WOODBOUND INN
Woodbound Rd (03452)
Rates: $65-$190
Tel: (800) 688-7770

KEARSARGE

ISAAC E. MERRILL HOUSE INN B & B
720 Kearsarge Rd (03847)
Rates: $49-$135
Tel: (603) 356-9041

KEENE

BEST WESTERN SOVEREIGN HOTEL
401 Winchester St (03431)
Rates: $69-$150
Tel: (603) 357-3038
(800) 528-1234

DAYS INN
175 Key Rd (03431)
Rates: $60-$88
Tel: (603) 352-7616
(800) 329-7466

THE MOTOR INN MOTEL
921 Main St, Rt 12 S (03431)
Rates: n/a
Tel: (603) 352-4138

VALLEY GREEN MOTEL
379 West St (03431)
Rates: $30-$69
Tel: (603) 352-7350

WINDING BROOK LODGE
Box 372 (03431)
Rates: $34-$50
Tel: (603) 352-3111

LACONIA

TIN WHISTLE INN
1047 Union Ave (03246)
Rates: n/a
Tel: (603) 528-4185

LANCASTER

LANCASTER MOTOR INN
P. O. Box 543 (03584)
Rates: $33-$49
Tel: (603) 788-4921

PINETREE MOTEL
RFD 2, Box 281 (03584)
Rates: $28-$40
Tel: (603) 636-2479

THE WOODPILE INN MOTEL
39 Portland St (03584)
Rates: $32-$50
Tel: (603) 788-2096

LEBANON

HOLIDAY INN
135 SR 120 (03766)
Rates: $55-$95
Tel: (603) 448-5070
(800) 465-4329

LINCOLN

PARKER'S MOTEL
Rt 3, Box 100 (03251)
Rates: $25-$75
Tel: (603) 745-8341

LITTLETON

**CONTINENTAL 93
MOTOR INN**
Lisbon Rd (03561)
Rates: $36-$79
Tel: (603) 444-5366

**EASTGATE
MOTOR INN**
RFD 1 (03561)
Rates: $39-$45
Tel: (603) 444-3971

LYME

LOCH LYME LODGE
NH 10, RFD 278
(03768)
Rates: $26-$65
Tel: (800) 423-2141

MANCHESTER

DAYS HOTEL
55 John E Devine Dr
(03103)
Rates: $63-$90
Tel: (603) 668-6110

ECONO LODGE
75 W Hancock St
(03102)
Rates: $40-$50
Tel: (603) 624-0111
(800) 424-4777

HOLIDAY INN
700 Elm St (03101)
Rates: $80-$115
Tel: (800) 465-4329

**HOWARD JOHNSON
HOTEL**
298 Queen City Ave
(03102)
Rates: $63-$126
Tel: (603) 668-2600
(800) 446-4656

MERRIMACK

**RESIDENCE INN
BY MARRIOTT**
246 Daniel Webster
Hwy (03054)
Rates: $69-$120
Tel: (603) 424-8100
(800) 331-3131

MOULTONBORO

**OLDE ORCHARD
INN B&B**
Old Rt 109 & Lee Rd
(03254)
Rates: $70-$90
Tel: (603) 476-5004

**ROB ROY
MOTOR LODGE**
P. O. Box 420 (03254)
Rates: $49-$75
Tel: (603) 476-5571

NASHUA

HOLIDAY INN
9 Northeastern Blvd
(03062)
Rates: $45-$120
Tel: (800) 465-4329

MOTEL 6
2 Progress Ave
(03062)
Rates: $40-$46
Tel: (603) 889-4151
(800) 440-6000

MARRIOTT HOTEL
2200 Southwood Dr
(03063)
Rates: $69-$119
Tel: (603) 880-9100
(800) 228-9290

RED ROOF INN
77 Spit Brook Rd
(03063)
Rates: $30-$58
Tel: (603) 888-1893
(800) 843-7663

NORTH CONWAY

MAPLE LEAF MOTEL
Box 917, Rt 16
(03860)
Rates: n/a
Tel: (603) 356-5388

**NORTH CONWAY
MOUNTAIN INN**
Main St (03860)
Rates: $69-$159
Tel: (603) 356-2803

NORTH WOODSTOCK

PITRE'S CABINS
Rt 112 West (03262)
Rates: n/a
Tel: (603) 745-8646

NORTHWOOD

**LAKE SHORE
FARM RESORT**
Jenness Pond Rd
(03261)
Rates: $285-$305
Tel: (603) 942-5921

OSSIPEE

PINE COVE MOTEL
Rts 16 & 28 (03864)
Rates: $45-$70
Tel: (603) 539-4491

PITTSBURG

THE GLEN
77 The Glen Rd
(03592)
Rates: $66-$160
Tel: (603) 538-6500

PORTSMOUTH

ANCHORAGE INN
417 Woodbury Ave
(03801)
Rates: $49-$79
Tel: (800) 370-8111

**HOWARD JOHNSON
HOTEL**
Interstate Traffic Cir
(03801)
Rates: $60-146
Tel: (603) 436-7600
(800) 446-4656

**THE PORT
MOTOR INN**
Portsmouth Circle
(03801)
Rates: $32-$98
Tel: (800) 282-7678

**WREN'S NEST
VILLAGE INN**
3548 Lafayette Rd
(03801)
Rates: $54-$129
Tel: (603) 436-2481

RINDGE

WOODBOUND INN
62 Woodbound Rd
(03641)
Rates: $65-$190
Tel: (603) 532-8341

ROCHESTER

ANCHORAGE INN
P. O. Box 7325
(03839)
Rates: $39-$60
Tel: (603) 332-3350

SALEM

HOLIDAY INN
1 Keewaydin Dr
(03079)
Rates: $35-$56
Tel: (603) 893-5511
(800) 465-4329

RED ROOF INN
15 Red Roof Ln
(03079)
Rates: $30-$54
Tel: (603) 898-6422
(800) 843-7663

SHELBURNE

PHILBROOK FARM INN
North Rd (03581)
Rates: $122-$475
Tel: (603) 466-3831

SUGAR HILL

THE HILLTOP INN
Main St (03585)
Rates: $50-$110
Tel: (603) 823-5695

THE HOMESTEAD INN
NH 117 & Sunset
Hill Rd (03585)
Rates: n/a
Tel: (603) 823-5564

SUNAPEE

BEST WESTERN SUNAPEE LAKE LODGE
1403 Rt 103 (03255)
Rates: $69-99
Tel: (603) 763-2010
(800) 606-5253

BURKEHAVEN RESORT
173 Burkehaven Hill
Rd (03782)
Rates: $60-$75
Tel: (603) 763-2788

DEXTER'S INN
P. O. Box 703A
(03782)
Rates: $90-$188
Tel: (603) 763-5571

THE OLD GOVERNORS HOUSE
Lower Main St
(03782)
Rates: n/a
Tel: (603) 763-9918

SEVEN HEARTHS INN B & B
26 Seven Hearths Ln
(03782)
Rates: $88-$138
Tel: (603) 763-5657

TAMWORTH

THE TAMWORTH INN
Main St (03886)
Rates: $80-$130
Tel: (603) 323-7721

TROY

THE INN AT EAST HILL FARM
Mountain Rd (03465)
Rates: n/a
Tel: (603) 242-6495

TUFTONBORO

19 MILE BAY LODGES
HC 69, Box 110
(03853)
Rates: n/a
Tel: (603) 569-3507

TWIN MOUNTAIN

CHARLMONT MOTOR INN
Rt 3, Box G (03595)
Rates: $35-$60
Tel: (603) 846-5549

WENTWORTH

HILLTOP ACRES B & B
Eastside & Buffalo
Rds (03282)
Rates: $65
Tel: (603) 764-5896

WEST LEBANON

ECONOMY INN AIRPORT
7 Airport Rd (03784)
Rates: $44-$65
Tel: (603) 298) 8888
(800) 433-3466

RADISSON INN NORTH COUNTRY
Exit 20 at Airport Rd
(03784)
Rates: $79-$140
Tel: (800) 333-3333

WILTON CENTER

AUK'S NEST BED & BREAKFAST
East Road, RFD 1
(03086)
Rates: $45-$60
Tel: (603) 878-3443

STEPPING STONES
Bennington Trail
(03086)
Rates: n/a
Tel: (603) 654-9048

WINNISQUAM

LYNNMERE MOTEL & COTTAGES
850 Laconia Rd
(03289)
Rates: $35-$65
Tel: (603) 524-0912

WOLFEBORO

MUSEUM LODGES
HC 69, P. O. Box 680
(03894)
Rates: $80-$130
Tel: (603) 569-1551

WOODSTOCK

WHEELOCK MOTOR COURT
Rt 3 (03293)
Rates: n/a
Tel: (603) 745-8771

WOODSVILLE

ALL SEASONS MOTEL
36 Smith St (03785)
Rates: $34-$54
Tel: (603) 747-2157

NEW JERSEY

ABSECON

DAYS INN
224 E White Horse
Pk (08201)
Rates: $40-$150
Tel: (609) 652-2200
(800) 329-7466

ATLANTIC CITY

RED CARPET INN
1630 N Albany Ave
(08401)
Rates: n/a
Tel: (609) 348-3171
(800) 251-1962

BELLMAWR

HOWARD JOHNSON HOTEL
341 S Black Horse
Pike (08031)
Rates: $40-$85
Tel: (609) 931-0700
(800) 446-4656

BEACH HAVEN

ENGLESIDE INN
30 Engleside Ave
(08008)
Rates: $65-$217
Tel: (609) 492-1251
(800) 762-2214

BLACKWOOD

HOJO INN
832 N Black Horse
Pk (08012)
Rates: $65-$95
Tel: (609) 228-4040
(800) 446-4656

BORDENTOWN

BEST WESTERN INN
1068 US 296 N
(08505)
Rates: $65-$115
Tel: (609) 298-8000
(800) 528-1234

DAYS INN
1073 US 206 N
(08505)
Rates: $55-$59
Tel: (609) 298-6100
(800) 329-7466

ECONO LODGE
187 US 130 N (08505)
Rates: $43-$125
Tel: (609) 298-5000
(800) 424-4777

RAMADA INN
1083 Rt 206 N
(08505)
Rates: $45-$105
Tel: (609) 298-3200
(800) 272-6232

CAPE MAY

MARQUIS DE LAFAYETTE
501 Beach Dr (08204)
Rates: $94-$238
Tel: (609) 884-3500

CARTERET

HOLIDAY INN
1000 Roosevelt Ave
(07008)
Rates: $90-$138
Tel: (201) 460-1777
(800) 465-4329

CHERRY HILL

HOLIDAY INN
Rt 70 & Sayer Ave
(08002)
Rates: $68-$78
Tel: (800) 465-4329

RESIDENCE INN BY MARRIOTT
1821 Old Cuthbert
Rd (08034)
Rates: $140-$170
Tel: (609) 429-6111
(800) 331-3131

CLIFTON

HOWARD JOHNSON HOTEL
680 W Rt 2 (07014)
Rates: $79-119
Tel: (201) 471-3800
(800) 446-4656

RAMADA HOTEL
265 Rt 3 E (07014)
Rates: $75-$125
Tel: (201) 778-6500
(800) 272-6232

COLESVILLE

HIGH POINT INN
1328 SR 23 N (07461)
Rates: $50-$65
Tel: (201) 702-1860

EAST BRUNSWICK

MOTEL 6
244 Rt 18 (08816)
Rates: $43-$49
Tel: (908) 390-4545
(800) 440-6000

EAST HANOVER

RAMADA HOTEL & CONF CTR
130 Rt 10 W (07936)
Rates: $89-$127
Tel: (201) 386) 5622
(800) 272-6232

EAST RUTHERFORD

DAYS INN-MEADOWLANDS
850 SR 120 (07073)
Rates: $52-$96
Tel: (201) 507-5222
(800) 329-7466

SHERATON-MEADOWLANDS
2 Meadowlands
Plaza (07073)
Rates: $79-$135
Tel: (201) 896-0500
(800) 325-3535

EAST WINDSOR

DAYS INN
460 Rt 33 (08520)
Rates: $49-$99
Tel: (609) 448-3200
(800) 329-7466

RAMADA INN
399 Monmouth St
(08520)
Rates: $59-$94
Tel: (609) 448-7000
(800) 272-6232

EATONTOWN

CROWN PLAZA AT RARITAN CENTER
125 Raritan Ctr
Pkwy (08837)
Rates: $115
Tel: (908) 225-8300

CRYSTAL MOTOR LODGE
170-174 Hwy 35
(07724)
Rates: $38-$66
Tel: (908) 542-4900
(800) 562-5290

EDISON

CLARION HOTEL & TOWERS
2055 Lincoln Hwy (08817)
Rates: $74-$119
Tel: (908) 287-3500
(800) 221-2222

RED ROOF INN
860 New Durham Rd (08817)
Rates: $35-$42
Tel: (908) 248-9300
(800) 843-7663

WELLESLEY INN
831 US 1S (08817)
Rates: $45-$70
Tel: (908) 287-0171
(800) 444-8888

ELIZABETH

CLARION HOTEL-AIRPORT
901 Spring St (07201)
Rates: $68-$108
Tel: (908) 527-1600
(800) 221-2222

HOLIDAY INN-JETPORT
1000 Spring St (07201)
Rates: $69-$109
Tel: (908) 355-1700
(800) 465-4329

ENGLEWOOD

RADISSON HOTEL
401 S Van Brunt St (07631)
Rates: $89-$189
Tel: (201) 871-2020
(800) 333-3333

FAIRFIELD

BEST WESTERN EXECUTIVE INN
216-234 Rt 46 E (07004)
Rates: $84-$163
Tel: (201) 575-7700
(800) 528-1234

RADISSON HOTEL & SUITES
690 US 46 E (07004)
Rates: $140-$185
Tel: (201) 227-9200
(800) 333-3333

RAMADA INN
38 Two Bridges Rd (07004)
Rates: $62-$119
Tel: (201) 575-1742
(800) 272-6232

FLEMINGTON

RAMADA INN
Route 202 & 31 (08822)
Rates: $76-$96
Tel: (908) 782-7472
(800) 272-6232

HAZLET

WELLESLEY INN
3215 Hwy 35 (07730)
Rates: $53-$79
Tel: (908) 888-2800
(800) 444-8888

HIGHTSTOWN

TOWN HOUSE MOTEL
SR 33 W (08520)
Rates: $59-$125
Tel: (609) 448-2400

HOPE

INN AT MILLRACE POND
Rt 519 (07844)
Rates: $85-$165
Tel: (908) 459-4884

JERSEY CITY

ECONO LODGE
750-762 Tonnelle Ave (07302)
Rates: $50-$60
Tel: (201) 420-9040
(800) 424-4777

LAKEWOOD

BEST WESTERN LEISURE INN
1600 Rt 70 (08701)
Rates: $69-$99
Tel: (908) 367-0900
(800) 528-1234

LAWRENCEVILLE

HOWARD JOHNSON LODGE
2995 Brunswick Pike (08648)
Rates: $63-$90
Tel: (800) 654-2000

RED ROOF INN
3203 Brunswick Pike (08648)
Rates: $45-$57
Tel: (609) 896-3388
(800) 843-7663

LYNDHURST

NOVOTEL-MEADOWLANDS
1 Polito Ave (07071)
Rates: $88-$120
Tel: (201) 896-6666

McAFEE

DAYS INN
Rt 23 & Rt 94 (07428)
Rates: $45-$125
Tel: (201) 827-4666
(800) 329-7466

MAHWAH

RAMADA INN
180 Rt 17 S (07430)
Rates: ($68-$109
Tel: (201) 529-5880
(800) 272-6232

SHERATON CROSSROADS HOTEL & TOWERS
1 International Blvd, Rt 17 (07495)
Rates: $109-$155
Tel: (201) 529-1660
(800) 325-3535

MAPLE SHADE

THE LANDMARK INN
Rts 73 & 38 (08052)
Rates: $50-$60
Tel: (609) 235-6400

MOTEL 6
Rt 73 (08052)
Rates: $40-$46
Tel: (609) 235-3550
(800) 440-6000

MARAMORA

ECONO LODGE
119 US 95 (08223)
Rates: $25-$100
Tel: (800) 424-4777

MIDDLETOWN

HOWARD JOHNSON LODGE
750 Hwy 35 S (07748)
Rates: $67-$99
Tel: (908) 671-3400
(800) 654-2000

MILLVILLE

MILLVILLE MOTOR INN
Rt 47, Delseas Dr (08332)
Rates: $54-$100
Tel: (800) 428-4373

MONMOUTH JUNCTION

RED ROOF INN
208 New Rd (08852)
Rates: $34-$44
Tel: (908) 821-8800
(800) 843-7663

MOUNT HOLLY

BEST WESTERN MOTOR INN
2020 Rt 541 (08060)
Rates: $55-$81
Tel: (609) 261-3800
(800) 528-1234

HOWARD JOHNSON LODGE
Mt. Holly Rd (08060)
Rates: $55-$86
Tel: (609) 267-6550
(800) 446-4656

MOUNT LAUREL

RED ROOF INN
603 Fellowship Rd (08054)
Rates: $35-$57
Tel: (609) 234-5589
(800) 843-7663

NEWARK

HOLIDAY INN-NORTH
160 Frontage Rd (07114)
Rates: $68-$84
Tel: (201) 589-1000
(800) 465-4329

MARRIOTT HOTEL-AIRPORT
Newark Intl Airport (07114)
Rates: $89-$159
Tel: (201) 623-0006
(800) 228-9290

RADISSON HOTEL-AIRPORT
128 Frontage Rd (07114)
Rates: $75-$145
Tel: (201) 690-5500
(800) 333-3333

RAMADA INN-AIRPORT
550 Rt 1 S (07114)
Rates: $70-$150
Tel: (201) 824-4000
(800) 272-6232

NORTH WILDWOOD

NEW ENGLAND MOTEL
106 W 11th St (08260)
Rates: $50-$150
Tel: (609) 522-7250
(800) 988-6243

NEW BRUNSWICK

ECONO LODGE
26 US 1 N (08901)
Rates: $47-$70
Tel: (908) 828-8000
(800) 424-4777

NORTH PLAINFIELD

HOWARD JOHNSON LODGE
US 22 W (07060)
Rates: $55-$85
Tel: (908) 753-6500
(800) 446-4656

OCEAN CITY

CROSSINGS MOTOR INN
3420 Haven Ave (08226)
Rates: $47-$139
Tel: (609) 396-4433

PARAMUS

HOWARD JOHNSON LODGE
393 SR 17 (07652)
Rates: $65-$90
Tel: (201) 265-4200
(800) 446-4656

RADISSON INN
601 From Rd (07652)
Rates: $125-$155
Tel: (201) 262-6900
(800) 333-3333

RED CARPET INN
211 Rt 17 (07652)
Rates: $42-$58
Tel: (201) 261-8686
(800) 251-1962

PARK RIDGE

MARRIOTT HOTEL
300 Brae Blvd (07656)
Rates: $84-$147
Tel: (201) 307-0800
(800) 228-9290

PARSIPPANY

DAYS INN
3159 Rt 46 (07054)
Rates: $56-$99
Tel: (201) 335-0200
(800) 329-7466

HILTON HOTEL
1 Hilton Court (07054)
Rates: $75-$155
Tel: (201) 267-7373
(800) 445-8667

HOWARD JOHNSON HOTEL
625 Rt 46 (07054)
Rates: $50-$60
Tel: (201) 882-8600
(800) 446-4656

RAMADA INN
949 Rt 46 (07054)
Rates: $65-$120
Tel: (201) 263-0404
(800) 272-6232

RED ROOF INN
855 Rt 46 (07054)
Rates: $38-$59
Tel: (201) 334-3737
(800) 843-7663

PENNS GROVE

WELLESLEY INN
517 S Pennsville Auburn Rd (08069)
Rates: n/a
Tel: (609) 299-3800
(800) 444-8888

PISCATAWAY

MOTEL 6
1012 Stelton Rd (08854)
Rates: $43-$49
Tel: (908) 981-9200
(800) 440-6000

PRINCETON

NOVOTEL HOTEL
100 Independence Way (08540)
Rates: $72-$109
Tel: (609) 520-1200

RESIDENCE INN BY MARRIOTT

4225 Rt 1 (08543)
Rates: $69-$149
Tel: (908) 329-9600
(800) 331-3131

SUMMERFIELD SUITES HOTEL
4375 US 1 S (08543)
Rates: $89-$179
Tel: (609) 951-0009
(800) 833-4353

RAMSEY

HOWARD JOHNSON LODGE
1255 Rt 17 S (07446)
Rates: $45-$90
Tel: (201) 327-4500
(800) 446-4656

WELLESLEY INN
946 Rt 17 N (07446)
Rates: $50-$75
Tel: (201) 934-9250
(800) 444-8888

ROCHELLE PARK

RAMADA HOTEL
375 W Passaic St (07866)
Rates: $60-$138
Tel: (201) 845-3400
(800) 272-6232

ROCKAWAY

HOWARD JOHNSON HOTEL
Green Pond Rd (07866)
Rates: $68-$88
Tel: (201) 625-1200
(800) 446-4656

RUNNEMEDE

HOLIDAY INN
109 9th Ave (08078)
Rates: $52-$62
Tel: (609) 939-4200
(800) 465-4329

SADDLE BROOK

HOLIDAY INN & CONFERENCE CTR
50 Kenney Pl (07662)
Rates: $69-$99
Tel: (201) 843-0600
(800) 465-4329

MARRIOTT HOTEL
I-80 & Garden State
Pkwy (07662)
Rates: $84-$120
Tel: (201) 843-9500
(800) 228-9290

SEASIDE HEIGHTS

SCOTTISH INNS
50 Lincoln Ave
(08751)
Rates: n/a
Tel: (908) 793-6999
(800) 251-1962

SECAUCUS

COURTYARD BY MARRIOTT
455 Harmon
Meadow Blvd
(07094)
Rates: $109-$119
Tel: (201) 617-8888
(800) 321-2211

HOLIDAY INN-HARMON MEADOW
300 Plaza Dr (07094)
Rates: $105-$115
Tel: (201) 348-2000
(800) 465-4329

RAMADA PLAZA SUITE HOTEL
350 Rt 3W, Mill
Creek Dr (07094)
Rates: $99-$159
Tel: (201) 863-8700
(800) 272-6232

RED ROOF INN
15 Meadowlands
Pkwy (07094)
Rates: $45-$61
Tel: (201) 319-1000
(800) 843-7663

SOMERS POINT

RESIDENCE INN BY MARRIOTT
900 Mays Landing
Rd (08244)
Rates: $93-$187
Tel: (609) 927-6400
(800) 331-3131

SOMERSET

RAMADA INN
60 Cottontail Ln
(08873)
Rates: $65-$125
Tel: (908) 560-9880
(800) 272-6232

SUMMERFIELD SUITES HOTEL
260 Davidson Ave
(08873)
Rates: $129-$159
Tel: (908) 356-8000
(800) 833-4353

SOUTH BRUNSWICK

DAYS INN
2316 US 130 (08810)
Rates: $54-$64
Tel: (908) 329-3000
(800) 329-7466

SOUTH PLAINFIELD

COMFORT INN
Stelton Rd & I-287
(07080)
Rates: $45-$70
Tel: (908) 561-4488
(800) 424-6423

HOLIDAY INN
4701 Stelton Rd
(07080)
Rates: $59-$89
Tel: (908) 753-5500
(800) 465-4329

SPRING LAKE

LA MAISON B & B
404 Jersey Ave
(07762)
Rates: $110-$225
Tel: (908) 449-0969

SPRINGFIELD

HOLIDAY INN
304 Rt 22 W (07081)
Rates: $73-$83
Tel: (201) 376-9400
(800) 465-4329

TINTON FALLS

RED ROOF INN
11 Center Plaza
(07724)
Rates: $40-$52
Tel: (908) 389-4646
(800) 843-7663

RESIDENCE INN BY MARRIOTT
90 Park Rd (07724)
Rates: $125-$138
Tel: (908) 389-8100
(800) 331-3131

SUNRISE SUITES HOTEL
3 Centre Plaza (07724)
Rates: $79-$159
Tel: (908) 389-4800

TOMS RIVER

HOLIDAY INN
290 Hwy 37 E (08753)
Rates: $74-$110
Tel: (908) 244-4000
(800) 465-4329

HOWARD JOHNSON LODGE
Rt 37, Hooper Ave
(08753)
Rates: $65-$80
Tel: (908) 244-1000
(800) 446-4656

RAMADA INN
2373 Rt 9 (08755)
Rates: $62-$199
Tel: (908) 905-2626
(800) 272-6232

VINELAND

RAMADA INN
2216 W Landis Ave
& Rt 55, Exit 32-A
(08360)
Rates: $50-$125
Tel: (609) 696-3800
(800) 272-6232

VOORHEES

HAMPTON INN
121 Laurel Oak Rd
(08043)
Rates: $84-$94
Tel: (609) 346-4500
(800) 426-7866

WAYNE

HOWARD JOHNSON LODGE
1850 Rt 23 & Ratzer
Rd (07470)
Rates: $69-$109
Tel: (201) 696-8050
(800) 446-4656

WEEHAWKEN

RAMADA SUITE HOTEL
500 Harbor Blvd
(07087)
Rates: $119-$189
Tel: (201) 617-5600
(800) 272-6232

WHIPPANY

HOWARD JOHNSON LODGE
1255 Rt 10 (07981)
Rates: $89-$129
Tel: (201) 539-8350
(800) 446-4656

WRIGHTSTOWN

DAYS INN
Wrightstown-Cookstown Rd
(08562)
Rates: $45-$85
Tel: (609) 723-6900
(800) 329-7466

NEW MEXICO

ALAMOGORDO

ALL AMERICAN INN
508 S White Sands
Blvd (88310)
Rates: $26-$32
Tel: (505) 437-1850

**BEST WESTERN
DESERT AIRE
MOTOR INN**
1021 S White Sands
Blvd (88310)
Rates: $47-$79
Tel: (505) 437-2110
(800) 528-1234

HOLIDAY INN
1401 S White Sands
Blvd (88310)
Rates: $47-$63
Tel: (800) 465-4329

MOTEL 6
251 Panorama Blvd
(88310)
Rates: $27-$33
Tel: (505) 434-5970
(800) 440-6000

SATELLITE INN
2224 N White Sands
Blvd (88310)
Rates: $30-$40
Tel: (505) 437-8454

SUPER 8 MOTEL
3204 N White Sands
(88310)
Rates: $32-$45
Tel: (505) 434-4205
(800) 800-8000

ALBUQUERQUE

**AMBERLEY
SUITE HOTEL**
7620 Pan American
Frwy NE (87109)
Rates: $70-$120
Tel: (800) 333-9806

**BEST WESTERN
AMERICAN
MOTOR INN**
12999 Central Ave
NE (87123)
Rates: $44-$78
Tel: (505) 298-7426
(800) 528-1234

**BEST WESTERN
FRED HARVEY
HOTEL**
2910 Yale Blvd SE
(87119)
Rates: $83-$123
Tel: (505) 843-7000
(800) 528-1234

BUDGETEL INN
7439 Pan American
Frwy NE (87109)
Rates: $40-$58
Tel: (505) 345-0010

**CASITA CHAMISA
BED & BREAKFAST**
850 Chamisal Rd
NW (87107)
Rates: n/a
Tel: (505) 897-4644

COMFORT INN
13031 Central Ave
NE (87123)
Rates: $37-$60
Tel: (505) 294-1800
(800) 221-2222

**COMFORT INN-
AIRPORT**
2300 Yale Blvd SE
(87106)
Rates: $53-$76
Tel: (505) 243-2244
(800) 221-2222

**COMFORT INN-
MIDTOWN**
2015 Menaul Blvd
NE (87107)
Rates: $49-$59
Tel: (505) 881-3210
(800) 221-2222

DAYS INN
6031 Iliff Rd NW
(87105)
Rates: $60-$100
Tel: (505) 836-3297
(800) 329-7466

DAYS INN
13317 Central Ave
NE (87123)
Rates: $45-$95
Tel: (505) 294-3297
(800) 329-7466

DAYS INN EUBANK
10321 Hotel Ave NE
(87123)
Rates: $55-$105
Tel: (505) 275-0599
(800) 329-7466

**DE ANZA
MOTOR LODGE**
4302 Central Ave NE
(87108)
Rates: $20-$37
Tel: (505) 255-1654

ECONO LODGE
13211 Central Ave
NE (87123)
Rates: $33-$96
Tel: (505) 292-7600
(800) 424-4777

HAMPTON INN
5101 Ellison NE
(87109)
Rates: $60-$67
Tel: (505) 344-1555
(800) 426-7866

HOJO INN
7640 Central SE
(87108)
Rates: $40-$50
Tel: (505) 265-9309
(800) 446-4656

**HOLIDAY INN
EXPRESS**
10330 Hotel Ave NE
(87123)
Rates: $55-$90
Tel: (505) 275-8900
(800) 465-4329

**HOLIDAY INN-
MIDTOWN**
2020 Menaul Blvd
NE (87107)
Rates: $89-$105
Tel: (505) 884-2511
(800) 465-4329

**HOLIDAY INN
PYRAMID HOTEL-
JOURNAL CENTER**
5151 San Francisco
Rd NE (87109)
Rates: $90-$140
Tel: (505) 821-3333
(800) 465-4329

**HOWARD JOHNSON
LODGE**
7630 Pan American
Frwy NE (87109)
Rates: $57-$64
Tel: (505) 828-1600
(800) 446-4656

**HOWARD JOHNSON
HOTEL**
15 Hotel Circle NE
(87123)
Rates: $50-$88
Tel: (505) 296-4852
(800) 446-4656

**LA QUINTA INN-
AIRPORT**
2116 Yale Blvd SE
(87106)
Rates: $48-$63
Tel: (505) 243-5500
(800) 531-5900

**LA QUINTA INN-
NORTH**
5241 San Antonio Dr
NE (87109)
Rates: $52-$65
Tel: (505) 821-9000
(800) 531-5900

LA QUINTA INN
2424 San Mateo Blvd
NE (87110)
Rates: $49-$64
Tel: (505) 884-3591
(800) 531-5900

LORLODGE MOTEL EAST
801 Central Ave NE (87102)
Rates: $20-$38
Tel: (505) 243-2891

MAGGIE'S RASPBERRY RANCH BED & BREAKFAST
9817 Eldridge Rd NW (87114)
Rates: n/a
Tel: (505) 897-1523
(800) 897-1523

MOTEL 6
3400 Prospect Ave NE (87107)
Rates: $30-$36
Tel: (505) 883-8813
(800) 440-6000

MOTEL 6
5701 Iliff Rd NW (87105)
Rates: $30-$36
Tel: (505) 831-8888
(800) 440-6000

MOTEL 6-EAST
13141 Central Ave NE (87123)
Rates: $30-$36
Tel: (505) 294-4600
(800) 440-6000

MOTEL 6-MIDTOWN
1701 University Blvd NE (87102)
Rates: $30-$36
Tel: (505) 843-9228
(800) 440-6000

MOTEL 6-PREMIER
6015 Iliff Rd NW (87121)
Rates: $30-$36
Tel: (505) 831-3400
(800) 440-6000

MOTEL 6-STADIUM
1000 Stadium Blvd SE (87102)
Rates: $30-$36
Tel: (505) 243-8017
(800) 440-6000

PARK INN INTERNATIONAL
601 Paisano NE (87123)
Rates: $35-$50
Tel: (505) 293-4444
(800) 437-7275

PINNACLE HOTEL FOUR SEASONS
2500 Carlisle Blvd NE (87110)
Rates: $74-$105
Tel: (505) 888-3311

PLAZA INN
900 Medical Arts NE (87120)
Rates: $65-$75
Tel: (505) 243-5693

RADISSON INN
1901 University Blvd SE (87106)
Rates: $59-$85
Tel: (505) 247-0512
(800) 333-3333

RAMADA INN
25 Hotel Circle NE (87123)
Rates: $63-83
Tel: (505) 271-1000
(800) 272-6232

RAMADA LIMITED-AIRPORT NORTH
Block 11, Yale & Ross Blvd (87106)
Rates: $45-$65
Tel: (505) 325-1191
(800) 272-6232

RESIDENCE INN BY MARRIOTT
3300 Prospect NE (87107)
Rates: $109-$135
Tel: (505) 881-2661
(800) 331-3131

RIO GRANDE INN
1015 Rio Grande Blvd NW (87104)
Rates: $41-$90
Tel: (800) 959-4726

ROYAL HOTEL
4119 Central Ave NE (87108)
Rates: $24-$49
Tel: (800) 843-8572

SUPER 8 MOTEL
2500 University Blvd NE (87107)
Rates: $37-$45
Tel: (505) 888-4884
(800) 800-8000

TRAVELODGE
13139 Central Ave NE (87123)
Rates: $40-$110
Tel: (505) 292-4878
(800) 578-7878

TRAVELODGE MIDTOWN
1635 Candelaria NE (87107)
Rates: $40-$115
Tel: (505) 344-5311
(800) 578-7878

THE W. E. MAUGER ESTATE B & B
701 Roma Ave NE (87102)
Rates: $55-$105
Tel: (505) 242-8755

ALTO

HIGH COUNTRY LODGE
N Hwy 48 (88312)
Rates: $59-$89
Tel: (505) 336-4321
(800) 845-7265

LA JUNTA GUEST RANCH
P. O. Box 139 (88312)
Rate: $70-$200
Tel: (800) 443-8423

ARTESIA

ARTESIA INN
1820 S 1st St (88210)
Rates: $30-$50
Tel: (505) 746-9801

AZTEC

THE STEP BACK INN
103 W Aztec Blvd (87410)
Rates: $58-$82
Tel: (505) 334-1200

BELEN

BEST WESTERN INN
2101 Sosimo Padilla Blvd (87002)
Rates: $59
Tel: (505) 861-0980
(800) 528-1234

BERNALILLO

LA HACIENDA GRANDE B & B
21 Baros Ln (87004)
Rates: $85-$109
Tel: (505) 867-1887

BLOOMFIELD

SUPER 8 MOTEL
525 W Broadway (87413)
Rates: $39-$53
Tel: (505) 632-8886
(800) 800-8000

CARLSBAD

BEST WESTERN STEVENS INN
1829 S Canal St (88220)
Rates: $45-$65
Tel: (505) 887-2851
(800) 528-1234

CONTINENTAL INN
3820 National Parks Hwy (88220)
Rates: $32-$42
Tel: (505) 887-0341

DAYS INN
3910 National Parks Hwy (88220)
Rates: $50-$95
Tel: (505) 887-7800
(800) 329-7466

LORLODGE
2019 S Canal St (88220)
Rates: $24-$42
Tel: (505) 887-1171

MOTEL 6
3824 National Parks Hwy (88220)
Rates: $26-$32
Tel: (505) 885-0011
(800) 440-6000

PARKVIEW MOTEL
401 E Greene St (88220)
Rates: $28-$39
Tel: (505) 885-3117

QUALITY INN
3706 National Parks Hwy (88220)
Rates: $48-$66
Tel: (800) 221-2222

STAGECOACH INN
1819 S Canal (88220)
Rates: $26-$50
Tel: (505) 887-1148

TRAVELODGE SOUTH
3817 National Parks Hwy (88220)
Rates: $29-$44
Tel: (505) 887-8888
(800) 578-7878

CHAMA

ELK HORN LODGE MOTEL
Rte 1, Box 45 (87520)
Rates: $38-$79
Tel: (800) 532-8874

CIMARRON

CIMARRON INN
P. O. Box 623 (87714)
Rates: $34-$48
Tel: (505) 376-2268

CLAYTON

BEST WESTERN KOKOPELLI LODGE
702 S First St (88415)
Rates: $44-$69
Tel: (505) 374-2589
(800) 528-1234

THRIFTLODGE
Hwy 87 NW (88415)
Rates: $35-$75
Tel: (505) 374-2558
(800) 525-9055

CLOUDCROFT

SUMMIT INN MOTEL
P. O. Box 627 (88317)
Rates: $38-$93
Tel: (505) 682-2814

CLOVIS

DAYS INN
1720 Mabry Dr (88101)
Rates: $35-$55
Tel: (505) 762-2971
(800) 329-7466

HOLIDAY INN
P. O. Box 973 (88101)
Rates: $45-$50
Tel: (800) 465-4329

MOTEL 6
2620 Mabry Dr (88101)
Rates: $26-$32
Tel: (505) 762-2995
(800) 440-6000

DEMING

BEST WESTERN MIMBRES VALLEY INN
1500 W Pine St (88030)
Rates: $42-$54
Tel: (505) 546-4544
(800) 528-1234

DAYS INN
1709 E Spruce St (88030)
Rates: $34-$44
Tel: (505) 546-8813
(800) 329-7466

DEMING MOTEL
500 W Pine St (88030)
Rates: $23-$30
Tel: (505) 546-2737

GRAND MOTOR INN
1721 E Spruce St (88030)
Rates: $38-$46
Tel: (505) 546-2632

HOLIDAY INN
P. O. Box 1138 (88031)
Rates: $44-$50
Tel: (800) 465-4329

MOTEL 6
I-10 & Motel Dr (88031)
Rates: $29-$35
Tel: (505) 546-2623
(800) 440-6000

WAGON WHEEL MOTEL
1109 W Pine St (88030)
Rates: $22-$29
Tel: (505) 546-2681

DULCE

BEST WESTERN JICARILLA INN
US 64 & Hawks Dr (87528)
Rates: $50-$68
Tel: (505) 759-3663
(800) 528-1234

ELEPHANT BUTTE

ELEPHANT BUTTE RESORT INN
P. O. Box E (87935)
Rates: $40-$59
Tel: (505) 744-5431

ESPANOLA

CHAMESA INN
920 N Riverside Dr (87532)
Rates: $53-$63
Tel: (505) 753-7291

COMFORT INN
2975 S Riverside Dr (87532)
Rates: $39-$69
Tel: (800) 221-2222

INN AT THE DELTA BED & BREAKFAST
304 Paseo de Onate (87532)
Rates: $85-$150
Tel: (505) 753-9466

SUPER 8 MOTEL
811 S Riverside Dr (87532)
Rates: $38-$59
Tel: (505) 753-5374
(800) 800-8000

FARMINGTON

BEST WESTERN INN
700 Scott Ave (87401)
Rates: $65-$119
Tel: (505) 327-5221
(800) 528-1234

COMFORT INN
555 Scott Ave (87401)
Rates: $49-$64
Tel: (800) 221-2222

HOLIDAY INN
600 E Broadway (87401)
Rates: $54-$64
Tel: (800) 465-4329

LA QUINTA INN
675 Scott Ave (87401)
Rates: $49-$55
Tel: (800) 531-5900

MOTEL 6
510 Scott Ave (87401)
Rates: $27-$33
Tel: (505) 327-0242
(800) 440-6000

MOTEL 6
1600 Bloomfield Hwy (87401)
Rates: $26-$32
Tel: (505) 326-4501
(800) 440-6000

GALLUP

AMBASSADOR MOTEL
1601 US 66 W (87301)
Rates: $27-$31
Tel: (505) 722-3843

BEST WESTERN INN
3009 W US 66 (87301)
Rates: $58-$149
Tel: (505) 722-2221
(800) 528-1234

BLUE SPRUCE LODGE
1119 US 66E (87301)
Rates: $18-$29
Tel: (505) 863-5211

COLONIAL MOTEL
1007 W Coal Ave (87301)
Rates: $18-$30
Tel: (505) 863-6821

COMFORT INN
3208 US 66 W (87305)
Rates: $40-$65
Tel: (800) 221-2222

DAYS INN CENTRAL
1603 US 66 W (87301)
Rates: $40-$50
Tel: (505) 863-3891
(800) 329-7466

DAYS INN WEST
3201 US 66 W
(87301)
Rates: $35-$50
Tel: (505) 863-6889
(800) 329-7466

ECONO LODGE
3101 US 66 W
(87301)
Rates: $37-$65
Tel: (505) 722-3800
(800) 424-4777

ECONOMY INN
1709 US 66 W
(87301)
Rates: $25-$45
Tel: (505) 863-9301

EL CAPITAN MOTEL
1300 US 66 E (87301)
Rates: $22-$36
Tel: (505) 863-6828

**EL RANCHO
HOTEL & MOTEL**
1000 US 66E (87301)
Rates: $36-$54
Tel: (505) 863-9311

**HOLIDAY INN
HOLIDOME**
2915 US 66 W
(87301)
Rates: $52-$67
Tel: (800) 465-4329

MOTEL 6
3306 US 66 W
(87301)
Rates: $32-$38
Tel: (505) 863-4492
(800) 440-6000

**ROAD RUNNER
MOTEL**
3012 US 66 E (87301)
Rates: $24-$34
Tel: (505) 863-3804

ROSEWAY INN
2003 Hwy 66 W
(87301)
Rates: $34-$44
Tel: (800) 454-5444

SLEEP INN
3820 US 66 E (87301)
Rates: $48-$58
Tel: (505) 863-3535
(800) 221-2222

GLENWOOD

**LOS OLMOS
GUEST RANCH**
P. O. Box 127 (88039)
Rates: $45-$80
Tel: (505) 539-2311

GRANTS

BEST WESTERN INN
1501 E Santa Fe Ave
(87020)
Rates: $59-$119
Tel: (505) 287-7901
(800) 528-1234

DAYS INN
1504 E Santa Fe Ave
(87020)
Rates: $49-$80
Tel: (505) 287-8883
(800) 329-7466

**HOLIDAY INN
EXPRESS**
1496 E Santa Fe Ave
(87020)
Rates: $49-$89
Tel: (505) 285-4676
(800) 465-4329

LEISURE LODGE
1204 E Santa Fe Ave
(87020)
Rates: $29-$38
Tel: (505) 287-2991

MOTEL 6
1505 E Santa Fe Ave
(87020)
Rates: $30-$36
Tel: (505) 285-4607
(800) 440-6000

RAMADA INN
1509 E Santa Fe Ave
(87020)
Rates: $50-$95
Tel: (505) 287-7700
(800) 272-6232

SANDS MOTEL
112 McArthur St
(87020)
Rates: $27-$43
Tel: (505) 287-2996

HOBBS

**BEST WESTERN
LEAWOOD
MOTOR INN**
1301 E Broadway
(88240)
Rates: $47-$63
Tel: (505) 393-4101
(800) 528-1234

DAYS INN
211 N Marland Blvd
(88240)
Rates: $33-$43
Tel: (505) 397-6541
(800) 329-7466

ECONO LODGE
619 N Marland Blvd
(88240)
Rates: $29-$40
Tel: (505) 397-3591
(800) 424-4777

MOTEL 6
1505 N Marland Blvd
(88240)
Rates: n/a
Tel: (505) 393-0221

RAMADA INN
501 N Marland Blvd
(88240)
Rates: $55-$95
Tel: (505) 397-3251
(800) 272-6232

SUPER 8 MOTEL
722 N Marland Blvd
(88240)
Rates: $26-41
Tel: (505) 397-7511
(800) 800-8000

ZIA MOTEL
619 N Marland Blvd
(88240)
Rates: $33-$39
Tel: (505) 397-3591

LAS CRUCES

**BEST WESTERN
MESILLA VALLEY
INN**
901 Avenida de
Mesilla (88005)
Rates: $44-$83
Tel: (505) 524-8603
(800) 528-1234

**BEST WESTERN
MISSION INN**
1765 S Main St
(88005)
Rates: $46-$72
Tel: (505) 524-8591
(800) 528-1234

DAYS INN
2600 S Valley Dr
(88001)
Rates: $41-$75
Tel: (505) 526-4441
(800) 329-7466

**DESERT LODGE
MOTEL**
1900 W Picacho St
(88005)
Rates: $19-$27
Tel: (505) 524-1925

HAMPTON INN
755 Avenida de
Mesilla (88005)
Rates: $56-$63
Tel: (505) 526-8311
(800) 426-7866

HILTON INN
705 S Telshor (88001)
Rates: $70-$90
Tel: (505) 522-4300

HOLIDAY INN
201 E University Ave
(88004)
Rates: $63-$69
Tel: (800) 465-4329

LA QUINTA INN
790 Avenida de
Mesilla (88005)
Rates: $48-$62
Tel: (800) 531-5900

**LUNDEEN INN
OF THE ARTS B & B**
618 S Alameda Blvd
(88005)
Rates: $53-$95
Tel: (505) 526-3327

MOTEL 6
235 La Posada Ln
(88001)
Rates: $33-$39
Tel: (505) 525-1010
(800) 440-6000

PLAZA SUITES
301 E University
(88001)
Rates: n/a
Tel: (505) 526-4411

ROYAL HOST MOTEL
2146 W Picacho St (88005)
Rates: $26-$34
Tel: (505) 524-8536

SUPER 8 MOTEL
245 La Posada Ln (88001)
Rates: $37-$97
Tel: (505) 523-8695
(800) 800-8000

WESTERN INN
2155 W Picacho Ave (88005)
Rates: $27-$42
Tel: (505) 523-5399

LAS VEGAS

EL CAMINIO MOTEL
1152 N Grand Ave (87701)
Rates: $30-$44
Tel: (505) 425-5994

HISTORIC PLAZA HOTEL
230 Old Town Plaza (87701)
Rates: $55-$110
Tel: (505) 425-3591
(800) 328-1882

INN ON THE SANTA FE TRAIL
1133 N Grand Ave (87701)
Rates: $39-$64
Tel: (505) 425-6791
(800) 425-6791

SCOTTISH INNS
1216 N Grand Ave (87701)
Rates: n/a
Tel: (505) 425-9357
(800) 251-1962

TOWN HOUSE MOTEL
1215 N Grand Ave (87701)
Rates: $26-$37
Tel: (505) 425-6717

LORDSBURG

BEST WESTERN AMERICAN MOTOR INN
994 E Motel Dr (88045)
Rates: $39-$54
Tel: (505) 542-3591
(800) 528-1234

BEST WESTERN WESTERN SKIES
1303 S Main (88045)
Rates: $46-$58
Tel: (505) 542-8807
(800) 528-1234

LOS ALAMOS

HILLTOP HOUSE MOTEL
Trinity Dr at Central (87544)
Rates: $68-$83
Tel: (505) 662-2441

LOVINGTON

DAYS INN
1600 W Ave D (88260)
Rates: $33-80
Tel: (505) 396-5346
(800) 329-7466

MESILLA

HAPPY TRAILS BED & BREAKFAST
1857 Paisaho Rd (88005)
Rates: $75-$100
Tel: (505) 527-8471

MORIARTY

DAYS INN
US 66 W (87035)
Rates: $40-$72
Tel: (505) 832-4451
(800) 329-7466

HOWARD JOHNSON
1316 Central Ave (87035)
Rates: $31-$62
Tel: (505) 832-4457
(800) 446-4656

SUNSET MOTEL
501 Old Rt 66 (87035)
Rates: $29-$35
Tel: (505) 832-4234

SUPER 8 MOTEL
1611 W Old Rt 66 (87035)
Rates: $37-$45
Tel: (505) 832-6730
(800) 800-8000

PLACITAS

HACIENDA DE PLACITAS B & B
491 Hwy 165 (87043)
Rates: $79-$150
Tel: (505) 867-0082

PORTALES

DUNES MOTEL
1613 West 2nd St (88130)
Rates: $26-$40
Tel: (505) 356-6668

PORTALES INN
218 West 3rd St (88130)
Rates: $29-$42
Tel: (505) 359-1208

RATON

CAPRI MOTEL
304 Canyon Dr (87740)
Rates: $29-$55
Tel: (505) 445-3641

HARMONY MOTOR MOTEL
351 Clayton Rd (87740)
Rates: $36-$58
Tel: (505) 445-2763

HOLIDAY CLASSIC MOTEL
P. O. Box 640 (87740)
Rates: $60-$73
Tel: (800) 255-8879

MELODY LANE MOTEL
136 Canyon Dr (87740)
Rates: $35-$45
Tel: (505) 445-3655
(800) 251-1962

MOTEL 6
1600 Cedar St (87740)
Rates: $28-$34
Tel: (505) 445-2777
(800) 440-6000

SUPER 8 MOTEL
1610 Cedar St (87740)
Rates: $36-$54
Tel: (505) 445-2355
(800) 800-8000

RED RIVER

RIO COLORADO LODGE
East Main St, Box 186 (87558)
Rates n/a
Tel: (505) 754-2212

TALL PINE RESORT
P. O. Box 567 (87558)
Rates: $60-$95
Tel: (505) 754-2241

TERRACE TOWERS LODGE
P. O. Box 149 (87558)
Rates: $34-$95
Tel: (800) 695-6343

RIO RANCHO

BEST WESTERN INN AT RIO RANCHO
1465 Rio Rancho Dr (87124)
Rates: $46-$65
Tel: (505) 892-1700
(800) 528-1234

DAYS INN
4200 Crestview Dr (87124)
Rates: $45-115
Tel: (505) 892-8800
(800) 329-7466

ROAD FORKS

DESERT WEST MOTEL
P. O. Box 2005 (88045)
Rates: $40-$45
Tel: (505) 542-8801

ROSWELL

**BEST WESTERN
EL RANCHO
PALACIO
MOTOR LODGE**
2205 N Main St
(88201)
Rates: $38-$56
Tel: (505) 622-2721
(800) 528-1234

**BEST WESTERN
SALLY PORT INN**
2000 N Main St
(88201)
Rates: $65-$105
Tel: (505) 622-6430
(800) 528-1234

BESTWAY INN
2052 Hwy 70 W
(88346)
Rates: $30-$88
Tel: (505) 378-8000

BUDGET INN
2101 N Main St
(88201)
Rates: $28-$38
Tel: (800) 752-4667

BUDGET INN WEST
2200 W 2nd St
(88201)
Rates: $27-$35
Tel: (505) 623-3811

COMFORT INN
2803 W 2nd
ST(88201)
Rates: $42-$48
Tel: (800) 221-2222

DAYS INN
1310 N Main St
(88201)
Rates: $38-$58
Tel: (505) 623-4021
(800) 329-7466

FRONTIER MOTEL
3010 N Main St
(88201)
Rates: $26-$39
Tel: (505) 622-1400

**LEISURE INNS
OF AMERICA**
2700 W 2nd St
(88201)
Rates: $25-$29
Tel: (505) 622-2575

NATIONAL 9 INN
2001 N Main St
(88201)
Rates: $28-$39
Tel: (505) 622-0110
(800) 524-9999

RAMADA INN
2803 W 2nd (88201)
Rates: $40-53
Tel: (505) 623-9440
(800) 272-6232

RUIDOSO

**BEST WESTERN
SWISS CHALET INN**
1451 Mechem
(88345)
Rates: $60-$106
Tel: (505) 258-3333
(800) 528-1234

**HIGH COUNTRY
LODGE**
P. O. Box 137 (88312)
Rates: $75-$79
Tel: (505) 336-4321

**INN AT PINE
SPRINGS**
P. O. Box 2100
(88346)
Rates: $40-$82
Tel: (505) 378-8100

**VILLAGE LODGE
AT INNSBROOK
RESORT**
1000 Mecham Dr
(88345)
Rates: $59-$89
Tel: (505) 258-5442

SANTA FE

**ALEXANDER'S INN
BED &BREAKFAST**
529 E Palace Ave
(87501)
Rates: $65-$140
Tel: (505) 986-1431

DAYS INN
3650 Cerrillos Rd
(87501)
Rates: $40-$165
Tel: (800) 329-7466

**DOUBLETREE
CLUB HOTEL**
3347 Cerrillos Rd
(87505)
Rates: $105-$145
Tel: (505) 473-2800
(800) 222-8733

ELDORADO HOTEL
309 W San Francisco
(87501)
Rates: $135-$210
Tel: (505) 988-4455

EL PARADERO INN
220 W Manhattan
(87501)
Rates: $50-$130
Tel: (505) 988-1177

**527 SANTA FE
APT MOTEL**
320 Artist Rd (87501)
Rates: $75-$130
Tel: (505) 982-6636
(800) 464-8005

HOLIDAY INN
4048 Cerrillos Rd
(87501)
Rates: $105-$275
Tel: (800) 465-4329

**HOMEWOOD
SUITES**
400 Griffin St (87501)
Rates: $140-170
Tel: (505) 988-3000
(800) 225-5466

HOTEL SANTA FE
1501 Paseo De
Peralta (87501)
Rates: $159-$199
Tel: (800) 825-9876

**INN ON THE
ALAMEDA**
303 E Alameda St
(87501)
Rates: $155-$330
Tel: (800) 289-2122

**INN OF THE
ANASAZI**
113 Washington Ave
(87501)
Rates: $195-$395
Tel: (800) 688-8100

LA QUINTA INN
4298 Cerrillos Rd
(87505)
Rates: $53-$74
Tel: (800) 531-5900

MOTEL 6-NORTH
3007 Cerrillos Rd
(87505)
Rates: $37-$43
Tel: (505) 473-1380
(800) 440-6000

MOTEL 6-SOUTH
3695 Cerrillos Rd
(87505)
Rates: $37-$43
Tel: (505) 471-4140
(800) 440-6000

PARK INN LIMITED
2900 Cerrillos Rd
(87501)
Rates: $39-$85
Tel: (505) 473-4281
(800) 279-0894

PRESTON HOUSE
106 Faithway St
(87501)
Rates: $58-$135
Tel: (505) 982-3465

QUALITY INN
3011 Cerillos Rd
(87501)
Rates: $63-$85
Tel: (800) 221-2222

RAMADA INN
2907 Cerrillos Rd
(87505)
Rates: $49-$70
Tel: (505) 471-3000
(800) 272-6232

**RESIDENCE INN
BY MARRIOTT**
1698 Galisteo St
(87505)
Rates: $89-$167
Tel: (505) 988-7300
(800) 331-3131

SANTA ROSA

**BEST WESTERN
ADOBE INN**
1501 E Will Rogers
Dr (88435)
Rates: $40-$55
Tel: (505) 472-3446
(800) 528-1234

**BEST WESTERN
SANTA ROSA INN**
3022 E Will Rogers
Dr (88435)
Rates: $42-$57
Tel: (505) 472-5877
(800) 528-1234

DAYS INN
1830 Will Rogers Dr
(88435)
Rates: $45-$65
Tel: (505) 472-5985
(800) 329-7466

HOLIDAY INN EXPRESS
3300 Will Rogers Dr
(88435)
Rates: $35-$56
Tel: (800) 465-4329

MOTEL 6
3400 Will Rogers Dr
(88435)
Rates: $28-$34
Tel: (505) 472-3045
(800) 440-6000

SUPER 8 MOTEL
1201 Will Rogers Dr
(88435)
Rates: $35-$43
Tel: (505) 472-5388
(800) 800-8000

SILVER CITY

BEAR MT. GUEST RANCH
2251 Bear Mt Rd
(88061)
Rates: $90-$105
Tel: (505) 538-2538

DAYS INN
3420 US Hwy 180
East (88061)
Rates: $45-$65
Tel: (505) 538-3711
(800)

THE DRIFTER MOTEL
711 Silver Heights
Blvd (88062)
Rates: $36-$43
Tel: (505) 538-2916

SUPER 8 MOTEL
1040 Hwy 180 E
(88061)
Rates: $38-$57
Tel: (505) 388-1983
(800) 800-8000

SOCORRO

BEST WESTERN GOLDEN MANOR
507 N California
(87801)
Rates: $45-$52
Tel: (505) (835-0230
(800) 528-1234

ECONO LODGE
713 NW California
St (87801)
Rates: $21-44
Tel: (505) 835-1500
(800) 424-4777

MOTEL 6
807 US Hwy 85
(87801)
Rates: $26-$32
Tel: (505) 835-4300
(800) 440-6000

TAOS

AUSTING HAUS INN
P. O. Box 8 (Ski
Valley 87525)
Rates: $88-$110
Tel: (800) 748-2932

CASA ENCANTADA BED &BREAKFAST
416 Liebert St
(87571)
Rates: $75-$125
Tel: (505) 758-7477

EL MONTE LODGE
317 E Kit Carson Rd
(87571)
Rates: $44-$105
Tel: (505) 758-3171

EL PUEBLO LODGE
412 Paseo del Pueblo
Norte (87571)
Rates: $40-$60
Tel: (505) 758-8700

EL RINCON BED & BREAKFAST
114 E Kit Carson Rd
(87571)
Rates: $49-$99
Tel: (505) 758-4874

HOLIDAY INN-DON FERNANDO DE TAOS
1005 Paseo del
Pueblo Sur (87571)
Rates: $69-$165
Tel: (800) 465-4329

INN ON THE RIO
910 E Kit Carson Rd
(87571)
Rates: $49-$79
Tel: (505) 758-7199

QUALITY INN
1043 Paseo del
Pueblo Sur (87571)
Rates: $55-$85
Tel: (800) 221-2222

RAMADA INN
615 Paseo del
Pueblo Sur (87571)
Rates: $79-$185
Tel: (505) 758-2900
(800) 272-6232

SAGEBRUSH INN
Paseo del Pueblo Sur
(87571)
Rates: $50-$100
Tel: (800) 428-3626

SUN GOD LODGE
919 Paseo del Pueblo
Sur (87571)
Rates: $40-$77
Tel: (505) 758-3162

TAOS MOTEL & RV PARK
Hwy 68 (87571)
Rates: n/a
Tel: (800) 323-6009

TRUTH OR CONSEQUENCES

ACE LODGE MOTEL
1302 Date St (87901)
Rates: $29-$60
Tel: (505) 894-2151

BEST WESTERN HOT SPRINGS MOTOR INN
2270 N Date St
(87901)
Rates: $47-$60
Tel: (505) 894-6665
(800) 528-1234

SUPER 8 MOTEL
2151 N Date St
(87901)
Rates: $40-$53
Tel: (505) 894-7888
(800)800-8000

TUCUMCARI

AMERICANA MOTEL
406 E Tucumcari
Blvd (88401)
Rates: $20-$38
Tel: (505) 461-0431

APACHE MOTEL
1106 E Tucumcari
Blvd (88401)
Rates: $20-$34
Tel: (505) 461-3367

BEST WESTERN ARUBA MOTEL
1700 E Tucumcari
Blvd (88401)
Rates: $42-$52
Tel: (505) 461-3335
(800) 528-1234

BEST WESTERN POW WOW INN
801 W Tucumcari
Blvd (88401)
Rates: $40-$125
Tel: (505) 461-0500
(800) 528-1234

BUCKAROO MOTEL
1315 W Tucumcari
Blvd (88401)
Rates: $18-$22
Tel: (505) 461-1650

COMFORT INN
2800 E Tucumcari
Blvd
(88401)
Rates: $44-$59
Tel: (800) 221-2222

DAYS INN
2623 S First St
(88401)
Rates: $30-$45
Tel: (505) 461-0330
(800) 329-7466

ECONO LODGE
3400 E Tucumcari
Blvd (88401)
Rates: $20-$44
Tel: (505) 461-4194
(800) 424-4777

FRIENDSHIP INN
315 E Tucumcari
Blvd (88401)
Rates: $20-$31
Tel: (800) 424-4777

HOLIDAY INN
3716 E Tucumcari
Blvd (88401)
Rates: $39-$79
Tel: (800) 465-4329

MOTEL 6
2900 E Tucumcari
Blvd (88401)
Rates: $26-$32
Tel: (505) 461-4791
(800) 440-6000

RELAX INN
1010 E Tucumcari
Blvd (88401)
Rates: $20-$30
Tel: (505) 461-3862

RODEWAY INN
1302 W Tucumcari
Blvd (88401)
Rates: $41-$55
Tel: (505) 461-3140
(800) 221-2000

ROYAL PALACIO MOTEL
1620 E Tucumcari
Blvd (88401)
Rates: $27-$35
Tel: (505) 461-1212

SAFARI MOTEL
722 E Tucumcari
Blvd (88401)
Rates: $23-$33
Tel: (505) 461-3642

SUPER 8 MOTEL
4001 E Tucumcari
Blvd (88401)
Rates: $35-$49
Tel: (505) 461-4444
(800) 800-8000

TRAVELODGE
1214 E Tucumcari
Blvd (88401)
Rates: $25-$75
Tel: (505) 461-1401
(800) 578-7878

VAUGHN

BEL AIR MOTEL
P. O. Box 68 (88353)
Rates: $28-$55
Tel: (505) 584-2241

WHITE ROCK

BANDELLER INN
Center SR 4 (87544)
Rates: $46-$69
Tel: (505) 672-3838

WHITE'S CITY

BEST WESTERN CAVERN INN
17 Carlsbad Caverns
Hwy (88268)
Rates: $55-$80
Tel: (505) 785-2291
(800) 528-1234

NEW YORK

ACRA

SLEEPY DUTCHMAN
Rt 23, Box 59B (12405)
Rates: n/a
Tel: (518) 622-2050

ALBANY

ECONO LODGE
1632 Central Ave
(12205)
Rates: $35-$52
Tel: (518) 456-8811
(800) 424-4777

HOWARD JOHNSON
1375 Washington
Ave (12206)
Rates: $54-$85
Tel: (518) 459-3100
(800) 446-4656

HOWARD JOHNSON
416 Southern Blvd
(12209)
Rates: $61-$150
Tel: (518) 562-6555
(800) 446-4656

MOTEL 6
100 Watervliet Ave
(12206)
Rates: $40-$46
Tel: (518) 438-7447
(800) 440-6000

QUALITY INN
1-3 Watervliet Ave
(12206)
Rates: $59-$95
Tel: (800) 221-2222

RAMADA INN-DOWNTOWN
300 Broadway (12207)
Rates: $62-$88
Tel: (518) 434-4111
(800) 272-6232

RESIDENCE INN BY MARRIOTT
1 Residence Inn Dr
(12110)
Rates: $135-$165
Tel: (518) 783-0600
(800) 331-3131

ALEXANDRIA BAY

RIVEREDGE RESORT & HOTEL
17 Holland St (13607)
Rates: $89-$218
Tel: (315) 482-9917
(800) ENJOY-US

ALTMAR

BRENDA' S MOTEL & CAMPGROUND
644 CR 48 (13302)
Rates: n/a:
Tel: (315) 298-2268

CANNON'S PLACE
P. O. Box 209, CR 48
(13302)
Rates: n/a
Tel: (315) 298-5054

FOX HOLLOW
2740 SR 13 (13302)
Rates: n/a:
Tel: (315) 298-2876

JAYHAWKERS BUNKHOUSE
CC Rd, Box 132
(13302)
Rates: n/a:
Tel: (315) 964-2557

AMENIA

DEER RUN
PO Box 302 (12501)
Rates: $50-99
Tel: (914) 373-9558

AMHERST

LORD AMHERST HOTEL
5000 Main St (14226)
Rates: $59-$99
Tel: (800) 544-2200

MARRIOTT HOTEL
1340 Millersport
Hwy (14221)
Rates: n/a
Tel: (716) 689-6900

MOTEL 6
4400 Maple Rd
(14226)
Rates: $36-$42
Tel: (716) 834-2231
(800) 440-6000

RED ROOF INN
42 Flint Rd (14226)
Rates: $39-$64
Tel: (716) 689-7474
(800) 843-7663

AMSTERDAM

VALLEY VIEW MOTOR INN
Rts 5 S & 30 (12010)
Rates: $31-$58
Tel: (518) 842-5637

ARMONK

RAMADA INN
94 Business Park Dr
(10504)
Rates: $79-$150
Tel: (914) 273-9090
(800) 272-6232

AUBURN

DAYS INN
37 William St (13021)
Rates: $49-$59
Tel: (315) 252-7567
(800) 329-7466

HOLIDAY INN
75 North St (13021)
Rates: $64-$101
Tel: (800) 465-4329

THE IRISH ROSE BED & BREAKFAST
102 South St (13021)
Rates: $55-$95
Tel: (315) 255-0196

AVOCA

GOODRICH CENTER MOTEL
8620 State Rt 415
(14809)
Rates: $35-$50
Tel: (607) 566-2216

BAINBRIDGE

ALGONKIN MOTEL
RDS Box 45, Rt 7
(13733)
Rates: n/a
Tel: (607) 967-5911

BALLSTON LAKE

WESTWOOD MOTEL
1012 Saratoga Rd
(12019)
Rates: $45-$80
Tel: (518) 339-3612

BATAVIA

BEST WESTERN BATAVIA INN
8204 Park Rd (14020)
Rates: $50-$80
Tel: (716) 343-1000
(800) 528-1234

DAYS INN
200 Oak St (14020)
Rates: $39-$78
Tel: (716) 343-1440
(800) 329-7466

RODEWAY INN
8212 Park Rd (14020)
Rates: $46-$79
Tel: (716) 343-2311
(800) 228-2000

BATH

DAYS INN
330 W Morris St
(14810)
Rates: $38-$63
Tel: (607) 776-7644
(800) 329-7466

OLD NATIONAL HOTEL
13 E Steuben St (14810)
Rates: $44-$50
Tel: (607) 776-4104

BELLPORT

THE GREAT SOUTH BAY INN B & B
160 S Country Rd (11713)
Rates: $80-$95
Tel: (516) 286-8588

BERLIN

THE SEDGWICK INN
P. O. Box 250 (12022)
Rates: $65-$95
Tel: (518) 658-2334

BERNHARDS BAY

SNUG HARBOR
Rt 9, Box 44 (13028)
Rates: n/a:
Tel: (315) 675-3527

BINGHAMTON

HOJO INN
690 Front St (13905)
Rates: $40-$70
Tel: (607) 724-1341
(800) 446-4656

HOLIDAY INN ARENA
2-8 Hawley St (13901)
Rates: $65-$79
Tel: (800) 465-4329

MOTEL 6
1012 Front St (13905)
Rates: $36-$42
Tel: (607) 771-0400
(800) 440-6000

SUPER 8 MOTEL
Box 196, E Side Sta (13904)
Rates: $44-$100
Tel: (800) 800-8000

BOONVILLE

HEADWATERS MOTOR LODGE
P. O. Box 404 (13309)
Rates: $43-$55
Tel: (315) 952-4493

BOWMANSVILLE

RED ROOF INN
146 Maple Dr (14026)
Rates: $27-$67
Tel: (716) 633-1100
(800) 843-7663

BRIGHTON

HAMPTON INN-SOUTH
717 E Henrietta Rd (14623)
Rates: $76-$88
Tel: (716) 272-7800
(800) 426-7866

WELLESLEY INN
797 E Henrietta Rd (14623)
Rates: $43-$85
Tel: (716) 427-0130
(800) 444-8888

BRISTOL CENTER

THE ACORN INN BED & BREAKFAST
4508 SR 64 S (14424)
Rates: $76-$140
Tel: (716) 229-2834

BROCKPORT

ECONO LODGE
6575 4th Section Rd (14420)
Rates: $44-$65
Tel: (716) 637-3157
(800) 424-4777

BUFFALO

BUFFALO EXIT 53 MOTOR LODGE
475 Dingens St (14206)
Rates: $40-$69
Tel: (716) 896-2800

HILTON HOTEL
120 Church St (14202)
Rates: $106-$160
Tel: (800) 445-8667

HOLIDAY INN-DOWNTOWN
620 Delaware Ave (14202)
Rates: $71-$93
Tel: (800) 465-4329

WELLESLEY INN
4630 Genesee St (14225)
Rates: $48-$68
Tel: (716) 631-8966
(800) 444-8888

CALCIUM

MICROTEL
8000 Virginia Smith Dr (13616)
Rates: $37-$41
Tel: (315) 629-5000

CAMBRIDGE

BLUE WILLOW MOTEL
51 S Park St (12816)
Rates: $35-$54
Tel: (518) 677-3552

CAMBRIDGE INN BED & BREAKFAST
16 W Main St (12816)
Rates" $45-$75
Tel: (518) 677-5741

TOWN HOUSE MOTOR INN
16 W Main (12816)
Rates: $45-$50
Tel: (518) 677-5524

CANANDAIGUA

ECONO LODGE
200 Robert Dann Dr (14870)
Rates: $39-$62
Tel: (607) 962-4444
(800) 424-4777

ECONO LODGE MUAR LAKE
170 Eastern Blvd (14424)
Rates: $50-$62
Tel: (716) 394-9000
(800) 424-4777

THE INN ON THE LAKE
770 S Main St (14424)
Rates: $68-$295
Tel: (716) 394-7800

RODEWAY INN
SR 96 & 21 (Manchester, 14504)
Rates: $40-$80
Tel: (716) 289-3811
(800) 424-4777

CANASTOGA

DAYS INN
NYS Rte 13 (13032)
Rates: $45-$70
Tel: (315) 697-3309
(800) 329-7466

CASTLETON

BELAIR MOTEL
1036 Rt 9 (12033)
Rates: $40-$55
Tel: (518) 732-7744

CATSKILL

DAYS INN
I-87/Exit 21 (12414)
Rates: $45-$75
Tel: (518) 943-5800
(800) 329-7466

CAZENOVIA

LINCKLAEN HOUSE
79 Albany St (13035)
Rates: $65-$130
Tel: (315) 655-3461

CENTRAL SQUARE

TOWN & COUNTRY MOTEL
1436 Brewerton Rd (13036)
Rates: n/a:
Tel: (315) 668-6751

CHAFFEE

JOSIE'S BROOKSIDE MOTEL
SR 16 & 39 (14030)
Rates: $29-$45
Tel: (716) 496-5057

CHEEKTOWAGA

BUFFALO EXIT 53 MOTOR LODGE
475 Dingens St (14206)
Rates: $50-$70
Tel: (716) 896-2800

HOLIDAY INN GATEWAY
601 Dingens St (14206)
Rates: $76-$87
Tel: (716) 896-2900
(800) 465-4329

RADISSON HOTEL & SUITES
4243 Genessee St (14225)
Rates: $129-$139
Tel: (716) 634-2300
(800) 333-3333

CLARENCE

HERITAGE HOUSE COUNTRY INN
8261 Main St (14221)
Rates: $53-$100
Tel: (716) 633-4900
(800) 283-3899

CLAY

RODEWAY INN
901 S Bay Rd (13041)
Rates: $39-$49
Tel: (315) 458-3510
(800) 228-2000

CLAYTON

(Thousand Islands)

WEST WINDS MOTEL
Box 56 RD 2 (13624)
Rates: $38-$67
Tel: (315) 686-3352

CLIFTON PARK

COMFORT INN
41 Fire Rd (12065)
Rates: $49-$135
Tel: (518) 234-4321
(800) 221-2222

COBLESKILL

BEST WESTERN INN
12 Campus Dr
Extenstion (12043)
Rates: $56-$94
Tel: (800) 528-1234

COHOES

HAMPTON INN
981 New Loudon Rd (12047)
Rates: $72-$82
Tel: (518) 785-0000
(800) 426-7866

INN AT THE CENTURY
997 New Loudon Rd (12047)
Rates: $72-$110
Tel: (518) 785-0931

COLD SPRING

HUDSON HOUSE INN
2 Main St (10516)
Rates: $70-$175
Tel: (914) 265-9355

COLONIE

MARRIOTT HOTEL
189 Wolf Rd (12205)
Rates: $109-$185
Tel: (518) 458-8444
(800) 228-9290

RED ROOF INN
188 Wolf Rd (12205)
Rates: $40-$81
Tel: (518) 459-1971
(800) 843-7663

RAMADA LIMITED
1630 Central Ave (12205)
Rates: $59-$79
Tel: (518) 456-0222
(800) 272-6232

COMMACK

HOWARD JOHNSON BED & BREAKFAST
450 Moreland Rd (11725)
Rates: $69-$135
Tel: (516) 864-8820
(800) 466-4656

COOPERS PLAINS

LAMPLITER MOTEL
9316 Victory Hwy (14870)
Rates" $30-$43
Tel: (607) 962-1184

STILES MOTEL
9239 Victory Hwy (14870)
Rates: $25-$47
Tel: (607) 962-5221
(800) 331-3920

COOPERSTOWN

AALSMEER MOTEL
Box 790, RD 2 (13326)
Rates: $75-$515:
Tel: (607) 547-8819

BEST WESTERN INN AT COMMONS
50 Commons Dr (13326)
Rates: $55-$150
Tel: (607) 547-9439
(800) 528-1234

CORFU

ECONO LODGE-DARIEN LAKES
8493 Rt 77 (14036)
Rates: $39-$60
Tel: (716) 599-4681
(800) 424-4777

CORNING

RADISSON HOTEL
125 Denison Pkwy E (14830)
Rates: $80-$158
Tel: (800) 333-3333

CORTLAND

ECONO LODGE
3775 US 11 (13045)
Rates: $40-$75
Tel: (607) 753-7594
(800) 424-4777

HOLIDAY INN
2 River St (13045)
Rates: $75-$129
Tel: (607) 756-4431
(800) 465-4329

SUPER 8 MOTEL
188 Clinton Ave (13045)
Rates: $49-71
Tel: (607) 756-5622
(800) 800-8000

WATERFALLS MOTEL
Rt 9A & Furnace
Dock Rd (10520)
Rates: $60-$70
Tel: (914) 271-4322

DANSVILLE

DAYSTOP
I-390, Exit 5 (14437)
Rates: $44-$55
Tel: (716) 335-6023
(800) 329-7466

DELHI

BUENA VISTA MOTEL
Box 212, Andes Rd (13753)
Rates: $38-$55
Tel: (607) 746-2135

DEPOSIT

ALEXANDER'S INN ON OQUAJA LAKE BED &BREAKFAST
770 Oquaja Lake Rd (13754)
Rates: $59-$99
Tel: (607) 467-6023

DIAMOND POINT

DIAMOND COVE COTTAGES
Lake Shore Dr (12845)
Rates: $55-$115
Tel: (518) 668-5787

DOVER PLAINS

OLD DROVERS INN
Old Rt 22 (12522)
Rates: $80-$180
Tel: (914) 832-9311

DUNKIRK

**DRAKES
MOTOR INN**
5361 West Lake Rd
(14048)
Rates: n/a
Tel: (716) 672-4867

RODEWAY INN
310 Lake Shore Dr
(14048)
Rates: $38-$58
Tel: (716) 366-2200
(800) 228-2000

**SHERATON
HARBORFRONT INN**
30 Lake Shore Dr E
(14048)
Rates: $65-$100
Tel: (716) 366-8350
(800) 325-3535

DURHAM

**GOLDEN HARVEST
BED & BREAKFAST**
37 Golden Hill Rd
(E Durham 12423)
Rates: n/a
Tel: (518) 634-2305

ROSE MOTEL
Rt 145 (12422)
Rates: n/a
Tel: (518) 239-8496

EAST GREENBUSH

**MOUNT VERNON
MOTEL**
576 Columbia Tpke
(12061)
Rates: n/a
Tel: (518) 477-9352

EAST HERKIMER

GLEN RIDGE MOTEL
Rt 5 (13350)
Rates: n/a
Tel: (315) 866-4149

EAST NORWICH

EAST NORWICH INN
SR 25A & SR 106
(11732)
Rates: $95-$125
Tel: (516) 922-1500

EAST SYRACUSE

EMBASSY SUITES
6646 Old Collamer
Rd (13057)
Rates: $99
Tel: (315) 446-3200
(800) 362-2779

**HOLIDAY INN EAST-
CARRIER CIRCLE**
6501 College Pt
(13057)
Rates: $80-$85
Tel: (800) 465-4329

MARRIOTT HOTEL
6302 Carrier Pkwy
(13057)
Rates: $79-$165
Tel: (315) 432-0200
(800) 228-9290

MICROTEL
6608 Old Collamer
Rd (13057)
Rates: $35-$39
Tel: (315) 437-3500
(800) 771-7171

MOTEL 6
6577 Court St Rd
(13057)
Rates: $33-$39
Tel: (315) 433-1300
(800) 440-6000

**RESIDENCE INN
BY MARRIOTT**
6420 Yorktown Cir
(13057)
Rates: $69-$139
Tel: (315) 432-4488
(800) 331-3131

EAST WINDHAM

**POINT LOOKOUT
INN**
Rt 23, Box 33 (12439)
Rates: $55-$125
Tel: (518) 734-3381

ELBRIDGE

COZY COTTAGE
4987 Kingston Rd
(13060)
Rates: n/a
Tel: (315) 689-2082

ELMHURST

**MARRIOTT HOTEL-
LA GUARDIA**
102-05 Ditmars Blvd
(11369)
Rates: $143-$175
Tel: (718) 565-8900
(800) 228-9290

**QUALITY HOTEL-
LA GUARDIA**
9500 Ditmars Blvd
(11369)
Rates: $99-$145
Tel: (800) 221-2222

ELMIRA

**COACHMAN
MOTOR LODGE**
908 Pennsylvania
Ave (14904)
Rates: $53-$63
Tel: (607) 733-5526

**HOLIDAY INN-
DOWNTOWN**
760 E Water St
(14901)
Rates: $65-$90
Tel: (607) 734-4211
(800) 465-4329

**NEW PLANTATION
MOTEL**
2046 Rt 17 (14901)
Rates: n/a
Tel: (607) 737-9008
(800) 836-0310

RED JACKET MOTEL
P. O. Box 489 (14902)
Rates: $35-$65
Tel: (607) 734-1616
(800) 562-5808

ENDICOTT

**BEST WESTERN
HOMESTEAD INN**
749 W Main St (13760)
Rates: $45-$63
Tel: (800) 528-1234

FALCONER

MOTEL 6
1980 E Main St
(14733)
Rates: $40-$46
Tel: (716) 665-3670
(800) 440-6000

FARMINGTON

**BEST WESTERN
SUNRISE HILL INN**
6108 Loomis Rd
(14425)
Rates: $39-$78
Tel: (716) 924-2131
(800) 528-1234

SUPER 8 MOTEL
6037 Rt 96 (14425)
Rates: $35-$75
Tel: (800) 800-8000

FISHKILL

**RESIDENCE INN
BY MARRIOTT**
2481 Rt 9 (12524)
Rates: $75-$129
Tel: (914) 896-5210
(800) 331-3131

WELLESLEY INN
2477 Rt 9 (12524)
Rates: $50-$80
Tel: (914) 896-4995
(800) 444-8888

FLEISCHMANNS

**RIVER RUN
BED & BREAKFAST**
Main St (12430)
Rates: $45-$95
Tel: (914) 254-4884

FREDONIA

DAYS INN
10455 Bennett Rd
(14063)
Rates: $40-$75
Tel: (716) 673-1351
(800) 329-7466

FREEPORT

**FREEPORT MOTOR
INN & BOATEL**
445 S Main St (11520)
Rates: $65-$75
Tel: (516) 623-9100

FULTON

**FULTON
MOTOR LODGE**
163 S 1st St (13069)
Rates: $48-$62
Tel: (315) 598-6100
(800) 223-6935

MINI MOTEL
RR 8, Box 160
(13069)
Rates: n/a:
Tel: (315) 592-7238

**192 EXECUTIVE
SUITES**
192 S 1st St (13069)
Rates: n/a:
Tel: (315) 593-6631
(315) 593-7304

**QUALITY INN-
RIVERSIDE**
930 S 1st St (13069)
Rates: $69-$79
Tel: (800) 221-2222

FULTONVILLE

THE POPLAR'S INN
Riverside Dr (12072)
Rates: $43-$60
Tel: (518) 853-4511

GANSEVOORT

**McGREGOR INN
MOTEL**
Rt 9 (12831)
Rates: n/a
Tel: (518) 587-1394

GARDEN CITY

**THE GARDEN CITY
HOTEL**
45 Seventh St (11530)
Rates: $160-$340
Tel: (516) 747-3000

GASPORT

HARTLAND MOTEL
8464 Ridge Rd (14067)
Rates: n/a
Tel: (716) 772-2266

GATES

MOTEL 6
155 Buell Rd (14624)
Rates: $36-$42
Tel: (716) 436-2170
(800) 440-6000

GENEVA

DAYSTOP
Rts 14 & 318 (14456)
Rates: $30-$85
Tel: (315) 789-4510
(800) 329-7466

MOTEL 6
485 Hamilton St
(14456)
Rates: $40-$46
Tel: (315) 789-4050
(800) 440-6000

**99 WILLIAM STREET
BED & BREAKFAST**
99 William St (14456)
Rates: $65
Tel: (315) 789-1273

GRAND GORGE

**GOLDEN ACRES
FARM RANCH**
Windy Ridge Rd
(12076)
Rates: $80-$330
Tel: (607) 588-7329

GRAND ISLAND

**CHATEAU
MOTOR LODGE**
1810 Grand Island
Blvd (14072)
Rates: $31-$69
Tel: (716) 773-2868

GREENPORT

SILVER SANDS MOTEL
P. O. Box 285 (11944)
Rates: $70-$100
Tel: (516) 477-0011

HAGUE

**TROUT HOUSE
VILLAGE**
Lake Shore Dr, Rt 9N
(12836)
Rates: n/a
Tel: (518) 543-6088

HAMBURG

HOJO INN
5245 Camp Rd
(14075)
Rates: $38-$75
Tel: (716) 648-2000
(800) 446-4656

RED ROOF INN
5370 Camp Rd
(14075)
Rates: $32-$59
Tel: (716) 648-7222
(800) 843-7663

HAMLIN

**SANDY CREEK
MANOR HOUSE
BED & BREAKFAST**
1960 Redman Rd
(14464)
Rates: n/a
716) 964-7528

HAMMONS-PORT

VINEHURST MOTEL
Box 203, Rt 54
(14840)
Rates: n/a
Tel: (607) 569-2300

HANCOCK

**SMITHS COLONIAL
MOTEL**
Rt 97, Box 172-D
(13783)
Rates: $38-$75
Tel: (607) 637-2989

HAUPPAUGE

**RADISSON
ISLANDIA**
3635 Express Dr N
(11788)
Rates: $105-$129
Tel: (800) 333-3333

HENRIETTA

MICROTEL
905 Lehigh Station
Rd (14467)
Rates: $35-$43
Tel: (716) 334-3400
(800) 771-7171

RED ROOF INN
4820 W Henrietta Rd
(14467)
Rates: $35-$60
Tel: (800) 843-7663

HERKIMER

HERKIMER MOTEL
100 Marginal Rd
(13350)
Rates: $38-$68
Tel: (315) 866-0490

INN TOWNE MOTEL
227 N Washington St
(13350)
Rates: $34-$54
Tel: (315) 866-1101

HIGHLAND FALLS

**BEST WESTERN
PALISADE MOTEL**
SR 218 (10928)
Rates: $65-$80
Tel: (914) 446-9400
(800) 528-1234

HILLSDALE

LINDEN VALLEY INN
E on NY 23 (12529)
Rates: $115-$145
Tel: (518) 325-7100

SWISS HUTTE MOTEL
Rt 23 (12529)
Rates: $75-$179
Tel: (518) 325-3333

HOLBROOK

RED CARPET INN
4444 Veterans
Memorial Hwy
(11741)
Rates: $47-$65
Tel: (516) 588-7700
(800) 251-1962

HORSEHEADS

**BEST WESTERN
MARSHALL MANOR**
3527 Watkins Glen
Rd (14845)
Rates: $34-$68
Tel: (607) 739-3891
(800) 528-1234

HOWARD JOHNSON
2671 Corning Rd
(14845)
Rates: $48-$80
Tel: (607) 739-5636
(800) 446-4656

MOTEL 6
4133 Rt 17 (14845)
Rates: $40-$46
Tel: (607) 739-2525
(800) 466-8356

HUNTER

**EVERGREEN
COTTAGES**
P.O. Box 161 (12442)
Rates: n/a
Tel: (518) 263-4932

ILION

WHIFFLETREE MOTEL
345 E Main St (13357)
Rates: $40-$75
Tel: (315) 895-7777

ITHACA

**BEST WESTERN
UNIVERSITY INN**
1020 Ellis Hollow Rd
(14850)
Rates: $88-$105
Tel: (607) 272-6100
(800) 528-1234

**COLLEGETOWN
MOTOR LODGE**
312 College Ave
(14850)
Rates: $57-$94
Tel: (800) 745-3542

ECONO LODGE
2303 N Triphammer
Rd (14850)
Rates: $42-$75
Tel: (607) 257-1400
(800) 424-4777

ECONOMY INN
658 Elmira Rd (14850)
Rates: $28-$85
Tel: (607) 277-0370
(800) 826-0778

**HOLIDAY INN-
EXECUTIVE TOWER**
222 S Cayuga St
(14850)
Rates: $65-$175
Tel: (800) 465-4329

**HOWARD JOHNSON
LODGE**
2300 N Triphammer
Rd (14850)
Rates: $45-$90
Tel: (607) 257-1212
(800) 446-4656

**LA TOURELLE
COUNTRY INN**
1150 Danby Rd
(14850)
Rates: $75-$180
Tel: (607) 273-2734

**MEADOW COURT
INN**
529 S Meadow St
(14850)
Rates: $35-$135
Tel: (607) 273-3885

**RAMADA INN
AIRPORT**
2310 N Triphammer
Rd (14850)
Rates: $80-$95
Tel: (607) 257-3100
(800) 272-6232

**SPRING WATER
MOTEL**
Rt 366 (14850)
Rates: $42-$70
Tel: (607) 272-3721

JAMAICA

**HILTON HOTEL-
JFK AIRPORT**
138-10 135th Ave
(11436)
Rates: $109-$169
Tel: (718) 322-8700

**PLAZA HOTEL-
JFK AIRPORT**
135-30 140th St
(11436)
Rates: n/a
Tel: (718) 659-6003

**TRAVELODGE-
JFK AIRPORT**
Belt Pkwy & Van
Wyck Expwy (11430)
Rates: $99-$119
Tel: (718) 995-9000
(800) 578-7878

JAMESTOWN

COMFORT INN
2800 N Main St Ext
(14701)
Rates: $51-$90
Tel: (716) 664-5920
(800) 221-2222

HOLIDAY INN
150 W 4th St (14701)
Rates: $62-$77
Tel: (716) 664-3400
(800) 465-4329

JOHNSON CITY

**BEST WESTERN
OF JOHNSON CITY**
569 Harry L Dr
(13790)
Rates: $45-$67
Tel: (607) 729-9194
(800) 528-1234

RED ROOF INN
590 Fairview St
(13790)
Rates: $40-$63
Tel: (607) 729-8940
(800) 843-7663

JOHNSTOWN

HOLIDAY INN
308 N Comrie Ave
(12095)
Rates: $52-$82
Tel: (518) 762-4686
(800) 465-4329

KENMORE

SUPER 8 MOTEL
1288 Sheridan Dr
(14217)
Rates: $40-$55
Tel: (716) 876-4020
(800) 800-8000

KINGSTON

DAYS INN
Rt 28 W (12401)
Rates: $44-$65
Tel: (914) 331-1919
(800) 329-7466

HOLIDAY INN
503 Washington Ave
(12401)
Rates: $66-$99
Tel: (914) 338-0400
(800) 465-4329

SUPER 8 MOTEL
487 Washington Ave
(12401)
Rates: $48-$70
Tel: (914) 338-3078
(800) 800-8000

LAKE GEORGE

BALMORAL MOTEL
444 Canada St
(12845)
Rates: $30-$98
Tel: (518) 668-2673

**GREEN HAVEN
RESORT MOTEL**
Rd 2, Box 2384
(12845)
Rates: $35-$70
Tel: (518) 668-2489

LAKE PLACID

**ART DEVLIN'S
OLYMPIC MOTOR INN**
350 Main St (12946)
Rates: $46-$106
Tel: (518) 523-3700

**BEST WESTERN
GOLDEN ARROW**
150 Main St (12946)
Rates: $60-$159
Tel: (518) 523-3353
(800) 528-1234

**EDGE OF
THE LAKE MOTEL**
56 Saranac Ave
(12946)
Rates: $38-$98
Tel: (518) 523-9430

**HOLIDAY INN
SUNSPREE RESORT**
1 Olympic Dr
(12946)
Rates: $49-$189
Tel: (518) 523-2556
(800) 874-1980

HOWARD JOHNSON
90 Saranac Ave
(12946)
Rates: $65-$105
Tel: (518) 523-9555
(800) 446-4656

THE NORTHWAY MOTEL
5 Wilmington Rd
(12946)
Rates: $40-$75
Tel: (518) 523-3500

RAMADA INN
8-12 Saranac Ave
(12946)
Rates: $45-$140
Tel: (518) 523-2587
(800) 272-6232

TOWN & COUNTRY MOTOR INN
67 Saranac Ave
(12946)
Rates: $42-$78
Tel: (518) 523-9268

LATHAM

COMFORT INN
866 Albany Shaker Rd (12110)
Rates: $56-$64
Tel: (518) 783-1900
(800) 221-2222

HOLIDAY INN EXPRESS
946 New Loudon Rd
(12110)
Rates: $67-$105
Tel: (800) 465-4329

HOWARD JOHNSON
611 Troy-Schenectady Rd
(12110)
Rates: $45-$99
Tel: (518) 785-5891
(800) 446-4656

MICROTEL
7 Rensselaer Ave
(12110)
Rates: $35-$50
Tel: (518) 782-9161
(800) 771-7171

QUALITY INN
622 Watervliet-Shaker Rd (12110)
Rates: $45-$99
Tel: (518) 785-1414
(800) 452-8426

LIBERTY

HOLIDAY INN EXPRESS
7 Rt 52 E (12754)
Rates: $55-$85
Tel: (914) 292-7171
(800) 465-4329

LITTLE FALLS

BEST WESTERN INN
20 Albany St (13365)
Rates: $52-$63
Tel: (315) 823-4954
(800) 528-1234

LIVERPOOL

DAYS INN-NORTH
400 7th North St
(13088)
Rates: $64-$76
Tel: (315) 451-1511
(800) 329-7466

ECONO LODGE NORTH
401 7th North St
(13088)
Rates: $40-$80
Tel: (315) 451-6000
(800) 424-4777

FOUR POINTS HOTEL
441 Electronics Pkwy(13088)
Rates: $83-$130
Tel: (315) 457-1122

FRIENDSHIP INN
629 Old Liverpool Rd (13088)
Rates: $39-$80
Tel: (800) 424-4777

HAMPTON INN
417 7th North St
(13088)
Rates: $58-$70
Tel: (315) 457-9900
(800) 426-7866

HOMEWOOD SUITES
275 Elwood Davis Rd (13088)
Rates: $89-$179
Tel: (315) 451-3800
(800) 225-5466

KNIGHTS INN
430 Electronics Pkwy (13088)
Rates: $36-$54
Tel: (315) 453-6330
(800) 843-5644

LIVINGSTON MANOR

LANZA'S INN
Rd 2, Box 446
(12758)
Rates: $54-$84
Tel: (914) 439-5070

LOCKPORT

TWIN OAKS MOTEL
4660 Ridge Rd
(14094)
Rates: n/a
Tel: (716) 433-2447

LONG LAKE

JOURNEY'S END COTTAGES
Deerland Rd, Rt 30
(12847)
Rates: $400-$550/(Weekly)
Tel: (518) 624-5381

LOWMAN

FOUNTAIN MOTEL
Rt 17, Box 11 (14861)
Rates: n/a
Tel: (607) 732-8617

LYONS

KREISS FARM B & B
2097 Highland Fruit Farm Rd (14489)
Rates: n/a
Tel: (315) 946-9448

MALONE

ECONO LODGE
227 W Main St
(12953)
Rates: $40-$50
Tel: (518) 483-0500
(800) 424-4777

FLANAGAN HOTEL
One Elm St (12953)
Rates: $30-$60
Tel: (518) 483-1400

FOUR SEASONS MOTEL
236 W Main St
(12953)
Rates: $40-$52
Tel: (518) 483-3490

SUPER 8 MOTEL AT JONS
Finny Blvd, Rt 30
(12953)
Rates: $44-$61
Tel: (518) 483-8123
(800) 800-8000

MALTA

POST ROAD LODGE
2865 Rt 9 (12020)
Rates: n/a
Tel: (518) 584-4169
(800) 836-2687

RIVIERA MOTEL
2539 Rt 9 (12020)
Rates: n/a
Tel: (518) 899-2600

MASONVILLE

MASON INN & MOTOR LODGE
Rt 206, Box 81
(13804)
Rates: $38-$45
Tel: (607) 265-3287

MASSENA

BOB'S MOTEL
Rt 2, Box 301 (13662)
Rates: n/a
Tel: (315) 769-9497

HILLSIDE MOTEL
15 Smith Rd (13662)
Rates: n/a
Tel: (315) 769-5403

NEW FLANDERS INN
Main & W Orvis Sts
(13662)
Rates: n/a
Tel: (315) 769-2441
(800) 654-6212

PARK INN MOTEL
528 CR 42 (13662)
Rates: n/a
Tel: (315) 769-7799

MAYBOOK

SUPER 8 MOTEL
207 Montgomery Rd
(12549)
Rates: $49-$55
Tel: (914) 457-3143
(800) 800-8000

MEXICO

STRIKE KING
LODGE
286 SR 104B (13114)
Rates: n/a:
Tel: (315) 963-7826

WALTON'S MOTEL
3210 US Rt 11, Box
92 (13114)
Rates: n/a
Tel: (315) 963-7120

MIDDLE GROVE

DAYBREAK MOTEL
2909 Rt 9 (12850)
Rates: $35-$125
Tel: (518) 882-6838

MIDDLEPORT

CANAL COUNTRY
INN
4021 Peet St (14105)
Rates: n/a
Tel: (716) 735-7572

MIDDLETOWN

MIDDLETOWN MOTEL
501 Rt 211 E (10940)
Rates: $43-$70
Tel: (914) 342-2535
(800) 343-2535

SUPER 8 LODGE
563 Rt 211 E (10940)
Rates: $47-$79
Tel: (914) 692-5828
(800) 800-8000

MILLBROOK

COTTONWOOD
MOTEL
RR2, Box 25 (12545)
Rates: $50-$99
Tel: (914) 677-3283

MONTAUK

SEPP'S SURF-
SOUND COTTAGES
Ditch Plains Rd
(11954)
Rates: $80+
Tel: (516) 668-2215

MONTGOMERY

SUPER 8 MOTEL
207 Montgomery Rd
(12549)
Rates: $43-$64
Tel: (914) 457-3143
(800) 800-8000

MONTOUR FALLS

FALLS MOTEL
239 N Genesee St
(14865)
Rates: $35-$49
Tel: (607) 535-7262

RELAX INN
100 Clawson Blvd
(14865)
Rates: $26-$59
Tel: (607) 535-7183

NANUET

ECONO LODGE
367 SR 59 (10954)
Rates: $57-$69
Tel: (914) 623-3838
(800) 424-4777

NEW HAMPTON

DAYS INN
Rt 17 M (10958)
Rates: $44-$119
Tel: (914) 374-2411
(800) 329-7466

NEW HARTFORD

HOLIDAY INN UTICA
1777 Burrstone Rd
(13413)
Rates: $88-$109
Tel: (315) 797-2131
(800) 465-4329

NEW YORK CITY
(and Vicinity)

THE CARLYLE
35 E 76th St
& Madison Ave
(10021)
Rates: $285-$420
Tel: (212) 744-1600

DELMONICO'S
SUITE HOTEL
502 Park Ave (10022)
Rates: $160-$285
Tel: (212) 486-0509

THE ESSEX HOUSE
160 Central Park S
(10019)
Rates: $198-$340
Tel: (212) 247-0300

FOUR SEASONS
HOTEL
57 E 57th St (10022)
Rates: $420-$550
Tel: (212) 758-5700
(800) 487-3769

HILTON & TOWERS
1335 Ave of the
Americas (10019)
Rates: $169-$305
Tel: (800) 445-8667

HOLIDAY INN-
CROWNE PLAZA
1605 Broadway
(10019)
Rates: $185-$235
Tel: (212) 977-4000

HOTEL PIERRE-
A FOUR SEASONS
HOTEL
2 E 61st St (10021)
Rates: $265-$490
Tel: (212) 838-8000

HOTEL PLAZA
ATHENEE
37 E 64th St (10021)
Rates: $240-$400
Tel: (212) 734-9100

LE PARKER MERIDIEN
118 W 57th St
(10019)
Rates: n/a
Tel: (212) 245-5000

THE LOWELL
28 E 63rd St (10021)
Rates: $260-$520
Tel: (212) 838-1400

LOEWS NEW YORK
569 Lexington Ave
(10022)
Rates: $169-$205
Tel: (212) 752-7000
(800) 23-LOEWS

MARRIOTT
MARQUIS
1535 Broadway
(10036)
Rates: $189-$239
Tel: (212) 398-1900

MAYFAIR HOTEL
610 Park Ave (10021)
Rates: $275-$1410
Tel: (212) 288-0800

THE MAYFLOWER
HOTEL ON THE PARK
15 Central Park W
(10023)
Rates: $145-$190
Tel: (212) 265-0060

MILLENIUM
BROADWAY HOTEL
145 W 44th St
(10036)
Rates: $215-$290
Tel: (212) 768-4400

MORGANS HOTEL
237 Madison Ave
(10016)
Rates: $195-$275
Tel: (212) 686-0300

**NOVOTEL
NEW YORK**
226 W 52nd St
(10019)
Rates: $119-$169
Tel: (212) 315-0100
(800) 221-4542

THE PENINSULA
700 5th Ave (10019)
Rates: $210-$550
Tel: (212) 247-2200

THE PLAZA HOTEL
5th Ave at 59th St
Central Park S
(10019)
Rates: $205-$475
Tel: (212) 759-3000

**THE REGENCY
HOTEL**
540 Park Ave (10021)
Rates: $250-$300
Tel: (212) 759-4100

**RENAISSANCE
HOTEL**
714 7th Ave (10036)
Rates: $165-$249
Tel: (212) 765-7676

**THE ROYALTON
HOTEL**
44 W 44th (10036)
Rates: $180-$325
Tel: (212) 869-4400

**SHERATON
MANHATTAN HOTEL**
790 7th Ave (10019)
Rates: $179-$305
Tel: (212) 581-3300
(800) 325-3535

**SHERATON
NEW YORK HOTEL
& TOWERS**
811 7th Ave (10019)
Rates: $179-$305
Tel: (212) 581-1000
(800) 325-3535

THE STANHOPE
995 Fifth Ave (10028)
Rates: $300-$2500
Tel: (212) 288-5800

WESTBURY HOTEL
15 E 69th St (10021)
Rates: $235-$1500
Tel: (212) 535-2000

NEWARK

QUALITY INN
125 N Main St (14513)
Rates: $63-$78
Tel: (315) 331-9500
(800) 221-2222

NEWBURGH

HOWARD JOHNSON
95 Rt 17K (12550)
Rates: $80-$130
Tel: (914) 564-4000
(800) 446-4656

**KELSAY'S HOUSE
OF NATIONS**
1 Scenic Dr (12550)
Rates: n/a
Tel: (914) 562-1477

NEWFANE

**LAKE ONTARIO
MOTEL**
3330 Lockport-
Olcott Blvd (14108)
Rates: n/a
Tel: (716) 778-5004
(800) 446-5767

NIAGARA FALLS
(New York, USA)

**BEST WESTERN
INN ON THE RIVER**
7001 Buffalo Ave
(14304)
Rates: $68-$138
Tel: (716) 283-7612
(800) 245-7612

**BEST WESTERN
SUMMIT INN**
9500 Niagara Falls
Blvd (14304)
Rates: $48-$118
Tel: (716) 297-5050
(800) 528-1234

BIT O' PARIS MOTEL
9890 Niagara Falls
Blvd (14304)
Rates: n/a
Tel: (716) 297-1710

**BOYLE'S HOUSE
BED & BREAKFAST**
2478 River Rd (14304)
Rates: n/a
Tel: (716) 693-3070

**BUDGET
HOST/AMERICANA
MOTOR INN**
9401 Niagara Falls
Blvd (14304)
Rates: n/a
Tel: (716) 297-2660
(800) 241-4927

CARAVAN MOTEL
6730 Niagara Falls
Blvd (14304)
Rates: n/a
Tel: (716) 236-0752

**THE COACHMAN
MOTEL**
523 Third St (14301)
Rates: $36-$109
Tel: (716) 285-2295
(800) 335-2295

**DAYS INN-
FALLS VIEW**
201 Rainbow Blvd
(14304)
Rates: $39-$219
Tel: (716) 285-9321
(800) 329-7466

DUNES MOTEL
5655 Niagara Falls
Blvd (14304)
Rates: n/a
Tel: (716) 283-6114

ECONO LODGE
7708 Niagara Falls
Blvd. (14304)
Rates: $39-$99
Tel: (716) 283-0621
(800) 424-4777

FALLS MOTEL
5820 Buffalo Ave
(14304)
Rates: n/a
Tel: (716) 283-3239

HOSPITALITY INN
6734 Niagara Falls
Blvd (14304)
Rates: n/a
Tel: (716) 283-8611

**HOWARD JOHNSON
LODGE AT THE FALLS**
454 Main St (14301)
Rates: $40-$125
Tel: (716) 285-5261
(800) 446-4656

**JUNIOR'S
MOTOR INN**
5647 Niagara Falls
Blvd (14304)
Rates: n/a
Tel: (716) 283-4914

**NIAGARA
RAINBOW MOTEL**
7900 Niagara Falls
Blvd (14304)
Rates: $25-$89
Tel: (716) 283-1760

PELICAN MOTEL
6817 Niagara Falls
Blvd (14304)
Rates: $29-$99
Tel: (716) 283-2278
(716) 283-3169

**PLAZA COURT
MOTEL**
7680 Niagara Falls
Blvd (14304)
Rates: n/a
Tel: (716) 283-2638
(716) 283-3151

RADISSON HOTEL
Third St & Old Falls
(14303)
Rates: $62-$129
Tel: (716) 285-3361
(800) 333-3333

SUNRISE INN
6225 Niagara Falls
Blvd (14304)
Rates: n/a
Tel: (716) 283-9952

**TRAVELERS
BUDGET INN**
9001 Niagara Falls
Blvd (14304)
Rates: $28-$79
Tel: (716) 297-3228

TRAVELODGE
200 Rainbow Blvd
(14303)
Rates: $40-$85
Tel: (716) 285-7316
(800) 578-7878

NIAGARA FALLS
(Ontario, Canada)

**BEST WESTERN
FALLVIEWS
MOTOR HOTEL**
5551 Murray St
(L2G 2J4)
Rates: $59-$169
Tel: (905) 356-0551
(800) 263-2580

CAMELOT INN
5640 Stanley Ave
(L2G 3X5)
Rates: $29-$75
Tel: (905) 354-3754

**COMFORT INN
ON THE RIVER**
4009 River Rd
(L2E 3E9)
Rates: $35-$128
Tel: (800) 221-2222

**FLAMINGO
MOTOR INN**
7701 Lundy's Ln
(L2H 1H3)
Rates: $32-$84
Tel: (416) 356-4646

GLENGATE MOTEL
5534 Stanley Ave
(L2G 3X2)
Rates: $24-$79
Tel: (416) 357-1333

**HOLIDAY INN-
BY THE FALLS**
5339 Murray Hill
(L2G 2J3)
Rates: $47-$150
Tel: (905) 356-1333
(800) 263-9393

MARCO POLO INN
5553 Ferry St
(L2G 1S3)
Rates: $30-$88
Tel: (905) 356-6959

**NIAGARA
FAMILY INN**
5612 Ellen Ave
(L2G 3P6)
Rates: $30-$64
Tel: (905) 354-9844

**NIAGARA PARKWAY
COURT MOTEL**
3708 Main St
(L2G 6B1)
Rates: $29-$89
Tel: (905) 295-3331

**QUALITY INN-
FALLSVIEW**
4946 Clifton Hill
(L2E 6S8)
Rates: $48-$118
Tel: (800) 263-7137

**RAMADA CORAL
INN RESORT**
7429 Lundy's Ln
(L2H 1G9)
Rates: $65-$99
Tel: (905) 356-6116
(800) 272-6232

SHERATON INN
6045 Stanley Ave
(L2G 3Y3)
Rates: $58-$209
Tel: (905) 374-4142
(800) 267-VIEW

SUNSET INN
5803 Stanley Ave
(L2G 3X8)
Rates: $29-$68
Tel: (905) 354-7513

VENTURE INN
4960 Clifton Hill
(L2E 6S8)
Rates: $49-$150
Tel: (905) 358-3293
(800) 263-2557

NORTH CREEK

**BLACK MOUNTAIN
SKI LODGE**
Star Rt (12853)
Rates: $55-$65
Tel: (518) 251-2800

**THE INN ON
GORE MOUNTAIN**
Peaceful Valley Rd
(12853)
Rates: $59-$75
Tel: (518) 251-2111

NORTH SYRACUSE

**BEST WESTERN INN-
AIRPORT**
Hancock Airport
(13212)
Rates: $78-$105
Tel: (315) 455-7362
(800) 528-1234

NORTH TONAWANDA

ROYAL MOTEL
3333 Niagara Falls
Blvd (14120)
Rates: n/a
Tel: (716) 692-2724
(716) 692-4546

STARFIRE MOTEL
3466 Niagara Falls
Blvd (14120)
Rates: n/a
Tel: (716) 694-3600

NORWICH

HOWARD JOHNSON
75 N Broad St
(13815)
Rates: $59-$95
Tel: (607) 334-2200
(800) 446-4656

OGDENSBURG

ALTA COURTS MOTEL
Riverside Dr (13669)
Rates: $35-$75
Tel: (315) 393-6860

DAYS INN
1200 Paterson St
(13669)
Rates: $45-$70
Tel: (315) 393-3200
(800) 329-7466

**QUALITY INN
GRAN-VIEW**
Rt 4, (13669)
Rates: $47-$95
Tel: (800) 221-2222

RODEWAY INN
Rt 4, Box 84 (13669)
Rates: $40-$54
Tel: (315) 393-3730
(800) 424-4777

**THE STONEFENCE
HOTEL**
Rt 4, Box 29 (13669)
Rates: $49-$95
Tel: (315) 393-1545

OLCOTT

**BAYSIDE
GUEST HOUSE**
1572 Lockport-Olcott
Rd (14126)
Rates: n/a
Tel: (716) 778-7767
(800) 438-2192

OLD FORGE

SUNSET MOTEL
Rt 28, Box 261
(13420)
Rates: $60-$72
Tel: (315) 369-6836

ONEONTA

CELTIC MOTEL
112 Oneida St
(13820)
Rates: n/a
Tel: (607) 432-0860

HOLIDAY INN
Box 634 (13820)
Rates: $69-$101
Tel: (800) 465-4329

SUPER 8 MOTEL
Rt 23 Southside
(13820)
Rates: $49-$86
Tel: (607) 432-9505
(800) 800-8000

OSWEGO

**CHESTNUT GROVE
INN**
7096 SR 104 W
(13126)
Rates: n/a
Tel: (315) 342-2547

ECONO LODGE
70 E 1st St (13126)
Rates: $55-90
Tel: (315) 343-1600
(800) 424-4777

K & G LODGE
94 Creamery Rd
(13126)
Rates: n/a:
Tel: (315) 343-8171

SUNSET CABINS
RR 10, Box 43
(13126)
Rates: n/a:
Tel: (315) 343-2166

THE THOMAS INN
309 W Seneca St
(13126)
Rates: n/a:
Tel: (315) 343-4900

TWIN PINES CABINS
1881 CR 1 (13126)
Rates: n/a:
Tel: (315) 343-2475

OWEGO

SUNRISE MOTEL
3778 Waverly Rd
(13827)
Rates: $32-$37
Tel: (607) 687-5666

PAINTED POST

**BEST WESTERN
LODGE ON THE
GREEN**
US 15 & SR 17
(14870)
Rates: $50-$99
Tel: (607) 962-2456
(800) 528-1234

ECONO LODGE
200 Robert Dann Dr
(14870)
Rates: $39-$65
Tel: (800) 424-4777

STILES MOTEL
9239 Victory Hwy
(14870)
Rates: $22-$42
Tel: (800) 331-3920

PALENVILLE

**HICKORY NOTCH
CABINS**
P.O. Box 279 (12463)
Rates: n/a
Tel: (518) 678-3259

PARISH

MONTCLAIR MOTEL
Rt 69 (13131)
Rates: $35-$40
Tel: (315) 625-7100

PARKSVILLE

**BEST WESTERN
PARAMOUNT**
Tanzman Rd (12768)
Rates: $60-$130
Tel: (914) 292-6700
(800) 528-1234

PEEKSKILL

PEEKSKILL INN
634 Main St (10566)
Rates: $63-$99
Tel: (914) 739-1500

PEMBROKE

**ECONO LODGE-
DARIEN LAKES**
8593 SR 77 (14036)
Rates: $45-$75
Tel: (716) 599-4681
(800) 424-4777

PENN YAN

VIKING MOTEL
680 E Lake Rd
(14527)
Rates: $42-$135
Tel: (315) 536-7061

PINE CITY

**RUFUS TANNER
HOUSE**
60 Sagetown Rd
(14871)
Rates: n/a
Tel: (607) 732-0213

PITTSFORD

THE DEPOT INN
41 N Main St (14534)
Rates: $68-$75
Tel: (716) 381-9900

PLAINVIEW

**RESIDENCE INN
BY MARRIOTT**
9 Gerhard Rd
(11803)
Rates: $133-$176
Tel: (516) 433-6200
(800) 331-3131

PLATTSBURGH

ECONO LODGE
610 Upper Cornelia
St (12901)
Rates: $37-$59
Tel: (518) 561-1500
(800) 424-4777

HOWARD JOHNSON
446 Rt 3, Cornelia St
(12901)
Rates: $52-$85
Tel: (518) 561-7750
(800) 446-4656

**PLATTSBURGH
HOTEL & CONF CTR**
412 Rt 3 (12901)
Rates: $65-$89
Tel: (518) 561-5000
(800) 431-5145

SUPER 8 MOTEL
7129 Rt 9 N (12901)
Rates: $41-$59
Tel: (518) 562-8888
(800) 800-8000

**PORT
JEFFERSON**

DANFORDS INN
25 E Broadway
(11777)
Rates: $100-$400
Tel: (800) 332-6367

PORT JERVIS

COMFORT INN
Rt 23 & Greenville
Tpk (12771)
Rates: $69-$89
Tel: (914) 856-6611
(800) 221-2222

PORT ONTARIO

**MANNING'S
PORT ONTARIO**
RS 1, Rt 3 (13142)
Rates: n/a:
Tel: (315) 298-2509

POUGHKEEPSIE

ECONO LODGE
426 South Rd (12601)
Rates: $44-$66
Tel: (914) 452-6600
(800) 424-4777

**HOLIDAY INN
EXPRESS**
341 South Rd (12601)
Rates: $69-$89
Tel: (914) 473-1151
(800) 465-4329

PULASKI

1880 HOUSE B & B
7536 S Jefferson St
(13142)
Rates: n/a:
Tel: (315) 298-6088

**BIG A SPORT
SHOP & LODGE**
7542 Salina St
(13142)
Rates: n/a
Tel: (315) 298-5509

CLARK'S COTTAGES
RD 2, Lake Rd
(13142)
Rates: n/a:
Tel: (315) 298-4778

**DOUBLE EAGLE
LODGE**
3268 SR 13 (13142)
Rates: n/a:
Tel: (315) 298-3326

DRIFTWOOD MOTEL
5240 US Rt 11
(13142)
Rates: n/a
Tel: (315) 298-5000

FISH HAWK LODGE
1091 Albion Cross
Rd (13142)
Rates: n/a:
Tel: (315) 298-5841

GOLDEN FISH CABINS
RD 1, Rt 3 (13142)
Rates: n/a:
Tel: (315) 298-6556

LAURDON HEIGHTS
7489-90 Lewis St
(13142)
Rates: n/a:
Tel: (315) 298-6091

MAPLE GROVE SPORT & ANGLER RESORT
2870 SR 13 (13142)
Rates: n/a
Tel: (315) 298-7256

PORT LODGE MOTEL
7469 Scenic Hwy
(13142)
Rates: n/a:
Tel: (315) 298-6876

PORTLY ANGLER LODGE
CR 2A at Rt 13
(13142)
Rates: n/a:
Tel: (315) 298-4773

RAINBOW SHORES HOTEL
RD 2 (13142)
Rates: n/a:
Tel: (315) 298-9982
(315) 298-5110

RAINBOW SHORES MOTEL
348 Rainbow Shores
Rd (13142)
Rates: n/a:
Tel: (315) 298-4407

REDWOOD MOTEL
P.O. Box 315 (13142)
Rates: n/a:
Tel: (315) 298-4717

RUPERT'S TRADING POST
7539 Rome St
(13142)
Rates: n/a:
Tel: (315) 298-4042

SEQUOIA INN
7686 N Jefferson St
(13142)
Rates: n/a:
Tel: (315) 298-4407
(315) 298-2460

WHITAKERS MOTEL
7700 Rome Rd
(13142)
Rates: n/a:
Tel: (315) 298-6162

WILD BILL'S LODGE
7453 Lewis St
(13142)
Rates: n/a:
Tel: (315) 298-2461

PURLING

BAVARIAN MANOR COUNTRY INN
CR 24 (12470)
Rates: n/a
Tel: (518) 622-3261

QUEENSBURY

WAKITA COURT MOTEL
Rd 5, Box 228
(12804)
Rates: $42-$106
Tel: (518) 792-0326
(800) 622-0938

RENSSELAER

FORT CRAILO MOTEL
110 Columbia Tpke
(12144)
Rates: $33-$65
Tel: (518) 472-1360

RHINEBECK

RHINEBECK MOTEL
117 Rt 9 (12572)
Rates: $40-99
Tel: (914) 876-5900

WHISTLE WOOD FARM
11 Pells Rd (12572)
Rates: $99-150
Tel: (914) 876-6838

RIPLEY

BUDGET HOST COLONIAL SQUIRE
Shortman Rd (14775)
Rates: $35-$52
Tel: (716) 736-8000
(800) 283-4678

ROCHESTER

COMFORT INN AIRPORT
395 Buell Rd (14624)
Rates: $33-$69
Tel: (800) 221-2222

COMFORT INN-WEST
1501 W Ridge Rd
(14615)
Rates: $50-$81
Tel: (800) 221-2222

ECONO LODGE-SOUTH
940 Jefferson Rd
(14623)
Rates: $39-$100
Tel: (716) 427-2700
(800) 424-4777

HAMPTON INN
717 E Henrietta Rd
(14623)
Rates: $73-$85
Tel: (716) 272-7800
(800) 426-7866

HAMPTON INN
500 Center Place Dr.
(14615)
Rates: $59-$79
Tel: (716) 663-6070
(800) 426-7866

HOLIDAY INN-GENESEE PLAZA
120 E Main St
(14604)
Rates: $99-$114
Tel: (800) 465-4329

MARRIOTT-AIRPORT
1890 W Ridge Rd
(14615)
Rates: $99-$140
Tel: (716) 225-6880
(800) 228-9290

MOTEL 6
155 Buell Rd (14624)
Rates: $38-$49
Tel: (716) 436-2170
(800) 440-6000

RADISSON INN
175 Jefferson Rd
(14623)
Rates: $79-$143
Tel: (716) 475-1910
(800) 333-3333

RAMADA INN AIRPORT
1273 Chill Ave
(14624)
Rates: $40-$90
Tel: (716) 464-8800
(800) 272-6232

RESIDENCE INN BY MARRIOTT
1300 Jefferson Rd
(14623)
Rates: $82-$170
Tel: (716) 272-8850
(800) 331-3131

TOWPATH MOTEL
2323 Monroe Ave
(14618)
Rates: $40-$46
Tel: (716) 271-2147

TRAIL BREAK MOTOR INN
7340 Pittsford-Palmyra Rd (14450)
Rates: $38-$47
Tel: (716) 223-1710

WELLESLEY INN-BRIGHTON
797 E Henrietta Rd
(14623)
Rates: $39-$62
Tel: (716) 427-0130
(800) 444-8888

WELLESLEY INN-GREECE
1635 W Ridge Rd
(14615)
Rates: $39-$85
Tel: (716) 621-2060
(800) 444-8888

ROCK HILL

HOWARD JOHNSON LODGE
P. O. Box 469 (12775)
Rates: $49-$99
Tel: (914) 796-3000
(800) 446-4656

ROCKVILLE CENTRE

HOLIDAY INN
173 Sunrise Hwy
(11570)
Rates: $95-$150
Tel: (516) 678-1300
(800) 465-4329

ROME

**ADIRONDACK
THIRTEEN PINES
MOTEL**
7353 River Rd
(13440)
Rates: $30-$55
Tel: (315) 337-4930

**AMERICAN
HERITAGE
MOTOR INN**
799 Lower Lawrence
St (13440)
Rates: $35-$45
Tel: (315) 339-3610
(800) 836-1203

**BEECHES-
PAUL REVERE
MOTOR LODGE**
7900 Turin Rd
(13440)
Rates: $54-$80
Tel: (315) 336-1776

**FAMILY INNS
OF AMERICA**
145 E Whitesboro St
(13440)
Rates: $39+
Tel: (315) 337-9400
(800) 348-3377

ROSCOE

ROSCOE MOTEL
Box 608 (12776)
Rates: $40-$55
Tel: (607) 498-5220

ROTTERDAM

BEST WESTERN INN
2788 Hamburg St
(12303)
Rates: $63-$93
Tel: (518) 355-1111
(800) 528-1234

SUPER 8 MOTEL
3083 Carman Rd
(12303)
Rates: $45-$49
Tel: (518) 355-2190
(800) 800-8000

SACKETS HARBOR

**ONTARIO PLACE
HOTEL**
103 General Smith
Dr (13685)
Rates: $49-$69
Tel: (315) 646-8000

SALAMANCA

DUDLEY HOTEL
132 Main St (14779)
Rates: $40-$50
Tel: (716) 945-3200

SANDY CREEK

HARRIS LODGING
P.O. Box 547 (13145)
Rates: n/a:
Tel: (315) 387-5907
(315) 387-5504

TUG HILL LODGE
216 Salisbury St
(13145)
Rates: n/a:
Tel: (315) 387-5326

SARANAC LAKE

**ADIRONDACK
COMFORT INN**
148 Lake Flower Ave
(12983)
Rates: $45-$115
Tel: (800) 221-2222

**ADIRONDACK
MOTEL**
23 Lake Flower Ave
(12983)
Rates: $38-$60
Tel: (518) 891-2116

**HOTEL SARANAC
OF PAUL SMITH'S
COLLEGE**
101 Main St (12983)
Rates: $48-$76
Tel: (518) 891-2200

LAKE SIDE MOTEL
27 Lake Flower Ave
(12983)
Rates: $50-$90
Tel: (518) 891-4333

THE POINT
HCR 1, Box 65
(12983)
Rates: $825-$1300
Tel: (518) 891-5674
(800) 255-3530

**SARA-PLACID
MOTOR INN**
120 Lake Flower Ave
(12983)
Rates: $35-$65
Tel: (518) 891-2729

SARATOGA SPRINGS

**ADIRONDACK
MOTEL**
230 West Ave (12866)
Rates: $49-$169
Tel: (518) 584-3510

**COMMUNITY COURT
MOTEL**
248 Broadway
(12866)
Rates: $40-$60+
Tel: (518) 584-6666

**COUNTRY CLUB
MOTEL**
306 Church St
(12866)
Rates: $55-$175
Tel: (518) 882-6838

**GRAND UNION
MOTEL**
92 S Broadway
(12866)
Rates: $42-$65
Tel: (518) 584-9000

HOLIDAY INN
232 Broadway
(12866)
Rates: $60-$195
Tel: (518) 584-4550
(800) 465-4329

**ROBIN HOOD
MOTEL**
2205 Rt 50 (12866)
Rates: n/a
Tel: (518) 885-8899

ST. CHARLES MOTEL
160 Broadway
(12866)
Rates: $45-$135
Tel: (518) 584-2050

ST. FRANCIS MOTEL
177 Broadway
(12866)
Rates: $55-$150
Tel: (518) 584-1275

**THOROBRED
MOTEL**
P.O. Box 195 (12866)
Rates: n/a
Tel: (518) 583-4903

**UNION GABLES
BED & BREAKFAST**
55 Union Ave
(12866)
Rates: $80-$220
Tel: (518) 584-1558
(800) 398-1558

SAUGERTIES

HOJO INN
2764 Rt 32 (12477)
Rates: $45-$77
Tel: (914) 246-9511
(800) 446-4656

SCHENECTADY

**BEST WESTERN
ROTTERDAM
MOTOR INN**
2788 Hamburg St
(12303)
Rates: $55-$150
Tel: (518) 355-1111
(800) 528-1234

HOLIDAY INN
100 Nott Ter (12308)
Rates: $69-$120
Tel: (518) 393-4141
(800) 465-4329

SCHROON LAKE

BLUE RIDGE MOTEL
RR 1, Box 321
(12870)
Rates: $36-$60
Tel: (518) 532-7521

DUN ROAMIN CABINS
Rt 9, P. O. Box 535
(12870)
Rates: $40-$75
Tel: (518) 532-7277

RAWLINS MOTEL AND CABINS
P.O. Box 9 (12870)
Rates: n/a
Tel: (518) 532-7907
(800) 901-5253

SHELTER ISLAND HEIGHTS

BEACH HOUSE INN
P. O. Box 648 (11965)
Rates: $90-$125
Tel: (516) 749-0264

SIDNEY

COUNTRY MOTEL
Rt 7 & E of Rt 8
(13838)
Rates: n/a
Tel: (607) 563-1035

SOUTH BUFFALO

HOWARD JOHNSON
5245 Camp Rd
(14075)
Rates: $38-$65
Tel: (800) 446-4656

SOUTHAMPTON

COLD SPRING BAY RESORT
Country Rd 39
(11968)
Rates: $90-$395
Tel: (516) 283-7600

SPRING GLEN

GOLD MOUNTAIN CHALET RESORT
P.O. Box 456 (12483)
Rates: $399-$499
(Two nights)
Tel: (914) 647-4332

SPRING VALLEY

ECONO LODGE
Rt 59 (10977)
Rates: $55-$61
Tel: (800) 424-4777

STAMFORD

RED CARPET MOTOR INN
5 Lake St (12167)
Rates: $48-$85
Tel: (607) 652-7394
(800) 251-1962

SUFFERN

WELLESLEY INN
17 N Airmont Rd
(10901)
Rates: $48-$70
Tel: (914) 368-1900
(800) 444-8888

SYRACUSE

BEST WESTERN INN UNIVERSITY TOWER
701 E Genesee St
(13210)
Rates: $69-$99
Tel: (315) 479-7000
(800) 528-1234

DAYS INN-EAST
6609 Thompson Rd
(13206)
Rates: $42-$69
Tel: (315) 437-5998
(800) 329-7466

HOLIDAY INN-FAIRGROUNDS AREA
100 Farrell Rd
(13209)
Rates: $54-$75
Tel: (800) 465-4329

JOHN MILTON INN
6578 Thompson Rd
(13206)
Rates: $35-$60
Tel: (315) 463-8555

RAMADA LIMITED UNIVERSITY
6590 Thompson Rd
N (13206)
Rates: $49-$99
Tel: (315) 463-0202
(800) 272-6232

RED CARPET INN
6590 Thompson Rd
(13206)
Rates: $36-$65
Tel: (315) 463-0202
(800) 251-1962

RED ROOF INN
6614 Thompson Rd
(13206)
Rates: $39-$70
Tel: (315) 437-3309
(800) 843-7663

TICONDEROGA

CIRCLE COURT MOTEL
440 Montcalm St
(12883)
Rates: $36-$59
Tel: (518) 585-7660

RANCH HOUSE AT BALDWIN
RR 1, 79 Baldwin Rd
(12883)
Rates: $69
Tel: (518) 585-6596

TONAWANDA

MICROTEL
1 Hospitality Centre
Way (14150)
Rates: $37-$41
Tel: (716) 693-8100
(800) 771-7171

TROY

BEST WESTERN RENSSELAER INN
1800 6th Ave (12180)
Rates: $54-$81
Tel: (518) 274-3210
(800) 528-1234

TUPPER LAKE

PINE TERRACE MOTEL & TENNIS CLUB
Moody Rd (12986)
Rates: $42-$450
Tel: (518) 359-9258

RED TOP INN
90 Moody Rd
(12986)
Rates: $40-$55
Tel: (518) 359-9209

SUNSET PARK MOTEL
De Mars Blvd
(12986)
Rates: $44-$56
Tel: (518) 359-3995

UNIONDALE

MARRIOTT HOTEL
101 James Doolittle
Blvd (11553)
Rates: $119-$135
Tel: (516) 794-3800
(800) 228-9290

UTICA

A-1 MOTEL
238 N Genesee St
(13502)
Rates: $30-$50
Tel: (315) 735-6698
(800) 809-6885

BEST WESTERN GATEWAY ADIRONDACK INN
175 N Genesee St
(13502)
Rates: $67-$119
Tel: (315) 732-4121
(800) 528-1234

HAPPY JOURNEY MOTEL
300 N Genesee St
(13502)
Rates: $28-$45
Tel: (315) 738-1959

HOWARD JOHNSON LODGE
302 N Genesee St
(13502)
Rates: $45-$85
Tel: (315) 724-4141
(800) 446-4656

MOTEL 6
150 N Genesee St
(13502)
Rates: $36-$42
Tel: (315) 797-8743
(800) 440-6000

RADISSON HOTEL
200 N Genesee St
(13502)
Rates: $91-$112
Tel: (800) 333-3333

RED ROOF INN
20 Weaver St (13502)
Rates: $39-$61
Tel: (315) 724-7128
(800) 843-7663

SUPER 8 MOTEL
309 N Genesse St
(13502)
Rates: $38-$55
Tel: (315) 797-0964
(800) 800-8000

VESTAL

HOWARD JOHNSON HOTEL
3601 Vestal Pkwy E
(13850)
Rates: $35-$65
Tel: (607) 729-6181
(800) 446-4656

RESIDENCE INN BY MARRIOTT
4610 Vestal Pkwy E
(13850)
Rates: $69-$150
Tel: (607) 770-8500
(800) 331-3131

VICTOR

MICROTEL
7498 Main St Fishers
(14564)
Rates: $34-$53
Tel: (716) 924-9240
(800) 771-7171

WADDINGTON

RIVERVIEW MOTEL & COTTAGES
RR 1, Box 14 (13694)
Rates: $38-$48
Tel: (315) 388-5912

WATERLOO

HOLIDAY INN
2568 SR 414 (13165)
Rates: $59-$85
Tel: (315) 539-5011
(800) 465-4329

WATERTOWN

CITY LINE MOTEL
19226 US Rt 11
(13601)
Rates: $24-$56
Tel: (315) 782-9619

ECONO LODGE
1030 Arsenal St
(13601)
Rates: $40-$60
Tel: (315) 762-5500
(800) 424-4777

NEW PARROT MOTEL
5791 Outer
Washington St
(13601)
Rates: $30-$52
Tel: (315) 788-5080

QUALITY INN
1190 Arsenal St
(13601)
Rates: $48-$72
Tel: (800) 221-2222

RAINBOW MOTEL
RD 6, Box 20 (13601)
Rates: n/a
Tel: (315) 788-2830

SUPER 8 MOTEL
104 Breen Ave
(13601)
Rates: $29-$70
Tel: (315) 786-6666
(800) 800-8000

WATKINS GLEN

CHALET LEON AT HECTOR FALLS
Box 388 (14891)
Rates: $40-$69
Tel: (607) 546-7171

GLEN MOTOR INN
3380 Rt 14 (14891)
Rates: $73-$90
Tel: (607) 535-2706

WAVERLY

O'BRIENS INN
6312 CR 60 (14892)
Rates: $38-$58
Tel: (607) 565-2817

WEEDSPORT

BEST WESTERN INN
2709 Erie Dr (13166)
Rates: $39-$80
Tel: (315) 834-6623
(800) 528-1234

PORT 40 MOTEL
9050 Rt 24 (13166)
Rates: $30-$66
Tel: (315) 834-6198

WEST NYACK

NYACK MOTOR LODGE
Rt 303 (10994)
Rates: $44-$68
Tel: (914) 358-4100

WESTBURY

ISLAND INN
Old Country Rd
(11590)
Rates: $99-$350
Tel: (516) 228-9500

WESTMORE-LAND

CARRIAGE MOTOR INN
P. O. Box 379 (13490)
Rates: $29-$42
Tel: (315) 853-3561

WHITE PLAINS

LA RESERVE SUITES
5 Barker Ave (10601)
Rates: $90-$200
Tel: (914) 761-7700

RESIDENCE INN
5 Barker Ave (10601)
Rates: n/a
Tel: (914) 761-7700
(800) 331-3131

WHITE PLAINS HOTEL
S Broadway & Lyon
Pl (10601)
Rates: $69-$79
Tel: (914) 761-8100

WHITEHALL

APPLE ORCHARD INN
Old Fairhaven Rd
(12887)
Rates: $65
Tel: (518) 499-0180

WILLIAMSVILLE

MICROTEL
50 Freemand Rd
(14221)
Rates: $34-$37
Tel: (716) 633-6200
(800) 771-7171

RESIDENCE INN BY MARRIOTT
100 Maple Rd
(14221)
Rates: $80-$200
Tel: (800) 331-3131

WILMINGTON

GRAND VIEW MOTEL
SR 86 (12987)
Rates: $44-$59
Tel: (518) 946-2209

HIGH VALLEY MOTEL
HCR 2, Box 13
(12997)
Rates: $40-$61
Tel: (518) 946-2355

HOLIDAY LODGE
P. O. Box 38 (12997)
Rates: $30-$90
Tel: (518) 946-2251

HUNGRY TROUT MOTOR INN
2 Mi W on Rt 86
(12997)
Rates: $49-$89
Tel: (518) 946-2217

LEDGE ROCK MOTEL
HCR 2, Box 34
(12997)
Rates: $49-$79
Tel: (518) 946-2302

WINKELMAN MOTEL
E of Jct NY 86
(12997)
Rates: $48-$56
Tel: (518) 946-7761

WILSON

FISHERMAN'S CHOICE B & B
4793 E Lake Rd
(14172)
Rates: n/a
Tel: (716) 751-9481

WOODBURY

QUALITY INN
7758 Jericho Tpk
(11797)
Rates: $65-$110
Tel: (800) 221-2222

RAMADA LIMITED
8030 Jericho Tpk
(11797)
Rates: $59-$179
Tel: (516) 921-8500
(800) 272-6232

YOUNGSTOWN

RIVER LOFT
425 Main St (14174)
Rates: n/a
Tel: (716) 745-3217

NORTH CAROLINA

ABERDEEN

BEST WESTERN PINEHURST MOTOR INN
1500 Sandhills Blvd (28315)
Rates: $65-$70
Tel: (910) 944-2367
(800) 528-1234

INN AT THE BRYANT HOUSE BED & BREAKFAST
214 N Poplar St (28315)
Rates: $40-$75
Tel: (919) 944-3300

MOTEL 6
1408 Sandhills Blvd (28315)
Rates: $30-$35
Tel: (910) 944-5633
(800) 440-6000

ALBERMARLE

COMFORT INN
735 SR 24/27 Bypass (28001)
Rates: $45-$59
Tel: (704) 983-6990
(800) 221-2222

RODEWAY INN
200 Henson St (28001)
Rates: $45-$65
Tel: (704) 982-3939
(800) 228-2000

ASHEVILLE

COMFORT SUITES
890 Brevard Rd (28806)
Rates: $55-$95
Tel: (704) 665-4000
(800) 221-2222

ECONO LODGE BILTMORE
190 Tunnel Rd (28805)
Rates: $40-$60
Tel: (704) 254-9521
(800) 424-4777

HOLIDAY INN-EAST
1450 Tunnel Rd (28805)
Rates: $55-$100
Tel: (704) 298-5611
(800) 465-4329

MOTEL 6
1415 Tunnel Rd (28805)
Rates: $28-$42
Tel: (704) 299-3040
(800) 466-8356

RED ROOF INN-WEST
16 Crowell Rd (28806)
Rates: $29-$59
Tel: (704) 667-9803
(800) 843-7663

BATTLEBORO

COMFORT INN
Rt 1, Box 153C (27809)
Rates: $40-$75
Tel: (919) 972-9426
(800) 221-2222

DAYS INN GOLDROCK
Rt 1, Box 155 (27809)
Rates: $39-$61
Tel: (919) 446-0621
(800) 329-7466

MASTERS ECONOMY INN
Rt 1, Box 162 (27809)
Rates: $26-$33
Tel: (919) 442-8075

MOTEL 6
Rt 1, Box 162A (27809)
Rates: $23-$27
Tel: (919) 977-3505
(800) 466-8356

RED CARPET INN
Rt 1, Box 162C (27809)
Rates: $20-$35
Tel: (919) 446-0771
(800) 251-1962

SCOTTISH INNS
Rt 1, Box 158 (27809)
Rates: $20-$32
Tel: (919) 446-1831
(800) 251-1962

BEECH MOUNTAIN

BEECH MOUNTAIN SLOPESIDE CHALETS
503 Beech Mtn Pkwy (28604)
Rates: n/a
Tel: (704) 387-4251
(800) 692-2061

BLACK MOUNTAIN

SUPER 8 MOTEL
101 Flat Creek Rd (28711)
Rates: $45-69
Tel: (704) 669-8076
(800) 800-8000

BOONE

GRANDMA JEAN'S BED & BREAKFAST
254 Meadowview Dr (28607)
Rates: $65
Tel: (305) 279-1775

SCOTTISH INNS
782 Blowing Rock Rd (28607)
Rates: $29-$64
Tel: (704) 264-2483
(800) 251-1962

BURLINGTON

COMFORT INN
978 Plantation Dr (27215)
Rates: $51-$64
Tel: (910) 227-3681
(800) 221-2222

ECONO LODGE
640 E Harden St (27253)
Rates: $32-$57
Tel: (910) 228-0231
(800) 424-4777

MOTEL 6
2155 Hanford Rd (27215)
Rates: $32-$36
Tel: (910) 226-1325
(800) 440-6000

CASHIERS

HIGH HAMPTON INN RESORT COMPLEX
P. O. Box 338 (28717)
Rates: $88-$188
Tel: (704) 743-2411

CHARLOTTE

BRADLEY MOTEL
4200 I-85S (28214)
Rates: $27-$36
Tel: (704) 392-3206

COMFORT INN-UNCC
5111 I-85 N Service Rd (28269)
Rates: $49-$125
Tel: (704) 598-0007
(800) 221-2222

CRICKET INN-COLISEUM
219 Archdale Dr (28217)
Rates: $32-$38
Tel: (704) 527-8500

DAYS INN
3482 Carowinds Blvd (29715)
Rates: $35-75
Tel: (803) 548-8000
(800) 329-7466

ECONO LODGE NORTH
I-85 Sugar Creek Rd (28213)
Rates: $36-$125
Tel: (704) 597-0470
(800) 424-4777

**HOLIDAY INN-
UNIVERSITY
EXECUTIVE PARK**
8520 University
Executive
Park Dr (28262)
Rates: $79-$99
Tel: (704) 547-0999
(800) 465-4329

HYATT-SOUTH PARK
5501 Carnegie Blvd
(28209)
Rates: $89-$165
Tel: (704) 554-1234
(800) 233-1234

**LA QUINTA INN-
AIRPORT**
3100 I-85 S Service
Rd (28208)
Rates: $45-$50
Tel: (704) 393-5306
(800) 531-5900

**LA QUINTA INN-
SOUTH**
7900 Nations Ford
Rd (28217)
Rates: $40-$57
Tel: (704) 522-7110
(800) 531-5900

MOTEL 6-SOUTH
3430 St. Vardell Ln
(28210)
Rates: $32-$36
Tel: (704) 527-0144
(800) 440-6000

**RED ROOF INN
AIRPORT**
3300 I-85 S (28208)
Rates: $29-$40
Tel: (704) 392-2316
(800) 843-7663

**RED ROOF INN
AT UNIVERSITY**
5116 I-85 N (28206)
Rates: $28-$40
Tel: (704) 596-8222
(800) 843-7663

**RED ROOF INN
COLISEUM**
131 Red Roof Dr
(28217)
Rates: $28-$42
Tel: (704) 529-1020
(800) 843-7663

**RESIDENCE INN
BY MARRIOTT**
8503 N Tryon St
(28262)
Rates: $99-139
Tel: (704) 547-1122
(800) 331-3131

**SHERATON
AIRPORT PLAZA**
3315 I-85 S
at Billy Graham
Pkwy (28208)
Rates: $129-$145
Tel: (704) 392-1200
(800) 325-3535

CHEROKEE

HAMPTON INN
P. O. Box 1926
(28719)
Rates: $74-$99
Tel: (704) 497-3115
(800) 426-7866

CORNELIUS

**HOLIDAY INN
LAKE NORMAN**
19901 Holiday Ln
(28031)
Rates: $79-$104
Tel: (704) 842-9120
(800) 465-4329

DUNN

BEST WESTERN INN
603 Spring Branch
Rd (28334)
Rates: $39-$59
Tel: (910) 892-2162
(800) 528-1234

DAYS INN
1125 East Broad St
(28334)
Rates: $40-$66
Tel: (910) 892-1293
(800) 329-7466

ECONO LODGE
513 Spring Branch
Rd (28334)
Rates: $36-$50
Tel: (910) 892-6181
(800) 424-4777

RAMADA INN
P. O. Box 729 (28334)
Rates: $59-$69
Tel: (910) 892-8101
(800) 272-6232

DURHAM

**BEST WESTERN
SKYLAND INN**
5400 US 70 (27705)
Rates: $56-$62
Tel: (919) 383-2508
(800) 528-1234

**CAROLINA DUKE
MOTOR INN**
2517 Guess Rd
(27705)
Rates: $34-$40
Tel: (919) 286-0771
(800) 438-1158

DAYS INN
I-85 & Redwood Rd
(27704)
Rates: $40-$70
Tel: (919) 688-4338
(800) 329-7466

HAMPTON INN
1816 Hillandale Rd
(27705)
Rates: $69-$87
Tel: (919) 471-6100
(800) 426-7866

HOWARD JOHNSON
1800 Hillandale Rd
(27705)
Rates: $40-$90
Tel: (919) 477-7381
(800) 446-4656

RED ROOF INN
5623 Chapel Hill
Blvd (27707)
Rates: $35-$44
Tel: (919) 489-9421
(800) 843-7663

RED ROOF INN
2000 I-85 Service Rd
(27705)
Rates: $38-$48
Tel: (919) 471-9882
(800) 843-7663

**RED ROOF INN
RESEARCH
TRIANGLE PARK**
4405 Hwy 55 E
(27713)
Rates: $32-$41
Tel: (919) 361-1950
(800) 843-7663

RESIDENCE INN
1919 Hwy 54 E
(27713)
Rates: $109-$142
Tel: (919) 361-1266
(800) 331-3131

FAYETTEVILLE

**HOLIDAY INN
BORDEAUX**
1707 Owen Dr
(28304)
Rates: $65-$71
Tel: (910) 323-0111
(800) 465-4329

**HOWARD JOHNSON
PLAZA HOTEL**
1965 Cedar Creek
Rd (28302)
Rates: $54-$88
Tel: (910) 323-8282
(800) 446-4656

MOTEL 6
2076 Cedar Creek
Rd (28301)
Rates: $30-$34
Tel: (910) 485-8122
(800) 440-6000

GASTONIA

DAYS INN
1700 N Chester St
(28052)
Rates: $35-$49
Tel: (704) 864-9981
(800) 329-7466

MOTEL 6
1721 Broadcast St
(28052)
Rates: $32-$36
Tel: (704) 868-4900
(800) 466-8356

GLENDALE SPRINGS

MOUNTAIN VIEW LODGE & CABINS
P. O. Box 90 (28629)
Rates: $50-$95
Tel: (910) 982-2233
(800) 209-8142

GOLDSBORO

BEST WESTERN INN
801 US 70 E Bypass
(27534)
Rates: $48-$64
Tel: (919) 735-7911
(800) 528-1234

HOLIDAY INN
P. O. Box 1973
(27530)
Rates: $58-$70
Tel: (919) 735-7901
(800) 465-4329

MOTEL 6
701 US 70 E Bypass
(27534)
Rates: $29-$33
Tel: (919) 734-4542
(800) 440-6000

GREENSBORO

DAYS INN
501 Regional Rd S
(27409)
Rates: $55-65
Tel: (910) 668-0476
(800) 329-7499

HOWARD JOHNSON
3030 High Point Rd
(27403)
Rates: $49-79
Tel: (910) 294-4920
(800) 446-4656

MOTEL 6-AIRPORT
605 Regional Rd S
(27409)
Rates: $32-$36
Tel: (910) 668-2085
(800) 440-6000

MOTEL 6-SOUTH
831 Greenhaven Dr
(27406)
Rates: $33-$37
Tel: (910) 854-0993
(800) 440-6000

RED ROOF INN-COLISEUM
2101 W Meadowview Rd
(27403)
Rates: $32-$41
Tel: (910) 852-6560
(800) 843-7663

RED ROOF INN
615 Regional Rd S
(27409)
Rates: $36-$70
Tel: (910) 271-2636
(800) 843-7663

SCOTTISH INNS
2608 Preddy Blvd
(27407)
Rates: $29-$70
Tel: (910) 299-6131
(800) 251-1962

GREENVILLE

HOWARD JOHNSON
702 S Memorial Dr
(27834)
Rates: $40-52
Tel: (919) 758-0643
(800) 446-4656

RED ROOF INN
301 SE Greenville
Blvd (27858)
Rates: $36-$70
Tel: (919) 756-2792

HENDERSON

DAYS INN
I-85 & Ruin Creek
Rd (27536)
Rates: $30-50
Tel: (919) 492-4041
(800) 329-7466

HENDERSON-VILLE

COMFORT INN
206 Mitchell Dr
(28739)
Rates: $44-$101
Tel: (704) 693-8800
(800) 221-2222

QUALITY INN
201 Sugarloaf Rd
(28792)
Rates: $39-$105
Tel: (704) 692-7231
(800) 221-2222

HICKORY

ECONO LODGE
325 US 70 SW
(28603)
Rates: $37-$61
Tel: (704) 328-2111
(800) 424-4777

HOWARD JOHNSON
483 Hwy 70 & 321
(28601)
Rates: $38-$56
Tel: (704) 322-1600
(800) 446-4656

RED ROOF INN
1184 Lenoir Rhyne
Blvd (28602)
Rates: $30-$44
Tel: (704) 323-1500
(800) 843-7663

HIGH POINT

MOTEL 6
200 Ardale Dr
(27260)
Rate: $27-$31
Tel: (910) 841-7717
(800) 440-6000

HOWARD JOHNSON
2000 Brentwood St
(27263)
Rates: $50-60
Tel: (910) 886-4141
(800) 446-4656

JACKSONVILLE

ONSLOW INN
201 Marine Blvd
(28540)
Rates: $37-$41
Tel: (800) 763-3151

SUPER 8 MOTEL
2149 N Marine Blvd
(28546)
Rates: $42-62
Tel: (910) 455-6888
(800) 800-8000

KENLY

ECONO LODGE
P. O. Box 577 (27542)
Rates: $34-$55
Tel: (919) 284-1000
(800) 424-4777

KILL DEVIL HILLS

HAMPTON INN
804 Virginia Dare Tr
(27948)
Rates: $49-$64
Tel: (919) 441-0411
(800) 426-7866

RAMADA INN-NAGS HEAD BEACH
1701 Virginia Dare
Tr (27948)
Rates: $49-$124
Tel: (919) 441-2151
(800) 272-6232

KINSTON

HAMPTON INN
1403 Richlands
(28501)
Rates: $59-$69
Tel: (919) 523-1400
(800) 426-7866

LAUREL SPRINGS

BURGISS FARM BED & BREAKFAST
Rt 1, Box 300 (28644)
Rates: $90
Tel: (910) 359-2995
(800) 233-1505

DOUGHTON HALL B & B INN
Rt 1, Box 1 (28644)
Rates: $75
Tel: (910) 359-2341

LAURINBURG

HAMPTON INN
115 Hampton Cir
(28352)
Rates: $58-$70
Tel: (910) 277-1516
(800) 426-7866

LENOIR

DAYS INN
206 Blowing Rock
Blvd (28645)
Rates: $38-$60
Tel: (704) 754-0731
(800) 329-7466

LUMBERTON

BEST WESTERN INN
201 Jackson Ct
(28358)
Rates: $55-$85
Tel: (910) 618-9799
(800) 528-1234

DAYS INN
3030 N Roberts Ave
(28359)
Rates: $47-$54
Tel: (910) 738-6401
(800) 329-7466

ECONO LODGE
3591 Lackey Rd
(28358)
Rates: $30-$55
Tel: (800) 424-4777

HOWARD JOHNSON
3530 Capuano Dr
(28358)
Rates: $35-$61
Tel: (910) 738-4281
(800) 446-4656

MOTEL 6
2361 Lackey Rd (28358)
Rates: $27-$31
Tel: (910) 738-2410
(800) 440-6000

QUALITY INN
3608 Kahn Dr(28358)
Rates: $35-$41
Tel: (910) 738-8261
(800) 221-2222

MARION

ECONO LODGE
2035 US 221 S (28752)
Rates: $36-$42
Tel: (704) 659-7940
(800) 424-4777

MOORESVILLE

RAMADA LIMITED
I-77 at Hwy 150
(28115)
Rates: $39-$100
Tel: (704) 664-6556
(800) 272-6232

MORGANTON

HOLIDAY INN
2400 S Sterling St
(28655)
Rates: $49-$54
Tel: (704) 437-0171
(800) 465-4329

RED CARPET INN
2217 S Sterling St
(28655)
Rates: $37-$48
Tel: (704) 437-6980
(800) 251-1962

MORRISVILLE

BUDGETEL INN
1001 Aerial Center
Pkwy (27560)
Rates: $43-$53
Tel: (919) 481-3600
(800) 428-3438

MURPHY

COMFORT INN
114 US 64 W (28906)
Rates: $40-$95
Tel: (704) 837-8030
(800) 221-2222

NAGS HEAD

**WELL BONE
MOTELS**
P. O. Box 1119
(27959)
Rates: $89-$99
Tel: (919) 441-7423

**WHALEBONE
MOTEL**
P. O. Box 185 (27959)
Rates: n/a
Tel: (919) 441-7423
(800) 845-6070

PINEBLUFF

**PINE CONE MANOR
BED & BREAKFAST**
450 E Philadelphia
Ave (28373)
Rates: n/a
Tel: (910) 281-5307

RAEFORD

DAYS INN
Hwy 401 Bypass &
Teal Dr (28376)
Rates: $40-$60
Tel: (910) 904-1050
(800) 329-7466

RALEIGH

**BEST WESTERN
CRABTREE**
6619 Glenwood Ave
(27612)
Rates: $68-$170
Tel: (919) 782-8650
(800) 528-1234

DAYS INN
6329 Glenwood Ave
(27612)
Rates: $55-$99
Tel: (919) 781-7904
(800) 329-7466

ECONO LODGE W
5110 Holly Ridge Dr
(27612)
Rates: $44-$52
Tel: (919) 782-3201
(800) 424-4777

HAMPTON INN
US 70 & 110
Drexmere St.
(Garner 27529)
Rates: $65-$70
Tel: (919) 772-6500
(800) 426-7866

HOWARD JOHNSON
3120 New Bern Ave
(27610)
Rates: $35-$65
Tel: (919) 231-3000
(800) 446-4656

**MOTEL 6-
NORTHWEST**
3921 Arrow Dr
(27612)
Rates: $34-$38
Tel: (919) 782-7071
(800) 440-6000

**MOTEL 6-
SOUTHWEST**
1401 Buck Jones Rd
(27606)
Rates: $37-$41
Tel: (919) 467-6171
(800) 440-6000

**THE PLANTATION
INN RESORT**
6401 Capital Blvd
(27604)
Rates: $50-$70
Tel: (919) 876-1411
(800) 992-9662

RED ROOF INN
3520 Maitland Dr
(27610)
Rates: $30-$46
Tel: (919) 231-0200
(800) 843-7663

**SUNDOWN INN
NORTH**
3801 Capital Blvd
(27612)
Rates: $39-$61
Tel: (919) 790-8480

VELVET CLOAK INN
1505 Hillsborough St
(27605)
Rates: $65-$85
Tel: (800) 334-4372

ROANOKE RAPIDS

HOLIDAY INN
100 Holiday Dr
(27870)
Rates: $62-$75
Tel: (919) 537-1031
(800) 465-4329

INTERSTATE INN
1606 Roanoke
Rapids Rd (27890)
Rates: $30-$40
Tel: (919) 536-4111

MOTEL 6
1911 Weldon Rd
(27870)
Rates: $28-$34
Tel: (919) 537-5252
(800) 466-8356

ROCKY MOUNT

SUNSET INN BED & BREAKFAST
1210 Sunset Ave
(27804)
Rates: $65-$125
Tel: (919) 446-9524

ROWLAND

DAYS INN
Rt 2 Box 187 (28383)
Rates: $25-$65
Tel: (910) 422-3366
(800) 329-7466

ROXBORO

DAYS INN
1006 N Madison
Blvd (27573)
Rates: $30-$45
Tel: (910) 599-9276
(800) 329-7466

SPECIAL OCCASIONS B & B
5111 Semora Rd
(27573)
Rates: n/a
Tel: (910) 597-2848

RUTHERFORD-TON

CARRIER HOUSES
423 N Main St
(28139)
Rates: $40-$60
Tel: (704) 287-4222

SALISBURY

DAYS INN
1810 Lutheran
Synod Dr (28144)
Rates: $30-$95
Tel: (704) 633-4211
(800) 329-7466

HAMPTON INN
1001 Klumac Rd
(28144)
Rates: $56-$63
Tel: (704) 637-8000
(800) 426-7866

HOLIDAY INN
530 Jake Alexander
Blvd (28144)
Rates: $61-$73
Tel: (704) 637-3100
(800) 465-4329

RODEWAY INN
321-R Bendix Dr.
(28146)
Rates: $49-$125
Tel: (704) 636-7065
(800) 228-2000

SANFORD

PALOMINO MOTEL
P. O. Box 777 (27330)
Rates: $34-$40
Tel: (919) 776-7531

SELMA

DAYS INN
I-95 & 70 (27576)
Rates: $23-$100
Tel: (919) 965-3762
(800) 329-7466

SKYLAND

GLENN & EDNA'S VACATION COTTAGE
P. O. Box 98 (28176)
Rates: n/a
Tel: (704) 684-9938

SMITHFIELD

HOWARD JOHNSON
I-96, Exit 95 & US 70
Business (27577)
Rates $33-$95
Tel: (919) 934-7176
(800) 446-4656

LOG CABIN MOTEL
Rt 2, Box 447 (27577)
Rates: $39-$54
Tel: (919) 934-1534

SOUTHPORT

PORT MOTEL
4821 Long Beach Rd
SE (28461)
Rates: $40
Tel: (910) 457-4800

STATESVILLE

RED ROOF INN
1508 E Broad St
(28677)
Rates: $28-$47
Tel: (704) 878-2051
(800) 843-7663

SUPER 8 MOTEL
1125 Greenland Dr
(28677)
Rates: $37-$70
Tel: (704) 878-9888
(800) 800-8000

TARBORO

LADY ANN OF HISTORIC TARBORO B & B
1205 Main St (27886)
Rates: $50-$70
Tel: (919) 641-1438

WADE

DAYS INN
Rt 1, Box 216-BB
(28395)
Rates: $37-$50
Tel: (910) 323-1255
(800) 329-7466

WADESBORO

DAYS INN
209 E Caswell St
(28170)
Rates: $40-$85
Tel: (704) 694-7070
(800) 329-7466

WASHINGTON

ECONO LODGE
1220 W 5th St
(27889)
Rates: $33-$45
Tel: (919) 946-7781
(800) 424-4777

WELDON

DAYS INN
1611 Roanoke
Rapids Rd (27890)
Rates: $37-$90
Tel: (919) 536-4867
(800) 329-7466

WILMINGTON

MOTEL 6
2828 Market (28403)
Rates: $30-$34
Tel: (910) 762-0120
(800) 440-6000

WATERWAY LODGE
7246 Wrightsville
Ave (28403)
Rates: $55-$90
Tel: (910) 256-3771
(800) 677-3771

WILSON

**QUALITY INN
SOUTH**
Hwy 301S (27893)
Rates: $48-$70
Tel: (919) 243-5165
(800) 221-2222

WINSTON-
SALEM

**HAWTHORNE INN
& CONF CTR**
420 High St (27101)
Rates: $62-$98
Tel: (910) 777-3000

**HOLIDAY INN
NORTH**
3050 University
Pkwy (27105)
Rates: $69-$120
Tel: (910) 723-2911
(800) 465-4329

MOTEL 6
3810 Patterson Ave
(27105)
Rates: $27-$31
Tel: (910) 661-1588
(800) 440-6000

**RAMADA INN-
AIRPORT**
531 Akron Dr
(27105)
Rates: $89-$94
Tel: (910) 767-8240
(800) 272-6232

RAMADA LIMITED 2
128 N Cherry St
(27101)
Rates: $60-$75
Tel: (910) 723-8861
(800) 272-6232

**RESIDENCE INN
BY MARRIOTT**
7835 N Point Blvd
(27106)
Rates: $99-$122
Tel: (910) 759-0777
(800) 331-3131

SALEM INN
127 S Cherry St
(27101)
Rates: $49-$55
Tel: (910) 725-8561

NORTH DAKOTA

BEACH

BUCKBOARD INN
HC2 Box 109A
(58621)
Rates: $29-$36
Tel: (701) 872-4794

BISMARCK

BEST WESTERN FLECK HOUSE MOTEL
122 E Thayer (58502)
Rates: $37-$53
Tel: (701) 255-1450
(800) 528-1234

BISMARCK MOTOR HOTEL
P. O. Box 1724
(58502)
Rates: $20-$32
Tel: (701) 223-2474

COMFORT INN
1030 Interstate Ave
(58501)
Rates: $36-$52
Tel: (800) 221-2222

DAYS INN
1300 Capitol Ave
(58501)
Rates: $35-$120
Tel: (701) 223-9151
(800) 329-7466

EXPRESSWAY INN
200 Bismarck Expwy
(58504)
Rates: $30-$48
Tel: (701) 222-2900

FAIRFIELD INN BY MARRIOTT NORTH
1120 Century Ave
(58501)
Rates: $40-$66
Tel: (701) 223-9077
(800) 228-2800

HOLIDAY INN
605 E Broadway
(58502)
Rates: $57-$83
Tel: (701) 255-6000
(800) 465-4329

KELLY INN
1800 N 12th St
(58501)
Rates: $42-$53
Tel: (701) 233-8001

MOTEL 6
2433 State St (58501)
Rates: $27-$31
Tel: (701) 255-6878
(800) 440-6000

RADISSON INN
800 S 3rd St (58504)
Rates: $65-$100
Tel: (701) 258-7700
(800) 333-3333

SELECT INN
1505 Interchange Ave (58501)
Rates: $28-$41
Tel: (701) 223-8060
(800) 641-1000

SUPER 8 MOTEL
1124 E Capitol Ave
(58501)
Rates: $38-$59
Tel: (701) 255-1314
(800) 800-8000

BOWMAN

BUDGET HOST 4U MOTEL
P. O. Box 590 (58623)
Rates: $23-$41
Tel: (701) 523-3243

EL VU MOTEL
Hwy 12 & 85 (58623)
Rates: n/a
Tel: (800) 521-0379

NORTH WINDS LODGE
P. O. Box 346 (58623)
Rates: $23-$36
Tel: (701) 523-5641

SUPER 8 MOTEL
P. O. Box 675 (58623)
Rates: $38-$54
Tel: (701) 523-5613
(800) 800-8000

CARRINGTON

CHIEFTAIN MOTOR LODGE
Hwy 281 (58421)
Rates: $31-$50
Tel: (701) 652-3131

DEVILS LAKE

COMFORT INN
215 Hwy 2 E (58301)
Rates: $39-$62
Tel: (701) 662-6760
(800) 221-2222

DAYS INN
Rt 5, Box 8 (58301)
Rates: $38-$56
Tel: (701) 662-5381
(800) 329-7466

SUPER 8 MOTEL
1001 Hwy E (58301)
Rates: $30-$50
Tel: (701) 662-8656
(800) 800-8000

TRAILS WEST MOTEL
P. O. Box 1113
(58301)
Rates: $29-$37
Tel: (701) 662-5011

DICKINSON

BUDGET INN
529 12th St W
(58601)
Rates: $31-$44
Tel: (701) 225-9123

COMFORT INN
493 Elk Dr (58601)
Rates: $27-$49
Tel: (701) 264-7300
(800) 221-2222

HOSPITALITY INN & CONVENTION CENTER
P. O. Box 1778
(58602)
Rates: $40-$59
Tel: (701) 227-1853

NODAK MOTEL
600 E Villard St
(58601)
Rates: $23-$38
Tel: (701) 225-5119

RODEWAY INN
1000 W Villard St
(58601)
Rates: $27-$75
Tel: (701) 225-6703
(800) 228-2000

SELECT INN
642 12 St W (58601)
Rates: $21-$34
Tel: (701) 227-1891
(800) 641-1000

DRAYTON

MOTEL 66
P. O. Box 116 (58225)
Rates: $27-$35
Tel: (701) 454-6464

FARGO
(and West Fargo)

AMERICINN MOTEL
1423 35th St SW
(58103)
Rates: $46-$67
Tel: (701) 234-9946

BEST WESTERN DOUBLEWOOD INN
3333 13th Ave S
(58103)
Rates: $68-$79
Tel: (701) 235-3333
(800) 528-1234

BEST WESTERN KELLY INN
3800 Main Ave
(58103)]
Rates: $55-$70
Tel: (701) 282-2143
(800) 528-1234

COMFORT INN EAST
1407 35th St S
(58103)
Rates: $36-$55
Tel: (701) 280-9666
(800) 221-2222

COMFORT INN WEST
3825 9th Ave SW
(58103)
Rates: $42-$70
Tel: (701) 282-9596
(800) 221-2222

COMFORT SUITES
1415 35th St S
(58103)
Rates: $46-$65
Tel: (701) 280-9666
(800) 237-5911

**COUNTRY SUITES
BY CARLSON**
3316 13th Ave S
(58103)
Rates: $65-$149
Tel: (701) 234-0565
(800) 456-4000

DAYS INN
901 38th St SW
(58103)
Rates: $39-$60
Tel: (701) 282-9100
(800) 329-7466

DAYS INN
1507 19th Ave N
(58102)
Rates: $40-$139
Tel: (701) 232-0000
(800) 329-7466

DAYS INN
525 E Main Ave
(West Fargo 58078)
Rates: $30-$47
Tel: (701) 281-0000
(800) 329-7466

ECONO LODGE
1401 35th St S
(58103)
Rates: $35-$60
Tel: (701) 232-3412
(800) 424-4777

**FAIRFIELD INN
BY MARRIOTT**
3902 9th Ave (58103)
Rates: $42-$70
Tel: (701) 281-0494
(800) 228-2800

HOLIDAY INN
3803 13th Ave
(58106)
Rates: $70-$95
Tel: (701) 282-2700
(800) 465-4329

MOTEL 6-WEST
1202 36th St S
(58103)
Rates: $26-$32
Tel: (701) 232-0251
(800) 440-6000

MOTEL 75
3402 14th Ave S
(58103)
Rates: $30-$39
Tel: (701) 232-1321

RADISSON HOTEL
201 5th St N (58102)
Rates: $65-$106
Tel: (701) 232-7363
(800) 333-3333

RODEWAY INN
2202 S University Dr
(58103)
Rates: $35-$56
Tel: (701) 239-8022
(800) 228-2000

SELECT INN
1025 38th St SW
(58103)
Rates: $32-$61
Tel: (701) 282-6300
(800) 641-1000

SUPER 8 MOTEL
3518 Interstate Blvd
(58103)
Rates: $34-$48
Tel: (701) 232-9202
(800) 800-8000

SUPER 8 MOTEL
301 3rd Ave N
(58102)
Rates: $45-$60
Tel: (701) 232-8851
(800) 800-8000

SUPER 8 MOTEL
825 E Main Ave (W
Fargo 58078)
Rates: $31-$43
Tel: (701) 282-7121
(800) 800-8000

GARRISON

GARRISON MOTEL
P. O. Box 999 (58540)
Rates: $25-$35
Tel: (701) 463-2858

GRAFTON

LEONARD MOTEL
Hwy 17 West (58237)
Rates: n/a
Tel: (701) 352-1730

GRAND FORKS

COMFORT INN
3251 30th Ave S
(58201)
Rates: $40-$71
Tel: (701) 775-7503
(800) 221-2222

**COUNTRY INN &
SUITES BY CARLSON**
3350 32nd Ave S
(58201)
Rates: $49-$82
Tel: (701) 775-5000
(800) 456-4000

DAYS INN
3101 34th St S (58201)
Rates: $44-$55
Tel: (701) 775-0600
(800) 329-7466

ECONO LODGE
900 N 43rd St
(58201)
Rates: $34-$54
Tel: (701) 746-4444
(800) 424-4777

**FAIRFIELD INN
BY MARRIOTT**
3051 S 34th St
(58201)
Rates: $40-$71
Tel: (701) 775-7910
(800) 228-2800

**IMA PLAINSMAN
MOTEL**
2201 Gateway Dr
(58203)
Rates: $29-$36
Tel: (701) 775-8134
(800) 341-8000

NORTH STAR INN
2100 S Washington
St (58201)
Rates: $34-$49
Tel: (701) 772-8151

RODEWAY INN
4001 Gateway Dr
(58203)
Rates: $32-$50
Tel: (701) 795-9960
(800) 228-2000

SELECT INN
1000 N 42nd St
(58203)
Rates: $26-$44
Tel: (701) 775-0555
(800) 641-1000

SUPER 8 MOTEL
1122 N 43rd St
(58203)
Rates: $38-$60
Tel: (701) 775-8138
(800) 800-8000

JAMESTOWN

**BEST WESTERN
DAKOTA INN**
Hwy 281 S (58401)
Rates: $38-$65
Tel: (701) 252-3611
(800) 726-7924

COMFORT INN
811 20 St SW (58401)
Rates: $37-$57
Tel: (701) 252-7125
(800) 221-2222

**GLADSTONE
SELECT HOTEL**
P. O. Box 989 (58402)
Rates: $42-$57
Tel: (701) 252-0700

**IMA RANCH HOUSE
MOTEL**
408 Business Loop
W (58401)
Rates: $28-$38
Tel: (701) 252-0222

LAKOTA

SUNLAC INN
P. O. Box 648 (58344)
Rates: $25-$34
Tel: (701) 701-2487

LANGDON

**LANGDON
MOTOR INN**
210 Ninth Ave
(58249)
Rates: $26-$34
Tel: (701) 256-3600

LINTON

WILLOWS MOTEL
P. O. Box 882 (58552)
Rates: $24-$38
Tel: (701) 254-4555

MANDAN

**BEST WESTERN
SEVEN SEAS INN**
2611 Old Red Tr
(58554)
Rates: $49-$59
Tel: (701) 663-7401
(800) 528-1234

MINOT

**BEST WESTERN
SAFARI INN**
1510 26th Ave SW
(58701)
Rates: $44-$75
Tel: (701) 852-4300
(800) 528-1234

CASA MOTEL
1900 US 2 & 52
Bypass (58701)
Rates: $22-$32
Tel: (701) 852-2352

COMFORT INN
1515 22nd Ave SW
(58701)
Rates: $40-$70
Tel: (701) 852-2201
(800) 221-2222

DAYS INN
2100 4th St SW
(58701)
Rates: $36-$60
Tel: (701) 852-3646
(800) 329-7466

**FAIRFIELD INN
BY MARRIOTT**
900 24 Ave SW
(58701)
Rates: $37-$68
Tel: (701) 838-2424
(800) 228-2800

HOLIDAY INN
2200 Burdick Expy
(58702)
Rates: $49-$75
Tel: (701) 852-2504
(800) 465-4329

SELECT INN
P. O. Box 460 (58702)
Rates: $26-$36
Tel: (701) 852-3411
(800) 641-1000

SUPER 8 MOTEL
1315 N Broadway
(58703)
Rates: $34-$51
Tel: (701) 852-1817
(800) 800-8000

PARSHALL

**PARSHALL
MOTOR INN**
North Main St,
Box 38 (58770)
Rates: n/a
Tel: (701) 862-3127

ROLLA

NORTHERN LIGHTS
Hwy 5 East (58367)
Rates: n/a
Tel: (701) 477-6164

RUGBY

ECONO LODGE
US 2 E (58368)
Rates: $36-$44
Tel: (701) 776-5776
(800) 424-4777

STEELE

LONE STEER MOTEL
I-94 Hwy #3 (58482)
Rates: n/a
Tel: (701) 475-2221

O K MOTEL
301 3rd Ave
Northeast (58482)
Rates: n/a
Tel: (701) 475-2440

VALLEY CITY

MID-TOWN MOTEL
906 E Main St
(58072)
Rates: $20-$30
Tel: (701) 845-2830

**WAGON WHEEL
INN**
930 4th Ave SW
(58072)
Rates: $29-$47
Tel: (701) 845-5333

WAHPETON

COMFORT INN
209 13th St S (58075)
Rates: $35-$55
Tel: (701) 642-1115
(800) 221-2222

SUPER 8 MOTEL
995 21st Ave N
(58075)
Rates: $41-$53
Tel: (701) 642-8731
(800) 800-8000

WASHBURN

**SCOT WOOD
MOTEL**
P. O. Box 1183
(58577)
Rates: $28-$35
Tel: (701) 462-8191

WATFORD CITY

MCKENZIE INN
120 SW 3rd St
(58854)
Rates: $25-$35
Tel: (701) 842-3980

WILLISTON

**AIRPORT
INTERNATIONAL
INN**
P. O. Box 1800
(58802)
Rates: $38-$70
Tel: (701) 774-0241

**EL RANCHO
MOTOR HOTEL**
P. O. Box 4277
(58802)
Rates: $34-$40
Tel: (701) 572-6321

SELECT INN
213 35th St W
(58801)
Rates: $29-$37
Tel: (701) 572-4242
(800) 641-1000

SUPER 8 LODGE
2324 2nd Ave W
(58801)
Rates: $29-$42
Tel: (701) 572-8371
(800) 800-8000

WEST FARGO

DAYS INN
525 E Main Ave
(58078)
Rates: $30-$47
Tel: (701) 281-0000
(800) 329-7466

SUPER 8 MOTEL
825 E Main Ave
(58078)
Rates: $31-$43
Tel: (701) 282-7121
(800) 800-8000

OHIO

AKRON

DAYS INN
3237 Arlington Rd
(44333)
Rates: $50-$75
Tel: (216) 644-1204
(800) 329-7466

HAMPTON INN
80 Springside Dr
(44333)
Rates: $57-$86
Tel: (330) 666-7361
(800) 426-7866

HOLIDAY INN
I-77 & Arlington Rd
(44312)
Rates: $70-$92
Tel: (216) 644-7126
(800) 465-4329

RED ROOF INN-SOUTH
2939 S Arlington Rd
(44312)
Rates: $35-$50
Tel: (216) 644-7748
(800) 843-7663

RESIDENCE INN BY MARRIOTT
120 W Montrose Ave
(44321)
Rates: $72-$145
Tel: (216) 666-4811
(800) 331-3131

SUPER 8 MOTEL
79 Rothrock Rd
(44321)
Rates: $36-$59
Tel: (216) 666-8887
(800) 800-8000

ALLIANCE

COMFORT INN
2500 W State St
(44601)
Rates: $47-$59
Tel: (330) 821-5555
(800) 221-2222

AMHERST

MOTEL 6
704 N Leavitt Rd
(44001)
Rates: $33-$39
Tel: (216) 988-3266
(800) 440-6000

TRAVELODGE
934 N Leavitt Rd
(44001)
Rates: $39-$72
Tel: (216) 985-1428
(800) 578-7878

ASHLAND

AMERIHOST INN
741 US 250E (44805)
Rates: $40-$90
Tel: (419) 281-8090

DAYS INN
1423 CR 1575 (44805)
Rates: $44-$65
Tel: (419) 289-0101
(800) 329-7466

TRAVELODGE
736 US 250 (44805)
Rates: $43-$65
Tel: (419) 281-0567
(800) 578-7878

ASHTABULA

HO HUM MOTEL
3801 N Ridge West
(44004)
Rates: $35-$50
Tel: (216) 969-1136

AURORA

AURORA INN
30 E Garfield Rd
(44202)
Rates: $75-$175
Tel: (216) 562-6121
(800) 444-6121

AUSTINTOWN

BUDGET LUXURY INN
5425 Clarkins Dr
(44515)
Rate: $30-$42
Tel: (330) 793-9806

KNIGHTS INN WEST
5431 76th Dr (44516)
Rates: $33-$41
Tel: (800) 843-5644

BEACHWOOD

MARRIOTT HOTEL
3663 E Park Dr
(44122)
Rates: $89-$149
Tel: (216) 464-5950
(800) 228-9290

BELLEFONTAINE

COMFORT INN
260 Northview
(43311)
Rates: $53-$63
Tel: (513) 599-5555
(800) 221-2222

HOLIDAY INN
1134 N Main St
(43311)
Rates: $69-$74
Tel: (513) 593-8515
(800) 465-4329

BLUFFTON

HOJO INN
855 SR 103 (45817)
Rates: $45-$65
Tel: (419) 358-7000
(800) 446-4656

BOARDMAN

DAYS INN
8392 Market St
(44512)
Rates: $34-$72
Tel: (216) 758-2371
(800) 329-7466

MICROTEL INN
7393 South Ave
(44512)
Rates: $37-$45
Tel: (330) 758-1816
(800) 804-8385

BOWLING GREEN

BEST WESTERN - FALCON PLAZA
1450 E Wooster St
(43402)
Rates: $56-$95
Tel: (419) 352-4671
(800) 528-1234

BUCKEYE BUDGET INN
1740 E Wooster St
(43402)
Rates: $38-$49
Tel: (419) 352-1520

HOLLEY LODGE
1630 E Wooster St
(43042)
Rates: $50-$70
Tel: (419) 352-2521
(800) 553-7829

BROADVIEW HEIGHTS

DAYS INN
4501 E Royalton Rd
(44147)
Rates: $40-$60
Tel: (216) 526-0640
(800) 329-7466

BUCYRUS

DAYS INN
1515 N Sandusky St
(44820)
Rates: $53-$95
Tel: (419) 562-3737
(800) 329-7466

BURBANK

MOTEL PLAZA
Rt 1, Box 8 (44214)
Rates: $27-$32
Tel: (216) 624-3012

CAMBRIDGE

BEST WESTERN INN
1945 Southgate
Pkwy (43725)
Rates: $30-$79
Tel: (614) 439-3581
(800) 528-1234

**CAMBRIDGE
FAIRDALE INN**
6405 Glenn Hwy
(43725)
Rates: $27-$32
Tel: (614) 432-2304

HOLIDAY INN
2248 Southgate
Pkwy (43725)
Rates: $53-$74
Tel: (614) 423-7313
(800) 465-4329

CANTON

**BEST SUITES
OF AMERICA**
4914 Everhard Rd
(44718)
Rates: $63-$91
Tel: (216) 499-1011

DAYS INN
3970 Convenience
Circle (44718)
Rates: $39-$55
Tel: (330) 493-8883
(800) 329-7466

**CANTON
FAIRFIELD INN**
5285 Broadmoor Cir
NW (44709)
Rates: $52-$58
Tel: (330) 493-7373
(800) 228-2800

HOLIDAY INN
4520 Everhard Rd
(44718)
Rates: $63-$98
Tel: (216) 494-2770
(800) 465-4329

MOTEL 6
6880 Sunset Strip
Ave NW (44720)
Rates: $33-$39
Tel: (216) 494-7611
(800) 440-6000

RED ROOF INN
5353 Inn Circle Ct
NW (44720)
Rates: $35-$56
Tel: (216) 499-1970
(800) 843-7663

**RESIDENCE INN
BY MARIOTT**
5280 Broadmoor Cir
NW (44709)
Rates: $59-$129
Tel: (330) 493-0004
(800) 331-3131

**SUPER 8 MOTEL-
NORTH**
3950 Convenience
Cir NW (44718)
Rates: $41-$70
Tel: (330) 492-5030
(800) 800-8000

CHILLICOTHE

CHRISTOPHER INN
30 N Plaza Blvd
(45601)
Rates: $70-$75
Tel: (614) 774-6835

COMFORT INN
20 N Plaza
Blvd(45601)
Rates: $55-$60
Tel: (800) 221-2222

DAYS INN
1250 N Bridge St
(45601)
Rates: $39-$85
Tel: (614) 775-7000
(800) 329-7466

TRAVELODGE
1135 E Main St
(45601)
Rates: $42-$69
Tel: (614) 775-2500
(800) 578-7878

CINCINNATI
(and Vicinity)

**AMERISUITES-
NORTH-WEST**
12001 Chase Plaza Dr
(Forest Park 45240)
Rates: $59-$129
Tel: (513) 825-9035
(800) 833-1516

**BEST WESTERN
BLUE ASH HOTEL**
5901 Pfieffer Rd
(45242)
Rates: $69-$109
Tel: (513) 793-4500
(800) 528-1234

COMFORT INN
9011 Fields-Ertel Rd
(45249)
Rates: $49-$115
Tel: (513) 683-9700
(800) 228-5150

DAYS INN
US 42, Exit 46 (45241)
Rates: $38-$62
Tel: (513) 554-1400
(800) 329-7466

DAYS INN-EAST
4056 Mt. Carmel-
Tobasco Rd (45255)
Rates: $43-$110
Tel: (513) 528-3800
(800) 329-7466

HOLIDAY INN
4501 Eastgate Blvd
(45245)
Rates: $79-$93
Tel: (513) 752-4400
(800) 465-4329

HOLIDAY INN-N
2235 Sharon Rd
(45241)
Rates: $99-$139
Tel: (513) 771-0700
(800) 465-4329

HOWARD JOHNSON
400 Glensprings Dr
(45246)
Rates: $46-$68
Tel: (513) 825-3129
(800) 446-4656

**IMPERIAL HOUSE-
WEST**
5510 Rybolt Rd
(45248)
Rates: $48-$58
Tel: (513) 574-6000

MOTEL 6
3960 Nine Mile Rd
(45255)
Rates: $36-$42
Tel: (513) 752-2262
(800) 440-6000

QUALITY HOTEL
4747 Montgomery
Rd (45212)
Rates: $79-$99
Tel: (513) 351-6600
(800) 221-2222

RED ROOF INN
5300 Kennedy Dr
(45213)
Rates: $50-$58
Tel: (513) 531-6589
(800) 843-7663

RED ROOF INN
11345 Chester Rd
(45246)
Rates: $25-$51
Tel: (513) 771-5141
(800) 843-7663

**RED ROOF INN-
EAST**
4035 Mt Carmel
Tobasco Rd (45255)
Rates: $30-$40
Tel: (513) 528-2741
(800) 843-7663

**RED ROOF INN-
NORTHEAST**
5900 Pfeiffer Rd
(45242)
Rates: $36-$52
Tel: (513) 793-8811
(800) 843-7663

REGAL HOTEL
150 W 5th St (45202)
Rates: $69-$159
Tel: (513) 352-2100
(800) 876-2100

**RESIDENCE INN
BY MARRIOTT**
11401 Reed Hartman
Hwy (45241)
Rates: $99-$140
Tel: (513) 530-5060
(800) 331-3131

RESIDENCE INN BY MARRIOTT
11689 Chester Rd (45246)
Rates: $59-$126
Tel: (513) 771-2525
(800) 331-3131

TRAVELODGE
3244 Central Pkwy (45225)
Rates: $41-$72
Tel: (513) 559-1800
(800) 578-7878

VILLAGER LODGE
7313 Kingsgate Way (45225)
Rates: $30-$70
Tel: (513) 777-5170

WESTIN HOTEL
At Fountain Square (45202)
Rates: $185-$205
Tel: (513) 621-7700
(800) 228-3000

CIRCLEVILLE

HOMETOWN INN
23897 US 23S (43113)
Rates: $34-$47
Tel: (614) 474-6006

MONTECELLO MOTEL
21530 US 23S (43113)
Rates: $30-$35
Tel: (614) 474-8884

TRAVELODGE
24701 US 23S (43113)
Rates: $39-$69
Tel: (614) 474-7511
(800) 578-7878

CLEVELAND

BUDGETEL INN-AIRPORT
4222 W 150th St (44135)
Rates: $49-$66
Tel: (216) 251-8500
(800) 428-3438

EMBASSY SUITES-DOWNTOWN
1701 E 12th St (44114)
Rates: $109-$189
Tel: (216) 523-8000
(800) 362-2779

HILTON INN-SOUTH
6200 Quarry Ln (44131)
Rates: $96-$152
Tel: (216) 447-1300
(800) 445-8667

MARRIOTT HOTEL-AIRPORT
4277 W 150th St (44135)
Rates: $118-$128
Tel: (216) 252-5333
(800) 228-9290

MARRIOTT-SOCIETY CENTER
127 Public Sq (44114)
Rates: $125-$156
Tel: (216) 696-9200
(800-228-9290

CLYDE

PLAZA MOTEL
500 E McPherson Hwy (43410)
Rates: $25-$52
Tel: (419) 547-6514

COLUMBUS

AMERISUITES
7490 Vantage Dr (43235)
Rates: $88-$98
Tel (614) 846-4355
(800) 833-1516

BEST WESTERN UNIVERSITY INN
3232 Olentangy River Rd (43202)
Rates: $54-$66
Tel: (614) 261-7141
(800) 528-1234

DAYS INN-EAST
5930 Scarborough Rd (43232)
Rates: $30-$55
Tel: (614) 868-9290
(800) 329-7466

DAYS INN FAIRGROUNDS
1700 Clara St (43211)
Rates: $35-$60
Tel: (614) 299-4300
(800) 329-8466

DAYS INN UNIVERSITY
3160 Olentangy River Rd (43202)
Rates: $39-$60
Tel: (614) 261-0523
(800) 329-7466

DAYS INN-WEST
1559 W Broad St (43222)
Rates: $30-$75
Tel: (614) 275-0388
(800) 329-7466

ECONO LODGE
920 Wilson Rd (43204)
Rates: $33-$66
Tel: (614) 274-8581
(800) 424-4777

HAMPTON INN
1100 Mediterranean Ave (43229)
Rates: $55-$67
Tel: (614) 848-9696
(800) 426-7866

HOLIDAY INN-AIRPORT
750 Stelzer Rd (43219)
Rates: $52-$62
Tel: (614) 237-6360
(800) 465-4329

HOLIDAY INN
175 Hutchinson Ave (43235)
Rates: $92-$96
Tel: (614) 885-3334
(800) 465-4329

HOLIDAY INN EAST I-70
4560 Hilton Corporate Dr (43232)
Rates: $59-$99
Tel: (614) 868-1380
(800) 465-4329

HOLIDAY INN ON THE LANE
328 W Lane Ave (43201)
Rates: $85-$90
Tel: (614) 294-4848
(800) 465-4329

HOMEWOOD SUITES
115 Hutchinson Ave (43235)
Rates: $95-$150
Tel: (614) 785-0001
(800) 225-5466

HOWARD JOHNSON
1070 Dublin-Grandview Ave (43215)
Rates: $49-$75
Tel: (614) 486-4554
(800) 446-4656

KNIGHTS INN-EAST
4320 Groves Rd (43232)
Rates: $30-$46
Tel: (614) 864-0600
(800) 843-5644

KNIGHTS INN
1300 Dublin-Granville Rd (43229)
Rates: $38-$46
Tel: (614) 846-7635
(800) 843-5644

LANSING ST B & B
180 Lansing St (43206)
Rates: $70
Tel: (614) 444-8488
(800) 383-7839

MARRIOTT NORTH
6500 Doubletree Ave (43229)
Rates: $114
Tel: (614) 885-1885

MICROTEL
7500 Vantage Dr (43235)
Rates: $32-$42
Tel: (614) 436-0556
(800) 433-3690

MOTEL 6
5500 Renner Rd (43228)
Rates: $33-$39
Tel: (614) 870-0993
(800) 440-6000

MOTEL 6-EAST
5910 Scarborough Blvd (43232)
Rates: $33-$39
Tel: (614) 755-2250
(800) 440-6000

MOTEL 6-NORTH
1289 Dublin-Granville Rd (43229)
Rates: $36-$42
Tel: (614) 846-9860
(800) 440-6000

PARKE UNIVERSITY HOTEL
3025 Olentangy
River Rd (43202)
Rates: $60-$125
Tel: (614) 267-1111
(800) 277-6158

RADISSON-NORTH
4900 Sinclair Rd
(43229)
Rates: $62-$175
Tel: (614) 846-0300
(800) 333-3333

RAMADA INN-WEST
4601 W Broad St
(43228)
Rates: $40-$125
Tel: (614) 878-5301
(800) 272-6232

RAMADA INN AIRPORT EAST 4
I-70 & Hamilton Rd
at Exit 107 (43232)
Rates: $59-$109
Tel: (614) 861-7220
(800) 272-6232

RED ROOF INN
750 Morse Rd
(43229)
Rates: $30-$48
Tel: (614) 846-8520
(800) 843-7663

RED ROOF INN-OSU
441 Ackerman Rd
(43202)
Rates: $34-$49
Tel: (614) 267-9941
(800) 843-7663

RED ROOF INN-WEST
5001 Renner Rd
(43228)
Rates: $36-$52
Tel: (614) 878-9245
(800) 843-7663

RED ROOF INN
7474 N High St
(43235)
Rates: $36-$46
Tel: (614) 846-3001
(800) 843-7663

RENAISSANCE DUBLIN HOTEL
600 N Metro Place
(43017)
Rates: $77-$159
Tel: (614) 764-2200
(800) 468-3571

RESIDENCE INN BY MARRIOTT
2084 S Hamilton Rd
(43232)
Rates: $121-$153
Tel: (614) 864-8844
(800) 331-3131

RESIDENCE INN BY MARRIOTT
6191 Zumstein Dr
(43229)
Rates: $119-$159
Tel: (614) 431-1819
(800) 331-3131

TRAVELODGE
7480 N High St
(43235)
Rates: $35-$68
Tel: (614) 431-2525
(800) 578-7878

VICTORIAN B & B
78 Smith Pl (43201)
Rates: n/a
Tel: (614) 299-1656

VILLAGE LODGE
5950 Scarborough
Blvd (43232)
Rates: $40-$80
Tel: (614) 864-4670
(800) 328-7829

COSHOCTON

TRAVELODGE
275 S Whitewoman
St (43812)
Rates: $54-$60
Tel: (614) 622-9823
(800) 578-7878

CURTICE

ECONO LODGE
10530 Corduroy Rd
(42413)
Rates: $20-$75
Tel: (419) 836-2822
(800) 424-4777

DAYTON
(and Vicinity)

COMFORT INN
7125 Miller Lane
(45414)
Rates: $55-$80
Tel: (513) 890-9995
(800) 221-2222

DAYS INN
100 Parkview Dr
(Brookville 45309)
Rates: $39-$59
Tel: (513) 833-4003
(800) 329-7466

ECONO LODGE
2140 Edwin C.
Moses Blvd (45408)
Rates: $39-$59
Tel: (513) 223-0166
(800) 424-4777

HOWARD JOHNSON
7575 Poe Ave (45414)
Rates: $50-$64
Tel: (513) 454-0550
(800) 446-4656

KNIGHTS INN-NORTH
3663 Maxton Rd
(45414)
Rates: $33-$41
Tel: (800) 843-5644

MARRIOTT HOTEL
1414 S Patterson
Blvd (45409)
Rates: $89-$120
Tel: (513) 223-1000
(800) 228-9290

MOTEL 6-NORTH
7130 Miller Lane
(45414)
Rates: $30-$36
Tel: (513) 898-3606
(800) 440-6000

QUALITY INN
1944 Miamisburg-
Centerville Rd
(45449)
Rates: $41-$52
Tel: (513) 435-1550
(800) 221-2222

RADISSON INN
2401 Needmore Rd
(45414)
Rates: $69-$89
Tel: (513) 278-5711
(800) 333-3333

RAMADA INN-AIRPORT
4079 Little York Rd
(45414)
Rates: $45-$85
Tel: (513) 890-9500
(800) 272-6232

RED ROOF INN-N
7370 Miller Ln
(45414)
Rates: $30-$47
Tel: (513) 898-1054
(800) 843-7663

RESIDENCE INN BY MARRIOTT
7070 Poe Ave (45414)
Rates: $111-$145
Tel: (513) 898-7764
(800) 331-3131

STOUFFER CENTER PLAZA HOTEL
5th & Jefferson Sts
(45402)
Rates: $79-$164
Tel: (513) 224-0800

TRAVELODGE
7911 Brandt Pike
(45424)
Rates: $35-$66
Tel: (513) 236-9361
(800) 578-7878

DEFIANCE

DAYS INN
1835 N Clinton St
(43512)
Rates: $42-$60
Tel: (419) 782-5555
(800) 329-7466

DELAWARE

TRAVELODGE
1001 US 23 N (43015)
Rates: $45-$65
Tel: (614) 369-4421
(800) 578-7878

DOVER

KNIGHTS INN
889 Commercial
Pkwy (44622)
Rates: $38-$50
Tel: (330) 364-7724
(800) 843-5644

DUBLIN

BUDGETEL INN
6145 Park Center Cir
(43017)
Rates: $40-$50
Tel: (614) 792-8300

RED ROOF INN
5125 Post Rd (43017)
Rates: $32-$53
Tel: (614) 764-3993
(800) 843-7663

RESIDENCE INN BY MARRIOTT
435 Metro Place S (43017)
Rates: $111-$154
Tel: (614) 791-0403
(800) 331-3131

STOUFFER DUBLIN HOTEL
600 Metro Place N (43017)
Rates: $74-$160
Tel: (614) 764-2200
(800) 468-3571

WOODFIN SUITES HOTEL
4130 Tuller Rd (43017)
Rates: $99-$189
Tel: (614) 766-7762
(800) 237-8811

EATON

ECONO LODGE
I-70 & US 127 (45320)
Rates: $33-$55
Tel: (513) 456-5959
(800) 424-4777

ELYRIA

COMFORT INN
739 Leona St (44035)
Rates: $38-$96
Tel: (216) 324-7676
(800) 221-2222

HOLIDAY INN
1825 Lorain Blvd (44035)
Rates: $79-$115
Tel: (216) 324-5411
(800) 465-4329

HOWARD JOHNSON
1724 Lorain Blvd (44035)
Rates: $40-$60
Tel: (216) 323-1515
(800) 446-4656

ENGLEWOOD

MOTEL 6
1212 S Main St (45322)
Rates: $30-$36
Tel: (513) 832-3770
(800) 440-6000

FAIRBORN

FAIRFIELD INN
2500 Paramount Pl (45324)
Rates: $60-$73
Tel: (513) 427-0800
(800) 228-2800

HAMPTON INN
2550 Paramount Pl (45324)
Rates: $64-$72
Tel: (513) 429-5505
(800) 426-7866

HOLIDAY INN
2800 Presidential Dr (45324)
Rates: $85-$115
Tel: (513) 426-7800
(800) 465-4329

HOMEWOOD SUITES
2750 Presidential Dr (45324)
Rates: $109-$119
Tel: (513) 429-0600
(800) 225-5466

RAMADA INN
800 N Broad St (45324)
Rates: $50-$60
Tel: (513) 879-3920
(800) 272-6232

RED ROOF INN
2580 Col. Glenn Hwy (45324)
Rates: $36-$49
Tel: (513) 426-6116
(800) 843-7663

FAIRLAWN

HILTON INN
3180 W Market St (44313)
Rates: $93-$143
Tel: (216) 867-5000
(800) 445-8667

RED ROOF INN
99 Rothrock Rd (44321)
Rates: $36-$58
Tel: (216) 666-0566
(800) 843-7663

FINDLAY

ECONO LODGE
316 Emma St (45840)
Rates: $28-$50
Tel: (419) 422-0154
(800) 424-4777

FAIRFIELD INN
2000 Tiffin Ave (45839)
Rates: $56-$66
Tel: (419) 424-9940
(800) 228-2800

FINDLAY INN & CONFERENCE CNTR
200 E Main Cross (45840)
Rates: $58-$85
Tel: (419) 422-5682

HAMPTON INN
921 Interstate Dr (45840)
Rates: $55-$74
Tel: (419) 422-5252
(800) 426-7866

RAMADA INN
820 Trenton Ave (45840)
Rates: $55-$71
Tel: (419) 423-8212
(800) 272-6232

SUPER 8 MOTEL
1600 Fox St (44830)
Rates: $37-$60
Tel: (419) 422-8863
(800) 800-8000

FOSTORIA

DAYS INN
601 Findlay St (44830)
Rates: $39-$64
Tel: (419) 435-6511
(800) 329-7466

FRANKLIN

COMFORT INN
3458 Commerce Dr (45005)
Rates: $43-$84
Tel:(513) 42-9378
(800) 221-2222

KNIGHTS INN
8500 Claude Thomas Rd (45005)
Rates: $32-$40
Tel: (800) 843-5644

OAKBROOK INN
6147 W SR 122 (45005)
Rates: $35-$58
Tel: (513) 424-1201

SUPER 8 MOTEL
3553 Commerce Dr (45005)
Rates: $39-$55
Tel: (513) 422-4888
(800) 800-8000

FREMONT

FREMONT TURNPIKE MOTEL
520 CR 89E (43420)
Rates: $30-$79
Tel: (419) 332-6489

HOLIDAY INN
3422 Port Clinton Rd (43420)
Rates: $79-$129
Tel: (419) 334-2682
(800) 465-4329

TRAVELODGE
1750 Cedar St (43420)
Rates: $41-$85
Tel: (419) 334-9517
(800) 578-7878

GALION

HOMETOWN INN
172 N Portland Way (44833)
Rates: $38-$63
Tel: (419) 468-9909

GALLIPOLIS

BEST WESTERN WILLIAM ANN
918 2nd Ave (45631)
Rates: $35-$45
Tel: (614) 446-3373
(800) 528-1234

GIRARD

DAYS INN
1610 Motor Inn Dr
(44420)
Rates: $39-$47
Tel: (330) 759-3410
(800) 329-7466

ECONO LODGE
1615 E Liberty St
(44420)
Rates: $29-$52
Tel: (330) 759-9820
(800) 424-4777

MOTEL 6
1600 Motor Inn Dr
(44420)
Rates: $24-$30
Tel: (216) 759-7833
(800) 440-6000

GROVE CITY

BEST WESTERN EXECUTIVE INN
4026 Jackpot Rd
(43123)
Rates: $45-$65
Tel: (614) 875-7770
(800) 528-1234

RED ROOF INN
1900 Stringtown Rd
(43123)
Rates: $34-$52
Tel: (614) 875-8543
(800) 843-7663

HAMILTON

HAMILTONIAN HOTEL
1 Riverfront Plaza
(45011)
Rates: $73-$81
Tel: (513) 896-6200
(800) 522-5570

HEATH

HOLIDAY INN
733 Hebron Rd
(43056)
Rates: $58-$67
Tel: (800) 465-4329

HOMETOWN INN
1266 Hebron Rd
(43056)
Rates: $36-$42
Tel: (614) 522-6112

SUPER 8 MOTEL
1177 S Hebron Rd
(43056)
Rates: $44-$57
Tel: (800) 800-8000

HEBRON

REGAL INN
4756 Keller Rd
(43025)
Rates: $25-$60
Tel: (614) 927-8011

HILLIARD

COMFORT INN
3831 Park Mill Run
Dr (43026)
Rates: $76
Tel: (614) 529-8118
(800) 240-2207

HOMEWOOD SUITES
3841 Park Mill Rd
(43026)
Rates: $99-$119
Tel: (614) 529-4100
(800) 225-5466

MOTEL 6
3950 Parkway Ln
(43026)
Rates: $33-$39
Tel: (614) 771-1500
(800) 440-6000

HOLLAND

RED ROOF INN
1214 Corporate Dr
(43528)
Rates: $34-$56
Tel: (419) 866-5512
(800) 843-7663

RESIDENCE INN BY MARRIOTT
6101 Trust Dr
(43528)
Rates: $101-$135
Tel: (419) 867-9555
(800) 331-3131

HUDSON

DAYS INN
344 E Hines Rd
(44236)
Rates: $39-$74
Tel: (216) 650-1100
(800) 329-7466

HURON

CLARION INN-TWINE HOUSE
132 N Main St
(44839)
Rates: $54-$149
Tel: (419) 433-8000
(800) 947-3400

PLANTATION MOTEL
2815 E Cleveland Rd
(44839)
Rates: $32-$91
Tel: (419) 433-4790

INDEPENDENCE

BUDGETEL INN
6161 Quarry Ln
(44131)
Rates: $48-$60
Tel: (216) 447-1133
(800) 428-3438

RED ROOF INN
6020 Quarry Ln
(44131)
Rates: $54-$65
Tel: (216) 447-0030
(800) 843-7663

RESIDENCE INN BY MARRIOTT
5101 W Creek Rd
(44131)
Rates: $79-$169
Tel: (216) 520-1450
(800) 331-3131

IRONTON

GRANDVIEW INN
154 County Rd
(45680)
Rates: $36-$69
Tel: (614) 377-4388
(800) 424-9849

JACKSON

COMFORT INN
605 E Main St (45640)
Rates: $60-$80
Tel: (614) 286-7581
(800) 221-2222

KENT

HOLIDAY INN
4363 SR 43 (44240)
Rates: $69-$95
Tel: (216) 678-0101
(800) 465-4329

THE INN OF KENT
303 E Main St (44240)
Rates: $42-$78
Tel: (216) 673-3411

KNIGHTS INN
4423 SR 43 (44240)
Rates: $38-$44
Tel: (216) 678-5250
(800) 843-5644

SUPER 8 MOTEL
4380 Edson Rd
(44240)
Rates: $42-$56
Tel: (330) 678-8817
(800) 800-8000

LAKEWOOD

DAYS INN
12019 Lake Ave
(44107)
Rates: $49-$59
Tel: (216) 226-4800
(800) 329-7466

LANCASTER

BEST WESTERN LANCASTER INN
1858 N Memorial Dr
(43130)
Rates: $52-$64
Tel: (614) 653-3040
(800) 528-1234

KNIGHTS INN
1327 River Valley Blvd (43130)
Rates: $37-$45
Tel: (614) 687-4823

LEBANON

BEST WESTERN HERITAGE INN
674 N Broadway (45036)
Rates: $35-$75
Tel: (513) 932-4111
(800) 528-1234

LIMA

COMFORT INN
10076 Market St (44452)
Rates: $45-$65
Tel: (330) 549-2187
(800) 221-2222

DAYS INN
1250 Neubrecht Rd (45801)
Rates: $30-$49
Tel: (419) 227-6515
(800) 329-7466

ECONO LODGE
1201 Neubrecht Rd (45801)
Rates: $43-$53
Tel: (419) 222-0596
(800) 424-4777

ECONOMY INN
10145 Market St (44452)
Rates: $40-$55
Tel: (330) 549-3224

HOLIDAY INN
1816 Harding Hwy (45804)
Rates: $82-$93
Tel: (419) 222-0004
(800) 465-4329

KNIGHTS INN
2285 N Eastown Rd (45807)
Rates: $32-$49
Tel: (419) 331-9215
(800) 843-5644

MOTEL 6
1800 Harding Hwy (45804)
Rates: $33-$39
Tel: (419) 228-0456
(800) 440-6000

RAMADA INN
3600 E Bluelick Rd (45801)
Rates: $45-$75
Tel: (800) 272-6232

LOGAN

SHAWNEE INN
30916 Lake Logan Rd (43138)
Rates: $35-$60
Tel: (614) 385-5674

LOUDONVILLE

LITTLE BROWN INN MOTEL
940 S Market St (44842)
Rates: $40-$55
Tel: (419) 994-5525

MACEDONIA

KNIGHTS INN
240 E Highland Rd (44056)
Rates: $34-$55
Tel: (216) 467-1981
(800) 843-5644

MOTEL 6
311 E Highland Rd (44056)
Rates: $36-$46
Tel: (216) 468-1670
(800) 440-6000

MANSFIELD

BEST WESTERN INN
880 Laver Rd (44905)
Rates: $53-$85
Tel: (419) 589-2200
(800) 528-1234

COMFORT INN
500 N Trimble Rd (44906)
Rates: $55-$60
Tel: (419) 529-1000
(800) 221-2222

DAYS INN
SR 13 & Hanley Rd E (44901)
Rates: $45-$100
Tel: (419) 756-6670
(800) 329-7466

ECONO LODGE
1017 Roogle Rd (44903)
Rates: $44-$68
Tel: (419) 589-3333
(800) 424-4777

FAIRFIELD INN
1065 Lexington Springmill Rd (44906)
Rates: $65-$120
Tel: (419) 747-2200
(800) 228-2800

42 MOTEL
2444 Lexington Ave (44907)
Rates: $33-$65
Tel: (419) 884-1315

HOLIDAY INN
116 W Park Ave (44902)
Rates: $62-$110
Tel: (419) 525-6000
(800) 465-4329

KNIGHTS INN
555 N Trimble Rd (44906)
Rates: $38-$53
Tel: (419) 529-2100
(800) 843-5644

PARK PLACE HOTEL
191 W Park Ave (44902)
Rates: $45-$55
Tel: (419) 522-7275
(800) 425-7275

SUPER 8 MOTEL
2425 Interstate Cir (44903)
Rates: $40-$60
Tel: (419) 746-8875
(800) 800-8000

TRAVELODGE
90 Hanley Rd (44903)
Rates: $38-$69
Tel: (419) 756-7600
(800) 578-7878

MARBLEHEAD

SURF MOTEL
230 E Main St (43440)
Rates: $45-$60
Tel: (419) 798-4823

MARIETTA

BEST WESTERN INN
279 Muskingum Dr (45750)
Rates: $48-$58
Tel: (614) 374-7211
(800) 528-1234

ECONO LODGE
702 Pike St (45750)
Rates: $50-$65
Tel: (614) 374-8481
(800) 424-4777

KNIGHTS INN
506 Pike St (45750)
Rates: $34-$56
Tel: (614) 373-7373
(800) 843-5644

LAFAYETTE HOTEL
101 Front St (45750)
Rates: $65-$200
Tel: (614) 373-5522
(800) 331-9336

MARION

COMFORT INN
256 James Way (43302)
Rates: $52-$65
Tel: (614) 398-5552
(800) 221-2222

FAIRFIELD INN BY MARRIOTT
227 James Way (43302)
Rates: $58-$78
Tel: (614) 389-6636
(800) 228-2800

HARDING MOTOR LODGE
1065 Delaware Ave (43302)
Rates: $37-$46
Tel: (614) 383-6771

L-K MOTEL
1838 Marion-Mt Gilead Rd (43302)
Rates: $34-$49
Tel: (614) 389-4651
(800) 282-5711

TRAVELODGE
1952 Marion-Mt Gilead Rd (43302)
Rates: $44-$76
Tel: (614) 389-4671
(800) 578-7878

MARYSVILLE

HOLIDAY INN
16510 Square Dr
(43040)
Rates: $41-$56
Tel: (513) 644-8821
(800) 848-5767

SUPER 8 MOTEL
10220 US 42 (43040)
Rates: $37-$58
Tel: (614) 873-4100
(800) 800-8000

MASON

**BEST WESTERN
KINGS ISLAND**
9847 Escort Dr
(45040)
Rates: $25-$150
Tel: (513) 398-3633
(800) 528-1234

**DAYS INN
KINGS ISLAND**
9735 Mason-
Montgomery Rd
(45040)
Rates: $36-$140
Tel: (513) 398-3297
(800) 329-7466

MAUMEE

COUNTRY INN
541 Dussel Dr
(43537)
Rates: $60-$110
Tel: (419) 893-8576
(800) 456-4000

DAYS INN
150 Dussel Dr
(43537)
Rates: $45-$59
Tel: (419) 893-9960
(800) 329-7466

KNIGHTS INN
1520 S Holland-
Sylvania Rd (43537)
Rates: $32-$51
Tel: (419) 865-1380
(800) 843-5644

RED ROOF INN
1570 Reynolds Rd
(43537)
Rates: $30-$48
Tel: (419) 893-0292
(800) 843-7663

**THARALDSON
INN & SUITES**
521 Dussel Dr
(43537)
Rates: $60-$110
Tel: (419) 897-0865

MAYFIELD HEIGHTS

BUDGETEL INN
1421 Golden Gate
Blvd (44124)
Rates: $49-$67
Tel: (216) 442-8400
(800) 428-3438

MENTOR

KNIGHTS INN
7677 Reynolds Rd
(44060)
Rates: $46-$66
Tel: (216) 946-0749
(800) 843-5644

KNIGHTS INN
8370 Broadmoor Rd
(44060)
Rates: $36-46
Tel: (216) 953-8835
(800) 843-5644

MIAMISBURG

MOTEL 6
8101 Springboro
Pike (45342)
Rates: $28-$41
Tel: (513) 434-8750
(800) 440-6000

RED ROOF INN
222 Byers Rd (45342)
Rates: $36-$55
Tel: (513) 866-0705
(800) 843-7663

**RESIDENCE INN
BY MARRIOTT**
155 Prestige Pl
(45342)
Rates: $110-$140
Tel: (513) 434-7881
(800) 331-3131

MIDDLEBURG HEIGHTS

MOTEL 6
7210 Engle Rd
(44130)
Rates: $29-$40
Tel: (216) 234-0990
(800) 440-6000

RED ROOF INN
17555 Bagley Rd
(44130)
Rates: $44-$76
Tel: (216) 243-2441
(800) 843-7663

**RESIDENCE INN
BY MARRIOTT**
17525 Rosbough Dr
(44130)
Rates: $129-$169
Tel: (216) 234-6688
(800) 331-3131

MIDDLETOWN

FAIRFIELD INN
6750 Roosevelt
Pkwy (45044)
Rates: $50-$125
Tel: (513) 424-5444
(800) 228-2800

MILAN

**COMFORT INN
CEDAR POINT**
11020 Milan Rd
(44846)
Rates: $46-$180
Tel: (419) 499-4681
(800) 221-2222

MONTPELIER

HOLIDAY INN
RR 3 (43543)
Rates: $63-$155
Tel: (419) 485-5555
(800) 465-4329

MORANE

**HOLIDAY INN-
SOUTH**
2455 Dryden Rd
(45439)
Rates: $75-$83
Tel: (513) 294-1471
(800) 465-4329

MOUNT GILEAD

DERRICK MOTEL
5898 SR 95 (43338)
Rates: $39-$50
Tel: (419) 946-6010

MOUNT VERNON

**CURTIS
MOTOR HOTEL**
6 Public Sq (43050)
Rates: $49-$56
Tel: (614) 397-4334
(800) 934-6835

**MOUNT VERNON
INN**
601 W High St
(43058)
Rates: $48-$78
Tel: (614) 392-9881

NAPOLEON

**PARAMOUNT
HOTEL**
P. O. Box 68 (43545)
Rates: $51-$57
Tel: (419) 592-5010

NEW PHILADELPHIA

HOLIDAY INN
131 Bluebell Dr
(44663)
Rates: $62-$100
Tel: (330) 339-7731
(800) 465-4329

MOTEL 6
181 Bluebell Dr
(44663)
Rates: $36-$42
Tel: (216) 339-6446
(800) 440-6000

TRAVEL LODGE
1256 W High Ave
(44663)
Rates: $40-$75
Tel: (330) 339-6671
(800) 578-7878

NEWARK

HOLIDAY INN
733 Hebron Rd
(43056)
Rates: $56-$64
Tel: (614) 522-1165
(800) 465-4329

HOWARD JOHNSON
775 Hebron Rd
(43055)
Rates: $46-$85
Tel: (614) 522-3191
(800) 446-4656

NORTH BALTIMORE

CROWN INN
P. O. Box 82 (45872)
Rates: $35-$40
Tel: (419) 257-3821

NORTH LIMA

ECONOMY INN
10145 Market St
(44452)
Rates: $30-$45
Tel: (330) 549-3224

NORTH RIDGEVILLE

TRAVELERS INN
32751 Lorain Rd
(44039)
Rates: $32-$62
Tel: (216) 327-6311

NORTHWOOD

COMFORT INN
2426 Oregon Rd
(43619)
Rates: $48-$86
Tel: (419) 666-2600
(800) 221-2222

NORWALK

L-K MOTEL
283 Benedict Ave
(44857)
Rates: $33-$68
Tel: (419) 668-8255
(800) 282-5711

OREGON

COMFORT INN EAST
2930 Navarre Ave
(43616)
Rates: $52-$79
Tel: (419) 691-8911
(800) 221-2222

ORRVILLE

ORRVILLE INN
10355 E Lincoln Way
(44667)
Rates: $32-$47
Tel: (330) 682-4080

OXFORD

COLLEGE VIEW MOTEL
4000 Oxford-Millville Rd (45056)
Rates: $32-$48
Tel: (513) 523-6311

SCOTTISH INNS
5235 College Corner Rd (45056)
Rates: $42-$52
Tel: (513) 523-6306
(800) 251-1962

PAINESVILLE

RIDER'S INN
792 Mentor Ave
(44077)
Rates: $75-$95
Tel: (216) 354-8200

PENINSULA

VIRGINIA MOTEL
5374 Akron-Cleveland Rd (44264)
Rates: $29-$50
Tel: (216) 650-0449

PERRYSBURG

DAYS INN
I-75 & US 20 (43551)
Rates: $45-$70
Tel: (419) 874-8771
(800) 329-7466

HOLIDAY INN
10621 Fremont Pike
(43551)
Rates: $65-$90
Tel: (419) 874-3101
(800) 465-4329

HOWARD JOHNSON
I-280 & Hanley Rd
(43551)
Rates: $33-$55
Tel: (419) 837-5245
(800) 446-4656

RED CARPET INN
26054 N Dixie Hwy
(43551)
Rates: n/a
Tel: (419) 872-2902
(800) 251-1962

PIQUA

COMFORT INN
987 E Ash St (45356)
Rates: $72-$102
Tel: (513) 778-8100
(800) 221-2222

HOWARD JOHNSON
902 Scot Dr (45356)
Rates: $29-$45
Tel: (513) 773-2314
(800) 446-4656

POLAND

FAIRFIELD INN
7397 S Tiffany (44514)
Rates: $60-$110
Tel: (330) 726-5979
(800) 228-2800

PORT CLINTON

L K INN
1811 E Perry St (43452)
Rates: $35-$100
Tel: (419) 732-2111
(800) 282-5711

PORTSMOUTH

HOLIDAY INN
P. O. Box 1190 (45662)
Rates: $55-$75
Tel: (614) 354-2851
(800) 465-4329

PUT-IN-BAY

PERRY HOLIDAY HOTEL
99 Concord Ave
(43456)
Rates: $65-$139
Tel: (419) 285-2107

REYNOLDS-BURG

BEST WESTERN COLUMBUS EAST
2100 Brice Rd
(43068)
Rates: $57-$64
Tel: (614) 864-1280
(800) 528-1234

LA QUINTA INN
2447 Brice Rd
(43068)
Rates: $45-$56
Tel: (614) 866-6456
(800) 531-5900

LENOX INN
P. O. Box 346 (43068)
Rates: $46-$66
Tel: (614) 861-7800

RED ROOF INN
2449 Brice Rd
(43068)
Rates: $26-$64
Tel: (614) 864-3683
(800) 843-7663

RICHFIELD

HOWARD JOHNSON
5171 Brecksville Rd
(44286)
Rates: $60-$90
Tel: (216) 659-6116
(800) 446-4656

RIO GRANDE

COLLEGE HILL MOTEL
10987 SR 588 (45674)
Rates: $32-$41
Tel: (614) 245-5326

ROSSFORD

KNIGHTS INN
1120 Buck Rd
(43460)
Rates: n/a
Tel: (800) 843-5644

ST. CLAIRSVILLE

FISCHER MOTEL
P. O. Box 63 (43950)
Rates: $28-$35
Tel: (614) 782-1715

KNIGHTS INN
51260 National Rd
(43950)
Rates: $30-$46
Tel: (614) 695-5038
(800) 843-5644

RED ROOF INN
68301 Red Roof Ln
(43950)
Rates: $30-$48
Tel: (614) 695-4057
(800) 843-7663

SUPER 8 MOTEL
68400 Matthews Dr
(43950)
Rates: $37-$59
Tel: (614) 695-1994
(800) 800-8000

TWIN PINES MOTEL
46079 National Rd
(43950)
Rates: n/a
Tel: (614) 695-3720

ST. MARYS

**S & W MOTEL
& SUITES**
1321 Celina Rd
(45885)
Rates: $49-$66
Tel: (419) 394-2341

SANDUSKY

AMERIHOST INN
1726 E Wyandot Ave
(Upper Sandusky
43351)
Rates: $48-$85
Tel: (419) 294-3919

BEST BUDGET INN
5918 Milan Rd
(44870)
Rates: $32-$118
Tel: (419) 625-7252

BEST WESTERN INN
1530 Cleveland Rd
(44870)
Rates: $49-$299
Tel: (419) 625-9234
(800) 528-1234

MECCA MOTEL
2227 Cleveland Rd
(44870)
Rates: $45-$99
Tel: (419) 626-1284
(800) 986-3222

**RADISSON
HARBOUR INN**
2001 ClevelandRd
(44870)
Rates: $99-$199
Tel: (419) 627-2500
(800) 333-3333

RODEWAY INN
2905 Milan Rd
(44870)
Rates: $32-$198
Tel: (419) 625-1291
(800) 424-4777

SHERATON INN
1119 Sandusky Mall
Blvd (44870)
Rates: $50-$120
Tel: (419) 625-6280
(800) 837-8886

SEAMAN

RODEWAY INN
55 Stern Dr.
P.O. Box 276 (45679)
Rates: $40-$65
Tel: (513) 386-2511
(800) 228-2000

SEVILLE

HOWARD JOHNSON
I-71 & I-76 (44273)
Rates: $30-$39
Tel: (216) 769-2053
(800) 446-4656

SHARONVILLE

HOLIDAY INN
3855 Hauck Rd
(45241)
Rates: $89-$129
Tel: (513) 563-8330
(800) 465-4329

**HOMEWOOD
SUITES-NORTH**
2670 E Kemper Rd
(45241)
Rates: $89-$115
Tel: (513) 772-8888
(800) 225-5466

MARRIOTT HOTEL
11320 Chester Rd
(45246)
Rates: $85-$125
Tel: (513) 772-1720
(800) 228-9290

MOTEL 6-EAST
3850 Hauck Rd
(45241)
Rates: $23-$47
Tel: (513) 563-1123
(800) 440-6000

MOTEL 6-WEST
2000 E Kemper Rd
(45241)
Rates: $25-$36
Tel: (513) 772-5944
(800) 440-6000

RED ROOF INN
2301 E Sharon Rd
(45241)
Rates: $25-$59
Tel: (800) 843-7663

SHELBY

**LODGE KEEPER
MOTEL**
178 Mansfield Ave
(44875)
Rates: n/a
Tel: (419) 347-2141
(800) 282-5711

SIDNEY

ECONO LODGE
2009 W Michigan St
(45365)
Rates: $36-$40
Tel: (513) 492-9164
(800) 424-4777

HOLIDAY INN
400 Folkerth Ave
(45365)
Rates: $57-$67
Tel: (513) 492-1131
(800) 465-4329

SOUTH POINT

**BEST WESTERN-
SOUTHERN HILLS
INN**
803 Solida Rd
(45680)
Rates: $48-$66
Tel: (614) 894-3391
(800) 528-1234

SPRINGDALE

BUDGETEL INN
12150 Springfield
Pike (45246)
Rates: $42-$53
Tel: (513) 671-2300
(800) 428-3438

SHERATON HOTEL
11911 Sheraton Ln
(45246)
Rates: $95-$160
Tel: (513) 671-6600
(800) 325-3535

SPRINGFIELD

**FAIRFIELD INN
BY MARRIOTT**
1870 W 1st St (45504)
Rates: $61-$77
Tel: (513) 323-9554
(800) 228-2800

RAMADA LIMITED
319 E Leffel Ln
(45505)
Rates: $49-$125
Tel: (513) 328-0123
(800) 272-6232

TOWNHOUSE MOTOR LODGE
2850 E Main St
(45503)
Rates: $36-$44
Tel: (513) 325-7661
(800) 561-2819

STEUBENVILLE

HOLIDAY INN
1401 University Blvd
(43952)
Rates: $52-$58
Tel: (614) 282-0901
(800) 465-4329

STOW

STOW INN
4601 Darrow Rd
(44224)
Rates: $50-$81
Tel: (216) 688-3508

STRONGSVILLE

DAYS INN
9029 Pearl Rd (44136)
Rates: $32-$50
Tel: (216) 234-3575
(800) 329-7466

RED ROOF INN
15385 Royalton Rd
(44136)
Rates: $35-$60
Tel: (216) 238-0170
(800) 843-7663

TIFFIN

TIFFIN MOTEL
315 West Market St
(44883)
Rates: n/a
Tel: (419) 447-7411

TOLEDO

BUDGET INN
2450 S Reynolds Rd
(43614)
Rates: $31-$41
Tel: (419) 865-0201

CLARION INN
3536 Secor Rd (43606)
Rates: $69-$180
Tel: (419) 535-7070
(800) 221-2222

COMFORT INN
3560 Secor Rd
(43606)
Rates: $45-$53
Tel: (419) 531-2666
(800) 221-2222

CROWN INN
1727 W Alexis Rd
(43613)
Rates: $38-$49
Tel: (419) 473-1485

MOTEL 6
5335 Heatherdowns
Blvd (43614)
Rates: $30-$36
Tel: (419) 865-2308
(800) 440-6000

RADISSON HOTEL
101 N Summit St
(43604)
Rates: $79-$119
Tel: (419) 241-3000
(800) 333-3333

RAMADA INN & CONF CTR
2429 S Reynolds Rd
(43614)
Rates: $70-$125
Tel: (419) 381-8765
(800) 272-6232

RED ROOF INN SECOR
3530 Executive
Pkwy (43606)
Rates: $26-$47
Tel: (419) 536-0118
(800) 843-7663

TROY

HAMPTON INN
45 Troy Town Dr.
(45373)
Rates: $55-$64
Tel: (513) 339-7801
(800) 426-7866

HOLIDAY INN
1375 SR 55 (45373)
Rates: $61-$73
Tel: (513) 335-0021
(800) 465-4329

KNIGHTS INN
30 Troy Town Dr
(45373)
Rates: $40-$54
Tel: (513) 339-1515
(800) 843-5644

MOTEL 6
1210 Brukner Dr
(45373)
Rates: $28-$30
Tel: (513) 335-0013
(800) 440-6000

TWINSBURG

SUPER 8 MOTEL
8848 Twin Hills Dr
(44087)
Rates: $43-$69
Tel: (216) 425-2889
(800) 800-8000

URBANA

LOGAN LODGE MOTEL
2551 SR 68 (43078)
Rates: $50-$60
Tel: (513) 652-2188

VAN WERT

DAYS INN
820 N Washington St
(45891)
Rates: $38-$90
Tel: (419) 238-5222
(800) 329-7466

LODGE KEEPER INN
875 N Washington St
(45891)
Rates: n/a
Tel: (419) 238-3700
(800) 282-5711

VANDALIA

PARK INN
75 Corporate Center
Dr (45377)
Rates: $46-$80
Tel: (513) 898-8321
(800) 437-7275

WADSWORTH

KNIGHTS INN
810 High St (44281)
Rates: $45-$60
Tel: (330) 336-6671
(800) 843-5644

WAPAKONETA

DAYS INN
1659 Bellefontaine St
(45895)
Rates: $32-$57
Tel: (419) 738-2184
(800) 329-7466

HOLIDAY INN
Box 1980 (45895)
Rates: $58-$68
Tel: (419) 738-8181
(800) 465-4329

SUPER 8 MOTEL
511 Lunar Dr (45895)
Rates: $40-$45
Tel: (419) 738-8810
(800) 800-8000

WARREN

BEST WESTERN INN
777 Mahoning Ave
NW (44483)
Rates: $53-$73
Tel: (216) 392-2515
(800) 528-1234

PARK HOTEL
136 N Park Ave
(44481)
Rates: $60-$70
Tel: (216) 393-1200

WASHINGTON COURT HOUSE

KNIGHTS INN
1820 Columbus Ave
(43160)
Rates: $42-$50
Tel: (614) 335-9133
(800) 843-5644

WAUSEON

ARROWHEAD MOTEL
8225 SR 108 (43567)
Rates: $36-$58
Tel: (419) 335-5811

WESTERVILLE

CORNELIA'S CORNER B & B
93 W College Ave (43081)
Rates: $60-$85
Tel: (614) 882-2678
(800) 745-2678

KNIGHTS INN
32 Heatherdown Dr (43081)
Rates: $40-$135
Tel: (614) 890-0426
(800) 843-5644

WESTLAKE

RED ROOF INN
29595 Clements Rd (44145)
Rates: $38-$63
Tel: (216) 892-7920
(800) 843-7663

RESIDENCE INN BY MARRIOTT
30100 Clemens Rd (44145)
Rates: $139-$169
Tel: (216) 892-2254
(800) 331-3131

WHITEHALL

QUALITY INN
4801 E Broad St (43213)
Rates: $39-$70
Tel: (614) 861-0321
(800) 221-2222

WICKLIFFE

PLAZA MOTEL
29152 Euclid Ave (44092)
Rates: $35-$42
Tel: (216) 943-0546
(800) 582-0843

WILLARD

LODGE KEEPER INN
117 E Walton (44890)
Rates: n/a
Tel: (419) 935-6321
(800) 282-5711

WILLOUGHBY

RED ROOF INN
4166 SR 306 (44094)
Rates: $40-$64
Tel: (216) 946-9872
(800) 843-7663

WILMINGTON

L-K MOTEL
264 W Curry Rd (45177)
Rates: $39-$59
Tel: (513) 382-6605
(800) 282-5711

WOOSTER

ECONO LODGE
2137 E Lincoln Way (44691)
Rates: $39-$54
Tel: (330) 264-8883
(800) 424-4777

THE WOOSTER INN
801 E Wayne Ave (44691)
Rates: $60-$120
Tel: (330) 264-2341

XENIA

BEST WESTERN REGENCY INN
600 Little Main St (45385)
Rates: $37-$49
Tel: (513) 372-9954
(800) 528-1234

YOUNGSTOWN

BEST WESTERN MEANDER INN
870 N Canfield-Niles Rd (44515)
Rates: $54-$75
Tel: (330) 544-2378
(800) 528-1234

DAYS INN
8392 Market St (44512)
Rates: $38-$75
Tel: (330) 758-2371
(800) 329-7466

SUPER 8 MOTEL
4250 Belmont Ave (44505)
Rates: $42-$54
Tel: (330) 793-7788
(800) 800-8000

WAGON WHEEL MOTEL
7015 Market St (44512)
Rates: $30-$55
Tel: (216) 758-4551

ZANESVILLE

FAIRFIELD INN
725 Zane St (43701)
Rates: $59-$69
Tel: (614) 453-8770
(800) 228-2800

HOLIDAY INN
4645 E Pike (43701)
Rates: $56-$99
Tel: (614) 453-0771
(800) 465-4329

SUPER 8 MOTEL
2440 National Rd (43701)
Rates: $50-$62
Tel: (614) 455-3124
(800) 800-8000

OKLAHOMA

ALTUS

DAYS INN
3202 N Main St
(73521)
Rates: $31-$39
Tel: (405) 477-2300
(800) 329-7466

RAMADA INN
2515 E Broadway
(73521)
Rates: $45-$76
Tel: (405) 477-3000
(800) 272-6232

ALVA

RANGER INN MOTEL
420 E Oklahoma Blvd (73717)
Rates: $26-$32
Tel: (405) 327-1981

WHARTON'S VISTA MOTEL
1330 W Oklahoma Blvd (73717)
Rates: $20-$29
Tel: (405) 327-3232

ANDARKO

ANDARKO MOTEL
1301 E Central (73006)
Rates: $24-$39
Tel: (405) 247-3315

ARDMORE

BEST WESTERN INN
6 Holiday Dr (73401)
Rates: $48-$81
Tel: (405) 223-7525
(800) 528-1234

COMFORT INN
2700 W Broadway (73401)
Rates: $49-$82
Tel: (405) 226-1250
(800) 221-2222

DAYS INN
2432 Veterans Blvd (73401)
Rates: $36-$60
Tel: (405) 223-7976
(800) 329-7466

HOLIDAY INN
2705 Holiday Dr (73401)
Rates: $53-$58
Tel: (405) 223-7130
(800) 465-4329

MOTEL 6
120 Holiday Dr (73401)
Rates: $26-$32
Tel: (405) 226-7666
(800) 440-6000

SUPER 8 MOTEL
2120 Veterans Blvd (73401)
Rates: $33-$43
Tel: (405) 223-2201
(800) 800-8000

ATOKA

BEST WESTERN INN
2101 S Mississippi (74525)
Rates: $45-$75
Tel: (405) 889-7381
(800) 528-1234

BARTLESVILLE

BEST WESTERN WESTON INN
222 SE Washington Blvd (74006)
Rates: $44-$99
Tel: (918) 335-7755
(800) 528-1234

HOLIDAY INN
1410 SE Washington Blvd (74006)
Rates: $48-$55
Tel: (918) 333-8320
(800) 465-4329

SUPER 8 MOTEL
211 SE Washington Blvd (74006)
Rates: $42-50
Tel: (918) 335-1122
(800) 800-8000

BLACKWELL

DAYS INN
4302 W Doolin (74631)
Rates: $33-$37
Tel: (405) 363-2911
(800) 329-7466

BOISE CITY

TOWNSMAN MOTEL
1205 E Main (73933)
Rates: $27-$35
Tel: (405) 544-2506

BROKEN ARROW

ECONO LODGE
1401 N Elm Pl (74012)
Rates: $39-$50
Tel: (918) 258-6617
(800) 424-4777

STRATFORD HOUSE INN
1301 N Elm Pl (74012)
Rates: $29-$34
Tel: (918) 258-7556

BROKEN BOW

CHARLES WESLEY MOTOR LODGE
302 N Park Dr (74728)
Rates: $30-$37
Tel: (405) 584-3303

END OF TRAIL MOTEL
11 N Park Dr (74728)
Rates: n/a
Tel: (405) 584-3350

CATOOSA

TRAVELERS INN
19250 Timbercrest Cir (74015)
Rates: $19-$35
Tel: (918) 266-7000

CHANDLER

ECONO LODGE
600 N Price (74834)
Rates: $36-$45
Tel: (405) 258-2131
(800) 424-4777

CHECOTAH

BEST WESTERN LA DONNA INN
P. O. Box 427 (74426)
Rates: $36-$60
Tel: (918) 473-2376
(800) 528-1234

I-40 INN
Old 69 Hwy & I-40 (74426)
Rates: n/a
Tel: (918) 473-2331

SHARPE HOUSE B & B
301 NW 2nd (74426)
Rates: $35-$50
Tel: (918) 473-2832

CHICKASHA

BEST WESTERN INN
2101 S 4th (73018)
Rates: $37-$53
Tel: (405) 224-4890
(800) 528-1234

DAYS INN
2701 S 4th St (73018)
Rates: $37-$47
Tel: (405) 222-5800
(800) 329-7466

SUPER 8 MOTEL
2728 S 4th St (73018)
Rates: $32-$45
Tel: (405) 222-3710
(800) 800-8000

CLAREMORE

**BEST WESTERN
WILL ROGERS INN**
940 S Lynn Riggs
Blvd (74017)
Rates: $41-$56
Tel: (918) 341-4410
(800) 528-1234

DAYS INN
Hwy 66 & Country
Club Dr (74017)
Rates: $45-$54
Tel: (918) 343-3297
(800) 329-7466

MOTEL CLAREMORE
812 E Will Rogers
Blvd (74017)
Rates: $35-$43
Tel: (918) 341-3254

CLINTON

**BEST WESTERN
TRADE WINDS INN**
2128 Gary Blvd
(73601)
Rates: $37-$80
Tel: (405) 323-2610
(800) 528-1234

BUDGET HOST INN
1413 Neptune Dr
(73601)
Rates: $16-$26
Tel: (800) 283-4678

PARK INN INTL
2140 Gary Blvd
(73601)
Rates: $28-$38
Tel: (405) 323-2010

RELAX INN
1116 S 10th St
(73601)
Rates: $20-$24
Tel: (405) 323-1888

DEL CITY

LA QUINTA INN
5501 Tinker
Diagonal (73115)
Rates: $47-$62
Tel: (405) 672-0067
(800) 531-5900

DUNCAN

DUNCAN INN
3402 N US 81 (73533)
Rates: $25-$36
Tel: (405) 252-5210

HILLCREST MOTEL
1417 S 81 Bypass
(73533)
Rates: $18-$20
Tel: (405) 255-1640

HOLIDAY INN
1015 N US 81
(73533)
Rates: $43-$53
Tel: (800) 465-4329

DURANT

**BEST WESTERN
MARKITA INN**
2401 W Main (74701)
Rates: $40-$100
Tel: (405) 924-7676
(800) 528-1234

DURANT INN
2121 W Main St
(74701)
Rates: $26-$35
Tel: (405) 924-5432

EDMOND

SEASONS INN
1005 Waterwood
Pkwy (73034)
Rates: $55-$150
Tel: (800) 322-4686

EL RENO

BEST WESTERN INN
I-40 & Country Club
Rd (73036)
Rates: $38-$57
Tel: (405) 262-6490
(800) 528-1234

DAYS INN
2700 S Country Club
Rd (73036)
Rates: $37-$45
Tel: (405) 262-8720
(800) 329-7466

RAMADA LIMITED
2851 Hwy 81 S
(73036)
Rates: $32-$58
Tel: (405) 262-1022
(800) 272-6232

RED CARPET INN
2640 S Country Club
Rd (73036)
Rates: $26-$32
Tel: (405) 262-1526
(800) 251-1962

SUPER 8 MOTEL
2820 Hwy 81 S
(73036)
Rates: $35-$47
Tel: (405) 262-8240
(800) 800-8000

ELK CITY

**BEST WESTERN
ELK CITY INN**
2015 W 3rd St
(73644)
Rates: $32-$48
Tel: (405) 225-2331
(800) 528-1234

DAYS INN
1100 Hwy 34 (73644)
Rates: $35-$75
Tel: (405) 225-9210
(800) 329-7466

ECONO LODGE
108 Meadow Ridge
(73644)
Rates: $33-$51
Tel: (405) 225-5120
(800) 424-4777

FLAMINGO INN
2000 W 3rd St
(73644)
Rates: $26-$40
Tel: (405) 225-1811

HOJO INN
2604 E Hwy 66
(73644)
Rates: $28-$39
Tel: (405) 225-2241
(800) 446-4656

HOLIDAY INN
P. O. Box 782 (73648)
Rates: $54-$67
Tel: (405) 225-6637
(800) 465-4329

MOTEL 6
2500 E Hwy 66
(73644)
Rates: $23-$29
Tel: (405) 225-6661
(800) 440-6000

QUALITY INN
P.O. Box 1025
(73644)
Rates: $30-$42
Tel: (405) 225-8140
(800) 221-2222

SUPER 8 MOTEL
2801 E Hwy 66
(73644)
Rates: $30-$46
Tel: (405) 225-9430
(800) 800-8000

TRAVELODGE
301 Sleepy Hollow
Ct (73644)
Rates: $27-$45
Tel: (405) 243-0150
(800) 578-7878

ENID

ECONO LODGE
2523 Mercer Rd
(73701)
Rates: $31-$43
Tel: (405) 237-3090
(800) 424-4777

HOLIDAY INN
2901 S Van Buren
(73703)
Rates: $34-$41
Tel: (800) 465-4329

RAMADA INN
3005 W Garriot Rd
(73703)
Rates: $45-$59
Tel: (405) 234-0440
(800) 272-6232

ERICK

COMFORT INN
P. O. Box 35 (73645)
Rates: $49-$69
Tel: (405) 526-3553
(800) 221-2222

DAYS INN
I-40 & Hwy 30
(73645)
Rates: $39-$52
Tel: (405) 526-3315
(800) 329-7466

EUFAULA

DAYS INN
Rt 2, Box 1199
(74426)
Rates: $35-$50
Tel: (918) 689-3999
(800) 329-7466

FREDERICK

SCOTTISH INNS
1015 S Main St
(73542)
Rates: $25-$32
Tel: (405) 335-2129
(800) 251-1962

GLENPOOL

BEST WESTERN INN
14831 S Casper St
(74033)
Rates: $45-$63
Tel: (405) 282-8831
(800) 528-1234

GUTHRIE

**BEST WESTERN
TERRITORIAL INN**
2323 Territorial Tr
(73044)
Rates: $40-$58
Tel: (405) 282-8831
(800) 528-1234

**HARRISON HOUSE
INN**
124 West Harrison
(73044)
Rates: $52-$87
Tel: (405) 282-1000
(800) 375-1001

**TOWN HOUSE
MOTEL**
221 E Oklahoma Ave
(73044)
Rates: $27-$39
Tel: (405) 282-2000

GUYMON

AMBASSADOR INN
P. O. Box 5 (73942)
Rates: $41-$50
Tel: (405) 338-5555

**BEST WESTERN
TOWNSMAN INN**
P. O. Box 159 (73942)
Rates: $40-$125
Tel: (405) 338-6556
(800) 528-1234

ECONO LODGE
923 Hwy 54 E (73942)
Rates: $37-$54
Tel: (405) 338-5431
(800) 424-4777

SUPER 8 MOTEL
1201 Hwy 54 E (73942)
Rates: $40-$56
Tel: (405) 338-0507
(800) 800-8000

HENRYETTA

HOJO INN
Hwy 75 & Trudgeon
St (74430)
Rates: $35-$45
Tel: (918) 652-4448
(800) 446-4656

LE BARON MOTEL
Rt 2, Box 170 (74437)
Rates: $28-$35
Tel: (918) 652-2531

HOOKER

SUNSET MOTEL
710 Hwy 54 (73945)
Rates: $23-$30
Tel: (405) 652-3250

KINGSTON

**LAKE TEXOMA
RESORT**
P. O. Box 41 (73439)
Rates: $62-$96
Tel: (800) 654-8240

LAWTON

**BEST WESTERN
SANDPIPER INN**
2202 N Hwy 277
(73507)
Rates: $36-$50
Tel: (405) 353-0310
(800) 528-1234

EXECUTIVE INN
3110 Cache Rd
(73505)
Rates: $39-$48
Tel: (405) 353-3104

HOSPITALITY INN
202 E Lee Blvd
(73501)
Rates: $33-$40
Tel: (405) 355-9765

HOWARD JOHNSON
1125 E Gore Blvd
(73501)
Rates: $46-$61
Tel: (405) 353-0200
(800) 446-4656

LONE WOLF

**QUARTZ
MOUNTAIN RESORT**
Rt 1 (73655)
Rates: $50-$88
Tel: (800) 654-8240

McALESTER

COMFORT INN
1215 George Nigh
Expwy (74502)
Rates: $40-$53
Tel: (918) 426-0115
(800) 221-2222

DAYS INN
1217 George Nigh
Expwy (74501)
Rates: $44-$64
Tel: (918) 426-5050
(800) 329-7466

HOLIDAY INN
1500 George Nigh
Expwy (74501)
Rates: $43-$50
Tel: (800) 465-4329

SUPER 8 MOTEL
2400 S Main Bus 69
(74501)
Rates: $33-$52
Tel: (918) 426-5400
(800) 800-8000

MIAMI

BEST WESTERN INN
2225 E Steve Owens
Blvd (74354)
Rates: $44-$64
Tel: (918) 542-6681
(800) 528-1234

MIDWEST CITY

COMFORT INN
5653 Tinker
Diagonal (73110)
Rates: $54-$66
Tel: (405) 733-1339
(800) 221-2222

HAMPTON INN
1833 Center Dr
(73110)
Rates: $63-$72
Tel: (405) 732-5500
(800) 426-7866

HOLIDAY INN-EAST
5701 Tinker
Diagonal (73110)
Rates: $56-$70
Tel: (405) 737-4481
(800) 465-4329

MOTEL 6
6166 Tinker
Diagonal (73110)
Rates: $32-$38
Tel: (405) 737-6676
(800) 466-8356

SUPER 8 MOTEL
6821 SE 29th St
(73110)
Rates: $35-$50
Tel: (405) 737-8880
(800) 800-8000

MOORE

**BEST WESTERN
CROSSROADS INN**
2600 N
Broadway(73160)
Rates: $42-$56
Tel: (405) 794-6611
(800) 528-1234

DAYS INN
1701 N Moore Ave
(73160)
Rates: $30-$60
Tel: (405) 794-5070
(800) 329-7466

MOTEL 6
1417 N Moore Ave
(73160)
Rates: $24-$28
Tel: (405) 799-6616
(800) 466-8356

SUPER 8 MOTEL
1520 N Moore Ave
(73160)
Rates: $40-$53
Tel: (405) 794-4030
(800) 800-8000

MUSKOGEE

**BEST WESTERN
TRADE WINDS INN**
534 S 32nd St (74401)
Rates: $42-$70
Tel: (918) 683-2951
(800) 528-1234

DAYS INN
900 S 32nd St (74401)
Rates: $38-$46
Tel: (918) 683-3911
(800) 329-7466

ECONO LODGE
2018 W Shawnee
Ave (74401)
Rates: $35-$60
Tel: (800) 424-4777

MOTEL 6
903 S 32nd St (74401)
Rates: $27-$33
Tel: (918) 683-8369
(800) 440-6000

QUALITY INN
2300 E Shawnee
(74403)
Rates: $36-$46
Tel: (918) 683-6551
(800) 221-2222

RAMADA INN
800 S 32nd St (74401)
Rates: $48-$135
Tel: (918) 682-4341
(800) 272-6232

NORMAN

DAYS INN
609 N Interstate Dr
(73069)
Rates: $40-$55
Tel: (405) 360-4380
(800) 329-7466

**RESIDENCE INN
BY MARRIOTT**
2681 Jefferson St
(73072)
Rates: $83-$115
Tel: (405) 366-0900
(800) 331-3131

**THE STRATFORD
HOUSE INN**
225 N Interstate Dr
(73069)
Rates: $34-$42
Tel: (405) 329-7194

OKLAHOMA CITY

APPLETREE SUITES
6022 1/2 NW 23rd
(73127)
Rates: $33-$44
Tel: (405) 495-3881

CARLYLE MOTEL
3600 NW 29th
Expwy (73112)
Rates: $28-$40
Tel: (405) 946-3355

**CENTURY CENTER
HOTEL**
1 N Broadway
(73102)
Rate: $109-$500
Tel: (800) 285-2780

CLARION INN
4445 N Lincoln Blvd
(73105)
Rates: $92-$106
Tel: (405) 528-2741
(800) 221-2222

COMFORT INN
4017 NW 39th
Expwy (73112)
Rates: $44-$85
Tel: (405) 947-0038
(800) 221-2222

COMFORT INN-SW
7800 C A Henderson
Blvd (73139)
Rates: $40-$58
Tel: (800) 221-2222

DAYS INN
122 Second St
(73131)
Rates: $41-$65
Tel: (800) 329-7466

DAYS INN AIRPORT
4712 W I-40 (73128)
Rates: $39-$50
Tel: (405) 947-8721
(800) 329-7466

DAYS INN NW
2801 NW 39th St
(73112)
Rates: $39-$65
Tel: (405) 946-0741
(800) 329-7466

DAYS INN SOUTH
2616 I-35 S (73129)
Rates: $41-$175
Tel: (405) 677-0521
(800) 329-7466

ECONO LODGE
8200 W I-40 (73128)
Rates: $30-$45
Tel: (405) 787-7051
(800) 424-4777

ECONO LODGE
820 S MacArthur
Blvd (73128)
Rates: $30-$45
Tel: (405) 947-8651
(800) 424-4777

EMBASSY SUITES
1815 S Meridian Ave
(73108)
Rates: $98-$125
Tel: (405) 682-6000
(800) 362-2779

**GOVERNORS
SUITES HOTEL**
2308 S Meridian Ave
(73108)
Rates: $54-$65
Tel: (405) 682-5299

HAMPTON INN
13500 Plaza Terrace
(73120)
Rates: $84-$100
Tel: (405) 752-7070
(800) 426-7866

HOLIDAY INN-N
12001 NE Expwy
(73131)
Rates: $60-$65
Tel: (405) 478-0400
(800) 465-4329

HOLIDAY INN-NW
3535 NW 39th
Expwy (73112)
Rates: $49-$56
Tel: (405) 947-2351
(800) 465-4329

HOLIDAY INN
801 S Meridian Ave
(73108)
Rates: $59-$76
Tel: (405) 942-8544
(800) 465-4329

HOWARD JOHNSON
1629 S Prospect
(73129)
Rates: $42-$58
Tel: (405) 677-0551
(800) 446-4656

HOWARD JOHNSON
400 S Meridian Ave
(73108)
Rates: $49-$65
Tel: (405) 943-9841
(800) 446-4656

**LA QUINTA INN-
SOUTH**
8315 I-35 S (73149)
Rates: $48-$64
Tel: (405) 631-8661
(800) 531-5900

MARRIOTT HOTEL
3233 NW Expwy
(73112)
Rates: $139-$145
Tel: (405) 842-6633
(800) 228-9290

MOTEL 6
12121 NE Expwy
(73131)
Rates: $28-$34
Tel: (405) 478-4030
(800) 440-6000

MOTEL 6-AIRPORT
820 S Meridian Ave
(73108)
Rates: $32-$38
Tel: (405) 946-6662
(800) 440-6000

MOTEL 6-NORTH
11900 NE Expwy
(73131)
Rates: $26-$32
Tel: (405) 478-8666
(800) 440-6000

MOTEL 6-WEST
4200 I-40 W (73108)
Rates: $30-$36
Tel: (405) 947-6550
(800) 440-6000

RADISSON INN
401 S Meridian Ave
(73108)
Rates: $59-$190
Tel: (800) 333-3333

RAMADA LIMITED
3709 NW 39th
Expwy (73112)
Rates: $38-$40
Tel: (405) 942-7730
(800) 272-6232

**RAMADA INN
AIRPORT S**
6800 I-35 S (73149)
Rates: $53-$64
Tel: (405) 631-3321
(800) 272-6232

RAMADA LIMITED 2
1400 63rd St (73111)
Rates: $45-$55
Tel: (405) 478-5221
(800) 272-6232

RED CARPET INN
8217 S I-35 (73149)
Rates: $21-$39
Tel: (405) 632-0807
(800) 251-1962

**RESIDENCE INN
BY MARRIOTT**
4361 W Reno (73107)
Rates: $95-$115
Tel: (405) 942-4500
(800) 331-3131

RICHMOND SUITES
1600 NW Expwy
(73118)
Rates: $72-$129
Tel: (405) 840-1440
(800) 843-1440

RODEWAY INN
4601 SW 3rd (73128)
Rates: $40-$65
Tel: (405) 947-2400
(800) 228-2000

SOUTHGATE INN
5245 S I-35 (73129)
Rates: n/a
Tel: (405) 672-5561

OKMULGEE

BEST WESTERN INN
3499 N Wood Dr
(74447)
Rates: $50-$95
Tel: (918) 756-9200
(800) 528-1234

DAYS INN
1221 S Wood Dr
(74447)
Rates: $38-$42
Tel: (918) 758-0660
(800) 329-7466

PAULS VALLEY

DAYS INN
Rt 3, Box 295-C
(73075)
Rates: $38-$58
Tel: (405) 238-7548
(800) 329-7466

**GARDEN INN
MOTEL**
P. O. Box 931 (73075)
Rates: $22-$31
Tel: (405) 238-7313

PERRY

**BEST WESTERN
CHEROKEE STRIP
MOTEL**
P. O. Box 529 (73077)
Rates: $45-$57
Tel: (405) 336-2218
(800) 528-1234

DAN-D-MOTEL
515 Fir St (73077)
Rates: $18-$24
Tel: (405) 336-4463

**FIRST INTERSTATE
INN**
P. O. Box 833 (73077)
Rates: $27-$32
Tel: (405) 336-2277

PONCA CITY

DAYS INN
1415 E Bradley
(74604)
Rates: $34-$46
Tel: (405) 767-1406
(800) 329-7466

POTEAU

**BEST WESTERN
TRADERS INN**
3111 N Broadway
(74953)
Rates: $40-$50
Tel: (918) 647-4001
(800) 528-1234

PRYOR

DAYS INN
Hwy 69 S & 69A
(74362)
Rates: $40-$55
Tel: (918) 825-7600
(800) 329-7466

HOLIDAY MOTEL
701 S Mill (74361)
Rates: $25-$39
Tel: (918) 825-1204

**PRYOR HOUSE
MOTOR INN**
123 S Mill (74361)
Rates: $32-$42
Tel: (918) 825-6677

PURCELL

ECONO LODGE
2500 Hwy 74 S
(73080)
Rates: $37-$50
Tel: (405) 527-5603
(800) 424-4777

SALLISAW

**BEST WESTERN
MOTOR INN**
706 S Kerr
(74955)
Rates: $35-$55
Tel: (918) 775-6294
(800) 528-1234

DAYS INN
Rt 2, Box 13 (74955)
Rates: $38-$60
Tel: (918) 775-4406
(800) 329-7466

ECONO LODGE
2403 E Cherokee
(74955)
Rates: $36-$45
Tel: (918) 775-7981
(800) 424-4777

GOLDEN SPUR INN
P. O. Box 828 (74955)
Rates: $26-$34
Tel: (918) 775-4443

MCKNIGHT MOTEL
1611 W Ruth St
(74955)
Rates: $30-$49
Tel: (800) 842-9442

RAMADA LIMITED
1300 E Cherokee
(74955)
Rates: $42-$48
Tel: (918) 775-7791
(800) 272-6232

SUPER 8 MOTEL
924 S Kerr (74955)
Rates: $33-$43
Tel: (918) 775-8900
(800) 800-8000

SAPULPA

SUPER 8 MOTEL
1505 New Sapulpa
Rd (74066)
Rates: $35-$48
Tel: (918) 227-3300
(800) 800-8000

SAVANNA

**BUDGET HOST
COLONIAL INN**
P. O. Box 323 (74565)
Rates: $22-$27
Tel: (800) 283-4678

SHAWNEE

**BEST WESTERN
CINDERELLA
MOTOR INN**
623 Kickapoo Spur
(74801)
Rates: $49-$72
Tel: (405) 273-7010
(800) 528-1234

HAMPTON INN
4851 N. Kickapoo
(49036)
Rates: $55-$69
Tel: (405) 275-1540
(800) 426-7866

MOTEL 6
4981 N Harrison St
(74801)
Rates: $30-$36
Tel: (405) 275-5310
(800) 440-6000

RODEWAY INN
12510 Valley View
Rd (74801)
Rates: $31-$40
Tel: (405) 275-1005
(800) 228-2000

STILLWATER

BEST WESTERN INN
600 E McElroy
(74075)
Rates: $45-$100
Tel: (405) 377-7010
(800) 528-1234

DAYS INN
5010 W 6th
(74074)
Rates: $32-$59
Tel: (405) 743-2570
(800) 329-7466

HOLIDAY INN
2515 W 6th
(74074)
Rates: $45-$62
Tel: (405) 372-0800
(800) 465-4329

MOTEL 6
5122 W 6th
(74074)
Rates: $25-$31
Tel: (405) 624-0433
(800) 440-6000

STROUD

BEST WESTERN INN
1200 N 8th Ave
(74079)
Rates: $47-$60
Tel: (918) 968-9515
(800) 528-1234

SULPHUR

SUPER 8 MOTEL
2110 W Broadway
(73086)
Rates: $36-$46
Tel: (405) 622-6500
(800) 800-8000

TAHLEQUAH

**TAHLEQUAH
MOTOR LODGE**
2501 S Muskogee
(74464)
Rates: $34-$52
Tel: (918) 456-2350

TONKAWA

WESTERN INN
Rt 1, Box 130 (74653)
Rates: $34-$44
Tel: (405) 628-2577

TULSA

**BEST WESTERN
TRADEWINDS
CENTRAL INN**
3141 E Skelly Dr
(74105)
Rates: $62-$90
Tel: (918) 749-5561
(800) 528-1234

**BEST WESTERN
TRADEWINDS
EAST INN**
3337 E Skelly Dr
(74135)
Rates: $51-$57
Tel: (918) 743-7931
(800) 528-1234

CAMELOT HOTEL
4956 S Peoria Ave
(74105)
Rates: $54-$69
Tel: (918) 747-8811

COMFORT INN
4717 S Yale Ave
(74135)
Rates: $38-$52
Tel: (918) 622-6776
(800) 221-2222

DAYS INN
5525 W Skelly Dr
(74107)
Rates: $32-$60
Tel: (918) 446-1561
(800) 329-7466

DAYS INN AIRPORT
1016 N Garnett Rd
(74116)
Rates: $36-$49
Tel: (918) 438-5050
(800) 329-7466

DOUBLETREE HOTEL
6110 S Yale Ave
(74136)
Rates: $69-$175
Tel: (918) 495-1000
(800) 222-8733

DOUBLETREE HOTEL
616 W 7th St (74127)
Rates: $69-$131
Tel: (918) 587-8000
(800) 222-8733

HAWTHORN SUITES
3509 S 79th East Ave
(74145)
Rates: $55-$110
Tel: (918) 663-3900
(800) 527-1133

**HOLIDAY INN
HOLIDOME**
8181 E Skelly Dr
(74129)
Rates: $56-$80
Tel: (800) 465-4329

**HOLIDAY INN
AIRPORT**
1010 N Garnett Rd
(74116)
Rates: $59-$85
Tel: (918) 437-7660
(800) 465-4329

HOWARD JOHNSON
4724 S Yale (74135)
Rates: $37-$55
Tel: (918) 496-1760
(800) 446-4656

HOWARD JOHNSON
17 W 7th St (74119)
Rates: $38-$65
Tel: (918) 585-5898
(800) 466-4656

LA QUINTA INN
10829 E 41st St S
(74146)
Rates: $46-$61
Tel: (918) 665-0220
(800) 531-5900

**LA QUINTA INN-
AIRPORT**
35 N Sheridan Rd
(74115)
Rates: $47-$62
Tel: (918) 836-3931
(800) 531-5900

**LA QUINTA INN-
SOUTH**
12525 E 52nd St
(74146)
Rates: $49-$52
Tel: (918) 254-1626
(800) 531-5900

MOTEL 6-EAST
1011 S Garnett Rd
(74128)
Rates: $27-$31
Tel: (918) 234-6200
(800) 440-6000

MOTEL 6-WEST
5828 W Skelly Dr
(74107)
Rates: $26-$30
Tel: (918) 445-0223
(800) 440-6000

**QUALITY INN
AIRPORT**
222 N Garnett Rd
(74116)
Rates: $40-$63
Tel: (918) 438-0780
(800) 221-2222

**RESIDENCE INN
BY MARRIOTT**
8181 E 41st St
(74145)
Rates: $99-$125
Tel: (918) 664-7241
(800) 331-3131

VINITA

PARK HILLS MOTEL
Rt 4, Box 292 (74301)
Rates: $20-$28
Tel: (918) 256-5511

SUPER 8 MOTEL
30954 S Hwy 69
(74301)
Rates: $34-$41
Tel: (800) 800-8000

WAGONOR

**INDIAN LODGE
MOTEL**
Rt 2, Box 393 (74467)
Rates: $32-$70
Tel: (918) 485-3184

SUPER 8
805 S Dewey (74467)
Rates: $35-$45
Tel: (918) 485-4818
(800) 800-8000

**WESTERN HILLS
GUEST RANCH**
P. O. Box 509 (74477)
Rates: $45-$98
Tel: (918) 772-2545

WATONGA

**ROMAN NOSE
RESORT**
Rt 1 (73772)
Rates: $45-$68
Tel: (405) 623-7281

WEATHERFORD

BEST WESTERN MARK MOTOR HOTEL
525 E Main St
(73096)
Rates: $39-$89
Tel: (405) 772-3325
(800) 528-1234

SCOTTISH INNS
616 E Main St
(73096)
Rates: $26-$36
Tel: (405) 772-3349
(800) 251-1962

TRAVEL INN
3401 E Main St
(73096)
Rates: $21-$25
Tel: (405) 772-6238

WEBBERS FALLS

SUPER 8
I-40 & Hwy 100
(74470)
Rates: $33-$45
Tel: (918) 464-2272
(800) 800-8000

WOODWARD

HOSPITALITY INN
4120 Williams Ave
(73801)
Rates: $24-$30
Tel: (405) 254-2964

NORTHWEST INN
Hwy 270 & 1st St
(73801)
Rates: $47-$72
Tel: (405) 256-7600

WAYFARER INN
2901 Williams Ave
(73801)
Rates: $32-$52
Tel: (405) 256-5553

YUKON

COMFORT INN-WEST
321 N Mustange Rd
(73099)
Rates: $40-$70
Tel: (405) 324-1000
(800) 221-2222

OREGON

AGNESS

LUCAS PIONEER RANCH & LODGE
03904 Cougar Ln (97406)
Rates: $30-$60
Tel: (541) 247-7443

SINGING SPRINGS RESORT
34501 Agness Illahe Rd (97406)
Rates: $30-$50
Tel: (541) 247-6162

ALBANY

BEST WESTERN PONY SOLDIER INN
315 Airport Rd SE (97321)
Rates: $69-$86
Tel: (541) 928-6322
(800) 528-1234

BUDGET INN
2727 Pacific Blvd SE (97321)
Rates: $36-$44
Tel: (541) 926-4246

CITY CENTER MOTEL
1730 Pacific Blvd SE (97321)
Rates: $27-$45
Tel: (541) 926-8442

COMFORT INN
251 Airport Way SE (97321)
Rates: $59-$90
Tel: (541) 928-0921
(800) 221-2222

HOLIDAY INN EXPRESS
1100 Price Rd SE (97321)
Rates: $40-$80
Tel: (541) 928-5050
(800) 928-5657

MARCO POLO MOTEL
2410 Pacific Blvd SE (97321)
Rates: $22-$40
Tel: (541) 926-4401

MOTEL ORLEANS
1212 Price Rd SE (97321)
Rates: $38-$44
Tel: (541) 926-0170
(800) 626-1900

PIONEER VILLA TRUCK PLAZA
Exit 216 I-5 (97321)
Rates: $34-$39
Tel: (541) 369-2801

STARDUST MOTEL
2735 E Pacific Blvd (97321)
Rates: $30-$65
Tel: (541) 926-4233

VALU-INN
3125 Santiam Hwy SE (97321)
Rates: $40-$80
Tel: (541) 926-1538

ARLINGTON

VILLAGE INN MOTEL
131 Beech St (97812)
Rates: $42+
Tel: (541) 454-2646

ASHLAND

ASHLAND MOTEL
1145 Siskiyou Blvd (97520)
Rates: $30-$43
Tel: (541) 482-2561

ASHLAND VALLEY INN
1193 Siskiyou Blvd (97520)
Rates: $38-$82
Tel: (541) 482-2641
(800) 547-6414

ASHLAND VILLAGE INN B & B
639 N Main St (97520)
Rates: $70-$150
Tel: (541) 482-9171

BEST WESTERN BARD'S INN
132 N Main St (97520)
Rates: $52-$125
Tel: (541) 482-0049
(800) 528-1234

BEST WESTERN HERITAGE INN
434 Valley View Rd (97520)
Rates: $46-$150
Tel: (541) 482-6932
(800) 528-1234

CEDARWOOD INN
1801 Siskiyou Blvd (97520)
Rates: $68+
Tel: (541) 488-2000
(800) 547-4141

GREEN SPRINGS INN
11470 Hwy 66 (97520)
Rates: $40-$99
Tel: (541) 482-0614

KNIGHTS INN MOTEL
2359 Hwy 66 (97520)
Rates: $32-$58
Tel: (541) 482-5111
(800) 547-4566

QUALITY INN FLAGSHIP
2520 Ashland St (97520)
Rates: $44-$113
Tel: (541) 488-2330
(800) 221-2222

WINDMILL'S ASHLAND HILLS INN
2525 Ashland St (97520)
Rates: $39-$109
Tel: (541) 482-8310
(800) 547-4747

ASTORIA

BAYSHORE MOTOR INN
555 Hamburg (97103)
Rates: $37-$60
Tel: (503) 325-2205
(800) 621-0641

CREST MOTEL
5366 Leif Erickson Dr (97103)
Rates: $65-$79
Tel: (503) 325-3141
(800) 421-3141

LAMPLIGHTER MOTEL
131 W Marine Dr (97103)
Rates: $34-$68
Tel: (503) 325-4051

RED LION INN
400 Industry St (97103)
Rates: $63-$88
Tel: (503) 325-7373
(800) 547-8010

ROSEBRIAR INN
636 14th St (97103)
Rates: $49-$129
Tel: (503) 325-7427
(800) 487-0224

BAKER CITY

BAKER CITY MOTEL
880 Elm St (97814)
Rates: $25-$33
Tel: (541) 523-6391
(800) 931-9229

EL DORADO MOTEL
695 Campbell (97814)
Rates: $36-$44
Tel: (541) 523-6494
(800) 537-5756

GEISER GRAND HOTEL
1996 Main St (97814)
Rates: $65-$125
Tel: (541) 523-1889

GREEN GABLES MOTEL
2533 10th St (97814)
Rates: $30+
Tel: (541) 523-5588

OREGON TRAIL MOTEL & RESORT
211 Bridge St (97814)
Rates: $32-$38
Tel: (541) 523-5844
(800) 628-3982

POWDER RIVER
BED & BREAKFAST
HCR 87, Box 500
(97814)
Rates: $60-$70
Tel: (541) 523-7143
(800) 600-7143

QUALITY INN
810 Campbell
(97814)
Rates: $40-$61
Tel: (541) 523-2244
(800) 221-2222

THE WESTERN MOTEL
3055 10th St (97814)
Rates: $28-$36
Tel: (541) 523-3700
(800) 481-3701

TRAIL MOTEL
2815 10th St (97814)
Rates: :n/a
Tel: (541) 523-4646

WARNERS SLOUGH
HOUSE B & B
Rt 2, Box 135 (97814)
Rates: n/a
Tel: (541) 523-6196

BANDON

BANDON BEACH
MOTEL
1140 Beach Loop Dr
(97411)
Rates: $45-$85
Tel: (541) 347-4430
(800) 822-8765

CAPRICE MOTEL
Rt 1, Box 530 (97411)
Rates: $38-$44
Tel: (541) 347-4494

DRIFTWOOD MOTEL
460 Hwy 101 (97411)
Rates: $35-$70
Tel: (541) 347-9022
(800) 341-8000

THE INN AT
FACE ROCK MOTEL
3225 Beach Loop Rd
(97411)
Rates: $49-$79
Tel: (541) 347-9441
(800) 638-3092

LA KRIS MOTEL
Hwy 101 S at 9th St
(97411)
Rates: $32-$65
Tel: (541) 347-3610

SUNSET
OCEANFRONT
ACCOMMODATIONS
Box 373 (97411)
Rates: $53-$175
Tel: (541) 347-2453
(800) 842-2407

TABLE ROCK MOTEL
840 Beach Loop Rd
(97411)
Rates: $30-$80
Tel: (541) 347-2700

BEAVERTON

GREENWOOD INN
10700 SW Allen Blvd
(97005)
Rates: $75-$102
Tel: (503) 643-7444
(800) 289-1300

PEPPERTREE MOTEL
10720 SW Allen Blvd
(97005)
Rates: $52-$69
Tel: (503) 641-7477
(800) 453-6219

SHILO INNS
9900 SW Canyon Rd
(97225)
Rates: $76-$105
Tel: (503) 297-2551
(800) 222-2244

VAL-U INN MOTEL
12255 SW Canyon
Rd (97005)
Rates: $36-$51
Tel: (503) 643-6621
(800) 443-7777

BEND

BEND RIVERSIDE
MOTEL & CONDO
1565 NW Hill St
(97702)
Rates: $49-$110
Tel: (541) 389-2363
(800) 284-2363

BEST WESTERN
ENTRADA LODGE
19221 Century Dr
(97702)
Rates: $55-$89
Tel: (541) 382-4080
(800) 528-1234

BEST WESTERN
INN & SUITES
721 NE 3rd (97701)
Rates: $55-$89
Tel: (541) 382-1515
(800) 528-1234

CASCADE MOTEL
LODGE
420 SE 3rd St (97702)
Rates: $42-$65
Tel: (541) 382-2612
(800) 852-6031

CASCADE VIEW
RANCH GUEST HOUSE
60435 Tekampe Rd
(97702)
Rates: $175-$285
Tel: (541) 388-5658

CHALET MOTEL
510 SE 3rd St (97702)
Rates: $32-$39
Tel: (541) 382-6124

CIMARRON
MOTOR INN
437 NE 3rd St
(97701)
Rates: $38-$63
Tel: (541) 382-7711
(800) 304-4050

COMFORT INN
61200 S Hwy 97
(97702)
Rates: $41-$130
Tel: (541) 388-2227
(800) 221-2222

CULTUS LAKE RESORT
P. O. Box 262 (97709)
Rates: $48-$81
Tel: (541) 389-3230

DESCHUTES RIVER
RANCH
20210 Swalley Rd
(97701)
Rates: $150
Tel: (541) 382-7240

GUEST HOUSE B & B
20020 Glen Vista Rd
(97702)
Rates: n/a
Tel: (541) 382-8565

HAMPTON INN
15 NE Butler Market
Rd (97701)
Rates: $56-$75
Tel: (541) 388-4114
(800) 426-7866

HOLIDAY MOTEL
880 SE 3rd St (97702)
Rates: $30-$34
Tel: (541) 382-4620
(800) 252-0121

MOTEL WEST
228 NE Irving
(97701)
Rates: $36-$40
Tel: (541) 389-5577
(800) 282-5577

PALMER'S COTTAGES
645 NE Greenwood
Ave (97701)
Rates: $20-$45
Tel: (541) 382-1197

PINES LODGE
61405 S Hwy 97
(97702)
Rates: $39-$79
Tel: (541) 389-5910
(800) 500-5910

PLAZA MOTEL
1430 NW Hill St
(97702)
Rates: $28-$60
Tel: (541) 389-0235

RED LION-SOUTH
849 NE 3rd St
(97701)
Rates: $74-$99
Tel: (541) 382-8384
(800) 733-5466

THE RIVERHOUSE
RESORT
3075 N Hwy 97
(97701)
Rates: $62-$69
Tel: (541) 389-3111
(800) 547-3928

SHILO INNS
SUITES HOTEL
3105 O B Riley Rd
(97701)
Rates: $83-$116
Tel: (541) 389-9600
(800) 222-2244

SONOMA LODGE
450 SE 3rd St (97702)
Rates: $30-$49
Tel: (541) 382-4891

SUPER 8 MOTEL
1275 S Hwy 97
(97702)
Rates: $48-$70
Tel: (541) 388-6888
(800) 800-8000

**SWALLOW RIDGE
BED & BREAKFAST**
65711 Twin Bridges
Rd (97701)
Rates: $45-$55
Tel: (541) 389-1913

TRAVELERS INN
3705 N Hwy 97
(97701)
Rates: $28-$85
Tel: (541) 382-2211
(800) 507-2211

**TWIN LAKES
RESORT**
11200 S Century Dr
(97702)
Rates: $60-$96
Tel: (541) 593-6526

**WESTWARD HO
MOTEL**
904 SE Third St
(97702)
Rates: $28-$115
Tel: (541) 382-2111
(800) 999-8143

BOARDMAN

DODGE CITY INN
1st Front St (97818)
Rates: $42-$46
Tel: (541) 481-2451

NUGGET INN
105 Front St SW
(97818)
Rates: $38-$48
Tel: (541) 481-2375
(800) 336-4485

RIVERVIEW MOTEL
200 Front St NE
(97818)
Rates: $32-$42
Tel: (541) 481-2775

BROOKINGS

**BEAVER STATE
MOTEL**
437 Chetco Ave
(97415)
Rates: $42-$55
Tel: (541) 469-5361

BONN MOTEL
1216 Chetco Ave
(97415)
Rates: $38-$48
Tel: (541) 469-2161

HARBOR INN MOTEL
15991 Hwy 101S
(97415)
Rates: $48-$70
Tel: (541) 469-3194
(800) 469-8884

PACIFIC SUNSET INN
1144 Chetco Ave
(97415)
Rates: $28-$53
Tel: (541) 469-2141
(800) 469-2141

BURNS

**BEST WESTERN
PONDEROSA**
577 W Monroe
(97720)
Rates: $38-$57
Tel: (541) 573-2047
(800) 528-1234

ROYAL INN
999 Oregon Ave
(97720)
Rates: $40-$48
Tel: (541) 573-5295

SILVER SPUR MOTEL
789 N Broadway
(97720)
Rates: $33-$38
Tel: (541) 573-2077
(800) 400-2077

**CAMP
SHERMAN**

**BLACK BUTTE
RESORT MOTEL**
35 Suttle-Sherman
Rd (97730)
Rates: $47-$57
Tel: (541) 595-6514

**COLD SPRINGS
RESORT & RV PARK**
Cold Springs Resort
Ln (97730)
Rates: $83-$91
Tel: (541) 595-6271

**CANNON
BEACH**

HALLMARK RESORT
1400 S Hemlock St
(97110)
Rates: $69-$189
Tel: (503) 436-1566
(800) 345-5675

**MCBEE MOTEL
COTTAGES**
888 S Hemlock St
(97110)
Rates: $39-$129
Tel: (503) 436-2569

**QUIET CANNON
LODGINGS**
372 N Spruce St
(97110)
Rates: $85-$95
Tel: (503) 436-1405

SURFS AND RESORT
Oceanfront & Gower
Sts (97110)
Rates: $119-$129
Tel: (503) 436-2274
(800) 546-6100

TWIN VIEW RESORT
HCR 2126 (97730)
Rates: $54-$98
Tel: (541) 595-6125

**CANNON BEACH
ECOLA CREEK LODGE**
208 5th St (97110)
Rates: $60-$99
Tel: (503) 436-2776
(800) 873-2749

**CANNON VILLAGE
MOTEL**
3163 S Hemlock St
(97110)
Rates: $65-$120
Tel: (503) 436-2317

HAYSTACK RESORT
3339 S Hemlock St
(97110)
Rates: $89-$159
Tel: (503) 436-1577
(800) 499-2220

TOLOVANA INN
3400 S Hemlock St
(97110)
Rates: $61-$239
Tel: (503) 436-2211
(800) 333-8890

VIKING MOTEL
Matanuska & S
Pacific (97110)
Rates: $139-$159
Tel: (503) 436-2274
(800) 547-6100

CANYONVILLE

LEISURE INN
P. O. Box 869 (97417)
Rates: $37-$55
Tel: (541) 839-4278

**CASCADE
LOCKS**

**BEST WESTERN
COLUMBIA RIVER
INN**
735 Wanapa St
(97014)
Rates: $54-$99
Tel: (541) 374-8777
(800) 595-7108

**BRIDGE OF THE
GODS MOTEL**
630 Wanapa St
(97014)
Rates: $46-$65
Tel: (541) 374-8628

**SCANDIAN
MOTOR LODGE**
P. O. Box 217 (97014)
Rates: $32-$48
Tel: (541) 374-8417

**CASCADE
SUMMIT**

**SHELTER COVE
RESORT**
Hwy 58, W Odell
Lake Rd
Rates: $60-$85
Tel: (541) 433-2548

CAVE JUNCTION

**COUNTRY HILLS
RESORT**
7901 Caves Hwy
(97523)
Rates: $40-$50
Tel: (541) 592-3406
(800) 997-8464

CHEMULT

CHEMULT MOTEL
US Hwy 97 (97731)
Rates: $38-$44
Tel: (541) 365-2228

CRATER LAKE MOTEL
Hwy 97,
P. O. Box 190 (97731)
Rates: $30-$50
Tel: (541) 365-2241

CHILOQUIN

MELITA'S MOTEL & RV PARK
39500 Hwy 97 N (97624)
Rates: $26-$53
Tel: (541) 783-2401

SPRING CREEK RANCH MOTEL
47600 Hwy 97 N (97624)
Rates: $24-$28
Tel: (541) 783-2775

CLACKAMAS

CASCADE MOTEL
10308 SE 82nd Ave (97266)
Rates: $38-$40
Tel: (503) 775-1571
(800) 972-4660

CLACKAMAS INN
16010 SE 82nd (97015)
Rates: $56-$93
Tel: (503) 650-5340
(800) 874-6560

CYPRESS INN
9040 SE Adams (97266)
Rates: $65-$77
Tel: (503) 655-0062
(800) 752-9991

COOS BAY

BEST WESTERN HOLIDAY MOTEL
411 N Bayshore Dr (97420)
Rates: $59-$110
Tel: (541) 269-5111
(800) 228-8655

COOS BAY MANOR BED & BREAKFAST
955 S 5th St (97420)
Rates: $65-$75
Tel: (541) 269-1224
(800) 269-1224

EDGEWATER INN
275 E Johnson St (97420)
Rates: $67-$72
Tel: (541) 267-0423

LAZY J MOTEL
1143 Hill St (97420)
Rates: n/a
Tel: (541) 269-9666

MOTEL 6
1445 N Bayshore Dr (97420)
Rates: $32-$42
Tel: (541) 267-7171
(800) 440-6000

PLAINVIEW MOTEL
2760 Cape Arago Hwy (97420)
Rates: $34-$38
Tel: (541) 888-5166

RED LION INN
1313 N Bayshore Dr (97420)
Rates: $69-$104
Tel: (541) 267-4141
(800) 547-8010

SEA PSALM MOTEL
1250 Cape Arago Hwy (97420)
Rates: $30-$35
Tel: (541) 888-9053

TIMBER LODGE MOTEL
1001 N Bayshore Dr (97420)
Rates: n/a
Tel: (541) 267-7066
(800) 782-7592

COQUILLE

MYRTLE LANE MOTEL
787 N Central (97423)
Rates: $35-$37
Tel: (541) 396-2102

CORVALLIS

ASHWOOD B & B
2940 NW Ashwood Dr (97330)
Rates: $51+
Tel: (541) 757-9772
(800) 306-5136

BUDGET INN
1480 SW 3rd St (97330)
Rates: $25-$35
Tel: (541) 752-8756

ECONO LODGE
345 NW 2nd St (97330)
Rates: $38
Tel: (541) 752-9601
(800) 424-4777

HARRISON HOUSE BED & BREAKFAST
2310 NW Harrison (97330)
Rates: $45-$60
Tel: (541) 752-6248

JASON INN
800 NW 9th St (97330)
Rates: $36-$48
Tel: (541) 753-7326
(800) 346-3291

MOTEL ORLEANS
935 NW Garfield (97330)
Rates: $36-$50
Tel: (541) 758-9125
(800) 626-1900

SHANICO INN
1113 NW 9th St (97330)
Rates: $44-$54
Tel: (541) 754-7474
(800) 432-1233

SUPER 8 MOTEL
407 NW 2nd St (97330)
Rates: $53-$73
Tel: (541) 758-8088
(800) 800-8000

TOWNE HOUSE MOTOR INN
350 SW 4th St (97330)
Rates: $36-$50
Tel: (541) 753-4496

COTTAGE GROVE

BEST WESTERN VILLAGE GREEN
725 Row River Rd (97424)
Rates: $59-$89
Tel: (541) 942-2491
(800) 528-1234

CITY CENTER MOTEL
737 Hwy 99 S (97424)
Rates: $25-$30
Tel: (541) 942-8322

COMFORT INN
845 Gateway Blvd (97424)
Rates: $47-$99
Tel: (541) 942-9747
(800) 221-2222

HOLIDAY INN
1601 Gateway Blvd (97424)
Rates: $40-$125
Tel: (800) 465-4329

RAINBOW MOTEL
1030 Pacific Hwy 99 N (97424)
Rates: $25-$30
Tel: (541) 942-5132

RIVER COUNTRY INN
71864 London Rd (97424)
Rates: $65
Tel: (541) 942-9334

STARDUST MOTEL
455 Bear Creek Rd (97424)
Rates: $25-$30
Tel: (541) 942-5706

CRATER LAKE

HOLIDAY VILLAGE MOTEL
Hwy 97, P. O. Box 95 (97604)
Rates: $28-$45
Tel: (541) 365-2394

WHISPERING PINES MOTEL
Diamond Lake Jct (97604)
Rates: $30-$35
Tel: (541) 365-2259

CRESCENT

WOODSMAN MOTEL
Hwy 97 (97733)
Rates: $35-$47
Tel: (541) 433-2710

CRESCENT LAKE

CRESCENT CREEK COTTAGES & RV PARK
Hwy 58, Milepost 71 (97425)
Rates: $30-$50
Tel: (541) 433-2324

ODELL LAKE RESORT
Hwy 58, Milesport 67 (97425)
Rates: $38-$50
Tel: (541) 433-2540

SHELTER COVE RESORT
W Odell Lake Rd, Hwy 58 (97425)
Rates: $65-$85
Tel: (541) 433-2548

WILLAMETTE PASS INN
Hwy 58, Milepost 69 (97425)
Rates: $58-$82
Tel: (541) 433-2211
(800) 301-2218

DALLAS

RIVERSIDE MOTEL
517 Main St (97338)
Rates: $35-$45
Tel: (541) 623-8163

DAYTON

WINE COUNTRY FARM
6855 Breyman Orchards Rd (97114)
Rates: $65-$125
Tel: (503) 864-3446
(800) 261-3446

DAYVILLE

FISH HOUSE INN
110 Franklin, Hwy 26 (97825)
Rates: $40-$65
Tel: (541) 987-2124

DEPOE BAY

HOLIDAY SURF LODGE & RV PARK
939 NW Hwy 101 (97341)
Rates: $39-335
Tel: (541) 765-2133
(800) 451-2108

INN AT ARCH ROCK
70 NW Sunset St (97341)
Rates: $45-$120
Tel: (541) 765-2560
(800) 765-8655

WHALE INN AT DEPOE BAY
416 Hwy 101 N (97341)
Rates: $50-$90
Tel: (541) 765-2789

DETROIT

ALL SEASONS MOTEL
130 Breitenbush Rd (97342)
Rates: $40-$80
Tel: (503) 854-3421

ELGIN

CITY CENTRE MOTEL
P. O. Box 207 (97827)
Rates: $37-$40
Tel: (541) 437-2441

MINAM MOTEL
72601 Hwy 72 (97827)
Rates: n/a
Tel: (541) 437-4475

ENTERPRISE

BOUCHER GUEST COTTAGE
83162 W Dorrance Ln (97828)
Rates: $55+
Tel: (541) 426-3209

PONDEROSA MOTEL
102 SE Greenwood (97828)
Rates: $42-$44
Tel: (541) 426-3186

SHILO INNS-WILDERNESS RETREAT
84570 Bartlett Rd (97828)
Rates: $39-$79
Tel: (503) 828-7741
(800) 222-2244

WILDERNESS INN
301 W North St (97828)
Rates: $44-$66
Tel: (541) 426-4535

EUGENE

ANGUS INN MOTEL
2121 Franklin Blvd (97403)
Rates: $36-$70
Tel: (541) 342-1243
(800) 456-6487

ATHERTON PLACE-A B & B INN
690 W Broadway (97402)
Rates: $50-$70
Tel: (541) 683-2674

BARRON'S MOTOR INN
1859 Franklin Blvd (97403)
Rates: $47-$61
Tel: (541) 342-6383
(800) 444-6383

BEST WESTERN NEW OREGON MOTEL
1655 Franklin Blvd (97403)
Rates: $52-$80
Tel: (541) 683-3669
(800) 528-1234

CAMILLE'S B & B
3277 Onyx Pl (97405)
Rates: $55-$70
Tel: (541) 344-9576

CAMPUS INN
390 East Broadway (97401)
Rates: $46-$56
Tel: (541) 343-3376
(800) 888-6313

CLASSIC RESIDENCE INN
1140 W 6th Ave (97401)
Rates: $26-$30
Tel: (541) 343-0730

COUNTRY SQUIRE INN
33100 Van Duyn Rd (97401)
Rates: $39-$100
Tel: (541) 484-2000

COURTESY INN
345 W 6th Ave (97401)
Rates: $40-$50
Tel: (541) 345-3391
(800) 459-3000

EUGENE MOTOR LODGE
476 E Broadway (97401)
Rates: $28-$60
Tel: (541) 344-5233

EUGENE TRAVELERS INN
540 E Broadway (97401)
Rates: $33-$49
Tel: (541) 342-1109
(800) 432-5999

HILTON HOTEL-EUGENE
66 E 6th & Oak Sts (97401)
Rates: $79-$129
Tel: (541) 342-2000
(800) 445-8667

HOLIDAY INN
225 Coburg Rd (97401)
Rates: $48-$61
Tel: (800) 465-4329

THE OVAL DOOR B & B INN
988 Lawrence (97401)
Rates: $64-$75
Tel: (541) 683-3160

PHOENIX INN
850 Franklin Blvd (97401)
Rates: $50-$129
Tel: (541) 344-0001
(800) 344-0131

RED LION HOTEL
205 Coburg Rd (97401)
Rates: $66-$97
Tel: (541) 342-5201
(800) 547-8010

RODEWAY INN
3480 Hutton St (97401)
Rates: $58-$64
Tel: (541) 746-8471
(800) 424-4777

SIXTY-SIX MOTEL
755 E Broadway (97401)
Rates: $24-$34
Tel: (541) 342-5041

TIMBERS MOTEL
1015 Pearl St (97401)
Rates: $32-$68
Tel: (541) 343-3345
(800) 643-4167

THE VALLEY RIVER INN
100 Valley River Way (97440)
Rates: $98-$300
Tel: (541) 687-0123
(800) 543-8266

FLORENCE

GULL HAVEN LODGE
94770 Hwy 101 (97439)
Rates: $35-$85
Tel: (541) 547-3583

MERCER LAKE RESORT
88875 Bay Berry Ln (97439)
Rates: $53-$65
Tel: (541) 997-3633
(800) 355-3633

MONEY SAVER MOTEL
170 Hwy 101 (97439)
Rates: $32-$58
Tel: (541) 997-7131

OCEAN BREEZE MOTEL
85165 Hwy 101 S (97439)
Rates: $50-$65
Tel: (541) 997-2642
(800) 997-2642

PARK MOTEL
85034 Hwy 101 (97439)
Rates: $34-$59
Tel: (541) 997-2634
(800) 392-0441

SILVER SANDS MOTEL
1449 Hwy 101 N (97439)
Rates: $34-$68
Tel: (541) 997-3459

VILLA WEST MOTEL
901 Hwy 101 (97439)
Rates: $35-$55
Tel: (541) 997-3457

FOREST GROVE

HOLIDAY MOTEL
3224 Pacific Ave (97116)
Rates: $33-$48
Tel: (541) 357-7411

FORT KLAMATH

CRATER LAKE RESORT
50711 Hwy 62 (97626)
Rates: $33-$48
Tel: (541) 381-2349

WILSON'S COTTAGES
57997 Hwy 62 (97626)
Rates: $30-$40
Tel: (541) 381-2209

GARIBALDI

HARBOR VIEW INN
302 Mooring Basin Rd (97118)
Rates: $45-$65
Tel: (503) 322-3251

TILLA-BAY MOTEL
8th & Hwy 101 (97118)
Rates: $39+
Tel: (503) 322-3405

GEARHART

GEARHART BY THE SEA
10th & N Marion (97138)
Rates: $71-$184
Tel: (503) 738-8331
(800) 547-0115

SURFSIDE CONDOS ON THE BEACH
P. O. Box 2591 (97138)
Rates: $69-$145
Tel: (503) 738-6384

WINDJAMMER MOTEL
4301 Hwy 101 N (97138)
Rates: $48-$117
Tel: (503) 738-3250
(800) 479-5191

GLADSTONE

BUDGET INN
19240 SE McLaughlin Blvd (97027)
Rates: $35-$85
Tel: (503) 656-1955
(800) 655-9368

GLENEDEN BEACH

SALISHAN LODGE
7760 Hwy 101 N (98388)
Rates: $110-$250
Tel: (431) 764-2371
(800) 452-2300

GOLD BEACH

BEST WESTERN INN OF THE BEACH-COMBER
29266 Ellensburg Ave (97444)
Rates: $53-$97
Tel: (541) 247-6691
(800) 528-1234

CITY CENTER MOTEL
150 Harlow St (97444)
Rates: $40-$80
Tel: (541) 247-6675

DRIFT IN MOTEL
715 North Ellensburg (97444)
Rates: $50-$64
Tel: (541) 247-4547
(800) 424-3833

INN AT GOLD BEACH
1435 S Ellensburg (97444)
Rates: $35-$125
Tel: (541) 247-6606
(800) 503-0833

IRELAND'S RUSTIC LODGES
1120 S Ellensburg (97444)
Rates: $30-$81
Tel: (541) 247-7718

JOT'S RESORT
94360 Wedderburn Loop Rd (97444)
Rates: $50-$115
Tel: (541) 247-6676
(800) 367-5687

KIMBALL CREEK BEND RESORT
97136 N Bank Rogue (97444)
Rates: $41-$70
Tel: (541) 247-7580

OREGON TRAIL LODGE
550 N Ellensburg Ave (97444)
Rates: $20-$50
Tel: (541) 247-6030

RIVER BRIDGE INN
1010 Jerry's Flat Rd (97444)
Rates: $45-$79
Tel: (503) 247-4533

ROGUE LANDING
94749 Jerry's Flat Rd (97444)
Rates: $20-$50
Tel: (541) 247-6105

SAND 'N SEA MOTEL
1040 S Ellensburg Ave (97444)
Rates: $41-$90
Tel: (541) 247-6658
(800) 808-7263

TU TU' TUN LODGE
96550 N Bank Rogue (97444)
Rates: $81-$91
Tel: (541) 247-6664

WESTERN VILLAGE MOTEL
975 S Ellensburg (97444)
Rates: $25-$59
Tel: (541) 247-6611

GOVERNMENT CAMP

MT HOOD INN
87450 E Government Camp Loop (97028)
Rates: $90-$135
Tel: (800) 443-7777

GRANTS PASS

BEST WESTERN INN AT THE ROGUE
8959 Rogue River Hwy (97527)
Rates: $45-$75
Tel: (541) 582-2200
(800) 238-0700

BUDGET INN
1253 NE 6th St (97526)
Rates: $40-$45
Tel: (541) 479-2952

CITY CENTER MOTEL
741 NE 6th St
(97526)
Rates: n/a
Tel: (541) 476-6134

FLAMINGO INN
728 NW 6th St
(97526)
Rates: $30-$42
Tel: (541) 476-6601

GOLDEN INN
1950 Northwest Vine
(97526)
Rates: $40-$48
Tel: (541) 479-6611

HOLIDAY INN EXPRESS
105 NE Agness
(97526)
Rates: $59-$84
Tel: (541) 471-6144
(800) 465-4329

KNIGHTS INN
104 SE 7th St (97526)
Rates: $38-$44
Tel: (541) 479-5595
(800) 843-5644

MOTEL ORLEANS
1889 NE 6th St
(97526)
Rates: $45-$63
Tel: (541) 479-8301
(800) 626-1900

REDWOOD MOTEL
815 NE 6th St
(97526)
Rates: $32-$56
Tel: (541) 476-0878

REGAL LODGE
1400 NW 6th St
(97526)
Rates: $35-$40
Tel: (541) 479-3305

RIVERSIDE INN
971 SE 6th St (97526)
Rates: $40-$96
Tel: (541) 476-6873
(800) 334-4567

ROD & REEL MOTEL
7875 Rogue River
Hwy (97526)
Rates: $40-$75
Tel: (541) 582-1516
 (800) 516-5557

ROGUE RIVER INN
6285 Rogue River
Hwy (97527)
Rates: $33-$81
Tel: (541) 582-1120
(800) 822-2895

ROGUE VALLEY MOTEL
7799 Rogue River
Hwy (97527)
Rates: $42-$72
Tel: (541) 582-3762

SHILO INNS
1880 NW 6th St
(97526)
Rates: $61-$76
Tel: (541) 479-8391
(800) 222-2244

SUPER 8 MOTEL
1949 NE 7th St
(97526)
Rates: $47-$53
Tel: (541) 474-0888
(800) 800-8000

THRIFTLODGE
748 SE 7th (97526)
Rates: n/a
Tel: (541) 476-7793
(800) 525-9055

WEASKU INN
5560 Rogue River
Hwy (97527)
Rates: $95-$250
Tel: (541) 476-4190
(800) 493-2758

GRESHAM

HOLIDAY INN EXPRESS
2323 NE 181st St
(97230)
Rates: $55-$79
Tel: (800) 465-4329

QUALITY INN
1545 NE Burnside
(97030)
Rates: $48-$85
Tel: (503) 666-9545
(800) 221-2222

HALFWAY

CLEAR CREEK FARM BED & BREAKFAST
Rt 1, Box 138 (97834)
Rates: $55-$60
Tel: (541) 742-2238

HARBOR

BEST WESTERN BEACHFRONT INN
16008 Boat Basin Rd
(97415)
Rates: $65-$172
Tel: (541) 469-7779
(800) 528-1234

HERMISTON

SANDS MOTEL
835 North First
(97838)
Rates: $33-$38
Tel: (541) 567-5516

THE WAY INN
635 S Hwy 395
(97838)
Rates: $32-$34
Tel: (541) 567-5561

HILLSBORO

RESIDENCE INN PORTLAND WEST
18855 NW
Tanasbourne Dr
(97214)
Rates: 89-$145
Tel: (503) 531-3200
(800) 331-3131

HOOD RIVER

COLUMBIA GORGE HOTEL
4000 Westcliff Dr
(97031)
Rates: $150-$270
Tel: (541) 386-5566
(800) 345-1931

HOOD RIVER HOTEL
102 Oak St (97031)
Rates: $49-$145
Tel: (541) 386-1900
(800) 386-1859

LOST LAKE RESORT
Mt Hood National
Forest (97031)
Rates: $45-$95
Tel: (541) 386-6366

MEREDITH GORGE MOTEL
4300 Westcliff Dr
(97031)
Rates: $34-$54
Tel: (541) 386-1515

SUNSET MOTEL
2300 W Cascade
(97031)
Rates: $50-$70
Tel: (541) 386-6027

THE UPPER ROOMS ON AVALON B & B
344 Avalon Dr
(97031)
Rates: $50-$65
Tel: (541) 386-2560

VAGABOND LODGE
4070 Westcliff Dr
(97031)
Rates: $33-$62
Tel: (503) 386-2992

IDLEYLD PARK

NORTH UMPQUA RESORT
23885 N Umpqua
Hwy (97447)
Rates: $29-$55
Tel: (541) 496-0149

JACKSONVILLE

THE STAGE LODGE
830 N 5th (97530)
Rates: $45-$69
Tel: (541) 899-3953
(800) 253-8254

JOHN DAY

BEST WESTERN INN
315 W Main (97845)
Rates: $52-$105
Tel: (541) 575-1700
(800) 528-1234

BUDGET 8 MOTEL
711 W Main (97845)
Rates: $38-$54
Tel: (541) 575-2155

BUDGET INN
250 E Main (97845)
Rates: $38-$43
Tel: (541) 575-2100
(800) 854-4442

DREAMERS LODGE
144 N Canyon Blvd
(97845)
Rates: $44-$48
Tel: (541) 575-0526
(800) 654-2849

SUNSET INN
390 W Main (97845)
Rates: $44-$56
Tel: (541) 575-1462
(800) 452-4899

JORDAN VALLEY

SAHARA MOTEL
607 Main, Hwy 95
(97910)
Rates: $36-$38
Tel: (541) 586-2810
(800) 828-4432

JOSEPH

DRAGON MEADOWS BED & BREAKFAST
504 N Lake St
(97846)
Rates: $65+
Tel: (541) 432-1027

INDIAN LODGE MOTEL
201 S Main St
(97846)
Rates: $36-$57
Tel: (541) 432-2651

JUNCTION CITY

GUEST HOUSE MOTEL
1335 Ivy St (97448)
Rates: $41-$67
Tel: (541) 998-6524
(800) 835-5170

KERBY

HOLIDAY MOTEL
24810 Redwood
Hwy (97531)
Rates: $44-$48
Tel: (503) 592-3003

KLAMATH FALLS

BEST WESTERN KLAMATH INN
4061 S 6th St (97603)
Rates: $59-$85
Tel: (541) 882-1200
(800) 528-1234

CIMARRON MOTOR INN
3060 S 6th St (97603)
Rates: $46-$59
Tel: (541) 882-4601
(800) 742-2648

DIAMOND LAKE RESORT
Diamond Lake
(97601)
Rates: $56-$135
Tel: (541) 793-3333
(800) 733-7593

HILL VIEW MOTEL
5543 S 6th St (97601)
Rates: $38-$40
Tel: (541) 883-7771

MAVERICK MOTEL
1220 Main St (97601)
Rates: $31-$39
Tel: (541) 882-6688
(800) 404-6690

OLYMPIC LODGE
3006 Green Springs
Dr (97601)
Rates: $36-$69
Tel: (541) 883-8800

OREGON MOTEL 8
5225 Hwy 97 N
(97601)
Rates: $27-$39
Tel: (541) 883-3431

QUALITY INN
100 Main St (97601)
Rates: $59-$72
Tel: (541) 882-466
(800) 221-2222

RED LION INN
3612 S 6th St (97603)
Rates: $56-$84
Tel: (541) 882-8864
(800) 547-8010

SHILO INNS
2500 Almond St
(97601)
Rates: $89-$119
Tel: (541) 885-7980
(800) 222-2244

SUPER 8 MOTEL
3805 Hwy 97 N
(97601)
Rates: $40-$56
Tel: (800) 800-8000

LA GRANDE

BEST WESTERN PONY SOLDIER MOTOR INN
2612 Island Ave
(97850)
Rates: $64-$85
Tel: (541) 963-7195
(800) 528-1234

BROKEN ARROW LODGE
2215 Adams Ave
(97850)
Rates: $32-$40
Tel: (541) 963-7116

GREENWELL MOTEL
305 Adams Ave
(97850)
Rates: $25-$30
Tel: (541) 963-4134
(800) 772-0991

MOON MOTEL
2116 Adams Ave
(97850)
Rates: n/a
Tel: (541) 963-2724

ORCHARD MOTEL
2206 Adams Ave
(97850)
Rates: $30-$39
Tel: (541) 963-6160

QUAIL RUN MOTOR INN
2400 Adams Ave
(97850)
Rates: $28-$30
Tel: (541) 963-3400

STARDUST LODGE
402 Adams Ave
(97850)
Rates: $30-$35
Tel: (541) 963-4166

WENDELL'S CORNER
2309 Adams Ave
(97850)
Rates: n/a
Tel: (541) 963-4424

LA PINE

DIAMOND STONE GUEST LODGE B & B
16696 Sprague Loop
(97739)
Rates: $75-$120
Tel: (541) 536-6263
(800) 600-6263

EAST LAKE RESORT
P. O. Box 95 (97739)
Rates: $58-$86
Tel: (541) 536-2230

HIGHLANDER MOTEL & RV PARK
51511 Hwy 97
(97739)
Rates: n/a
Tel: (541) 536-2131

LAMPLITER MOTEL & RV PARK
51526 Hwy 97
(97739)
Rates: $32-$36
Tel: (541) 536-2931

PAULINE LAKE RESORT
P. O. Box 7 (97739)
Rates: $60-$125
Tel: (541) 536-2240

TIMBERCREST INN
52560 Hwy 97
(97739)
Rates: $33-$42
Tel: (541) 536-1737

WEST VIEW MOTEL
51371 Hwy 97
(97739)
Rates: $36-$44
Tel: (541) 536-2115
(800) 440-2115

LAKE OSWEGO

BEST WESTERN SHERWOOD INN
15700 SW Upper
Boones Ferry Rd
(97034)
Rates: $50-$85
Tel: (503) 620-2980
(800) 528-1234

CROWNE PLAZA
14811 Kruse Oaks
Blvd (97035)
Rates: $95-$135
Tel: (503) 624-8400
(800) 227-6963

HOWARD JOHNSON PLAZA HOTEL
14811 Kruse Oaks
Blvd (97035)
Rates: $85-$125
Tel: (800) 654-2000

PHOENIX INN
14905 SW Bangy Rd
(97034)
Rates: $54-$60
Tel: (503) 624-7400

RESIDENCE INN PORTLAND SOUTH
15200 SW Bangy Rd
(97035)
Rates: $108-$142
Tel: (503) 684-2603
(800) 331-3131

LAKESIDE

LAKESHORE LODGE
290 S 8th St (97449)
Rates: $34-$49
Tel: (541) 759-3161
(800) 759-3951

**SEADRIFT MOTEL
& CAMPGROUND**
11022 Coast Hwy
101 (97449)
Rates: $36-$44
Tel: (541) 759-3102

LAKEVIEW

**A A MOTEL
& APARTMENTS**
411 North F St
(97630)
Rates: $30-$36
Tel: (541) 947-2201

**HUNTER'S HOT
SPRINGS RESORT**
Hwy 395 N (97630)
Rates: $45-$55
Tel: (541) 948-4800

**INTERSTATE 8
MOTEL**
354 North K St
(97630)
Rates: $34-$40
Tel: (541) 947-3341

**LAKEVIEW LODGE
MOTEL**
301 North G St
(97630)
Rates: $32-$60
Tel: (541) 947-2181

RIM ROCK MOTEL
727 South F St
(97630)
Rates: $30-$34
Tel: (541) 947-2185

LEBANON

**CASCADE CITY
CENTER MOTEL**
1296 Main St (97355)
Rates: $32-$45
Tel: (541) 258-8154

SHANICO INN
1840 Main St (97355)
Rates: $40-$46
Tel: (541) 259-2601

LINCOLN CITY

**ANCHOR MOTEL
AND LODGE**
4417 SW Hwy 101
(97367)
Rates: $40-$60
Tel: (541) 996-3810
(800) 582-8611

BEL-AIRE MOTEL
2945 NW Hwy 101
(97367)
Rates: n/a
Tel: (541) 994-2984

**BEST WESTERN
LINCOLN SANDS
INN**
535 NW Inlet St
(97367)
Rates: $75-$160
Tel: (541) 994-4227
(800) 528-1234

**BLUE HERON
LANDING MOTEL**
4006 W Devils Lake
Rd (97367)
Rates: $54-$58
Tel: (541) 994-4708

CAPTAIN COOK INN
2626 NE Hwy 101
(97367)
Rates: $39-$59
Tel: (541) 994-2522
(800) 994-2522

CITY CENTER MOTEL
1014 NE Hwy 101
(97367)
Rates: $28-$32
Tel: (541) 994-2612

COHO INN
1635 NW Harbor
(97367)
Rates: $62-$78
Tel: (541) 994-3684
(800) 848-7006

**DOCK OF
THE BAY MOTEL**
1116 SW 51st St
(97367)
Rates: $89-$149
Tel: (541) 996-3549
(800) 362-5229

DOLPHIN MOTEL
1018 SE Hwy 101
(97367)
Rates: n/a
Tel: (541) 996-2124

EDGECLIFF MOTEL
3733 SW Hwy 101
(97367)
Rates: $50-$95
Tel: (541) 996-2055

**ENCHANTED
COTTAGE B & B**
4507 SW Coast (97367)
Rates: n/a
Tel: (541) 996-4101

ESTER LEE MOTEL
3803 SW Hwy 101
(97367)
Rates: $40-$95
Tel: (541) 996-3606

**HIDEAWAY
OCEANFRONT
MOTEL**
810 SW 10th St
(97367)
Rates: n/a
Tel: (541) 994-8874

OVERLOOK MOTEL
3521 SW Anchor
(97367)
Rates: n/a
Tel: (541) 996-3300

RODEWAY INN
861 SW 51st St
(97367)
Rates: $40-$85
Tel: (541) 996-3996
(800) 228-2000

SAILOR JACK MOTEL
1035 NW Harbor
Ave (97367)
Rates: $49-$99
Tel: (541) 994-3696
(800) 724-5671

SEA ECHO MOTEL
3510 NE Hwy 101
(97367)
Rates: $35-$55
Tel: (541) 994-2575

**SEA HORSE
OCEANFRONT
MOTEL**
2039 N Harbor Dr
(97367)
Rates: $45-$125
Tel: (541) 994-2101
(800) 996-2101

SEA REST MOTEL
1249 NW 15th St
(97367)
Rates: n/a
Tel: (541) 994-3053

**SEAGULL BEACH-
FRONT MOTEL**
1511 NW Harbor
Ave (97367)
Rates: $45-$120
Tel: (541) 994-2948
(800) 422-0219

SHILO INNS
1501 NW 40th St
(97367)
Rates: $54-$175
Tel: (541) 994-3655
(800) 222-2244

**SURFTIDES BEACH
RESORT**
2945 NW Jetty Ave
(97367)
Rates: $52-$95
Tel: (541) 994-2191
(800) 452-2159

**WESTSHORE
OCEANFRONT
MOTEL**
3127 SW Anchor Ave
(97367)
Rates: $59-$65
Tel: (541) 996-2091
(800) 621-3187

WHISTLING WINDS
3264 NW Jetty Ave
(97367)
Rates: n/a
Tel: (541) 994-6155

MADRAS

**BEST WESTERN
RAMA INN**
12 SW 4th (97741)
Rates: $31-$39
Tel (541) 475-6141

GOFFY'S MOTEL
600 N Hwy 26
(97741)
Rates: $32-$98
Tel: (541) 475-4633
(800) 227-6865

JUNIPER MOTEL
414 N Hwy 26
(97741)
Rates: n/a
Tel: (541) 475-6186
(800) 244-1399

ROYAL DUTCH MOTEL
1101 SW Hwy 97
(97741)
Rates: $30+
Tel: (541) 475-2281

SONNY'S MOTEL
1539 SW Hwy 97
(97741)
Rates: $46-$50
Tel: (541) 475-7217
(800) 624-6137

MANZANITA

SUNSET SURF MOTEL
248 Ocean Rd
(97130)
Rates: $55-$119
Tel: (541) 368-5224
(800) 243-8035

MAUPIN

DESCHUTES MOTEL
Rt 1, Box 10, Hwy
197 (97037)
Rates: $35-$40
Tel: (541) 395-2626

THE OASIS RESORT
609 Hwy 197 (97037)
Rates: $35-$55
Tel: (541) 395-2611

McKENZIE BRIDGE

THE COUNTRY PLACE
56245 Delta Dr
(97413)
Rates: $63-$200
Tel: (541) 822-6008

McKENZIE RIVER

EAGLE ROCK LODGE RESORT BED & BREAKFAST
49198 McKenzie
Hwy (97489)
Rates: $65-$129
Tel: (541) 822-3962

McMINNVILLE

BEST WESTERN VINEYARD INN
2035 SW 99W
(97128)
Rates: $62-$70
Tel: (503) 472-4900
(800) 285-6242

PARAGON MOTEL
2065 Hwy 99 West
(97128)
Rates: $39-$91
Tel: (503) 472-9493
(800) 525-5469

MEDFORD

BEST WESTERN PONY SOLDIER INN
2340 Crater Lake
Hwy (97504)
Rates: $69-$86
Tel: ((541) 779-2011
(800) 528-1234

CAPRI MOTEL
250 Barnett Rd
(97504)
Rates: $29-$38
Tel: (541) 773-7796

CEDAR LODGE MOTOR INN
518 N Riverside
(97501)
Rates: $37-$62
Tel: (541) 773-7361
(800) 282-3419

HORIZON MOTOR INN
1150 E Barnett Rd
(97501)
Rates: $55-$646
Tel: (541) 779-5085
(800) 452-2255

MOTEL ORLEANS
850 Alba Dr (97504)
Rates: $35-$39
Tel: (541) 779-6730
(800) 626-1900

PEAR TREE MOTEL
3730 Fern Valley Rd
(97504)
Rates: $55-$58
Tel: (541) 535-4445

RED LION INN
200 N Riverside
(97501)
Rates: $82-$164
Tel: (541) 779-5811
(800) 547-8010

RESTON HOTEL
2300 Crater Lake
Hwy (97504)
Rates: $52-$72
Tel: (541) 779-3141
(800) 779-STAY

TRAVELODGE
2111 Biddle Rd
(97504)
Rates: $49-$80
Tel: (541) 620-6574
(800) 578-7878

WINDMILL INN OF MEDFORD
1950 Biddle Rd
(97504)
Rates: $54-$70
Tel: (541) 779-0050
(800) 547-4747

MILTON-FREEWATER

OUT WEST MOTEL
Hwy 11 (97862)
Rates: $33-$40
Tel: (541) 938-6647
(800) 881-6647

MILWAUKIE

MILWAUKIE INN
14015 SE
McLoughlin Blvd
(97267)
Rates: $35-$65
Tel: (503) 659-2125
(800) 255-1553

MOLALLA

STAGE COACH INN MOTEL
415 Grange St
(97038)
Rates: $42-$65
Tel: (503) 829-4382

MONMOUTH

COURTESY INN
270 N Pacific Hwy
(97361)
Rates: $45-$60
Tel: (541) 838-4438

MOSIER

HEWETT'S B & B
501 Third St (97040)
Rates: $45-$75
Tel: (541) 478-3455

MT. HOOD

MT. HOOD INN
87450 E Government
Camp Loop (97028)
Rates: $95-$135
Tel: (503) 272-3205
(800) 443-7777

SHAMROCK FOREST INN
59550 E Hwy 26
(97028)
Rates: $38-$69
Tel: (503) 622-4003

MYRTLE POINT

MYRTLE TREES MOTEL
1010 8th St (97458)
Rates: $30-$39
Tel: (541) 572-5811

NESKIA BEACH

BREAKER HOUSE AT NESKIA BEACH
32864 Neskia Beach
Rd (97444)
Rates: $80-$145
Tel: (541) 247-6670

NESKOWIN

THE BREAKERS CONDOMINUMS
48060 Breakers Blvd
(97149)
Rates: $75-$190
Tel: (503) 392-3417

NETARTS

TERIMORE LODGING BY THE SEA
5105 Crab Ave
(97143)
Rates: $40-$80
Tel: (503) 842-4623
(800) 635-1821

THREE CAPES INN AT NETARTS
4800 Netarts Hwy W
(97143)
Rates: $45-$60
Tel: (503) 842-4003

NEWBERG

SHILO INNS
501 Sitka Ave (97132)
Rates: $59-$75
Tel: (503) 537-0303
(800) 222-2244

NEWPORT

**AGATE BEACH
OCEAN FRONT**
175 NW Gilbert Way
(97365)
Rates: $90-$100
Tel: (541) 265-8746
(800) 755-5674

**BEST WESTERN
HALLMARK RESORT**
744 SW Elizabeth St
(97365)
Rates: $79-$239
Tel: (541) 265-2600
(800) 528-1234

CITY CENTER MOTEL
538 SW Coast Hwy
(97365)
Rates: $38-$65
Tel: (541) 265-7381
(800) 628-9665

**DRIFTWOOD
VILLAGE MOTEL**
7947 N Coast Hwy
(97365)
Rates: $50-$125
Tel: (541) 265-5738

MONEY SAVER MOTEL
861 SW Coast Hwy
101 (97365)
Rates: n/a
Tel: (541) 265-2277

**NEWPORT
MOTOR INN**
1311 N Hwy 101
(97365)
Rates: $40-$42
Tel: (541) 265-8516

PENNY SAVER MOTEL
710 N Hwy 101
(97365)
Rates: $38-$65
Tel: (541) 265-6631
(800) 477-3669

**SANDS
MOTOR LODGE**
206 N Coast Hwy
(97365)
Rates: $36-$48
Tel: (541) 265-5321

SHILO INNS
536 SW Elizabeth
(97365)
Rates: $76-$164
Tel: (541) 265-7701
(800) 222-2244

**SURF 'N SAND
MOTEL**
8143 N Hwy 101
(97365)
Rates: $62-$96
Tel: (541) 265-2215

TIDES INN MOTEL
715 SW Bay St
(97365)
Rates: $30-$80
Tel: (541) 265-7202

VAL-U INN MOTEL
531 SW Fall St
(97365)
Rates: $65-$125
Tel: (541) 265-6203
(800) 443-7777

VIKINGS COTTAGES
729 NW Coast St
(97365)
Rates: $55-75
Tel: (541) 265-2477
(800) 480-2477

WAVES MOTEL
820 NW Coast St
(97365)
Rates: $48-$150
Tel: (541) 265-4661
(800) 282-6993

WEST WIND MOTEL
747 SW Coast Hwy
(97365)
Rates: $40-$55
Tel: (541) 265-5388
(800) 305-5388

WHALER MOTEL
155 SW Elizabeth
(97365)
Rates: $88-$120
Tel: (541) 265-9261
(800) 443-9444

WILLER'S MOTEL
754 SW Coast Hwy
(97365)
Rates: $38-$80
Tel: (541) 265-2241
(800) 945-5377

NORTH BEND

BAY BRIDGE MOTEL
33 US 101 (97459)
Rates: $41-$65
Tel: (541) 756-3151
(800) 557-3156

**ITTY BITTY INN
B & B MOTEL**
1504 Sherman Ave
(97459)
Rates: $38-$42
Tel: (541) 756-6398

PARKSIDE INN
1480 Sherman Ave
(97459)
Rates: n/a
Tel: (541) 756-4124

**PONY VILLAGE
MOTOR LODGE**
Virginia Ave (97459)
Rates: $41-$59
Tel: (541) 756-3191

NORTH POWDER

**POWDER RIVER
MOTEL**
850 2nd St (97867)
Rates: n/a
Tel: (541) 898-2829

OAKLAND

RANCH MOTEL
581 John Long Rd
(97470)
Rates: $27-$75
Tel: (541) 849-2126

OAKRIDGE

ARBOR INN
48229 Hwy 58
(97463)
Rates: $27-$32
Tel: (541) 782-2611
(800) 505-9047

**BEST WESTERN
OAKRIDGE INN**
47433 Hwy 58
(97463)
Rates: $45-$62
Tel: (541) 782-2212
(800) 528-1234

OAKRIDGE MOTEL
48197 Hwy 58
(97463)
Rates: $29-$35
Tel: (541) 782-2432

ONTARIO

BUDGET INN
1737 N Oregon St
(97914)
Rates: $35-$80
Tel: (541) 889-3101
(800) 905-0024

CARLILE MOTEL
589 N Oregon St
(97914)
Rates: $30-$35
Tel: (541) 889-8658
(800) 640-8658

**HOLIDAY
MOTOR INN**
615 E Idaho (97914)
Rates: $34-$48
Tel: (541) 889-9188

HOWARD JOHNSON
1249 Tapadera Ave
(97914)
Rates: $52-$62
Tel: (541) 889-8621
(800) 654-2000

**OREGON TRAIL
MOTEL**
92 E Idaho (97914)
Rates: $28-$75
Tel: (541) 889-8633
(800) 895-7945

**REGENCY CREST
INN MOTEL**
88 N Oregon St
(97914)
Rates: $35-$65
Tel: (541) 889-6449
(800) 889-6449

STOCKMAN'S MOTEL
81 SW 1st St (97914)
Rates: $28-$50
Tel: (541) 889-4446

OREGON CITY

VAL-U INN MOTEL
1900 Clackamette Dr
(97045)
Rates: $54-$68
Tel: (503) 655-7141
(800) 443-7777

OTTER ROCK

ALPINE CHALETS
7045 Otter Crest
Loop (97369)
Rates: $75-$90
Tel: (541) 765-2572
(800) 825-5768

PACIFIC CITY

**ANCHORAGE
MOTEL**
6585 Pacific Ave
(97135)
Rates: $35-$49
Tel: (503) 965-6773

INN AT PACIFIC CITY
35215 Brooten Rd
(97135)
Rates: $44-$59
Tel: (503) 965-6366

PARKDALE

**MOUNT HOOD
BED & BREAKFAST**
8885 Cooper Spur
Rd (97041)
Rates: $90-$124
Tel: (541) 352-6885
(800) 557-8885

PENDLETON

CHAPARRAL MOTEL
620 SW Tutuilla
(97801)
Rates: $45
Tel: (541) 276-8654

**LET 'ER BUCK
MOTEL**
205 SE Dorion Ave
(97801)
Rates: $26-$32
Tel: (541) 276-3293

LONGHORN MOTEL
411 SW Dorion Ave
(97801)
Rates: $31-$35
Tel: (541) 276-7531

RED LION HOTEL
304 SE Nye Ave
(97801)
Rates: $63-$80
Tel: (541) 276-6141
(800) 733-5466

7 INN
I-84 Exit 202 (97801)
Rates: $31-$84
Tel: (541) 276-4711

SUPER 8 MOTEL
601 SE Nye Ave
(97801)
Rates: $43-$59
Tel: (541) 276-8881
(800) 800-8000

**TAPADERA
MOTOR INN**
105 SE Court (97801)
Rates: $34-$58
Tel: (541) 276-3231
(800) 722-8277

PILOT ROCK

PILOT ROCK MOTEL
362 NE 4th St
(97868)
Rates: n/a
Tel: (541) 443-2851

PORT ORFORD

**CASTAWAY-
BY-THE-SEA MOTEL**
545 W 5th St (97465)
Rates: $45-$75
Tel: (541) 332-4502

SHORELINE MOTEL
206 6th (97465)
Rates: $32-$39
Tel: (541) 332-2903

PORTLAND

**ALADDIN
MOTOR INN**
8905 SW 30th AVe
(97219)
Rates: $34-$65
Tel: (503) 246-8241
(800) 292-4466

**AMERICAN BUDGET
INN-6TH AVE**
2221 SW 6th Ave
(97201)
Rates: $37-$44
Tel: (503) 226-2979

THE BENSON HOTEL
309 SW Broadway at
Oak (97205)
Rates: $165-$600
Tel: (503) 228-2000
(800) 426-0670

BEST VALUE INN
3310 SE 82nd Ave
(97266)
Rates: 33-$50
Tel: (503) 777-4786
(800) 358-5066

**BEST WESTERN
HERITAGE INN**
4319 NW Yeon
(97210)
Rates: $54-$115
Tel: (503) 497-9044
(800) 528-1234

**BEST WESTERN INN
CONV. CENTER**
420 NE Holladay St
(97232)
Rates: $60-$85
Tel: (503) 233-6331
(800) 528-1234

**BEST WESTERN INN
AT THE MEADOWS**
1215 N Hayden
Meadows Dr (97217)
Rates: $80-$150
Tel: (503) 286-9600
(800) 528-1234

**BUDGET VALUE
VIKING MOTEL**
6701 N Interstate
Ave (97217)
Rates: $38-$42
Tel: (503) 285-6687
(800) 308-5097

**CLARION HOTEL
AIRPORT**
6233 NE 78th Ct
(97218)
Rates: $79-$104
Tel: (503) 251-2000
(800) 994-7878

**COMFORT INN-
LLOYD CENTER**
431 NE Multnomah
St (97232)
Rates: $56-$99
Tel: (503) 233-7933
(800) 221-2222

**CYPRESS INN-
DOWNTOWN**
809 SW King St
(97205)
Rates: $45-$80
Tel: (503) 252-8247
(800) 225-4205

**DAYS INN
CITY CENTER**
1414 SW 6th Ave
(97201)
Rates: $66-$93
Tel: (503) 221-1611
(800) 899-0248

**DAYS INN
AIRPORT**
3828 NE 2nd Ave
(97220)
Rates: $55-85
Tel: (503) 256-2550
(800) 329-7466

DELTA INN
9930 N Whitaker
(97217)
Rates: $55-$65
Tel: (503) 289-1800
(800) 833-1800

FIFTH AVENUE SUITES
521 SW 5th Ave
(97204)
Rates: $155-$165
Tel: (503) 222-0001
(800) 711-2971

4TH AVENUE MOTEL
1889 SW 4th Ave
(97201)
Rates: $40-$45
Tel: (503) 226-7646

**HISTORIC HOTEL
VINTAGE PLAZA**
422 SW Broadway
(97205)
Rates: $155-$245
Tel: (503) 228-1212
(800) 243-0555

**HOLIDAY INN
EXPRESS**
2323 NE 181st St
(97230)
Rates: $65-$75
Tel: (503) 492-4000
(800) 465-4329

**HOLIDAY IN
AIRPORT**
8439 NE Columbia
Blvd (97220)
Rates: $79-$89
Tel: (503) 256-5000
(800) 465-4329

HOLIDAY MOTEL
8050 NE Martin
Luther King (97211)
Rates: $35-$45
Tel: (503) 285-3661

HOWARD JOHNSON AIRPORT
7101 NE 82nd Ave (97220)
Rates: $77-$88
Tel: (503) 255-6722
(800) 446-4656

IMPERIAL HOTEL
400 SW Broadway & Stark St (97205)
Rates: $87-$109
Tel: (503) 228-7221
(800) 452-2323

MALLORY HOTEL
729 SW 15th (97205)
Rates: $65-$110
Tel: (503) 223-6311
(800) 228-8657

THE MARK SPENCER HOTEL
409 SW 11th Ave (97205)
Rates: $57-$98
Tel: (503) 224-3293
(800) 548-3934

MARRIOTT PORTLAND
1401 SW Front Ave (97201)
Rates: $137-$500
Tel: (503) 226-7600

MEL'S MOTOR INN
5205 N Interstate Ave (97217)
Rates: $36-$55
Tel: (503) 285-2556

OXFORD SUITES
12226 N Jantzen Dr (97217)
Rates: $66-$77
Tel: (503) 283-3030
(800) 548-7848

PORTLAND CENTER APARTMENTS
200 SW Harrison St (97201)
Rates: n/a
Tel: (503) 224-3030

RANCH INN MOTEL
10138 SW Barbur Blvd (97219)
Rates: $33-$40
Tel: (503) 246-3375

RESIDENCE INN PORTLAND WEST
18855 NW Tanasbourne Dr (97229)
Rates: $79-$110
Tel: (503) 531-3200
(800) 331-3131

THE RIVERSIDE INN
50 SW Morrison St (97204)
Rates: $79-$129
Tel: (503) 221-0711
(800) 899-0247

ROSE MANOR INN
4546 SE McLoughlin Blvd (97202)
Rates: $30-$51
Tel: (503) 236-4175
(800) 252-8222

ROSE MOTEL
8920 SW Barbur (97219)
Rates: n/a
Tel: (503) 244-0107

QUALITY INN AIRPORT
8247 NE Sandy Blvd (97220)
Rates: $70-$125
Tel: (503) 256-4111
(800) 221-2222

RED LION HOTEL COLUMBIA RIVER
1401 N Hayden Island Dr (97217)
Rates: $103-$145
Tel: (503) 283-2111
(800) 547-8010

RED LION HOTEL DOWNTOWN
310 SW Lincoln (97201)
Rates: $98-$118
Tel: (503) 221-0450
(800) 547-8010

RED LION HOTEL JANTZEN BEACH
909 N Hayden Island Dr (97217)
Rates: $98-$130
Tel: (503) 283-4466
(800) 547-8010

RED LION INN COLISEUM
1224 N Thunderbird Way (97227)
Rates: $60-$88
Tel: (503) 235-8311
(800) 547-8010

RIVER PLACE HOTEL
1510 SW Harbor Way (97201)
Rates: $165-$600
Tel: (503) 228-3233
(800) 227-1333

RODEWAY INN LLOYD CENTER
1506 NE 2nd Ave (97232)
Rates: $55-$75
Tel: (503) 231-7665
(800) 228-2000

SIXTH AVENUE MOTEL
2221 SW 6th Ave (97201)
Rates: $36-$43
Tel: (503) 226-2979

VALUE INN DOWNTOWN
415 SW Montgomery St (97201)
Rates: $35-$60
Tel: (503) 226-4751

PORT ORFORD

CASTAWAY BY THE SEA
P. O. Box 844 (97465)
Rates: $52-$69
Tel: (541) 332-4502

SEA CREST MOTEL
P. O. Box C (97465)
Rates: $30-$55
Tel: (541) 332-3040

PRINEVILLE

CAROLINA MOTEL
1050 E 3rd St (97754)
Rates: $26-$59
Tel: (541) 447-4152

CITY CENTER MOTEL
509 E 3rd St (97754)
Rates: $28-$45
Tel: (541) 447-5522

OCHOCO INN & MOTEL
123 E 3rd St (97754)
Rates: $36-$40
Tel: (541) 447-6231

RUSTLERS ROOST MOTEL
960 W 3rd St (97754)
Rates: $36-$40
Tel: (541) 447-4185

PRAIRIE CITY

STRAWBERRY MOUNTAIN INN
HCR 77, 940 Hwy 26 E (97869)
Rates: $55-$85
Tel: (541) 820-4522
(800) 545-6913

PROSPECT

PROSPECT HISTORICAL HOTEL
391 Mill Creek Dr (97536)
Rates: $50-$85
Tel: (541) 560-3664
(800) 994-6490

REDMOND

HUB MOTEL
1128 N Hwy 97 (97756)
Rates: $38-$42
Tel: (541) 548-2101
(800) 784-3482

REDMOND INN
1545 Hwy 97 (97756)
Rates: $44-$58
Tel: (541) 548-1091
(800) 833-3259

REEDSPORT

ANCHOR BAY INN
1821 Winchester Ave (97467)
Rates: $32-$52
Tel: (541) 271-2149
(800) 767-1821

BEST BUDGET INN
1894 Winchester Ave (97467)
Rates: $30-$75
Tel: (541) 271-3686

BEST WESTERN SALBASGEON INN
1400 Hwy Ave 101 (97467)
Rates: $56-$86
Tel: (541) 271-4831
(800) 528-1234

DOUGLAS COUNTRY INN
1894 Winchester Ave (97467)
Rates: $34-$36
Tel: (541) 271-3686

FIR GROVE MOTEL
2178 Winchester Ave (97467)
Rates: $32-$42
Tel: (541) 271-4848

SALBASGEON INN OF THE UMPQUA
45209 SR 38 (97467)
Rates: $65-$85
Tel: (541) 271-2025

SALTY SEAGULL MOTEL
1806 Winchester Ave (97467)
Rates: $29-$44
Tel: (541) 271-3729
(800) 476-8336

TROPICANA MOTEL
1593 Highway Ave (97467)
Rates: $32-$49
Tel: (541) 271-3671
(800) 799-9970

ROCKAWAY BEACH

BROADWATER VACATION RENTALS
438 Hwy 101 (97136)
Rates: $59-$149
Tel: (503) 355-2248

GETAWAY MOTEL ON THE BEACH
621 S Pacific (97136)
Rates: $40-$120
Tel: (503) 355-2501
(800) 756-5552

OCEAN LOCOMOTION MOTEL
19130 Alder Ave (97136)
Rates: $45-$87
Tel: (503) 355-2093

OCEAN SPRAY MOTEL
505 N Pacific Ave (97136)
Rates: $40-$60
Tel: (503) 355-2237

101 MOTEL
530 N Hwy 101 (97136)
Rates: $25-$55
Tel: (503) 355-2420

SAND DOLLAR MOTEL
105 NW 23rd Ave (97136)
Rates: $40-$80
Tel: (503) 355-2301

SEA TREASURES INN
301 N Miller St (97136)
Rates: $40-$70
Tel: (503) 355-8220
(800) 444-1864

SILVER SANDS MOTEL
215 S Pacific (97136)
Rates: $62-$78
Tel: (503) 355-2206
(800) 457-8972

SURFSIDE RESORT MOTEL
101 NW 11th Ave (97136)
Rates: $48-$149
Tel: (503) 355-2312
(800) 243-7786

TRADEWINDS MOTEL
523 N Pacific St (97136)
Rates: $55-$150
Tel: (503) 355-2112
(800) 824-0938

ROSEBURG

BEST WESTERN DOUGLAS INN MOTEL
511 SE Stephens St (97470)
Rates: $40-$72
Tel: (541) 673-6625
(800) 528-1234

BEST WESTERN GARDEN VILLA MOTEL
760 NW Garden Valley Blvd (97470)
Rates: $52-$86
Tel: (541) 672-1601
(800) 528-1234

BUDGET 16 MOTEL
1067 NE Stephens St (97470)
Rates: $40-$46
Tel: (541) 673-5556

CASA LOMA MOTEL
1107 NE Stephens St (97470)
Rates: $27-$35
Tel: (541) 673-5569

DUNES MOTEL
610 W Madrone St (97470)
Rates: $40-$56
Tel: (541) 672-6684
(800) 260-9973

HOLIDAY INN EXP.
375 W Harvard Blvd (97470)
Rates: $52-$87
Tel: (541) 673-7517
(800) 465-4329

HOWARD JOHNSON
978 NE Stephens St (97470)
Rates: $58-$90
Tel: (541) 673-5082
(800) 446-4656

MOTEL ORLEANS
427 NW Garden Valley Rd (97470)
Rates: $40-$49
Tel: (541) 673-5561
(800) 626-1900

SYCAMORE MOTEL-NATIONAL 9
1627 SE Stephens St (97470)
Rates: n/a
Tel: (541) 672-3354
(800) 524-9999

WINDMILL INN
1450 NW Mulholland Dr (97470)
Rates: $50-$71
Tel: (541) 673-0901
(800) 547-4747

ST. HELENS

BEST WESTERN OAK MEADOWS INN
585 S Columbia River Hwy (97501)
Rates: $55-$65
Tel: (503) 397-3000
(800) 528-1234

VILLAGE INN MOTEL
535 S Hwy 30 (97501)
Rates: $34-$43
Tel: (503) 397-1490

SALEM

CITY CENTRE MOTEL
510 Liberty St SE (97301)
Rates: $42-$52
Tel: (503) 364-0121
(800) 289-0121

GRAND MOTEL
1555 State St (97301)
Rates: $36-$45
Tel: (503) 581-2466

HOLIDAY LODGE
1400 Hawthorne (97301)
Rates: $40-$48
Tel: (503) 585-2323
(800) 543-5071

MOTEL 6
2250 Mission St SE (97302)
Rates: $31-$37
Tel: (503) 588-7191
(800) 440-6000

PHOENIX INN
4370 Commercial SE (97308)
Rates: $53-$105
Tel: (503) 588-9220
(800) 445-4498

QUALITY HOTEL
3301 Market St NE (97301)
Rates: $61-$125
Tel: (503) 370-7888
(800) 221-2222

SILVER MOUNTAIN BED & BREAKFAST
4672 Drift Creek Rd SE (97301)
Rates: $60-$70
Tel: (503) 769-7127
(800) 952-3905

TIKI LODGE MOTEL
3705 Market St NE (97301)
Rate: $31-$59
Tel: (503) 581-4441
(800) 438-8458

TRAVELODGE
1875 Fisher Rd NE
(97305)
Rates: $31-$47
Tel: (503) 588-5423

SANDY

**BEST WESTERN
SANDY INN**
37465 Hwy 26
(97055)
Rates: $49-$95
Tel: (503) 668-7100
(800) 528-1234

**MOUNT HOOD
SHAMROCK FOREST
MOTEL INN**
59550 E Hwy 26
(97055)
Rates: $30-$51
Tel: (503) 622-4911

SEASIDE

**BEST WESTERN
OCEAN VIEW
RESORT**
414 N Promenade
(97138)
Rates: $90-$124
Tel: (503) 738-3334
(800) 234-8439

CITY CENTER MOTEL
250 1st Ave (97138)
Rates: $48-$149
Tel: (503) 738-6377
(800) 479-5191

COAST RIVER INN
800 S Holladay Dr
(97138)
Rates: $55-$75
Tel: (503) 738-8474
(800) 479-5191

**COMFORT INN
BOARDWALK**
545 Broadway
(97138)
Rates: $65-$95
Tel: (503) 738-3011
(800) 228-5150

**COUNTRY RIVER
INN**
1020 N Holladay Dr
(97138)
Rates: $40-$80
Tel: (503) 738-8049
(800) 605-3337

**EDGEWATER INN
PROMENADE**
341 S Promenade
(97138)
Rates: $69-$159
Tel: (503) 738-4142
(800) 822-3170

**INN ON THE
PROMENADE**
361 S Promenade
(97138)
Rates: $50-$140
Tel: (503) 738-5241
(800) 654-2506

THE LANAI MOTEL
3140 Sunset Blvd
(97138)
Rates: $45-$85
Tel: (503) 738-6343
(800) 738-2683

SEASIDER MOTEL
110 5th Ave (97138)
Rates: $35-$135
Tel: (503) 738-7764
(800) 840-7764

SEASIDER II MOTEL
210 N Downing
(97138)
Rates: $35-$70
Tel: (503) 738-7622

SEAVIEW INN
120 9th Ave (97138)
Rates: $54-484
Tel: (503) 738-5371
(800) 479-5191

SISTERS

**BEST WESTERN
PONDEROSA
LODGE**
500 Hwy 20 W
(97759)
Rates: $64-$74
Tel: (541) 549-1234
(800) 528-1234

BLUE LAKE RESORT
Blue Lake Dr,
Hwy 20/126 (97759)
Rates: $68-$108
Tel: (541) 595-6671

**CASCADE COUNTRY
INN**
15870 Barclay Dr
(97759)
Rates: $100-$125
Tel: (541) 549-4666
(800) 316-0089

COMFORT INN
540 Hwy 20 W
(97759)
Rates: $59-$74
Tel: (541) 549-7829
(800) 221-2222

SPRINGFIELD

**RED LION INN/
EUGENE-
SPRINGFIELD**
3280 Gateway Rd
(97477)
Rates: $61-$94
Tel: (541) 726-8181
(800) 547-8010

RODEWAY INN
3480 Hutton St
(97477)
Rates: $56-$66
Tel: (541) 746-8471
(800) 228-2000

SHILO INNS
3350 Gateway Rd
(97477)
Rates: $49-$63
Tel: (541) 747-0332
 (800) 222-2244

SUTTON MOTEL
1152 Main St (97477)
Rates: $31-$32
Tel: (541) 747-5621

**VILLAGE INN
MOTEL**
1875 Mohawk Blvd
(97477)
Rates: $42-$47
Tel: (541) 747-4546
(800) 327-6871

STAYTON

**GARDNER HOUSE
BED & BREAKFAST**
633 N 3rd Ave
(97383)
Rates: $55-$65
Tel: (503) 769-5478

SUBLIMITY

**BEST WESTERN
SUNRISE INN**
300 Sublimity Blvd
(97385)
Rates: $45-$89
Tel: (503) 769-9579
(800) 528-1234

SUMMER LAKE

**THE LODGE
AT SUMMER LAKE**
36980 Hwy 31
(97640)
Rates: $34-$45
Tel: (541) 943-3993

SUMMER LAKE B & B
D7 Ranch (97640)
Rates: $50-$85
Tel: (541) 943-3983
(800) 261-2778

SUMPTER

SUMPTER B & B
344 NE Columbia St
(97877)
Rates: n/a
Tel: (541) 894-2229
(800) 640-3184

SUNNY VALLEY

**SUNNY VALLEY
MOTEL**
I-5 Exit 71 (97497)
Rates: $30-$45
Tel: (541) 476-9217

SUNRIVER

**TWIN LAKES
RESORT**
11200 S Century Dr
(97707)
Rates: $62-$96
Tel: (541) 593-6526

**VILLAGE
PROPERTIES**
P. O. Box 3055
(97707)
Rates: $70-$285
Tel: (541) 593-1653
(800) 786-7483

SUTHERLIN

**TOWN AND
COUNTRY MOTEL**
1386 W Central Ave
(97479)
Rates: $43-$52
Tel: (541) 459-9615
(800) 459-9615

SWEET HOME

PORTA VIA MOTEL
805 Long St (97386)
Rates: $42-$59
Tel: (541) 367-5137

WILLOW MOTEL
3026 Hwy 20 (97386)
Rates: $22-$40
Tel: (541) 367-2206

THE DALLES

BEST EASTERN OREGON MOTOR MOTEL
200 W 2nd St (97058)
Rates: $39-$49
Tel: (541) 296-9111

BEST WESTERN TAPADERA INN
112 W 2nd (97058)
Rates: $59-$69
Tel: (541) 296-9107
(800) 528-1234

CAPTAIN GRAY'S GUEST HOUSE
210 W 4th St (97058)
Rates: $40-$50
Tel: (541) 298-2222
(800) 448-4729

DAYS INN
2500 W 6th (97058)
Rates: $49-$59
Tel: (541) 296-1191
(800) 329-7466

THE INN AT THE DALLES
3550 SE Frontage Rd (97058)
Rates: $35-$46
Tel: (541) 296-1167
(800) 982-3496

LONE PINE MOTEL
351 Lone Pine Dr (97058)
Rates: $42-$58
Tel: (541) 298-2800

QUALITY INN
2114 W 6th (97058)
Rates: $59-$69
Tel: (541) 298-5161
(800) 221-2222

SHAMROCK MOTEL
118 W 4th St (97058)
Rates: $28-$38
Tel: (541) 296-5464

SHILO INNS
3223 NE Bret Clodfelter Way (97058)
Rates: $59-$83
Tel: (541) 298-5502
(800) 222-2244

TIGARD

BEST WESTERN INN CHATEAU 290
17993 Lower Boones Ferry Rd (97224)
Rates: $52-$90
Tel: (503) 620-2030
(800) 528-1234

EMBASSY SUITES HOTEL
9000 SW Washington Sq Rd (97223)
Rates: $132-$142
Tel: (503) 644-4000
(800) 772-3897

MOTEL 6
17950 SW McEwan Rd (97224)
Rates: $36-$46
Tel: (503) 620-2066
(800) 440-6000

MOTEL 6
17959 SW McEwan Rd (97224)
Rates: $35-47
Tel: (503) 684-0760
(800) 440-6000

QUALITY INN PORTLAND I-5 SOUTH
7300 SW Hazelfern Rd (97223)
Rates: $59-$89
Tel: (503) 620-3460
(800) 228-5151

SHILO INNS WASHINGTON SQUARE
10830 SW Greenburg Rd (97223)
Rates: $58-$76
Tel: (800) 222-2244

TILLAMOOK

SHILO INNS
2515 N Main (97141)
Rates: $62-$89
Tel: (800) 222-2244

WESTERN ROYAL INN
1125 N Main (97141)
Rates: $45-$74
Tel: (503) 842-8844

TROUTDALE

SHILO INNS
2522 NE 238th Dr (97060)
Rates: $45-$69
Tel: (503) 667-1414
(800) 222-2244

PHOENIX INN
477 NW Phoenix Dr (97060)
Rates: $50-$61
Tel: (503) 669-6500
(800) 824-6824

TUALATIN

SWEETBRIER INN
7125 SW Nyberg Rd (97062)
Rates: $55-$78
Tel: (503) 692-5800
(800) 692-5800

UMATILLA

HEATHER INN
705 Willamette Ave (97882)
Rates: $41-$60
Tel: (541) 922-4871
(800) 447-7529

REST-A-BIT MOTEL
1370 6th St (97882)
Rates: $26-$44
Tel: (541) 922-3271
(800) 423-9913

UNION

ANGLE FARM COUNTRY INN B & B
1782 S Main (97883)
Rates: n/a
Tel: (541) 562-5671

VIDA

WAYFARER RESORT
46725 Goodpasture Rd (97488)
Rates: $70-$190
Tel: (541) 896-3613

WALDPORT

ALSEA MANOR MOTEL
190 SW Hwy 101 (97394)
Rates: $52-$58
Tel: (541) 563-3249

EDGEWATER COTTAGES
3978 SW 101 (97394)
Rates: $50-$150
Tel: (541) 563-2240

SEA STONES COTTAGES
6317 SW 101 (97394)
Rates: $31-$66
Tel: (541) 547-3118

SUNDOWN MOTEL
5050 SW PCH 101 (97394)
Rates: $39-$79
Tel: ((541) 563-3018
(800) 535-0192

WALDPORT MOTEL
170 SW Arrow (97394)
Rates: $30-$50
Tel: (541) 563-3035

WALLOWA

MINGO MOTEL & HOT TUB
102 N Alder (97885)
Rates: $36-$38
Tel: (541) 886-2021

WALLOWA LAKE

STEIN'S CABINS
84681 Ponderosa Ln (97846)
Rates: $55-$85
Tel: (541) 432-2391

WARRENTON

RAY'S MOTEL
45 NE Skipanon Dr
(97146)
Rates: $32-$43
Tel: (503) 861-2566
(800) 348-2566

SHILO INNS
1609 E Harbor Dr
(97146)
Rates: $74-$130
Tel: (503) 861-2181
(800) 222-2244

WARM SPRINGS

**KAH-NEE-TA
VILLAGE**
100 Main St (97761)
Rates: $90-$110
Tel: (541) 553-1112
(800) 831-1071

WARRENTON

SHILO INNS
1609 E Harbor Dr
(97146)
Rates: $63-$121
Tel: (503) 861-2181
(800) 222-2244

WELCHES

MT. HOOD VILLAGE
65000 E Hwy 26
(97067)
Rates: n/a
Tel: (503) 622-4011

**OLD WELCHES INN
BED & BREAKFAST**
26401 E Welches Rd
(97067)
Rates: $75-$130
Tel: (503) 622-3574

WESTLAKE

**SILTCOOS LAKE
RESORT**
82855 Fir St (97493)
Rates: $60-$75
Tel: (541) 997-3741

WESTPORT

WESTPORT MOTEL
Hwy 30 (97016)
Rates: 38-$78
Tel: (503) 455-2212

WHEELER

**WHEELER ON
THE BAY LODGE**
580 Marine Dr
(97147)
Rates: $80-$112
Tel: (503) 368-5858
(800) 469-3204

WILSONVILLE

**BEST WESTERN
WILLAMETTE INN**
30800 SW Parkway
Ave (97070)
Rates: $64-$85
Tel: (503) 682-2288
(800) 528-1234

**HOLIDAY INN
PORTLAND SOUTH**
25425 SW Boones
Ferry Rd (97070)
Rates: $59-$125
Tel: (503) 682-2211
(800) 465-4329

MOTEL ORLEANS
8815 SW Sun Place
(97070)
Rates: $33-$68
Tel: (503) 682-3184
(800) 626-1900

SUPER 8 MOTEL
25438 SW Parkway
Ave (97070)
Rates: $41-$51
Tel: (800) 800-8000

WINCHESTER BAY

FRIENDSHIP INN
390 Broadway
(97467)
Rates: $48-$85
Tel: (541) 271-4871
(800) 424-4777

WOODBURN

COMFORT INN
120 NE Arney Rd
(97071)
Rates: $55-$75
Tel: (503) 982-1727
(800) 221-2222

**FAIRWAY INN
MOTEL**
2450 Country Club
Ct (97071)
Rates: $32-$50
Tel: (503) 981-3211
(800) 981-2466

**HOLIDAY INN
EXPRESS**
2887 Newberg Hwy
(97071)
Rates: $59-$79
Tel: (503) 982-6515

YACHATS

THE ADOBE RESORT
1555 Hwy 101
(97498)
Rates: $58-$95
Tel: (541) 547-3141
(800) 522-3623

FIRESIDE MOTEL
1881 Hwy 101 N
(97498)
Rates: $48-$80
Tel: (541) 547-3636
(800) 336-3573

**GULL HAVEN
LODGE**
94770 Hwy 101 N
(97498)
Rates: $35-$85
Tel: (541) 547-3583

**HOLIDAY INN
MARKET & MOTEL**
5933 Hwy 101 N
(97498)
Rates: $50-$60
Tel: (541) 547-3120

OCEAN COVE INN
Prospect & Hwy 101
(97498)
Rates: $55-$80
Tel: (541) 547-3900

**ROCK PARK
COTTAGES**
431 West 2nd St
(97498)
Rates: $46-$56
Tel: (541) 547-3214

**SHAMROCK
LODGETTES
RESORT & SPA**
105 Hwy 101 S
(97498)
Rates: $65-$99
Tel: (541) 547-3312
(800) 845-5028

SILVER SURF MOTEL
3767 Hwy 101 N
(97498)
Rates: $69-$89
Tel: (541) 547-3175
(800) 281-5723

THE SEE VUE
95590 Hwy 101
(97498)
Rates: $42-$65
Tel: (541) 547-3227

YA-TEL MOTEL
640 Hwy 101 (97498)
Rates: $44-$60
Tel (541) 547-3225

YACHATS INN
331 Hwy 101 S
(97498)
Rates: $58-$83
Tel: (541) 547-3456

YAMHILL

**FLYING M GUEST
RANCH**
23029 NW Flying M
Rd (97148)
Rates: $50-$200
Tel: (503) 662-3222

PENNSYLVANIA

ADAMSTOWN

BLACK FOREST INN
P. O. Box 457 (19501)
Rates: $37-$89
Tel: (717) 484-4801

ALLENTOWN

ALLENWOOD MOTEL
1058 Hausman Rd (18104)
Rates: $39+
Tel: (215) 395-3707

COMFORT INN
7625 Imperial Way (18106)
Rates: $35-$80
Tel: (610) 391-0344
(800) 221-2222

DAYS INN
Rt 22 & 309 (18104)
Rates: $45-$100
Tel: (610) 395-3731
(800) 329-7466

ECONO LODGE
2115 Downyflake Ln (18103)
Rates: $43-$95
Tel: (610) 797-2200
(800) 424-4777

HOWARD JOHNSON
3220 Hamilton Blvd (18103)
Rates: $48-95
Tel: (610) 439-4000
(800) 446-4656

MICROTEL-ALLENTOWN
1880 Steelstone Rd (18103)
Rates: $36-$43
Tel: (610) 266-9070

RED ROOF INN
1846 Catasauqua Rd (18103)
Rates: $37-$58
Tel: (610) 264-5404
(800) 843-7663

ALTOONA

ECONO LODGE
2906 Pleasant Vly Blvd (16601)
Rates: $38-$52
Tel: (814) 944-3555
(800) 424-4777

HOJO INN
1500 Sterling St (16602)
Rates: $39-$55
Tel: (814) 946-7601
(800) 446-4656

RAMADA INN
Rt 220, Plank Rd Exit (16601)
Rates: $54-$99
Tel: (814) 946-1631
(800) 272-6232

ALUM BANK

WEST VU MOTEL
RD 1, Box 366 (15521)
Rates: $25-$34
Tel: (814) 839-2632

BARKEYVILLE

DAYS INN
I-80 & Rt 8 (16038)
Rates: $44-$51
Tel: (814) 786-7901
(800) 329-7466

BEAVER FALLS

BEAVER VALLEY MOTEL
SR 18 (15010)
Rates: $37-$52
Tel: (412) 843-0630

HOLIDAY INN
P. O. Box 696 (15010)
Rates: $68-$86
Tel: (412) 646-3700
(800) 465-4329

BEDFORD

ECONO LODGE
Rd 2, Box 28, Transport St (15522)
Rates: $34-$46
Tel: (814) 623- 5174
(800) 424-4777

JANEY LYNN MOTEL
RD 5, Box 367 (15522)
Rates: $24-$39
Tel: (814) 623-9515

MOTEL TOWN HOUSE
200 S Richard St (15522)
Rates: $28-$50
Tel: (814) 623-5138
(800) 879-8696

QUALITY INN
RD 2, Box 171 (15522)
Rates: $54-$66
Tel: (814) 623-5188
(800) 221-2222

SUPER 8 MOTEL
Bus Rt 220 N (15522)
Rates: $40-$56
Tel: (814) 849-8840
(800) 800-8000

BENSALEM

COMFORT INN
3660 Street Rd (19020)
Rates: $56-$99
Tel: (800) 221-2222

BERWYN

RESIDENCE INN BY MARRIOTT
600 W Swedesford Rd (19312)
Rates: $79-$130
Tel: (610) 640-9494
(800) 331-3131

BETHLEHEM

COMFORT INN
3191 Highfield Dr (18017)
Rates: $53-$85
Tel: (610) 865-6300
(800) 221-2222

COMFORT SUITES
120 W 3rd St (18015)
Rates: $75-$103
Tel: (610) 882-9700
(800) 221-2222

HOTEL BETHLEHEM
437 Main St (18017)
Rates: n/a
Tel: (215) 867-3711

BLOOMSBURG

ECONO LODGE
189 Columbia Mall Dr (17815)
Rates: $43-$65
Tel: (717) 387-0490
(800) 424-4777

THE INN AT TURKEY HILL
991 Central Rd (17815)
Rates: $79-$175
Tel: (717) 387-1500

MAGEE'S MAIN STREET
20 W Main St (17815)
Rates: $55-$150
Tel: (800) 331-9815

QUALITY INN
1 Buckhorn Rd (17815)
Rates: $50-$70
Tel: (717) 784-5300
(800) 221-2222

BREEZEWOOD

COMFORT INN
P. O. Box 309 (15533)
Rates: $43-$70
Tel: (814) 735-2200
(800) 221-2222

PENN AIRE MOTEL
P. O. Box 156 (15533)
Rates: $36-$46
Tel: (814) 735-4351

WILTSHIRE MOTEL
Star Rt 2, Box 1 (15533)
Rates: $24-$36
Tel: (814) 735-4361

BRIDGEVILLE

KNIGHTS INN
111 Hickory Grade
Rd (15017)
Rates: $33-$46
Tel: (412) 221-8110
(800) 843-5644

BROOKVILLE

**BUDGET HOST
GOLD EAGLE INN**
RD 3, Box 358
(15825)
Rates: $30-$54
Tel: (814) 849-7344
(800) 283-4678

DAYS INN
230 Allegheny Blvd
(15825)
Rates: $39-$75
Tel: (814) 849-8001
(800) 329-7466

HOWARD JOHNSON
245 Allegheny Blvd
(15825)
Rates: $38-$49
Tel: (814) 849-3335
(800) 446-4656

RAMADA LIMITED
235 Allegheny Blvd
(15825)
Rates: $40-$65
Tel: (814) 849-8381
(800) 272-6232

SUPER 8 MOTEL
251 Allegheny Blvd
(15825)
Rates: $37-$59
Tel: (814) 849-8840
(800) 800-8000

BURNHAM

HOLIDAY INN
Rt 322 (17009)
Rates: $39-$65
Tel: (717) 248-4961
(800) 465-4329

BUTLER

DAYS INN
139 Pittsburgh Rd
(16001)
Rates: $32-$79
Tel: (412) 287-6761
(800) 329-7466

SUPER 8 MOTEL
138 Pittsburgh Rd
(16001)
Rates: $41-$59
Tel: (412) 287-8888
(800) 800-8000

CARLISLE

ALBRIGHT MOTEL
1165 Harrisburg Pike
(17013)
Rates: $25-$28
Tel: (717) 249-4380

BEST WESTERN INN
1245 Harrisburg
Pike (17013)
Rates: $50-$73
Tel: (717) 243-5411
(800) 528-1234

**COAST TO COAST
BUDGET HOST INN**
1252 Harrisburg
Pike (17013)
Rates: $32-$76
Tel: (717) 243-8585
(800) 283-4678

DAYS INN
101 Alexander
Springs Rd (17013)
Rates: $50-$125
Tel: (717) 258-4147
(800) 329-7466

ECONO LODGE
1460 Harrisburg
Pike (17013)
Rates: $38-$80
Tel: (717) 249-7775
(800) 424-4777

HOLIDAY INN
1450 Harrisburg
Pike (17013)
Rates: $55-$72
Tel: (717) 245-2400
(800) 465-4329

HOWARD JOHNSON
1255 Harrisburg
Pike (17013)
Rates: $39-$80
Tel: (717) 243-6000
(800) 446-4656

RODEWAY INN
1239 Harrisburg
Pike (17013)
Rates: $39-$79
Tel: (717) 249-2800
(800) 228-2000

CHADDS FORD

**BRANDYWINE RIVER
HOTEL**
US 1 & SR 100
(19317)
Rates: $99-$130
Tel: (610) 388-1200

CHALK HILL

**LODGE AT
CHALK HILL**
Rt 40E, Box 240
(15421)
Rates: $54-$71
Tel: (412) 438-8880
(800) 833-4283

CHAMBERS-BURG

DAYS INN
30 Falling Springs
Rd (17201)
Rates: $58-64
Tel: (717) 263-1288
(800) 329-7466

HOLIDAY INN
1095 Wayne Ave
(17201)
Rates: $55-$72
Tel: (717) 263-3400
(800) 465-4329

FRIENDSHIP INN
1620 Lincoln Way E
(17201)
Rates: $31-$43
Tel: (717) 264-4108
(800) 228-2000

TRAVELODGE
565 Lincoln Way E
(17201)
Rates: $45-$75
Tel: (717) 264-4187
(800) 578-7878

CHESTER

HOWARD JOHNSON
1300 Providence Rd
(19013)
Rates: $58-$80
Tel: (610) 876-7211
(800) 446-4656

CLARION

DAYS INN
Rt 68 & I-80 (16214)
Rates: $38-$120
Tel: (814) 226-8682
(800) 329-7466

HOLIDAY INN
Rt 68 & I-80 (16214)
Rates: $65-$77
Tel: (814) 226-8850
(800) 465-4329

SUPER 8 MOTEL
Rt 3 & Rt 68 (16214)
Rates: $38-$61
Tel: (814) 226-4550
(800) 800-8000

CLARKS SUMMIT

SUMMIT INN
649 Northern Blvd
(18411)
Rates: $35-$59
Tel: (717) 586-1211

CLEARFIELD

BEST WESTERN INN
P. O. Box 286 (16830)
Rates: $51-$68
Tel: (814) 765-2441
(800) 528-1234

DAYS INN
RR 2, Box 245B
(16830)
Rates: $39-$80
Tel: (814) 765-5381
(800) 329-7466

FRIENDSHIP INN
Rd 2, Box 297-B
(16830)
Rates: $40-$70
Tel: (814) 765-7587
(800) 228-2000

ROYAL 9 MOTOR INN
Rt 322 E (16830)
Rates: $25-$36
Tel: (814) 765-2639

SUPER 8 MOTEL
RR 2, Box 242-C
(16830)
Rates: $42-$56
Tel: (814) 768-7580
(800) 800-8000

COOKSBURG

FOREST VIEW CABINS
Box 105 (16217)
Rates: n/a
Tel: (814) 744-8413

COOPERSBURG

TRAVELODGE
321 South 3rd St
(18036)
Rates: $39-$95
Tel: (610) 282-1212
(800) 578-7878

CORAOPOLIS

EMBASSY SUITES
550 Cherrington
Pkwy (15108)
Rates: $99-$137
Tel: (412) 269-9070
(800) 362-2779

LA QUINTA INN-AIRPORT
1433 Beers School
Rd (15108)
Rates: $53-$67
Tel: (412) 269-0400
(800) 531-5900

MARRIOTT-AIRPORT
100 Aten Rd (15108)
Rates: $89-$124
Tel: (412) 788-8800
(800) 228-9290

MOTEL 6
1170 Thorn Run Rd
(15108)
Rates: $36-$42
Tel: (412) 269-0990
(800) 440-6000

RED ROOF INN-AIRPORT
1454 Beers School
Rd (15108)
Rates: $39-$47
Tel: (412) 264-5678
(800) 843-7663

ROYCE HOTEL-AIRPORT
1160 Thorn Run Rd
(15108)
Rates: $119-$129
Tel: (412) 262-2400

CRANBERRY

RED ROOF INN
20009 Rt 19 (16046)
Rates: $45-$55
Tel: (800) 843-7663

RESIDENCE INN
1306 Freedom Rd
(16066)
Rates: n/a
Tel: (412) 779-1000
(800) 331-3131

DANVILLE

COUNTRYSIDE INN
180 & Rt 54, Exit 33
(17821)
Rates: $33-$39
Tel: (717) 275-4640

RED ROOF INN
300 Red Roof Inn Rd
(17821)
Rates: $34-$53
Tel: (717) 275-7600
(800) 843-7663

DELMONT

SUPER 8 MOTEL
180 Sheffield Dr
(15626)
Rates: $42-$58
Tel: (412) 468-4888
(800) 800-8000

DENVER

BLACK HORSE LODGE & SUITES
2180 N Reading Rd
(17517)
Rates: $57-$119
Tel: (717) 336-7563

COMFORT INN
2015 N Reading Rd
(17517)
Rates: $34-$89
Tel: (717) 336-4649

HOLIDAY INN
P. O. Box 129 (17517)
Rates: $48-$106
Tel: (717) 336-7541
(800) 465-4329

PENNSYLVANIA DUTCH MOTEL
2275 N Reading Rd
(17517)
Rates: $36-$50
Tel: (717) 267-5559

RED CARPET INN
2069 N Reading Rd
(17517)
Rates: n/a
Tel: (717) 336-5254
(800) 251-1962

DOUGLASS-VILLE

ECONO LODGE
387 Ben Franklin
Hwy (19518)
Rates: $40-$55
Tel: (610) 385-3016
(800) 424-4777

DRUMS

DAYS INN
RR 2, Box 304
(18227)
Rates: $55-$69
Tel: (717) 788-5887
(800) 329-7466

ECONO LODGE
SR 309 & I-80 (18222)
Rates: $39-$59
Tel: (717) 788-4121
(800) 424-6423

DUBOIS

DU BOIS MANOR MOTEL
525 Liberty Blvd
(15801)
Rates: $30-$45
Tel: (814) 371-5400
(800) 336-7701

HOLIDAY INN
US 219 & I-80
(15801)
Rates: $55-$82
Tel: (814) 371-5100
(800) 465-4329

RAMADA INN
Rt 255 & I-80 Exit 17
(15801)
Rates: $51-$72
Tel: (814) 371-7070
(800) 228-2828

DUNMORE

DAYS INN
1100 O'Neill Hwy
(18512)
Rates: $54-$79
Tel: (717) 348-6101
(800) 329-7466

EASTON

DAYS INN
2555 Nazareth Rd
(18042)
Rates: $45-$95
Tel: (610) 253-0546
(800) 329-7466

BEST WESTERN EASTON INN
185 S 3rd St (18042)
Rates: $60-$98
Tel: (610) 253-9131
(800) 528-1234

EBENSBURG

COMFORT INN
SR 22 (15931)
Rates: $47-$69
Tel: (814) 472-6100
(800) 221-2222

THE COTTAGE RESTAURANT & INN
RD 4, Box 50 (15931)
Rates: $48-$64
Tel: (814) 472-8002

EDINBORO

RAMADA INN & CONF CTR
Rt 6N (16412)
Rates: $65-$150
Tel: (814) 734-5650
(800) 272-6232

ENOLA

QUALITY INN
501 N Enola Rd
(17025)
Rates: $50-$73
Tel: (800) 221-2222

EPHRATA

**SMITHTON
COUNTRY INN**
900 W Main St
(17522)
Rates: $55-$150
Tel: (717) 733-6094

ERIE

DAYS INN
7415 Schultz Rd
(16509)
Rates: $46-$89
Tel: (814) 868-8521
(800) 329-7466

HOLIDAY INN
18 W 18th St (16501)
Rates: $49-$89
Tel: (814) 456-2961
(800) 465-4329

**HOLIDAY INN-
SOUTH**
8040 Perry Hwy
(16509)
Rates: $64-$73
Tel: (814) 864-4911
(800) 465-4329

HOWARD JOHNSON
7575 Peach St (16509)
Rates: $45-$96
Tel: (814) 864-4811
(800) 446-4656

MICROTEL-ERIE
8100 Peach St (16509)
Rates: $32-$49
Tel: (814) 864-1010

RAMADA INN
6101 Wattsburg Rd
(16509)
Rates: $50-$70
Tel: (814) 825-3100
(800) 272-6232

RED ROOF INN
7865 Perry Hwy
(16509)
Rates: $39-$70
Tel: (814) 868-5246
(800) 843-7663

SUPER 8 MOTEL
8052 Perry Hwy
(16506)
Rates: $40-$57
Tel: (800) 800-8000

ESSINGTON

**HOLIDAY INN-
AIRPORT**
45 Industrial Hwy
(19029)
Rates: $69-$79
Tel: (610) 521-2400
(800) 685-6110

MOTEL 6-AIRPORT
43 Industrial Hwy
(19029)
Rates: $50-$56
Tel: (215) 521-6650
(800) 440-6000

**RED ROOF INN-
AIRPORT**
49 Industrial Hwy
(19029)
Rates: $46-$56
Tel: (610) 521-5090
(800) 843-7663

FAYETTEVILLE

RITE SPOT MOTEL
5651 Lincoln Way E
(17222)
Rates: $34-$44
Tel: (717) 352-2144

FOGELSVILLE

CLOVERLEAF MOTEL
327 Star Rd (18051)
Rates: $39-$43
Tel: (610) 395-3367

FRACKVILLE

ECONO LODGE
501 S Middle St
(17931)
Rates: $36-$50
Tel: (717) 874-3838
(800) 424-4777

FRANKLIN

FRANKLIN MOTEL
1421 Liberty St
(16323)
Rates: n/a
Tel: (814) 437-3061

FRYSTOWN

**MOTEL OF
FRYSTOWN**
90 Fort Motel Dr
(17067)
Rates: $30-$40
Tel: (717) 933-4613

GALETON

OX YOKE INN
RD 1, Route 6
(16922)
Rates: n/a
Tel: (814) 435-6522

PINE LOG MOTEL
P. O. Box 151 (16922)
Rates: $30-$36
Tel: (814) 435-6400

GETTYSBURG

**BUDGET HOST
THREE CROWNS
MOTOR LODGE**
205 Steinwehr Ave
(17325)
Rates: $45-$62
Tel: (800) 729-6564

ECONO LODGE
945 Baltimore Pike
(17325)
Rates: $33-$73
Tel: (800) 424-4777

**HERITAGE
MOTOR LODGE**
64 Steinwehr Ave
(17325)
Rates: $30-$56
Tel: (717) 334-9281

HOLIDAY INN
516 Baltimore Pike
(17325)
Rates: $42-$88
Tel: (717) 334-6211
(800) 465-4329

HOWARD JOHNSON
301 Steinwehr Ave
(17325)
Rates: $55-$79
Tel: (717) 334-1188
(800) 654-2000

QUALITY INN
380 Steinwehr Ave
(17325)
Rates: $46-$89
Tel: (717) 334-1103
(800) 221-2222

GLEN ROCK

**ROCKY RIDGE
MOTEL**
Rt 216, Steaks Run
Rd (17327)
Rates: $28-$38
Tel: (717) 235-5646

GRANTVILLE

HOLIDAY INN
P. O. Box 179 (17028)
Rates: $86-$170
Tel: (717) 469-0661
(800) 465-4329

GREENCASTLE

ECONO LODGE
735 Buchanan Trail E
(17225)
Rates: $35-$51
Tel: (800) 424-4777

GROVE CITY

**SNOW GOOSE INN
BED & BREAKFAST**
112 E Main St
(16127)
Rates: $55
Tel: (412) 458-4644

HARRISBURG
(and Vicinity)

**BEST WESTERN
CAPITAL PLAZA**
150 Nationwide Dr
(17110)
Rates: $47-$59
Tel: (717) 545-9089
(800) 528-1234

**BEST WESTERN
COUNTRY OVEN**
300 N Mountain Rd
(17112)
Rates: $61-$89
Tel: (717) 652-7180
(800) 528-1234

**BEST WESTERN
HOTEL CROWN PARK**
765 Eisenhower Blvd
(17111)
Rates: $69-$119
Tel: (717) 558-9500
(800) 528-1234

BUDGETEL INN
990 Eisenhower Blvd
(17111)
Rates: $28-$55
Tel: (717) 939-8000
(800) 428-3438

BUDGETEL INN
200 N Mountain Rd
(17112)
Rates: $48-$63
Tel: (717) 540-9339
(800) 428-3438

COMFORT INN EAST
4021 Union Deposit
Rd (17109)
Rates: $53-$78
Tel: (717) 561-8100
(800) 221-2222

DAYS INN
353 Lewisberry Rd
(17070)
Rates: $43-$80
Tel: (717) 774-4156
(800) 329-7466

HOJO INN
1450 N 7th St (17102)
Rates: $40-$75
Tel: (800) 446-4656

**HOLIDAY INN-
AIRPORT**
4751 Lindle Rd
(17111)
Rates: $102-$114
Tel: (800) 637-4817

MOTEL 6
200 Commerce Dr
(New Cumberland,
17070)
Rates: $32-38
Tel: (717) 774-8910
(800) 466-8356

QUALITY INN
525 S Front St
(17104)
Rates: $46-$70
Tel: (717) 233-1611
(800) 221-2222

**RADISSON PENN
HARRIS HOTEL**
1150 Camp Hill
Bypass (17011)
Rates: $80-$108
Tel: (800) 333-3333

RAMADA HOTEL
PA Trpk, Exit 18 & 1
(17070)
Rates: $54-$119
Tel: (717) 657-1445
(800) 272-6232

RED ROOF INN-N
400 Corporate Cir
(17110)
Rates: $38-$57
Tel: (717) 657-1445
(800) 843-7663

RED ROOF INN-S
950 Eisenhower Blvd
(17111)
Rates: $30-$49
Tel: (717) 939-1331
(800) 843-7663

**RESIDENCE INN
BY MARRIOTT**
4480 Lewis Rd
(17111)
Rates: $98-$134
Tel: (717) 561-1900
(800) 331-3131

SHERATON INN
800 East Park Dr
(17111)
Rates: $75-$135
Tel: (717) 561-2800
(800) 325-3535

**SUPER 8 MOTEL-
NORTH**
4125 N Front St
(17110)
Rates: $42-$63
Tel: (717) 233-5891
(800) 800-8000

HAZLETON

**BEST WESTERN
GENETTI
MOTOR LODGE**
RR 1, Box 37 (18201)
Rates: $45-$150
Tel: (717) 454-2494
(800) 528-1234

COMFORT INN
RR 1, Box 301
(18201)
Rates: $62-$98
Tel: (717) 455-9300
(800) 221-2222

FOREST HILL INN
RD 1, Box 262
(18201)
Rates: $44-$49
Tel: (717) 459-2730

HAMPTON INN
RR 1, Box 273A
(18201)
Rates: $47-$52
Tel: (717) 454-3449
(800) 426-7866

HOLIDAY INN
Rt 309 S (18201)
Rates: $69-$75
Tel: (717) 455-1451
(800) 465-4329

**MOUNT LAUREL
MOTEL**
1039 S Church St
(18201)
Rates: $38-$55
Tel: (717) 455-6391

HERMITAGE

HOLIDAY INN
3200 S Hermitage Rd
(16159)
Rates: $63-$74
Tel: (412) 981-1530
(800) 465-4329

ROYAL MOTEL
301 S Hermitage Rd
(16148)
Rates: $33-$39
Tel: (412) 347-5546
(800) 831-8348

HERSHEY

ECONO LODGE
115 Lucy Ave (17033)
Rates: $40-$50
Tel: (717) 533-2515
(800) 424-4777

HORSHAM

**RESIDENCE INN
BY MARRIOTT**
3 Walnut Grove Dr
(19044)
Rates: $105-$133
Tel: (215) 443-7330
(800) 331-3131

HUNTINGDON

DAYS INN
RD 1, Box 353
(16652)
Rates: $39-$65
Tel: (814) 643-3934
(800) 329-7466

**HUNTINGDON
MOTOR INN**
P. O. Box 353 (16652)
Rates: $35-$54
Tel: (814) 643-1133

JOHNSTOWN

COMFORT INN
455 Theatre Dr
(15904)
Rates: $51-$62
Tel: (814) 266-3678
(800) 221-2222

DAYS INN
1540 Scalp Ave
(15904)
Rates: $40-$80
Tel: (814) 269-3366
(800) 329-7466

HOLIDAY INN
250 Market St
(15901)
Rates: $59-$79
Tel: (814) 535-7777
(800) 465-4329

HOLIDAY INN EXP.
1440 Scalp Ave
(15904)
Rates: $39-$54
Tel: (814) 266-8789
(800) 465-4329

KANE

KANE VIEW MOTEL
RD 1, Box 91A
(16735)
Rates: $33-$48
Tel: (814) 837-8600

KEMPTON

HAWK MT. INN B&B
RD 1, Box 186
(19529)
Rates: n/a
Tel: (215) 756-4224

KING OF PRUSSIA

HOLIDAY INN
260 Mall Blvd
(19406)
Rates: $95-$105
Tel: (800) 465-4329

KINTNERSVILLE

LIGHTFARM B & B
2042 Berger Rd
(18930)
Rates: $85-$150
Tel: (610) 847-3276

KITTANNING

RODEWAY INN
422 E. Friendship
Plaza (16201)
Rates: $42-$52
Tel: (412) 543-1100
(800) 228-2000

KULPSVILLE

HOLIDAY INN
1750 Sumneytown
Pike (19443)
Rates: $71-$95
Tel: (215) 368-3800
(800) 465-4329

KUTZTOWN

CAMPUS INN
15080 Kutztown Rd
(19530)
Rates: $40-$75
Tel: (610) 683-8721

LINCOLN MOTEL
RD 4, Box 171
(19530)
Rates: $35-$70
Tel: (610) 683-3456

LANCASTER

BEST WESTERN EDEN INN
222 Eden Rd (17601)
Rates: $79-$149
Tel: (717) 569-6444
(800) 528-1234

BRUNSWICK HOTEL
P. O. Box 749 (17603)
Rates: $48-$68
Tel: (717) 397-4801

COMFORT INN
500 Centerville Rd
(17601)
Rates: $49-$98
Tel: (717) 898-2431
(800) 221-2222

SUPER 8 MOTEL
2129 E Lincoln Hwy
(17602)
Rates: $34-$79
Tel: (717) 393-8888
(800) 800-8000

TRAVELODGE
2101 Columbia Ave
(17603)
Rates: $42-$92
Tel: (717) 397-4201
(800) 578-7878

LANGHORNE

RED ROOF INN
3100 Cabot Blvd W
(19047)
Rates: $58-$70
Tel: (215) 750-6200
(800) 843-7663

LENHARTSVILLE

TOP MOTEL
RD 1, Box 834
(19534)
Rates: n/a
Tel: (215) 756-6021

LESTER

ECONO LODGE-AIRPORT
600 SR 291 (19029)
Rates: $46-$62
Tel: (610) 521-3900
(800) 424-4777

LEVITTOWN

COMFORT INN
6401 Bristol Pk
(19057)
Rates: $50-$95
Tel: (215) 547-5000
(800) 221-2222

LEWISBURG

DAYS INN
US Rt 15 (17837)
Rates: $53-$126
Tel: (717) 523-1171
(800) 329-7466

LIONVILLE

COMFORT INN
5 N Pottstown Pike
(19341)
Rates: $58-$64
Tel: (610) 524-8811
(800) 221-2222

HAMPTON INN
4 N Pottstown Pike
(19341)
Rates: $58-$74
Tel: (610) 363-5555
(800) 426-7866

HOLIDAY INN
815 N Pottstown
Pike (19341)
Rates: $65-$95
Tel: (610) 363-1100
(800) 465-4329

LITITZ

GENERAL SUTTER INN
14 E Main St (17543)
Rates: $65-$100
Tel: (717) 626-2115

LOCK HAVEN

BEST WESTERN
101 E Walnut St
(17745)
Rates: $49-$80
Tel: (717) 748-3297
(800) 528-1234

MANHEIM

RODEWAY INN
2931 Lebanon Rd
(17545)
Rates: $38-$52
Tel: (717) 665-2755
(800) 228-2000

MT. HOPE MOTEL
2845 Lebanon Rd
(17545)
Rates: $25-$35
Tel: (717) 665-3118

MANSFIELD

COMFORT INN
300 Gateway Dr
(16933)
Rates: $49-$80
Tel: (717) 662-3000
(800) 822-5470

MANSFIELD INN
26 S Main St (16933)
Rates: $45-$65
Tel: (717) 662-2136

OASIS MOTEL
RD 1, Box 90 (16933)
Rates: $30-$40
Tel: (717) 659-5576

WEST'S DELUXE MOTEL
RD 1, Box 97 (16933)
Rates: $32-$45
Tel: (717) 659-5141
(800) 995-9378

MARS

DAYS INN
909 Sheraton Dr
(16046)
Rates: $50-$78
Tel: (412) 772-2700
(800) 329-7466

MOTEL 6-NORTH
Rt 19, Box 1316
(16046)
Rates: $29-$38
Tel: (412) 776-4333
(800) 440-6000

OAK LEAF MOTEL
US Rt 19 (16046)
Rates: n/a
Tel: (412) 776-1551

MEADVILLE

DAVID MEAD INN
455 Chestnut St
(16335)
Rates: n/a
Tel: (814) 336-1692

DAYS INN
240 Conneaut Lake
Rd (16335)
Rates: $45-$90
Tel: (814) 337-4264
(800) 329-7466

SUPER 8 MOTEL
845 Conneaut Lake
Rd (16335)
Rates: $43-$65
Tel: (814) 333-8883
(800) 800-8000

MECHANICS-BURG

ECONO LODGE
650 Gettysburg Rd
(17055)
Rates: $30-$50
Tel: (717) 766-4728
(800) 424-4777

HOLIDAY INN
5401 Carlisle Pike
(17055)
Rates: $75-$85
Tel: (717) 697-0321
(800) 465-4329

MERCER

COLONIAL INN MOTEL
383 N Perry Hwy
(16137)
Rates: $22-$36
Tel: (412) 662-5600

HOWARD JOHNSON
835 Perry Hwy
(16137)
Rates: $67-$78
Tel: (412) 748-3030
(800) 542-7674

MIDDLETOWN

RODEWAY INN
800 Eisenhower Blvd
(17057)
Rates: $39-$75
Tel: (717) 939-4147

MIFFLINVILLE

SUPER 8 MOTEL
I-80, Exit 37, Box E
(18631)
Rates: $36-$56
Tel: (717) 759-6778
(800) 800-8000

MILESBURG

DAYS INN
P. O. Box 538 (16853)
Rates: $42-$100
Tel: (814) 355-7521
(800) 329-7466

MILL HALL

COMFORT INN
RR 3, Box 600 (17751)
Rates: $39-$100
Tel: (717) 726-4901
(800) 221-2222

MONROEVILLE

DAYS INN
2727 Mosside Blvd
(15146)
Rates: $47-$61
Tel: (412) 856-1610
(800) 329-7466

RADISSON HOTEL
101 Mall Blvd
(15146)
Rates: $75-$135
Tel: (800) 333-3333

RED ROOF INN
2729 Mosside Blvd
(15146)
Rates: $41-$59
Tel: (412) 856-4738
(800) 843-7663

WM PENN MOTEL
4139 Wm Penn Hwy
(15146)
Rates: $36-$47
Tel: (412) 373-0700

MONTGOMERY VILLE

COMFORT INN
678 Bethlehem Pike
(18936)
Rates: $70-$89
Tel: (800) 221-2222

MORGANTOWN

CONESTOGA WAGON MOTEL
Rt 23 (19543)
Rates: n/a
Tel: (215) 286-5061

HOLIDAY INN-HOLIDOME
N of Exit 22 off PA
Tpk (19543)
Rates: $65-$95
Tel: (610) 286-3000
(800) 465-4329

NEW BERLINVILLE

MEL-DOR MOTEL
P. O. Box 349 (19545)
Rates: $35-$45
Tel: (610) 367-2626

NEW CASTLE

COMFORT INN
1740 New Butler Rd
(16101)
Rates: $47-$59
Tel: (412) 658-7700
(800) 221-2222

NEW COLUMBIA

COMFORT INN
P. O. Box 62 (17856)
Rates: $49-$63
Tel: (717) 568-8000
(800) 221-2222

NEW CUMBERLAND

KNIGHTS INN
300 Commerce Dr
(17070)
Rates: $28-$36
Tel: (717) 774-5990
(800) 843-5644

MOTEL 6
200 Commerce Dr
(17070)
Rates: $32-$38
Tel: (717) 774-8910
8(88) 466-8356

NEW HOPE

AARON BURR HOUSE B & B
80 W Bridge St
(18938)
Rates: $90-$190
Tel: (215) 862-2343

HOLIDAY INN
P. O. Box 419 (18938)
Rates: $85-$105
Tel: (800) 465-4329

WEDGEWOOD INN BED & BREAKFAST
111 W Bridge St
(18938)
Rates: $70-$190
Tel: (215) 862-2570

NEW KENSINGTON

DAYS INN
300 Tarentum
Bridge Rd (15068)
Rates: $50-$75
Tel: (412) 335-9171
(800) 329-7466

NEW STANTON

CARDINAL MOTEL
P. O. Drawer B
(15672)
Rates: $30-$36
Tel: (412) 925-2162

HOWARD JOHNSON
112 W Byers Ave
(15672)
Rates: $38-$74
Tel: (412) 925-3511
(800) 446-4656

NORTH EAST

RED CARPET INN
12264 E Main St
(16428)
Rates: $36-$49
Tel: (800) 251-1962

OAKDALE

COMFORT INN
7011 Old
Stuebeuville Pike
(15071)
Rates: $53-$95
Tel: (412) 787-2600
(800) 221-2222

HOWARD JOHNSON
2101 Montour
Church Rd (15071)
Rates: $42-$53
Tel: (412) 923-2244
(800) 446-4656

OAKLAND

HAMPTON INN
3315 Hamlet St
(15213)
Rates: $69-$84
Tel: (412) 681-1000
(800) 426-7866

OIL CITY

HOLIDAY INN
1 Seneca St (16301)
Rates: $62-$79
Tel: (814) 677-1221
(800) 465-4329

PHILADELPHIA

BARCLAY HOTEL
237 S 18th St (19103)
Rates: $135-$400
Tel: (800) 421-6662

**CHESTNUT HILL
HOTEL**
8229 Germantown
Ave (19118)
Rates: $110-$150
Tel: (215) 242-5905
(800) 628-9744

**FOUR SEASONS
HOTEL**
1 Logan Sq (19103)
Rates: $175-$355
Tel: (215) 963-1500
(800) 332-3442

HOLIDAY INN
18th & Market Sts
(19103)
Rates: $79
Tel: (800) 465-4329

HILTON-AIRPORT
4509 Island Ave
(19153)
Rates: $109
Tel: (215) 365-4150
(800) 445-8667

**RESIDENCE INN
BY MARRIOTT**
4630 Island Ave
(19153)
Rates: $88-$130
Tel: (215) 492-1611
(800) 331-3131

**THE RITTENHOUSE
HOTEL**
210 W Rittenhouse
Sq (19103)
Rates: $140-$270
Tel: (215) 546-9000

TRAVELODGE
2015 Penrose Ave
(19145)
Rates: $49-$104
Tel: (215) 755-6500
(800) 578-7878

PHILIPSBURG

HARBOR INN
Rts 322 & 53 (16866)
Rates: $48-$59
Tel: (814) 342-0250

MAIN LINER MOTEL
RD 3, Box 115
(16866)
Rates: $28-$39
Tel: (814) 342-2004

PINE GROVE

COMFORT INN
Rt 443 & I-81 (17963)
Rates: $40-$115
Tel: (717) 345-8031
(800) 424-6423

ECONO LODGE
RD 1, Box 581
(17963)
Rates: $40-$50
Tel: (717) 345-4099
(800) 424-4777

PITTSBURGH

DAYS INN
Rt 28 & PA tpk
(15238)
Rates: $48-$76
Tel: (412) 828-5400
(800) 329-7466

DAYS INN
100 Kisow Dr
(15205)
Rates: $35-$50
Tel: (412) 922-0120
(800) 329-7466

**HAMPTON INN
HOTEL**
555 Trumbull Dr
(15205)
Rates: $69-$79
Tel: (412) 922-0100
(800) 426-7866

HAWTHORN SUITES
700 Mansfield Ave
(15205)
Rates: $116-$146
Tel: (412) 279-6300
(800) 527-1133

HILTON & TOWERS
Gateway Center
(15222)
Rates: $80-$219
Tel: (412) 391-4600
(800) 445-8667

HOLIDAY INN
4859 McKnight Rd
(15237)
Rates: $59-$109
Tel: (412) 366-5200
(800) 465-4329

HOLIDAY INN
401 Holiday Dr
(15220)
Rates: $79-$122
Tel: (412) 922-6100
(800) 465-4329

HOLIDAY INN
100 Lytton Ave
(15213)
Rates: $109-$122
Tel: (800) 465-4329

HOLIDAY INN-S
164 Ft Couch Rd
(15241)
Rates: $67-$105
Tel: (412) 833-5300
(800) 465-4329

HOWARD JOHNSON
5300 Clairton Blvd
(15236)
Rates: $69-$89
Tel: (412) 884-6000
(800) 446-4656

**MARRIOTT
GREENTREE**
101 Marriott Dr
(15205)
Rates: $65-$117
Tel: (412) 922-8400
(800) 228-9290

MOTEL 6-AIRPORT
211 Beecham Dr
(15205)
Rates: $32-$38
Tel: (412) 922-9400
(800) 440-6000

RED ROOF INN
6404 Steubenville
Pike (15205)
Rates: $30-$56
Tel: (412) 787-7870
(800) 843-7663

SUPER 8 MOTEL
Rt 286 & Old
Frankstown Rd
(15239)
Rates: $42-$58
Tel: (800) 800-8000

TRAVELODGE
4800 Steubenville
Pike (15205)
Rates: $32-$38
Tel: (412) 922-6900
(800) 578-7878

**THE WESTIN
WILLIAM PENN**
530 William Penn Pl
(15219)
Rates: $204-$274
Tel: (412) 281-7100
(800) 228-3000

PITTSTON

HOWARD JOHNSON
347 Rt 315 (18640)
Rates: $47-$65
Tel: (717) 654-3301
(800) 446-4656

KNIGHTS INN
310 Rt 315 (18640)
Rates: $33-$46
Tel: (717) 654-6020
(800) 843-5644

POCONO MOUNTAINS AREA

BEST WESTERN INN-HUNT'S LANDING
900 Rt 6 & 209
(Matamoras 18336)
Rates: $55-$87
Tel: (717) 491-2400
(800) 528-1234

BUDGET MOTEL
P. O. Box 216
(Stroudsburg 18301)
Rates: $33-$68
Tel: (717) 424-5451
(800) 233-8144

COMFORT INN
I-84 & SR 191
(Hamlin 18436)
Rates: $46-$99
Tel: (717) 689-4148
(800) 221-2222

COMFORT INN-
SR 611, P.O. Box 184
(Bartonsville 18321)
Rates: $45-$161
Tel: (717) 476-1500
(800) 221-2222

DAYS INN-POCONO
Rt 940, HCR 1,
Box 35
(White Haven 18661)
Rates: $55-$115
Tel: (717) 443-0391
(800) 329-7466

FIFE & DRUM MOTOR INN
100 terrace St (18431)
Rates: $32-$75
Tel: (717) 253-1392

HOLIDAY INN
Rt 611 & I-80
(Bartonsville 18321)
Rates: $62-$109
Tel: (717) 424-6100
(800) 465-4329

HOWARD JOHNSON
1220 W Main St
(Stroudsburg 18360)
Rates: $75-$109
Tel: (714) 424-1930
(800) 777-5453

POCONO MOUNTAIN LODGE
Rt 940 (White Haven 18661)
Rates: $50-$68
Tel: (800) 443-4049

SUPER 8 MOTEL
340 Green Tree Dr
(E Stroudsburg 18301)
Rates: $41-$56
Tel: (717) 424-7411
(800) 800-8000

POTTSTOWN

COMFORT INN
99 Robinson ST
(19464)
Rates: $54-$69
Tel: (610) 326-5000
(800) 221-2222

DAYS INN
29 High St (19464)
Rates: $39-$65
Tel: (610) 970-1101
(800) 329-7466

HOLIDAY INN EXPRESS
1600 Industrial Hwy
(19464)
Rates: $56-$66
Tel: (610) 327-3300
(800) 465-4329

PUNSUTAWNEY

COUNTRY VILLA MOTEL
Rd 1, Box 77 (15767)
Rates: $30-$44
Tel: (814) 938-8330

PANTALL HOTEL
135 E Mahoning
(15767)
Rates: $47-$93
Tel: (814) 938-6600
(800) 872-6825

QUAKERTOWN

ECONO LODGE
1905 Rt 663 (18951)
Rates: $40-$70
Tel: (215) 538-3000
(800) 424-4777

RODEWAY INN
1920 SR 663 (18951)
Rates: $35-$75
Tel: (215) 536-7600
(800) 228-2000

READING

DUTCH COLONY INN
4635 Perkiomen Ave
(19606)
Rates: $53-$85
Tel: (610) 779-2345
(800) 828-2830

ECONO LODGE
2310 Fraver Dr
(19605)
Rates: $38-$60
Tel: (610) 378-1145
(800) 424-4777

ECONO LODGE
635 Spring St (19610)
Rates: $34-$60
Tel: (610) 378-5105
(800) 424-4777

HOLIDAY INN-N
2545 5th St (19605)
Rates: $64-$129
Tel: (610) 929-4741
(800) 465-4329

WELLESLEY INN
910 Woodland Ave
(19610)
Rates: n/a
Tel: (610) 374-1500
(800) 444-8888

ST. MARY'S

BEST WESTERN EXECUTIVE INN
1002 Earth Rd & Rt 255 (15857)
Rates: $45-$64
Tel: (814) 834-0000
(800) 528-1234

SCRANTON

ECONO LODGE
1175 Kane St (18505)
Rates: $35-$75
Tel: (717) 346-8782
(800) 424-4777

SELINSGROVE

COMFORT INN
P. O. Box 299 (17870)
Rates: $48-$70
Tel: (717) 374-8880
(800) 221-2222

SEWICKLEY

SEWICKLEY COUNTRY INN
801 Ohio River Blvd
(15143)
Rates: $64-$80
Tel:(412) 741-4300
(800) 835-6072

SHAMOKIN DAM

DAYS INN
Rt 11 & 15 (17876)
Rates: $39-$79
Tel: (717) 743-1111
(800) 329-7466

SHARTLESVILLE

DUTCH MOTEL
Motel Rd (19554)
Rates: $30-$45
Tel: (610) 488-1479

SOMERSET

DAYS INN
220 Waterworks Rd
(15501)
Rates: $51-$90
Tel: (814) 445-9200
(800) 329-7466

KNIGHTS INN
I-76/I-70, Exit 10
(15501)
Rates: $37-$64
Tel: (814) 445-8933
(800) 843-5644

RAMADA INN
P. O. Box 511 (15501)
Rates: $64-$98
Tel: (814) 443-4646
(800) 272-6232

SUPER 8 MOTEL
I-70/76, Exit 10
(15501)
Rates: $41-$58
Tel: (814) 445-8788
(800) 800-8000

STATE COLLEGE

**DAYS INN-
PENN STATE**
240 S Pugh St
(16801)
Rates: $55-$105
Tel: (814) 238-8454
(800) 329-7466

HAMPTON INN
1101 E College Ave
(16801)
Rates: $55-$78
Tel: (814) 231-1590
(800) 426-7866

HOLIDAY INN
1450 S Atherton St
(16801)
Rates: $62-$69
Tel: (814) 238-3001
(800) 465-4329

STRASBURG

**STRASBURG INN
HISTORIC**
1 Historic Dr (17579)
Rates: $55-$109
Tel: (717) 687-7691
(800) 872-0201

STROUDSBURG

SUPER 8 MOTEL
340 Green Tree Dr E
(18301)
Rates: $46-$66
Tel: (717) 424-7411
(800) 800-8000

TANNERSVILLE

HOWARD JOHNSON
I-80 & Rt 715 (18372)
Rates: $50-$140
Tel: (717) 629-4100
(800) 446-4656

TOWANDA

TOWANDA MOTEL
383 York Ave (18848)
Rates: $39-$70
Tel: (717) 265-2178

TREVOSE

RED ROOF INN
3100 Lincoln Hwy
(19053)
Rates: $44-$53
Tel: (215) 244-9422
(800) 843-7663

TURTLE CREEK

JAMES STREET B & B
553 James St (15145)
Rates: $35-$55
Tel: (412) 372-8060

ULYSSES

PINE LOG MOTEL
Rt 1, Box 15 (16948)
Rates: $32-$38
Tel: (814) 435-6400

VALLEY FORGE

MOTEL 6
815 W Dekaib Pike
(King of Prussia
19406)
Rates: $46-$52
Tel: (610) 265-7200
(800) 466-8356

WARREN

HOLIDAY INN
210 Ludlow St
(16365)
Rates: $55-$71
Tel: (814) 726-3000
(800) 465-4329

SUPER 8 MOTEL
204 Struthers St
(16365)
Rates: $40-$64
Tel: (814) 723-8881
(800) 800-8000

WASHINGTON

HOLIDAY INN
340 Race Track Rd
(15301)
Rates: $79-$94
Tel: (412) 222-6200
(800) 465-4329

KNIGHTS INN
125 Knights Inn Dr
(15301)
Rates: $41-$47
Tel: (800) 843-5644

MOTEL 6
1283 Motel 6 Dr
(15301)
Rates: $40-$46
Tel: (412) 223-8040
(800) 466-8356

RED ROOF INN
1399 W Chestnut St
(15301)
Rates: $40-$47
Tel: (412) 228-5750
(800) 843-7663

WAYNESBORO

BEST WESTERN INN
239 W Main St
(17268)
Rates: $51-$71
Tel: (717) 762-9113
(800) 528-1234

WAYNESBURG

ECONO LODGE
350 Miller Ln (15370)
Rates: $40-$54
Tel: (412) 627-5544
(800) 424-4777

SUPER 8 MOTEL
80 Miller Ln (15370)
Rates: $41-$61
Tel: (412) 627-8880
(800) 800-8000

WELLSBORO

CANYON MOTEL
18 East Ave (16901)
Rates: $25-$49
Tel: (717) 724-1681
(800) 255-2718

FOXFIRE B & B
RD 2, Box 439
(16901)
Rates: $36-$65
Tel: (717) 724-5175

SHERWOOD MOTEL
2 Main St (16901)
Rates: $25-$49
Tel: (717) 724-3424
(800) 626-5802

WEST CHESTER

**ABBEY GREEN
MOTOR LODGE**
1036 Wilmington
Pike (19382)
Rates: $39-$57
Tel: (610) 692-3310

HOLIDAY INN
943 S High St (19382)
Rates: $75-$119
Tel: (610) 692-1900
(800) 465-4329

WEST MIDDLESEX

COMFORT INN
Rt 18 & Wilson Rd
(16159)
Rates: $45-$70
Tel: (412) 342-7200
(800) 221-2222

RADISSON HOTEL
P. O. Box 596 (16159)
Rates: $80-$98
Tel: (412) 528-2501
(800) 272-6232

WEXFORD

ECONO LODGE
107 V.I.P. Dr (15090)
Rates: $45-$57
Tel: (800) 424-4777

WILKES-BARRE

**BEST WESTERN
GENETTI HOTEL**
77 E Market St
(18701)
Rates: $69-$74
Tel: (717) 823-6152
(800) 833-6152

DAYS INN
760 Kidder St
(18702)
Rates: $40-$61
Tel: (717) 826-0111
(800) 329-7466

HAMPTON INN
1063 Hwy 315
(18702)
Rates: $55-$71
Tel: (717) 825-3838
(800) 426-7866

RED CARPET INN
400 Kidder St
(18702)
Rates: $33-$60
Tel: (717) 823-2171
(800) 251-1962

RED ROOF INN
1035 Hwy 315
(18702)
Rates: $40-$63
Tel: (717) 829-6422
(800) 843-7663

WILLIAMSPORT

BING'S MOTEL
2961 Lycoming
Creek Rd (17701)
Rates: $28-$34
Tel: (717) 494-0601

CITY VIEW INN
RD 4, Box 550
(17701)
Rates: $42-$48
Tel: (717) 326-2601

ECONO LODGE
2401 E 3rd St (17701)
Rates: $40-50
Tel: (717) 326-1501
(800) 424-4777

GENETTI HOTEL
200 W 4th St (17701)
Rates: $29-$79
Tel: (717) 326-6600
(800) 321-1388

HOLIDAY INN
1840 E 3rd St (17701)
Rates: $64-$74
Tel: (717) 326-1981
(800) 329-7466

RIDGEMONT MOTEL
RD 4, Box 536
(17701)
Rates: $33-$37
Tel: (717) 321-5300

SHERATON HOTEL
100 Pine St (17701)
Rates: $79-$95
Tel: (717) 327-8231
(800) 325-3535

WIND GAP

TRAVEL INN
499 E Moorestown
Rd (18091)
Rates: $42-$62
Tel: (610) 863-4146

WORMLEYS-BURG

FRIENDSHIP INN
US 15 & 11 (17043)
Rates: $28-$70
Tel: (800) 424-4777

WYOMISSING

THE INN AT READING
1040 Park Rd (19610)
Rates: $68-$110
Tel: (610) 372-7811

SHERATON HOTEL
422 W Papermill Rd
(19610)
Rates: $85-$115
Tel: (610) 376-3811

WELLESLEY INN
910 Woodland Ave
(19610)
Rates: $35-$75
Tel: (610) 374-1500
(800) 444-8888

YORK

DAYS INN
222 Arsenal Rd
(17402)
Rates: $49-$79
Tel: (717) 843-9971
(800) 329-7466

HAMPTON INN
1550 Mt. Zion Rd
(17402)
Rates: $71-$83
Tel: (717) 840-1500
(800) 426-7866

HOLIDAY INN
2600 E Market St
(17402)
Rates: $69-$79
Tel: (717) 755-1966
(800) 465-4329

MOTEL 6
125 Arsenal Rd
(17404)
Rates: $35-$46
Tel: (717) 846-6260
(800) 440-6000

RED ROOF INN
323 Arsenal Rd
(17402)
Rates: $41-$56
Tel: (717) 843-8181
(800) 843-7663

SUPER 8 MOTEL
40 Arsenal Rd
(17404)
Rates: $34-$64
Tel: (717) 852-8686
(800) 800-8000

TRAVELODGE
132-140 N George St
(17401)
Rates: $35-$50
Tel: (717) 843-8974
(800) 578-7878

RHODE ISLAND

CRANSTON

DAYS INN
101 New London
Ave (02920)
Rates: $47-$79
Tel: (401) 942-4200
(800) 329-7466

EAST PROVIDENCE

**NEW YORKER
MOTOR LODGE**
400 Newport Ave
(02916)
Rates: n/a
Tel: (401) 434-8000

MIDDLETOWN

**CARLTON
PINEAPPLE INN**
1225 Aquidneck Ave
(02842)
Rates: $25-$70
Tel: (401) 847-8400

NEWPORT

**ANNA'S VICTORIAN
CONNECTION**
5 Fowler Ave (02840)
Rates: n/a
Tel: (401) 849-2489

BUDGET INN
1185 W Main Rd
(02840)
Rates: $36-$108
Tel: (401) 849-4700
(800) 862-2006

**HARBOR-BASE
PINEAPPLE INN**
372 Coddington
Hwy (02840)
Rates: $25-$70
Tel: (401) 847-2600

HOWARD JOHNSON
351 W Main Rd
(02842)
Rates: $34-$99
Tel: (401) 849-2000
(800) 446-4656

MOTEL 6
249 J T Connell Hwy
(02840)
Rates: $30-$36
Tel: (401) 848-0600
(800) 440-6000

PORTSMOUTH

**FOUNDER'S BROOK
MOTEL**
314 Boyd's Ln
(02871)
Rates: $59-$149
Tel: (401) 683-1244
(800) 334-8765

PROVIDENCE

MARRIOTT HOTEL
Charles & Orms Sts
(02904)
Rates: $115-$300
Tel: (401) 272-2400
(800) 228-9290

**PROVIDENCE
BILTMORE**
Kennedy Plaza
(02903)
Rates: $134-$299
Tel: (401) 421-0700

WESTIN HOTEL
1 W Exchange St
(02903)
Rates: $99-$190
Tel: (401) 598-8000

WAKEFIELD

**LARCHWOOD INN
& HOLLY HOUSE**
521-522 Main St
(02879)
Rates: $75-$110
Tel: (401) 783-5454

WARWICK

**HOLIDAY INN
AT THE CROSSINGS**
801 Greenwich Ave
(02886)
Rates: $119-$175
Tel: (800) 465-4329

**MASTER HOSTS
INNS**
2138 Post Rd (02886)
Rates: $55-$75
Tel: (401) 737-7400
(800) 251-1962

MOTEL 6
20 Jefferson Blvd
(Warwick, 02888)
Rates: $50-$56
Tel: (401) 467-9800
(800) 466-8356

WESTERLY

THE VILLA INN
190 Shore Rd (02891)
Rates: $85-$165
Tel: (800) 722-9240

SOUTH CAROLINA

AIKEN

DAYS INN
1204 Richland Ave
W (29801)
Rates: $30-$110
Tel: (803) 649-5524
(800) 329-7466

DELUXE INN
P. O. Box 2875
(29801)
Rates: $27-$44
Tel: (803) 642-2840

RAMADA INN
Hwy 19 & I-20
(29801)
Rates: $40
Tel: (803) 648-4272
(800) 272-6232

RAMADA LIMITED
1850 Richland Ave
W (29801)
Rates: $32-$38
Tel: (803) 648-6821
(800) 272-6232

WILLCOX INN
100 Colleton Ave SW
(29801)
Rates: $69-$135
Tel: (803) 649-1377

ANDERSON

DAYS INN
1007 Smith Mill Rd
(29625)
Rates: $58-$85
Tel: (803) 375-0375

HOLIDAY INN
3025 N Main St
(29621)
Rates: $59-$95
Tel: (864) 226-6051
(800) 465-4329

**HOLIDAY INN
EXPRESS**
103 Anderson
Business Pk (29621)
Rates: $59-$62
Tel: (864) 231-0231
(800) 465-4329

LA QUINTA INN
3430 Clemson Blvd
(29621)
Rates: $49-$66
Tel: (864) 225-3721
(800) 531-5900

QUALITY INN
3509 Clemson Blvd
(29621)
Rates: $49-$54
Tel: (864) 226-1000
(800) 221-2222

**ROYAL AMERICAN
MOTOR INN**
4515 Clemson Blvd
(29621)
Rates: $33-$42
Tel: (803) 226-7236

SUPER 8 MOTEL
3302 Cinema Ave
(29621)
Rates: $41-$61
Tel: (864) 225-8384
(800) 800-8000

BEAUFORT

BATTERY CREEK INN
102 B Marina Blvd
(29902)
Rates: $70+
Tel: (803) 521-1441

DAYS INN
1809 S Ribaut
(Port Royal 29902)
Rates: $42-$59
Tel: (803) 524-1551
(800) 329-7466

HOLIDAY INN
2001 Boundary St
(29902)
Rates: $50-$60
Tel: (803) 524-2144
(800) 465-4329

**HOWARD
JOHNSON LODGE**
3651 Trask Pkwy
(29902)
Rates: $45-$50
Tel: (803) 524-6020
(800) 446-4656

RAMADA LIMITED
US Hwy 21 & SC 170
(29903)
Rates: $38-$65
Tel: (803) 524-3322
(800) 272-6232

SCOTTISH INNS
2623 Hwy 21 (29902)
Rates: $28-$50
Tel: (803) 521-1555
(800) 251-1962

BISHOPVILLE

ECONO LODGE
1153 S Main St
(29010)
Rates: $35-$85
Tel: (805) 428-3200
(800) 424-4777

CAMDEN

COLONY INN
2020 W DeKalb St
(29020)
Rates: $35-$51
Tel: (803) 342-5508

GREENLEAF INN
1310 N Broad St
(29020)
Rates: $45-$70
Tel: (803) 425-1806

PARKVIEW MOTEL
1039 W DeKalb St
(29020)
Rates: $21-$27
Tel: (803) 432-7687

CAYCE

KNIGHTS INN
1987 Airport Blvd
(29033)
Rates: $31-$42
Tel: (803) 794-0222
(800) 843-5644

**MASTERS
ECONOMY INN**
2125 Commerce Dr
(29033)
Rates: $24-$35
Tel: (803) 791-5850

TREMONT INN
111 Knox Abbott Dr
(29033)
Rates: $30-$38
Tel: (803) 796-6240

CHARLESTON

BEST WESTERN INN
1540 Savannah Hwy
(29407)
Rates: $45-$109
Tel: (803) 571-6100
(800) 528-1234

COMFORT INN
5055 N Arco Ln
(29418)
Rates: $35-$65
Tel: (803) 554-6485
(800) 221-2222

DAYS INN-AIRPORT
2998 W Montague
Ave (29418)
Rates: $42-$68
Tel: (803) 747-4101
(800) 329-7466

ECONO LODGE
3668 Dorchester Rd
(29405)
Rates: $38-$99
Tel: (803) 747-0961
(800) 424-4777

HAWTHORN SUITES
181 Church St
(29401)
Rates: $89-$190
Tel: (803) 577-2644
(800) 527-1133

HOJO INN
3640 Dorchester Rd
(29405)
Rates: $29-55
Tel: (803) 554-4140
(800) 4465-4656

HOWARD JOHNSON
2512 Ashley
Phosphate Rd
(29418)
Rates: $31-$50
Tel: (803) 797-6864
(800) 446-4656

HOLIDAY INN EXPRESS
2070 McMillan Ave (29405)
Rates: $40-$53
Tel: (800) 465-4329

HOLIDAY INN-RIVERVIEW
301 Savannah Hwy (29407)
Rates: $49-$99
Tel: (803) 556-7100
(800) 465-4329

INDIGO INN B & B
1 Maiden Ln (29401)
Rates: $90-$160
Tel: (803) 577-5900
(800) 845-7639

LA QUINTA INN
2499 La Quinta Ln (29418)
Rates: $46-$74
Tel: (803) 797-8181
(800) 531-5900

MARRIOTT HOTEL
4770 Marriott Dr (29406)
Rates: $94
Tel: (803) 747-1900
(800) 228-9290

MASTERS ECONOMY INN
6100 Rivers Ave (29406)
Rates: $39-$48
Tel: (800) 633-3434

MIDDLETON INN
Ashley River Rd (29414)
Rates: $109-$139
Tel: (803) 446-0500
(803) 556-0500

MOTEL 6-NORTH
2551 Ashley Phosphate Rd (29418)
Rates: $28-$32
Tel: (803) 572-6590
(800) 440-6000

MOTEL 6-SOUTH
2058 Savannah Hwy (29407)
Rates: $32-$36
Tel: (803) 556-5144
(800) 440-6000

ORCHARD INN
4725 Saul White Blvd (29418)
Rates: $36-$57
Tel: (803) 747-3671

RED ROOF INN
7480 Northwoods Blvd (29418)
Rates: $34-$45
Tel: (800) 843-7663

RESIDENCE INN BY MARRIOTT
7645 Northwoods Blvd (29406)
Rates: $90-$130
Tel: (803) 572-5757
(800) 331-3131

RODEWAY INN-COLISEUM NORTH
5020 Rivers Ave (29418)
Rates: $39-$65
Tel: (803) 554-4982
(800) 228-2000

SUPER 8 MOTEL
2311 Ashley Phosphate Rd(29406)
Rates: $40-$54
Tel: (803) 572-2228
(800) 800-8000

TOWN & COUNTRY INN
2008 Savannah Hwy (29407)
Rates: $59-$106
Tel: (803) 571-1000

CHERAW

INN CHERAW
321 Second St (29520)
Rates: $38-$70
Tel: (803) 537-2011

CLEMSON

COMFORT INN
1305 Tiger Blvd (29633)
Rates: $45-$85
Tel: (864) 653-3600
(800) 221-2222

DAYS INN
1387 Tiger Blvd (29631)
Rates: $40-$55
Tel: (864) 653-4411
(800) 329-7466

HOLIDAY INN
894 Tiger Blvd (29633)
Rates: $49-$59
Tel: (864) 654-4450
(800) 465-4329

CLINTON

COMFORT INN
Rt 5, Box 478 (29325)
Rates: $39-$58
Tel: (864) 833-5558
(800) 221-2222

DAYS INN
I-26 & SR 56 (29325)
Rates: $42-$57
Tel: (803) 833-6600
(800) 329-7466

HOLIDAY INN
P.O. Box 926 (29325)
Rates: $49-$65
Tel: (803) 833-4900
(800) 465-4329

COLUMBIA

ADAMS MARK HOTEL
1200 Hampton St (29201)
Rates: $69-$134
Tel: (803) 771-7000
(800) 444-2326

AMERISUITES
7525 Two Notch Rd (29223)
Rates: $48-$53
Tel: (803) 736-6666

BUDGETEL INN
1538 Horseshoe Dr (29204)
Rates: $36-$49
Tel: (803) 736-6400
(800) 428-3438

BUDGETEL INN WEST
911 Bush River Rd (29210)
Rates: $34-$53
Tel: (803) 798-3222
(800) 428-3438

COMFORT INN
2025 Main St (29201)
Rates: $40-$59
Tel: (803) 252-6321
(800) 424-6323

DAYS INN
133 Plumbers Rd (29203)
Rates: $34-$150
Tel: (803) 754-4408
(800) 329-7466

DAYS INN
827 Bush River Rd (29210)
Rates: $32-$43
Tel: (803) 772-9672
(800) 329-7466

ECONOMY INNS
1776 Burning Tree Rd (29210)
Rates: $29-$36
Tel: (803) 798-9210
(800) 826-0778

HAMPTON INN
7333 Garners Ferry Rd. (29209)
Rates: $58-$81
Tel: (803) 783-5410
(800) 426-7866

HOLIDAY INN-AIRPORT
500 Chris Dr (29169)
Rates: $75-$82
Tel: (803) 794-9440
(800) 465-4329

HOLIDAY INN-COLISEUM
630 Assembly St (29201)
Rates: $45-$70
Tel: (803) 779-7800
(800) 465-4329

HOLIDAY INN-NE
7510 Two Notch Rd (29223)
Rates: $72-$88
Tel: (803) 736-3000
(800) 465-4329

KNIGHTS INN-NW
1803 Bush River Rd (29210)
Rates: $27-$40
Tel: (803) 772-0022
(800) 843-5644

LA QUINTA INN
1335 Garner Ln (29210)
Rates: $43-$55
Tel: (803) 798-9590
(800) 531-5900

RED ROOF INN-EAST
7580 Two Notch Rd (29223)
Rates: $34-$44
Tel: (803) 736-0850
(800) 843-7663

RED ROOF INN-WEST
10 Berryhill Rd
(29210)
Rates: $29-$40
Tel: (803) 798-9220
(800) 843-7663

RESIDENCE INN BY MARRIOTT
150 Stoneridge Dr
(29210)
Rates: $87-$117
Tel: (803) 779-7000
(800) 331-3131

SUPER 8 MOTEL
5719 Fairfield Rd
(29204)
Rates: $40-$55
Tel: (803) 735-0008
(800) 800-8000

DILLON

COMFORT INN
Rt 1, Box 69-B
(29536)
Rates: $50-$69
Tel: (803) 774-4137
(800) 424-6423

DAYS INN
818 Rudford Blvd
(29536)
Rates: $28-$65
Tel: (803) 774-6041
(800) 329-7466

HOLIDAY INN EXPRESS
Rt 1, Box 73 (29536)
Rates: $45-$90
Tel: (803) 774-5111
(800) 465-4329

SUPER 8 MOTEL
I-95, Exit 193 (29536)
Rates: $36-$46
Tel: (803) 774-4161
(800) 800-8000

EASLEY

DAYS INN
121 Days Inn Dr
(29640)
Rates: $43-$51
Tel: (803) 859-9902
(800) 329-7466

FLORENCE

COMFORT INN
P. O. Box 5688
(29502)
Rates: $38-$55
Tel: (800) 221-2222

DAYS INN NORTH
2111 W Lucas St
(29501)
Rates: $35-$69
Tel: (803) 665-4444
(800) 329-7466

DAYS INN SOUTH
P.O. Box 3806 (29502)
Rates: $29-$59
Tel: (803) 665-8550
(800) 329-7466

ECONO LODGE
I-95 & US 52 (29502)
Rates: $35-$110
Tel: (803) 665-8558
(800) 424-4777

ECONO LODGE-SOUTH
3932 W Palmetto St
(29501)
Rates: $32-$50
Tel: (803) 662-7712
(800) 424-4777

HAMPTON INN
1826 W Lucas St
(29501)
Rates: $69+
Tel: (803) 662-7000
(800) 426-7866

HOJO LODGE
3821 Bancroft Rd
(29503)
Rates: $33-$66
Tel: (803) 664-9494
(800) 446-4656

MOTEL 6
1834 W Lucas Rd
(29501)
Rates: $28-$32
Tel: (803) 667-6100
(800) 440-6000

PARK INN INTERNATIONAL
831 S Irby St (29501)
Rates: $34-$43
Tel: (803) 662-9421
(800) 437-7275

QUALITY INN I-95
3024 TV Rd (29501)
Rates: $35-$45
Tel: (800) 221-2222

RAMADA INN
I-95 & US 52, Exit
164 (29501)
Rates: $53-$75
Tel: (803) 669-4241
(800) 272-6232

RED ROOF INN
2690 David McLeod
Blvd (29501)
Rates: $26-$39
Tel: (803) 678-9000
(800) 843-7663

SHONEY'S INN
I-95 & US 52 (29501)
Rates: $44-$54
Tel: (803) 669-1921
(800) 222-2222

SUPER 8 MOTEL
1832 W Lucas St
(29501)
Rates: $42-$55
Tel: (803) 661-7267
(800) 800-8000

THUNDERBIRD MOTOR INN
P. O. Box 3909
(29502)
Rates: $34-$47
Tel: (803) 669-1611

YOUNG'S PLANTATION INN
P. O. Box 3806
(29502)
Rates: $25-$35
Tel: (803) 669-4171
(800) 476-2299

FORT MILL

DAYS INN
3482 Carowinds
Blvd (29715)
Rates: $35-$75
Tel: (803) 548-8000
(800) 329-7466

RAMADA INN - CAROWINDS 3
225 Carowinds Blvd
(29715)
Rates: $71-$145
Tel: (803) 548-2400
(800) 272-6232

GAFFNEY

COMFORT INN
143 Corona Dr
(29341)
Rates: $45-$60
Tel: (864) 487-4200
(800) 221-2222

DAYS INN
136 Peachoid Rd
(29341)
Rates: $39-$53
Tel: (803) 489-7172
(800) 329-7466

GEORGETOWN

DESEASONS MOTEL
412 St. James St
(29440)
Rates: n/a
Tel: (803) 546-4117

GREENVILLE

DAYS INN
3905 Augusta Rd
(29605)
Rates: $30-$50
Tel: (803) 277-4010
(800) 329-7466

DAYS INN
831 Congaree Rd
(29607)
Rates: $50-$109
Tel: (803) 288-6221
(800) 329-7466

HOLIDAY INN EXPRESS
5009 Pelham Rd
(29615)
Rates: $59+
Tel: (803) 297-5353
(800) 465-4329

HOLIDAY INN EXPRESS
27 S Pleasantburg Dr
(29607)
Rates: $50-$70
Tel: (803) 232-3339
(800) 465-4329

HOLIDAY INN I-85
4295 Augusta Rd
(29605)
Rates: $52-$68
Tel: (803) 277-8921
(800) 465-4329

HOWARD JOHNSON
2756 Laurens Rd
(29607)
Rates: $59-$64
Tel: (803) 288-6900
(800) 446-4656

LA QUINTA INN
31 Old Country Rd
(29607)
Rates: $48-$59
Tel: (803) 297-3500
(800) 531-5900

MOTEL 6
224 Bruce Rd (29605)
Rates: $27-$31
Tel: (803) 277-8630
(800) 440-6000

THE PHOENIX INN
P. O. Box 5064 Sta B
(29606)
Rates: $46-$95
Tel: (864) 233-4651
(800) 257-3529

QUALITY INN
50 Orchard Park Dr
(29615)
Rates: $39-$66
Tel: (800) 221-2222

RAMADA INN DOWNTOWN
1001 S Church St
(29601)
Rates: $55-$116
Tel: (803) 232-7666
(800) 272-6232

RAMADA LIMITED SOUTH
1314 S Pleasantburg
Dr (29605)
Rates: $41-$119
Tel: (803) 277-3734
(800) 272-6232

RED ROOF INN
2801 Laurens Rd
(29607)
Rates: $28-$39
Tel: (803) 297-4458
(800) 843-7663

RESIDENCE INN BY MARRIOTT
48 McPrice Ct
(29615)
Rates: $89-$109
Tel: (803) 297-0099
(800) 331-3131

GREENWOOD

ECONO LODGE
719 Bypass 25 NE
(29646)
Rates: $40-$96
Tel: (864) 229-5329
(800) 424-4777

HARDEEVILLE

DAYS INN STATELINE
I-95 & US 17 (29927)
Rates: $39-$99
Tel: (803) 784-2281
(800) 329-7466

ECONOMY INN
101 Frontage Rd
(29927)
Rates: $26-$33
Tel: (803) 784-2201

HOWARD JOHNSON LODGE
I-95 & US Hwy 17
(29927)
Rates: $33-$79
Tel: (803) 784-2271
(800) 446-4656

RAMADA LIMITED
I-95 & Rd 88, Exit 98
(29927)
Rates: $30-$40
Tel: (803) 784-3192
(800) 272-6232

SUPER 8 MOTEL
Hwy 17 & I-95
(29927)
Rates: $28-$51
Tel: (803) 784-2151
(800) 800-8000

THUNDERBIRD LODGE
P. O. Box 1126
(29927)
Rates: $22-$38
Tel: (803) 784-2196

HARTSVILLE

LANDMARK INN
1301 S 4th St (29550)
Rates: $52-$68
Tel: (803) 332-2611

HILTON HEAD ISLAND

MOTEL 6
830 Wm Hilton
Pkwy (29928)
Rates: $36-$42
Tel: (803) 785-2700
(800) 440-6000

RED ROOF INN
5 Regency Pkwy
(29928)
Rates: $29-$50
Tel: (803) 686-6808
(800) 843-7663

SHONEY'S INN
200 Museum St
(29926)
Rates: $62-$95
Tel: (803) 681-3655
(800) 222-2222

LANCASTER

DAYS INN
1100 N Main St
(29720)
Rates: $36-$54
Tel: (803) 286-6441
(800) 329-7466

LATTA

PATRICK HENRY MOTOR LODGE
203 N Richardson St
(29565)
Rates: $20-$35
Tel: (803) 752-5861

LITTLE RIVER

HARBOR INN
1564 US 17 Hwy N
(29566)
Rates: $33-$63
Tel: (800) 292-0404

LUGOFF

DAYS INN
529 Hwy 601 (29078)
Rates: $48-$75
Tel: (803) 438-6990
(800) 329-7466

HOLIDAY INN
P. O. Box 96 (29078)
Rates: $49-$85
Tel: (803) 438-9441
(800) 465-4329

MANNING

BUDGET INN
I-95 & US 301
(29102)
Rates: $19-$27
Tel: (803) 473-2561

COMFORT INN
P.O. Box 57 (29102)
Rates: $40-$75
Tel: (803) 473-7550
(800) 221-2222

DAYS INN
Rt 5, Box 442 (29102)
Rates: $30-$55
Tel: (803) 473-2596
(800) 329-7466

ECONOMY INN
P. O. Box 490 (29102)
Rates: $28-$44
Tel: (803) 473-4021

MT PLEASANT

COMFORT INN EAST
310 Hwy 17 Bypass
(29464)
Rates: $59-$109
Tel: (803) 884-5853
(800) 221-2222

DAYS INN
261 Johnnie Dodds
Blvd (29464)
Rates: $45-$82
Tel: (803) 881-1800
(800) 329-7466

GUILDS INN
101 Pitt St (29464)
Rates: $85-$140
Tel: (803) 881-0510

MASTERS ECONOMY INN
300 Wingo Way
(29464)
Rates: $36-$64
Tel: (803) 884-2814
(800) 633-3434

MYRTLE BEACH

**DAYS INN-
WACCAMAW**
3650 Hwy 501
(29577)
Rates: $40-$95
Tel: (803) 236-1950
(800) 329-7466

EL DORADO MOTEL
2800 S Ocean Blvd
(29577)
Rates: $25-$65
Tel: (803) 626-3559

KNIGHTS INN
3622 Hwy 501
(29577)
Rates: $30-$60
Tel: (803) 236-7400
(800) 843-5644

**MARINER
APARTMENT MOTEL**
7003 N Ocean Blvd
(29572)
Rates: $31-$94
Tel: (803) 449-5281

RED ROOF INN
2801 S Kings Hwy
(29577)
Rates: $40-$96
Tel: (803) 626-4444
(800) 843-7663

ST JOHN'S INN
6803 N Ocean Blvd
(29572)
Rates: $35-$140
(803) 449-5251

SEA MIST RESORT
1200 S Ocean Blvd
(29577)
Rates: $29-$145
Tel: (803) 448-1551

SUPER 8 MOTEL
3450 Hwy 17S
Bypass (29577)
Rates: $37-$67
Tel: (803) 293-6100
(800) 800-8000

WATERSIDE INN
2000 N Ocean Blvd
(29577)
Rates: $61-$154
Tel: (803) 448-5935

NEWBERRY

BEST WESTERN INN
11701 S Hwy 34
(29108)
Rates: $38-$54
Tel: (803) 276-5850
(800) 528-1234

COMFORT INN
1147 Wilson Rd
(29108)
Rates: $38-$70
Tel: (800) 221-2222

DAYS INN
Rt 1, Box 407-B
(29108)
Rates: $34-$45
Tel: (803) 276-2294
(800) 329-7466

ORANGEBURG

BEST WESTERN INN
826 John C Calhoun
Dr (29115)
Rates: $43-$49
Tel: (803) 534-7630
(800) 528-1234

HOLIDAY INN
415 John C Calhoun
Dr (29115)
Rates: $54-$72
Tel: (803) 531-4600
(800) 465-4329

HOWARD JOHNSON
3608 Old St
Matthews Rd (29115)
Rates: $40-$70
Tel: (803) 531-4900
(800) 446-4656

RUSSELL STREET INN
491 N Russell St
(29115)
Rates: $35-$64
Tel: (803) 531-2030

SUN INN
895 John C Calhoun
Dr (29115)
Rates: $34-$38
Tel: (800) 488-5368

RICHBURG

DAYS INN
I-77, Exit 65 (29729)
Rates: $31-$55
Tel: (803) 789-5555
(800) 329-7466

ECONO LODGE
Rt 1, Box 182 (29729)
Rates: $35-$75
Tel: (803) 789-3000
(800) 424-4777

RELAX INN
Rt 1, Box 1830
(29729)
Rates: $25-$95
Tel: (803) 789-6363

SUPER 8 MOTEL
Rt 1, Box 181-C
(29729)
Rates: $41-$49
Tel: (803) 789-7888
(800) 800-8000

RIDGELAND

**BEST WESTERN
POINT SOUTH**
Drawer AA (29936)
Rates: $42-$98
Tel: (800) 528-1234

COMFORT INN
P. O. Drawer J
(29936)
Rates: $43-$92
Tel: (803) 726-2121
(800) 221-2222

ECONO LODGE
516 E Main St
(29936)
Rates: $40-$45
Tel: (800) 424-4777

PALMS MOTEL
P. O. Box 547 (29936)
Rates: $23-$30
Tel: (803) 726-5511

QUALITY INN
P. O. Box AA (29936)
Rates: $44-$98
Tel: (803) 726-8101
(800) 221-2222

RIDGE SPRING

**SOUTHWOOD
MANOR B & B**
100 E Main St
(29129)
Rates: $65-$75
Tel: (803) 685-5100

RIDGEWAY

RIDGEWAY MOTEL
P. O. Box 472 (29130)
Rates: $26-$29
Tel: (803) 337-3238

ROCK HILL

BEST WESTERN INN
1106 Anderson Rd
(29730)
Rates: $52-$62
Tel: (803) 329-1330
(800) 528-1234

BOOK & SPINDLE B & B
626 Oakland Ave
(29730)
Rates: $50-$75
Tel: (803) 328-1913

ECONO LODGE
962 Riverview Rd
(29730)
Rates: $37-$95
Tel: (803) 329-3232
(800) 424-4777

HOLIDAY INN
2640 Cherry Rd
(29730)
Rates: $55-$70
Tel: (803) 329-1122
(800) 465-4329

HOWARD JOHNSON
2625 Cherry Rd
(29730)
Rates: $48-$72
Tel: (803) 329-3121
(800) 446-4656

RODEWAY INN
656 Anderson Rd.
(29730)
Rates: $30-$85
Tel: (803) 329-2100
(800) 228-2000

ST. GEORGE

BEST WESTERN INN
P. O. Box 386 (29477)
Rates: $40-$72
Tel: (803) 563-2277
(800) 528-1234

ECONO LODGE
I-95 & US 78 (29477)
Rates: $21-$45
Tel: (803) 563-4027
(800) 424-4777

ECONOMY MOTEL
125 Motel Dr (29477)
Rates: $27-$37
Tel: (803) 563-2360

HOLIDAY INN
I-95 & US 78 (29477)
Rates: $41-$55
Tel: (800) 465-4329

**ST. GEORGE
MOTOR INN**
215 S Parler Ave
(29477)
Rates: $16-$20
Tel: (803) 563-3029

SOUTHERN INN II
P. O. Box 375 (29477)
Rates: $20-$29
Tel: (803) 563-3775

SUPER 8 MOTEL
114 Winningham Rd
(29477)
Rates: $31-$59
Tel: (803) 563-5551
(800) 800-8000

SANTEE

CLARK'S INN
114 Bradford Blvd
(29142)
Rates: $37-$48
Tel: (800) 345-7888

COMFORT INN
265 Britain St (29142)
Rates: $40-$65
Tel: (803) 854-3221
(800) 221-2222

DAYS INN
P. O. Box 9 (29142)
Rates: $39-$58
Tel: (803) 854-2175
(800) 329-7466

ECONOMY INN
626 Bass Dr (29142)
Rates: $30-$42
Tel: (803) 854-2107

HOWARD JOHNSON
I-95 Exit 102 Rd 400
(29142)
Rates: $26-$60
Tel: (803) 478-7676
(800) 446-4656

RAMADA INN
Rt 6, P.O. Box 501
(29142)
Rates: $38-$68
Tel: (803) 854-2191
(800) 272-6232

SUPER 8 MOTEL
9125 Old Hwy 6
(29142)
Rates: $30-$44
Tel: (803) 854-3456
(800) 800-8000

SIMPSONVILLE

COMFORT INN
600 Fairview Rd
(29681)
Rates: $49-$100
Tel: (864) 963-2777
(800) 221-2222

SPARTANBURG

**BEST WESTERN
SPARTAN INN**
I-85 Bus at Exit 6
(29303)
Rates: $44-$74
Tel: (864) 578-5400
(800) 528-1234

**DAYS INN-
DOWNTOWN**
578 N Church St
(29303)
Rates: $32-$52
Tel: (864) 585-4311
(800) 329-7466

ECONO LODGE
710 Sunbeam Rd
(29303)
Rates: $30-$80
Tel: (864) 578-9450
(800) 424-7770

MOTEL 6
105 Jones Rd (29303)
Rates: $30-$34
Tel: (803) 573-6383
(800) 440-6000

QUALITY HOTEL
7136 Asheville Hwy
(29303)
Rates: $52-$105
Tel: (864) 503-0780
(800) 221-2222

RAMADA INN
1000 Hearon Cir
(29303)
Rates: $59-$125
Tel: (864) 503-9048
(800) 272-6232

**RESIDENCE INN
BY MARRIOTT**
9011 Fairforest Rd
(29301)
Rates: $49-$184
Tel: (803) 576-3333
(800) 331-3131

**SPARTAN INN &
CONF CTR**
700 Sunbeam Rd
(29303)
Rates: $46-$59
Tel: (803) 578-5400

**WILSON WORLD
HOTEL**
9027 Fairforest Rd
(29301)
Rates: $69-$94
Tel: (803) 574-2111

SUMMERTON

SUMMERTON INN
P. O. Box 640 (29148)
Rates: $17-$39
Tel: (803) 485-2635

SUMMERVILLE

ECONO LODGE
110 Holiday Inn Dr
(29483)
Rates: $40-$50
Tel: (803) 875-3022
(800) 424-7777

HOLIDAY INN
120 Holiday Inn Dr
(29483)
Rates: $56-$67
Tel: (803) 875-3300
(800) 465-4329

SUMTER

ECONOMY INN
P. O. Box 704 (29150)
Rates: $35-$39
Tel: (803) 469-4740

RAMADA INN
226 N Washington St
(29151)
Rates: $49-$69
Tel: (803) 775-2323
(800) 272-6232

TURBEVILLE

EXIT INN
P. O. Box 289 (29162)
Rates: $30-$43
Tel: (803) 659-8060

WALTERBORO

BEST WESTERN INN
1140 Snider's Hwy
(29488)
Rates: $46-$62
Tel: (803) 538-3600
(800) 528-1234

COMFORT INN
1109 Snider's Hwy
(29488)
Rates: $37-$71
Tel: (803) 538-5403
(800) 221-2222

ECONO LODGE
1057 Sniders Hwy
(29488)
Rates: $ 30-$39
Tel: (803) 538-3830
(800) 424-7777

HOLIDAY INN
1120 Snider's Hwy
(29488)
Rates: $52-$68
Tel: (803) 538-5473
(800) 465-4329

HOWARD JOHNSON
1305 Bells Hwy
(29488)
Rates: $25-$55
Tel: (803) 538-3948
(800) 446-4656

RICE PLANTERS INN
P. O. Box 529 (29488)
Rates: $24-$35
Tel: (803) 538-8964

SUPER 8 MOTEL
Rt 3, Box 760 (29488)
Rates: $31-$44
Tel: (803) 538-5383
(800) 800-8000

THUNDERBIRD INN
P. O. Box 815 (29488)
Rates: $21-$30
Tel: (803) 538-2503

WINNSBORO

DAYS INN
Hwy 34 & 321 Byp
(29180)
Rates: $25-$75
Tel: (803) 635-1447
(800) 329-7466

FAIRFIELD MOTEL
115 S 321 Bypass
(29180)
Rates: $25-$29
Tel: (800) 292-1509

YEMASSEE

DAYS INN
Jct US 17 & I-95
(29945)
Rates: $34-$59
Tel: (803) 726-8156
(800) 329-7466

**HOLIDAY INN
EXPRESS**
40 Frampton Dr
(29945)
Rates: $49-$59
Tel: (803) 726-9400
(800) 465-4329

PALMETTO LODGE
P. O. Box 218 (29945)
Rates: $20-$32
Tel: (803) 589-2361

**SOUTHERN
COMFORT INN**
P. O. Box 574 (29945)
Rates: $18-$25
Tel: (803) 589-2015

SUPER 8 MOTEL
Hwy 68 & I-95
(29945)
Rates: $24-$46
Tel: (803) 589-2177
(800) 800-8000

YORK

DAYS INN
1568 Alexander Love
Hwy (29745)
Rates: $38-$60
Tel: (803) 684-2525
(800) 329-7466

SOUTH DAKOTA

ABERDEEN

BEST WESTERN RAMKOTA
1400 8th Ave NW (57401)
Rates: $54-$63
Tel: (605) 229-4040
(800) 528-1234

BREEZE-INN MOTEL
1216 6th Ave SW (57401)
Rates: $24-$34
Tel: (605) 225-4222
(800) 341-8000

BUDGET SAVER MOTEL
1409 6th Ave SE (57401)
Rates: n/a
Tel: (605) 225-5300

COMFORT INN
2923 6th Ave SE (57401)
Rates: $40-$57
Tel: (605) 226-0097
(800) 221-2222

HOLIDAY INN
P. O. Box 1007 (57401)
Rates: $40-$70
Tel: (800) 465-4329

SUPER 8 MOTEL-EAST
2405 6th Ave SE (57401)
Rates: $38-$55
Tel: (605) 229-5005
(800) 800-8000

SUPER 8 MOTEL-NORTH
770 NW Hwy 281 (57401)
Rates: $32-$49
Tel: (605) 226-2288
(800) 800-8000

SUPER 8 MOTEL-WEST
714 S Hwy 281 (57401)
Rates: $32-$49
Tel: (605) 225-1711
(800) 800-8000

WHITE HOUSE INN
500 6th Ave SW (57401)
Rates: $30-$46
Tel: (605) 225-5000
(800) 225-6000

BADLANDS NATIONAL PARK

BADLANDS INN
Box 103 (Interior 57750)
Rates: $28-$45
Tel: (605) 433-5401

BUDGET HOST MOTEL
HC 54, Box 115 (Interior 57750)
Rates: $37-$48
Tel: (605) 433-5335
(800) 283-4678

CEDAR PASS LODGE
P. O. Box 5 (Interior 57750)
Rates: $35-$45
Tel: (605) 433-5460

BELLE FOURCHE

ACE MOTEL
109 6th Ave (57717)
Rates: $20-$50
Tel: (605) 892-2612

BEST WESTERN KINGS INN
518 National St (57717)
Rates: $30-$110
Tel: (605) 892-2691
(800) 528-1234

MOTEL LARIAT
1033 Elkhorn (57717)
Rates: $24-$51
Tel: (605) 892-2601

SUNSET MOTEL
HCR 30, Box 65 (57717)
Rates: $25-$55
Tel: (605) 892-2508

SUPER 8 MOTEL
501 National St (57717)
Rates: $33-$53
Tel: (605) 892-3361
(800) 800-8000

BERESFORD

CROSSROADS MOTEL
1409 W Cedar (57004)
Rates: $22-$32
Tel: (605) 763-2020

BROOKINGS

BEST WESTERN STAUROLITE INN
2515 E 6th St (57006)
Rates: $45-$75
Tel: (605) 692-9421
(800) 528-1234

HOLIDAY INN
2500 E 6th St (57006)
Rates: $49-$61
Tel: (800) 465-4329

SUPER 8 MOTEL
3034 LeFevre Dr (57006)
Rates: $40-$55
Tel: (605) 692-6920
(800) 800-8000

WAYSIDE MOTEL
1430 6th St (57006)
Rates: $26-$30
Tel: (800) 658-4577

BUFFALO

TIPPERARY LODGE
P. O. Box 247 (57720)
Rates: $30-$38
Tel: (605) 375-3721

CANISTOTA

BEST WESTERN U-BAR MOTEL
130 Ash St (57012)
Rates: $23-$45
Tel: (605) 296-3466
(800) 528-1234

CHAMBERLAIN

BEL AIRE MOTEL
312 E King St (57325)
Rates: $35-$48
Tel: (605) 734-5595

LAKE SHORE MOTEL
115 N River St (57325)
Rates: $30-$44
Tel: (605) 734-5566

RADISSON RESORT
101 Goe Mickleson Shoreline Dr (57325)
Rates: $69-$189
Tel: (605) 734-6376
(800) 333-3333

CORSICA

IMA PARKWAY MOTEL
Hwy 281 (57328)
Rates: $21-$35
Tel: (605) 946-5230
(800) 341-8000

CUSTER

AMERICAN PRESIDENTS CABINS
P. O. Box 446 (57730)
Rates: $24-$59
Tel: (605) 673-3373

BAVARIAN INN MOTEL
P. O. Box 152 (57730)
Rates: $24-$79
Tel: (605) 673-2802
(800) 657-4312

BLACK HILLS BALLOONS B & B
Rt 1, Box 10 (57730)
Rates: $65-$75
Tel: (605) 673-2520

BLUE BELL LODGE & RESORT
HCR 83, Box 63 (57730)
Rates: $75-$100
Tel: (605) 255-4531

CHIEF MOTEL
120 Mt. Rushmore
Rd (57730)
Rates: $26-$65
Tel: (605) 673-2318

LEGION LAKE RESORT
HCR 83, Box 67
(57730)
Rates: $69-$110
Tel: (800) 658-3530

ROCKET MOTEL
211 Mt. Rushmore
Rd (57730)
Rates: $30-$58
Tel: (605) 673-4401

THE ROOST RESORT
HCR 83, Box 120
(57730)
Rates: $34-$58
Tel: (605) 673-2326

DAKOTA DUNES

COUNTRY INN
151 Tower Rd
(57049)
Rates: $59-$79
Tel: (605) 232-3500

DEADWOOD

DAYS INN
68 Main St (57732)
Rates: $35-$99
Tel: (605) 578-3476
(800) 329-7466

DEADWOOD GULCH RESORT
P.O. Box 643 (57732)
Rates: $54-$95
Tel: (605) 578-1294

FIRST GOLD HOTEL
270 Main St (57732)
Rates: $47-$77
Tel: (605) 578-9777
(800) 274-1876

EAGLE BUTTE

SUPER 8 MOTEL
P.O. Box 180 (57625)
Rates: $37-$52
Tel: (605) 964-8888
(800) 800-8000

EUREKA

LAKEVIEW MOTEL
RR 1, Box 49 (57437)
Rates: $24-$35
Tel: (605) 284-2681

FAITH

PRAIRIE VISTA INN
P. O. Box 575 (57626)
Rates: $37-$53
Tel: (605) 967-2343
(800) 341-8000

FAULKTON

SUPER 8 MOTEL
700 Main St (57438)
Rates: $33-$53
Tel: (605) 598-4567
(800) 800-8000

FORT PIERRE

FORT PIERRE MOTEL
211 S First St (57532)
Rates: $26-$36
Tel: (605) 223-3111

FREEMAN

FENSEL'S MOTEL
Hwy 81 (57029)
Rates: n/a
Tel: (605) 925-4204

GETTYSBURG

HARER LODGE B & B
RR 1, Box 87A
(57442)
Rates: n/a
Tel: (605) 765-2167

IMA TRAIL MOTEL
211 E Garfield
(57442)
Rates: $23-$38
Tel: (605) 765-2482
(800) 341-8000

HILL CITY

BEST WESTERN GOLDEN SPIKE INN
106 Main St (57745)
Rates: $34-$105
Tel: (605) 574-2577
(800) 528-1234

LANTERN INN MOTEL
P. O. Box 744 (57745)
Rates: $38-$76
Tel: (605) 574-2582

PALMER GULCH LODGE
Box 295, Hwy 244
(57745)
Rates: $64-$91
Tel: (605) 574-2525
(800) 233-4331

ROBINS ROOST CABINS
HCR 87, Box 62
(57745)
Rates: n/a
Tel: (605) 574-2252

HOT SPRINGS

BEST WESTERN INN
602 W River St
(57747)
Rates: $38-$94
Tel: (605) 745-4292
(800) 528-1234

BISON MOTEL
646 S 5th St (57747)
Rates: n/a
Tel: (605) 745-5191

COMFORT INN
737 S 6th St (57747)
Rates: $49-$94
Tel: (605) 745-7378
(800) 221-2222

EL RANCHO MOTEL
640 S 6th St (57747)
Rates: $28-$60
Tel: (800) 341-8000

SUPER 8 MOTEL
800 Mammoth St
(57747)
Rates: $37-$60
Tel: (605) 745-3888
(800) 800-8000

HURON

BEST WESTERN OF HURON
2000 Dakota Ave S
(57350)
Rates: $47-$52
Tel: (605) 352-2000
(800) 528-1234

THE CROSSROADS HOTEL
100 4th SDt SW
(57350)
Rates: $51-$61
Tel: (605) 352-3204

TRAVELER MOTEL
241 Lincoln NW
(57350)
Rates: n/a
Tel: (605) 352-6401

KADOKA

BEST WESTERN H & H EL CENTRO MOTEL
P. O. Box 37 (57543)
Rates: $38-$100
Tel: (605) 837-2287
(800) 528-1234

CUCKLEBURR MOTEL
P. O. Box 575 (57543)
Rates: $22-$45
Tel: (605) 837-2151

HILLTOP MOTEL
E 225 Hwy 16
(57543)
Rates: $25-$48
Tel: (605) 837-2216

IMA DAKOTA INN
I-90 Exit 150 (57543)
Rates: $24-65
Tel: (605) 837-2151
(800) 341-8000

WEST MOTEL
P. O. Box 247 (57543)
Rates: $24-$56
Tel: (605) 837-2427

KENNEBEC

BUDGET HOST INN
Box 141 (57544)
Rates: $21-$36
Tel: (800) 283-4678

KING'S MOTEL
HC 81, Box 30
(57544)
Rates: $25-$38
Tel: (605) 869-2270

KEYSTONE

BED & BREAKFAST INN
P. O. Box 662 (57751)
Rates: $43-$84
Tel: (605) 666-4490

BEST WESTERN FOUR PRESIDENTS MOTEL
P. O. Box 690 (57751)
Rates: $50-$92
Tel: (605) 666-4472
(800) 528-1234

ECONO LODGE
SR 40 E (57751)
Rates: $29-$59
Tel: (605) 666-4417
(800) 424-4777

THE FIRST LADY INN
P. O. Box 677 (57751)
Rates: $47-$87
Tel: (800) 252-2119

HILLSIDE COUNTRY COTTAGES
13315 S Hwy 16 (57701)
Rates: $34-$60
Tel: (605) 342-4121

IMA KELLY INN
P. O. Box 654 (57751)
Rates: $30-$67
Tel: (605) 666-4483
(800) 341-8000

POWDER HOUSE LODGE
P. O. Box 714 (57751)
Rates: $30-$95
Tel: (605) 666-4646

RUSHMORE MANOR INN
115 Swanzey St (57751)
Rates: $40-$80
Tel: (605) 666-4443

TRIPLE R RANCH
Hwy 16A (57751)
Rates: n/a
Tel: (605) 666-4605

KIMBALL

TRAVELERS MOTEL
P.O. Box 457 (57355)
Rates: $27-$44
Tel: (605) 778-6215

LEAD

BEST WESTERN GOLDEN HILLS RESORT
900 Miners Ave (57754)
Rates: $69-$185
Tel: (605) 584-1800
(800) 528-1234

LEMMON

IMA PRAIRIE MOTEL
115 E 10th (57638)
Rates: $22-$29
Tel: (605) 374-3304
(800) 341-8000

LOWER BRULE

IMA GOLDEN BUFFALO RESORT
120 Crazy Horse St (57548-0250)
Rates: $40-$60
Tel: (605) 473-5506
(800)341-8000

MADISON

LAKE PARK MOTEL
P. O. Box 47 (57042)
Rates: $35-$50
Tel: (605) 256-3524
(800) 341-8000

SUPER 8 MOTEL
P. O. Box 5 (57042)
Rates: $33-$44
Tel: (605) 256-6931
(800) 800-8000

MILBANK

LANTERN MOTEL
RR 2, Box 281 (57252)
Rates: $28-$42
Tel: (605) 432-4591

IMA MANOR MOTEL
P. O. Box 26 (57252)
Rates: $30-$42
Tel: (605) 432-4527
(800) 341-8000

MITCHELL

BEST WESTERN INN
1001 S Burr (57301)
Rates: $32-$75
Tel: (605) 996-5536
(800) 528-1234

BUDGET HOST INN
1313 S Ohlman St (57301)
Rates: $33-$43
Tel: (605) 996-6647
(800) 283-4678

COACHLIGHT MOTEL
P. O. Box 416 (57301)
Rates: $31-$41
Tel: (605) 996-5686

HOLIDAY INN
1525 W Havens St (57301)
Rates: $55-$85
Tel: (605) 996-6501
(800) 465-4329

MOTEL 6
1309 S Ohlman St (57301)
Rates: $27-$33
Tel: (605) 996-0530
(800) 440-6000

SIESTA MOTEL
1210 W Havens St (57301)
Rates: $30-$48
Tel: (605) 996-5544
(800) 424-0537

MOBRIDGE

IMA WRANGLER MOTOR INN
820 West Grand Cir (57601)
Rates: $44-$69
Tel: (605) 645-3641
(800) 341-8000

SUPER 8 MOTEL
Box 156 (57601)
Rates: $26-$52
Tel: (605) 845-7215
(800) 800-800

MURDO

ANDERSON MOTEL
408 Lincoln (57559)
Rates: n/a
Tel: (605) 669-2448

BEST WESTERN GRAHAM'S
301 W 5th St (57559)
Rates: $28-$78
Tel: (605) 669-2441
(800) 528-1234

HOSPITALITY INN
302 W 5th St (57559)
Rates: $25-$68
Tel: (605) 669-2425

SUPER 8 MOTEL
604 E 5th (57559)
Rates: $29-$47
Tel: (605) 669-2437
(800) 800-8000

NORTH SIOUX CITY

SUPER 8 MOTEL
1300 River Dr (57049)
Rates: $40-$56
Tel: (605) 332-4716
(800) 800-8000

OACOMA

DAYS INN
I-90, Exit 260 (57365)
Rates: $34-$70
Tel: (605) 734-4100
(800) 329-7466

IMA OASIS INN
P. O. Box 39 (57365)
Rates: $35-$60
Tel: (605) 734-6061
(800) 341-8000

OACOMA INN
P. O. Box 38 (57365)
Rates: $28-$69
Tel: (605) 734-5593

PICKSTOWN

FORT RANDALL INN
P. O. Box 108 (57367)
Rates: $35-$50
Tel: (605) 487-7801
(800) 553-3003

PIEDMONT

ELK CREEK RESORT & LODGE
P. O. Box 8486 (57769)
Rates: $25-$89
Tel: (800) 846-2267

PIERRE

BEST WESTERN RAMKOTA
920 W Sioux (57501)
Rates: $59-$72
Tel: (605) 224-6877
(800) 528-1234

BUDGET HOST MOTEL
640 N Euclid Ave (57501)
Rates: $27-$51
Tel: (605) 224-5896

CAPITOL INN MOTEL
815 Wells Ave (57501)
Rates: $26-$30
Tel: (800) 658-3055

DAYS INN
520 W Sioux (57501)
Rates: $32-$50
Tel: (605) 224-0411
(800) 329-7466

GOVERNOR'S INN
700 W Sioux (57501)
Rates: $38-$51
Tel: (605) 224-4200
(800) 341-8000

KELLY INN
713 W Sioux (57501)
Rates: $39-$47
Tel: (605) 224-4140

SUPER 8 MOTEL
320 W Sioux (57501)
Rates: $29-$52
Tel: (605) 224-1617
(800) 800-8000

PLANKINTON

SUPER 8 MOTEL
801 S Main, Box 1C (57368)
Rates: $40-$77
Tel: (605) 942-7722
(800) 800-8000

PLATTE

KINGS INN
P. O. Box 54 (57369)
Rates: $22-$34
Tel: (605) 337-3385

PRESHO

HUTCH'S MOTEL
P. O. Box 449 (57568)
Rates: $28-$46
Tel: (605) 895-2591
(800) 341-8000

RAPID CITY

BIG SKY MOTEL
4080 Tower Rd (57701)
Rates: $25-$52
Tel: (605) 348-3200

CASTLE INN
15 E North St (57701)
Rates: $29-$90
Tel: (800) 658-5464

DAYS INN
125 Main St (57701)
Rates: $43-$150
Tel: (605) 343-5501
(800) 329-7466

ECONO LODGE
625 E Disk Dr (57701)
Rates: $24-$149
Tel: (605) 342-6400
(800) 424-4777

FAIR VALUE INN
1607 La Crosse St (57701)
Rates: $25-$65
Tel: (605) 342-8118

FOOTHILLS INN
1625 La Crosse St (57701)
Rates: $30-$120
Tel: (605) 348-5640

GOLD NUGGET MOTEL
13470 S Hwy 16 (57701)
Rates: $39-$59
Tel: (605) 348-2082

GOLD STAR MOTEL
801 E North (57701)
Rates: $26-$62
Tel: (605) 341-7051

HILLSIDE COUNTRY COTTAGES
13315 S Hwy 16 (57701)
Rates: $25-$55
Tel: (605) 342-4121

HILTON INN
445 Mt. Rushmore Rd (57701)
Rates: $75-$250
Tel: (605) 348-8300

HOLIDAY INN
505 N Fifth St (57701)
Rates: $80-$105
Tel: (605) 348-4000
(800) 465-4329

HOLIDAY INN I-90
1902 La Crosse St (57701)
Rates: $59-$99
Tel: (605) 348-1230
(800) 465-4329

LAZY U MOTOR LODGE
2215 Mt. Rushmore Rd (57701)
Rates: $22-$69
Tel: (605) 343-4242

MOTEL 6
620 E Latrobe St (57701)
Rates: $29-$35
Tel: (605) 343-3687
(800) 440-6000

QUALITY INN
2208 Mt. Rushmore Rd (57701)
Rates: $39-$119
Tel: (605) 342-3322
(800) 221-2222

RAMADA INN
1721 La Crosse St (57701)
Rates: $49-$169
Tel: (605) 342-1300
(800) 272-6232

ROCKERVILLE TRADING POST & MOTEL
13525 Main St (57701)
Rates: $30-$59
Tel: (605) 341-4880

SUPER 8 MOTEL
2124 La Crosse St (57701)
Rates: $28-$62
Tel: (605) 348-8070
(800) 800-8000

THRIFTY MOTOR INN
1303 La Crosse St (57701)
Rates: $22-$69
Tel: (605) 342-0551

TIP-TOP MOTOR HOTEL
405 St Joseph St (57701)
Rates: $32-$74
Tel: (605) 343-3901
(800) 341-8000

TRADEWINDS MOTEL
420 East North St (57701)
Rates: n/a
Tel: (605) 342-4153

REDFIELD

COACHMAN INN
826 4th St (57469)
Rates: $23-$38
Tel: (800) 382-8000

SELBY

SUPER 8 MOTEL
5000 Hwy 12 & 83 (57472)
Rates: $37-$61
Tel: (605) 649-7979
(800) 800-8000

SIOUX FALLS

BEST WESTERN RAMKOTA
2400 N Louise Ave (57107)
Rates: $65-$229
Tel: (605) 336-0650
(800) 528-1234

BEST WESTERN TOWN HOUSE
400 S Main (57102)
Rates: $50-$70
Tel: (605) 336-2740
(800) 528-1234

BRIMARK INN
3200 W Russell St (57101)
Rates: $39-$56
Tel: (605) 332-2000

BUDGETEL INN
3200 Meadow Ave
(57106)
Rates: $35-$53
Tel: (605) 362-0835

COMFORT INN-NORTH
5100 N Cliff Ave
(57104)
Rates: $35-$53
Tel: (605) 331-4490
(800) 221-2222

COMFORT INN-SOUTH
3216 S Carolyn Ave
(57106)
Rates: $40-$71
Tel: (605) 361-2822
(800) 221-2222

COMFORT SUITES
3208 S Carolyn Ave
(57106)
Rates: $50-$80
Tel: (605) 362-9711
(800) 221-2222

EXEL INN
1300 W Russell St
(57104)
Rates: $31-$44
Tel: (605) 331-5800
(800) 356-8013

FAIRFIELD INN BY MARRIOTT
4501 W Empire Pl
(57116)
Rates: $43-$57
Tel: (605) 361-2211
(800) 228-2800

KELLY INN
3101 W Russell St
(57107)
Rates: $39-$54
Tel: (605) 338-6242

MOTEL 6
3009 W Russell St
(57107)
Rates: $30-$36
Tel: (605) 336-7800
(800) 440-6000

RAMADA INN CONVENTION CENTER
1301 W Russell St
(57104)
Rates: $59-$84
Tel: (605) 336-1020
(800) 272-6232

RAMADA LIMITED
12th & South Lyons
Ave (57104)
Rates: $35-$75
Tel: (605) 330-0000
(800) 272-6232

RESIDENCE INN
4509 W Empire Pl
(57116)
Rates: $89-$139
Tel: (605) 361-2202

RODEWAY INN
809 West Ave N
(57104)
Rates: $44-$59
Tel: (605) 336-0230
(800) 228-2000

SELECT INN
3500 S Gateway Blvd
(57106)
Rates: $30-$41
Tel: (605) 361-1864
(800) 641-1000

SLEEP INN
1500 N Kiwanis Ave
(57107)
Rates: $46-$60
Tel: (605) 339-3992
(800) 221-2222

SUPER 8 MOTEL
1508 W Russell St
(57104)
Rates: $36-$57
Tel: (605) 339-9330
(800) 800-8000

SISSETON

HOLIDAY MOTEL
E of Jct US 127
(57262)
Rates: $22-$30
Tel: (605) 698-7644

IMA I-29 MOTEL
I-29 Jct SD 10E
(57262)
Rates: $30-$38
Tel: (605) 698-4314
(800) 341-8000

VIKING MOTEL
West Hwy 10 (57262)
Rates: n/a
Tel: (605) 698-7663

SPEARFISH

BEST WESTERN INN
346 W Kansas
(57783)
Rates: $39-$89
Tel: (605) 642-4676
(800) 528-1234

COMFORT INN
2725 1st Ave (57783)
Rates: $49-$75
Tel: (605) 642-2337
(800) 221-2222

FAIRFIELD INN
2720 1st Ave (57783)
Rates: $41-$91
Tel: (605) 642-3500

IMA KELLY INN
540 E Jackson Blvd
(57783)
Rates: $45-$80
Tel: (605) 642-7795
(800) 635-3559

QUEEN'S MOTEL
305 Main St (57783)
Rates: $24-$49
Tel: (605) 642-2631

RAMADA INN - NORTHERN BLACK HILLS
I-90 & Exit 14
(57783)
Rates: $46-$91
Tel: (605) 642-4683
(800) 272-6232

ROYAL REST MOTEL
444 Main St (57783)
Rates: $25-$45
Tel: (605) 642-3842

SHADY PINES CABINS
514 Mason St (57783)
Rates: n/a
Tel: (800) 551-8920

SHERWOOD LODGE
231 West Jackson
Blvd (57783)
Rates: n/a
Tel: (605) 642-4688

STURGIS

BEST WESTERN OF STURGIS
2431 S Junction
(57785)
Rates: $35-$89
Tel: (605) 347-3604
(800) 528-1234

JUNCTION INN
1802 S Junction Ave
(57785)
Rates: $29-$69
Tel: (605) 347-5675

NATIONAL 9 STARLITE INN
2426 Junction Ave
(57785)
Rates: $29-$63
Tel: (605) 347-2506

SUPER 8 MOTEL
P. O. Box 306 (57785)
Rates: $32-$44
Tel: (605) 347-4447
(800) 800-8000

VERMILLION

COMFORT INN
701 W Cherry St
(57069)
Rates: $39-$55
Tel: (605) 624-8333
(800) 221-2222

SUPER 8 MOTEL
1208 E Cherry St
(57069)
Rates: $36-$50
Tel: (605) 624-8005
(800) 800-8000

WALL

BEST WESTERN PLAINS MOTEL
712 Glenn St (57790)
Rates: $38-$95
Tel: (605) 279-2145
(800) 528-1234

ELK MOTEL
South Blvd (57790)
Rates: $26-$62
Tel: (605) 279-2127
(800) 782-9402

HITCHING POST MOTEL
211 10th Ave (57790)
Rates: $27-$63
Tel: (605) 279-2133

KINGS INN MOTEL
608 Main St (57790)
Rates: $35-$56
Tel: (605) 279-2178

SANDS MOTOR INN
804 Glenn St (57790)
Rates: $32-$79
Tel: (605) 279-2121
(800) 341-8000

WATERTOWN

BEST WESTERN RAMKOTA
1901 9th Ave SW
(57201)
Rates: $50-$69
Tel: (605) 886-8011
(800) 528-1234

COMFORT INN
800 35th St Cir
(57201)
Rates: $42-$58
Tel: (605) 886-3010
(800) 221-2222

DRAKE MOTOR INN
P. O. Box 352 (57201)
Rates: $27-$37
Tel: (800) 821-8695

GUEST HOUSE INN
P. O. Box 1147
(57201)
Rates: $32-$37
Tel: (605) 886-8061

TRAVEL HOST MOTEL
1714 9th Ave SW
(57201)
Rates: $29-$44
Tel: (605) 886-6120

WEBSTER

SUPER 8 MOTEL
P. O. Box 592 (57274)
Rates: $32-$80
Tel: (605) 345-4701
(800) 800-8000

WINNER

IMA BUFFALO TRAIL MOTEL
950 W 1st (57580)
Rates: $32-$80
Tel: (605) 842-2212
(800) 341-8000

SUPER 8 MOTEL
902 E Hwy 44
(57580)
Rates: $29-$90
Tel: (605) 842-0991
(800) 800-8000

WARRIOR INN MOTEL
Hwys 44 & 118
(57580)
Rates: $34-$70
Tel: (800) 658-4705

YANKTON

BROADWAY MOTEL
1210 Broadway
(57078)
Rates: $25-$33
Tel: (605) 665-7805

COMFORT INN
2118 Broadway
(57078)
Rates: $40-$52
Tel: (605) 665-8053
(800) 221-2222

LEWIS & CLARK RESORT
P. O. Box 754 (57078)
Rates: $35-$80
Tel: (605) 665-2680

MULBERRY INN
512 Mulberry St
(57078)
Rates: $25-$48
Tel: (605) 665-7116

SUPER 8 MOTEL
Rt 4, Box 36 (57078)
Rates: $32-$43
Tel: (605) 665-6510
(800) 800-8000

YANKTON INN & CONV CTR
1607 Hwy 50 E
(57078)
Rates: $42-$59
Tel: (605) 665-2906

TENNESSEE

ANTIOCH

DAYS INN
I-24 & Bell Rd
(37013)
Rates: $41-$60
Tel: (615) 731-7800
(800) 329-7466

HAMPTON INN
210 Crossings Place
(37013)
Rates: $60-$65
Tel: (615) 731-0229
(800) 426-7866

ASHLAND CITY

**BIRD SONG
COUNTRY INN
BED & BREAKFAST**
1306 Hwy 49 E
(37015)
Rates: n/a
Tel: (615) 792-4005

ATHENS

**DAYS INN
OF ATHENS**
2541 Decatur Pike
(37302)
Rates: $34-$48
Tel: (423) 745-5800
(800) 329-7466

**HOLIDAY INN
ATHENS I-75**
I-75 & Mt. Verd Rd
(37303)
Rates: $35-$46
Tel: (423) 745-1212
(800) 465-4329

**HOMESTEAD INN
EAST**
1827 Holiday Dr
(37303)
Rates: $30-$42
Tel: (423) 744-9002

**HOMESTEAD INN
WEST**
2808 Decatur Pike
(37303)
Rates: $31-$37
Tel: (423) 745-9002

SCOTTISH INNS
2620 Decatur Pike
(37303)
Rates: n/a
Tel: (423) 744-8200
(800) 251-1962

SUPER 8 MOTEL
2539 Decatur Pike
(37303)
Rates: $36-$55
Tel: (423) 745-4500
(800) 800-8000

BLOUNTVILLE

SUPER 8 MOTEL
131 Airport Cir
(37617)
Rates: $37-$100
Tel: (423) 323-4155
(800) 800-8000

BRENTWOOD

AMERISUITES
202 Summit View Dr
(37027)
Rates: $82-$90
Tel: (615) 661-9477

**ENGLISH MANOR
BED & BREAKFAST**
6304 Murray Ln
(37027)
Rates: n/a
Tel: (615) 373-4627
(800) 332-4640

HILTON SUITES
9000 Overlook Blvd
(37027)
Rates: $99-$109
Tel: (615) 370-0111
(800) 445-8667

**RESIDENCE INN
BY MARRIOTT**
206 Ward Cir (37027)
Rates: $93-$153
Tel: (615) 371-0100
(800) 331-3131

BRISTOL

**ECONO LODGE
MEDICAL CENTER**
3281 W State St
(37621)
Rates: $40-$90
Tel: (423) 968-9119
(800) 424-4777

HOJO INN
975 Volunteer Pkwy
(37620)
Rates: $38-$135
Tel: (423) 968-9474

HOLIDAY INN I-81
111 Holiday Dr
(37620)
Rates: $44-$62
Tel: (423) 968-1101
(800) 465-4329

QUALITY INN
P. O. Box 1016
(37621)
Rates: $42-$55
Tel: (423) 968-9119
(800) 221-2222

BROWNSVILLE

DAYS INN
2530 Anderson Ave
(38012)
Rates: $40-$60
Tel: (901) 772-3297
(800) 329-7466

BUCHANAN

CYPRESS BAY RESORT
110 Cypress Resort
Loop (38222)
Rates: n/a
Tel: (901) 232-8221

**PARIS LANDING
MOTEL**
Rt 1 Box 84B (38222)
Rates: n/a
Tel: (901) 642-5590

SHAMROCK RESORT
220 Shamrock Rd
(38222)
Rates: n/a
Tel: (901) 232-8211
(800) 852-7885

CAMDEN

**BIRDSONG RESORT/
MARINA &
CAMPGROUND**
255 Marina Rd
(38320)
Rates: n/a
Tel: (901) 584-7880
(800) 225-7469

PASSPORT INN
Hwy 70 E (38320)
Rates: $39-$45
Tel: (901) 584-3111
(800) 251-1962

CARTHAGE

**DEFEATED CREEK
MARINA**
156 Marina Ln
(37030)
Rates: n/a
Tel: (615) 774-3131

CARYVILLE

BUDGET HOST INN
101 Tennessee Dr
(37714)
Rates: $24-$31
Tel: (423) 562-9595
(800) 283-4678

**HOLIDAY INN
COVE LAKE**
Rt 1, Box 14 (37714)
Rates: $43-$55
Tel: (423) 562-8476
(800) 465-4329

CELINA

CEDAR HILL RESORT
2371 Cedar Hill Rd
(38551)
Rates: $35-$110
Tekl: (615) 243-3201
(800) 872-8393

**DALE HOLLOW
MARINA**
99 Arlon Webb Dr
(38551)
Rates: n/a
Tel: (615) 243-2211

CENTERVILLE

BUCKSNORT MOTEL
I-40 Exit 152 (37140)
Rates: n/a
Tel: (615) 729-5450
(800) 841-5813

CHATTANOOGA

**BEST WESTERN
AIRPORT INN**
6650 Ringgold Rd
(37412)
Rates: $39-$99
Tel: (423) 894-1860
(800) 528-1234

**BEST WESTERN-
HERITAGE INN**
7641 Lee Hwy (37421)
Rates: $39-$95
Tel: (423) 899-3311
(800) 528-1234

**BEST WESTERN-
ROYAL INN**
3644 Cummings
Hwy (37419)
Rates: $43-$120
Tel: (423) 821-6840
(800) 528-1234

COMFORT INN
7717 Lee Hwy (37421)
Rates: $52-$77
Tel: (423) 894-5454
(800) 221-2222

DAYS INN
7725 Lee Hwy (37421)
Rates: $44-$74
Tel: (615) 899-2288
(800) 329-7466

DAYS INN
5435 Alabama Hwy
(Ringgold GA 30736)
Rates: $69-$275
Tel: (706) 965-5730
(800) 329-7466

**DAYS INN
CONVENTION CENTRE**
1400 Mack Smith Rd
(37412)
Rates: $40-$150
Tel: (423) 894-0440
(800) 329-7466

**DAYS INN
LOOKOUT
MOUNTAIN**
3801 Cummings
Hwy (37419)
Rates: $38-$68
Tel: (615) 821-6044
(800) 329-7466

**DAYS INN
RIVERGATE**
901 Carter St (37402)
Rates: $45-$109
Tel: (423) 266-7331
(800) 329-7466

ECONO LODGE
1417 St. Thomas St
(37412)
Rates: $30-$45
Tel: (423) 894-1417
(800) 424-4777

**HOLIDAY INN
EXPRESS**
7024 McCutcheon
Rd (37421)
Rates: $64-$69
Tel: (423) 490-8560
(800) 465-4329

**HOLIDAY INN I-75
AIRPORT**
2345 Shallowford
Village Dr (37421)
Rates: $63-$77
Tel: (423) 855-2898
(800) 465-4329

**HOLIDAY INN-
SOUTHEAST**
6700 Ringgold Rd
(37412)
Rates: $55-$71
Tel: (423) 893-8100
(800) 465-4329

**KINGS LODGE
MOTEL**
2400 Westside Dr
(37404)
Rates: $32-$50
Tel: (423) 698-8944
(800) 251-7702

MOTEL 6
7707 Lee Hwy (37421)
Rates: $34-$47
Tel: (615) 892-7707
(800) 466-8356

**QUALITY INN-
SOUTH**
6710 Ringgold Rd
(37412)
Rates: $44-$59
Tel: (423) 894-6820
(800) 424-6423

**RAMADA INN I-75
SOUTH**
6639 Capehart Ln
(37412)
Rates: $48-$56
Tel: (423) 894-6110
(800) 228-2825

RAMADA INN 5
100 W 21st St (37408)
Rates: $48-$78
Tel: (423) 265-3151
(800) 272-6232

RED ROOF INN
7014 Shallowford Rd
(37421)
Rates: $37-$65
Tel: (423) 899-0143
(800) 843-7663

SUPER 8 MOTEL
1401 Mack Smith Rd
(37412)
Rates: $45-$60
Tel: (423) 892-3888
(800) 800-8000

CLARKSVILLE

A&W MOTEL
1505 Madison St
(37043)
Rates: n/a
Tel: (615) 647-3545

DAYS INN
1100 Hwy 76 (37043)
Rates: $40-$70
Tel: (615) 358-3194
(800) 329-7466

HOLIDAY INN I-24
3095 Wilma Rudolph
Blvd (37040)
Rates: $49-$66
Tel: (615) 648-4848
(800) 465-4329

**RAMADA INN
RIVERVIEW**
50 College St (37040)
Rates: $44-$85
Tel: (615) 552-3331
(800) 272-6232

RAMADA LIMITED
3100 Wilma Rudolph
Blvd (37040)
Rates: $36-$49
Tel: (615) 552-0098
(800) 272-6232

SKYWAY MOTEL
2581 Ft. Campbell
Blvd (37042)
Rates: $23-$35
Tel: (615) 431-5225

TRAVELODGE
3075 Wilma Rudolph
Blvd (37040)
Rates: $50-$55
Tel: (615) 645-1400

CLEVELAND

**BEST WESTERN
CLEVELAND INN**
156 James Asberry
Dr (37311)
Rates: $37-$69
Tel: (423) 457-2233
(800) 528-1234

BUDGETEL INN
107 Interstate Dr
NW (37312)
Rates: $34-$47
Tel: (423) 339-1000
(800) 428-3438

COLONIAL INN
1555 25th St (37311)
Rates: $22-$32
Tel: (423) 472-6845

DAYS INN
2550 Georgetown Rd
(37311)
Rates: $30-$65
Tel: (423) 476-2112
(800) 329-7466

EXCLUSIVE QUARTERS
210 James Ashbury Dr NW (37812)
Rates: $49-$54
Tel: (423) 479-1333

HOLIDAY INN NORTH
I-75 & SR 60 (37320)
Rates: $45-$65
Tel: (423) 472-1504
(800) 465-4329

QUALITY INN
2595 Georgetown Rd (37311)
Rates: $47-$125
Tel: (423) 479-3720
(800) 221-2222

RAMADA INN
I-75 & SR 64 Bypass (37320)
Rates: $40-453
Tel: (423) 479-4531
(800) 272-6232

RED CARPET INN
1501 25th St (37311)
Rates: $25-$29
Tel: (423) 476-6514
(800) 251-1962

TRAVEL INN
3000 Valley Hills Tr NW (37311)
Rates: $26-$42
Tel: (615) 472-2185

COLLIERVILLE

PLANTATION INN
1230 W Poplar (38017)
Rates: $38-$45
Tel: (901) 853-1235

COLUMBIA

ECONO LODGE
1548 Bear Creek Pkwy (38401)
Rates: $40-$60
Tel: (615) 381-1410
(800) 424-4777

JAMES K POLK MOTEL
1111 Nashville Hwy (38401)
Rates: $30-$40
Tel: (615) 388-4913

OAK SPRINGS INN & GALLERY
1512 Williamsport Pike (38401)
Rates: n/a
Tel: (615) 388-7539
(800) 542-7698

RAMADA INN
1208 Nashville Hwy (38401)
Rates: $46-$75
Tel: (615) 388-2720
(800) 272-6232

COOKEVILLE

BEST WESTERN THUNDERBIRD MOTEL
900 S Jefferson Ave (38501)
Rates: $35-$60
Tel: (615) 526-7115
(800) 528-1234

DAYS INN
1292 Bunker Hill Rd (38501)
Rates: $30-$65
Tel: (615) 528-1511
(800) 329-7466

EASTWOOD INN
1646 E Spring St (38506)
Rates: n/a
Tel: (615) 526-6158

HAMPTON INN
340 Interstate Dr (38301)
Rates: $55-$75
Tel: (615) 520-1117
(800) 426-7866

HOLIDAY INN
970 S Jefferson Ave (38501)
Rates: $61-$68
Tel: (615) 526-7125
(800) 465-4329

HOWARD JOHNSON MOTOR LODGE
2021 E Spring St (38501)
Rates: $32-$46
Tel: (615) 526-3333
(800) 446-4656

STAR MOTOR INN
1115 S Willow Ave (38501)
Rates: n/a
Tel: (615) 526-9511
(800) 842-1685

CORDOVA

BEST SUITES OF AMERICA
8166 Varnavas Dr (38018)
Rates: $67-$93
(901) 386-4600

COVINGTON

BEST WESTERN INN
873 Hwy 51 N (38019)
Rates: $39-$49
Tel: (901) 476-8561
(800) 528-1234

CROSSVILLE

CAPRI TERRACE MOTEL
714 N Main St (38555)
Rates: n/a
Tel: (615) 484-7561

EXECUTIVE INN
3114 N Main St (38555)
Rates: n/a
Tel: (615) 484-9691
(800) 626-9432

HERITAGE INN
317 Hwy 127 (38555)
Rates: n/a
Tel: (615) 484-9505
(800) 762-7065

RAMADA INN
SR 127 & I-40 (38555)
Rates: $44-$59
Tel: (615) 484-7581
(800) 272-6232

CUMBERLAND GAP

CUMBERLAND GAP INN
630 Brooklyn St (37724)
Rates: $60-$70
Tel: (423) 869-9172

HOLIDAY INN
US Hwy 25 (37724)
Rates: $45-$64
Tel: (423) 869-3631
(800) 465-4329

DANDRIDGE

COMFORT INN
620 Green Valley Dr (37725)
Rates: $39-$149
Tel: (423) 397-2090
(800) 221-2222

MOUNTAIN HARBOR INN
1199 Hwy 139 (37725)
Rates: $60-$115
Tel: (423) 397-3345

TENNESSEE MOUNTAIN INN
531 Patriot Dr (37725)
Rates: $35-$69
Tel: (423) 397-9437
(800) 235-9440

DAYTON

BEST WESTERN DAYTON INN
7835 Rhea County Hwy (37321)
Rates: $42-$100
Tel: (423) 775-6560
(800) 528-1234

DAYS INN
3914 Rhea County Hwy (37321)
Rates: $45-$85
Tel: (423) 775-9718
(800) 329-7466

DICKSON

COMFORT INN
2325 Hwy 46 S (37055)
Rates: $40-$75
Tel: (615) 446-2423
(800) 221-2222

DAYS INN
Hwy 46 & I-40 (37055)
Rates: $29-$69
Tel: (615) 446-7561
(800) 329-7466

HOLIDAY INN
2420 Hwy 46 S (37055)
Rates: $52-$70
Tel: (615) 446-9081
(800) 465-4329

DYERSBURG

DAYS INN
2600 Lake Rd
(38024)
Rates: $39-$50
Tel: (901) 287-0888
(800) 329-7466

RAMADA INN
2331 Lake Rd
(38024)
Rates: $35-$45
Tel: (901) 287-0044
(800) 272-6232

ELKTON

ECONOMY INN
I-65 & Bryson Rd
(38455)
Rates: n/a
Tel: (615) 468-2594

FARRAGUT

BUDGETEL INN
11341 Campbell
Lakes Dr (37922)
Rates: $52-$61
Tel: (423) 671-1010

FAYETTEVILLE

**BEST WESTERN
FAYETTEVILLE INN**
3021 Thornton
Taylor
Pkwy (37334)
Rates: $48-$125
Tel: (615) 433-0100
(800) 528-1234

DAYS INN
1651 Huntsville
Hwy (37334)
Rates: $37-$59
Tel: (615) 433-6121
(800) 329-7466

FRANKLIN

**BEST WESTERN
FRANKLIN INN**
1308 Murfreesboro
Rd (37064)
Rates: $42-$75
Tel: (615) 790-0570
(800) 251-3200

BUDGETEL INN
4207 Franklin
Commons Ct (37064)
Rates: $37-$54
Tel: (615) 791-7700
(800) 428-3438

COMFORT INN
4206 Franklin
Commons Ct (37064)
Rates: $55-$85
Tel: (615) 791-6675
(800) 221-2222

DAYS INN
4217 S Carothers Rd
(37064)
Rates: $42-$175
Tel: (800) 329-7466

GOOSECREEK INN
2404 Goose Creek
Bypass (37064)
Rates: n/a
Tel: (615) 794-7200

**NAMASTE ACRES
BARN B & B**
5436 Leipers Creek
(37064)
Rates: $60-$85
Tel: (615) 791-0333

GALLATIN

SHONEY'S INN
221 W Main St
(37066)
Rates: $36-$42
Tel: (615) 452-5433
(800) 222-2222

GATLINBURG

ALTO MOTEL
P. O. Box 1277
(37738)
Rates: $60-$70
Tel: (615) 436-5175

**BON AIR
MOUNTAIN INN**
950 Parkway (37738)
Rates: $43-$95
Tel: (423) 436-4857
(800) 848-4857

**COX'S GATEWAY
MOTEL**
1100 Parkway
(37738)
Rates: $48-$150
Tel: (615) 436-5656

**CREEKSTONE
MOTEL**
104 Oglewood Ln
(37738)
Rates: $32-$54
Tel: (800) 572-7770

GRANDVIEW INN
335 E Holly Ridge
Rd (37738)
Rates: $80-$100
Tel: (615) 436-3161
(800) 578-4330

**HIGHLAND
MOTOR INN**
131 Parkway (37738)
Rates: $30-$68
Tel: (423) 436-4110
(800) 635-8874

**HOLIDAY INN
RESORT**
520 Airport Rd
(37738)
Rates: $49-$99
Tel: (423) 436-9201
(800) 435-9201

MARGIE'S CHALETS
P.O. Box 288 (37738)
Rates: n/a
Tel: (615) 436-9475
(800) 264-9475

MICROTEL
211 Airport Rd
(37738)
Rates: $35-$80
Tel: (615) 436-0107

PARK VISTA HOTEL
P.O. Box 30 (37738)
Rates: $69-$129
Tel: (423) 436-9211
(800) 421-7175

**RAMADA INN
FOUR SEASONS**
756 Parkway (37738)
Rates: n/a
Tel: (423) 436-7881
(800) 272-6232

RODEWAY INN
1109 Parkway
(37738)
Rates: $44-$125
Tel: (423) 436-5811

GERMANTOWN

**BEST INNS
OF AMERICA**
7787 Wolf River Blvd
(38138)
Rates: $51-$74
Tel: (901) 757-7800

HOMETOWN SUITES
7855 Wolf River Blvd
(38138)
Rates: $99-$114
Tel: (901) 751-2500

GOODLETTS-VILLE

**BUDGETEL INN
NASHVILLE NORTH**
120 Cartwright Ct
(37072)
Rates: $50-$68
Tel: (615) 851-1891

COMFORT INN
925 Conference Dr
(37072)
Rates: $35-$90
Tel: (615) 859-5400
(800) 221-2222

**ECONO LODGE
RIVERGATE**
320 Long Hollow
Pike
(37072)
Rates: $30-50
Tel: (615) 859-4988
(800) 424-4777

MOTEL 6-
323 Cartwright St
(37072)
Rates: $25-$33
Tel: (615) 859-9674
(800) 466-8356

RED ROOF INN
110 Northgate Dr
(Goodlettsville
37072)
Rates: $40-$51
Tel: (615) 859-2537
(800) 843-7663

RODEWAY INN
650 Wade Cir
(Goodlettsville
37072)
Rates: $34-$44
Tel: (615) 859-1416
(800) 228-2000

GREENVILLE

ANDREW JOHNSON INN
2145 E Andrew
Johnson Hwy
(37745)
Rates: $33-$39
Tel: (423) 638-8124

DAYS INN
935 E Andrew
Johnson Hwy
(37743)
Rates: $35-$75
Tel: (615) 639-2156
(800) 329-7466

HOLIDAY INN
1780 E Andrew
Johnson Hwy
(37743)
Rates: $37-$52
Tel: (423) 639-4185
(800) 465-4329

HARRIMAN

BEST WESTERN SUNDANCER MOTOR LODGE
P. O. Box 1421
(37748)
Rates: $38-$55
Tel: (423) 882-6200
(800) 528-1234

SCOTTISH INNS
1867 S Roane St
(37748)
Rates: $28-$50
Tel: (423) 882-6600
(800) 251-1962

HERMITAGE

HERMITAGE INN
4144 Lebanon Rd
(37076)
Rates: $30-$64
Tel: (615) 883-7444

RAMADA LIMITED 9
I-40 E & Old
Hickory Blvd
(37076)
Rates: $38-$65
Tel: (615) 889-8940
(800) 272-6232

HOHENWALD

NATCHEZ TRACE BED & BREAKFAST
P.O. Box 193 (38461)
Rates: n/a
Tel: (615) 285-2777
(800) 377-2770

RIDGETOP BED & BREAKFAST
Hwy 412 (38461)
Rates: n/a
Tel: (615) 285-2777
(800) 3777-2770

HORNBEAK

BOARDMAN RESORT
813 Lake Dr (38232)
Rates: n/a
Tel: (901) 538-2112

HUNTSVILLE

HOLIDAY INN
11597 Scott Hwy
(37756)
Rates: $49-$59
Tel: (423) 663-4100
(800) 465-4329

HURRICANE MILLS

BEST WESTERN INN
15542 Hwy 13 S
(37078)
Rates: $39-$110
Tel: (615) 296-4251
(800) 528-1234

DAYS INN
15415 Hwy 13 S
(37078)
Rates: $38-$56
Tel: (615) 296-7647
(800) 329-7466

SUPER 8 MOTEL
Rt 1, Box 79 (37078)
Rates: $30-$55
Tel: (615) 296-2432
(800) 800-8000

JACKSON

BEST WESTERN OLD HICKORY INN
1849 Hwy 45 Bypass
(38305)
Rates: $44-$51
Tel: (901) 668-4222
(800) 528-1234

BUDGETEL INN
2370 N Highland
Ave (38305)
Rates: $29-$46
Tel: (901) 664-1800

COMFORT INN
1963 US 45 Bypass
(38305)
Rates: $34-$59
Tel: (901) 664-1800
(800) 221-2222

DAYS INN
1919 US 45 Bypass
(38305)
Rates: $28-$44
Tel: (901) 688-3444
(800) 329-7466

DAYS INN-WEST
2239 N Hollywood
Dr (38305)
Rates: $30-$48
Tel: (901) 664-4840
(800) 329-7466

ECONO LODGE
1936 US 45 (38305)
Rates: $29-$50
Tel: (901) 664-3030
(800) 424-4777

ECONO LODGE JACKSON WEST
196 Providence Rd
(Denmark 38391)
Rates: $28-$60
Tel: (901) 427-2778
(800) 424-4777

SUPER 8 MOTEL
2295 N Highland
Ave (38305)
Rates: $33-$53
Tel: (901) 668-1145
(800) 800-8000

TRAVELERS MOTEL
2247 N Highland
Ave (38305)
Rates: $24-$71
Tel: (901) 668-0542

JASPER

DAYS INN
Hwy 72 Dixie Lee
Junction (37347)
Rates: $29-$58
Tel: (423) 837-7933
(800) 329-7466

JELLICO

BEST WESTERN HOLIDAY PLAZA MOTEL
P. O.Box 177 (37766)
Rates: $30-$50
Tel: (423) 784-7241
(800) 528-1234

DAYS INN
P. O. Box 299 (37762)
Rates: $38-$54
Tel: (423) 784-7281
(800) 329-7466

JOELTON

DAYS INN
201 Gifford Pl
(37080)
Rates: $35-$65
Tel: (615) 876-3261
(800) 329-7466

JOHNSON CITY

COMFORT INN
1900 S Roan St
(37604)
Rates: $50-$60
Tel: (423) 928-9600
(800) 221-2222

DAYS INN
2312 Brown's Mill
Rd (37601)
Rates: $40-$55
Tel: (423) 282-3211
(800) 329-7466

GARDEN PLAZA HOTEL
211 Mockingbird Ln
(37604)
Rates: $72-$83
Tel: (423) 929-2000
(800) 342-7336

HAMPTON INN
508 N State of
Franklin Rd (37604)
Rates: $51-$67
Tel: (423) 929-8000

HOLIDAY INN
101 W Springbrook
Dr (37604)
Rates: $73-$79
Tel: (423) 282-4611
(800) 465-4329

QUALITY INN
2406 N Roan St
(37601)
Rates: $50-$65
Tel: (423) 282-2161
(800) 221-2222

RED ROOF INN
210 Broyles Dr
(37601)
Rates: $31-$40
Tel: (423) 282-3050
(800) 843-7663

SUPER 8 MOTEL
108 Wesley St
(37601)
Rates: $34-$54
Tel: (432) 282-8818
(800) 800-8000

KINGSPORT

COMFORT INN
100 Indian Center Ct
(37660)
Rates: $47-$125
Tel: (423) 378-4418
(800) 221-2222

ECONO LODGE
1704 E Stone Dr
(37660)
Rates: $36-$42
Tel: (423) 245-0286
(800) 424-4777

LA QUINTA INN
10150 Airport Pkwy
(37663)
Rates: $50-$57
Tel: (423) 323-0500

MICROTEL
1708 E Stone Dr
(37660)
Rates: $36-$40
Tel: (615) 378-9220

KINGSTON

DAYS INN
495 Gallaher Rd
(37763)
Rates: $34-$70
Tel: (423) 376-2069
(800) 329-7466

HOWARD JOHNSON
1200 N Kentucky St
(37763)
Rates: $35-60
Tel: (615) 376-3477
(800) 446-4656

KINGSTON SPRINGS

ECONO LODGE
123 Luyben Hills Rd
(37082)
Rates: $35-$75
Tel: (615) 952-2900
(800) 228-2000

SCOTTISH INNS
116 Luyden Hills Rd
(37082)
Rates: 33-$56
Tel: (615) 952-3115
(800) 251-1962

KNOXVILLE

**BEST WESTERN
WEST**
500 Lovell Rd
(37932)
Rates: $40-$70
Tel: (423) 675-7666
(800) 528-1234

BUDGETEL INN
11341 Cambell Lakes
Dr (37922)
Rates: $47-$71
Tel: (423) 671-1010
(800) 428-3438

COMFORT INN
2306 Airport Hwy
(Alcoa 37701)
Rates: $46-$85
Tel: (423) 970-3140
(800) 221-2222

COMFORT INN
323 Emory Rd
(37949)
Rates: $38-$88
Tel: (423) 938-5500
(800) 221-2222

DAYS INN
1706 W Cumberland
Ave (37916)
Rates: $43-$129
Tel: (423) 521-5000
(800) 329-7466

DAYS INN WEST
200 Lovell Rd
(37922)
Rates: $40-$75
Tel: (423) 966-5801
(800) 329-7466

ECONO LODGE
5505 Merchant Ctr.
Blvd. (37912)
Rates: $37-$80
Tel: (423) 687-5680
(800) 424-4777

**HAMPTON INN
NORTH**
119 Cedar Ln (37912)
Rates: $54-$63
Tel: (423) 689-1011
(800) 426-7866

**HOLIDAY INN-
NORTHWEST**
5335 Central Ave
Pike (37912)
Rates: $68
Tel: (423) 688-9110
(800) 465-4329

HOLIDAY INN-WEST
1315 Kirby Rd
(37909)
Rates: $78-$104
Tel: (423) 584-3911
(800) 465-4329

**HOWARD JOHNSON
MOTOR LODGE**
118 Merchants Dr
(37912)
Rates: $45-$75
Tel: (423) 688-3141
(800) 446-4656

LA QUINTA INN
258 N Peters Rd
(37923)
Rates: $49-$63
Tel: (423) 690-9777
(800) 531-5900

MICROTEL
309 N Peters Rd
(37922)
Rates: $36-$55
Tel: (615) 531-8041

MOTEL 6
402 Lovell Rd
(37922)
Rates: $29-$33
Tel: (423) 675-7200
(800) 440-6000

**QUALITY INN
NORTH**
6712 Central Ave
Pike (37912)
Rates: $35-$65
Tel: (423) 693-8111
(800) 221-2222

QUALITY INN WEST
7621 Kingston Pike
(37919)
Rates: $61-$86
Tel: (423) 693-8111
(800) 221-2222

RAMADA INN
323 Cedar Bluff Rd
(37923)
Rates: $43-$59
Tel: (423) 693-7330
(800) 272-6232

RAMADA INN EAST
1500 Cherry St
(37917)
Rates: $28-$79
Tel: (423) 547-7110
(800) 272-6232

**RAMADA LIMITED -
EAST 3**
722 Brakebill Rd
(37924)
Rates: $35-$84
Tel: (423) 546-7271
(800) 272-6232

**RAMADA LIMITED
WEST**
11748 Snyder Rd
(37922)
Rates: $36-$95
Tel: (423) 675-5566
(800) 272-6232

**RED ROOF INN-
NORTH**
5640 Merchants
Center Blvd (37912)
Rates: $30-$51
Tel: (423) 689-7100
(800) 843-7663

RED ROOF INN-W
209 Advantage Pl
(37922)
Rates: $32-$51
Tel: (423) 691-1664
(800) 843-7663

RODEWAY INN
6730 Central Ave
(Pike 37918)
Rates: $29-$59
Tel: (423) 687-3500
(800) 228-2000

SCOTTISH INNS
9340 Park West Blvd
(37923)
Rates: n/a
Tel: (423) 693-6061
(800) 251-1962

SCOTTISH INNS-NORTH
301 Callahan Dr
(37912)
Rates: $26-$44
Tel: (800) 251-1962

SUPER 8 MOTEL
6200 Paper Mill Rd
(37919)
Rates: $35-$59
Tel: (423) 584-8511
(800) 800-8000

LAKE CITY

THE LAMB'S INN
602 N Main (37769)
Rates: $24-$42
Tel: (423) 426-2171

LAKELAND

SUPER 8 MOTEL
9779 Huff & Puff Rd
(38002)
Rates: $35-$55
Tel: (901) 372-4575
(800) 800-8000

LEBANON

COMFORT INN
829 S Cumberland St
(37087)
Rates: $34-$64
Tel: (615) 444-1001
(800) 221-2222

DAYS INN
I-24 & Hwy 53
(37355)
Rates: $35-$70
Tel: (615) 728-6023
(800) 329-7466

DAYS INN
231 Murfreesboro
Rd (37087)
Rates: $30-$60
Tel: (615) 444-5635
(800) 329-7466

HAMPTON INN
704 S. Cumberland
St. (37087)
Rates: $45-$59
Tel: (615) 444-7400
(800) 426-7866

HOLIDAY INN EXPRESS
641 S Cumberland St
(37087)
Rates: $38-$50
Tel: (615) 444-7020
(800) 465-4329

SUPER 8 MOTEL
914 Murfreesboro
Rd (37090)
Rates: $35-$55
Tel: (615) 444-5637
(800) 800-8000

LENOIR

CROSSROADS INN
1110 Hwy 321N
(37771)
Rates: $25-$40
Tel: (423) 986-2011

LOUDON

HOLIDAY INN EXPRESS
12452 Hwy 72N
(37774)
Rates: $38-$44
Tel: (423) 458-5668
(800) 465-4329

KNIGHTS INN
15100 Hwy 72
(37774)
Rates: $30-$45
Tel: (423) 458-5855

MANCHESTER

AMBASSADOR INN
Rt 6, Box 6022
(37355)
Rates: $35-$100
Tel: (800) 237-9228

COMFORT INN
2314 Hillsboro Blvd
(37355)
Rates: $37-$47
Tel: (615) 728-0800
(800) 221-2222

DAYS INN
890 Interstate Dr
(37355)
Rates: $35-$50
Tel: (615) 728-6023
(800) 329-7466

ECONO LODGE
Rt 8, Box 8131
(37355)
Rates: $25-$32
Tel: (615) 728-9530
(800) 424-4777

HAMPTON INN
Rt 6, Box 6009
(37355)
Rates: $45-$55
Tel: (615) 728-3300
(800) 426-7866

HOLIDAY INN
I-24 & US 41 (37355)
Rates: $39-$46
Tel: (615) 728-9651
(800) 465-4329

SCOTTISH INNS
2457 Hillsboro Blvd
(37355)
Rates: $23-$53
Tel: (615) 728-0506
(800) 251-1962

SUPER 8 MOTEL
2430 Hillsboro Blvd
(37355)
Rates: $33-$48
Tel: (615) 728-9720
(800) 800-8000

MARTIN

UNIVERSITY LODGE
P. O. Box 50 (38237)
Rates: $36-$41
Tel: (901) 587-9577

McKENZIE

MCKENZIE MOTOR INN
121 Highland Dr
(38201)
Rates: n/a
Tel: (901) 352-3325

McMINNVILLE

SCOTTISH INNS
1105 Sparta St
(37110)
Rates: $20-$29
Tel: (615) 473-2181
(800) 251-1962

SHONEYS INN
508 Sunnyside
Heights (37110)
Rates: $38-$51
Tel: (615) 473-4446
(800) 222-2222

MEMPHIS

BEST WESTERN RIVERBLUFF
340 W Illinois Ave
(38106)
Rates: $50-$67
Tel: (901) 948-9005
(800) 528-1234

BEST WESTERN INN
8945 Hamilton Rd
(Southaven, MS
38671)
Rates: $39-$75
Tel: (800) 528-1234

BEST WESTERN TRAVELERS INN
5024 Hwy 78 (38118)
Rates: $62-$95
Tel: (901) 363-8430
(800) 528-1234

BROWNESTONE HOTEL
300 N 2nd (38105)
Rates: $75-$275
Tel: (901) 525-2511
(800) 468-3515

BUDGETEL INN
6020 Shelby Oaks Dr
(38134)
Rates: $43-$55
Tel: (901) 377-2233

BUDGETEL INN MEMPHIS AIRPORT
3005 Millbranch Rd
(38116)
Rates: $42-$60
Tel: (901) 396-5411

COMFORT INN AIRPORT/ GRACELAND
1581 E Brooks Rd (38116)
Rates: $42-$55
Tel: (901) 345-3344
(800) 221-2222

COMFORT INN EAST
5877 Poplar Ave (38119)
Rates: $52-$60
Tel: (901) 767-6300
(800) 221-2222

COMFORT INN HOTEL
2411 Winchester Rd (38116)
Rates: $72-$82
Tel: (901) 332-2370
(800) 221-2222

COUNTRY SUITES BY CARLSON
4300 American Way (38118)
Rates: $61-$76
Tel: (901) 366-9333
(800) 456-4000

DAYS INN
3839 Elvis Presley Blvd (38116)
Rates: $40-$75
Tel: (901) 346-5500
(800) 329-7466

DAYS INN AIRPORT
1533 E Brooks Rd (38116)
Rates: $42-$60
Tel: (901) 345-2470
(800) 329-7466

DAYS INN
2949 Airways Blvd (38116)
Rates: $36-$59
Tel: (901) 345-8554
(800) 329-7466

DRURY INN
1556 Sycamore View (38134)
Rates: n/a
Tel: (800) 325-8300

ECONO LODGE
2315 S Service Rd (W Memphis, AR 72303)
Rates: $32-$38
Tel: (800) 424-4777

HAMPTON INN-POPLAR
5320 Poplar Ave (38119)
Rates: n/a
Tel: (901) 683-8500
(800) 426-7866

HAMPTON INN WALNUT GROVE
33 Humphreys Center Dr (38120)
Rates: $56-$70
Tel: (901) 747-3700
(800) 426-7866

HOLIDAY INN CROWNE PLAZA
250 N Main (38103)
Rates: $105-$125
Tel: (901) 527-7300
(800) 465-4329

HOLIDAY INN EAST
5795 Poplar Ave (38119)
Rates: $86-$99
Tel: (901) 682-7881
(800) 465-4329

HOLIDAY INN MEDICAL CENTER
1837 Union Ave (38104)
Rates: $69-$86
Tel: (901) 278-4100
(800) 465-4329

HOMEWOOD SUITES
5811 Poplar Ave (38119)
Rates: $89-$149
Tel: (901) 763-0500

HOWARD JOHNSON LODGE EAST
1541 Sycamore View (38134)
Rates: $45-$75
Tel: (901) 388-1300
(800) 654-2000

LA QUINTA INN-AIRPORT
2745 Airways Blvd (38132)
Rates: $50-$69
Tel: (901) 396-1000
(800) 531-5900

LA QUINTA INN-EAST
6068 Macon Cove (38134)
Rates: $47-$60
Tel: (901) 382-2323
(800) 531-5900

LA QUINTA INN-MEDICAL CENTER
42 S Camilla St (38104)
Rates: $40-$53
Tel: (901) 526-1050
(800) 531-5900

MEMPHIS AIRPORT HOTEL
2240 Democrat Rd (38132)
Rates: $50-$275
Tel: (901) 332-1130

MEMPHIS INN EAST
6050 Macon Cove (38134)
Rates: $29-$53
Tel: (901) 375-9898
(800) 770-4667

MOTEL 6-EAST
1321 Sycamore View Rd (38134)
Rates: $30-$50
Tel: (901) 382-8572
(800) 466-8359

MOTEL 6-GRACELAND EAST
1117 E Brooks Rd (38116)
Rates: $30-$39
Tel: (901) 346-0992
(800) 466-8359

RED ROOF INN-EAST
6055 Shelby Oaks Dr (38134)
Rates: $38-$62
Tel: (901) 388-6111
(800) 843-7663

RED ROOF INN MEDICAL CENTER
210 S Pauline (38104)
Rates: $37-$50
Tel: (901) 528-0650
(800) 843-7663

RED ROOF INN-SOUTH
3875 American Way (38118)
Rates: $38-$58
Tel: (901) 363-2335
(800) 843-7663

RESIDENCE INN BY MARRIOTT
6141 Poplar Pike (38119)
Rates: $115-$159
Tel: (901) 685-9595
(800) 331-3131

SUPER 8 MOTEL
6015 Macon Cove Rd (38134)
Rates: $40-$62
Tel: (501) 373-4888
(800) 800-8000

SUPER 8-WEST MEMPHIS
901 Club Rd (W Memphis, AR 72301)
Rates: $39-$52
Tel: (901) 735-8818
(800) 800-8000

SUPER 8 MOTEL
3280 Elvis Presley Blvd (38116)
Rates: $36-$56
Tel: (901) 345-1425
(800) 800-8000

SUPER 8 MOTEL
4060 Lamar Ave (38118)
Rates: $36-$83
Tel: (800) 800-8000

MILAN

RAMADA LIMITED
US Hwy 70/79 & 45 (38358)
Rates: n/a
Tel: (901) 686-3345
(800) 272-6232

MILLINGTON

BEST WESTERN INN
7726 Hwy 51 N (38053)
Rates: $45-$50
Tel: (901) 873-2222
(800) 528-1234

ECONO LODGE
8193 Hwy 51 N (38053)
Rates: $34-$41
Tel: (901) 873-4400
(800) 424-4777

MONTEAGLE

**ADAMS
EDGEWORTH INN**
Monteagle Assembly
(37356)
Rates: $70-$145
Tel: (615) 924-4000

DAYS INN
102 College St
(37356)
Rates: n/a
Tel: (615) 924-2900
(800) 329-7466

DAYS INN
742 Dixie Lee Ave
(37356)
Rates: $24-$70
Tel: (615) 924-2900
(800) 329-7466

**JIM OLIVER'S
SMOKE HOUSE
MOTOR LODGE**
US Hwy 64-41 A
(37356)
Rates: $24-$159
Tel: (615) 924-2268
(800) 678-0997

MORRISTOWN

DAYS INN
2512 E Andrew
Johnson Hwy
(37814)
Rates: $32-$52
Tel: (423) 587-2200
(800) 329-7466

**RAMADA INN &
CONFERENCE
CENTER**
I-81 & US 25 E
(37815)
Rates: $54-$90
Tel: (423) 587-2400

SUPER 8 MOTEL
2430 E Andrew
Johnson Hwy
(37814)
Rates: $34-$48
Tel: (423) 586-8880
(800) 800-8000

MT. JULIET

**NATUREVIEW INN
BED & BREAKFAST**
3354 Old Lebanon
Dirt Rd (37122)
Rates: n/a
Tel: (615) 758-4439
(800) 758-7972

MOUNTAIN CITY

DAYS INN
Hwy 421, Rt 4
(37683)
Rates: $39-$70
Tel: (615) 727-7311
(800) 329-7466

MURFREESBORO

**BEST WESTERN
CHAFFIN INN**
168 Chaffin Pl
(37129)
Rates: $37-$59
Tel: (615) 895-3818
(800) 528-1234

DAYS INN
2036 S Church St
(37130)
Rates: $25-$60
Tel: (615) 893-1090
(800) 329-7466

**GARDEN PLAZA
HOTEL**
1850 Old Fort Pkwy
(37129)
Rates: $65-$75
Tel: (615) 895-5555
(800) 342-7336

HAMPTON INN
2230 Old Fort Pkwy
(37129)
Rates: $59-$66
Tel: (615) 896-1172
(800) 426-7866

**HOLIDAY INN
HOLIDOME**
2227 Old Fort Pkwy
(37130)
Rates: $53-$66
Tel: (615) 896-2420
(800) 465-4329

**HOWARD JOHNSON
LODGE**
2424 S Church St
(37130)
Rates: $36-$55
Tel: (615) 896-5522
(800) 446-4656

MOTEL 6
114 Chaffin Pl
(37129)
Rates: $28-$34
Tel: (615) 890-8524

**MURFREESBORO
MOTEL**
1150 NW Broad St
(37129)
Rates: $25-$38
Tel: (615) 893-2100

QUALITY INN
118 Westgate (37130)
Rates: $29-$85
Tel: (615) 848-9030
(800) 221-2222

RAMADA LIMITED
1855 S Church St
(37130)
Rates: $40-$85
Tel: (615) 896-5080
(800) 272-6232

SCOTTISH INNS
2029 S Church St
(37130)
Rates: $23-$55
Tel: (615) 896-3210
(800) 251-1962

TRAVELODGE
2025 S Church St
(37130)
Rates: $38-$125
Tel: (615) 896-2320
(800) 578-7878

NASHVILLE
(and Vicintiy)

**BEST SUITES
OF AMERICA**
2521 Elm Hill Pike
(37214)
Rates: $69-$95
Tel: (615) 391-3919

**BEST WESTERN
CALUMET INN**
701 Stewart's Ferry
Pike (37214)
Rates: $46-$163
Tel: (615) 889-9199
(800) 528-1234

**BUDGETEL INN
AIRPORT**
531 Donelson Pike
(37214)
Rates: $40-$60
Tel: (615) 885-3100
(800) 428-3438

**BUDGETEL INN
NASHVILLE NORTH**
120 Cartwright Ct
(Goodlettsville 37072)
Rates: $50-$68
Tel: (615) 851-1891

**BUDGETEL INN
NASHVILLE WEST**
5612 Lenox Ave
(37209)
Rates: $48-$84
Tel: (615) 353-0700

COMFORT INN
2306 Brick Church
Pike (37207)
Rates: $35-$55
Tel: (615) 226-9560
(800) 221-2222

COMFORT INN
925 Conference Dr
(Goodlettsville
37072)
Rates: $35-$90
Tel: (615) 859-5400
(800) 221-2222

**COMFORT INN
SOUTHEAST**
97 Wallace Rd
(37211)
Rates: $37-$57
Tel: (615) 833-6860
(800) 221-2222

DAYS INN
1400 Brick Church
Pike (37207)
Rates: $34-$65
Tel: (615) 228-5977
(800) 329-7466

DAYS INN
1300 Plaza Dr
(37167)
Rates: $48-$150
Tel: (615) 355-6161
(800) 329-7466

**DRURY INN-
AIRPORT**
837 Briley Pkwy
(37217)
Rates: $51-$72
Tel: (615) 361-6999
(800) 325-8300

DRURY INN-SOUTH
341 Harding Pl
(37211)
Rates: $54-$72
Tel: (615) 834-7170
(800) 325-8300

ECONO LODGE
2403 Brick Church
Pike (37207)
Rates: $27-$68
Tel: (800) 424-4777

ECONO LODGE-OPRYLAND
2460 Music Valley
Dr (37214)
Rates: $46-$80
Tel: (615) 889-0090
(800) 424-4777

ECONO LODGE RIVERGATE
320 Long Hollow
Pike
(Goodlettsville
37072)
Rates: $30-50
Tel: (615) 859-4988
(800) 424-4777

EMBASSY SUITES
10 Century Blvd
(37214)
Rates: $99-$139
Tel: (615) 871-0033
(800) 362-2779

HAMPTON INN
2350 Elm Hill Pike
(37214)
Rates: $65-$77
Tel: (615) 871-0222
(800) 426-7866

HILLSBORO HOUSE B & B
1933 20th Ave S
(37212)
Rates: n/a
Tel: (615) 292-5501
(800) 228-7851

HILTON SUITES-BRENTWOOD
9000 Overlook Blvd
(Brentwood 37027)
Rates: $99-$109
Tel: (800) 445-8667

HOJO INN
323 Harding Pl
(37211)
Rates: $39-$55
Tel: (615) 834-0570
(800) 446-4656

HOLIDAY INN EXPRESS
2516 Music Valley
Dr (37214)
Rates: $59-$74
Tel: (615) 889-0086
(800) 465-4329

HOLIDAY INN EXPRESS-AIRPORT
1111 Airport Center
Dr (37214)
Rates: $65
Tel: (615) 883-1366
(800) 465-4329

HOLIDAY INN EXPRESS-SE AIRPORT
981 Murfreesboro
Rd (37217)
Rates: $51-$57
Tel: (615) 327-9150
(800) 465-4329

HOLIDAY INN VANDERBILT
2613 W End Ave
(37203)
Rates: $75-$125
Tel: (615) 327-4707
(800) 465-4329

HOWARD JOHNSON
6834 Charlotte Pike
(37209)
Rates: $55-75
Tel: (615) 352-7080
(800) 446-4656

HOWARD JOHNSON
2600 Music Valley
Dr (37214)
Rates: $49-69
Tel: (615) 889-8235
(800) 446-4656

HOWARD JOHNSON
970 Murfreesboro
Rd (37217)
Rates: $39-69
Tel: (615) 367-6119
(800) 446-4656

LA QUINTA INN-AIRPORT
2345 Atrium Way
(37214)
Rates: $53-$72
Tel: (615) 885-3000
(800) 221-4731

LA QUINTA INN-METRO CENTER
2001 Metro Center
Blvd (37228)
Rates: $52-$75
Tel: (615) 259-2130
(800) 221-4731

LA QUINTA MOTOR INN-SOUTH
4311 Sidco Dr
(37204)
Rates: $59-$84
Tel: (615) 834-6900
(800) 221-4731

MOTEL 6-AIRPORT
420 Metroplex Dr
(37211)
Rates: $36-$50
Tel: (615) 833-8887
(800) 466-8356

MOTEL 6-GOODLETTSVILLE
323 Cartwright St
(Goodlettsville
37072)
Rates: $25-$33
Tel: (615) 859-9674
(800) 466-8356

MOTEL 6-NORTH
311 W Trinity Ln
(37207)
Rates: $30-$36
Tel: (615) 227-9696
(800) 466-8356

MOTEL 6-SOUTH
95 Wallace Rd
(37211)
Rates: $38-$50
Tel: (615) 333-9933
(800) 466-8356

NASHVILLE MEDICAL CENTER INN
1909 Hayes St
(37203)
Rates: $64-$84
Tel: (615) 329-1000

PEAR TREE INN SOUTH
343 Harding Pl
(37211)
Rates: $49-$65
Tel: (615) 834-4242
(800) 282-8733

QUARTERS MOTOR INN
1100 Bell Rd (37013)
Rates: $49-$53
Tel: (615) 731-5990

RAMADA INN SUITES
2425 Atrium Way
(37214)
Rates: $58-$106
Tel: (615) 883-5201
(800) 272-6232

RED ROOF INN
110 Northgate Dr
(Goodlettsville
37072)
Rates: $40-$51
Tel: (615) 859-2537
(800) 843-7663

RED ROOF INN #206
510 Claridge Dr
(37214)
Rates: $46-$52
Tel: (615) 872-0735
(800) 843-7663

RED ROOF INN SOUTH
4271 Sidco Dr
(37204)
Rates: $36-$66
Tel: (615) 832-0093
(800) 843-7663

RESIDENCE INN
2300 Elm Hill Pike
(37214)
Rates: $99-$159
Tel: (615) 889-8600

RODEWAY INN
650 Wade Cir
(Goodlettsville
37072)
Rates: $34-$44
Tel: (615) 859-1416
(800) 228-2000

RODEWAY INN
625 N Gallatin
(Madison 37115)
Rates: $38-$50
Tel: (615) 865-2323
(800) 228-2000

SCOTTISH INNS - HALLMARK INN
1501 Dickerson Rd
(37207)
Rates: n/a
Tel: (615) 226-6940
(800) 251-1962

SHERATON MUSIC CITY HOTEL
777 McGavock Pike
(37214)
Rates: $125-$550
Tel: (615) 885-2200
(800) 325-3535

SHONEY'S INN
1521 Demonbreun St (37203)
Rates: n/a
Tel: (615) 255-9977
(800) 222-2222

SUPER 8 MOTEL
412 Robertson Ave (37209)
Rates: $41-$64
Tel: (615) 356-0888
(800) 800-8000

SUPER 8 MOTEL
350 Harding Pl (37211)
Rates: $49-$54
Tel: (615) 834-0620
(800) 800-8000

TRAVEL PARK HOLIDAY
2572 Music Valley Dr (37214)
Rates: $24-$28
Tel: (615) 889-4225

TWELVE OAKS MOTEL
656 W Iris Dr (37204)
Rates: n/a
Tel: (615) 385-1323

UNION STATION HOTEL
1001 Broadway (37203)
Rates: $70-$150
Tel: (615) 726-1001
(800) 331-2123

WYNDHAM GARDEN HOTEL
1112 Airport Center Dr (37214)
Rates: $74-$109
Tel: (615) 889-9090

NEWPORT

BEST WESTERN INN
P. O. Box 382 (37821)
Rates: $36-$99
Tel: (423) 623-8713
(800) 528-1234

HOLIDAY INN
I-40 & Hwy 32 (37821)
Rates: $39-$64
Tel: (423) 623-8622
(800) 465-4329

RELAX INN
1848 W Knoxville Hwy (37821)
Rates: $24-$85
Tel: (615) 625-1521

NORMANDY

PARIS PATCH FARM & INN
625 Cortner Rd (37360)
Rates: n/a
Tel: (615) 857-3017
(800) 876-3017

OAK RIDGE

COMFORT INN
433 S Rutgers Ave (37830)
Rates: $55-$82
Tel: (423) 481-8200
(800) 221-2222

DAYS INN
206 S Illinois (37830)
Rates: $39-$57
Tel: (423) 483-5615
(800) 329-7466

GARDEN PLAZA HOTEL
215 S Illinois (37830)
Rates: $75-$87
Tel: (423) 481-2468
(800) 342-7336

SUPER 8 MOTEL
1590 Oak Ridge Tpk (37830)
Rates: $44-$49
Tel: (423) 483-1200
(800) 800-8000

ONEIDA

THE GALLOWAY INN
Hwy 27 S, Box 4525 (37841)
Rates: $25-$31
Tel: (423) 569-8835

ONLY

BUDGET HOST INN AT BUCKSNORT
Rt 1 (37140)
Rates: $30-$49
Tel: (800) 283-4678

OOLTEWAH

SUPER 8 MOTEL
5111 Hunter Rd (37363)
Rates: $40-$55
Tel: (423) 238-5951
(800) 251-1962

PARIS

AVALON MOTEL
1315 Wood St (38242)
Rates: n/a
Tel: (901) 642-4121

BEST WESTERN TRAVELERS INN
1297 E Wood St (38242)
Rates: $38-$44
Tel: (901) 642-8881
(800) 528-1234

PIGEON FORGE

ECONO LODGE
2440 Parkway (37863)
Rates: $70-$102
Tel: (423) 438-1231
(800) 424-4777

THE GRAND HOTEL & CONV. CENTER
3171 Parkway (37863)
Rates: $29-$99
Tel: (423) 453-1000
(800) 251-4444

HEARTLANDER COUNTRY RESORT
2385 Parkway (37863)
Rates: $30-$110
Tel: (423) 453-4106
(800) 453-4106

MICROTEL
202 Emert St (37863)
Rates: $36-$62
Tel: (423) 429-0150
(800) 431-7666

PORTLAND

BUDGET HOST INN
5339 Long Rd (37148)
Rates: $29-$42
Tel: (615) 325-2005
(800) 283-4678

POWELL

COMFORT INN
323 E Emory Rd (37849)
Rates: $40-$76
Tel: (423) 938-5500
(800) 221-2222

PULASKI

SANDS MOTOR HOTEL
P.O. Box 408 (38478)
Rates: $34-$45
Tel: (615) 363-4501

SUPER 8 MOTEL
2400 Hwy 64 (38478)
Rates: $45-$50
Tel: (615) 363-4501
(800) 800-8000

RICEVILLE

RELAX INN
Rt 2, Box 278-A (37370)
Rates: $20-$25
Tel: (615) 745-5893

SAMBURG

BILL NATION'S CAMP
244 W Lakeview Dr (38232)
Rates: n/a
Tel: (901) 538-2177

BOARDMAN'S RESORT
813 Lake Dr (38232)
Rates: n/a
Tel: (901) 538-2112

DUCK INN
218 Church (38254)
Rates: n/a
Tel: (901) 538-2364

HAMILTON'S RESORT
4992 Hamilton Rd (38232)
Rates: n/a
Tel: (901) 538-2325

SAMBURG MOTEL
100 Lakeview St (38254)
Rates: n/a
Tel: (901) 538-2467
(800) 742-0385

SAVANNAH

SAVANNAH MOTEL
105 Adams St
(38372)
Rates: n/a
Tel: (901) 925-3392

**SHAWS KOMFORT
MOTEL**
2302 Wayne Rd
(38372)
Rates: n/a
Tel: (901) 925-3977

SEVIERVILLE

**BEST WESTERN
DUMPLIN VALLEY
INN**
3426 Winfield Dunn
Pkwy (37764)
Rates: $30-$90
Tel: (423) 933-3467
(800) 528-1234

**SPRING GAP
LOG CABINS**
3054 Kulpan Way
(37862)
Rates: $85-$95
Tel: (423) 453-0829

SHELBYVILLE

**BEST WESTERN
CELEBRATION INN**
724 Madison St
(37160)
Rates: $55-$165
Tel: (615) 684-2378
(800) 528-1234

SHELBYVILLE INN
317 N Cannon Blvd
(37160)
Rates: $49-$68
Tel: (615) 684-6050

SMYRNA

DAYS INN
1300 Plaza Dr
(37167)
Rates: $48-$85
Tel: (615) 355-6161
(800) 329-7466

SOMERVILLE

PLEASANT RETREAT
420 Hotel St (38076)
Rates: n/a
Tel: (901) 465-4599
(901) 465-3916

SPRING HILL

HOLIDAY INN
Kedron Rd & US
Hwy 31 (37174)
Rates: $60-$100
Tel: (615) 486-1234
(800) 465-4329

SPRINGFIELD

**BEST WESTERN
SPRINGFIELD**
2001 Memorial Blvd
(37172)
Rates: $53-$135
Tel: (615) 384-1234
(800) 528-1234

HILL TOP LODGE
Rt 3, Antioch Rd
(38256)
Rates: n/a
Tel: (901) 644-2049

HOWELL'S RESORT
Rt 1 Box 409A
(38256)
Rates: n/a
Tel: (901) 642-7442

**MANSARD ISLAND
RESORT**
Rt 1 Box 261 (38256)
Rates: n/a
Tel: (901) 642-5590

SWEETWATER

BUDGET HOST INN
Rt 5, Box 52 (37874)
Rates: $27-$63
Tel: (423) 337-9357
(800) 283-4678

COMFORT INN
803 S Main St
(37874)
Rates: $36-$69
Tel: (423) 337-6646
(800) 221-2222

**COMFORT INN-
WEST**
Rt 5, Box 48 (37874)
Rates: $34-$65
Tel: (423) 337-3353
(800) 221-2222

DAYS INN
Rt 5, Box 46 (37874)
Rates: $29-$45
Tel: (423) 337-4200
(800) 329-7466

QUALITY INN
P. O. Box 6655
(37874)
Rates: $42-$68
Tel: (423) 337-3541
(800) 221-2222

**SWEETWATER
HOTEL
& CONVENTION
CENTER**
180 Hwy 68 (37874)
Rates: $36-$39
Tel: (615) 337-03511

TIPTONVILLE

GRAY'S CAMP
Rt 1 Box 280 (38079)
Rates: n/a
Tel: (901) 253-7813

RAY'S CAMP
Rt 1 Box 5B-1 (38079)
Rates: n/a
Tel: (901) 253-7765

TOWNSEND

**BEST WESTERN
VALLEY VIEW
LODGE**
Hwy 321 (37882)
Rates: $35-$99
Tel: (423) 448-2237
(800) 528-1234

DAYS INN
P.O. Box 148 (37882)
Rates: $33-$80
Tel: (423) 448-2211
(800) 329-7466

**WEAR'S MOTEL
& COTTAGES**
8270 Hwy 73 (37882)
Rates: $45-$80
(423) 448-2296

UNION CITY

**CULTRA
MOTOR INN**
1221 Reelfoot Ave
(38261)
Rates: n/a
Tel: (901) 885-6610

HAMPTON INN
2201 Reelfoot Ave
(38261)
Rates: n/a
Tel: (901) 885-8850

SUPER 8 MOTEL
1400 Vaden Ave
(38261)
Rates: $37-$48
Tel: (901) 885-4444
(800) 800-8000

WHITE PINE

DAYS INN
3670 Roy Messer
Hwy (37890)
Rates: $36-$79
Tel: (423) 674-2573
(800) 329-7466

WILDERSVILLE

**BEST WESTERN
CROSSROADS INN**
21045 Hwy 22 N
(38388)
Rates: $32-$56
Tel: (901) 968-2532
(800) 528-1234

WINCHESTER

**FRASSRAND
TERRACE MOTEL**
700 S College St
(37398)
Rates: $24-$50
Tel: (615) 967-3856

TEXAS

ABILENE

BEST WESTERN COLONIAL INN
3210 Pine St (79601)
Rates: $36-$50
Tel: (915) 677-2683
(800) 528-1234

BEST WESTERN MALL SOUTH
3950 Ridgemont Dr (79606)
Rates: $44-$50
Tel: (915) 695-1262
(800) 528-1234

COMFORT INN
1758 I-20 E (79601)
Rates: $53-$79
Tel: (915) 676-0203
(800) 228-5150

DAYS INN
17021 I-20 E (79601)
Rates: $42-$60
Tel: (915) 672-6433
(800) 329-7466

ECONO LODGE
1633 W Stamford (79601)
Rates: $26-$40
Tel: (915) 673-5424
(800) 424-4777

EMBASSY SUITES HOTEL
4250 Ridgemont Dr (79606)
Rates: $83-$93
Tel: (915) 698-1234
(800) 362-2779

FAIRFIELD INN BY MARRIOTT
3902 Turner Plaza (79606)
Rates: $53-$59
Tel: (915) 695-2448
(800) 228-2800

HAMPTON INN
3917 Ridgemont Dr (79606)
Rates: $53-$69
Tel: (915) 695-0044
(800) 426-7866

HOLIDAY INN EXPRESS
1625 SR 351 (79601)
Rates: $47-$51
Tel: (915) 673-5271
(800) 465-4329

KIVA MOTEL
5403 S 1st St (79605)
Rates: $49-$125
Tel: (915) 695-2150
(800) 592-4466

LA QUINTA INN
3501 W Lake Rd (79601)
Rates: $47-$59
Tel: (915) 676-1676
(800) 531-5900

MOTEL 6
4951 W Stamford (79603)
Rates: $24-$28
Tel: (915) 672-8462
(800) 440-6000

QUALITY INN
505 Pine St (79601)
Rates: $41-$46
Tel: (915) 676-0222
(800) 221-2222 (800) 588-0222 (TX)

RAMADA INN
3450 S Clack (79606)
Rates: $45-$50
Tel: (915) 695-7700
(800) 272-6232

RED CARPET INN
2202 I-20 (79603)
Rates: $35-$42
Tel: (915) 677-2463
(800) 251-1962

ROYAL INN
5695 S 1st St (79605)
Rates: $29-$40
Tel: (915) 692-3022
(800) 588-4386

SUPER 8 MOTEL
1525 E I-20 (79601)
Rates: $34-$38
Tel: (915) 673-5251
(800) 800-8000

ADDISON

COMFORT INN
14975 Landmark Blvd (75248)
Rates: $65
Tel: (214) 701-0881
(800) 228-5150

HAMPTON INN
4555 Beltway Rd (75244)
Rates: $55-$72
Tel: (214) 991-2800
(800) 426-7866

HARVEY HOTEL
14315 Midway Rd (75244)
Rates: $55-$106
Tel: (214) 980-8877
(800) 922-9222

HOMEWOOD SUITES
4451 Beltline Rd (75244)
Rates: $79-$117
Tel: (214) 788-1342
(800) 225-5466

MARRIOTT HOTEL QUORUM
14901 Dallas Pkwy (75240)
Rates: $79-$139
Tel: (214) 661-2800
(800) 228-9290

MOTEL 6
4325 Beltline Rd (75244)
Rates: $31-$37
Tel: (214) 386-4577
(800) 440-6000

ALICE

DAYS INN
555 N Johnson St (78332)
Rates: $35-$45
Tel: (512) 664-8016
(800) 329-7466

KINGS INN MOTEL
815 Hwy 281 S (78332)
Rates: $30-$35
Tel: (512) 664-4351

ALPINE

BEST WESTERN ALPINE CLASSIC INN
2401 E Hwy 90 (79830)
Rates: $65-$95
Tel: (915) 837-1530
(800) 528-1234

THE CORNER HOUSE BED & BREAKFAST
801 E Avenue (79830)
Rates: $27-$65
Tel: (915) 837-7161
(800) 585-7795

DAYS INN
2000 E Hwy 90 (79831)
Rates: $28-$58
Tel: (915) 837-3417
(800) 329-7466

HIGHLAND INN
1404 E Hwy 90 (79830)
Rates: $40-$45
Tel: (915) 837-5811

LONGHORN RANCH MOTEL
HC 65, P. O. Box 267 (79830)
Rates: $45-$55
Tel: (915) 371-2541

RAMADA LIMITED
2800 W Hwy 90 (79830)
Rates: $55+
Tel: (915) 837-1100
(800) 272-6232

SUNDAY HOUSE INN MOTEL
P. O. Box 578 (79830)
Rates: $34-$42
Tel: (915) 837-3363
(800) 510-3363

TERLINGUA RANCH LODGE
HC 65, Box 220, (79830)
Rates: $38
Tel: (915) 371-2416

ALVIN

HOMEPLACE INN
1588 S Hwy 35
Bypass (77511)
Rates: $48-$59
Tel: (713) 331-0335

AMARILLO

**BEST WESTERN
SANTA FE INN**
4600 I-40 E (79120)
Rates: $47-$61
Tel: (806) 372-1885
(800) 528-1234

**THE BIG TEXAN
MOTEL**
7701 I-40 E (79120)
Rates: $40-$50
Tel: (806) 372-5000
(800) 657-7177

**BUDGET HOST
LA PALOMA INN**
2915 I-40 E (79104)
Rates: $40-$80
Tel: (806) 372-8101
(800) 283-4678

COMFORT INN-WEST
2100 S Coulter Dr
(79106)
Rates: $38-$54
Tel: (806) 358-6141
(800) 228-5150

**CROWN PLAZA
HOTEL**
3100 I-40 W (79102)
Rates: $69-$99
Tel: (806) 358-6161
(800) 817-0521

ECONO LODGE
1803 Lakeside Dr
(79120)
Rates: $33-$42
Tel: (806) 335-1561
(800) 424-4777
(800) 847-6556 (TX)

HAMPTON INN
1700 I-40E (79103)
Rates: $43-$60
Tel: (806) 372-1425
(800) 426-7866

HOLIDAY INN I-40
1911 I-40 at Ross-
Osage (79102)
Rates: $75-$85
Tel: (806) 372-8741
(800) 465-4329

**LA QUINTA INN-
AIRPORT**
1708 I-40 E (79103)
Rates: $44-$58
Tel: (806) 373-7486
(800) 531-5900

**LA QUINTA INN
MEDICAL CENTER**
2108 S Coulter St
(79106)
Rates: $45-$60
Tel: (806) 352-6311
(800) 531-5900

MOTEL 6-AIRPORT
4301 I-40 E (79104)
Rates: $25-$34
Tel: (806) 373-3045
(800) 440-6000

MOTEL 6-CENTRAL
2032 Paramount
Blvd (79109)
Rates: $24-$34
Tel: (806) 355-6554
(800) 440-6000

MOTEL 6-EAST
3930 I-40 E (79103)
Rates: $24-$33
Tel: (806) 374-6444
(800) 440-6000

MOTEL 6-WEST
6040 I-40 W (79106)
Rates: $27-$35
Tel: (806) 359-7651
(800) 440-6000

**RADISSON INN
AIRPORT**
7090 I-40 E (79104)
Rates: $65-$105
Tel: (806) 373-3303
(800) 333-3333

RAMADA INN EAST
2501 I-40 E (79104)
Rates: $69-$75
Tel: (806) 379-6555
(800) 272-6232

RAMADA INN WEST
6801 I-40 W (79106)
Rates: $50-$85
Tel: (806) 358-7881
(800) 272-6232

**RODEWAY INN
MEDICAL CENTER**
6005 Amarillo Blvd
W (79106)
Rates: $29-$36
Tel: (806) 355-3321
(800) 424-4777

TRAVELODGE-EAST
3205 I-40 E, Tee
Anchor Blvd (79104)
Rates: $32-$38
Tel: (806) 372-8171
(800) 578-7878

ANGLETON

HOMEPLACE INN
1235 N Velasco
(77515)
Rates: $46-$53
Tel: (409) 849-2465

ANTHONY

**SUPER 8 MOTEL
WEST**
100 Park North Dr
(79821)
Rates: $38-$46
Tel: (915) 886-2888
(800) 800-8000

ARANSAS PASS

HOMEPORT INN
1515 W Wheeler Ave
(78336)
Rates: $30-$36
Tel: (512) 758-3213

ARLINGTON

**BEST WESTERN-
GREAT SOUTHWEST
INN**
3501 E Division St
(76011)
Rates: $42-$74
Tel: (817) 640-7722
(800) 528-1234

**BUDGETEL INN-
SIX FLAGS**
2401 Diplomacy Dr
(76011)
Rates: $52-$59
Tel: (800) 428-3438

COMFORT INN
1601 E Division St
(76011)
Rates: $42-$74
Tel: (817) 261-2300
(800) 221-2222

**DAYS INN AIRPORT
SOUTH-SIX FLAGS**
1195 N Watson Rd
(76011)
Rates: $35-$68
Tel: (817) 649-8881
(800) 329-7466

**DAYS INN BALLPARK
AT ARLINGTON-
SIX FLAGS**
910 N Collins St
(76011)
Rates: $35-$75
Tel: (817) 261-8444
(800) 329-7466

**DAYS INN
RANGER STADIUM**
2001 E Copeland Rd
(76011)
Rates: $38-$85
Tel: (817) 461-1122
(800) 329-7466

**HAWTHORN SUITES
HOTEL**
2401 Brookhollow
Plaza Dr (76011)
Rates: $70-$160
Tel: (817) 640-1188
(800) 225-5466
(800) 527-1133 (TX)

HOWARD JOHNSON
903 N Collins St
(76011)
Rates: $65-$75
Tel: (817) 261-3621
(800) 654-2000

INN TOWNE LODGE
1181 N Watson Rd
(76006)
Rates: $32-$46
Tel: (817) 649-0993

LESTER MOTOR INN
2725 W Division St
(76012)
Rates: $20-$35
Tel: (817) 275-5496

MOTEL 6
2626 E Randol Mill
Rd (76011)
Rates: $28-$38
Tel: (817) 649-0147
(800) 440-6000

OASIS MOTEL
818 W Division St
(76011)
Rates: $23-$40
Tel: (817) 274-1616

PARK INN LIMITED
703 Benge Dr (76013)
Rates: $35-$40
Tel: (817) 860-2323
(800) 437-7275

RAMADA INN
700 E Lamar Blvd
(76011)
Rates: $40-$45
Tel: (817) 265-7711
(800) 228-2828

**RESIDENCE INN
BY MARRIOTT**
1050 Brookhollow
Plaza Dr (76006)
Rates: $66+
Tel: (817) 640-5151
(800) 331-3131

VALUE INN
820 N Watson Rd
(76011)
Rates: $20-$45
Tel: (817) 640-5151

ATHENS

**SPANISH TRACE INN
MOTEL**
716 E Tyler St
(75751)
Rates: $41-$76
Tel: (903) 675-5173
(800) 488-5173

ATLANTA

THE BUTLER'S INN
1100 W Main St
(75551)
Rates: $29-$37
Tel: (903) 796-8235
(800) 338-0297

AUBREY

**THE GUEST HOUSE
BED & BREAKFAST**
Rt 1, Box 203 (76227)
Rates: $55-$75
Tel: (817) 440-2076

AUSTIN

BALCOR SUITES
11215 Research Blvd
(78759)
Rates: $55-$75
Tel: (512) 343-0584

BEL-AIR MOTEL
3400 S Congress
(78704)
Rates: $20-$38
Tel: (512) 444-5973

**BEST WESTERN
ATRIUM NORTH**
7928 Gessner Dr
(78753)
Rates: $40-$125
Tel: (512) 339-7311
(800) 528-1234
(800) 468-3708 (TX)

**BEST WESTERN
SEVILLE PLAZA INN**
4323 I-35 S (78744)
Rates: $40-$45
Tel: (512) 447-5511
(800) 528-1234

**BEST WESTERN
SOUTH**
3401 I-35 S (78741)
Rates: $39-$53
Tel: (512) 448-2444
(800) 528-1234

**THE BROOK HOUSE
BED & BREAKFAST**
609 W 33rd St
(78705)
Rates: $69-$99
Tel: (512) 459-0534

**CAPITOL
MOTOR INN**
2525 I-35 S (78741)
Rates: $40-$45
Tel: (512) 441-0143

**CARRINGTON'S INN
BED & BREAKFAST**
1900 David St
(78705)
Rates: $69-$99
Tel: (512) 479-0638
(800) 871-8908

CORPORATE SUITES
4815 W Braker
(78759)
Rates: $69-$149
Tel: (512) 345-8822

COUNTRY INN
5656 I-35 N (78751)
Rates: $34+
Tel: (512) 452-1177
(800) 544-1404

**COURTYARD
BY MARRIOTT**
5660 I-35 N (78751)
Rates: $79-$89
Tel: (512) 458-2340
(800) 321-2211

DAYS INN NORTH
8210 I-35 N (78753)
Rates: $33-$45
Tel: (512) 835-2200
(800) 329-7466

**DOUBLETREE GUEST
SUITES**
303 W 15th St
(78701)
Rates: $89-$169
Tel: (512) 478-7000
(800) 222-8733

**DOUBLETREE
HOTEL**
6505 I-35 N (78752)
Rates: $74
Tel: (512) 454-3737
(800) 222-8733

**DRURY INN
HIGHLAND MALL**
919 E Koenig Ln
(78751)
Rates: $50-$63
Tel: (512) 454-1144
(800) 325-8300

DRURY INN-NORTH
6511 I-35 N (78752)
Rates: $37-$74
Tel: (512) 467-9500
(800) 325-8300

ECONO LODGE
6201 US 290 E
(78723)
Rates: $40-$99
Tel: (512) 458-4759
(800) 424-4777

**EMBASSY SUITES
AIRPORT NORTH**
5901 I-35 N (78723)
Rates: $113-$123
Tel: (512) 454-8004
(800) 362-2779

EXEL INN
2711 I-35 S (78741)
Rates: $30-$56
Tel: (512) 462-9201
(800) 356-8013

**FOSONS REGENT
HOTEL**
98 San Jacinto Blvd
(78701)
Rates: $132-$1185
Tel: (512) 478-4500
(800) 332-3442

**GOVERNOR'S INN
BED & BREAKFAST**
611 W 22nd St
(78705)
Rates: $69-$99
Tel: (512) 477-0711
(800) 871-8908

**GREENSHORES
ON LAKE AUSTIN**
6900 Greenshores Rd
(78730)
Rates: $65-$125
Tel: (512) 346-0011

**HABITAT SUITES
HOTEL**
500 Highland Mall
Blvd (78752)
Rates: $89-$129
Tel: (512) 467-6000
(800) 535-4663

**HAWTHORN SUITES
CENTRAL**
935 La Posada Dr
(78752)
Rates: $69-$123
Tel: (512) 459-3335
(800) 527-1133

**HAWTHORN SUITES
SOUTH**
4020 I-35 S (78704)
Rates: $99-$139
Tel: (512) 440-7722
(800) 527-1133

**HEART OF TEXAS
MOTEL**
5303 US 290 W
(78735)
Rates: $50-$65
Tel: (512) 892-0644

**HILTON & TOWERS
NORTH**
6000 Middle
Fiskville Rd (78752)
Rates: $69-$250
Tel: (512) 451-5757
(800) 445-8667

**HOLIDAY INN
AIRPORT
HIGHLAND MALL**
6911 I-35 N (78752)
Rates: $65-$75
Tel: (512) 459-4251
(800) 465-4329

**HOLIDAY INN
AUSTIN SOUTH**
3401 I-35 S (78741)
Rates: $69-$120
Tel: (512) 448-4999
(800) 465-4329

HOLIDAY INN NORTHWEST PLAZA
8901 Business Park Dr (78759)
Rates: $75-$80
Tel: (512) 343-0888
(800) 465-4329

HOWARD JOHNSON PLAZA HOTEL
7800 I-35 N (78753)
Rates: $58-$84
Tel: (512) 836-8520
(800) 446-4656

LA QUINTA INN-BEN WHITE
4200 I-35 S (78745)
Rates: $50-$60
Tel: (512) 443-1774
(800) 531-5900

LA QUINTA INN-CAPITOL
300 E 11th St (78701)
Rates: $61-$83
Tel: (512) 476-1166
(800) 531-5900

LA QUINTA INN-HIGHLAND MALL/AIRPORT
5812 I-35 N (78751)
Rates: $51-$64
Tel: (512) 459-4381
(800) 531-5900

LA QUINTA INN-NORTH
7100 I-35 N (78752)
Rates: $50-$55
Tel: (512) 452-9401
(800) 531-5900

LA QUINTA INN-OLTORF
1603 E Oltorf Blvd (78741)
Rates: $50-$62
Tel: (512) 447-6661
(800) 531-5900

LAKE AUSTIN SPA RESORT
1705 Quinlan Park Rd (78732)
Rates: $225+
Tel: (512) 266-2444
(800) 847-5637

MASTER HOSTS INN-CHARIOT INN
7300 I-35 N (78752)
Rates: $38-$51
Tel: (512) 452-9371
(800) 251-1962

MOTEL 6-AIRPORT
5330 Interregional Hwy N (78751)
Rates: $35-$41
Tel: (512) 467-9111
(800) 440-6000

MOTEL 6-CENTRAL
8010 I-35 N (78753)
Rates: $29-$35
Tel: (512) 837-9890
(800) 440-6000

MOTEL 6-NORTH
9420 I-35 N (78753)
Rates: $29-$35
Tel: (512) 339-6161
(800) 440-6000

MOTEL 6-SOUTH
2707 Interregional Hwy S (78741)
Rates: $29-$35
Tel: (512) 444-5882
(800) 440-6000

NEW AUSTIN MOTEL
2607 I-35 S (78741)
Rates: $26-$34
Tel: (512) 443-4242

OMNI SOUTHPARK HOTEL
4140 Governor's Row (78744)
Rates: $119-$350
Tel: (512) 448-2222
(800) 843-6664

PEACEFUL HILL BED & BREAKFAST
10817 Ranch Rd 2222 (78730)
Rates: $60
Tel: (512) 338-1817

QUALITY INN AIRPORT
909 E Koenig Ln (78751)
Rates: $43-$48
Tel: (512) 452-4200
(800) 221-2222

QUALITY INN-SOUTH
2200 I-35 S (78704)
Rates: $51-$64
Tel: (512) 444-0561
(800) 221-2222

RAMADA INN SOUTH
1212 W Ben White Blvd (78704)
Rates: $80-$85
Tel: (512) 447-0151
(800) 272-6232

RAMADA LIMITED
5526 I-35 N (78751)
Rates: $42-$56
Tel: (512) 451-7001
(800) 272-6232

RED LION HOTEL AIRPORT
6121 I-35 N (78752)
Rates: $75-$131
Tel: (512) 323-5466
(800) 733-5466

RENAISSANCE STOUFFER HOTEL
9721 Arboretum Blvd (78759)
Rates: $142-$215
Tel: (512) 343-2626
(800) 468-3571

RESIDENCE INN BY MARRIOTT
3713 Tudor Blvd (78759)
Rates: $99
Tel: (512) 502-8200
(800) 331-3131

RESIDENCE INN BY MARRIOTT
4537 I-35 S (78744)
Rates: $69-$129
Tel: (512) 912-1100
(800) 331-3131

STARS PASSPORT INN UNIVERSITY
3105 I-35 N (78722)
Rates: $28-$49
Tel: (512) 478-1631
(800) 725-7666

TOWN LAKE MOTOR INN
2915 I-35 S (78741)
Rates: $30-$36
Tel: (512) 444-8432

TRAVELODGE SUITES
8300 I-35 N (78752)
Rates: $39-$69
Tel: (512) 835-5050
(800) 578-7878

WALNUT FOREST MOTEL
11506 I-35 N (78753)
Rates: $22-$28
Tel: (512) 835-0864

BALLINGER

BALLINGER CLASSIC MOTEL
1005 Hutchings (76821)
Rates: $34-$40
Tel: (915) 365-5717

DESERT INN MOTEL
Hwy 67 W (76821)
Rates: $25-$32
Tel: (915) 365-2518

STONEWALL MOTEL
201 N Broadway (76821)
Rates: $26-$36
Tel: (915) 895-7760

BANDERA

COOL WATER ACRES BED & BREAKFAST
Rt 1, Box 785 (78003)
Rates: $50-$75
Tel: (210) 796-4866

RIVER FRONT MOTEL
Main St
P. O. Box 2609 (78003)
Rates: $49-$63
Tel: (210) 796-3093
(800) 870-5671

BASTROP

BASTROP INN MOTEL
102 Childers Dr (78602)
Rates: $30-$35
Tel: (512) 321-3949

BAYTOWN

BEST WESTERN BAYTOWN INN
5021 I-10 E (77521)
Rates: $40-$100
Tel: (713) 421-2233
(800) 528-1234

BUDGETEL INN
5215 I-10 E (77521)
Rates: $40-$57
Tel: (713) 421-7300
(800) 428-3438

HOLIDAY INN
300 S Hwy 146 (77520)
Rates: $46-$51
Tel: (713) 427-7481
(800) 465-4329

LA QUINTA INN
4911 I-10 E (77521)
Rates: $52-$66
Tel: (713) 421-5566
(800) 531-5900

MOTEL 6
8911 Hwy 146
(77520)
Rates: $29-$33
Tel: (713) 576-5777
(800) 440-6000

BEAUMONT

**BEST WESTERN
BEAUMONT INN**
2155 N 11th St
(77703)
Rates: $39-$45
Tel: (409) 898-8150
(800) 528-1234

**BEST WESTERN
JEFFERSON INN**
1610 I-10 S (77707)
Rates: $38-$44
Tel: (409) 842-0037
(800) 528-1234

DAYS INN
30 I-10 N (77702)
Rates: $29-$32
Tel: (409) 838-0581
(800) 329-7466

ECONO LODGE
1155 I-10 S (77701)
Rates: $29-$44
Tel: (409) 835-5913
(800) 424-4777

**GRAND DUERR
BED & BREAKFAST**
2298 McFaddin at
7th (77701)
Rates: $99-$159
Tel: (409) 833-9600

HILTON HOTEL
2355 I-10 S (77705)
Rates: $62-$72
Tel: (409) 842-3600
(800) 445-8667

**HOLIDAY INN
BEAUMONT PLAZA**
3950 I-10 S (77705)
Rates: $70-$99
Tel: (409) 842-5995
(800) 465-4329

**HOLIDAY INN
I-10 MIDTOWN**
2095 N 11th St
(77703)
Rates: $55-$67
Tel: (409) 892-2222
(800) 465-4329

J & J MOTEL
6675 Eastex Frwy
(77705)
Rates: $24+
Tel: (409) 892-4241

LA QUINTA INN
220 I-10 N (77702)
Rates: $43-$58
Tel: (409) 838-9991
(800) 531-5900

QUALITY INN
1295 N 11th St
(77702)
Rates: $43-$48
Tel: (409) 892-7722
(800) 221-2222

RAMADA HOTEL
2525 N 11th St
(77703)
Rates: $55-$60
Tel: (409) 898-2111
(800) 272-6232

**ROAD RUNNER
MOTEL**
3985 College St
(77707)
Rates: $28-$36
Tel: (409) 842-4420

RODEWAY INN
4085 I-10 S (77705)
Rates: $24-$39
Tel: (409) 842-9341
(800) 424-4777

SUPER 8 MOTEL
2850 I-10 E (77703)
Rates: $41-$43
Tel: (409) 899-3040
(800) 800-8000

BEDFORD

LA QUINTA INN
1450 W Airport
Frwy (76022)
Rates: $47-$53
Tel: (817) 267-5200
(800) 531-5900

BEEVILLE

**BEST WESTERN
DRUMMERS INN**
400 US 181 S (78102)
Rates: $40-$46
Tel: (512) 358-4000
(800) 528-1234

EL CAMINO MOTEL
1500 N Washington
(78102)
Rates: $27-$35
Tel: (512) 358-2141

EXECUTIVE INN
1601 N St. Mary
(78102)
Rates: $36-$40
Tel: (512) 358-0022

BELLMEAD

MOTEL 6
1509 Hogan Ln
(76705)
Rates: $24-$29
Tel: (817) 799-4957
(800) 440-6000

BELTON

**BEST WESTERN
RIVER FOREST
MOTEL**
1414 E 6th Ave
(76513)
Rates: $35-$50
Tel: (817) 939-5711
(800) 528-1234

**BUDGET HOST-
THE BELTON INN**
1520 I-35 S (76513)
Rates: $35-$47
Tel: (817) 939-0744
(800) 283-4678

RAMADA LIMITED
1102 E 2nd Ave
(76513)
Rates: $30-$35
Tel: (817) 939-3745
(800) 272-6232

BIG BEND NATIONAL PARK

**CHISOS MOUN-
TAINS LODGE**
Basin Rural Station
(79834)
Rates: $59-$69
Tel: (915) 477-2291

BIG SPRING

**DAYS INN BIG
SPRING**
300 Tulane Ave
(79720)
Rates: $42-$48
Tel: (915) 263-7621
(800) 329-7466

ECONO LODGE
804 I-20 W (79720)
Rates: $38-$69
Tel: (915) 263-5200
(800) 424-4777

MOTEL 6
600 I-20 W (79720)
Rates: $25-$29
Tel: (915) 267-1695
(800) 440-6000

**PONDEROSA
MOTOR INN**
2701 S Gregg St
(79720)
Rates: $24-$31
Tel: (915) 267-5237

BIG SURF

ECONO LODGE
804 I-20 W (79720)
Rates: $39-$69
Tel: (915) 263-5200
(800) 424-4777

BLANCO

**CREEKWOOD
COUNTRY INN
BED & BREAKFAST**
P. O. Box 1357
(78606)
Rates: $75-$85
Tel: (210) 833-2248

SWISS LODGE
1206 N Main (78606)
Rates: $43-$45
Tel: (210) 833-5528

BOERNE

**BEST WESTERN
TEXAS COUNTRY INN**
35150 I-10 W (78006)
Rates: $48-$72
Tel: (210) 249-9791
(800) 528-1234

**BOERNE LAKE
LODGE
BED & BREAKFAST
RESORT**
310 Lakeview Dr
(78006)
Rates: $150-$250
Tel: (210) 816-6060
(800) 809-5050

**KEY TO THE HILLS
MOTEL**
1228 S Main St
(78006)
Rates: $48-$60
Tel: (210) 249-3562
(800) 690-5763

BONHAM

DAYS INN
1515 Old Ector Rd
(75418)
Rates: $38-$40
Tel: (903) 583-3121
(800) 329-7466

BORGER

**THE INN PLACE
OF BORGER**
100 Bulldog Blvd
(79007)
Rates: $39-$46
Tel: (806) 273-9556

BOWIE

DAYS INN
RR 5, Box 138
(76230)
Rates: $30-$53
Tel: (817) 872-5426
(800) 329-7466

PARK LODGE
708 Park Ave (76230)
Rates: $28-$46
Tel: (817) 872-1111

BRADY

PLATEAU MOTEL
2023 S Bridge
(76825)
Rates: $27-$38
Tel: (915) 597-2185

SUNSET INN
2108 S Bridge
(76825)
Rates: $40-$44
Tel: (915) 597-0789

BRECKENRIDGE

RIDGE MOTEL
Hwy 180,
P. O. Box 312 (76424)
Rates: $28-$40
Tel: (817) 559-2244
(800) 462-5308

BRENHAM

THE BRENHAM INN
2217 S Market (77833)
Rates: $41-$46
Tel: (409) 836-1300
(800) 275-2539

BROADDUS

**COUNTRY INN
"A MOTEL"**
P. O. Box 428,
Hwy 147 (75929)
Rates: $35-$70
Tel: (409) 872-3691

BROOKSHIRE

BRAZOS VALLEY INN
217 Waller Ave
(77423)
Rates: $36-$49
Tel: (713) 934-3122

BUDGET INN
542 Koomey Rd
(77423)
Rates: $29-$40
Tel: (713) 934-4477

**DAYS INN
BROOKSHIRE**
RM 359 & I-10
(77423)
Rates: $42-$45
Tel: (713) 934-3122
(800) 329-7466

BROWNFIELD

**BEST WESTERN
CAPROCK INN**
321 Lubbock Rd
(79316)
Rates: $38-$46
Tel: (806) 637-9471
(800) 528-1234

BROWNSVILLE

**HOLIDAY INN
FORT BROWN
HOTEL & RESORT**
1900 E Elizabeth St
(78520)
Rates: $69-$200
Tel: (210) 546-2201
(800) 465-4329

HOWARD JOHNSON
1945 N Expwy
(78520)
Rates: $50-$99
Tel: (210) 546-4591
(800) 446-4656

LA QUINTA INN
55 Sam Perl Blvd
(78520)
Rates: $43-$55
Tel: (210) 546-0381
(800) 531-5900

MOTEL 6
2250 N Expwy
(78521)
Rates: $28-$34
Tel: (210) 546-4699
(800) 440-6000

SHERATON INN
3777 N Expwy (78520)
Rates: $80-$101
Tel: (210) 350-9191
(800) 325-3535

BROWNWOOD

**BEST WESTERN
BROWNWOOD**
410 E Commerce
(76801)
Rates: $40-$49
Tel: (915) 646-3511
(800) 528-1234

DAYS INN
1204 C C Wodson Rd
(76801)
Rates: $39-$48
Tel: (915) 643-5611
(800) 329-7466

GATE I MOTOR INN
4410 Hwy 377 S
(76801)
Rates: $34
Tel: (915) 643-5463

**GOLD KEY INN
MOTEL**
515 E Commerce
(76801)
Rates: $29-$44
Tel: (915) 646-2551
(800) 646-0912

BRYAN

**FAIRFIELD INN
BY MARRIOTT**
4613 S Texas Ave
(77802)
Rates: $46-$54
Tel: (409) 268-1552
(800) 228-2800

PREFERENCE INN
1601 S Texas Ave
(77802)
Rates: $35-$60
Tel: (409) 822-6196

BUFFALO

**BEST WESTERN
CRAIG'S INN**
P. O. Box 667 (75831)
Rates: $37-$41
Tel: (903) 322-5831
(800) 528-1234

BURLESON

DAYS INN
329 S Burleson Blvd
(76028)
Rates: $38-$50
Tel: (817) 447-1111
(800) 329-7466

BURNET

**ROCKY REST
COUNTRY INN**
404 S Water St
(78611)
Rates: $55-$60
Tel: (512) 756-2600

CALDWELL

THE SURREY INN
403 E Hwy 21
(77836)
Rates: $37-$40
Tel: (409) 567-3221

VARSITY INN CALDWELL
705 Hwy 36 N
(77836)
Rates: $33-$49
Tel: (409) 567-4661

CAMERON

VARSITY MOTEL
1004 E 1st St (76520)
Rates: $34-$40
Tel: (817) 697-6446

CANTON

BEST WESTERN CANTON INN
Rt 2, Box 6-B (75103)
Rates: $40-$82
Tel: (903) 567-6591
(800) 528-1234

DAYS INN
Hwy 19, I-20 (75103)
Rates: $35-$48
Tel: (903) 567-6588
(800) 339-7466

CANYON LAKE

MARICOPA RANCH RESORT
P. O. Box 1659
(78130)
Rates: $57+
Tel: (210) 964-3731

CARROLLTON

RED ROOF INN
1720 S Broadway
(75006)
Rates: $31-$47
Tel: (214) 245-1700
(800) 843-7663

CARTHAGE

CARTHAGE MOTEL
321 S Shelby (75633)
Rates: $28-$35
Tel: (903) 693-3814

CASTROVILLE

BEST WESTERN ALSATIAN INN
1650 Hwy 90 W
(78009)
Rates: $45-$59
Tel: (210) 538-2262
(800) 528-1234

CENTER

BEST WESTERN CENTER INN
1005 Hurst St
(75935)
Rates: $36-$51
Tel: (409) 598-3384
(800) 528-1234

CENTER POINT

MARIANNE'S BED & BREAKFAST
Rt 1, Box 527 (78010)
Rates: $70+
Tel: (210) 634-7489

CENTERVILLE

DAYS INN
P. O. Box 729 (75833)
Rates: $35-$50
Tel: (903) 536-7175
(800) 329-7466

CHANNELVIEW

BEST WESTERN HOUSTON EAST
15919 I-10 E (77530)
Rates: $32-$47
Tel: (713) 452-1000
(800) 528-1234

DAYS INN
15545 I-10 E (77530)
Rates: $40-$55
Tel: (713) 457-3000
(800) 329-7466

HOLIDAY INN
15157 I-10 E (77530)
Rates: $49+
Tel: (713) 452-7304
(800) 465-4329

CHILDRESS

BEST WESTERN CLASSIC INN
1805 Ave F NW
(79201)
Rates: $43-$51
Tel: (817) 937-6353
(800) 528-1234

COMFORT INN
1804 Ave F NW
(79201)
Rates: $39-$49
Tel: (817) 937-6363
(800) 221-2222

ECONO LODGE
1612 Ave F NW
(79201)
Rates: $33-$46
Tel: (817) 937-3695
(800) 424-4777

CISCO

OAK MOTEL
300 I-20 E (76437)
Rates: $20-$29
Tel: (817) 442-2100

RODEWAY WHITE ELEPHANT INN
1898 Hwy 206 W
(76437)
Rates: $39-$42
Tel: (817) 442-3735
(800) 621-2457

CLARENDON

WESTERN SKIES MOTEL
800 W 2nd St (79226)
Rates: $35-$42
Tel: (806) 874-3501

CLAUDE

L A MOTEL
200 E 1st St (79019)
Rates: $22-$35
Tel: (806) 226-4981

CLEBURNE

BUDGET HOST INN
2107 N Main (76031)
Rates: $36-$48
Tel: (817) 556-3631
(800) 283-4678

DAYS INN
101 N Ridgeway Dr
(76031)
Rates: $40-$65
Tel: (817) 645-8836
(800) 329-7466

CLIFTON

THE RIVER'S BEND BED & BREAKFAST
P. O. Box 228 (76634)
Rates: $75-$150
Tel: (817) 675-4936

CLUTE

LA QUINTA INN
1126 Hwy 332 W
(77531)
Rates: $47-$60
Tel: (409) 265-7461
(800) 531-5900

MOTEL 6
1000 Hwy 332 W
(77531)
Rates: $26-$30
Tel: (409) 265-4764
(800) 440-6000

COLDSPRING

SAN JACINTO INN
P. O. Box 459 (77331)
Rates: $34-$39
Tel: (409) 653-3008

COLLEGE STATION

COMFORT INN
104 Texas Ave S
(77840)
Rates: $54-$170
Tel: (409) 846-7333
(800) 221-2222

HILTON HOTEL & CONF. CENTER
801 University Dr E
(77840)
Rates: $68-$104
Tel: (409) 693-7500
(800) 445-8667

HOLIDAY INN-COLLEGE STATION
1503 Texas Ave S
(77840)
Rates: $49-$61
Tel: (409) 693-1736
(800) 465-4329

LA QUINTA INN
607 Texas Ave S
(77840)
Rates: $51-$65
Tel: (409) 696-7777
(800) 531-5900

MANOR HOUSE MOTOR INN
2504 Texas Ave S
(77840)
Rates: $49-$54
Tel: (409) 764-9540
(800) 231-4100

MOTEL 6
2327 Texas Ave S
(77840)
Rates: $28-$32
Tel: (409) 696-3379
(800) 440-6000

RAMADA INN MOTOR HOTEL
1502 Texas Ave S
(77840)
Rates: $38-$100
Tel: (409) 693-9891
(800) 272-6232

COLORADO CITY

DAYS INN
Rt 1, Box 293 (79512)
Rates: $35-$63
Tel: (915) 728-2638
(800) 329-7466

VILLA INN MOTEL
2310 Hickory St
(79512)
Rates: $29-$36
Tel: (915) 728-5217

COLUMBUS

COLUMBUS INN
2208 Hwy 71 S
(78934)
Rates: $40-$45
Tel: (409) 732-5723

HOMEPLACE INN
2436 Hwy 71 S
(78934)
Rates: $44-$52
Tel: (409) 732-6293

COMANCHE

GUEST HOUSE-HERITAGE HILL BED & BREAKFAST
Hwy 36 E, Rt 3
P.O. Box 221 (76442)
Rates: $40-$70
Tel: (915) 356-3397

COMFORT

MOTOR INN AT COMFORT
32 Hwy 87 & I-10
(78013)
Rates: $50+
Tel: (210) 995-3822

IDLEWILDE BED & BREAKFAST
115 Hwy 473 (78013)
Rates: $63-$93
Tel: (210) 995-3844

KLEINA HIMMUL BED & BREAKFAST
Rt 1, Box 127-B
(78013)
Rates: $75-$85
Tel: (210) 995-2003

CONROE

HEATHER'S GLEN-A BED & BREAKFAST
200 E Phillips
(77301)
Rates: $75-$95
Tel: (409) 441-6611
(800) 665-2643

HOLIDAY INN
1601 I-45 S (77301)
Rates: $59-$65
Tel: (409) 756-8941
(800) 465-4329

MOTEL 6
820 I-45 S (77304)
Rates: $29-$35
Tel: (409) 760-4003
(800) 440-6000

RAMADA INN
1520 S Frazier
(77301)
Rates: $61+
Tel: (409) 756-8939
(800) 272-6232

CORPUS CHRISTI

BEST WESTERN GARDEN INN
11217 I-37 (78410)
Rates: $49-$65
Tel: (512) 241-6675
(800) 528-1234

DAYS INN
901 Navigation Blvd
(78408)
Rates: $35-$85
Tel: (512) 888-8599
(800) 329-7466

DRURY INN
2021 N Padre Island
Dr (78408)
Rates: $52-$67
Tel: (512) 289-8200
(800) 325-8300

EMBASSY SUITES HOTEL
4337 S Padre Island
Dr (78411)
Rates: $110-$125
Tel: (512) 853-7899
(800) 362-2779

FAIRFIELD INN BY MARRIOTT
5217 Blanche Moore
Dr (78411)
Rates: $52-$80
Tel: (512) 985-8393
(800) 228-2800

GULF BEACH-II LUXURY MOTOR INN
3500 Surfside Blvd
(78402)
Rates: $45-$70
Tel: (512) 882-3500

HAMPTON INN
5209 Blanche Moore
Dr (78411)
Rates: $54-$87
Tel: (512) 985-8395
(800) 426-7866

HAMPTON INN
5501 Interstate 37 at
McBride (78408)
Rates: $59-$84
Tel: (512) 289-5861
(800) 426-7866

HOLIDAY INN-AIRPORT
5549 Leopard St
(78408)
Rates: $69-$75
Tel: (512) 289-5100
(800) 465-4329

HOLIDAY INN EMERALD BEACH
1102 S Shoreline
Blvd (78401)
Rates: $79-$115
Tel: (512) 883-5731
(800) 465-4329

HOLIDAY INN NORTH PADRE ISLAND RESORT
15202 Windward Dr
(78418)
Rates: $89-$250
Tel: (512) 949-8041
(800) 465-4329

HOWARD JOHNSON
300 N Shoreline Blvd
(78403)
Rates: $89-$109
Tel: (512) 883-5111
(800) 446-4656

LA QUINTA INN-NORTH
5155 I-37 N (78408)
Rates: $54-$64
Tel: (512) 888-5721
(800) 531-5900

LA QUINTA INN-SOUTH
6225 S Padre Island
Dr (78412)
Rates: $60-$65
Tel: (512) 991-5730
(800) 531-5900

MOTEL 6-EAST
8202 S Padre Island
Dr (78412)
Rates: $28-$36
Tel: (512) 991-8858
(800) 440-6000

MOTEL 6-NORTH-WEST
845 Lantana St
(78408)
Rates: $26-$30
Tel: (512) 289-9397
(800) 440-6000

RED ROOF INN
6301 I-37 (78409)
Rates: $29-$53
Tel: (512) 289-6925
(800) 843-7663

**RESIDENCE INN
BY MARRIOTT**
5229 Blanche Moore
Dr (78411)
Rates: $89-$139
Tel: (512) 985-1113
(800) 331-3131

**SURFSIDE
CONDOMINIUM
APARTMENTS**
15005 Windward Dr
(78418)
Rates: $75-$100
Tel: (512) 949-8128
(800) 548-4585

**TRAVELODGE
AIRPORT**
910 Corn Products
Rd (78409)
Rates: $49-$59
Tel: (512) 289-5666
(800) 578-7878

VAL-U-INN
5224 I-37 at
Navigation Blvd
(78407)
Rates: $37-$45
Tel: (512) 883-2951
(800) 443-7777

CORSICANA

SUPER 8 MOTEL
2021 Regal Dr
(75110)
Rates: $29-$33
Tel: (903) 874-4751
(800) 800-8000

COTULLA

RODEWAY INN
1100 W FM 468
(78014)
Rates: $37-$52
Tel: (210) 879-2311
(800) 424-4777

CROCKETT

CROCKETT INN
1600 Loop 304 E
(75835)
Rates: $35+
Tel: (409) 544-5611
(800) 633-9518

EMBERS MOTOR INN
1401 Loop 304 E
(75835)
Rates: $25-$36
Tel: (409) 544-5681

CUERO

**SANDS MOTEL
& RV PARK**
2117 N Esplanade
(77954)
Rates: $32-$38
Tel: (512) 275-3437

DALHART

**BEST WESTERN
NURSANICKEL
MOTEL**
Hwy 87 S (79022)
Rates: $31-$51
Tel: (806) 249-5637
(800) 528-1234

**BEST WESTERN
SKIES MOTOR INN**
623 Denver Ave
(79022)
Rates: $32-$49
Tel: (806) 249-4538
(800) 528-1234

COMFORT INN
HCR 2, Box 22
(79022)
Rates: $32-$55
Tel: (806) 249-8585
(800) 221-2222

DAYS INN
701 Liberal St
54 E (79022)
Rates: $45-$95
Tel: (806) 249-5246
(800) 229-3297

ECONO LODGE
123 Liberal St
(79022)
Rates: $28-$37
Tel: (806) 249-6464
(800) 424-4777

FRIENDSHIP INN
400 Liberal St (79022)
Rates: $24-$69
Tel: (806) 249-4557
(800) 424-4777

SANDS MOTEL
301 Liberal St (79022)
Rates: $19-$35
Tel: (806) 249-4568

SUPER 8 MOTEL
E Hwy 54
P. O. Box 1325 (79022)
Rates: $32-$40
Tel: (806) 249-8526
(800) 800-8000

DALLAS

**BEST WESTERN
PRESTON SUITES
HOTEL**
6104 LBJ Frwy
(75240)
Rates: $130-$210
Tel: (214) 458-2626
(800) 528-1234

BRISTOL SUITES
7800 Alpha Rd
(75240)
Rates: $79-$119
Tel: (214) 233-7600
(800) 922-9222

CLARION HOTEL
1241 W Mockingbird
Ln (75247)
Rates: $84-$104
Tel: (214) 630-7000
(800) 221-2222

COMFORT INN
8901 East R L
Thornton Frwy
(75228)
Rates: $49-$59
Tel: (214) 324-4475
(800) 221-2222

**CRESCENT COURT
HOTEL**
400 Crescent Court
(75210)
Rates: $230-$320
Tel: (214) 871-3200
(800) 654-6541

DAYS INN
8312 S Lancaster Rd
(75241)
Rates: $40-$125
Tel: (214) 224-3196
(800) 329-7466

DAYS INN CENTRAL
4150 N Central
Expwy (75204)
Rates: $45-$95
Tel: (214) 827-6080
(800) 329-7466

**DOUBLETREE HOTEL
AT CAMPBELL
CENTRE**
8250 N Central
Expwy (75206)
Rates: $54-$104
Tel: (214) 691-8700
(800) 222-8733

**DRURY INN-
DALLAS NORTH**
2421 Walnut Hill Ln
(75229)
Rates: $58-$77
Tel: (214) 484-3330
(800) 325-8300

ECONO LODGE
Airport I-35 N
(75234)
Rates: $42-52
Tel: (214) 243-5500
(800) 424-4777

**EMBASSY SUITES
HOTEL-DALLAS/
PARK CENTRAL**
13131 N Central
Expwy (75243)
Rates: $119-$169
Tel: (214) 234-3300
(800) 362-2779

EXECUTIVE INN
3232 W Mockingbird
Ln (75235)
Rates: $36-$72
Tel: (214) 357-5601

**EXEL INN
OF DALLAS EAST**
8510 East R L
Thornton Frwy
(75228)
Rates: $38-$75
Tel: (214) 328-8500
(800) 356-8013

GRAND HOTEL
1914 Commerce St
(75201)
Rates: $110-$550
Tel: (214) 747-7000

HAMPTON INN
1015 Elm (75202)
Rates: $74-82
Tel: (214) 742-5678
(800) 426-7866

HAMPTON INN-DALLAS NORTH
11069 Composite Dr (75229)
Rates: $58-$73
Tel: (214) 484-6557
(800) 426-7866

HARVEY HOTEL-BROOKHOLLOW
7050 Stemmons Frwy (75247)
Rates: $79-$107
Tel: (214) 630-8500
(800) 922-9222

HARVEY HOTEL-DALLAS
7815 LBJ Frwy at Colt Rd (75240)
Rates: $49-$79
Tel: (214) 960-7000
(800) 922-9222

HARVEY HOTEL DOWNTOWN
400 N Olive St (75201)
Rates: $79-$140
Tel: (214) 922-8000
(800) 922-9222

HAWTHORN SUITES
7900 Brookriver Dr (75247)
Rates: $89-$119
Tel: (214) 688-1010
(800) 527-1133

HOLIDAY INN NORTH PARK PLAZA
10650 N Central Expwy (75231)
Rates: $55
Tel: (214) 373-6000
(800) 465-4329

HYATT REGENCY DALLAS AT REUNION
300 Reunion Blvd (75207)
Rates: $94-$150
Tel: (214) 651-1234
(800) 233-1234

LA QUINTA INN-CENTRAL
4440 N Central Expwy (75206)
Rates: $52-$64
Tel: (214) 821-4220
(800) 531-5900

LA QUINTA INN-EAST
8303 E Thornton Frwy (75228)
Rates: $60-$150
Tel: (214) 324-3731
(800) 531-5900

LA QUINTA INN NORTHPARK
10001 N Central Expwy (75231)
Rates: $52-$65
Tel: (214) 361-8200
(800) 531-5900

LA QUINTA INN REGAL ROW
1625 Regal Row (75247)
Rates: $53-$65
Tel: (214) 630-5701
(800) 531-5900

MARRIOTT PARK CENTRAL
7750 LBJ Frwy (75251)
Rates: $70-$104
Tel: (214) 233-4421
(800) 228-9290

MOTEL 6
2660 Forest Ln (75234)
Rates: $30-$38
Tel: (214) 484-9111
(800) 440-6000

MOTEL 6
2753 Forest Ln (75234)
Rates: $27-$35
Tel: (214) 620-2828
(800) 440-6000

MOTEL 6-SOUTHEAST
4220 Independence Dr (75237)
Rates: $26-$33
Tel: (214) 296-3331
(800) 440-6000

PLAZA AMERICAS HOTEL
650 N Pearl St (75201)
Rates: $170-$230
Tel: (214) 979-9000

QUALITY INN
2015 Market Center Blvd (75207)
Rates: $69-$109
Tel: (214) 741-7481
(800) 228-5151

RADISSON-CENTRAL
6060 N Central Expwy (75206)
Rates: $79-$109
Tel: (214) 750-6060
(800) 333-3333

RADISSON HOTEL & SUITES DALLAS
2330 W Northwest Hwy (75220)
Rates: $99-$139
Tel: (214) 351-4477
(800) 333-3333

RADISSON MOCKINGBIRD WEST
1893 W Mockingbird Ln (75235)
Rates: $54-$115
Tel: (214) 634-8850
(800) 333-3333

RAMADA HOTEL DOWNTOWN
1011 S Akard St (75215)
Rates: $45-$125
Tel: (214) 421-1083
(800) 272-6232

RAMADA HOTEL MARKET CENTER
1055 Regal Row (75247)
Rates: $79-$350
Tel: (214) 634-8550
(800) 272-6232

RED ROOF INN DALLAS EAST
8108 E.Thornton Frwy (75228)
Rates: $28-$44
Tel: (214) 388-8741
(800) 843-7663

RED ROOF INN MARKET CENTER
1550 Empire Central Dr (75235)
Rates: $29-$41
Tel: (214) 638-5151
(800) 843-7663

RED ROOF INN-NORTHWEST
10335 Gardner Rd (75220)
Rates: $29-$41
Tel: (214) 506-8100
(800) 843-7663

RESIDENCE INN BY MARRIOTT/CENTRAL-N.PARK
10333 N Central Expwy (75231)
Rates: $75-$139
Tel: (214) 750-8220
(800) 331-3131

RESIDENCE INN BY MARRIOTT-MARKET CENTER
6950 N Stemmons Frwy (75247)
Rates: $99-$130
Tel: (214) 631-2472
(800) 331-3131

RESIDENCE INN BY MARRIOTT-NORTH
13636 Goldmark Dr (75240)
Rates: $100-$130
Tel: (214) 669-0478
(800) 331-3131

RODEWAY INN
2026 Market Center Blvd (75207)
Rates: $52-$78
Tel: (214) 748-2243
(800) 424-4777

SHERATON PARK CENTRAL
12720 Merit Dr (75251)
Rates: $69-$160
Tel: (214) 385-3000
(800) 325-3535

STOUFFER RENAISSANCE HOTEL MARKET CENTER
2222 Stemmons Frwy (75207)
Rates: $89-$189
Tel: (214) 631-2222
(800) 228-9898

TRAVELODGE
3140 W Mockingbird Ln (75235)
Rates: $38-$59
Tel: (214) 357-1701
(800) 578-7878

THE WESTIN HOTEL GALLERIA DALLAS
13340 Dallas Pkwy (75240)
Rates: $109-$185
Tel: (214) 934-9494
(800) 228-3000

DECATUR

BEST WESTERN INN
1801 Hwy 287 S (76234)
Rates: $35-$49
Tel: (817) 627-5982
(800) 528-1234

COMFORT INN
1709 Hwy 287 S
(76234)
Rates: $36-$50
Tel: (817) 627-6919
(800) 221-2222

DEL RIO

AMISTAD LODGE MOTEL
Hwy 90 W, HCR 3,
Box 25 (78840)
Rates: $31+
Tel: (210) 775-8591

ANGLER'S LODGE MOTEL
Hwy 90 W, HCR 3,
Box 25 (78840)
Rates: $27+
Tel: (210) 775-1586

BEST WESTERN INN OF DEL RIO
810 Ave F (78840)
Rates: $43-$61
Tel: (210) 775-7511
(800) 528-1234
(800) 336-3537 (TX)

BEST WESTERN LA SIESTA
2000 Ave F (78840)
Rates: $46-$73
Tel: (210) 775-6323
(800) 528-1234
(800) 336-3537 (TX)

DAYS INN
3808 Hwy 90 W
(78840)
Rates: $25-$40
Tel: (210) 775-1511
(800) 329-7466

DEL RIO MOTOR LODGE
1300 Ave F (78840)
Rates: $20+
Tel: (210) 775-2486
(800) 882-9826

DESERT HILLS MOTEL
1912 Ave F (78840)
Rates: $20-$28
Tel: (210) 775-3548

LA QUINTA INN
2005 Ave F (78840)
Rates: $40-$53
Tel: (210) 775-7591
(800) 531-5900

LAKEVIEW INN DIABLO EAST
Hwy 90 W, HCR 3,
Box 38 (78840)
Rates: $27-$45
Tel: (210) 775-9521
(800) 344-0109

MOTEL 6
2115 Ave F (78840)
Rates: $25-$29
Tel: (210) 774-2115
(800) 440-6000

RED TOP INN/ ECONOMY INN
3811 Hwy 90 W
(78840)
Rates: $22+
Tel: (210) 775-7414

ROUGH CANYON INN MOTEL
Hwy 277 N, RR 2
(78840)
Rates: $27+
Tel: (210) 774-6266

WESTERN MOTEL
1203 Ave F (78840)
Rates: $20+
Tel: (210) 774-4661

DENISON

RAMADA INN
1600 S Austin Ave
(75021)
Rates: $59-$69
Tel: (903) 465-6800
(800) 272-6232

DENTON

DAYS INN OF DENTON
601 I-35 E (76205)
Rates: $40-$45
Tel: (817) 566-1990
(800) 329-7466

DENTON INN
820 S I-35 E (76205)
Rates: $46-$49
Tel: (817) 387-0591

DESERT SANDS MOTOR INN
611 S I-35 E (76205)
Rates: $28-$50
Tel: (817) 387-6181

ECONO LODGE
3116 Bandera Dr
(76207)
Rates: $29-59
Tel: (800) 424-4777

EXEL INN OF DENTON
4211 N I-35 E (76201)
Rates: $27-$40
Tel: (817) 383 1471
(800) 356-8013

HOLIDAY LODGE
1112 E University
(76205)
Rates: $25-$31
Tel: (817) 382-9688

LA QUINTA INN
700 Fort Worth Dr
(76201)
Rates: $41-$46
Tel: (817) 387-5840
(800) 531-5900

MOTEL 6
5125 N I-35 (76207)
Rates: $26-$32
Tel: (817) 566-4798
(800) 440-6000

ROYAL HOTEL & SUITES
1210 N I-35 E (76205)
Rates: $32-$59
Tel: (817) 383-2007

WESTERN INN
3116 Bandera Dr
(76207)
Rates: $28-$34
Tel: (817) 383-1681

DESOTO

HOLIDAY INN
1515 N Beckley Ave
(75115)
Rates: $67-$77
Tel: (214) 224-9100
(800) 465-4329

DUMAS

BEST WESTERN DUMAS INN MOTEL
1712 S Dumas Ave
(79029)
Rates: $49-$77
Tel: (806) 935-6441
(800) 528-1234

COMFORT INN
1620 S Dumas Ave
(79029)
Rates: $45-$85
Tel: (806) 935-6988
(800) 228-5150

DAYS INN OF DUMAS
1701 S Dumas Ave
(79029)
Rates: $51-$61
Tel: (806) 935-9644
(800) 329-7466

ECONO LODGE OLD TOWN INN
1719 S Dumas Ave
(79029)
Rates: $27-$57
Tel: (806) 935-9098
(800) 424-4777

HOLIDAY INN
1525 S Dumas Ave
(79029)
Rates: $55
Tel: (806) 935-4000
(800) 465-4329

PHILLIPS MANOR MOTEL
18721 S Dumas Ave
(79029)
Rates: $28-$44
Tel: (806) 935-9281

SUPER 8 MOTEL
119 W 17th (79029)
Rates: $33-$52
Tel: (806) 935-6222
(800) 800-8000

DUNCANVILLE

HAMPTON INN
4154 Preferred Pl
(75237)
Rates: $47-$59
Tel: (214) 298-4747
(800) 426-7866

HOLIDAY INN- DALLAS SW
711 E Camp Wisdom
Rd (75116)
Rates: $55-$70
Tel: (214) 298-8911
(800) 465-4329

MOTEL 6- DUNCANVILLE
202 Jellison Rd
(75116)
Rates: 30-$34
Tel: (214) 296-0345
(800) 440-6000

EAGLE LAKE

THE FARRIS 1912 INN
201 N McCarty St
(77434)
Rates: $40-$95
Tel: (409) 234-2546

EAGLE PASS

BEST WESTERN EAGLE PASS
1923 Loop 431
(78852)
Rates: $62-$74
Tel: (210) 758-1234
(800) 528-1234

EAGLE PASS INN
2150 N Hwy 277
(78852)
Rates: $28-$45
Tel: (210) 773-9531
(800) 272-9786

HOLLY INN
2421 E Main St
(78852)
Rates: $39-$44
Tel: (210) 773-9261
(800) 424-8125

LA QUINTA INN
2525 E Main St
(78852)
Rates: $47-$64
Tel: (210) 773-7000
(800) 531-5900

EASTLAND

BUDGET HOST INN
P. O. Box 108 (76448)
Rates: $34-$40
Tel: (817) 629-2655
(800) 283-4678

ECONO LODGE
2001 I-20 W (76448)
Rates: $33-$39
Tel: (817) 629-3324
(800) 424-4777

SUPER 8 MOTEL & RV PARK
3900 I-20 E (76448)
Rates: $23-$33
Tel: (817) 629-3336
(800) 800-8000

EL CAMPO

EL CAMPO INN
210 W Hwy 59
(77437)
Rates: $34-$48
Tel: (409) 543-1110

EL PASO

AMERICANA INN
14387 Gateway Blvd
W (79927)
Rates: $34-$48
Tel: (915) 852-3025

BEST WESTERN AIRPORT INN
7144 Gateway Blvd
E (79915)
Rates: $39-$71
Tel: (915) 779-7700
(800) 528-1234
(800) 295-7276 (TX)

BUDGETEL INN
7620 N Mesa St
(79912)
Rates: $37-$48
Tel: (915) 585-2999
(800) 428-3438

BUDGET LODGE MOTEL
1301 N Mesa St
(79902)
Rates: $23-$37
Tel: (915) 533-6821

CAMINO REAL HOTEL
101 S El Paso St
(79901)
Rates: $125-$275
Tel: (915) 534-3000
(800) 722-6466

COMFORT INN AIRPORT EAST
900 N Yarborough St
(79915)
Rates: $39-$89
Tel: (915) 594-9111
(800) 221-2222
(800) 497-1347 (TX)

DAYS INN EL PASO
9125 Gateway Blvd
W (79925)
Rates: $51-$55
Tel: (915) 593-8400
(800) 329-7466

ECONO LODGE
6363 Montana St
(79925)
Rates: $36-$40
Tel: (915) 779-6222:
(800) 424-4777

EMBASSY SUITES HOTEL
6100 Gateway Blvd
E (79905)
Rates: $89-$99
Tel: (915) 779-6222
(800) 362-2779

HILTON-EL PASO AIRPORT
2027 Airway Blvd
(79925)
Rates: $85-$95
Tel: (915) 778-4241
(800) 445-8667
(800) 742-7248 (TX)

HOWARD JOHNSON LODGE
8887 Gateway Blvd
W (79925)
Rates: $40-$71
Tel: (915) 591-9471
(800) 446-4656

INTERNATIONAL HOTEL
113 W Missouri
(79901)
Rates: $55-$130
Tel: (915) 544-3300
(800) 228-2828

LA QUINTA INN-AIRPORT
6140 Gateway Blvd
E (79905)
Rates: $49-$64
Tel: (915) 778-9321
(800) 531-5900

LA QUINTA INN-LOMALAND
11033 Gateway Blvd
W (79935)
Rates: $47-$60
Tel: (915) 591-2244
(800) 531-5900

LA QUINTA INN-WEST
7550 Remcon Cir
(79912)
Rates: $48-$71
Tel: (915) 833-2522
(800) 531-5900

MARRIOTT-EL PASO
1600 Airway Blvd
(79925)
Rates: $49-$119
Tel: (915) 779-3300
(800) 228-9290

MOTEL 6
1330 Lomaland Dr
(79935)
Rates: $30-$36
Tel: (915) 592-6386
(800) 440-6000

MOTEL 6-CENTRAL
4800 Gateway Blvd
E (79905)
Rates: $32-$38
Tel: (915) 533-7521
(800) 440-6000

MOTEL 6-EAST
11049 Gateway Blvd
W (79935)
Rates: $29-$35
Tel: (915) 594-8533
(800) 440-6000

MOTEL 6-WEST
7840 N Mesa St
(79932)
Rates: $28-$34
Tel: (915) 584-2129
(800) 440-6000

PEAR TREE APARTMENTS
222 Bartlett (79912)
Rates: $44-$77
Tel: (915) 833-7327

QUALITY INN
6201 Gateway Blvd
W (79925)
Rates: $45-$50
Tel: (915) 778-6611
(800) 228-5151

ELGIN

RAGTIME RANCH BED & BREAKFAST
P. O. Box 575 (78621)
Rates: $95
Tel: (800) 899-4538

ENNIS

QUALITY INN
107 Wagon Wheel
Dr (75119)
Rates: $44-$59
Tel: (214) 875-9641
(800) 228-5151

EULESS

LA QUINTA INN-DFW AIRPORT WEST
1001 W Airport
Frwy (76040)
Rates: $49-$64
Tel: (817) 540-0233
(800) 531-5900

MOTEL 6-DFW AIRPORT
110 W Airport Frwy
(76039)
Rates: $26-$32
Tel: (817) 545-0141
(800) 440-6000

RAMADA INN-DFW WEST
2155 W Airport
Frwy (76040)
Rates: $50-$95
Tel: (817) 283-2400
(800) 272-6232

FALFURRIAS

DAYS INN
Hwy 281 S, Rt 2, Box
208-D (78355)
Rates: $42-$45
Tel: (512) 325-2515
(800) 329-7466

FARMERS BRANCH

BEST WESTERN OAK TREE INN
13333 N Stemmons
Frwy (75234)
Rates: $50+
Tel: (214) 241-8521
(800) 528-1234

DOUBLETREE AT PARK WEST
1590 LBJ Frwy
(75234)
Rates: $68-$99
Tel: (214) 869-4300
(800) 222-8733

ECONO LODGE DALLAS AIRPORT
2275 Valley View Ln
(75234)
Rates: $44+
Tel: (214) 243-5500
(800) 424-4777

LA QUINTA INN NORTHWEST
13235 N Stemmons
Frwy (75234)
Rates: $48-$66
Tel: (214) 620-7333
(800) 531-5900

FORT DAVIS

HISTORIC LIMPIA HOTEL
P. O. Box 822
On the Town Square
(79734)
Rates: $49-$65
Tel: (915) 426-3237
(800) 662-5517

FORT HANCOCK

FORT HANCOCK MOTEL
P. O. Box 250 (79839)
Rates: $35-$42
Tel: (915) 769-3981
(800) 553-4654

FORT STOCKTON

BEST WESTERN SWISS CLOCK INN
3201 W Dickinson
Blvd (79735)
Rates: $38-$52
Tel: (915) 336-8521
(800) 528-1234

COMFORT INN
3200 W Dickinson
Blvd (79735)
Rates: $29-$43
Tel: (915) 336-8531
(800) 221-2222

DAYS INN
1408 N Hwy 285
(79735)
Rates: $38-$59
Tel: (915) 336-7500
(800) 329-7466

ECONO LODGE
800 E Dickinson
Blvd (79735)
Rates: $38-$58
Tel: (915) 336-9711
(800) 424-4777

LA QUINTA INN
2601 I-10 W (79735)
Rates: $42-$61
Tel: (915) 336-9781
(800) 531-5900

MOTEL 6
3001 W Dickinson
Blvd (79735)
Rates: $26-$30
Tel: (915) 336-9737
(800) 440-6000

SANDS MOTEL
1801 W Dickinson
Blvd (79735)
Rates: $26-$30
Tel: (915) 336-2274

FORT WORTH

BEST WESTERN WEST BRANCH INN
7301 W Frwy (76116)
Rates: $38-$58
Tel: (817) 244-7444
(800) 528-1234

CARAVAN MOTOR HOTEL
P. O. Box 10128
(76114)
Rates: $28-$42
Tel: (817) 626-1951

COMFORT INN
2050 Beach St
(76103)
Rates: $54
Tel: (817) 535-2591
(800) 221-2222

DAYS INN
1010 Houston St
(76102)
Rates: $45-$75
Tel: (817) 336-2011
(800) 329-7466

DAYS INN WEST
8500 I-30 W &
Las Vegas Tr (76108)
Rates: $38-$48
Tel: (817) 246-4961
(800) 329-7466

GREEN OAKS INN & CONF.CENTER
6901 W Frwy (76116)
Rates: $61-$98
Tel: (817) 738-7311
(800) 433-2174
(800) 772-7341 (TX)

HAMPTON INN
4799 SW Loop 820
(76132)
Rates: $66-92
Tel: (817) 346-7845
(800) 426-7866

HOLIDAY INN S & CONF CENTER
100 Altamesa Blvd E
(76134)
Rates: $75-$80
Tel: (817) 293-3088
(800) 465-4329

LA QUINTA INN WEST
7888 I-30 W (76108)
Rates: $46-$57
Tel: (817) 246-5511
(800) 531-5900

MOTEL 6-EAST
1236 Oakland Blvd
(76103)
Rates: $27-$34
Tel: (817) 834-7361
(800) 440-6000

MOTEL 6-NORTH
3271 I-35 W (76106)
Rates: $26-$32
Tel: (817) 625-4359
(800) 440-6000

MOTEL 6-SOUTH
6600 S Frwy (76134)
Rates: $26-$32
Tel: (817) 293-8595
(800) 440-6000

MOTEL 6-SE
4433 S Frwy (76115)
Rates: $26-$32
Tel: (817) 921-4900
(800) 440-6000

MOTEL 6-WEST
8701 I-30 W (76116)
Rates: $26-$32
Tel: (817) 244-9740
(800) 440-6000

RADISSON PLAZA HOTEL
815 Main St (76102)
Rates: $79-$107
Tel: (817) 870-2100
(800) 333-3333

RAMADA HOTEL DOWNTOWN
1701 Commerce St
(76102)
Rates: $62-$84
Tel: (817) 335-7000
(800) 272-6232

**RAMADA INN-
MIDTOWN**
1401 S University Dr
(76107)
Rates: $50-$55
Tel: (817) 336-9311
(800) 272-6232

**RESIDENCE INN
BY MARRIOTT**
1701 S University Dr
(76107)
Rates: $95-$105
Tel: (817) 870-1011
(800) 331-3131

**ROYAL WESTERN
SUITES**
8401 I-30 W (76116)
Rates: $46-$52
Tel: (817) 560-0060

SUPER 8 MOTEL
7960 I-30 W (76108)
Rates: $40-$63
Tel: (817) 246-7168
(800) 800-8000

**WORTHINGTON
HOTEL**
200 Main St (76102)
Rates: $129-$159
Tel: (817) 870-1000
(800) 433-5677

FREDERICKS-
BURG

**ALFRED HAUS
BED & BREAKFAST**
231 W Main St
(78624)
Rates: $74+
Tel: (210) 997-5612

**ALLEGANI'S
LITTLE HORSE INN**
307 S Creek (78624)
Rates: $75-$95
Tel: (210) 997-7448

**BEST WESTERN
SUNDAY HOUSE
INN**
501 E Main St
(78624)
Rates: $54-$110
Tel: (210) 997-4484
(800) 528-1234

**BUDGET HOST
DELUXE INN**
901 E Main St
(78624)
Rates: $28-$60
Tel: (210) 997-3344
(800) 283-4678

COMFORT INN
908 S Adams St
(78624)
Rates: $54-$64
Tel: (210) 997-9811
(800) 228-5150

**COUNTRY INN
MOTEL**
Hwy 290 W (78624)
Rates: $35-$58
Tel: (210) 997-2185

DIETZEL MOTEL
909 W Main St (78624)
Rates: $32-$49
Tel: (210) 997-3330

ECONO LODGE
810 S Adams St
(78624)
Rates: $39-$59
Tel: (210) 997-3437
(800) 424-4777
(800) 553-2666 (TX)

**FREDERICKSBURG
INN & SUITES**
201 S Washington
(78624)
Rates: $59-$75
Tel: (210) 977-0202
(800) 446-0202

**FRONTIER INN
MOTEL**
Rt 2, Box 99 (78624)
Rates: $30+
Tel: (210) 997-4389

**THE GARDEN HOUSE
BED & BREAKFAST**
104 N Adams St
(78624)
Rates: $69
Tel: (210) 990-8455
(800) 745-3591

**MAGNOLIA HOUSE
BED & BREAKFAST**
101 E Hackberry
(78624)
Rates: $80-$110
Tel: (210) 997-0306

MILLER'S INN MOTEL
910 E Main St (78624)
Rates: $36-$50
Tel: (210) 997-2244

**MISS TOODLES INN
BED & BREAKFAST**
104 N Adams St
(78624)
Rates: $115+
Tel: (210) 990-8455
(800) 745-3591

PEACH TREE INN
401 S Washington
(78624)
Rates: $28-$66
Tel: (210) 997-2117
(800) 843-4666

**RIVER VIEW
INN & FARM**
Hwy 16 S (78624)
Rates: $55-$65
Tel: (210) 997-8555

**ROCK HOUSE
ON ACORN
BED & BREAKFAST**
231 W Main St
(78624)
Rates: $85+
Tel: (210) 997-5612

**ROCKY TOP
BED & BREAKFAST**
RR 965, Enchanted
Rock Rd (78624)
Rates: $70
Tel: (210) 997-8145

SAVE INN MOTEL
514 E Main St
(78624)
Rates: $43-$58
Tel: (210) 997-6568

**SCHMIDT BARN
BED & BREAKFAST**
231 W Main St
(78624)
Rates: $79+
Tel: (210) 997-5612

**SETTLERS CROSSING
HISTORIC GUEST
HOUSES**
Rt 1, Box 315 (78624)
Rates: $85-$119
Tel: (210) 997-2722
(800) 874-1020

**STONEWALL VALLEY
RANCH HOUSE**
104 N Adams St
(78624)
Rates: $85
Tel: (210) 990-8455
(800) 745-3591

**STRACKBEIN-ROEDER
SUNDAY HAUS
BED & BREAKFAST**
231 W Main St
(78624)
Rates: $100+
Tel: (210) 997-5612

SUNSET INN
900 S Adams St
(78624)
Rates: $32-$45
Tel: (210) 997-9581

**WATKINS HILL-
FREDERICKSBURG'S
GUEST HOUSE**
608 E Creek St
(78624)
Rates: $100-$225
Tel: (210) 997-6739
(800) 899-1672

**WEST MAIN HAUS
BED & BREAKFAST**
231 W Main St
(78624)
Rates: $75+
Tel: (210) 997-5612

**WOLF CREEK BARN
BED & BREAKFAST**
231 W Main St
(78624)
Rates: $98+
Tel: (210) 997-5612

FREEPORT

**COUNTRY HEARTH
INN**
1015 W 2nd at
Velasco (77541)
Rates: $46-$67
Tel: (409) 239-1602
(888) 443-2784

FULTON

**BAY FRONT
COTTAGES**
309 S Fulton Beach
Rd (78382)
Rates: $45-$54
Tel: (512) 729-6693

**BEST WESTERN
INN BY THE BAY**
3902 I-35 N (78358)
Rates: $39-$70
Tel: (512) 729-8351
(800) 528-1234

**HARBOR LIGHTS
COTTAGES**
108 Laurel (78358)
Rates: $41+
Tel: (512) 729-6770

KONTIKI BEACH RESORT MOTEL
2290 Fulton Beach Rd (78358)
Rates: $60-$65
Tel: (512) 729-4975
(800) 242-3407

REEF MOTEL
3rd & Broadway (78358)
Rates: $40+
Tel: (512) 729-6955

SPORTSMAN MANOR
4170 I-35 N (78358)
Rates: $36-$44
Tel: (512) 729-5331
(800) 224-6684

GAINESVILLE

BEST WESTERN SOUTH WINDS MOTEL
2103 I-35 N (76240)
Rates: $32-$39
Tel: (817) 665-7737
(800) 528-1234

BUDGET HOST
Rt 2, Box 120 (76240)
Rates: $32-$40
Tel: (817) 665-2856
(800) 283-4678

COMFORT INN
1936 I-35 N (76240)
Rates: $38-$45
Tel: (817) 665-5599
(800) 221-2222

DAYS INN
Rt 2, Box 13-A (76240)
Rates: $32-$42
Tel: (817) 665-5555
(800) 329-7466

HOLIDAY INN
600 Fair Park Blvd (76240)
Rates: $45-$50
Tel: (817) 665-8800
(800) 465-4329

GALVESTON

COMFORT INN
2300 Seawall Blvd (77550)
Rates: $35-$125
Tel: (409) 762-1166
(800) 221-2222

ECONO LODGE
2825 61st St (77551)
Rates: $30-$99
Tel: (409) 744-7133
(800) 424-4777

HILLTOP MOTEL
8828 Seawall Blvd (77554)
Rates: $35-$65
Tel: (409) 744-4423

LA QUINTA INN
1402 Seawall Blvd (77550)
Rates: $72-$109
Tel: (409) 763-1224
(800) 531-5900

MOTEL 6
7404 Ave J Broadway (77554)
Rates: $27-$42
Tel: (409) 740-3794
(800) 440-6000

GARLAND

DAYS INN-
6222 Beltline Rd (75043)
Rates: $40-$45
Tel: (214) 226-7621
(800) 329-7466

LA QUINTA INN
12721 I-635 (75041)
Rates: $43-$59
Tel: (214) 271-7581
(800) 531-5900

MOTEL 6
436 W I-30 & Beltline (75043)
Rates: $28-$32
Tel: (214) 226-7140
(800) 440-6000

GATESVILLE

BEST WESTERN CHATEAU VILLE MOTOR INN
2501 E Main St (76528)
Rates: $33-$47
Tel: (817) 865-2281
(800) 528-1234

GEORGETOWN

COMFORT INN
1005 Leander Rd (78628)
Rates: $39-$59
Tel: (512) 863-7504
(800) 221-2222

DAYS INN
209 I-35 N (78628)
Rates: $35-$65
Tel: (512) 863-5572
(800) 329-7466

LA QUINTA INN
333 I-35 N (78628)
Rates: $49-$65
Tel: (512) 869-2541
(800) 531-5900

GIDDINGS

BEST WESTERN CLASSIC INN
3556 E Austin (78942)
Rates: $35-$47
Tel: (409) 542-5791
(800) 528-1234

ECONO LODGE
Rt 3, Box 461 (78942)
Rates: $27-$39
Tel: (409) 542-9666
(800) 424-4777

GIDDINGS SANDS MOTEL
1600 E Austin (78942)
Rates: $31-$46
Tel: (409) 542-3111

GLEN ROSE

HIDEAWAY COUNTRY LOG CABIN BED & BREAKFAST
P. O. Box 430 (76043)
Rates: $70-$93
Tel: (817) 823-6606

GRAHAM

GATEWAY INN
1401 Hwy 16 S (76450)
Rates: $32-$39
Tel: (817) 549-0222

RODEWAY INN
1919 Hwy 16 S (76450)
Rates: $31-$44
Tel: (817) 549-8320
(800) 424-4777

GRANBURY

BEST WESTERN CLASSIC INN
1209 N Plaza Dr (76048)
Rates: $40-$64
Tel: (817) 573-8874
(800) 528-1234
(800) 523-5170 (TX)

DAYS INN OF GRANBURY
1339 N Plaza Dr (76048)
Rates: $59-$69
Tel: (817) 573-2691
(800) 329-7466
(800) 858-8607 (TX)

PLANTATION INN ON THE LAKE
1451 E Pearl St (76048)
Rates: $60-$75
Tel: (817) 573-8846
(800) 422-2402

GRAND PRAIRIE

HAMPTON INN DFW AIRPORT
2050 N Hwy 360 (75050)
Rates: $63-$69
Tel: (214) 988-8989
(800) 426-7866

LA QUINTA INN
1410 NW 19th St (75050)
Rates: $43-$78
Tel: (214) 641-3021
(800) 531-5900

MOTEL 6
406 E Safari Blvd (75050)
Rates: $29-$35
Tel: (214) 642-9424
(800) 440-6000

RAMADA INN
402 E Safari Blvd (75050)
Rates: $50-$75
Tel: (214) 263-4421
(800) 272-6232

GREENVILLE

**BEST WESTERN
INN & SUITES**
1216 I-30 W (75402)
Rates: $40-$45
Tel: (903) 454-1792
(800) 528-1234

BUDGET HOST INN
5118 I-30 & US 69
(75401)
Rates: $27-$42
Tel: (903) 455-8462
(800) 283-4678

HOLIDAY INN
1215 I-30 E (75401)
Rates: $41-$46
Tel: (903) 454-7000
(800) 465-4329

MOTEL 6
5109 I-30 & US 69
(75402)
Rates: $23-$29
Tel: (903) 455-0515
(800) 440-6000

ROYAL INN
I-30 & US 69 (75401)
Rates: $27-$40
Tel: (903) 455-9600

GROOM

CHALET INN
FM 2300 I-40 (79039)
Rates: $35-$40
Tel: (806) 248-7524
(800) 472-1122

GROVES

MOTEL 6
5201 E Pkwy (77619)
Rates: $24-$28
Tel: (409) 962-6611
(800) 440-6000

HAMILTON

**HAMILTON
GUEST HOTEL
BED & BREAKFAST**
109 N Rice (76351)
Rates: $49-$79
Tel: (817) 386-8977
(800) 876-2502

**VALUE LODGE INN
MOTEL**
Rt 3, Box 319 (76351)
Rates: $25-$40
Tel: (817) 386-8959

HARLINGEN

**BEST WESTERN
HARLINGEN INN**
6779 US 83 W
Expwy (78552)
Rates: $51-$65
Tel: (210) 425-7070
(800) 528-1234

DAYS INN
1901 W Tyler St
(78550)
Rates: $55-$81
Tel: (210) 425-1810
(800) 329-7466

LA QUINTA INN
1002 US 83 S Expwy
(78552)
Rates: $50-$65
Tel: (210) 428-6888
(800) 531-5900

MOTEL 6
224 US 77 S Expwy
(78550)
Rates: $30-$36
Tel: (210) 421-4200
(800) 440-6000

SUPER 8 MOTEL
1115 US 77 & 83 S
Expwy (78550)
Rates: $40-$60
Tel: (210) 412-8873
(800) 800-8000

HASKELL

**BEVERS HOUSE
ON BRICK ST
BED & BREAKFAST**
311 N Ave F (79521)
Rates: $50-$75
Tel: (817) 864-3284
(800) 580-3284

HEARNE

EXECUTIVE INN
Hwy 6 at FM 485
(77859)
Rates: $30-$55
Tel: (409) 279-5345

HEBBRONVILLE

**TEXAS EXECUTIVE
INN**
1302 N Smith (78361)
Rates: $36-$52
Tel: (512) 527-4082
(800) 870-7689

HENDERSON

**BEST WESTERN INN
OF HENDERSON**
1500 Hwy 259 S
(75652)
Rates: $40-$50
Tel: (903) 657-9561
(800) 528-1234

HEREFORD

**BEST WESTERN
RED CARPET INN**
830 W 1st St (79045)
Rates: $32-$48
Tel: (806) 364-0540
(800) 528-1234

HILLSBORO

**BEST WESTERN
HILLSBORO INN**
P. O. Box 632 (76645)
Rates: $38-$56
Tel: (817) 582-8465
(800) 528-1234

RAMADA INN
I-35 & Hwy 22
(76645)
Rates: $36-$51
Tel: (817) 582-3493
(800) 272-6232

HONDO

WHITETAIL LODGE
P. O. Box 110
Hwy 90 E (78861)
Rates: $42-$56
Tel: (210) 426-3031
(800) 375-4065

HOUSTON

COMFORT INN
715 Hwy 6 S (77079)
Rates: $55-$68
Tel: (713) 493-0444
(800) 221-2222

**COMFORT INN-
HOBBY AIRPORT**
9000 Airport Blvd
(77031)
Rates: $56-$72
Tel: (713) 943-0035
(800) 221-2222

DAYS INN
4640 S Main St
(77002)
Rates: $45-$89
Tel: (713) 523-3777
(800) 329-7466

DAYS INN-AIRPORT
17607 Eastex Frwy
(77396)
Rates: $39-$45
Tel: (713) 446-4611
(800) 329-7466

**DAYS INN-
ASTRODOME**
8500 Kirby Dr (77054)
Rates: $59-$72
Tel: (713) 796-8383
(800) 329-7466

**DAYS INN
HOUSTON NORTH**
9025 N Frwy (77037)
Rates: $37-$43
Tel: (713) 820-1500
(800) 329-7466

DAYS INN & SUITES
9041 Westheimer Rd
(77063)
Rates: $51-$165
Tel: (713) 783-1400
(800) 329-7466

DAYS INN-WEST
9799 Katy Frwy
(77024)
Rates: $47-$53
Tel: (713) 468-7801
(800) 329-7466

**DOUBLETREE
GUEST SUITES**
5353 Westheimer Rd
(77056)
Rates: $124-$154
Tel: (713) 961-9000
(800) 222-8733
(800) 772-7666 (TX)

**DOUBLETREE HOTEL
AT ALLEN CENTER**
400 Dallas St (77002)
Rates: $72-$160
Tel: (713) 759-0202
(800) 222-8733
(800) 772-7666 (TX)

DRURY INN
1615 W Loop 610 S
(77027)
Rates: $68-$83
Tel: (713) 963-0700
(800) 325-8300

**DRURY INN
HOUSTON HOBBY**
7902 Mosley Rd
(77017)
Rates: $62-$80
Tel: (713) 941-4300
(800) 325-8300

**DRURY INN
I-10 WEST**
1000 N Hwy 6
(77079)
Rates: $59-$82
Tel: (713) 558-7007
(800) 325-8300

**ECONO LODGE-
WEST**
9535 Katy Frwy
(77024)
Rates: $29-$44
Tel: (713) 467-4411
(800) 424-4777

FAIRFIELD INN
3131 W Loop S
(77027)
Rates: $66+
Tel: (713) 961-1690
(800) 228-2800

**FOUR SEASONS
HOTEL-
HOUSTON CENTER**
1300 Lamar St
(77010)
Rates: $90-$260
Tel: (713) 650-1300
(800) 332-3442

**HAMPTON INN
I-10 EAST**
828 Mercury Dr
(77013)
Rates: $52-$62
Tel: (713) 673-4200
(800) 426-7866

HAMPTON INN
10155 E Frwy
(77029)
Rates: $49-$55
Tel: (713) 675-2711
(800) 426-7866

HARVEY HOTEL
2712 Southwest
Frwy (77098)
Rates: $59-$114
Tel: (713) 523-8448
(800) 922-9222

**HAWTHORN SUITES
HOTEL**
6910 Southwest
Frwy (77074)
Rates: $109-$139
Tel: (713) 785-3415
(800) 527-1133

**HILTON
HOBBY AIRPORT**
8181 Airport Blvd
(77061)
Rates: $80-$134
Tel: (713) 645-3000
(800) 445-8667
(800) 695-2740 (TX)

**HILTON & TOWERS-
WESTCHASE**
9999 Westheimer Rd
(77042)
Rates: $82-$127
Tel: (713) 974-1000
(800) 445-8667

**HILTON-UNIVERSITY
CONF. CENTER**
4800 Calhoun Rd
(77004)
Rates: $79-$89
Tel: (713) 743-2610
(800) 445-8667

HOJO INN
4602 Katy Frwy
(77007)
Rates: $45-$55
Tel: (713) 861-9000
(800) 446-4656

**HOLIDAY INN-
GALLERIA**
7787 Katy Frwy
(77024)
Rates: $49-$81
Tel: (713) 681-5000
(800) 465-4329

**HOLIDAY INN-
HOBBY AIRPORT**
9100 Gulf Frwy
(77017)
Rates: $96-$116
Tel: (713) 943-7979
(800) 465-4329

**HOLIDAY INN
HOUSTON AIRPORT**
15222 JFK Blvd (77032)
Rates: $83+
Tel: (713) 449-2311
(800) 465-4329

**HOLIDAY INN
MEDICAL CENTER**
6701 S Main St
(77030)
Rates: $65-$70
Tel: (713) 797-1110
(800) 465-4329

**HOWARD JOHNSON
HOBBY AIRPORT**
7777 Airport Blvd
(77061)
Rates: $56+
Tel: (713) 644-1261
(800) 446-4656

**HOWARD JOHNSON
LODGE-CENTER**
4225 N Freeway
(77022)
Rates: $42-$58
Tel: (713) 695-6011
(800) 446-4656

**HYATT REGENCY
HOUSTON**
1200 Louisiana St
(77002)
Rates: $150-$206
Tel: (713) 654-1234
(800) 233-1234

**INTERSTATE
MOTOR LODGE**
13213 I-10 E (77015)
Rates: $31-$40
Tel: (713) 453-6353

**J W MARRIOTT
HOUSTON**
5150 Westheimer Rd
(77056)
Rates: $139-$149
Tel: (713) 961-1500
(800) 231-6058

**THE LANCASTER
HISTORIC HOTEL**
701 Texas at
Louisiana (77002)
Rates: $95-$185
Tel: (713) 228-9500
(800) 231-0336

**LA QUINTA INN-
ASTRODOME**
9911 Buffalo
Speedway (77054)
Rates: $56-$82
Tel: (713) 668-8082
(800) 531-5900

**LA QUINTA INN-
AIRPORT**
6 N Belt E (77060)
Rates: $53-$66
Tel: (713) 447-6888
(800) 531-5900

**LA QUINTA INN-
LOOP 1960**
17111 N Frwy
(77090)
Rates: $52-$74
Tel: (713) 444-7500
(800) 531-5900

**LA QUINTA INN-
BROOKHOLLOW**
11002 Northwest
Frwy (77092)
Rates: $53-$64
Tel: (713) 688-2581
(800) 531-5900

**LA QUINTA INN-
CY FAIR**
13290 FM 1960W
(77065)
Rates: $57-$72
Tel: (713) 469-4018
(800) 531-5900

**LA QUINTA INN
GREENWAY PLAZA**
4015 Southwest
Frwy (77027)
Rates: $61-$76
Tel: (713) 623-4750
(800) 531-5900

**LA QUINTA INN
HOBBY AIRPORT**
9902 Gulf Frwy
(77034)
Rates: $60-$75
Tel: (713) 941-0900
(800) 531-5900

**LA QUINTA INN-
EAST**
11999 E Frwy (77029)
Rates: $52-$66
Tel: (713) 453-5425
(800) 531-5900

**LA QUINTA INN
SHARPSTOWN**
8201 Southwest
Frwy (77074)
Rates: $55-$70
Tel: (713) 772-3626
(800) 531-5900

LA QUINTA INN-SOUTHWEST FRWY/BELTWAY
10552 Southwest Frwy (77074)
Rates: $50-$64
Tel: (713) 270-9559
(800) 531-5900

LA QUINTA INN-WEST
11113 Katy Frwy (77079)
Rates: $57-$72
Tel: (713) 932-0808
(800) 531-5900

LA QUINTA INN-WIRT RD
8017 Katy Frwy (77024)
Rates: $54-$67
Tel: (713) 688-8941
(800) 531-5900

THE LOVETT INN-HISTORIC BED & BREAKFAST
501 Lovett Blvd (77006)
Rates: $75-$150
Tel: (713) 522-5224
(800) 779-5224

MARRIOTT NORTH AT GREENSPOINT
255 N Sam Houston Pkwy E (77060)
Rates: $59-$119
Tel: (713) 875-4000
(800) 228-9290

MARRIOTT-WEST LOOP-BY THE GALLERIA
1750 W Loop S (77027)
Rates: $89-$139
Tel: (713) 960-0111
(800) 228-9290

MARRIOTT WESTSIDE
13210 Katy Frwy (77079)
Rates: $119-$130
Tel: (713) 558-8338
(800) 228-9290

MEDALLION HOTEL HOUSTON
3000 N Loop W (77092)
Rates: $105-$115
Tel: (713) 688-0100
(800) 688-3000

MOTEL 6
16884 Northwest Frwy (77040)
Rates: $33-$40
Tel: (713) 937-7056
(800) 440-6000

MOTEL 6
14833 Katy Frwy (77094)
Rates: $32-$43
Tel: (713) 497-5000
(800) 440-6000

MOTEL 6
5555 W 34th St (77092)
Rates: $31-$43
Tel: (713) 682-8588
(800) 440-6000

MOTEL 6-ASTRODOME
3223 S Loop W (77025)
Rates: $32-$38
Tel: (713) 664-6425
(800) 440-6000

MOTEL 6-SOUTHEAST
8800 Airport Blvd (77061)
Rates: $33-$39
Tel: (713) 941-0990
(800) 440-6000

MOTEL 6-SOUTHWEST
9638 Plainfield Rd (77036)
Rates: $31-$37
Tel: (713) 778-0008
(800) 440-6000

OMNI HOUSTON
4 Riverway (77056)
Rates: $130-$150
Tel: (713) 871-8181
(800) 843-6664

QUALITY INN-AIRPORT
6115 Will Clayton Pkwy (77205)
Rates: $59-$79
Tel: (713) 446-9131
(800) 221-2222
(800) 231-6134 (TX)

QUALITY INN-NASA
904 NASA Rd One (77058)
Rates: $58+
Tel: (713) 333-3737
(800) 221-2222

RADISSON SUITE HOTEL HOUSTON
1400 Old Spanish Tr (77054)
Rates: $62+
Tel: (713) 796-1000
(800) 333-3333

RAMADA HOTEL ASTRODOME
2100 S Braeswood Blvd (77030)
Rates: $65-$79
Tel: (713) 797-9000
(800) 272-6232

RAMADA INN SOUTH/NASA
1301 NASA Rd One (77058)
Rates: $78-$87
Tel: (713) 488-0220
(800) 272-6232
(800) 255-7345 (TX)

RAMADA LIMITED 1960
15725 Bammel Village Dr (77014)
Rates: $48-$52
Tel: (713) 893-5224
(800) 272-6232
(800) 201-3201 (TX)

RAMADA PLAZA HOTEL
12801 Northwest Frwy (77040)
Rates: $78-$88
Tel: (713) 462-9977
(800) 272-6232

RED ROOF INN HOBBY
9005 Airport Blvd (77061)
Rates: $69-$89
Tel: (713) 943-3300
(800) 843-7663

RESIDENCE INN BY MARRIOTT-ASTRODOME
7710 S Main St (77030)
Rates: $62-$160
Tel: (713) 660-7993
(800) 331-3131

RESIDENCE INN BY MARRIOTT-GALLERIA
2500 McCue (77056)
Rates: $99-$129
Tel: (713) 840-9757
(800) 331-3131

RESIDENCE INN HOUSTON CLEAR LAKE
525 Bay Area Blvd (77058)
Rates: $79-$140
Tel: (713) 486-2424
(800) 331-3131

ROBIN'S NEST BED & BREAKFAST INN
4104 Greeley (77006)
Rates: $65-$110
Tel: (713) 528-5821
(800) 622-8343

RODEWAY INN-SW FREEWAY
3135 Southwest Frwy (77098)
Rates: $40-$54
Tel: (713) 526-1071
424-4777

SHONEY'S INN-ASTRODOME
2364 SouthLoop W (77054)
Rates: n/a
Tel: (713) 799-2436
(800) 222-2222

SHONEY'S INN
12323 Katy Frwy (77079)
Rates: n/a
Tel: (713) 493-5626
(800) 222-2222

SHONEY'S INN
14444 SW Frwy (77487)
Rates: n/a
Tel: (713) 565-6655
(800) 222-2222

SHERATON GRAND HOTEL
2525 W Loop S (77027)
Rates: $136-$169
Tel: (713) 961-3000
(800) 325-3535

STOUFFER RENAISSANCE HOUSTON
6 Greenway Plaza E (77046)
Rates: $79-$169
Tel: (713) 629-1200
(800) 468-3571

TRAVELODGE
4204 Hwy 6 N (77084)
Rates: $35-$40
Tel: (713) 859-2233
(800) 578-7878

**TRAVELODGE
FM 1960**
4726 FM 1960 W
(77069)
Rates: $45-$51
Tel: (713) 587-9171
(800) 578-7878

**THE WESTIN
GALLERIA**
5060 W Alabama St
(77056)
Rates: $90-$140
Tel: (713) 960-8100
(800) 228-3000

WESTIN OAKS
5011 Westheimer
(77056)
Rates: $183-218
Tel: (713) 960-8100
(800) 228-3000

HUNTSVILLE

ECONO LODGE
1501 I-45 N (77340)
Rates: $30-$36
Tel: (409) 295-6401
(800) 424-4777

MOTEL 6
1607 I-45 N (77340)
Rates: $27-$33
Tel: (409) 291-6927
(800) 440-6000

**PARK INN
INTERNATIONAL**
1407 I-45 N (77340)
Rates: $42-$57
Tel: (409) 295-6454
(800) 437-7275

RODEWAY INN
3211 I-45 S, Exit 114
(77340)
Rates: $32-$79
Tel: (409) 295-7595
(800) 424-4777
(800) 228-2000 (TX)

SAM HOUSTON INN
3296 I-45 S, Exit 114
(77340)
Rates: $44-$54
Tel: (409) 295-9151
(800) 395-9151

INGRAM

**HUNTER HOUSE
MOTOR INN**
310 Hwy 39 W
(78025)
Rates: $44-$99
Tel: (210) 367-2377
(800) 655-2377

IRVING

**COMFORT INN
DFW AIRPORT**
8205 Esters Blvd
(75063)
Rates: $55+
Tel: (214) 929-0066
(800) 221-2222

**DAYS INN
TEXAS STADIUM**
2200 E Airport Frwy
(75062)
Rates: $45-$62
Tel: (214) 438-6666
(800) 329-7466

**DRURY INN-
DFW AIRPORT**
4210 W Airport
Frwy (75062)
Rates: $65-$71
Tel: (214) 986-1200
(800) 325-8300

**FOUR SEASONS
RESORT & CLUB**
4150 N MacArthur
Blvd (75038)
Rates: $150-$290
Tel: (214) 717-0700
(800) 332-3442

HAMPTON INN-DFW
4340 W Airport
Frwy (75061)
Rates: $65-$85
Tel: (214) 986-3606
(800) 426-7866

**HARVEY HOTEL-
DFW AIRPORT**
4545 W John
Carpenter Frwy
(75063)
Rates: $69-$164
Tel: (214) 929-4500
(800) 922-9222

HARVEY SUITES
4550 W John
Carpenter Frwy
(75063)
Rates: $79-$144
Tel: (214) 929-4499
(800) 922-9222

**HOMEWOOD
SUITES
LAS COLINAS**
4300 Wingren Rd
(75039)
Rates: $69-$150
Tel: (214) 556-0665
(800) 225-5466

IRVING INN SUITES
909 W Airport Frwy
(75062)
Rates: $30-$50
Tel: (214) 255-7108

**LA QUINTA INN
DFW AIRPORT**
4105 W Airport
Frwy (75062)
Rates: $52-$68
Tel: (214) 252-6546
(800) 531-5900

MOTEL 6
510 S Loop 12
(75060)
Rates: $28-$34
Tel: (214) 438-4227
(800) 440-6000

**OMNI MANDALAY
HOTEL-LAS COLINAS**
221 E Las Colinas
Blvd (75039)
Rates: $89-$180
Tel: (214) 556-0800
(800) 843-6664

**RED ROOF INN-
DFW AIRPORT**
8150 Esters Blvd
(75063)
Rates: $40-$59
Tel: (214) 929-0020
(800) 843-7663

**RED ROOF INN-
DFW SOUTH**
2611 W Airport
Frwy (75062)
Rates: $38-$54
Tel: (214) 570-7500
(800) 843-7663

**RESIDENCE INN
BY MARRIOTT**
950 Walnut Hill Ln
(75038)
Rates: $75-$160
Tel: (214) 580-7773
(800) 331-3131

**SHERATON
GRAND HOTEL**
4440 W Carpenter
Frwy (75261)
Rates: $120-$140
Tel: (214) 929-8400
(800) 325-3535
(800) 345-5251 (TX)

SKYWAY INN
110 W Airport Frwy
(75062)
Rates: $30-$50
Tel: (214) 438-2000

SUITES INN
1701 W Airport
Frwy (75062)
Rates: $30-$50
Tel: (214) 255-1133

**WILSON WORLD
MOTOR HOTEL**
4600 W Airport
Frwy (75062)
Rates: $72-$130
Tel: (214) 513-0800
(800) 333-9457

JACKSBORO

JACKSBORO INN
704 S Main St
(76458)
Rates: $30-$38
Tel: (817) 567-3751

JACKSONVILLE

**BEST WESTERN INN
OF JACKSONVILLE**
1407 E Rusk St
(75766)
Rates: $42-$56
Tel: (903) 586-9842
(800) 528-1234

JASPER

**BEST WESTERN
INN OF JASPER**
205 W Gibson (75951)
Rates: $45-$49
Tel: (409) 384-7767
(800) 528-1234

RAMADA INN
239 E Gibson (75951)
Rates: $54-$75
Tel: (409) 384-9021
(800) 272-6232

JEFFERSON

BEST WESTERN INN
400 S Walcott (75657)
Rates: $46-$100
Tel: (903) 665-3983
(800) 528-1234

JOHNSON CITY

**DREAM CATCHER
BED & BREAKFAST**
Rt 1, Box 345 (78636)
Rates: $60-$85
Tel: (210) 868-4875

SAVE INN MOTEL
107 Hwy 281 & 290 S
(78636)
Rates: $36-$55
Tel: (210) 868-4044

JUNCTION

CAROUSEL INN
1908 Main St (76849)
Rates: $24-$38
Tel: (915) 446-3301

DAYS INN
111 St. Martinez St
(76849)
Rates: $45-$60
Tel: (915) 446-3730
(800) 329-7466

THE HILLS MOTEL
1520 Main St (76849)
Rates: $27-$36
Tel: (915) 446-2567

LA VISTA MOTEL
2040 N Main St
(76849)
Rates: $26-$34
Tel: (915) 446-2191

KATY

**BEST WESTERN
HOUSTON WEST INN**
22455 I-10 W (77450)
Rates: $45-$52
Tel: (713) 392-9800
(800) 528-1234

SUPER 8 MOTEL
22157 Katy Frwy
(77450)
Rates: $40-$50
Tel: (713) 395-5757
(800) 800-8000

KERRVILLE

**BEST WESTERN
SUNDAY HOUSE INN**
2124 Sidney Baker St
(78028)
Rates: $59-$98
Tel: (210) 896-1313
(800) 528-1234
(800) 677-9477 (TX)

**DIETERT HAUS
BED & BREAKFAST**
710 Mockingbird
(78028)
Rates: $80
Tel: (210) 895-2235

FLAGSTAFF INN
906 Junction Hwy
(78028)
Rates: $40+
Tel: (210) 792-4449

HILLCREST INN
1508 Sidney Baker St
(78028)
Rates: $34-$58
Tel: (210) 896-7400

**HOLIDAY INN-Y.O.
RANCH HOTEL &
CONF CENTER**
2033 Sidney Baker St
(78028)
Rates: $65-$100
Tel: (210) 257-4440
(800) 465-4329
(800) 531-2800 (TX)

**INN OF THE HILLS
RIVER RESORT**
1001 Junction Hwy
(78028)
Rates: $50-$85
Tel: (210) 895-5000
(800) 292-5690

**LA REATA RANCH
BED & BREAKFAST**
225 Junction Hwy
(78028)
Rates: $75
Tel: (210) 896-5503

**RAMADA HILL
COUNTRY INN**
2127 Sidney Baker St
(78028)
Rates: $36-$46
Tel: (210) 896-1511
(800) 272-6232

SAVE INN MOTEL
1804 Sidney Baker St
(78028)
Rates: $28-$59
Tel: (210) 896-8200
(800) 219-8158

SHONEY'S INN
2145 Sidney Baker St
(78028)
Rates: $32-$55
Tel (210) 896-1711
(800) 222-2222
(800) 225-1374 (TX)

KILGORE

RAMADA INN
3501 Hwy 259 N
(75662)
Rates: $40-$66
Tel: (903) 983-3456
(800) 272-6232

KILLEEN

LA QUINTA INN
1112 S Ft Hood St
(76541)
Rates: $44-$57
Tel: (817) 526-8331
(800) 531-5900

RAMADA INN
1100 S Ft Hood St
(76541)
Rates: $40-$51
Tel: (817) 634-3101
(800) 272-6232

KINGSVILLE

**B BAR B RANCH
BED & BREAKFAST**
Rt 1, Box 457 (78363)
Rates: $75-$100
Tel: (512) 296-3331

**BEST WESTERN
KINGSVILLE INN**
2402 E King Ave
(78363)
Rates: $45-$55
Tel: (512) 595-5656
(800) 528-1234

COMFORT INN
2502 E Kennedy
(78363)
Rates: $34-$39
Tel: (512) 595-7000
(800) 221-2222

HOWARD JOHNSON
105 Hwy 77 (78363)
Rates: $48-$55
Tel: (512) 592-6471
(800) 446-4656

**LA CUPULA
MOTOR INN**
3430 Hwy 77 S
(78363)
Rates: $40-$45
Tel: (512) 595-5753

MOTEL CARBY
1415 S 14th St
(78363)
Rates: $24-$30
Tel: (512) 592-5214

MOTEL 6
101 Hwy 77 N
(78363)
Rates: $26-$30
Tel: (512) 592-5106
(800) 440-6000

MOTEL 77
716 S 14th St (78363)
Rates: $23-$30
Tel: (512) 592-4322

QUALITY INN
221 Hwy 77 S
Bypass (78363)
Rates: $47-$95
Tel: (512) 592-5251
(800) 221-2222

KOUNTZE

**LITTLE HOUSE
ON TIMBER RIDGE**
Hwy 92 & Hwy
1943, P. O. Box 115
(77625)
Rates: $75+
Tel: (409) 246-3107

LA GRANGE

**NORTHPOINTE
EXECUTIVE SUITES**
202 Northpointe Ave
(78945)
Rates: $42-$55
Tel: (409) 968-6406

LA PORTE

LA QUINTA INN
1105 Hwy 146 S
(77571)
Rates: $58-$74
Tel: (713) 470-0760
(800) 531-5900

LAKE JACKSON

**BEST WESTERN
LAKE JACKSON INN**
915 Hwy 332 W
(77566)
Rates: $45-$50
Tel: (409) 297-3031
(800) 528-1234

RAMADA INN
925 Hwy 332 W
(77566)
Rates: $68-$92
Tel: (409) 297-1161
(800) 272-6232
(800) 544-2119 (TX)

LAKE LBJ

**TROPICAL HIDEAWAY
BEACH RESORT**
604 Highcrest Dr
(78654)
Rates: $85-$250
Tel: (210) 598-9896
(800) 662-4431

LAMAR

SEA GUN RESORT
5868 I-35 N (77710)
Rates: $40-$82
Tel: (512) 729-3292
(800) 224-2232

LAMESA

SHILOH INN
1707 Lubbock Hwy
(79331)
Rates: $35-$44
Tel: (806) 872-6721
(800) 222-2244

LAMPASAS

CIRCLE MOTEL
1502 S Key Ave
(76550)
Rates: $40-$52
Tel: (512) 556-6201
(800) 521-5417

SARATOGA MOTEL
1408 S Key Ave
(76550)
Rates: $30-$60
Tel: (512) 556-6244

LAREDO

**BEST WESTERN
FIESTA INN**
5240 San Bernardo
Ave (78040)
Rates: $49-$64
Tel: (210) 723-3603
(800) 528-1234

**FAMILY GARDENS
INN**
5830 San Bernardo
Ave (78041)
Rates: $48-$55
Tel: (210) 723-5300
(800) 292-4053

**HOLIDAY INN ON
THE RIO GRANDE**
1 S Main Ave (78040)
Rates: $59-$110
Tel: (210) 722-2411
(800) 465-4329

LA QUINTA INN
3610 Santa Ursula
Ave (78041)
Rates: $58-$77
Tel: (210) 722-0511
(800) 531-5900

MOTEL 6-NORTH
5920 San Bernardo
Ave (78041)
Rates: $33-$39
Tel: (210) 722-8133
(800) 440-6000

MOTEL-SOUTH
5310 San Bernardo
Ave (78041)
Rates: $32-$38
Tel: (210) 725-8187
(800) 440-6000

LEAGUE CITY

**SOUTH SHORE
HARBOUR RESORT**
2500 S Shore Blvd
(77573)
Rates: $115-$155
Tel: (713) 344-1000
(800) 442-5005

LEAKEY

**WHISKEY
MOUNTAIN INN
BED & BREAKFAST**
HCR 1, Box 555
(78873)
Rates: $50-$80
Tel: (210) 232-6797
(800) 370-6797

LEWISVILLE

COMFORT SUITES
755A Vista Ridge
Mall Dr (75067)
Rates: $64-$89
Tel: (214) 315-6464
(800) 220-5150

**COUNTRY INN &
SUITES**
755 Vista Ridge
Mall Dr (75067)
Rates: $50-$60
Tel: (214) 315-6565
(800) 456-4000

DAYS INN
1401 S Stemmons
Frwy (75067)
Rates: $40-$46
Tel: (214) 436-0080
(800) 329-7466

LA QUINTA INN
1657 N Stemmons
Frwy (75067)
Rates: $40-$54
Tel: (214) 221-7525
(800) 531-5900

LITTLEFIELD

**CRESCENT PARK
MOTEL**
2000 Hall Ave
(79339)
Rates: $35-$45
Tel: (806) 385-4464
(800) 658-9960

LIVINGSTON

ECONO LODGE
117 Hwy 59 at Hwy
190 (77351)
Rates: $33-$35
Tel: (409) 327-2451
(800) 424-4777

**PARK INN
INTERNATIONAL**
2500 Hwy 59 S
(77351)
Rates: $34-$40
Tel: (409) 327-2525
(800) 437-7275

LLANO

**THE BADU HOUSE
HISTORIC BED &
BREAKFAST**
601 Bessemer St
(78643)
Rates: $55-$65
Tel: (915) 247-4304

**BEST WESTERN
CLASSIC INN**
901 W Young St
(78643)
Rates: $40-$48
Tel: (915) 247-4101
(800) 528-1234

LOCKHART

**BEST WESTERN
PLUM CREEK**
2001 Hwy 183 S
(78644)
Rates: $42-$61
Tel: (512) 398-4911
(800) 528-1234

LOCKHART INN
1207 Hwy 183 S
(78644)
Rates: $25-$34
Tel: (512) 398-5201

LONGVIEW

COMFORT SUITES
3307 N 4th St (75605)
Rates: $49-$125
Tel: (903) 663-4991
(800) 228-5150

DAYS INN OF LONGVIEW
3103 Estes Pkwy
(75602)
Rates: $45
Tel: (903) 758-1113
(800) 329-7466

ECONO LODGE
3120 Estes Pkwy
(75607)
Rates: $36-$39
Tel: (903) 753-4884
(800) 424-4777

FAIRFIELD INN BY MARRIOTT
3305 N 4th St (75605)
Rates: $52-$58
Tel: (903) 663-1995
(800) 228-2800

HAMPTON INN
112 S Access Rd
(75603)
Rates: $62-$66
Tel: (903) 758-0959
(800) 426-7866

HOLIDAY INN
3119 Estes Pkwy
(75602)
Rates: $59-$79
Tel: (903) 758-0700
(800) 465-4329

LA QUINTA INN
502 S Access Rd
(75602)
Rates: $57-$80
Tel: (903) 757-3663
(800) 531-5900

LONGVIEW INN
605 Access Rd
(75602)
Rates: $40-$55
Tel: (903) 753-0350
(800) 733-1139

MOTEL 6
110 W Access Rd
(75603)
Rates: $26-$30
Tel: (903) 758-5256
(800) 440-6000

SUPER 8 MOTEL
3304 S Eastman Rd
(75602)
Rates: $38-$60
Tel: (903) 758-5199
(800) 800-8000

LUBBOCK

BEST WESTERN LUBBOCK REGENCY
6624 I-27 (79404)
Rates: $58-$73
Tel: (806) 745-2208
(800) 528-1234
(800) 588-5677 (TX)

HAMPTON INN
4003 Loop 289 S
(79401)
Rates: $56-$95
Tel: (806) 795-1080
(800) 426-7866

HOLIDAY INN CIVIC CENTER
801 Ave Q (79401)
Rates: $70-$95
Tel: (806) 763-1200
(800) 465-4329

HOLIDAY INN-LUBBOCK PLAZA HOTEL
3201 Loop 289 S
(79423)
Rates: $75-$89
Tel: (806) 797-3241
(800) 465-4329

MOTEL 6
909 66th St (79412)
Rates: $27-$33
Tel: (806) 745-5541
(800) 440-6000

RESIDENCE INN BY MARRIOTT
2551 Loop 289 S
(79423)
Rates: $95-$125
Tel: (806) 745-1963
(800) 331-3131

SHERATON INN
505 Ave Q (79401)
Rates: $69-$79
Tel: (806) 747-0171
(800) 325-3535

SUPER 8 MOTEL
5410 I-27 (79412)
Rates: $46-$70
Tel: (806) 762-8400
(800) 800-8000

SUPER 8 MOTEL
501 Ave Q (79401)
Rates: $44-$50
Tel: (806) 762-8726
(800) 800-8000

LUCKENBACH

THE LUCKENBACH INN BED & BREAKFAST
HC 13, Box 9 (78624)
Rates: $95-$125
Tel: (210) 997-2205
(800) 997-1124

LUFKIN

BEST WESTERN EXPO INN
4200 N Medford Dr
(75901)
Rates: $39-$47
Tel: (409) 632-7300
(800) 528-1234

DAYS INN
2130 S 1st St (75901)
Rates: $41-$49
Tel: (409) 639-3301
(800) 329-7466

HOLIDAY HOUSE MOTEL
308 N Timberland Dr (75901)
Rates: $22-$28
Tel: (409) 634-6626

HOLIDAY INN
4306 S 1st St (75901)
Rates: $40-$65
Tel: (409) 639-3333
(800) 465-4329

LA QUINTA INN
2119 S 1st St (75901)
Rates: $48-$63
Tel: (409) 634-3351
(800) 531-5900

MOTEL 6
1110 S Timberland Dr (75901)
Rates: $24-$28
Tel: (409) 637-7850
(800) 440-6000

LYTLE

BEST WESTERN LA VILLA
19525 McDonald St
(78052)
Rates: $44-$69
Tel: (210) 772-4777
(800) 528-1234

MADISONVILLE

BEST WESTERN OF MADISONVILLE
3305 E Main (77864)
Rates: $37-$46
Tel: (409) 348-3606
(800) 528-1234

MANSFIELD

DAYS INN
1560 E Broad St
(76063)
Rates: $34-$49
Tel: (817) 473-6118
(800) 329-7466

MARATHON

THE GAGE HOTEL
102 Hwy 90 W
(79842)
Rates: $40-$60
Tel: (915) 386-4205
(800) 884-4243

MARBLE FALLS

BEST WESTERN MARBLE FALLS INN
1403 Hwy 281
(78654)
Rates: $49-$68
Tel: (210) 693-5122
(800) 528-1234

MARSHALL

BEST WESTERN OF MARSHALL
5555 E End Blvd S
(75670)
Rates: $46-$56
Tel: (903) 935-1941
(800) 528-1234

ECONOMY INN
6002 E End Blvd S
(75670)
Rates: $30-$36
Tel: (903) 935-1184
(800) 826-0778

LA MAISON MALFACON COUNTRY INN
700 E Rusk St
(75670)
Rates: $45-$60
Tel: (903) 938-3600

**MEREDITH HOUSE
BED & BREAKFAST**
410 E Meredith St
(75670)
Rates: $40-$80
Tel: (903) 935-7147

MOTEL 6
300 I-20 E (75670)
Rates: $25-$29
Tel: (903) 935-4393
(800) 440-6000

RAMADA INN
5301 E End Blvd S
(75670)
Rates: $48-$57
Tel: (903) 938-9261
(800) 272-6232

MATHIS

**MATHIS
MOTOR INN
& RV PARK**
1223 N Front St
(78368)
Rates: $27-$36
Tel: (512) 547-3272
(800) 251-7531

McALLEN

**CASA DE PALMAS
DOUBLETREE**
101 Main St (78501)
Rates: $62-$99
Tel: (210) 653-1101
(800) 274-1102

DRURY INN
612 W Expwy 83
(78501)
Rates: $59-$85
Tel: (210) 687-5100
(800) 325-8300

HAMPTON INN
300 W Expwy 83
(78501)
Rates: $59-$85
Tel: (210) 682-4900
(800) 426-7866

**HOLIDAY INN
AIRPORT**
2000 S 10th St
(78502)
Rates: $56-$72
Tel: (210) 686-1741
(800) 465-4329

LA QUINTA INN
1100 S 10th St
(78501)
Rates: $51-$69
Tel: (210) 687-1101
(800) 531-5900

MOTEL 6
700 Hwy 83 Expwy
(78501)
Rates: $24-$30
Tel: (210) 687-3700
(800) 440-6000

RODEWAY INN
1421 S 10th St
(78501)
Rates: $36-$50
Tel: (210) 686-1586
(800) 424-4777

THRIFTY INN
620 Hwy 83 Expwy
(78501)
Rates: $40-$55
Tel: (210) 631-6700

McKINNEY

COMFORT INN
2104 N Central
Expwy (75070)
Rates: $37-$47
Tel: (214) 548-8888
(800) 221-2222

WOODS MOTEL
1431 N Tennessee St
(75070)
Rates: $30-$41
Tel: (214) 542-4469

MEMPHIS

**BEST WESTERN
DE VILLE MOTEL**
Hwy 287 N (79245)
Rates: $42-$52
Tel: (806) 259-3583
(800) 528-1234

MERCEDES

DAYS INN
Mile 2 W &
Expwy 83 (78570)
Rates: $44-$64
Tel: (210) 565-3121
(800) 329-7466

MESQUITE

DAYS INN
3601 Hwy 80 E
(75150)
Rates: $32-$40
Tel: (214) 279-6561
(800) 329-7466

MOTEL 6
3629 Hwy 80 E
(75150)
Rates: $26-$30
Tel: (214) 613-1662
(800) 440-6000

MIDLAND

BEST WESTERN INN
3100 W Wall St
(79701)
Rates: $48-$56
Tel: (915) 699-4144
(800) 528-1234

DAYS INN
4714 W Hwy 80
(79703)
Rates: $27-$32
Tel: (915) 699-7727
(800) 329-7466

HAMPTON INN
3904 W Wall St
(79703)
Rates: $45-$51
Tel: (915) 694-7774
(800) 426-7866

HILTON HOTEL
117 W Wall St
(79701)
Rates: $79-$99
Tel: (915) 683-6131
(800) 445-8667 (800)
722-6131 (TX)

**HOLIDAY INN
COUNTRY VILLA**
4300 W Wall St
(79703)
Rates: $54-$159
Tel: (915) 697-3181
(800) 465-4329

LA QUINTA INN
4130 W Wall St
(79703)
Rates: $45-$57
Tel: (915) 697-9900
(800) 531-5900

**LEXINGTON HOTEL
SUITES**
1003 S Midkiff Rd
(79701)
Rates: $44-$60
Tel: (915) 697-3155

MOTEL 6
1000 S Midkiff Rd
(79701)
Rates: $23-$27
Tel: (915) 697-3197
(800) 440-6000

**RAMADA INN
AIRPORT**
100 S Airport Plaza
Dr (79711)
Rates: $45-$50
Tel: (915) 561-8000
(800) 272-6232

SUPER 8 MOTEL
1000 I-20 W (79701)
Rates: $29-$39
Tel: (915) 684-8888
(800) 800-8000

MIDLOTHIAN

**BEST WESTERN
MIDLOTHIAN INN**
220 N Hwy 67
(76065)
Rates: $37-$50
Tel: (214) 775-1891
(800) 528-1234

MINERAL WELLS

DAYS INN
3701 E Hubbard
(76067)
Rates: $40-$49
Tel: (817) 325-6961
(800) 329-7466

HOJO INN
2809 Hwy 180 W
(76067)
Rates: $42-$55
Tel: (817) 328-1111
(800) 446-4656

**12 OAKS INN
MOTEL**
4103 Hwy 180 E
(76067)
Rates: $38-$42
Tel: (817) 325-6956

MISSION

MISSION INN
1786 W Hwy 83
(78572)
Rates: $46
Tel: (210) 581-7451

MONAHANS

BEST WESTERN COLONIAL INN
702 I-20 W (79756)
Rates: $39-$46
Tel: (915) 943-4345
(800) 528-1234

MOUNT PLEASANT

DAYS INN
2501 W Ferguson
(75455)
Rates: $45-$59
Tel: (903) 577-0152
(800) 329-7466

LAKEWOOD MOTEL
2214 Lakewood Dr
(75455)
Rates: $27-$35
Tel: (903) 572-9808

TANKERSLEY GARDENS BED & BREAKFAST
Rt 7, Box 696 (85455)
Rates: $45-$110
Tel: (903) 572-0567

MOUNTAIN HOME

Y. O. RANCH
Hwy 41 W (78058)
Rates: $65-$95
Tel: (210) 640-3222
(800) 967-2624

MULESHOE

HERITAGE HOUSE INN
2301 W American
Blvd (79347)
Rates: $40-$50
Tel: (806) 272-7575
(800) 253-5896

NACOGDOCHES

BEST WESTERN INN
3428 South St
(75962)
Rates: $48-$52
Tel: (409) 560-4900
(800) 528-1234

EAGLE'S AERIE BED & BREAKFAST
12 E Lake Estates,
Rt 3 (75964)
Rates: $55+
Tel: (409) 564-7995
(800) 754-3906

ECONO LODGE
2020 NW Stallings
Dr (75961)
Rates: $42+
Tel: (409) 569-0880
(800) 424-4777

THE FREDONIA HISTORIC HOTEL
200 N Fredonia St
(75961)
Rates: $59-$89
Tel: (409) 564-1234
(800) 594-5323

HARDEMAN GUEST HOUSE-HISTORIC BED & BREAKFAST
316 N Church St
(75961)
Rates: $65-$80
Tel: (409) 569-1947
(800) 884-1947

LA QUINTA INN
3215 South St
(75961)
Rates: $46-$59
Tel: (409) 560-5453
(800) 531-5900

NAVASOTA

BEST WESTERN NAVASOTA INN
818 Hwy 6 Loop S
(77868)
Rates: $34-$44
Tel: (409) 825-7775
(800) 528-1234

NEDERLAND

BEST WESTERN AIRPORT INN
200 Memorial Hwy
69 (77627)
Rates: $38-$50
Tel: (409) 727-1631
(800) 528-1234

NEW BOSTON

BEST WESTERN INN
1024 N Center
(75570)
Rates: $43-$89
Tel: (903) 628-6999
(800) 528-1234

NEW BRAUNFELS

CAMP HUACO SPRINGS CABINS
1405 Gruene Rd
(78130)
Rates: $25-$95
Tel: (210) 625-5411
(800) 553-5628

HOLIDAY INN
1051 I-35 E (78130)
Rates: $65-$85
Tel: (210) 625-8017
(800) 465-4329

KUEBLER-WALDRIP HAUS BED & BREAKFAST
1620 Hueco Springs
Loop (78132)
Rates: $89-$200
Tel: (210) 625-8372
(800) 299-8372

RAMADA LIMITED
815 I-35 W (78130)
Rates: $35-$89
Tel: (210) 625-6201
(800) 272-6232

RODEWAY INN
1209 I-35 S (78130)
Rates: $42-$77
Tel: (210) 629-6991
(800) 424-4777
(800) 967-1168 (TX)

NOCONA

NOCONA HILLS MOTEL & RESORT
100 E Huron Circle
(76255)
Rates: $25-$30
Tel: (817) 825-3161

NORTH RICHLAND HILLS

LA QUINTA INN NORTHEAST
7920 Bedford-Euless
Rd (76180)
Rates: $45-$56
Tel: (817) 485-2750
(800) 531-5900

LEXINGTON INN-DFW WEST
8709 Airport Frwy
(76180)
Rates: $45-$61
Tel: (817) 656-8881
(800) 656-8886

MOTEL 6
7804 Bedford-Euless
Rd (76180)
Rates: $29-$41
Tel: (817) 485-3000
(800) 440-6000

ODEM

DAYS INN
1505 Voss Ave
(78370)
Rates: $30-$62
Tel: (512) 368-2166
(800) 329-7466

ODESSA

BEST WESTERN GARDEN OASIS
110 I-20 W (79761)
Rates: $45-$68
Tel: (915) 337-3006
(800) 528-1234

CLASSIC SUITES
3031 I-20 E Business
(79761)
Rates: $27-$32
Tel: (915) 333-9678

DAYS INN
3075 E Hwy 80
(79761)
Rates: $38-$52
Tel: (915) 335-8000
(800) 329-7466

ECONO LODGE
1518 S Grant (79763)
Rates: $30-$38
Tel: (915) 333-1485
(800) 424-4777

HOLIDAY INN CENTRE
6201 Hwy 80 E
(79760)
Rates: $55-$160
Tel: (915) 362-2311
(800) 465-4329

LA QUINTA INN
5001 Hwy 80 E
(79761)
Rates: $60-$67
Tel: (915) 333-2820
(800) 531-5900

MOTEL 6-SOUTH
200 E I-20 Service Rd
(79766)
Rates: $24-$28
Tel: (915) 333-4025
(800) 440-6000

PARKWAY INN
3071 Hwy 80 E
(79761)
Rates: $28-$33
Tel: (915) 332-4224
(800) 926-6760

SUPER 8 MOTEL
6713 I-20 E (79762)
Rates: $30-$35
Tel: (915) 363-8281
(800) 800-8000

VILLA WEST INN
300 I-20 W (79760)
Rates: $19-$29
Tel: (915) 335-5055

ORANGE

BEST WESTERN INN OF ORANGE
2630 I-10 (77630)
Rates: $45-$65
Tel: (409) 883-6616
(800) 528-1234

HOLIDAY INN
2900 I-10 (77630)
Rates: $49+
Tel: (409) 883-9981
(800) 465-4329

KING'S INN MOTEL
2208 I-10 W (77630)
Rates: $36+
Tel: (409) 883-6701

MOTEL 6
4407 27th St (77630)
Rates: $23-$27
Tel: (409) 883-4891
(800) 440-6000

RAMADA INN
2610 I-10 W (77630)
Rates: $60-$135
Tel: (409) 993-0231
(800) 272-6232

OZONA

DAYSTOP
820 Loop 466 W
(76943)
Rates: $27-$47
Tel: (915) 392-2631
(800) 329-7466

FLYING W LODGE
Eight 11th St (76943)
Rates: $27-$35
Tel: (915) 392-2656

PALESTINE

BEST WESTERN PALESTINE INN
1601 W Palestine
Ave (75801)
Rates: $39-$44
Tel: (903) 723-4655
(800) 528-1234

DAYS INN
1100 E Palestine Ave
(75801)
Rates: $54-$61
Tel: (903) 729-3151
(800) 329-7466
(800) 944-1143 (TX)

PANHANDLE

S & S MOTOR INN
Rt 2, Box 58 (79068)
Rates: $26-$40
Tel: (806) 537-5111

PARIS

BEST WESTERN INN OF PARIS
3755 NE Loop 286
(75460)
Rates: $34-$40
Tel: (903) 785-5566
(800) 528-1234

DAYS INN
2650 N Main (75460)
Rates: $35-$45
Tel: (903) 784-8164
(800) 329-7466

HOLIDAY INN
3560 NE Loop 286
(75460)
Rates: $47-$68
Tel: (903) 785-5545
(800) 465-4329

VICTORIAN INNS
425 NE 35th St
(75460)
Rates: $32-$38
Tel: (903) 785-3871
(800) 935-0863

PASADENA

ECONO LODGE
823 W Pasadena
Frwy (77506)
Rates: $40-$45
Tel: (713) 477-4266
(800) 424-4777

RAMADA INN
114 S Richy (77506)
Rates: $55-$65
Tel: (713) 477-6871
(800) 272-6232

PEARSALL

EXECUTIVE INN
613 North Oak
(78061)
Rates: $30-$34
Tel: (210) 334-3693

PECOS

BEST WESTERN SWISS CLOCK INN
900 W Palmer
(79772)
Rates: $35-$62
Tel: (915) 447-2215
(800) 528-1234

MOTEL 6
3002 S Cedar St
(79772)
Rates: $24-$28
Tel: (915) 445-9034
(800) 440-6000

PLAINVIEW

BEST WESTERN CONESTOGA INN
600 I-27 N (79072)
Rates: $44-$90
Tel: (806) 293-9454
(800) 528-1234

DAYS INN
3600 Olton Rd
(79072)
Rates: $32-$46
Tel: (806) 293-2561
(800) 329-7466

HOLIDAY INN
4005 Olton Rd
(79073)
Rates: $43-$45
Tel: (806) 293-4181
(800) 465-4329

PLANO

BEST WESTERN PARK SUITES HOTEL
640 Park Blvd E
(75074)
Rates: $69-$80
Tel: (214) 578-2243
(800) 528-1234

COMFORT INN
621 Central Pkwy E
(75074)
Rates: $37-$47
Tel: (214) 424-5568
(800) 221-2222

HARVEY HOTEL
1600 N Central
Expwy (75074)
Rates: $49-$83
Tel: (214) 578-8555
(800) 922-9222

LA QUINTA INN
1820 N Central
Expwy (75074)
Rates: $42-$55
Tel: (214) 423-1300
(800) 531-5900

MOTEL 6
2550 N Central
Expwy (75074)
Rates: $29-$38
Tel: (214) 578-1626
(800) 440-6000

SLEEP INN
4801 W Plano Pkwy
(75093)
Rates: $49-$84
Tel: (214) 867-1111
(800) 221-2222

PORT ARANSAS

**BEACHGATE
CONDOMINIUMS**
2000 On The Beach
(78373)
Rates: $65-$110
Tel: (512) 749-5900

BELLE'S INN MOTEL
710 Station at Ave G
(78373)
Rates: $35-$65
Tel: (512) 749-6138

**EXECUTIVE KEYS
APARTMENT MOTEL**
820 Access Rd 1A
(78373)
Rates: $38-$172
Tel: (512) 749-6272
(800) 248-1095

**HARBOR VIEW
MOTEL**
121 W Cotter (78373)
Rates: $35
Tel: (512) 749-6391

**PARADISE ISLE
MOTEL**
314 Cutoff Rd
(78373)
Rates: $40
Tel: (512) 749-6993

ROCK COTTAGES
603 E Ave G (78373)
Rates: $39-$45
Tel: (512) 749-6360

SEA HORSE LODGE
503 E Ave G (78373)
Rates: $65-$95
Tel: (512) 749-5513

**SEA & SANDS
COTTAGES**
410 10th St (78373)
Rates: $60
Tel: (512) 749-5191

SEASIDE MOTEL
500 Sandcastle Dr
(78373)
Rates: $39-$180
Tel: (512) 749-4105
(800) 765-3101

SUNDAY VILLAS
1900 S 11th St
(78373)
Rates: $70
Tel: (512) 749-6480

**TROPIC ISLAND
MOTEL**
315 Cutoff Rd
(78373)
Rates: $55-$105
Tel: (512) 749-6128

PORT ARTHUR

RAMADA INN
3801 Hwy 73 (77643)
Rates: $50-$135
Tel: (409) 962-9858
(800) 272-6232

PORT ISABEL

SOUTHWIND INN
600 Davis St (78578)
Rates: $29-$50
Tel: (210) 943-3392

YACHT CLUB HOTEL
700 Yturria St
(78578)
Rates: $35-$99
Tel: (210) 943-1301

PORT LAVACA

DAYS INN
2100 N Bypass 35
(77979)
Rates: $46-$58
Tel: (512) 552-4511
(800) 329-7466

PORTLAND

COMFORT INN
1703 N Hwy 181
(78374)
Rates: $47-$75
Tel: (512) 643-2222
(800) 221-2222

QUANAH

**QUANAH PARKER
INN**
1405 W 11th St
(79252)
Rates: $27-$40
Tel: (817) 663-6366
(800) 441-7971

QUEEN CITY

DAYS INN
301 Hwy 59 (75572)
Rates: $30-$55
Tel: (903) 796-7191
(800) 329-7466

RAINBOW

**RAINBOW'S END
BED & BREAKFAST**
County Road 312
(76077)
Rates: $90+
Tel: (817) 897-2238

RANGER

DAYS INN
I-20 Ex 349,
Box 160-C (76470)
Rates: $36-$50
Tel: (817) 647-1176
(800) 329-7466

RICHARDSON

CLARION HOTEL
1981 N Central
Expwy (75080)
Rates: $49-$129
Tel: (214) 444-4000
(800) 285-3434

**HAWTHORN SUITES
HOTEL**
250 Municipal Dr
(75080)
Rates: $90-$130
Tel: (214) 669-1000
(800) 527-1133

LA QUINTA INN
13685 N Central
Expwy (75243)
Rates: $49-$67
Tel: (214) 234-0682
(800) 531-5900

OMNI HOTEL
701 E Campbell Rd
(75080)
Rates: $69-$175
Tel: (214) 231-9600
(800) 843-6664

SLEEP INN
2650 N Central
Expwy (75080)
Rates: $49-$67
Tel: (214) 470-9440
(800) 626-5337

RICHMOND

EXECUTIVE INN
26035 Southwest
Frwy (77469)
Rates: $31-$40
Tel: (713) 342-5387

ROBSTOWN

DAYS INN
320 Hwy 77 S
(78380)
Rates: $27-$35
Tel: (512) 387-9416
(800) 329-7466

ECONO LODGE
2225 Hwy 77 N
(78380)
Rates: $36-$48
Tel: (512) 387-9444
(800) 424-4777

ROCKPORT

ANCHOR MOTEL
1204 E Market
(78382)
Rates: $40-$60
Tel: (512) 729-3249

**ANTHONY'S
BY THE SEA
BED & BREAKFAST**
732 S Pearl St (78382)
Rates: $55-$95
Tel: (512) 729-6100
(800) 460-2557

**BIG TREE TRAILER
INN & COTTAGES**
HC 04, Box 146
(77710)
Rates: $20-$40
Tel: (512) 729-8708

DAYS INN
1212 Laurel (78382)
Rates: $50-$80
Tel: (512) 729-6379
(800) 329-7466

**DEL CAMINO
APARTMENT MOTEL**
1009 I-35 N (78382)
Rates: $65
Tel: (512) 729-2510

**HOLIDAY LODGE
MOTEL**
1406 I-35 N (78382)
Rates: $34-$40
Tel: (512) 729-3433

**HUNT'S COURT
MOTEL-WATER-
FRONT**
901 S Water St
(78382)
Rates: $40-$69
Tel: (512) 729-2273

**KEY ALLEGRO
RENTALS**
1798 Bayshore
(78382)
Rates: $110
Tel: (512) 729-2333
(800) 348-1627

**LAGUNA REEF
APARTMENT MOTEL**
1021 Water St
(78382)
Rates: $50-$60
Tel: (512) 729-1742
(800) 248-1057

LAS BRIZAS MOTEL
1155 I-35 N (78382)
Rates: $35
Tel: (512) 729-9112

**OCEAN VIEW
MOTEL**
1131 S Water St
(78382)
Rates: $34-$46
Tel: (512) 729-3326

PELICAN MOTEL
1011 E Market St
(78382)
Rates: $40-$55
Tel: (512) 729-3837
(800) 248-1057

ROCKPORTER INN
813 S Church St
(78382)
Rates: $40
Tel: (512) 729-9591

**ROD AND REEL
MOTEL**
1105 E Market St
(78382)
Rates: $31-$54
Tel: (512) 729-2028
(888) 729-2028

**SANDOLLAR
RESORT
MOTEL & RV**
HC O1, Box 30
(78382)
Rates: $44-$59
Tel: (512) 729-2381

**SANDRA BAY
COTTAGES**
1801 Broadway
(78382)
Rates: $45+
Tel: (512) 729-6257

SUN TAN MOTEL
1805 Broadway
(78382)
Rates: $39-$60
Tel: (512) 729-2179

SUNSET INN
800 S Church St
(78382)
Rates: $26-$35
Tel: (512) 729-4792

ROSENBERG

**BEST WESTERN
SUNDOWNER
MOTOR INN**
28382 Southwest
Frwy (77471)
Rates: $34-$50
Tel: (713) 342-6000
(800) 528-1234

ROUND ROCK

LA QUINTA INN
2004 I-35 N (78681)
Rates: $51-$63
Tel: (512) 255-6666
(800) 531-5900

RAMADA LIMITED
1400 I-35 N (78681)
Rates: $49-$51
Tel: (512) 255-4437
(800) 272-6232

SAN ANGELO

**BEST WESTERN INN
OF THE WEST**
415 W Beauregard
(76901)
Rates: $39-$44
Tel: (915) 653-2995
(800) 528-1234

DAYS INN
4613 S Jackson
(76903)
Rates: $35-$45
Tel: (915) 658-6594
(800) 329-7466

EL PATIO MOTEL
1901 W Beauregard
St (76901)
Rates: $20-$35
Tel: (915) 655-5711
(800) 677-7735

HAMPTON INN
2959 Loop 306
(76902)
Rates: $63-83
Tel: (915) 942-9622
(800) 426-7866

**HOLIDAY INN
CONV. CENTER
HOTEL**
441 Rio Concho Dr
(76903)
Rates: $48-$67
Tel: (915) 658-2828
(800) 465-4329

**INN OF
THE CONCHOS**
2021 N Bryant Blvd
(76903)
Rates: $36-$46
Tel: (915) 658-2811
(800) 621-6041

LA QUINTA INN
2307 Loop 306
(76904)
Rates: $48-$60
Tel: (915) 949-0515
(800) 531-5900

MOTEL 6
311 N Bryant Blvd
(76903)
Rates: $24-$28
Tel: (915) 658-8061
(800) 440-6000

**OLE COACH
MOTOR INN**
4205 S Bryant Blvd
(76903)
Rates: $29-$39
Tel: (915) 653-6966
(800) 227-6456

**SANTA FE
JUNCTION
MOTOR INN**
410 W Ave L (76903)
Rates: $33-$38
Tel: (915) 655-8101

SUPER 8 MOTEL
1601 S Bryant Blvd
(76903)
Rates: $39-$54
Tel: (915) 653-1323
(800) 800-8000

SAN ANTONIO

ALOHA INN
1435 Austin Hwy
(78209)
Rates: $35-$42
Tel: (210) 828-0933
(800) 752-6354

**BEST WESTERN
FIESTA INN**
13535 I-10 W (78249)
Rates: $45-$89
Tel: (210) 697-9761
(800) 528-1234

**BEST WESTERN
INGRAM PARK INN**
6855 NW Loop 410
(78238)
Rates: $49-$89
Tel: (210) 520-8080
(800) 528-1234

**BEST WESTERN
LACKLAND INN &
SUITES**
6815 Hwy 90 W
(78227)
Rates: $48-$78
Tel: (210) 675-9690
(800) 528-1234

**COACHMAN INN
BROOKS FIELD**
3180 Gollard Rd
(78223)
Rates: $36-$52
Tel: (210) 337-7171

**COMFORT INN
AIRPORT NORTH-
EAST**
2635 NE Loop 410
(78217)
Rates: $55-$95
Tel: (210) 653-9110
(800) 221-2222

**COMFORT INN I-10
EAST**
4403 I-10 E (78219)
Rates: $38-$70
Tel: (210) 333-9430
(800) 221-2222

COMFORT INN-NW
4 Plano Pl (78229)
Rates: $49-$109
Tel: (210) 684-8606
(800) 221-2222

COMFORT SUITES
6350 I-35 N (78218)
Rates: $49-$139
Tel: (210) 646-6600
(800) 221-2222

COMFORT SUITES
Northbrook Dr
(78232)
Rates: $79-$145
Tel: (210) 494-9000
(800) 221-2222

COMFORT SUITES
6901 I-10 W (78201)
Rates: $74-$95
Tel: (210) 738-1100
(800) 221-2222

DAYS INN EAST
439 E Houston St
(78220)
Rates: $35-$98
Tel: (210) 333-9100
(800) 329-7466

DAYS INN-NE
3443 I-35 N (78219)
Rates: $32-$74
Tel: (210) 225-4521
(800) 329-7466
(800) 548-2626 (TX)

DAYS IN NORTHSIDE
11202 I-35 N (78233)
Rates: $46-$86
Tel: (210) 655-4311
(800) 329-7466

DRURY INN EAST
8300 I-35 N (78239)
Rates: $58-$73
Tel: (210) 654-1144
(800) 325-8300

DRURY SUITES
8811 Jones
Maltsberger (78216)
Rates: $79-$89
Tel: (210) 308-8100
(800) 325-8300

**EMBASSY SUITES
HOTEL-AIRPORT**
10110 Hwy 281 N
(78216)
Rates: $109-$169
Tel: (210) 525-9999
(800) 362-2779

**EXECUTIVE GUEST-
HOUSE HOTEL**
12828 Hwy 281 N
(78216)
Rates: $74-$124
Tel: (210) 494-7600
(800) 362-8700

**FAMILY GARDENS
COUNTRY SUITES**
2383 NE Loop 410
(78217)
Rates: $65
Tel: (210) 599-4204
(800) 314-3424

**HAMPTON INN
AIRPORT**
8818 Jones
Maltsberger (78216)
Rates: $68-$83
Tel: (210) 366-1800
(800) 426-7866

**HAMPTON INN-
NORTHEAST**
4900 Crestwind
(78239)
Rates: $62-$75
Tel: (210) 657-1107
(800) 429-7866

HAWTHORN SUITES
4041 Bluemel Rd
(78240)
Rates: $85-$175
Tel: (210) 561-9660
(800) 527-1133

**HILTON HOTEL&
CONFERENCE
CENTER-AIRPORT**
611 NW Loop 410
(78216)
Rates: $109-$124
Tel: (210) 340-6060
(800) 445-8667

**HILTON
PALACIO DEL RIO**
200 S Alamo St
(78205)
Rates: $163-$215
Tel: (210) 222-1400
(800) 445-8667

**HOLIDAY INN-
DOWNTOWN-
MARKET SQUARE**
318 W Durango
(78204)
Rates: $79-$119
Tel: (210) 225-3211
(800) 465-4329

**HOLIDAY INN
EXPRESS
AIRPORT**
95 NE Loop 410
(78216)
Rates: $75-$85
Tel: (210) 308-6700
(800) 465-4329

**HOLIDAY INN
NORTHEAST**
3855 I-35 N (78219)
Rates: $58-$88
Tel: (210) 226-4361
(800) 465-4329

**HOLIDAY INN
RIVERWALK**
217 N St. Mary's St
(78205)
Rates: $115-$129
Tel: (210) 224-2500
(800) 465-4329

HOWARD JOHNSON
9603 I-35 N (78233)
Rates: $35-$75
Tel: (210) 655-2120
(800) 654-2000

**HYATT
REGENCY HILL
COUNTRY RESORT**
9800 Hyatt Resort Dr
(78251)
Rates: $190-$220
Tel: (210) 647-1234
(800) 233-1234

**HYATT REGENCY
SAN ANTONIO**
123 Losoya St
(78205)
Rates: $119-$214
Tel: (210) 222-1234
(800) 233-1234

LA MANSION DEL RIO HOTEL
112 College St (78205)
Rates: $155-$290
Tel: (210) 225-2581
(800) 531-7208
(800) 292-7300 (TX)

LA QUINTA INN-AIRPORT E.
333 NE Loop 410 (78216)
Rates: $61-$79
Tel: (210) 828-0781
(800) 531-5900

LA QUINTA INN-AIRPORT W.
219 NE Loop 410 (78216)
Rates: $58-$75
Tel: (210) 342-4291
(800) 531-5900

LA QUINTA INN CONV. CENTER
1001 E Commerce St (78205)
Rates: $85-$92
Tel: (210) 222-9181
(800) 531-5900

LA QUINTA INN INGRAM PARK
7134 NW Loop 410 (78238)
Rates: $67-$74
Tel: (210) 680-8883
(800) 531-5900

LA QUINTA INN-LACKLAND
6511 Military Dr W (78227)
Rates: $49-$69
Tel: (210) 674-3200
(800) 531-5900

LA QUINTA INN MARKET SQUARE
900 Dolorosa St (78207)
Rates: $76-$83
Tel: (210) 271-0001
(800) 531-5900

VLA QUINTA INN-SOUTH
7202 S Pan American Expwy (78224)
Rates: $58-$67
Tel: (210) 922-2111
(800) 531-5900

LA QUINTA INN TOEPPERWEIN
12822 I-35 N (78233)
Rates: $73+
Tel: (210) 657-5500
(800) 531-5900

LA QUINTA INN VANCE JACKSON
5922 NW Expwy (78201)
Rates: $52-$69
Tel: (210) 734-7931
(800) 531-5900

LA QUINTA INN WINDSOR PARK
6410 I-35 N (78218)
Rates: $51-$72
Tel: (210) 653-6619
(800) 531-5900

LA QUINTA INN-WURZBACH
9542 I-10 W (78230)
Rates: $54-$75
Tel: (210) 593-0338
(800) 531-5900

MARRIOTT RIVERCENTER
101 Bowie St (78205)
Rates: $160-$180
Tel: (210) 223-1000
(800) 228-9290
(800) 648-4462 (TX)

MARRIOTT RIVERWALK
711 E Riverwalk (78205)
Rates: $135-$170
Tel: (210) 224-4555
(800) 228-9290
(800) 648-4462 (TX)

MOTEL 6-EAST
138 N WW White Rd (78219)
Rates: $29-$38
Tel: (210) 333-1850
(800) 440-6000

MOTEL 6-FIESTA
16500 I-10 W (78257)
Rates: $32-$44
Tel: (210) 697-0731
(800) 440-6000

MOTEL 6 NORTHEAST
4621 E Rittiman Rd (78218)
Rates: $31-$39
Tel: (210) 665-8088
(800) 440-6000

MOTEL 6-FT. SAM HOUSTON
5522 N Pan Am Expwy (78218)
Rates: $29-$38
Tel: (210) 661-8791
(800) 440-6000
(800) 466-8356 (TX)

MOTEL 6-NORTH
9503 I-35 N (78233)
Rates: $28-$36
Tel: (210) 650-4419
(800) 440-6000

MOTEL 6-NORTHWEST
9400 Wurzbach Rd (78240)
Rates: $40-$46
Tel: (210) 593-0013
(800) 440-6000

MOTEL 6-RIVERWALK
211 N Pecos St (78207)
Rates: $38-$44
Tel: (210) 225-1111
(800) 440-6000

MOTEL 6-WEST
2185 SW Loop 410 (78227)
Rates: $30-$42
Tel: (210) 673-9020
(800) 440-6000

OAK MOTOR LODGE
150 Humphreys Ave (78209)
Rates: $29-$75
Tel: (210) 826-6368
(800) 385-9568

PEAR TREE INN
143 NE Loop 410 (78216)
Rates: $66-$83
Tel: (210) 366-4300
(800) 282-8733

PLAZA SAN ANTONIO HOTEL
555 S Alamo St (78205)
Rates: $140-$500
Tel: (210) 229-1000
(800) 421-1172

QUALITY INN & CONF CENTER
10811 I-35 N (78233)
Rates: $39-$69
Tel: (210) 590-4646
(800) 221-2222

QUALITY INN & SUITES
3817 N Pam Am Expwy (78219)
Rates: $55-$75
Tel: (210) 224-3030
(800) 221-2222

RAMADA HOTEL AIRPORT
1111 NE Loop 410 (78209)
Rates: $66-$89
Tel: (210) 828-9031
(800) 272-6232

RAMADA LIMITED WINDSOR PARK
6370 I-35 N (78218)
Rates: $42-$70
Tel: (210) 646-6336
(800) 272-6232

RELAY STATION MOTEL
5530 I-10 E (78219)
Rates: $32-$47
Tel: (210) 662-6691
(800) 735-2981

RESIDENCE INN BY MARRIOTT
1014 NE Loop 410 (78209)
Rates: $99-$139
Tel: (210) 805-8118
(800) 331-3131

RESIDENCE INN BY MARRIOTT
628 S Santa Rosa Blvd (78204)
Rates: $139
Tel: (210) 231-6000
(800) 331-3131

RODEWAY INN
900 N Main Ave (78212)
Rate: $38-$99
Tel: (210) 223-2951
(800) 424-4777

RODEWAY INN CROSSROADS
6804 NW Expwy (78201)
Rates: $36-$55
Tel: (210) 734-7111
(800) 424-4777

**RODEWAY INN-
DOWNTOWN**
1500 I-35 S (78204)
Rates: $48-$90
Tel: (210) 271-3334
(800) 424-4777

**RODEWAY INN-
FIESTA PARK**
19793 I-10 W (78257)
Rates: $36-$100
Tel: (210) 698-3991
(800) 424-4777

**SCOTSMAN INN
EAST**
211 N WW White Rd
(78219)
Rates: $36-$42
Tel: (210) 359-7268
(800) 677-7268

**SEVEN OAKS
RESORT
& CONFERENCE
CENTER**
1400 Austin Hwy
(78209)
Rates: $50-$65
Tel: (210) 824-5371
(800) 346-5866

**SHONEY'S INN-
AIRPORT**
8600 Jones
Maltsberger Rd
(78216)
Rates: $59-$69
Tel: (210) 342-1400
(800) 222-2222

**ST. ANTHONY
HOTEL**
300 E Travis St
(78205)
Rates: $125-$190
Tel: (210) 227-4392
(800) 338-1338

SUPER 8 MOTEL
11027 I-35 N (78233)
Rates: $35-$50
Tel: (210) 637-1022
(800) 800-8000

SUPER 8 MOTEL
5336 Wurzbach Rd
(78238)
Rates: $38-$48
Tel: (210) 520-0888
(800) 800-8000

**SUPER 8 MOTEL
DOWNTOWN
NORTH**
3617 N Pan Am
Expwy (78219)
Rates: $41-$51
Tel: (210) 227-8888
(800) 800-8000

**SUPER 8 MOTEL
FIESTA TEXAS**
5319 Casa Bella
(78249)
Rates: $55-$72
Tel: (210) 696-6916
(800) 800-8000

**TERRELL CASTLE
COUNTRY INN**
950 E Grayson St
(78208)
Rates: $50-$92
Tel: (210) 271-9145

**THRIFTY INN
NORTHWEST**
9806 I-10 W (78230)
Rates: $41-$80
Tel: (210) 696-0810

SAN MARCOS

DAYS INN
1005 I-35 N (78666)
Rates: $35-$79
Tel: (512) 353-5050
(800) 329-7466

**EXECUTIVE HOUSE
HOTEL**
1433 I-35 N (78666)
Rates: $30-$65
Tel: (512) 353-7770

HOLIDAY INN
1635 Aquarena
Springs Dr (78666)
Rates: $47-$62
Tel: (512) 353-801
(800) 465-4329

HOMEPLACE INN
1429 I-35 N (78666)
Rates: $40-$62
Tel: (512) 396-0400

LA QUINTA INN
1619 I-35 N (78666)
Rates: $68-$88
Tel: (512) 392-8800
(800) 531-5900

**LONESOME DOVE
BED & BREAKFAST**
407 Oakwood Loop
(78666)
Rates: $65-$85
Tel: (512) 392-2921

MOTEL 6
1321 I-35 N (78666)
Rates: $27-$34
Tel: (512) 396-8705
(800) 440-6000

RODEWAY INN
801 I-35 N (78666)
Rates: $35-$116
Tel: (512) 353-1303
(800) 424-4777

SANDERSON

DESERT AIR MOTEL
P. O. Box 326 (79848)
Rates: $22-$34
Tel: (915) 345-2572

SCHULENBURG

**OAKRIDGE
MOTOR INN**
P. O. Box 43 (78956)
Rates: $42-$45
Tel: (409) 743-4192

SEALY

RODEWAY INN
2021 Meyers St
(77474)
Rates: $35-$42
Tel: (409) 885-7407
(800) 424-4777

SEGOVIA

**BEST WESTERN
RIVER VALLEY INN**
HC 10, Box 138
(76849)
Rates: $45-$79
Tel: (915) 446-3331
(800) 528-1234

SEGUIN

ECONO LODGE
3013 N Hwy 123
Bypass (78155)
Rates: $30-$79
Tel: (210) 372-3990
(800) 424-4777

SEMINOLE

SEMINOLE INN
2000 Hobbs Hwy
(79360)
Rates: $35-$40
Tel: (915) 758-9881
(800) 658-9985

SHAMROCK

**BEST WESTERN
IRISH INN**
301 I-40 E (79079)
Rates: $38-$54
Tel: (806) 256-2106
(800) 528-1234

ECONO LODGE
1006 E 12th St
(79079)
Rates: $29-$46
Tel: (806) 256-2111
(800) 424-4777

**THE WESTERN
MOTEL**
104 E 12th St (79079)
Rates: $20-$32
Tel: (806) 256-3244

SHERMAN

**BEST WESTERN
GRAYSON HOUSE
INN**
2105 Texoma Pkwy
(75090)
Rates: $43-$61
Tel: (903) 892-2161
(800) 528-1234
(800) 723-4194 (TX)

CROSSROADS INN
2424 Texoma Pkwy
(75090)
Rates: $26+
Tel: (903) 893-0184

ECONOMY INN
1530 Texoma Pkwy
(75090)
Rates: $30-$35
Tel: (903) 893-7666
(800) 826-0778

HOLIDAY INN
3605 Hwy 75 S
(75090)
Rates: $56-$69
Tel: (903) 868-0555
(800) 465-4329

INN OF SHERMAN
1831 Texoma Pkwy
(75090)
Rates: $44-$38
Tel: (903) 892-0422
(800) 255-1011

SHERWOOD INN
401 S Sam Rayburn
Frwy (75090)
Rates: $38
Tel: (903) 893-6581

SMITHVILLE

**THE KATY HOUSE
BED & BREAKFAST**
201 Ramona St
(78957)
Rates: $65-$85
Tel: (512) 237-4262
(800) 843-5289

SNYDER

**PURPLE SAGE
MOTEL**
1501 E Coliseum Dr
(79549)
Rates: $35-$65
Tel: (915) 573-5491
(800) 545-5792

WILLOW PARK INN
1137 E Hwy 180 & 84
(79549)
Rates: $48-$58
Tel: (915) 573-1961

SONORA

**DEVIL'S RIVER
MOTEL**
1312 N Service Rd
(76950)
Rates: $32-$42
Tel: (915) 387-3516

**HOLIDAY HOST
MOTEL**
Hwy 290 E (76950)
Rates: $26-$33
Tel: (915) 387-2532

TWIN OAKS MOTEL
907 N Crockett Ave
(76950)
Rates: $28-$40
Tel: (915) 387-2551

SOUTH PADRE ISLAND

**BEST WESTERN
FIESTA ISLES**
5701 Padre Blvd
(78597)
Rates: $54-$118
Tel: (210) 761-4913
(800) 528-1234

CASTAWAYS
3700 Gulf Blvd
(78597)
Rates: $95+
Tel: (210) 761-1903

**CONTINENTAL
CONDOMINIUMS**
4908 Gulf Blvd
(78597)
Rates: $84+
Tel: (210) 761-1306

DAYS INN
3913 Padre Blvd
(78597)
Rates: $47-$120
Tel: (210) 761-7831
(800) 329-7466

LA INTERNATIONAL
5008 Gulf Blvd
(78597)
Rates: $75+
Tel: (210) 761-1306

MOTEL 6
4013 Padre Blvd
(78597)
Rates: $36-$42
Tel: (210) 761-7911
(800) 440-6000

PALMS RESORT
3616 Gulf Blvd
(78597)
Rates: $44+
Tel: (210) 761-1316

RADISSON RESORT
500 Padre Blvd
(78597)
Rates: $89-$330
Tel: (210) 761-6511
(800) 333-3333

**SAND CASTLE
MOTEL**
200 W Kingfish
(78597)
Rates: $46-$64
Tel: (210) 761-1321

**SERVICE 24
CONDO RENTALS**
108 W Pompano
P. O. Box 2938
(78597)
Rates: $69-$445
Tel: (210) 761-1487
(800) 828-4287

**THE TIKI
APARTMENT HOTEL**
6608 Padre Blvd
(78597)
Rates: $62-$132
Tel: (210) 761-2694

SPRING

MOTEL 6
19606 Cypresswood
Ct (77388)
Rates: $33-$39
Tel: (713) 350-6400
(800) 440-6000

STAFFORD

LA QUINTA INN
12727 Southwest
Frwy (77477)
Rates: $59-$73
Tel: (713) 240-2300
(800) 531-5900

STEPHENVILLE

**BEST WESTERN
CROSS TIMBERS**
1625 S Loop (76401)
Rates: $39-$45
Tel: (817) 968-2114
(800) 528-1234

**BUDGET HOST
TEXAN MOTOR INN**
3030 W Washington
(76401)
Rates: $33-$40
Tel: (817) 968-5003
(800) 283-4678

DAYS INN
701 S Loop (76401)
Rates: $33-$46
Tel: (817) 968-3392
(800) 329-7466

HOLIDAY INN
2865 W Washington
(76401)
Rates: $40-$150
Tel: (817) 968-5256
(800) 465-4329

SULPHUR SPRINGS

HOLIDAY INN
1495 E Industrial
(75482)
Rates: $43-$54
Tel: (915) 236-6887
(800) 465-4329

SURFSIDE BEACH

ANCHOR MOTEL
1302 Bluewater Hwy
(77541)
Rates: $35-$55
Tel: (409) 239-3543

SWEETWATER

BEST WESTERN SUNDAY HOUSE INN
701 SW Georgia St (79556)
Rates: $46-$68
Tel: (915) 235-4853
(800) 528-1234

HOLIDAY INN
500 NW Georgia St (79556)
Rates: $44-$58
Tel: (915) 236-6887
(800) 465-4329

MOTEL 6
510 NW Georgia St (79556)
Rates: $21-$27
Tel: (915) 235-4387
(800) 440-6000

MULBERRY MANOR BED & BREAKFAST
1400 Sam Houston (79556)
Rates: $50-$75
Tel: (915) 235-3811

RANCH HOUSE MOTEL
301 SW Georgia St (79556)
Rates: $26-$40
Tel: (915) 236-6341
(800) 622-5361

TEMPLE

BEST WESTERN INN AT SCOTT & WHITE
2625 S 31st St (765604)
Rates: $51-$62
Tel: (817) 778-5511
(800) 528-1234

ECONO LODGE
1001 N General Bruce Dr (76504)
Rates: $30-$45
Tel: (817) 771-1688
(800) 424-4777

FAIRFIELD INN BY MARRIOTT
1402 SW H.K. Dodgen Lp (76504)
Rates: $51-$60
Tel (817) 771-3030
(800) 228-2800

HAMPTON INN
1414 SW H.K. Dodgen Lp (76504)
Rates: $47-$61
Tel: (817) 778-6700:
(800) 426-7866

LA QUINTA INN
1604 W Barton Ave (76504)
Rates: $47-$59
Tel: (817) 771-2980
(800) 531-5900

MOTEL 6
1100 N General Bruce Dr (76504)
Rates: $26-$30
Tel: (817) 778-0272
(800) 440-6000

QUALITY INN
802 N General Bruce Dr (76504)
Rates: $46-$64
Tel: (817) 778-4411
(800) 221-2222

RODEWAY INN SCOTT & WHITE
400 SW HK Dodgen Lp 363 (76504)
Rates: $46-$59
Tel: (817) 773-1515
(800) 424-4777

SUPER 8 MOTEL
5505 S General Bruce Dr (76504)
Rates: $34-$53
Tel: (817) 778-0962
(800) 800-8000

TERLINGUA

BIG BEND MOTOR INN
P. O. Box 336, Hwy 118 & 170 (79852)
Rates: $50-$65
Tel: (915) 371-2218
(800) 848-2363

CHISOS MINING COMPANY MOTEL
Box 228, Hwy 170 (79852)
Rates: $30-$45
Tel: (915) 371-2254

LAJITAS ON THE RIO GRANDE
Star Rt 70, Box 400 (79852)
Rates: $48-$65
Tel: (915) 424-3471

TERRELL

BEST WESTERN LA PIEDRA INN
309 I-20 E (75160)
Rates: $36-$50
Tel: (214) 563-2676
(800) 528-1234

DAYS INN
1618 Hwy 34 S (75160)
Rates: $38-$85
Tel: (214) 551-1170
(800) 329-7466

TEXARKANA

BEST WESTERN KINGS ROW INN
4200 N State Line Ave (75502)
Rates: $40-$44
Tel: (501) 773-0593
(800) 528-1234
(800) 643-5464 (TX)

BEST WESTERN NORTHGATE MOTOR LODGE
400 W 53rd St (75502)
Rates: $40-$45
Tel: (903) 793-6565
(800) 528-1234
(800) 262-0048 (TX)

BUDGETEL INN
5012 N State Line Ave (75502)
Rates: $33-$49
Tel: (501) 773-1000
(800) 428-3438

COMFORT INN
5105 N State Line Ave (75501)
Rates: $42-$75
Tel: (903) 792-3366
(800) 221-2222

HOLIDAY INN EXPRESS
5401 N State Line Ave (75503)
Rates: $44-$51
Tel: (903) 792-3366
(800) 465-4329

LA QUINTA INN
5201 N State Line Ave (75503)
Rates: $41-$53
Tel: (903) 794-1900
(800) 531-5900

MOTEL 6-EAST
900 Realtor Ave (75502)
Rates: $25-$31
Tel: (501) 772-0678
(800) 440-6000

MOTEL 6-WEST
1924 Hampton Rd (75503)
Rates: $25-$31
Tel: (903) 793-1413
(800) 440-6000

SHONEY'S INN
5210 N State Line Ave (75504)
Rates: $39-$89
Tel: (501) 772-0070
(800) 222-2222

TEXAS CITY

HAMPTON INN
2320 FM 2004 (77591)
Rates: $60-$76
Tel: (409) 986-6686
(800) 426-7866

LA QUINTA INN
1121 Hwy 146 N (77590)
Rates: $54-$79
Tel: (409) 948-3101
(800) 531-5900

THE WOODLANDS

LA QUINTA INN
28673 I-45 N (77381)
Rates: $57-$78
Tel: (713) 367-7722
(800) 531-5900

RED ROOF INN
24903 I-45 N (77380)
Rates: $45-$60
Tel: (713) 367-5040
(800) 843-7663

THE WOODLANDS RESORT
2301 N Millbend Dr
(77380)
Rates: $125-$225
Tel: (713) 367-1100
(800) 433-2624

THREE RIVERS

NOLAN RYAN'S BASS INN
HCR 71, Box 390
(78071)
Rates: $38-$99
Tel: (512) 786-3521
(800) 803-3340

TOMBALL

BEST WESTERN TOMBALL INN
30130 State Hwy 249
(77375)
Rates: $48-$53
Tel: (713) 351-9700
(800) 528-1234

TULIA

BEST WESTERN INN
Rt 1, Box 60 (79088)
Rates: $45-$64
Tel: (806) 995-2738
(800) 528-1234

TYLER

BEST WESTERN INN & SUITES
2828 W NW Loop
323 (75702)
Rates: $42-$93
Tel: (903) 595-2681
(800) 528-1234

DAYS INN
3300 Mineola Hwy
(75702)
Rates: $44-$90
Tel: (903) 595-2451
(800) 329-7466

ECONO LODGE
3209 W Gentry
Pkwy (75702)
Rates: $32-$37
Tel: (903) 593-0103
(800) 424-4777

FAIRFIELD INN BY MARRIOTT
1945 W SW Loop
323 (75701)
Rates: $52-$58
Tel: (903) 561-2535
(800) 228-2800

HOLIDAY INN SOUTHEAST CROSSING
3310 Troup Hwy
(75701)
Rates: $60-$75
Tel: (903) 593-3600
(800) 465-4329

HOWARD JOHNSON
2843 W NW Loop
323 (75712)
Rates: $45-$55
Tel: (903) 597-1301
(800) 446-4656

LA QUINTA INN
1601 W SW Loop
323 (75701)
Rates: $53-$66
Tel: (903) 561-2223
(800) 531-5900

MOTEL 6
3236 Brady Gentry
Pkwy (75702)
Rates: $27-$31
Tel: (903) 595-6691
(800) 440-6000

RESIDENCE INN BY MARRIOTT
3303 Troup Hwy
(75701)
Rates: $86-$102
Tel: (903) 595-5188
(800) 331-3131

RODEWAY INN
2739 W NW Loop
323 (75710)
Rates: $55-$70
Tel: (903) 531-9513
(800) 424-4777

STRATFORD HOUSE INN MOTEL
2600 W NW Loop
323 (75702)
Rates: $31-$35
Tel: (903) 597-2756

SUPER 8 MOTEL
2616 N NW Loop
323 (75702)
Rates: $38-$66
Tel: (903) 593-8361
(800) 800-8000

UNCERTAIN

MOSSY BRAKE LODGE BED & BREAKFAST
Rt 2, Box 63AB
(75661)
Rates: $65
Tel: (903) 789-3440
(800) 607-6002

UNIVERSAL CITY

CLARION SUITES HOTEL
13101 E Loop, 1604
N (78233)
Rates: $79-$139
Tel: (210) 655-9491
(800) 221-2222
(800) 537-4238 (TX)

UVALDE

BEST WESTERN CONTINENTAL INN
701 E Main St
(78801)
Rates: $35-$50
Tel: (210) 278-5671
(800) 528-1234

VAN HORN

BEST WESTERN AMERICAN INN
1309 W Broadway
(79855)
Rates: $28-$46
Tel: (915) 283-2030
(800) 528-1234

BEST WESTERN INN OF VAN HORN
1705 W Broadway
(79855)
Rates: $37-$44
Tel: (915) 283-2410
(800) 528-1234
(800) 367-7589 (TX)

COMFORT INN
1601 W Broadway
(79855)
Rates: $38-$58
Tel: (915) 283-2211
(800) 221-2222

DAYS INN
600 E Broadway St
(79855)
Rates: $35-$45
Tel: (915) 283-2401
(800) 329-7466

ECONOMY INN
P. O. Box 622, Hwy
80 N (79855)
Rates: $22-$42
Tel: (915) 283-2754
(800) 826-0778

FREEWAY INN MOTEL
505 Van Horn Dr
(79855)
Rates: $21-$29
Tel: (915) 283-2939

HOLIDAY INN EXPRESS
1905 SW Frontage
Rd (79855)
Rates: $41-$55
Tel: (915) 283-7444
(800) 465-4329

HOWARD JOHNSON
P. O. Box 776,
Hwy 80 (79855)
Rates: $31-$42
Tel: (915) 283-2780
(800) 446-4656

RODEWAY INN
1805 W Broadway
(79855)
Rates: $30-$45
Tel: (915) 283-2992
(800) 424-4777

SUPER 8 MOTEL
1807 E Service Rd
(79855)
Rates: $36-$41
Tel: (915) 283-2282
(800) 800-8000

VEGA

**BEST WESTERN
COUNTRY INN**
1800 Vega Blvd
(79092)
Rates: $46-$50
Tel: (806) 267-2131
(800) 528-1234

VERNON

**BEST WESTERN
VILLAGE INN**
1615 Expressway
(76384)
Rates: $44-$50
Tel: (817) 552-5417
(800) 528-1234
(800) 600-5417 (TX)

DAYS INN
3110 Expwy (76384)
Rates: $36-$65
Tel: (817) 552-9982
(800) 329-7466

ECONO LODGE
4100 Hwy 287 NW
(76384)
Rates: $29-$48
Tel: (817) 553-3384
(800) 424-4777

GREENTREE INN
3029 Morton (76384)
Rates: $31-$44
Tel: (817) 552-5421
(800) 600-5421

SUPER 8 MOTEL
1829 Exp Hwy 287
(76384)
Rates: $33-$43
Tel: (817) 552-9321
(800) 800-8000

WESTERN MOTEL
715 Wilbarger St
(76384)
Rates: $21-$30
Tel: (817) 552- 2531

VICTORIA

**FAIRFIELD INN
BY MARRIOTT**
7502 N Navarro St
(77904)
Rates: $55-$60
Tel: (512) 582-0660
(800) 228-2800

HAMPTON INN
3112 E Houston
Hwy (77901)
Rates: $39-$47
Tel: (512) 578-2030
(800) 426-7866

**HOLIDAY INN
HOLIDOME**
2705 E Houston
Hwy (77901)
Rates: $50+
Tel: (512) 575-0251
(800) 465-4329

LA QUINTA INN
7603 N Navarro St
(77904)
Rates: $47-$65
Tel: (512) 572-3585
(800) 531-5900

MOTEL 6
3716 E Houston
Hwy (77901)
Rates: $26-$30
Tel: (512) 573-1273
(800) 440-6000

RAMADA INN
3901 E Houston
Hwy (77901)
Rates: $42-$49
Tel: (512) 578-2723
(800) 272-6232

WACO

**BEST WESTERN
OLD MAIN LODGE**
I-35 & 4th St,
Box 174 (76703)
Rates: $49-$55
Tel: (817) 753-0316
(800) 528-1234
(800) 299-9226 (TX)

**BEST WESTERN
WACO MALL**
6624 Hwy 84 W
(76712)
Rates: $42-$48
Tel: (817) 776-3194
(800) 528-1234

ECONO LODGE
500 I-35 E (76704)
Rates: $35-$52
Tel: (817) 756-5371
(800) 424-4777

**FAIRFIELD INN
BY MARRIOTT**
5805 N Woodway Dr
(76712)
Rates: $52-$58
Tel: (817) 776-7821
(800) 228-2800

HILTON INN
113 S University
Parks Dr (76701)
Rates: $69-$79
Tel: (817) 754-8484
(800) 445-8667

**HOLIDAY INN-
WACO I-35**
1001 Lake Brazos Dr
(76704)
Rates: $59-$69
Tel: (817) 753-0261
(800) 465-4329

LA QUINTA INN
1110 S 9th St (76706)
Rates: $50-$64
Tel: (817) 752-9741
(800) 531-5900

MOTEL 6 PREMIER
3120 Jack Kultgen
Frwy (76706)
Rates: $27-$34
Tel: (817) 662-4622
(800) 440-6000

RAMADA INN
4201 Franklin Ave
(76710)
Rates: $48-$56
Tel: (817) 772-9440
(800) 272-6232

RIVERPLACE INN
101 I-35 N (76704)
Rates: $28-$46
Tel: (817) 752-8333

WAXAHACHIE

**BONNYNOOK INN
BED & BREAKFAST**
414 W Main (75165)
Rates: $75-$105
Tel: (214) 938-7207
(800) 486-5936

COMFORT INN
200 N I-35 E (75165)
Rates: $42-$54
Tel: (214) 937-4202
(800) 221-2222

RAMADA LIMITED
795 S I-35 E (75165)
Rates: $34-$48
Tel: (214) 937-4982
(800) 272-6232

TRAVELODGE
803 S I-35 E (75165)
Rates: $42-$53
Tel: (214) 937-8223
(800) 578-7878

WEATHERFORD

**BEST WESTERN
SANTA FE INN**
1927 Santa Fe Dr
(76086)
Rates: $39-$48
Tel: (817) 594-7401
(800) 528-1234

COMFORT INN
809 Palo Pinto St
(76086)
Rates: $48-$56
Tel: (817) 599-8683
(800) 221-2222

SUPER 8 MOTEL
111 I-20 W (76087)
Rates: $37-$52
Tel: (817) 594-8702
(800) 800-8000

WEBSTER

MOTEL 6
1001 W NASA Rd
One (77598)
Rates: $32-$36
Tel: (713) 332-4581
(800) 440-6000

WEST COLUMBIA

HOMEPLACE INN
714 Columbia Dr
(77486)
Rates: $44-$55
Tel: (409) 345-2399

WESTLAKE

MARRIOTT SOLANA DALLAS/FW
5 Village Cir (76262)
Rates: $59-$109
Tel: (817) 430-3848
(800) 228-9290

WHARTON

HOMEPLACE INN
1808 FM 102 (77488)
Rates: $42-$52
Tel: (409) 532-1152

WICHITA FALLS

BEST WESTERN TOWNE CREST INN
1601 8th St (76301)
Rates: $29-$35
Tel: (817) 322-1182
(800) 528-1234

DAYS INN
1211 Central Expwy
(76305)
Rates: $42-$78
Tel: (817) 723-5541
(800) 329-7466

FAIRFIELD INN BY MARRIOTT
4414 Westgate Dr
(76307)
Rates: $45-$52
Tel: (817) 691-1066
(800) 228-2800

LA QUINTA INN
1128 Central Frwy
(76305)
Rates: $42-$57
Tel: (817) 322-6971
(800) 531-5900

MOTEL 6
1812 Maurine St
(76304)
Rates: $29-$35
Tel: (817) 322-8817
(800) 440-6000

SHERATON INN
100 Central Frwy
(76305)
Rates: $59-$72
Tel: (817) 761-6000
(800) 325-3535

WIMBERLEY

HOMESTEAD BED & BREAKFAST
RR 2 at Scudder Ln
(78676)
Rates: $85-$95
Tel: (512) 847-8788
(800) 918-8788

7A RANCH RESORT
333 Wayside Dr
(78676)
Rates: $50-$86
Tel: (512) 847-2517

WINNIE

BEST WESTERN GULF COAST INN
46310 I-10 E
P. O. Box 697 (77665)
Rates: $36-$55
Tel: (409) 296-9292
(800) 528-1234

WINNSBORO

THEE HUBBELL HOUSE BED & BREAKFAST
307 West Elm
(75494)
Rates: $75-$175
Tel: (800) 227-0639

WOODVILLE

WOODVILLE INN
201 N Magnolia
(75979)
Rates: $34-$42
Tel: (409) 283-3741

ZAPATA

BASS LAKE SUNDOME MOTEL
Rt 1, Box 200 (78076)
Rates: $25-$49
Tel: (210) 765-4961

BEST WESTERN INN BY THE LAKE
Star Rt 1, Box 252
(78076)
Rates: $35-$64
Tel: (210) 765-8403
(800) 528-1234

FALCON EXECUTIVE INN
P. O. Box 686
Hwy 83 (78076)
Rates: $38-$42
Tel: (210) 765-6982

UTAH

ALTAMONT

MOON LAKE RESORT
P.O. Box 70
(Mountain Home 84001)
Rates: $50-$75
Tel: (801) 454-3475

BEAVER

BEAVER LODGE
355 Main St, Box 406
(84713)
Rates: n/a
Tel: (801) 438-2462

BEST WESTERN PAICE INN
161 S Main St
(84713)
Rates: $50-$75
Tel: (801) 438-2438
(800) 528-1234

BEST WESTERN PARADISE INN
1451 N 300 (84713)
Rates: $50-$75
Tel: (801) 438-2455
(800) 528-1234

COUNTRY INN
1450 N 300 W
(84713)
Rates: $40-$49
Tel: (801) 438-2484
(800) 754-2484

DELANO MOTEL
480 N Main St
(84713)
Rates: $22-$39
Tel: (801) 438-2418

GRANADA INN
75 S Main, Box K
(84713)
Rates: $40-$49
Tel: (801) 438-2292

PAICE MANSFIELD MOTEL
10 W Center,
Box 777 (84713)
Rates: $40-$49
Tel: (801) 438-2410
(801) 438-2486

SLEEPY LAGOON MOTEL
882 S Main St (84713)
Rates: $30-$45
Tel: (801) 438-5681

BICKNELL

AQUARIUS MOTEL
240 W Main St (84715)
Rates: $19-$42
Tel: (801) 425-3835
(800) 833-5379

SUNGLOW MOTEL
63 E Main St (84715)
Rates: $27-$37
Tel: (801) 425-3821

BIG WATER

HIGHWAY HOST MOTEL
Hwy 89, Box 4 (84741)
Rates: $50-$75
Tel: (801) 675-3731
(800) 748-5034

WARM CREEK MOTEL
Hwy 89, Box 410004
(84741)
Rates: $50-$75
Tel: (801) 675-9199
(800) 748-5065

BLANDING

BEST WESTERN
88 E Center (84511)
Rates: $50-$75
Tel: (801) 678-2278
(800) 528-1234

SUNSET INN
88 W Center
Box 119-3 (84512)
Rates: $40-$49
Tel: (801) 678-3323

BLUFF

KOKOPELLI INN
Hwy 191 (84512)
Rates: $50-$75
Tel: (801) 672-2322
(800) 541-8854

RECAPTURE LODGE
P. O. Box 309 (84512)
Rates: $50-$75
Tel: (801) 672-2281

RIVER HOUSE INN
Box 310252 (84512)
Rates: $40-$49
Tel: (801) 672-2217

BOULDER

BOULDER MOUNTAIN LODGE
P.O. Box 1397 (84716)
Rates: $50-$150
Tel: (801) 335-7460
(800) 556-3446

BOULDER MOUNTAIN RANCH
Hell's Backbone Rd
Box 1373 (84716)
Rates: $50-$75
Tel: (801) 335-7480

CIRCLE CLIFFS MOTEL
52 N Main St
Box 1399 (84716)
Rates: $40-$49
Tel: (801) 335-7353

BRIGHAM CITY

BUSHNELL LODGE
115 E 700 S (84302)
Rates: $50-$75
Tel: (801) 723-8575

CRYSTAL INN
480 Westland Dr
(84302)
Rates: $75-$150
Tel: (801) 723-0440
(800) 408-0440

HOWARD JOHNSON
1167 S Main St (84302)
Rates: $50-$80
Tel: (801) 723-8511
(800) 446-4656

BRYCE CANYON NATIONAL PARK

BEST WESTERN RUBY'S INN
Hwy 63,
Box 1 (84764)
Rates: $44-$130
Tel: (801) 834-5341
(800) 528-1234

BRYCE PIONEER VILLAGE
80 S Main, Box 119
(Tropic 84776)
Rates: $50-$75
Tel: (801) 679-8654
(800) 222-0381

DOUG'S COUNTRY INN MOTEL
141 N Main, Box 157
(Tropic 84776)
Rates: $49-$75
Tel: (801) 679-8600
(800) 993-6847

PINK CLIFFS VILLAGE
13500 E Hwy 12
Box 640006 (84717)
Rates: $75-$150
Tel: (801) 834-5351
(800) 834-0043

WORLD HOST BRYCE VALLEY INN
200 N Main St, Box
A (Tropic 84776)
Rates: $50-$150
Tel: (801) 679-8811
(800) 442-1890

CAPITAL REEF NATIONAL PARK

CAPITOL REEF INN & CAFE
Box 100 (Torrey 84775)
Rates: $45-$55
Tel: (801) 425-3271

CASTLE DALE

VILLAGE INN MOTEL
P.O. Box 1244 (84513)
Rates: $40-$49
Tel: (801) 381-2309

CEDAR BREAKS NATIONAL MONUMENT

ASPEN WHISPERING PINES LODGE
P. O. Box 1001
(84762)
Rates: $85-$135
Tel: (801) 682-2378

CEDAR CITY

ASTRO BUDGET INN
323 S Main St
(84720)
Rates: $26-$58
Tel: (801) 586-6557

COMFORT INN
250 N 1100 West
(84720)
Rates: $33-$75
Tel: (801) 586-2082
(800) 221-2222

ECONOMY HOTEL
443 S Main (84720)
Rates: $21-$42
Tel: (801) 586-4461

HOLIDAY INN-CONVENTION CTR
1575 W 200 North
(84720)
Rates: $50-$100
Tel: (801) 586-8888
(800) 465-4329

RAYCAP MOTEL
2555 N Main St
(84720)
Rates: $35-$47
Tel: (801) 586-7435
(800) 574-4507

RODEWAY INN
281 S Main St
(84720)
Rates: $44-$76
Tel: (801) 586-9916
(800) 228-2000

SUPER 8 MOTEL
145 N 1550 W
(84720)
Rates: $41-$63
Tel: (801) 586-8880
(800) 800-8000

VALU INN
344 S Main St (84720)
Rates: $23-$55
Tel: (801) 586-9114

CIRCLEVILLE

THE BUNKHOUSE
400 S 303 W, Box 85
(84723)
Rates: $40-$75
Tel: (801) 577-2522

CLEARFIELD

SUPER 8 MOTEL
572 N Main (84015)
Rates: $40-$55
Tel: (801) 825-8000
(800) 800-8000

COALVILLE

A COUNTRY PLACE
99 S Main, Box 894
(84017)
Rates: $40-$75
Tel: (801) 336-2451
(800) 371-2451

DELTA

BEST WESTERN MOTOR INN
527 E Topaz Blvd
(84624)
Rates: $42-$68
Tel: (801) 864-3882
(800) 528-1234

BUDGET MOTEL
75 South 350 E
(84624)
Rates: $25-$45
Tel: (801) 864-4533

DRAPER

ECONO LODGE
12605 S Minuteman
Dr (84020)
Rates: $48-$70
Tel: (801) 571-1122
(800) 424-4777

DUCHESNE

RIO DAMIAN MOTEL
23 W Main St,
Box 166 (84021)
Rates: $50-$75
Tel: (801) 738-2217

DUCK CREEK VILLAGE

DUCK CREEK VILLAGE INN
Hwy 14, Box 1149
(84762)
Rates: $50-$75
Tel: (801) 682-2568

MEADEAU VIEW LODGE
Movie Ranch Rd
Box 1331 (84762)
Rates: $50-$75
Tel: (801) 682-2495
(800) 332-0568

WHISPERING PINES LODGE
116 Color Country
Rd (84762)
Rates: $75-$150
Tel: (801) 682-2378

DUTCH JOHN

RED CANYON LODGE
790 Red Canyon Rd
(84023)
Rates: $75-$150
Tel: (801) 889-3759

ECHO

KOZY CAFE & MOTEL
24 Echo Main St
(84024)
Rates: $30-$49
Tel: (801) 336-5641

EDEN

SNOWBERRY INN B & B
1315 N Hwy 158
Box 795 (84310)
Rates: $75-$150
Tel: (801) 745-2634

EPHRAIM

IRON HORSE MOTEL
670 N Main, Box 226
(84627)
Rates: $50-$75
Tel: (801) 283-4223
(800) 339-4201

TRAVEL INN MOTEL
330 N Main St
(84627)
Rates: $49+
Tel: (801) 283-4071

ESCALANTE

CIRCLE D MOTEL
475 W Main St,
Box 305 (84726)
Rates: $40-$75
Tel: (801) 826-4297

QUIET FALLS MOTEL
75 S 100 W (84726)
Rates: $40-$49
Tel: (801) 826-4250

RAINBOW COUNTRY B & B
585 E 300 S (84726)
Rates: $50-$75
Tel: (801) 826-4567

FAIRVIEW

SKYLINE MOTEL
236 N State St
(84629)
Rates: $40-$49
Tel: (801) 427-3312

FILLMORE

BEST WESTERN PARADISE INN
1025 N Main St
(84631)
Rates: $48-$62
Tel: (801) 743-6895
(800) 528-1234

FILLMORE MOTEL
61 N Main St (84631)
Rates: $25-$42
Tel: (801) 743-5454

SPINNING WHEEL MOTEL
65 S Main St (84631)
Rates: $25-$36
Tel: (801) 743-6260

GARDEN CITY

BEAR LAKE MOTOR LODGE
50 S Bear Lake Blvd
(84028)
Rates: $50-$75
Tel: (801) 946-3271

BLUE WATER RESORT
2126 S Bear Lake
Blvd (84028)
Rates: $75-$150
Tel: (801) 946-3333

HARBOR VILLAGE RESORT
900 N Bear Lake
Blvd (84028)
Rates: $75-$300
Tel: (801) 946-3448
(800) 324-6840

GREEN RIVER

BUDGET HOST BOOKCLIFF LODGE
395 E Main (84525)
Rates: $30-$95
Tel: (801) 561-3406
(800) 283-4678

BUDGET INN MOTEL
60 E Main (84525)
Rates: $30-$75
Tel: (801) 564-3441

MANCOS ROSE MOTEL
20 W Main (84525)
Rates: $40-$49
Tel: (801) 564-9660

MOTEL 6
946 E Main (84525)
Rates: $28-$44
Tel: (801) 564-3436
(800) 466-8356

NATIONAL 9 INN
456 W Main (84525)
Rates: $40-$49
Tel: (801) 564-8237
(800) 474-3304

HANKSVILLE

POOR BOY MOTEL
264 E 100 N (84734)
Rates: $40-$49
Tel: (801) 542-3471

HATCH

GALAXY MOTEL
216 N Main (84735)
Rates: $49-$76
Tel: (801) 735-4327

MT. RIDGE MOTEL 7 RV PARK
106 S Main (84735)
Rates: $50-$75
Tel: (801) 735-4258
(800) 870-4258

NEW BRYCE MOTEL
227 W Main (84735)
Rates: $37-$47
Tel: (801) 735-4265

RIVERSIDE MOTEL
P.O. Box 521 (84735)
Rates: $28-$52
Tel: (801) 735-4223

HEBER CITY

DANISH VIKING LODGE
999 S Main (84032)
Rates: $39-$50
Tel: (801) 654-2202
(800) 544-4066

HEBER VALLEY RV PARK & RESORT
7000 N Old Hwy 40
(80432)
Rates: $50-$75
Tel: (801) 654-4049

HY LANDER MOTEL
425 S Main (84032)
Rates: $30-$48
Tel: (801) 654-2150
(800) 932-0355

SWISS ALPS INN
167 S Main (84032)
Rates: $29-$47
Tel: (801) 654-0722

HUNTINGTON

VILLAGE INN MOTEL
307 S Main (84528)
Rates: $40-$49
Tel: (801) 687-9888

HUNTSVILLE

JACKSON FORK INN
7345 E 900 S (84317)
Rates: $75-$150
Tel: (801) 745-0051
(800) 255-0672

HURRICANE

BEST WESTERN WESTON'S LAMPLIGHTER
280 W State (84737)
Rates: $40-$65
Tel: (801) 635-4647
(800) 528-1234

PAH TEMPE HOT SPRINGS RESORT B & B
825 N 800 E (84737)
Rates: $50-$75
Tel: (801) 635-2353

PARK VILLA MOTEL
650 W State (84737)
Rates: $28-$58
Tel: (801) 635-4010
(800) 682-6336

JORDAN

SUPER 8 MOTEL
10722 S 300 W
(84095)
Rates: $57-$85
Tel: (801) 553-8888
(800) 800-8000

JUNCTION

JUNCTION MOTEL
300 S Main (84740)
Rates: $40-$49
Tel: (801) 577-2629

KANAB

AIKENS LODGE-NATIONAL 9
79 W Center St
(84741)
Rates: $30-$50
Tel: (801) 644-2625
(800) 524-9999

BUNKHOUSE MOTEL
6676 E Hwy 89
(84741)
Rates: $40-$75
Tel: (801) 644-8805

COLOR COUNTRY INN
1550 S Hwy 89A
(84741)
Rates: $50-$75
Tel: (801) 644-2164
(800) 473-2164

CORAL SANDS MOTEL
60 S 100 E (84741)
Rates: $40-$75
Tel: (801) 644-2616
(800) 654-0805

BRANDON MOTEL BED & BREAKFAST
223 West Center St
(84741)
Rates: $50-$75
Tel: (801) 644-2631

FOUR SEASONS MOTOR INN
36 North 300 W
(84741)
Rates: $59-$67
Tel: (801) 644-2635

K MOTEL
330 S 100 E (84741)
Rates: $40-$150
Tel: (801) 644-2611
(800) 283-4678

PARRY LODGE
89 E Center St (84741)
Rates: $41-$65
Tel: (801) 644-2601

RIDING'S BON-BON INN MOTEL
171 W 200 S (84741)
Rates: $40-$49
Tel: (801) 644-5094
(801) 644-3069

RIDING'S QUAIL PARK LODGE
125 North 300 W
(84741)
Rates: $35-$55
Tel: (801) 644-2639
(800) 644-8115

SHILO INNS
296 West 100 N
(84741)
Rates: $63-$89
Tel: (801) 644-2562
(800) 222-2244

SUN-N-SAND MOTEL
347 S 100 E (84741)
Rates: $50-$75
Tel: (801) 644-5050
(800) 644-5050

TREASURE TRAIL MOTEL
150 W Center St
(84741)
Rates: $39-$58
Tel: (801) 644-2687
(800) 603-2687

KOOSHAREM

GRASS VALLEY GUEST RANCH MOTEL
P.O. Box 440071 (84744)
Rates: $40-$49
Tel: (801) 638-7322

LAKE POWELL

DEFIANCE HOUSE- BULLFROG MARINA
Bullfrog Marina (84533)
Rates: $69-$116
Tel: (801) 684-2233

LAYTON

LA QUINTA INN
1965 N 1200 West (84041)
Rates: $56-$71
Tel: (801) 776-6700
(800) 221-4731

VALLEY VIEW MOTEL
1560 N Main St (84041)
Rates: $40-$49
Tel: (801) 825-1632

LEHI

BEST WESTERN TIMPANOGOS INN
195 S 850 E (84043)
Rates: $61-$84
Tel: (801) 768-1400
(800) 528-1234

MANILA

NIKI'S INN
P. O. Box 340 (84046)
Rates: $35-$47
Tel: (801) 784-3117

VACATION INN
Hwy 43,
P. O. Box 306 (84046)
Rates: $43-$59
Tel: (801) 784-3259
(800) 662-4327

MANTI

MANTI COUNTRY VILLAGE
145 N Main St (84642)
Rates: $37-$48
Tel: (801) 835-9300
(800) 452-0787

MANTI MOTEL
445 N Main St (84642)
Rates: $50-$75
Tel: (801) 835-8533

MARYSVALE

MARYSVALE MINERS LODGE
315 N Main St (84750)
Rates: $40-$75
Tel: (801) 326-4258

MEXICAN HAT

BURCH'S TRADING CO. & MOTEL
P.O. Box 310-337 (84531)
Rates: $50-$75
Tel: (801) 683-2221

SAN JUAN INN
US 163, P. O. Box 535 (84531)
Rates: $45-$60
Tel: (801) 683-2220
(800) 683-2220

MIDVALE

LA QUINTA INN
530 Catalpa Rd (84047)
Rates: $75-$150
Tel: (801) 566-3291
(800) 531-5900

MOTEL 6
496 N Catalpa Rd (84047)
Rates: $36-$45
Tel: (801) 561-0058
(800) 440-6000

MILFORD

THE STATION MOTEL
485 S 100 W (84751)
Rates: $50-$75
Tel: (801) 387-2481

MOAB

APACHE MOTEL
166 S 400 East (84532)
Rates: $30-$65
Tel: (801) 259-5755
(800) 228-6882

ARCHES INN
41 W 100 N (84532)
Rates: $50-$150
Tel: (801) 259-5191
(800) 421-5614

BOWEN MOTEL
169 N Main St (84532)
Rates: $30-$60
Tel: (801) 259-7132
(800) 874-5439

COMFORT SUITES
800 S Main St (84532)
Rates: $85-$95
Tel: (801) 259-5252
(800) 221-2222

ENTRADA RANCH
P.O. Box 567 (84532)
Rates: $50-$150
Tel: (801) 259-5796

HOTEL OFF CENTER
96 E Center St (84532)
Rates: $50-$75
Tel: (801) 259-4244
(800) 237-4685

KOKOPELLI LODGE
72 S 100 East (84532)
Ratews: $45-$55
Tel: (801) 259-7615
(800) 505-5343

MOAB VALLEY INN
711 S Main (84532)
Rates: $75-$150
Tel: (801) 259-4419
(800) 831-6622

PIONEER SPRINGS BED & BREAKFAST
1275 S Boulder (84532)
Rates: $50-$75
Tel: (801) 259-4663

PACK CREEK RANCH
La Sal Pass Rd (84532)
Rates: $90-$200
Tel: (801) 259-5505

RED STONE INN
535 S Main St (84532)
Rates: $43-$49
Tel: (801) 259-3500
(800) 772-1972

ROSE TREE INN
481 Rose Tree Ln (84532)
Rates: $50-$75
Tel: (801) 259-4305

SLICKROCK CABINS
1301 1/2 N Hwy 191 (84532)
Rates: n/a
Tel: (801) 259-7660
(801) 259-4152

SUNSET MOTEL
41 W 100 N (84532)
Rates: $50-$150
Tel: (801) 259-5192
(800) 421-5614

THE VIRGINIAN MOTEL
70 E 200 St S (84532)
Rates: $30-$55
Tel: (801) 259-5951
(800) 261-2063

MONTICELLO

CANYONLANDS MOTOR INN
197 N Main (84535)
Rates: $22-$55
Tel: (801) 587-2266
(800) 952-6212

MOUNT CARMEL JUNCTION

BEST WESTERN THUNDERBIRD RESORT
Hwy 9 & 89 (84755)
Rates: $60-$70
Tel: (801) 648-2203
(800) 528-1234

GOLDEN HILLS MOTEL
125 E State St (84755)
Rates: $22-$49
Tel: (801) 648-2268

MURRAY

RESTON HOTEL
5335 College Dr
(84123)
Rates: $50-$75
Tel: (801) 264-1054
(800) 231-9710

NEPHI

BEST WESTERN PARADISE INN
1025 S Main (84648)
Rates: $44-$62
Tel: (801) 623-0642
(800) 528-1234

SAFARI HOTEL
413 S Main (84648)
Rates: $27-$49
Tel: (801) 623-1071

STARLITE MOTEL
675 S Main (84648)
Rates: $40-$49
Tel: (801) 623-1937

TEMPLE VIEW LODGE
260 E Main (84642)
Rates: $50-$75
Tel: (801) 835-6663

WHITMORE MANSION B & B
110 S Main (84648)
Rates: $75-$150
Tel: (801) 623-2047

OGDEN

BEST WESTERN HIGH COUNTRY INN
1335 W 12th St
(84404)
Rates: $48-$72
Tel: (801) 391-9474
(800) 528-1234

BEST WESTERN OGDEN PARK HOTEL
247 24th St (84401)
Rates: $79-$109
Tel: (801) 627-1190
(800) 528-1234

BIG Z MOTEL
1123 West 2100 S
(84401)
Rates: $27-$32
Tel: (801) 394-6632

COLONIAL MOTEL
1269 Washington
Blvd (84404)
Rates: $40-$49
Tel: (801) 399-5851

COMFORT SUITES OF OGDEN
1150 W 2150 S
(84404)
Rates: $50-$75
Tel: (801) 621-2545
(800) 462-9925

FLYING J INN
1206 W 21st St
(84404)
Rates: $45-$49
Tel: (801) 393-8644
(800) 343-8644

MILLSTREAM
1450 Washington
Blvd (84404)
Rates: $50-$75
Tel: (801) 394-9425

MOTEL 6-DOWNTOWN
1455 Washington
Blvd (84404)
Rates: $30-$35
Tel: (801) 627-4560
(800) 466-8356

MOTEL 6-RIVERDALE
1500 W Riverdale Rd
(84405)
Rates: $33-$39
Tel: (801) 627-2880
(800) 466-8356

SLEEP INN
1155 S 1700 W (84401)
Rates: $50-$75
Tel: (801) 731-6500
(800) 221-2222

SUPER 8 MOTEL
1508 W 2100 S
(84401)
Rates: $36-$45
Tel: (801) 731-7100
(800) 800-8000

TRAVELODGE
2110 Washington
Blvd (84401)
Rates: $45-$57
Tel: (801) 394-4563
(800) 578-7878

WESTERN COLONY INN
234 24th St (84401)
Rates: $50-$75
Tel: (801) 627-1332

ORDERVILLE

PARKWAY MOTEL
74 E State St (84758)
Rates: $40-$49
Tel: (801) 648-2380

STARLITE MOTEL
Hwy 89,
Box 58 (84758)
Rates: $40-$75
Tel: (801) 648-2060

PANGUITCH

BLUE PINE MOTEL
130 N Main St
(87459)
Rates: $28-$45
Tel: (801) 676-8197

BRYCE WAY MOTEL
429 N Main St
(84759)
Rates: $22-$52
Tel: (801) 676-2400

CAMERON MOTEL
78 W Center St
(84759)
Rates: $50-$75
Tel: (801) 676-8840
(800) 537-9212

COLOR COUNTRY MOTEL
526 N Main (84759)
Rates: $25-$53
Tel: (801) 676-2386
(800) 225-6518

DEER TRAIL LODGE
P.O. Box 647 (84759)
Rates: $50-$150
Tel: (801) 676-2211

HORIZON MOTEL
730 N Main St
(84759)
Rates: $25-$69
Tel: (801) 676-2651

MARIANNA INN MOTEL
699 N Main (84759)
Rates: $27-$59
Tel: (801) 676-8844
(800) 331-7407

RUSTIC LODGE
186 S Westshore Rd
(84759)
Rates: $50-$150
Tel: (801) 676-2627

SANDS MOTEL
390 N Main (84759)
Rates: n/a
Tel: (801) 676-8874
(800) 497-9261

SPORTSMAN'S PARADISE CABINS
Hwy 89,
Box 655 (84759)
Rates: n/a
Tel: (801) 676-8348

PARK CITY

BEST WESTERN LANDMARK INN
6560 N Landmark
Dr (84060)
Rates: $69-$164
Tel: (801) 649-7300
(800) 528-1234

BLUE CHURCH LODGE
424 Park Ave
Box 1720 (84060)
Rates: $150-$300
Tel: (801) 649-8009
(800) 626-5467

RADISSON INN
2121 Park Ave
(84060)
Rates: $75-$150
Tel: (801) 649-5000
(800) 333-3333

PAROWAN

BEST WESTERN SWISS VILLAGE INN
580 N Main St
(84761)
Rates: $41-$70
Tel: (801) 477-3391
(800) 528-1234

DAY'S INN
625 West 200 S
(84761)
Rates: $40-$75
Tel: (801) 477-3326
(800) 329-7466

PAYSON

COMFORT INN
830 N Main (84651)
Rates: $75-$150
Tel: (801) 465-4861
(800) 221-2222

PINE VALLEY

PINE VALLEY LODGE
960 E Main St (84722)
Rates: $50-$75
Tel: (801) 574-2544

PRICE

GREENWELL INN
655 E Main (84501)
Rates: $25-$47
Tel: (801) 637-3520
(800) 666-3520

NATIONAL 9 INN
641 W Price River Dr
(84501)
Rates: $29-$49
Tel: (801) 637-7000
(800) 524-9999

PRICE BUDGET HOST
145 N Carbonville
Rd (84501)
Rates: $40-$49
Tel: (801) 637-2424
(800) 283-4678

SHAMAN LODGE
3769 W Garden
Creek Rd (84501)
Rates: $75-$300
Tel: (801) 637-7489

PROVO

**COLONY INN
SUITES-NATIONAL 9**
1380 S University
Ave (84601)
Rates: $30-$65
Tel: (801) 374-6800
(800) 524-9999

**COMFORT INN
UNIVERSITY**
1555 N Canyon Rd
(84604)
Rates: $53-$90
Tel: (801) 374-6020
(800) 221-2222

DAYS INN
1675 North 200 W
(84604)
Rates: $52-$65
Tel: (801) 375-8600
(800) 329-7466

HAMPTON INN
1511 South 40 E
(84601)
Rates: $61-$78
Tel: (801) 377-6396
(800) 426-7866

HOWARD JOHNSON
1292 S University
Ave (84601)
Rates: $75-$150
Tel: (801) 374-2500
(800) 446-4656

MOTEL 6
1600 S University
Ave (84601)
Rates: $49+
Tel: (801) 375-5064
(800) 440-6000

**PROVO PARK
HOTEL**
101 W 100 N (84601)
Rates: $75-$150
Tel: (801) 377-4700
(800) 777-7144

RESIDENCE INN
295 W 2230 N
(84601)
Rates: n/a
Tel: (800) 331-3131

SLEEP INN
1505 S 40th E (84606)
Rates: $40-$49
Tel: (801) 377-6396
(800) 627-5337

UPTOWN MOTEL
469 W Center St
(84601)
Rates: $30-$53
Tel: (801) 373-8248

VALLEY INN MOTEL
1425 S State St
(84606)
Rates: $40-$49
Tel: (801) 377-3804

RICHFIELD

**BEST WESTERN
APPLE TREE INN**
145 S Main St
(84701)
Rates: $42-$100
Tel: (801) 896-5481
(800) 528-1234

**BUDGET HOST
KNIGHTS INN**
69 S Main St (84701)
Rates: $34-$62
Tel: (800) 525-9024

DAYS INN
333 N Main St
(84701)
Rates: $56-$68
Tel: (801) 896-6476
(800) 329-7466

**GRAND WESTERN
HOTEL**
575 S Main St
(84701)
Rates: $40-$49
Tel: (801) 896-6948

JENSEN MOTEL
290 S Main St
(84701)
Rates: $40-$49
Tel: (801) 896-5447

MONTAIR MOTEL
190 S Main St
(84701)
Rates: $40-$49
Tel: (801) 896-4415

NEW WEST MOTEL
447 S Main St
(84701)
Rates: $49+
Tel: (801) 896-4076

ROMANICO INN
1170 S Main St
(84701)
Rates: $30-$46
Tel: (801) 896-8471
(800) 948-0001

WESTON INN
647 S Main St
(84701)
Rates: $50-$75
Tel: (801) 896-9271
(800)333-7819

ROOSEVELT

BEST WESTERN INN
Rt 2,
Box 2860 (84066)
Rates: $40-$65
Tel: (801) 722-4644
(800) 528-1234

FRONTIER MOTEL
75 S 200 East St
(84066)
Rates: $30-$46
Tel: (801) 722-3640
(800) 248-1014

**WESTERN HILLS
MOTEL**
737 E 200 S (84066)
Rates: $40-$49
Tel: (801) 722-5115

ST. GEORGE

**AN OLDE PENNY
FARTHING INN**
278 N 100 W (84770)
Rates: $50-$150
Tel: (801) 673-7755

ANCESTOR INN
60 W St George Blvd
(84770)
Rates: $26-$46
Tel: (801) 673-4666

THE BLUFFS MOTEL
1140 S Bluff (84770)
Rates: $39-$69
Tel: (801) 628-6699
(800) 832-5833

BUDGET INN
1221 S Main St
(84770)
Rates: $40-$50
Tel: (801) 673-6661
(800) 929-0790

DESERT EDGE INN
525 E St. George
Blvd (84770)
Rates: n/a
Tel: (801) 673-6137

ECONO LODGE
460 E St. George
Blvd (84770)
Rates: $40-$70
Tel: (801) 673-4861
(800) 424-4777

HILTON INN
1450 S Hilton Dr
(84770)
Rates: $49-$99
Tel: (801) 628-0463
(800) 662-2525

**HOLIDAY
INN/HOLIDOME**
850 S Bluff St (84770)
Rates: $75-$150
Tel: (801) 628-4235
(800) 465-4329

MOTEL 6
205 N. 1000 E
(84770)
Rates: $35-$38
Tel: (801) 628-7979
(800) 440-6000

SANDS MOTEL
581 E St. George
Blvd (84770)
Rates: $50-$150
Tel: (801) 673-3501

SOUTHSIDE INN
750 E St. George
Blvd (84770)
Rates: $40-$49
Tel: (801) 628-9000

SUN TIME INN
420 E St. George
Blvd (84770)
Rates: $50-$75
Tel: (801) 673-3232
(800) 237-6253

SINGLETREE INN
260 E. St. George
Blvd (84770)
Rates: $40-$62
Tel: (801) 673-6161
(800) 528-8890

SUPER 8 MOTEL
915 S Bluff (84770)
Rates: $40-$46
Tel: (801) 628-4251
(800) 800-8000

**THUNDERBIRD
LODGE**
150 N 1000 E (84770)
Rates: $40-$57
Tel: (801) 673-6123

**TRAVELODGE
MOTEL**
175 N 1000 East St
(84770)
Rates: $35-$79
Tel: (801) 673-4621
(800) 574-8552

SALINA

**BUDGET HOST
SCENIC HILLS
MOTEL**
75 East 1500 S
(84654)
Rates: $30-$52
Tel: (801) 529-7483
(800) 283-4678

HENRY'S HIDEAWAY
60 N State St (84654)
Rates: $35-$57
Tel: (801) 529-7467

SAFARI MOTEL
1425 S State St
(84654)
Rates: $35-$60
Tel: (801) 529-7447

SALT LAKE CITY

ALL-STAR
754 W North Temple
(84116)
Rates: $40-$49
Tel: (801) 531-7300

COLONIAL VILLAGE
1530 S Main (84115)
Rates: $40-$49
Tel: (801) 486-8171

**COMFORT INN
AIRPORT**
200 N Admiral Byrd
Rd (84116)
Rates: $70-$150
Tel: (801) 537-7444
(800) 221-2222

**CONTINENTAL
MOTEL**
819 W North Temple
(84116)
Rates: $40-$49
Tel: (801) 363-4546

**COVERED WAGON
MOTEL**
230 W North Temple
(84103)
Rates: $40-$49
Tel: (801) 533-9100

DAYS INN AIRPORT
1900 W North
Temple St (84116)
Rates: $50-$80
Tel: (801) 539-8538
(800) 329-7466

DAYS INN CENTRAL
315 W 33rd South
(84115)
Rates: $49-$89
Tel: (801) 486-8780
(800) 329-7466

ECONO LODGE
715 W N Temple
(84116)
Rates: $48-$65
Tel: (801) 363-0062
(800) 424-4777

HILTON AIRPORT
5151 Wiley Post Way
(84116)
Rates: $75-$150
Tel: (801) 539-1515
(800) 999-3736

HILTON HOTEL
150 West 500 S
(84101)
Rates: $95-$130
Tel: (801) 532-3344
(800) 445-8667

HOWARD JOHNSON
122 W South Temple
(84101)
Rates: $79-$250
Tel: (801) 521-0130
(800) 446-4656

**LOG CABIN ON
THE HILL B & B**
2275 E 6200 S (84121)
Rates: $50-$150
Tel: (801) 272-2969

MARRIOTT HOTEL
75 S W Temple
(84101)
Rates: $69-$166
Tel: (801) 531-0800
(800) 345-4754

**MOTEL 6
AIRPORT WEST**
1990 W North
Temple St (84116)
Rates: $35-$45
Tel: (801) 364-1053
(800) 440-6000

**MOTEL 6
DOWNTOWN**
176 W 6th South St
(84101)
Rates: $36-$42
Tel: (801) 531-1252
(800) 440-6000

**QUALITY INN CITY
CENTER**
154 West 600 S
(84101)
Rates: $49-$108
Tel: (801) 521-2930
(800) 221-2222

RAMADA INN
230 West 600 S
(84101)
Rates: $70-$87
Tel: (801) 364-5200
(800) 272-6232

RED BUTTE B & B
1731 E 900 S (84105)
Rates: $300+
Tel: (801) 582-5356

RED LION HOTEL
255 S W Temple
(84101)
Rates: $74-$135
Tel: (801) 328-2000
(800) 547-8010

**RESIDENCE INN
BY MARRIOTT**
765 East 400 S
(84102)
Rates: $125-$176
Tel: (801) 532-5511
(800) 331-3131

RESTON HOTEL
5335 College Dr
(84123)
Rates: $62-$71
Tel: (801) 264-1054

**ROYAL EXECUTIVE
INN**
121 N 300 W (84103)
Rates: $40-$59
Tel: (801) 521-3450
(800) 541-7639

SHILO INNS
206 SW Temple
(84101)
Rates: $90-$105
Tel: (800) 222-2244

SKYLINE INN
2475 East 1700 S
(84108)
Rates: $45-$58
Tel: (801) 582-5350

SUPER 8 MOTEL
616 South 200 W
(84101)
Rates: $45-$56
Tel: (801) 534-0808
(800) 800-8000

SUPER 8 MOTEL
223 N Jimmy
Doolittle Rd (84116)
Rates: $65-$80
Tel: (801) 533-8878
(800) 800-8000

TRAVELODGE
524 S W Temple St
(84101)
Rates: $50-$75
Tel: (801) 531-7100
(800) 578-7878

SANDY

BEST WESTERN COTTON TREE
10695 S Auto Mall Dr (84054)
Rates: $69-$87
Tel: (801) 523-8484
(800) 528-1234

MAJESTIC ROCKIES MOTEL
8901 S State (84111)
Rates: $40-$49
Tel: (801) 255-2313

SCIPIO

HOTEL SCIPIO
195 N State,
Box 75 (84656)
Rates: $40-$49
Tel: (801) 758-2450

SPANISH FORK

IDEAL MOTEL
150 S Main St
(84660)
Rates: $40-$49
Tel: (801) 798-1900

SPRING CITY

HORSESHOE MOUNTAIN B & B
310 S Main, Box 84
(84662)
Rates: $50-$75
Tel: (801) 462-2871

SPRINGDALE

BLUE HOUSE B & B
125 E Main St
(Rockville 84767)
Rates: $50-$75
Tel: (801) 772-3912

BEST WESTERN DRIFTWOOD LODGE
1515 Zion Park Blvd
(84767)
Rates: $54-$80
Tel: (801) 772-3262
(800) 528-1234

BUMBLEBERRY INN
897 Zion Park Blvd
(84767)
Rates: $45-$63
Tel: (801) 772-3224
(800) 828-1534

CANYON RANCH MOTEL
668 Zion Park Blvd
(84767)
Rates: $50-$150
Tel: (801) 772-3357

CLIFFROSE LODGE
281 Zion Park Blvd
(84767)
Rates: $45-$135
Tel: (801) 772-3234
(800) 243-8824

EL RIO LODGE IN ZION CANYON
995 Zion Park Blvd
(84767)
Rates: $50-$75
Tel: (801) 772-3205

ZION PARK INN
1215 Zion Park Blvd
(84767)
Rates: $50-$150
Tel: (801) 772-3200
(800) 934-7275

TOQUERVILLE

YOUR INN
650 Spring Dr
(84774)
Rates: $40-$150
Tel: (801) 635-9964

TORREY

CAPITOL REEF INN
360 W Main St
(84775)
Rates: $40-$75
Tel: (801) 425-3271

CHUCK WAGON LODGE
12 W Main (84774)
Rates: $50-$75
Tel: (801) 425-3335
(800) 863-3288

LUNA MESA OASIS
P.O. Box 140 (84774)
Rates: $40-$49
Tel: (801) 456-9122
(800) 629-9141

RIM ROCK RUSTIC INN
Hwy 24, Box 750264
(84774)
Rates: $50-$75
Tel: (801) 425-3843
(800) 243-0786

TORREY TRADING POST
75 W Main St
(84774)
Rates: $40-$49
Tel: (801) 425-3716

TREMONTON

MARBLE MOTEL
116 N Tremonton St
(84337)
Rates: $30-$35
Tel: (801) 257-3524

SANDMAN MOTEL
585 W Main St
(84337)
Rates: $34-$40
Tel: (801) 257-7149

VERNAL

ECONO LODGE
311 E Main St
(84078)
Rates: $34-$46
Tel: (801) 789-2000
(800) 424-4777

RODEWAY INN
590 W Main St.
(84078)
Rates: $37-$53
Tel: (801) 789-8172
(800) 228-2000

SPLIT MOUNTAIN MOTEL
1015 E Hwy 40
(84078)
Rates: $40-$49
Tel: (801) 789-9020

WELLINGTON

NATIONAL 9 INN
50 South 700 E
(84542)
Rates: $25-$50
Tel: (801) 637-7980
(800) 524-9999

WENDOVER

HERITAGE MOTEL
505 E Wendover Blvd (84083)
Rates: $50-$75
Tel: (801) 665-7744

MOTEL 6
561 E. Wendover Blvd (84083)
Rates: $27-$40
Tel: (801) 665-2267
(800) 440-6000

WESTERN RIDGE MOTEL
895 E Wendover
(84083)
Rates: $49-$150
Tel: (801) 665-2211

WEST VALLEY CITY

SLEEP INN
3440 S 2200 W
(84119)
Rates: $40-$75
Tel: (801) 975-1888

WOODS CROSS

MOTEL 6
2433 S 800 W (84087)
Rates: $32-$42
Tel: (801) 298-0289
(800) 440-6000

HAMPTON INN
2393 South 800 West
(84087)
Rates: $65-$79
Tel: (801) 296-1211
(800) 426-7866

VERMONT

ALBURG

**YE OLDE
GRAYSTONE B & B**
RFD 1, Box 76
(05440)
Rates: $50-$55
Tel: (802) 796-3911

ANDOVER

INN AT HIGH VIEW
East Hill Rd (05143)
Rates: $95-$135
Tel: (802) 875-2724

ARLINGTON

**ARLINGTON
MANOR HOUSE
BED & BREAKFAST**
Buck Hill Rd (05250)
Rates: $45-$130
Tel: (802) 375-6784

**CUTLEAF MAPLES
MOTEL**
Rt 7A (05250)
Rates: n/a
Tel: (802) 375-2725

HILL FARM INN
RR 2, Box 2015
(05250)
Rates: $70-$85
Tel: (802) 375-2269
(800) 882-2545

VALHALLA MOTEL
Historic Rt 7A
(05250)
Rates: n/a
Tel: (802) 375-2212
(800) 258-2212

BARNET

**INN AT MAPLE-
MONT FARM**
Rt. 5,(05821)
Rates: $65-$80
Tel: (802) 633-4880
(800) 230-1617

BARRE

BUDGET INN
573 N Main St
(05641)
Rates: $35-$49
Tel: (802) 479-3333
(800) 446-4656

HOJO INN
573 N Main St
(05641)
Rates: $36-$80
Tel: (802) 479-3333
(800) 446-4656

**HOLLOW INN
& MOTEL**
278 S Main St
(05641)
Rates: $75-$94
Tel: (802) 479-9313
(800) 998-9444

BARTON

**PINE CREST
MOTEL & CABINS**
RR 1, Box 279
(05822)
Rates: $35-$50
Tel: (802) 525-3472

BELLOWS FALLS

**WHIPPOWIL
COTTAGES**
US Rt 5 (05101)
Rates: n/a
Tel: (802) 463-3442

BENNINGTON

**APPLEY VALLEY
INN & CAFE**
Rt 7 (05201)
Rates: $35-$85
Tel: (802) 442-6588

**BENNINGTON
MOTOR INN**
143 W Main St
(05201)
Rates: $48-$90
Tel: (802) 442-5479
(800) 359-9900

**FIFE 'N DRUM
MOTEL**
Rt 7S, RR 1, Box 4340
(05201)
Rates: $34-$69
Tel: (802) 442-4074

**KNOTTY PINE
MOTEL**
130 Northside Dr
(05201)
Rates: $38-$64
Tel: (802) 442-5487

**PLEASANT VALLEY
MOTEL**
Pleasant Valley Rd
(05201)
Rates: $40-$48
Tel: (802) 442-6222

RAMADA INN
US 7 at Kocher Dr
(05201)
Rates: $65-$150
Tel: (802) 442-8145
(800) 272-6232

**SOUTH GATE
MOTEL**
P. O. Box 1073
(05201)
Rates: $32-$64
Tel: (802) 447-7525

**VERMONTER
MOTOR LODGE**
RR 1, Box 2377
(05201)
Rates: $43-$80
Tel: (802) 442-2529
(800) 382-3175

BETHEL

GREENHURST INN
River St, RD 2
Box 60 (05032)
Rates: n/a
Tel: (802) 234-9474

**POPLAR MANOR
BED & BREAKFAST**
Rt 107 & 12 (05032)
Rates: $42-$44
Tel: (802) 234-5426

BOLTON VALLEY

TRAILSIDE CONDOS
HC 33, Box 751
(05477)
Rates: $190-$454
Tel: (802) 434-2769
(800) 451-5025

BONDVILLE

BROMLEY VIEW INN
Rt 30, Box 161
(05340)
Rates: $60-$90
Tel: (802) 297-1459
(800) 297-1459

BRADFORD

BRADFORD MOTEL
P. O. Box 250 (05033)
Rates: $35-$70
Tel: (802) 222-4467

BRANDON

**BRANDON
MOTOR LODGE**
Rt 7 South (05733)
Rates: $38-$70
Tel: (802) 247-9594
(800) 675-7614

**GINGERBREAD
HOUSE FINE ARTS
BED & BREAKFAST**
RR 3, Rt 73 E
Box 3241 (05733)
Rates: $60-$150
Tel: (802) 247-3380

**HIVUE
BED & BREAKFAST
TREE FARM**
Highpond Rd (05733)
Rates: $50+
Tel: (802) 247-3042
(800) 880-3042

BRATTLEBORO

BRATTLEBORO INN
1380 Putney Rd
(05301)
Rates: $129-$149
Tel: (802) 254-8701

COLONIAL MOTEL
Putney Rd (05301)
Rates: $32-$65
Tel: (802) 257-7733
(800) 239-0032

MOLLY STARK MOTEL
829 Marlboro Rd
(05301)
Rates: $37-$56
Tel: (802) 254-2440

MOTEL 6
Putney Rd, Rt 5N
(05301)
Rates: $40-$46
Tel: (802) 254-6007
(800) 440-6000

BRIDGEWATER CORNERS

THE CORNERS INN & RESTAURANT
Rt 4 & Upper Rd
(05035)
Rates: $45-$85
Tel: (802) 672-9968

BRISTOL

BRISTOL COMMONS INN
Jct 17 & 116 (05443)
Rates: $39-$68
Tel: (802) 453-2326

FIREFLY RANCH BED & BREAKFAST
P. O. Box 152 (05443)
Rates: $65-$105
Tel: (802) 453-2223

BROWNSVILLE

BURTON FARM LODGE B & B
RFD 1, Box 558
(05089)
Rates: $60-$70
Tel: (802) 484-3300

THE POND HOUSE AT SHATTUCK HILL FARM BED & BREAKFAST
P. O. Box 234 (05037)
Rates: $85-$115
Tel: (802) 484-0011

MILLBROOK B & B
P. O. Box 410 (05037)
Rates: n/a
Tel: (802) 484-7934

BURKE

OLD CUTTER INN
RR 1, Box 62 (05832)
Rates: $52-$64
Tel: (802) 626-5152
(800) 295-1943

BURLINGTON
(and South Burlington)

ANCHORAGE INNS
108 Dorset St
(S Burlington 05403)
Rates: $36-$80
Tel: (802) 863-7000

ECONO LODGE
1076 Williston Rd
(S Burlington 05403)
Rates: $50-$79
Tel: (802) 863-1125
(800) 424-4777

ETHAN ALLEN MOTEL
1611 Williston Rd
(S Burington 05403)
Rates: n/a
Tel: (802) 863-4573

FRIENDSHIP LAKE VIEW INN
1860 Shelburne Rd
(S Burlington 05403)
Rates: $34-$84
Tel: (800) 424-6423

HARBOR SUNSET MOTEL
1700 Shelburne Rd
(S Burlington 05403)
Rates: $25-$45
Tel: (802) 864-5080

HO HUM MOTEL-ROUTE 2
1660 Williston Rd
(05401)
Rates: $32-$96
Tel: (802) 863-4551

HOLIDAY INN
1068 Williston Rd
(S Burlington 05403)
Rates: $72-$100
Tel: (802) 863-6363
(800) 465-4329

HOWARD JOHNSON
1 Dorset St (05402)
Rates: $52-$90
Tel: (802) 863-5541
(800) 446-4656

HOWARD JOHNSON
1720 Shelburne Rd
(S Burlington 05403)
Rates: $95-120
Tel: (802) 860-6000
(800) 446-4656

RAMADA INN
1117 Williston Rd
(S Burlington 05403)
Rates: $54-$99
Tel: (802) 658-0250
(800) 272-6232

RODEWAY INN
1860 Shelburne Rd
(05401)
Rates: $39-$98
Tel: (802) 862-0230
(800) 228-2000

SHERATON HOTEL
870 Williston Rd
(S Burlington 05403)
Rates: $79-$137
Tel: (802) 865-6600
(800) 325-3535

SUPER 8 MOTEL
1016 Shelburne Rd
(05403)
Rates: $35-$80
Tel: (802) 862-6421
(800) 800-8000

TOWN & COUNTRY MOTEL
490 Shelburne Rd
(05401)
Rates: $32-$75
Tel: (802) 862-5786

CAMBRIDGE

4 PAUSE BED & BREAKFAST
RR 1, Box 765
(05444)
Rates: $50-$65
Tel: (802) 899-3927

CANAAN

LAKE WALLACE MOTEL
Rt 114 (05903)
Rates: n/a
Tel: (802) 266-3311

COLCHESTER

DAYS INN
23 College Pkwy
(05446)
Rates: $35-$125
Tel: (802) 655-0900
(800) 329-7466

HAMPTON INN
8 Mountain View Dr
(05446)
Rates: $69-$99
Tel: (802) 655-6177
(800) 426-7866

CRAFTSBURY COMMON

THE INN ON THE COMMON
Main St (05827)
Rates: $135-$270
Tel: (802) 586-9619
(800) 521-2233

DANBY

TUCKER INN
RFD 1, Box 100
(05739)
Rates: $40-$60
Tel: (802) 293-5835

DANVILLE

INJUNJOE COURT
US Rt 2, Box 126
(W Danville, 05873)
Rates: $40-$75
Tel: (802) 684-3430

DERBY

THE BORDER MOTEL
135 N Main (05829)
Rates: $42-$49
Tel: (802) 766-2088
(800) 280-1898

DORSET

BARROWS HOUSE
Rt 30 (05251)
Rates: $120-$235
Tel: (802) 867-4455
(800) 639-1620

EAST BURKE

OLD CUTTER INN
RR 1, Box 52 (05832)
Rates: $42-$140
Tel: (802) 626-5152

ESSEX

**VERMONT CNTR POINT
BED & BREAKFAST
RESERVATION SERVICE**
P.O. Box 8513
(05451)
Rates: n/a
Tel: (800) 449-2745

THE WILSON INN
10 Kellog Rd (05452)
Rates: $81-$101
Tel: (802) 879-1515
(800) 879-1515

FAIRLEE

**SILVER MAPLE LODGE
& COTTAGES B & B**
RR 1, Box 8 (05045)
Rates: $46-$64
Tel: (802) 333-4326
(800) 666-1946

FRANKLIN

**FAIR MEADOWS
FARM B & B**
Box 430, Rt 235
(05457)
Rates: n/a
Tel: (802) 285-2132

GRAFTON

THE HAYES HOUSE
Bear Hill Rd (05146)
Rates: n/a
Tel: (802) 843-2461

HARDWICK

**BRICK HOUSE
GUESTS**
2 Brick House Rd
(05836)
Rates: $45-$70
Tel: (802) 472-5512

ISLAND POND

LAKEFRONT MOTEL
P. O. Box 161 (05846)
Rates: $55-$60
Tel: (802) 723-6507

JEFFERSONVILLE

**DEER RUN
MOTOR INN**
RR 1, Box 260
(05464)
Rates: $50-$85
Tel: (802) 644-8866
(800) 354-2728

**THE HIGHLANDER
MOTEL**
RR 1, Box 436
(05464)
Rates: $42-$64
Tel: (802) 644-2725
(800) 367-6471

**THE JEFFERSON
HOUSE**
Main St, Box 288
(05464)
Rates: n/a
Tel: (802) 644-2030

JERICHO

**HOMEPLACE
BED & BREAKFAST**
Old Pump Rd
(05465)
Rates: $45-$55
Tel: (802) 899-4694

KILLINGTON

**BUTTERNUT
ON THE MOUNTAIN**
Box 306, Killington
Rd (05751)
Rates: $54-$140
Tel: (802) 422-2000
(800) 524-7654

**THE CASCADES
LODGE**
RR 1, P. O. Box 2848
(05751)
Rates: $51-$198
Tel: (802) 422-3731
(800) 345-0113

CEDARBROOK
MOTOR INN
US 4 & SR 100 S
(05751)
Rates: $30-$99
Tel: (802) 422-9666
(800) 446-1088

CORTINA INN
US Rte 4 (05751)
Rates: $136-$302
Tel: (802) 773-3333
(800) 451-6108

**EDELWEISS
MOTEL & CHALETS**
US Rt 4 (05751)
Rates: $38-$90
Tel: (802) 775-5577
(800) 479-2863

**MENDON
MOUNTAINVIEW
RESORT**
Rt 4E, Box 32 HCR
34 (05751)
Rates: $49-$140
Tel: (802) 773-4311
(800) 368-4311

LONDONDERRY

WHITE PINE LODGE
Rt 11 West (05148)
Rates: n/a
Tel: (802) 824-3909

LUDLOW

**CAVENDISH POINTE
HOTEL**
Rt 103 (05149)
Rates: $54-$105
Tel: (802) 226-7688
(800) 438-7908

**THE COMBES
FAMILY INN**
953 E Lake Rd
(05149)
Rates: $90-$102
Tel: (802) 228-8799
(800) 822-8799

**HAPPY TRAILS
MOTEL**
Rt 103 S (05149)
Rates: $49-$119
Tel: (802) 228-8888
(800) 228-9984

TIMBER INN MOTEL
RR 1, Box 1003
(05149)
Rates: $40-$95
Tel: (802) 228-8666

LYNDONVILLE

LYNBURKE MOTEL
RR 1, Box 377
(05851)
Rates: $35-$50
Tel: (802) 626-3346

MANCHESTER

**AVALANCHE
MOTOR LODGE**
Rt 11 & 30 (05254)
Rates: $55-$75
Tel: (802) 362-2622
(800) 592-2622

**BRITTANY INN
MOTEL**
Rt 7A, Box 760
(05255)
Rates: $48-$68
Tel: (802) 362-1033

MANCHESTER
CENTER

**WEDGEWOOD
MOTEL**
RR 1, Box 2295
(05255)
Rates: $40-$68
Tel: (802) 362-2145
(800) 254-2145

MARLBORO

WHETSTONE INN
Off Hwy 9 (05344)
Rates: $30-$85
Tel: (802) 254-2500

MENDON

**RED CLOVER
HISTORIC
COUNTRY INN**
Woodward Rd
(05701)
Rates: $140-$265
Tel: (802) 775-2290
(800) 752-0571

MIDDLEBURY

THE MIDDLEBURY INN
Court Square (05753)
Rates: $68-$170
Tel: (802) 388-4961
(800) 842-4666

SUGARHOUSE MOTOR INN
Rt 7 (05753)
Rates: $50-$60
Tel: (802) 388-2770
(800) 784-2746

MONTPELIER

ECONO LODGE
101 Northfield St (05602)
Rates: $45-$85
Tel: (802) 223-5258
(800) 424-4777

NEWFANE

FOUR COLUMNS INN
230 West St (05345)
Rates: $100-$275
Tel: (802) 365-7713

NEWPORT

TOP O' THE HILLS MOTEL & INN
HCR 61, Box 14 (05855)
Rates: $43-$70
Tel: (802) 334-2452
(800) 258-6748

NORTH HERO

SHORE ACRES INN
RR 1, Box 3, US 2 (05475)
Rates: $55-$115
Tel: (802) 372-8722

PERKINSVILLE

GWENDOLYN'S BED & BREAKFAST INN
Rt 106 (05151)
Rates: $55-$92
Tel: (802) 263-5248

PERU

JOHNNY SEESAW'S BED & BREAKFAST
SR 11 ,Bromley Mtn (05152)
Rates: $48-$120
Tel: (802) 824-5533
(800) 424-2729

PITTSFIELD

CLEAR RIVER INN & TAVERN
Rt 100 (05762)
Rates: $38-$85
Tel: (802) 746-7916
(800) 746-7916

POULTNEY

STONEBRIDGE INN BED & BREAKFAST
3 Beaunau St (05764)
Rates: $60-$84
Tel: (802) 287-9849
(800) 308-7001

PUTNEY

PUTNEY INN
Depot Rd (05346)
Rates: $58-$78
Tel: (802) 387-5517
(800) 653-5517

READING

BAILEY'S MILL BED & BREAKFAST
Bailey's Mill Rd (05062)
Rates: $75-$125
Tel: (802) 484-7809
(800) 639-3437

ROCHESTER

HARVEY'S MOUNTAIN VIEW INN
RR 1, Box 53 (05767)
Rates: $28-$68
Tel: (802) 767-4273

RUTLAND

DAYS INN
253 S Main St (05701)
Rates: $49-$129
Tel: (802) 773-3361
(800) 329-7466

ECONO LODGE-PICO
Rt 4, Box 7650 (05701)
Rates: $41-$65
Tel: (802) 773-6644
(800) 424-4777

GREEN-MONT MOTEL
138 Main St (05701)
Rates: $35-$80
Tel: (802) 775-2575
(800) 774-2575

HIGHLANDER MOTEL
203 N Main St (05701)
Rates: $36-$65
Tel: (802) 773-6069
(800) 884-6069

HOJO INN
378 S Main St (05701)
Rates: $39-$109
Tel: (802) 775-4303
(800) 446-4656

HOLIDAY INN
411 S Main St (05701)
Rates: $74-$149
Tel: (802) 775-1911
(800) 465-4329

RED CLOVER INN
RR 2, Box 7450 (05701)
Rates: $140-$255
Tel: (802) 775-2290

SUNSET MOTEL
238 S Main St (05701)
Rates: $35-$68
Tel: (802) 773-2784
(800) 231-1709

TYROL MOTOR INN
RR 2, Box 7602 (05701)
Rates: $40-$106
Tel: (802) 773-7485

ST. ALBANS

CADILLAC MOTEL
213 Main St (05478)
Rates: $43-$70
Tel: (802) 524-2191

ECONO LODGE
287 Main St (05478)
Rates: $47-$73
Tel: (800) 424-4777

ST. JOHNSBURY

AIME'S MOTEL
RFD 1, Box 332 (05819)
Rates: $35-$60
Tel: (802) 748-3194

SAXTONS RIVER

THE INN AT SAXTONS RIVER
27 Main St (05154)
Rates: $78-$98
Tel: (802) 869-2110

SHAFTSBURY

BAYBERRY MOTEL
Rt 7A, Box 137 (05262)
Rates: $38-$75
Tel: (802) 447-7180

HILLBROOK MOTEL
Rt 7A (05262)
Rates: $32-$48
Tel: (802) 447-7201

KIMBERLY COTTAGE
Myers Rd, Box 345 (05262)
Rates: $50-$125
Tel: (802) 442-4354

SERENITY MOTEL
RR1 Box 281 (05262)
Rates: $40-$60
Tel: (802) 442-6490

SHARON

COLUMNS MOTOR LODGE
Rt 14 (05065)
Rates: $36-$42
Tel: (802) 763-7040

SHELBURNE

ECONO LODGE
1961 Shelburne Rd
(05482)
Rates: $39-$55
Tel: (802) 985-3377
(800) 424-4777

SHOREHAM

**INDIAN TRAIL FARM
BED & BREAKFAST**
Box 49, Smith St
(05770)
Rates: $50+
Tel: (802) 897-5292

SOUTH HERO

**SANDBAR
MOTOR INN**
US Rt 2 (05486)
Rates: $48-$85
Tel: (802) 372-6911

SOUTH
WOODSTOCK

**KEDRON VALLEY
INN**
Rt 106 (05071)
Rates: $120-$194
Tel: (802) 457-1473
(800) 836-1193

SPRINGFIELD

**THE ABBY-LYN
MOTEL**
RD 1, Box 80 (05150)
Rates: $38-$60
Tel: (802) 886-2223

HOWARD JOHNSON
818 Charlestown Rd
(05156)
Rates: $69-$95
Tel: (802) 885-4516
(800) 446-4656

PA-LO-MAR MOTEL
2 Linhale Dr (05156)
Rates: $30-$56
Tel: (802) 885-4142

STOCKBRIDGE

**CHASE INN
BED & BREAKFAST**
Rt 100 (05772)
Rates: $20-$40
Tel: (802) 746-8972
(800) 746-8972

STOWE

**ANDERSON LODGE-
AN AUSTRIAN INN**
3430 Mountain Rd
(05672)
Rates: $58-$72
Tel: (802) 253-7336
(800) 336-7336

**BURGUNDY ROSE
MOTOR INN**
Rt 100 (05672)
Rates: $45-$85
Tel: (802) 253-7768
(800) 989-7768

COMMODORES INN
Rt 100 (05672)
Rates: $52-$122
Tel: (802) 253-7131
(800) 447-8693

1860 HOUSE B & B
P.O. Box 276 (05672)
Rates: n/a
Tel: (802) 253-7351
(800) 248-1860

**GOLDEN KITZ
LODGE & MOTEL**
1965 Mountain Rd
(05672)
Rates: $17-$40
Tel: (802) 253-4217
(800) 548-7568

**GREEN MOUNTAIN
INN**
Main St (05672)
Rates: $75-$220
Tel: (802) 253-7301
(800) 253-7302

HOB KNOB INN
2364 Mountain Rd
(05672)
Rates: $50-$130
Tel: (802) 253-8549
(800) 245-8540

**INN AT TURNER
MILL B & B**
56 Turner Mill Ln
(05672)
Rates: $35-$50
Tel: (802) 253-2062
(800) 992-0016

INNSBRUCK INN
4361 Mountain Rd
(05672)
Rates: $45-$134
Tel: (802) 253-8582
(800) 827-8582

**MIGUEL'S
STOWE AWAY INN**
3148 Mountain Rd
(05672)
Rates: $49-$90
Tel: (802) 253-7574
(800) 245-1240

**MOUNTAIN ROAD
RESORT**
1007 Mountain Rd
(05672)
Rates: $60-$170
Tel: (802) 253-4566
(800) 367-6873

MOUNTAINEER INN
3343 Mountain Rd
(05672)
Rates: $35-$85
Tel: (802) 253-7525

**NOTCH BROOK
CONDOMINIUMS**
1229 Notch Brook
Rd (05672)
Rates: $59-$98
Tel: (802) 253-4882
(800) 253-4882

THE SALZBURG INN
Mountain Rd, Rt 108
(05672)
Rates: $58-$78
Tel: (805) 253-8541
(800) 448-4554

**STOWE INN
AT LITTLE RIVER**
123 Mountain Rd
(05672)
Rates: $50-$175
Tel: (802) 253-4836
(800) 227-1108

**STOWE MOUNTAIN
RESORT**
5781 Mountain Rd
(05672)
Rates: $85-$205
Tel: (802) 253-3000
(800) 253-4754

TEN ACRES LODGE
14 Barrows Rd
(05672)
Rates: $60-$220
Tel: (802) 253-7638

**TOPNOTCH AT
STOWE RESORT**
4000 Mountain Rd
(05672)
Rates: $118-$660
Tel: (802) 253-8585
(800) 451-8686

**WALKABOUT CREEK
LODGE B & B**
199 Edson Hill Rd
(05672)
Rates: $70-$130
Tel: (802) 253-7354
(800) 426-6697

**YE OLDE ENGLAND
INNE**
433 Mountain Rd
(05672)
Rates: $85-$225
Tel: (802) 253-7558
(800) 477-3771

STRATTON
MOUNTAIN

BIRKENAUS HOTEL
Stratton Mt Rd
(05155)
Rates: $50-$149
Tel: (802) 297-2000

**LIFTLINE LODGE
RESORT HOTEL**
Stratton Mtn Rd
(05155)
Rates: $59-$145
Tel: (802) 297-2600
(800) 597-5438

TAFTSVILLE

**APPLEBUTTER INN
BED & BREAKFAST**
Happy Valley Rd
(05073)
Rates: $35-$65
Tel: (802) 457-4158

VERGENNES

**BASIN HARBOR
CLUB RESORT**
Basin Harbor Rd
(05491)
Rates: $165-$375
Tel: (802) 475-2311
(800) 622-4000

WHITFORD HOUSE INN
RR 1, Box 1490 (05491)
Rates: $70-$150
Tel: (802) 758-2704
(800) 746-2704

WAITSFIELD

THE GARRISON HOTEL
Box 539-C (05673)
Rates: $60-$190
Tel: (802) 496-2352
(800) 766-7829

MILLBROOK INN
RFD Box 62 (05673)
Rates: n/a
Tel: (802) 496-2405
(800) 477-2809

SUGARBUSH RESORT
RR 1, Box 35 (05674)
Rates: n/a
Tel: (802) 583-3333
(800) 537-8427

SUGARBUSH VILLAGE CONDOS
RR 1, Box 68-12 (05674)
Rates: n/a
Tel: (802) 583-3000
(800) 451-4326

TUCKER HILL LODGE
Rt 17, Box 147 (05673)
Rates: $40-$55
Tel: (802) 496-3984
(800) 543-7841

WARREN

GOLDEN LION RIVERSIDE INN
Sugarbush Access Rd, Rt 100 (05674)
Rates: $25-$42
Tel: (802) 496-3084

POWDERHOUND RESORT
Rt 100, Box 369 (05674)
Rates: $65-$130
Tel: (802) 496-5100
(800) 548-4022

WATERBURY

HOLIDAY INN
Blush Hill Rd (05676)
Rates: $69-$133
Tel: (802) 244-7822
(800) 465-4329

1836 CABINS
Box 128-T
Stowe Rd (05677)
Rates: $79-$99
Tel: (802) 244-8533

THE OLD STAGE-COACH INN B & B
18 N Main St (05676)
Rates: $45-$110
Tel: (802) 244-5056
(800) 262-2206

WELLS RIVER

BIRCHWOOD MOTOR INN
RR 1, Box 2 (45081)
Rates: n/a
Tel: (802) 757-2274
(800) 895-2277

WESTON

DARLING FAMILY INN BED & BREAKFAST
815 Rt 100 (05161)
Rates: $75-$110
Tel: (802) 824-3223

WHITE RIVER JUNCTION

BEST WESTERN AT THE JUNCTION
Rt 5, I-91 Exit 11 (05001)
Rates: $49-$125
Tel: (802) 295-3015
(800) 528-1234

HOLIDAY INN
Holiday Inn Dr (05001)
Rates: $70-$125
Tel: (802) 295-3000
(800) 465-4329

HOTEL COOLIDGE
17 S Main St (05001)
Rates: n/a
Tel: (802) 295-3118
(800) 622-1124

WILDER

WILDER MOTEL
319 Hartford Ave (05088)
Rates: n/a
Tel: (802) 295-9793

WILLIAMSTOWN

THE AUTUMN CREST INN
RFD 1, Box 1540, (05679)
Rates: $88-$148
Tel: (802) 433-6627
(800) 339-6627

WILLISTON

RESIDENCE INN BY MARRIOTT
1 Hurricane Ln (05495)
Rates: $70-$172
Tel: (802) 878-2001
(800) 331-3131

WILMINGTON

VINTAGE MOTEL
Rt 9 W (05363)
Rates: $27-$38
Tel: (802) 464-8824
(800) 899-9660

WOODSTOCK

BRAESIDE MOTEL
P. O. Box 411 (05091)
Rates: $48-$88
Tel: (802) 457-1366
(800) 303-1366

KEDRON VALLEY INN
Rt 106 (05071)
Rates: $93-$249
Tel: (802) 457-1473
(800) 836-1193

THREE CHURCH STREET B & B
3 Church St (05091)
Rates: $70-$105
Tel: (802) 457-1925
(800) 457-1925

THE WINSLOW HOUSE B & B
38 US 4 (05091)
Rates: $68-$95
Tel: (802) 457-1820

VIRGINIA

ALDIE

THE CASTLE
Rt 15, Box 28K
Rates: n/a
Tel: (703) 327-4113

ALEXANDRIA

ALEXANDRIA HOTEL
801 N Fairfax St
(22314)
Rates: n/a
Tel: (703) 549-1000
(800) 296-1000

CLASSIC B & B
6216 Saddle Tree Dr
(22340)
Rates: $100
Tel: (703) 922-7836

COMFORT INN
5716 S Van Dorn St
(22310)
Rates: $56-$85
Tel: (703) 922-9200
(800) 221-2222

**COMFORT INN
MT VERNON**
7212 Richmond
Hwy (22306)
Rates: $50-$80
Tel: (703) 765-9000
(800) 221-2222

DAYS INN
110 S Bragg St
(22312)
Rates: $46-$61
Tel: (703) 354-4950
(800) 329-7466

DAYS INN
6100 Richmond
Hwy (22303)
Rates: $50-$67
Tel: (703) 329-0500
(800) 329-7466

**DOUBLETREE
SUITES**
100 S Reynolds St
(22304)
Rates: $89-$99
Tel: (703) 370-9600
(800) 424-2900

ECONO LODGE-
8849 Richmond Hwy
(22309)
Rates: $45-$65
Tel: (703) 780-0300
(800) 424-4777

**ECONO LODGE-
OLD TOWN**
700 N Washington St
(22314)
Rates: $55-$80
Tel: (703) 836-5100
(800) 424-4777

**GUEST QUARTERS
SUITE HOTEL**
100 S Reynolds St
(22304)
Rates: $89
Tel: (703) 370-9600

HOLIDAY INN
480 King St (22314)
Rates: $99-$250
Tel: (703) 549-6080
(800) 465-4329

HOWARD JOHNSON
5821 Richmond
Hwy (22303)
Rates: $55-$98
Tel: (703) 329-1400
(800) 446-4656

QUALITY INN
6461 Edsall Rd
(22312)
Rates: $55-$99
Tel: (800) 221-2222

RAMADA HOTEL
901 N Fairfax St
(22314)
Rates: $106-$250
Tel: (703) 683-6000
(800) 272-6232

RAMADA INN
4641 Kenmore Ave
(22304)
Rates: $64-$104
Tel: (703) 751-4510
(800) 272-6232

RED ROOF INN
5975 Richmond
Hwy (22303)
Rates: $49-$62
Tel: (703) 960-5200
(800) 843-7663

SHERATON SUITES
801 N St. Asaph St
(22314)
Rates: $99-$164
Tel: (703) 836-4700

ALTAVISTA

**COMFORT SUITES
HOTEL**
1558 Main St (24517)
Rates: $53-$90
Tel: (804) 369-4000
(800) 221-2222

AMHERST

FAIRVIEW B & B
Rt 4, Box 117 (25421)
Rates: $65-$70
Tel: (804) 277-8500

APPOMATTOX

BUDGET INN
714 W Confederate
Blvd (24522)
Rates: $28-$42
Tel: (804) 352-7451

SUPER 8 MOTEL
Rt 4, Box 100 (24522)
Rates: $39-$60
Tel: (804) 352-2339
(800) 800-8000

ARLINGTON

**DOUBLETREE HOTEL
NATIONAL AIRPORT**
300 Army Navy Dr
(22202)
Rates: $65-$155
Tel: (800) 222-8733

ECONO LODGE-N
3335 Lee Hwy
(22207)
Rates: $35-$65
Tel: (800) 424-4777

HOLIDAY INN
1489 Jefferson Davis
Hwy (22202)
Rates: n/a
Tel: (800) 465-4329

HOLIDAY INN
1850 St. Myers Dr
(22209)
Rates: n/a
Tel: (800) 465-4329

HOLIDAY INN
4610 N Fairfax Dr
(22203)
Rates: $79-$132
Tel: (800) 465-4329

HOWARD JOHNSON
5821 Richmond
Hwy (22303)
Rates: $59-$99
Tel: (703) 329-1400
(800) 446-4656

**HOWARD JOHNSON
NATL AIRPORT**
2650 Jefferson Davis
Hwy (22202)
Rates: $79-$145
Tel: (703) 684-7200
(800) 446-4656

**HYATT ARLINGTON
AT KEY BRIDGE**
1325 Wilson Blvd
(22209)
Rates: $69-$181
Tel: (703) 525-1234

**MARRIOTT CRYSTAL
GATEWAY HOTEL**
1700 Jefferson Davis
Hwy (22202)
Rates: $105-$192
Tel: (703) 920-3230

**MARRIOTT
KEY BRIDGE**
1401 Lee Hwy
(22209)
Rates: $164-$184
Tel: (703) 524-6400

**RAMADA
RENAISSANCE
ARLINGTON HOTEL**
950 N Stafford St
(22203)
Rates: $120-$180
Tel: (703) 528-6000

STOUFFER CONCOURSE HOTEL
2399 Jefferson Davis Hwy (22202)
Rates: $89-$240
Tel: (703) 418-6800

ASHLAND

COMFORT INN
101 Cottage Greene Dr (23005)
Rates: $47-$69
Tel: (804) 752-7777
(800) 221-2222

ECONO LODGE
I-95 & SR 54 (23005)
Rates: $27-$73
Tel: (804) 798-9221
(800) 424-4777

BAILEYS CROSS-ROADS

ECONO LODGE-PENTAGON
5666 Columbia Pike (22041)
Rates: $60-$65
Tel: (703) 820-5600
(800) 424-4777

BEDFORD

BEST WESTERN TERRACE HOUSE
921 Blue Ridge Ave (24523)
Rates: $41-$52
Tel: (540) 586-8266
(800) 528-1234

BERRYVILLE

BLUE RIDGE B & B RESERVATIONS
Rt 2, Box 3895 (22611)
Rates: n/a
Tel: (703) 955-1246
(800) 296-1246

BIG STONE GAP

COUNTRY INN MOTEL
627 Gilley Ave (24219)
Rates: $28-34
Tel: (703) 523-0374

BLACKSBURG

BEST WESTERN RED LION INN
900 Plantation Rd (24060)
Rates: $45-$61
Tel: (540) 552-7770
(800) 528-1234

BRUSH MOUNTAIN INN
3030 Mt. Tabor Rd (24062)
Rates: n/a
Tel: (703) 951-7530

BUDGET HOST INN
3333 S Main St (24060)
Rates: $32-$48
Tel: (540) 951-4242
(800) 446-4656

COMFORT INN
3705 S Main St (24060)
Rates: $51-$85
Tel: (540) 951-1500
(800) 221-2222

HOLIDAY INN
3503 Holiday Ln (24060)
Rates: $48-$60
Tel: (540) 951-1330
(800) 465-4329

MARRIOTT HOTEL
900 Prices Fork Rd (24060)
Rates: $69-$79
Tel: (703) 552-7001
(800) 228-9290

BLAND

BIG WALKER MOTEL
P. O. Box 155 (24315)
Rates: $26-$33
Tel: (703) 688-3331

BOYCE

RIVER HOUSE
Rt 2, Box 135 (22620)
Rates: n/a
Tel: (703) 837-1476

BRACEY

DAYS INN
2850 Hwy 903 (23919)
Rates: $47-$75
Tel: (804) 689-2000
(800) 329-7466

BRANDY STATION

BLUE HAVEN B & B
14648 Carrico Mills Rd (22714)
Rates: $65-$85
Tel: (540) -825-0716

BRISTOL

ECONO LODGE
912 Commonwealth Ave (24201)
Rates: $65-$80
Tel: (540) 466-2112
(800) 424-4777

LA QUINTA INN
1014 Old Airport Rd (24201)
Rates: $45-$52
Tel: (540) 669-9353

RED CARPET INN
15589 Lee Hwy (24202)
Rates: n/a
Tel: (703) 669-1151
(800) 251-1962

SKYLAND MOTEL
15545 Lee Hwy (24201)
Rates: $20-$45
Tel: (703) 669-0166

SUPER 8 MOTEL
2139 Lee Hwy (24201)
Rates: $39-$63
Tel: (540) 466-8800
(800) 800-8000

BUCHANAN

WATTSTULL INN
Rt 1, Box 21 (24066)
Rates: $42-$45
Tel: (703) 254-1551

BUENA VISTA

BUENA VISTA MOTEL
477 E 29th St (24416)
Rates: $40-$48
Tel: (703) 261-2138

CAPE CHARLES

DAYS INN
29106 Lankford Hwy (23310)
Rates: $40-$69
Tel: (804) 331-1000
(800) 329-7466

CHANTILLY

COMFORT INN DULLES AIRPORT
4050 Westfax Dr (22021)
Rates: n/a
Tel: (703) 818-8200
(800) 221-2222

WASHINGTON DULLES AIRPORT MARRIOTT
333 W Service Rd (22021)
Rates: $59-$110
Tel: (703) 471-9500

CHARLOTTES-VILLE

BEST WESTERN CAVALIER INN
105 Emmet St (22905)
Rates: $54-$75
Tel: (804) 296-8111
(800) 528-1234

BEST WESTERN MOUNT VERNON
1613 Emmet St (22906)
Rates: $49-$58
Tel: (804) 296-5501
(800) 528-1234

BOAR'S HEAD INN
200 Ednam Dr (22901)
Rates: n/a
Tel: (800) 476-1988

CAMPS & COTTAGES OF CHARLOTTESVILLE
Rt 6, Box 260A
(22902)
Rates: n/a
Tel: (804) 293-2529

COMFORT INN
1807 Emmet St (22901)
Rates: $49-$73
Tel: (804) 293-6188
(800) 221-2222

ECONO LODGE
400 Emmet St (22903)
Rates: $60-$75
Tel: (804) 296-2104
(800) 424-4777

ECONO LODGE-N
2014 Holiday Dr
(22901)
Rates: $60-$75
Tel: (804) 295-3185
(800) 424-4777

ENGLISH INN
2000 Morton Dr
(22901)
Rates: n/a
Tel: (804) 971-9900

HOLIDAY INN-N
US N & Hwy 250
Bypass (22901)
Rates: $58-$68
Tel: (804) 293-9111
(800) 465-4329

KNIGHTS INN
1300 Seminole Tr
(22901)
Rates: $41-$58
Tel: (804) 973-8133
(800) 843-5644

OMNI CHARLOTTESVILLE
235 W Main St
(22901)
Rates: n/a
Tel: (804) 971-5500

QUALITY INN
1600 Emmet St
(22901)
Rates: 49-$69
(804) 971-3746
(800) 221-2222

SUPER 8 MOTEL
390 Greenbrier Dr
(22901)
Rates: $40-$79
Tel: (804) 973-0888
(800) 800-8000

CHESAPEAKE

DAYS INN
1439 George
Washington Hwy
(23323)
Rates: $34-$44
Tel: (804) 487-8861
(800) 329-7466

ECONO LODGE
4725 Military Hwy
W (23321)
Rates: $31-$43
Tel: (804) 488-4963
(800) 424-4777

ECONO LODGE
2222 Military Hwy S
(23320)
Rates: $37-$70
Tel: (804) 543-2200
(800) 424-4777

ECONO LODGE
3244 Western Branch
(23321)
Rates: $37-$50
Tel: (804) 484-6143
(800) 424-4777

MOTEL 6
701 Woodlake Dr
(23320)
Rates: $36-$42
Tel: (804) 420-2976
(800) 440-6000

RED ROOF INN
724 Woodlake Dr
(23320)
Rates: $32-$42
Tel: (804) 523-0123
(800) 843-7663

SUPER 8 MOTEL
100 Red Cedar Ct
(23320)
Rates: $40-$57
Tel: (804) 547-8880
(800) 800-8000

WELLESLEY INN
1750 Sara Dr (23320)
Rates: $40-$80
Tel: (804) 366-0100
(800) 444-8888

CHESTER

COMFORT INN
2100 W Hundred Rd
(23831)
Rates: $57-$105
Tel: (804) 751-0000
(800) 221-2222

DAYS INN
P. O. Box AN (23831)
Rates: $42-$78
Tel: (804) 748-5871
(800) 329-7466

HOWARD JOHNSON
2401 W Hundred Rd
(23831)
Rates: $52-$70
Tel: (804) 748-6321
(800) 446-4656

RED CARPET INN
2300 W Hundred Rd
(23831)
Rates: $25-$37
Tel: (804) 748-2237
(800) 251-1962

SUPER 8 MOTEL
2421 Southland Dr
(23831)
Rates: $42-$59
Tel: (804) 748-0050
(800) 800-8000

CHINCOTEAGUE

BEACH ROAD MOTEL
6151 Maddox Blvd
(23336)
Rates: $35-$79
Tel: (804) 336-6562

CHRISTIAN- BURG

DAYS INN
P. O. Box 768 (24073)
Rates: $40-$60
Tel: (540) 382-0261
(800) 329-7466

ECONO LODGE
2430 Roanoke St
(24073)
Rates: $36-$48
Tel: (540) 382-6161
(800) 424-4777

HOWARD JOHNSON
100 Bristol Dr
(24073)
Rates: $33-$60
Tel: (540) 381-0150
(800) 446-4656

SUPER 8 MOTEL
55 Laurel St NE
(24073)
Rates: $38-$60
Tel: (540) 382-5813
(800) 800-8000

CLAYPOOL HILL

SUPER 8 MOTEL
US Rt 19 (24609)
Rates: $42-$60
Tel: (540) 964-9888
(800) 800-8000

COLLINSVILLE

DUTCH INN MOTEL
633 Virginia Ave
(24078)
Rates: $46-$69
Tel: (540) 647-3721

ECONO LODGE
800 S Virginia Ave
(24078)
Rates: $30-$66
Tel: (540) 647-3941
(800) 424-4777

FAIRYSTONE MOTEL
626 Virginia Ave
(24078)
Rates: $37-$48
Tel: (540) 647-3941

COLONIAL BEACH

DAYS INN
30 Colonial Ave
(22443)
Rates: $50-$74
Tel: (804) 224-0404
(800) 329-7466

COLONIAL HEIGHTS

DAYS INN
2310 Indian Hill Rd
(23834)
Rates: $36-$54
Tel: (804) 520-1010
(800) 329-7466

COVINGTON

BEST WESTERN MOUNTAINVIEW
820 E Madison St
(24426)
Rates: $62-$90
Tel: (540) 962-4951
(800) 528-1234

COMFORT INN
203 Interstate Dr
(24426)
Rates: $52-$72
Tel: (540) 962-2141
(800) 221-2222

HOLIDAY INN
P. O. Box 920 (24426)
Rates: $58-$99
Tel: (540) 962-4951
(800) 465-4329

KNIGHTS COURT
908 Valley Ridge Rd
(24426)
Rates: $45-$53
Tel: (540) 962-7600
(800) 843-5644

CULPEPER

COMFORT INN
890 Willis Ln (22701)
Rates: $49-$65
Tel: (540) 825-4900
(800) 221-2222

HOLIDAY INN
P. O. Box 1206
(22701)
Rates: $55-$59
Tel: (540) 825-1253
(800) 465-4329

SUPER 8 MOTEL
889 Willis Lane
(22701)
Rates: $38-$60
Tel: (540) 825-8088
(800) 800-8000

DANVILLE

DAYS INN
1390 Piney Forest Dr
(24540)
Rates: $45-75
Tel: (804) 836-6745
(800) 329-7466

SUPER 8 MOTEL
2385 Riverside Dr
(24541)
Rates: $38-$59
Tel: (804) 799-5845
(800) 800-8000

DOSWELL

BEST WESTERN-KINGS QUARTERS
P. O. Box 100 (23047)
Rates: $32-$88
Tel: (804) 876-3321
(800) 528-1234

DUMFRIES

HOLIDAY INN EXPRESS
17133 Dumfries Rd
(22026)
Rates: $57-$65
Tel: (703) 221-1141
(800) 465-4329

EMPORIA

COMFORT INN
1411 Skippers Rd
(23847)
Rates: $41-$53
Tel: (804) 348-3282
(800) 221-2222

DAYS INN
921 W Atlantic St
(23847)
Rates: $40-$66
Tel: (804) 634-9481
(800) 329-7466

ECONO LODGE
3173 Susset Dr
(23847)
Rates: $28-$44
Tel: (804) 535-8535
(800) 424-4777

HAMPTON INN
1207 W Atlantic St
(23847)
Rates: $54-$65
Tel: (804) 634-9200
(800) 426-7866

HOLIDAY INN
P. O. Box 827 (23847)
Rates: $51-$57
Tel: (804) 634-4191
(800) 465-4329

RED CARPET INN
1586 Skippers Rd
(23847)
Rates: $29-$37
Tel: (804) 634-4181
(800) 251-1962

FAIRFAX

HOLIDAY INN
3535 Chain Bridge
Rd (22030)
Rates: $65-$89
Tel: (703) 591-5500
(800) 465-4329

HOLIDAY INN FAIR OAKS
11787 Lee Jackson
Hwy (22033)
Rates: $69-$115
Tel: (703) 352-2525
(800) 465-4329

HYATT FAIR LAKES
12777 Fair Lakes Cir
(22033)
Rates: $59-$79
Tel: (703) 818-1234

WELLESLEY INN
10327 Lee Hwy
(22030)
Rates: $46-$70
Tel: (703) 359-2888
(800) 444-8888

FALLS CHURCH

MARRIOTT HOTEL
3111 Fairview Park
Dr (22042)
Rates: $142-$500
Tel: (703) 849-9400
(800) 228-9290

QUALITY INN EXECUTIVE
6111 Arlington Blvd
(22044)
Rates: $60-$70
Tel: (703) 534-9100

RAMADA INN-TYSONS CORNER
7801 Leesburg Pike
(22043)
Rates: $96-$129
Tel: (703) 675-3693
(800) 272-6232

FARMVILLE

SUPER 8 MOTEL
HC 6, Box 1755
(23901)
Rates: $39-$60
Tel: (804) 392-8196
(800) 800-8000

FORT HAYWOOD

INN AT TABB'S CREEK LANDING
P.O. Box 219 (23138)
Rates: n/a
Tel: (804) 725-5136

FREDERICKSBURG

BEST WESTERN INN
2205 William St
(22401)
Rates: $38-$69
Tel: (703) 786-5050
(800) 528-1234

BEST WESTERN-JOHNNY APPLESEED
543 Warrenton Rd
(22405)
Rates: $35-$58
Tel: (540) 373-0000
(800) 528-1234

BEST WESTERN-THUNDERBIRD INN
3000 Plank Rd
(22401)
Rates: $36-$59
Tel: (703) 786-7404
(800) 528-1234

DAYS INN-NORTH
14 Simpson Rd
(22405)
Rates: $36-$45
Tel: (540) 373-5340
(800) 329-7466

DAYS INN-SOUTH
5316 Jefferson Davis
Hwy (22401)
Rates: $36-$45
Tel: (540) 898-6800
(800) 329-7466

DUNNING MILLS INN
2305 Jefferson Davis
Hwy (22401)
Rates: $55-$90
Tel: (703) 373-1256

ECONO LODGE
5321 Jefferson Davis
Hwy (22408)
Rates: $45-$65
Tel: (540) 898-5440
(800) 424-4777

HAMPTON INN
2310 Plank Rd
(22401)
Rates: $46-$55
Tel: (703) 371-0220
(800) 426-7866

HERITAGE INN
5308 Jefferson Davis
Hwy (22402)
Rates: $30-$59
Tel: (540) 898-1000

HOLIDAY INN-S
5324 Jefferson Davis
Hwy (22401)
Rates: $59-$69
Tel: (540) 898-1102
(800) 465-4329

HOLIDAY INN-N
564 Warrenton Rd
(22405)
Rates: $35-$62
Tel: (540) 371-5550
(800) 465-4329

HOWARD JOHNSON
386 Warrenton Rd
(22405)
Rates: $30-$60
Tel: (540) 371-6000
(800) 446-4656

HOWARD JOHNSON
5327 Jefferson Davis
Hwy (22408)
Rates: $50-$65
Tel: (540) 898-1800
(800) 446-4656

MOTEL 6
401 Warrenton Rd
(22405)
Rates: $32-$38
Tel: (540) 371-5443
(800) 440-6000

RAMADA INN
I-95, Exit 130-B
(22404)
Rates: $45-$75
Tel: (540) 786-8361
(800) 272-6232

SHERATON INN
P. O. Box 618 (22404)
Rates: $59-$99
Tel: (703) 786-8321
(800) 325-3535

SUPER 8 MOTEL
3002 Mall Court
(22401)
Rates: $38-$59
Tel: (540) 786-8881
(800) 800-8000

FRONT ROYAL

BUDGET INN
1122 N Royal St
(22630)
Rates: $24-$48
Tel: (540) 635-2196

CENTER CITY MOTEL
416 S Royal Ave
(22630)
Rates: $25-$45
Tel: (540) 635-4050

SCOTTISH INNS
533 S Royal Ave
(22630)
Rates: $39-$52
Tel: (540) 636-6168
(800) 251-1962

SUPER 8 MOTEL
111 South St (22630)
Rates: $40-$68
Tel: (540) 636-4888
(800) 800-8000

GLEN ALLEN

AMERISUITES
4100 Cox Rd (23060)
Rates: $82-$92
Tel: (804) 747-9644

GLADE SPRING

ECONOMY INN
P. O. Box 453 (24340)
Rates: $30-$42
Tel: (703) 429-5131
(800) 826-0778

GORDONSVILLE

**SLEEPY HOLLOW
FARM B & B**
16280 Blue Ridge
Turnpike (22942)
Rates: $85
Tel: (540) 832-5555
(800) 215-4804

GOSHEN

**THE HUMMINGBIRD
INN**
P.O. Box 147 (24439)
Rates: $95-$155
Tel: (800) 397-3214

HAMPTON

ARROW INN
7 Semple Farm Rd
(23666)
Rates: $37-$59
Tel: (804) 865-0300
(800) 833-2520

**COLISEUM
INTERSTATE INN**
2000 W Mercury
Blvd (23666)
Rates: n/a
Tel: (804) 838-7070

DAYS INN
1918 Coliseum Dr
(23666)
Rates: $38-$71
Tel: (804) 826-4810
(800) 329-7466

**ECONO LODGE-
COLISEUM**
2708 W Mercury
Blvd (23666)
Rates: $33-$50
Tel: (804) 826-8970
(800) 424-7777

HAMPTON INN
1813 W Mercury
Blvd (23666)
Rates: $49-$55
Tel: (804) 838-8484
(800) 426-7866

HOLIDAY INN
1815 W Mercury
Blvd (23666)
Rates: $68-$88
Tel: (804) 838-0200
(800) 465-4329

LA QUINTA INN
2138 W Mercury
Blvd (23666)
Rates: $40-$57
Tel: (804) 827-8680
(800) 531-5900

QUALITY INN
1809 W Mercury
Blvd (23666)
Rates: $69-$74
Tel: (804) 838-5011
(800) 221-2222

RED ROOF INN
1925 Coliseum Dr
(23666)
Rates: $34-$45
Tel: (804) 838-1870
(800) 843-7663

**SHERATON INN-
COLISEUM**
1215 W Mercury
Blvd (23666)
Rates: $59-$99
Tel: (804) 838-5011

HARRISON-
BURG

COMFORT INN
1440 E Market St
(22801)
Rates: $49-$59
Tel: (540) 433-6066
(800) 221-2222

DAYS INN
1131 Forest Hill Rd
(22801)
Rates: $40-$55
Tel: (540) 433-9353
(800) 329-7466

ECONO LODGE
US 33 & I-81 (22801)
Rates: $36-$66
Tel: (540) 438-2576
(800) 424-4777

HOJO INN
605 Port Republic
Rd (22801)
Rates: $40-$60
Tel: (540) 434-6771
(800) 446-4656

KNIGHT'S INN
10 Linda Ln (22801)
Rates: n/a
Tel: (703) 433-2538

MOTEL 6
10 Linda Ln (22801)
Rates: $36-$42
Tel: (703) 433-6939
(800) 440-6000

RAMADA INN
1 Pleasant Valley Rd
(22801)
Rates: $35-$65
Tel: (540) 434-9981
(800) 272-6232

RED CARPET INN
3210 S Main St
(22801)
Rates: $25-$38
Tel: (703) 434-6704
(800) 251-1962

ROCKINGHAM MOTEL
4035 S Main St
(22801)
Rates: $30-$37
Tel: (703) 433-2538

SCOTTISH INNS
Rt 11 N (22801)
Rates: $26-$53
Tel: (703) 434-5301
(800) 251-1962

SHERATON INN
1400 E Market St
(22801)
Rates: $57-$80
Tel: (703) 433-2521
(800) 325-3535

SUPER 8 MOTEL
3330 S Main (22801)
Rates: $40-$60
Tel: (540) 433-8888
(800) 800-8000

VILLAGE INN
Rt 1, Box 76 (22801)
Rates: $34-$50
Tel: (703) 434-7355
(800) 736-7355

HERNDON

HILTON HOTEL AIRPORT
13869 Park Center Rd (22071)
Rates: $79-$129
Tel: (703) 478-2900
(800) 445-8677

HOLIDAY INN EXPRESS
485 Elden St (22070)
Rates: $54-$80
Tel: (703) 478-9777
(800) 465-4329

RENAISSANCE HOTEL DULLES INTL AIRPORT
13869 Park Center Rd (22071)
Rates: $59-$79
Tel: (703) 478-2900

RESIDENCE INN BY MARRIOTT
315 Elden St (22070)
Rates: $57-$143
Tel: (703) 435-0044
(800) 331-3131

SUMMERFIELD SUITES HOTEL
13700 Coopermine Rd (22071)
Rates: n/a
Tel: (703) 713-6800

HILLSVILLE

DOE RUN AT GROUNDHOG MOUNTAIN
Mile Post 189 Blue Ridge Pkwy (24343)
Rates: $80-$109
Tel: (703) 398-2212

ECONO LODGE
I-77 & US 58 (24343)
Rates: $32-$87
Tel: (540) 728-9118
(800) 424-4777

HOLIDAY INN EXPRESS
Rt 1, Box 361 (24343)
Rates: $55-$81
Tel: (540) 728-2120
(800) 465-4329

HOPEWELL

INNKEEPER
3852 Courthouse Rd (23860)
Rates: n/a
Tel: (804) 458-2600

HOT SPRINGS

ROSELOE MOTEL
Rt 2, Box 590 (24445)
Rates: $34-$44
Tel: (540) 839-5373

IRVINGTON

TIDES INN
P.O. Box 480 (22480)
Rates: $130-$450
Tel: (804) 438-5000

TIDES LODGE
P.O. Box 309 (22480)
Rates: $105-$325
Tel: (804) 438-6000

KEYSVILLE

SHELDON'S MOTEL
Rt 2, Box 189 (23947)
Rates: $48-$54
Tel: (804) 736-8434

LEESBURG

COLONIAL INN
19 S King St (22075)
Rates: n/a
Tel: (703) 777-5000

DAYS INN
721 E Market St (22075)
Rates: $46-$58
Tel: (703) 777-6622
(800) 329-7466

LAUREL BRIGADE INN
20 W Market St (22075)
Rates: n/a
Tel: (703) 777-1010

LEESBURG WEST-PARK HOTEL
59 Club House Dr SW (22075)
Rates: n/a
Tel: (703) 777-1910

LITTLE ROCK MOTEL
Rt 4, Box 608 (22075)
Rates: n/a
Tel: (703) 777-3499

PIEDMONT MOTEL
Rt 2, Box 230 (22075)
Rates: n/a
Tel: (703) 777-3361

LEXINGTON

COMFORT INN-VIRGINIA HORSE CENTER
P. O. Box 905 (24450)
Rates: $59-$74
Tel: (540) 463-7311
(800) 221-2222

DAYS INN-KEYDET GENERAL
Rt 6, Box 31 (24450)
Rates: $38-$70
Tel: (540) 463-2143
(800) 329-7466

ECONO LODGE
I-64 & US 11 (24450)
Rates: $50-$75
Tel: (540) 463-7371
(800) 424-4777

HOLIDAY INN
I-64, Exit 55 (24450)
Rates: $56-$74
Tel: (540) 463-7351
(800) 465-4329

HOWARD JOHNSON
I-81 & US 11 (24450)
Rates: $58-$75
Tel: (540) 463-9181
(800) 446-4656

RAMADA INN
US 11, Rt I-81 & A5 (24450)
Rates: $53-$90
Tel: (540) 463-6400
(800) 272-6232

RED OAK INN
US 11, Exit 53 (24450)
Rates: n/a
Tel: (703) 463-9131

SUPER 8 MOTEL
Rt 7, Box 99 (24450)
Rates: $42-$63
Tel: (540) 463-7858
(800) 800-8000

THE KEEP
116 Lee Ave (24450)
Rates: n/a
Tel: (540) 463-3560

THRIFTY INN
820 S Main St (24450)
Rates: $29-$49
Tel: (540) 463-2151

LOUISA

GINGER HILL B & B
Rt 5, Box 33E (23093)
Rates: $75-$130
Tel: (703) 967-3260

LURAY

BEST WESTERN INTOWN OF LURAY
410 W Main St
(22835)
Rates: $38-$90
Tel: (540) 743-6511
(800) 528-1234

CARDINAL MOTEL
US Bus 211 (22835)
Rates: n/a
Tel: (703) 743-5010

INTOWN MOTEL
410 W Main St
(22835)
Rates: $38-$85
Tel: (540) 743-6511

LURAY CAVERNS MOTEL WEST
US 211 Bypass
(22835)
Rates: n/a
Tel: (703) 743-4536

LURAY INN & CONFERENCE CENTER
US 211, Box 389
(22835)
Rates: n/a
Tel: (703) 743-4521

LYNCHBURG

COMFORT INN
Odd Fellows Rd
(24506)
Rates: $39-$94
Tel: (804) 847-9041
(800) 221-2222

HOLIDAY INN
P. O. Box 11768
(24506)
Rates: $65-$85
Tel: (804) 847-4424
(800) 465-4329

HOLIDAY INN SELECT
601 Main St (24504)
Rates: $69-$89
Tel: (804) 528-2500
(800) 465-4329

HOWARD JOHNSON
US 29 N (24506)
Rates: $46-$68
Tel: (804) 845-7041
(800) 446-4656

RAMADA LIMITED
1500 Main St (24504)
Rates: $38-$48
Tel: (804) 845-5975
(800) 272-6232

MANASSAS

RED ROOF INN
10610 Automotive
Dr (22110)
Rates: $38-$47
Tel: (703) 335-9333
(800) 843-7663

MARION

BEST WESTERN MARION
1424 N Main St
(24354)
Rates: $61-$68
Tel: (540) 783-3193
(800)528-1234

VIRGINIA HOUSE MOTOR INN
1419 N Main St
(24354)
Rates: $37-$41
Tel: (703) 783-5112

MARTINSVILLE

BEST WESTERN INN
P. O. Box 1183
(24114)
Rates: $45-$68
Tel: (540) 632-5611
(800) 528-1234

SUPER 8 MOTEL
960 N Memorial
Blvd (24112)
Rates: $39-$59
Tel: (540) 666-8888
(800) 800-8000

MAX MEADOWS

GATEWAY MOTEL
Rt 3, Box 488 (24360)
Rates: $25-$36
Tel: (703) 637-3119

McCLEAN

THE RITZ-CARLTON TYSONS CORNER
1700 Tysons Blvd
(22102)
Rates: $135-$210
Tel: (703) 506-4300

TYSONS WESTPARK HOTEL
8401 Westpark Dr
(22102)
Rates: $59-$89
Tel: (703) 734-2800

McKENNEY

SCOTTISH INNS
21723 Boydton
Plank Rd (23872)
Rates: $30-$40
Tel: (804) 478-4481
(800) 251-1962

MEADOWS OF DAN

WOODBERRY INN
P.O. Box 908 (24120)
Rates: n/a
Tel: (703) 593-2567

MELFA

CAPTAIN'S QUARTERS MOTEL
Rt 13, Box D (23410)
Rates: n/a
Tel: (804) 787-4545

MILLBORO

FORT LEWIS LODGE
HCR 3, Box 21A
(24460)
Rates: n/a
Tel: (703) 925-2314

MONTROSS

THE INN AT MONTROSS
P. O. Box 908 (22520)
Rates: $65-$125
Tel: (804) 493-9097
(800) 321-0979

MOUNT JACKSON

BEST WESTERN INN
250 Conickville Rd
(22842)
Rates: $39-$67
Tel: (703) 477-2911
(800) 528-1234

THE WIDOW KIP'S COUNTRY INN
335 Orchard Dr
(22842)
Rates: $65-$70
Tel: (540) 477-2400
(800) 478-8714

NATURAL BRIDGE

BUDGET INN
US 11 (24578)
Rates: $28-$62
Tel: (703) 291-2143

FANCY HILL MOTEL
US 11 (24578)
Rates: n/a
Tel: (703) 291-2143

WATTSTULL INN
Blue Ridge Pkwy
Exit Rt 43 (24578)
Rates: n/a
Tel: (703) 254-1551

NEW CHURCH

THE GARDEN & THE SEA B & B
P.O. Box 275 (23415)
Rates: $60-$165
Tel: (804) 824-0672
(800) 824-0672

NEW MARKET

BUDGET INN
2192 Old Valley Pike
(22844)
Rates: $20-$48
Tel: (540) 740-3105
(800) 296-6835

DAYS INN
9360 George C
Collins Pkwy (22844)
Rates: $39-$70
Tel: (540) 740-4100
(800) 329-7466

NEWPORT NEWS

COMFORT INN
12330 Jefferson Ave
(23602)
Rates: $58-$72
Tel: (804) 249-0200
(800) 221-2222

DAYS INN
14747 Warwick Blvd
(23602)
Rates: $38-$56
Tel: (757) 874-0201
(800) 329-7466

HOST INN
985 J Clyde Morris
Blvd (23601)
Rates: $39-$45
Tel: (804) 599-3303
(800) 747-3303

**KING JAMES
MOTOR HOTEL**
6045 Jefferson Ave
(23605)
Rates: $30-$50
Tel: (804) 245-2801

MOTEL 6
797 J Clyde Morris
Blvd (23601)
Rates: $32-$38
Tel: (804) 595-6336
(800) 440-6000

TRAVELODGE
6128 Jefferson Ave
(23605)
Rates: $39-$60
Tel: (804) 826-4500
(800) 578-7878

NORFOLK

ANCHORAGE INN
929 E Ocean View
Ave (23503)
Rates: n/a
Tel: (804) 583-2605

**BEACHCOMBER
MOTEL**
2090 E Ocean View
Ave (23503)
Rates: n/a
Tel: (804) 583-2605

**COMFORT INN
TOWN POINT**
930 Virginia Beach
Blvd (23504)
Rates: $35-$55
Tel: (804) 623-5700
(800) 221-2222

DAYS INN
1631 Bayville St
(23503)
Rates: $38-$100
Tel: (757) 583-4521
(800) 329-7466

**DAYS INN
MILITARY CIRCLE**
5701 Chambers St
(23502)
Rates: $38-$62
Tel: (804) 461-0100
(800) 329-7466

ECONO LODGE
3343 N Military
Hwy (23518)
Rates: $33-$59
Tel: (804) 855-3116
(800) 424-4777

ECONO LODGE
1850 E Little Creek
(23518)
Rates: $31-$46
Tel: (804) 588-8888
(800) 424-4777

ECONO LODGE
865 N Military Hwy
(23502)
Rates: $40-$60
Tel: (804) 461-4865
(800) 424-4777

ECONO LODGE
9601 4th View St
(23503)
Rates: $43-$54
Tel: (804) 480-9611
(800) 424-4777

HILTON
1500 N Military
Hwy (23502)
Rates: n/a
Tel: (804) 466-8000

HOWARD JOHNSON
700 Monticello Ave
(23510)
Rates: $51-$85
Tel: (804) 627-5555
(800) 446-4656

LAFAYETTE
4233 Granby St
(23504)
Rates: n/a
Tel: (804) 622-5383

**LODGE AT
LITTLE CREEK**
7969 Shore Dr
(23518)
Rates: n/a
Tel: (804) 588-3600

**MARRIOTT HOTEL
WATERSIDE**
235 E Main St
(23510)
Rates: n/a
Tel: (804) 627-4200

MOTEL 6
853 N Military Hwy
(23502)
Rates: $36-$42
Tel: (804) 461-2380
(800) 440-6000

QUALITY INN
719 E Ocean View
Ave (23503)
Rates: n/a
Tel: (804) 583-5211

QUALITY INN
6280 Northampton
Blvd (23502)
Rates: $55-$95
Tel: (804) 461-6251
(800) 221-2222

SCOTTISH INNS
1001 N Military
Hwy (23502)
Rates: $25-$44
Tel: (800) 251-1962

SHERATON INN
Military Hwy &
Virginia Beach
(23518)
Rates: n/a
Tel: (804) 461-9192

NORTON

SUPER 8 MOTEL
425 Wharton Lane
(24273)
Rates: $43-$64
Tel: (540) 679-0893
(800) 800-8000

ONLEY

ANCHOR MOTEL
P.O. Box 69 (23418)
Rates: $42-$58
Tel: (804) 787-8000

PETERSBURG

AMERICAN INN
2209 County Dr
(23803)
Rates: $31-$37
Tel: (804) 733-2800

BEST WESTERN INN
405 E Washington St
(23803)
Rates: $39-$95
Tel: (804) 733-1776
(800) 528-1234

CALIFORNIA INN
2214 Country Dr
(23803)
Rates: n/a
Tel: (804) 732-5500

COMFORT INN
11974 S Crater Rd
(23805)
Rates: $37-$60
Tel: (804) 732-2900
(800) 221-2222

DAYS INN
P.O. Box 1509
(23805)
Rates: $39-$65
Tel: (804) 733-4400
(800) 329-7466

**ECONO LODGE-
SOUTH**
16905 Parkdale Rd
(23805)
Rates: $33-$66
Tel: (804) 862-2717
(800) 424-4777

FLAGSHIP INN
815 S Crater Rd
(23803)
Rates: $32-$52
Tel: (804) 861-3470

**HOLIDAY INN-
NORTH**
501 E Washington St
(23803)
Rates: $49-$75
Tel: (804) 733-0730
(800) 465-4329

QUALITY INN
11205 S Crater Rd
(23805)
Rates: $35-$60
Tel: (804) 733-0600
(800) 221-2222

RAMADA INN
501 E Washington St
(23803)
Rates: $40-$76
Tel: (804) 733-0730
(800) 272-6232

STAR MOTEL
39 S Crater Rd
(23803)
Rates: n/a
Tel: (804) 733-3600

SUPER 8 MOTEL
555 Wythe St E
(23803)
Rates: $33-$50
Tel: (804) 861-0793
(800) 800-8000

TRAVELODGE-NORTH
2201 Ruffinmill Rd
(23834)
Rates: $32-$48
Tel: (804) 526-4611
(800) 578-7878

PORTSMOUTH

DAYS INN
1031 London Blvd
(23704)
Rates: $35-$99
Tel: (757) 399-4414
(800) 329-7466

HOLIDAY INN-WATERFRONT
8 Crawford Pkwy
(23704)
Rates: $75-$88
Tel: (804) 393-2573
(800) 465-4329

SUPER 8 MOTEL
925 London Blvd
(23704)
Rates: $40-$58
Tel: (804) 398-0612
(800) 800-8000

PULASKI

RED CARPET INN
I-81, Exit 94 (24301)
Rates: $28-$46
Tel: (703) 980-2230
(800) 251-1962

RADFORD

BEST WESTERN INN
1501 Tyler Ave
(24141)
Rates: $56-$90
Tel: (540) 639-3000
(800) 528-1234

COMFORT INN
1501 Tyler Ave
(24141)
Rates: $45-$66
Tel: (540) 639-4800
(800) 221-2222

DOGWOOD LODGE
7073 Lee Hwy
(24141)
Rates: $24-$34
Tel: (540) 639-9338

SUPER 8 MOTEL
1600 Tyler Ave
(24141)
Rates: $38-$60
Tel: (540) 731-9355
(800) 800-8000

RAPHINE

DAYS INN
Rt 2, Box 438 (24472)
Rates: $34-84
Tel: (540) 377-2604
(800) 329-7466

RICHMOND

DAYS INN
1600 Robin Hood Rd
(23220)
Rates: $38-$70
Tel: (804) 353-1287
(800) 329-7466

DAYS INN
2100 Dickens Rd
(23230)
Rates: $46-$81
Tel: (804) 282-3300
(800) 329-7466

ECONO LODGE-SOUTH
2125 Willis Rd
(23237)
Rates: $33-$47
Tel: (804) 271-6031
(800) 424-4777

ECONO LODGE-WEST
6523 Midlothian Tpk
(23225)
Rates: $31-$45
Tel: (804) 276-8241
(800) 424-4777

HOJO INN
801 E Parham Rd
(23227)
Rates: $40-$51
Tel: (804) 266-8753
(800) 446-4656

HOLIDAY INN-CROSSROADS
2000 Staples Mill Rd
(23230)
Rates: $70-$75
Tel: (804) 359-6061
(800) 465-4329

HOLIDAY INN-DOWNTOWN
301 W Franklin St
(23220)
Rates: $65-$75
Tel: (804) 644-9871
(800) 465-4329

HOLIDAY INN
6531 W Broad St
(23230)
Rates: $62-$94
Tel: (804) 282-5642
(800) 465-4329

HOWARD JOHNSON
4303 Commerce Rd
(23234)
Rates: $65-$69
Tel: (800) 446-4656

MARRIOTT HOTEL
500 E Broad St
(23219)
Rates: $94+
Tel: (804) 643-3400
(800) 228-9290

PARK SUITES HOTEL
9th & Bank St
(23219)
Rates: n/a
Tel: (804) 343-7300

RAMADA INN - SOUTH
2126 Willis Rd
(23237)
Rates: $53-$64
Tel: (804) 271-1281
(800) 272-6232

RAMADA LIMITED 3
5221 Brook Rd
(23227)
Rates: $34-$58
Tel: (800) 272-6232

RED ROOF INN
4350 Commerce Rd
(23234)
Rates: $31-$43
Tel: (804) 271-9240
(800) 843-7663

RED ROOF INN
100 Greshamwood
Pl (23225)
Rates: $26-$46
Tel: (804) 745-0600
(800) 843-7663

RESIDENCE INN BY MARRIOTT
2121 Dickens Rd
(23230)
Rates: $67-$162
Tel: (804) 285-8200
(800) 331-3131

SHERATON AIRPORT INN
4700 S Laburnom
Ave (23231)
Rates: $59-$105
Tel: (804) 226-4300
(800) 325-3535

SHERATON PARK SOUTH
9901 Midlothian
Tpke (23235)
Rates: $59-$99
Tel: (804) 323-1144

SUPER 8 MOTEL
5615 Chamberlayne
Rd (23227)
Rates: $43-$61
Tel: (804) 262-8880
(800) 800-8000

SUPER 8 MOTEL
5110 Williamsburg
Rd (23231)
Rates: $44-$62
Tel: (804) 222-8008
(800) 800-8000

SUPER 8 MOTEL
8620 Midlothian
Tpke (23235)
Rates: $42-$60
Tel: (804) 320-2823
(800) 800-8000

SUPER 8 MOTEL
7200 W Broad St
(23294)
Rates: $44-$62
Tel: (804) 672-8128
(800) 800-8000

ROANOKE

**COMFORT INN
AIRPORT**
3695 Thirlane Rd
NW (24019)
Rates: $44-$57
Tel: (800) 221-2222

**DAYS INN
CIVIC CENTER**
535 Orange Ave NE
(24016)
Rates: $52-$67
Tel: (540) 342-4551
(800) 329-7466

**HOLIDAY INN
CIVIC CENTER**
501 Orange Ave NE
(24016)
Rates: $50-$68
Tel: (540) 342-8961
(800) 465-4329

**HOLIDAY INN
TANGLEWOOD**
4468 Starkey Rd SW
(24014)
Rates: $75-$85
Tel: (540) 774-4400
(800) 465-4329

**MARRIOTT HOTEL-
AIRPORT**
2801 Hershberger
Rd NW (24017)
Rates: $58-$129
Tel: (540) 563-9300
(800) 228-9290

**RAMADA INN-
RIVER'S EDGE**
1927 Franklin Rd SW
(24014)
Rates: $43-$55
Tel: (540) 343-0121
(800) 272-6232

**ROANOKER
MOTOR LODGE**
7645 Williamson Rd
(24019)
Rates: $32-$37
Tel: (540) 362-3344
(800) 355-3010

**RODEWAY INN-
CIVIC CENTER**
526 Orange Ave NE
(24016)
Rates: $36-$65
Tel: (540) 981-9341
(800) 228-2000

**SHERATON INN-
AIRPORT**
2727 Ferndale Dr
NW (24017)
Rates: $68-$75
Tel: (540) 372-4500
(800) 325-3535

SUPER 8 MOTEL
6616 Thirlane Rd
(24019)
Rates: $41-$61
Tel: (540) 563-8888
(800) 800-8000

ROCKY MOUNT

FRANKLIN MOTEL
RFD 1 (24151)
Rates: $29-$33
Tel: (540) 483-9962
(800) 775-3506

RUTHER GLEN

**COMFORT INN-
CARMEL CHURCH**
P. O. Box 105 (22546)
Rates: $42-$72
Tel: (804) 448-2828
(800) 221-2222

**DAYS INN-
CARMEL CHURCH**
P. O. Box 70 (22546)
Rates: $35-$85
Tel: (804) 448-2011
(800) 329-7466

HOWARD JOHNSON
23786 Rogers Clark
Blvd (22546)
Rates: $45-$60
Tel: (804) 448-2499
(800) 446-4656

SALEM

BUDGET HOST INN
5399 W Main St
(24153)
Rates: $28-$65
Tel: (540) 380-2080
(800) 283-4678

HOLIDAY INN
1671 Skyview Rd
(24153)
Rates: $52-$78
Tel: (540) 389-7061
(800) 465-4329

KNIGHTS INN
301 Wildwood Rd
(24153)
Rates: $37-$45
Tel: (540) 389-0280
(800) 843-5644

QUALITY INN
179 Sheraton Dr
(24153)
Rates: $44-$57
Tel: (540) 562-1912
(800) 221-2222

SUPER 8 MOTEL
300 Wildwood Rd
(24153)
Rates: $36-$53
Tel: (540) 389-0297
(800) 800-8000

SANDSTON

**BEST WESTERN
AIRPORT INN**
5700 Williamsburg
Rd (23150)
Rates: $39-$44
Tel: (804) 222-2780
(800) 528-1234

DAYS INN-AIRPORT
5500 Williamsburg
Rd (23150)
Rates: $55-$71
Tel: (804) 222-2041
(800) 329-7566

**ECONO LODGE-
AIRPORT**
5408 Williamsburg
Rd (23150)
Rates: $33-$47
Tel: (804) 222-1020
(800) 424-4777

KNIGHT'S INN
5252 Airport Square
Ln (23150)
Rates: n/a
Tel: (804) 226-4519

LEGACY INN
5252 Airport Square
Ln (23150)
Rates: $30-$46
Tel: (804) 226-4519

MOTEL 6
5704 US Hwy 60
(23150)
Rates: $33-$42
Tel: (804) 222-7600
(800) 440-6000

SCOTTSVILLE

CHESTER INN
Rt 4, Box 57 (24590)
Rates: n/a
Tel: (804) 286-2218

**HIGH MEADOWS
INN**
High Meadows Ln
(24590)
Rates: $85-$235
Tel: (804) 286-2218

SKIPPERS

ECONO LODGE
I-95 S & SR 629
(23879)
Rates: $29-$66
Tel: (804) 634-6124
(800) 424-4777

SOUTH BOSTON

**BEST WESTERN
HOWARD HOUSE INN**
2001 Seymour Dr
(24592)
Rates: $55-$63
Tel: (804) 572-4311
(800) 528-1234

SUPER 8 MOTEL
1040 Bill Tuck Hwy
(24592)
Rates: $41-$62
Tel: (804) 572-8868
(800) 800-8000

SOUTH HILL

**BEST WESTERN
SOUTH HILL**
P.O. Box 594 (23970)
Rates: $61-75
Tel: (804) 447-3123
(800) 528-1234

ECONO LODGE
623 E Atlantic St
(23970)
Rates: $40-$68
Tel: (804) 447-7116
(800) 424-4777

HOLIDAY INN
US 58 & I-85 (23970)
Rates: $55-$65
Tel: (804) 447-3123
(800) 465-4329

SUPER 8 MOTEL
922 E Atlantic St
(23970)
Rates: $38-$56
Tel: (804) 447-7655
(800) 800-8000

SPERRYVILLE

**THE CONYERS
HOUSE B & B**
Rt 1, Box 157 (22740)
Rates: $90-$195
Tel: (703) 987-8025

SPRINGFIELD

RAMADA INN
6868 Springfield
Blvd
(22150)
Rates: $49-119
Tel: (703) 644-5311
(800) 272-6232

**SPRINGFIELD
HILTON**
6550 Loisdale Rd
(22150)
Rates: $70-$130
Tel: (703) 971-8900

STANLEY

**JORDAN HOLLOW
FARM INN**
Rt 2, Box 375 (22851)
Rates: n/a
Tel: (703) 778-2209

STAUNTON

COMFORT INN
1302 Richmond
(24401)
Rates: $50-$65
Tel: (540) 886-5000
(800) 221-2222

DAYS INN
Rt 2, Box 414 (24401)
Rates: $45-$69
Tel: (540) 337-3031
(800) 329-7466

ECONO LODGE
Rt 2, Box 364 (24401)
Rates: $32-$55
Tel: (540) 337-1231
(800) 424-4777

ECONO LODGE
1031 Richmond
(24401)
Rates: $38-$64
Tel: (540) 885-5158
(800) 424-4777

STEPHENS CITY

COMFORT INN
167 Town Run Lane
(22655)
Rates: $43-$75
Tel: (540) 869-6500
(800) 221-2222

STERLING

**HAMPTON INN
DULLES AIRPORT**
45440 Holiday Dr
(22170)
Rates: $77-$85
Tel: (703) 471-4300
(800) 426-7866

HOLIDAY INN
1000 Sully Rd
(22170)
Rates: $75-$125
Tel: (703) 471-7411
(800) 465-4329

STRASBURG

HOTEL STRASBURG
201 Holliday St
(22657)
Rates: $69-$149
Tel: (540) 465-9191
(800) 348-8327

SUFFOLK

HOLIDAY INN
2864 Pruden Blvd
(23434)
Rates: $64-$72
Tel: (804) 934-2311
(800) 465-4329

SYRIA

**GRAVES MOUNTAIN
LODGE GUEST
RANCH**
Hwy 670 (22743)
Rates: $75-$200
Tel: (703) 923-4231

TROUTDALE

FOX HILL INN
Rt 2, Box 1A1
(24378)
Rates: n/a
Tel: (703) 677-3313

TROUTVILLE

COMFORT INN
2654 Lee Hwy
(24175)
Rates: $45-$65
Tel: (540) 992-5600
(800) 221-2222

HOWARD JOHNSON
P. O. Box 100 (24175)
Rates: $42-$70
Tel: (703) 992-3000
(800) 446-4656

TRAVELODGE
2444 Lee Hwy
(24175)
Rates: $40-$65
Tel: (703) 992-6700
(800) 578-7878

VERONA

SCOTTISH INNS
P. O. Box 586 (24482)
Rates: $30-$38
Tel: (703) 248-8981
(800) 251-1962

VIENNA

**RESIDENCE INN
TYSONS CORNER**
8616 Westwood
Center Dr (22182)
Rates: $129-$169
Tel: (800) 331-3131

**TYSONS CORNER
MARRIOTT HOTEL**
8028 Leesburg Pike
(22182)
Rates: $36-$172
Tel: (703) 734-3200

VIRGINIA
BEACH

ALICIA'S COTTAGES
304-306 24th St
(23451)
Rates: n/a
Tel: (804) 340-8890

**ANGIE'S GUEST
COTTAGE**
302 24th St (23451)
Rates: n/a
Tel: (804) 428-4690

AQUARIUS MOTEL
20th & Oceanfront
(23451)
Rates: n/a
Tel: (804) 425-0650

BEACH CABANA
23rd & Oceanfront
(23451)
Rates: n/a
Tel: (804) 428-8188

CORAL SAND MOTEL
23rd & Pacific
(23451)
Rates: n/a
Tel: (804) 425-0872

ECONO LODGE
2968 Shore Dr
(23451)
Rates: $40-$64
Tel: (804) 481-0666
(800) 424-4777

ECONO LODGE
3637 Bonney Rd
(23452)
Rates: $30-$50
Tel: (804) 486-5711
(800) 424-4777

ECONO LODGE
5819 Northampton
Blvd (23455)
Rates: $33-$51
Tel: (804) 464-9306
(800) 424-4777

EXECUTIVE INN
717 S Military Hwy
(23464)
Rates: $29-$69
Tel: (804) 420-2120
(800) 678-3466

HOLIDAY INN
5655 Greenwich Rd
(23462)
Rates: $75-$99
Tel: (804) 499-4400
(800) 465-4329

**HOLLY KOVE
EFFICIENCIES**
395 Norfolk Ave
(23451)
Rates: n/a
Tel: (804) 425-8374

HOWARD JOHNSON
1801 Atlantic Ave
(23451)
Rates: $59-$129
Tel: (804) 437-9100
(800) 446-4656

**LA COQUILLE
MOTEL APARTMENTS**
314 16th St (23451)
Rates: $45-$88
Tel: (804) 422-3889

LA QUINTA INN
192 Newtown Rd
(23462)
Rates: $43-$60
Tel: (804) 497-6620
(800) 531-5900

LAKESIDE MOTEL
2572 Virginia Beach
Blvd (23452)
Rates: n/a
Tel: (804) 340-3211

LOTUS POND B & B
1324 Sandbridge Rd
(23456)
Rates: n/a
Tel: (804) 426-7164

MARDI GRAS MOTEL
28th & Atlantic
(23451)
Rates: n/a
Tel: (804) 428-3434

**OCEAN HOLIDAY
HOTEL**
2417 Atlantic Ave
(23451)
Rates: $40-$120
Tel: (804) 425-6920
(800) 345-7263

**RAMADA INN
AIRPORT SOUTH 3**
5725 Northampton
Blvd (23455)
Rates: $45-$65
Tel: (804) 464-9351
(800) 272-6232

RED CARPET INN
2700 Pacific Ave
(23451)
Rates: $39+
Tel: (804) 425-9330
(800) 251-1962

RED ROOF INN
196 Ballard Ct (23462)
Rates: $33-$52
Tel: (804) 490-0225
(800) 843-7663

SANDPIPER MOTEL
1112 Pacific Ave
(23451)
Rates: n/a
Tel: (804) 422-0001

**SUNDOWNER
MOTEL**
27th & Pacific Ave
(23451)
Rates: n/a
Tel: (804) 428-3011

**THUNDERBIRD
MOTOR LODGE**
35th & Oceanfront
(23451)
Rates: $35-$110
Tel: (804) 428-3024
(800) 633-6669

TRAVELODGE
4600 Bonney Rd
(23462)
Rates: $35-$87
Tel: (804) 473-9745
(800) 578-7878

WARRENTON

COMFORT INN
6633 Lee Hwy
(22186)
Rates: $59-$74
Tel: (540) 349-8900
(800) 221-2222

HAMPTON INN
501 Blackwell Rd
(22186)
Rates: $57-$75
Tel: (540) 349-4200
(800) 426-7866

HOJO INN
6 Broadview Ave
(22186)
Rates: $32-$49
Tel: (703) 347-4141
(800) 446-4656

WARM SPRINGS

**MEADOW LANE
LODGE**
Star Rt A, Box 110
(24484)
Rates: n/a
Tel: (703) 839-5959

THREE HILLS INN
P.O. Box 9 (24484)
Rates: $49-$149
Tel: (540) 839-5381

WARSAW

**BEST WESTERN
WARSAW**
4522 Richmond Rd
(22572)
Rates: $40-$105
Tel: (800) 528-1234

WAYNESBORO

BEST WESTERN INN
15 Windigrove Dr
(22960)
Rates: $45-$85
Tel: (800) 528-1234

COMFORT INN
640 W Broad St
(22980)
Rates: $38-$65
Tel: (540) 942-1171
(800) 221-2222

DAYS INN
2060 Rosser Ave
(22980)
Rates: $42-$89
Tel: (703) 942-1171
(800) 329-7466

**DELUXE BUDGET
MOTEL**
2112 W Main St
(22980)
Rates: $25-$55
Tel: (540) 949-8253

SUPER 8 MOTEL
2045 Rosser Ave
(22980)
Rates: $40-$61
Tel: (540) 943-3888
(800) 800-8000

WILLIAMSBURG

BEST WESTERN
Rt 60 & Hwy 199
(23187)
Rates: $59-$79
Tel: (804) 229-3003
(800) 528-1234

**BEST WESTERN-
COLONIAL
CAPITOL INN**
111 Penniman Rd
(23187)
Rates: $55-$99
Tel: (804) 253-1222
(800) 528-1234

**BEST WESTERN-
PATRICK HENRY INN**
York & Page Sts
(23187)
Rates: $49-$119
Tel: (804) 229-9540
(800) 528-1234

**BEST WESTERN-
VIRGINIA INN**
900 Capital Landing
Rd (23187)
Rates: $49-$69
Tel: (804) 229-1655
(800) 528-1234

**BEST WESTERN
WILIAMSBURG
WESTPARK HOTEL**
1600 Richmond Rd
(23185)
Rates: $34-$79
Tel: (800) 528-1234

**COMMONWEALTH
INN**
1233 Richmond Rd
(23185)
Rates: $30-$59
Tel: (804) 253-1087
(800) 344-0046

DAYS INN
902 Richmond Rd
(23185)
Rates: $30-$65
Tel: (757) 229-5060
(800) 329-7466

DAYS INN POTTERY
6488 Richmond Rd
(23185)
Rates: $27-$78
Tel: (804) 565-0900
(800) 329-7466

ECONO LODGE-CENTRAL
1900 Richmond Rd
(23185)
Rates: $30-$60
Tel: (804) 229-6600
(800) 424-4777

ECONO LODGE POTTERY
7051 Richmond Rd
(23188)
Rates: $25-$50
Tel: (804) 564-3341
(800) 424-4777

GEORGE WASHINGTON INN
500 Merrimac Tr
(23185)
Rates: $39-$109
Tel: (804) 220-1410
(800) 444-4678

GOVERNOR'S INN
504 N Henry St
(23185)
Rates: $45-$100
Tel: (804) 229-1000
(800) 447-4329

HERITAGE INN
1324 Richmond Rd
(23185)
Rates: $32-$66
Tel: (804) 229-6220
(800) 782-3800

HOLIDAY INN PATRIOT
3032 Richmond Rd
(23185)
Rates: $48-$129
Tel: (804) 565-2600
(800) 446-6001

MOTEL 6
3030 Richmond Rd
(23185)
Rates: $32-$38
Tel: (804) 565-3433
(800) 440-6000

QUALITY INN POTTERY
5351 Richmond Rd
(23188)
Rates: n/a
Tel: (804) 565-2000

QUARTERPATH INN
620 York St (23185)
Rates: $33-$65
Tel: (804) 220-0960
(800) 446-9222

RAMADA INN
351 York St (23185)
Rates: $45-$198
Tel: (804) 229-4100
(800) 272-6232

SUPER 8 MOTEL
304 2nd St (23185)
Rates: $40-$55
Tel: (804) 229-2981
(800) 800-8000

THOMAS JEFFERSON INN
7247 Pocahontas Tr
(23185)
Rates: n/a
Tel: (804) 220-2000

TRAVELODGE SUITES
1420 Richmond Rd
(23185)
Rates: $30-$150
Tel: (804) 229-2981
(800) 578-7878

WILLIS WHARF

BALLARD HOUSE
12527 Ballard Dr
(23486)
Rates: $50
Tel: (804) 442-2206

WINCHESTER

BEST WESTERN LEE JACKSON
711 Millwood Ave
(22601)
Rates: $42-$54
Tel: (540) 662-4154
(800) 528-1234

BUDGETEL INN
800 Millwood Ave
(22601)
Rates: $43-$60
Tel: (540) 678-0800
(800) 428-3438

DAYS INN
2951 Valley Ave
(22601)
Rates: $38-$60
Tel: (540) 667-1200
(800) 329-7466

ECHO VILLAGE MOTEL
US Rt 11 (22603)
Rates: n/a
Tel: (703) 869-1900

HOLIDAY INN
1017 Millwood Pike
(22601)
Rates: $49-$71
Tel: (540) 667-3300
(800) 465-4329

HOWARD JOHNSON
2549 Valley Ave
(22601)
Rates: $35-$58
Tel: (540) 662-2521
(800) 446-4656

MOHAWK MOTEL
2754 Northwestern
Pike (22603)
Rates: $25-$32
Tel: (540) 667-1410

QUALITY INN EAST
603 Millwood Ave
(22601)
Rates: $40-$55
Tel: (540) 667-2250
(800) 221-2222

SUPER 8 MOTEL
1077 Millwood Pike
(22602)
Rates: $39-$59
Tel: (540) 665-4450
(800) 800-8000

TOURIST CITY MOTEL
214 Millwood Ave
(22601)
Rates: $25-$33
Tel: (540) 662-9011

TRAVELODGE
160 Front Royal Pike
(22602)
Rates: $43-$70
Tel: (540) 665-0685
(800) 578-7878

WOODBRIDGE

DAYS INN
14619 Potomac Mills
Rd (22192)
Rates: $58-$96
Tel: (703) 494-4433
(800) 329-7466

ECONO LODGE
13317 Gordon Blvd
(22191)
Rates: $48-$70
Tel: (703) 491-5196
(800) 424-4777

FRIENDSHIP INN
13964 Jefferson
Davis Hwy
(22191)
Rates: $43-$58
Tel: (703) 494-4144
(800) 453-4511

SCOTTISH INNS
951 Annapolis Way
(22191)
Rates: $40-$42
Tel: (703) 490-3400
(800) 251-1962

WOODSTOCK

BUDGET HOST INN
1290 S Main St
(22664)
Rates: $29-$41
Tel: (540) 459-4086
(800) 283-4678

WYTHEVILLE

BEST WESTERN WYTHEVILLE INN
355 Nye Rd (24382)
Rates: $39-$109
Tel: (540) 228-7300
(800) 528-1234

DAYS INN
150 Malin Dr (24382)
Rates: $39-$59
Tel: (540) 228-5500
(800) 329-7466

ECONO LODGE
1190 E Main St
(24382)
Rates: $31-$55
Tel: (540) 228-5517
(800) 424-4777

HOLIDAY INN
P. O. Box 697 (24382)
Rates: $43-$70
Tel: (540) 228-5483
(800) 465-4329

**INTERSTATE
MOTOR LODGE**
705 Chapman Rd
(24382)
Rates: $25-$52
Tel: (540) 228-8618

MOTEL 6
220 Lithia Rd (24382)
Rates: $30-$36
Tel: (540) 228-7988
(800) 466-8356

RED CARPET INN
280 Lithia Rd (24382)
Rates: $32-$52
Tel: (540) 228-5525
(800) 251-1962

SUPER 8 MOTEL
130 Nye Cir (24382)
Rates: $38-$53
Tel: (540) 228-6620
(800) 800-8000

WASHINGTON

ABERDEEN

CENTRAL PARK MOTEL
6504 Olympic Hwy (98520)
Rates: $30-$45
Tel: (360) 533-1210

NORDIC INN
1700 S Boone St (98520)
Rates: $35-$64
Tel: (360) 533-0100

OLYMPIC INN
616 W Heron St (98520)
Rates: $39-$92
Tel: (360) 533-4200

RED LION INN
521 W Wishkah (98520)
Rates: $50-$75
Tel: (360) 532-5210
(800) 547-8010

THUNDERBIRD MOTEL
410 W Wishkah (98520)
Rates: $46-$64
Tel: (360) 532-3153

TOWNE MOTEL
712 W Wishkah (98520)
Rates: n/a
Tel: (360) 533-2340

TRAVELURE MOTEL
623 W Wishkah (98520)
Rates: $37-$62
Tel: (360) 532-3280

AIRWAY HEIGHTS

HEIGHTS MOTEL
13504 W Hwy 2 (99001)
Rates: n/a
Tel: (509) 244-2072

LANTERN PARK MOTEL
W 13820 Sunset Hwy (99001)
Rates: $29-$57
Tel: (509) 244-3653

AMANDA PARK

AMANDA PARK MOTEL
P. O. Box 624 (98526)
Rates: $35
Tel: (800) 410-2237

ANACORTES

ANACORTES INN
3006 Commercial Ave (98221)
Rates: $45-$125
Tel: (360) 293-3153
(800) 327-7976

ISLANDS INN
3401 Commercial Ave (98221)
Rates: $60-$100
Tel: (360) 293-4644

OLD BOOK INN BED & BREAKFAST
530 Old Brook Ln (98221)
Rates: $70-$80
Tel: (800) 503-4768

SAN JUAN MOTEL
1103 6th St (98221)
Rates: $35-$56
Tel: (360) 293-5105
(800) 533-8009

SHIP HARBOR INN
5316 Ferry Terminal Rd (98221)
Rates: $49-$85
Tel: (360) 293-5177
(800) 852-8568

ARLINGTON

ARLINGTON MOTOR INN
2214 SR 530 (98223)
Rates: $44-$98
Tel: (360) 652-9595

SMOKEY POINT MOTOR INN
17329 Smokey Point Dr (98223)
Rates: $39-$55
Tel: (360) 659-8561

ASHFORD

CABINS AT THE BERRY
37221 Hwy 706 E (98304)
Rates: n/a
Tel: (360) 569-2628

MT. RAINIER COUNTRY CABINS
38624 SR 706 E (98304)
Rates: $55-$70
Tel: (360) 569-2355

AUBURN

BEST WESTERN-PONY SOLDIER INN
1521 D St NE (98002)
Rates: $71-$89
Tel: (206) 939-5950
(800) 528-1234

NENDELS AUBURN
102 15th St NE (98802)
Rates: $48-$56
(206) 833-8007

VAL-U INN
9 14th Ave NW (98001)
Rates: $56-$69
Tel: (206) 735-9600
(800) 443-7777

BAINBRIDGE ISLAND

BAINBRIDGE INN BED & BREAKFAST
9200 Hemlock Ave NE (98110)
Rates: n/a
Tel: (360) 842-7564

FROG ROCK INN BED & BREAKFAST
15576 Washington Ave NE (98110)
Rates: $60-$75
Tel: (206) 842-2761

MONARCH MANOR BED & BREAKFAST
7656 Yeomalt Pt Dr NE (98110)
Rates: $75-$250
Tel: (206) 780-0112

BEAVER

BEAR CREEK MOTEL & RV PARK
MP 206, Hwy 101 W (98306)
Rates $42-$48
Tel: (360) 327-3660

BELLEVUE

BELLEVUE B & B
830 100th Ave SE (98004)
Rates: $60-$100
Tel: (206) 453-1048

BEST WESTERN BELLEVUE INN
11211 Main St (98004)
Rates: $100-$125
Tel: (206) 455-5240
(800) 528-1234

KANES MOTEL
14644 SE Eastgate SE Way (98007)
Rates: $36-$45
Tel: (206) 746-8201

LA RESIDENCE SUITE HOTEL
475 100th Ave NE (98004)
Rates: n/a
Tel: (206) 455-1475

RED LION INN-BELLEVUE CENTER
818 112th Ave NE (98004)
Rates: $74-$112
Tel: (206) 455-1515
(800) 547-8010

**RESIDENCE INN
BY MARRIOTT**
14455 29th Pl NE
(98007)
Rates: $80-$195
Tel: (206) 882-1222
(800) 331-3131

**WEST COAST
BELLEVUE HOTEL**
625 116th Ave NE
(98004)
Rates: $62-$91
Tel: (206) 455-9444
(800) 426-0670

BELLINGHAM

**BAY CITY
MOTOR INN**
116 N Samish Way
(98225)
Rates: n/a
Tel: (360) 676-0332

BELL MOTEL
208 N Samish Way
(98225)
Rates: n/a
Tel: (360) 733-2520

COACHMAN INN
120 N Samish Way
(98225)
Rates: n/a
Tel: (360) 671-9000

DAYS INN
125 E Kellogg Rd
(98226)
Rates: $44-84
Tel: (360) 671-8200
(800) 329-7466

**HOLIDAY INN
EXPRESS**
4160 Guide
Meridian (98226)
Rates: $45-$62
Tel: (360) 671-4800
(800) 465-4329

LIONS INN MOTEL
2419 Elm St (98225)
Rates: $44-$48
Tel: (360) 733-2330

MAC'S MOTEL
1215 E Maple
(98225)
Rates: n/a
Tel: (360) 734-7570

MOTEL 6
3701 Byron (98225)
Rates: $30-$36
Tel: (360) 671-4494
(800) 440-6000

PARK MOTEL
101 N Samish Way
(98225)
Rates: $40-$60
Tel: (360) 733-8280

QUALITY INN
100 E Kellogg Rd
(98226)
Rates: $49-$89
Tel: (360) 647-8000
(800) 221-2222

RODEWAY INN
3710 Meridian St
(98225)
Rates: $45-$64
Tel: (360) 738-6000
(800) 424-4777

SHAMROCK MOTEL
4133 W Maplewood
Ave (98226)
Rates: n/a
Tel: (360) 676-1050

**SHANGRI-LA
DOWNTOWN
MOTEL**
611 E Holly St
(98225)
Rates: $28-$35
Tel: (360) 733-7050

VAL-U INN
805 Lakeway Dr
(98226)
Rates: $44-$63
Tel: (360) 671-9600
(800) 443-7777

BINGEN

CITY CENTER MOTEL
208 W Steuben
(98605)
Rates: n/a
Tel: (509) 493-2445

BLAINE

**THE INN
AT SEMIAHMOO**
9565 Semiahmoo
Pkwy (98230)
Rates: $115-$275
Tel: (360) 371-2000
(800) 770-7992

**NORTHWOODS
MOTEL**
288 D St (98230)
Rates: $35-$50
Tel: (360) 332-5603

WESTVIEW MOTEL
1300 Peace Portal Dr
(98230)
Rates: n/a
Tel: (360) 332-5501

BOTHELL

**RESIDENCE INN
BY MARRIOTT**
11920 NE 195th St
(98011)
Rates: $100-$145
Tel: (206) 485-3030
(800) 331-3131

BREMERTON

**THE CHIEFTAN
MOTEL**
600 National Ave N
(98312)
Rates: n/a
Tel: (206) 479-3111

DUNES MOTEL
3400 11th St (98312)
Rates: $43-$51
Tel: (360) 377-0093

FLAGSHIP INN
4320 Kitsap Way
(98312)
Rates: $60-$75
Tel: (360) 479-6566

MIDWAY INN
2909 Wheaton Way
E (98310)
Rates: $50-$60
Tel: (360) 479-2909
(800) 231-1576

OYSTER BAY INN
4412 Kitsap Way
(98312)
Rates: $47-$75
Tel: (360) 377-5510

QUALITY INN
4303 Kitsap Way
(98312)
Rates: $65-$120
Tel: (800) 776-2291

SUPER 8 MOTEL
5068 Kitsap Way
(98310)
Rates: $44-$60
Tel: (360) 377-8881
(800) 800-8000

BREWSTER

BREWSTER MOTEL
801 S Bridge St
(98812)
Rates: $30-$50
Tel: (509) 689-2625

BRIDGEPORT

4 MOTEL
2138 Columbia
(98816)
Rates: $35-$42
Tel: (509) 686-2002

STIRLING MOTEL
1717 Foster Creek
Ave (98813)
Rates: n/a
Tel: (509) 686-4821

BUCKLEY

COMFORT INN
100 410 Hwy (98321)
Rates: $59-$69
Tel: (800) 221-2222

MT. VIEW INN
29405 Hwy 410
(98321)
Rates: $45-$65
Tel: (360) 829-1100
(800) 582-4111

BURLINGTON

STERLING MOTOR INN
866 S Burlington
Blvd (98233)
Rates: $35-$55
Tel: (206) 757-0071

CARNATION

RIVER INN SNOQUALMIE VALLEY B & B
4548 Tolt River Rd
(98014)
Rates: $65-$185
Tel: (206) 333-6000

CARSON

CARSON MINERAL HOT SPRINGS
P.O. Box 1169 (98610)
Rates: $30-$100
Tel: (509) 427-8292
(800) 607-3678

CASTLE ROCK

MOUNT ST. HELENS MOTEL
1340 Mt St. Helens
Way NE (98611)
Rates: $30-$48
Tel: (360) 274-7721

7 WEST MOTEL
864 Walsh Ave NE
(98611)
Rates: n/a
Tel: (360) 274-7526

TIMBERLAND INN
1271 Mt St. Helens
Way (98611)
Rates: $40-$98
Tel: (360) 274-6002

CATHLAMET

NASSA POINT MOTEL
851 E Hwy 4 (98612)
Rates: $28-$45
Tel: (360) 795-3941

CENTRALIA

DAYS INN
702 Harrison Ave
(98531)
Rates: $45-$70
Tel: (360) 736-2875
(800) 329-7466

FERRYMAN'S INN
1003 Eckerson Rd
(98531)
Rates: $36-$42
Tel: (360) 330-2094

LAKE SHORE MOTEL
1325 Lakeshore Dr
(98531)
Rates: n/a
Tel: (360) 736-9344

MOTEL 6
1310 Belmont Ave
(98531)
Rates: $30-$40
Tel: (360) 330-2057
(800) 440-6000

PARK MOTEL
1011 Belmont Ave
(98531)
Rates: $29-$38
Tel: (206) 736-9333

PEPPERTREE WEST MOTOR INN
1208 Alder St (98531)
Rates: $30-$46
Tel: (360) 736-1124
(800) 795-1124

CHEHALIS

RELAX INN
550 SW Parkland Dr
(98532)
Rates: $30-$51
Tel: (360) 748-8608

CHELAN

BRICKHOUSE INN BED & BREAKFAST
304 Wapato St
(98816)
Rates: n/a
Tel: (509) 682-4791

CABANA MOTEL
420 Manson Rd
(98816)
Rates: $63-$112
Tel: (509) 682-2233
(800) 799-2332

KELLY'S RESORT
12801 S Lakeshore
Rd (98816)
Rates: $90-$150
Tel: (509) 687-3220

LAKE CHELAN MOTEL
2044 W Woodin Ave
(98816)
Rates: n/a
Tel: (509) 682-2742

MIDTOWNER MOTEL
721 E Woodin Ave
(98816)
Rates: n/a
Tel: (509) 682-4051

CHENEY

ROSEBROOK INN
304 W 1st (99004)
Rates: n/a
Tel: (509) 235-6538

WILLOW SPRINGS MOTEL
5 B St (99004)
Rates: $37-$45
Tel: (509) 235-5138

CHEWELAH

NORDLIG MOTEL
101 W Grant St
(99109)
Rates: $35-$43
Tel: (509) 935-6704

49ER MOTEL & RV PARK
311 S Park St (99109)
Rates: n/a
Tel: (509) 935-8613

CLARKSTON

ASTOR MOTEL
1201 Bridge St
(99403)
Rates: n/a
Tel: (509) 758-2509

MOTEL 6
222 Bridge St (99403)
Rates: $32-$38
Tel: (509) 758-1631
(800) 440-6000

GOLDEN KEY MOTEL
1376 Bridge St
(99403)
Rates: n/a
Tel: (509) 758-5566

HACIENDA LODGE MOTEL
812 Bridge St (99403)
Rates: n/a
Tel: (800) 600-5583

HIGHLAND HOUSE BED & BREAKFAST
707 Highland
(99403)
Rates $35-$80
Tel: (509) 758-3126

SUNSET MOTEL
1200 Bridge St
(99403)
Rates: n/a
Tel: (800) 845-5223

CLEELUM

BONITA MOTEL
906 E First St (98922)
Rates: n/a
Tel: (509) 674-2380

CEDARS MOTEL
1001 E First St
(98922)
Rates: $38-$50
Tel: (509) 674-5535

CHALET MOTEL
800 E First St (98922)
Rates: n/a
Tel: (509) 674-2320

MUS MOTEL & ANTIQUES
521 E First St (98922)
Rates: $30-$55
Tel: (509) 674-2551

STEWART LODGE
805 W First St
(98922)
Rates: $43-$60
Tel: (509) 674-4548

TIMBER LODGE MOTEL
301 W First St
(98922)
Rates: $43-$56
Tel: (509) 674-5966

WIND BLEW INN
811 Hwy 970 (98922)
Rates: n/a
Tel: (509) 674-2294

COLVILLE

BEAVER LODGE RESORT
2430 Hwy 20 East
(99114)
Rates: n/a
Tel: (509) 684-5657

BENNY'S COLVILLE INN
915 S Main St
(99114)
Rates: $40-$105
Tel: (509) 684-2517

DOWNTOWN MOTEL
369 S Main St (99114)
Rates: $30-$50
Tel: (509) 684-2565

MAPLE AT SIXTH BED & BREAKFAST
407 E 6th (99114)
Rates: $45-$55
Tel: (800) 446-2750

CONCONULLY

CONCONULLY LAKE RESORT
102 Sinlahekin Rd
(98819)
Rates: $45
Tel: (800) 850-0813

CONCONULLY MOTEL
P. O. Box 181 (98819)
Rates: n/a
Tel: (509) 826-1610

GIBSON'S NORTH FORK LODGE
100 W Boone (98819)
Rates: n/a
Tel: (509) 826-1475

LIAR'S COVE RESORT
1835 A Conconully
Rd (98819)
Rates: $40-$50
Tel: (800) 830-1288

SHADY PINES RESORT
125 W Fork Salmon
Creek Rd
(98819)
Rates: $54-$60
Tel: (800) 552-2287

CONNELL

M & M MOTEL
730 S Columbia Ave
(99326)
Rates: n/a
Tel: (509) 234-8811

TUMBLEWOOD MOTEL
433 S Columbia
(99326)
Rates: $22-$35
Tel: (509) 234-2081

COPALIS BEACH

BEACHWOOD RESORT
SR 109 (98536)
Rates: n/a
Tel: (360) 289-2177

LINDA'S LOW TIDE MOTEL
14 McCullough Rd
(98535)
Rates: $30-$60
Tel: (360) 289-3450

ROD'S BEACH RESORT
2961 SR 109 (98535)
Rates: n/a
Tel: (360) 289-2222

SHADES BY THE SEA MOTEL
3208 Hwy 109
(98535)
Rates: $30-$70
Tel: (360) 289-3358

COULEE CITY

BLUE TOP MOTEL
109 N 6th St (99115)
Rates: $27-$48
Tel: (509) 632-5596

COULEE LODGE RESORT
33017 Park Lake Rd
NE (99115)
Rates: $27-$53
Tel: (509) 632-5565

LAKEVIEW MOTEL
HCR 1, Box 11
(99115)
Rates: n/a
Tel: (509) 632-5792

LAUREN'T SUN VILLAGE RESORT
33575 Park Lake Rd
NE (99115)
Rates: $42-$95
Tel: (509) 632-5664

COULEE DAM

COULEE HOUSE MOTEL
110 Roosevelt Way
(99116)
Rates: $46-$110
Tel: (509) 633-1101
(800) 715-7767

PONDEROSA MOTEL
10 Lincoln St (99116)
Rates: $36-$56
Tel: (509) 633-2100
(800) 633-6421

CURLEW

BLUE COUGAR MOTEL
2141 Hwy 21 N
(99118)
Rates: n/a
Tel: (509) 779-4817

CUSICK

THE OUTPOST RESORT & RV PARK
405351 Hwy 20
(99119)
Rates)
Tel: (509) 445-1317

DAYTON

BLUE MOUNTAIN MOTEL
414 W Main St
(99328)
Rates: n/a
Tel: (509) 382-3040

THE PURPLE HOUSE BED & BREAKFAST
415 E Clay St (99328)
Rates: $85-$125
Tel: (800) 486-2574

THE WEINHARD HOTEL
235 E Main St
(99328)
Rates: $65-$110
Tel: (509) 382-4032

DEER PARK

LOVE'S VICTORIAN BED & BREAKFAST
North 31317 Cedar
Rd (99006)
Rates: n/a
Tel: (509) 276-6939

DEMING

THE GUEST HOUSE BED & BREAKFAST
5723 Schornbush Rd
(98244)
Rates: $60
Tel: (360) 592-2343

THE LOGS RESORT
9002 Mt. Baker Hwy
(98244)
Rates: n/a
Tel: (360) 599-2711

DES MOINES

KINGS ARMS MOTEL APARTMENT
23226 30th Ave S
(98198)
Rates: n/a
Tel: (206) 824-0300

EAST WENATCHEE

FOUR SEASONS INN
11 W Grant Rd
(98802)
Rates: $44-$62
Tel: (509) 884-6611

EATONVILLE

HENLEY'S SILVER LAKE RESORT
40718 S Silver Lake
Rd E (98328)
Rates: n/a
Tel: (360) 832-3580

LAGRANDE MOTEL
46719 Mt Hwy East
(98348)
Rates: n/a
Tel: (206) 832-4912

EDMONDS

K & E MOTOR INN
23921 Hwy 99
(98020)
Rates: $42-$62
Tel: (206) 778-2181

ELBE

HOBO INN
P. O. Box 20 (98330)
Rates: $70-$85
Tel: (360) 569-2500

ELK

JERRY'S LANDING RESORT
N 41114 Lakeshore
(99009)
Rates: n/a
Tel: (509) 292-2337

ELLENSBURG

BEST WESTERN INN
1700 Canyon Rd
(98926)
Rates: $52-$72
Tel: (509) 925-9801
(800) 528-1234

HAROLDS MOTEL
601 N Water (98926)
Rates: $31-$49
Tel: (509) 925-4141

I-90 INN MOTEL
1390 Dollar Way Rd
N (98926)
Rates: $33-$48
Tel: (509) 925-9844

NITES INN MOTEL
1200 S Ruby (98926)
Rates: $36-$45
Tel: (509) 962-9600

REGAL LODGE
300 W 6th St (98926)
Rates: $35-$155
Tel: (509) 925-3116

SUPER 8 MOTEL
1500 Canyon Rd
(98926)
Rates: $46-$62
Tel: (509) 962-6888
(800) 800-8000

THUNDERBIRD MOTEL
403 W 8th Ave
(98926)
Rates: $35-$55
Tel: (800) 843-3492

ENUMCLAW

BEST WESTERN PARK CENTER HOTEL
1000 Griffin Ave
(98022)
Rates: $64-$80
Tel: (360) 825-4490
(800) 528-1234

EPHRATA

COLUMBIA MOTEL
1257 Basin St SW
(98823)
Rates: $32-$42
Tel: (509) 754-5226

LARIAT MOTEL
1639 Basin St SW
(98823)
Rates: n/a
Tel: (509) 754-2437

EVERETT

CHERRY MOTEL
8421 Evergreen Way
(98208)
Rates: $29-$46
Tel: (206) 347-1100

CYPRESS INN
12619 4th Ave W
(98208)
Rates: $59-$69
Tel: (206) 347-9099
(800) 752-9991

HOLIDAY INN
101 128th St SE
(98208)
Rates: $69-$101
Tel: (206) 337-2900
(800) 465-4329

HOWARD JOHNSON
3501 Pine St (98201)
Rates: $100-110
Tel: (206) 339-3333
(800) 446-4656

MOTEL 6
10006 Everett Way
(98204)
Rates: $29-$35
Tel: (206) 347-2060
(800) 440-6000

MOTEL 6-SOUTH
224 128th St SW
(98204)
Rates: $38-$44
Tel: (206) 353-8120
(800) 440-6000

RAMADA INN
9602 19th Ave SE
(98208)
Rates: $45-$70
Tel: (206) 337-9090
(800) 272-6232

TRAVELODGE
3030 Broadway
(98201)
Rates: $44-$66
Tel: (206) 259-6141
(800) 578-7878

WAITS MOTEL
1301 Lombard Ave
(98201)
Rates: $30-$40
Tel: (206) 252-3166

WELCOME MOTOR INN
1205 N Broadway
(98201)
Rates: $37-$52
Tel: (206) 252-8828

FEDERAL WAY

BEST WESTERN FEDERAL WAY EXECUTEL
21611 20th Ave S
(98003)
Rates: $89-$99
Tel: (206) 941-6000
(800) 528-1234

ROADRUNNER MOTEL
1501 350th St S
(98003)
Rates: n/a
Tel: (800) 828-7202

SUPER 8 MOTEL
1688 348th St S
(98003)
Rates: $46-$65
Tel: (206) 838-8808
(800) 800-8000

FERNDALE

SCOTTISH LODGE MOTEL
5671 Riverside Dr
(98248)
Rates: n/a
(360) 384-4040

SUPER 8 MOTEL
5788 barrett Ave
(98248)
Rates: $45-$61
Tel: (360) 384-8881
(800) 800-8000

FIFE

BEST WESTERN EXECUTIVE INN
5700 Pacific Hwy E
(98424)
Rates: $65-$87
Tel: (206) 922-0080
(800) 938-8500

DAYS INN-PORTAGE INN
3021 Pacific Hwy E
(98424)
Rates: $40-$70
Tel: (206) 922-3500
(800) 329-7466

ECONO LODGE
3518 Pacific Hwy E
(98424)
Rates: $33-$59
Tel: (206) 922-0550
(800) 424-4777

HOMETEL INN
3520 Pacific Hwy E
(98424)
Rates: $30-$40
Tel: (800) 258-3520

KINGS MOTOR INN
5115 Pacific Hwy E
(98424)
Rates: n/a
Tel: (800) 929-3509

MOTEL 6
5201 20th St E (98424)
Rates: $32-$38
Tel: (206) 922-1270
(800) 440-6000

ROYAL COACHMAN INN
5805 Pacific Hwy E
(98424)
Rates: $49-$120
Tel: (206) 922-2500
(800) 422-3051

COMFORT INN
5601 Pacific Hwy E
(98424)
Rates: $46-$56
Tel: (206) 926-2301
(800) 221-2222

FORKS

BAGBY'S TOWN MOTEL
1080 Forks Ave S
(98331)
Rates: n/a
Tel: (800) 742-2429

FORKS MOTEL
351 Forks Ave S
(98331)
Rates: $39-$69
Tel: (360) 374-6243
(800) 544-3416

HOH HUMM RANCH
171763 Hwy 101
(98331)
Rates: n/a
Tel: (360) 374-5337

KALALOCH LODGE
15715 Hwy 101
(98331)
Rates: $70-$150
Tel: (360) 962-2271

MANITOU LODGE
P. O. Box 600 (98331)
Rates: $53-$65
Tel: (360) 374-6295

MILL CREEK INN BED & BREAKFAST
Hwy 101 (98331)
Rates: n/a
Tel: (360) 374-5873

MILLER TREE INN BED & BREAKFAST
654 E Division St
(98331)
Rates: $55-$70
Tel: (360) 374-6806

THREE RIVERS RESORT
7764 LaPush Rd
(98331)
Rates: $35-$45
Tel: (360) 374-5300

TOWN MOTEL
HC 80, Box 350
(98331)
Rates: n/a
Tel: (360) 374-6231

GIG HARBOR

DAVENPORT HOTEL BED & BREAKFAST
7501 Artondale
(98335)
Rates: $65-$75
Tel: (206) 851-8527

NO CABBAGES BED & BREAKFAST
7712 Goodman Dr
NW (98332)
Rates: $50+
Tel: (206) 858-7797

THE PARSONAGE BED & BREAKFAST
4107 Burnham Dr
(98332)
Rates: n/a
Tel: (206) 851-8654

WESTWYND MOTEL
6703 144 St NW
(98332)
Rates: n/a
Tel: (206) 857-4047

GLACIER

GLACIER CREEK MOTEL & CABINS
10036 Mt. Baker
Hwy (98244)
Rates: n/a
Tel: (360) 599-2991

MT BAKER CHALET
9857 Mt Baker Hwy
(98244)
Rates: $50-$150
Tel: (360) 599-2405

GOLDENDALE

BARCHRIS MOTEL
128 N Academy
(98620)
Rates: n/a
Tel: (509) 773-4325

PONDEROSA MOTEL
775 E Broadway St
(98620)
Rates: $42-$70
Tel: (509) 773-5842

GRAND COULEE

TRAIL WEST MOTEL
108 Spokane Way
(99133)
Rates: $32-$39
Tel: (509) 633-3155

UMBRELLA MOTEL
404 Spokane Way
(99133)
Rates: $25-$50
Tel: (509) 633-1691

GRANDVIEW

GRANDVIEW MOTEL
522 E Wine Country
Rd (98930)
Rates: $26-$39
Tel: (509) 882-1323

GRAYLAND

GRAYLAND MOTEL & COTTAGES
2013 Hwy 105
(98547)
Rates: n/a
Tel: (360) 267-2395

OCEAN SPRAY MOTEL
1757 Hwy 105
(98547)
Rates: $45-$70
Tel: (360) 267-2205

SURF MOTEL & COTTAGES
2029 Hwy 105
(98547)
Rates: $56-$67
Tel: (360) 267-2244

WALSH MOTEL
1593 Hwy 105
(98547)
Rates: n/a
Tel: (360) 267-2191

GREEN ACRES

ALPINE MOTEL
18815 E Cataldo
(99016)
Rates: $32-$72
Tel: (509) 928-2700

GREENWATER

ALTA CRYSTAL RESORT/MT. RAINIER
68317 SR 410 E
(98022)
Rates: $69-$159
Tel: (360) 663-2500

THE INN AT THE RANCH CABIN
16423 Mountain Side
Dr (98022)
Rates: $75-$150
Tel: (360) 663-2667

HANSVILLE

GUEST HOUSE AT TWIN SPITS B & B
2570 NE Twin Spits
Rd (98340)
Rates: $60-$75
Tel: (360) 638-1001

HOME VALLEY

HOME VALLEY BED & BREAKFAST
P. O. Box 377 (98648)
Rates: n/a
Tel: (509) 427-7070

HOODSPORT

CANAL CREEK MOTEL
N 27131 Hwy 101
(98548)
Rates: $38-$52
Tel: (360) 877-6770

**SUNRISE MOTEL
& RESORT**
N 24520 Hwy 101
(98548)
Rates: n/a
Tel: (360) 877-5301

HOQUIAM

**SNORE & WHISKER
MOTEL**
3031 Simpson Ave
(98550)
Rates: $30-$60
Tel: (360) 532-5060

STOKEN MOTEL
504 Perry Ave
(98550)
Rates: n/a
Tel: (360) 532-4300

TIMBERLINE INN
415 Perry Ave
(98550)
Rates: $35-$75
Tel: (360) 533-8048

WEST WOOD INN
910 Simpson Ave
(98550)
Rates: $40-$75
Tel: (360) 532-8161
(800) 562-0994

ILWACO

A-CO-HO MOTEL
Port of Ilwaco (98624)
Rates: n/a
Tel: (360) 642-3333

COL-PACIFIC MOTEL
P. O. Box 34 (98624)
Rates: n/a
Tel: (360) 642-3177

HEIDI'S INN MOTEL
126 Spruce St (98624)
Rates: $36-$65
Tel: (360) 642-2387
(800) 642-2387

INCHELIUM

**HARTMAN'S
LOG CABIN RESORT**
HCR 156 Twin Lakes
(99138)
Rates: n/a
Tel: (509) 722-3543

**RAINBOW BEACH
RESORT**
HC1, Box 146 (99138)
Rates: n/a
Tel: (509) 722-5901

INDEX

**BUSH HOUSE
COUNTRY INN**
300 5th St (98256)
Rates: n/a
Tel: (360) 793-2312

**THE CABIN
AT INDEX B & B**
52525 Riverside Rd
(98256)
Rates: $80-$95
Tel: (206) 827-2102

IONE

IONE MOTEL
301 S 2nd (99139)
Rates: $32-$65
Tel: (509) 442-3213

PEND OREILLE INN
107 Riverside (99139)
Rates: n/a
Tel: (509) 442-3418

PLAZA MOTEL
103 S 2nd (99139)
Rates: $30-$40
Tel: (509) 442-3534

ISSAQUAH

MOTEL 6
1885 15th Pl NW
(98027)
Rates $38-$44
Tel: (206) 392-8405
(800) 440-6000

KALALOCH

KALALOCH LODGE
57151 Hwy 101
(98331)
Rates: $55-$125
Tel: (360) 962-2271

KALAMA

**COLUMBIA INN
MOTEL**
602 N Frontage Rd
(98625)
Rates: $30-$39
Tel: (360) 673-2855

KELSO

**BEST WESTERN
ALADDIN
MOTOR INN**
310 Long Ave
(98626)
Rates: $46-$80
Tel: (360) 425-9660
(800) 528-1234

BUDGET INN
505 N Pacific (98626)
Rates: $31-$40
Tel: (360) 636-4610

MOTEL 6
106 Minor Rd
(98626)
Rates: $40-$46
Tel: (360) 425-3229
(800) 440-6000

RED LION INN
510 Kelso Dr (98632)
Rates: $66-$99
Tel: (360) 636-4400
(800) 547-8010

SUPER 8 MOTEL
250 Kelso Dr (98626)
Rates: $46-$62
Tel: (360) 423-8880
(800) 800-8000

KENNEWICK

**BEST WESTERN
KENNEWICK**
4001 W 27th Ave
(99336)
Rates: $56-$76
Tel: (800) 528-1234

**CAVANAUGH'S-
COLUMBIA CENTER**
1101 N Columbia
Center Blvd (99336)
Rates: $62-$280
Tel: (509) 783-0611
(800) 843-4667

CLEARWATER INN
5616 W Clearwater
Ave (99336)
Rates: $47-$52
Tel: (509) 735-2242

COMFORT INN
7801 W Quinault
Ave (99336)
Rates: $46-$68
Tel: (509) 783-8396
(800) 221-2222

**GREEN GABLE
MOTEL**
515 W Columbia Dr
(99336)
Rates: n/a
Tel: (509) 582-5811

**HOLIDAY INN
EXPRESS**
4220 W 27th Pl
(99337)
Rates: $49-$89
Tel: (509) 736-3326
(800) 465-4329

NENDELS INN
2811 W 2nd St
(99336)
Rates: n/a
Tel: (509) 735-9511

SHANIKO INN
321 N Johnson St
(99336)
Rates: $45-$53
Tel: (509) 735-6385

SUPER 8 MOTEL
626 N Columbia
Center Blvd (99336)
Rates: $44-$64
Tel: (509) 736-6888
(800) 800-8000

**TAPADERA
BUDGET INN**
311 N Ely Hwy 395
(99336)
Rates: $36-$58
Tel: (509) 783-6191
(800) 722-8277

KENT

THE BEST INN
23408 30th Ave
(98032)
Rates: $39-$65
Tel: (206) 870-1280

**BEST WESTERN
PONY SOLDIER INN**
1233 N Central
(98032)
Rates: $71-$88
Tel: (206) 852-7224
(800) 528-1234

CYPRESS INN
22218 84th Ave S
(98032)
Rates: $67-$89
Tel: (206) 395-0219
(800) 752-9991

DAYS INN
1711 W Meeker St
(98032)
Rates: $45-$85
Tel: (206) 854-1950
(800) 329-7466

**GOLDEN KENT
MOTEL**
22203 84th Ave S
(98032)
Rates: $40-$55
Tel: (206) 872-8372

**HOMECOURT
ALL SUITE HOTEL**
6329 S 212th (98032)
Rates: $70-$85
Tel: (800) 426-0670

VAL U INN
22420 84th Ave S
(98032)
Rates $48-$66
Tel: (206) 872-5525
(800) 443-7777

KETTLE FALLS

BARNEY'S MOTEL
395 & 20 Jct (99141)
Rates: n/a
Tel: (509) 738-6546

**BULL HILL
RANCH & RESORT**
3738 Bull Hill Rd
(99141)
Rates: $85-$140
Tel: (509) 732-4355

**GRANDVIEW INN
MOTEL & RV PARK**
978 Hwy 395 N
(99141)
Rates: n/a
Tel: (509) 738-6733

KETTLE FALLS INN
205 E 3rd St (99141)
Rates: $37-$48
Tel: (509) 738-6514
(800) 341-8000

KINGSTON

**KINGSTON HOUSE
BED & BREAKFAST**
26117 Ohio Ave NE
(98346)
Rates: $85-$180
Tel: (360) 297-8818

**SMILEY'S
COLONIAL MOTEL**
11067 Hwy 104
(98346)
Rates: $30-$59
Tel: (360) 297-3622

KIRKLAND

BEST WESTERN INN
12223 116th NE
(98034)
Rates: $60-$84
Tel: (206) 822-2300
(800) 332-4200

LA QUINTA INN
10530 NE Northup
Way (98033)
Rates: $61-$124
Tel: (206) 828-6585
(800) 531-5900

MOTEL 6
12010 120th Pl NE
(98034)
Rates: $38-$44
Tel: (206) 821-5618
(800) 440-6000

LA CONNER

ART'S PLACE B & B
511 Talbott St (98257)
Rates: $60
Tel: (360) 466-3033

**HERON/LA CONNER
BED & BREAKFAST**
117 Maple Ave (98257)
Rates: $45-$135
Tel: (360) 466-4626

**LA CONNER
COUNTRY INN**
107 S 2nd St (98257)
Rates: $84-$136
Tel: (360) 466-3101

LA PUSH

**OCEAN PARK
RESORT**
700 Main St (98350)
Rates: $36-$125
Tel: (800) 487-1267

LACEY

CAPITOL INN MOTEL
120 College St SE
(98503)
Rates: $52-$66
Tel: (360) 493-1991
(800) 282-7028

SUPER 8 MOTEL
4615 Martin Way
(98503)
Rates: $52-$68
Tel: (360) 459-8888
(800) 800-8000

LAKE STEVENS

**PEONY HOUSE
BED & BREAKFAST**
1602 E Lakeshore
(98258)
Rates: n/a
Tel: (206) 334-1046

LAKEWOOD

**BEST WESTERN
LAKEWOOD
MOTOR INN**
6125 Motor Ave SW
(98499)
Rates: $58-$79
Tel: (206) 584-2212
(800) 528-1234

WESTERN INN
9920 S Tacoma Way
(98499)
Rates: $38-$52
Tel: (206) 588-5241

LEAVENWORTH

**BAYERN ON
THE RIVER**
1505 Alpen See
Strasse (98826)
Rates: $50-$79
Tel: (509) 548-5875
(800) 873-3960

**BUDGET HOST
CANYONS INN**
185 Hwy 2 (98826)
Rates: $61-$120
Tel: (509) 548-7992
(800) 693-1225

**DER RITTERHOF
MOTOR INN**
Hwy 2, Box 307
(98826)
Rates: $66-$170
Tel: (509) 548-5845
(800) 255-5845

THE EVERGREEN INN
1117 Front St (98826)
Rates: $60-$125
Tel: (509) 548-5515
(800) 327-7212

**LAKE WENATCHEE
HIDE-A-WAYS**
2511 Kinnikinick Dr
(98826)
Rates: $95-$135
Tel: (800) 883-2611

NATAPOC LODGING
12338 Bretz Rd
(98826)
Rates: $130
Tel: (509) 763-3313

**OBERTAL
MOTOR INN**
922 Commercial St
(98826)
Rates: $61-$99
Tel: (509) 548-5208
(800) 537-9382

**PHIPPEN'S
BED & BREAKFAST**
10285 Ski Hill Dr
(98826)
Rates: $70-$90
Tel: (800) 666-9806

**RIVER'S EDGE
LODGE**
8401 Hwy 2 (98826)
Rates: $40-$80
Tel: (509) 548-7612

**SAIMON'S
HIDE-A-WAYS**
16408 River Rd
(98826)
Rates: $85-$125
Tel: (800) 845-8638

SQUIRREL TREE INN
15251 Hwy 2 (98826)
Rates: n/a
Tel: (509) 763-3157

**TYROLEAN
RITZ HOTEL**
633 Front St (98826)
Rates: $60-$120
Tel: (509) 548-5455
(800) 854-6365

LILLIWAUP

**MIKE'S
BEACH RESORT**
N 38470 Hwy 101
(98555)
Rates: n/a
Tel: (800) 231-5324

LONG BEACH

**ANCHORAGE
MOTOR COURT**
2209 Boulevard N
(98631)
Rates: $48-$116
Tel: (360) 642-2351
(800) 646-2351

**ARCADIA COURT
MOTEL**
401 Boulevard N
(98631)
Rates: $37-$85
Tel: (360) 642-2613

BOULEVARD MOTEL
301 Ocean Blvd N
(98631)
Rates: $30-$95
Tel: (360) 642-2434

BREAKERS MOTEL
26th St & Hwy 103
(98631)
Rates: $54-$160
Tel: (800) 288-8890

**CHAUTAUQUA
LODGE**
305 14th NW (98631)
Rates: $50-$150
Tel: (800) 869-8401

**DRIFTWOOD RV
PARK & CABINS**
Box 296 (98631)
Rates: $47-$57
Tel: (360) 642-2711

LIGHT HOUSE MOTEL
Rt 1, Box 527 (98631)
Rates: $47-$59
Tel: (360) 642-3622

**LONG BEACH
MOTEL**
12th South & Pacific
(98631)
Rates: n/a
Tel: (206) 642-3500

OCEAN LODGE
101 Boulevard N
(98631)
Rates: $38-$75
Tel: (360) 642-2777

**OUR PLACE
AT THE BEACH**
1309 Boulevard S
(98631)
Rates: $37-$70
Tel: (360) 642-3793
(800) 538-5107

PACIFIC VIEW MOTEL
203 Bolstad St
(98631)
Rates: $42-$72
Tel: (360) 642-2415

RIDGE COURT MOTEL
201 Boulevard N
(98631)
Rates: $30-$80
Tel: (360) 642-2412

SAND LO MOTEL
1910 N Pacific Hwy
(98631)
Rates: n/a
Tel: (360) 642-2600

THE SANDS MOTEL
Box 531, Rt 1 (98631)
Rates: n/a
Tel: (360) 642-2100

SHAMAN MOTEL
115 3rd St SW
(98631)
Rates: $49-$84
Tel: (800) 753-3750

WHALE'S TALE MOTEL
P. O. Box 418 (98631)
Rates: $55-$75
Tel: (360) 642-3455
(800) 559-4253

LOON LAKE

**SHORE ACRES
RESORT**
41987 Shore Acres
Rd (99148)
Rates: n/a
Tel: (800) 900-2474

LONGVIEW

**HUDSON MANOR
MOTEL**
1616 Hudson St
(98632)
Rates: $28-$43
Tel: (360) 425-1100

**TOWN CHALET
MOTEL**
1822 Washington
Way (98632)
Rates: $31-$46
Tel: (360) 423-2020

THE TOWNHOUSE
744 Washington Way
(98632)
Rates: $26-$38
Tel: (360) 423-7200

LYNDEN

**WINDMILL INN
MOTEL**
8022 Guide
Meridian Rd (98264)
Rates: $34-$47
Tel: (360) 354-3424

LYNNWOOD

**BEST WESTERN
LANDMARK HOTEL**
4300 200th St SW
(98036)
Rates: $65-$105
Tel: (206) 775-7447
(800) 528-1234

**RESIDENCE INN
BY MARRIOTT**
18200 Alderwood
Mall Blvd (98037)
Rates: $90-$150
Tel: (206) 771-1100
(800) 331-3131

ROSE MOTEL
20222 Hwy 99
(98036)
Rates: n/a
Tel: (206) 771-9962

SILVER CLOUD INN
19332 36th Ave W
(98036)
Rates: $49-$86
Tel: (206) 775-7600
(800) 205-6935

MAPLE FALLS

**THURSTON
BED & BREAKFAST**
9512 Silver Lake Rd
(98266)
Rates: n/a
Tel: (360) 599-2261

**YODELER INN
BED & BREAKFAST**
7485 Mt. Baker Hwy
(98266)
Rates: $65
Tel: (800) 642-9033

MARYSVILLE

**BEST WESTERN-
TUALIP INN**
P. O. Box 426 (98270)
Rates: $61-$71
Tel: (800) 528-1234

**VILLAGE
MOTOR INN**
235 Beach St (98270)
Rates: $48-$65
Tel: (360) 659-0005

MAZAMA

LOST RIVER RESORT
Harts Pass Hwy
(98833)
Rates: $50-$75
Tel: (800) 996-2537

MERCER ISLAND

**MERCER ISLAND
HIDEAWAY**
8820 SE 63rd St
(98040)
Rates: $50-$75
Tel: (206) 232-1092

METALINE FALLS

CIRCLE MOTEL
HCZ Box 616,
Hwy 31 (99153)
Rates: $26-$35
Tel: (509) 446-4343

MOCLIPS

BARNACLE MOTEL
4816 Pacific Ave
(98562)
Rates: n/a
Tel: (360) 276-4318

HI TIDE OCEAN BEACH RESORT
4890 Railroad Ave
(98562)
Rates: $84-$159
Tel: (360) 276-4142
(800) 662-5477

MOCLIPS MOTEL
4852 Pacific Ave
(98562)
Rates: n/a
Tel: (360) 276-4228

MOONSTONE BEACH MOTEL
4849 Pacific Ave
(98562)
Rates: n/a
Tel: (360) 276-4346

WEEKENDER MOTEL
4675 Hwy 109
(98562)
Rates: n/a
Tel: (360) 276-4670

MONROE

BEST WESTERN BARON INN
19233 Hwy 2 (98272)
Rates: $56-$150
Tel: (360) 794-3111
(800) 528-1234

BROOKSIDE MOTEL
19930 Hwy 2 (98272)
Rates: n/a
Tel: (360) 794-8832

FAIRGROUNDS INN MOTEL
18950 Hwy 2 (98272)
Rates: n/a
Tel: (360) 794-5401

MONTESANO

MONTE SQUARE MOTEL
518 1/2 South 1st St
(98563)
Rates: n/a
Tel: (206) 249-4424

SYLVAN HAUS-MURPHY B & B
P. O. Box 416 (98563)
Rates: n/a
Tel: (360) 249-3453

MORTON

EVERGREEN MOTEL
121 Front St (98356)
Rates: n/a
Tel: (360) 496-5407

RESORT OF THE MOUNTAINS
1130 Morton Rd
(98356)
Rates: n/a
Tel: (360) 496-5885

ROY'S MOTEL
161 2nd St, Hwy 7
(98356)
Rates: n/a
Tel: (360) 496-5000

SEASONS MOTEL
200 Westlake (98356)
Rates: $50-$60
Tel: (360) 496-6835

STILTNER MOTEL
30 Morton Rd
(98356)
Rates: n/a
Tel: (360) 496-5103

MOSES LAKE

EL RANCHO MOTEL
1214 S Pioneer Way
(98837)
Rates: $28-$50
Tel: (509) 765-7193
(800) 341-8000

HOLIDAY INN EXPRESS
1735 E Kittleson
(98837)
Rates: $65-$80
Tel: (509) 766-2000
(800) 465-4329

INTERSTATE INN
2801 W Broadway
(98837)
Rates: $36-$54
Tel: (509) 765-1777

LAKESIDE MOTEL
802 W Broadway
(98837)
Rates: n/a
Tel: (509) 765-8651

LAKE SHORE MOTEL
3206 W Lakeshore
Dr (98837)
Rates: $34+
Tel: (509) 765-9201

MAPLES MOTEL
1006 W 3rd (98837)
Rates: n/a
Tel: (509) 765-5665

MOTEL 6
2822 Wapato Dr
(98837)
Rates: $30-$40
Tel: (509) 766-0250
(800) 440-6000

OASIS BUDGET INN
466 Melva Ln
(98837)
Rates: n/a
Tel: (509) 765-8636

SAGE "N" SAND MOTEL
1011 S Pioneer Way
(98837)
Rates: $32-$52
Tel: (800) 336-0454

SHILO INNS
1819 E Kittleson
(98837)
Rates: $68-$76
Tel: (509) 765-9317
(800) 222-2244

SUNLAND MOTOR INN
309 E Third Ave
(98837)
Rates: $32-$52
Tel: (509) 765-1170
(800) 220-4403

SUPER 8 MOTEL
449 Melva Ln
(98837)
Rates: $46-$62
Tel: (509) 765-8886
(800) 800-8000

TRAVELODGE
316 S Pioneer Way
(98837)
Rates: $44-$66
Tel: (509) 765-8631
(800) 578-7878

MOUNT VERNON

BEST WESTERN COLLEGE WAY INN
300 W College Way
(98273)
Rates: $45-$70
Tel: (360) 424-4287
(800) 528-1234

BEST WESTERN COTTONTREE INN
2300 Market St
(98273)
Rates: $64-$75
Tel: (360) 428-5678
(800) 528-1234

DAYS INN
2009 Riverside Dr
(98273)
Rates: $35-$150
Tel: (360) 424-4141
(800) 329-7466

HILLSIDE MOTEL
2300 Bonnie View
Rd (98273)
Rates: n/a
Tel: (360) 445-3252

WEST WINDS MOTEL
2020 Riverside Dr
(98273)
Rates: n/a
Tel: (360) 424-4224

WHISPERING FIRS
1957 Kanako Ln
(98273)
Rates: n/a
Tel: (360) 428-1990
(800) 428-1992

THE WHITE SWAN INN
1388 Moore Rd
(98273)
Rates: $75-$95
Tel: (206) 445-6805

NACHES

SILVER BEACH MOTEL
40380 Hwy 12
(98937)
Rates: n/a
Tel: (509) 672-2500

**SQUAW ROCK
RESORT**
15070 SR 410 (98937)
Rates: n/a
Tel: (509) 658-2926

TROUT LODGE
27090 Hwy 12
(98937)
Rates: $40-$55
Tel: (509) 672-2211

NASELLE

**SLEEPY HOLLOW
MOTEL**
HCR 78 (98638)
Rates: n/a
Tel: (360) 484-3232

NEAH BAY

THE CAPE MOTEL
Bay View Ave
(98357)
Rates: n/a
Tel: (360) 645-2250

**SILVER SALMON
RESORT**
Bayview &
Roosevelt (98357)
Rates: n/a
Tel: (360) 645-2388

TYEE MOTEL
P. O. Box 193 (98357)
Rates: n/a
Tel: (360) 645-2233

NEWPORT

**GOLDEN SPUR
MOTEL**
924 W Hwy 2
(99156)
Rates: n/a
Tel: (509) 447-3823

**MARSHALL LAKE
RESORT**
1301 Marshall Lake
Rd (99156)
Rates: n/a
Tel: (509) 447-4158

NORTH BEND

EDGEWICK INN
14600 468th Ave SE
(98045)
Rates: $48-$53
Tel: (206) 888-9000

OAK HARBOR

**BEST WESTERN
HARBOR PLAZA**
33175 SR 20 (98277)
Rates: $70-110
Tel: (360) 679-4567
(800) 528-1234

OCEAN CITY

**NORTH BEACH
MOTEL**
2601 SR 109 (98569)
Rates: $30-$55
Tel: (360) 289-4116
(800) 640-8053

**PACIFIC SANDS
MOTEL**
2687 SR 109 (98569)
Rates: $40-$56
Tel: (360) 289-3588

**WEST WINDS
RESORT MOTEL**
Rt 4, Box 160 (98569)
Rates: $32-$100
Tel: (360) 289-3448
(800) 867-3448

OCEAN PARK

**COASTAL
COTTAGES**
P. O. Box 888 (98640)
Rates: $50-$65
Tel: (360) 665-4658
(800) 200-0424

**OCEAN PARK
RESORT**
259th "R" St (98640)
Rates: $55-$85
Tel: (360) 665-4585
(800) 835-4634

**SUNSET VIEW
RESORT**
P. O. Box 399 (98640)
Rates: $64-$159
Tel: (360) 665-4494

**SHAKTI COVE
COTTAGES**
253rd at Park (98640)
Rates: $54-$64
Tel: (360) 665-4000

**WESTGATE MOTEL
& TRAILER COURT**
20803 Pacific Hwy
(98640)
Rates: $42-$55
Tel: (360) 665-4211

OCEAN SHORES

**BEACH FRONT
VACATION RENTALS**
759 Ocean Shores
Blvd (98569)
Rates: $65-$225
Tel: (800) 544-8887

**CASA DEL ORO
MOTEL**
665 Point Brown Ave
NW (98569)
Rates: $85-$120
Tel: (360) 289-2281
(800) 291-2281

**CHALET VILLAGE
MOTEL**
659 Ocean Shores
Blvd (98569)
Rates: $75-$85
Tel: (360) 289-4297
(800) 303-4297

DISCOVERY INN
1031 Discovery Ave
SE (98569)
Rates: $42-$78
Tel: (360) 289-3371

EBB TIDE MOTEL
839 Ocean Shores
Blvd (98569)
Rates: n/a
Tel: (360) 289-3700

THE GREY GULL
651 Ocean Shores
Blvd (98569)
Rates: $98-$315
Tel: (360) 289-3381

**NAUTILUS
CONDOMINIUMS**
835 Ocean Shores
Blvd (98569)
Rates: $100-$140
Tel: (800) 221-4511

**OCEAN SHORES
MOTEL**
681 Ocean Shores
Blvd (98569)
Rates: $40-$125
Tel: (360) 289-3351

**ROYAL PACIFIC
MOTEL**
781 Ocean Shores
Blvd NW (98569)
Rates: $39-$129
Tel: (360) 289-3306
(800) 562-9748

SANDS RESORT
801 Ocean Shores
Blvd (98569)
Rates: $49-$125
Tel: (360) 289-2444

SILVER KING MOTEL
1070 Discovery Ave
SE (98569)
Rates: $45-$50
Tel: (360) 289-3386
(800) 562-6001

SURFVIEW CONDOS
656 Ocean Court
(98569)
Rates: $55-$70
Tel: (360) 289-3077

WESTERLY MOTEL
870 Ocean Shores
Blvd (98569)
Rates: $30-$50
Tel: (360) 289-3711

ODESSA

ODESSA MOTEL
601 E First Ave
(99159)
Rates: $37-$43
Tel: (509) 982-2412

OKANOGAN

**CARIBOO INN
MOTEL**
233 Queen St (98840)
Rates: n/a
Tel: (509) 422-6109

CEDARS INN
One Apple Way
(98840)
Rates: $45-$51
Tel: (509) 422-6431

**PONDEROSA
MOTOR LODGE**
1034 S 2nd Ave
(98840)
Rates: $37-$42
Tel: (509) 422-0400
(800) 732-6702

U & I MOTEL
838 2nd St N (98840)
Rates: n/a
Tel: (509) 422-2920

OLALLA

**OLALLA ORCHARD
BED & BREAKFAST**
12530 Orchard Ave
SE (98359)
Rates: $76-$100
Tel: (206) 857-5915

OLYMPIA

BAILEY MOTOR INN
3333 Martin Way
(98506)
Rates: n/a
Tel: (360) 491-7515

**BEST WESTERN-
ALADDIN
MOTOR INN**
900 S Capitol Way
(98501)
Rates: $60-$79
Tel: (360) 352-7200
(800) 528-1234

DAYS INN
120 College St SE
(98503)
Rates: $56-$60
Tel: (360) 493-1991
(800) 329-7466

DEEP LAKE RESORT
12405 Tilley Rd S
(98512)
Rates: $53-$85
Tel: (360) 352-7388

**HOLIDAY INN
SELECT**
2300 Evergreen Park
Dr (98502)
Rates: $78+
Tel: (360) 943-4000
(800) 465-4329

HOLLY MOTEL
2816 Martin Way
(98506)
Rates: n/a
Tel: (360) 943-3000

LEE STREET SUITES
348 Lee St SW
(98501)
Rates: n/a
Tel: (360) 943-8391

SHALIMAR SUITES
5895 Capital Blvd S
(98501)
Rates: n/a
Tel: (360) 943-8391

TYEE HOTEL
500 Tyee Dr (98502)
Rates: $70-$78
Tel: (360) 352-0511
(800) 648-6440

OLYMPIC
NATIONAL PARK

**LAKE CRESCENT
LODGE**
HC 62, Box 11
(Port Angeles 98362)
Rates: $68-$121
Tel: (360) 928-3211

LOG CABIN RESORT
6540 E Beach Rd
(98362)
Rates: $50-$75
Tel: (360) 928-3325

OMAK

OMAK INN
912 Koala Dr (98841)
Rates: $60-$69
Tel: (509) 826-3822

ROYAL MOTEL
514 E Riverside Dr
(98841)
Rates: n/a
Tel: (509) 826-5715

STAMPEDE MOTEL
215 W 4th St (98841)
Rates: n/a
Tel: (800) 639-1161

THRIFTLODGE
122 N Main (98841)
Rates: $29-49
Tel: (800) 578-7878

ORCAS ISLAND

**ROSARIO
RESORT & SPA**
One Rosario Way
(Eastsound 98245)
Rates: $63-$220
Tel: (800) 562-8820

WEST BEACH RESORT
Rt 1, Box 510
(Eastsound 98245)
Rates: $105-$150
Tel: (360) 376-2240

OROVILLE

RED APPLE INN
1815 Main St (98844)
Rates: $32-$49
Tel: (509) 476-3694

OTHELLO

**ALADDIN
MOTOR INN**
1020 E Cedar St
(99344)
Rates: $35-$49
Tel: (509) 488-5671

CABANA MOTEL
665 E Windsor St
(99344)
Rates: $32-$80
Tel: (800) 442-4581

MAR DON RESORT
8198 Hwy 262 E
(99344)
Rates: n/a
Tel: (509) 346-2651

PACIFIC BEACH

**SAND DOLLAR
MOTEL**
53 Central (98571)
Rates: $43-$100
Tel: (360) 276-4525

**SANDPIPER BEACH
RESORT**
4159 SR 109 (98571)
Rates: $55-$160
Tel: (360) 276-4580
(800) 567-4737

SHORELINE MOTEL
12 1st St South (98571)
Rates: $45-$75
Tel: (800) 233-3365

PACKWOOD

**MOUNTAIN VIEW
LODGE MOTEL**
13163 Hwy 12
(98361)
Rates: $28-$70
Tel: (360) 494-5555

**TATOOSH
MEADOWS RESORT**
102 E Main (98361)
Rates: $100-$250
Tel: (800) 294-2311

PASCO

AIRPORT MOTEL
2532 N 4th (99301)
Rates: n/a
Tel: (509) 545-1460

**KING CITY
TRUCK STOP MOTEL**
2100 E Hillsboro Rd
(99301)
Rates: $38-$48
Tel: (509) 547-3475

MOTEL 6
1520 N Oregon St
(99301)
Rates: $32-$38
Tel: (509) 546-2010
(800) 440-6000

RED LION INN
2525 N 20th Ave
(99301)
Rates: $85-$105
Tel: (509) 547-0701
(800) 547-8010

SAGE 'N SUN MOTEL
1232 S 10th St
(99301)
Rates: $28-$48
Tel: (800) 391-9188

**THUNDERBIRD
MOTEL**
414 W Columbia
(99301)
Rates: n/a
Tel: (509) 547-9506

TRAVEL INN MOTEL
725 W Lewis (99301)
Rates: n/a
Tel: (509) 547-7791

TRI-MARK MOTEL
720 W Lewis (99301)
Rates: n/a
Tel: (509) 547-7766

THE VINEYARD INN
1800 W Lewis
(99301)
Rates: $39-$55
Tel: (509) 547-0791
(800) 824-5457

PATEROS

**LAKE PATEROS
MOTOR INN**
115 Lakeshore Dr
(98846)
Rates: $51-$59
Tel: (509) 923-2207
(800) 444-1985

PESHASTIN

TIMBERLINE HOTEL
8284 Hwy 2 (98847)
Rates: n/a
Tel: (509) 548-7415

POINT ROBERTS

**CEDAR HOUSE INN
BED & BREAKFAST**
1534 Gulf Rd (98281)
Rates: $36-$49
Tel: (360) 945-0284

POMEROY

PIONEER MOTEL
1201 Main St,
Box 579 (99347)
Rates: $35-$50
Tel: (509) 843-1312

PORT ANGELES

AGGIE'S INN
602 E Front St
(98362)
Rates: $46-$68
Tel: (360) 457-0471

CHINOOK MOTEL
1414 E 1st St (98362)
Rates: n/a
Tel: (360) 452-2336

DAN DEE MOTEL
132 E Lauridsen
Blvd (98362)
Rates: n/a
Tel: (206) 457-5404

**HISTORIC
LAKE CRESCENT
LODGE RESORT**
416 Lake Crescent
Rd (98362)
Rates: $64-$114
Tel: (360) 928-3211

**INDIAN VALLEY
MOTEL**
7020 Hwy 101
(98362)
Rates: n/a
Tel: (206) 928-3266

LOG CABIN RESORT
3183 E Beach Rd
(98363)
Rates: $40-$100
Tel: (360) 928-3325

THE POND MOTEL
1425 W Hwy 101
(98362)
Rates: $27-$63
Tel: (360) 452-8422

**RED LION
BAYSHORE INN**
221 N Lincoln St
(98362)
Rates: $80-$125
Tel: (360) 452-9215
(800) 547-8010

**SOL DUC HOT
SPRINGS RESORT**
P. O. Box 2169
(98362)
Rates: $78-$128
Tel: (360) 327-3583

SUPER 8 MOTEL
2104 E 1st St (98362)
Rates: $43-$63
Tel: (360) 452-8401
(800) 800-8000

UPTOWN MOTEL
101 E 2nd St (98362)
Rates: $35-$125
Tel: (360) 457-9434
(800) 858-3812

PORT HADLOCK

PORT HADLOCK INN
201 Alcohol Loop Rd
(98339)
Rates: n/a
Tel: (206) 385-5801

PORT LUDLOW

**ALADDIN
MOTOR INN**
2333 Washington
(98365)
Rates: $50-$99
Tel: (360) 385-3747
(800) 281-3747

**ANNAPURNA INN
BED & BREAKFAST**
538 Adams (98365)
Rates: $65-$115
Tel: (360) 385-2909
(800) 868-2662

**THE CABIN
GETAWAY**
839 Jacob Miller
(98365)
Rates: $95
Tel: (360) 385-5571

**COMMANDER'S
HOUSE GETAWAY**
Point House (98365)
Rates: $49-$125
Tel: (360) 385-2828
(800) 826-3854

GAIA'S GETAWAY
4343 Haines (98365)
Rates: $60-$80
Tel: (360) 385-1194

**INN AT LUDLOW
BAY RESORT**
One Heron Rd
(98365)
Rates: $165-$450
Tel: (360) 437-0411

**NORTH BEACH
RETREAT**
510 56th St (98365)
Rates: $50
Tel: (360) 385-1621

**PILOT HOUSE
GETAWAY**
327 Jackson (98365)
Rates: $60-$95
Tel: (360) 379-0811

**POINT HUDSON
RESORT & MARINA**
Point Hudson
(98365)
Rates: $45-$85
Tel: (360) 385-2828
(800) 826-3854

PORT ORCHARD

**CEDAR HOLLOW
GUEST HOUSE**
3875 Locker Rd
(98366)
Rates: $75
Tel: (360) 871-1527

**NORTHWEST
INTERLUDE B & B**
3377 Sarann Ave E
(98366)
Rates: $55-$75
Tel: (360) 871-4676

VISTA MOTEL
1090 Bethel (98366)
Rates: $30-$59
Tel: (360) 876-8046

PORT TOWNSEND

**ALADDIN
MOTOR INN**
2333 Washington St
(98368)
Rates: n/a
Tel: (360) 385-3747

**BISHOP VICTORIAN
GUEST SUITES**
714 Washington St
(98368)
Rates: $54-$98
Tel: (360) 385-6122
(800) 824-4738

**THE ENGLISH INN
BED & BREAKFAST**
718 "F" St (98368)
Rates: $65-$95
Tel: (800) 254-5302

HARBORSIDE INN
330 Benedict St
(98368)
Rates: $64-$98
Tel: (800) 942-5960

**JAMES SWAN
HOTEL**
222 Monroe (98368)
Rates: n/a
Tel: (800) 776-1718

**POINT HUDSON
RESORT & MARINA**
Point Hudson
Harbor (98368)
Rates: $45-$90
Tel: (800) 826-3854

PORT TOWNSEND INN
2020 Washington St (98368)
Rates: $58-$78
Tel: (360) 385-2211
(800) 822-8696

PUFFIN & GULL APARTMENT MOTEL
825 Washington St (98368)
Rates: n/a
Tel: (360) 385-1475

SALMON BERRY FARM B & B
2404 35th St (98368)
Rates: $75
Tel: (360) 385-1517

THE TIDES INN
1807 Water St (98368)
Rates: $58-$105
Tel: (360) 385-0595
(800) 822-8696

WATER STREET HOTEL
635 Water St (98368)
Rates: $40-$60
Tel: (360) 385-5467

POULSBO

CYPRESS INN
19801 NE 7th (98370)
Rates: $54-$89
Tel: (360) 697-2119
(800) 752-9991

POULSBO INN
18680 Hwy 305 (98370)
Rates: $53-$105
Tel: (360) 779-3921

PROSSER

BEST WESTERN INN
225 Merlot Dr (99350)
Rates: $52-$57
Tel: (509) 786-7977
(800) 528-1234

PROSSER MOTEL
120 Wine Country Rd (99350)
Rates: $24-$35
Tel: (509) 786-2555

PULLMAN

AMERICAN TRAVEL INN
515 S Grand Ave (99163)
Rates: $35-$55
Tel: (509) 334-3500

COUNTRY B & B
Rt 2, Box 666 (99163)
Rates: $40-$100
Tel: (509) 334-4453

HOLIDAY INN EXPRESS
SE 1190 Bishop (99163)
Rates: $64-$89
Tel: (509) 334-4437
(800) 46504329

MANOR LODGE MOTEL
SE 455 Paradise (99163)
Rates: n/a
Tel: (509) 334-2511

QUALITY INN-PARADISE CREEK
SE 1050 Bishop (99163)
Rates: $58-$135
Tel: (509) 332-0500
(800) 221-2222

PUYALLUP

MOTEL PUYALLUP
1412 S Meridian St (98371)
Rates: $39-$64
Tel: (206) 845-8825

NORTHWEST MOTOR INN
1409 S Meridian St (98371)
Rates: $40-$56
Tel: (206) 841-2600

QUILCENE

MAPLE GROVE MOTEL
61 Maple Grove Rd (98376)
Rates: $40-$50
Tel: (360) 765-3410

QUINAULT

LAKE QUINAULT LODGE
345 S Shore Rd (98575)
Rates: $90-$115
Tel: (360) 288-2571
(800) 562-6672

QUINCY

THE SUNDOWNER MOTEL
414 F St SE (98848)
Rates: n/a
Tel: (509) 787-3587

TRADITIONAL INNS
500 F St SW (98848)
Rates: $37-$77
Tel: (509) 787-3525

RANDLE

MEDICI MOTEL
471 Cispus Rd (98377)
Rates: $45
Tel: (360) 497-7700
(800) 697-7750

TALL TIMBER
10023 Hwy 12 (98377)
Rates: n/a
Tel: (360) 497-5908

RAYMOND

MAUNU'S MOUNTCASTLE MOTEL
524 3rd St (98577)
Rates: $32-$45
Tel: (360) 942-5571

WILLIS MOTEL
425 3rd St (98577)
Rates: n/a
Tel: (360) 942-5313

REDMOND

REDMOND INN
17601 Redmond Way (98052)
Rates: $55-$100
Tel: (800) 634-8080

SILVER CLOUD INN
15304 NE 21st St (98052)
Rates: $54-$69
Tel: (206) 746-8200
(800) 205-6934

RENTON

HOLIDAY INN
800 S Rainier Ave (98055)
Rates: $99-$119
Tel: (206) 226-7700
(800) 465-4329

NENDEL'S INN
3700 E Valley Rd (98055)
Rates: $45-$66
Tel: (206) 251-9591
(800) 547-0106

SILVER CLOUD INN
1850 Maple Valley Hwy (98055)
Rates: $52-$70
Tel: (206) 226-7600

REPUBLIC

FISHERMAN'S COVE RESORT
1157 Fisherman's Cove Rd (99166)
Rates: $25-$65
Tel: (509) 775-3641

FRONTIER INN OTEL
979 S Clark Ave (99166)
Rates: $34-$57
Tel: (509) 775-3361

K-DIAMOND-K RANCH B & B
404 Hwy 21 S (99166)
Rates: $60
Tel: (509) 775-3536

KLONDIKE MOTEL
150 N Clark Ave (99166)
Rates: n/a
Tel: (509) 775-3555

TIFFANYS RESORT
1026 Tiffany Rd (99166)
Rates: $42-$112
Tel: (509) 775-3152

RICHLAND

BALI HI MOTEL
1201 George
Washington Way
(99352)
Rates: $37-$44
Tel: (509) 943-3101

**COLUMBIA CENTER
DUNES MOTEL**
1751 Fowler Ave
(99352)
Rates: $35-$45
Tel: (509) 783-8181
(800) 638-6168

NENDEL'S INN
615 Jadwin Ave
(99352)
Rates: $37-$43
Tel: (509) 943-4611
(800) 547-0106

**RED LION INN-
HANFORD HOUSE**
802 George
Washington Way
(99352)
Rates: $79-$99
Tel: (509) 946-7611
(800) 547-8010

**SHILO INNS
RIVERSHORE**
50 Comstock St
(99352)
Rates: $52-$83
Tel: (509) 946-4661
(800) 222-2244

VAGABOND INN
515 George
Washington
Way (99352)
Rates: $32-$58
Tel: ((509) 946-6117
(800) 552-1555

RIMROCK

**GAME RIDGE
MOTEL & LODGE**
27350 Hwy 12
(98937)
Rates: $38-$79
Tel: (509) 672-2212

RITZVILLE

**BEST WESTERN
HERITAGE INN**
1405 Smitty's Blvd
(99169)
Rates: $47-$145
Tel: (509) 659-1007
(800) 528-1234

**COLWELL
MOTOR INN**
501 W 1st Ave
(99169)
Rates: $52-$125
Tel: (509) 659-1620
(800) 341-8000

COTTAGE MOTEL
508 E 1st Ave (99169)
Rates: n/a
Tel: (509) 569-0721

TOP HAT MOTEL
210 E 1st St (99169)
Rates: $35-$42
Tel: (509) 659-1100

WEST SIDE MOTEL
407 W 1st St (99169)
Rates: n/a
Tel: (509) 659-1164

ROCKPORT

**CLARK'S SKAGIT
RIVER CABINS**
5675 Hwy 20 (98283)
Rates: $50-$100
Tel: (360) 873-2250
(800) 273-2606

**DIABLO LAKE
RESORT**
Hwy 20 Mile 127
1/2 (98283)
Rates: n/a
Tel: (206) 386-4429

**TOTEM TRAIL
MOTEL**
5551 Hwy 20 (98283)
Rates: $35-$50
Tel: (360) 873-4535

ROSLYN

THE ROSLYN INNS
P. O. Box 386 (98941)
Rates: n/a
Tel: (509) 649-2936

SAN JUAN
ISLANDS

BLAIR HOUSE B & B
345 Blair Ave
(Friday Harbor
98250)
Rates: $75-$125
Tel: (360) 378-5907

**DOE BAY VILLAGE
RESORT**
Star Rt, Box 85
(Olga 98279)
Rates: $40-$92
Tel: (360) 376-2291

**FRIDAY HARBOR
HOUSE MOTEL**
130 West St (Friday
Harbor 98250)
Rates: $165-$325
Tel: (360) 378-8455

**INN AT FRIDAY
HARBOR**
410 Spring St (Friday
Harbor 98250)
Rates: $49-$130
Tel: (360) 378-4000
(800) 552-1457

**INN AT FRIDAY
HARBOR SUITES**
680 Spring St
(Friday Harbor
98250)
Rates: $59-$188
Tel: (360) 378-3031
(800) 752-5752

L'AERIE B & B
HC 1, Box 147
(Eastsound 98245)
Rates: $75-$95
Tel: (360) 376-4647

LAKEDALE LODGE
2627 Roche Harbor
Rd (Friday Harbor
98250)
Rates: $75-$125
Tel: (800) 617-2267

NORTH BEACH INN
P. O. Box 80
(Eastsound 98245)
Rates: $65-$175
Tel: (360) 376-2660

**NORTH SHORE
COTTAGES**
P. O. Box 1273
(Eastsound 98245)
Rates: $120
Tel: (360) 376-5131

SAN JUAN INN
50 Spring St
(Friday Harbor
98250)
Rates: $70-$175
Tel: (360) 378-2070
(800) 742-8210

**SNUG HARBOR
RESORT & MARINA**
2371 Mitchell Bay
Rd (Friday Harbor
98250)
Rates: $30-$200
Tel: (360) 378-4762

**TUCKER HOUSE
BED & BREAKFAST**
260 B St (Friday
Harbor 98250)
Rates: $70-$135
Tel: (360) 378-2783
(800) 965-0123

**WEST BEACH
RESORT**
Rt 1, Box 510
(Eastsound 98245)
Rates: $80-$110
Tel: (360) 376-2240

WESTWINDS B & B
4909 H-Hannah Rd
(Friday Harbor
98250)
Rates: $165-$245
Tel: (360) 378-5283

WHARFSIDE B & B
On the Jacqueline,
Slip K-13
(Friday Harbor
98250)
Rates: $80-$85
Tel: (360) 378-5661

SEABECK

**SUMMER SONG
BED & BREAKFAST**
P. O. Box 82 (98380)
Rates: n/a
Tel: (206) 830-5089

SEATAC

**CONTINENTAL
COURT ALL SUITES
MOTEL**
17223 32nd Ave S
(98188)
Rates: $40-$60
Tel: (800) 233-1501

**HILTON INN
SEATTLE AIRPORT**
17620 Pacific Hwy S
(98188)
Rates: $114-$134
Tel: (206) 244-4800
(800) 445-8667

LA QUINTA INN
2824 S 188th St
(98188)
Rates: $53-$76
Tel: (206) 241-5211
(800) 221-4731

**MARRIOTT
SEA-TAC AIRPORT**
3201 S 176th St
(98188)
Rates: $79-$129
Tel: (206) 241-2000
(800) 228-9290

**MOTEL 6-
SEA-TAC AIRPORT**
16500 Pacific Hwy S
(98188)
Rates: $35-$41
Tel: (206) 246-4101
(800) 440-6000

**MOTEL 6-
SEA-TAC SOUTH**
18900 47th Ave S
(98188)
Rates: $32-$38
Tel: (206) 241-1648
(800) 440-6000

**RED LION-SEATTLE
AIRPORT HOTEL**
18740 Pacific Hwy S
(98188)
Rates: $149-$156
Tel: (206) 433-1881
(800) 547-8010

**SEA-TAC CREST
MOTOR INN**
18845 Int'l Blvd
(98188)
Rates: $42-$59
Tel: (206) 433-0999

SHADOW MOTEL
2930 S 176th St
(98188)
Rates: n/a
Tel: (206) 246-9300

THRIFTLODGE
17108 Pacific Hwy S
(98199)
Rates: $34-$62
Tel: (206) 244-1230
(800) 578-7878

SEATTLE

THE ALEXIS HOTEL
1007 First Ave
(98104)
Rate: $165-$335
Tel: (206) 624-4844

AURORA NITES INN
11746 Aurora Ave N
(98133)
Rates: n/a
Tel: (206) 365-3216

**AURORA SEAFAIR
INN**
9100 Aurora Ave N
(98103)
Rates: $55-$85
Tel: (206) 522-3754

**BEECH TREE
MANOR INN B & B**
1405 Queen Anne
Ave N (98109)
Rates: $45-$79
Tel: (206) 281-7037

**BEST WESTERN-
AIRPORT EXECUTEL**
20717 Pacific Hwy S
(98198)
Rates: $95-$125
Tel: (206) 878-3300
(800) 528-1234

**BEST WESTERN
EXECUTIVE INN**
200 Taylor Ave N
(98109)
Rates: $88-$148
Tel: (206) 448-9444
(800) 528-1234

**CAVANAUGH'S INN
ON FIFTH AVENUE**
1415 Fifth Ave (98101)
Rates: n/a
Tel: (800) 843-4667

CITY CENTER MOTEL
226 Aurora Ave N
(98109)
Rates: n/a
Tel: (206) 441-0266

**DAYS INN
TOWN CENTER**
2205 7th Ave (98121)
Rates: $64-$99
Tel: (206) 448-3434
(800) 329-7466

**DOUBLETREE INN
HOTEL**
205 Strander Blvd
(98188)
Rates: $69-$108
Tel: (206) 575-8220
(800) 228-8733

ECONO LODGE
13910 Pacific Hwy
(98168)
Rates: $54-$69
Tel: (206) 922-0550
(800) 424-4777

**EMBASSY SUITES
HOTEL**
15920 West Valley
Hwy (98188)
Rates: $109-$179
TeL: (206) 227-8844
(800) 362-2779

EMERALD INN
8512 Aurora Ave N
(98103)
Rates: $44-$70
Tel: (206) 522-5000

**EXECUTIVE
RESIDENCE**
2601 Elliott Ave
#3152 (98121)
Rates: $49-$99
Tel: (800) 428-3867

**EXECUTIVE
RESIDENCE
ON ELLIOTT BAY**
2400 Elliott Ave
(98121)
Rates: $109-$195
Tel: (206) 329-8000

**FOUR SEASONS-
OLYMPIC HOTEL**
411 University St
(98101)
Rates: $135-$290
Tel: (206) 621-1700
(800) 332-3442

**GEISHA
MOTOR INN**
9613 Aurora Ave N
(98103)
Rates: n/a
Tel: (206) 524-8880

LEGEND MOTEL
22204 Pacific Hwy S
(98198)
Rates: n/a
Tel: (206) 878-0366

**MARRIOTT
RESIDENCE INN-
SEATTLE SOUTH**
16201 W Valley Hwy
(98188)
Rates: $120-$185
Tel: (800) 331-3131

**MAYFLOWER PARK
HISTORIC HOTEL**
405 Olive Way
(98101)
Rates: $115-$155
Tel: (206) 623-8700

**MOTEL 6-
SOUTH SEATTLE**
20651 Military Rd
(98188)
Rates: $37-$43
Tel: (206) 824-9902
(800) 440-6000

**PENSIONE
NICHOLAS B & B**
9123 First Ave
(98101)
Rates: $60-$160
Tel: (206) 441-7125

**QUALITY INN
CITY CENTER**
2224 8th Ave (98121)
Rates: $74-$150
Tel: (206) 624-6820
(800) 221-2222

**RAMADA INN
NORTHGATE**
2140 N Northgate
Way (98133)
Rates: $105-$132
Tel: (206) 365-0700
(800) 272-6232

RESIDENCE INN
16201 W Valley Hwy
(98188)
Rates: n/a
Tel: (206) 226-5500
(800) 331-3131

**RESIDENCE INN
BY MARRIOTT**
800 Fairview Ave N
(98109)
Rates: $100-$350
Tel: (206) 624-6000
(800) 331-3131

RODESIDE LODGE
12501 Aurora Ave N
(98133)
Rates: $39-$65
Tel: (206) 364-7771
(800) 227-7771

SANDPIPER VILLAS FAMILY MOTEL
11000 1st Ave SW (98146)
Rates: $39-$59
Tel: (206) 242-8883

SEATTLE INN
225 Aurora Ave N (98109)
Rates: n/a
Tel: (206) 728-7666

SHAFER BAILLIE MANSION B & B
907 14th Ave E (98112)
Rates: $69-$95
Tel: (206) 322-4654

SHORELINE MOTEL
16526 Aurora Ave N (98133)
Rates: n/a
Tel: (206) 542-7777

SUN HILL MOTEL
8517 Aurora Ave N (98103)
Rates: n/a
Tel: (206) 525-1205

SUPER 8 MOTEL
3100 S 192nd (98188)
Rates: $62-$86
Tel: (206) 433-8188
(800) 800-8000

TRAVELODGE SPACE NEEDLE
200 6th Ave N (98109)
Rates: $68-$123
Tel: (206) 441-7878
(800) 578-7878

VAGABOND INN
325 Aurora Ave N (98109)
Rates: $59-$79
Tel: (206) 441-0400
(800) 522-1555

WARWICK HOTEL
401 Lenora St (98121)
Rates: $90-$190
Tel: (206) 443-4300
(800) 426-9280

WESTCOAST ROOSEVELT HOTEL
1531 Seventh Ave (98101)
Rates: n/a
Tel: (206) 621-1200

THE WESTIN HOTEL
1900 5th Ave (98101)
Rates: $190-$270
Tel: (206) 728-1000
(800) 228-3000

SEAVIEW

SEAVIEW COHO MOTEL
3701 Pacific Hwy (98644)
Rates: $40-$130
Tel: (360) 642-2531
(800) 681-8153

SOU'WESTERN LODGE & CABINS
Beach Access Rd-38th Pl (98644)
Rates: $35-$105
Tel: (360) 642-2542

SEDRO WOOLLEY

SKAGIT MOTEL
1977 Hwy 20 (98284)
Rates: n/a
Tel: (360) 856-6001

THREE RIVERS INN MOTEL
210 Ball St (98284)
Rates: $46-$65
Tel: (360) 855-2626
(800) 221-5122

SEKIU

CURLEY'S RESORT
291 Front St (98381)
Rates: n/a
Tel: (360) 963-2281

OLSON'S RESORT
Front St #444 (98381)
Rates: $50-$85
Tel: (360) 963-2311

STRAITSIDE RESORT MOTEL
241 Front St (98381)
Rate: $30-$70
Tel: (360) 963-2100

VAN RIPER'S RESORT
Front & Rice Sts (98381)
Rates: n/a
Tel: (360) 963-2334

SEQUIM

BEST WESTERN SEQUIM BAY LODGE
268522 Hwy 101 E (98382)
Rates: $55-$140
Tel: (360) 683-0691
(800) 528-1234

ECONO LODGE
801 E Washington St (98382)
Rates: $49-$85
Tel: (360) 683-7113
(800) 424-4777

GROVELAND COTTAGE B & B
4861 Sequim-Dungeness Way (98382)
Rates: $55-$90
Tel: (206) 683-3565
(800) 879-8859

HIDDEN MEADOW INN B & B
901 W Sequim Bay Rd (98382)
Rates: $79-$89
Tel: (360) 681-2577

JUAN DE FUCA COTTAGES
182 Marine Dr (98382)
Rates: $90-$110
Tel: (360) 683-4433

RED RANCH INN
830 W Washington St (98382)
Rates: $40-$100
Tel: (360) 683-4195
(800) 777-4193

SUNDOWNER MOTEL
364 W Washington St (98382)
Rates: $45-$69
Tel: (206) 683-5532

SHELTON

CITY CENTER BEST RATES MOTEL
128 E Alder (98584)
Rates: $32-$40
Tel: (360) 426-3397

LAKE NAHWATZEL RESORT
W 12900 Shelton-Matlock Rd (98584)
Rates: $30-$50
Tel: (360) 426-8323

REST FULL FARM BED & BREAKFAST
W 2230 Shelton Valley Rd (98584)
Rates: $60-$70
Tel: (360) 426-8774

SUPER 8 MOTEL
2943 Northview Circle (98584)
Rates: $44-$68
Tel: (360) 426-1654
(800) 800-8000

SILVER CREEK

LAKE MAYFIELD MOTEL
2911 US Hwy 12 (98585)
Rates: n/a
Tel: (360) 985-2484

SILVER LAKE

SILVER LAKE MOTEL & RESORT
3201 Spirit Lake Hwy (98645)
Rates: $30-$75
Tel: (360) 274-6141

SILVERDALE

SEABREEZE BEACH COTTAGE & SPA
16609 Olympic View Rd NW (98383)
Rates: $139-$169
Tel: (360) 692-4648

SKYKOMISH

CASCADIA B & B
210 Railroad Ave (98288)
Rates: n/a
Tel: (360) 677-2390

SKYMOISH HOTEL
102 Railroad Ave (98288)
Rates: n/a
Tel: (360) 677-2477

SKYRIVER INN
333 River Dr E
(98288)
Rates: $53-$65
Tel: (360) 677-2261
(800) 367-8194

SNOHOMISH

**SNOHOMISH
GRAND HOTEL
BED & BREAKFAST**
901 1/2 1st St
(98290)
Rates: $50-$75
Tel: (360) 568-8854

SNOQUALMIE

**IDYL INN ON THE
RIVER B & B**
4548 Tolt River Rd
(98014)
Rates: $55-$225
Tel: (206) 868-2000

**THE OLD HONEY
FARM B & B**
8910 384th Ave SE
(98065)
Rates: $45-$55
Tel: (206) 888-1637

SALISH LODGE
37807 SE Fall City
(98065)
Rates: $145-$450
Tel: (206) 888-2556
(800) 826-6124

SNOQUALMIE PASS

**BEST WESTERN
SUMMITT INN**
SR 906 (98068)
Rates: $69-$84
Tel: (206) 434-6300
(800) 528-1234

SOAP LAKE

ROYAL VIEW MOTEL
Hwy 17 & 4th Sts
(98851)
Rates: n/a
Tel: (509) 246-1831

SOUTH BEND

H & H MOTEL
P. O. Box 613,
Hwy 101 (98586)
Rates: n/a
Tel: (360) 875-5523

SEAQUEST MOTEL
801 West First St
(98586)
Rates: n/a
Tel: (800) 624-7006

SPOKANE

AL'S MOTEL
N 1421 Division St
(99202)
Rates: $35-$59
Tel: (509) 328-6054

**APPLE TREE INN
MOTEL**
N 9508 Division St
(99218)
Rates: n/a
Tel: (800) 323-5796

ARNOLD'S MOTEL
N 6217 Division St
(99207)
Rates: n/a
Tel: (509) 487-1619

BEL AIR MOTEL 7
1303 E Sprague Ave
(99202)
Rates: $33-$49
Tel: (509) 535-1677

BELL MOTEL
W 9030 Sunset Hwy
(99204)
Rates: n/a
Tel: (800) 223-1388

**BEST WESTERN
NORTHPOINTE**
9601 N Newport
Hwy (99218)
Rates: $49-$130
Tel: (509) 468-4201
(800) 528-1234

**BEST WESTERN
THUNDERBIRD INN**
W 120 Third Ave
(99204)
Rates: $51-$76
Tel: (509) 747-2011
(800) 578-2473

**BEST WESTERN
TRADE WINDS N**
N 3033 Division St
(99207)
Rates: $56-$76
Tel: (509) 326-5500
(800) 528-1234

BROADWAY MOTEL
6317 E Broadway
(99212)
Rates: $66-$74
Tel: (509) 535-2442

**CARROLL'S BUDGET
SAVER MOTEL**
E 1234 Sprague Ave
(99202)
Rates: $29-$65
Tel: (509) 534-0669

**CAVANAUGH'S
AT THE PARK**
W 303 North River
Dr (99201)
Rates: $80-$800
Tel: (509) 326-8000
(800) 843-4667

**CAVANAUGH'S
FOURTH AVENUE**
110 E 4th Ave
(99202)
Rates: $50-$76
Tel: (509) 838-6101
(800) 843-4667

**CAVANAUGH'S
RIVER INN**
N 700 Division St
(99202)
Rates: $70-$98
Tel: (509) 326-5577
(800) 843-4667

**CAVANAUGH'S
VALUE INNS**
W 1203 Fifth Ave
(99204)
Rates: $34-$68
Tel: (800) 843-4667

**CLINIC CENTER
MOTEL**
S 702 McClellan
(99204)
Rates: n/a
Tel: (509) 747-6081

**COMFORT INN
BROADWAY**
6309 E Broadway
(99212)
Rates: $51-$79
Tel: (509) 535-7185
(800) 221-2222

**COMFORT INN
NORTH**
7111 N Division St
(99208)
Rates: $55-$105
Tel: (800) 221-2222

**COMFORT INN
VALLEY**
P. O. Box 141152
(99214)
Rates: $61-$86
Tel: (509) 924-3838

DAYS INN
1919 N Hutchinson
Rd (99212)
Rates: $47-$72
Tel: (509) 926-5399
(800) 329-7466

HOLIDAY INN WEST
4212 W Sunset Blvd
(99204)
Rates: $42-$58
Tel: (509) 747-2021
(800) 465-4329

LIBERTY MOTEL
6801 N Division St
(99208)
Rates: $38-$60
Tel: (509) 467-6000

MAPLETREE MOTEL
E 4824 Sprague Ave
(99212)
Rates: $28-$45
Tel: (509) 535-5810

MOTEL 6
1508 S Rustle St
(99204)
Rates: $33-$39
Tel: (509) 459-6120
(800) 440-6000

NENDELS VALU INN
W 1420 Second Ave
(99204)
Rates: $38-$52
Tel: (509) 838-2026

PARK LANE MOTEL & SUITES
4412 E Sprague Ave (99212)
Rates: n/a
Tel: (800) 533-1626

QUALITY INN-VALLEY SUITES
I-90 Argonne
Exit 287 (99212)
Rates: $69-$350
Tel: (509) 928-5218
(800) 424-6420

RAMADA INN AIRPORT
Spokane Int'l Airport (99219)
Rates: $59-$125
Tel: (509) 838-5211
(800) 272-6232

RANCH MOTEL
S 1609 Lewis St (99204)
Rates: $25-$32
Tel: (800) 871-8919

RED LION SPOKANE CITY CENTER
322 N Spokane Falls Ct (99201)
Rates: $98-$118
Tel: (509) 455-9600
(800) 733-5466

RED LION SPOKANE VALLEY
N 1100 Sullivan Rd (99220)
Rates: $82-$109
Tel: (509) 925-9000
(800) 547-8010

RED TOP MOTEL
7217 E Trent Ave (99212)
Rates: $42-$105
Tel: (509) 926-5728

RODEWAY INN
4301 W Sunset Hwy (99210)
Rates: $50-$105
Tel: (509) 838-1471
(800) 228-2000

RODEWAY INN CITY CENTER
827 W 1st Ave (99204)
Rates: $39-$69
Tel: (509) 838-8271
(800) 424-4777

ROYAL SCOT MOTEL
W 20 Houston (99208)
Rates: n/a
Tel: (509) 467-6672

SHAMROCK MOTEL
E 1629 Sprague Ave (99202)
Rates: $40-$60
Tel: (509) 535-0388

SHANGRI-LA MOTEL
2922 W Government Way (99204)
Rates: $33-$43
Tel: (509) 747-2066

SHERATON SPOKANE HOTEL
N 322 Spokane Falls Ct (99201)
Rates: n/a
Tel: (800) 848-9600

SHILO INNS
E 923 3rd Ave (99202)
Rates: $58-$62
Tel: (509) 535-9000
(800) 222-2244

SUNTREE INN
S 123 Post St (99204)
Rates: $33-$50
Tel: (800) 888-6630

SUNTREE INN
211 S Division St (99202)
Rates: $39-$64
Tel: (509) 838-6630
(800) 888-6630

SUPER 8 MOTEL
11102 W Westbow Blvd (99204)
Rates: $50-$70
Tel: (509) 838-8800
(800) 800-8000

SUPER 8 MOTEL
2020 N Argonne Rd (99212)
Rates: $38-$66
Tel: (509) 928-4888
(800) 800-8000

WESTCOAST RIDPATH HOTEL
515 W Sprague Ave (99204)
Rates: $55-$150
Tel: (509) 838-2711
(800) 426-0670

WOLFF LODGING
1825 N Hutchison Rd (99212)
Rates: $35-$64
Tel: (800) 528-9519

SPRAGUE

LAST ROUNDUP MOTEL & RV
312 E First (99032)
Rates: n/a
Tel: (509) 257-2593

PURPLE SAGE MOTEL
405 W First (99032)
Rates: n/a
Tel: (509) 257-2507

STEVENSON

ECONO LODGE
40 NE 2nd St (98648)
Rates: $45-$55
Tel: (509) 427-5628
(800) 424-4777

SUMAS

BB BORDER INN MOTEL
121 Cleveland (98295)
Rates: n/a
Tel: (360) 988-5800

SULTAN

DUTCH CUP MOTEL
918 Main St (98294)
Rates: $40-$51
Tel: (360) 793-2215

SUNNYSIDE

SUN VALLEY INN
724 Yakima Valley Hwy (98944)
Rates: $34-$75
Tel: (509) 837-4721

RED APPLE MOTEL
412 Yakima Valley Hwy (98944)
Rates: n/a
Tel: (509) 839-2100

TOWN HOUSE MOTEL
509 Yakima Valley Hwy (98944)
Rates: $38-$52
Tel: (509) 837-5500
(800) 342-4435

TRAVELODGE
408 Yakima Valley Hwy (98944)
Rates: $41-$110
Tel: (509) 837-7878
(800) 578-7878

TACOMA

BEST WESTERN EXECUTIVE INN
5700 Pacific Hwy E (98424)
Rates: $65-$87
Tel: (800) 938-8500

BEST WESTERN TACOMA INN
8726 S Hosmer St (98444)
Rates: $64-$160
Tel: (206) 535-2880
(800) 528-1234

BLUE SPRUCE MOTEL
12715 Pacific Ave (98444)
Rates: n/a
Tel: (206) 531-6111

BUDGET INN-SOUTH TACOMA
9915 S Tacoma Way (98499)
Rates: n/a
Tel: (206) 588-6615

CORPORATE SUITES
219 Division Ct E (98499)
Rates: n/a
Tel: (800) 255-6058

COMFORT INN
5601 Pacific Hwy E (98424)
Rates: $48-$65
Tel: (206) 926-2301
(800) 221-2222

DAYS INN
3021 Pacific Hwy E (98424)
Rates: $45-$80
Tel: (206) 922-3500
(800) 329-7466

GOLDEN LION MOTOR INN
9021 S Tacoma Way (98499)
Rates: n/a
Tel: (206) 588-2171

HIDDEN MAPLE BED & BREAKFAST
4616 N 46th (98407)
Rates: $75-$95
Tel: (206) 756-2094

HOWARD JOHNSON
8702 S Hosmer (98444)
Rates: $55-110
Tel: (206) 535-3100
(800) 446-4656

LA QUINTA INN
1425 E 27th St (98421)
Rates: $67-$83
Tel: (206) 383-0146
(800) 531-5900

MADIGAN MOTEL
12039 Pacific Hwy SW (98499)
Rates: $40-$50
Tel: (206) 588-8697

MOTEL 6-SOUTH
1811 S 76th St (98408)
Rates: $30-$40
Tel: (206) 473-7100
(800) 440-6000

RAMADA INN TACOMA DOME-CIVIC CENTER
2611 East E St (98421)
Rates: $62-$250
Tel: (206) 572-7272
(800) 272-6232

ROYAL COACHMAN INN
5805 Pacific Hwy E (98424)
Rates: $49-$120
Tel: (206) 922-2500
(800) 422-3051

SHERATON HOTEL
1320 Broadway Plaza (98402)
Rates: $110-$140
Tel: (206) 572-3200

SHILO INNS
7414 S Hosmer St (98408)
Rates: $68-$87
Tel: (206) 475-4020
(800) 222-2244

WESTERN INN
9920 S Tacoma Way (98499)
Rates: $36-$52
Tel: (206) 588-5241

THORP

CIRCLE H HOLIDAY RANCH RESORT
810 Watt Canyon Rd (98946)
Rates: n/a
Tel: (509) 964-2000

TOKELAND

TRADEWINDS ON THE BAY MOTEL
4305 Pomeroy Ave (98590)
Rates: n/a
Tel: (360) 267-7500

TOLEDO

COWLITZ MOTEL & RV PARK
162 Cowlitz Loop Rd (98591)
Rates: n/a
Tel: (360) 864-6611

TONASKET

BONAPARTE LAKE RESORT
695 Bonaparte Lake Rd (98855)
Rates: n/a
Tel: (509) 486-2828

RAINBOW RESORT
761 Loomis Hwy (98855)
Rates: n/a
Tel: (509) 223-3700

RED APPLE INN
Hwy 97 & 1st St (98855)
Rates: $36-$46
Tel: (509) 486-2119

SPECTACLE FALLS RESORT MOTEL
879 Loomis Hwy (98855)
Rates: n/a
Tel: (509) 223-4141

SPECTACLE LAKE RESORT
10 McCammon Rd (98855)
Rates: $30-$100
Tel: (509) 223-3433

TOPPENISH

EL CORRAL MOTEL
61731 Hwy 97 (98948)
Rates: $32
Tel: (509) 865-2365

OXBOW MOTOR INN
511 S Elm St (98948)
Rates: $39-$69
Tel: (509) 865-5800
(800) 222-3161

TOPPENISH INN MOTEL
515 S Elm St (98948)
Rates: $39-$56
Tel: (509) 865-7444

TROUT LAKE

THE FARM B & B
490 Sunnyside Rd (98650)
Rates: $65-$75
Tel: (509) 395-2488

MIO AMORE PENSIONE B & B
53 Little Mountain Rd (98650)
Rates: $60-$135
Tel: (509) 395-2264

TUKWILA

BEST WESTERN SOUTHCENTER
15901 W Valley Hwy (98188)
Rates: $72-$125
Tel: (206) 226-1812
(800) 544-9863

HAMPTON INN
7200 S 156th St (98188)
Rates: $65-$83
Tel: (206) 228-5800
(800) 426-7866

HOMEWOOD SUITES HOTEL
6955 Fort Dent Way (98188)
Rates: $109-$159
Tel: (206) 433-8000

RESIDENCE INN BY MARRIOTT
16201 W Valley Hwy (98188)
Rates: $124-$185
Tel: (206) 226-5500
(800) 331-3131

SOUTH CITY MOTEL
14242 S Pacific Hwy (98168)
Rates: n/a
Tel: (206) 243-0222

TOWN & COUNTRY SUITES
14800 Interurban Ave S (98168)
Rates: $47-$49
Tel: (206) 246-2323

TUMWATER

BEST WESTERN TUMWATER INN
5188 Capitol Blvd (98501)
Rates: $54-$66
Tel: (360) 956-1235
(800) 528-1234

MOTEL 6
400 W Lee St (98501)
Rates: $30-$40
Tel: (360) 754-7320
(800) 440-6000

TWISP

IDLE-A-WHILE MOTEL
505 North Hwy 20 (98856)
Rates: $40-$53
Tel: (509) 997-3222

SPORTSMAN MOTEL
1010 E Hwy 20 (98856)
Rates: n/a
Tel: (509) 997-2911

WAGON WHEEL MOTEL
HCR 73, Box 57 (98856)
Rates: n/a
Tel: (509) 997-4671

UNION

ALDERBROOK RESORT
E 7101 Hwy 106 (98592)
Rates: $49-$99
Tel: (360) 898-2200
(800) 622-9370

ROBIN HOOD VILLAGE
E 6780 Hwy 106 (98592)
Rates: $55-$185
Tel: (360) 898-2163

UNION GAP

DAYS INN
2408 Rudkin Rd (98903)
Rates: $40-$60
Tel: (509) 248-9700
(800) 329-7466

LA CASA MOTEL
2703 Main St (98903)
Rates: n/a
Tel: (509) 457-6147

QUALITY INN
12 E Valley Mall Blvd (98903)
Rates: $46-$59
Tel: (509) 248-6924
(800) 221-2222

SUPER 8 MOTEL
2605 Rudkin Rd (98903)
Rates: $45-$51
Tel: (509) 248-8880
(800) 800-8000

USK

THE INN AT USK
410 River Rd (99180)
Rates: n/a
Tel: (509) 445-1526

VALLEY

TEAL'S WAITTS LAKE RESORT
3365 Waitts Lake Rd (99181)
Rates: n/a
Tel: (509) 937-2400

VANCOUVER

BEST WESTERN FERRYMAN'S INN
7901 NE 6th Ave (98665)
Rates: $54-$78
Tel: (360) 574-2151
(800) 528-1234

BEST WESTERN GREENWOOD LODGE
780 NE Greenwood Dr (98662)
Rates: $68-$133
Tel: (360) 254-3100
(800) 528-1234

THE FORT MOTEL
500 E 13th St (98662)
Rates: n/a
Tel: (360) 694-3327

RED LION INN AT THE QUAY
100 Columbia St (98660)
Rates: $74-$111
Tel: (360) 694-8341
(800) 733-733-5466

RESIDENCE INN PORTLAND NORTH
8005 NE Parkway Dr (98662)
Rates: $119-$155
Tel: (360) 253-4800
(800) 331-3131

RODEWAY INN CASCADE PARK
221 NE Chalkov Dr (98684)
Rates: $55-$75
Tel: (360) 256-7044
(800) 426-5110

SHILO INNS DOWNTOWN
401 E 13th St (98686)
Rates: $58-$91
Tel: (360) 696-0411
(800) 222-2244

SHILO INNS HAZEL DELL
13206 Hwy 99 (98686)
Rates: $58-$65
Tel: (360) 573-0511
(800) 222-2244

SUNNYSIDE MOTEL
12200 NE Hwy 99 (98686)
Rates: n/a
Tel: (206) 573-4141

VALUE MOTEL
708 NE 78th St (98665)
Rates: n/a
Tel: (360) 574-2345

VANCOUVER LODGE
601 Broadway (98660)
Rates: $40-$60
Tel: (360) 693-3668

VASHON ISLAND

ANGELS OF THE SEA B & B
26431 99th Ave SW (98070)
Rates: $75-$130
Tel: (800) 798-9249

CASTLE HILL B & B
26734 94th Ave SW (98070)
Rates: $65+
Tel: (206) 463-5491

THE ISLAND WITHIN BED & BREAKFAST
P. O. Box 2241 (98070)
Rates: $100+
Tel: (206) 567-4177

PEABODY'S B & B
23007 64th Ave SW (98070)
Rates: $70+
Tel: (206) 463-3506

SOJOURN HOUSE
27415 94th Ave SW (98070)
Rates: $650+ week
Tel: (206) 463-5193

SWALLOW'S NEST GUEST COTTAGES
6030 248th St SW (98070)
Rates: $50-$150
Tel: (206) 463-2646
(800) 269-6378

WAITSBURG

WAITSBURG MOTEL
711 Coppei (99361)
Rates: n/a
Tel: (509) 337-8103

WALLA WALLA

A & H MOTEL
2599 Isaacs (99362)
Rates: n/a
Tel: (509) 529-0560

BEST WESTERN WALLA WALLA SUITES
7 E Oak St (99362)
Rates: $57-$75
Tel: (509) 525-4700
(800) 528-1234

CAPRI MOTEL
2003 Melrose St (99362)
Rates: $42-$46
Tel: (509) 525-1130

CITY CENTER MOTEL
627 W Main St (99362)
Rates: n/a
Tel: (509) 529-2660

COMFORT INN
520 N 2nd Ave (99362)
Rates: $52-$125
Tel: (509) 525-2522
(800) 221-2222

PONY SOLDIER MOTOR INN
326 E Main St (99362)
Rates: $67-$83
Tel: (509) 529-4360
(800) 634-7669

SICYON GALLERY BED & BREAKFAST
1283 Star (99362)
Rates: n/a
Tel: (509) 525-2964

SUPER 8 MOTEL
2315 Eastgate St N (99362)
Rates: $44-$62
Tel: (509) 525-8800
(800) 800-8000

TAPADERA BUDGET INN
211 N 2nd St (99362)
Rates: $31-$54
Tel: (800) 722-8277

WHITMAN INN
107 N 2nd St (99362)
Rates: $43-$99
Tel: (509) 525-2200

WASHOUGAL

ECONO LODGE
544 6th St (98671)
Rates: $40-$55
Tel: (360) 835-8591
(800) 424-4777

WENATCHEE

AVENUE MOTEL
720 N Wenatchee
Ave (98801)
Rates: $30-$65
Tel: (509) 663-7161
(800) 733-8981

**BEST WESTERN
HERITAGE INN**
1905 N Wenatchee
Ave (98801)
Rates: $63-$99
Tel: (509) 664-6565
(800) 528-1234

CHIEFTAN MOTEL
1005 N Wenatchee
Ave (98801)
Rates: $45-$80
Tel: (509) 663-8141

**FORGET ME NOT
BED & BREAKFAST**
1133 Washington St
(98801)
Rates: n/a
Tel: (509) 663-6114

HILL CREST MOTEL
2921 School St (98801)
Rates: n/a
Tel: (509) 663-5157

HOLIDAY LODGE
610 N Wenatchee
Ave (98801)
Rates: $36-$75
Tel: (509) 662-8167
(800) 722-0852

MOTEL LYLES
924 N Wenatchee
Ave (98801)
Rates: $36-$85
Tel: (800) 582-3788

ORCHARD INN
1401 N Miller St
(98801)
Rates: $47-$63
Tel: (509) 662-3443
(800) 368-4571

RED LION INN
1225 N Wenatchee
Ave (98801)
Rates: $69-$99
Tel: (509) 663-0711
(800) 547-8010

**THE UPTOWNER
MOTEL**
101 N Mission
(98801)
Rates: n/a
Tel: (509) 288-5279

VAGABOND INN
700 N Wenatchee
Ave (98801)
Rates: $30-$70
Tel: (509) 663-8133
(800) 522-1555

**WEST COAST
WENATCHEE
CENTER HOTEL**
201 N Wenatchee
Ave (98801)
Rates: $77-$92
Tel: (509) 663-1234
(800) 426-0670

WESTPORT

ALBATROSS MOTEL
200 E Dock St
(98595)
Rates: $46-$62
Tel: (360) 268-9235

BREAKERS MOTEL
971 Montesano
(98595)
Rates: n/a
Tel: (360) 268-0848

CHINOOK MOTEL
707 N Montesano
(98595)
Rates: n/a
Tel: (360) 268-9623

**CRANBERRY MOTEL
& RV PARK**
920 S Montesano
(98595)
Rates: n/a
Tel: (360) 268-0807

FRANK L MOTEL
725 S Montesano
(98595)
Rates: n/a
Tel: (360) 268-9200

HARBOR RESORT
871 Neddie Rose Dr
(98595)
Rates: n/a
Tel: (360) 268-0169

MARINERS COVE INN
303 Ocean Ave
(98595)
Rates: $42-$57
Tel: (360) 268-0531

OCEAN AVE INN
275 Ocean Ave (98595)
Rates: n/a
Tel: (360) 268-9278

SANDS MOTEL
1416 Montesano
(98595)
Rates: n/a
Tel: (800) 654-5250

SHIPWRECK MOTEL
2653 Nyhus (98595)
Rates: n/a
Tel: (360) 268-9151

WHIDBEY ISLAND

**ACORN
MOTOR INN**
8066 80th St NW
(Oak Harbor 98277)
Rates: $44-$85
Tel: (360) 675-6646

**BEST WESTERN
HARBOR PLAZA**
5691 SR Hwy 20
(Oak Harbor 98277)
Rates: $63-$97
Tel: (360) 679-4567
(800) 927-5478

**CASCADE SUNRISE
BED & BREAKFAST**
5730 S Summerhill
Dr (Langley 98260)
Rates: n/a
Tel: (360) 241-8501

**DRAKE'S LANDING
BED & BREAKFAST**
203 Wharf St
(Langley 98260)
Rates: $45-$55
Tel: (360) 221-3999

**HARBOUR INN
MOTEL**
1606 E Main St
(Freeland 98249)
Rates: $35-$62
Tel: (360) 331-6900

ISLAND TYME B & B
4940 S Bayview Rd
(Langley 98260)
Rates: $85-$135
Tel: (360) 221-5078
(800) 898-8936

**UNCLE JOHN'S
COTTAGES B & B**
1762 E Lancaster Rd
(Freeland 98249)
Rates: $60-$90
Tel: (360) 331-5623
(800) 779-5623

**THE VICTORIAN
BED & BREAKFAST**
602 N Main St
(Coupeville 98239)
Rates: $65-$100
Tel: (360) 678-5305

WHITE PASS

**GAME RIDGE
MOTEL & LODGE**
27350 Hwy 12
(98937)
Rates: $39-$82
Tel: (509) 672-2212

WHITE SALMON

**INN OF THE
WHITE SALMON
BED & BREAKFAST**
172 W Jewett (98672)
Rates: $89-$115
Tel: (509) 492-2335

WILBUR

SETTLE INN
303 NE Main (99185)
Rates: $35-$42
Tel: (509) 647-2100

WINLOCK

SUNRISE MOTREL
663 SR 505 (98596)
Rates: $38
Tel: (360) 785-4343

WINTHROP

**BEST WESTERN
CASCADE INN**
960 Hwy 20,
Box 813 (98862)
Rates: $45-$85
Tel: (800) 468-6754
(800) 528-1234

**THE CHEWUCH
INN MOTEL**
223 White Ave
(98862)
Rates: $55-$70
Tel: (509) 996-3107

MARIGOT HOTEL
960 Hwy 20 S
(98861)
Rates: $48-$85
Tel: (509) 996-3100
(800) 468-6754

**THE VIRGINIAN
RESORT**
808 N Cascade Hwy
(98862)
Rates: $40-$75
Tel: (509) 996-2535

WINTHROP INN
E Thinthrop,
Hwy 20 (98862)
Rates: $50-$75
Tel: (509) 996-2217
(800) 444-1972

**WOLFRIDGE
RESORT**
412B Wolf Creek Rd
(98862)
Rates: n/a
Tel: (509) 996-2828

WOODLAND

HANSEN'S MOTEL
1215 Pacific (98674)
Rates: n/a
Tel: (360) 225-7018

LAKESIDE MOTEL
785 Lake Shore Dr
(98674)
Rates: n/a
Tel: (360) 225-8240

LEWIS RIVER INN
1100 Lewis River Rd
(98674)
Rates: $42-$60
Tel: (360) 225-6257

SCANDIA MOTEL
1123 Hoffman St
(98674)
Rates: $36-$42
Tel: (360) 225-8006

WOODLANDER INN
1500 Atlantic St
(98674)
Rates: $42-$60
Tel: (360) 225-6548
(800) 444-9667

YAKIMA

BALI HAI MOTEL
710 N 1st St (98901)
Rates: $23-$43
Tel: (509) 452-7178

DAYS INN
2408 Rudkin Rd
(98903)
Rates: $50-$150
Tel: (509) 248-9700
(800) 329-7466

**CAVANAUGH'S
AT YAKIMA CENTER**
607 E Yakima Ave
(98901)
Rates: $58-$98
Tel: (509) 248-5900
(800) 843-4667

**COLONIAL
MOTOR INN**
1405 N 1st St (98901)
Rates: $39-$47
Tel: (509) 453-8981

HOLIDAY INN
9 N 9th St (98901)
Rates: $61-$91
Tel: (509) 452-6511
(800) 465-4329

MOTEL 6
1104 N 1st St (98901)
Rates: $33-$39
Tel: (509) 454-0080
(800) 440-6000

RED APPLE MOTEL
416 N 1st St (98901)
Rates: n/a
Tel: (509) 248-7150

**RED CARPET
MOTOR INN**
1608 Fruitvale Blvd
(98902)
Rates: $31-$41
Tel: (509) 457-1131
(800) 251-1962

RED LION INN
818 N 1st St (98901)
Rates: $59-$890
Tel: (509) 453-0391
800) 547-8010

**RED LION INN/
YAKIMA VALLEY**
1507 N 1st St (98901)
Rates: $77-$130
Tel: (509) 248-7850
(800) 547-8010

**TOURIST
MOTOR INN**
1223 N 1st St (98901)
Rates: n/a
Tel: (509) 452-6551

VAGABOND INN
510 N 1st St (98901)
Rates: $40-$50
Tel: (509) 457-6155

YELM

PRAIRIE MOTEL
700 Prairie Park Ln
(98597)
Rates: n/a
Tel: (360) 458-8300

**SALSICH MANSION
BED & BREAKFAST**
10808 Vail Rd SE
(98597)
Rates: n/a
Tel: (360) 458-7741

WEST VIRGINIA

BECKLEY

BECKLEY HOTEL & CONFERENCE CTR
1940 Harper Rd (25801)
Rates: $65-$200
Tel: (800) 274-6010

BEST WESTERN FOUR SEASONS INN
1939 Harper Rd (25801)
Rates: $40-$60
Tel: (304) 252-0671
(800) 528-1234

CHARLES HOUSE MOTEL
223 S Heber St (25801)
Rates: n/a
Tel: (304) 253-8318

COMFORT INN
1909 Harper Rd (25801)
Rates: $49-$64
Tel: (304) 255-2161
(800) 221-2222

HOWARD JOHNSON
1907 Harper Rd (25801)
Rates: $48-$64
Tel: (800) 446-4656

SHONEY'S INN
2033 Harper Rd (25313)
Rates: n/a
Tel: (304) 255-9091
(800) 222-2222

SUPER 8 MOTEL
2014 Harper Rd (25801)
Rates: $44-$61
Tel: (304) 253-0802
(800) 800-8000

BERKELEY SPRINGS

PARK HAVEN MOTOR LODGE
Rt 1, Box 298, Rt 522 S (25411)
Rates: n/a
Tel: (304) 258-1734

BLUEFIELD

ECONO LODGE
3400 Cumberland Rd (24701)
Rates: $39-$55
Tel: (304) 327-8171
(800) 424-4777

HOLIDAY INN
US 460, (24701)
Rates: $55-$80
Tel: (800) 465-4329

RAMADA INN - E RIVER MOUNTAIN
3175 E Cumberland Rd (24701)
Rates: $45-$60
Tel: (304) 325-5421
(800) 272-6232

BRIDGEPORT

HEDGES MOTEL
Rt 50 East (26330)
Rates: n/a
Tel: (304) 842-2811

HOLIDAY INN
100 Lodgeville Rd (26330)
Rates: $49-$85
Tel: (304) 842-5411
(800) 465-4329

KNIGHTS INN
1235 W Main St (26330)
Rates: $39-$44
Tel: (304) 842-7115
(800) 843-5644

SUPER 8 MOTEL
Meadowbrook Rd SR 2, Box 168 (26330)
Rates: $43-$59
Tel: (304) 842-7381
(800) 800-8000

BUCKHANNON

BAXA HOTEL-MOTEL
21 N Kanawha St (26201)
Rates: $29-$38
Tel: (304) 472-2500

COLONIAL MOTEL
24 N Kanawha St (26201)
Rates: n/a
Tel: (304) 472-3000

BURNSVILLE

BURNSVILLE MOTEL
5th & Main (26335)
Rates: $26-$31
Tel: (304) 853-2918

CHAPMANVILLE

RODEWAY INN
P. O. Box 4545 (25508)
Rates: $49-$54
Tel: (304) 855-7182
(800) 228-2000

CHARLESTON

DAYS INN
6400 MacCorkle Ave (25304)
Rates: $43-$62
Tel: (304) 925-1010
(800) 329-7466

HAMPTON INN
#1 Preferred Place (25309)
Rates: $67-90
Tel: (304) 746-4646
(800) 426-7866

KNIGHTS INN
6401 MacCorkle Ave SE (25304)
Rates: $37-$45
Tel: (304) 925-0451
(800) 843-5644

MOTEL 6
6311 MacCorkle Ave SE (25304)
Rates: $34-$40
Tel: (304) 925-0471
(800) 440-6000

RED ROOF INN
6305 MacCorkle Ave SE (25304)
Rates: $42-$60
Tel: (304) 925-6953
(800) 843-7663

CLARKSBURG

TERRACE MOTEL
1202 E Pike St (26301)
Rates: n/a
Tel: (304) 622-6161

CROSS LANES

MOTEL 6
330 Goff Mountain Rd (25313)
Rates: $34-$40
Tel: (304) 776-5911
(800) 440-6000

DAVIS

DEERFIELD VILLAGE RESORT
Cortland Ln (26260)
Rates: $105-$125
Tel: (304) 866-4698
(800) 342-3217

HIGHLANDER VILLAGE
P. O. Box 656 (26260)
Rates: $32-$39
Tel: (304) 259-5551

DUNBAR

SUPER 8 MOTEL
911 Dunbar Ave (25064)
Rates: $40-$60
Tel: (304) 768-6888
(800) 800-8000

ELKINS

BEST WESTERN INN
P. O. Box 1878 (26241)
Rates: $45-$100
Tel: (304) 636-7711
(800) 528-1234

CHEAT RIVER LODGE
Rt 1, Box 115 (26241)
Rates: n/a
Tel: (304) 636-2301

DAYS INN
1200 Harrison Ave (26241)
Rates: $49-$74
Tel: (304) 637-4667
(800) 329-7466

ECONO LODGE
Rt 1, Box 15 (26241)
Rates: $37-$58
Tel: (304) 636-5311
(800) 424-4777

MOUNTAIN SPLENDOR INN
P. O. Box 1802 (26241)
Rates: n/a
Tel: (304) 636-8111

SUPER 8 MOTEL
Box 284, Rt 3 (26241)
Rates: $39-$60
Tel: (304) 636-6500
(800) 800-8000

FAIRMONT

COUNTRY CLUB MOTOR LODGE
1499 Locust Ave (26554)
Rates: $23-$30
Tel: (304) 366-4141

ECONO LODGE
226 Middletown Rd (26554)
Rates: $41-$61
Tel: (304) 366-5995
(800) 424-4777

HOLIDAY INN
I-79 & E Grafton Rd (26554)
Rates: $39-$80
Tel: (304) 366-5500
(800) 465-4329

RED ROOF INN
50 Middletown Rd (26554)
Rates: $30-$41
Tel: (304) 366-6800
(800) 843-7663

SUPER 8 MOTEL
I-79, Kingmont Exit (26554)
Rates: $47-$65
Tel: (800) 800-8000

FAYETTEVILLE

COMFORT INN-NEW RIVER
US 19 & Laurel Creek Rd (25840)
Rates: $35-$75
Tel: (304) 574-3443
(800) 221-2222

FRANKLIN

MT. STATE MOTEL
Rt 220 North (26807)
Rates: n/a
Tel: (304) 358-2084

GHENT

ECONO LODGE
I-77 exit 28, Odd Rd (25843)
Rates: $39-$50
Tel: (304) 787-3250
(800) 424-4777

HARPERS FERRY

CLIFFSIDE INN & CONF. CENTER
US Rt 340 (25425)
Rates: $45-$71
Tel: (800) 786-9437

HILLSBORO

THE CURRENT
Denmar Rd (24946)
Rates: n/a
Tel: (304) 653-4722

HUNTINGTON

DAYS INN
5196 US 60 E (25705)
Rates: $49-$60
Tel: (304) 733-4477
(800) 329-7466

ECONO LODGE
3325 US 60 E (25705)
Rates: $35-$46
Tel: (304) 529-1331
(800) 424-4777

RADISSON HOTEL
1001 3rd Ave (25701)
Rates: $78-$88
Tel: (304) 525-1001
(800) 333-3333

RED ROOF INN
5190 US 60 E (25705)
Rates: $44-$52
Tel: (304) 733-3737
(800) 843-7663

HURRICANE

RAMADA LIMITED
419 Hurricane Creek Rd (25526)
Rates: $35-$65
Tel: (304) 562-3346
(800) 272-6232

RED ROOF INN
I-64 at SR 34 (25526)
Rates: $33-$42
Tel: (304) 757-6392
(800) 843-7663

JANE LEW

WILDERNESS PLANTATION INN
P. O. Drawer 96 (26378)
Rates: $42-$51
Tel: (304) 884-7806

KEYSER

ECONO LODGE
US 220 S (26726)
Rates: $45-$78
Tel: (304) 788-0913
(800) 424-4777

LEWISBURG

BRIER INN
540 N Jefferson St (24901)
Rates: $42-$47
Tel: (304) 645-7722

BUDGET HOST
204 N Jefferson St (24901)
Rates: $32-$65
Tel: (304) 645-3055
(800) 678-3055

DAYS INN
635 N Jefferson St (24901)
Rates: $45-$75
Tel: (304) 645-2345
(800) 329-7466

GENERAL LEWIS INN
301 E Washington St (24901)
Rates: $54-$92
Tel: (304) 645-2600

SUPER 8 MOTEL
550 N Jefferson St (24901)
Rates: $42-$65
Tel: (304) 647-3188
(800) 800-8000

LOGAN

SUPER 8 MOTEL
316 Riverview Ave (25601)
Rates: $49-$66
Tel: (304) 752-8787
(800) 800-8000

MARLINTON

MARLINTON MOTOR INN
US 219 N (24954)
Rates: $38+
Tel: (304) 799-4711

MARTINSBURG

DAYS INN
209 Viking Way (25401)
Rates: $49-$68
Tel: (304) 263-1800
(800) 329-7466

ECONO LODGE
I-81 & Spring Mills Rd (25401)
Rates: $47-$64
Tel: (304) 274-2181
(800) 424-4777

KNIGHTS INN
1599 Edwin Miller Blvd (25401)
Rates: $40-$55
Tel: (304) 267-2211
(800) 843-5644

KRISTA LITE MOTEL
Rt 1 (25401)
Rates: $35-$39
Tel: (304) 263-0906

HAMPTON INN
975 Foxcroft Ave. (25401)
Rates: $63-69
Tel: (304) 267-2900
(800) 426-7866

HOLIDAY INN
301 Foxcroft Ave
(25401)
Rates: $65-$75
Tel: (304) 267-5500
(800) 465-4329

PIKESIDE MOTEL
2138 Winchester Ave
(25401)
Rates: n/a
Tel: (304) 263-5189

SCOTTISH INNS
1024 Winchester Ave
(25401)
Rates: $30-$48
Tel: (304) 267-2935
(800) 251-1962

MORGANTOWN

**ECONO LODGE
COLISEUM**
3506 Monongahela
Blvd (26505)
Rates: $59
Tel: (304) 599-8181
(800) 424-4777

**FRIENDSHIP INN-
MOUNTAINEER**
452 Country Club
Rd (26505)
Rates: $38-$44
Tel: (304) 599-4850
(800) 453-4511

HOLIDAY INN
1400 Saratoga Ave
(26505)
Rates: $45-$95
Tel: (304) 599-1680
(800) 465-4329

NEW CREEK

TOLL GATE MOTEL
HC 72, Box 121
(26743)
Rates: $27-$34
Tel: (304) 788-5100

NITRO

BEST WESTERN INN
4115 1st Ave (25143)
Rates: $44-$60
Tel: (304) 755-8341
(800) 528-1234

OCEANA

OCEANA MOTEL
Cook Parkway
(24870)
Rates: n/a
Tel: (304) 682-6186

PARKERSBURG

BEST WESTERN INN
US 50 (26101)
Rates: $36-$59
Tel: (304) 485-6551
(800) 528-1234

ECONO LODGE
US 50 (26101)
Rates: $30-$65
Tel: (800) 424-4777

RED ROOF INN
3714 E 7th St (26101)
Rates: $44-$47
Tel: (304) 485-1741
(800) 843-7663

THE STABLES LODGE
3604 7th St (26101)
Rates: n/a
Tel: (304) 424-5100

PENCE SPRINGS

**PENCE SPRINGS
HOTEL**
P. O. Box 90 (24962)
Rates: $45-$300
Tel: (304) 445-2606

PRINCETON

DAYS INN
P. O. Box 830 (24740)
Rates: $55-$82
Tel: (304) 425-8100
(800) 329-7466

**TOWN-N-COUNTRY
MOTEL**
805 Oakvale Rd
(24740)
Rates: $30-$45
Tel: (304) 425-8156

RAVENSWOOD

SCOTTISH INNS
Rt 2, Box 33 (20164)
Rates: $28-$35
Tel: (304) 273-2830
(800) 251-1962

RICHWOOD

**FOUR SEASONS
LODGE**
39-55 Rt Marlinton
Rd (26261)
Rates: n/a
Tel: (304) 846-4605

RIPLEY

ECONO LODGE
1 Hospitality Dr
(25271)
Rates: $36-$47
Tel: (304) 372-5000
(800) 424-4777

SUPER 8 MOTEL
102 Duke Dr (25271)
Rates: $39-$59
Tel: (304) 372-8880
(800) 800-8000

ST. ALBANS

DAYS INN
6210 MacCorkle Ave
SW (25177)
Rates: $39-$49
Tel: (304) 766-6231
(800) 329-7466

SOUTH
CHARLESTON

MICROTEL
600 Second St (25303)
Rates: $30-$42
Tel: (304) 744-4900
(800) 771-7177

**RAMADA PLAZA
HOTEL**
2nd Ave & B St
(25303)
Rates: $52-$125
Tel: (304) 744-4641
(800) 272-6232

RED ROOF INN
4006 MacCorkle Ave
SW (25309)
Rates: $44-$48
Tel: (304) 744-1500
(800) 843-7663

SUMMERSVILLE

BEST WESTERN INN
1203 S Broad St (26651)
Rates: $36-$60
Tel: (304) 872-6900
(800) 528-1234

COMFORT INN
903 Industrial Dr N
(26651)
Rates: $43-$58
Tel: (304) 872-6500
(800) 221-2222

SLEEP INN
701 Professional
Park Dr (26651)
Rates: $38-$53
Tel: (304) 872-4500
(800) 221-2222

SUPER 8 MOTEL
306 Merchants Walk
(26651)
Rates: $38-$59
Tel: (304) 872-4888
(800) 800-8000

SUTTON

ELK MOTOR COURT
35 Camden Ave
(26601)
Rates: n/a
Tel: (304) 765-7173

TRIADELPHIA

COMFORT INN
RD 1, Box 258
(26059)
Rates: $42-$105
Tel: (304) 547-1380
(800) 221-2222

DAYS INN
RD 1, Box 292
(26059)
Rates: $44-$47
Tel: (800) 329-7466

WESTON

COMFORT INN
I-79 & US 33 (26452)
Rates: $48-$58
Tel: (304) 269-7000
(800) 221-2222

SUPER 8 MOTEL
12 Market Pl (26452)
Rates: $40-$62
Tel: (304) 269-1086
(800) 800-8000

WHEELING

**WILSON LODGE
AT OGLEBY**
SR 88 N (26003)
Rates: $88-$124
Tel: (304) 243-4000
(800) 624-6988

WILLIAMSTOWN

COMFORT INN
RD 1, Box 258
(26187)
Rates: $42-$70
Tel: (304) 547-1380
(800) 221-2222

WHITE SULPHUR SPRINGS

BUDGET INN
830 E Main St
(24986)
Rates: $28-$60
Tel: (304) 536-2121

OLD WHITE MOTEL
865 E Main St
(24986)
Rates: $30-$65
Tel: (304) 536-2441

WISCONSIN

ABBOTSFORD

CEDAR CREST MOTEL
207 N 4th St (54405)
Rates: $24-$38
Tel: (715) 223-3661

HOME MOTEL
412 N 4th St (54405)
Rates: $28-$40
Tel: (715) 223-6343

ABRAMS

**FOSTER
FARM HOUSE
VACATION HOME**
4991-Hwy 41 (54101)
Rates: $50-$75
Tel: (414) 826-7570

ALGOMA

**ALGOMA BEACH
MOTEL**
1500 Lake St (54201)
Rates: $32-$95
Tel: (414) 487-2828

BARBIE ANN MOTEL
533 4th St (54201)
Rates: $30-$45
Tel: (414) 487-5561

HARBOR INN MOTEL
99 Michigan St
(54201)
Rates: $42-$52
Tel: (414) 487-5241

RIVER HILLS MOTEL
820 N Water St
(54201)
Rates: $30-$54
Tel: (414) 487-3451
(800) 236-3451

SCENIC SHORE INN
2221 Lake St (54201)
Rates: $30-$50
Tel: (414) 487-3214

**WEST WIND
SHORES COTTAGES**
N6870 Hwy 42
(54201)
Rates: $50-$80
Tel: (414) 487-5867

ALLENTON

**ADDISON HOUSE
BED & BREAKFAST**
6373 Hwy 175
(53002)
Rates: $45-$85
Tel: (414) 629-9993

ALMA

**REIDT'S MOTEL
& CABINS**
S1638 SR 35 (54610)
Rates: $30-$60
Tel: (608) 685-4843

AMERY

**AMERY'S CAMELOT
MOTEL**
359 S Keller Ave
(54001)
Rates: $23-$37
Tel: (715) 268-8194

**FORREST INN
MOTEL**
1045 River Place Dr
(54001)
Rates: $40-$60
Tel: (715) 268-4100
(800) 763-1263

ANTIGO

SUPER 8 MOTEL
535 Century Ave
(54409)
Rates: $39-$64
Tel: (715) 623-4188
(800) 800-8000

APPLETON

**BEST WESTERN
MIDWAY HOTEL**
3033 W College Ave
(54914)
Rates: $75-$103
Tel: (414) 731-4141
(800) 528-1234

BUDGETEL INN
3920 W College Ave
(54914)
Rates: $42-$53
Tel: (414) 734-6070
(800) 428-3438

**COMFORT SUITES
COMFORT DOME**
3809 W Wisconsin
Ave (54914)
Rates: $74-$160
Tel: (414) 730-3800
(800) 228-5150

**EXEL INN
OF APPLETON**
210 N Westhill Blvd
(54914)
Rates: $37-$52
Tel: (414) 733-5551

FAIRFIELD INN
132 Mall Dr (54915)
Rates: $49-$85
Tel: (414) 954-0202
(800) 228-2800

RESIDENCE INN
310 Metro Dr (54915)
Rates: n/a
Tel: (414) 954-0570
(800) 331-3131

ROADSTAR INN
3623 W College Ave
(54914)
Rates: $32-$44
Tel: (414) 731-5271

SNUG INN MOTEL
3437 N Richmond
(54914)
Rates: $35-$65
Tel: (414) 739-7316
(800) 236-4444

WOODFIELD SUITES
3730 W College Ave
(54914)
Rates: $80-$120
Tel: (414) 734-7777
(800) 338-0008

ARCADIA

RKD MOTEL
915 E Main Hwy 95
(54612)
Rates: $30-$45
Tel: (608) 323-3338

ASHLAND

**ANDERSON'S
CHEQUAMEGON
MOTEL**
2200 W Lakeshore
Dr (54806)
Rates: $29-$60
Tel: (715) 682-4658

ASHLAND MOTEL
2300 W Lakeshore
Dr (54806)
Rates: $35-$65
Tel: (715) 682-5503

BAYVIEW MOTEL
2419 E Lakeshore Dr
(54806)
Rates: $25-$45
Tel: (715) 682-5253
(800) 249-3200

**BEST WESTERN
HOLIDAY HOUSE
MOTEL**
Hwy 2, Lakeshore
Dr (54806)
Rates: $40-$100
Tel: (715) 682-5235
(800) 528-1234

CREST MOTEL
Sanborn Ave
& Hwy 2 (54806)
Rates: $38-$65
Tel: (715) 682-6603

HARBOR MOTEL
1200 W Lakeshore
Dr (54806)
Rates: $25-$55
Tel: (715) 682-5211

**HOTEL
CHEQUAMEGON**
101 Lakeshore Dr
(54806)
Rates: $50-$85
Tel: (715) 682-9095

LAKE AIRE MOTOR INN
US 2 & Hwy 13 (54806)
Rates: $28-$75
Tel: (715) 682-4551

SUPER 8 MOTEL
1610 W Lakeshore Dr (54806)
Rates: $41-$73
Tel: (715) 682-9377
(800) 800-8000

TOWN MOTEL
920 W Lakeshore Dr (54806)
Rates: $39-$59
Tel: (715) 682-5555

BAILEYS HARBOR

JOURNEY'S END MOTEL
2528 Cty F (54202)
Rates: $36-$53
Tel: (414) 839-2887
(800) 944-3582

PARENT MOTEL & COTTAGES
8404 Hwy 57 (54202)
Rates: $55-$68
Tel: (414) 839-2218

RIDGES RESORT & GUEST HOUSE LAKESIDE GOLF ACADAMY
8252 Hwy 57 (54202)
Rates: $38-$150
Tel: (414) 839-2288

SANDS RESORT MOTEL
2371 Ridges Dr (54202)
Rates: $50-$110
Tel: (414) 839-2401

BALDWIN

COLONIAL MOTEL
I-94 & US 63 (54002)
Rates: $30-$50
Tel: (715) 684-3351

BALSAM LAKE

BALSAM LAKE MOTEL
501 W Main St (54810)
Rates: $34-$45
Tel: (715) 485-3501

FOX DEN MOTEL & RESORT
101 County Rd 1 (54810)
Rates: $30-$40
Tel: (715) 485-3400

BARABOO

BEST WESTERN INN
725 W Pine (53913)
Rates: $53-$97
Tel: (608) 356-1100
(800) 528-1234

4 WINDS MOTEL
S 4090 A Hwy 12 (53913)
Rates: $35-$100
Tel: (608) 356-9481

GARDEN GATE BED & BREAKFAST
220 8th St (53913)
Rates: $65-$120
Tel: (608) 356-0963

HOWARD JOHNSON
750 W Pine (53913)
Rates: $32-$175
Tel: (608) 356-8366
(800) 446-4656

QUALITY INN
W Hwy 12 (53913)
Rates: $55-$150
Tel: (608) 356-6422
(800) 355-6422

SPINNING WHEEL MOTEL
809 8th St (53913)
Rates: $33-$85
Tel: (608) 356-3933

SUNSET RESORT BED & BREAKFAST
HCR 61 Box 6325 (54873)
Rates: $55-$65
Tel: (715) 795-2449

BEAVER DAM

GRAND VIEW MOTEL
1510 N Center (53916)
Rates: $26-$38
Tel: (414) 885-9208

SWANSON'S DOWNTOWN MOTOR COURT
414 8th Ave (53913)
Rates: $29-$60
Tel: (608) 356-4005

THUNDERBIRD MOTOR INN
1013 8th St (53913)
Rates: $38-$85
Tel: (608) 356-7757
(800) 233-0827

BAYFIELD

APPLE TREE INN
Rt 1, Box 251 (54814)
Rates: $69-$84
Tel: (715) 779-5572

BAY VILLA MOTEL
Rte 1 Box 33 (54814)
Rates: $48-$84
Tel: (715) 779-3252

BAYWOOD PLACE BED & BREAKFAST
20 N 3rd St (54814)
Rates: $55-$70
Tel: (715) 779-3690

HARBOR'S EDGE MOTEL
33 N Front St (54814)
Rates: $42-$89
Tel: (715) 779-3962

MORNING GLORY BED & BREAKFAST
119 S 6th St (54814)
Rates: $60-$77
Tel: (715) 779-5621

SEAGULL BAY MOTEL
Rt 1 Box 314, Hwy 13 & S 7th St (54814)
Rates: $30-$65
Tel: (715) 779-5558

WINFIELD INN
Rt 1, Box 33 (54814)
Rates: $32-$105
Tel: (715) 779-5180

SUPER 8 MOTEL

SUPER 8 MOTEL
711 Park Ave (53916)
Rates: $43-$62
Tel: (414) 887-8880
(800) 800-8000

BELGIUM

QUARRY INN MOTEL
690 Hwy D (53004)
Rates: $29-57
Tel: (414) 285-3475

BELOIT

COMFORT INN
2786 Milwaukee Rd (53511)
Rates: $48-$81
Tel: (608) 362-2666
(800) 221-2222

DRIFTWOOD MOTEL
1826 Riverside Dr (53511)
Rates: $26-$36
Tel: (608) 364-4081

ECONO LODGE
2956 Milwaukee Rd (53511)
Rates: $35-$42
Tel: (608) 364-4000
(800) 424-4777

IKE'S MOTEL
114 Dearborn Ave (53511)
Rates: $30-$80
Tel: (608) 362-3423

BERLIN

TRAVELER'S REST MOTEL
227 Ripon Rd (54923)
Rates: $35-$50
Tel: (414) 361-4441

BLACK RIVER FALLS

AMERICAN BUDGET INN
919 Hwy 54 (54615)
Rates: $41-$66
Tel: (715) 284-4333

**BEST WESTERN-
ARROWHEAD
LODGE**
I-94 & Hwy 54
(54615)
Rates: $49-$165
Tel: (715) 284-9471
(800) 528-1234

**FALLS ECONOMY
MOTEL**
512 E 2nd St (54615)
Rates: $30-$50
Tel: (715) 284-9919

**PINES
MOTOR LODGE**
I-94 & Hwy 12 N
(54615)
Rates: $35-$50
Tel: (715) 284-5311
(800) 345-7463

**RIVER CREST
RESORT**
N 6978 Hwy 12
(54615)
Rates: $59-$79
Tel: (715) 284-4763
(800) 863-4764

BLOOMER

OASIDE MOTEL
2407 Woodard Dr
(54724)
Rates: $32-$65
Tel: (715) 568-3234
(800) 322-7995

BOSCOBEL

HUBL'S MOTEL
RR 2 Hwy 60 (53805)
Rates: $25-$75
Tel: (608) 375-4277

BOULDER JUNCTION

WILDCAT LODGE
Hwy M, P6500
(54512)
Rates: $60-$150
Tel: (715) 385-2421

**ZASTROWS
LYNX LAKE LODGE**
P. O. Box 277 (54512)
Rates: $249
Tel: (715) 686-2249
(800) 882-5969

BRANTWOOD

PALMQUIST'S FARM
Rt 1, Box 134 (54513)
Rates: $49-$59
Tel: (715) 564-2558

BRILLION

SANDMAN MOTEL
550 W Ryan St
(54110)
Rates: $28-$50
Tel: (414) 756-2106

BROOKFIELD

MARRIOTT HOTEL
375 S Moorland Rd
(53005)
Rates: $69-$129
Tel: (414) 786-1100
(800) 228-9290

MOTEL 6
20300 W Bluemound
Rd (53045)
Rates: $30-$37
Tel: (414) 786-7337
(800) 466-8356

**RESIDENCE INN
BY MARRIOTT**
950 S Pinehurst Ct
(53005)
Rates: $85-$165
Tel: (414) 782-5990
(800) 331-3131

BURLINGTON

RAINBOW MOTEL
733 Milwaukee Ave
(53105)
Rates: $46-$68
Tel: (414) 763-2491

CABLE

**LAKEWOODS
RESORT**
HC 73, Box 715
(54821)
Rates: $45-$250
Tel: (715) 794-2561
(800) 255-593

CAMP DOUGLAS

K & K MOTEL
Rt 2, Box 242A (54618)
Rates: $30-$53
Tel: (608) 427-3100

CAMPBELL-SPORT

MIELKE-MAUK HOUSE
W 977 Hwy F (53010)
Rates: $60-$90
Tel: (414) 533-8602

NEWCASTLE PINES
N1499 Highway 45
(53010)
Rates: $75-$95
Tel: (414) 533-5252

CASCADE

**HOEFT'S RESORT
& CAMPGROUND**
W 9070 Crooked
Lake Dr (53011)
Rates: $65
Tel: (414) 626-2221

TIMBERLAKE INN
311 Madison Ave
(53011)
Rates: $60-$90
Tel: (414) 528-8481

CASHTON

**CANNONDALEN
BED & BREAKFAST**
Rt 1, Box 58 (54619)
Rates: $50-$65
Tel: (608) 269-2886

THE GEIGER HOUSE
401 Dennsiton St
(53806)
Rates: $45-$60
Tel: (608) 725-5419

CASSVILLE

**EAGLES ROOST
RESORT**
1034 Jack Oak Rd
(53806)
Rates: $30-$100
Tel: (608) 725-5553

SAND BAR MOTEL
1115 E Bluff St
(53806)
Rates: $30-$50
Tel: (608) 725-5300

CHILTON

**THUNDERBIRD
MOTEL**
121 E Chestnut
(53014)
Rates: $36-$50
Tel: (414) 849-4216

CHIPPEWA FALLS

AMERICINN MOTEL
11 W South Ave
(54729)
Rates: $48-$63
Tel: (715) 723-5711

**COUNTRY VILLA
MOTEL**
Rt 3 Box 40 (54729)
Rates: $26-$40
Tel: (715) 288-6376

**IMA INDIANHEAD
MOTEL**
501 Summit Ave
(54729)
Rates: $35-$40
Tel: (715) 723-9171
(800) 341-8000

LAKE AIRE MOTEL
5732 Sandburst Ln
(54729)
Rates: $30-$50
Tel: (715) 723-2231
(800) 236-2231

CLEAR LAKE

**ATHLETIC CLUB
MOTEL**
200 Digital Dr
(54005)
Rates: $35-$65
Tel: (715) 263-3111

CLINTONVILLE

**CLINTONVILLE
MOTEL**
297 S Main St
(54929)
Rates: n/a
Tel: (715) 823-6565

COLUMBUS

DERING HOUSE
251 W James St
(53925)
Rates: $35-$90
Tel: (414) 623-2015

CRANDON

LAKELAND MOTEL
400 S Lake Ave
(54520)
Rates: $28-$40
Tel: (715) 478-2423

RUSTIC HAVEN RESORT
Rt 1 Box 93 (54520)
Rates: $50-$90
Tel: (715) 478-2255

CRIVITZ

BONNIE BELL MOTEL
1450 US Hwy 141
(54114)
Rates: $29-$60
Tel: (715) 854-7395

THE PINES MOTEL
7968 N Hwy 141
(54114)
Rates: $30-$60
Tel: (715) 854-7987

SHAFFER PARK MOTEL
Rt 3 (54114)
Rates: $42-$45
Tel: (715) 854-2186

DARLINGTON

TOWNE MOTEL
245 W Harriet St
(53530)
Rates: n/a
Tel: (608) 776-2661

DICKEYVILLE

PLAZA MOTEL
203 S Main (53808)
Rates: $25-$48
Tel: (608) 568-7562
(800) 545-4061

DODGEVILLE

BEST WESTERN QUIET HOUSE
Hwy 18, Johns St
(53533)
Rates: $63-$145
Tel: (800) 528-1234

SUPER 8 MOTEL
1308 Johns St (53533)
Rates: $39-$67
Tel: (618) 935-3888
(800) 800-8000

DRESSER

VALLEY MOTEL
211 State Rd 35
(54009)
Rates: $35-$75
Tel: (715) 755-2781

DUNBAR

RICHARDS' MOTEL
11466 W Hwy 8
(54119)
Rates: $27-$38
Tel: (715) 324-5444

DURAND

DURAND MOTEL
610-11th Ave (54736)
Rates: $22-$35
Tel: (715) 755-2781
(800) 545-6107

DYCKESVILLE

GYPSY VILLA RESORT
950 Circle Dr (54217)
Rates: $69-$310
Tel: (715) 479-8644
(800 232-9714

HIAWATHA MOTOR INN
1982 N Hwy 45
(54217)
Rates: $30-$80
Tel: (715) 479-6431
(800) 645-4370

PINE-AIRE RESORT & CAMPGROUND
4443 Chain O'Lakes
Rd (54217)
Rates: $75-$139
Tel: (715) 479-9208
(800) 597-6777

SUNSET BEACH MOTEL & CONDO
8931 N Hwy 57
(54217)
Rates: $39-$129
Tel: (414) 866-2978

EAGLE RIVER

AMERICAN BUDGET INN
780 Hwy 45 N
(54521)
Rates: $52-$78
Tel: (715) 479-5151

EAGLE RIVER INN
5260 Hwy 70 W
(54521)
Rates: $69-$169
Tel: (715) 479-2000

THE EDGEWATER INN
5054 Hwy 70 W
(54521)
Rates: $39-$59
Tel: (715) 479-4011

GYPSY VILLA RESORT
950 Circle Dr (54521)
Rates: $350+
Tel: (800) 232-9714

RIVERSIDE MOTEL RESORT
5012 Hwy 70 (54521)
Rates: n/a
Tel: (800) 530-0019

WHITE EAGLE MOTEL
4948 Hwy 70 (54521)
Rates: $30-$51
Tel: (715) 479-4426

EAST TROY

MITTEN FARM B & B
W2452 County Rd J
(53120)
Rates: $50
Tel: (414) 642-5530

EAU CLAIRE

BEST WESTERN WHITE HOUSE INN
1828 S Hastings Way
(54701)
Rates: $40-$80
Tel: (715) 832-8356
(800) 528-1234

COMFORT INN
3117 Craig Rd
(54701)
Rates: $45-$80
Tel: (715) 833-9798
(800) 221-2222

DAYS INN-WEST
6319 Traux Ln
(54703)
Rates: $50-$80
Tel: (715) 874-5550
(800) 329-7466

EAU CLAIRE MOTEL
3210 E Clairemont
Ave (54701)
Rates: $27-$41
Tel: (715) 835-5148
(800) 624-3763

EXEL INN OF EAU CLAIRE
2305 Craig Rd
(54701)
Rates: $34-$48
Tel: (715) 834-3193

HEARTLAND INN
4075 Commonwealth
Ave (54701)
Rates: $42-$57
Tel: (715) 839-7100

HIGHLANDER INN
1135 W MacArthur
Ave (54701)
Rates: $27-$35
Tel: (715) 835-2261

HOLIDAY INN
2703 Craig Rd
(54701)
Rates: $59-$70
Tel: (715) 835-2211
(800) 465-4329

HOLIDAY INN CONVENTION CENTER
205 S Barstow St
(54701)
Rates: $61-$71
Tel: (715) 835-6121
(800) 465-4329

MAPLE MANOR MOTEL
2507 S Hastings Way
(54701)
Rates: $30-$49
Tel: (715) 834-2618
(800) 624-3763

QUALITY INN
809 W Clairmont
Ave (54701)
Rates: $56-$99
Tel: (715) 834-6611
(800) 221-2222

ROADSTAR INN
1151 W MacArthur
Ave (54701)
Rates: $30-$40
Tel: (715) 832-9731

SUPER 8 MOTEL
6260 Texaco Dr
(54703)
Rates: $38-$54
Tel: (715) 874-6868
(800) 800-8000

EDGERTON

TOWNE EDGE MOTEL
1104 N Main St
(53534)
Rates: $23-$40
Tel: (608) 884-9328

EGG HARBOR

**THE ALPINE INN
& COTTAGES**
7715 Alpine Rd
(54209)
Rates: $67-$905
Tel: (414) 868-3000

ELLISON BAY

**ANDERSON'S
RETREAT**
12621 Woodland Dr
(54210)
Rates: $48-$375
Tel: (414) 854-2746

**ELLISON BAY
COTTAGES**
12039 Hwy 42
(54210)
Rates: $60-$80
Tel: (414) 854-4109

ELM GROVE

**SLEEPY HOLLOW
MOTEL**
12600 W Bluemound
Rd (53122)
Rates: $39-$96
Tel: (414) 782-8333
(800) 341-8000

ELROY

ELROY VALLEY INN
Hwy 80 & 82 (53929)
Rates: $30-$50
Tel: (608) 462-8251

FERRRYVILLE

GRANDVIEW MOTEL
RR 1 Box 280 (54628)
Rates: $30-$65
Tel: (608) 734-3235

**MISSISSIPPI HUMBLE
BUSH B & B**
Main St, Box 297
(54628)
Rates: $65
Tel: (608) 734-3022

FENNIMORE

**FENMORE HILLS
MOTEL**
5814 Hwy 18 W
(53809)
Rates: $37-$57
Tel: (608) 822-3281

FOND DU LAC

BUDGETEL INN
77 Holiday Ln
(54935)
Rates: $40-$100
Tel: (414) 921-4000
(800) 428-3438

DAYS INN
107 N Pioneer Rd
(54937)
Rates: $36-$50
Tel: (414) 923-6790
(800) 329-7466

ECONO LODGE
649 W Johnson St
(54935)
Rates: $38-$54
Tel: (414) 923-2020
(800) 424-4777

HOLIDAY INN
625 Rolling
Meadows Dr (54935)
Rates: $75-$135
Tel: (414) 923-1440
(800) 465-4329

MOTEL 6
738 W Johnson St
(54935)
Rates: $25-$31
Tel: (414) 923-0678
(800) 466-8356

NORTHWAY MOTEL
301 S Pioneer Rd
(54935)
Rates: $27-$60
Tel: (414) 921-7975

SUPER 8 MOTEL
Pioneer Rd (54935)
Rates: $40-$58
Tel: (414) 922-1088
(800) 800-8000

TRAVELERS INN
1325 S Main St
(54935)
Rates:$32-$50
Tel: (414) 923-0223

FREDERIC

FREDERIC MOTEL
Hwy 35 (54837)
Rates: n/a
Tel: (715) 327-4496

GERMANTOWN

SUPER 8 MOTEL
N96 W 17490
County Q (53022)
Rates: $45-$67
Tel: (414) 255-0880
(800) 800-8000

GILLS ROCK

**HARBOR HOUSE
INN**
12666 SR 42 (54210)
Rates: $49-$110
Tel: (414) 854-5196

**WINDSIDE
COTTAGES**
12714 Hwy 42
(54210)
Rates: $50-$90
Tel: (414) 854-4871

GLENDALE

**BUDGETEL INN
NORTHEAST**
5110 N Port
Washington Rd
(53217)
Rates: $43-$53
Tel: (414) 964-8484
(800) 428-3448

**EXEL INN
NORTHEAST**
5485 N Port
Washington Rd
(53217)
Rates: $40-$57
Tel: (414) 961-7272

**RESIDENCE INN
BY MARRIOTT**
7275 N Port
Washington Rd
(53217)
Rates: $136-$162
Tel: (414) 352-0070
(800) 331-3131

GRANTSBURG

WOOD RIVER INN
703 W SR 70 (54840)
Rates: $32-$45
Tel: (715) 463-2541

GREEN BAY

**BARTH'S TOWER
MOTEL**
2625 Humboldt Rd
(54311)
Rates: $40-$65
Tel: (414) 468-1242

BAY MOTEL
1301 S Military Ave
(54304)
Rates: $35-$59
Tel: (414) 494-3441

**BEST WESTERN
DOWNTOWNER**
321 S Washington St
(54301)
Rates: $45-$80
Tel: (414) 437-8771
(800) 528-1234

BUDGETEL INN
2840 S Oneida
(54304)
Rates: $49-$64
Tel: (414) 494-7887
(800) 428-3438

COMFORT INN
2841 Ramada Way
(54304)
Rates: $47-$99
Tel: (414) 498-2060
(800) 221-2222

DAYS INN
1978 Gross Ave
(54304)
Rates: $37-$109
Tel: (414) 498-8088
(800) 329-7466

DAYS INN DOWNTOWN
406 N Washington St
(54301)
Rates: $45-$95
Tel: (414) 435-4484
(800) 329-7466

EXEL INN
2870 Ramada Way
(54304)
Rates: $40-$55
Tel: (414) 499-3599

HOLIDAY INN-CITY CENTER
200 Main St (54301)
Rates: $62-$95
Tel: (414) 437-5900
(800) 465-4329

MOTEL 6
1614 Shawano Ave
(54303)
Rates: $26-$32
Tel: (414) 494-6730
(800) 466-8356

RESIDENCE INN BY MARRIOTT
335 W St. Joseph St
(54301)
Rates: $65-$150
Tel: (414) 435-2222
(800) 331-3131

SUPER 8 MOTEL
2868 S Oneida St
(54304)
Rates: $50-$74
Tel: (414) 494-2042
(800) 800-8000

VALLEY MOTEL
116 N Military Ave
(54303)
Rates: $35-$44
Tel: (414) 494-3455

HARTFORD

SUPER 8 MOTEL
1539 E Sumner St
(53027)
Rates: $41-$59
Tel: (414) 673-7431
(800) 800-8000

HAYWARD

COUNTRY INN
P.O. Box 1010 (54843)
Rates: $58-$68
Tel: (715) 634-4100

NORTHWOODS MOTEL
Rt 6, Box 6453
(54843)
Rates: $43-$48
Tel: (715) 634-8088

ROSS' TEAL LAKE LODGE
Rt 7A (54843)
Rates: $110-$160
Tel: (715) 462-3631

SUPER 8 MOTEL
317 S Hwy 27
(54843)
Rates: $45-$63
Tel: (715) 634-2646
(800) 800-8000

HAZELHURST

HAZELHURST INN
6941 Hwy 51 (54531)
Rates: $45-$65
Tel: (715) 356-6571

HILLSBORO

TIGER INN
629 High Ave
(54634)
Rates: $49-$62
Tel: (608) 489-2918

HUDSON

BEST WESTERN HUDSON HOUSE INN
1616 Crest View Dr
(54016)
Rates: $51-$160
Tel: (715) 386-2394
(800) 528-1234

COMFORT INN
811 Dominion Dr
(54016)
Rates: $48-$75
Tel: (715) 386-6355
(800) 221-2222

FAIRFIELD INN BY MARRIOTT
2400 Center Dr
(54016)
Rates: $46-$90
Tel: (715) 386-6688
(800) 228-2800

SUPER 8 MOTEL
808 Dominion Dr
(54016)
Rates: $52-$65
Tel: (715) 386-8800
(800) 800-8000

HURLEY

AMERICAN BUDGET INN
850 10th Ave N
(54534)
Rates: $39-$81
Tel: (715) 561-3500

HOLIDAY INN
1000 10th Ave (54534)
Rates: $48-$62
Tel: (715) 561-3030
(800) 465-4329

JANESVILLE

BUDGETEL IN
616 Midland Rd
(53546)
Rates: $40-$59
Tel: (608) 758-4545

MOTEL 6
3907 Milton Ave
(53546)
Rates: $27-$35
Tel: (608) 756-1742
(800) 466-8356

SELECT INN
3520 Milton Ave
(53545)
Rates: $30-$48
Tel: (608) 754-0251
(800) 641-1000

SUPER 8 MOTEL
3430 Milton Ave
(53545)
Rates: $39-$61
Tel: (608) 756-2040
(800) 800-8000

JOHNSON CREEK

COLONIAL INN MOTEL
Hwy 26 & B (53038)
Rates: $24-$50
Tel: (414) 699-3518

DAYS INN
W 4545 Linmar Ln
(53038)
Rates: $52-$180
Tel: (414) 699-8000
(800) 329-7466

KAUKAUNA

SETTLE INN
1201 Maloney Dr
(54130)
Rates: $41-$52
Tel: (414) 766-0088

KENOSHA

BUDGETEL INN
7540 118th Ave
(53142)
Rates: $42-$65
Tel: (414) 857-7911

DAYS INN
12121 75th St (53142)
Rates: $49-$69
Tel: (414) 857-2311
(800) 329-7466

KNIGHTS INN WEST
7221 122nd Ave
(53142)
Rates: $40-$60
Tel: (414) 857-2622
(800) 843-5644

KEWASKUM

COUNTRY RIDGE INN B & B
4134 Ridge Rd
(53040)
Rates: $50-$65
Tel: (414) 626-4853

THE DOCTORS INN
1121 Fond du Lac
Ave (53040)
Rates: $45-$65
Tel: (414) 626-2666

LA CROSSE

BLUFF VIEW INN
3715 Mormon
Coulee Rd (54601)
Rates: $27-$75
Tel: (608) 788-0600

DAYS INN
101 Sky Harbour Dr
(54603)
Rates: $49-$149
Tel: (608) 783-1000
(800) 329-7466

EXEL INN
2150 Rose St (54603)
Rates: $33-$51
Tel: (608) 781-0400

RADISSON HOTEL
200 Harborview
Plaza (54601)
Rates: $79-$119
Tel: (608) 784-6680
(800) 333-3333

ROADSTAR INN
2622 Rose St (54603)
Rates: $35-$41
Tel: (608) 781-3070

SUPER 8 MOTEL
1625 Rose St (54603)
Rates: $47-$65
Tel: (608) 781-8880
(800) 800-8000

LAC DU FLAMBEAU

**DILLMAN'S
SAND LAKE LODGE**
3305 Sand Lake Ln
(54538)
Rates: $55-$400
Tel: (715) 588-3143

TY-BACH B & B
3104 Simpson Ln
(54538)
Rates: $55-$70
Tel: (715) 588-7851

LADYSMITH

AMERICINN MOTEL
800 W College Ave
(54848)
Rates: $48-$70
Tel: (715) 532-6650

**BEST WESTERN
EL RANCHO MOTEL**
8500 W Flambeau
Ave (54848)
Rates: $44-$60
Tel: (715) 532-6666
(800) 528-1234

EVERGREEN MOTEL
Hwy 8, W of Hwy
27 (54848)
Rates: $30-$48
Tel: (715) 532-5611

LAKE GENEVA

**LAKEWOOD INN
MOTEL**
1150 Wells St (53147)
Rates: $32-$100
Tel: (414) 248-6773

**T C SMITH
HISTORIC INN B & B**
865 Main St (53147)
Rates: $95-$350
Tel: (414) 248-1097
(800) 423-0233

LANCASTER

MARTHA'S B & B
7867 University
Farm Rd (53813)
Rates: $50
Tel: (608) 723-4711

LAND O' LAKES

SUNRISE LODGE
5900 W Shore Dr
(54540)
Rates: $47-$68
Tel: (715) 547-3684
(800) 221-9689

LA POINTE

**MADELINE ISLAND
MOTEL**
P. O. Box 51 (54850)
Rates: $40-$70
Tel: (715) 747-3000

LODI

LODI VALLEY SUITES
N 1440 Hwy 113
(53555)
Rates: $39-$67
Tel: (608) 592-7331

**PRAIRIE GARDEN
BED & BREAKFAST**
W13172 Hwy 188
(53555)
Rates: $47-$87
Tel: (608) 592-5187
(800) 380-8427

LOMIRA

**THE WINE &
SHUTTERS B & B**
W265 County Trunk
H (53048)
Rates: $50-$75
Tel: (414) 269-4056

LUCK

LUCK COUNTRY INN
Hwy 35 & 48 (54853)
Rates: $42-$75
Tel: (715) 472-2000

MADISON

**BEST WESTERN
WEST TOWNE SUITES**
650 Grand Canyon
Dr (53719)
Rates: $60-$75
Tel: (608) 833-4200
(800) 528-1234

**BUDGETEL
INN/BUDGET DOME**
8102 Excelsior Dr
(53717)
Rates: $58-$98
Tel: (608) 831-7711
(800) 428-3438

**COLLINS HOUSE
BED & BREAKFAST**
704 E Gorham St
(53703)
Rates: $59-$140
Tel: (608) 255-4230

DAYS INN
4402 E Broadway
(53704)
Rates: $52-$110
Tel: (608) 223-1800
(800) 329-7466

**EAST TOWNE
SUITES**
4801 Annamark Dr
(53704)
Rates: $61-$149
Tel: (608) 244-2020
(800) 950-1919

ECONO LODGE
4726 E Washington
Ave (53704)
Rates: $37-$60
Tel: (608) 241-4171
(800) 424-4777

EDGEWATER HOTEL
666 Wisconsin Ave
(53703)
Rates: $95-$155
Tel: (608) 256-9071
(800) 922-5512

EXEL GRAND HOTEL
722 John Nolen Dr
(53713)
Rates: $57-$84
Tel: (608) 255-7400

EXEL INN
4202 E Towne Blvd
(53704)
Rates: $33-$110
Tel: (608) 241-3861
(800) 356-8013

**HOLIDAY INN-
EAST TOWNE**
4402 E Washington
Ave (53704)
Rates: $90+
Tel: (800) 465-4329

**HOMEWOOD
SUITES**
501 D'Onofrio Dr
(53719)
Rates: $79-$119
Tel: (608) 833-8333
(800) 225-5466

**IMA EDGEWOOD
MOTEL**
101 W Broadway
(53716)
Rates: $32-$39
Tel: (608) 222-8601
(800) 341-8000

**MADISON
CONCOURSE HOTEL**
1 W Dayton St
(53703)
Rates: $82-$145
Tel: (608) 257-6000

MOTEL 6-NORTH
1754 Thierer Rd
(53704)
Rates: $29-$37
Tel: (608) 241-8101
(800) 466-8356

MOTEL 6-SOUTH
6402 E Broadway
(53704)
Rates: $29-$37
Tel: (608) 221-0415
(800) 466-8356

QUALITY INN-SOUTH
4916 E Broadway
(53716)
Rates: $64-$69
Tel: (608) 222-5501
(800) 221-2222

RAMADA LIMITED
3841 E Washington
Ave (53704)
Rates: $50-$90
Tel: (608) 244-2481
(800) 272-6232

RED ROOF INN
4830 Hayes Rd
(53704)
Rates: $31-$53
Tel: (608) 241-1787
(800) 843-7663

**RESIDENCE INN
BY MARRIOTT**
4862 Hayes Rd
(53704)
Rates: $95-$150
Tel: (608) 244-5047
(800) 331-3131

**ROADSTAR-WEST
TOWNE**
6900 Seybold Rd
(53719)
Rates: $38-$62
Tel: (608) 274-6900

SELECT INN
4845 Hayes Rd
(53704)
Rates: $32-$46
Tel: (608) 249-1815

SUPER 8 MOTEL
1602 W Beltline Hwy
(53713)
Rates: $48-$66
Tel: (608) 258-8882
(800) 800-8000

UNIVERSITY INN
441 N Francis St
(53703)
Rates: $58-$68
Tel: (608) 257-4881

MANITOWISH WATERS

**VOSS' BIRCHWOOD
LODGE**
P. O. Box 456 (54545)
Rates: $52-$79
Tel: (715) 543-8441

MANITOWOC

COMFORT INN
2200 S 44th St
(54220)
Rates: $47-$96
Tel: (414) 683-0220
(800) 221-2222

DAYS INN
908 Washington St
(54220)
Rates: $38-$125
Tel: (414) 682-8271
(800) 329-7466

**IMA WESTMOOR
MOTEL**
4626 Calumet Ave
(54220)
Rates: $30-$48
Tel: (414) 684-3374
(800) 341-8000

**INN ON
MARITIME BAY**
101 Maritime Dr
(54220)
Rates: $69-$95
Tel: (414) 682-7000
(800) 654-5353

MARINETTE

CHALET MOTEL
1301 Marinette Ave
(54143)
Rates: $34-$44
Tel: (715) 735-6687

SUPER 8 MOTEL
1508 Marinette Ave
(54143)
Rates: $42-$51
Tel: (715) 735-7887
(800) 800-8000

MARSHFIELD

**BEST WESTERN
MARSHFIELD
INNKEEPER**
2700 S Roddis Ave
(54449)
Rates: $50-$68
Tel: (715) 387-1761
(800) 528-1234

**DOWNTOWN
MOTEL**
750 S Central Ave
(54449)
Rates: $36-$56
Tel: (715) 387-1111

MARSHFIELD INN
116 W Ives (54449)
Rates: $43-$53
Tel: (715) 387-6381
(800) 851-8669

MAUSTON

**COUNTRY INN
BY CARLSON**
P. O. Box 25 (53948)
Rates: $44-$70
Tel: (608) 847-5959

MEDFORD

MEDFORD INN
321 N 8th St (54451)
Rates: $30-$39
Tel: (715) 748-4420

MENOMONIE

**BOLO COUNTRY
INN**
207 Pine Ave W
(54751)
Rates: $49-$80
Tel: (715) 235-5596

**CEDAR TRAIL
GUESTHOUSE**
E4761 County Rd C
(54751)
Rates: $45-$65
Tel: (715) 664-8828

SUPER 8 MOTEL
1622 N Broadway
(54751)
Rates: $44-$70
Tel: (715) 235-8889
(800) 800-8000

MEQUON

**BREEZE INN
TO THE CHALET
MOTEL 40**
10401 N Port
Washington Rd
(53092)
Rates: $44-$64
Tel: (414) 241-4510
(800) 343-4510

**PORT ZEDLER
MOTEL**
10036 N Port
Washington Rd
(53092)
Rates: $33-$90
Tel: (414) 241-5850

MERCER

**GREAT NORTHERN
MOTEL**
Hwy 51S (54547)
Rates: $39-$59
Tel: (715) 476-2440

MERRILL

BRICK HOUSE B & B
108 S Cleveland St
(54452)
Rates: $40-$60
Tel: (715) 536-3230

MILTON

**CHASE ON THE HILL
BED & BREAKFAST**
11624 State Rd 26
(53563)
Rates: $45-$60
Tel: (608) 868-6646

MILWAUKEE

BUDGETEL INN
7141 S 13th St
(53154)
Rates: $36-$51
Tel: (414) 762-2266
(800) 428-3438

**BUDGETEL INN
NORTHWEST**
5442 N Lovers Ln
(53225)
Rates: $42-$53
Tel: (414) 535-1300
(800) 428-3438

ECONO LODGE
6541 S 13th St
(53221)
Rates: $33-$49
Tel: (414) 764-2510
(800) 424-4777

EXEL INN-MILWAUKEE SOUTH
1201 W College Ave
(53221)
Rates: $31-$45
Tel: (414) 764-1776

EXEL INN-MILWAUKEE WEST
115 N Mayfair Rd
(Wauwatosa 53226)
Rates: $33-$47
Tel: (414) 257-0140

HOLIDAY INN-SOUTH
6331 S 13th St
(53221)
Rates: $65-$95
Tel: (414) 764-1500
(800) 465-4329

HOTEL WISCONSIN
720 N Old World
Third St (53202)
Rates: $49-$69
Tel: (414) 271-4900

MOTEL 6
5037 S Howell Ave
(53207)
Rates: $26-$34
Tel: (414) 482-4414
(800) 466-8356

PORT MOTEL
9717 W Appleton
Ave (53225)
Rates: $33-$46
Tel: (414) 466-4728

RAMADA INN SOUTH-AIRPORT
6401 S 13th St
(53221)
Rates: $58-$110
Tel: (414) 764-5300
(800) 272-6232

SUPER 8 MOTEL-AIRPORT
5253 S Howell Ave
(53207)
Rates: $52-$60
Tel: (414) 481-8488
(800) 800-8000

SUPER 8 MOTEL
8698 N Servite Dr
(53223)
Rates: $40-$54
Tel: (414) 354-5354
(800) 800-8000

MINOCQUA

AQUA AIRE MOTEL
806 Hwy 51 N
(54548)
Rates: $25-$59
Tel: (715) 356-3433

BEST WESTERN-LAKEVIEW MOTOR LODGE
311 Park St & Hwy
51 (54548)
Rates: $33-$109
Tel: (715) 356-5208
(800) 528-1234

COMFORT INN
8729 Hwy 51 N
(54548)
Rates: $47-$75
Tel: (715) 358-2588
(800) 221-2222

CROSS TRAILS MOTOR LODGE
8644 Hwy 51 N
(54548)
Rates: $30-$69
Tel: (715) 356-5202
(800) 841-5261

SUPER 8 MOTEL
Hwy 51 & 70 W
(54548)
Rates: $45-$65
Tel: (715) 356-9541
(800) 800-8000

NEKOOSA

SHERMALOT MOTEL
1148 Queensway
(54457)
Rates: $31-$38
Tel: (715) 325-2626

NEW GLARUS

SWISS AIRE MOTEL
1200 Hwy 69 (53574)
Rates: $40-$95
Tel: (608) 527-2138
(800) 798-4391

NEW LISBON

EDGE O' THE WOOD MOTEL
W 7396 Frontage Rd
(53950)
Rates: $25-$44
Tel: (608) 562-3705
(800) 638-4929

OAK CREEK

RED ROOF INN
6360 S 13th St
(53154)
Rates: $32-$54
Tel: (414) 764-3500
(800) 843-7663

KNIGHTS INN SOUTH
9420 S 20th St
(53154)
Rates: $42-$57
Tel: (414) 761-3807
(800) 843-5644

OCONO-MOWOC

INN AT PINE TERRACE
351 E Lisbon Rd
(53066)
Rates: $60-$120
Tel: (800) 421-4667

OLYMPIA RESORT & CONFERENCE CENTER
1350 Royale Mile Rd
(53066)
Rates: $59-$229
Tel: (800) 558-9573

ONALASKA

COMFORT INN
1223 Crossing
Meadows Dr (54650)
Rates: $50-$75
Tel: (608) 781-7500
(800) 221-2222

IMA ONALASKA INN
651 2nd Ave S
(54650-3219)
Rates: $25-$45
Tel: (608) 783-2270
(800) 341-8000

IMA SHADOW RUN LODGE
710 2nd Ave N
(54650)
Rates: $25-$45
Tel: (608) 783-0020
(800) 341-8000

ONTARIO

THE INN AT WILD-CAT MOUNTAIN
Hwy 33,
P.O. Box 112
Rates: $50-$75
Tel: (608) 337-4352

OSHKOSH

BUDGETEL INN
1950 Omro Rd
(54901)
Rates: $42-$53
Tel: (414) 233-4190
(800) 428-3438

FAIRFIELD INN BY MARRIOTT
1800 S Koeller Rd
(54901)
Rates: $46-$80
Tel: (414) 233-8504
(800) 228-2800

HILTON & CONVENTION CENTER
1 N Main St (54901)
Rates: $83-$94
Tel: (414) 231-5000
(800) 445-8667

HOLIDAY INN
500 S Koeller Rd
(54901)
Rates: $56-$71
Tel: (414) 233-1511
(800) 465-4329

HOWARD JOHNSON
1919 Omro Rd
(54901)
Rates: $40-$80
Tel: (414) 233-1200
(800) 446-4656

MOTEL 6
1015 S Washburn St
(54904)
Rates: $25-$31
Tel: (414) 235-0265
(800) 466-8356

SUPER 8 MOTEL
P.O. Box 3168 (54903)
Rates: $42-$58
Tel: (414) 426-2885
(800) 800-8000

OSSEO

**BUDGET HOST
TEN-SEVEN INN**
1994 E 10th St
(54758)
Rates: $29-$50
Tel: (715) 597-3114
(800) 888-2199

**RODEWAY INN-
ALAN HOUSE
MOTEL**
P. O. Box 7 (54758)
Rates: $48-$55
Tel: (715) 597-3175
(800) 228-2000

PARK FALLS

**NORTHWAY
MOTOR LODGE**
Hwy 13S (54552)
Rates: $44-$49
Tel: (715) 762-2406
(800) 844-7144

SUPER 8 MOTEL
1212 Hwy 13S
(54552)
Rates: $48-$65
Tel: (715) 762-3383
(800) 800-8000

PEMBINE

GRAND MOTEL
Jct 8 & 141 (54156)
Rates: $25-$42
Tel: (715) 324-5417

PHILLIPS

SKYLINE MOTEL
804 N Lake Ave
(54555)
Rates: $39-$56
Tel: (715) 339-3086
(800) 596-0407

TIMBER INN
606 N Lake Ave
(54555)
Rates: $41-$47
Tel: (715) 339-3071

PLATTEVILLE

**BEST WESTERN
GOVERNOR DODGE
MOTOR INN**
W Hwy 151 (53818)
Rates: $58-$73
Tel: (608) 348-2301
(800) 528-1234

MOUND VIEW INN
1755 E Hwy 151
(53818)
Rates: $35-$85
Tel: (608) 348-9518

SUPER 8 MOTEL
100 Hwy 80-81 S
(53818)
Rates: $41-$64
Tel: (608) 348-8800
(800) 800-8000

PLOVER

DAYS INN
5253 Harding Ave
(54467)
Rates: $40-$95
Tel: (715) 341-7300
(800) 329-7466

**ELIZABETH INN &
CONVENTION
CENTER**
5246 Harding Ave
(54467)
Rates: $35-$72
Tel: (715) 341-3131
(800) 472-8322

PLYMOUTH

**BEVERLY'S LOG
GUEST HOUSE**
W6926 Stoney Ridge
Ln (53073)
Rates: $65-$75
Tel: (414) 892-6064

**PORT
WASHINGTON**

**BEST WESTERN
HARBORSIDE
MOTOR INN**
135 E Grand Ave
(53024)
Rates: $49-$149
Tel: (414) 284-9461
(800) 528-1234

**PORT WASHINGTON
INN**
308 W Washington
St (53074)
Rates: $75-$125
Tel: (414) 284-5583

PORTAGE

RIDGE MOTOR INN
2900 New Pinery Rd
(53901)
Rates: $35-$135
Tel: (608) 742-5306

SUPER 8 MOTEL
3000 New Pinery Rd
(53901)
Rates: $49-$59
Tel: (608) 742-8330
(800) 800-8000

POYNETTE

JAMIESON HOUSE
407 N Franklin St
(53955)
Rates: $65-$130
Tel: (608) 635-4100

**PRAIRIE
DU CHIEN**

**BEST WESTERN-
QUIET HOUSE
SUITES**
Hwy 18/35 & 60 S
(53821)
Rates: $66-$153
Tel: (608) 326-4777
(800) 528-1234

BRIDGEPORT INN
Hwy 18/35 & 60 S
(53821)
Rates: $62-$110
Tel: (608) 326-6082
(800) 234-6082

**BRISBOIS
MOTOR INN**
533 N Marquette Rd
(53821)
Rates: $39-$74
Tel: (608) 326-8404
(800) 356-5850

DELTA MOTEL
Hwy 18 & 35 S
(53821)
Rates: $28-$59
Tel: (608) 326-4951

HOLIDAY MOTEL
1010 S Marquette Rd
(53821)
Rates: $24-$55
Tel: (608) 326-2448

**NEUMANN HOUSE
BED & BREAKFAST**
121 N Michigan St
(53821)
Rates: $53-$68
Tel: (608) 326-8104

PRAIRIE MOTEL
1616 S Marquette Rd
(53821)
Rates: $24-$55
Tel: (608) 326-6461

SUPER 8 MOTEL
Hwy 18/35 & 60 S
(53821)
Rates: $50-$80
Tel: (608) 326-8777
(800) 800-8000

PRENTICE

**COUNTRYSIDE
MOTEL**
W 5370 Greenberg
Rd (54556)
Rates: $34-$42
Tel: (715) 428-2333

RACINE

**FAIRFIELD INN
BY MARRIOTT**
6421 Washington
Ave (53406)
Rates: $48-$65
Tel: (414) 886-5000
(800) 228-2800

**HOLIDAY INN-
RIVERSIDE**
3700 Northwestern
Ave (53405)
Rates: $49-$90
Tel: (800) 465-4329

KNIGHTS INN
1149 Oakes Rd
(53406)
Rates: $42-$60
Tel: (800) 843-5644

MARRIOTT HOTEL
7111 Washington
Ave (53406)
Rates: $59-$99
Tel: (414) 886-6100
(800) 228-9290

SUPER 8 MOTEL
7141 Kinzie Ave
(53406)
Rates: $42-$60
Tel: (414) 884-0486
(800) 800-8000

REEDSBURG

COPPER SPRINGS MOTEL
E7278 Hwy 23 & 33
(53959)
Rates: $29-$48
Tel: (608) 524-4312

MOTEL REEDSBURG
1133 E Main St
(53959)
Rates: $24-$63
Tel: (608) 524-2306
(800) 526-6835

RHINELANDER

BEST WESTERN-CLARIDGE MOTOR INN
70 N Stevens St
(54501)
Rates: $53-$74
Tel: (715) 362-7100
(800) 528-1234

FEASE'S SHADY REST LODGE
8440 Shady Rest Rd
(54501)
Rates: $298-$1070
Tel: (715) 282-5231
(800) 261-1500

HOLIDAY ACRES RESORT
4060 S Shore Dr
(54501)
Rates: $59-$213
Tel: (715) 369-1500
(800) 261-1500

KAFKA'S RESORT
4281 W Lake George Rd (54501)
Rates: $65-$105
Tel: (715) 369-2929
(800) 426-6674

SUPER 8 MOTEL
667 W Kemp St
(54501)
Rates: $37-$60
Tel: (715) 369-5880
(800) 800-8000

RIB LAKE

OLKIVES LAKEVIEW RESORT
N9503 Spirit Lake Rd (54470)
Rates: n/a
Tel: (715) 427-3344

RICE LAKE

CURRIER'S LAKE-VIEW RESORT MOTEL
2010 E Sawyer St
(54868)
Rates: $40-$87
Tel: (715) 234-7474
(800) 433-5253

SUPER 8 MOTEL
2401 S Main St
(54868)
Rates: $41-$63
Tel: (715) 234-6956
(800) 800-8000

RICHLAND CENTER

STARLITE MOTEL
Rt 2 Hwy 14 East
(53581)
Rates: $25-$34
Tel: (608) 647-6158

SUPER 8 MOTEL
100 Foundry Dr
(53581)
Rates: $46-$61
Tel: (608) 647-8988
(800) 800-8000

RIVER FALLS

SUPER 8 MOTEL
1207 St. Croix St
(54022)
Rates: $54-$64
Tel: (715) 425-8388
(800) 800-8000

ST. CROIX FALLS

IMA DALLES HOUSE MOTEL
Hwy 8 & Hwy 35 S
(54024)
Rates: $46-$53
Tel: (715) 483-3206
(800) 341-8000

ST. GERMAIN

ST. GERMAIN B & B
6255 Hwy 70 E
(54558)
Rates: $45-$70
Tel: (715) 479-8007

ST. GERMAIN MOTEL & RESORT
170 Hwy 70 (54558)
Rates: $360-$650/weekly
Tel: (715) 542-3535

SAYNER

FROELICH'S SAYNER LODGE
P. O. Box 100 (54560)
Rates: $60-$100
Tel: (715) 542-3261
(800) 553-9695

SHAWANO

SUPER 8 MOTEL
211 Waukechon St
(54166)
Rates: $39-$61
Tel: (715) 526-6688
(800) 800-8000

SHEBOYGAN

BUDGETEL INN
2932 Kohler Memorial Dr (53081)
Rates: $40-$52
Tel: (414) 457-2321
(800) 528-3438

COMFORT INN
4332 N 40th St
(53083)
Rates: $36-$61
Tel: (800) 221-2222

PARKWAY MOTEL
3900 Motel Rd
(53081)
Rates: $41-$55
Tel: (414) 458-8338
(800) 341-8000

RAMADA INN - HARBOR CENTRE
723 Center Ave
(53081)
Rates: $45-$85
Tel: (414) 458-1400
(800) 272-6232

SELECT INN
930 N 8th St (53081)
Rates: $35-$40
Tel: (414) 458-4641

SIREN

PINE WOOD MOTEL
23862 Hwy 35
(54872)
Rates: $33-$45
Tel: (715) 349-5225

SISTER BAY

EDGE OF TOWN MOTEL
11092 Hwy 42
(54234)
Rates: $30-$70
Tel: (414) 854-2012

JUST-N-TRAILS BED & BREAKFAST
RR 1, Box 274
(54656)
Rates: $70-$250
Tel: (608) 269-4522
(800) 488-4521

SPARTA

BEST NIGHTS INN
303 W Wisconsin St
(54656)
Rates: $32-$89
Tel: (608) 269-3066

COUNTRY INN BY CARLSON
737 Avon Rd (54656)
Rates: $45-$57
Tel: (800) 456-4000

DOWNTOWN MOTEL
509 S Water St
(54656)
Rates: $28-$40
Tel: (608) 269-3138

HERITAGE MOTEL
704 W Wisconsin St
(54656)
Rates: $32-$54
Tel: (608) 269-6991
(800) 658-9484

SPOONER

AMERICAN BUDGET INN
101 Maple St (54801)
Rates: $50-$73
Tel: (715) 635-9770

COUNTRY HOUSE MOTEL
717 S River St (54801)
Rates: $35-$65
Tel: (715) 635-8721

GREEN ACRES MOTEL
N 4809 Hwy 63 S & 253 (54801)
Rates: $45-$89
Tel: (715) 635-2177

STEVENS POINT

BUDGETEL INN
4917 Main St (54481)
Rates: $35-$45
Tel: (715) 344-1900
(800) 428-3438

FAIRFIELD INN
5317 Hwy 10 E (54481)
Rates: $43-$65
Tel: (715) 342-9300

HOLIDAY INN
1501 N Point Dr (54481)
Rates: $70-$90
Tel: (715) 341-9446
(800) 465-4329

POINT MOTEL
209 Division St (54481)
Rates: $34-$46
Tel: (715) 344-8312
(800) 344-3093

TRAVELER MOTEL
3350 Church (54481)
Rates: $28-$50
Tel: (715) 344-6455
(800) 341-8000

STOCKHOLM

PINE CREEK LODGE
N447 244th St (54769)
Rates: $85
Tel: (715) 448-3203

STODDARD

WATER'S EDGE MOTEL
201 N Pearl St (54658)
Rates: n/a
Tel: (608) 457-2126

STURGEON BAY

CARL'S OLD BRIDGE MOTEL
114 N Madison Ave (54235)
Rates: $30-$70
Tel: (414) 743-1245

COMFORT INN
923 Greenbay (54235)
Rates: $40-$100
Tel: (414) 743-7486
(800) 221-2222

HOLIDAY MOTEL
29 N 2nd Ave (54235)
Rates: $25-$75
Tel: (414) 743-5571

NIGHTENGALE MOTEL
1547 Egg Harbor Rd (54235)
Rates: $25-$62
Tel: (414) 743-7633

QUIET COTTAGE
4608 Glidden Dr (54235)
Rates: $65-$80
Tel: (414) 743-4526

SNUG HARBOR INN
1627 Memorial Dr (54235)
Rates: $39-$140
Tel: (414) 743-2337

SUN PRAIRIE

MCGOVERN'S MOTEL & SUITES
820 W Main St (53590)
Rates: $31-$58
Tel: (608) 837-7321

SUPERIOR

BEST WESTERN BAY WALK INN
1405 Susquehanna Ave (54880)
Rates: $45-$89
Tel: (715) 392-7600
(800) 528-1234

BUDGET UPTOWN MOTEL
104 E 5th St (54880)
Rates: $38-$55
Tel: (715) 394-4449

DRIFTWOOD INN
2200 E 2nd St (54880)
Rates: $28-$72
Tel: (715) 398-6661

STOCKADE MOTEL
1610 E 2nd St (54880)
Rates: $27-$50
Tel: (715) 398-3585

SUPERIOR INN
525 Hammond Ave (54880)
Rates: $35-$62
Tel: (715) 394-7706

THREE LAKES

ONEIDA VILLAGE INN
1785 Superior St (54562)
Rates: $28-$80
Tel: (715) 546-3373
(800) 374-7443

TOMAH

BUDGET HOST DAYBREAK INN
Hwys 12 & 16 (54660)
Rates: $32-$58
Tel: (608) 372-5946
(800) 999-7088

COMFORT INN
305 Wittig Rd (54660)
Rates: $39-$79
Tel: (608) 372-6600
(800) 221-2222

CRANBERRY SUITES
319 Wittig Rd (54660)
Rates: $45-$60
Tel: (608) 374-2801

ECONO LODGE
2005 N Superior Ave (54660)
Rates: $32-$52
Tel: (800) 424-4777

HOWARD JOHNSON
I-90 & Hwy 131 (54660)
Rates: $46-$80
Tel: (608) 372-4500
(800) 446-4656

LARK INN
229 N Superior Ave (54660)
Rates: $40-$60
Tel: (608) 372-5981
(800) 447-5275

PARK MOTEL
1515 Kilbourne Ave (54660)
Rates: $24-$46
Tel: (608) 372-4655

SUPER 8 MOTEL
P. O. Box 48 (54660)
Rates: $49-$50
Tel: (608) 372-3901
(800) 800-8000

TREVOR

STATE LINE MOTEL
23610 128th St (53179)
Rates: n/a
Tel: (414) 396-9561

TWO RIVERS

COOL CITY MOTEL
3009 Lincoln Ave (54241)
Rates: $24-$45
Tel: (414) 793-2244
(800) 729-1520

VILLAGE INN MOTEL
3310 Memorial Dr (54241)
Rates: $40-$55
Tel: (414) 794-8818

VIROQUA

DOUCETTE'S HICKORY HILL MOTEL
SR 27 & 82 (54665)
Rates: $30-$65
Tel: (608) 637-3104

WASHBURN

REDWOOD MOTEL & CHALETS
26 W Bayfield St
(54891)
Rates: $30-$61
Tel: (715) 373-5512

SUPER 8 MOTEL
Harbor View Dr
(54891)
Rates: $40-$60
Tel: (715) 373-5671
(800) 800-8000

WASHINGTON ISLAND

DOR-CROS CHALET MOTEL
P. O. Box 249 (54246)
Rates: $49-$64
Tel: (414) 847-2126

FINDLAY'S HOLIDAY INN
Detroit Harbor
(54246)
Rates: $60-$100
Tel: (414) 847-2526

VIKING VILLAGE MOTEL
P. O. Box 135 (54246)
Rates: $48-$85
Tel: (414) 847-2551

WATERTOWN

FLAGS INN MOTEL
N627 Hwy 26 (53094)
Rates: n/a
Tel: (414) 261-9400

HERITAGE INN
700 E Main St (53094)
Rates: $44-$49
Tel: (414) 261-9010

KARLSHUEGEL INN
749 N Church St
(53098)
Rates: $60-$85
Tel: (414) 261-3980

SUPER 8 MOTEL
1730 S Church St
(53094)
Rates: $51-$63
Tel: (414) 261-1188
(800) 800-8000

WAUKESHA

SELECT INN
2510 Plaza Ct
(53072)
Rates: $34-$57
Tel: (414) 786-6015
(800) 641-1000

WAUPACA

BEST WESTERN GRAND SEASONS HOTEL
110 Grand Season Dr
(54981)
Rates: $49-$66
Tel: (715) 258-9212
(800) 528-1234

VILLAGE INN MOTEL
1060 W Fulton
(54981)
Rates: $38-$80
Tel: (715) 258-8526
(800) 626-6391

WAUSAU

ACE MOTEL
2211 Stewart Ave
(54401)
Rates: n/a
Tel: (715) 845-4261

BEST WESTERN MIDWAY HOTEL
2901 Martin Ave
(54401)
Rates: $75-$99
Tel: (715) 842-1616
(800) 528-1234

BUDGETEL INN
1910 Stewart Ave
(54401)
Rates: $42-$52
Tel: (715) 842-0421
(800) 428-3448

EXEL INN OF WAUSAU
116 S 17th Ave
(54401)
Rates: $33-$49
Tel: (715) 842-0641

MARLENE MOTEL
2010 Stewart Ave
(54401)
Rates: $31-$37
Tel: (715) 845-6248
(800) 835-0180

RIB MOUNTAIN INN
2900 Rib Mountain
Way (54401)
Rates: $47-$122
Tel: (715) 848-2802

SKI INN HOTEL & CONF CENTER
201 N 17th Ave
(54401)
Rates: $39-$61
Tel: (715) 845-4341

WAUSAU INN & CONF CENTER
2001 N Mountain Rd
(54401)
Rates: $55-$63
Tel: (800) 928-7281

WAUTOMA

SUPER 8 MOTEL
P.O. Box 578 (54982)
Rates: $44-$67
Tel: (414) 787-4811
(800) 800-8000

WEST BEND

SUPER 8 MOTEL
2433 W Washington
St (53095)
Rates: $46-$61
Tel: (414) 335-6788
(800) 800-8000

WESTBY

WESTBY HOUSE
200 W State St (54667)
Rates: $60-$80
Tel: (608) 634-4112

WESTFIELD

MARTHA'S ETHNIC BED & BREAKFAST
259 2nd St (53964)
Rates: $40-$60
Tel: (608) 296-3361

WEYERHAEUSER

COUNTRY VIEW MOTEL
W14691 Hwy 8
(54895)
Rates: $24-$30
Tel: (715) 353-2780

WHITE LAKE

JESSE'S WOLF RIVER LODGE
N2119 Taylor Rd
(54491)
Rates: $80-$120
Tel: (715) 882-2182

WHITEWATER

BLACK STALLION INN
Rt 1 US Hwy 12
(53190)
Rates: n/a
Tel: (414) 473-7700

WILLARD

THE BARN OF CLARK COUNTY
N7890 Bachelors Ave
(54493)
Rates: $59-$79
Tel: (715) 267-3215

WINDSOR

SUPER 8 MOTEL
4506 Lake Cir
(53598)
Rates: $41-$56
Tel: (608) 846-3971
(800) 800-8000

WISCONSIN DELLS

INTERNATIONAL MOTEL
1311 E Broadway
(53965)
Rates: $30-$100
Tel: (608) 254-2431

SUPER 8 MOTEL
800 Co Hwy H
(53965)
Rates: $40-$65
Tel: (608) 254-6464
(800) 800-8000

WISCONSIN RAPIDS

BEST WESTERN-RAPIDS MOTOR INN
911 Huntington Ave
(54494)
Rates: $46-$58
Tel: (715) 423-3211
(800) 528-1234

CAMELOT MOTEL
9210 Hwy 13 S
(54494)
Rates: $25-$42
Tel (715) 325-5111

MEAD INN
451 E Grand Ave
(54494)
Rates: $51-$83
Tel: (715) 423-1500
(800) 843-6323

SUPER 8 MOTEL
3410 8th St S (54494)
Rates: $39-$62
Tel: (715) 423-8080
(800) 800-8000

WYOMING

AFTON

**BEST WESTERN
HI COUNTRY INN**
P. O. Box 0907
(83110)
Rates: $45-$60
Tel: (307) 886-3856
(800) 528-1234

THE CORRAL
689 S Washington
(83110)
Rates: $30-$42
Tel: (307) 886-5424

MOUNTAIN INN
US 89, Rt 1 (83110)
Rates: $42-$52
Tel: (307) 886-3156

ALPINE

**ALPEN HAUS
HOTEL & RESORT**
Hwy 89 & 26 (83128)
Rates: $50-$75
Tel: (307) 654-7545
(800) 343-6755

**BEST WESTERN
FLYING SADDLE
LODGE**
Hwy 89 & 26 (83128)
Rates: $66-$150
Tel: (307) 654-7561
(800) 528-1234

LAKESIDE MOTEL
Box 238 (83128)
Rates: n/a
Tel: (307) 654-7507

**THREE RIVERS
MOTEL**
US Hwy 89 (83128)
Rates: n/a
Tel: (307) 654-7551

ATLANTIC CITY

**ATLANTIC CITY
MERCHANTILE**
100 Main St (82520)
Rates: n/a
Tel: (307) 332-5143

BAGGS

DRIFTERS INN
Hwy 789 (82321)
Rates: n/a
Tel: (307) 383-2015

BASIN

LILAC MOTEL
710 W C St (82410)
Rates: n/a
Tel: (307) 568-3355

BEULAH

**WINDY ACRES
RANCH B & B**
5480 Hwy 14 (82712)
Rates: n/a
Tel: (307) 283-2909

BONDURANT

**HOBACK VILLAGE
MOTEL**
Hwy 191 (82922)
Rates: n/a
Tel: (307) 733-3631

SMILING S
33 Mi S of Jackson,
Box 171 (82922)
Rates: n/a
Tel: (307) 733-3457

TRIANGLE F LODGE
Box 159 (82922)
Rates: n/a
Tel: (307) 733-2836

BUFFALO

**ARROWHEAD
MOTEL**
749 Fort St (82834)
Rates: $20-$35
Tel: (307) 684-9453

**BLUE GABLES
MOTEL**
662 N Main St
(82834)
Rates: n/a
Tel: (307) 684-7822

COMFORT INN
65 US 16 E (82834)
Rates: $29-$149
Tel: (302) 684-9564
(800) 221-2222

CROSSROADS INN
75 N Bypass (82834)
Rates: $28-$78
Tel: (307) 684-2256
(800) 852-2302

ECONO LODGE
333 Hart St (82834)
Rates: $31-$37
Tel: (307) 684-2219
(800) 424-4777

**MANSION HOUSE
MOTEL**
313 N Main St
(82834)
Rates: n/a
Tel: (307) 684-2218

**MOUNTAIN VIEW
MOTEL**
585 Fort St (82834)
Rates: $26-$44
Tel: (307) 684-2881

SOUTH FORK INN
16 mi W of Buffalo
on US 16 (82834)
Rates: n/a
Tel: (307) 684-9609

WYOMING MOTEL
610 E Hart St (82834)
Rates: $22-$89
Tel: (307) 684-5505
(800) 666-5505

IMA Z-BAR MOTEL
626 Fort St (82834)
Rates: $29-$45
Tel: (307) 684-5535
(800) 341-8000

CASPER

BEST WESTERN INN
2325 E Yellowstone
Hwy (82602)
Rates: $47-$84
Tel: (307) 234-3541
(800) 528-1234

COMFORT INN
480 Lathrop (82601)
Rates: $41-$64
Tel: (307) 235-3038
(800) 221-2222

COMMERICAL INN
5755 CY Ave (82601)
Rates: n/a
Tel: (307) 235-6688
(800) 738-6689

FIRST INTERSTATE INN
205 E Wyoming Blvd
(82601)
Rates: $29-$45
Tel: (307) 234-9125

HAMPTON INN
400 West F St (82601)
Rates: $52-$68
Tel: (307) 235-6668
(800) 426-7866

HILTON INN
I-25 & N Poplar
(82601)
Rates: $61-$175
Tel: (307) 266-6000
(800) 445-8667

HOLIDAY INN
300 W F St (82601)
Rates: $65-$71
Tel: (307) 235-2531
(800) 465-4329

KELLY INN
821 N Poplar (82601)
Rates: $36-$44
Tel: (307) 266-2400
(800) 635-3559

LA QUINTA INN
301 East E St (82601)
Rates: $33-$38
Tel: (307) 234-1159
(800) 531-5900

MOTEL 6
1150 Wilkins Cir
(82601)
Rates: $28-$34
Tel: (307) 234-3903

PARKWAY PLAZA
123 W East St
(82601)
Rates: 42+
Tel: (307) 235-1777
(800) 270-7829

RANCH HOUSE MOTEL
1130 E F St (82601)
Rates: n/a
Tel: (307) 266-4044

RED ARROW MOTEL
W Yellowstone &
Wyo Blvd (82601)
Rates: n/a
Tel: (307) 234-5293

ROYAL INN
440 East A St (82601)
Rates: $20-$36
Tel: (307) 234-3501
(800) 967-6925

SHILO INNS
739 Luker Ln (82601)
Rates: $47-$72
Tel: (307) 237-1335
(800) 222-2244

SHOWBOAT MOTEL
100 West F St (82601)
Rates: $22-$44
Tel: (307) 235-2711
(800) 524-9999

SUPER 8
3838 CY Ave (82601)
Rates: $34-$52
Tel: (307) 266-3480
(800) 800-8000

TOPPER MOTEL
728 E A St (82601)
Rates: n/a
Tel: (307) 237-8407

TRAVELIER MOTEL
500 E 1st St (82601)
Rates: $19-$22
Tel: (307) 237-9343

VIRGINIAN MOTEL
830 E A St (82601)
Rates: n/a
Tel: (307) 266-9731

WESTRIDGE MOTEL
955 CY Ave (82601)
Rates: $38-$58
Tel: (307) 234-8911
(800) 341-8000

YELLOWSTONE MOTEL
1610 E Yellowstone (82601)
Rates: n/a
Tel: (307) 234-9174
(800) 531-9257

CENTENNIAL

CENTENNIAL VALLEY TRADING POST
2755 Hwy 130 (82055)
Rates: n/a
Tel: (307) 721-5074

FRIENDLY FLY STORE & MOTEL
WYO 130, Box 195 (82055)
Rates: n/a
Tel: (307) 742-6033

THE OLD CORRAL MOUNTAIN LODGE
Main St (82055)
Rates: n/a
Tel: (307) 745-5918

RAINBOW VALLEY RESORT
75 Rainbow Valley Rd (82055)
Rates: n/a
Tel: (307) 745-0368

SNOWY MOUNTAIN LODGE
3474 Hwy 130 (82055)
Rates: n/a
Tel: (307) 742-7669

CHEYENNE

A DRUMMOND'S RANCH B & B
399 Happy Jack Rd (82007)
Rates: $60-$125
Tel: (307) 634-6042

ADVENTURERS COUNTRY B & B
3803 I-80 S Service Rd (82001)
Rates: n/a
Tel: (307) 632-4087

ATLAS MOTEL
1524 W Lincolnway (82001)
Rates: n/a
Tel: (307) 632-9214

BEST WESTERN-HITCHING POST INN
1700 W Lincolnway (82001)
Rates: $60-$98
Tel: (307) 638-3301
(800) 528-1234

BIG HORN MOTEL
2004 E Lincolnway (82001)
Rates: n/a
Tel: (307) 632-3122

CHEYENNE MOTEL
1601 E Lincolnway (82001)
Rates: n/a
Tel: (307) 778-7664

COMFORT INN
2245 Etchepare Dr (82007)
Rates: $35-$50
Tel: (307) 638-7202
(800) 221-2222

DAYS INN
2360 W Lincolnway (82003)
Rates: $35-$60
Tel: (307) 778-8877
(800) 329-7466

FAIRFIELD INN
1415 Stillwater Ave (82001)
Rates: $48-$62
Tel: (307) 637-4070
(800) 228-2800

FIREBIRD MOTEL
1905 E Lincolnway (82001)
Rates: n/a
Tel: (307) 632-5505

FRONTIER MOTEL
1400 W Lincolnway (82001)
Rates: n/a
Tel: (307) 634-7961

HOLIDAY INN
204 W Fox Farm Rd (82007)
Rates: $63-$125
Tel: (307) 638-4468
(800) 465-4329

HOME RANCH MOTEL
2414 E Lincolnway (82001)
Rates: n/a
Tel: (307) 634-3575

HOWDY PARDNERS BED & BREAKFAST
1920 Tranquility Rd (82009)
Rates: n/a
Tel: (406) 259-7993
(307) 634-6493

KNIGHTS INN
3839 E Lincolnway (82001)
Rates: n/a
Tel: (307) 634-2171

LA QUINTA INN
2410 W Lincolnway (82001)
Rates: $47-$61
Tel: (307) 632-7117
(800) 531-5900

LINCOLN COURT
1700 W Lincolnway (82001)
Rates: $39-$160
Tel: (307) 638-3307
(800) 221-0125

MOTEL 6
1735 Westland Rd (82001)
Rates: $28-$34
Tel: (307) 635-6806
(800) 440-6000

PORCH SWING BED & BREAKFAST
712 E 20th St (82001)
Rates: $43-$58
Tel: (307) 778-7182

QUALITY INN
5401 Walker Rd (82001)
Rates: n/a
Tel: (307) 632-8901
(800) 876-8901

RANGER MOTEL
909 W 16th St (82001)
Rates: n/a
Tel: (307) 634-7995

ROUNDUP MOTEL
403 S Greeley Hwy (82001)
Rates: n/a
Tel: (307) 634-7741

SAPP BROS. BIG C
I-80 & Archer (82001)
Rates: n/a
Tel: (307) 632-6000
(800) 788-4671

STAGECOACH MOTEL
1515 W Lincolnway (82001)
Rates: n/a
Tel: (307) 634-4495

SUPER 8 MOTEL
1900 W Lincolnway
(82001)
Rates: $37-$56
Tel: (307) 635-8741
(800) 843-1991

TWIN CHIMNEYS MOTEL
2405 E Lincolnway
(82001)
Rates: n/a
Tel: (307) 632-8921

WINDY HILLS GUEST HOUSE
393 Happy Jack Rd
(82007)
Rates: $65-$75
Tel: (307) 632-6423

WYOMING MOTEL
1401 W Lincolnway
(82001)
Rates: n/a
Tel: (307) 632-8104

CHUGWATER

BUFFALO LODGE
100 Buffalo Dr (82210)
Rates: $37-$58
(307) 422-3248

CLEARMONT

RBL BISON RANCH BED & BREAKFAST
4355 US Hwy 14-16
E (82835)
Rates: n/a
Tel: (307) 758-4387

CODY

BEST BET INN
1701 17th St (82414)
Rates: n/a
Tel: (307) 587-9009

BEST WESTERN-SUNRISE MOTOR INN
1407 8th St (82414)
Rates: $42-$89
Tel: (307) 587-5566
(800) 528-1234

BEST WESTERN-SUNSET MOTOR INN
1601 8th St (82414)
Rates: $32-$110
Tel: (307) 587-4265
(800) 528-1234

BIG BEAR MOTEL
139 W Yellowstone
Hwy (82414)
Rates: $25-$52
Tel: (307) 587-3117
(800) 325-7163

CARRIAGE HOUSE MOTEL
1816 8th St (82414)
Rates: n/a
Tel: (307) 587-2572

CARTER MOUNTAIN MOTEL
1701 Central (82414)
Rates: n/a
Tel: (307) 587-4295

GATEWAY MOTEL
203 Yellowstone Ave
(82414)
Rates: n/a
Tel: (307) 587-2561

GOFF CREEK LODGE RESORT
P. O. Box 155A
(82414)
Rates: $60-$100
Tel: (307) 587-3753
(800) 859-3985

HIGH COUNTRY MOTOR INN
405 Yellowstone Ave
(82414)
Rates: n/a
Tel: (307) 587-5960

KELLY INN
2513 Greybull Hwy
(82414)
Rates: $40-$78
Tel: (307) 527-5505
(800) 635-3559

MOUNTAIN VIEW INN
N Fork Star Rt
(82414)
Rates: $45-$100
Tel: (307) 587-2081

PARKWAY INN
720 Yellowstone Ave
(82414)
Rates: n/a
Tel: (307) 587-4208

SEVEN K'S MOTEL
232 W Yellowstone
Ave (82414)
Rates: n/a
Tel: (307) 587-5890
(800) 223-9204

SHOSHONE LODGE/RANCH
P. O. Box 790-T
(82414)
Rates: $46-$80
Tel: (307) 587-4044

SKYLINE MOTOR INN
1919 17th St (82414)
Rates: $26-$60
Tel: (307) 587-4201
(800) 843-8809

STAGE STOP
502 Yellowstone Ave
(82414)
Rates: n/a
Tel: (307) 587-2804

SUPER 8 MOTEL
730 Yellowstone Ave
(82414)
Rates: $31-$59
Tel: (307) 527-6214
(800) 800-8000

TRAIL INN & MOTEL
2750 N Fork Hwy
(82414)
Rates: n/a
Tel: (307) 587-3741

TROUT CREEK INN
Yellowstone Hwy W
(82414)
Rates: $28-$64
Tel: (307) 587-6288
(800) 341-8000

UPTOWN MOTEL
1562 Sheridan Ave
(82414)
Rates: n/a
Tel: (307) 587-4245

WESTERN 6 GUN MOTEL
423 Yellowstone Ave
(82414)
Rates: n/a
Tel: (307) 587-4835
(800) 231-6486

WISE CHOICE INN
2908 N Fork Hwy
(82414)
Rates: $66-$75
Tel: (307) 587-6288

YELLOWSTONE VALLEY INN
3324 N Fork Hwy
(82414)
Rates: n/a
Tel: (307) 587-3961

COKEVILLE

HIDEOUT MOTEL
245 S Hwy 30 N
(83114)
Rates: n/a
Tel: (307) 279-3281

VALLEY HI MOTEL
Hwy 30 & 89 (83114)
Rates: n/a
Tel: (307) 279-3251

DAYTON

FOOTHILLS MOTEL
101 N Main (82836)
Rates: n/a
Tel: (307) 655-2547

DIAMONDVILLE

ENERGY INN
P. O. Box 494 (83116)
Rates: $30-$38
Tel: (307) 877-6901

DOUGLAS

ALPINE INN
2310 E Richards
(82633)
Rates: n/a
Tel: (307) 358-4780

BEST WESTERN DOUGLAS INN
1450 Riverbend Dr
(82633)
Rates: $55-97
Tel: (307) 358-9790
(800) 528-1234

CHIEFTAIN MOTEL
815 Richards (82633)
Rates: $29-$43
Tel: (307) 358-2673

FIRST INTERSTATE INN
2349 E Richards
(82633)
Rates: $27-$44
Tel: (307) 358-2833
(800) 992-9026

4 WINDS MOTEL
615 E Richards
(82633)
Rates: n/a
Tel: (307) 358-2322

PLAINS MOTEL
628 Richards E
(82633)
Rates: n/a
Tel: (307) 358-4484

SUPER 8 MOTEL
314 Russell Ave
(82633)
Rates: $37-$53
Tel: (307) 358-6800
(800) 800-8000

VAGABOND MOTEL
430 E Richards
(82633)
Rates: n/a
Tel: (307) 358-9414

DUBOIS

**BLACK BEAR
COUNTRY INN**
505 N Ramshorn St
(82513)
Rates: $28-$40
Tel: (307) 455-2344
(800) 873-2327

**BRANDING IRON
MOTEL**
401 N Ramshorn St
(82513)
Rates: $26-$41
Tel: (307) 455-2893
(800) 341-8000

**CHINOOK WINDS
MOTEL**
640 S 1st St (82513)
Rates: $25-$55
Tel: (307) 455-2987

DUNLOGGIN B & B
305 S 1st St (82513)
Rates: n/a
Tel: (307) 455-2445

LAZY L & B RANCH
Route 66 (82513)
Rates: $595-$825
Tel: (307) 455-2839

**PINNACLE BUTTES
LODGE**
3577 Hwy 26 (82513)
Rates: $29-$47
Tel: (307) 455-2506

**RED ROCK RANCH
MOTEL**
2 Mi E on US 26
(82513)
Rates: n/a
Tel: (307) 455-2337

**RENDEZVOUS
MOTEL**
1349 W Ramshorn St
(82513)
Rates: $42-$80
Tel: (307) 455-2844
(800) 682-9323

**STAGECOACH
MOTOR INN**
103 E Ramshorn St
(82513)
Rates: $30-$46
Tel: (307) 455-2303

**TWIN PINES
LODGE & CABINS**
218 W Ramshorn St
(82513)
Rates: $27-$45
Tel: (307) 455-2600

WIND RIVER MOTEL
519 W Ramshorn St
(82513)
Rates: n/a
Tel: (307) 455-2611

EDGERTON

**TEAPOT
MOTOR LODGE**
Hwy 387 (82635)
Rates: n/a
Tel: (307) 437-6541

ENCAMPMENT

ELK HORN MOTEL
Box 666 (82325)
Rates: n/a
Tel: (307) 327-5110

RIVERSIDE CABINS
Star Rt, Box 15
(82325)
Rates: n/a
Tel: (307) 327-5361

**RUSTIC MOUNTAIN
LODGE B & B**
Star Rt 49 (82325)
Rates: n/a
Tel: (307) 327-5539

EVANSTON

ALEXANDER MOTEL
Box 181 (82930)
Rates: n/a
Tel: (307) 789-2346

BEAR RIVER INN
261 Bear River Dr
(82930)
Rates: n/a
Tel: (307) 789-0791

**BEST WESTERN
DUNMAR INN**
1601 Harrison Dr
(82930)
Rates: $60-$90
Tel: (307) 780-3770
(800) 528-1234

BIG HORN MOTEL
202 Bear River Dr
(82930)
Rates: $20-$40
Tel: (307) 789-6830

DAYS INN
339 Wasatch Rd
(82930)
Rates: $45-$75
Tel: (307) 789-2220
(800) 357-2220

HILLCREX DC MOTEL
1725 Harrison Dr
(82930)
Rates: n/a
Tel: (307) 789-1111

**PINE GABLES INN-
HISTORIC B & B**
1049 Center St
(82930)
Rates: $31-$53
Tel: (307) 789-2069

PRAIRIE INN MOTEL
264 Bear River Dr
(82930)
Rates: $34-$42
Tel: (307) 789-2920

SUPER 8 MOTEL
70 Bear River Dr
(82930)
Rates: $33-$47
Tel: (307) 789-7510
(800) 800-8000

**WESTON PLAZA
HOTEL**
1983 Harrison Dr
(82930)
Rates: $44-$49
Tel: (307) 789-0783
(800) 255-9840

**WESTON SUPER
BUDGET INN**
1936 Harrison Dr
(82930)
Rates: n/a
Tel: (307) 789-2810
(800) 255-9840

EVANSVILLE

SHILO INNS
739 Luker Ln (82636)
Rates: $41-$51
Tel: (800) 222-2244

FARSON

SITZMAN'S MOTEL
Box 25 (82932)
Rates: n/a
Tel: (307) 273-9241

FORT BRIDGER

**WAGON WHEEL
MOTEL**
270 N Main (82933)
Rates: n/a
Tel: (307) 782-6361

GILLETTE

ARROWHEAD MOTEL
202 Emerson (82716)
Rates: n/a
Tel: (307) 686-0909

**BEST WESTERN
TOWER WEST
LODGE**
109 N Hwy 14-16
(82716)
Rates: $43-$87
Tel: (307) 686-2210
(800) 528-1234

CIRCLE L MOTEL
410 E 2nd (82716)
Rates: n/a
Tel: (307) 682-9375

DAYS INN
910 E Boxelder
(82716)
Rates: $38-$80
Tel: (800) 329-7466

HOLIDAY INN
2009 S Douglas Hwy
59 (82716)
Rates: $62-$78
Tel: (307) 686-3000
(800) 686-3368

MOTEL 6
2105 Rodgers Dr
(82716)
Rates: $26-$32
Tel: (307) 686-8600
(800) 440-6000

MUSTANG MOTEL
922 E 3rd St (82716)
Rates: n/a
Tel: (307) 682-4784

RAMADA LIMITED
608 E 2nd St (82716)
Rates: $28-$50
Tel: (307) 682-9341
(800) 272-6232

RODEWAY INN
1020 Hwy 51 E
(82716)
Rates: $36-$56
Tel: (307) 682-5111
(800) 424-4777

ROLLING HILLS MOTEL
409 Butler-Spaeth Rd
(82716)
Rates: n/a
Tel: (307) 682-4757
(800) 551-8707

SUPER 8 MOTEL
208 S Decker Ct
(82716)
Rates: $27-$44
Tel: (307) 682-8078
(800) 800-800

THRIFTY INN
1004 E Hwy 14-16
(82716)
Rates: n/a
Tel: (307) 621-2616
(800) 621-2182

GLENROCK

GLENROCK MOTEL
108 S 3rd St (82637)
Rates: n/a
Tel: (307) 436-2772

GRAND TETON NATIONAL PARK

ATKINSON'S MOTEL
Box 108 (83013)
Rates: n/a
Tel: (307) 543-2442

COLTER BAY VILLAGE
P. O. Box 240
(Moran 83013)
Rates: $48-$94
Tel: (307) 543-2811

FLAGG RANCH VILLAGE
P. O. Box 187 (83013)
Rates: $65-$82
Tel: (307) 543-2861
(800) 443-2311

JACKSON LAKE LODGE
P. O. Box 240
(Moran 83013)
Rates: $85-$155
Tel: (307) 543-2855

SIGNAL MOUNTAIN LODGE
P. O. Box 50
(Moran 83013)
Rates: $65-$140
Tel: (307) 543-2831

TOGWOTEE MOUNTAIN LODGE
P. O. Box 91-A
(Moran 83013)
Rates: $49-$208
Tel: (800) 543-2847

GREEN RIVER

COACHMAN INN
470 E Flaming Gorge
Way (82935)
Rates: $25-$38
Tel: (307) 875-3681

DESMOND MOTEL
140 N 7th W (82935)
Rates: $26-$36
Tel: (307) 875-3701

FLAMING GORGE MOTEL
316 E Flaming Gorge
Way (82935)
Rates: n/a
Tel: (307) 875-4190

SUPER 8 MOTEL
280 W Flaming Gorge
Way (82935)
Rates: $31-$45
Tel: (307) 875-9330
(800) 800-8000

WESTERN MOTEL
890 Flaming Gorge
Way (82935)
Rates: $28-$40
Tel: (307) 875-2840

GREYBULL

ANTLER MOTEL
1116 N 6th St (82426)
Rates: $25-$50
Tel: (307) 765-4404

K-BAR MOTEL
300 Greybull Ave
(82426)
Rates: $28-$48
Tel: (307) 765-4426
(800) 690-4426

SAGE MOTEL
1135 N 6th St (82426)
Rates: $28-$32
Tel: (307) 765-4443

WHEELS MOTEL
1324 N 6th (82426)
Rates: n/a
Tel: (307) 765-2105

YELLOWSTONE MOTEL
247 Greybull Ave
(82426)
Rates: $30-$60
Tel: (307) 765-4456

GUERNSEY

ANNETTE'S B & B
Box 31 (82214)
Rates: n/a
Tel: (307) 836-2148

BUNKHOUSE HOTEL
380 W Whalen
(82214)
Rates: $28-$36
Tel: (307) 836-2356

HANNA

GOLDEN RULE MOTEL
305 S Adams (82327)
Rates: n/a
Tel: (307) 325-6525

HELL'S HALF ACRE

HELL'S HALF ACRE MOTEL
Hwys 20 & 26
(82648)
Rates: n/a
Tel: (307) 472-0018

HULETT

HULETT MOTEL
202 Main St (82720)
Rates: n/a
Tel: (307) 467-9900
(800) 451-4332

MOTEL PIONEER
119 Hunter (82720)
Rates: $24-$39
Tel: (307) 467-5656

JACKSON

ALIPINE MOTEL
70 Jean St (83001)
Rates: n/a
Tel: (307) 739-3200

ANTLER MOTEL
43 W Pearl St (83001)
Rates: $72-$104
Tel: (307) 733-2535

DON'T FENCE ME INN
2350 N Moose-
Wilson Rd (83001)
Rates: n/a
Tel: (307) 733-7979

ELK COUNTRY INN
480 W Pearl St
(83001)
Rates: n/a
Tel: (307) 733-2364

FLAT CREEK MOTEL
1935 N US 89 (83001)
Rates: $65-$95
Tel: (307) 733-5276
(800) 438-9338

FORTY-NINER MOTEL
330 W Pearl St (83001)
Rates: $38-$94
Tel: (307) 733-7550
(800) 451-2980

JACKSON HOLE LODGE
40 W Broadway
(83001)
Rates: $65-$185
Tel: (307) 733-2992

JACKSON HOLE RACQUET CLUB RESORT
Star Rt 362A (83001)
Rates: n/a
Tel: (307) 733-3990
(800) 443-8616

MAD DOG RANCH
6 mi NW of Jackson,
Box 1645 (83001)
Rates: n/a
Tel: (307) 733-3729

MOTEL 6
600 S Hwy 89 (83001)
Rates: $32-$48
Tel: (307) 733-1620
(800) 440-6000

PAINTED BUFFALO INN
400 W Broadway
(83001)
Rates: $59-$105
Tel: (307) 733-4340
(800) 288-3866

PROSPECTOR MOTEL
155 N Jackson St
(83001)
Rates: $35-$125
Tel: (307) 733-4858
(800) 851-0070

SASSY MOOSE INN
HC 362, Teton
Village Rd (83001)
Rates: n/a
Tel: (307) 733-1277

SNOW KING RESORT
400 E Snow King
Ave (83001)
Rates: $100-$490
Tel: (307) 733-5200
(800) 522-5464

TETON GABLES MOTEL
Jct 191-189-22
(83001)
Rates: n/a
Tel: (307) 733-3723

TWIN MOUNTAIN RIVER RANCH B & B
Star Rt 40 (83001)
Rates: n/a
Tel: (307) 733-1168

VIRGINIAN MOTEL
750 W Broadway
(83001)
Rates: $44-$80
Tel: (307) 733-2792
(800) 262-4999

WESTERN MOTEL
225 S Glenwood,
Box 1569 (83001)
Rates: n/a
Tel: (307) 733-3291

WILSON MOTEL
980 E Pearl St
(83001)
Rates: n/a
Tel: (307) 733-2956

WYOMING INN OF JACKSON
930 Broadway
(83001)
Rates: $79-$209
Tel: (307) 734-0035
(800) 844-0035

KAYCEE

CASSIDY INN MOTEL
326 Nolan Ave (82426)
Rates: n/a
Tel: (307) 738-2250

GRAVES B & B
1729 Barnum Rd
(82639)
Rates: n/a
Tel: (307) 738-2319

SIESTA MOTEL
255 Nolan Ave (82639)
Rates: n/a
Tel: (307) 738-2291

KEMMERER

ANTLER MOTEL
419 Coral St (83101)
Rates: n/a
Tel: (307) 877-4461

FAIRVIEW MOTEL
Hwy N 30 at 89
(83101)
Rates: $30-$44
Tel: (307) 877-3578

FOSSIL BUTTE MOTEL
1424 Central Ave
(83101)
Rates: n/a
Tel: (307) 877-3996

LAKE VIVA NAUGHTON MARINA MOTEL
Hwy 233 (83101)
Rates: n/a
Tel: (307) 877-9669

RAILWAY INN MOTEL
1427 W 5th Ave
(83101)
Rates: n/a
Tel: (307) 877-3544

LAGRANGE

BEAR MOUNTAIN BACK TRAILS
Box 37 (82221)
Rates: n/a
Tel: (307) 834-2281

LANDER

BEST WESTERN - THE INN AT LANDER
260 Grand View Dr
(82520)
Rates: $46-$100
Tel: (307) 332-2847
(800) 528-1234

BUNK HOUSE B & B
2024 Mortimore Ln
(82520)
Rates: n/a
Tel: (307) 332-5624

DOWNTOWN MOTEL
569 Main St (82520)
Rates: n/a
Tel: (307) 332-5220

HOLIDAY LODGE
210 McFarlane Dr
(82520)
Rates: $26-$45
Tel: (307) 332-2511
(800) 624-1974

MAVERICK
808 Main St (82520)
Rates: n/a
Tel: (307) 332-2821

PIECE OF CAKE BED & BREAKFAST
2343 Baldwin Creek
Rd (82520)
Rates: n/a
Tel: (307) 332-7608

PRONGHORN LODGE
150 E Main St
(82520)
Rates: $27-$46
Tel: (307) 332-3940
(800) 283-4678

SILVER SPUR MOTEL
340 N 10th (82520)
Rates: $28-$44
Tel: (307) 332-5189
(800) 922-7831

TETON MOTEL
586 Main St (82520)
Rates: n/a
Tel: (307) 332-3582

LARAMIE

BEST WESTERN FOSTER'S COUNTRY INN
1561 Snowy Range
Rd (82070)
Rates: $44-$93
Tel: (307) 742-8371
(800) 526-5145

BEST WESTERN GAS LITE MOTEL
960 N 3rd St (82070)
Rates: $39-$79
Tel: (307) 742-6616
(800) 528-1234

DOWNTOWN MOTEL
165 N 3rd St (82070)
Rates: $29-$59
Tel: (307) 742-6671
(800) 942-6671

ECONO LODGE
1470 McCue St
(82070)
Rates: $29-$79
Tel: (307) 745-8900
(800) 424-4777

HOLIDAY INN
2313 Soldier Springs
(82070)
Rates: $50-$80
Tel: (307) 742-6611
(800) 465-4329

LARAMIE INN
421 Boswell Dr
(82070)
Rates: $28-$66
Tel: (307) 742-3721
(800) 642-4212

MOTEL 6
621 Plaza Ln (82070)
Rates: $24-$33
Tel: (307) 742-2307
(800) 440-6000

MOTEL 8
501 Boswell Dr
(82070)
Rates: n/a
Tel: (307) 745-4856

**PRAIRIE BREEZE
BED & BREAKFAST**
718 Ivinson Ave
(82070)
Rates: n/a
Tel: (307) 745-5482
(800) 840-2170

RANGER MOTEL
453 N 3rd (82070)
Rates: n/a
Tel: (307) 742-6677

SUNSET INN
1104 S 3rd St (82070)
Rates: $28-$70
Tel: (307) 742-3741

**THUNDERBIRD
LODGE**
1369 N 3rd (82070)
Rates: n/a
Tel: (307) 745-4871

UNIVERSITY INN
1720 Grand Ave
(82070)
Rates: $35-$69
Tel: (307) 721-8855
(800) 869-9466

LOVELL

CATTLEMEN MOTEL
470 Montana Ave
(82431)
Rates: $36-$46
Tel: (307) 548-2296

**HORSESHOE BEND
MOTEL**
375 E Main St
(82431)
Rates: $34-$40
Tel: (307) 548-2221

SUPER 8 MOTEL
595 E Main St
(82431)
Rates: $31-45
Tel: (307) 548-2725
(800) 800-8000

WESTERN MOTEL
180 W Main St (82431)
Rates: n/a
Tel: (307) 548-2781

LUSK

RAWHIDE MOTEL
805 S Main St (82225)
Rates: n/a
Tel: (307) 334-2440

**SAGE & CACTUS
VILLAGE**
Star Rt 1, Box 158
(82225)
Rates: n/a
Tel: (307) 663-7653

**TOWN HOUSE
MOTEL**
525 S Main St (82225)
Rates: $32-$46
Tel: (307) 334-2376

TRAIL MOTEL
305 W 8th St (82225)
Rates: $32-$50
Tel: (307) 334-2530
(800) 333-5875

LYMAN

VALLEY WEST MOTEL
Main St (82937)
Rates: n/a
Tel: (307) 787-3700

MEDICINE BOW

TRAMPAS LODGE
Box 66 (82329)
Rates: n/a
Tel: (307) 379-2280

VIRGINIAN HOTEL
404 Lincoln Hwy,
Box 127 (82329)
Rates: n/a
Tel: (307) 379-2377

MEETEETSE

OASIS MOTEL
1702 State St (82433)
Rates: n/a
Tel: (307) 868-2551

VISION QUEST INN
2207 State St (82433)
Rates: n/a
Tel: (307) 868-2512
(800) 668-9061

MOORCROFT

**KEYHOLE MOTEL
MARINA**
213 McKean Rd
(82721)
Rates: n/a
Tel: (307) 756-9529

MOORCOURT MOTEL
Hwy 14 & Devils
Tower Rd (82721)
Rates: $35-$65
Tel: (307) 756-3411

NEWCASTLE

AUTO INN MOTEL
2503 W Main (82701)
Rates: n/a
Tel: (307) 746-2734

CAMBRIA INN
Box 158, 8 mi N on
Hwy 85 (82701)
Rates: n/a
Tel: (307) 746-2096

**FLYING V CAMBRIA
INN**
23726 Hwy 85 (82701)
Rates: n/a
Tel: (307) 746-2096

**FOUNTAIN INN-
CRYSTAL PARK
RESORT**
2 Fountain Plaza
(82701)
Rates: $42-$62
Tel: (307) 746-4426
(800) 882-8858

**FOUR CORNERS
GENERAL STORE**
24713 US Hwy 85 N
(82701)
Rates: n/a
Tel: (307) 746-4776

HILL TOP MOTEL
1121 S Summit
(82701)
Rates: n/a
Tel: (307) 746-4494

**MALLO CAMP
& RESORT**
Box 233 (82701)
Rates: n/a
Tel: (307) 746-4094
(800) 835-0157

MORGAN MOTEL
205 S Spokane
(82701)
Rates: n/a
Tel: (307) 746-2715

PINES MOTEL
248 E Wentworth
(82701)
Rates: $26-$55
Tel: (307) 746-4334

SAGE MOTEL
1227 S Summit Ave
(82701)
Rates: $31-$35
Tel: (307) 746-2724

STARDUST MOTEL
833 S Summit Ave
(82701)
Rates: n/a
Tel: (307) 746-4719

SUNDOWNER INN
451 W Main (82701)
Rates: n/a
Tel: (307) 746-2796

PINE BLUFFS

SUNSET MOTEL
316 W 3rd (82082)
Rates: n/a
Tel: (307) 245-3591

**GATOR'S TRAVELYN
MOTEL**
515 W 7th St (82082)
Rates: n/a
Tel: (307) 245-3226

PINEDALE

**BEST WESTERN
PINEDALE INN**
850 W Pine St
(82941)
Rates: $39-$89
Tel: (307) 367-6869
(800) 528-1234

**BOULDER LAKE
LODGE**
Box 1100 (82941)
Rates: n/a
Tel: (307) 537-4300

**CAMP O'THE
PINES MOTEL**
38 N Fremont
(82941)
Rates: n/a
Tel: (307) 367-4536

CHAMBERS HOUSE
111 W Magnolia St
(82041)
Rates: n/a
Tel: (307) 367-2168
(800) 567-2168

HALF MOON LODGE MOTEL
46 N Sublett Ave (82941)
Rates: n/a
Tel: (307) 367-2851

LAKESIDE LODGE RESORT MARINA
99 FSR 111 on Fremont Lake (82941)
Rates: n/a
Tel: (307) 367-2221

LOG CABIN MOTEL
49 E Magnolia (82941)
Rates: n/a
Tel: (307) 367-4579

PINE CREEK INN
650 W Pine St (82941)
Rates: n/a
Tel: (307) 367-2191

POLE CREEK RANCH BED & BREAKFAST
244 Pole Creek Rd (82941)
Rates: n/a
Tel: (307) 367-4433

RIVERA LODGE
442 W Marilyn (82941)
Rates: n/a
Tel: (307) 367-2424

SUN DANCE MOTEL
148 E Pine (82941)
Rates: $34-$55
Tel: (307) 367-4336

TETON COURT MOTEL
123 E Magnolia St (82941)
Rates: n/a
Tel: (307) 367-4317

WINDOW ON THE WINDS BED & BREAKFAST
10151 Hwy 191 (82941)
Rates: $45-$60
Tel: (307) 367-2600

THE ZZZZ INN
327 S Hwy 191 (82941)
Rates: $50-$75
Tel: (307) 367-2121

POWELL

BEST CHOICE MOTEL
337 E 2nd St (82435)
Rates: n/a
Tel: (307) 754-2243

BEST WESTERN KINGS INN
777 E 2nd St (82435)
Rates: $38-$81
Tel: (307) 754-5117
(800) 528-1234

JOANN RANCH
137 Rd 8VE (82435)
Rates: n/a
Tel: (307) 645-3109

PARK MOTEL
715 E 2nd St (82435)
Rates: n/a
Tel: (307) 754-2233

SUPER 8 MOTEL
845 E Coulter (82435)
Rates: $31-$45
Tel: (307) 754-7231
(800) 800-8000

RANCHESTER

WESTERN MOTEL
350 Dayton St (82839)
Rates: $25-$51
Tel: (307) 655-2212
(800) 341-8000

RAWLINS

BEST WESTERN-COTTONTREE INN
P.O. Box 387 (82301)
Rates: $56-$85
Tel: (307) 324-2737
(800) 528-1234

BRIDGER INN
1904 E Cedar St (82301)
Rates: $26-$34
Tel: (307) 328-1401

DAYS INN
2222 E Cedar St (82301)
Rates: $45-$55
Tel: (307) 324-6615
(800) 329-7466

KEY MOTEL
1806 E Cedar St (82301)
Rates: $26-$38
Tel: (307) 324-2728

RAWLINS MOTEL
905 W Spruce St (82301)
Rates: $28-$42
Tel: (307) 324-3456

SLEEP INN
1400 Higley Blvd (82301)
Rates: $39-$44
Tel: (307) 328-1732
(800) 221-2222

SUNSET MOTEL
1302 W Spruce St (82301)
Rates: $22-$35
Tel: (307) 324-3448
(800) 336-6752

WESTON INN
1801 E Cedar St (82301)
Rates: n/a
Tel: (307) 324-2783
(800) 255-9840

RIVERTON

DAYS INN
909 W Main St (82501)
Rates: $35-$55
Tel: (307) 856-9677
(800) 329-7466

HI-LO MOTEL
414 N Federal Blvd (82501)
Rates: $24-$33
Tel: (307) 856-9223

HOLIDAY INN
900 E Sunset (82501)
Rates: $47-$56
Tel: (307) 856-8100
Tel: (800) 465-4329

JACK PINE MOTEL
120 S Federal Blvd (82501)
Rates: n/a
Tel: (307) 856-9251

MOUNTAIN VIEW MOTEL
720 W Main St (82501)
Rates: n/a
Tel: (307) 856-2418

SUNDOWNER STATION MOTEL
1616 N Federal Blvd (82501)
Rates: $42-$48
Tel: (307) 856-6503
(800) 874-1116

SUPER 8 MOTEL
1040 N Federal Blvd (82501)
Rates: $35-$53
Tel: (307) 857-2400
(800) 800-8000

THUNDERBIRD MOTEL
302 E Fremont (82501)
Rates: $25-$40
Tel: (307) 856-9201

WYOMING MOTEL
319 N Federal Blvd (82501)
Rates: n/a
Tel: (307) 856-6549

ROCK SPRINGS

COMFORT INN
1670 Sunset Blvd (82901)
Rates: $38-$55
Tel: (307) 382-9490
(800) 221-2222

DAYS INN
1545 Elk St (82901)
Rates: $47-$72
Tel: (307) 362-5646
(800) 329-7466

ECONO LODGE
1635 N Elk (82901)
Rates: $34-48
Tel: (307) 382-4217
(800) 424-4777

HOLIDAY INN
1675 Sunset Dr (82901)
Rates: $54-$75
Tel: (307) 382-9200
(800) 465-4329

THE INN AT ROCK SPRINGS
2518 Foothill Blvd (82901)
Rates: $48-$71
Tel: (307) 362-9600
(800) 442-9692

IRWIN HOTEL
138 Elk St (82901)
Rates: n/a
Tel: (307) 382-9817

LA QUINTA INN
2717 Dewar Dr
(82901)
Rates: $39-$54
Tel: (307) 362-1770
(800) 531-5900

MOTEL 6
2615 Commercial
Way (82901)
Rates: $28-$40
Tel: (307) 362-1850
(800) 440-6000

MOTEL 8
108 Gateway Blvd
(82901)
Rates: n/a
Tel: (307) 362-8200

RODEWAY INN
1004 Dewar Dr
(82901)
Rates: $40-$59
Tel: (307) 362-6673
(800) 228-2000

SPRINGS MOTEL
1525 9th St (82901)
Rates: $30-$40
Tel: (307) 362-6683

SARATOGA

**CARY'S SAGE
& SAND MOTEL**
311 S 1st (82331)
Rates: n/a
Tel: (307) 326-8339

HACIENDA MOTEL
Hwy 130 S (82331)
Rates: $32-$55
Tel: (307) 326-5751

RIVIERA LODGE
303 N 1st (82331)
Rates: n/a
Tel: (307) 326-5651

SARATOGA INN
Box 869 (82331)
Rates: n/a
Tel: (307) 326-5261

SILVER MOON
412 E Bridge (82331)
Rates: n/a
Tel: (307) 326-5974

SHELL

**WAGON WHEEL
LODGE**
Hwy 14 (82441)
Rates: n/a
Tel: (307) 765-2561

SHERIDAN

ALAMO MOTEL
1326 N Main (82801)
Rates: n/a
Tel: (307) 672-2455

BRAMBLE MOTEL
2366 N Main (82801)
Rates: n/a
Tel: (307) 674-4902

COMFORT INN
1450 E Brundage Ln
(82801)
Rates: $40-$80
Tel: (307) 672-5098
(800) 221-2222

EVERGREEN INN
580 E 5th St (82801)
Rates: n/a
Tel: (307) 672-9757

**FOOTHILLS RANCH
BED & BREAKFAST**
521 Pass Creek Rd
(Parkman 82838)
Rates: n/a
Tel: (307) 655-9362

**IMA GUEST HOUSE
MOTEL**
2007 N Main (82801)
Rates: $33-$44
Tel: (307) 674-7496
(800) 341-8000

HOLIDAY INN
1809 Sugarland Dr
(82801)
Rates: $48-$130
Tel: (307) 672-8931
(800) 465-4329

HOLIDAY LODGE
625 Coffeen Ave
(82801)
Rates: n/a
Tel: (307) 672-2407

PARKWAY MOTEL
2112 Coffeen Ave
(82801)
Rates: n/a
Tel: (307) 674-7259

RANCHER MOTEL
1552 Coffeen Ave
(82801)
Rates: n/a
Tel: (307) 672-2428

ROCK TRIM MOTEL
449 Coffeen Ave
(82801)
Rates: $26-$38
Tel: (307) 672-2464

SUPER 8 MOTEL
2435 N Main St
(82801)
Rates: $32-$43
Tel: (307) 672-9725
(800) 800-8000

SUPER SAVER INN
1789 N Main (82801)
Rates: n/a
Tel: (307) 672-0471

TRAILS END MOTEL
2125 N Main St
(82801)
Rates: $34-$526
Tel: (307) 672-2477

TRIANGLE MOTEL
540 Coffeen Ave
(82801)
Rates: n/a
Tel: (307) 674-8031

XL MOTEL
907 N Broadway
(82801)
Rates: n/a
Tel: (307) 674-6458

SHOSHONI

DESERT INN MOTEL
605 W 2nd (82649)
Rates: n/a
Tel: (307) 876-2273

STORY

**WAGON BOX
SUPPER CLUB INN**
Box 248 (82842)
Rates: n/a
Tel: (307) 683-2444

SUNDANCE

BEST WESTERN INN
26 S Hwy 585
(82729)
Rates: $35-$99
Tel: (307) 283-2800
(800) 528-1234

TEN SLEEP

CIRCLE S MOTEL
Box 50 (82442)
Rates: n/a
Tel: (307) 366-2320

FLAGSTAFF MOTEL
Box 376 (82442)
Rates: n/a
Tel: (307) 366-2745

**MEADOWLARK
LAKE RESORT**
26 mi E on Hwy 16,
Box 86 (82442)
Rates: n/a
Tel: (307) 366-2424
(800) 858-5672

TETON VILLAGE

**CRYSTAL SPRINGS
INN**
3285 W McCollister
Dr (83025)
Rates: $46-$84
Tel: (307) 733-4423

THE HOSTEL
Box 546 (83025)
Rates: n/a
Tel: (307) 733-3415

THERMOPOLIS

EL RANCHO MOTEL
924 Shoshoni Rd
(82443)
Rates: $25-$42
Tel: (307) 864-2341

**HOLIDAY INN
OF THE WATERS**
P. O. Box 1323 (82443)
Rates: $49-$88
Tel: (307) 864-3131
(800) 465-4329

**PLAZA INN
THE PARK**
116 E Park St (82443)
Rates: n/a
Tel: (307) 864-2251

RAINBOW MOTEL
408 Park St (82443)
Rates: n/a
Tel: (307) 864-2129
(800) 554-8815

ROUNDTOP MOUNTAIN MOTEL
412 N 6th (82443)
Rates: n/a
Tel: (307) 864-3126

SUPER 8 MOTEL
Lane 5, Hwy 20 S (82443)
Rates: $47-$56
Tel: (307) 864-5515
(800) 800-8000

WIND RIVER MOTEL
501 S 6th St (82443)
Rates: n/a
Tel: (307) 864-2325

TORRINGTON

BLUE LANTERN MOTEL
1402 S Main (82240)
Rates: n/a
Tel: (307) 532-8999

KING'S INN
1555 S Main (82240)
Rates: $38-$76
Tel: (307) 532-4011

MAVERICK MOTEL
US 26 & 85 (82240)
Rates: $27-$32
Tel: (307) 532-4064

OREGON TRAIL LODGE
710 East Valley Blvd (82240)
Rates: n/a
Tel: (307) 532-2101

WAPITI

ABSAROKA MOUNTAIN RANCH
1231 Yellowstone Park Hwy (82450)
Rates: $49-$88
Tel: (307) 587-3963

ELEPHANT HEAD LODGE
1170 Yellowstone Park Hwy (82450)
Rates: $58-$82
Tel: (307) 587-3980

HALF MILE CREEK RANCH
P. O. Box 48 (82450)
Rates: $60
Tel: (307) 587-9513

YELLOWSTONE VALLEY INN
3324 Yellowstone Park Hwy (82414)
Rates: $29-$59
Tel: (307) 587-3961

WHEATLAND

BLACKBIRD INN
1101 11th St (82201)
Rates: n/a
Tel: (307) 322-4540

BEST WESTERN TORCHLIGHT MOTOR INN
1809 N 16th St (82201)
Rates: $41-$80
Tel: (307) 322-4070
(800) 528-1234

PLAINS MOTEL
208 16th St (82201)
Rates: n/a
Tel: (307) 322-3416

VIMBO'S MOTEL
203 16th St (82201)
Rates: $32-$41
Tel: (307) 322-3842

WEST WINDS MOTEL
1756 South Rd (82201)
Rates: $27-$52
Tel: (307) 322-2705

WYOMING MOTEL
1101 9th St (82201)
Rates: n/a
Tel: (307) 322-5383

WORLAND

BEST WESTERN SETTLERS INN
2200 Big Horn Ave (82401)
Rates: $44-$54
Tel: (307) 347-8201
(800) 528-1234

DAYS INN
500 N 10th (82401)
Rates: $34-$48
Tel: (307) 347-4251
(800) 329-7466

SUPER 8 MOTEL
2500 Big Horn Ave (82401)
Rates: $31-$46
Tel: (307) 347-9236
(800) 800-8000

TOWN & COUNTRY MOTEL
1021 Russell Ave (82401)
Rates: n/a
Tel: (307) 347-3249

TOWN HOUSE MOTOR INN
119 N 10th (82401)
Rates: n/a
Tel: (307) 347-2426

YELLOWSTONE NATIONAL PARK

CANYON VILLAGE LODGE & CABINS
Yellowstone National Park (82190)
Rates: $43-$80
Tel: (303) 297-2757

GRANT VILLAGE
Yellowstone National Park (82190)
Rates: $56-$66
Tel: (303) 297-2757

LAKE LODGE & CABINS
Yellowstone National Park (82190)
Rates: $39-$79
Tel: (303) 297-2757

LAKE YELLOWSTONE HOTEL & CABINS
Yellowstone National Park (82190)
Rates: $49-$253
Tel: (303) 297-2757

MAMMOTH HOT SPRINGS HOTEL
Yellowstone National Park (82190)
Rates: $24-$158
Tel: (303) 297-2757

OLD FAITHFUL INN
P. O. Box 165 (82190)
Rates: $47-$210
Tel: (307) 344-7311

OLD FAITHFUL LODGE CABINS
P. O. Box 165 (82190)
Rates: $22-$38
Tel: (307) 344-7311

OLD FAITHFUL SNOW LODGE & CABINS
P. O. Box 165 (82190)
Rates: $47-$63
Tel: (307) 344-7311

STATE DEPARTMENTS OF TOURISM

Alabama 800-252-2262	**Kentucky** 800-225-8747	**North Dakota** 800-435-5663
Alaska 800-280-2267	**Louisiana** 800-334-8626	**Ohio** 800-282-5393
Arizona 888-520-3434	**Maine** 207-623-0363	**Oklahoma** 800-652-6552
Arkansas 800-628-8725	**Maryland** 800-543-1036	**Oregon** 800-547-7842
California 800-862-2543	**Massachusetts** 800-447-6277	**Pennsylvania** 800-847-4872
Colorado 303-866-3437	**Michigan** 800-543-2937	**Rhode Island** 800-556-2484
Connecticut 800-282-6863	**Minnesota** 800-657-3700	**South Carolina** 803-734-0122
Delaware 800-441-8846	**Mississippi** 800-927-6378	**South Dakota** 800-732-5682
Dist. of Columbia 202-724-4091	**Missouri** 800-877-1234	**Tennessee** 800-836-6200
Florida 904-487-1462	**Montana** 800-847-4868	**Texas** 800-452-9292
Georgia 800-847-4842	**Nebraska** 800-228-4307	**Utah** 801-538-1030
Hawaii 808-587-0300	**Nevada** 800-638-2328	**Vermont** 802-828-3236
Idaho 800-635-7820	**New Hampshire** 800-258-3608	**Virginia** 800-847-4882
Illinois 800-233-0121	**New Jersey** 800-537-7397	**Washington** 206-461-5840
Indiana 800-289-6646	**New Mexico** 800-545-2040	**West Virginia** 800-225-5982
Iowa 800-345-4692	**New York** 800-225-5692	**Wisconsin** 800-432-8747
Kansas 800-252-6727	**North Carolina** 800-847-4862	**Wyoming** 800-225-5996

HOTEL/MOTEL
800 Numbers

AUBERGES WANDLYN INNS
800-561-0000

BEST WESTERN
800-528-1234

BUDGET HOST
800-283-4678
800-BUD-HOST

CLARION INNS
800-252-7466
800-4-CHOICE
800-424-6423

COMFORT INNS
800-221-2222
800-4-CHOICE
800-424-6423

DAYS INN
800-329-7466
800-DAYS-INN

DOUBLETREE
800-222-8733
800-222-TREE

DRURY INNS
800-325-8300
(Midwest only)

ECONO LODGE
800-424-4777
800-4-CHOICE
800-424-6423

ECONOMY INNS
800-826-0778

EMBASSY SUITES
800-362-2779
800-EMBASSY

**FAIRFIELD INN
BY MARRIOTT**
800-228-2800

FRIENDSHIP INNS
800-424-4777
800-4-CHOICE

HAMPTON INNS
800-426-7866
800-HAMPTON

HEARTLAND INNS
800-334-3277
(mainly Iowa)

HILTON HOTELS
800-445-8667
800-HILTONS

HOLIDAY INNS
800-465-4329
800-HOLIDAY

HOMEWOOD SUITES
800-225-5466
800-CALLHOME

HOWARD JOHNSON
800-446-4656
800-IGO-HOJO
800-654-2000

HYATT HOTELS
800-233-1234

KNIGHTS COURT
800-843-5644

KNIGHTS INNS
800-843-5644

KNIGHTS STOP
800-843-5644

LA QUINTA INNS
800-531-5900

LEES INN
800-733-5337
(Midwest only)

QUALITY INNS
800-221-2222
800-4-CHOICE
800-424-6423

RADISSON SUITES
800-333-3333
800-RADISON

RAMADA INNS
800-272-6232
800-2-RAMADA
800-228-2828

RED CARPET INNS
800-251-1962

RED LION INNS
800-547-8010
800-RED-LION

RED ROOF INNS
800-843-7663
800-THE-ROOF
(No CA)

**RESIDENCE INN
BY MARRIOTT**
800-331-3131

RODEWAY INNS
800-424-4777
800-4-CHOICE

SANDMAN INNS
800-726-3626

SCOTTISH INNS
800-251-1962

SHILO INNS
800-222-2244

SLEEP INNS
800-221-2222
800-4-CHOICE
800-424-6423

SUPER 8 MOTELS
800-800-8000

VAGABOND INNS
800-522-1555

**TRAVELODGE/
THRIFTLODGE**
800-578-7878

WYNDHAM HOTELS
800-922-9222

SHERATON HOTELS
800-325-3535

MOTEL 6
800-440-6000
505-891-6161

MARRIOTT HOTEL
800-228-9290

IMA HOTELS
800-341-8000

CROWN STERLING SUITES
800-433-4600

RITZ-CARLTON
800-241-3333

RENAISSANCE HOTELS
800-468-3571
1-800-HOTEL

WESTIN HOTELS
800-228-3000

WOODFIN SUITES
800-237-8811

CANADIAN DIRECTORY OF PET-FRIENDLY LODGING

TRAVELING BETWEEN THE UNITED STATES AND CANADA

Dogs and cats

If you intend to travel into Canada with either a dog or a cat, your animal must have a certificate signed by a licensed veterinarian. This certificate must clearly describe the animal and validate that the animal has been vaccinated against rabies within the past 36 months. The certificate will also be needed for your animal's re-entry into the United States. Make certain that the rabies vaccination does not expire while you're touring Canada. Exemptions from this rule: Seeing eye dogs, puppies and kittens under three months, provided they are healthy at the time of importation.

Passports and proof of citizenship

United States citizens are not required to have a passport to enter Canada or return to the United States. Proof of citizenship in the form of a birth certificate, voter's certificate or baptismal certificate are normally all you'll need. If you're a naturalized citizen, carry your naturalization papers. U.S. resident aliens must have an Alien Registration Receipt Card. If minors are traveling with you, or on their own, they must present a notarized letter of consent signed by both parents or guardians in addition to providing proof of citizenship.

You should know that Canadian customs can stop a person traveling with a minor from entering Canada if customs has been advised that a divorced or separated parent is attempting to cross the border with a minor child without the written permission of the absent parent.

The Canadian GST

Beginning January 1, 1991, the Canadian government established a 7% Goods and Services Tax (GST) which is levied on most items sold and most services rendered. Non-Canadians may apply for a rebate on many items, among them short-term accommodations. There is a minimum rebate claim of $7 and evidence of purchase is required. Penalties apply and vary by province and territory. Be prepared and avoid penalties and delays.

Brochures explaining the GST and containing a rebate form are available in Canada at the land border as well as in airport duty-free shops, information centers, custom offices and many individual hotels. For additional information, write: Revenue Canada, Customs & Excise, Visitor's Rebate Program, Ottawa, ON, Canada K1A 1J5. Or call toll-free from Canada (800) 66VISIT. Outside Canada: (616) 991-3346.

Personal baggage may be brought into Canada on a temporary basis without payment of duties and taxes. Infrequently, a refundable security deposit may be required by customs at the time of your entry. All items brought into the country must accompany you on your departure.

Personal baggage can include clothing, personal effects, sporting goods, cars, vessels, aircraft, snowmobiles, cameras, food products and those items that would be considered appropriate for the purpose and length of your stay.

There are some limitations as follows: Tobacco products are limited to 50 cigars, 200 cigarettes and 400 grams (14 oz.) of tobacco per person. Alcoholic beverages are limited to 1.14 litres (40 oz.) of liquor or wine or 8.5 litres (300 oz.) of beer or ale, (the equivalent of 24 bottles/cans). A minimum stay of 24 hours is normally required when transporting liquor or tobacco products into Canada.

Liquor and tobacco products exceeding the allowable quantities are subject to federal duty and taxes as well as provincial liquor fees. In addition, you must be 18 or 19 (depending on the province or territory) to bring alcohol into Canada and be at least 16 to import tobacco and related products.

Gifts

With the exception of tobacco, alcoholic beverages and advertising matter, gifts taken into or mailed to Canada are allowed free entry as long as the value of the gift doesn't exceed $60 (Canadian currency). Gifts with a higher value are subject to duty and taxes on the excess amount.

Plants and fruits

House plants may be admitted into Canada. Other plants and plant material need a permit from Agriculture Canada and a state or federal phytosanitary certificate obtained from the plant health authority of origin.

Fresh fruits and vegetables not typically grown in Canada, i.e., tropical and subtropical items, may be imported. However, they may be inspected by a plant health inspector at the time of entry. Fresh fruit and vegetables commonly grown in Canada, may be refused entry, depending on the original and final destination of the fruits or vegetables. For further information, contact the Plant Health Division, Food Production and Inspection Branch, Agriculture Canada, Ottawa, ON, Canada K1A 0C6.

Employment of visitors

Without employment authorization prior to entry into Canada, employment of visitors is not permitted. In order to secure employment, a permit for a specific job for a specific period of time must be obtained from the Canadian Department of Manpower and Immigration. You will be denied entry into Canada if it is your intention to finance your visit by seeking a paying job.

U.S. customs regulations

Exemptions granted to returning residents of the United States include a $400 exemption if not used within the prior 30 days for residents who have been in Canada no less than 48 hours. Based on retail value, the exemptions apply only to goods acquired for personal or household use or as gifts - not intended for resale. Exemptions for a family can be combined, i.e. a family of four would be entitled to a $1,600 duty-free exemption on one declaration even if the articles declared by one member of the family exceeded that individual's $400 exemption.

Evidence of retail value will be needed. Keep all sales slips. The goods for which the exemption is claimed must be with you at the time of re-entry.

You can also send gifts to friends and relatives in the United States free of duty and taxes. However, the retail value of any one gift may not exceed more than $40. Only one gift per day can be received by any one recipient. Tobacco products, alcoholic beverages and perfume containing alcohol with a value of more than $5 retail are excluded from this provision. The package containing the gift must be marked "Unsolicited Gift" and include the contents and retail value on the outside of the package. These gifts are not considered part of your $400 exemption. You do not have to declare them upon your return to the United States.

If you qualify for the $400 exemption, you may include 100 cigars and 200 cigarettes duty free. Cigarettes may be subject to state or local tax. If you're over 21, you may include 1 litre in your $400 exemption from tax and duty. In all cases, state liquor laws are enforced by customs.

When your stay in Canada has been less than 48 hours, you may return with duty and tax free merchandise that has a maximum value of $25. This exemption must not include more than 50 cigarettes, 10 cigars, 150 millilitres of alcohol or 150 millilitres of perfume containing alcohol. Members of a family unit may NOT combine their purchases under this exemption. All goods must be declared.

National Park entrance fees

Daily or annual permits are available to Canadian National Parks that charge entrance fees. The annual permit is $30 per fiscal year and admits the private vehicle and all occupants to all national parks. The daily permit fee varies by park but averages $5 and is valid only on the date of purchase. Canadian citizens age 65 and over can obtain free annual permits by presenting proof of age and motor vehicle registration at any park entrance where fees are collected.

FOR YOUR INFORMATION:

Seat Belts: The use of seat belts is mandatory in all vehicles traveling in or through Canada.

Radar Detectors: The possession and use of radar detection devices is illegal in Manitoba, Newfoundland, Northwest Territories, Ontario, Prince Edward Island, Quebec and Yukon Territory.

Currency: Prices and admission fees are in Canadian dollars. It is financially advantageous to use Canadian currency when traveling in Canada. You can obtain the official exchange rate of U.S. funds at a bank in Canada or purchase traveler's checks in Canadian currency.

Legal Questions: Persons with felony convictions, DWI's or other offenses may be denied entry into Canada. For further info, contact Canada Customs, Communications Branch, Ottawa, ON, Canada K1A 0L5; (613) 957-0275.

ALBERTA

ATHABASCA

HILL SIDE MOTEL
48A Ave (T0G 0B0)
Tel: (403) 675-5111

BANFF

BEST WESTERN
453 Marten St
(T0L 0C0)
Tel: (800) 528-1234

CASTLE MOUNTAIN VILLAGE
Box 1655 (T0L 0C0)
Tel: (403) 762-3868

MOUNT ROYAL HOTEL
138 Banff Ave,
Box 550 (T0L 0C0)
Tel: (403) 762-3331

RED CARPET INN
425 Banff Ave,
Box 1800 (T0L 0C0)
Tel: (403) 762-4184

BARRHEAD

DALLAS HOTEL
5211 49th St,
Box 1690 (T0G 0E0)
Tel: (403) 674-2444

BASHAW

BASHAW MOTOR INN
Box 534 on Hwy 21
(T0B 0H0)
Tel: (403) 372-4024

BASSANO PRAIRIE SCHOONER INN
Box 489 (T0J 0B0)
Tel: (403) 641-3978

BLAIRMORE

CEDAR RIVERSIDE BEST CANADIAN MOTOR INN
11217 21st Ave
(T0K 0E0)
Tel: (403) 562-8851

BONNYVILLE

BONNYVILLE CENTER INN
5316A 50 Ave
(T9N 1Y8)
Tel: (403) 826-3336

BONNYVILLE NEIGHBOURHOOD INN
5011 66 St (T9N 2L9)
Tel: (403) 826-3309

SOUTHVIEW MOTEL
5401 50 Ave
(T9N 1Z7)
Tel: (403) 826-3321

BOWDEN

CALBODEERO MOTEL
Hwy 2, Box 158
(T0M 0K0)
Tel: (403) 224-3332

BOYLE

BOYLE HOTEL
5505-5501 Railway
Ave (T0A 0M0)
Tel: (403) 689-3777

BROOKS

DOUGLAS COUNTRY INN
Box 463 (T0J 0J0)
Tel: (403) 362-2873

PLAINSMAN MOTOR INN
1119 2nd St W
(T0J 0J0)
Tel: (403) 362-3407

SUPER 8 MOTEL
1240 Cassils Rd E,
Box 729 (T1R 1B6)
Rates: $59-65
Tel: (403) 362-8000
(800) 800-8000

CALGARY

AMBASSADOR MOTOR INN
802 16 Ave NE
(T2E 1K8)
Tel: (800) 661-1447

AVONDALE MOTOR INN
2231 Banff Trail NW
(T2M 4L2)
Tel: (403) 289-1921

BEST WESTERN AIRPORT INN
1947 18th Ave NE
(T2E 7T8)
Rates: $59-119
Tel: (403) 250-5015
(800) 528-1234

BLACKFOOT INN
5940 Blackfoot Trail SE
(T2H 2B5)
Tel: (800) 661-1151

BUDGET HOST MOTOR INN
4420 16 Ave NW
(T3B 0M4)
Tel: (800) 661-3772

CALGARY CHATEAU AIRPORT
2001 Airport Rd NE
(T2E 6Z8)
Tel: (800) 441-1414

CARRIAGE HOUSE
9030 MacLeod Trail S
(T2H 0M4)
Tel: (800) 661-9566

CEDAR RIDGE MOTEL
5307 MacLeod Trail
SW (T2H 0J3)
Tel: (403) 258-1064

CLARION HOTEL-AIRPORT
4804 Edmonton Trail
NE (T2E 3V2)
Tel: (800) 221-2222

DAYS INN
2369 Banff Trail NW
(T2M 4L2)
Rates: 45-69
Tel: (403) 289-5571
(800) 329-7466

DELTA BOW VALLEY
209 4th Ave SE
(T2G 0C6)
Tel: (800) 268-1133

ECONO LODGE
101 St & Trans
Canada Hwy
(T2M 4N3)
Tel: (800) 424-4777

ECONO LODGE
2440 16th Ave NW
(T2M 0M5)
Rates: $58-68
Tel: (403) 289-2561
(800) 424-4777

ECONO LODGE
5307 MacLeod Trail
S (T2H 0J3)
Rates: $45-69
Tel: (403) 258-1064
(800) 424-4777

ECONO LODGE
2231 Banff Trail
(T2M 4L2)
Rates: $49-63
Tel: (403) 289-1921
(800) 424-4777

FLAMINGO MOTOR HOTEL
7505 MacLeod Trail S
(T2H 0L8)
Tel: (403) 252-4401

HOWARD JOHN-SON
4510 S Macleod Trail
(T2G 0A4)
Tel: (403) 243-1700
(800) 446-4656

OLYMPIA MOTEL
5020 16th Ave NW
(T3B 0N3)
Tel: (403) 288-4461

POINTE INN
1808 19 St NE
(T2E 4Y3)
Tel: (800) 661-8164

PORT O'CALL INN
1935 McKnight Blvd
(T2E 6V4)
Tel: (800) 661-1161

**QUALITY INN
MOTEL VILLAGE**
2359 Banff Trail NW
(T2M 4L2)
Tel: (800) 661-4667

RAMADA HOTEL
708 8th Ave SW
(T2P 1H2)
Tel: (800) 661-8684

RAMADA INN
1250 McKinnon Dr
NE (T2E 7T7)
Tel: (800) 228-5151

**RAMADA
CROWCHILD INN**
5353 Crowchild Tr
NW (T3A 1W9)
Rates: $75-105
Tel: (403) 288-5353
(800) 272-6232

**RELAX INN-
CALGARY AIRPORT**
2750 Sunridge Blvd
NE (T1Y 3C2)
Tel: (800) 667-3529

**RELAX INN-
CALGARY SOUTH**
9206 McLeod Trail S
(T2J 0P5)
Tel: (800) 667-3529

**ROYAL PACIFIC
HOTEL**
1330 8 St SW
(T2R 1B6)
Tel: (800) 567-8877

SANDMAN HOTEL
888 7th Ave (T2P 3J3)
Tel: (800) 663-6900

SHERATON CAVALIER
2620 32nd Ave NE
(T1Y 6B8)
Tel: (800) 325-3535

STAMPEDER INN
3828 MacLeod Trail
S (T2G 2R2)
Tel: (403) 243-5531

SUPER 8 MOTEL
1904 Crowchild Tr
NW (T2M 3Y7)
Rates: $49-69
Tel: (403) 289-9211
(800) 800-8000

WESTIN HOTEL
320 4th Ave SW
(T2P 2S6)
Tel: (800) 228-3000

CANMORE

A-1 MOTEL
Box 339 (T0L 0M0)
Tel: (403) 678-5200

AKAI MOTEL
1715 Mountain Ave
(T0L 0M0)
Tel: (403) 678-4664

CEE-DER CHALETS
Box 525 (T0L 0M0)
Tel: (403) 678-5251

**VISCOUNT MOTOR
INN**
Box 790 (T0L 0M0)
Tel: (403) 678-5221

CARDSTON

TRAILS END MOTEL
37 8 Ave, Box 308
(T0K 0K0)
Tel: (403) 653-4481

CAROLINE

GATEWAY MOTEL
Box 699 (T0M 0M0)
Tel: (403) 722-3322

CARSTAIRS

**GOLDEN WEST
MOTOR INN**
Box 1060 (T0M 0N0)
Tel: (403) 337-3333

CLARESHOLM

BLUEBIRD MOTEL
Box 1888 (T0L 0T0)
Tel: (800) 661-4891

DAYSLAND

**DAYSLANDER
MOTEL**
Box 10 (T0B 1A0)
Tel: (403) 374-3645

DEVON

DEVON INN
Box 280 (T0C 1E0)
Tel: (403) 987-2511

DONALDA

DONALDA INN
Box 269 (T0B 1H0)
Tel: (403) 883-2201

DRAYTON VALLEY

**DRAYTON VALLEY
HOTEL**
Box 7590 (T0E 0M0)
Tel: (403) 542-5351

VALLEY MOTOR INN
5403 59 St (T0E 0M0)
Tel: (403) 542-4451

DRUMHELLER

**BEST WESTERN
JURASSIC INN**
1103 Hwy 9 S
(T0J 0Y0)
Rates: $63-108
Tel: (403) 823-7700
(800) 528-1234

HOO-DOO MOTEL
Box 310 (T0J 0Y0)
Tel: (403) 823-5662

EDMONTON

**ARGYLL PLAZA
HOTEL**
9933 63 Ave
(T6E 6C9)
Tel: (800) 661-6454

AURORA MOTEL
15145 111 Ave
(T5M 2R1)
Tel: (403) 489-2581

**BEST WESTERN CITY
CENTRE INN**
11310 - 109 St (T5G
2T7)
Rates: $62-89
Tel: (403) 479-2042
(800) 666-5026

**BEVERLY CREST-
TRAVELODGE**
3414 118 Ave
(T5W 0Z4)
Tel: (800) 255-3050

CHATEAU LOUIS
11727 Kingsway
(T5G 3A1)
Tel: (800) 661-9843

COMFORT INN
17510 100th Ave
(T5S 1S9)
Tel: (800) 221-2222

DAYS INN
10041 106 St (T5J
1G3)
Rates: $54-89
Tel: (403) 423-1925
(800) 329-7466

DERRICK MOTEL
3925 Calgary Trail N
(T6J 5H2)
Tel: (403) 434-1402

DOVER HOTEL
12704 120 St
(T5B 4P3)
Tel: (403) 471-2610

**EASTGLEN MOTOR
INN**
6918 118 Ave
(T5B 4P3)
Tel: (403) 471-2610

ECONO LODGE
4009 Calgary Trail N
(T6J 5H2)
Rates: $39-45
Tel: (403) 435-4877
(800) 424-4777

ECONO LODGE
10209 100th Ave (T5J
0A1)
Rates: $90-100
Tel: (403) 428-6442
(800) 424-4777

**EDMONTON
YELLOWHEAD HOTEL**
15004 Yellowhead
Trail
(T5V 1A1)
Tel: (403) 447-2400

**HOLIDAY INN-
CROWNE PLAZA**
101 St at Bellamy
Hill (T5J 1H7)
Tel: (800) 465-4329

**HOWARD
JOHNSON**
10010-104 St
(T5J 0Z1)
Tel: (403) 423-2450
(800) 446-4656

INN ON 7TH HOTEL
10001 107 St (T5J 1J1)
Tel: (800) 661-7327

KINGSWAY INNS
10812 Kingsway Ave
(T5G 0W9)
Tel: (403) 479-4266

LODGE MOTOR INN
18125 Stony Plain Rd
(T5S 1B1)
Tel: (403) 489-3321

MAYFIELD INN
16615 109 Ave
(T5P 4K8)
Tel: (403) 484-0821

NISKU INN
P. O. Box 9801
(T5J 2T2)
Tel: (800) 661-6966

OUTLOOK MOTEL
1850 Yellowhead
Trail NE (T6S 1B4)
Tel: (403) 467-7613

QUALITY INN
10209 100th Ave (T5J 0A1)
Tel: (800) 221-2222

RELAX TRAVELODGE-EDMONTON WEST
18320 Stony Plain
Rd (T5S 1A7)
Tel: (800) 661-9563

RENFORD INN ON WHYTE
10620 82 Ave
(T6E 2A7)
Tel: (800) 661-6498

RIVER VALLEY APARTMENTS
9710 105 St
(T5K 1A4)
Tel: (800) 661-7385

SAXONY MOTOR INN
15540 Stony Plain Rd
(T5P 3Z2)
Tel: (403) 484-3331

SOUTHBEND MOTEL
5130 Calgary Trail
Northbound
(T6H 2H4)
Tel: (403) 434-1418

SUPER BUDGET HOTEL
17817 Stony Plain
Rd (T5S 1B4)
Tel: (403) 483-0019

TOWER ON THE PARK
9715 110 St
(T5K 2M1)
Tel: (800) 661-6454

TRAILWAY MOTEL
3815 Calgary Trail
NW (T6J 5H2)
Tel: (403) 435-3863

WESTRIDGE MOTORLODGE
2161 Stony Plain Rd
(T5T 5X8)
Tel: (403) 447-452

WESTIN HOTEL
10135 100th St
(T5J 0N7)
Tel: (800) 228-3000

EDSON

EDSON MOTOR HOTEL
Box 7920 (T7E 1V9)
Tel: (403) 723-3381

ODYSSEY MOTOR INN
5601 2nd Ave
(T7E 1L7)
Tel: (403) 723-5505

SUPER 8 MOTEL
4300 2nd Ave, Box
6867 (T7E 1V2)
Rates: $59-65
Tel: (403) 723-2500
(800) 800-8000

FALHER

GERRY'S SUITE & HOTEL
Box 524 (T0H 1M0)
Tel: (403) 837-2513

FORT ASSINIBOINE

FORT MOTOR INN
Box 88 (T0G 1A0)
Tel: (403) 584-3883

FORT MCLEOD

RED COAT INN
Box 516 (T0L 0Z0)
Tel: (403) 553-4434

FORT MCMURRAY

MACKENZIE PARK INN
424 Gregoire Dr
(T9H 3R2)
Tel: (800) 582-3273

MCMURRAY MOTOR INN
9906 Saunderson
Ave (T9H 1R9)
Tel: (403) 743-1700

RUSTY'S MOTOR INN
385 Gregoire Dr
(T9H 4K7)
Tel: (403) 791-4646

FOX CREEK

GUEST HOUSE
Box 470 (T0H 1P0)
Tel: (403) 622-3821

GRAND CENTRE

BEEJAY MOTOR INN
P. O. Box 245
(T0A 1T0)
Tel: (403) 495-4466

EL LOBO MOTEL
Box 1050 (T0A 1T0)
Tel: (403) 594-7521

IMPERIAL MOTOR INN
Hwy 28 N, Box 1830
(T0A 1T0)
Tel: (403) 594-7133

KING'S COURT MOTEL
Hwy 28, Box 1830
(T0A 1T0)
Tel: (403) 594-4408

LAKELAND INN
Box 1050 (T0A 1T0)
Tel: (403) 594-3311

GRAND PRAIRIE

ALPINE MOTOR INN
10901 100 Ave
(T8V 3J9)
Tel: (403) 532-1680

SUPER 8 MOTEL
10050 116 Ave
(T8V 4K5)
Rates: $69-89
Tel: (403) 532-8288
(800) 800-8000

GRIMSHAW

DEE-JAY MOTEL
Box 236 (T0H 1W0)
Tel: (403) 332-4298

MILE ZERO MOTOR INN
Box 263 (T0H 1W0)
Tel: (403) 332-4606

HANNA

WEST VIEW MOTEL
P. O. Box 1107
(T0J 1P0)
Tel: (403) 854-3232

HIGH PRAIRIE

RAVEN MOTOR INNS
Box 883 (T0G 1E0)
Tel: (403) 523-3350

HINTON

ALPINE PARK MOTOR INN & RV PARK
Hwy 16, P. O. Box
2058 (T0E 1C0)
Tel: (403) 865-5099

PINES MOTEL
Box 6296 (T7X 1X6)
Tel: (403) 865-2624

JASPER

AMETHYST LODGE
P. O. Box 1200
(T0E 1E0)
Tel: (800) 661-9935

LOBSTICK LODGE
P. O. Box 1200
(T0E 1E0)
Tel: (800) 661-9317

MARMOT LODGE
P. O. Box 687
(T0E 1E0)
Tel: (800) 661-6521

OVERLANDER COUNTRY INN
Box 1552 (T0E 1E0)
Tel: (403) 866-3790

LAKE LOUISE

CHATEAU LAKE LOUISE
(T0L 1E0)
Tel: (800) 828-7447

LAKE LOUISE INN
P. O. Box 209
(T0L 1E0)
Tel: (800) 661-9237

LEDUC

RELAX INN INT'L AIRPORT
5705 50th St,
Box 3538 (T9E 6M3)
Tel: (800) 667-3529

LETHBRIDGE

CHINOOK MOTEL
1245 Mayor Magrath
Dr (T1K 2B1)
Tel: (403) 329-0555

COUNTRY LODGE
2210 7 Ave S
(T1J 1M7)
Tel: (800) 661-8091

DAYS INN
100 3rd Ave S
(T1J 4L2)
Rates: $53-105
Tel: (403) 327-6000

EL RANCHO MOTOR HOTEL
526 Mayor Magrath
Dr (T1J 3M2)
Tel: (403) 321-5701

PARK N' SLEEP
1125 Mayor Magrath
Dr (T1K 2P8)
Tel: (800) 661-8091

PEPPER TREE INN
1142 Mayor Magrath
Dr (T1K 2P8)
Tel: (403) 328-4436

SUPER 8 MOTEL
2210 - 7th Ave S
(T1J 1M7)
Rates: $51-65
Tel: (403) 329-0100
(800) 800-8000

LLOYDMINSTER

LODGE MOTEL
6301 44 St (T9V 2G6)
Tel: (403) 875-1919

TROPICAL INN
5621 44 St (T9V 0B2)
Tel: (403) 875-7000

WEST HARVEST INN
5620 44 St (T9V 0B6)
Tel: (403) 875-6113

MANNVILLE

MANNVILLE MOTEL
P. O. Box 538
(T0B 2W0)
Tel: (403) 763-3800

MEDICINE HAT

BEST WESTERN INN
722 Redcliff Dr
(T1A 5E3)
Tel: (800) 528-1234

CIRCLE T LODGE
1100 Redcliff Dr SW
(T1A 5E5)
Tel: (800) 255-3050

IMPERIAL MOTOR INN
3282 13th Ave SE
(T1B 1H8)
Tel: (403) 527-8811

MEDICINE HAT INN
530 4th St SE
(T1A 0K8)
Tel: (403) 526-1313

MEDICINE HAT LODGE
1051 Ross Glen Dr
SE (T1B 3T8)
Tel: (800) 661-8095

QUALITY INN
954 7th St SW
(T1A 7R7)
Tel: (800) 221-2222

SUPER 8 MOTEL
1280 Trans-Canada
Way (T1B 1J5)
Rates: $46-67
Tel: (403) 528-8888
(800) 800-8000

MILK RIVER

MILK RIVER INN
104 Main St, Box 116
(T0K 1M0)
Tel: (403) 647-3818

SOUTHGATE INN
Box 66 (T0K 1M0)
Tel: (403) 647-3733

MILLET

PIPESTONE MOTEL
Box 729 (T0C 1Z0)
Tel: (403) 387-4000

MORLEY

NAKODA LODGE
P. O. Box 149
(T0L 1N0)
Tel: (403) 881-3949

NORDEGG

NORDEGG RESORT LODGE
General Delivery
(T0M 2H0)
Tel: (403) 721-3757

OLDS

BEST WESTERN OF OLDS
Hwy 27 & Hwy 2A
(T4H 1P7)
Rates: $55-130
Tel: (403) 556-5900
(800) 528-1234

PATRICIA

PATRICIA HOTEL
Box 24 (T0J 2K0)
Tel: (403) 378-4647

PEACE RIVER

THE CRESCENT MOTEL
9810 98th St
(T8S 1J3)
Tel: (403) 624-2586

PINCHER CREEK

BLUE MOUNTAIN MOTEL
Box 2416 (T0K 1W0)
Tel: (403) 627-5335

SUPER 8 MOTEL
1307 Freebairn Ave,
Box 1628 (T0K 1W0)
Rates: $53-67
Tel: (403) 627-5671
(800) 800-8000

PROVOST

GREENHEAD MOTEL
Box 324 (T0B 3S0)
Tel: (403) 753-2201

HORIZON MOTEL
Hwy 13 E, Box 697
(T0B 3S0)
Tel: (403) 753-2285

RED DEER

ALADDIN MOTOR INN
7444 Gaetz Ave
(T4P 1X7)
Tel: (403) 343-2711

FRIENDSHIP INN
4124 Gaetz Ave.
(T4N 3Z2)
Rates: $43-58
Tel: (403) 342-6969
(800) 453-4511

GREAT WEST INN
6500 67 St (T4P 1A2)
Tel: (800) 661-4961

HOLIDAY HOUSE MOTEL
RR 4, Hwy 2 S
(T4N 5E4)
Tel: (403) 346-4188

NORTH HILL INN
7150 Gaetz Ave
(T4N 6A5)
Tel: (403) 343-8800

RED DEER LODGE
4311-49th Ave
(T4N 5Y7)
Tel: (403) 346-8841

SLEEPY'S INN SOUTH
2807 Gaetz Ave
(T4R 1H1)
Tel: (403) 346-2011

**TRAVELODGE
HOTEL**
2807 50 Ave (T4R
1H6)
Rates: $50-90
Tel: (403) 346-2011
(800) 578-7878

REDCLIFF

PALS MOTEL
1210 Highway Ave
(T0J 2P0)
Tel: (403) 548-7455

ROCKY MOUNTAIN HOUSE

ALPINE MOTEL
Hwy 11, Box 148
(T0M 1T0)
Tel: (403) 845-3325

VOYAGEUR MOTEL
Box 1376 (T0M 1T0)
Tel: (403) 845-3381

RYCROFT

**LEPRECHAUN
MOTOR LODGE**
4753 48th Ave
(T0H 3A0)
Tel: (403) 765-9910

ST. MICHAEL

ST. MICHAEL HOTEL
Box 87 (T0B 4B0)
Tel: (403) 896-2363

ST. PAUL

GALAXY MOTEL
Box 1265 (T0A 3A0)
Tel: (403) 645-4441

**WOODLAND
MOTOR INN**
4417 50 Ave
(T0A 3A3)
Tel: (403) 645-2245

SANGUDO

ARCADIAN MOTEL
Box 88 (T0E 2A0)
Tel: (403) 785-2277

SHERWOOD PARK

FRANKLIN'S INN
2016 Sherwood Dr
(T8A 3X3)
Tel: (403) 467-1234

SPRUCE GROVE

GROVE MOTOR INN
Box 4175 (T7X 3B4)
Tel: (403) 962-5000

STONY PLAIN

STONY MOTOR INN
4801 48 St, Box 1799
(T0E 2G0)
Tel: (403) 963-3444

STRATHMORE

**BEST WESTERN
STRATHMORE INN**
550 Hwy 1
(T1P 1M6)
Rates: $49-87
Tel: (403) 934-5777
(800) 528-1234

**WHEATLAND
COUNTY INN**
960 Westridge Rd
(T1P 1H8)
Tel: (403) 934-4000

SUNDEE

**PARKWOOD
MOTOR INN**
307 Main Ave W,
Box 11
(T0M 1X0)
Tel: (403) 638-4424

SYLVAN LAKE

**RACOON LODGE
MOTEL**
4515 Lakeshore Dr
(T0M 1Z0)
Tel: (403) 887-5423

TABER

HERITAGE INN
4830 46 Ave, Box 100
(T0K 2G0)
Tel: (403) 223-4424

TABER MOTEL
Box 2496 (T0K 2G0)
Tel: (403) 223-4411

VALLEYVIEW

**RAVEN MOTOR
INNS**
Box 816 (T0H 2N0)
Tel: (403) 524-3383

VEGREVILLE

VISTA MOTEL
4797 50th Ave
(T0B 4L0)
Tel: (403) 632-3288

VIKING

**CALEDONIA
MOTOR INN**
Hwys 36 & 14
(T0B 4N0)
Tel: (403) 336-2400

WAINWRIGHT

BISON MOTEL
601 14 Ave, Box 2047
(T0B 4P0)
Tel: (403) 842-4416

**BUFFALO SPRINGS
MOTOR INN**
Box 1646 (T0B 4P0)
Tel: (403) 842-3371

**PLAINS WEST
MOTOR INN**
Box 1680 (T0B 4P0)
Tel: (403) 842-4436

WANHAM

**GRIZZLY BEAR
MOTOR INN**
Box 191 (T0H 3P0)
Tel: (403) 694-3888

WASKATENAU

**WASKATENAU
MOTEL**
Box 304 (T0A 3P0)
Tel: (403) 358-2801

WESTLOCK

EAST GLEN MOTEL
Hwy 44, Box 1019
(T0G 2L0)
Tel: (403) 349-3138

WESTLOCK INN
Box 309 (T0G 2L0)
Tel: (403) 349-4483

WETASKIWIN

**WETASKIWIN
MOTEL**
4705 56 St (T9A 1V6)
Tel: (403) 352-7141

WHITECOURT

RENFORD INN
Box 1616 (T7S 1P4)
Tel: (800) 661-6498

ROYAL OAK INN
P. O. Box 1628
(T7S 1P4)
Tel: (403) 778-4443

SMITTY'S INN
P. O. Box 570
(T7S 1N6)
Tel: (403) 778-5055

WHITE-KAPS MOTEL
Box 1586 (T7S 1P4)
Tel: (403) 778-2246

BRITISH COLUMBIA

ABBOTSFORD

BEST WESTERN REGENCY INN
32080 Marshall Rd
(V2T 1A1)
Tel: (800) 528-1234

ECONO LODGE
32111 Marshall Rd
(V2T 1A3)
Rates: $45-69
Tel: (604) 859-3171
(800) 424-4777

FRASER VALLEY INN
33790 Essendene Ave
(V2S 2H2)
Tel: (604) 853-3307

MOTEL RIO
31399 Livington Ave
(V2S 1M3)
Tel: (604) 859-9673

QUALITY INN
1881 Sumas Way
(V2S 4L5)
Tel: (800) 221-2222

AGASSIZ

PATHFINDER MOTEL & RV PARK
6110 Lougheed Hwy
7 (V0M 1A0)
Tel: (603) 796-9345

AINSWORTH HOT SPRINGS

AINSWORTH MOTEL
Hwy 31, Box 1276
(V0G 1A0)
Tel: (604) 229-4711

MERMAID LODGE & MOTEL
North St, Box 1333
(V0G 1A0)
Tel: (604) 229-4969

WOODBURY RESORT & MARINA
Hwy 31, Box 1262
(V0G 1A0)
Tel: (604) 353-7717

ALBERT BAY

BAYSIDE INN HOTEL
Box 492, 81 Fir St
(V0N 1A0)
Tel: (604) 974-5857

ANAHIM LAKE

BAXTER'S MOTOR INN
10 Anahim St,
General Delivery
(V0L 1C0)
Tel: (604) 742-3200

AVOLA

AVOLA MOUNTAIN MOTEL
Yellowhead Hwy 5,
Box 35 (V0E 1C0)
Tel: (604) 678-5340

BALFOUR

BALFOUR BEACH INN & MOTEL
Hwy 3A, Box 5
(V0G 1C0)
Tel: (604) 229-4235

SUNNY SLOPE RESORT
General Delivery
(V0G 1C0)
Tel: (604) 229-4777

BAMFIELD

BAMFIELD TRAILS MOTEL
Frigape Rd, Box 7
(V0R 1B0)
Tel: (604) 728-3231

BARRIERE

MONTE CARLO MOTEL
380 Hwy 5, Box 941
(V0E 1E0)
Tel: (604) 672-9676

Y-5 MOTEL
Hwy 5, Box 628
(V0E 1E0)
Tel: (604) 672-9739

BEAR LAKE

GRIZZLY INN MOTEL
Hart Lake Rd, Box 1838
(V0J 3G0)
Tel: (604) 972-4436

BEAVERDELL

BEAVERDELL HOTEL
Hwy 33, Box 40
(V0H 1A0)
Tel: (604) 484-5513

BELLA COOLA

BAY MOTOR HOTEL
Hwy 20,
Hagensborg,
c/o Box 216
(V0T 1C0)
Tel: (604) 982-2212

BELLA COOLA MOTEL
Clayton St, Box 188
(V0T 1C0)
Tel: (604) 799-5323

BLUE RIVER

BLUE RIVER MOTEL
Spruce St, Box 48
(V0E 1J0)
Tel: (604) 673-8387

SANDMAN INN
Hwy 5, Box 31 (V0E 1J0)
Tel: (800) 726-3626

VENTURE LODGE
Yellowhead Hwy 5,
Box 37 (V0E 1J0)
Tel: (604) 673-8384

BOSTON BAR

CANYON ALPINE MOTEL
50530 Trans Canada Hwy,
Box 395 (V0K 1C0)
Tel: (604) 867-9295

CHARLES HOTEL
Box 190 (V0K 1C0)
Tel: (604) 867-9221

WHITEWATER MOTEL
50885 Trans Canada Hwy,
Box 352 (V0K 1C0)
Tel: (604) 867-8831

BOSWELL

HEIDELBERG INN
12862 Hwy 3A, RR 1
(V0B 1A0)
Tel: (604) 223-8263

HOLBROOK FALLS MOTEL
10135 Hwy 3A,
Box 7
(V0B 1A0)
Tel: (604) 223-8427

MTN SHORES RESORT
Hwy 3A, RR 1,
Site 9,
Comp 6 (V0B 1A0)
Tel: (604) 223-8258

BOWSER

MAPLEGUARD RESORT MOTEL
151 Burne Rd, Deep Bay,
c/o RR 1, Site 160
(V0R 1G0)
Tel: (604) 757-9211

SHADY SHORES FISHING RESORT
6695 Island Hwy,
Box 18,
Site 118 (V0R 1G0)
Tel: (604) 757-8595

BRENTWOOD BAY

BRENTWOOD INN RESORT
7172 Brentwood Dr,
Box 396 (V0S 1A0)
Tel: (604) 652-2912

BRIDAL FALLS

BRIDAL FALLS MOTEL
53680 Bridal Falls Rd,
Rosedale (V0X 1X0)
Tel: (604) 794-7710

BURNABY

HOLIDAY INN-METROTOWN
4405 Central Blvd
(V5H 4M3)
Tel: (800) 465-4395

METRO CENTRE HOTEL
4561 Kingsway
(V5H 2B3)
Tel: (604) 433-0551

BURNS LAKE

BURNS LAKE MOTOR INN
Hwy 16 E (V0J 1E0)
Tel: (800) 663-2968

LAKELAND HOTEL
329 Yellowhead 16
(V0J 1E0)
Tel: (800) 663-2969

CACHE CREEK

BONAPARTE MOTEL
Hwy 97 N, Box 487
(V0K 1H0)
Tel: (604) 457-9693

CACHE CREEK MOTOR INN
Box 699 (V0K 1H0)
Tel: (800) 663-4900

DESERT MOTEL
1069 S Trans Canada
Hwy, P. O. Box 339
(V0K 1H0)
Tel: (800) 663-0212

SANDMAN INN
Hwy 1, Box 278
(V0K 1H0)
Tel: (800) 726-3626

SLUMBER LODGE
1085 Trans Canada Hwy,
Box 158 (V0K 1H0)
Tel: (800) 663-2831

TUMBLEWEED MOTEL
Box 287, 1221 Quartz
Rd(V0K 1H0)
Tel: (604) 457-6522

CAMPBELL RIVER

ABOVE TIDE MOTEL
361 Island Hwy
(V9W 2B5)
Tel: (604) 286-6231

ANCHOR INN
261 Island Hwy
(V9W 2B3)
Tel: (800) 663-7227

AUSTRIAN CHALET VILLAGE
462 S Island Hwy
(V9W 1A5)
Tel: (604) 923-4231

BACHMAIR'S BAVARIAN-HOTEL
492 S Island Hwy
(V9W 1A5)
Tel: (604) 923-2848

BENNETT'S POINT RESORT & MOTEL
4383 S Island Hwy,
RR 1,Site 113
(V9W 3S4)
Tel: (604) 923-4281

BEST WESTERN AUSTRIAN CHALET
462 South Island
Hwy (V9W 1A5)
Rates: $69-149
Tel: (250) 923-4231
(800) 528-1234

BIG ROCK MOTEL
1020 S Island Hwy
(V9W 1B3)
Tel: (604) 923-4211

COAST DISCOVERY INN
975 Shoppers Row
(V9W 2C5)
Tel: (800) 663-1144

EDGEWATER MOTEL
4073 S Island Hwy,
RR 1 (V9W 3S4)
Tel: (604) 923-5421

ELK FALLS FISHING RESORT MOTEL
2320 Campbell River
Rd (V9W 4N7)
Tel: (604) 286-6796

OCEAN FRONT MOTEL
934 S Island Hwy
(V9W 1A8)
Tel: (604) 923-6409

RUSTIC MOTEL
2140 N Island Hwy
(V9W 2G7)
Tel: (604) 286-6295

SEASIDE MOTEL
87 S Island Hwy
(V9W 1A2)
Tel: (604) 287-3343

SUPER 8 MOTEL
340 S Island Hwy
(V9W 1A5)
Tel: (800) 800-8000

CASTLEGAR

COZY PINES MOTEL
2100 Crestview Cres
(V1N 3B3)
Tel: (604) 365-5613

FIRESIDE MOTOR INN
1810 8th Ave (V1N 2Y2)
Tel: (604) 365-2128

FLAMINGO MOTEL
1660 Columbia Ave
(V1N 1H9)
Tel: (604) 365-7978

SANDMAN INN
1944 Columbia Ave
(V1N 2W7)
Tel: (800) 726-3626

TWIN RIVERS MOTEL
1485 Columbia Ave
(V1N 1H8)
Tel: (604) 365-6900

CHASE

CHASE COUNTRY INN & RV PARK
807 Cedar Ave,
Box 1031 (V0E 1M0)
Tel: (604) 679-3333

OVERLANDER MOTEL
181 Shuswap Ave,
Box 92 (V0E 1M0)
Tel: (604) 679-8633

ST. IVES ON SHUSWAP
Anglemont,
c/o RR 1, Site 30-11
(V0E 1M0)
Tel: (604) 942-0455

CHEMAINUS

HORSESHOE BAY INN
9576 Chemainuis Rd,
Box 359 (V0R 1K0)
Tel: (604) 246-3425

CHETWYND COUNTRY SQUIRE MOTOR INN
Box 146 (V0C 1J0)
Tel: (800) 668-3101

PINECONE MOTOR INN
5224 53rd Ave,
Box 686 (V0C 1J0)
Tel: (800) 663-8082

STAGECOACH INN
5413 S Access Rd,
Box 927 (V0C 1J0)
Tel: (800) 663-2744

WINDREM MOTEL
5201 S Access Rd,
Box 604 (V0C 1J0)
Tel: (604) 788-2460

CHILLIWACK

BEST WESTERN RAINBOW INN
43971 Industrial Way
(V2R 3A4)
Rates: $74-99
Tel: (604) 795-3828
(800) 665-1030

CHILLIWACK MOTOR INN
8120 Young Rd S
(V2P 6H3)
Tel: (604) 792-8501

COUNTRY INNS MOTOR HOTEL
45944 Yale Rd W (V2P 2M3)
Tel: (604) 792-0661

HOLIDAY INN
45920 1st Ave (V2P 7K1)
Tel: (604) 795-4788

JOURNEY'S END MOTEL
45405 Luckakuck Way (V0X 2E0)
Tel: (604) 858-0636

MALIBU MOTEL
46607 Yale Rd (V2P 2R6)
Tel: (604) 792-9375

PARKWOOD MOTOR HOTEL
8600 Young Rd (V2P 4P4)
Tel: (604) 795-9155

RAINBOW MOTEL
45620 Yale Rd W (V2P 2N2)
Tel: (604) 792-6412

TRAVELODGE
45466 Yale Rd W (V2R 1A3)
Rates: $60-145
Tel: (604) 792-4240
(800) 578-7878

CHRISTINA LAKE

CHRISTINA LAKE MOTOR INN
19 Westlake Dr, Box 510 (V0H 1E0)
Tel: (604) 447-9421

LAKEVIEW MOTEL
1658 Hwy 3, Box 296 (V0H 1E0)
Tel: (604) 447-9358

NEW HORIZON MOTEL
2037 Hwy 3, Box 1094 (V0H 1E0)
Tel: (604) 447-9312

TOTEM RESORT & TRAILER PARK
61 Kingsley Rd, Box 6 (V0H 1E0)
Tel: (604) 447-9322

CLEARBROOK

ALPINE MOTOR INN
32111 Marshall Rd (V2T 1A3)
Tel: (604) 859-3171

COUNTRY INN MOTOR HOTEL
2073 Clearbrook Rd (V2T 2X1)
Tel: (800) 665-7252

CLEARWATER

CLEARWATER COUNTRY INN & RV PARK
449 Yellowhead Hwy 5,RR 1, Box 1626 (V0E 1N0)
Tel: (604) 674-3121

DUTCH LAKE MOTEL
333 Roy Rd, Box 5116,RR 2 (V0E 1N0)
Tel: (604) 674-3325

DUTCH LAKE RESORT
RR 2, Box 2160 (V0E 1N0)
Tel: (604) 674-3351

JASPER WAY INN MOTEL
57 E Old N Thompson Hwy, Box 2127 (V0E 1N0)
Tel: (604) 674-3345

SYLVAN COURT MOTEL
734 Clearwater Village Rd, Box 1104 (V0E 1N0)
Tel: (604) 674-2334

WELLS GRAY INN
Box 280 (V0E 1N0)
Tel: (604) 674-2214

CLINTON

THE CARIBOO LODGE
Box 450 (V0K 1K0)
Tel: (604) 459-7992

NOMAD MOTEL
Cariboo Hwy, Box 142 (V0K 1K0)
Tel: (604) 459-2214

ROUND UP MOTEL
1214 Kelly Lake Rd, Box 310 (V0K 1K0)
Tel: (604) 459-2226

CLOVERDALE

THE CLYDESDALE INN
17630 56th Ave (V3S 1C5)
Tel: (604) 576-2826

COAL RIVER

SUMMIT LAKE LODGE
Mile 392, Alaska Hwy (V1G 4J8)
Tel: (604) 232-5531

COMOX

PORT AUGUSTA RESORT MOTEL
2082 Comox Ave (V9N 4A7)
Tel: (604) 339-2277

COQUITLAM

COQUITLAM SLUMBER LODGE
730 Clarke Rd (V3J 3Y1)
Tel: (800) 667-5955

DAYS INN COQUITLAM
725 Brunette Ave (V3K 1C3)
Tel: (800) 325-2525

CORTES ISLAND

CORTES ISLAND MOTEL
Manson's Landing, Box 76 (V0P 1K0)
Tel: (604) 935-6363

COURTENAY

ANCO MOTEL
1885 Cliffe Ave (V9N 2K9)
Tel: (604) 334-2451

ARBUTUS PACIFIC HOTEL
275 8th St (V9N 1N4)
Tel: (800) 663-2146

COLLINGWOOD INN
1675 Cliffe Ave (V9N 2K6)
Tel: (800) 663-7922

THE ECONOMY INN
2605 Island Hwy (V9N 2L8)
Tel: (604) 334-4491

KINGFISHER BEACH RESORT & RV PARK
4330 S Island Hwy, RR 6, Site 672 (V9N 8H9)
Tel: (604) 338-1323

RIVER HEIGHTS MOTEL
1820 Cliffe Ave (V9N 2K8)
Tel: (604) 338-8932

SLEEPY HOLLOW INN
1190 Cliffe Ave (V9N 2K1)
Tel: (604) 334-4476

THE WASHINGTON INN
1001 Ryan Rd (V9N 3R6)
Tel: (604) 338-5441

COWICHAN BAY

INN AT THE WATER RESORT
1681 Botwood Lane, Box 58 (V0R 1N0)
Tel: (604) 748-6222

CRANBROOK

ALMO COURT MOTEL
Van Horne & Second St S (V1C 1C3)
Tel: (604) 426-3213

BEST WESTERN COACH HOUSE MOTOR INN
1417 Cranbrook St N (V1C 3S7)
Tel: (800) 528-1234

CRANBROOK MOTOR INN
621 Cranbrook St N (V1C 3R8)
Tel: (604) 426-8231

G.E. MOTELS
58 Cobham Ave W (V1C 4G4)
Tel: (604) 426-3516

HERITAGE ESTATE MOTEL
362 Van Horne St SW (V1C 1Z5)
Tel: (604) 426-3862

HOSPITALITY LODGE
1209 Cranbrook St N (V1C 3S6)
Tel: (604) 489-4124

INN OF THE SOUTH
803 Cranbrook St N (V1C 3S2)
Tel: (800) 663-2708

NOMAD MOTEL
910 Cranbrook St N (V1C 3S3)
Tel: (800) 663-7417

PONDEROSA MOTEL
590 Van Horne St S (V1C 4H3)
Tel: (604) 426-6114

SANDMAN INN
405 Cranbrok St N (V1C 3R7)
Tel: (800) 726-3626

STARLIGHT MOTEL
1111 Cranbrook St (V1C 3S4)
Tel: (800) 663-7417

TRAVELLERS MOTEL
2000 Cranbrook St (V1C 3T1)
Tel: (604) 426-4208

CRESTON

ALBERTA MOTEL
RR 2, Site 27, Box 13 (V0B 1G0)
Tel: (604) 428-4418

BAVARIAN ORCHARD MOTEL
3111 Hwy 3, Box 1364 (V0B 1G0)
Tel: (604) 428-9935

BUDGET HOST SUNSET MOTEL
2705 Hwy 3, Box 2186 (V0B 1G0)
Tel: (800) 663-7082

CITY CENTRE MOTEL
220 15th Ave N, Box 40 (V0B 1G0)
Tel: (604) 428-2257

CRESTON VALLEY MOTEL
1809 Canyon St, Box 1699 (V0B 1G0)
Tel: (604) 428-9823

DOWNTOWNER MOTOR INN
1218 Canyon St, Box 490 (V0B 1G0)
Tel: (800) 665-9904

HACIENDA INN
800 North West Blvd, Box 2070 (V0B 1G0)
Tel: (800) 567-2215

SIESTA MOTEL
320 20th Ave S, Box 1188 (V0B 1G0)
Tel: (604) 428-2640

SKIMMER HORN INN
2711 Hwy 3 E, Box 262 (V0B 1G0)
Tel: (800) 663-7082

STARLITE MOTEL
RR 1, Site 12, Box 10 (V0B 1G0)
Tel: (604) 428-9921

VALLEY VIEW MOTEL
216 Valleyview, Box 3 (V0B 1G0)
Tel: (604) 428-2336

CROFTON

CROFT INN MOTEL
1568 Chaplin St, Box 372 (V0R 1R0)
Tel: (604) 246-9222

TWIN GABLES MOTEL
1508 Joan Ave, Box 39 (V0R 1R0)
Tel: (604) 246-3112

DAWSON CREEK

CEDAR LODGE MOTEL
801 110th Ave (V1G 2V9)
Tel: (604) 782-8531

CENTRAL MOTEL
1301 101 Alaska Ave (V1G 1Z4)
Tel: (604) 782-8525

DAWSON CREEK SLUMBER LODGE
10600 8th St (V1G 3R3)
Tel: (604) 782-8136

DAWSON CREEK TRAVELLERS INN
800 112th Ave (V1G 2Y2)
Tel: (604) 782-5551

ECONO LODGE
832 103rd Ave (V1G 2E8)
Tel: (604) 782-9181

GEORGE DAWSON INN
11705 8th St (V1G 4N9)
Tel: (604) 782-9151

NORTH COUNTRY INN
800 120th Ave (V1G 4P9)
Tel: (604) 782-9404

PEACE VILLA MOTEL
1641 Alaska Ave (V1G 1Z9)
Tel: (604) 782-8175

TRAIL MOTEL
1748 Alaska Ave, Box 667 (V1G 4H7)
Tel: (800) 663-2749

VOYAGEUR MOTEL
801 111 Ave (V1G 2Z1)
Tel: (604) 782-1020

DEASE LAKE

NORTHWAY MOTOR INN
Boulder Ave, General Delivery (V0C 1L0)
Tel: (604) 771-5341

DELTA

BEST WESTERN TSAWWASSEN INN
1665 56th St (V4L 2B2)
Tel: (604) 943-8221

DELTA TOWN & COUNTRY INN
6005 Hwy 17 (V4K 4E2)
Tel: (604) 946-4404

TSAWWASSEN MOTEL
6574 Ladner Trunk Rd, Box 69 (V4K 3N5)
Tel: (604) 946-4288

DUNCAN

BEST WESTERN COWICHAN VALLEY INN
6464 Trans Canada Hwy (V9L 3W8)
Tel: (800) 528-1234

SILVER BRIDGE INN
140 Trans Canada Hwy (V9L 3P7)
Tel: (604) 748-4311

THE VILLAGE GREEN INN
141 Trans Canada Hwy (V9L 3P8)
Tel: (604) 746-5126

YORK TOWN INN
5325 Trans Canada Hwy, Box 395 (V9L 3X5)
Tel: (604) 748-0331

ELKFORD

ELKFORD MOTOR INN
Box 1060 (V0B 1H0)
Tel: (604) 865-2211

ENDERBY

CEDAR PARK INN
6376 Hwy 97A (V0E 1V0)
Tel: (604) 838-7895

FORTUNES LANDING MOTOR INN
Hwy 97 N, Box 168
(V0E 1V0)
Tel: (604) 838-6825

PARK MOTEL
Hwy 97, RR 1, Site 15A,Comp 9
(V0E 1V0)
Tel: (604) 838-7895

FAIRMONT HOT SPRINGS

FAIRMONT MOUNTAIN BUNGALOWS
Hwy 93/95, Box 100
(V0B 1L0)
Tel: (604) 345-6365

SPRUCE GROVE RESORT
Hwy 93/95, Box 118
(V0B 1L0)
Tel: (604) 345-6561

FALKLAND

THE HIGHLAND MOTEL
Adelphi St, Box 26
(V0E 1W0)
Tel: (604) 379-2249

FANNY BAY

PACIFIC VILLAGE RESORT AND MARINA
Island Hwy, RR 1
(V0R 1W0)
Tel: (604) 335-2333

FERNIE

CEDAR LODGE
Hwy 3, Box 1477
(V0B 1M0)
Tel: (604) 423-4622

MOUNTAIN SHADOWS INN
RR 1 (V0B 1M0)
Tel: (604) 423-7703

SNOW VALLEY MOTEL& RV PARK
1043 7th Ave, Box 1530
(V0B 1M0)
Tel: (604) 423-4421

3 SISTERS MOTEL
441 Hwy 3, Box 1349
(V0B 1M0)
Tel: (604) 423-4438

SUPER 8 MOTEL
Hwy # 3 (V0B 1M1)
Rates: $60-78
Tel: (604) 423-6788
(800) 800-8000

FIELD

WEST LOUISE LODGE
c/o Box 9,
Lake Louise, AB
(T0L 1E0)
Tel: (604) 343-6311

FORT NELSON

COACHOUSE INN
4711 50th Ave S,
Box 27 (V0E 1R0)
Tel: (604) 774-3911

PROVINCIAL MOTEL
Mile 300, Box 690
(V0C 1R0)
Tel: (800) 663-1144

SHANNON MOTEL
Mile 300, Alaska Hwy,
Box 480 (V0C 1R0)
Tel: (604) 774-6000

FORT ST. JAMES

CHUNDOO MOTOR INN
290 E Stuart Dr,
Box 130 (V0J 1P0)
Tel: (604) 996-8216

PITKA BAY RESORT
Pitka Bay Rd, Box 242
(V0J 1P0)
Tel: (604) 996-8585

FORT ST. JOHN

CEDAR LODGE MOTOR INN
9824 99th Ave
(V1J 5A5)
Tel: (604) 785-8107

THE COACHMAN INN
8540 Alaska Rd
(V1T 5L6)
Tel: (604) 787-0651

FORT ST. JOHN MOTOR INN
10707 102nd St
(V1J 2E8)
Tel: (604) 787-0411

FOUR SEASONS MOTOR INN
9810 100th St
(V1J 3Y1)
Tel: (604) 785-6647

NORTHWOODS INN
10627 Alaska Rd
(V1J 5P4)
Tel: (800) 663-8316

PIONEER INN
9830 100th Ave
(V1J 1Y5)
Tel: (800) 663-8312

THE ROOST MOTEL
9207 Alaska Rd
(V1J 1A2)
Tel: (604) 785-2906

THE SHEPHERD'S INN
Mile 72, Alaska Hwy,
Box 6425 (V1J 4H8)
Tel: (604) 827-3676

FRASER LAKE

ORANGE VALLEY MOTEL & CAMPGROUND
Hwy 16, Box 392
(V0J 1S0)
Tel: (604) 699-6350

FRUITVALE

BEAVER VALLEY MOTOR INN
290 Hwy Dr, Box 1022
(V0G 1L0)
Tel: (604) 367-7664

GANGES

ARBUTUS COURT MOTEL
770 Vesuvious Bay Rd, RR 1, Comp 1
(V0S 1E0)
Tel: (604) 537-5415

GARIBALDI HIGHLANDS

DRYDEN CREEK RESORTS
Depot Rd & Hwy 99,
Bracendale, Box 1012
(V0N 1T0)
Tel: (604) 898-9726

GIBSONS

CEDAR'S INN
895 Sunshine Hwy 101,
Box 739 (V0N 1V0)
Tel: (604) 886-3008

SUNNY CREST MOTOR MOTEL
835 Hwy 101, Box 856
(V0N 1V0)
Tel: (604) 886-2419

SUNSHINE LODGE
679 North Rd, Box 1768
(V0N 1N0)
Tel: (604) 886-3321

UPTOWN MOTEL & RV PARK
710 North Rd, Box 425
(V0N 1V0)
Tel: (604) 886-2957

GOLD BRIDGE

GOLD BRIDGE HOTEL
General Delivery
(V0K 1P0)
Tel: (800) 663-1144

PEPPERCORN TRAIL MOTEL & RV PARK
Mill Rd, Box 23
(V0P 1G0)
Tel: (604) 283-2443

GOLDEN

ARL INN TOWNER
915 10th Ave S, Box
629 (V0A 1H0)
Tel: (604) 344-2291

**BEST WESTERN
MOUNTAINVIEW
INN**
1024 - 11th St N
(V0A 1H0)
Rates: $69-180
Tel: (250) 344-2333
(800) 528-1234

**THE BIG BEND
HOTEL**
429 North 9th Ave
(V0A 1H0)
Tel: (604) 344-5951

BROOKSIDE MOTEL
1301 11th Ave N,
Box 1739 (V0A 1H0)
Tel: (604) 344-2359

**GOLDEN LION
MOTEL**
Trans Canada Hwy 1,
Box 296 (V0A 1H0)
Tel: (604) 344-2251

**GOLDEN RIM
MOTOR INN**
1416 Golden View
Rd,
Box 510 (V0A 1H0)
Tel: (604) 344-2216

**GOLDEN VILLAGE
MOTOR INN**
Box 371 (V0A 1H0)
Tel: (604) 344-5996

MARY'S MOTEL
8th Ave N, Box 322
(V0A 1H0)
Tel: (604) 344-7111

**PONDEROSA
MOTOR INN**
1206 Trans Canada
Hwy, Box 303
(V0A 1H0)
Tel: (604) 344-2205

RONDO MOTEL
904 Park Dr, Box 258
Tel: (604) 344-5295

SELKIRK INN
Trans Canada Hwy,
Box 70 (V0A 1H0)
Tel: (604) 344-6315

SOUTHWIND MOTEL
773 Nicholson Rd,
Box 4126 (V0A 1H0)
Tel: (604) 344-2356

SPORTSMAN MOTEL
1200 12th St N,
Box 4016 (V0A 1H0)
Tel: (604) 344-2915

SUPER 8 MOTEL
1047 Trans CN Hwy
(V0A 1H0)
Rates: $50-85
Tel: (604) 344-0888
(800) 800-8000

GRAND FORKS

BON AIR MOTEL
1531 Central Ave,
Box 986 (V0H 1H0)
Tel: (604) 442-8218

IMPERIAL MOTEL
7389 Riverside,
Box 2558 (V0H 1H0)
Tel: (604) 442-8236

JOHNNY'S MOTEL
7291 Hwy 3, Box 876
(V0H 1H0)
Tel: (604) 442-8242

PINEGROVE MOTEL
2091 Central Ave,
Box 927 (V0H 1H0)
Tel: (604) 442-8203

RIVERSIDE MOTEL
7351 Hwy 3, Box
1027 (V0H 1H0)
Tel: (604) 442-2259

**WESTERN
TRAVELLER MOTEL**
1591 Central Ave,
Box 1780 (V0H 1H0)
Tel: (604) 442-5566

GRANISLE

**GRANISLE VILLAGE
INN**
Hagan St (V0J 1W9)
Tel: (800) 661-8577

GREENWOOD

**BOUNDARY CREEK
MOTEL**
Box 104 (V0H 1J0)
Tel: (604) 445-6641

**EVENING STAR
MOTEL**
798 N Government
St,
Box 287 (V0H 1J0)
Tel: (604) 445-6733

**GREENWOOD
MOTEL& RV PARK**
256 N Copper St,
Box 428 (V0H 1J0)
Tel: (604) 445-6363

HAGENSBORG

**GLACIER VIEW
MOTEL
& CAMPGROUND**
Hwy 20, Box 239
(V0T 1H0)
Tel: (604) 982-2615

HARRISON HOT SPRINGS

**BUNGALOW
MOTOR COURT**
511 Lillooet Ave,
Box 377 (V0M 1K0)
Tel: (604) 796-3536

GLENCOE MOTEL
259 Hot Springs Rd,
Box 181 (V0M 1K0)
Tel: (604) 796-2574

**HARRISON HOT
SPRINGS
HOTEL**
100 Esplanade
(V0M 1K0)
Tel: (800) 663-2266

LAKESHORE MOTEL
338 Esplanade Ave,
Box 38 (V0M 1K0)
Tel: (604) 796-2441

SPA MOTEL
140 Esplanade Ave,
Box 23 (V0M 1K0)
Tel: (604) 796-2828

HEDLEY

CORONA MOTEL
Box 165, Hwy 3
(V0X 1K0)
Tel: (604) 292-8302

HERIOT BAY

HERIOT BAY INN
Heriot Bay Rd,
Box 100
(V0P 1H0)
Tel: (604) 285-3322

HIXON

**CARIBOO
SHAMROCK
MOTEL & CAMPSITE**
Hwy 97 S, Box 151
(V0K 1S0)
Tel: (604) 998-4414

VON-LIENEN MOTEL
Colgrove Rd,
Box 456
(V0K 1S0)
Tel: (604) 998-4685

HOLBERG

HOLBERG MOTEL
50 E Hardy Way,
Box 23 (V0N 1Z0)
Tel: (604) 288-3424

HOPE

CITY CENTRE MOTEL
455 Wallace St,
Box 96 (V0X 1L0)
Tel: (604) 889-5411

COQUIHALLA INN
559 Hope-Princeton
Hwy,
Box 1657 (V0X 1L0)
Tel: (604) 869-7177

FLAMINGO MOTEL
724 Hope-Princeton
Hwy,
Box 288 (V0X 1L0)
Tel: (604) 869-9610

**HOLIDAY MOTEL
& CAMPGROUND**
63950 Old Yale Rd,
RR 2 (V0X 1L0)
Tel: (604) 869-5352

IMPERIAL MOTEL
350 Hope-Princeton
Hwy,
(V0X 1L0)
Tel: (604) 869-9951

INN TOWNE MOTEL
510 Trans Canada
Hwy 1,
Box 1037 (V0X 1L0)
Tel: (604) 869-7276

LAKE OF THE WOODS RESORT
Trans Canada Hwy,
Box 6 (V0X 1L0)
Tel: (604) 869-9211

LUCKY STRIKE MOTEL
504 Old Hope-
Princeton Hwy,
Box 498 (V0X 1L0)
Tel: (604) 869-5715

MAPLE LEAF MOTOR INN
377 Old Hope-
Princeton Hwy,
Box 438 (V0X 1L0)
Tel: (604) 869-7107

MOUNT HOPE MOTEL
318 Hope-Princeton
Hwy,
Box 288 (V0X 1L0)
Tel: (604) 869-5502

PARK MOTEL
832 Fourth Ave,
Box 1388 (V0X 1L0)
Tel: (604) 869-5891

ROYAL LODGE MOTEL
580 Hope/
Princeton Hwy,
Box 398 (V0X 1L0)
Tel: (604) 869-5358

SLUMBER LODGE
250 Fort St
(V0X 1L0)
Tel: (800) 663-2831

SWISS CHALETS MOTEL
456 Trans Canada
Hwy 1,
Box 308 (V0X 1L0)
Tel: (604) 869-9020

THUNDERBIRD MOTEL
63030 Flood Hope
Rd, RR 2, Box 4
(V0X 1L0)
Tel: (604) 869-2711

WINDSOR MOTEL
778 3rd Ave
(V0X 1L0)
Tel: (604) 869-9944

HOUSTON

HOUSTON MOTOR INN
Hwy 16, Box 1110
(V0J 1Z0)
Tel: (604) 845-7112

PLEASANT VALLEY MOTEL
Hwy 16, Box 1110
(V0J 1Z0)
Tel: (604) 845-2246

HUDSON'S HOPE

PEACE GLEN HOTEL
Dudley Dr, Box 248
(V0C 1V0)
Tel: (604) 783-9966

SPORTSMAN'S INN
Box 209 (V0C 1V0)
Tel: (604) 783-5523

INVERMERE

LEE-JAY MOTEL
1015 13th St,
Box 1020 (V0A 1K0)
Tel: (604) 342-9227

THE TOWNE HOUSE MOTEL
1201 12th St,
Box 2218 (V0K 1K0)
Tel: (604) 342-6618

ISKUT

BLACK SHEEP MOTEL
Box 120 (V0J 1K0)
Tel: (604) 234-3141

KAMLOOPS

ACADIAN MOTEL
1390 Columbia St
(V2C 2W8)
Tel: (604) 374-5591

BAMBI MOTEL
1084 Battle St (V2C
2N3)
Tel: (604) 372-7626

CASA MARQUIS MOTOR INN
530 Columbia St
(V2C 2V1)
Tel: (604) 372-7761

COAST CANADIAN INN
339 St. Paul St
(V2C 2J5)
Tel: (800) 663-1144

COUNTRY MANOR MOTEL
176 Comazetto Rd
(V2C 6L6)
Tel: (604) 374-7222

DAVY CROCKETT MOTEL
1893 Trans Canada
Hwy E
(V2C 3Z9)
Tel: (604) 372-2122

THE DOME MOTOR INN
555 W Columbia St
(V2C 1K7)
Tel: (604) 374-0358

EL CAMINO MOTEL
2505 Trans Canada
Hwy E (V2C 4A9)
Tel: (604) 374-7114

FOUNTAIN MOTEL
506 Columbia St
(V2C 2V1)
Tel: (604) 374-4451

4 SEASONS MOTEL
1767 Trans Canada
Hwy E
(V2C 3Z6)
Tel: (604) 372-2313

GRANDVIEW MOTEL
463 Grandview Ter
(V2C 3Z3)
Tel: (604) 372-1312

HOSPITALITY INN
500 W Columbia St
(V2C 1K6)
Tel: (604) 374-4164

KAMLOOPS THRIFT INN
2459 Trans Canada
Hwy E (V2C 4A9)
Tel: (604) 374-2488

KINGS MOTOR INN
1775 Trans Canada
Hwy E (V2C 3Z6)
Tel: (604) 372-2800

LAC LE JEUNE RESORT
Box 3215 (V2C 6B8)
Tel: (604) 372-2722

LAMPLIGHTER MOTEL
1901 Trans Canada
Hwy E
(V2C 3Z9)
Tel: (604) 372-3386

MONTE VISTA MOTEL
2349 Trans Canada
Hwy E
(V2C 4A8)
Tel: (604) 372-3033

PANORAMA INN
610 W Columbia St
(V2C 1L1)
Tel: (800) 663-3813

THE PLACE INN
1285 Trans Canada
Hwy W
(V2E 2J7)
Tel: (604) 374-5911

QUALITY INN
650 Victoria St
(V2C 2B4)
Tel: (800) 221-2222

THE RANCHLAND MOTEL
2357 Trans Canada
Hwy E
(V2C 4A8)
Tel: (800) 663-4902

RIDER'S MOTOR INN
1759 Trans Canada
Hwy E
(V2C 3Z6)
Tel: (604) 374-2144

RIVERLAND MOTEL
1530 River St (V2C
1Y9)
Tel: (800) 663-1530

SAGEBRUSH MOTEL
660 W Columbia St
(V2C 1L1)
Tel: (604) 372-3151

SANDMAN INN
550 Columbia St
(V2C 1V1)
Tel: (800) 726-3626

SCOTT'S MOTOR INN
551 11th Ave &
Columbia
(V2C 3Y1)
Tel: (800) 665-3343

SKYLINE MOTEL
1763 Trans Canada
Hwy E (V2C 3Z6)
Tel: (604) 374-8944

SLUMBER LODGE
775 W Columbia St
(V2C 1K9)
Tel: (800) 667-5955

STOCKMEN'S HOTEL
540 Victoria St
(V2C 2B2)
Tel: (800) 663-2837

SUPER 8 MOTEL
1521 Hugh Allan Dr
(V1S 1P4)
Rates: $47-77
Tel: (604) 374-8688
(800) 800-8000

**TRAVELODGE
HOTEL**
430 Columbia St
(V2C 2T5)
Tel: (800) 255-3050

**WHISTLER INN
APARTMENT HOTEL**
505 Saint Paul St,
Box 478 (V2C 5L2)
Tel: (604) 828-1322

KASLO

**BEACHCOMBER'S
MARINA**
551 Rainbow Dr,
Box 999 (V0G 1M0)
Tel: (604) 353-7777

KASLO MOTEL
330 D Ave, Box 697
(V0G 1M0)
Tel: (604) 353-2431

LAKEWOOD INN
Box 459, Kohle Rd
(V0G 1M0)
Tel: (604) 353-2395

**MARINER INN
HOTEL**
430 Front St, Box 606
(V0G 1M0)
Tel: (604) 353-7171

**SUNNY BLUFFS
MOTEL**
434 N Marine Dr,
Box 1060 (V0G 1M0)
Tel: (604) 353-2277

KELOWNA

**ABBOTT VILLA
MOTOR INN**
1627 Abbott St (V1Y
1A9)
Tel: (604) 763-7771

**BIG WHITE MOTOR
LODGE**
1891 Parkinson Way
(V1Y 7V6)
Tel: (800) 663-8603

CHINOOK MOTEL
1864 Gordon Dr
(V1Y 3H7)
Tel: (604) 763-3657

**COAST ROYAL
ANNE HOTEL**
348 Bernard Ave
(V1Y 6N5)
Tel: (800) 663-1144

DAYS INN
2649 Hwy 79 N
(V1X 4J6)
Rates: $55-75
Tel: (604) 868-3297
(800) 329-7466

**KELOWNA SLUMBER
LODGE MOTEL**
2486 Hwy 97 N
(V1X 4J3)
Tel: (604) 860-5703

**LA MISSION
MOTOR INN**
579 Truswell Rd
(V1Y 1X5)
Tel: (604) 64-4127

LODGE MOTOR INN
2170 Harvey Ave
(V1Y 6G8)
Tel: (800) 665-2518

OASIS MOTOR INN
1884 Gordon Dr
(V1Y 3H7)
Tel: (604) 763-5396

**OKANAGAN
SEASONS
RESORT MOTEL**
1580 Hwy 33 W
(V1X 1Z9)
Tel: (604) 860-5707

**THE PARK LAKE
HOTEL**
1675 Abbott St (V1Y
8S3)
Tel: (604) 860-7900

RAINBOW MOTEL
1810 Gordon Dr
(V1Y 3H6)
Tel: (604) 763-3544

SAFARI MOTOR INN
1651 Powick Rd
(V1X 4L1)
Tel: (604) 860-8122

SANDMAN INN
2130 Harvey Ave
(V1Y 6G8)
Tel: (800) 726-3626

THRIFT INN
2592 Hwy 97 N
(V1X 4J4)
Tel: (604) 762-8222

**WAYSIDE MOTOR
INN**
2639 Hwy 97 N
(V1X 4J6)
Tel: (604) 860-4454

**WESTERN BUDGET
MOTEL**
2679 Hwy 97 N
(V1X 4J6)
Tel: (604) 763-2484

WILLOW INN HOTEL
235 Queensway Ave
(V1Y 6S4)
Tel: (604) 762-2122

KEREMEOS

ALPINE INN
Hwy 3, RR 1, Site 45,
Comp 10 (V0X 1N0)
Tel: (604) 499-5244

ELK MOTEL
310 7th Ave, RR 1,
Hwy 3 W,
P. O. Box 361
(V0X 1N0)
Tel: (604) 499-2043

OASIS MOTEL
Hwy 3A, RR 1, Site
65, Comp 6
(V0X 1N0)
Tel: (604) 499-5857

PARK'S MOTEL
RR 1, Hwy 3
(V0X 1N0)
Tel: (604) 499-5834

SIMILKAMEEN MOTEL
Hwy 3 W, RR 1, Site
35, Comp 1
(V0X 1N0)
Tel: (604) 499-5984

KIMBERLEY

**KIMBERLEY PALACE
HOTEL**
2665 Warren Ave
(V1A 1T6)
Tel: (604) 427-7848

NORTH STAR MOTEL
Hwy 95A, Site 20,
Box 6, SS 1
(V1A 2Y3)
Tel: (604) 427-5633

**SILVER BIRCH
RESORT CHALETS**
Dewdney Way,
Box 339
(V1A 2Y9)
Tel: (604) 427-5385

SYLVIA MOTEL
455 Ross St
(V1A 2C5)
Tel: (604) 427-2203

KITIMAT

KITIMAT MOTEL
656 Dadook Cres,
Box 477 (V8C 2R9)
Tel: (604) 632-6677

LAC LA HACHE

**KOKANEE BAY
MOTEL
& TRAILER COURT**
Hwy 97, RR 1,
Comp 1 (V0K 1T0)
Tel: (604) 396-7345

**LAC LA HACHE
MOTEL**
Hwy 97 N, Box 152
(V0K 1T0)
Tel: (604) 396-4422

LAKE
COWICHAN

**SOUTHSHORE
MOTEL**
266 Southshore Rd
(V0R 2G0)
Tel: (604) 749-6482

LANGLEY

LANGLEY MOTOR INN
21653 Fraser Hwy
(V3A 4H1)
Tel: (604) 533-4431

TRAVELODGE
20470 88th Ave
(V1M 2Y6)
Rates: $60-85
Tel: (604) 888-4891
(800) 578-7878

WEST COUNTRY HOTEL
20222 56th Ave
(V3A 3Y5)
Tel: (604) 530-5121

WESTWARD INN
19650 Fraser Hwy
1A (V3A 4C7)
Tel: (604) 534-9238

LIKELY

HIGH COUNTRY MOTOR INN
Box 52 (V0L 1N0)
Tel: (604) 790-2335

LILLOOET

4 PINES MOTEL
108 8th Ave, Box 70
(V0K 1V0)
Tel: (604) 256-4247

HOTEL VICTORIA
667 Main St, Box
1480 (V0K 1V0)
Tel: (604) 256-4112

JAY-GEE MOTEL
Bouvette Rd, Box
307 (V0K 1V0)
Tel: (604) 256-7525

MILE-O-MOTEL
616 Main St, Box 295
(V0K 1V0)
Tel: (604) 256-7511

LITTLE FORT

**MOUNT OLIE MOTEL
& CAMPGROUND**
Hwy 5, Box 916
(V0E 2C0)
Tel: (604) 677-4323

RIVERMOUNT MOTEL
Hwy 5, Box 273
(V0E 2C0)
Tel: (604) 677-4244

LOGAN LAKE

COPPER VALLEY MOTOR INN
19 Apex Dr, Box 790
(V0K 1W0)
Tel: (604) 523-9433

LUMBY

DIAMOND MOTOR INN
1643 Vernon St,
Box 721 (V0E 2G0)
Tel: (604) 547-9221

LYTTON

BRAEDEN LODGE MOTEL
223 Main St, Box 250
(V0K 1Z0)
Tel: (604) 455-2334

LYTTON HOTEL
Box 113, Main St
(V0K 1Z0)
Tel: (604) 455-2211

LYTTON PINES MOTEL
Trans Canada Hwy,
Box 249 (V0K 1Z0)
Tel: (604) 455-2322

TOTEM MOTEL & LODGE
320 Fraser St, Box 5
(V0K 1Z0)
Tel: (604) 455-2321

MACKENZIE

ALEXANDER MACKENZIE HOTEL
403 Mackenzie Blvd,
Box 40 (V0J 2C0)
Tel: (604) 997-3266

TIMBERMAN INN MOTEL
Box 40 (V0J 2C0)
Tel: (604) 997-6464

WILLISTON LAKE LODGE
305 Mackenzie Blvd,
Box 626 (V0J 2C0)
Tel: (604) 997-3131

MADEIRA PARK

PARK MOTEL
Hwy 101, Box 131
(V0N 2H0)
Tel: (604) 883-9040

MALAHAT

MALAHAT MOUNTAIN OCEANVIEW MOTEL
231 Trans Canada
Hwy,
Box 397 (V0R 2L0)
Tel: (604) 478-9231

MAPLE RIDGE

BEST WESTERN MOTOR LODGE
21735 Lougheed
Hwy 7 (V2X 2S2)
Tel: (800) 528-1234

TRAVELODGE
21650 Lougheed
Hwy (V2X 2S1)
Tel: (800) 255-3050

MARA

ROGERS FALLS RESORT
RR 1, Hwy 97A
(V0E 2K0)
Tel: (604) 838-6294

MASSET

NAIKOON PARK MOTEL
Tow Hill Rd, Lot 14,
Box 467 (V0T 1M0)
Tel: (604) 626-5187

MCBRIDGE

LOG-TEL MOTEL
Bridge Rd, Box 308
(V0J 2E0)
Tel: (604) 569-2633

SANDMAN INN
Hwy 16, Box 548
(V0J 2E0)
Tel: (800) 726-3626

MCLEESE LAKE

MCLEESE LAKE BEACH RESORT
Hwy 97 N, Box 39
(V0L 1P0)
Tel: (604) 297-6525

MERRITT

COPPER VALLEY MOTEL
2276 Nicola Ave,
Box 670 (V0K 2B0)
Tel: (604) 378-9214

DAYS INN
3350 Voght St
(V1K 1C7)
Rates: $55-100
Tel: (604) 378-2292
(800) 329-7466

DOUBLE D INN
1502 Nicola Ave, RR
1, Site 10, Comp 11
(V0K 2B0)
Tel: (604) 378-5112

DOUGLAS MOTEL
2702 Nicola Ave,
Box 1100 (V0K 2B0)
Tel: (604) 378-9244

GRASSLANDS MOTOR HOTEL
Hwy 5, RR 1 (V0K
2B0)
Tel: (604) 378-2292

INN TOWNE MOTEL
2261 Voght St (V0K
2B0)
Tel: (604) 378-4291

ROAD RUNNER MOTEL
2701 Nicola Ave, Box
1269
(V0K 2B0)
Tel: (604) 378-4201

SPORTSMANS MOTEL
3463 Voght St, RR 1
(V0K 2B0)
Tel: (800) 663-6868

VALNICOLA MOTOR HOTEL
2350 Voght St,
Box 2640
(V0K 2B0)
Tel: (604) 378-2254

MEZIADIN LAKE

NECHAKO NORTHCOAST INN
Hwy 37A, Box 1
(V0J 3S0)
Tel: (604) 636-9222

MIDWAY

MIDWAY MOTOR INN
622 Palmerston St,
Box 330 (V0H 1M0)
Tel: (604) 449-2662

MISSION

MISSION INN
34551 Lougheed
Hwy, RR 6
(V2V 6B2)
Tel: (604) 826-2023

MUNCHO LAKE

DOUBLE 'G' SERVICE & MOTEL
Mile 456,
Alaska Hwy
(V0C 1Z0)
Tel: (604) 776-3411

HIGHLAND GLEN LODGE
Mile 462,
Alaska Hwy
(V0C 1Z0)
Tel: (604) 776-3481

J & H WILDERNESS MOTEL & FISHING CAMP
Mile 463, Box 38,
Alaska Hwy
(V0C 1Z0)
Tel: (604) 776-3453

MUNCHO LAKE LODGE
Mile 463,
Alaska Hwy
(V0C 1Z0)
Tel: (604) 776-3456

NAKUSP

CANYON COURT
937 Canyon Rd,
Box 727 (V0G 1R0)
Tel: (604) 265-3737

SELKIRK INN
210 6th Ave W,
Box 370 (V0G 1R0)
Tel: (604) 265-3666

NANAIMO

BEST WESTERN NORTH GATE
6450 Metral Dr
(V9T 2L8)
Tel: (800) 661-0061

BIG 7 ECONOMY MOTEL
736 Nicol St
(V9R 4V1)
Tel: (604) 754-2328

BLUEBIRD MOTEL
995 N Terminal Ave
(V9S 4K3)
Tel: (604) 753-4151

BUCCANEER MOTEL
1577 Stewart Ave
(V9S 4E3)
Tel: (604) 753-1246

COAST BASTION INN
11 Bastion St
(V9R 2Z9)
Tel: (800) 663-1144

DAYS INN
809 Island Hwy S
(V9R 5K1)
Rates: $55-116
Tel: (604) 754-8171
(800) 329-7466

DEPARTURE BAY MOTEL
2011 Estevan Rd,
Island Hwy N (V9S 3Y9)
Tel: (604) 754-2161

DIPLOMAT MOTEL
333 Nicol St,
Island Hwy S
(V9R 4T5)
Tel: (604) 743-3261

DORCHESTER HOTEL
70 Church St
(V9R 5H4)
Tel: (604) 754-6835

HARBOURVIEW DAYS INN
809 Island Hwy S,
RR 1 (V9R 5K1)
Tel: (800) 325-2525

HIGHLANDER MOTOR INN
96 N Terminal Ave
(V9S 4J2)
Tel: (604) 754-6355

MOBY DICK BOATEL
1000 Stewart Ave
(V9S 4C9)
Tel: (604) 753-7111

PORT-O-CALL MOTEL
505 N Terminal Ave
(V9S 4K1)
Tel: (604) 753-3421

THE ROYAL MOTEL
335 N Terminal Ave
(V9S 4J6)
Tel: (604) 753-1171

WESTWARD HO MOTEL
250 N Terminal Ave
(V9S 4J5)
Tel: (604) 754-4202

NELSON

ALPINE MOTEL
1120 Hallmines Rd
(V1L 1G6)
Tel: (800) 665-0310

LAKESIDE MOTEL
805 Nelson Ave (V1L 2N8)
Tel: (800) 663-0102

NORTH SHORE INN
687 Hwy 3A, Box 39
(V1L 5P7)
Tel: (604) 352-6606

QUEEN'S HOTEL
621 Baker St
(V1L 4J3)
Tel: (604) 352-5351

SLUMBER LODGE
153 Baker St
(V1L 4H1)
Tel: (800) 663-2831

VIKING MOTEL
1301 Front St
(V1L 4C5)
Tel: (800) 663-0102

VILLA MOTEL
655 Hwy 3A,
Box 770
(V1L 5R4)
Tel: (800) 665-0310

WILLOW BAY MOTEL
2619 Hwy 3A, RR 1
(V1L 5P4)
Tel: (800) 663-0102

NEW DENVER

LUCERNE MOTEL
504 Slocan Ave,
Box 330 (V0G 1S0)
Tel: (604) 358-2228

NEW HAZELTON

BULKLEY VALLEY MOTEL
Box 177 (V0J 2J0)
Tel: (604) 842-5224

ROBBERS ROOST LODGE
Hwy 16, Box 555
(V0J 2J0)
Tel: (604) 842-6916

28 INN MOTEL
4545 Yellowhead,
Hwy 16 (V0J 2J0)
Tel: (604) 842-6006

NIMPO LAKE

THOMSONS COUNTRY INN
Hwy 20, General
Delivery
(V0L 1R0)
Tel: (604) 742-3331

NORTH VANCOUVER

CANYON COURT MOTEL
1748 Capilano Rd
(V7P 3B4)
Tel: (604) 988-3181

LYNNWOOD INN
1515 Barrow St
(V2J 1B7)
Tel: (800) 663-0466

MAPLES MOTOR LODGE
1800 Capilano Rd
(V7P 3B6)
Tel: (604) 987-4461

VANCOUVER LIONS GATE TRAVELODGE
2060 Marine Dr
(V7P 1V7)
Tel: (800) 268-3330

OKANAGAN FALLS

LAKEVIEW MOTEL & CAMPSITE
2151 9th Ave, Box 257
(V0H 1R0)
Tel: (604) 497-5175

SUNOKA MOTOR INN
Box 253, Hwy 97
(V0H 1R0)
Tel: (604) 497-5258

OLIVER

BEL AIR CEDAR MOTEL
Hwy 97S, RR 1
(V0H 1T0)
Tel: (604) 498-2443

MOUNT VIEW MOTEL
34226 97th St, Box 1406
(V0H 1T0)
Tel: (604) 498-3446

PINE BLUFF MOTEL
Hwy 97N, RR 2
(V0H 1T0)
Tel: (604) 498-3377

SOUTHWIND MOTOR INN
34017 Hwy 97S, Box 1500 (V0H 1T0)
Tel: (604) 498-3442

VALLEY MOTEL
34469 97th St, Box 107 (V0H 1T0)
Tel: (604) 498-2225

100 MILE HOUSE

BEST WESTERN 108 RESORT
Telqua Dr, RR 1, Comp 2,
108 Ranch (V0K 2E0)
Tel: (604) 791-5211

IMPERIAL MOTEL
250 Hwy 97, Box 113
(V0K 2E0)
Tel: (604) 395-2471

99 MILE MOTEL
896 Alpine, Hwy 97, Box 2140 (V0K 2E0)
Tel: (604) 395-2255

100 MILE HOUSE SLUMBER LODGE
350 Cariboo Hwy 2, Box 1328 (V0K 2E0)
Tel: (800) 663-2831

100 MILE MOTEL & RV PARK
310 Hwy 97 S, Box 112 (V0K 2E0)
Tel: (604) 395-2234

RED COACH FLAG INN
170 N Cariboo Hwy, Box 760 (V0K 2E0)
Tel: (800) 663-8422

OSOYOOS

AVALON MOTEL
Hwy 3, Box 92
(V0H 1V0)
Tel: (604) 495-6334

BELLA VILLA MOTEL
6904 64th Ave, RR 1
(V0H 1V0)
Tel: (604) 495-6751

BOUNDARY MOTEL
Hwy 97, RR 2
(V0H 1V0)
Tel: (604) 495-6050

FALCON MOTEL
7106 62nd Ave, Hwy 3 E, RR 1 (V0H 1V0)
Tel: (604) 495-7544

HIGHLAND INN
5912 62nd Ave, RR 1, Box 6 (V0H 1V0)
Tel: (604) 495-6919

MOUNT KOBAU MOTEL
9013 103 St, Box 431
(V0H 1V0)
Tel: (604) 495-7322

RICHTER PASS MOTOR INN
7506 62nd Ave, Box 480 (V0H 1V0)
Tel: (604) 495-7229

RIVIERA MOTEL
6512 64th Ave, RR 1
(V0H 1V0)
Tel: (604) 495-6551

THE SAHARA MOTEL
67 St E, Box 530
(V0H 1V0)
Tel: (604) 495-7211

SANDY BEACH MOTEL
6702 64th Ave, Box 257 (V0H 1V0)
Tel: (604) 495-6931

SPANISH FIESTA MOTEL
7104 62nd Ave, Hwy 3E,
RR 1 (V0H 1V0)
Tel: (604) 495-6833

STARLITE MOTOR INN
Hwy 3, Box 1019
(V0H 1V0)
Tel: (604) 495-7223

SUNBEACH MOTEL
RR 1 (V0H 1V0)
Tel: (604) 495-7766

OYAMA SOUTH

SWISS VILLAGE RESORT AND MOTEL
Hwy 97, RR 1
(V0H 1W0)
Tel: (604) 548-3516

PARKSVILLE

THE ROADHOUSE INN
1223 Smithers Rd
(V2P 2C1)
Tel: (604) 248-2912

SKYLITE MOTEL
459 E Island Hwy,
Box 398 (V9P 2G5)
Tel: (604) 248-4271

VANCOUVER ISLAND PARKSVILLE MOTEL
414 W Island Hwy
(V9P 2G3)
Tel: (800) 663-7300

PEACHLAND

BAYVIEW MOTEL
Hwy 97, RR 1,
Site 17,
Comp 24 (V0H 1X0)
Tel: (604) 767-2265

DAVIS COVE RESORT
3701 Beach Ave, RR 2,
Site 22, Comp 5
(V0H 1X0)
Tel: (604) 767-2355

PEACHLAND MOTEL
5956 Hwy 97 S, Box 798
(V0H 1X0)
Tel: (604) 767-2205

PEACHLAND TOTEM INN HOTEL
Beach Ave, Box 679
(V0H 1X0)
Tel: (604) 767-9191

PEMBERTON

PEMBERTON HOTEL
Frontier St, Box 128
(V0N 2L0)
Tel: (604) 894-6313

PENTICTON

AIRPORT SKYTEL
Airport Rd, RR 3,
Site 30,
Comp 4 (V2A 6J7)
Tel: (604) 492-0127

BEL AIR MOTEL
2670 Skaha Lake Rd
(V2A 6G1)
Tel: (604) 492-6111

BEST WESTERN TELSTAR INN
3180 Skaha Lake Rd
(V2A 6G4)
Tel: (604) 493-0311

BLACK FOREST MOTEL
707 Westminster Ave
W (V2A 1K9)
Tel: (604) 492-0028

BLACK SEA MOTEL
988 Lakeshore Dr
(V2A 1C1)
Tel: (604) 492-5722

BOWMONT MOTEL
80 Riverside Dr
(V2A 5Y3)
Tel: (604) 492-0112

CARMI MOTEL
1473 Main St
(V2A 5G4)
Tel: (604) 492-4143

COAST LAKESIDE RESORT
21 Lakeshore Dr W
(V2A 7M5)
Tel: (800) 663-1144

CROWN MOTEL
950 Lakeshore Dr
(V2A 1C1)
Tel: (604) 492-4092

EDGEWATER MOTEL
3833 Skaha Lake Rd
(V2A 6G8)
Tel: (604) 492-4337

5000 MOTEL
1742 Main St (V2A
5G8)
Tel: (604) 492-8747

FLAMINGO MOTEL
2387 Skaha Lake Rd
(V2A 6E8)
Tel: (604) 492-8333

GOLDEN SANDS MOTOR INN
1028 Lakeshore Dr
(V2A 1C1)
Tel: (604) 492-4210

GRANADA MOTOR INN
2593 Skaha Lake Rd
(V2A 6G1)
Tel: (604) 493-2144

HIGHLAND MOTEL
1140 Burnaby Ave
(V2A 1G9)
Tel: (604) 492-7002

JUBILEE MOTEL
2475 Skaha Lake Rd
(V2A 6E8)
Tel: (604) 432-7206

KREEKSIDE MOTEL
1706 Main St
(V2A 5G8)
Tel: (604) 492-3829

LAKESIDE VILLA
Skaha Lake Rd, RR
2, Site 40, Comp 9
(V2A 6J7)
Tel: (604) 492-7111

LOG CABIN MOTEL
3287 Skaha Lake Rd
(V2A 6G5)
Tel: (604) 492-3155

MAJESTIC FLAG INN
152 Riverside Dr
(V2A 5Y4)
Tel: (604) 493-6616

PARADISE VALLEY MOTEL
3118 Skaha Lake Rd
(V2A 6G4)
Tel: (604) 492-2756

PASS MOTOR INN
2307 Skaha Lake Rd
(V2A 6E8)
Tel: (604) 492-0323

RAMADA COURT-YARD INN
1050 Eckhardt Ave
W (V2A 2C3)
Rates: $99-250
Tel: (604) 492-8926
(800) 272-6232

THE ROCHESTER MOTEL
970 Lakeshore Dr
(V2A 1C1)
Tel: (604) 493-1128

SANDMAN INN
939 Burnaby Ave W
(V2A 1G7)
Tel: (800) 726-3626

THE SHIELINGS MOTEL
2509 S Main St
(V2A 5J4)
Tel: (604) 492-7118

SPANISH VILLA
890 Lakeshore Dr
(V2A 1C1)
Tel: (604) 492-2922

STARDUST MOTOR INN
1048 Westminster
Ave (V2A 1L5)
Tel: (604) 492-7015

SUN VALLEY MOTEL
2784 Skaha Lake Rd
(V2A 6G1)
Tel: (604) 492-3806

SWISS SUNSET INN
2604 Skaha Lake Rd
(V2A 6G1)
Tel: (604) 492-8209

WATERFRONT INN
3688 Parkview St
(V2A 6H1)
Tel: (800) 563-6006

WESTERN MOTEL
38 Warren Ave
(V2A 3L8)
Tel: (604) 493-1677

WOODLOCK INNS
2406 Skaha Lake Rd
(V2A 6E9)
Tel: (604) 492-3029

PINK MOUNTAIN

SPORTSMAN'S INN
Mile 143, Alaska
Hwy (V0C 2B0)
Tel: (604) 772-3220

PORT ALBERNI

COAST HOSPITALITY INN
3835 Redford St
(V9Y 3S2)
Tel: (800) 663-6677

HARBOUR WAY MOTEL
3805 Redford St
(V9Y 3S2)
Tel: (604) 723-9405

MAPLES RESORT MOTEL
9624 Lakeshore Rd,
RR 3 (V9Y 7L7)
Tel: (604) 723-7533

REDFORD MOTOR INN
3723 Redford St
(V9Y 3S3)
Tel: (604) 724-0121

SOMASS MOTEL
5279 River Rd
(V9Y 6Z3)
Tel: (604) 724-3236

TIMBERLODGE & RV CAMPGROUND
Site 210, Comp 12,
Hwy 4 (V9Y 7L6)
Tel: (604) 723-9415

TYEE VILLAGE MOTEL
4151 Redford St
(V9Y 3R6)
Tel: (800) 663-6876

PORT ALICE

QUATSINO CHALET HOTEL
111 Nigel St
(V0N 2N0)
Tel: (604) 284-3318

PORT CLEMENTS

GOLDEN SPRUCE MOTEL
2 Grouse St,
Box 296 (V0T 1R0)
Tel: (604) 557-4325

PORT COQUITLAM

BEST WESTERN POCO INN
1545 Lougheed Hwy
(V3B 1A5)
Rates: $79-159
Tel: (604) 941-6216
(800) 528-1234

PORT HARDY

AIRPORT INN
4030 Byng Rd,
Box 2039 (V0N 2P0)
Tel: (604) 949-9434

GLEN LYON INN
6435 Hardy Bay Rd,
Box 103 (V0N 2P0)
Tel: (604) 949-7115

NORTH SHORE INN
7370 Market St,
Box 1888 (V0N 2P0)
Tel: (604) 949-8500

THE PIONEER INN
4965 Byng Rd,
Box 699 (V0N 2P0)
Tel: (604) 949-7271

PORT HARDY INN
9040 Granville St,
Box 1798 (V0N 2P0)
Tel: (604) 949-8525

THUNDERBIRD INN
7050 Rupert St,
Box 88 (V0N 2P0)
Tel: (604) 949-7767

PORT MCNEILL

DALEWOOD INN
1703 Broughton
Blvd,
Box 280 (V0N 2R0)
Tel: (604) 956-3304

**HAIDA-WAY MOTOR
INN**
1817 Campbell Way,
Box 399 (V0N 2R0)
Tel: (604) 956-3373

POWELL RIVER

**HYATT MOTOR
LODGE**
6255 Marine Ave
(V8A 4K6)
Tel: (604) 483-3113

**THE INN AT WEST-
VIEW**
7050 Alberni at Joyce
(V8A 2C3)
Tel: (604) 485-6281

MARINE INN
4429 Marine Ave
(V8A 2J9)
Tel: (604) 485-4242

MARLAND MOTEL
7156 Thunder Bay
Rd
(V8A 1E6)
Tel: (604) 485-4435

**OLD COURTHOUSE
MANOR HOTEL**
6243 Walnut St
(V8A 4K4)
Tel: (604) 483-4000

**SEASIDE VILLA
MOTEL
& TRAILER PARK**
7274 Hwy 101, RR 1
(V8A 4Z2)
Tel: (604) 485-2911

**WESTVIEW
CENTRE MOTEL**
4534 Marine Ave
(V8A 2K4)
Tel: (604) 485-4023

PRINCE GEORGE

ANCO MOTEL
1630 Central St
(V2M 3C2)
Tel: (604) 563-3671

**BEDNESTI LAKE
RESORT**
Box 308, Sta A
(V2L 4S3)
Tel: (604) 563-0689

CAMELOT COURT
1600 Central St
(V2M 3C2)
Tel: (604) 563-0661

**COAST INN
OF THE NORTH**
770 Brunswick St
(V2L 2C2)
Tel: (800) 663-1144

**CONNAUGHT
MOTOR INN**
1550 Victoria St
(V2L 2L3)
Tel: (800) 663-6620

**DOWNTOWN
MOTEL**
650 Dominion St
(V2L 1T8)
Tel: (604) 563-9241

**GOLDCAP MOTOR
INN**
1458 7th Ave (V2L
3P2)
Tel: (604) 563-0666

GRAMA'S INN
901 Central St (V2M
3C8)
Tel: (604) 563-7174

HOLIDAY INN
444 George St (V2L
1R6)
Tel: (800) 465-4329

JACOB'S INN
1401 Queensway
(V2L 1L4)
Tel: (604) 563-9236

NECHAKO INN
1915 3rd Ave (V2M
1G6)
Tel: (604) 563-7106

P.G. HI-WAY MOTEL
1737 20th Ave (V2L
4B9)
Tel: (604) 564-6869

**QUEENSWAY
COURT MOTEL**
1616 Queensway St
(V2L 1L7)
Tel: (604) 562-5068

**RAMADA HOTEL -
DOWNTOWN**
444 George St
(V2L 1R6)
Rates: $71-145
Tel: (604) 563-0055
(800) 272-6232

**RED CEDAR INN
& CAMPGROUND**
5580 Bear Rd, SS-2,
Site 3, Comp 1
(V2N 2K6)
Tel: (604) 964-4427

ROBLYN MOTEL
3755 John Hart Hwy
(V2K 2Z4)
Tel: (604) 962-7081

SANDMAN INN
1650 Central St
(V2M 3C2)
Tel: (800) 726-3626

SLUMBER LODGE
910 Victoria St (V2L
2K8)
Tel: (800) 663-2831

SPRUCELAND INN
1391 Central St
(V2M 3E2)
Tel: (800) 663-3295

**WEST HEIGHTS
MOTEL**
Box 2002 (V2N 2J6)
Tel: (604) 964-4708

PRINCE RUPERT

ALEEDA MOTEL
900 3rd Ave W
(V8J 1M8)
Tel: (604) 627-1367

**CREST MOTOR
HOTEL**
222 1st Ave W,
Box 277 (V8J 3P6)
Tel: (800) 663-8150

HIGHLINER INN
815 1st Ave W
(V8J 1B3)
Tel: (800) 663-8158

**NEPTUNE MOTOR
INN**
1051 Chamberlin
Ave (V8J 4J5)
Tel: (604) 627-1377

**PARKSIDE RESORT
MOTEL**
101 11th Ave & Hwy 16
(V8J 2W2)
Tel: (604) 624-9131

**PRINCE RUPERT
HOTEL**
2nd Ave & 6th St,
Box 338 (V8J 3P9)
Tel: (604) 624-6711

RAFFLES INN
1080 W 3rd Ave
(V8J 1N1)
Tel: (604) 624-9161

**TOTEM LODGE
MOTEL**
1335 Park Ave
(V8J 1K3)
Tel: (604) 624-6761

PRINCETON

THE CEDARS MOTEL
139 3rd St, Box 567
(V0X 1W0)
Tel: (604) 295-3237

**COPPER TOWN
MOTEL**
Hwy 3 W, Box 404
(V0X 1W0)
Tel: (604) 295-3288

EVERGREEN MOTEL
250 Hwy 3 E,
Box 546 (V0X 1W0)
Tel: (604) 295-7179

PONDEROSA MOTEL
130 Bridge St,
Box 238 (V0X 1W0)
Tel: (604) 295-6941

RIVERSIDE MOTEL
307 Thomas Ave,
Box 368 (V0X 1W0)
Tel: (604) 295-6232

SANDMAN INN
Hwy 3, Box 421
(V0X 1W0)
Tel: (800) 726-3626

QUADRA ISLAND

WHISKEY POINT LODGE
725 Quathiaski Cove Rd,
Box 309 (V0P 1N0)
Tel: (604) 285-2201

QUALICUM BEACH

CASA DEL MAR MOTEL
6115 W Island Hwy,
RR 3,
Site 353, Comp 1
(V0R 2T0)
Tel: (604) 757-8776

CRESCENT RESORT MOTEL
431 W Crescent Rd
(V0R 2T0)
Tel: (604) 752-9551

THE GEORGE INN
532 Memorial Ave,
Box 2280 (V0R 2T0)
Tel: (604) 752-9236

OLD DUTCH INN
2690 Island Hwy,
Box 1240 (V9K 1T3)
Tel: (604) 752-6914

QUALICUM COLLEGE INN
427 College Rd,
Box 99 (V0R 2T0)
Tel: (800) 663-7306

RIVERSIDE RESORT
3506 W Island Hwy,
Box 1859 (V0R 2T0)
Tel: (604) 752-9544

THE SHOREWATER MOTEL
3295 W Island Hwy,
RR 1,Site 136,
Comp 2 (V0R 2T0)
Tel: (800) 663-7307

QUEEN CHARLOTTE CITY

GRACIE'S PLACE
3113 3rd Ave,
Box 447 (V0T 1S0)
Tel: (604) 559-4262

HECATE INN
321 3rd Ave,
Box 124 (V0T 1S0)
Tel: (604) 559-4543

PREMIER HOTEL
3101 3rd Ave,
Box 268 (V0T 1S0)
Tel: (604) 559-8415

QUESNEL

CARAVAN MOTEL
202 Hwy 97 S
(V2J 4C5)
Tel: (604) 747-3111

FOUNTAIN MOTEL
524 Front St
(V2J 2K6)
Tel: (604) 992-7071

THE GOLD PAN MOTEL
855 Front St
(V2J 2L3)
Tel: (604) 992-2107

GOOD KNIGHT INN
176 Davie St
(V2J 2S7)
Tel: (800) 663-1585

QUESNEL AIRPORT INN MOTEL & RV
4051 Hwy 97 N,
Box 4422 (V2J 3J4)
Tel: (604) 992-5942

SYLVAN MOTEL
955 Front St
(V2J 2Y2)
Tel: (604) 992-5611

VALHALLA MOTEL
Valhalla Rd,
Box 4625 (V2J 3J8)
Tel: (604) 747-1111

THE WILLOW INN MOTEL
856 Front St
(V2J 2L5)
Tel: (800) 663-8921

RADIUM HOT SPRINGS

CEDAR MOTEL
Hwy 93/95, Box 157
(V0A 1M0)
Tel: (604) 347-9463

KOOTENAY MOTEL
Box 7, Hwy 93
(V0A 1M0)
Tel: (604) 347-9490

LIDO MOTEL
McKay St, Box 36
(V0A 1M0)
Tel: (604) 347-9533

MOUNTAIN VIEW MOTEL
Radium Ave, Box 143 (V0A 1M0)
Tel: (604) 347-9654

RADIUM HOT SPRINGS LODGE
Kootenay National Park (V0A 1M0)
Tel: (604) 347-9622

SKYVIEW MOTEL
Box 26 (V0A 1M0)
Tel: (604) 347-9698

SUNSET MOTEL
McKay St, Box 86
(V0A 1M0)
Tel: (604) 347-9863

TUK-IN MOTEL
Hwy 92/95 S, Box 57
(V0A 1M0)
Tel: (604) 347-9464

WAYSIDE MOTEL
Joseph St, Box 71
(V0A 1M0)
Tel: (604) 347-9332

REVELSTOKE

ALPINE MOTEL
1001 W 2nd St,
Box 414 (V0E 2S0)
Tel: (604)837-2116

BEST WESTERN WAYSIDE INN
1901 Laforme Blvd,
Box 59 (V0E 2S0)
Tel: (800) 528-1234

CAT POWER SKI LODGE
1601 3rd St W,
Box 1479 (V0E 2S0)
Tel: (604) 837-5151

COLUMBIA MOTEL
1601 2nd St W,
Box 421 (V0E 2S0)
Tel: (800) 663-5303

FRONTIER MOTEL
122 N Nakusp-Mica Creek Hwy,
Box 1239 (V0E 2S0)
Tel: (604) 837-5119

HIDDEN MOTEL
1855 Big Eddy Rd,
Box 9159 (V0E 3K0)
Tel: (604) 837-4240

HIGHWAY HAVEN MOTEL & CAMPGROUND
Hwy 1, Box 2098
(V0E 2S0)
Tel: (604) 837-2525

MOUNTAIN VIEW MOTEL
1017 First St W,
Box 3079 (V0E 2S0)
Tel: (604) 837-4900

PEAKS LODGE
Trans Canada Hwy,
Box 1061 (V0E 2S0)
Tel: (604) 837-2176

REGENT INN
112 First St E,
Box 582 (V0E 2S0)
Tel: (604) 837-2107

REVELSTOKE LODGE
601 1st St W,
Box 650 (V0E 2S0)
Tel: (604) 837-2181

SANDMAN INN
1821 Fraser St,
Box 2329 (V0E 2S0)
Tel: (800) 726-3626

SWISS CHALET MOTEL
1101 Victoria Rd,
Box 359 (V0E 2S0)
Tel: (604) 837-4650

RICHMOND

BEST WESTERN RICHMOND INN
7551 Westminster Hwy (V6X 1A3)
Tel: (800) 663-0299

DELTA PACIFIC RESORT
1021 St. Edwards Dr (V6X 2M9)
Tel: (800) 268-1133

DELTA RIVER INN
3500 Cessna Dr (V7B 1C7)
Tel: (800) 268-1133

GRANADA INN
9020 Bridgeport Rd (V6X 1S1)
Tel: (800) 663-2337

RELAX HOTEL VANCOUVER-AIRPORT
3071 St. Edwards Dr (V6X 3K4)
Tel: (800) 667-3529

SKYLINE AIRPORT HOTEL
3031 3 Rd (V6X 2B6)
Tel: (800) 663-0974

ROCK CREEK

EDELWEISS INN & MOTEL
Hwy 3, RR 2 (V0H 1Y0)
Tel: (604) 446-2400

ROGERS PASS

BEST WESTERN GLACIER PARK LODGE
Trans Canada Hwy, Glacier National Park (V0E 2S0)
Tel: (800) 528-1234

ROSSLAND

RED MOUNTAIN RESORT MOTEL
Red Muntain Rd, Box 816 (V0G 1Y0)
Tel: (604) 362-9000

ROSSLAND MOTEL
Box 1141 (V0G 1Y0)
Tel: (604) 362-7218

SCOTSMAN MOTEL
1199 Nancy Greene Hwy,
Box 1071 (V0G 1Y0)
Tel: (800) 663-0203

SAANICHTON

SUPER 8 MOTEL
2477 Mt. Newton Cross Rd (V8M 2B7)
Rates: $47-77
Tel: (604) 652-6888
(800) 800-8000

WADDLING DOG INN
2476 Mount Newton Cross Rd (V0S 1M0)
Tel: (604) 652-1146

SALMO

SALCREST MOTEL
110 Motel Ave,
Box 519 (V0G 1Z0)
Tel: (604) 357-9557

SELKIRK MOTEL
307 Second Relief Rd,
Box 862 (V0G 1Z0)
Tel: (604) 357-2346

SALMON ARM

BEST WESTERN VILLAGER WEST MOTOR INN
61 10th St SW (V1E 4M2)
Tel: (800) 528-1234

DOUBLE 'M' MOTEL, CAMPGROUND & RV PARK
6000 50 St NE (V1E 4M4)
Tel: (604) 832-6955

ORCHARD MOTEL
1460 Trans Canada HwyNE (V1E 4N1)
Tel: (604) 832-6025

SALMON ARM MOTOR HOTEL
551 Trans Canada Hwy NE,
Box 909 (V1E 4P1)
Tel: (800) 663-5308

SALMON ARM SUPER 8 MOTEL
2901 10th Ave NE (V1E 4N1)
Tel: (800) 800-8000

SALMON ARM TRAVELODGE
2401 Trans Canada Hwy W,
Box 1661 (V1E 4P7)
Tel: (604) 832-9721

SALMON RIVER MOTEL & CAMPGROUND
910 40 St SW (V1E 4M2)
Tel: (604) 832-3065

THE SHUSWAP INN MOTOR HOTEL
200 Trans Canada Hwy W,
Box 1540 (V1E 4P6)
Tel: (800) 661-4355

STARDUST MOTEL
4061 Trans Canada Hwy NE (V1E 4M4)
Tel: (604) 832-4672

SUPER 8 MOTEL
2901 10th Ave NE (V1E 4N1)
Rates: $47-77
Tel: (604) 832-8812
(800) 800-8000

VIEW POINT MOTEL
6871 Trans Canada Hwy NW (V1E 4M2)
Tel: (604) 832-2833

SARDIS

BEST WESTERN RAINBOW COUNTRY INN
43971 Industrial Way (V2R 1A9)
Tel: (604) 795-3828

COMFORT INN
45405 Luckakuck Way (V2R 3C7)
Tel: (800) 221-2222

SLEEP EZEE MOTEL
44477 Yale Rd W, RR 1 (V2R 1A9)
Tel: (604) 792-2178

SAYWARD

SALMON RIVER MOTEL & RV PARK
(V0P 1P0)
Tel: (604) 282-3364

SCOTCH CREEK

3 GABLES MOTEL
Anglemont Squilax Hwy,
RR 1, Site 14, Comp 1 (V0E 1M0)
Tel: (604) 955-6377

SECHELT

BLUE SKY MOTEL
4726 Hwy 101, Box 472 (V0N 3A0)
Tel: (604) 885-9987

COZY COURT MOTEL
5522 Inlet Ave, Box 1534 (V0N 3A0)
Tel: (604) 885-9314

ROYAL BEACH MOTEL & MARINA
5758 Wharf Rd, Box 2648 (V0N 3A0)
Tel: (604) 885-7844

SICAMOUS

ALPINER MOTEL
Box 288 (V0E 2V0)
Tel: (604) 836-2290

CEDARS MOTEL
1210 Paradise, Box 294 (V0E 2V0)
Tel: (604) 836-3175

MONASHEE MOTOR INN
Hwy 1, Box 249 (V0E 2V0)
Tel: (604) 836-2575

PARADISE MOTEL
Main St, Box 100 (V0E 2V0)
Tel: (604) 836-2525

SICAMOUS INN
1304 Rauma Rd,
Box 910 (V0E 2V0)
Tel: (604) 836-4117

SUNSHINE MOTEL
529 Main St,
Box 939 (V0E 2V0)
Tel: (604) 836-3302

**WHISPERING PINES
MOTEL**
473 Main St, Box 374
(V0E 2V0)
Tel: (604) 836-2556

**WILLOW LODGE
MOTEL**
1321 Trans Canada
Hwy 1,
Box 134 (V0E 2V0)
Tel: (604) 836-2546

SIDNEY

**BEST WESTERN
EMERALD ISLE INN**
2306 Beacon Ave
(V8L 1X2)
Rates: $69-260
Tel: (250) 656-4441
(800) 528-1234

CEDARWOOD MOTEL
9522 Lochside Dr
(V8L 1N8)
Tel: (604) 656-5551

**VICTORIA AIRPORT
TRAVELODGE**
2280 Beacon Ave
(V8L 1X1)
Tel: (800) 255-3050

**WATERFRONT
HOTEL SIDNEY**
2537 Beacon Ave
(V8L 1X3)
Tel: (604) 656-1131

SLOCAN

SLOCAN INN
Slocan St, Box 330
(V0G 2C0)
Tel: (604) 355-2223

SMITHERS

ASPEN MOTOR INN
4268 Hwy 16, Box
756 (V0J 2N0)
Tel: (800) 663-7676

CAPRI MOTOR INN
3984 Hwy 16 W,
Box 3418 (V0J 2N0)
Tel: (604) 847-4226 '

FLORENCE MOTEL
Hwy 16 W, Box 516
(V0J 2N0)
Tel: (604) 847-2678

**HUDSON BAY
LODGE**
3251 E Hwy 16,
Box 3636 (V0J 2N0)
Tel: (604) 847-4581

JUNIPER LODGE
Box 444 (V0J 2N0)
Tel: (604) 847-2601

SANDMAN INN
3932 Hwy 16,
Box 935 (V0J 2N0)
Tel: (800) 726-3626

**SLUMBER LODGE
MOTEL**
1515 Main St
(V0J 2N0)
Tel: (800) 663-2831

SMITHERS HOTEL
3771 Broadway Ave,
Box 2110 (V0J 2N0)
Tel: (604) 847-3441

SORENTO MOTEL
4435 Hwy 16,
Box 444 (V0J 2N0)
Tel: (604) 847-2601

SOINTULA

**MALCOLM ISLAND
INN**
1st St, Box 380
(V0N 3E0)
Tel: (604) 973-6366

SOOKE

**SOOKE HARBOUR
HOUSE**
1528 Whiffen Spit
Rd,
RR 4 (V0S 1N0)
Tel: (604) 642-3421

SORRENTO

**SHUSWAP LAKE
MOTEL
AND RESORT**
Pachendale Rd &
Trans Canada
Hwy, Box 250
(V0E 2W0)
Tel: (604) 675-2420

**SORRENTO MOTOR
INN**
Trans Canada Hwy,
Box 30 (V0E 2W0)
Tel: (604) 675-2454

SOUTH
HAZELTON

**GRANDVIEW INN
HOTEL**
Box 130 (V0J 2R0)
Tel: (604) 842-5221

SPENCES BRIDGE

SPORTSMAN MOTEL
Box 68 (V0K 2L0)
Tel: (604) 458-2212

SUMMERLAND

**BALCARRA MOTEL
& CAMPGROUND**
9315 Pineo St,
Box 644 (V0H 1Z0)
Tel: (604) 494-4201

**PLEASANT VIEW
MOTEL & RV PARK**
13608 Hwy 97,
Box 959 (V0H 1Z0)
Tel: (604) 494-7406

**SUMMERLAND
MOTEL**
Hwy 97, RR 4 (V0H
1Z0)
Tel: (604) 494-4444

SURREY

RAMADA LIMITED
19225 hwy 10
(V3S 8V9)
Rates: $72-95
Tel: (604) 576-8388
(800) 272-6232

SURREY INN
9850 King George
Hwy (V3T 4Y3)
Tel: (604) 588-9511

TAHSIS

**COAST TAHSIS
CHALET**
Box 400 (V0P 1X0)
Tel: (800) 663-1144

TAKYSIE LAKE

**TAKYSIE LAKE
RESORT & MOTEL**
(V0J 2V0)
Tel: (604) 694-3367

TATLA LAKE

GRAHAM INN
General Delivery,
Hwy 20 (V0L 1V0)
Tel: (604) 476-1112

TELKWA

DOUGLAS MOTEL
Hwy 16 W, Box 291
(V0J 2X0)
Tel: (604) 846-5679

TERRACE

THE CEDARS MOTEL
4830 Hwy 16 W
(V8G 1L6)
Tel: (604) 635-2258

**COPPER RIVER
MOTEL**
4113 Hwy 16 E
(V8G 3N4)
Tel: (604) 635-6124

INN OF THE WEST
4620 Lakelse Ave
(V8G 1R1)
Tel: (800) 772-5555

KALUM MOTEL
5522 Hwy 16 W,
Box 593 (V8G 4B5)
Tel: (604) 635-2362

THE RAINBOW INN
5510 Hwy 16 W
(V8G 4R6)
Tel: (604) 635-6415

**REEL INN MOTEL
& TRAIL PARK**
5508 Hwy 16 W,
RR 3 (V8G 4R6)
Tel: (604) 635-2803

SANDMAN INN
4828 Hwy 16 W
(V8G 1L6)
Tel: (800) 726-3626

TERRACE INN
4551 Grieg Ave
(V8G 1M7)
Tel: (800) 663-8156

WILD DUCK MOTEL
5504 Hwy 16 W
(V8G 4R6)
Tel: (604) 635-9798

TOFINO

DOLPHIN MOTEL
1190 Pacific Rim
Hwy,
Box 116 (V0R 2Z0)
Tel: (604) 725-3377

TRAIL

RAY-LYN MOTEL
118 Wellington St
(V1R 2K2)
Tel: (604) 368-5541

TRAIL MOTEL
3080 Highway Dr
(V1R 2T3)
Tel: (604) 368-8844

TROUT LAKE

WINDSOR HOTEL
Kelly St, Box 49
(V0G 1R0)
Tel: (604) 369-2244

TUMBLER RIDGE

**TUMBLER RIDGE
INN**
Box 99 (V0C 2W0)
Tel: (604) 242-4277

UCLUELET

**ISLAND WEST
RESORT
RV PARK & MARINA**
140 Bay St, Box 32
(V0R 3A0)
Tel: (604) 726-7515

SEA SIDE MOTEL
160 Hemlock St,
Box 32 (V0R 3A0)
Tel: (604) 726-4624

THORNTON MOTEL
1861 Peninsula Rd,
Box 490 (V0R 3A0)
Tel: (604) 726-7725

**UCLUELET LODGE
HOTEL**
250 Main St,
Box 10 (V0R 3A0)
Tel: (604) 726-4324

VALEMOUNT

ALPINE MOTEL
1470 5th Ave,
Box 228
(V0E 2Z0)
Tel: (604) 566-4471

MOUNTAINEER INN
Yellowhead Hwy 5,
Box 217 (V0E 2Z0)
Tel: (800) 663-4462

RAMAKADA MOTEL
1275 Juniper St,
Box 220 (V0E 2Z0)
Tel: (604) 566-4555

SARAK MOTEL
Karas Dr, Box 339
(V0E 2Z0)
Tel: (800) 663-4465

**SWIFT CREEK
MOTEL**
1310 2nd Ave,
Box 428 (V0E 2Z0)
Tel: (604) 566-4366

TETE JAUNE LODGE
Hwy 16, Tete Jaune
Cache,
Box 879 (V0E 2Z0)
Tel: (604) 566-9815

**YELLOWHEAD
MOTEL**
5th Ave, Box 547
(V0E 2Z0)
Tel: (604) 566-4411

VANCOUVER

**BOSMAN'S MOTOR
HOTEL**
1060 Howe St
(V6Z 1P5)
Tel: (800) 663-7840

**BURRARD MOTOR
INN**
1100 Burrard St
(V6Z 1Y7)
Tel: (800) 663-0366

**CARIBOO MOTEL
& TRAILER PARK**
2555 Kingsway
(V5R 5H3)
Tel: (604) 435-2251

**CENTURY PLAZA
HOTEL**
1015 Burrard St
(V6Z 1Y5)
Tel: (800) 663-1818

**COAST VANCOUVER
AIRPORT HOTEL**
1041 SW Marine Dr
(V6P 6L6)
Tel: (800) 663-1144

DELTA PLACE
645 Howe St
(V6C 2Y9)
Tel: (800) 268-1133

DUFFERIN HOTEL
900 Seymour St
(V6B 3L9)
Tel: (604) 683-4251

**ELDORADO MOTOR
HOTEL**
2330 Kingsway
(V5R 5G9)
Tel: (604) 434-1341

**FOUR SEASONS
HOTEL**
791 W Georgia St
(V6C 2T4)
Tel: (800) 332-3442
(US)

**GEORGIAN COURT
HOTEL**
773 Beatty St (V6B
2M4)
Tel: (800) 663-1155

HOLIDAY INN
1110 Howe St (V6Z
1R2)
Tel: (800) 465-4329

HOLIDAY INN
711 W Broadway
Ave
(V5Z 3Y2)
Tel: (800) 465-4329

HOTEL VANCOUVER
900 W Georgia St
(V6C 2W6)
Tel: (800) 441-1414

**LONDON GUARD
MOTEL**
2227 Kingsway
(V5N 2T6)
Tel: (604) 430-4646

**OCEANSIDE
APARTMENT HOTEL**
1847 Pendrell St
(V6G 1T3)
Tel: (604) 682-5641

**OLD ENGLISH B & B
REGISTRY**
1226 Silverwood
Crescent (N
Vancouver, V7P 1J3)
Rates: $85-125
Tel: (604) 986-5069

**PAN PACIFIC
VANCOUVER HOTEL**
300 999 Canada Pl
(V6C 3B5)
Tel: (800) 663-1515

**QUALITY INN-
DOWNTOWN**
1335 Howe St
(V6Z 1R7)
Tel: (800) 221-2222

**QUALITY INN-
METROTOWN**
3484 Kingsway
(V5R 5L6)
Tel: (800) 221-2222

**RIVIERA MOTOR
INN**
1431 Robson St
(V6G 1C1)
Tel: (604) 685-1301

SYLVIA HOTEL
1154 Gilford St
(V6G 2P6)
Tel: (604) 681-9321

TRAVELODGE
1304 Howe St
(V6Z 1R6)
Rates: $79-119
Tel: (604) 682-2767
(800) 578-7878

TRAVELODGE
2060 Marine Dr (N
Vancouver, V7P 1V7)
Rates: $62-120
Tel: (604) 985-5311
(800) 578-7878

2400 MOTEL
2400 Kingsway
(V5R 5G9)
Tel: (604) 434-2464

**VANCOUVER
SANDMAN HOTEL**
180 W Georgia St
(V6B 4P4)
Tel: (800) 726-3626

WESTIN BAYSHORE
1601 W Georgia St
(V6G 2V4)
Tel: (800) 228-3000

YMCA HOTEL
955 Burrard St
(V6Z 1Y2)
Tel: (604) 681-0221

VANDERHOOF

**BUENA VISTA
MOTEL**
2110 Hwy 16,
Box 376
(V0J 3A0)
Tel: (604) 567-2296

HILLVIEW MOTEL
Hwy 16 E, Box 279
(V0J 3A0)
Tel: (604) 567-4468

**NECHAKO RIVER
MOTEL**
Loop Rd, Box 28
(V0J 3A0)
Tel: (604) 567-2717

**VANDERHOOF
HOTEL**
2351 Church St,
Box 1217 (V0J 3A0)
Tel: (604) 567-3188

VERNON

**BEST WESTERN
LODGE**
3914 32 St (V1T 5P1)
Rates: $57-119
Tel: (250) 545-3385
(800) 528-1234

BLUE STREAM MOTEL
4202 32nd St
(V1T 5P4)
Tel: (604) 545-2221

**COLDSTREAM
BEACH RESORT**
12408 Kalamalka Rd
(V1B 1M7)
Tel: (604) 545-0677

THE GLOBE MOTEL
3900 33rd St
(V1T 5T7)
Tel: (604) 542-2327

**HILLSIDE PLAZA
MOTEL**
4100 32nd St
(V1T 5P1)
Tel: (604) 549-1211

THE KICKWILLIE INN
9883 Pinnacles Rd,
Box 7,
Silver Star Mtn
(V0E 1G0)
Tel: (604) 542-4548

**LAKESIDE MARINA
HOTEL**
Okanagan Landing
Rd, RR 6,
Site 6, Comp 21
(V1T 6Y5)
Tel: (604) 542-2377

THE PINNACLES
9889 Pinnacles Rd,
Box 8,
Silver Star Mtn
(V0E 1G0)
Tel: (604) 542-4548

POLSON PARK MOTEL
3201 24th Ave
(V1T 1L4)
Tel: (604) 549-2231

SANDMAN INN
4201 32nd St
(V1T 5P3)
Tel: (800) 726-3626

SCHELL MOTEL
2810 35th St
(V1T 6B5)
Tel: (604) 545-1351

**SWISS HOTEL
SILVER LODGE INN**
Silver Star Mountain
Rd,
Box 5 (V0E 1G0)
Tel: (604) 549-5105

TEL-A-FREND MOTEL
1501 32nd St
(V1T 5K4)
Tel: (604) 545-1779

**TIKI VILLAGE
MOTOR INN**
2408 34th St
(V1T 5W8)
Tel: (604) 545-2268

**VERNON SLUMBER
LODGE**
3602 32nd St
(V1T 5N3)
Tel: (800) 663-2831

**VERNON
TRAVELODGE**
3000 28th Ave
(V1T 1W1)
Tel: (800) 255-3050

**WESTGATE MOTOR
INN**
4204 32nd St
(V1T 4P4)
Tel: (800) 663-4427

WILLY'S MOTOR INN
3309 39th Ave
(V1T 3W2)
Tel: (800) 661-4003

VICTORIA

ADMIRAL MOTEL
257 Belleville St
(V8V 1X1)
Tel: (604) 388-6267

CAPTAIN'S PALACE
309 Belleville St
(V8V 1X2)
Tel: (604) 388-9191

CHERRY BEND MOTEL
4879 Cherry Tree
Bend Rd
(V8Y 1S1)
Tel: (604) 658-5611

**CHESTNUT GROVE
MOTEL**
210 Gorge Rd E
(V9A 1L5)
Tel: (604) 385-3488

**COLONY MOTOR
INN**
2852 Douglas St
(V8T 4M5)
Tel: (604) 385-2441

DAFFODIL INN
680 Garbally Rd
(V8T 2K2)
Tel: (604) 386-8351

**DASHWOOD
MANOR**
1 Cook St (V8V 3W6)
Tel: (604) 385-5517

DOMINION HOTEL
759 Yates St
(V8W 1L6)
Tel: (800) 663-6101

DORIC MOTEL
3025 Douglas St
(V8T 4N2)
Tel: (604) 386-2481

DOUGLAS HOTEL
1450 Douglas St
(V8W 2G1)
Tel: (604) 383-4157

DUTCHMAN INN
2828 Rock Bay Ave
(V8T 4S1)
Tel: (604) 386-7557

THE EMPRESS
721 Government St
(V8W 1W5)
Tel: (800) 268-9411

**EXECUTIVE HOUSE
HOTEL**
777 Douglas St
(V8W 2B5)
Tel: (800) 663-7001

GORGE MOTEL
7 Gorge Rd W
(V9A 1L9)
Tel: (604) 384-6675

HARBOUR TOWERS
345 Quebec St
(V8V 1W4)
Tel: (800) 663-5896

**HOLIDAY COURT
MOTEL**
740 Hillside Ave
(V8T 1Z4)
Tel: (604) 385-7741

IMPERIAL INN
1961 Douglas St
(V8T 4K7)
Tel: (604) 382-2111

INGRAHAM HOTEL
2915 Douglas St
(V8T 4M8)
Tel: (800) 228-2000

LAUREL POINT INN
680 Montreal St
(V8V 1Z8)
Tel: (800) 663-7667

MAYFAIR MOTEL
650 Speed Ave
(V8Z 1A4)
Tel: (604) 388-7337

QUALITY HOTEL
4550 Cordova Bay
Rd (V8X 3V5)
Tel: (800) 221-2222

RAMADA INN
3010 Blanshard St
(V8T 5B5)
Tel: (800) 228-2828

ROBIN HOOD MOTEL
136 Gorge Rd E
(V9A 1L4)
Tel: (604) 388-4302

RODEWAY INN
2915 Douglas St.
(V8T 4M8)
Rates: $39-79
Tel: (604) 385-6731
(800) 228-2000

ROYAL VICTORIAN INN
230 Gorge Rd E
(V9A 1L5)
Tel: (604) 385-5771

SCOTSMAN MOTEL
490 Gorge Rd E (V8T 2W4)
Tel: (604) 388-7358

SHAMROCK MOTEL
675 Superior St
(V8V 1V1)
Tel: (604) 385-8768

SLUMBER LODGE
3110 Douglas St
(V8Z 3K4)
Tel: (800) 663-2831

STAY 'N SAVE MOTOR INN
3233 Maple St
(V8X 4Y9)
Tel: (800) 663-0298

TALLY-HO PACIFIC MOTOR INN
3020 Douglas St
(V8T 4N4)
Tel: (800) 663-5660

WASA

WASA LAKE RESORT
Box 184 (V0B 2K0)
Tel: (604) 422-3427

WELLS

HUBS MOTEL
Barkerville Hwy,
Box 116 (V0K 2R0)
Tel: (800) 663-3292

WELLS HOTEL & GALLERY
Box 134 (V0K 2R0)
Tel: (604) 994-3427

WHITE CAP MOTOR INN
Ski Hill Rd, Box 153
(V0K 2R0)
Tel: (604) 994-3489

WEST VANCOUVER

HORSESHOE BAY MOTEL
6588 Royal Ave
(V7W 2B6)
Tel: (604) 921-7454

WHISTLER

BEST WESTERN LISTEL WHISTLER HOTEL
4121 Village Green
(V0N 1B4)
Rates: $99-249
Tel: (604) 932-1133
(800) 663-5472

CHATEAU WHISTLER RESORT
4599 Chateau Blvd,
Box 100 (V0N 1B0)
Tel: (800) 268-9411

DELTA MOUNTAIN INN
4050 Whistler Way,
Box 550 (V0N 1B0)
Tel: (800) 268-1133

WHISTLER FAIRWAYS HOTEL
4005 Whistler Way
(V0N 1B0)
Tel: (800) 663-5644

WHITE ROCK

BAY MOTOR INN
15611 Marine Dr
(V4B 1E1)
Tel: (604) 531-5557

1799 MOTEL
1799 King George
Hwy 99A (V4A 4Z9)
Tel: 604) 531-3786

WILLIAMS LAKE

CAESER INN
55 S 6th Ave
(V2G 1K8)
Tel: (800) 663-6893

DRUMMOND LODGE MOTEL
1405 Cariboo Hwy E
(V2G 2W3)
Tel: (800) 667-4555

FRASER INN
285 Donald Rd
(V2G 4K4)
Tel: (800) 452-6789

JAMBOREE MOTEL
845 Carson Dr
(V2G 3N7)
Tel: (604) 398-8208

LAKESIDE RESORT MOTEL
1505 Cariboo Hwy S
(V2G 2W3)
Tel: (800) 663-4938

OVERLANDER MOTOR INN
1118 Lakeview Cres
(V2G 1A3)
Tel: (800) 663-6898

SANDMAN INN
664 Oliver St
(V2G 1M6)
Tel: (800) 726-3626

SLUMBER LODGE
27 Seventh Ave S
(V2G 1L2)
Tel: (800) 663-2831

STAMPEDER MOTEL
2 Lakeview Ave
(V2G 1B2)
Tel: (604) 392-4496

SUPER 8 MOTEL
1712 Broadway Ave
S (V2G 2W4)
Tel: (800) 800-8000

VALLEY VIEW MOTEL
1523 Cariboo Hwy
(V2G 2W3)
Tel: (604) 392-4655

WINDERMERE

SKOOKUM INN
Hwy 93, Box 68
(V0B 2L0)
Tel: (604) 342-6293

WINFIELD

BELVEDERE RESORT MOTEL
3570 Woodsdale Rd,
RR 2, Site 38
(V0H 2C0)
Tel: (604) 766-2693

WONOWON

BLUEBERRY MOTEL
Mile 101, Alaska
Hwy,
Box 28 (V0C 2N0)
Tel: (604) 772-3322

PINE HILL MOTEL
Mile 102, Alaska
Hwy,
Box 30 (V0C 2N0)
Tel: (604) 772-3340

YAHK

BOB'S MOTEL
Box 26 (V0B 2P0)
Tel: (604) 424-5581

KAE'S MOTEL
Hwy 3/95 (V0B 2P0)
Tel: (604) 424-5554

YALE

COLONIAL INN
35185 Trans Canada Hwy,
RR 1 (V0K 2S0)
Tel: (604) 863-2277

FORT YALE MOTEL
13265 Trans Canada Hwy,
Box 44 (V0K 2S0)
Tel: (604) 863-2216

YOUBOU

SASEENOS BAY MOTEL
8405 Bremner Rd,
Box 175 (V0R 3E0)
Tel: (604) 745-6222

ZEBALLOS

ZEBALLOS HOTEL
148 Maquinna St,
P. O. Box 69
(V0P 2A0)
Tel: (604) 7614275

MANITOBA

ALONSA

ALONSA HOTEL
(R0H 0A0)
Tel: (204) 767-2013

ALTONA

FOUR WINDS MOTEL
Box 1809 (R0G 0B0)
Tel: (204) 324-5305

ANOLA

ANOLA VILLAGE INN
(R0E 0A0)
Tel: (204) 866-3580

ARBORG

THE TRAVELLING INN
Box 1037 (R0C 0A0)
Tel: (204) 376-5261

ZAN'S FAMILY INN
Box 1026 (R0C 0A0)
Tel: (204) 376-5255

ASHERN

INTERLAKE MOTEL
Box 220 (R0C 0E0)
Tel: (204) 768-2817

SHARPTAIL MOTOR INN
Box 100 (R0C 0E0)
Tel: (204) 768-2319

BALDUR

BALDUR MOTOR HOTEL
Box 88 (R0K 0B0)
Tel: (204) 535-2049

BIRTLE

BIRTLE HOTEL
Box 400 (R0M 0C0)
Tel: (204) 842-5253

BOISSEVAIN

BOISSEVAIN MOTOR HOTEL
Box 700 (R0K 0E0)
Tel: (204) 534-2406

GARDEN MOTEL 78
Box 583 (R0K 0E0)
Tel: (204) 534-2438

BRANDON

CANADIAN INN
150 5th St (R7A 3K4)
Tel: (204) 727-6404

CASA BLANCA MOTOR LODGE
2728 Victoria Ave
(R7B 0M8)
Tel: (204) 728-1500

COLONIAL INN
1944 Queens Ave,
Box 952 (R7A 5Z9)
Tel: (204) 728-8532

COMFORT INN
925 Middleton Ave
(R7C 1A8)
Tel: (800) 221-2222

HILLCREST MOTEL
Hwy 1A, 1st St N,
Box 91 (R7A 5Y6)
Tel: (204) 725-1550

JOURNEY'S END MOTEL
925 Middleton Ave,
Box 248 (R7A 5Y8)
Tel: (800) 668-4200

KEYSTONE MOTOR INN
1050 18th St,
Box 254 (R7A 5C1)
Tel: (204) 728-6620

THE LITTLE CHALET
Trans Canada Hwy
&18th St (R7C 1A7)
Tel: (204) 725-1574

MID-WAY MOTEL
Hwy 1A, 2st St N,
Box 451 (R7A 5Z4)
Tel: (204) 725-1560

REDWOOD MOTOR INN
345 18th St N,
Box 815 (R7A 5Z8)
Tel: (800) 665-6372

RODEWAY INN MOTEL
300 18th St N (R7A 6Z2)
Tel: (204) 728-7230

ROYAL OAK INN
3130 Victoria Ave,
Box 670 (R7A 5Z7)
Tel: (204) 728-5775

SUPER 8 MOTEL
Intersection #'s1 & 10
S (R7C 1A7)
Rates: $57-77
Tel: (800) 800-8000

VICTORIA INN
3550 Victoria Ave W,
Box 458 (R7A 5Z4)
Tel: (204) 725-1532

WESTERN MOTEL
1148 18th St
(R7A 5C2)
Tel: (204) 728-5761

CARBERRY

4-WAY HOTEL
Box 86 (R0K 0H0)
Tel: (204) 834-2878

CARMAN

CARMAN MOTOR INN
Box 666 (R0G 0J0)
Tel: (204) 745-3733

CHURCHILL

THE ARCTIC INN
Box 306 (R0B 0E0)
Tel: (204) 675-8204

POLAR MOTEL
15 Franklin St,
Box 1031 (R0B 0E0)
Tel: (204) 675-8878

TUNDRA INN

34 Franklin St,
Box 999 (R0B 0E0)
Tel: (800) 661-1460

DAUPHIN

DAUPHIN INN MOTEL
35 Memorial Blvd
(R7N 2A5)
Tel: (204) 638-4430

RODEWAY INN MOTEL
Box 602 (R7N 2V4)
Tel: (204) 638-5102

TWEEN LAKES MOTEL
Box 744 (R7N 3B3)
Tel: (204) 638-4233

DELORAINE

DELORAINE MOTOR INN
(R0M 0M0)
Tel: (204) 747-2416

DOMINION CITY

QUEEN'S HOTEL
(R0A 0H0)
Tel: (204) 427-2307

ELKHORN

ELKHORN MOTOR HOTEL
Box 68 (R0M 0N0)
Tel: (204) 845-2505

EMERSON

MAPLE LEAF MOTEL
Box 55 (R0A 0L0)
Tel: (204) 373-2594

ERICKSON

NORDIC INN
Box 266 (R0J 0P0)
Tel: (204) 636-2601

FLIN FLON

VICTORIA INN
Box 220 (R8A 1M9)
Tel: (204) 687-7555

GILBERT PLAINS

**GILBERT PLAINS
HOTEL**
(R0L 0X0)
Tel: (204) 548-2337

GILLAM

NEW GILLAM HOTEL
Box 68 (R0B 0L0)
Tel: (204) 652-2670

GIMLI

COUNTRY RESORT
10 Centre St,
Box 1860 (R0C 1B0)
Tel: (204) 642-8565

NORSEMAN MOTEL
71 6th Ave,
Box 131 (R0C 1B0)
Tel: (204) 642-5181

GLADSTONE

GLADSTONE MOTEL
Box 531 (R0J 0T0)
Tel: (204) 385-2770

GLENBORO

**SPRUCE WOODS
INN LTD.**
Box 430 (R0K 0X0)
Tel: (204) 827-2648

GLENELLA

CORONA HOTEL
Box 37 (R0J 0V0)
Tel: (204) 352-4221

GRAND RAPIDS

HILLTOP MOTEL
(R0C 1E0)
Tel: (204) 639-2370

GRANDVIEW

PARKVIEW MOTEL
Box 570 (R0L 0Y0)
Tel: (204) 546-2178

GRETNA

**GRETNA BORDER
INN**
Box 369 (R0G 0V0)
Tel: (204) 327-5228

HADASHVILLE

DAWSON TRAIL INN
(R0E 0X0)
Tel: (204) 426-5371

PARKVIEW INN
(R0E 0X0)
Tel: (204) 426-5441

ILFORD

GOLD TRAIL LODGE
(R0B 0S0)
Tel: (204) 288-4380

KILLARNEY

EMERALD ISLE MOTEL
Box 1600 (R0K 1G0)
Tel: (204) 523-4215

ERIN INN
Box 1418 (R0K 1G0)
Tel: (204) 523-4651

LA RIVIERE

**HOLIDAY MOUN-
TAIN MOTEL**
Box 89 (R0G 1A0)
Tel: (204) 242-2172

LAC DU BONNET

**LAKEVIEW MOTOR
MOTEL**
Box 189 (R0E 1A0)
Tel: (204) 345-8661

LANGRUTH

RIDGE HOTEL
Box 130 (R0H 0N0)
Tel: (204) 445-2332

LAURIER

LAURIER HOTEL
(R0J 1A0)
Tel: (204) 447-2505

LEAF RAPIDS

WHITEWATER INN
Box 130 (R0B 1W0)
Tel: (204) 473-2451

LETELLIER

LETELLIER HOTEL
Box 246 (R0G 1C0)
Tel: (204) 737-2630

LYNN LAKE

WOLVERINE MOTEL
510 Halstead Ave,
Box 353 (R0B 0W0)
Tel: (204) 356-2496

MACGREGOR

J. K.'S MOTEL
Box 432 (R0H 0H0)
Tel: (204) 685-2585

MANITOU

**MANITOU MOTOR
INN**
(R0G 1G0)
Tel: (204) 242-2830

MARIAPOLIS

**MARIAPOLIS
MOTOR HOTEL**
Box 2 (R0K 1K0)
Tel: (204) 836-2758

MCCREARY

**MCCREARY
CHALET & HOTEL**
Box 460 (R0J 1B0)
Tel: (204) 835-2203

MELITA

**MELITA
DREAMLAND MOTEL**
Box 414 (R0M 1L0)
Tel: (204) 522-3245

MELITA MOTEL
Box 456 (R0M 1L0)
Tel: (204) 522-3261

MINIOTA

**MINIOTA MOTOR
HOTEL**
Box 4 (R0M 1M0)
Tel: (204) 567-3776

MINNEDOSA

GATEWAY MOTEL
Box 325 (R0J 1E0)
Tel: (204) 867-2729

MORDEN

STAR MOTEL
Box 2540 (R0G 1J0)
Tel: (204) 822-4494

MORRIS

BURKE'S MOTEL
Box 428 (R0G 1K0)
Tel: (204) 746-2222

**COLONIAL INN
MOTOR HOTEL**
Box 248 (R0G 1K0)
Tel: (204) 746-2335

NEEPAWA

NEEPAWA MOTEL
Box 1622 (R0J 1H0)
Tel: (204) 476-2331

VIVIAN MOTOR HOTEL
236 Hamilton St (R0J
1H0)
Tel: (204) 476-5089

NEWDALE

LEISURE INN
(R0J 1J0)
Tel: (204) 849-2182

NINETTE

NINETTE MOTOR HOTEL
(R0K 1R0)
Tel: (204) 528-3331

NORTH SHORE LODGE
Box 120 (R0K 1R0)
Tel: (204) 528-3412

NORWAY HOUSE

PLAYGREEN INN
(R0B 1B0)
Tel: (204) 359-6321

NOTRE DAME DE LOURDES CAPRI-CORNE MOTEL
Box 266 (R0G 1M0)
Tel: (204) 248-2012

OAK RIVER

BLANCHARD HOTEL
(R0K 1T0)
Tel: (204) 566-2421

OAKVIEW

LAKE MANITOBA NARROWS LODGE
(R0C 2K0)
Tel: (204) 768-2749

OAKVILLE

OAKVILLE MOTOR HOTEL
(R0H 0Y0)
Tel: (204) 267-2533

ONANOLE

SOUTHGATE MOTOR HOTEL
(R0J 1N0)
Tel: (204) 848-2542

PINEY

PINEY HOTEL
(R0A 1K0)
Tel: (204) 423-2021

PORTAGE LA PRAIRIE

HI-WAY MOTEL
2010 Saskatchewan Ave W (R1N 0P2)
Tel: (204) 857-8771

MANITOBAH INN
Box 867 (R1N 3C3)
Tel: (204) 857-9791

WESTGATE INN MOTEL
1010 Saskatchewan Ave W (R1N 0K1)
Tel: (204) 239-5200

WESTWARD VILLAGE INN
2401 Saskatchewan Ave W (R1N 3L5)
Tel: (204) 857-9745

RAPID CITY

QUEEN'S HOTEL
450 2nd Ave E,
Box 249 (R0K 1W0)
Tel: (204) 826-2626

RESTON

RESTON MOTOR HOTEL
(R0M 1X0)
Tel: (204) 877-3383

RICHER

RICHER INN MOTOR HOTEL
Box 100 (R0E 1S0)
Tel: (204) 422-5482

RIDING MOUNTAIN

RIDING MOUNTAIN INN
Box 31 (R0J 1T0)
Tel: (204) 967-2211

ROBLIN

EASTWAY MOTEL
Box 1023 (R0L 1P0)
Tel: (204) 937-830102

1 PARKWAY INN
(R0L 1P0)
Tel: (204) 937-2130

SATURN MOTOR HOTEL
(R0L 1P0)
Tel: (204) 937-4300

RORKETON

RORKETON HOTEL
(R0L 1R0)
Tel: (204) 732-2042

ROSSBURN

ROSSBURN HOTEL
(R0J 1V0)
Tel: (204) 859-2561

RUSSELL

THE JOLLY LODGER
Box 35 (R0J 1W0)
Tel: (204) 773-2177

RUSSELL INN
Box 578 (R0J 1W0)
Tel: (204) 773-2186

SELKIRK

DAERWOOD MOTOR INN
162 Main St
(R1A 1R3)
Tel: (204) 482-7722

LORD SELKIRK HOTEL& MOTEL
420 Main St (R1A 1V3)
Tel: (204) 785-8669

SEVEN SISTERS FALLS

OTTER FALLS RESORT
(R0E 1Y0)
Tel: (204) 348-7216

RIVERVIEW LODGE
Box 114 (R0E 1Y0)
Tel: (204) 348-7607

SEVEN SISTERS MOTEL
(R0E 1Y0)
Tel: (204) 348-2269

SHERRIDON

REDWOOD INN
(R0B 1L0)
Tel: (204) 472-3364

SHILO

SHILO INN
General Delivery
(R0K 2A0)
Tel: (204) 765-2157

SHOAL LAKE

HUNTER'S PARADISE MOTEL
Box 396 (R0J 1Z0)
Tel: (204) 759-2047

SOURIS

SOURIS MOTOR INN
(R0K 2C0)
Tel: (204) 483-2175

SPRAGUE

SPRAGUE HOTEL
Box 66 (R0A 1Z0)
Tel: (204) 437-2245

STONY MOUNTAIN

STONY MOUNTAIN MOTOR INN
Box 321 (R0C 3A0)
Tel: (204) 344-5511

SWAN RIVER SKYLINE MOTEL
Box 628 (R0L 1Z0)
Tel: (204) 734-3471

THUNDERHILL MOTEL
Box 1948 (R0L 1Z0)
Tel: (204) 734-4104

TWILIGHT MOTEL
Box 2263 (R0L 1Z0)
Tel: (204) 734-3424

TWO-MORROWS INN
1570 Main St E,
Box 2261 (R0L 1Z0)
Tel: (204) 734-3451

WASHENFELDER'S VALLEY HOTEL
703 Main St E,
Box 1239 (R0L 1Z0)
Tel: (204) 734-2058

WESTWOOD INN
P. O. Box 2050
(R0L 1Z0)
Tel: (204) 734-4548

TEULON

TEULON INN MOTOR HOTEL
Box 240 (R0C 3B0)
Tel: (204) 886-2263

THE PAS

GOLDEN ARROW MOTEL
Box 2855 (R9A 1M6)
Tel: (204) 623-5451

LA VERENDRYE MOTEL
Box 510 (R9A 1K6)
Tel: (204) 623-3431

TAMARACK MOTEL
Box 3074 (R9A 1L7)
Tel: (204) 623-7406

THOMPSON

COUNTRY INN & SUITES
70 Thompson Dr N
(R8N 0C3)
Tel: (800) 456-4000

TREHERNE

BIRCH MOTEL
Box 116 (R0G 2V0)
Tel: (204) 723-2535

VIRDEN

COUNTRYSIDE INN MOTEL
Box 1150 (R0M 2C0)
Tel: (204) 748-1244

VIRDEN MOTEL
Box 1259 (R0M 2C0)
Tel: (204) 748-2424

WABOWDEN

SASAGIU RAPIDS LODGE
(R0B 1S0)
Tel: (204) 677-9351

WARREN

WOODLANDS MOTOR HOTEL
(R0C 3E0)
Tel: (204) 322-5318

WASAGAMING

MANIGAMING MOTEL
137 Ta-Wa-Pit
(R0J 2H0)
Tel: (204) 848-2459

MOOSWA MOTEL
Box 39 (R0J 2H0)
Tel: (204) 848-2533

THE NEW CHALET
Box 100 (R0J 2H0)
Tel: (204) 848-2892

WAWANESA

OAKLAND INN
Box 100 (R0K 2G0)
Tel: (204) 824-2501

WHITESHELL

PROV. PARK INVERNESS FALLS RESORT
Rennie P.O.
(R0E 1R0)
Tel: (204) 369-5336

WINKLER

WINKLER MOTOR INN
Box 968 (R0G 2X0)
Tel: (204) 325-7388

WINNIPEG BEACH

HAMILTON HOUSE MOTEL
Box 399 (R0C 3G0)
Tel: (204) 389-2169

WINNIPEG

AIRPORT HOTEL
1800 Ellice Ave
(R3H 0B7)
Tel: (204) 783-7035

BALMORAL MOTOR HOTEL
Balmoral & Notre
Dame Ave (R3B 2R4)
Tel: (204) 943-1544

BEST WESTERN CARLTON INN
220 Carlton St
(R3C 1P5)
Tel: (800) 528-1234

BEST WESTERN INTERNATIONAL INN
1808 Wellington Ave
(R3H 0G3)
Tel: (800) 528-1234

CANADIANA MOTOR HOTEL
1400 Notre Dame
Ave (R3E 3G5)
Tel: (204) 786-3471

CHARLESWOOD MOTOR HOTEL
3425 Robin Blvd
(R3R 0C6)
Tel: (204) 837-1391

CHARTERHOUSE HOTEL
330 York Ave
(R3C 0N9)
Tel: (204) 942-0101

COMFORT INN
3109 Pembina Hwy
(R3T 4R6)
Tel: (800) 221-2222

COMFORT INN-AIRPORT
1770 Sargent Ave
(R3H 0C8)
Tel: (800) 221-2222

COUNTRY INNS & SUITES BY CARLSON
730 King Edward St
(R3H 1B4)
Tel: (800) 456-4000

DELTA WINNIPEG
288 Portage Ave
(R3C 0B8)
Tel: (800) 268-1133

GRANT MOTOR INN
635 Pembina Hwy
(R3M 2L4)
Tel: (204) 453-8247

HOLIDAY INN CROWNE PLAZA
350 St. Mary's Ave
(R3C 3J2)
Tel: (800) 465-4329

HOLIDAY INN WINNIPEG SOUTH
1330 Pembina Hwy
(R3T 2B4)
Tel: (800) 465-4329

INTERNATIONAL INN
1808 Wellington Ave
(R3H 0G3)
Tel: (800) 528-1234

JOURNEY'S END HOTEL
1770 Sargent Ave
(R3H 0B5)
Tel: (800) 668-4200

JOURNEY'S END HOTEL
3109 Pembina Hwy
(R3T 4R6)
Tel: (800) 668-4200

KIRKFIELD MOTOR HOTEL
3317 Portage Ave
(R3K 0W8)
Tel: (204) 837-1314

LAKE HAVEN RESORT MOTEL
854 Furby St
(R3A 1L7)
Tel: (204) 783-1980

MARLBOROUGH INN
331 Smith St
(R3B 2G9)
Tel: (204) 942-6411

MARYLAND MOTOR HOTEL
Notre Dame &
Maryland
(R3E 0L7)
Tel: (204) 785-5981

MATHER MOTEL
2672 Portage Ave
(R3J 0R1)
Tel: (204) 832-1344

NORLANDER INN MOTOR HOTEL
1792 Pembina Hwy
(R3T 2G2)
Tel: (204) 269-6955

OSBORNE VILLAGE MOTOR INN
160 Osborne
(R3L 1Y6)
Tel: (204) 452-9824

PALOMINO PLAINS MOTEL
2583 Pembina Hwy
(R3T 2H5)
Tel: (204) 269-2526

POLO PARK INN
1405 St. Matthews
Ave
(R3G 0K5)
Tel: (800) 665-0033

PORTAGE VILLAGE INN
311 Portage Ave
(R3B 2B9)
Tel: (204) 947-1568

RAMADA INN
1824 Pembina Hwy
(R3T 2G2)
Tel: (800) 268-8998

RAMADA INN
1824 Pembina Hwy
(R3T 2G2)
Tel: (800) 268-8998

RAMADA MARLBOROUGH HOTEL
331 Smith St
(R3B 2G9)
Rates: $73-135
Tel: (204) 942-6411
(800) 272-6232

RODEWAY INN-DOWNTOWN
367 Ellice Ave (R3B 1Y1)
Tel: (800) 221-2222

ST. NORBERT MOTOR HOTEL
3540 Pembina Hwy
(R3V 1A6)
Tel: (204) 269-1290

SHERATON WINNIPEG
161 Donald St
(R3C 1M3)
Tel: (800) 325-3535

SHERBROOK INN
685 Westminster Ave
(R3C 1Z4)
Tel: (204) 786-5851

STOCK EXCHANGE HOTEL
1105 Arlington St
(R3E 3L1)
Tel: (204) 786-6601

SUPER 8 MOTEL
1484 Niakwa Rd E
(R2J 3T3)
Rates: $43-59
Tel: (204) 253-1935
(800) 800-8000

TRAVELODGE HOTEL-DOWNTOWN WINNIPEG
360 Colony St (R3B 2P3)
Tel: (800) 667-3529

WESTIN HOTEL
2 Lombard Pl
(R3B 0Y3)
Tel: (800) 228-3000

WINNIPEGOSIS

WINNIPEGOSIS MOTOR INN
Box 430 (R0L 2G0)
Tel: (204) 656-4955

NEW BRUNSWICK

ATHOLVILLE

FUNDY LINE MOTEL
P. O. Box 490,
Notre Dame St
(E0K 1A0)
Tel: (506) 753-3395

BATHURST

BEST WESTERN DANNY'S INN
St. Peter Ave W,
P. O. Box 180
(E2A 3Z2)
Tel: (800) 528-1234

COMFORT INN
1170 St. Peter Ave
(E2A 2Z9)
Tel: (800) 221-2222

COUNTRY INN & SUITES
777 St. Peter Ave
(E2A 1Y9)
Tel: (800) 456-4000

BELLEDUNE

E & M MOTEL
RR 1, Box 7
(E0B 1G0)
Tel: (506) 522-5506

BOUCTOUCHE

HILLTOP MOTEL
P. O. Box 182
(E0A 1G0)
Tel: (506) 743-5003

CAMPBELLTON

COMFORT INN
3 Sugarloaf St W
(E3N 3G9)
Tel: (800) 221-2222

HOWARD JOHNSON
157 Water St
(E3N 3H2)
Tel: (506) 753-4133
(800) 446-4656

CAMPOBELLO

FRIAR'S BAY MOTOR LODGE
Welshpool
(E0G 3H0)
Tel: (506) 752-2058

POLLOCK COVE COTTAGES
Wilson's Beach
(E0G 3L0)
Tel: (506) 752-2300

CAP-PELE

HERITAGE MOTEL
889 Ch. Acadia W,
C.P. 506 (E0A 1J0)
Tel: (506) 577-2211

COLES ISLAND

CANNAN GAME LODGE
(E0E 1G0)
Tel: (506) 362-2901

DALHOUSIE ART'S MOTEL
P. O. Box 1678
(E0K 1B0)
Tel: (506) 684-3334

DUMFRIES

MOONLIGHT MOTEL
P. O. Box 101
(E0H 1S0)
Tel: (506) 575-8116

EDMUNDSTON

AUBERGE WANDLYN INN
919 Canada Rd,
P. O. Box 68
(E3V 3K5)
Tel: (506) 735-5525

COMFORT INN
5 Bateman Ave
(E3V 3L1)
Tel: (800) 221-2222

HOWARD JOHNSON
100 Rice St
(E3V 1T4)
Tel: (800) 654-2000

LA ROMA MOTEL
RR 4 (E3V 3V7)
Tel: (506) 735-3305

LYNN MOTEL
20 Church St
(E3V 1J2)
Tel: (506) 735-8851

MOTEL GUY
RR 3 (E3V 3K5)
Tel: (506) 735-4253

MOTEL LE BRAYON & CHALETS
Rue du Rocher St.
Basile(E0L 1H0)
Tel: (506) 263-5656

FLORENCEVILLE

BEECHWOOD MOTEL
RR 2, Wicklow
(R0J 1K0)
Tel: (506) 278-3289

FREDERICTON

AUBERGE WANDLYN INN
58 Prospect St W,
P. O. Box 214
(E3B 2T8)
Tel: (506) 452-8937

COMFORT INN
255 Prospect St W
(E3B 5Y4)
Tel: (800) 221-2222

CONDOR MOTOR LODGE
P. O. Box 801
(E3B 5B4)
Tel: (506) 450-9911

DUTCH INN
P. O. Box 282 (E3B 4Y9)
Tel: (506) 357-8456

THE FREDERICTON INN
1315 Regent St
(E3C 1A1)
Tel: (506) 455-1430

HOWARD JOHNSON
Lower St. Mary's,
Trans Canada Hwy
#2 (E3B 5E3)
Tel: (506) 472-0480
(800) 446-4656

KEDDY'S INN
368 Forest Hill Rd,
P. O. Box 1510
(E3B 5G2)
Tel: (800) 561-7666

KINGSCLEAR HOTEL & RESORT
RR 6 (E3B 4X7)
Tel: (800) 561-5111

ROADSIDE MOTEL
RR 6 (E3B 4X7)
Tel: (506) 450-2080

SHERATON INN FREDERICTON
225 Woodstock Rd
(E3B 2H8)
Tel: (800) 325-3535

GRAND FALLS

MOTEL LEO LA RENAISSANCE
P. O. Box 2784
(E0J 1M0)
Tel: (800) 661-0077

SCENIC MOTEL
P. O. Box 1378, TCH
(E0J 1M0)
Tel: (506) 473-2211

GRAND MANAN

MARATHON INN
North Head (E0G 2M0)
Tel: (506) 662-8144

SURFSIDE MOTEL
North Head
(E0G 2M0)
Tel: (506) 662-8156

HARTLAND

JA-SA-LE MOTEL
P. O. Box 418
(E0J 1N0)
Tel: (506) 375-4419

MCADAM

LAKELAND MOTEL
Saunders Rd
(E0H 1K0)
Tel: (506) 784-3173

MONCTON

**AUBERGE
WANDLYN INN**
RR 8, Magnetic Hill
(E1C 8K2)
Tel: (506) 384-3554

COLONIAL INNS
42 Highfield St,
P. O. Box 1381
(E1C 8T6)
Tel: (800) 561-4667

COMFORT INN
20 Maplewood Dr
(E1A 6P9)
Tel: (800) 221-2222

COMFORT INN
2495 Mountain Rd,
RR 8 (E1C 8K2)
Tel: (800) 221-2222

**COUNTRY INN &
SUITES**
2475 Mountain Rd,
P. O. Box 2340
(E1C 8J3)
Tel: (800) 456-4000

HOTEL BEAUSEJOUR
750 Main St
(E1C 1E6)
Tel: (800) 441-1414

JONES LAKE MOTEL
1650 Main St
(E1E 1G6)
Tel: (506) 389-1718

**KEDDY'S
BRUNSWICK HOTEL**
1005 Main St,
P. O. Box 828
(E1C 8N6)
Tel: (800) 561-7666

KEDDY'S MOTOR INN
RR 6, Shediac Rd
(E1C 8K1)
Tel: (800) 561-7666

MIDTOWN MOTEL
61 Weldon St (E1C
5V9)
Tel: (506) 388-5000

MITCHELL'S MOTEL
Rte 2 (E1C 8J5)
Tel: (506) 858-8877

SCENIC MOTEL
Box 2862 (E1C 8T8)
Tel: (506) 858-8878

TRAVELODGE
434 Main St
(E1C 1B9)
Rates: $51-97
Tel: (506) 382-1664
(800) 578-7878

NEWCASTLE

**AUBERGE
WANDLYN INN**
365 Water St,
P. O. Box 411
(E1V 3M5)
Tel: (506) 622-3870

COMFORT INN
201 Edward St
(E1V 2Y7)
Tel: (800) 221-2222

FUNDY LINE MOTEL
869 King George
Hwy (E1V 1P9)
Tel: (506) 622-3650

HALFWAY INN
Renous Hwy,
P. O. Box 655
(E1V 3T7)
Tel: (506) 551-1492

THE WHARF INN
1 Jane St P. O. Box
474 (E1V 3M6)
Tel: (800) 561-2111

NORTH
COCAGNE

**COCAGNE MOTEL
DE COCAGNE**
P. O. Box 119
(E0A 1K0)
Tel: (506) 576-6657

OROMOCTO

OROMOCTO HOTEL
100 Hersey St
(E2V 1J3)
Tel: (506) 357-8424

PENNFIELD

SMITTY'S MOTEL
Rte 1 (E0G 2R0)
Tel: (506) 755-3034

PERTH-
ANDOVER

**PERTH-ANDOVER
MOTOR INN**
P. O. Box 898
(E0J 1V0)
Tel: (506) 273-2224

PETIT-ROCHER

**MOTEL CHATEAU
MARITIME**
P. O. Box 938
(E0B 2E0)
Tel: (506) 783-4297

PLASTER ROCK

**NORTHERN
WILDNERNESS LODGE**
P. O. Box 571
(E0J 1W0)
Tel: (506) 356-8327

TOBIQUE VIEW MOTEL
P. O. Box 571
(E0J 1W0)
Tel: (506) 356-2684

SACKVILLE

BORDENS MOTEL
P. O. Box 26
(E0A 3C0)
Tel: (506) 536-1066

MARSHLANDS INN
Robson Ave,
P. O. Box 1440
(E0A 3C0)
Tel: (506) 536-1327

**SLUMBERLAND
MOTEL**
RR 3 (E0A 3C0)
Tel: (506) 536-1657

SAINT JOHN

COLONIAL INN
175 City Rd,
P. O. Box 2149
(E2L 3T5)
Tel: (800) 561-4667

COMFORT INN
1155 Fairville Blvd,
P.O Box 3925, Stn B
(E2M 5E6)
Tel: (800) 221-2222

**COUNTRY INN &
SUITES**
1011 Fairville Blvd,
P.O.Box 3547, Stn B
(E2M 4Y2)
Tel: (800) 456-4000

COURTENAY BAY INN
350 Haymarket Sq
(E2L 3P1)
Tel: (800) 565-7666

DELTA BRUNSWICK
39 King St
(E2L 4W3)
Tel: (800) 268-1133

**DONNER'S HOUSE-
KEEPING CABINS**
1121 Manawagonish
Rd (E2M 3X5)
Tel: (506) 672-1375

FAIRPORT MOTEL
1360 Manawagonish
Rd (E2M 3Y1)
Tel: (506) 635-8300

FUNDY LINE MOTEL
2149 Ocean West
Way (E2M 5H6)
Tel: (506) 672-2493

FUNDY LINE MOTEL
532 Rothesay Ave
(E2J 2C7)
Tel: (506) 633-7733

HILLCREST MOTEL
1315 Manawagonish
Rd (E2M 3X3)
Tel: (506) 672-5310

HILLSIDE MOTEL
1131 Manawagonish
Rd (E2M 3X5)
Tel: (506) 672-1273

HOWARD JOHNSON
400 Main St,
Chelsey Dr
(E2K 4N5)
Tel (506) 642-2622

ISLAND VIEW MOTEL
1726 Manawagonish
Rd (E2M 3Y5)
Tel: (506) 672-1381

**KEDDY'S
FORT HOWE HOTEL**
Main & Portland St
(E2K 4H8)
Tel: (800) 561-7666

LEECROFT COURT
2181 Ocean West
Way (E2M 5H6)
Tel: (506) 672-1056

TERRACE MOTEL
2131 Ocean West
Way, P.O.Box 3782,
Stn B (E2M 5H6)
Tel: (506) 672-9670

VALLEY VIEW MOTEL
1309 Manawagonish
Rd (E2M 3X8)
Tel: (506) 672-6060

SAINT-LEONARD

DAIGLE'S MOTEL
68 Bridge St
(E0L 1M0)
Tel: (506) 423-6351

SAINT-LOUIS DE-KENT

**PARK WOODLAND
MOTEL**
P. O. Box 218
(E0A 2Z0)
Tel: (506) 876-24

SAINT-QUENTIN

**MOTEL HOTEL
VICTORIA**
P. O. Box 207
(E0K 1J0)
Tel: (506) 235-2002

ST. ANDREWS

**BEST WESTERN
SHIRETOWN INN**
218 Water St,
P. O. Box 145
(E0G 2X0)
Tel: (800) 528-1234

**ST. ANDREWS
MOTOR INN**
111 Water St
(E0G 2X0)
Tel: (506) 529-4571

ST. STEPHEN

**AUBERGE
WANDLYN INN**
99 King St,
P. O. Box 99
(E3L 2C6)
Tel: (506) 466-1814

**BUSY BEE MOTEL
& CABINS**
Bay Rd, RR 3
(E3L 2Y1)
Tel: (506) 466-2938

FUNDY LINE MOTEL
198 King St
(E3L 2E2)
Tel: (506) 466-2130

**LAKE DIDGEGUASH
FOUR SEASONS
CHALETS**
148 Pleasant St
(E3L 2X2)
Tel: (506) 755-2737

STE-ANNE-DE-MADAWASKA

MOTEL NEW MOON
RR 1 (E0L 1G0)
Tel: (506) 445-2262

SHEFFIELD

RIVERVIEW MOTEL
RR 2 (E3B 4X3)
Tel: (506) 357-5167

STANLEY

**CORNISH CORNER
INN**
Main St,
P. O. Box 40
(E0H 1T0)
Tel: (506) 367-2239

SUSSEX

**FAIRWAY MOTOR
INN**
Box 1757 (E0E 1P0)
Tel: (506) 433-3470

**TIMBERLAND
MOTOR INN**
P. O. Box 802
(E0E 1P0)
Tel: (506) 433-2480

WATERBOR-OUGH

MCINTYRE'S MOTEL
(E0E 1S0)
Tel: (506) 362-2913

WOODSTOCK

**AUBERGE WANDLYN
INN**
P. O. Box 1191
(E0J 2B0)
Tel: (506) 328-8876

**COSY CABINS &
MOTEL**
RR 1 (E0J 2B0)
Tel: (506) 328-3344

PANORAMA MOTEL
(E0J 2B0)
Tel: (506) 328-3315

**STILES MOTEL
HILLVIEW**
827 Main St,
P. O. Box 1390 (E0J
2B0)
Tel: (506) 328-6671

YOUNGS COVE ROAD

MCCREADY'S MOTEL
(E0E 1S0)
Tel: (506) 362-2916

NEWFOUNDLAND

ARNOLD'S COVE

TANKER INN
P. O. Box 130
(A0B 1A0)
Tel: (709) 463-2313

BONAVISTA BAY

COZY CABINS RESORT
Traytown (A0G 4K0)
Tel: (709) 533-6601

EASTPORT EFFICIENCY UNITS
Eastport (A0G 1Z0)
Tel: (709) 677-2458

YELLOW TEAPOT INN
Brookfield
(A0G 1B0)
Tel: (709) 536-5858

BOTWOOD

ATLANTIC HOTEL
P. O. Box 50
(A0H 1E0)
Tel: (709) 257-2242

CARBONEAR

CARBONEAR MOTEL
P. O. Box 719
(A0A 1T0)
Tel: (709) 596-5662

FONG'S MOTEL
Rt 70, P. O. Box 329
(A0A 1T0)
Tel: (709) 596-5114

CLARENVILLE

HOLIDAY INN
Trans Canada Hwy,
Rt 1 (A0E 1J0)
Tel: (800) 465-4329

CONCEPTION BAY

MAKINSON MOTEL
Rt 71, P. O. Box 401,
Clarke's Beach
(A0A 1W0)
Tel: (709) 786-2310

CORMACK

FUNLAND RESORT
P. O. Box 145
(A0K 2E0)
Tel: (709) 635-7372

CORNER BROOK

BEST WESTERN MAMA TEEK INN
Maple Valley Rd,
Box 787,
Rt 1, Corner Brook
(A1H 6G7)
Tel: (709) 639-8901

COMFORT INN
41 Maple Valley Rd,
P. O. Box 1142
(A2H 6P2)
Tel: (800) 221-2222

GLYNMILL INN
Cobb Lane,
P. O. Box 550
(A2H 6E6)
Tel: (800) 563-4400

HOLIDAY INN
48 West St
(A2H 2Z2)
Tel: (800) 465-4329

HOTEL CORNER BROOK
Main St,
P. O. Box 398
(A2H 6E3)
Tel: (709) 634-8211

COW HEAD

SHALLOW BAY MOTEL & CABINS
P. O. Box 44
(A0K 2A0)
Tel: (709) 243-2471

DEER LAKE

DEER LAKE MOTEL
P. O. Box 820, Rt 1
(A0K 2E0)
Tel: (709) 635-2108

ROCKY BROOK CABINS
Rt 422, Veterans Dr,
RR 2, Box 8
(A0K 2E0)
Tel: (709) 635-7255

FORTUNE

FAIR ISLE MOTEL
Fortune Hwy,
P. O. Box 520
(A0E 1P0)
Tel: (709) 832-1010

GANDER

ALBATROSS MOTEL
Rt 1, P. O. Box 450
(A1V 1W8)
Tel: (709) 256-3956

COUNTRY INN
315 Gander Bay Rd,
P. O. Box 154 (A1V 1W6)
Tel: (709) 256-4005

HOLIDAY INN
1 Caldwell St
(A1V 1T6)
Tel: (800) 465-4329

HOTEL GANDER
100 Trans Canada
Hwy(A1V 1P5)
Tel: (709) 256-3931

SINBAD'S MOTEL
Bennett Dr,
P. O. Box 450
(A1V 1W8)
Tel: (800) 563-4900

GRAND FALLS

MOUNT PETYON HOTEL-MOTEL
Rt 1, 214 Lincoln Rd
(A2A 1P8)
Tel: (800) 563-4900

MARYSTOWN

MOTEL MORTIER
P. O. Box 487
(A0E 2M0)
Tel: (709) 279-1600

MOUNT PEARL

GREENWOOD LODGE & MOTEL
53 Greenwood Cres
(A1N 3J1)
Tel: (709) 364-5300

NOTRE DAME BAY

CARMANVILLE OLDE INN
P. O. Box 16
(A0G 1N0)
Tel: (709) 534-2544

PARADISE

KARWOOD HOLIDAY RESORT
P. O. Box 821
(A1L 1E2)
Tel: (709) 782-1094

PASADENA

LAKELAND LODGE & MOTEL
P. O. Box 250
(A0L 1K0)
Tel: (709) 686-2242

PORT AUX BASQUES

HOTEL PORT AUX BASQUES
P. O. Box 400
(A0M 1C0)
Tel: (709) 695-2171

WALKER'S MOTEL
Marine Dr,
P. O. Box 865
(A0M 1C0)
Tel: (709) 695-7355

ROCKY HARBOUR

GROS MORNE CABINS
P. O. Box 151
(A0K 4N0)
Tel: (709) 458-2020

OCEAN VIEW MOTEL
P. O. Box 129 (A0K 4N0)
Tel: (709) 458-2730

ST. JOHN'S

AIRPORT INN
Airport Rd,
P. O. Box 9432
(A1A 2Y3)
Tel: (709) 753-3500

BEST WESTERN TRAVELLERS INN
199 Kenmount Rd
(A1B 3P9)
Tel: (800) 528-1234

CENTER CITY MOTEL
389 Elizabeth Ave
(A1B 1V1)
Tel: (709) 726-0092

HOLIDAY INN GOVERNMENT CENTRE
180 Portugal Cove Rd (A1B 2N2)
Tel: (800) 465-4329

QUALITY HOTEL
2 Hill O'Chips
(A1C 6B1)
Tel: (800) 221-2222

RADISSON PLAZA HOTEL
120 New Gower St
(A1C 6K4)
Tel: (800) 333-3333

TREPASSEY

TREPASSEY MOTEL
Rt 10 (A0A 4B0)
Tel: (709) 438-2934

NORTHWEST TERRITORIES

BAKER LAKE

IGLU HOTEL
Box 179 (X0C 0A0)
Tel: (819) 793-2801

FORT PROVIDENCE

SNOWSHOE INN
(X0E 0L0)
Tel: (403) 699-3511

HAY RIVER

MACKENZIE PLACE
Box 1880 (X0E 0R0)
Tel: (403) 874-2535

MIGRATOR MOTEL
Box 1847 (X0E 0R0)
Tel: (403) 874-6792

PTARMIGAN INN
Box 1000 (X0E 0R0)
Tel: (403) 874-6781

HOLMAN

ARCTIC CHAR INN
General Delivery
(X0E 0S0)
Tel: (403) 396-3531

IQALUIT

NAVIGATOR INN
P. O. Box 158
(X0A 0H0)
Tel: (819) 979-6201

NORMAN WELLS

RAYUKA INN
Box 308 (X0E 0V0)
Tel: (403) 587-2354

YELLOWKNIFE

YELLOWKNIFE INN
P. O. Box 490
(X1A 2N4)
Tel: (403) 873-2601

NOVA SCOTIA

AMHERST

AUBERGE WANDLYN INN
Box 275, Hwy 104
(B4H 3Z2)
Tel: (902) 667-3331

COMFORT INN
143 S Albion St
(B4H 2X2)
Tel: (800) 221-2222

FUNDY WINDS FAMILY MOTEL
Box 1136 (B4H 3Y6)
Tel: (902) 667-3881

PIED PIPER MOTEL
Upper Nappan,
RR 6 (B4H 2Y4)
Tel: (902) 667-3891

TRANTRAMAR MOTEL
Box 724 (B4H 4B9)
Tel: (902) 667-3838

ANNAPOLIS ROYAL

AUBERGE WANDLYN ROYAL ANNE MOTEL
P. O. Box 628
(B0S 1A0)
Tel: (902) 532-2323

CHAMPLAIN MOTEL
RR 2 (B0S 1A0)
Tel: (902) 5342-5473

ANTIGONISH

AUBERGE WANDLYN INN
158 Main St
(B2G 2B7)
Tel: (902) 863-4001

THE DINGLE MOTEL
RR 7 (B2G 2L4)
Tel: (902) 863-3730

BADDECK

INVERARY INN RESORT
Box 190 (B0E 1B0)
Tel: (902) 295-2674

TELEGRAPH HOUSE
Chebucto St, Box 8
(B0E 1B0)
Tel: (902) 295-9988

BEDORD

STARDUST MOTEL
1067 Bedford Hwy
(B4A 2X3)
Tel: (902) 835-3316

TRAVELERS MOTEL
773 Bedford Hwy
(B4A 1A4)
Tel: (902) 835-3394

BLACK POINT

GRAND VIEW MOTEL
(B0J 1B0)
Tel: (902) 857-9776

BRAS D'OR

MACNEIL'S MOTEL
(B0C 1B0)
Tel: (902) 736-9106

BRIDGETOWN

BRIDGETOWN MOTOR HOTEL
396 Granville St E
(B0S 1C0)
Tel: (902) 665-4491

CARLETON MOTEL & CABINS
4101 Hwy 201,
RR 3 (B0S 1C0)
Tel: (9020 665-4716

BRIDGEWATER

AUBERGE WANDLYN INN
50 North St, Box 40
(B4V 2W6)
Tel: (902) 543-7131

BRIDGEWATER MOTOR INN
35 High St
(B4V 1V8)
Tel: (800) 528-1234

COMFORT INN
49 North St
(B4V 2V7)
Tel: (800) 221-2222

THE MARINER INN
324 Aberdeen Rd
(B4V 2T2)
Tel: (902) 543-5545

CHESTER

WINDJAMMER MOTEL
P. O. Box 240, Rt 3
(B0J 1J0)
Tel: (902) 275-3567

DARTMOUTH

AMBASSADOR ALL-SUITE APARTMENT HOTEL
356 Windmill Rd
(B2A 1J3)
Tel: (800) 565-1565

AUBERGE WANDLYN INN
739 Windmill Rd
(B3B 1C1)
Tel: (902) 469-0810

BEST WESTERN MIC MAC HOTEL
313 Prince Albert Rd
(B2Y 1N3)
Rates: $49-99
Tel: (902) 469-5850
(800) 528-1234

COMFORT INN
456 Windmill Rd
(B3A 1J7)
Tel: (800) 221-2222

COUNTRY INN & SUITES
P. O. Box 57
(B2Y 3Y2)
Tel: (800) 456-4000

4 SEASONS MOTOR INN
40 Lakecrest Dr,
Box 10 (B3L 4J7)
Tel: (902) 435-0060

FUTURE INNS
20 Highfield Park Dr
(B3A 4S8)
Tel: (902) 465-6555

KEDDY'S DARTMOUTH INN
9 Braemer Dr
(B2H 3H6)
Tel: (800) 561-7666

RAMADA RENAISSANCE HOTEL
240 Brownlow Ave
(B3B 1X6)
Rates: $105-170
Tel: (902) 468-8888
(800) 272-6232

DEBERT

MASSTOWNER MOTEL
RR 1 (B0M 1G0)
Tel: (902) 662-2500

DIGBY

ADMIRAL DIGBY INN
Shore Rd, Box 608
(B0V 1A0)
Tel: (902) 245-2531

KINGFISHER MOTEL
Warwick St, Box 280
(B0V 1A0)
Tel: (902) 245-4747

SIESTA MOTEL
81 Montague Row,
Box 250 (B0V 1A0)
Tel: (902) 245-2568

ENFIELD

**AIRPORT HOTEL
HALIFAX**
P. O. Box 250
(B0N 1N0)
Tel: (800) 667-3333

HALIFAX

**AUBERGE
WANDLYN INN**
50 Bedford Hwy
(B3M 2J2)
Tel: (902) 443-0416

**BICENTENNIAL
MOTEL**
4 Melrose Ave,
Box 10, Armdale
(B3L 4J7)
Tel: (902) 443-9341

BLUENOSE DAYS INN
636 Bedford Hwy
(B3M 2L8)
Tel: (800) 235-2525

CAT & FIDDLE INN
1946 Oxford St
(B3H 4A2)
Tel: (902) 422-3222

CITADEL INN
1960 Brunswick St
(B3J 2G7)
Tel: (800) 565-7162

DAYS INN
636 Bedford Hwy
(B3M 2L8)
Rates: $49-89
Tel: (902) 443-3171
(800) 329-7466

DELTA BARRINGTON
1875 Barrington St
(B3J 3L6)
Tel: (800) 268-1133

**DOUBLETREE
CHATEAU HALIFAX**
1990 Barrington St
(B3J 1P2)
Tel: (800) 828-7447

ECONO LODGE
560 Bedford Hwy
(B3M 2L8)
Tel: (800) 424-4777

HALIFAX HILTON
1181 Hollis St
(B3H 2P6)
Tel: (800) 268-9275

**HOLIDAY INN-
DARTMOUTH**
99 Wyse Rd
(B3A 1L9)
Tel: (800) 465-4329

**HOLIDAY INN-
HALIFAX CENTRE**
1980 Robie St
(B3H 3G5)
Tel: (800) 465-4329

**KEDDY'S
HALIFAX HOTEL**
20 St. Margarets Bay
Rd (B3N 1J4)
Tel: (800) 561-7666

**THE LORD NELSON
HOTEL**
1515 S Park St,
Box 700 (B3J 2T3)
Tel: (800) 565-2020

**PRINCE GEORGE
HOTEL**
1725 Market St
(B3J 3N9)
Tel: (800) 565-1567

**SHERATON
HALIFAX**
1919 Upper Water St
(B3J 3J5)
Tel: (800) 325-3535

HUBBARDS

**ANCHORAGE
HOUSE & CABINS**
Shore Club Rd
(B0J 1T0)
Tel: (902) 857-9402

INGONISH
BEACH

INGONISH CHALETS
Box 196 (B0C 1L0)
Tel: (902) 285-2008

THE ISLAND INN
Box 116 (B0C 1L0)
Tel: (902) 285-2404

KENTVILLE

ALLEN'S MOTEL
384 Park St (B4N
1M9)
Tel: (902) 678-2683

LIVERPOOL

**WHITE POINT BEACH
LODGE RESORT**
Box 9000 (B0T 1G0)
Tel: (902) 354-2711

LOUISBOURG

**LOUISBOURG
MOTEL**
1225 Main St
(B0A 1M0)
Tel: (902) 733-2844

LUNENBURG

HOME PORT MOTEL
167 Victoria Rd,
P. O. Box 1510
(B0J 2C0)
Tel: (902) 634-8234

TOPMAST MOTEL
Box 958 (B0J 2C0)
Tel: (902) 634-4661

MERIGOMISH

COUNTRY INN
RR 1 (B0K 1G0)
Tel: (902) 926-2335

MUSQUODOBOIT
HARBOUR

CAMELOT INN
Box 31, Hwy 7 E
(B0J 2L0)
Tel: (902) 889-2198

NEW GLASGOW

COMFORT INN
740 Westville Rd
(B2H 2J8)
Tel: (800) 221-2222

NEW MINAS

WHITE SPOT MOTEL
9060 Commercial St
(B4N 3E4)
Tel: (902) 681-3244

NORTH SYDNEY

CLANSMAN MOTEL
Peppett St
(B2A 3M3)
Tel: (902) 794-7226

NORTH STAR INN
39 Forrest St,
P. O. Box 157
(B2A 3M3)
Tel: (902) 794-8581

OXFORD

PARKSIDE MOTEL
Main St, Box 109
(B0M 1P0)
Tel: (902) 447-2258

PICTOU

WILLOW HOUSE INN
3 Willow St,
Box 1272
Tel: (902) 485-5740

PORT
HAWKESBURY

**AUBERGE
WANDLYN INN**
689 Reeves St,
Box 759 (B0E 2V0)
Tel: (902) 625-0320

**PORT HAWKESBURY
MOTEL**
Box 549 (B0E 2V0)
Tel: (902) 625-2480

SHELBURNE

**CAPE COD
COLONY MOTEL**
235 Water St,
Box 34 (B0T 1W0)
Tel: (902) 875-3411

LOYALIST INN
160 Water St,
Box 245 (B0T 1W0)
Tel: (902) 875-2343

STELLARTON

**HEATHER
MOTOR HOTEL**
Box 2090 (B0K 1S0)
Tel: (800) 565-4500

SYDNEY

COMFORT INN
368 Kings Rd
(B1S 1A8)
Tel: (800) 221-2222

HOLIDAY INN
480 Kings Rd
(B1S 1A8)
Tel: (800) 465-4329

JACQUES-CARTIER MOTEL
P. O. Box 555
(B1P 6H4)
Tel: (902) 539-4375

SYDNEY MINES

GOWRIE HOUSE COUNTRY INN
139 Shore Rd
(B1V 1A6)
Tel: (902) 544-1050

TRURO

BEST WESTERN GLENGARRY MOTEL
150 Willow St
(B2N 4Z6)
Tel: (800) 528-1234

COMFORT INN
12 Meadow Dr
(B2N 5V4)
Tel: (800) 221-2222

KEDDY'S TRURO INN
437 Prince St
(B2N 1E6)
Tel: (800) 561-7666

WAVERLY

INN ON THE LAKE
Box 29 (B0N 2S0)
Tel: (902) 861-3480

WEST BAY

DUNDEE RESORT
RR 3 (B0E 3K0)
Tel: (902) 345-2649

WESTERN SHORE

OAK ISLAND INN & MARINA
Box 6 (B0J 3M0)
Tel: (800) 565-5075

WHYCOCOMAGH FAIR ISLE MOTEL
Trans Canada Hwy,
P. O. Box 53
(B0E 3M0)
Tel: (902) 756-2291

WINDSOR

DOWNEAST MOTEL
P. O. Box 2048
(B0N 2T0)
Tel: (902) 798-8374

WOLFVILLE

VICTORIA'S HISTORIC INN
416 Main St,
Box 308 (B0P 1X0)
Tel: (902) 542-5744

YARMOUTH

BEST WESTERN MERMAID MOTEL
545 Main St
(B5A 1J6)
Tel: (800) 528-1234

CAPRI MOTEL
577 Main St
(B5A 1J6)
Tel: (902) 742-7168

COMFORT INN
96 Starrs Rd
(B5A 2T5)
Tel: (800) 221-2222

MIDTOWN MOTEL
13 Parade St
(B5A 3A5)
Tel: (902) 742-5333

RODD COLONY HARBOUR INN
6 Forest St (B5A 3K7)
Tel: (902) 742-9194

RODD GRAND HOTEL
4117 Main St,
P. O. Box 220
(B5A 4B2)
Tel: (902) 742-2446

ONTARIO

ALGOMA MILLS

TRAPPER JACK'S MOTEL
Box 105 (P0R 1A0)
(705) 849-2341

ALLISTON

RED PINE MOTOR INN
497 Victoria St E,
Box 5 (L0M 1A0)
Tel: (705) 435-4381

ANGUS

ANGUS VILLAGE MOTEL
174 Mill St
(L0M 1B0)
Tel: (705) 424-6362

APSLEY

JACK'S LAKE LODGE
Box 69 (K0L 1A0)
Tel: (705) 656-4291

ARDEN

GULL LAKE COTTAGES
RR 1 (K0H 1B0)
Tel: (613) 336-2341

LAND O'LAKES MOTEL
RR 4 (K0H 1B0)
Tel: (613) 355-2684

ARKONA

ROCK GLEN MOTEL
Box 217, RR 1,
Hwy 7 (N0M 1B0)
Tel: (519) 828-3838

ARNPRIOR

CEDAR COVE PARK
Box 158 (K7S 3H4)
Tel: (613) 623-3133

TWIN MAPLES MOTEL
175 Daniel St S
(K1S 2L9)
Tel: (613) 623-4271

VACATION INN
70 Madawaska Blvd
(K7S 1S5)
Tel: (613) 623-7991

ATIKOKAN

INDIAONTA RESORT
Box 1289 (P0T 1C0)
Tel: (807) 947-2581

THE PINES MOTEL
RR 11 (P0T 1C0)
Tel: (807) 597-6767

WHITE OTTER INN
710 MacKenzie
Ave E,
Box 27 (P0T 1C0)
Tel: (807) 597-2747

AYLMER

ELM MOTEL
530 Talbot St E
(N5H 2W2)
Tel: (519) 773-8136

BAILIEBORO

MAYES FAMILY COTTAGES
Box 10, RR 1
(K0L 1B0)
Tel: (705) 939-6490

BANCROFT

BEST WESTERN SWORD MOTOR INN
146 Hastings St N,
Box 28 (K0L 1C0)
Tel: (800) 528-1234

SOMERSET INN
RR 3 (K0L 1C0)
Tel: (613) 339-3100

BARRIE

BARRIE HURONIA MOTEL
240 Bradford St
(L4N 3B6)
Tel: (705) 728-3340

BARRIE TRAVELODGE
55 Hart St
(L4N 5M3)
Tel: (800) 255-3050

BEST WESTERN ROYAL OAK INN
35 Hart Dr
(L4N 5M3)
Tel: (800) 528-1234

COMFORT INN
75 Hart Dr
(L4N 5M3)
Tel: (800) 221-2222

HOLIDAY INN
20 Fairview Rd
(L4M 6E7)
Tel: (800) 465-4329

LAKE SIMCOE MOTEL
114 Blake St
(L4M 1K3)
Tel: (705) 728-3704

WHITE TOWERS MOTEL
120 Donald St
(L4N 5G7)
Tel: (705) 726-0208

BARRY'S BAY

MOUNTAIN VIEW MOTEL
Box 101, RR 2
(K0J 1B0)
Tel: (613) 756-2757

BEARDMORE

CRESTWIND HOTEL
Box 149 (P0T 1G0)
Tel: (807) 875-2132

BELLE RIVER

GREEN ACRES MOTEL
Box 426 (N0R 1A0)
Tel: (519) 727-6102

BELLEVILLE

BEST WESTERN BELLEVILLE
387 Front St N
(K8P 3C8)
Tel: (613) 969-1112

COMFORT INN
200 Park St N
(K8P 2Y9)
Tel: (800) 221-2222

QUALITY INN
407 Front St N
(K8P 3C8)
Tel: (800) 221-2222

QUEEN'S MOTOR INN
400 Dundas St E
(K8N 1E8)
Tel: (613) 966-1211

RAMADA INN
11 Bay Bridge Rd,
Hwy 62 (K8N 4Z1)
Tel: (800) 228-2828

VOYAGER MOTOR INN
RR 5 (K8N 4Z5)
Tel: (613) 962-8641

BLIND RIVER

AUBERGE ELDO INN
Box 156 (P0R 1B0)
Tel: (7050 356-2255

MACIVER'S MISSISAUGUA MOTEL
Box 502 (P0R 1B0)
Tel: (705) 356-7411

FRIENDSHIP INN
181 Causley St,
Hwy 1 (P0R 1B0)
Tel: (705) 356-2249

OLD MILL MOTEL
Woodward Ave,
Hwy 17,
Box 251 (P0R 1B0)
Tel: (705) 356-2274

BLOOMFIELD

BLOOMFIELD INN
29 Stanley St W,
Box 16 (K0K 1G0)
Tel: (613) 393-3301

BOBCAYGEON

BLUE TOP VILLA
RR 3 (K0M 1A0)
Tel: (705) 738-2840

**KEEWANEE LODGE
MOTEL**
RR 1 (K0M 1A0)
Tel: (705) 738-2878

RIVERSIDE LODGE
84 Front St E,
Box 903 (K0M 1A0)]
Tel: (705) 738-2193

BONFIELD

SUNNYSIDE CAMP
Box 53 (P0H 1E0)
Tel: (705) 776-2401

BRAMPTON

HOLIDAY INN
30 Peel Centre Dr
(L6T 4G3)
Tel: (800) 465-4329

WELCOMINN
30 Clark Blvd
(L6W 1X3)
Tel: (416) 454-1300

BRANTFORD

BELL CITY MOTEL
901 Colborne St E
(N3S 3T3)
Tel: (519) 756-5236

**BEST WESTERN
BRANT PARK INN**
19 Holiday Dr,
Box 1900 (N3T 5W5)
Tel: (800) 528-1234

COMFORT INN
58 King George Rd
(N3R 5K4)
Tel: (800) 221-2222

DAYS INN
460 Fairview Dr
(N3R 7A9)
Tel: (519) 759-2700

QUALITY INN
666 Colborne St E
(N3S 3P8)
Tel: (800) 221-2222

TRAVELODGE
664 Colborne St
(N3S 3P8)
Rates: $46-149
Tel: (519) 753-7371
(800) 578-7878

BRIGHTON

**HARBOURVIEW
MOTEL & MARINA**
Box 1719 (K0K 1H0)
Tel: (613) 475-1515

**PRESQU'ILE BEACH
MOTEL**
243 Main St W,
RR 4 (K0K 1H0)
Tel: (613) 475-1010

BRITT

BRITT MOTOR INN
RR 1 (P0G 1A0)
Tel: (705) 383-2343

**LONG BRANCH
HOTEL**
Hwy 69, RR 1
(P0G 1A0)
Tel: (705) 383-2352

M & R MOTEL
Box 144 (P0G 1A0)
Tel: (705) 383-2491

BROCKVILLE

COMFORT INN
7777 Kent Blvd
(K6V 5V5)
Tel: (800) 221-2222

SEAWAY MOTEL
Box 11, RR 1
(K6V 5T1)
Tel: (613) 342-1357

BRUCE MINES

BAVARIAN INN
49 Taylor St
(P0R 1C0)
Tel: (705) 785-3447

BURKS FALLS

**RUSS HAVEN
RESORT**
Pickerel Lake Rd,
RR 2 (P0A 1C0)
Tel: (705) 382-2027

**SILVER SPRINGS
MOTOR COURT**
Box 190 (P0A 1C0)
Tel: (705) 382-2513

BURLINGTON

COMFORT INN
3290 S Service Rd
(L7N 3M6)
Tel: (800) 221-2222

CRESTWOOD MOTEL
527 Plains Rd E
(L7T 2E2)
Tel: (416) 634-6119

HOLIDAY INN
3063 S Service Rd
(L7N 3E9)
Tel: (800) 465-4329

**TOWN & COUNTRY
MOTEL**
517 Plains Rd E
(L7T 2E2)
Tel: (416) 634-2383

**TRAVELODGE
BURLINGTON**
950 Walkers Line
(L7N 2G2)
Tel: (800) 255-3050

**VENTURE INN
BURLINGTON**
2020 Lakeshore Rd
(L7S 1Y2)
Tel: (416) 681-0762

CALABOGIE

BARRYVALE LODGE
RR 2 (K0J 1H0)
Tel: (613) 752-2392

**JOCKO'S BEACH
MOTEL**
RR 3 (K0J 1H0)
Tel: (613) 752-2107

CAMBRIDGE

COMFORT INN
220 Holiday Inn Dr
(N3C 1Z4)
Tel: (800) 221-2222

DAYS INN
650 Hespeler Rd
(N1R 6J8)
Rates: $59-100
Tel: (519) 622-1070

DESERT INN
605 Hespeler Rd
(N1R 6J3)
Tel: (519) 622-1180

HOLIDAY INN
200 Holiday Inn Dr,
P. O. Box 820
(N3C 1Z4)
Tel: (800) 465-4329

CAMPBELLFORD

MOTEL RIVIERA
352 Front St N,
Box 569 (K0L 1L0)
Tel: (705) 653-1771

**TRENT HOUSE
MOTEL**
149 Queen St N
(K0L 1L0)
Tel: (705) 653-2190

CAPREOL

MCKEE'S CAMP
Box 1113 (P0M 1H0)
Tel: (705) 858-3529

CARLETON
PLACE

CEDARS MOTEL
RR 2 (K7C 3P2)
Tel: (613) 257-2047

**TWIN OAKS MOTOR
HOTEL**
Box 434 (K7C 3P5)
Tel: (613) 257-1020

CHAPLEAU

MOTEL CHAPLEAU
72 Cedar St,
Box 727 (P0M 1K0)
Tel: (705) 864-0290

RIVERSIDE MOTEL
116 Cherry St,
Box 699 (P0M 1K0)
Tel: (705) 864-0440

CHATHAM

BELLA DONNA MOTEL
510 Grand Ave E
(N7L 3Z3)
Tel: (519) 352-4670

CHATHAM MOTEL
659 Grand Ave E
(N7L 1X6)
Tel: (519) 352-4670

COMFORT INN
1100 Richmond St
(N7M 5J5)
Tel: (800) 221-2222

FLAMINGO MOTEL
421 Grand Ave E
(N7L 1X4)
Tel: (519) 354-5130

KENT MOTEL
420 Grand Ave E
(N7L 1X2)
Tel: (519) 352-9222

LUXURY INN
25 Michener Rd
(N7L 4B8)
Tel: (519) 354-3366

RAINBOW MOTEL
RR 1 (N7M 5J1)
Tel: (519) 352-6610

TRAVELLERS MOTEL
RR 5 (N7M 5J5)
Tel: (519) 351-3874

CHATSWORTH

KEY MOTEL
RR 3 (N0H 1G0)
Tel: (519) 794-2350

CLEARWATER

TUDOR LODGE MOTEL
1665 London Rd
(N7T 7H2)
Tel: (519) 542-7716

CLOYNE

CLOYNE MOTOR INN
Box 130 (K0H 1K0)
Tel: (613) 336-8779

GLENCANNON RESORT
RR 2 (K0H 1K0)
Tel: (613) 336-2425

MARBLE LAKE LODGE
RR 2 (K0H 1K0)
Tel: (613) 336-2213

COBOURG

BEST WESTERN MOTOR INN
930 Burnham St
(K3A 2X9)
Tel: (800) 528-1234

COMFORT INN
121 Densmore Rd
(K9A 4J9)
Tel: (800) 221-2222

HILLSIDE MOTEL
Box 351 (K9A 4K8)
Tel: (416) 372-2158

TOM'S MOTEL
428 King St E (K9A 1M6)
Tel: (416) 372-9421

COCHRANE

CHIMO MOTEL
Box 2326 (P0L 1C0)
Tel: (705) 272-6555

GOLDEN GATE MOTEL
Box 1930 (P0L 1C0)
Tel: (705) 272-5498

COE HILL

ISLAND VIEW COTTAGES
Box 179, RR 2
(K0L 1P0)
Tel: (613) 337-5533

COLDWATER

COLDWATER MOTEL
Box 148 (K0K 1E0)
Tel: (705) 835-3388

SEVERN FALLS MOTEL
Box 315, RR 1
(L0K 1E0)
Tel: (705) 686-7955

COLLINGWOOD

BLUE MOUNTAIN MOTEL
Box 2152, RR 2
(L9Y 3Z1)
Tel: (705) 445-1146

HIGHWAYMAN INN
1 Balsam St (L9Y 3J4)
Tel: (705) 444-2144

MARINER MOTOR HOTEL
305 Hume St
(L9Y 1W2)
Tel: (705) 445-3330

MOORE'S MOTEL
RR 3 (L9Y 3Z2)
Tel: (705) 445-2478

SEA & SKI MOTEL
530 First St
(L9Y 1C1)
Tel: (705) 445-2061

VACATION INN RESORT
Box 4517 (L9Y 4J9)
Tel: (705) 445-9422

THE VILLAGE MOTEL
RR 3 (L9Y 3Z2)
Tel: (705) 445-1617

COMBERMERE

SAND BAY CAMP
RR 2 (K0J 1L0)
Tel: (613) 756-5060

CONESTOGO

BLACK FOREST INN
26 King St
(N0B 1N0)
Tel: (519) 664-2223

CORBEIL

BIRCH HILL CAMP
Box 118, RR 1
(P0H 1K0)
Tel: (705) 752-1273

CORNWALL

ANCHOR MOTEL
1123 Brookdale Ave
(K6J 4P6)
Tel: (613) 932-0783

BEST WESTERN PARKWAY INN
1515 Vincent Massey Dr (K6H 5R6)
Tel: (613) 932-0451

CARDINAL MOTEL
2405 Vincent Massey Dr (K6J 5N4)
Tel: (613) 933-2557

CENTURY MOTEL
1209 Brookdale Ave
(K6J 4P7)
Tel: (613) 932-1430

COMFORT INN
1625 Vincent Massey Dr, RR 2 (K6H 5R6)
Tel: (800) 221-2222

COSEY CORNER MOTEL
1613 2nd St W
(K6J 1J6)
Tel: (613) 938-1258

ECONO LODGE
1750 Vincent Massey Dr (K6H 5R8)
Tel: (800) 424-4777

HOLIDAY INN
805 Brookdale Ave
(K6J 4P3)
Tel: (800) 465-4329

MARTIN'S INN
220 Vincent Massey Dr (K6H 5R6)
Tel: (613) 933-6897

**MURRAY HILL
MOTOR HOTEL**
1620 Vincent Massey
Dr (K6H 5R6)
Tel: (613) 933-1650

TRAVELODGE HOTEL
1142 Brookdale Ave
(K6J 4P4)
Tel: (800) 255-3050

COURTICE

PINE RIDGE MOTEL
1607 King St E
(L1E 2R7)
Tel: (416) 436-2080

DORION

TRILLIUM MOTEL
RR 1 (P0T 1K0)
Tel: (807) 857-2268

DORNOCH

DORNOCH INN
RR 1, Durham
(N0G 1R0)
Tel: (519) 794-3550

DORSET

**THE TOM SALMON
INN**
Box 38, 3 Main St
(P0A 1E0)
Tel: (705) 766-2261

DOWLING

**DOWLING MOTOR
HOTEL**
Box 245 (P0M 1R0)
Tel: (705) 855-3123

DRYDEN

**BEST WESTERN
MOTOR INN**
349 Government Rd,
Box 904 (P8N 2Z5)
Tel: (800) 528-1234

CEDAR MOTEL
Box 843 (P8N 2Z5)
Tel: (807) 938-6373

COMFORT INN
522 Government Rd
(P8N 2P5)
Tel: (800) 221-2222

**EVENING STAR
MOTEL**
Box 524, RR 1
(P8N 2Z2)
Tel: (807) 937-5268

HIDEAWAY MOTEL
Box 14, RR 1
(P8N 2Y4)
Tel: (807) 223-5329

HILLCREST MOTEL
130 Grand Trunk
Ave (P8N 2W5)
Tel: (807) 223-6283

**TIMBERLAND
MOTEL**
406 Government Rd
(P8N 2P5)
Tel: (800) 465-8629

**TOWN & COUNTRY
MOTEL**
500 Government Rd
(P8N 2P7)
Tel: (807) 223-2377

**TRANS CANADA
MOTEL**
149 Third St
(P8N 2V8)
Tel: (807) 223-2251

DUNNVILLE

**COUNTRY INN
MOTEL**
RR 5 (N1A 2W4)
Tel: (416) 774-7363

RIVERVIEW MOTEL
642 Main St W
(N1A 1W7)
Tel: (416) 774-5634

DURHAM

CARDINAL MOTEL
RR 3 (N0G 1R0)
Tel: (519) 369-3300

DWIGHT

CURV-INN
RR 1 (P0A 1H0)
Tel: (705) 635-1892

**DWIGHT VILLAGE
MOTEL**
Box 15 (P0A 1H0)
Tel: (705) 635-2400

EAGLE RIVER

**FIN & FEATHER
RESORT**
General Delivery
(P0V 1S0)
Tel: (807) 755-5200

EAR FALLS

**MANITOU FALLS
CAMP**
Box 236 (P0V 1T0)
Tel: (807) 222-3214

TRILLIUM MOTEL
Box 400 (P0V 1T0)
Tel: (807) 222-3126

EGANVILLE

PINE TREE MOTEL
Hwy 60 & 41, RR 6
(K0J 1T0)
Tel: (613) 628-2724

ELK LAKE

MOOSEHORN MOTEL
1 First St, Box 278
(P0J 1G0)
Tel: (705) 678-2400

ELLIOT LAKE

DUNLOP LODGE
Box 277 (P5A 2J7)
Tel: (705) 848-8090

INN ON THE LAKE
Hwy 108 (P5A 2T1)
Tel: (705) 848-3611

ROADHOUSE INN
220 Ontarior Ave
(P5A 1Y5)
Tel: (705) 461-3711

ELORA

CHEVY'S MOTEL
77 Victoria St
(N0B 1S0)
Tel: (519) 846-5333

THE VILLAGE INN
66 Guelph Rd,
Box 308 (N0B 1S0)
Tel: (519) 846-5333

EMO

EMO INN
Box 598 (P0W 1E0)
Tel: (807) 482-2272

ENGLEHART

OLDE TOWNE INN
Box 988 (P0J 1H0)
Tel: (705) 544-2225

ENGLISH RIVER

**ENGLISH RIVER
MOTEL**
Box 998, Ignace
(P0T 1T0)
Tel: (807) 986-2434

ESPANOLA

ALTA VISTA MOTEL
Box 950 (P0P 1C0)
Tel: (705) 869-2520

**GOODMAN'S
MOTEL**
Box 878 (P0P 1C0)
Tel: (705) 869-1020

**PINEWOOD MOTOR
INN**
Box 1578, 278 Station
Rd, Hwy 5 (P0P 1C0)
Tel: (705) 869-3460

QUEENSWAY MOTEL
287 Queensway Rd,
Box 1519 (P0P 1C0)
Tel: (705) 869-1065

ETOBICOKE

**RAMADA HOTEL -
TORONTO AIRPORT**
2 Holiday Dr
(M9C 2Z7)
Rates: $79-143
Tel: (416) 621-2121
(800) 272-6232

EVANSVILLE

TWILIGHT ISLE RESORT
General Delivery
(P0P 1E0)
Tel: (705) 282-2871

FENELON FALLS

BALSAM RESORT
RR 1 (K0M 1N0)
Tel: (705) 887-5040

ROSEDALE MOTEL
RR 1 (K0M 1N0)
Tel: (705) 887-2491

ROYAL RESORT
RR 1 (K0M 1N0)
Tel: (705) 454-8004

SUNDIAL MOTEL
157 Lindsay St
(K0M 1N0)
Tel: (705) 887-2400

FERGUS

THE HIGHLANDER INN
280 Bridge St
(N1M 1T6)
Tel: (519) 843-3115

FIELD

CAMP HORIZON
Box 160 (P0H 1M0)
Tel: (705) 758-6741

FLESHERTON

FORT GARRY MOTEL
Hwy 10 N, Box 298
(N0C 1E0)
Tel: (519) 924-2532

FOLEYET

MOOSE LAND RESORT
Box 70 (P0M 1T0)
Tel: (705) 899-2300

RED PINE LODGE
Box 94 (P0M 1T0)
Tel: (705) 899-2875

FONTHILL

HIPWELL'S MOTEL
299 Hwy 10 W,
Box 253 (L0S 1E0)
Tel: (416) 892-3588

FOREST

FOREST GOLF & COUNTRY HOTEL
102 Main St S,
Box 445 (N0N 1J0)
Tel: (519) 786-2397

RAVENSWOOD INN
RR 2, Box 13
(N0N 1J0)
Tel: (519) 243-2240

FORT ERIE

COMFORT INN
1 Journey's End Dr
(L2A 6G1)
Tel: (800) 221-2222

GATEWAY MOTEL
315 Garrison Rd
(L2A 1M9)
Tel: (416) 871-4438

HAVEN MOTEL
215 Garrison Rd
(L2A 1M6)
Tel: (416) 871-2171

LAKEVIEW INN MOTEL
139 Garrison Rd
(L2A 1M3)
Tel: (416) 871-6806

QUALITY INN
20 Central Ave S
(L2A 6C1)
Tel: (800) 221-2222

FORT FRANCES

MAKABI INN MOTEL
325 Scott St (P9A 1H1)
Tel: (807) 274-9874

MIDTOWN MOTEL
417 Portage Ave,
Box 416 (P9A 2A1)
Tel: (807) 274-9814

REID'S VOYAGEUR INN
525 Portage Ave
(P9A 2A2)
Tel: (807) 274-9805

FRENCH RIVER

BEAUSEJOUR HOTEL
RR 1, Alban
(P0M 1A0)
Tel: (705) 857-2193

FRENCH RIVER INN
RR 2, Hwy 69 S,
Alban (P0M 1A0)
Tel: (705) 857-2788

GANANOQUE

APPLEBY MOTEL
480 King St E
(K7G 1G8)
Tel: (613) 382-4402

CAN-AM MOTOR LODGE
641 King St E
(K7G 1H4)
Tel: (613) 382-3311

COLONIAL RESORT
780 King St W
(K7G 2H5)
Tel: (613) 382-4677

1000 ISLANDS MOTEL
550 King St E
(K7G 1H2)
Tel: (613) 382-3911

TRINITY HOUSE
90 Stone St S
(K7G 1Z8)
Tel: (613) 382-8383

GERALDTON

CROWN & ANCHOR MOTEL
1801 Main St
(P0T 1M0)
Tel: (807) 854-1211

GOLD NUGGET MOTEL
509 Main St, Box 580
(P0T 1M0)
Tel: (807) 854-0740

PARK BAY VIEW MOTEL
Box 338 (P0T 1M0)
Tel: (807) 854-1716

SILVER NUGGET MOTOR HOTEL
1311 Main St, Box 380 (P0T 1M0)
Tel: (807) 854-0911

WHITE WOLF RESORT
Box 921 (P0T 1M0)
Tel: (807) 854-0618

GLOUCESTER

RELAX INN OTTAWA EAST - GLOUCESTER
1486 Innes Rd
(K1B 3V5)
Tel: (800) 667-3529

TRAVELODGE
1486 Innes Rd
(K1B 3V5)
Rates: $65-73
Tel: (613) 745-1133
(800) 578-7878

GODERICH

BEDFORD ARMS MOTEL
242 Bayfield Rd
(N7A 3G6)
Tel: (519) 524-7348

BLUFFS MOTEL
RR 2 (N7A 3X8)
Tel: (519) 524-7396

CHERRYDALE FARMS
RR 4 (N7A 3Y1)
Tel: (519) 524-2191

COUNTRY 21 MOTEL
RR 2 (N7A 3X8)
Tel: (519) 524-7302

GARDINER'S MOTEL
400 Bayfield Rd
(N7A 4E7)
Tel: (519) 524-7302

GOGAMA

MANDERLEY MANOR RESORT
Box 237 (P0M 1W0)
Tel: (705) 894-2300

MINAKWA LODGE
Box 58 (P0M 1W0)
Tel: (705) 894-2294

GOLDEN LAKE

**GOLDEN SANDS
VACATIONLAND**
RR 1 (K0J 2X0)
Tel: (613) 625-2525

GRAVENHURST

**CANOKA MOTEL
& OLD BAVARIA INN**
Box 1589 (P0C 1G0)
Tel: (705) 687-2209

OAKWOOD MOTEL
1060 Muskoka Rd S,
Box 1869 (P0C 1G0)
Tel: (705) 687-4224

SKYWAYS MOTEL
RR 1 (P0C 1G0)
Tel: (705) 687-6608

THREE COINS MOTEL
RR 2, Kilworthy
(P0E 1G0)
Tel: (705) 689-2361

GUELPH

**BEST WESTERN
CARDEN PLACE**
106 Carden St
(NiH 3A3)
Rates: $67-119
Tel: (613) 632-5941
(800) 528-1234

COLLEGE INN
Stone Rd & Gordon
St (N1G 1Y6)
Tel: (519) 836-1240

COMFORT INN
480 Silvercreek
Pkwy (N1H 7R5)
Tel: (800) 221-2222

DAYS INN
785 Gordon St
(N1G 1Y8)
Rates: $56-76
Tel: (519) 822-9112
(800) 329-7466

HOLIDAY INN
601 Scottsdale Rd
(N1G 3E7)
Tel: (800) 465-4329

HOWARD JOHNSON
112 E King Street,
(L8N 1A8)
Tel: (905) 546-8111
(800) 446-4656

HAGAR

MANOR MOTEL
Hwy 17 E (P0M 1X0)
Tel: (705) 967-2803

HAILEYBURY

EDGEWATER MOTEL
1267 Lakeshore Rd,
RR 1 (P0J 1K0)
Tel: (705) 647-8588

LEISURE INN
509 Ferguson Ave,
Box 218 (P0J 1K0)
Tel: (705) 672-5084

HALIBURTON

**HALIBURTON
FOREST**
RR 1 (K0M 1S0)
Tel: (705) 754-2198

**HILLCREST HAVEN
RESORT**
RR 1 (K0M 1S0)
Tel: (705) 754-2521

**SILVER MAPLE
MOTEL**
Box 365 (K0M 1S0)
Tel: (705) 457-2607

HAMILTON

**BEST WESTERN
HOTEL STRATA**
51 Keefer Crt
(L8E 4V4)
Tel: (416) 578-1212

CITY MOTOR HOTEL
1620 Main St E
(L8H 1C6)
Tel: (416) 549-1371

COMFORT INN
183 Centennial
Pkwy N
(L8E 1H8)
Tel: (800) 221-2222

HOLIDAY INN
150 King St E (L8N
1B2)
Tel: (800) 465-4329

HOWARD JOHNSON
1333 E Weber St
(N2A 1C2)
Tel: (519) 893-1234
(800) 446-4656

HOWARD JOHNSON
112 E King Street,
(L8N 1A8)
Tel: (905) 546-8111
(800) 446-4656

**MOUNTAINVIEW
MOTEL**
1870 Main St W
(L8S 1H7)
Tel: (416) 528-7521

PINES MOTEL
395 Centennial
Pkwy (L8E 2X6)
Tel: (416) 561-5652

RAMADA HOTEL
150 King St E
(L8N 1B2)
Rates: $70-110
Tel: (905) 528-3451
(800) 272-6232

**ROYAL CONNAUGHT
HOTEL**
112 King St E
(L8N 1A8)
Tel: (416) 546-8111

**SHERATON
HAMILTON HOTEL**
116 King St W
(L8P 4V3)
Tel: (800) 325-3535

VISITORS INN
649 Main St W
(L8S 1A2)
Tel: (416) 529-6979

HARCOURT

**ELEPHANT LAKE
LODGE**
Box 16 (K0L 1X0)
Tel: (705) 448-2861

HAWKESBURY

**BEST WESTERN
MOTEL L'HERITAGE**
1575 Tupper St,
P. O. Box 890
(K6A 3E1)
Tel: (800) 528-1234

BLACK HORSE INN
Box 372 (K6A 2S2)
Tel: (613) 632-2783

HEARST

**NORTHERN
SEASONS MOTEL**
915 George St,
Box 823 (P0L 1N0)
Tel: (705) 362-4281

VILLA MOTEL
Hwy 11 W, Box 1823
(P0L 1N0)
Tel: (705) 362-4331

HILTON BEACH

**HILTON BEACH
HOTEL**
Box 113 (P0R 1G0)
Tel: (705) 246-9905

HORNEPAYNE

**HALLMARK CENTRE
INN**
200 Front St,
Box 630 (P0M 1Z0)
Tel: (807) 868-2008

HUNTSVILLE

COMFORT INN
86 King William St
(P0A 1K0)
Tel: (800) 221-2222

**FRIENDLY ACRES
RESORT**
RR 4 (P0A 1K0)
Tel: (705) 635-2522

OX BOW LODGE
RR 4, Group Box 201
(P0A 1K0)
Tel: (705) 635-2514

RAINBOW MOTEL
32 King William St,
Box 418 (P0A 1K0)
Tel: (705) 789-5514

RAYMOR MOTEL
117 Main ST W,
Box 218 (P0A 1K0)
Tel: (705) 789-6784

TALLY-HO INN
Box 1718 (P0A 1K0)
Tel: (705) 635-2281

TULIP MOTOR INN
RR 3 (P0A 1K0)
Tel: (800) 565-4001

IGNACE

**NORTH WOODS
MOTOR INN**
Box 128 (P0T 1T0)
Tel: (807) 934-2296

**TRADING POST
MOTEL**
Box 402 (P0T 1T0)
Tel: (807) 934-2386

INGERSOLL

RELAX INN
20 Samnah Cres
(N5C 3J7)
Tel: (800) 667-3529

INGLESIDE

LAKESIDE INN
General Delivery
(K0C 1M0)
Tel: (613) 537-2158

IRON BRIDGE

IRON BRIDGE MOTEL
Box 40 (P0R 1H0)
Tel: (705) 843-2115

**PARKER'S MOTEL
& COTTAGES**
Box 219 (P0R 1H0)
Tel: (705) 843-2233

**IROQUOIS
FALLS**

**GLENDALE
MOTOR HOTEL**
697 Ambridge Dr,
Box 756 (P0K 1G0)
Tel: (705) 232-4041

JARVIS

STAR MOTEL
RR 1 (N0A 1J0)
Tel: (519) 587-2541

**KAKABEKA
FALLS**

THE CASCADES MOTEL
Box 9 (P0T 1W0)
Tel: (807) 473-9012

TELSTAR MOTEL
Box 39 (P0T 1W0)
Tel: (807) 473-9141

KANATA

COMFORT INN-WEST
222 Hearst Way
(K2L 3A2)
Tel: (800) 221-2222

KAPUSKASING

APOLLO MOTEL
Box 519, RR 2
(P5N 2X8)
Tel: (705) 335-6084

**CHAIN OF LAKES
MOTEL**
470 Government Rd
(P5N 2X7)
Tel: (705) 335-2213

COMFORT INN
172 Government Rd E
(P5N 2W9)
Tel: (800) 221-2222

MATTAGAMI MOTEL
25 Kolb St
(P5N 1G2)
Tel: (705) 335-6171

KATHRINE

CAMP DOE-MIS-CO
Box 68, Doe Lake Rd
(P0A 1L0)
Tel: (705) 382-3427

KEARNEY

THE BEEHIVE
Box 144 (P0A 1M0)
Tel: (705) 636-7766

KEEWATIN

GAYLES MOTEL
Hwy 17 W
(P0X 1C0)
Tel: (807) 547-2667

KEMPTVILLE

EVERGREEN MOTEL
Box 693, Vista Crt
(K0G 1J0)
Tel: (613) 258-2642

KENORA

ANCHOR INN MOTEL
Box 542 (P9N 3X5)
Tel: (807) 468-6861

**BEST WESTERN
BECKETT'S VILLAGE**
920 Hwy 17 E,
Box 121 (P9N 3X1)
Tel: (800) 528-1234

COMFORT INN
1230 Hwy 17 E
(P9N 1L9)
Tel: (807) 221-2222

DAYS INN
920 Hwy 17 E
(P9N 1L9)
Rates: $58-75
Tel: (807) 468-2003
(800) 329-7466

INN OF THE WOODS
470 1st Ave S
(P9N 1W5)
Tel: (807) 468-5521

**KENORA INN
MOTEL**
1429 River St
(P9N 1K6)
Tel: (807) 468-5261

**KENORA TRAV-
ELODGE**
800 Sunset Strip
(P9N 1L9)
Tel: (800) 255-3050

KENRICIA HOTEL
155 Main St (P9N
1T1)
Tel: (807) 468-6461

KENWOOD HOTEL
15 Chipman St
(P9N 1V5)
Tel: (807) 468-8913

LAKE-VU MOTEL
740 Lakeview Dr
(P9N 3P7)
Tel: (807) 468-5501

LAURENSIDE INN
1404 River St
(P9N 1K5)
Tel: (807) 468-6065

LUTHER VILLAGE
Box 2040 (P9N 3X8)
Tel: (807) 543-4052

MACKENZIE LODGE
RR 2, Site 200,
Comp. 1 (P9N 3W8)
Tel: (807) 548-5171

**WHISPERING PINES
MOTEL**
Hwy 17 E (P0X 1H0)
Tel: (807) 548-4025

KILWORTHY

KAHSHE MOTEL
RR 2 (P0E 1G0)
Tel: (705) 689-2774

**THREE COINS
MOTOR MOTEL**
RR 2 (P0E 1G0)
Tel: (705) 689-2361

KINCARDINE

BROADWAY MOTEL
481 Broadway St
(N2Z 2C2)
Tel: (519) 396-3413

KINCARDINITE MOTEL
319 Kincardine Ave
(N2Z 2R2)
Tel: (519) 396-7511

TRIANGLE MOTEL
612 King St (N2Z
2C5)
Tel: (519) 396-3487

KINGSTON

AMBASSADOR HOTEL
1550 Princess St,
Box 787 (K7L 4X6)
Tel: (613) 548-3605

BEAVER MOTEL
RR 2 Hwy 15
(K7L 5H6)
Tel: (613) 546-6674

COMFORT INN
1454 Princess St
(K7M 3E5)
Tel: (800) 221-2222

COMFORT INN
55 Warne Crescent
(K7L 4V4)
Tel: (800) 221-2222

ECONO LODGE
2327 Princess St
(K7M 3G1)
Rates: $40-67
Tel: (613) 546-2691
(800) 424-4777

EMBASSY MOTEL
2404 Princess St W
(K7M 3G4)
Tel: (613) 546-4271

EXECUTIVE MOTEL
RR 1 (K7L 4V1)
Tel: (613) 549-1620

GLEN MANOR MOTEL
1155 Princess St
(K7M 3E1)
Tel: (613) 546-4285

GREEN ACRES INN
2480 Princess St
(L7M 3G4)
Tel: (613) 546-1796

**THE HIGHLAND
MOTEL**
RR 1/Hwy 15 S
(K7L 5H6)
Tel: (800) 267-1048

HOLIDAY INN
1 Princess St (K7L
1A1)
Tel: (800) 465-4329

**HOWARD JOHNSON
CONFEDERATION
PLACE**
237 Ontario St
(K7L 2Z4)
Tel: (800) 654-2000

**JOURNEY'S END
MOTEL**
Box 5, RR 8,
55 Warne Cres
(K7L 4V4)
Tel: (613) 546-9500

**LORD NELSON
MOTEL**
Box 2, RR 2
(K7L 5H6)
Tel: (613) 542-2883

**PRINCE GEORGE
HOTEL**
200 Ontario St
(K7L 2Y9)
Tel: (613) 549-5440

**SEVEN OAKES
MOTOR INN**
2331 Princess St
(K7M 3G1)
Tel: (613) 546-3655

KIRKLAND LAKE

BON AIR MOTOR INN
50 Government Rd E
(P2N 1A5)
Tel: (705) 567-3241

COMFORT INN
455 Government Rd
W (P0K 1A0)
Tel: (800) 221-2222

PARKER'S MOTEL
Box 353 (P2N 3J1)
Tel: (705) 567-9246

KITCHENER

**BARONS MOTOR
INN**
901 Victoria St N
(N2B 3C3)
Tel: (519) 744-2215

COMFORT INN
2899 King St E
(N2A 1A6)
Tel: (800) 221-2222

EMBASSY MOTEL
4521 King St E,
RR 3 (N2G 3W6)
Tel: (519) 653-3176

HOLIDAY INN
30 Fairway Rd S
(N2A 2N2)
Tel: (800) 465-4329

HOWARD JOHNSON
Hwy 2,
P. O. Box 1140
(K0C 1X0)
Tel: (613) 543-3788
(800) 446-4656

HOWARD JOHNSON
1333 E Weber St
(N2A 1C2)
Tel: (519) 893-1234
(800) 446-4656

KITCHENER MOTEL
1485 Victoria St N
(N2B 3E4)
Tel: (519) 745-1177

**RELAX HOTEL
KITCHENER**
2960 King St E
(N2A 1A9)
Tel: (800) 667-3529

RODEWAY SUITES
55 New Dundee Rd.
(N2G 3W5)
Rates: $40-66
Tel: (519) 895-2272
(800) 228-2000

SHAMROCK MOTEL
1575 Victoria St N
(N2B 3E6)
Tel: (519) 743-4361

VALHALLA INN
Box 4, 105 King St E
(N2G 3W9)
Tel: (519) 744-4141

**WALPER TERRACE
HOTEL**
1 King St W
(N2G 1A1)
Tel: (519) 745-4321

LAKEFIELD

**BLUE MOUNTAIN
MARINA**
RR 2 (K0L 2H0)
Tel: (705) 877-2159

BURNHAM LODGE
RR 2 (K0L 2H0)
Tel: (705) 877-2822

LANCASTER

IMPALA MOTEL
Box 103 (K0C 2C0)
Tel: (613) 347-2028

LATCHFORD

**FRONTIERSMAN
MOTEL**
Box 81 (P0J 1N0)
Tel: (705) 676-2424

LEAMINGTON

COMFORT INN
279 Erie St S
(N8H 3C4)
Tel: (800) 221-2222

MANERY'S MOTEL
161 Talbot St E
(N8H 1L8)
Tel: (519) 326-3336

**SUN PARLOR
MOTEL**
135 Talbot St W
(N8H 1N2)
Tel: (519) 326-6131

**WIGLE'S
COLONIAL MOTEL**
133 Talbot St E
(N8H 1L6)
Tel: (519) 326-3265

LINDSAY

**LYN PARK SPANISH
VILLA**
220 Lindsay St S
(K9V 2N3)
Tel: (705) 324-9101

VICTORIA MOTEL
RR 5 (K9V 4R5)
Tel: (705) 324-3537

LITTLE CURRENT

BRIDGEWAY MOTEL
Box 333, Hwy 6
(P0P 1K0)
Tel: (705) 368-2230

LIVELY

THE VILLAGE INN
RR 1 (P0M 2E0)
Tel: (705) 692-5021

WESTWAY MOTEL
Reg Rd 55, RR 1
(P0M 2E0)
Tel: (705) 692-3222

LOMBARDY

BASS LAKE LODGE
RR 1 (K0G 1L0)
Tel: (613) 283-0136

LONDON

AMERICAN MOTEL
2031 Dundas St E
(N5V 1P6)
Tel: (519) 451-2030

BEST WESTERN LAMPLIGHTER INN
591 Wellington Rd S
(N6C 4R3)
Tel: (800) 528-1234

BRIARWOOD INN
299 King St
(N6B 1S1)
Tel: (519) 673-3300

QUALITY INN
1156 Wellington Rd
(N6E 1M3)
Tel: (800) 221-2222

ECONO LODGE
1170 Wellington Rd
S (N6E 1M3)
Tel: (800) 424-4777

HORSESHOE DAYS INN
1100 Wellington Rd
S (N6E 1M2)
Tel: (519) 681-1240

HOWARD JOHN-SON HOTEL
1150 Wellington Rd
S (N6E 1M3)
Tel: (800) 446-4656

HYLAND MOTEL
750 Wharncliffe Rd S
(N6J 2N4)
Tel: (519) 681-5901

THE NATIONAL TRAVELLER HOTEL
636 York St
(N5W 2S7)
Tel: (519) 433-8161

QUALITY SUITES
1120 Dearness Dr
(N6E 1N9)
Tel: (800) 221-2222

QUALITY SUITES-DOWNTOWN
374 Dundas St (N6B 1V7)
Tel: (800) 221-2222

RADISSON HOTEL LONDON CITY CENTRE
300 King St
(N6B 1S2)
Tel: (800) 333-3333

RAINBOW MOTEL
1100 Wharnclifee Rd
(N6A 4B5)
Tel: (519) 685-3772

RAMADA INN
817 Exeter Rd
(N6E 1W1)
Rates: $70-109
Tel: (519) 681-4900
(800) 272-6232

RAMADA HOTEL DOWNTOWN
186 King St
(N6A 1C7)
Tel: (800) 228-2828

RELAX HOTEL LONDON
855 Wellington Rd S
(N6E 3N5)
Tel: (800) 667-3529

SHERATON ARMOURIES HOTEL-LONDON
325 Dundas St
(N6B 1T9)
Tel: (519) 679-6111

STATION PARK INN
242 Pall Mall St
(N6A 5P6)
Tel: (519) 642-4444

LONG SAULT

LION MOTEL
Box 610 (K0C 1P0)
Tel: (613) 534-2119

LONGLAC

L'OREE DES BOIS MOTEL
Box 971 (P0T 2A0)
Tel: (807) 876-2252

WOODLANDS INN
Box 1030,
130 Queen St (P0T 1A0)
Tel: (807) 876-2264

MABERLY

SILVER LAKE LODGE
RR 3 (K0H 2B0)
Tel: (613) 268-2511

MACKEY

HILLTOP MOTEL
General Delivery
(K0J 2B0)
Tel: (613) 586-2576

MACTIER

AVON MOTEL
RR 1 (P0C 1H0)
Tel: (705) 375-3000

H & H MARINA AND RESORT
Box 179 (P0C 1H0)
Tel: (705) 375-5323

SUNSET POINT COTTAGES
Box 93 (P0C 1H0)
Tel: (705) 375-5367

MADOC

COLONIAL INN MOTEL
Box 250 (K0K 2K0)
Tel: (613) 473-2221

MOIRA LAKE LODGE
Box 549 (K0K 2K0)
Tel: (613) 473-2744

MANITOUWADGE

MANITOUWADGE MOTOR HOTEL
46 Manitou Rd,
Box 278 (P0T 2C0)
Tel: (807) 826-4502

MANITOWANING

HEMBRUFF'S MOTEL
Box 250 (P0P 1N0)
Tel: (705) 859-3515

THE WAYSIDE MOTEL
Box 250 (P0P 1N0)
Tel: (705) 859-3515

MAPLE LEAF

LAKEVIEW RESORT
RR 1 (K0L 2R0)
Tel: (613) 338-5593

MARATHON

PIC MOTEL
Box 928 (P0T 2E0)
Tel: (807) 229-0130

MARKHAM

HOWARD JOHNSON
555 Cochrane Dr
(L3R 8E3)
Tel: (416) 479-5000

JOURNEY'S END MOTEL
8330 Woodbine Ave
(L3R 2N8)
Tel: (800) 668-4200

MARMORA

BELLE VISTA MOTEL
Box 487 (K0K 2M0)
Tel: (613) 472-3333

NU AVALON MOTEL
RR 2 (K0K 2M0)
Tel: (613) 472-2536

MARTEN RIVER

ROCK PINE MOTEL
General Delivery
(P0H 1T0)
Tel: (705) 892-2211

MARYSVILLE

GENERAL WOLFE HOTEL
Box 100, Wolfe Island
(K0H 2Y0)
Tel: (613) 385-2611

MASSEY

MOHAWK MOTEL
335 Sauble St,
Box 429 (P0P 1P0)
Tel: (705) 865-2722

WAYSIDE MOTEL
Box 717 (P0P 1P0)
Tel: (705) 865-2500

MATACHEWAN

CAMP MATACHEWAN
Box 10 (P0K 1M0)
Tel: (705) 565-2240

MATHESON

BEL AIR MOTEL
351 4th Ave,
Box 219 (P0K 1N0)
Tel: (705) 273-2757

KISS MOTEL
RR 2 (P0K 1N0)
Tel: (705) 273-2812

SLEEPY OWL MOTEL
Box 337 (P0K 1N0)
Tel: (705) 273-2933

VI-MAR MOTEL
Box 496 (P0K 1N0)
Tel: (705) 273-2535

MATTAWA

TWO RIVERS MOTEL
Box 483 (P0H 1V0)
Tel: (705) 744-2403

VALOIS MOTEL
701 Valois Dr,
Box 360 (P0H 1V0)
Tel: (705) 744-5583

MATTICE

MATTICE MOTEL
Con. 3, Lot 24E
(P0L 1T0)
Tel: (call operator:
Mattice 5441)

MEAFORD

BAY-VUE MOTEL
(N0H 1Y0)
Tel: (519) 538-3490

**FISHERMAN'S
WHARF MOTEL**
12 Bayfield St,
Box 374 (N0H 1Y0)
Tel: (519) 538-1390

HILLTOP MOTEL
300 Sykes St S,
Box 609 (N0H 1Y0)
Tel: (519) 538-1700

MEAFORD MOTEL
128 Sykes St N
(N0H 1Y0)
Tel: (519) 538-2611

MIDLAND

CHALET MOTEL
748 Young St
(L4R 2E5)
Tel: (705) 526-6571

COMFORT INN
980 King St
(L4R 4K5)
Tel: (800) 221-2222

KING'S MOTEL
751 King St,
Box 23 (L4R 4K8)
Tel: (705) 526-7744

MIDWAY MOTEL
69 Vinden St E,
Box 1, SS-9
(L4R 4L9)
Tel: (705) 526-7481

PANORAMA MOTEL
Box 396 (L4R 4L1)
Tel: (705) 526-5441

MILTON

**FIFTH WHEEL
TRUCK STOPS**
40 Chisholm Dr,
Box 160 (L9T 4N9)
Tel: (416) 878-8441

**HALTON COUNTRY
INN**
RR 3 (L9T 2X7)
Tel: (416) 878-6701

HERITAGE INN
161 Chisholm Dr
(L9T 4A6)
Tel: (416) 878-2825

MINAKI

**FOUR SEASONS'
NORTHLAND RESORT-
MINAKI LODGE**
P. O. Box 26
(P0X 1J0)
Tel: (800) 468-3331

GUNN LAKE LODGE
General Delivery
(P0X 1J0)
Tel: (807) 224-2321

MINDEN

HUGGY BEAR'S
RR 2 (K0M 2K0)
Tel: (705) 489-3111

MISSISSAUGA

COMFORT INN
1230 Journey's End
Cir (L3Y 7V1)
Tel: (800) 221-2222

RAMADA HOTEL
2501 Argentia Rd
(L5N 4G8)
Rates: $70-145
Tel: (905) 858-2424
(800) 272-6232

MONTEVILLE

SHUSWAP LODGE
RR 1 (P0M 2K0)
Tel: (705) 898-2485

MOONBEAM

BLUE MOON MOTEL
205 Government Rd
W,Box 149 (P0L 1V0)
Tel: (705) 367-2335

MORRISBURG

HOWARD JOHNSON
Hwy 2, P. O. Box
1140 (K0C 1X0)
Tel: (613) 543-3788
(800) 446-4656

PARKWAY MOTEL
RR 1 (K0C 1X0)
Tel: (613) 543-2533

**UPPER CANADA
MOTEL**
RR 1 (K0C 1X0)
Tel: (613) 543-3711

MORSON

**BUENA VISTA
RESORT**
RR 1, Sleeman
(P0W 1M0)
Tel: (807) 488-5652

MOUNTAIN GROVE

EVERGREEN MOTEL
RR 3 (K0H 2C0)
Tel: (613) 335-2603

NAPANEE

**MASTERSON'S
MOTEL**
Box 157, Hwy 41 N
(K7R 3M3)
Tel: (613) 354-9392

NAPANEE MOTEL
361 Dundas St W
(K7R 2B5)
Tel: (613) 354-5200

TWIN PEAKS MOTEL
353 Dundas St W
(K7R 2B5)
Tel: (613) 354-4066

NEPAN

**MONTEREY MOTOR
INN**
2259 Hwy 16
(K2E 6Z8)
Tel: (613) 226-5813

NESTOR FALLS

**CLARKE & CROMBIE
CAMP**
Box 38, Hwy 71
(P0K 1K0)
Tel: (807) 484-2114

NEW LISKEARD

**ALL SEASONS
MOTOR INN**
Box 187 (P0J 1P0)
Tel: (705) 647-6705

**GLEN AURA
COTTAGES**
Box 373 (P0J 1P0)
Tel: (705) 647-6153

HUSKY MOTEL
Box 916 (P0J 1P0)
Tel: (705) 647-6721

WATERFRONT INN
2 Cedar St, Box 2734
(P0J 1P0)
Tel: (705) 647-8711

WHEEL INN MOTEL
208 Armstrong
(P0J 1P0)
Tel: (705) 647-6116

NEWBORO

STAGECOACH INN
General Delivery
(K0G 1P0)
Tel: (613) 272-2900

NEWMARKET

JOURNEY'S END MOTEL
1230 Journey's End Cir (L3Y 7V1)
Tel: (800) 668-4200

VOYAGEUR PLACE HOTEL
17565 Yonge St
(L3Y 5H6)
Tel: (416) 895-2131

NIAGARA FALLS

ASHBURY MOTEL
7800 Lundy's Lane
(L2H 1H1)
Tel: (416) 356-8280

ASTON VILLA MOTEL
7939 Lundy's Lane
(L2H 1H3)
Tel: (416) 357-3535

BEST WESTERN MOTOR HOTEL
5551 Murray St
(L2G 2J4)
Tel: (416) 356-0551

CARAVAN MOTEL
8511 Lundy's Lane
(L2H 1H5)
Tel: (416) 357-1104

CLARION OLD STONE INN
5425 Robinson St
(L2G 7L6)
Tel: (416) 357-1234

COMFORT INN
5640 Stanley Ave
(L2G 3X5)
Tel: (800) 221-2222

COMFORT INN ON THE RIVER
4009 River Rd (L2E 3E4)
Tel: (800) 221-2222

CONTINENTAL INN
5756 Ferry St
(L2G 1S7)
Tel: (416) 356-2449

DAYS INN BY THE FALLS
4029 River Rd
(L2E 3E5)
Tel: (416) 356-6666

DIPLOMAT INN
5983 Stanley Ave
(L2G 3Y2)
Tel: (416) 357-9564

EDGECLIFFE MOTEL
4615 Cataract Ave
(L2E 3M3)
Tel: (416) 354-1688

EMPIRE MOTEL
5046 Centre St
(L2G 3N9)
Tel: (416) 357-2550

FALLS MANOR MOTEL
7104 Lundy's Lane
(L2G 1W2)
Tel: (416) 358-3211

FIDDLER'S GREEN-AFFORDABLE INNS
7720 Lundy's Lane
(L2H 1H1)
Tel: (416) 358-9833

THE GARDENS MOTEL
13055 Lundy's Lane
(L2E 6S4)
Tel: (416) 227-0891

GLENGATE MOTEL
5534 Stanley Ave
(L2G 3X2)
Tel: (416) 357-1333

HONEYMOON CITY MOTEL
4943 Clifton Hill
(L2G 3N5)
Tel: (416) 357-4330

INN ON THE HILL
5785 Ferry St
(L2G 1S8)
Tel: (416) 358-3559

KINGS BRIDGE INN
3516 Main St
(L2G 6A6)
Tel: (416) 295-4552

LA RIVIERA MOTEL
5427 Ferry St
(L2G 1S2)
Tel: (416) 356-0211

LIBERTY INNS
6408 Stanley Ave
(L2G 3Y5)
Tel: (416) 356-5877

MAYSIDE MOTEL
5450 Kitchener St
(L2G 1B8)
Tel: (416) 358-7844

MELODY MOTEL
13065 Lundy's Lane
(L2E 6S4)
Tel: (416) 227-1023

NIAGARA CLIFTON MOTOR INN
4945 Clifton Hill
(L2G 3N5)
Tel: (416) 356-8212

NIAGARA GATEWAY MOTEL
4745 Bender Hill
(L2G 3K4)
Tel: (416) 358-6811

NIAGARA PARKWAY COURT
3708 Main St
(L2G 6B1)
Tel: (416) 295-4374

OAKES INN
6546 Buchanan Ave
(L2G 3W2)
Tel: (416) 356-4514

OLYMPIA MOTEL
5099 Centre St
(L2G 3P1)
Tel: (416) 356-2614

RAMADA CORAL INN
7429 Lundy's Lane
(L2H 1G9)
Tel: (800) 854-7854

SCOTSMAN MOTEL
6179 Lundy's Lane
(L2G 1T4)
Tel: (416) 374-0041

SIESTA MOTEL
5703 Thorold Stone
(L2J 1A1)
Tel: (416) 356-7299

SKYLINE BROCK HOTEL
5685 Falls Ave
(L2E 6W7)
Tel: (416) 374-4445

SKYLINE FOXHEAD HOTEL
5685 Falls Ave
(L2E 6W7)
Tel: (416) 374-4444

SUNSET INN
5803 Stanley Ave
(L2G 3X8)
Tel: (416) 354-7513

THRIFTLODGE
6000 Stanley Ave
(L2G 3Y1)
Rates: $45-130
Tel: (905) 358-6243
(800) 578-7878

VACATION INNS
6519 Stanley Ave
(L2G 7L2)
Tel: (416) 356-1722

WILLOW MOTEL
8646 Lundy's Ln
(L2H 1H4)
Tel: (416) 374-2664

NIAGARA-ON-THE-LAKE

THE OBAN INN
160 Front St,
Box 94 (L0S 1J0)
Tel: (416) 468-2165

NIPIGON

BEAVER MOTOR HOTEL
RR 1 (P0T 2J0)
Tel: (807) 887-2914

NORTHLAND MOTEL
Box 736 (P0T 2J0)
Tel: (807) 887-2032

TOWN & COUNTRY MOTEL
Box 460 (P0T 2J0)
Tel: (807) 887-2382

NOELVILLE

BEAR LAKE LODGE
Box 125 (P0M 2N0)
Tel: (705) 898-2759

NOLALU

COME BY CHANCE RESORT
RR 2, Box 10
(P0T 2K0)
Tel: (807) 475-8788

NORTH BAY

AMBASSADOR MOTEL
666 Lakeshore Dr
(P1A 2G2)
Tel: (705) 472-3340

BAY MOTEL
RR 2, Box 6
(P1B 8G3)
Tel: (705) 472-7422

BAYSHORE MOTEL
566 Lakeshore Dr
(P1A 2E6)
Tel: (705) 472-5350

BEST WESTERN
700 Lakeshore Dr
(P1A 2G4)
Tel: (800) 528-1234

BO-MARK MOTEL
RR 2, Hwy 11 N
(P1B 8G3)
Tel: (705) 474-3100

COMFORT INN
676 Lakeshore Dr
(P1A 2G4)
Tel: (800) 221-2222

COMFORT INN
1200 O'Brien St
(P1B 9B3)
Tel: (800) 221-2222

DOLPHIN MOTEL & COTTAGES
549 Lakeshore Dr
(P1A 2E5)
Tel: (705) 472-5370

EMPIRE HOTEL
425 Fraser St
(P1B 3X1)
Tel: (705) 472-8200

FIFTH WHEEL TRUCK STOP
Pinewood Park Dr
(P1B 8Z4)
Tel: (705) 476-2372

HOWARD JOHNSON
425 Fraser St
(P1B 3X1)
Tel: (705) 472-8200
(800) 446-4656

HOWARD JOHNSON
425 Fraser St
(P1B 3X1)
Tel: (705) 472-8200
(800) 446-4656

HYLAND MOTEL
104 Highland Rd
(P1B 6K4)
Tel: (705) 472-2450

MANITOU MOTEL
710 Lakeshore Dr
(P1A 2G4)
Tel: (705) 472-1900

PINEWOOD PARK INN
201 Pinewood Dr,
Box 687 (P1B 8J8)
Tel: (800) 461-9592

RELAX INN NORTH BAY
1525 Seymour St,
Box 748 (P1B 8J8)
Tel: (800) 667-3529

SANDS MOTOR INN
366 McIntyre St E
(P1B 1C8)
Tel: (705) 472-2890

VENTURE INN
718 Lakeshore Dr
(P1A 2G4)
Tel: (705) 472-7171

WHITE FAWN MOTEL
4319 Hwy 11 N,
RR 2 (P1B 8G3)
Tel: (705) 497-3150

NORTH COBALT

COBALT TRUCK STOP
Box 147 (P0J 1R0)
Tel: (705) 679-8185

MAIDEN BAY CAMP
Box 218, RR 1
(P0J 1R0)
Tel: (705) 647-8533

OAKVILLE

HOLIDAY INN
360 Iroquois Shore
Rd (L6H 1M4)
Tel: (800) 465-4329

HOWARD JOHNSON
590 Argus Rd
(L6J 3J3)
Tel: (800) 654-2000

OMPAH

PALMERSTON MOTEL
RR 1 (K0H 2J0)
Tel: (613) 479-2888

ONAPING FALLS

WINDY LAKE MOTEL
Box 596, Hwy 144
(P0M 2C0)
Tel: (705) 966-3967

ORANGEVILLE

NORPEEL MOTEL
RR 4, Hwy 10 (L9W
2Y9)
Tel: (519) 941-0840

ORILLIA

CHIEFTAIN MOTEL
RR 3 (L3V 6H3)
Tel: (705) 325-7471

COMFORT INN
75 Progress Dr
(L3V 6V7)
Tel: (800) 221-2222

HOLIDAY MOTEL
436 Laclie St
(L3V 4P6)
Tel: (705) 325-1316

KNIGHT'S INN
285 Memorial Ave
(L3V 5X8)
Tel: (705) 326-3554

LAKELAND INN
400 Memorial Ave
L3V 6K3)
Tel: (705) 325-9511

MAPLES MOTEL
107 Meywash St
(L3V 1X6)
Tel: (705) 326-3561

NORTHCOURT MOTEL
320 Laclie St
(L3V 4P1)
Tel: (705) 325-2751

SUNDIAL INN
600 Sundial Dr
(L3V 6H3)
Tel: (705) 325-2233

ORONO

SONRISE MOTEL
4177 Hwy 35 & 115
(L0B 1M0)
Tel: (416) 983-5219

TWIN OAKS MOTEL
3511 Conc. Rd 4
(L0B 1M0)
Tel: (416) 983-5856

OSHAWA

COMFORT INN
605 Bloor St W
(L1J 5Y6)
Tel: (800) 221-2222

HOLIDAY INN
1011 Bloor St E
(L1H 7K6)
Tel: (800) 465-4329

OSHAWA TRAVELODGE
940 Champlain Ave
(L1J 7A6)
Tel: (800) 255-3050

RODEWAY SUITES
1910 Simcoe St. N.
(L1G 4Y3)
Rates: $54-72
Tel: (905) 404-8700
(800) 228-2000

OTTAWA

BEACON ARMS HOTEL
88 Albert St
(K1P 5E9)
Tel: (613) 235-1413

BEACON HILL MOTEL
1668 Montreal Rd
(K1J 6N5)
Tel: (613) 745-6818

COMFORT INN
1242 Michael St
(K1J 7T1)
Tel: (800) 221-2222

DELTA OTTAWA
361 Queen St
(K1R 7S9)
Tel: (800) 268-1133

**EMBASSY WEST
MOTOR HOTEL**
1400 Carling Ave
(K1Z 7L8)
Tel: (800) 267-8696

HOLIDAY INN
350 Dalhousie St
(K1N 7E9)
Tel: (800) 465-4329

HOTEL ROXBOROUGH
123 Metcalfe St
(K1P 5L9)
Tel: (613) 237-5171

HOWARD JOHNSON
140 Slater St
(K1P 5H6)
Tel: (800) 654-2000

LORD ELGIN HOTEL
100 Elgin St
(K1P 5K8)
Tel: (800) 267-4298

MINTO PLACE HOTEL
433 Laurier Ave W
(K1R 7Y1)
Tel: (613) 232-2200

**NOVOTEL HOTEL
OTTAWA**
33 Nicholas St
(K1N 9M7)
Tel: (613) 230-3033

OTTAWA HILTON
150 Albert St
(K1P 5G2)
Tel: (613) 238-1500

PARI'S MOTEL
665 Montreal Rd
(K1K 0T1)
Tel: (613) 745-6891

PARK LANE HOTEL
111 Cooper St
(K2P 2E3)
Tel: (800) 267-8378

QUALITY HOTEL
290 Rideau St (K1N
5Y3)
Tel: (800) 221-2222

**RADISSON HOTEL
OTTAWA CENTRE**
100 Kent St
(K1P 5R7)
Tel: (800) 333-3333

**RAMADA HOTEL &
SUITES**
111 Cooper St
(K2P 2E3)
Rates: $70-115
Tel: (613) 238-1331
(800) 272-6232

**RELAX HOTEL
OTTAWA-
DOWNTOWN**
402 Queen St
(K1R 5A7)
Tel: (800) 667-3529

THE SKYLINE OTTAWA
101 Lyon St
(K1R 5T9)
Tel: (613) 237-3600

SOUTHWAY INN
2431 Bank St
(K1V 8R9)
Tel: (613) 737-0811

SWISS INN MOTEL
5023 Bank St
(K1G 3N4)
Tel: (613) 822-0392

**TALISMAN MOTOR
HOTEL**
1376 Carling Ave
(K1Z 7L5)
Tel: (613) 722-7600

**TOWN HOUSE
MOTOR HOTEL**
319 Rideau St
(K1N 5Y4)
Tel: (613) 789-5555

TRAVELODGE
2098 Montreal Rd
(K1J 6M8)
Rates: $49-123
Tel: (613) 745-1531
(800) 578-7878

VENTURE INN
480 Metcalfe St
(K1S 3N6)
Tel: (613) 237-5500

WEBB'S MOTEL
1705 Carling Ave
(K2A 1C8)
Tel: (613) 728-1881

WESTIN HOTEL
11 Colonel By Dr
(K1N 9H4)
Tel: (800) 228-3000

OWEN SOUND

COMFORT INN
955 9th Ave E (N4K
6N4)
Tel: (800) 221-2222

DERBY INN-MOTEL
Box 1108, RR 5
(N4K 5N7)
Tel: (519) 376-2580

ECONO LODGE
485 9th Ave E
(N4K 3E2)
Rates: $48-69
Tel: (519) 371-
3011(800) 424-4777

HOLIDAY INN
950 6th St E
(N4K 1H1)
Tel: (800) 465-4329

HWY 70 MOTEL
RR 5 (N4K 5N7)
Tel: (519) 376-5841

PAKENHAM

PAKENHAM INN
RR 1 (K0A 2X0)
Tel: (613) 624-5376

PALMER RAPIDS

THE WINGLE INN
RR 2 (K0J 2E0)
Tel: (613) 758-2072

PARIS

ROSE COURT MOTEL
12 Paris Rd
(N3L 3H8)
Tel: (519) 442-2122

PARRY SOUND

BIG WHEEL MOTEL
RR 2 (P2A 2W8)
Tel: (705) 378-2895

COMFORT INN
118 Bowes St
(P2A 2L7)
Tel: (800) 221-2222

**CRANE LAKE
HOUSE RESORT**
Rosseau Rd
(P0C 1K0)
Tel: (705) 378-2206

ELL MAR MOTEL
RR 2 (P2A 2W8)
Tel: (705) 378-2391

GEORGIAN INN
48 Joseph St
(P2A 2G5)
Tel: (705) 746-2118

**KITCHENER MOTOR
INN**
24 Gibson St
(P2A 1W8)
Tel: (705) 746-2171

MAPLES MOTEL
RR 2 (P2A 2W8)
Tel: (705) 378-2342

SHERWOOD MOTEL
RR 2 (P2A 2W8)
Tel: (705) 378-2848

**SUNNY POINT
COTTAGES & INN**
Box P, Rosseau Rd
(P0C 1K0)
Tel: (800) 265-0432

**TRAVELLERS
MOTOR HOTEL**
36 Mary St
(P2A 1E4)
Tel: (705) 746-9307

WHITFIELD LODGE
RR 2, Hwy 69 S
(P2A 2W8)
Tel: (705) 378-2277

PEFFERLAW

**EAGLEWOOD
COTTAGES**
Box 256, RR 2
(L0E 1N0)
Tel: (705) 437-1634

PEMBROKE

BAYVIEW INN MOTEL
845 Pembroke St E
(K8A 3M3)
Tel: (613) 732-7759

BEST WESTERN PEMBROKE INN
1 International Dr
(K8A 6X9)
Tel: (800) 567-2378

COLONIAL INN
1350 Pembroke St W
(K8A 7A3)
Tel: (613) 732-3623

COMFORT INN
959 Pembroke St E
(K8A 3M3)
Tel: (800) 221-2222

COPELAND CHAMPLAIN MOTOR HOTEL
1325 Pembroke St W
(K8A 5R3)
Tel: (613) 732-2889

FLAMINGO MOTEL
655 Hwy 17 W
(K8A 7H2)
Tel: (613) 732-4521

FOREST LEA INN
1433 Pembroke St W
(K8A 7A5)
Tel: (613) 732-9981

SCENIC MOTEL
788 Hwy 17 W
K8A 7H7)
Tel: (613) 735-3171

SLEEPY HAVEN
1207 Pembroke St E
(K8A 7R6)
Tel: (613) 732-9953

TRAVELLER'S INN
1044 Pembroke St E
(K8A 6Z3)
Tel: (613) 732-9901

PERTH

AQUARIUS MOTEL
2 Lanark Rd
(K7H 2S1)
Tel: (613) 267-4261

FRIENDSHIP INN
125 Dufferin St.
(K7H 3A5)
Rates: $39-89
Tel: (613) 267-3300
(800) 453-4511

MCCREARY'S BEACH RESORT
RR 6 (K7H 3C8)
Tel: (613) 267-4450

PETERBOROUGH

BLUE JAY MOTEL
RR 7 (K9J 6X8)
Tel: (705) 743-2160

CLEAR VIEW TERRACE MOTEL
RR 7 (K9J 6X8)
Tel: (705) 745-4621

COMFORT INN
1209 Landsdowne St
(K9J 7M2)
Tel: (800) 221-2222

HOLIDAY INN
150 George St N
(K9J 3G5)
Tel: (800) 465-4329

QUALITY INN
1074 Landsdowne St
(K9J 1Z9)
Tel: (800) 221-2222

RAMADA INN
100 Charlotte St
(K9J 7L4)
Rates: $75-115
Tel: (705) 743-7272
(800) 272-6232

PICKERING

JOURNEY'S END MOTEL
533 Kingston Rd
(L1V 3N7)
Tel: (416) 831-6200

PICKLE LAKE

PICKLE LAKE HOTEL
Box 440 (P0V 3A0)
Tel: (807) 928-2581

PICTON

TIP OF THE BAY MOTOR HOTEL
35 Bridge St,
Box 3159 (K0K 2T0)
Tel: (613) 476-2156

PLANTAGENET

MOTEL DE CHAMPLAIN
Box 294 (K0B 1L0)
Tel: (613) 673-5220

PORCUPINE

TRILLIUM MOTEL
Box 172 (P0N 1C0)
Tel: (705) 235-3839

PORT ELGIN

COLONIAL MOTEL
235 Goderich St S
(N0H 2C1)
Tel: (519) 832-2021

JK MOTEL
764 Goderich St S
(N0H 2C0)
Tel: (519) 389-4837

SAUGEEN TRAILS MOTEL
RR 3 (N0H 2C7)
Tel: (519) 389-4233

PORT HOPE

COMFORT INN
P. O. Box 86
(L1A 3V9)
Tel: (800-221-2222

GREENWOOD TOWER INN
162 Peter St
(L1A 3V9)
Tel: (416) 885-7283

PORT LORING

DRIFTWOOD MOTEL
Box 69 (P0H 1Y0)
Tel: (705) 757-2636

ROGERSON'S LODGES
Box 26 (P0H 1Y0)
Tel: (705) 757-2050

PORT PERRY

RAILROADHOUSE MOTOR MOTEL
Box 804, Scugog St,
Hwy 7A (L9L 1A7)
Tel: (416) 985-8131

PORT SEVERN

ALLCOVE RESORT
Box 76 (L0K 1S0)
Tel: (705) 538-2511

PORT SEVERN MOTOR HOTEL
General Delivery
(L0K 1S0)
Tel: (705) 538-0255

POWASSAN

WASSI LODGE RESORT
Rr 4 (P0H 1Z0)
Tel: (705) 724-2032

PRESCOTT

GLEN MOTEL
RR 3 (K0E 1T0)
Tel: (613) 925-4215

ISLE OF REST MOTEL
RR 1 (K0E 1T0)
Tel: (613) 925-3228

JOHNSTOWN MOTEL
Grp. Box 85, RR 3
(K0E 1T0)
Tel: (613) 657-3548

PROVIDENCE BAY

HURON SANDS MOTEL
20 Sunova Beach Rd
(P0P 1T0)
Tel: (705) 377-4616

RAINY RIVER

THE ROAD RUNNER MOTEL
Box 103 (P0W 1L0)
Tel: (807) 852-3296

RAMORE

ROLLY'S MOTEL
Box 218 (P0K 1R0)
Tel: (705) 236-4004

RENFREW

DAYS INN VALLEY MOTEL
Box 355 (K7V 4A4)
Tel: (613) 432-3636

LA CASA MOTOR INN
RR 1 (K7V 3Z4)
Tel: (613) 432-4866

THE RENFREW INN
760 Gibbons Rd,
Box 99 (K7V 4A2)
Tel: (613) 432-8109

SUNSET MOTEL
409 Stewart St N
(K7V 1Y4)
Tel: (613) 432-5801

RICHMOND

RICHMOND INN
Box 100, Perth St
(K0A 2Z0)
Tel: (613) 838-2121

RICHMOND HILL

SUMMIT MOTEL
11610 Yonge St
(L4C 4Y6)
Tel: (416) 884-9011

RIDGETOWN

BATEMAN MOTOR INN
RR 3 (N0P 2C0)
Tel: (519) 674-5454

ROLPHTON

ROLPHTON MOTEL
Box 103 (K0J 2H0)
Tel: (613) 586-2223

ST. CHATHARINES

COMFORT INN
2 Dunlop Dr
(L2R 1A2)
Tel: (800) 221-2222

HOLIDAY INN
2 N Service Rd (L2N 4G9)
Tel: (800) 465-4329

HOWARD JOHNSON
89 Meadowvale Dr
(L2N 3Z8)
Tel: (800) 654-2000

LEONARD HOTEL & MOTOR INN
259 St. Paul St
(L2R 3M7)
Tel: (4160 685-5455

ST. THOMAS

COMFORT INN
100 Centennial Ave
(N5R 5B2)
Tel: (800) 221-2222

NU-ELGIN MOTEL
RR 7 (N5P 3T2)
Tel: (519) 633-0580

WESTERN CHELSEA INN
292 Wellington St
(N5R 2S9)
Tel: (519) 631-2860

SARNIA

BEST WESTERN GUILDWOOD INN
1400 Venetian Blvd
(N7T 7W6)
Tel: (519) 337-7577

CHIPICAN MOTEL
1144 Christina St
(N7V 3C3)
Tel: (519) 336-4153

COMFORT INN
505 Harbour Rd
(N7T 5R8)
Tel: (800) 221-2222

402 MOTOR INN
751 Christina St N
(N7V 1X5)
Tel: (519) 344-1157

HOLIDAY INN
1498 Venetial Blvd,
Box 2290 (N7T 7W6)
Tel: (800) 465-4329

SAUBLE BEACH

GOLDEN EAGLE MOTEL & COTTAGES
323 Main St
(N0H 2G0)
Tel: (519) 422-1164

SAULT STE. MARIE

ALGOMA'S WATER TOWER INN
360 Great Northern
Rd (P6A 5N3)
Tel: (800) 461-0800

AMBASSADOR MOTEL
1275 Hwy 17 N
(P6A 5K7)
Tel: (705) 759-6199

BEL AIR MOTEL
398 Pim St (P6B 2V1)
Tel: (705) 945-7950

COMFORT INN
333 Great Northern
Rd (P6B 4Z8)
Tel: (800) 221-2222

HEYDEN MOTEL
RR 2 (P6A 5K7)
Tel: (705) 777-2082

HOLIDAY INN
208 St. Mary's River
Dr (P6A 5V4)
Tel: (800) 465-4329

LINCOLN MOTEL
21 Hwy 17E
(P6A 3S2)
Tel: (705) 253-4091

NORWEST HOTEL & INN
138 East St, Box 1360
(P6A 6N2)
Tel: (705) 942-1970

PINE GROVE MOTEL
1515 Trunk Rd
(P6A 5K9)
Tel: (705) 759-1202

RAMADA INN
229 Great Northern
Rd (P6B 4Z2)
Tel: (800) 228-2828

SATELITE MOTEL SAULT
248 Great Northern
Rd (P6B 4Z6)
Tel: (705) 256-6215

SHADY REST MOTEL APARTMENTS
1547 Trunk Rd
(P6A 5K9)
Tel: (705) 759-2316

TRAVELLERS MOTEL
859 Trunk Rd
(P6A 3T3)
Tel: (705) 946-6433

SAVANT LAKE

FOUR WINDS MOTOR HOTEL
General Delivery
(P0V 2S0)
Tel: (807) 584-2223

SCHREIBER

BIRCH GROVE MOTEL
316 Walker St, Box
277 (P0T 2S0)
Tel: (807) 824-2800

CIRCLE ROUTE MOTEL
Box 758 (P0T 2S0)
Tel: (807) 824-2452

CLIFFSIDE MOTEL
106 Quebec St,
Box 332 (P0T 2S0)
Tel: (807) 824-2754

NOR-WEST MOTEL
Box 288 (P0T 2S0)
Tel: (807) 824-2501

RONGIE LAKE MOTEL
Box 70 (P0T 2S0)
Tel: (807) 824-2742

SEELEYS BAY

THE BAY MOTEL
Box 42, RR 1
(K0H 2N0)
Tel: (613) 387-3800

SHANNONVILLE

SALMON RIVER MOTEL
RR 2 (K0K 3A0)
Tel: (613) 962-4735

SHARBOT LAKE

SHARBOT LAKE MOTOR INN
General Delivery
(K0H 2P0)
Tel: (613) 279-2198

SHEBANDOWAN

CEDAR HILL RESORT
Box 29 (P0T 2T0)
Tel: (807) 926-2871

SHELBURNE

HY-LAND MOTEL
RR 4 (L0N 1S0)
Tel: (519) 925-5552

**SHINING TREE-
THE COUNTRY
LODING**
General Delivery
(P0M 2X0)
Tel: (705) 263-2021

SIMCOE

**BEST WESTERN
LITTLE RIVER INN**
203 Queensway W
(N3Y 2M9)
Rates: $58-78
Tel: (519) 426-2125
(800) 5281234

COMFORT INN
85 The Queensway E
(N3Y 4M5)
Tel: (800) 221-2222

**THE LITTLE RIVER
INN**
203 Queensway W
(N3Y 2M9)
Tel: (519) 426-2125

QUEENSWAY MOTEL
139 Queensway W
(N3Y 2M8)
Tel: (519) 426-3658

SIOUX LOOKOUT

**WELCOME MOTOR
HOTEL**
Box 1287 (P0V 2T0)
Tel: (807) 737-1330

SIOUX NARROWS

**CRYSTAL HARBOUR
RESORT**
Box 278 (P0X 1N0)
Tel: (807) 226-5233

MAPLE LEAF MOTEL
Box 212 (P0X 1N0)
Tel: (807) 226-5696

SMITHS FALLS

**DAVES HOLIDAY
MOTEL**
RR 3 (K7A 4S4)
Tel: (613) 283-7147

SOUTH RIVER

POCONO LODGE
RR 1 (P0A 1X0)
Tel: (705) 386-2834

SOUTHAMPTON

**SAUGEEN MARINA
MOTEL**
Box 1120 (N0H 2L0)
Tel: (519) 797-2817

SPRAGGE

ROYS MOTEL
Box 1 (P0R 1K0)
Tel: (705) 849-2482

SPRUCEDALE

**THE GROVE
COTTAGES**
RR 1 (P0A 1Y0)
Tel: (705) 685-7055

STOKES BAY

GOOD ACRES CAMP
General Delivery
(N0H 2M0)
Tel: (519) 592-5866

STRATFORD

NORETTA MOTEL
691 Ontario St
(N5A 3J6)
Tel: (519) 271-6110

ROSECOURT MOTEL
599 Erie St
(N5A 2N9)
Tel: (519) 271-6005

TRAVELLERS MOTEL
784 Ontario St
(N5A 3K1)
Tel: (519) 271-3830

**TWENTY THREE
ALBERT PLACE**
23 Albert St
(N5A 3K2)
Tel: (519) 273-5800

STRATHROY

4 CORNERS MOTEL
RR 6 (N7G 3H7)
Tel: (519) 245-4495

STUREGON FALLS

CHAMPLAIN MOTEL
155 Front St,
Box 1078 (P0H 2G0)
Tel: (705) 753-1300

LINCOLN MOTEL
Box 2606 (P0H 2G0)
Tel: (705) 753-0880

**MOULIN ROUGE
MOTEL**
175 Front St,
Box 38 (P0H 2G0)
Tel: (705) 753-2020

RED ROCK MOTEL
Box 2050 (P0H 2G0)
Tel: (705) 753-3006

SUDBURY

BELMONT INN
340 York St
(P3E 2A7)
Tel: (705) 673-1131

BUTCHART'S CAMP
RR 2 (P3E 4M9)
Tel: (705)522-8900

**CARDINAL MOTOR
INN**
1500 Regent St S
(P3E 3Z6)
Tel: (705) 522-8900

**CHATEAU GUAY
MOTEL**
2865 Kingsway
(P3B 2G4)
Tel: (705) 566-1501

COMFORT INN
440 2nd Ave N,
Box 2490, Stn A
(P3A 4S9)
Tel: (800) 221-2222

COMFORT INN
2171 Regent St S
(P3E 5V3)
Tel: (800) 221-2222

**ESTAIRE MOTOR
HOTEL**
Site 33, Box 14,
RR 3 (P3E 4N1)
Tel: (705) 695-2124

HOLIDAY INN
85 St. Anne Rd,
Box 1033 (P3E 4S4)
Tel: (800) 485-4329

**HOWARD
JOHNSON**
390 S Elgin St
(P3B 1B4)
Tel: (705) 675-1273
(800) 446-4656

NORTHWAY MOTEL
2689 Kingsway
(P3B 2G1)
Tel: (705) 566-1284

**RAMADA INN
CITY CENTRE**
85 Ste Anne Rd
(P3E 4S4)
Rates: $70-102
Tel: (705) 675-1123
(800) 272-6232

**RELAX INN
SUDBURY**
1401 Paris St
(P3E 3B6)
Tel: (800) 667-3529

**RICHARD LAKE
MOTEL**
RR 3, Site 14, Box 4,
Hwy 69 S (P3E 4N1)
Tel: (705) 522-3788

**SENATOR MOTOR
HOTEL**
390 Elgin St S
(P3B 1B1)
Tel: (706) 675-1273

**SPORTSMAN'S
LODGE**
Box 475 (P0M 1V0)
Tel: (705) 853-4434

VENTURE INN
1956 Regent St S
(P3E 3Z9)
Tel: (705) 522-7600

SUNDRIDGE

SHADY MAPLES MOTEL
Box 135 (P0A 1Z0)
Tel: (705) 384-5188

SUTTON

SOUTH SHORE MOTEL
1745 Baseline Rd
(L0E 1R0)
Tel: (416) 722-3287

TEMAGAMI

ANGUS LAKE LODGE & MOTEL
RR 1 (P0H 2H0)
Tel: (705) 569-3868

NORTHLAND PARADISE LODGE
Box 472, Stevens Rd
(P0H 2H0)
Tel: (705) 569-3791

SCANDIA INN
Box 70 (P0H 2H0)
Tel: (705) 569-3644

TEMAGAMI SHORES INN & RESORT
Box 68 (P0H 2H0)
Tel: (705) 569-3200

TERRACE BAY

RED DOG INN
Box 607 (P0T 2W0)
Tel: (807) 825-3285

THESSALON

CAROLYN BEACH MOTEL
Hwy 17B W, Box 10
(P0R 1L0)
Tel: (705) 842-3330

THOMASBURG

SUNRISE MOTEL
Box 4 (K0K 3H0)
Tel: (613) 478-2326

THORNBURY

BEAVER MOTEL
161 King St E,
Box 457 (N0H 2P0)
Tel: (519) 599-3054

THOROLD

LOCK 7 MOTEL
24 Chapel St S
(L2V 2C6)
Tel: (416) 227-6177

THUNDER BAY

AIRLANE MOTOR HOTEL
698 W Arthur St
(P7E 5R8)
Tel: (807) 577-1181

BEST WESTERN CROSSROADS MOTOR INN
655 W Arthur St
(P7E 5R6)
Tel: (807) 528-1234

BOB'S MOTEL
235 Arthur St W
(P7E 5P7)
Tel: (807) 475-4546

CIRLCE INN
686 Memorial Ave
(P7B 3Z5)
Tel: (807) 344-5744

COMFORT INN
660 W Arthur St
(P7E 5R8)
Tel: (800) 221-2222

CREST MOTOR HOTEL
875 Red River Rd
(P7B 1K3)
Tel: (807) 767-1627

EMPIRE MOTEL
387 N Cumberland
St (P7A 4P6)
Tel: (807) 345-6561

FORT MOTEL
627 Kingsway Ave
(P7E 2A6)
Tel: (807) 623-4544

HOLIDAY INN MOTEL
375 Kingsway Ave
(P7E 2A6)
Tel: (807) 623-2514

KINGS MOTEL
540 N Cumberland
St (P7A 4S3)
Tel: (807) 344-7269

KINGSWAY MOTEL
345 Kingsway Ave
(P7E 2A6)
Tel: (807) 623-1223

LAKEHEAD MOTEL
421 N Cumberland
St (P7A 4P9)
Tel: (807) 345-4487

LAKEVIEW MOTEL
391 N Cumberland
St (P7A 4P7)
Tel: (807) 345-1711

LANDMARK INN
1010 Dawson Rd
(P7B 5J4)
Tel: (800) 465-3950

OLD COUNTRY MOTEL
500 N Cumberland
St (P7A 4R8)
Tel: (807) 344-2511

OVERPASS MOTEL
2410 W Arthur St
(P7C 4V1)
Tel: (807) 475-7758

PRINCE ARTHUR HOTEL
17 N Cumberland St
(P7A 4K8)
Tel: (807) 345-5411

SHORELINE HOTEL
Box 3105 (P7A 4L7)
Tel: (807) 344-9661

SUPERIOR MOTEL
446 N Cumberland
St (P7A 4R2)
Tel: (807) 345-1408

VALHALLA INN
1 Valhalla Inn Rd
(P7E 6J1)
Tel: (807) 577-1121

VENTURE INN
450 Memorial Ave
(P7B 3Y7)
Tel: (807) 345-2343

VOYAGEUR MOTEL
177 Powley St
(P7A 2K8)
Tel: (807) 345-4786

TILBURY

CEDAR INN MOTEL
RR 5 (N0P 2L0)
Tel: (519) 682-1140

TILLSONBURG

HILLTOP MOTEL
50 Simcoe St
(N4G 2H5)
Tel: (519) 842-5966

SUPER 8 MOTEL
92 Simcoe St
(N4G 2J1)
Rates: $57-78
Tel: (519) 842-7366
(800) 800-8000

TIMMINS

BEST WESTERN
1800 Riverside Dr
(P4N 7J5)
Rates: $55-89
Tel: (705) 267-6241
(800) 528-1234

COMFORT INN
939 Algonquin Blvd E
Box 1190 (P4N 7J5)
Tel: (800) 221-2222

PINE RIDGE MOTEL
RR 2 (P4N 7C3)
Tel: (705) 268-9508

RIVERSIDE INN
1800 Riverside Dr,
Box 1223 (P4N 7J5)
Tel: (705) 267-6241

SENATOR HOTELS
14 Mountjoy St S
(P4N 1S4)
Tel: (705) 267-6211

VENTURE INN TIMMINS
730 Algonquin Blvd E
(P4N 7G2)
Tel: (705) 268-7171

TORONTO
(Metro Area)

BEACH MOTEL
2183 Lakeshore Blvd
W (M8V 1A1)
Tel: (416) 259-3296

**BEST WESTERN
CARLTON PLACE
HOTEL**
33 Carlston Crt
(M9W 6H5)
Tel: (416) 675-1234

**BEST WESTERN
HOTEL STRATA**
30 Norfinch Dr
(M3N 1X1)
Tel: (416) 665-3500

**BOND PLACE
HOTEL**
65 Dundas St E
(M5B 2G8)
Tel: (416) 362-6061

**THE BRISTOL PLACE
HOTEL**
950 Dixon Rd
(M9W 5N4)
Tel: (416) 675-9444

**CARLINGVIEW
AIRPORT INN**
221 Carlingview Dr
(M9W 5E8)
Tel: (416) 675-3303

CELEBRITY INN
6355 Airport Rd
(L4V 1E4)
Tel: (416) 677-7331

**COMFORT INN-
BRAMPTON**
5 Rutherford Rd S
(L6W 3J3)
Tel: (800) 221-2222

**COMFORT INN-
DOWNSVIEW**
66 Norfinch Dr
(M3N 1X1)
Tel: (800) 221-2222

COMFORT INN-EAST
3306 Kingston Rd
(M1M 1P8)
Tel: (800) 221-2222

**COMFORT INN-
NORTHEAST**
8330 Woodbine Ave
(L3R 2N8)
Tel: (800) 221-2222

**COMFORT INN-
PICKERING**
533 Kingstn Rd
(L1V 3N7)
Tel: (800) 221-2222

COMFORT INN-WEST
1500 Matheson Blvd
(L4W 3Z4)
Tel: (800) 221-2222

**DAYS INN
TORONTO WEST**
4635 Tomken Rd
(L4W 1J9)
Tel: (800) 325-2525

**DAYS INN TORONTO
DOWNTOWN**
30 Carlton St
(M5B 2E9)
Tel: (800) 325-2525

DELTA CHELSEA INN
33 Gerrard St W
(M5G 1Z4)
Tel: (800) 268-1133

**DELTA MEADOW-
VALE INN**
6750 Mississauga Rd
(L5N 2L3)
Tel: (800) 268-1133

**DELTA TORONTO
AIRPORT**
801 Dixon Rd
(M9W 1J5)
Tel: (800) 268-1133

**DODGE SUITES
HOTEL**
5050 Orbitor Dr
(L4W 4X2)
Tel: (416) 238-9600

EXECUTIVE INN
621 King St W
(M5V 1M5)
Tel: (416) 362-7441

**FOUR SEASONS
HOTEL**
21 Avenue Rd
(M5R 2G1)
Tel: (800) 332-3442

**FOUR SEASONS
INN ON THE PARK**
1100 Eglinton Ave E
(M3C 1H8)
Tel: (800) 332-3442

HILLCREST MOTEL
2143 Lakeshore Blvd
W (M8V 1A1)
Tel: (416) 255-7711

HOLIDAY INN
2125 N Sheridan
Way (L5K 1A3)
Tel: (418) 855-2000

**HOLIDAY INN
TORONTO AIRPORT**
970 Dixon Rd
(M9W 1J9)
Tel: (416) 465-4329

**HOLIDAY INN
DOWNTOWN**
89 Chestnut St
(M5G 1R1)
Tel: (800) 465-4329

**HOLIDAY INN
TORONTO
AIRPORT SOUTH**
2 Holiday Inn Dr
(M9C 2Z7)
Tel: (800) 465-4329

**HOLIDAY INN
TORONTO EAST**
22 Metropolitan Rd
(M1R 2T6)
Tel: (800) 465-4329

**HOLIDAY INN
TORONTO YORKDALE**
3450 Duffering St
(M6A 2V1)
Tel: (800) 465-4329

HOTEL IBIS
240 Jarvis St
(M5B 2B8)
Tel: (416) 593-9400

**HOTEL
INTER-CONTINENTAL**
220 Bloor St W
(M5S 1T8)
Tel: (416) 960-5200

HOTEL STRATA
5585 Ambler Dr
(L4W 3Z1)
Tel: (416) 238-3500

HOWARD JOHNSON
2420 Surveyor Rd
(L5N 4E6)
Tel: (416) j858-8600

HOWARD JOHNSON
40 Progress Crt
(M1G 3T5)
Tel: (800) 446-4656

HOWARD JOHNSON
475 Younge St
(M4Y 1X7)
Tel: (416) 924-0611
(800) 446-4656

HOWARD JOHNSON
2737 Keele St
(M2M 2E9)
Tel: (416) 636-4656
(800) 446-4656

HOWARD JOHNSON
600 Dixon Rd
(M9W 1J1)
Tel: (416) 240-7511
(800) 446-4656

HOWARD JOHNSON
555 Cochrane Dr
(L3R 8E3)
Tel: (905) 479-5000
(800) 446-4656

HOWARD JOHNSON
15520 Yonge St
(L4G 1P2)
Tel: (905) 727-1312
(800) 446-4656

HOWARD JOHNSON
430 Ouellette Ave
(N9A 1B2)
Tel: (519) 256-4656
(800) 446-4656

IDLEWOOD INN
4212 Kingston Rd
(M1E 2M6)
Tel: (416) 286-6862

KING EDWARD HOTEL
37 King St E
(M5C 1E9)
Tel: (416) 863-9700

**NOVOTEL
MISSISSAUGA**
3670 Hurontario St
(L5B 1P3)
Tel: (800) 221-4542

**NOVOTEL
NORTH YORK**
3 Park Home Ave
(M2N 6L3)
Tel: (800) 221-4542

**NOVOTEL-
TORONTO AIRPORT**
135 Carlingview Dr
(M9W 5E7)
Tel: (800) 221-4542

**NOVOTEL-
TORONTO CENTRE**
45 The Esplanade
(M5E 1W2)
Tel: (800) 221-4542

PARK PLAZA HOTEL
4 Avenue Rd
(M5R 2E8)
Tel: (416) 924-5471

**QUALITY HOTEL-
AIRPORT EAST**
2180 Islington Ave
(M9P 3P1)
Tel: (800) 221-2222

**QUALITY HOTEL-
DOWNTOWN**
111 Lombard St
(M5C 2T9)
Tel: (800) 221-2222

**QUALITY HOTEL-
MIDTOWN**
280 Bloor St
(M5S 1V8)
Tel: (800) 221-2222

**QUALITY SUITES-
AIRPORT**
262 Carlingview Dr
(M9W 5G1)
Tel: (800) 221-2222

RADISSON HOTEL
1250 Eglinton Ave E
(M3C 1J3)
Tel: (800) 333-3333

**RAMADA HOTEL-
AIRPORT WEST**
5444 Dixie Rd
(L4W 2L2)
Tel: (800) 854-7854

**RAMADA INN
400/401**
1677 Wilson Ave
(M3L 1A5)
Tel: (800) 228-2828

**RELAX HOTEL-
TORONTO AIRPORT**
445 Rexdale Blvd
(M9W 6K5)
Tel: (800) 667-3529

**RELAX INN
TORONTO EAST-
SCARBOROUGH**
20 Milner Business
Crt (M1B 3C6)
Tel: (800) 667-3529

**RELAX INN
TORONTO NORTH-
NORTH YORK**
50 Forfinch Dr
(M3N 1X1)
Tel: (800) 667-3529

**RELAX INN
TORONTO WEST-
MISSISSAUGA**
5599 Ambler Dr
(L4W 3Z1)
Tel: (800) 667-3529

**ROEHAMPTON
HOTEL**
808 Mt. Pleasant Rd
(M4P 2L2)
Tel: (416) 487-5101

ROYAL YORK HOTEL
100 Front St W
(M5J 1E3)
Tel: (416) 368-2511

**SHERATON CENTRE
HOTEL & TOWERS**
123 Queen St W
(M5H 2M9)
Tel: (800) 325-3535

**SHERATON
TORONTO EAST-
HOTEL & TOWERS**
2035 Kennedy Rd
(M1T 3G2)
Tel: (416) 299-1500

SKYDOME HOTEL
45 Peter St S
(M5V 3B4)
Tel: (416) 360-7100

**SWISSOTEL
TORONTO AIRPORT**
Box 3000, Toronto
AMF (L5P 1C4)
Tel: (416) 672-7000

**TORONTO AIRPORT
HILTON**
5875 Airport Rd
(L4V 1N1)
Tel: (416) 677-9900

**TORONTO AIRPORT
MARRIOTT HOTEL**
901 Dixon Rd (M9W
1J5)
Tel: (416) 674-9400

VALHALLA INN
1 Valhalla Inn Rd
(M9B 1S9)
Tel: (416) 239-2391

**VENTURE INN
SCARBOROUGH**
50 Estate Dr
(M1H 2Z1)
Tel: (416) 439-9666

**VENTURE INN
YORKVILLE**
89 Avenue Rd
(M5R 2G3)
Tel: (416) 964-1220

**WESTIN HARBOUR
CASTLE**
1 Harbour Sq
(M5J 1A6)
Tel: (800) 228-3000

TRENTON

ALJAN MOTEL
RR 2, SS-2 (K8V 5P5)
Tel: (613) 392-9281

COMFORT INN
68 Monogram Pl
(K8V 6E6)
Tel: (800) 221-2222

**COPPERFIELD'S
DAYS INN**
10 Trenton St
(K8V 4M9)
Tel: (613) 392-9291

DAYS INN
10 Trenton St
(K8V 4M9)
Rates: $54-95
Tel: (613) 392-9291

MERMAID MOTEL
RR 4 (K8V 5P7)
Tel: (613) 392-2200

RAMADA INN
Hwy 401 & Glen
Miller Rd,
Box 70 (K8V 5R1)
Tel: (800) 228-2828

SUNRISE MOTEL
289 Dundas St E
(K8V 1M1)
Tel: (613) 394-4444

TWEED

PARK PLACE MOTEL
43 Victoria St,
Box 257 (K0K 3J0)
Tel: (613) 478-3134

UPSALA

PARKVIEW MOTEL
General Delivery
(P0T 2Y0)
Tel: (807) 986-2366

**SAVANNAE RIVER
RESORT**
Box B (P0T 2Y0)
Tel: (807) 986-2484

UTTERSON

**BIRCHDALE
COTTAGES**
RR 2 (P0B 1M0)
Tel: (705) 769-2046

**GREEN VALLEY
COTTAGES**
RR 3 (P0B 1M0)
Tel: (705) 789-7931

VAL RITA

**AUBERGE OWENS
INN**
Box 178 (P0L 2G0)
Tel: (705) 335-8575

VANIER

CONCORDE MOTEL
333 Montreal Rd
(K1L 6B4)
Tel: (613) 745-2112

VERMILLION
BAY

**BAYVIEW
HOTEL/MOTEL**
35 Spruce St (P0V
2V0)
Tel: (807) 227-2603

NORTHSIDE MOTEL
Box 132, Hwy 17
(P0V 2V0)
Tel: (807) 227-5339

**PINE GROVE MOTEL-
NORTHWINDS**
Box 40 (P0V 2V0)
Tel: (807) 227-2013

THE PINES
Box 40 (P0V 2V0)
Tel: (807) 227-2091

WABIGOON

LANG'S MOTEL
Box 16 (P0V 2W0)
Tel: (807) 938-6423

WAHNAPITAE

NORVIC MOTEL
Box 353, RR 1
(P0M 3C0)
Tel: (705) 694-4818

WALLACEBURG

SKYEVIEW MOTEL
RR 4, Kent Rd 33
(N8A 4L1)
Tel: (519) 677-5998

WASAGA BEACH

ALBATROSS MOTEL
Box 225, 160 Main St
(L0L 2P0)
Tel: (705) 429-4000

MAPLE MOTEL
Box 261 (L0L 2P0)
Tel: (705) 429-2676

WATERLOO

COMFORT INN
190 Weber St N (N2J 3H4)
Tel: (800) 221-2222

WAUBAUSHENE

TAY MOTEL
Box 88 (L0K 2C0)
Tel: (705) 538-2261

WAWA

CAMP HIGH FALLS
Box 1102 (P0S 1K0)
Tel: (705) 856-4496

LAKEVIEW HTEL
25 Broadway Ave,
Box 265 (P0S 1K0)
Tel: (705) 856-2625

NORTHERN LIGHTS MOTEL
Box 1241 (P0S 1K0)
Tel: (705) 856-2205

PARKWAY MOTEL
Box 784 (P0S 1K0)
Tel: (705) 856-7020

SPORTSMAN'S MOTEL
45 Mission Rd,
Box 219 (P0S 1K0)
Tel: (705) 856-2272

WABATONGUSHI LODGE
Box 1017 (P0S 1K0)
Tel: (705) 884-2487

WEBBWOOD

CELTIC MOTEL
Box 124, Hwy 17 W
(P0P 2G0)
Tel: (705) 869-1771

WELLAND

BEST WESTERN ROSE CITY SUITES
300 Prince Charles
Dr (L3C 7B3)
Tel: (800) 528-1234

COMFORT INN
870 Niagara St
(L3C 1M3)
Tel: (800) 221-2222

WHEATLEY

LAKESIDE VILLAGE MOTEL
RR 1, 1262 Hwy 3
(N0P 2P0)
Tel: (519) 825-4307

WHITBY

QUALITY SUITES-EAST
1700 Champlain Ave
(L1N 6A7)
Tel: (800) 221-2222

WHITEFISH

BIL MUR MOTEL
Box 160 (P0M 3E0)
Tel: (705) 866-0378

WHITNEY

ALGONQUIN EAST GATE MOTEL
Box 193 (K0J 2M0)
Tel: (613) 637-2652

WIARTON

PACIFIC HOTEL
Box 209, 624 Berford
St (N0H 2T0)
Tel: (519) 534-1370

SHENSTONE MOTOR INN
RR 1 (N0H 2T0)
Tel: (519) 534-1831

SPIRIT ROCK MOTEL
877 Berford St
(N0H 2T0)
Tel: (519) 534-1645

TOP NOTCH MOTEL
General Delivery,
Hwy 6 (N0H 2T0)
Tel: (519) 534-1310

WILLARD LAKE

WILLARD LAKE RESORT MOTEL
General Delivery
(P0X 1H0)
Tel: (807) 468-0314

WINDSOR

AMBASSADOR MOTEL
1864 Huron Church
Rd (N9C 2L5)
Tel: (519) 969-6502

BEST WESTERN ROSE CITY INN
430 Ouellette Ave
(N9A 1B2)
Tel: (519) 253-7281

COMFORT INN
2765 Huron Church
Rd (N9E 3Y7)
Tel: (800) 221-2222

COMFORT INN
2955 Dougall Ave
(N9E 1S1)
Tel: (800) 221-2222

DAYS INN
675 Goyeau St
(N9A 1H3)
Rates: $65-95
Tel: (519) 258-8411

HILTON WINDSOR
277 Riverview Dr W
(N9A 5K4)
Tel: (519) 973-5555

HURON MOTEL
1980 Huron Church
Rd (N9C 2L5)
Tel: (519) 966-2080

THE INNKEEPER MOTEL
2098 Division Rd
(N8W 1Z9)
Tel: (519) 966-3845

KENORA MOTEL
2030 Huron Church
Rd (N9C 2L5)
Tel: (519) 969-7500

PRINCETON MOTEL
3032 Dougall
(N9E 1S4
Tel: (519) 969-2750

QUALITY SUITES-DOWNTOWN
250 Dougall Ave
(N9A 7C6)
Tel: (800) 221-2222

RAMADA INN
480 Riverside Dr W
(N9A 5K6)
Tel: (800) 268-8998

RELAX HOTEL DOWNTOWN
33 Riverside Dr E
(N9A 2S4)
Tel: (800) 667-3529

RELAX INN WIND-SOR
2330 Huron Church
Rd W (N9E 3S6)
Tel: (800) 667-3529

ROYAL WINDSOR HOTEL
675 Goyeau St
(N9A 1H3)
Tel: (519) 258-8411

SKYLINE MOTEL
1425 Division Rd
(N9A 6J3)
Tel: (519) 969-1060

WOLFE ISLAND

GENERAL WOLFE HOTEL
Box 100 (K0H 2Y0)
Tel: (613) 385-2611

WOODBRIDGE

NEW WOODBINE MOTEL
7242 Hwy 27
(L4L 1A5)
Tel: (416) 851-2876

WOODSTOCK

CROWN MOTEL
RR 5, 1275 Dundas
St E (N4S 7V9)
Tel: (519) 537-3446

MARINER MOTEL
1252 Dundas St E
(N4S 8H4)
Tel: (519) 537-5332

QUALITY INN & CONV. CENTER
580 Bruin Blvd
(N4S 7Z5)
Tel: (800) 221-2222

PRINCE EDWARD ISLAND

BORDEN

CARLETON MOTEL
RR 1 (C0B 1X0)
Tel: (902) 855-2644

CARDIGAN

RODD BRUDENELL RIVER RESORT
Box 67 (C0A 1G0)
Tel: (902) 652-2332

CAVENDISH

LAKEVIEW LODGE & COTTAGES
Rt 6 (C0A 1N0)
Tel: (902) 963-2436

SEASIDE MOTEL & COTTAGES
(C0A 1N0)
Tel: (902) 963-2724

CHARLOTTETOWN

AUBERGE WANDLYN INN
Box 9500 (C1A 8L4)
Tel: (902) 892-1201

BEST WESTERN MACLAUCHLAN'S MOTOR INN
238 Grafton St
(C1A 1L5)
Tel: (800) 528-1234

COMFORT INN
112 Trans Canada Hwy (C1E 1E7)
Tel: (800) 221-2222

DOUBLETREE-PRINCE EDWARD HOTEL
18 Queen St
(C1A 8B9)
Tel: (800) 828-7447

HOLIDAY ISLAND MOTOR LODGE
307 University Ave
(C1A 4M5)
Tel: (902) 892-4141

ISLANDER MOTOR LODGE
146 - 148 Pownal St
(C1A 3W6)
Tel: (902) 892-1217

KIRKWOOD MOTOR HOTEL
455 University Ave
(C1A 4N8)
Tel: (902) 892-4206

RODD CONFEDERATION INN
Trans Canada Hwy,
P. O. Box 651
(C1A 7L3)
Tel: (800) 565-7633

ROYALTY MAPLES COURT
RR 7, West Royalty
(C1A 7J9)
Tel: (902) 368-1030

SOUTHPORT MOTEL
20 Stratford Rd
(C1A 7B7)
Tel: (902) 569-2287

THRIFTLODGE
Highway 1
(C1A 7L3)
Rates: $68-96
Tel: (902) 892-2481
(800) 578-7878

TRAVELODGE
Intersection of Hwys
1 & 2 (C1A 8C2)
Rates: $71-132
Tel: (902) 894-8566
(800) 578-7878

CORNWALL

MCCRADY'S GREEN ACRES
RR 2, Meadow Bank
(C0A 1H0)
Tel: (902) 566-4938

WINDSOR MOTEL
RR 3, New Haven
(C0A 1H0)
Tel: (902) 675-2186

CRAPAUD

DESABLE MOTEL
Trans Canada Hwy,
RR 1 (C0A 1J0)
Tel: (902) 658-2387

RED ROOSTER MOTEL
Trans Canada Hwy
(C0A 1J0)
Tel: (902) 658-2834

FLAT RIVER

OLD WATER WHEEL MOTEL
Rt 261 (C0A 1B0)
Tel: (902) 659-2033

HUNTER RIVER

ANDREW LODGE
RR 2, New Glasgow
(C0A 1N0)
Tel: (902) 964-2508

LITTLE YORK

DALVAY BY THE SEA HOTEL
Box 8, Grand
Tracadie
(C0A 1P0)
Tel: (902) 672-2048

STANHOPE BY THE SEA

Box 9 (C0A 1P0)
Tel: (902) 672-2047

LOWER NEWTOWN

LINDEN LODGE COUNTRY INN
Belfast, RR 3
(C0A 1A0)
Tel: (902) 659-2716

MONTAGUE

LOBSTER SHANTY NORTH
P. O. Box 158
(C0A 1R0)
Tel: (902) 838-2463

SHADY REST MOTEL
RR 2, Rt 17
(C0A 1R0)
Tel: (902) 838-4298

THE SULKY INN
4 Rink St, Box 286
(C0A 1R0)
Tel: (902) 838-4100

MOUNT STEWART

RIVERVIEW MOTEL
Rt 22 (C0A 1T0)
Tel: (902) 676-2349

MURRAY HARBOUR

ALPHA & OMEGA MOTEL
RR 1 (C0A 1V0)
Tel: (902) 962-2494

NORTH LAKE HARBOUR

BLUEFIN MOTEL
(C0A 1K0)
Tel: (902) 357-2599

NORTH RIVER

HOWARD JOHNSON
Trans Canada Hwy
(C0A 1H0)
Tel: (902) 566-2211
(800) 446-4656

ST. ELEANORS

GREEN ACRES MOTEL
115 Bayview Dr
(C1N 4A2)
Tel: (902) 436-3508

TRAVELLERS INN
80 All Weather Hwy
(C1N 5L3)
Tel: (902) 436-9100

ST. PETERS

THE NOR'EASTER LODGE
(C0A 2A0)
Tel: (902) 961-2613

SHERWOOD

PRINCESS MOTEL
Brackley Pt. Rd
(C0A 2H0)
Tel: (902) 566-3373

SOURIS

LIGHTHOUSE & BEACH MOTEL
Box 134 (C0A 2B0)
Tel: (902) 687-2339

SINGING SANDS SEA BREEZE MOTEL
Rr 2, Rt 16,
Kingsboro (C0A 2B0)
Tel: (902) 357-2371

SOURIS WEST MOTEL
RR 4, Souris West
(C0A 2B0)
Tel: (902) 687-2676

SUMMERSIDE

BEST WESTERN LINKLETTER INN
311 Market St
(C1N 1K8)
Tel: (800) 528-1234

DYNASTY SPA RESORT
Box 64 (C1N 4P6)
Tel: (800) 363-8800

MULBERRY MOTEL
6 Water St E
(C1N 1A1)
Tel: (902) 436-2520

PARKVIEW MOTEL & COTTAGES
RR 2 (C1N 4J8)
Tel: (902) 436-6146

QUALITY INN GARDEN OF THE GULF
618 Water St E (C1N 2V5)
Tel: (800) 221-2222

TIGNISH

ISLAND'S END INN
P. O. Box 88
(C0B 2B0)
Tel: (902) 882-3554

MCRAE MOTEL
P. O. Box 161
(C0B 2B0)
Tel: (902) 882-3260

TYNE VALLEY
Box 32 (C0B 2C0)
Tel: (902) 831-2042

VERNON BRIDGE

DUNVEGAN FARM MOTEL
RR 2, Rt 24, Uigg
(C0A 2E0)
Tel: (902) 651-2833

WILMOT

BAKER'S LIGHTHOUSE MOTEL
802 Water St
(C1N 4J6)
Tel: (902) 436-2992

WINSLOE

FAIR ISLE MOTEL
RR 1, Brackley Pt.
Rd
(C0A 2H0)
Tel: (902) 368-8259

IDA & ERROLL'S BLUE HERON MOTEL
RR 9 (C1E 1Z3)
Tel: (902) 621-0145

MILLSTREAM RESORT
RR 1, Brackley Beach
(C0A 2H0)
Tel: (902) 672-2186

PEACEFUL ACRES MOTEL
RR 1, Harrington
(C0A 2H0)
Tel: (902) 672-2646

SHERWOOD MOTEL
Brackley Pt. Rd
(C1E 1Z3)
Tel: (902) 892-1622

WOODSTOCK

LEWIS MOTEL
Rt 2, O'LKeary RR 3
(C0B 1V0)
Tel: (902) 859-2396

QUEBEC

ALMA

COMFORT INN
870 Ave du Pont St
(G8B 2V8)
Tel: (800) 221-2222

ANCIENNE LORETTE

HOTEL LE LUXEMBOURG
6001 Boul Hamel W
(G2E 2H3)
Tel: (800) 463-7229

COMFORT INN-WEST
1255 Boul Duplessis
(G2G 2B4)
Tel: (800) 221-2222

ARUNDEL

WHISKY JACK INN
RR 2 (J0T 1A0)
Tel: (819) 687-2625

BAI COMEAU

COMFORT INN
745 Boul Lafleche
(G5C 1C6)
Tel: (800) 221-2222

MOTEL LASALLE
196 Boul LaSalle
(G4Z 1S6)
Tel: (418) 296-6601

BEAUCE

CHATEAU BLANC
Rt 108, St. Ephren
(G0M 1R0)
Tel: (418) 484-2112

BEAUPORT

COMFORT INN-EAST
240 Boul Sainte-Anne (G1E 3L7)
Tel: (800) 221-2222

MOTEL AIGLE D'OR
1165 Boul Ste-Anne
(G1E 5N6)
Tel: (418) 666-7622

MOTEL COLONIAL
142 du Manege
(G1E 5H5)
Tel: (418) 667-3652

MOTEL DE LA CAPITALE
1082 Boul Ste-Anne
(G1E 3M3)
Tel: (418) 663-0587

BIC

MOTEL BIC
3260 Rt 132 W
(G0L 1B0)
Tel: (418) 736-4439

BLAINVILLE

ROUSSILLON MIRABEL
1136 Boul Labelle
(J7C 3J4)
Tel: (800) 561-8719

BOUCHERVILLE

COMFORT INN-SOUTH SHORE
96 Boul de Mortagne
(J4B 5M7)
Tel: (800) 221-2222

MOTEL BISCAYNE
8900 Taschereau
(J4X 1C2)
Tel: (514) 466-2169

MOTEL DES NATIONS
7355 Marie Victorin
(J4W 1A6)
Tel: (516) 671-3751

CAP-DE-LA-MADELEINE

MOTEL BOULEVARD
381 Boul Ste-Madeleine
(G8T 3M6)
Tel: (819) 378-3816

MOTEL PARI
43 - Be Rue Ste-Marthe(G8T 4K5)
Tel: (819) 375-4727

CHARLEMAGNE

TRAVELODGE
115 Rue Copin St,
Suite 106 (J52 4P8)
Rates: $65-140
Tel: (514) 582-5933
(800) 578-7878

CHATEAU RICHER

MOTEL SPRING
Rt 138, Blvd Ste.
Anne (G0A 1N0)
Rates: $30+
Tel: (418) 824-4953

CHEVERY

OCEAN VIEW HOTEL
Box 89 (G0G 1G0)
Tel: (418) 787-2233

CHICOUTIMI

COMFORT INN
1595 Boul Talbot
(G7H 4C3)
Tel: (800) 221-2222

DAYS INN
250 des Saguenéens
(G7H 3A4)
Rates: $60-95
Tel: (418) 545-8326

CLOVA

HOTEL TAMARAC
(G0X 3M0)
Tel: (819) 662-3319

COTEAU DU LAC

MOTEL DES ERABLES
44 Rte 201 (J0P 1B0)
Tel: (514) 763-5714

DOLBEAU

AUBERGE LA DILIGENCE
414 de la Friche
(G8L 2R1)
Tel: (800) 463-9651

MOTEL DU BOULEVARD
1610 Boul Wallberg
(G8L 1H4)
Tel: (418) 276-8207

DORION

MOTEL SEIGNEURIE VAUDREUIL
154 Boul Harwood
(J7V 1Y2)
Tel: (514) 455-3368

DORVAL

HOTEL BEAUSEJOUR
1010 Herron Rd
(H9S 1B3)
Tel: (514) 631-4537

COMFORT INN-AEROPORT
340 Ave Michel
Jasmin(H9P 1C1)
Tel: (800) 221-2222

QUALITY HOTEL-DORVAL AEROPORT
770 Cote de Liesse
(H4T 1E7)
Tel: (800) 221-2222

QUALITY INN-AEROPORT
6755 Cote de Liesse
(H4T 1E5)
Tel: (800) 221-2222

DRUMMOND-VILLE

COMFORT INN
1055 Rue Hains
(J2C 5L3)
Tel: (800) 221-2222

MOTEL ALOUETTE
1975 Boul Mercure
(J2B 3P3)
Tel: (819) 478-4166

GASPE

AUBERGE DES COMMANDANTS
CP 470 (G0C 1R0)
Tel: (418) 368-3355

GATINEAU

ADAM MOTEL
100 Boul Greber
(J8T 3P8)
Tel: (819) 561-3600

COMFORT INN
630 Boul la Gappe
(J8T 9Z6)
Tel: (800) 221-2222

GRANBY

HOTEL ROUSSILLON GRANBY
34 Rue Principale
(J2G 2T4)
Tel: (800) 363-6057

MOTEL DU LAC
255 Denison E (J2G 8C7)
Tel: (514) 372-5930

GRAND-REMOUS

LA POINTE A DAVID
CP 100 (J0W 1E0)
Tel: (819) 438-2844

HULL

QUALITY INN-LE MARQUIS
131 rue Laurier
(J8X 3W3)
Tel: (800) 221-2222

IBERVILLE

MOTEL BELLE RIVIERE
93 Bord de L'Eau
(J2X 4J3)
Tel: (514) 347-5561

JONQUIERE

MOTEL RICHELIEU
3075 Boul Boyaume
(G7X 7V3)
Tel: (418) 548-8265

LA MARTRE GITE DU PASSANT DEL'AUBERGE
8 Ave Keable
(G0E 2H0)
Tel: (418) 288-5533

LAC MEGANTIC

PANORAMA MOTEL
3284 Laval
(G6B 1A4)
Tel: (819) 583-2110

LAC SIMON

AUBERGE EVASION
80 Tour du Lac
(J0V 1E0)
Tel: (819) 428-4444

LAVAL

COMFORT INN
2055 Route des
Laurentides
(H7S 1Z6)
Tel: (800) 221-2222

QUALITY SUITES
2035 Route des
Laurentides
(H7S 1Z6)
Tel: (800) 221-2222

MOTEL LE VICOMTE DE LAVAL
1313 Boul des
Laurentides
(H7M 2Y2)
Tel: (514) 669-1794

MOTEL LIDO
1354 Boul des
Laurentides
(H7N 4Y4)
Tel: (514) 669-2601

MOTEL MARINA
3375-2ieme Rue
(H7R 2X3)
Tel: (514) 627-4050

RELAX HOTEL MONTREAL-LAVAL
2900 Boul le Carrefour
(H7T 2K9)
Tel: ((800) 667-3529

SHERATON LAVAL
2440 Autoroute des
Laurentides
(H7T 1X5)
Tel: (800) 325-3535

LEBEL SUR QUEVILLON

HOTEL-MOTEL QUEVILLON
CP 340 (J0Y 1X0)
Tel: (819) 755-4815

MOTEL OSCAR
1018 Boul Quevillon
(J0Y 1X0)
Tel: (819) 755-4807

LENNOXVILLE

MOTEL LA PAYSANNE
42 Queen (J1M 1H9)
Tel: (819) 569-5585

MOTEL LENNOXVILLE
94 Queen (J1M 1J4)
Tel: (819) 563-7525

LEVIS

COMFORT INN
10 du Vallon E
(G0R 2K0)
Tel: (800) 221-2222

HOTEL-MOTEL ROUND-POINT
53 Rte Kennedy
(G6V 6C7)
Tel: (800) 463-4451

LONGUEUIL

HOLIDAY INN
999 de Serigny (J4K 2T1)
Tel: (800) 465-4329

RAMADA HOTEL
999 De Serigny
(J4K 2T1)
Rates: $70-145
Tel: (514) 670-3030
(800) 272-6232

LOURDES-DE-BLANC-SABLON

MOTEL ANSE AUX CAILLOUX
CP 148 (G0G 1W0)
Tel: (418) 461-2112

MAGOG

MOTEL DE L'OUTLET
480 Rue Hatley W
(J1X 3G4)
Tel: (819) 847-2609

MOTEL FLEUR DE LYS
2074 Rte 112, RR 4
(J1X 5R9)
Tel: (819) 843-5508

METIS BEACH

PLACE PETIT MIAMI
1101 Rte 132
(G0J 1W0)
Tel: (418) 936-3411

MONT LAURIER

ECONO LODGE
700 Blvd Paquette
(J9L 1L4)
Rates: $49-65
Tel: (819) 623-6465
(800) 424-4777

MONTMAGNY

MAISON ROUSSEAU
100 St-Jean-Baptiste
E (G5V 1K3)
Tel: (418) 248-8822

MONTREAL

DAYS INN LE SEVILLE
4545 Cote Vertu W
(H4S 1C8)
Tel: (800) 329-2525

DELTA MONTREAL
450 Rue Sherbrooke
W (H3A 2T4)
Tel: (800) 268-1133

**FOUR SEASONS
HOTEL**
1050 Sherbrooke St
W (H3A 2R6)
Tel: (800) 332-3442

**HOLIDAY INN
CROWNE PLAZA-
METRO CENTRE**
505 Sherbrooke St E
(H2L 1K2)
Tel: (800) 465-4329

**HOLIDAY INN
CROWNE PLAZA-
DOWNTOWN**
420 Sherbrooke St W
(H3A 1B4)
Tel: (800) 465-4329

HOTEL DE PARIS
901 Sherbrooke St E
(H2L 1L3)
Tel: (514) 522-6861

**HOTEL DU MANOIR
ST. DENIS**
2006 St. Denis
(H2X 3K7)
Tel: (514) 843-3670

**HOTEL LE SAINT-
ANDRE**
1285 Rue Saint-
Andre (H2L 3T1)
Tel: (514) 849-7070

**HOTEL MERIDIEN
MONTREAL**
4 Complexe
Desjardins (H5B 1E5)
Tel: (800) 361-8234

HOWARD JOHNSON
475 Rue Sherbrooke
Quest (H3A 2L9)
Tel: (514) 842-3961
(800) 446-4656

HOWARD JOHNSON
6600 Cote de Liesse
(H4T 1E3)
Tel: (514) 735-7788
(800) 446-4656

**JOURNEY'S END
HOTEL**
3440 Ave du Parc
(H2X 2H5)
Tel: (800) 668-4200

**LA CHATEAU
CHAMPLAIN**
1 Place du Canada
(H3B 4C9)
Tel: (514) 878-9000

**LE WESTIN
MONT-ROYAL**
1050 Sherbrooke St
W (H3A 2R6)
Rates: $250-310
Tel: (514) 284-1110
(800) 228-3000

**RAMADA
RENAISSANCE**
3625 Ave du Parc
(H2X 3P8)
Tel: (800) 228-2828

RITZ-CARLTON
1228 Sherbrooke St
(H3G 1H6)
Tel: (800) 363-0366

THRIFTLODGE
1600 St Hubert
(H2L 3Z3)
Tel: (514) 849-3214
(800) 578-7878

TRAVELODGE
1010 Herron Rd
(Dorval, H9S 1B3)
Rates: $63-105
Tel: (514) 631-4537
(800) 578-7878

**TRAVELODGE
HOTEL**
50 Blvd René-
Lévesque W
(H2Z 1A2))
Rates: $55-82
Tel: (514) 874-9090
(800) 578-7878

NEW
RICHMOND

**HOTEL MOTEL
FRANCIS**
210 Pandiac
(G0C 2B0)
Tel: (418) 392-4485

POINTE CLAIRE

COMFORT INN
700 Bul Saint-Jean
(H9R 3K2)
Tel: (800) 221-2222

HOLIDAY INN
6700 Trans Canada
Hwy (H9R 1C2)
Tel: (800) 465-4329

**QUALITY SUITES-
WEST ISLAND**
6300 Trans Canada
Hwy (H9R 1B9)
Tel: (800) 221-2222

QUEBEC CITY

DAYS INN
7300 Boul Wilfred-
Hamel Ouest
(Ste Foy, G2R 1C8)
Rates: $48-80
Tel: (418) 877-2226

HOLIDAY INN QUEBEC
395 de la Couronne,
CP 30237 (G1K 8Y2)
Tel: (800) 465-4329

**HOTEL
LA MAISON DOYON**
109 Rue Ste-Anne
(G1R 3X6)
Tel: (418) 694-1720]

**HOTEL-MOTEL
LE VOYAGEUR**
2250 Boul Ste-Anne
(G1J 1Y2)
Tel: (800) 463-5568

L'HOTEL BELLEY
249 Rue St. Paul
(G1K 3W5)
Tel: (418) 692-1694

**LOEWS
LE CONCORDE**
1225 Place Montcalm
(G1R 4W6)
Tel: (800) 463-5256

MOTEL CARL
4415 Buol Hamel
(G1P 2J7)
Tel: (418) 872-9649

**MOTEL
VALON LEVIS**
208 Rte Kennedy
(G0R 2K0)
Tel: (418) 837-8841

QUALITY SUITES
1600 Rue Bouvier
(G2K 1N8)
Tel: (800) 221-2222

QUEBEC HILTON
3 Place Quebec
(G1K 7M9)
Tel: (800) 268-9275

**RAMADA HOTEL -
DOWNTOWN**
395 Rue De La
Couronne (G1K 8Y2)
Rates: $69-135
Tel: (418) 647-2611
(800) 272-6232

RAWDON

AUBERGE STEWART
4333 Ch Brennan
(J0K 1S0)
Tel: (514) 834-8210

RICHMOND

**MOTEL LE MARQUIS
DE RICHEMONT**
836 Rue Craig E,
CP 1865 (J0B 2H0)
Tel: (819) 826-3765

RIMOUSKI

COMFORT INN
455 Boul St-Germain
(G5L 3P2)
Tel: (800) 221-2222

RIVIERE-DU-
LOUP

COMFORT INN
85 Boul Cartier
(G5R 4X4)
Tel: (800) 221-2222

DAYS INN
182 Fraser (G2R 1C8)
Rates: $49-109
Tel: (418) 862-6354

**MOTEL
AU VIEUX PILOTEUX**
185 Fraser (G5R 1E2)
Tel: (418) 867-2635

MOTEL LOUPI
50 Ancrage
(G5R 3Y5)
Tel: (418) 862-6898

ROCK FOREST

COMFORT INN
4295 Boul Bourque,
P. O. Box 1816
(J1N 1C3)
Tel: (800) 221-2222

LE MOTEL LE CHATILLON
5050 Boul Bourque
(J1N 2K7)
Tel: (819) 564-4474

ROUYN-NORANDA

COMFORT INN
1295 Ave Lariviere
(J9X 6M6)
Tel: (800) 221-2222

ST. ANDRE AVELLIN

MOTEL BAR SALON ST-ANDRE AVELLIN
15 Rang Ste-Julie E
(J0V 1W0)
Tel: (819) 983-2313

ST-BASILE-LE GRAND

MOTEL ST. BASILE
121 Laurier (J0L 1S0)
Tel: (514) 464-3039

ST-DAVID

MOTEL HOSPITALITE
3500 Boul Rive S
(G6W 6N7)
Tel: (418) 837-6664

ST-FAUSTIN

HOTEL MONTAGNARD DE ST. FAUSTIN
800 Rue St-Faustin
(J0T 2G0)
Tel: (819) 688-2801

ST. FERREOL-LES-NEIGES

AUBERGE LE REFUGE DU PARC
186 Rte St-Julien
(G0A 3R0)
Tel: (418) 826-2363

ST. GEORGES

AUBERGE MOTEL BENEDICT ARNOLD
18255 Boul Lacroix
(G5Y 5C4)
Tel: (800) 361-6162

ST. HILAIRE

MOTEL ORCHIDEE
725 Ave du Cine
Parc(J3G 4S6)
Tel: (514) 464-2585

ST. JEAN-SUR RICHELIEU

COMFORT INN
700 Rue Gadbois
(J3A 1V1)
Tel: (800) 221-2222

MIRIFIK INN/HARRIS
576 Champlain St
(J3B 6X1)
Tel: (514) 348-3821

ST. LAURENT

ECONO LODGE
6755 Cote de Liesse
(H4T 1E5)
Rates: $65
Tel: (514) 735-5702
(800) 424-4777

RAMADA HOTEL - MONTREAL AIRPORT
7300 Cote de Liesse
(H4T 1E7)
Rates: $92-119
Tel: (514) 733-8818
(800) 272-6232

ST. LEONARD

ECONO LODGE
4645 Metropolitan E
(H1R 1Z4)
Rates: $53
Tel: (514) 725-3671
(800) 424-4777

LIDO MOTEL
5905 Boul
Metropolitan E
(H1P 1Y3)
Tel: (514) 321-8840

ST. MATHIEU DE BELOEIL

MOTEL BELOEIL
4180 Bernard Pilon
(J3G 4S5)
Tel: (514) 467-1373

STE. ANNE DEBEAUPRE

MOTEL ST-LOUIS
9657 Boul Ste-Anne
(G0A 3C0)
Tel: (418) 827-4298

STE. ANNE DES MONTS

MANOIR SUR MER
475 1ere Ave W (G0E 2G0)
Tel: (418) 763-7844

STE. BEATRIX

MOTEL STE-BEATRIX
247 Ch. Ste-Beatrix
(J0K 1Y0)
Tel: (514) 883-5881

STE. FOY

COMFORT INN
7320 Boul Wilfred-Hamel
(G2G 1C1)
Tel: (800) 221-2222

MOTEL L'ABITATION
2828 Boul Laurier
(G1V 2M1)
Tel: (800) 567-7267

MOTEL ONCLE SAM
7025 Boul Hamel W
(G2G 1B6)
Tel: (418) 872-1488

MOTEL SONIA
7082 Boul Hamel W
(G2G 1B5)
Tel: (418) 872-4127

STE. HELENE DE BAGOT

DAYS INN
410 Couture
(J0H 1M0)
Rates: $49-130
Tel: (514) 791-2580

MOTEL PRESTIGE
Exit 152, Hwy 20
(J0H 1M0)
Tel: (514) 791-2580

STE. MARTHE-DU-CAP

MOTEL CANADIEN
1821 Notre-Dame
(G8T 8B2)
Tel: (819) 375-5542

MOTEL LE HAVRE
1360 Notre-Dame
(G8T 4J3)
Tel: (819) 378-4597

MOTEL VALLEY INN
3070 Notre-Dame,
Rte 138 (G8T 7V7)
Tel: (819) 376-3803

SEIGNEURIE

HOLIDAY INN
7300 Cote de Liesse
(H4T 1E7)
Tel: (800) 465-4329

SEPT. ILES

COMFORT INN
854 Boul Laure (G4R 1Y7)
Tel: (800) 221-2222

MOTEL SEPT-ILES
1100 Laure
(G4S 1C2)
Tel: (418) 962-7047

SHAWINIGAN

MOTEL SAFARI
4500 12e Ave
(G9N 6T5)
Tel: (819) 536-2664

SHAWVILLE

**ED & ELLEN PLACE
MOTEL**
Box 39 (J0X 2Y0)
Tel: (819) 647-2287

SUTTON

HOTEL HORIZON
297 Maple (J0E 2K0)
Tel: (514) 538-3212

TADOUSSAC

**MOTEL DE L'ANSE A
L'EAU**
173 Rue Pionniers
(G0T 2A0)
Tel: (418) 235-4313

THETFORD MINES

COMFORT INN
123 Boul Smith S
(G6G 7S7)
Tel: (800) 221-2222

TRACY

COMFORT INN
7075 Av de la Plaza
(J3R 4X9)
Tel: (800) 221-2222

TROIS-RIVIERES OUEST

COMFORT INN
6255 Rue Corbeil
(G8Z 4P8)
Tel: (800) 221-2222

DEAUVILLE MOTEL
4696 Boul Royal
(G9A 4N1)
Tel: (819) 375-9691

**VAL DAVID
MOTEL AU FOYER**
929 Rte 117 (J0T
2N0)
Tel: (819) 322-5995

**MOTEL LE
RADISSON
DE VAL DAVID**
1480 Rte 117,
B.G.A. 8
(J0T 2N0)
Tel: (819) 322-2727

VAL D'OR

COMFORT INN
1665 3ieme Ave
(J9P 1V9)
Tel: (800) 221-2222

VILLE-MARIE

**HOTEL-MOTEL
CAROLINE**
P. O. Box 1210
(J0Z 3W0)
Tel: (819) 629-2965

SASKATCHEWAN

ABBEY

ABBEY HOTEL
Box 99 (S0N 0A0)
Tel: (306) 689-2470

ALAMEDA

ALAMEDA HOTEL
4th St, Box 238
(S0C 0A0)
Tel: (306) 489-9080

ANEROID

PEG HOTEL
Box 31 (S0N 0C0)
Tel: (306) 588-9281

ANNAHEIM

THE POST HOTEL
Box 113 (S0K 0G0)
Tel: (306) 598-2055

ARCOLA

ARCOLA HOTEL
Railway St, Box 390
(S0C 0G0)
Tel: (306) 455-2319

ASSINIBOIA

**ASSINIBOIA
LODGE HOTEL**
122-3rd Ave W
(S0H 0B0)
Tel: (306) 642-3386

ASSINBOIA MOTEL
137 Centre St,
Box 640(S0H 0B0)
Tel: (306) 642-3515

**FRANKLIN MOTOR
HOTEL**
137 Centre St,
Box 640
(S0H 0B0)
Tel: (306) 642-3515

WHEEL INN MOTEL
Hwy 13 E, Box 1660
(S0H 0B0)
Tel: (306) 642-3308

BALCARRES

**COUNTRY INN
HOTEL**
Main St, Box 356
(S0G 0C0)
Tel: (306) 334-2605

BALGONIE

**BALGONIE
AUTO COURT
MOTEL**
Hwy 1 E, Box 112
(S0G 0E0)
Tel: (306) 771-2510

BEAUVAL

INN ON THE LAKE
Bag Service 23
(S0M 0G0)
Tel: (306) 288-2323

BEECHY

BEECHY HOTEL
Main St, General
Del. (S0L 0C0)
Tel (306) 859-2233

BENGOUGH

BIG MUDDY INN
Main St, Box 190
(S0C 0K0)
Tel: (306) 268-2175

BETHUNE

BETHUNE MOTEL
Box 179 (S0G 0H0)
Tel: (306) 638-3023

BIG RIVER

BIG RIVER HOTEL
Box 131 (S0J 0E0)
Tel: (306) 469-2030

**TIMBERLAND
LODGE**
Hwy 55, Box 730
(S0J 0E0)
Tel: (306) 469-4888

BIGGAR

BIGGAR HOTEL
1st Ave W, Box 1647
(S0K 0M0)
Tel: (306) 948-3641

HOMESTYLE MOTEL
801 Main St, Box 935
(S0K 0M0)
Tel: (306) 948-2225

**WESTWINDS
MOTOR HOTEL**
Box 902 (S0K 0M0)
Tel: (306) 948-3301

BLADWORTH

**COMMERCIAL
HOTEL**
Main St, Box 118
(S0G 0J0)
Tel: (306) 567-5576

BRADWELL

BRADWELL HOTEL
Struan St, Box 65
(S0K 0P0)
Tel: (306) 257-4100

CRAIK HOTEL
Main St, Box 100
(S0K 0P0)
Tel: (306) 734-2206

BROADVIEW

EDWARD'S MOTEL
Hwy 1 E, Box 844
(S0G 0K0)
Tel: (306) 696-2755

BUFFALO NARROWS

**BUFFALO
NARROWS
MOTOR INN**
Main St, Box 85
(S0M 0J0)
Tel: (306) 235-4214

BURSTALL

BURSTALL HOTEL
Main St, Box 280
(S0N 0H0)
Tel: (306) 679-2223

CABRI

CABRI HOTEL
Box 509 (S0N 0J0)
Tel: (306) 587-2400

CANDLE LAKE

**SHIP'S LANTERN
RESORT HOTEL**
General Delivery
(S0J 3E0)
Tel: (306) 929-4555

CANORA

GATEWAY MOTEL
General Delivery
(S0A 0L0)
Tel: (306) 563-5661

PINE GROVE MOTEL
Box 1499 (S0A 0L0)
Tel: (306) 563-5493

CANWOOD

**CANWOOD VILLA
HOTEL**
Main St, Box 158
(S0J 0K0)
Tel: (306) 468-2256

CARLYLE

SKYLINE MOTOR INN
Box 385 (S0C 0R0)
Tel: (306) 453-6745

SKYLINE OASIS MOTEL
106 3rd St W, Box 575 (S0C 0R0)
Tel: (306) 453-6714

CARNDUFF

AVONMORE HOTEL
Broadway Ave, Box 213 (S0C 0S0)
Tel: (306) 482-3655

CARNDUFF MOTEL
Railway Ave, Box 213 (S0C 0S0)
Tel: (306) 482-3655

CARONPORT

CARONPORT MOTEL
Trans Canad Hwy 1, General Delivery (S0H 0S0)
Tel: (306) 756-3334

CARROT RIVER

EMPRESS HOTEL & MOTEL
Box 1119 (S0E 0L0)
Tel: (306) 768-2733

PASQUIA MOTEL
Hwy 23 S, Box 247 (S0E 0L0)
Tel: (306) 768-2738

CENTRAL BUTTE

CENTRAL BUTTE HOTEL
Main St, Box 388 (S0H 0T0)
Tel: (306) 796-9090

CHITEK LAKE

CHITEK LAKE LODGE
Hwy 24, Box 47 (S0J 0L0)
Tel: (306) 984-2266

L & D VENTURE INN
Box 44 (S0J 0L0)
Tel: (306) 984-2345

CLAIR

CLAIR HOTEL
Hwy 5, Box 122 (S0A 0N0)
Tel: (306) 383-4082

CLAVET

CLAVET MOTOR INN
91 Campbell Cres (S0K 0Y0)
Tel: (306) 242-2848

COLONSAY

COLONSAY HOTEL
Main St, Box 86 (S0K 0Z0)
Tel: (306) 255-2171

CONQUEST

MERCHANT'S HOTEL
Main St, Box 34 (S0L 0L0)
Tel: (306) 856-2006

CORONACH

COUNTRY BOY MOTEL
Hwy 18, Box 459 (S0H 0Z0)
Tel: (306) 267-3267

CRAIK

ROADSIDE MOTEL
Hwy 11, Box 68 (S0G 0V0)
Tel: (306) 734-2330

CREIGHTON

R J'S MOTEL
225 Creighton Ave, Box 584 (S0P 0A0)
Tel: (306) 688-2957

CUDWORTH

COUNTRY MOTOR INN
Main St, Box 280 (S0K 1B0)
Tel: (306) 256-7055

CUT KNIFE

LUCERNE HOTEL
Main St, Box 398 (S0M 0N0)
Tel: (306) 398-4761

DAVIDSON

C & T MOTEL
Hwy 44, Box 501 (S0G 1A0)
Tel: (306) 567-2033

DAVIDSON HOTEL-MOTEL
Railway St, Box 849 (S0G 1A0)
Tel: (306) 567-3131

JUBILEE MOTOR INN
Box 636 (S0G 1A0)
Tel: (306) 567-3000

DELISLE

DELISLE HOTEL
502 1st St W, Box 157 (S0L 0P0)
Tel: (306) 493-2462

DEMAINE

DEMAINE HOTEL
Main St, Box 181 (S0L 0R0)
Tel: (306) 858-2027

DENZIL

DENZIL HOTEL
Main St, Box 117 (S0L 0S0)
Tel: (306) 358-2044

DILKE

DILKE HOTEL
Box 130 (S0G 1C0)
Tel: (306) 488-4909

DINSMORE

DINSMORE HOTEL
Main St, Box 505 (S0L 0T0)
Tel: (306) 846-2238

DODSLAND

DODSLAND HOTEL
Box 280 (S0L 0V0)
Tel: (306) 356-2012

DOLLARD

DOLLARD HOTEL
Box 65 (S0N 0S0)
Tel: (306) 297-2013

DUNDURN

LAZY J MOTEL
Box 235 (S0K 1K0)
Tel: (306) 492-2023

DUVAL

DUVAL HOTEL
Main St, Box 130 (S0G 1G0)
Tel: (306) 725-9043

EASTEND

CYPRESS HOTEL
Box 487 (S0N 0T0)
Tel: (306) 295-3505

RIVERSIDE MOTEL
Hwy 13, Red Coast Trail, Box 3 (S0N 0T0)
Tel: (306) 295-3630

ELBOW

SPORTSMAN JUBILEE HOTEL
Saskatchewan St, Box 267 (S0H 1J0)
Tel: (306) 854-2202

ENDEAVOUR

PIONEER HOTEL
Box 160 (S0A 0W0)
Tel: (306) 547-4229

ENGLEFELD

ENGLEFELD HOTEL
Hwy 5, Box 147
(S0K 1N0)
Tel: (306) 287-3141

LAZY ACRES MOTEL
Box 125 (S0K 1N0)
Tel: (306) 287-3710

EASTERHAZY

PLUS 2 MOTOR INN
Box 1180 (S0A 0X0)
Tel: (306) 745-6627

ESTEVAN

BEEFEATER MOTOR INN
Box 505 (S4A 2A5)
Tel: (306) 634-6456

CIRCLE 6 MOTEL
206-4th St (S4A 0T6)
Tel: (306) 634-2637

ESTEVAN MOTEL
905 4th St (S4A 0W2)
Tel: (306) 634-2609

FAI'S MOTEL
South Service Rd,
Box 684 (S4A 2A6)
Tel: (306) 634-2693

SUPER 6 MOTEL
Hwy 39 W, Box 812
(S4A 2A7)
Tel: (306) 634-2691

FIFE LAKE

FIFE LAKE HOTEL
Main St, Box 86
(S0H 1N0)
Tel: (306) 476-2605

FOAM LAKE

LA VISTA MOTEL
Hwy 16, Box 608
(S0A 1A0)
Tel: (306) 272-3341

TRI-R MOTEL
Hwy 16, Box 760
(S0A 1A0)
Tel: (306) 272-4220

FORT QU'APPELLE

HILLCREST MOTEL
Box 1746 (S0G 1S0)
Tel: (306) 332-5635

FOSSTON

GLOBE HOTEL
Railway Wve, Box
62 (S0E 0V0)
Tel: (306) 322-4416

FOX VALLEY

FOX DEN MOTEL
Railway St, Box 158
(S0N 0V0)
Tel: (306) 666-2040

GLENTWORTH

ROYAL HOTEL
Main St, Box 34
(S0H 1V0)
Tel: (306) 266-4822

GOODSOIL

GOODSOIL HOTEL
Main St, Box 217
(S0M 1A0)
Tel: (306) 238-2055

AMBASSADOR HOTEL
Main St, Box 30
(S0H 1X0)
Tel: (306) 648-3550

MAYFAIR MOTEL
4th Ave E, Box 930
(S0H 1X0)
Tel: (306) 648-3138

GRENFELL

GRANITE HOTEL
1209 Front St, Box 40
(S0G 2B0)
Tel: (306) 697-3486

HOMESTEAD MOTEL
Box 1077 (S0G 2B0)
Tel: (306) 697-2846

GULL LAKE

CLARENDON HOTEL
Box 615 (S0N 1A0)
Tel: (306) 672-3303

GULL MOTEL
Hwy 1, Box 630
(S0N 1A0)
Tel: (306) 672-4184

LAZY DEE MOTEL
Box 119 (S0N 1A0)
Tel: (306) 672-3870

HANLEY

HANLEY HOTEL
Box 520 (S0G 2E0)
Tel: (306) 544-2246

HERBERT

HERBERT MOTOR HOTEL
Box 729 (S0H 2A0)
Tel: (306) 784-2559

LONE EAGLE MOTEL
Hwy 1, Box 54
(S0H 2A0)
Tel: (306) 784-2223

HERSCHEL

HERSCHEL VILLAGE INN
Main St, Box 98
(S0L 1L0)
Tel: (306) 377-4770

HUDSON BAY

TREE LINE MOTEL
Box 727 (S0E 0Y0)
Tel: (306) 865-2228

HUMBOLDT

BELLA VISTA INN
Hwy 5 W, Box 2317
(S0K 2A0)
Tel: (800) 687-0790

PIONEER MOTOR HOTEL
9th St, Box 1060
(S0K 2A0)
Tel: (306) 682-2638

WINDSOR HOTEL
Box 2470 (S0K 2A0)
Tel: (306) 682-2112

HYAS

HYAS HOTEL
Main St, Box 39
(S0A 1K0)
Tel: (306) 594-2840

INDIAN HEAD

SHAYNE INN
Hwy 1, Box 1240
(S0G 2K0)
Tel: (306) 695-3702

JANSEN

JANSEN HOTEL
Main St, Box 90
(S0K 2B0)
Tel: (306) 364-2062

KAMSACK

DUCK MOUNTAIN MOTOR HOTEL
Queen Elizabeth
Blvd E,
Hwy 5, Box 1600
(S0A 1S0)
Tel: (306) 542-2656

WOODLANDER INN
Box 788 (S0A 1S0)
Tel: (306) 542-2125

KELVINGTON

SPORTSMAN MOTEL
Hwy 38, Box 928
(S0A 1W0)
Tel: (306) 327-4455

KENOSEE LAKE

KENOSEE GARDENS
General Delivery
(S0C 2S0)
Tel: (306) 577-2211

KENOSEE MOTEL
Moose Mountain
Prov Park,
Box 130 (S0C 2S0)
Tel: (306) 577-2264

KINDERSLEY

**BEST WESTERN
WESTRIDGE MOTOR
INN**
Box 1657 (S0L 1S0)
Tel: (800) 528-1234

**CROSSROADS
MOTEL**
Box 1495 (S0L 1S0)
Tel: (306) 463-2664

**PRAIRIE ROSE
MOTEL**
2nd St E, Box 906
(S0L 1S0)
Tel: (306) 463-2678

**PRAIRIE TRAIL
MOTEL**
Box 2229 (S0L 1S0)
Tel: (306) 463-2633

KIPLING

**KIPLING MOTOR
INN**
Hwy 48, Box 806
(S0G 2S0)
Tel: (306) 736-2557

KUROKI

**EL KUROKI MOTOR
HOTEL**
Main St, Box 160
(S0A 1Y0)
Tel: (306) 338-2593

KYLE

SAPHIRE MOTEL
Hwy 4, Box 369
(S0L 1T0)
Tel: (306) 375-2335

LA LOCHE

**NORTHERN LIGHTS
MOTEL**
Box 365 (S0M 1G0)
Tel: (306) 822-2222

LA RONGE

DRIFTER'S MOTEL
Hwy 2, Box 303
(S0J 1L0)
Tel: (306) 425-2224

HARBOUR INN
1327 La Ronge Ave,
Box 1140 (S0J 1L0)
Tel: (800) 667-4097

**NORTHLAND
MOTOR HOTEL**
Box 340 (S0J 1L0)
Tel: (306) 425-2323

RED'S CAMPS
Main St, Box 67
(S0J 1L0)
Tel: (306) 425-2163

RIVERSIDE MOTEL
Hwy 2, Box 255
(S0J 1L0)
Tel: (306) 425-2150

LAC VERT

LAC VERT HOTEL
Main St, Box 39
(S0K 2G0)
Tel: (306) 874-5682

LAKE LENORE

LAKE LENORE HOTEL
Main St, Box 128
(S0K 2J0)
Tel: (306) 368-2301

LAMPMAN

LAMPMAN HOTEL
Main St, Box 148
(S0C 1N0)
Tel: (306) 487-2414

LANCER

LANCER HOTEL
Hwy 32, Box 128
(S0N 1G0)
Tel: (306) 689-2973

LANGENBURG

**LANGENBURG
COUNTRY INN**
Hwy 16 E, Box 279
(S0A 2A0)
Tel: (306) 743-2638

LANIGAN

LAGANS HOTEL
Hwy 16, Box 429
(S0K 2M0)
Tel: (306) 365-2916

LEADER

FOUR L MOTEL
Box 609 (S0N 1H0)
Tel: (306) 628-3834

LEROSS

LEROSS HOTEL
Main St, Box 23
(S0A 2C0)
Tel: (306) 675-4502

LIBERTY

**LIBERTY MOTOR
HOTEL**
Hwy 2, Box 10
(S0G 3A0)
Tel: (306) 847-2122

LLOYDMINSTER

CAPRI MOTOR INN
4615 50 Ave
(S9V 0P4)
Tel: (306) 825-5591

CEDAR INN MOTEL
4526 44th St
(S9V 0G4)
Tel: (306) 825-6155

**THE GOOD KNIGHT
INN**
4729 44th St
(S9V 0G6)
Tel: (306) 825-0124

**IMPERIAL 400
MOTEL**
4320 44th St,
Box 2070
(S9V 1R5)
Tel: (306) 825-4400

VOYAGEUR MOTEL
4724 44th St (S9V
0G6)
Tel: (306) 825-2248

LUCKY LAKE

LUCKY LAKE HOTEL
Main St, Box 278
(S0L 1Z0)
Tel: (306) 858-9090

LUMSDEN

LUMSDEN HOTEL
Box 527 (S0G 3C0)
Tel: (306) 731-2411

MACKLIN

MACKLIN HOTEL
Box 356 (S0L 2C0)
Tel: (306) 753-2419

MACRORIE

MACRORIE HOTEL
Box 148 (S0L 2E0)
Tel: (306) 243-2112

MAIDSTONE

MAIDSTONE HOTEL
Hwy 16, Box 415
(S0M 1M0)
Tel: (306) 893-2242

SANDPIPER MOTEL
Box 299 (S0M 1M0)
Tel: (306) 893-2635

MAKWA

MAKWA HOTEL
Hwy 304, Box 114
(S0M 1N0)
Tel: (306) 236-4022

MANITOU BEACH

SHADY REST MOTEL
Regina St, Box 11,
RR 1 (S0K 4T0)
Tel: (306) 946-2741

MANOR

MANOR HOTEL
Box 291 (S0C 1R0)
Tel: (306) 448-2050

MAPLE CREEK

COMMERCIAL HOTEL
Hwy 21, Pacific Ave,
Box 1959 (S0N 1N0)
Tel: (306) 662-2673

JACK'S MOTOR HOTEL
Box 969 (S0N 1N0)
Tel: (306) 662-4431

MAPLE GROVE MOTEL
Hwy 21, Box 34
(S0N 1N0)
Tel: (306) 662-2658

PRAIRIE PRIDE MOTEL
Hwy 1, Box 1648
(S0N 1N0)
Tel: (306) 662-2626

MARENGO

MARENGO HOTEL
Main St, Box 22
(S0L 2K0)
Tel: (306) 968-2929

MARKINCH

MARKINCH HOTEL
Box 34 (S0G 3J0)
Tel: (306) 726-4474

MARSDEN

MARSDEN HOTEL
Railway Ave,
Box 175
(S0M 1P0)
Tel: (306) 826-5245

MARYFIELD

ARLINGTON HOTEL
Main St, Box 399
(S0G 3K0)
Tel: (306) 646-2230

MCLEAN

MCLEAN MOTOR HOTEL
Main St, Box 148
(S0G 3E0)
Tel: (306) 699-2810

MEADOW LAKE

CAPRI MOTOR INN
101 1st St E,
Box 327 (S0M 1V0)
Tel: (306) 236-3101

EMPIRE HOTEL & MOTEL
Box 1200 (S0M 1V0)
Tel: (306) 236-5696

FOUR SEASONS MOTEL
Hwy 4, Box 1180
(S0M 1V0)
Tel: (306) 236-4493

NOR'WESTER MOTOR INN
Hwy 4, Box 1180
(S0M 1V0)
Tel: (306) 236-4424

MELFORT

CARRA VALLA INN
708 Saskatchewan
Ave E,
Box 3668 (S0E 1A0)
Tel: (306) 752-2828

HI-LO MOTOR INN
Box 412 (S0E 1A0)
Tel: (306) 752-2836

MELVILLE

MELSASK MOTEL
465 3rd Ave W,
Box 1689 (S0A 2P0)
Tel: (306) 728-4433

PRINCE WILLIAM INN
Box 2999 (S0A 2P0)
Tel: (306) 728-5416

MILDEN

MILDEN HOTEL
Box 88 (S0L 2L0)
Tel: (306) 935-2022

MILESTONE

MILESTONE HOTEL
Main St, Box 547
(S0G 3L0)
Tel: (306) 436-2041

MONT NEBO

MONT NEBO HOTEL
Main St, Box 65
(S0J 1X0)
Tel: (306) 468-2879

MONTMARTRE

CANDIAC HOTEL
Main St, Box 460
(S0G 3N0)
Tel: (306) 424-2931

MOOSE JAW

BEST WESTERN DOWNTOWN MOTOR LODGE
45 Athabasca St E
(S6H 0L3)
Tel: (800) 528-1234

BEST WESTERN HERITAGE INN
1590 Main St N,
Box 2020 (S6H 7N7)
Tel: (800) 528-1234

DREAMLAND MOTEL
1035 Athabasca St E
(S6H 0N1)
Tel: (306) 692-1878

HARWOOD MOOSE JAW INN
24 Fairford St E (S6H 0C7)
Tel: (306) 691-5440

KNOWLES MOTEL
Hwy 1, Box 936
(S6H 4P6)
Tel: (306) 693-3601

MATADOR INN MOTEL
50 McDonald St W
(S6H 6H1)
Tel: (306) 692-6411

MAYNARD MOTEL
1230 Main St N (S6H 3L1)
Tel: (306) 692-7414

PARKE LODGE MOTOR INN
Box 1106 (S6H 4P8)
Tel: (306) 692-0647

PRAIRIE OASIS TOURIST COMPLEX
Box 250 (S6H 4N9)
Tel: (306) 693-8888

ROYAL HOTEL
69 River St W
(S6H 1R3)
Tel: (306) 693-5618

SUPER 8 MOTEL
1706 Main St N, Box
452 (S6H 4P1)
Rates: $48-67
Tel: (306) 692-8888
(800) 800-8000

MOOSOMIN

MOOSOMIN TWI-LITE MOTEL
Hwy 1, Box 1500
(S0G 3N0)
Tel: (306) 435-3321

PRAIRIE PRIDE MOTEL
Hwy 1, Box 1235
(S0G 3N0)
Tel: (306) 435-3394

MORSE

MOTEL 9
Hwy 1, Box 118
(S0H 3C0)
Tel: (306) 629-3383

MOSSBANK

EMPRESS HOTEL
3rd St, Box 392
(S0H 3G0)
Tel: (306) 354-2471

MUENSTER

MUENSTER HOTEL
Railway St, Box 159
(S0K 2Y0)
Tel: (306) 682-2889

NAICAM

NAICAM MOTEL
Hwy 6, Box 610 (S0K 2Z0)
Tel: (306) 874-2371

NETHERHILL

NETHERHILL HOTEL
Main St, Box 69
(S0L 2M0)
Tel: (3060 463-3354

NIPAWIN

AVENUE HOTEL
101 1st St W, Box 786
(S0E 1E0)
Tel: (306) 862-9877

CUMBERLAND HOUSE HOTEL
Box 786 (S0E 1E0)
Tel: (306) 888-2266

GREEN GROVES MOTEL
Hwy 35 S, Box 897
(S0E 1E0)
Tel: (306) 862-4633

KINGFISHER INN
Hwy 35 S, Box 849
(S0E 1E0)
Tel: (306) 862-9801

TOBIN LAKE MOTEL
Box 1420 (S0E 1E0)
Tel: (306) 862-4681

NOKOMIS

NOKOMIS MOTEL
Main St, Box 399
(S0G 3R0)
Tel: (306) 528-2055

NORTH BATTLEFORD

BATTLEFORDS INN
11212 Railway Ave
N (S9A 2R7)
Tel: (306) 445-1515

BEAVER BROOK LODGE MOTEL
Hwy 16, Box 1627
(S9A 3W2)
Tel: (306) 445-7747

CAPRI MOTOR HOTEL
992 101st St
(S9A 2Z6)
Tel: (306) 445-9425

HITCHING POST LODGE
Hwy 16, Box 1690
(S9A 3W2)
Tel: (306) 445-9464

SUPER 8 MOTEL
Hwy 16, Box 1690
(S9A 3W2)
Tel: (800) 800-8000

TROPICAL INN
1001 Hwy, 16 Bypass
(S9A 2W3)
Tel: (306) 446-4700

OGEMA

OGEMA MOTOR INN
Box 298 (S0C 1Y0)
Tel: (306) 459-2455

OUTLOOK

IRRIGATION CENTRE MOTEL
610 McKenzie St,
Box 789 (S0L 2N0)
Tel: (306) 867-8633

RAYLEN MOTEL
522 McKenzie St,
Box 400 (S0L 2N0)
Tel: (306) 867-8661

RED WHEEL MOTEL
509 Saskatchewan
Ave E,
Box 613 (S0L 2N0)
Tel: (306) 867-8374

OXBOW

BOW MANOR MOTOR HOTEL
Hwy 18 E, Box 475
(S0C 2B0)
Tel: (306) 483-2991

PELLY

FORT LIVINGSTONE HOTEL
Main St, Box 186
(S0A 2Z0)
Tel: (306) 595-2146

PENNANT

PENNANT HOTEL '85
Hwy 32, Box 38
(S0N 1X0)
Tel: (306) 626-3303

PERDUE

PERDUE HOTEL
Hwy 14, Box 218
(S0K 3C0)
Tel: (306) 237-4224

PILGER

PILGER HOTEL
Main St, Box 73
(S0K 3G0)
Tel: (306) 367-4273

PLEASANTDALE

PLEASANTDALE HOTEL
Main St, Box 36
(S0K 3H0)
Tel: (306) 874-5758

PONTEIX

PONTEIX MOTOR INN
120 Centre St,
Box 697 (S0N 1Z0)
Tel: (306) 625-3501

PORCUPINE PLAIN CONORA HOTEL
McCallister St,
Box 158
(S0E 1H0)
Tel: (306) 278-2427

PORCUPINE MOTEL
Hwy 23, Box 27
(S0E 1H0)
Tel: (306) 278-2244

PREECEVILLE

GOLDEN WEST HOTEL
Box 647 (S0A 3B0)
Tel: (306) 547-2015

PRINCE ALBERT

CHRISTOPHER HOTEL
Main Rd, Box 1535
(S6V 5T1)
Tel: (306) 982-2112

CORONET MOTOR INN
3551 2nd Ave W
(S6V 5G1)
Tel: (306) 764-6441

IMPERIAL 400 MOTEL
3580 2nd Ave W
(S6V 5G2)
Tel: (306) 764-6881

JOURNEY'S END MOTEL
3863 2nd Ave W
(S6W 1A1)
Tel: (800) 668-4200

MADISON INN
Box 1613 (S6V 5T2)
Tel: (306) 922-9595

MARLBORO INN
67 13th St E
(S6V 1C7)
Tel: (800) 661-7666

PORTER'S MOTEL
Hwy 2 S, RR 2
(S6V 5P9)
Tel: (306) 764-2374

PRINCE ALBERT INN
3680 2nd Ave W
(S6V 5G2)
Tel: (306) 922-5000

SOUTH HILL INN
3245 2nd Ave W
(S6V 5G1)
Tel: (306) 922-1333

TWILITE MOTEL
Hwy 2, RR 2, Site 3,
Box 41 (S6V 5P9)
Tel: (306) 764-1491

QUILL LAKE

CENTENNIAL MOTEL
Hwy 5, Box 190
(S0A 3E0)
Tel: (306) 383-2322

QUINTON

QUINTON MOTOR INN
Hwy 15, Box 190
(S0A 3G0)
Tel: (306) 835-2086

RAMA

RAMA HOTEL
Box 206 (S0A 3H0)
Tel: (306) 593-6048

RAYMORE

RAYMORE HOTEL
Box 37 (S0A 3J0)
Tel: (306) 746-2009

WESTVIEW MOTEL
Hwy 6, Box 220
(S0A 3J0)
Tel: (306) 746-2124

REDVERS

REDVERS MOTOR HOTEL
Railway Ave,
Box 725
(S0C 2H0)
Tel: (306) 452-3282

REGINA BEACH

LAKESHORE INN
Box 480 (S0G 4C0)
Tel: (306) 729-2020

REGINA

BEST WESTERN SEVEN OAKS INN
777 Albert St
Rates: $58-175
Tel: (306) 757-0121
(800) 528-1234

CHELTON INN
1907 11th Ave (S4P 0J2)
Tel: (800) 667-9922

COMFORT INN
3221 E Eastgate Dr
(S4Z 1A4)
Tel: (800) 221-2222

COUNTRY INNS & SUITES
3321 Eastgate Bay
(S4Z 1A4)
Tel: (800) 456-4000

DELTA REGINA
1818 Victoria Ave
(S4P 0R1)
Tel: (800) 268-1133

HOWARD JOHNSON
1717 Victoria Ave
(S4P 0P9)
Tel: (306) 569-4656
(800) 446-4656

IMPERIAL 400 MOTEL
4255 Albert St S
(S4S 3R6)
Tel: (306) 584-8800

INNTOWNER MOTOR INN
1009 Albert St
(S4R 2P9)
Tel: (800) 667-7785

KATEPWA BEACH HOTEL
Box 944 (S4P 3B2)
Tel: (306) 332-4696

LANDMARK INN
4150 Albert St S
(S4S 3R8)
Tel: (800) 667-8191

PLAINS MOTOR HOTEL
1965 Albert St
(S4P 2T5)
Tel: (306) 757-8661

PRAIRIE INN MOTEL
1020 Albert St
(S4R 2P8)
Tel: (306) 525-3535

REGINA INN
1975 Broad St
(S4P 1Y2)
Tel: (800) 667-8162

REGINA SUPER 8 MOTEL
2730 Victoria Ave E
(S4N 6M5)
Tel: (800) 800-8000

RELAX INN REGINA
1110 E Victoria Ave
(S4N 7A9)
Tel: (800) 667-3529

RELAX INN REGINA SOUTH WEST
4025 Albert St
(S4S 3R6)
Tel: (800) 667-3529

SEVEN OAKS MOTOR INN
777 Albert St
(S4R 2P6)
Tel: (800) 667-8063

SIESTA MOTEL
641 Victoria Ave E
(S4N 0P1)
Tel: (306) 525-8142

TRAVELODGE
1110 Victoria Ave
(S4N 7A9)
Rates: $50-75
Tel: (306) 565-0455
(800) 578-7878

VICTORIA INN
1717 Victoria Ave
(S4P 0P9)
Tel: (800) 667-8190

RICHMOUND

RICHMOUND HOTEL
Main St, Box 180
(S0N 2E0)
Tel: (306) 669-2022

RIVERHURST

RIVERSIDE INN
Main St, Box 40
(S0H 3P0)
Tel: (306) 353-2211

ROCKGLEN

ROCKGLEN HOTEL
Box 430 (S0H 3R0)
Tel: (306) 476-2311

VALLEY CITY MOTEL
Hwy 2 N, Box 70
(S0H 3R0)
Tel: (306) 476-2277

ROSE VALLEY

ROSE VALLEY HOTEL
Main St, Box 217
(S0E 1M0)
Tel: (306) 322-2021

ROSETOWN

ROSETOWN MOTEL
Box 551 (S0L 2V0)
Tel: (306) 882-2212

ROSTHERN

PARKLAND HOTEL
Hwy 312, Box 452
(S0K 3R0)
Tel: (306) 232-4464

ROSTHERN HOTEL
8016 Saskatchewan Ave,
Box 547 (S0K 3R0)
Tel: (306) 232-4841

ST. WALBURG

ST. WALBURG INN
26-1st St E, Box 208
(S0M 2T0)
Tel: (306) 248-3414

SASKATOON

BEST WESTERN YELLOWHEAD MOTOR INN
1715 Idylwyld Dr N
(S7L 1B4)
Tel: (800) 528-1234

COMFORT INN
2155 Northridge Dr
(S7L 6X6)
Tel: (800) 221-2222

CONFEDERATION INN
3330 Fairlight Dr
(S7M 3Y4)
Tel: (306) 384-2882

COUNTRY INNS & SUITES
617 Cynthia St
(S7L 6B7)
Tel: (800) 456-4000

DELTA BESSBOROUGH
601 Spadina Cres E
(S7K 3G8)
Tel: (800) 268-1133

HOLIDAY INN
90 22nd St E
(S7K 3X6)
Tel: (800) 465-4329

IDYLWYLD MOTEL
1825 Idylwyld Dr N
(S7L 1B6)
Tel: (306) 244-2191

IMPERIAL 400 MOTEL
610 Idylwyld Dr N
(S7L 0Z2)
Tel: (306) 244-2901

NORTHGATE MOTOR INN
706 Idylwyld Dr N
(S7L 0Z2)
Tel: (306) 664-4414

PARKTOWN MOTOR HOTEL
924 Spadina Cres E
(S7K 3H5)
Tel: (800) 667-3999

PATRICIA HOTEL
345 2nd Ave N
(S7K 2B8)
Tel: (306) 242-8861

RAMADA RENAISSANCE HOTEL
405 20th St E
(S7K 6X6)
Tel: (800) 268-9889

RAMADA HOTEL SASKATOON
90 - 22nd St E
(S7K 3X6)
Rates: $71-118
Tel: (306) 244-2311
(800) 272-6232

RELAX INN-AIRPORT
102 Cardinal Cres
(S7L 6H6)
Tel: (800) 667-3529

RIVIERA MOTOR INN
2001 Ave B N (S7L 1H7)
Tel: (306) 242-7272

SANDS HOTEL
806 Idylwyld Dr N
(S7L 0Z6)
Tel: (306) 665-6500

SASKATOON INN
2002 Airport Dr
(S7L 6M4)
Tel: (800) 667-8789

SHERATON CAVALIER
612 Spadina Cres E
(S7K 3G9)
Tel: (800) 325-3535

TRAV-A-LEER MOTEL
3301 22nd St W
(S7M 0W1)
Tel: (306) 384-1957

WESTGATE INN
2501 22nd St W
(S7M 0V9)
Tel: (800) 667-5268

SENLAC

SUNSET MOTEL
Box 22 (S0L 2Y0)
Tel: (306) 228-3004

SHAUNAVON

INN OF THE SOUTH
Box 538 (S0N 2M0)
Tel: (306) 297-2686

SHAUNAVON HOTEL
189 Centre St,
Box 727 (S0N 2M0)
Tel: (306) 297-3855

STARDUST MOTEL
493 3rd Ave W
(S0N 2M0)
Tel: (306) 297-2613

SHELLBROOK

SHELLBROOK HOTEL
Box 698 (S0J 2E0)
Tel: (306) 747-2233

SHELLBROOK MOTEL
Box 684 (S0J 2E0)
Tel: (306) 747-2631

SIMPSON

SIMPSON HOTEL
Railway Ave,
Box 215
(S0G 4M0)
Tel: (306) 836-2088

SONNINGDALE

SONNINGDALE HOTEL
Main St, Box 119
(S0K 4B0)
Tel: (306) 237-4543

SOUTHEY

SOUTHEY HOTEL
126 Keats St, Box 9
(S0G 4P0)
Tel: (306) 726-2055

SPALDING

SPALDING HOTEL
Main St, Box 309
(S0K 4C0)
Tel: (306) 872-2232

SPIRITWOOD

SPIRITWOOD MOTOR INN
Hwy 3, Box 629
(S0J 2M0)
Tel: (306) 883-2112

WELCOME INN HOTEL
Main St, Box 820
(S0J 2M0)
Tel: (306) 883-2058

STOUGHTON

CROSS ROADS INN
Main St, Box 27
(S0G 4T0)
Tel: (306) 457-2230

STRASBOURG

ROYAL HOTEL
Main St, Box 33
(S0G 4V0)
Tel: (306) 725-3630

STURGIS

BLUE GRASS MOTEL
Box 448 (S0A 4A0)
Tel: (306) 548-2965

SWIFT CURRENT

BEST WESTERN INN
105 George St W
(S9H 0K4)
Rates: $55-125
Tel: (306) 773-4660
(800) 528-1234

CARAVEL MOTEL
N Service Rd
(S9H 3X6)
Tel: (306) 773-8385

CENTRAL MOTEL
77 Begg St W
(S9H 3X6)
Tel: (306) 773-1906

CITY CENTRE MOTEL
Hwy 1 E, S Service
Rd (S9H 3X6)
Tel: (306) 773-4422

COMFORT INN
1510 S Service Rd E
(S9H 3X6)
Tel: (800) 221-2222

FRIENDSHIP INN-SWIFT HOTEL
160 Begg St W
(S9H 0K4)
Tel: (800) 424-4777

IMPERIAL 400 MOTEL
1150 Begg St E
(S9H 3X6)
Tel: (306) 773-2033

IMPERIAL HOTEL
2 Central Ave N
(S9H 0K7)
Tel: (306) 306) 773-8327

K MOTEL
Hwy 1 W, NW
Service Rd,
Box 695 (S9H 3W7)
Tel: (306) 773-4657

RAINBOW MOTEL
Hwy 1 E, S Service
Rd (S9H 3X6)
Tel: (306) 773-8351

RODEWAY INN MOTEL
1200 Begg St E
(S9H 3X6)
Tel: (306) 773-4664

SAFARI INN MOTEL
810 Begg St E
(S9H 3X6)
Tel: (306) 773-4608

WESTWIND MOTEL
155 Begg St NW
(S9H 3S8)
Tel: (306) 773-1441

SYLVANIA

SYLVANIA HOTEL
Main St, Box 16
(S0E 1S0)
Tel: (306) 873-5319

TISDALE

COUNTRYSIDE INN
Hwy 3 E, Box 2035
(S0E 1T0)
Tel: (306) 873-5603

CROWN HOTEL
Box 1838 (S0E 1T0)
Tel: (306) 873-2934

PARK MOTEL
Box 2229 (S0E 1T0)
Tel: (306) 873-2607

TISDALE HOTEL
1001 100th Ave,
Box 1748 (S0E 1T0)
Tel: (306) 873-2134

TOMPKINS

PRAIRIE VIEW MOTEL
Hwy 1, Box 267
(S0N 2S0)
Tel: (306) 622-2012

TOMPKINS HOTEL
Box 159 (S0N 2S0)
Tel: (306) 622-2002

TUGASKE

TUGASKE HOTEL
Main St, Box 189
(S0H 4B0)
Tel: (306) 759-2300

UNITY

ARMADA INN
Box 1642 (S0K 4L0)
Tel: (306) 228-2603

SELKIRK HOTEL & MOTEL
Main St, Box 595
(S0K 4L0)
Tel: (306) 228-2664

VANGUARD

VANGUARD HOTEL
Railway St, Box 160
(S0N 2V0)
Tel: (306) 582-9082

VANSCOY

VANSCOY MOTOR HOTEL
Hwy 7, Box 178
(S0L 3J0)
Tel: (306) 668-2124

VISCOUNT

VISCOUNT HOTEL
306 Amhurst Ave,
Box 68 (S0K 4M0)
Tel: (306) 944-4262

WADENA KOZY MOTEL
Hwy 35, Box 726
(S0A 4J0)
Tel: (306) 338-2566

WADENA LODGE MOTOR INN
Hwy 35 W, Box 1090
(S0A 4J0)
Tel: (306) 338-2509

WAKAW

WAKAW LODGE MOTEL
Box 399 (S0K 4P0)
Tel: (306) 233-4345

WAPELLA

COMMERCIAL HOTEL
Box 142 (S0G 4Z0)
Tel: (306) 532-4253

CURRIN'S MOTEL & CAMPGROUND
5th Ave N, Box 124
(S0G 4Z0)
Tel: (306) 532-4366

WATROUS

SALTY SURF INN
Box 37, RR 1
(S0K 4T0)
Tel: (306) 946-2110

SUNDOWN MOTEL
Hwy 2 E, Box 955
(S0K 4T0)
Tel: (306) 948-3347

WAYSIDE INN MOTEL
802 1st Ave E,
Box 477
(S0K 4T0)
Tel: (306) 946-3383

WAWOTA

VILLAGE INN
Box 328 (S0G 5A0)
Tel: (306) 739-2229

WAWOTA HOTEL
Box 620 (S0G 5A0)
Tel: (306) 739-2551

WEYBURN

BIG J MOTEL
Hwy 39 NW, Box 69
(S4H 2J8)
Tel: (306) 842-2691

CIRCLE 6 MOTEL
140 Sims Ave
(S4H 2H5)
Tel: (306) 842-4528

EL RANCHO MOTEL
53 Government Rd S
(S4H 2A2)
Tel: (306) 842-1411

WEYBURN INN
5 Government Rd
(S4H 0N8)
Tel: (306) 842-6543

WHITE CITY

GREAT PLAINS MOTEL
Hwy 1, Box 530
(S0G 5B0)
Tel: (306) 791-7464

WHITE FOX

WHITE FOX HOTEL
Box 69 (S0J 3B0)
Tel: (306) 276-2086

WHITEWOOD

TRIPLE G MOTEL
Box 607 (S0G 5C0)
Tel: (306) 735-2627

WHITEWOOD HOTEL
Lalonde St, Box 820
(S0G 5C0)
Tel: (306) 735-2323

WHITKOW

WHITKOW HOTEL
Hwy 378, Box 17,
RR 1 (S0M 1S0)
Tel: (306) 445-9834

WILCOX

WILCOX MOTOR INN
Hwy 39, Box 276
(S0G 5E0)
Tel: (306) 732-2022

WINDTHORST

WINDTHORST HOTEL
Main St, Box 100
(S0G 5G0)
Tel: (306) 224-2178

WOOD MOUNTAIN

TRAIL'S END HOTEL
Box 26 (S0H 4L0)
Tel: (306) 266-4844

WYNYARD

ARROWHEAD MOTOR INN
Hwy 16, Box 1210
(S0A 4T0)
Tel: (306) 554-2507

SOUTHSHORE MOTOR LODGE
505 Main St, Box 1330
(S0A 4T0)
Tel: (306) 554-2516

YELLOW GRASS

YELLOW GRASS HOTEL
102 Railway Ave,
Box 300
(S0G 5J0)
Tel: (306) 465-2425

YORKTON

CORONA MOTOR INN
345 Broadway W
(S3N 0N8)
Tel: (306) 783-6571

HOLIDAY INN
100 Broadway
(S3N 2V6)
Tel: (800) 667-1585

IMPERIAL 400 MOTEL
207 Broadway E
(S3N 2V6)
Tel: (306) 783-6581

REDWOOD MOTEL
317 W Broadway
(S3N 0N8)
Tel: (306) 783-3663

YORKE INN MOTEL
418 W Broadway
(S3N 0P2)
Tel: (306) 782-2251

YOUNG

YOUNG HOTEL
Main St, Box 208
(S0K 4Y0)
Tel: (306) 259-2233

YUKON

CARCROSS

CARIBOU HOTEL
Box 136 (Y0B 1B0)
Tel: (403) 821-3391

DAWSON CITY

TRIPLE J HOTEL
5th Ave, & Queen,
P. O. Box 359
(Y0B 1G0)
Tel: (403) 993-5323

DESTRUCTION BAY

TALBOT ARM MOTEL
(Y0B 1H0)
Tel: (403) 841-4461

SWIFT RIVER

SWIFT RIVER LODGE
Mile 733, Alaska
Hwy
(Y0A 1A0)
Tel: (403) 851-6401

WATSON LAKE

GATEWAY MOTOR INN
Box 560
(Y0A 1C0)
Tel: (403) 536-7744

UPPER LIARD RESORT
Mile 642,
Alaska Hwy,
P. O. Box 209
(Y0A 1C0)
Tel: (403) 536-2271

WATSON LAKE HOTEL
Box 370 (Y0A 1C0)
Tel: (403) 536-7781

WHITEHORSE

AIRLINE INN
16 Burns Rd
(Y1A 4Y9)
Tel: (403) 668-4400

AIRPORT CHALET
Mile 916, Alaska
Hwy
(Y1A 3E4)
(403) 668-2166

CHIKOOT TRAIL INN
4190 4th Ave
(Y1A 4T4)
Tel: (403) 668-4190

FORT YUKON HOTEL
2163 2nd Ave
(Y1A 3T7)
Tel: (403) 667-2595

KLUANE VILLAGE
Mile 1118, Alaska
Hwy
(Y1A 3V4)
Tel: (403) 841-4141

REGINA HOTEL
102 Wood St
(Y1A 2E3)
Tel: (403) 667-7801

STEWART CROSSING LODGE
Mile 213, Klondike
Hwy
(Y1A 4N1)
Tel: (403) 996-2501

TAKU HOTEL
4109 4th Ave
(Y1A 1H6)
Tel: (403) 668-4545

TOWN & MOUNTAIN HOTEL
401 Main St
(Y1A 2B6)
Tel: (403) 668-7644

TRAILS NORTH
Mile 922, Alaska
Hwy
(Y1A 3Y8)
Tel: (403) 633-2327

WESTMARK KLONDIKE INN
2288 Second Ave
(Y1A 1C8)
Tel: (403) 668-4747

WHITEHORSE CENTER MOTOR INN
206 Jarvis St
(Y1A 2H1)
Tel: (403) 668-4567

YUKON INN
4220 4th Ave
(Y1A 1K1)
Tel: (800) 661-0454

CANADA TOURISM DEPARTMENTS

Alberta
800-661-8888

British Columbia
800-663-6000

Manitoba
800-665-0040
Ext. E30

New Brunswick
800-561-0123

Newfoundland/ Labrador
800-563-6353

Northwest Territory
800-661-0788

Nova Scotia
800-341-6096

Ontario
800-668-2746

Prince Edward Island
800-463-4734

Quebec
800-363-7777

Saskatchewan
800-667-7191

Yukon Territory
403-667-5340
800-661-0408
(in Yukon Territory)

PET-FRIENDLY PUBLICATIONS

Pet-Friendly Publications is the country's premier publisher of pet travel guide books and directories. Pet-Friendly books are sold throughout the United States at all Major bookstores.

Vacationing With Your Pet Travel Series

Where To Stay, What To Do and How To Do It With Your Pooch.

Eileen's *Arizona, California* and *Texas* Directories of dog-friendly lodging and outdoor adventure are for travelers who want to bring their canine companions along when they vacation or travel. Each 700-page, illustrated book describes thousands of dog-friendly day hikes, parks, beaches, forest trails, lakes, deserts, B&B's, budget motels, 5-star resorts and more. Over 200 pages of valuable travel and training information also included.

To Order From Publisher
1-800-638-3637
(8:30-5:00 MST)

Use your Visa or
MasterCard,
or send $19.95 + $3.95
S&H per book to:

Pet-Friendly Publications,
P. O. Box 8459,
Scottsdale, AZ 85252,
or visit our *Web site* at
www.travelpet.com.

**VACATIONING
WITH YOUR PET!** ™

VACATIONER'S PET SHOP ™

Neat Travel Stuff for Pets!

DEAR PET LOVER...

Whether you're a seasoned veteran who's been vacationing with your dog for years, or a first-time adventurer, vacationing with your pet is a special experience that requires the appropriate gear to make travel time more enjoyable. Take a little time to think about what you'll need while away from home with your pet. There's  *nothing more frustrating than spending valuable vacation time driving from one shopping center to another, trying to locate what you've forgotten.*

In the years that Rosie, Max and I have been on the road, we've learned a great deal about pet travel. And we've collected a number of pet-travel accessories that will make your travels more enjoyable. You'll find a representative selection of these products here in the VACATIONER's PET SHOP CATALOG.

BE PREPARED!

Now that you're a part of the latest travel phenomena, you'll want to be sure that you're properly equipped - not only for your dog's comfort, but for his safety as well. I've tried many products over the past few years and I'd like to introduce you to some of my favorites and explain a little about each.

CALL 1-800-638-3637 TO ORDER

PET-FRIENDLY PUBLICATIONS
P.O. BOX 8459
SCOTTSDALE, AZ 85252
ALL PRICES QUOTED INCLUDE SHIPPING COSTS.

THE TRIP BEGINS

While we're talking safety and protection, here are some great safety items I came across during one of my trips...

Let's think about what else you might need to make your journey more pleasurable. Anticipate your needs and the needs of your dog so that every vacation will be a memorable one.

PET PROTECT... FIRST AID KIT FOR PETS

With this kit, you'll have what it takes to save the life of your pet. Rosie and Max are such an important part of my life that I wouldn't travel without the Pet Protect First Aid Kit For Pets. Not only does it include over 30 essential items for emergency needs but it also contains an easy to follow Pet Emergency and Care Guide that can save the life of your pet.

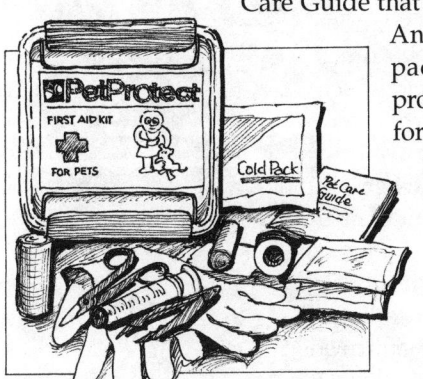

And everything comes neatly packaged in a rugged waterproof case which makes it great for home or travel. I keep one in the glove compartment of my Tahoe and another in the medicine cabinet at home.

"This makes a perfect gift for friends who own pets."

Pet Protect (First Aid Kit)...................**$35**

Buy two...
Only $59
SAVE $11

> *Whenever we travel for a weekend or an overnight, this is the bag I choose. I even use one for all the incidentals that I normally packed in a shopping bag. All of our personal needs are combined in one handy, easy to use and economical bag.*

Get your act together!

THE ULTIMATE TRAVEL BAG

What about those quick day trips where you're just going off to spend the afternoon at a friend's? Or an overnight or weekend jaunt that includes your dog? If you're anything like me, you probably end up with an armload of shopping bags. If that description fits, I know you're going to love the weekend tote I came across in my travels. It's the handiest carryall I've ever used. Large enough to hold all the supplies you'll need for your dog. It comes complete with built-in wheels which pop out to make it easy to roll, freeing your hands to hold onto your dog. The bag is easy to use and when your trip is over, it folds down to about the size of an 8"x10" note pad. And it's not much heavier than that either. Available in Ink Blue with Fire Engine Red trim, this bag will suit your needs and look good too.

The Ultimate Travel Bag.................$29

Buy two... Only $49 SAVE $9

TRAINING ... A WELL-TRAINED PET IS THE BEST TRAVELING COMPANION.

PET AGREE ... THE ULTRA SOUND TRAINING METHOD

Pet Agree brings out the best in your pet. It's safe, silent, effective and the most humane way to train your pets and make them more a part of your world. Whether you're beginning with a puppy or if you want to retrain an older pet, Pet Agree will make your training tasks easy. Instead of spending weeks or months on training, in many cases, just minutes with Pet Agree will do the job. Pet Agree emits a silent, humane, high frequency sound that emphasizes verbal commands. Clearly audible to dogs and cats, the sound cannot be heard by humans. The ultra sound gets the attention of your pet in the same way your voice does but the distinct ultrasound of Pet Agree keeps the attention of your

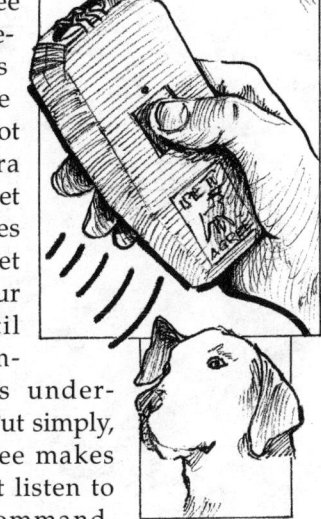

pet until the command is understood. Put simply, Pet-Agree makes your pet listen to your command. Just give a verbal command as you simultaneously press the Pet Agree button for one or two seconds. Repeated use reinforces your training efforts.

Use Pet-Agree to:

- *Reinforce basic commands; Sit, Stay, Heel, and Come.*
- *Help with housebreaking*
- *Stay off furniture*
- *Stop jumping*
- *Stop excessive barking*
- *Stop cats from wailing*
- *Stop chasing cars*
- *Stop biting or scratching*
- *Stop digging*
- *Stay out of an area*
- *Stop clawing or chewing*

Pet Agree..................$34

TATTLE TALE... YOUR PORTABLE SOLUTION TO TRAINING AND SAFETY

TATTLE TALE is a vibration alarm that keeps your pets off the furniture and safeguards your home or hotel room when you travel. By using structural vibration technology, *TATTLE TALE* can detect vibration in an object or surface without any apparent motion. When it does, *TATTLE TALE* sounds a distinct 3-second alarm. You can use it to keep

And for safety when you're travelling, it can't be beat. Hang the TATTLE TALE to detect tampering of doors, windows, even drawers. Imagine the security you'll have if you know the entry areas to your room or home are secure. A single 9V battery offers long life continuous operation. Buy more than one and give yourself complete security.

pets off furniture, countertops, and beds. Keep pets away from plant stands and garbage cans. Why, it can even prevent

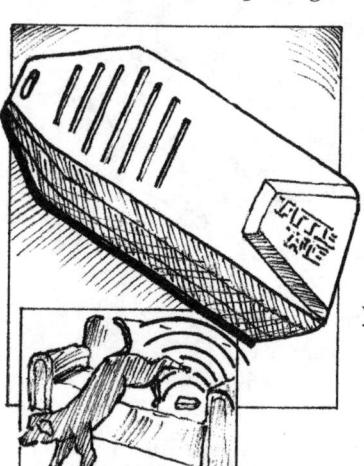

scratching, climbing and clawing. Hang it or set it anywhere, it works in any position. For example, if you want to make sure that your pet stays off the hotel room bed, just put *TATTLE TALE* on your pillow. When your pet jumps on the bed, the alarm will sound and your pet will be warned away.

Tattle Tale..................$34

PET TRAINING
Keeps Pets Off:
• Furniture
• Counter Tops
• Beds
• Plant Stands
• Garbage Cans
• Car Hoods

PREVENTS
• Scratching
• Clawing
• Climbing

MANY USES
• Home
• Camping
• Travel

Buy two...
Only $59
SAVE $9

FLUORESCENT DOG SAFETY VEST

This vest is perfect to use at home or away. How often have you walked your dog at night and then suddenly realized how invisible he is to traffic? I remember one vacation when Rosie ran off while we were walking her. Luckily, we found her but I wouldn't want to relive that experience again. When I saw this vest, I knew I knew it would become standard nighttime

attire for Rosie and Max. It goes on in seconds and secures with Velcro closures. It's so lightweight and comfortable that your dog won't realize he's wearing it. The orange fluorescent mesh glows when light hits it, offering instant protection. Oncoming traffic will spot them in a flash. So whether you're on the road or taking a leisurely walk around your block, insure the safety of your pooch with this high visibility vest.

Dog Safety Vest...................$ 9

Specify Sm. (up to 30 lbs), Med. (up to 60 lbs) or Lg. (over 60 lbs)

BLINKING SAFETY LIGHT

NEVER LOSE SIGHT OF YOUR PET
MAKE YOUR PET VISIBLE TO CARS
USE FOR NIGHTTIME SAFETY

• Lightweight
• Flashing light attracts attention
• Visible for over 2,000 feet
• Off/On waterproof switch
  and long lasting battery

Blinking Safety Light.......$12

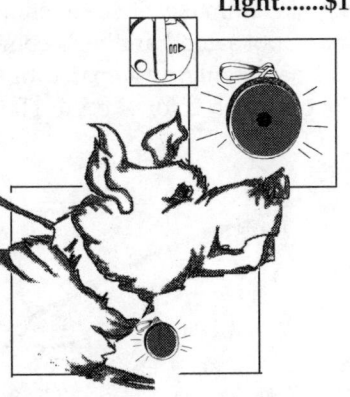

Our new Blinking Safety Light is truly hot! This is a remarkable lifesaving device designed to provide nighttime visibility for your precious pet. It comes with a easy-on, easy-off clip-on hook that attaches to your pet's collar. The blinking red light brightly illuminates your pet's position, making your pet ultra visible to cars.

POOCH POUCH ... A MUST FOR EVERY DOG WALKER

What a handy little fanny pouch this is. You can carry everything you'll need to walk your dog... and still have room for some things you hadn't even thought of. Attractive, lightweight, it's made of a stain resistant fabric. Easy to wear because of its adjustable waist straps - wear it on one walk and you'll never walk without it. There's a large carrying compartment for extras like a ball ,a soft frisbee or an extra pair of sun-

glasses. Include a drink for yourself if you like - there's room. There's even a side pocket so you can take along treats and have easy access to them when you want to reward your dog. And more! A dog shield repellent in a holster for quick use. Even a zippered compartment for your wallet and keys. Why, there's even a multi-purpose key ring. What else? A scooper for cleaning up after your dog, utility snaps for an extra leash, and a reflective patch for nighttime visibility. I know what you're thinking. This pouch must be gigantic. It's not. What makes it so functional is its design. It goes on in a snap, looks good and feels comfortable too. If you like to walk and hate being unprepared or hate those bulging pockets, the Pooch Pouch is for you. You'll never leave home without it.

Pooch Pouch.................$45

H APPY TAILS TO YOU AND YOUR POOCH!

FROM THE PEOPLE AND POOCHES OF PET-FRIENDLY PUBLICATIONS

Well, that's about it for now. Rosie, Maxwell and I hope that you've found our directory and little pet travel catalog to be enlightening and helpful. During future journeys, we'll continue to search out ways to make traveling with your pet easier and more enjoyable. Until then... happy trails to you on your next trip. Have fun and enjoy your canine and feline companions. They're your best friends... don't leave home without them.

Fondly,
Eileen, Rosie & Maxwell